Paust & Upp Bus.Law 2d Ed. MTB—a

BUSINESS LAW TEXT

SECOND EDITION

By

DR. JORDAN L. PAUST
Ph.B., M.A., J.D.
Chairman, Law Department, Los Angeles City College
Attorney at Law
Member, California and Wisconsin Bars

and

DR. ROBERT D. UPP
B.S.J., M.A., M.S., J.D.
Professor of Law, Los Angeles City College
Attorney at Law
Member of California Bar

ST. PAUL, MINN.
WEST PUBLISHING CO.
1974

Library of Congress Catalog Card Number: 73–92587

Paust & Upp Bus.Law 2d Ed. MTB
3rd Reprint—1976

PREFACE

In completing this revised and updated edition of our text, we are indebted to the following business law experts for their many suggestions and invaluable contributions: Paul Cummings (J.D., Boston College), Louis Igo (J.D., University of Tulsa), Randal Lease (J.D., University of South Dakota), Mary Ellen Pangonis (J.D., University of Southern California), Jordan J. Paust (J.D., University of California at Los Angeles, LL.M., University of Virginia), Andrew Peters (J.D., University of West Virginia), Burwell Rudulph (J.D., Harvard University), and John Weaver (J.D., University of Arizona). We express our deep gratitude for their assistance.

We have followed the same simple format used in the original edition. Each chapter begins with an outlined summary of the important points of law relevant to the subject matter of that chapter. This is followed by what we believe to be important, practical, and interesting cases carefully edited to pinpoint the specific legal point involved. At the end of each chapter are short factual situation problems designed to stimulate the students' logical thought processes. There is an italicized heading preceding each case which indicates the rule of law involved. For further simplification, citations and footnotes have been omitted from the body of the edited cases. Great care has been used to locate factual situations of a nature and subject matter with which beginning college students can identify.

At Los Angeles City College we utilize this book for a two semester course, covering the Introduction, Contracts and Sales in Law 1, and the balance in Law 2. However, the material can easily be compressed into a single semester. There is a workbook available to accompany this text which is most useful for preparation, review, and examination. Our experience has been that this combination facilitates the teaching of the material and motivates the students' interest.

J.L.P.
R.D.U.

Los Angeles, California
January, 1974

*

SUMMARY OF CONTENTS

PART 1. THE LAW AND THE COURTS

SUMMARY OF CONTENTS

PART 6. PARTNERSHIPS

PART 7. CORPORATIONS

PART 8. NEGOTIABLE INSTRUMENTS

APPENDICES

TABLE OF CONTENTS

PART 1. THE LAW AND THE COURTS

PART 2. THE LAW OF CONTRACTS

TABLE OF CONTENTS

TABLE OF CONTENTS

TABLE OF CONTENTS

TABLE OF CONTENTS

TABLE OF CONTENTS

TABLE OF CONTENTS

TABLE OF CONTENTS

PART 6. PARTNERSHIPS

PART 7. CORPORATIONS

TABLE OF CONTENTS

APPENDICES

BUSINESS LAW

Part 1

THE LAW AND THE COURTS

Chapter 1

INTRODUCTION

How shall we define the term "law" ? For our purposes in the field of business law, we can define law as that body of rules made by human beings which regulate them in their relationships with each other and with society as a whole.

Its function is to establish order. Imagine the chaos in our society if each of us had the complete freedom to act as we pleased. For example, think of the confusion that would result if everyone could drive an automobile on either side of the road at any time, or if anyone could drive at any speed one desired at any place and at any time. Imagine the confusion and accidents that would occur if we had complete freedom at intersections. In the area of disputes, imagine the confusion in our society if there were no rules to settle disputes. Finally, think of the chaos if there were no penal laws for our protection.

The law varies from state to state and even between governing bodies within the same state. The reasons are often obvious; such as climate, terrain, religion, population and the historical background of the people in the particular area. Let us turn to the field of criminal law to illustrate how the background of the people can affect the law. In the eastern part of the United States before a person can defend himself, he must act the part of a gentleman and must "retreat to the wall"; however, in the western part of the United States where the original settlors had to be rough and tough a person can defend himself without retreating, and in fact can pursue his aggressor until he is reasonably safe from further aggression. Climate and terrain can make a difference in the law. In California water is very scarce in the desert areas but very plentiful in other areas, thus a great deal of law has developed on the subject of water. In states like Wisconsin, Illinois, Ohio, Michigan, and Minnesota, water is so plentiful that there is relatively little law on the subject.

The student should keep in mind that the law is made by human beings for human beings. Naturally, this results in mistakes. Also, this results in change. This is because as society changes so does the law. Consider the change in the laws relating to the automobile. With the replacement of the horse and buggy, we developed a whole new body of law which is contained in the Vehicle Code. As the automobile became more powerful and faster, we had to change the laws to keep pace with the new power and speed. This, in turn, developed new types of roads and highways and thus the Streets and Highways Code. Other examples of changes in the law or new laws resulting from changes in society can be found in the fields of civil rights, social security, foods and drugs, welfare, unemployment insurance, monopolies, insurance, and general business (e.g., the Uniform Commercial Code).

Law is not a subject that can be learned once for all time; and no one is safe in assuming that he knows the rule as to any point unless the law has been checked to date for possible modifications.

As a student, you may tend to become frustrated because there is a certain amount of confusion in the law, but you will not really understand the law until you see the confusion and the reason for it. It should be realized that there is often more than one answer to the same legal problem, each of which can be correct, depending upon the particular circumstances, time, and place. Law is not like arithmetic where there is almost always only one correct answer to a problem. As a student, you will be unhappy if you must have one definite answer to every legal problem because very often there is more than one answer, or there is no answer at all. Also, remember that you must always remain completely objective. Remember that there are always two or more sides to every legal problem. When reading the cases, you will note that the court seldom explains the loser's legal position. This is only natural as we cannot expect the court to expound on the loser's legal position and then hold the other way; however, remember there were two attorneys in court, and the loser must have had a good reason for being there since it costs a great deal of money to appeal a case. Try to figure the loser's position. His position might become the law tomorrow. Also, perhaps the court erred in its decision. After all, judges are only human beings subject to the same frailties and errors as the rest of us. If you do not agree with a case or rule, you should not hesitate to express your dissent, assuming you do so with good reasoning, for the history of the law is full of examples of the dissent becoming the majority.

Chapter 2

SOURCES OF THE LAW

Western civilization developed two systems of law under which most of the civilized world now lives. The Roman or Civil Law system is the older of the two and is found in all of the Continental European countries and in those areas which were colonized or controlled by the nations of Continental Europe. The younger system is the English or Common Law system which is followed by all of the English-speaking countries of the world and by the countries colonized or controlled by them.

A. CIVIL LAW

This is a legislative system based on written codes or statutes coming down through generations from the compilation of Justinian and his successors comprising the Institutes, Code, Digest and Novels, and collectively denominated the "Corpus Juris Civilis". The rules change, but the fundamental legal principles remain fairly continuous. There is little lawmaking for judges in this system. Their main function is to apply the proper code provision to the factual situation that has come before the court. This is a system of "written law" as compared to law made by court decisions.

B. COMMON LAW

The common law originated in England's feudal society. It was brought to England by the Norman conquerors who followed a different procedure than the Romans in making law. A system of courts and traveling judges was established in which the judges were left to their own devices in making the law in that they were expected to make law by deciding what the law should be in a particular case as it was tried before them. This was judge-made law or case law. It is referred to as the "unwritten law" although voluminously recorded and in great part republished in statutory or code form in subsequent years. To give continuity to this system, the judges imposed on themselves an unwritten rule called STARE DECISIS, which means to stand by decided cases. For example, a case would be tried before a judge involving a legal problem which had never been decided upon before. The judge's decision was called a "precedent" or an original rule of law. In later cases involving the same problem, other judges would follow the same rule whether or not they agreed with it. The result was that the precedent became the law. It was called the common law since it was applied to all persons and was, therefore, a law common to all people. The doctrine of STARE DECISIS is not, however, completely rigid. There are certain elements of elasticity that keep the common law changing. For example, the reason for the original decision may have changed so that the judge would not be bound to follow the decision. The factual situation before the judge might be different than the one in the original case so that the judge would not have to follow the same rule. Finally, the later judge might feel that the original decision was wrong and so he refuses to follow it. The result of these later decisions is the making of new and conflicting law which creates a certain amount of confusion until a higher court decides which ruling is better and hence "the law".

C. EQUITY

The common law judges had limited authority to grant relief. They could only award money damages or restoration of property. If a person wanted to enjoin another from doing a certain act, such as a nuisance, or he wanted the other party to a contract to specifically perform that contract, he had to go to the King for relief. The King, of course, had the power to grant specific performance or to enjoin a nuisance. This relief was known as a dispensation of equity or equitable relief. However, the King did not have time to handle all of the cases presented to him so he appointed a high churchman as his agent to conduct these cases. This man was called a Chancellor, and the court he presided over was called the Court of Chancery. Soon the cases became so numerous that there arose from the Court of Chancery the courts of equity to handle all cases where the relief in the common law courts was inadequate. Thus there grew up, side by side, the two systems, the common law courts and the courts of equity. The common law courts gave relief in the form of money or restoration of property, and the equity courts gave relief in the areas of specific performance, injunction, rescission, and relief from forfeiture. In most states in the United States, however, the distinction between law and equity courts has been abolished which means that one court can administer both types of relief.

D. UNITED STATES

The two main sources of law in the United States are judicial decisions, also called case law, and legislative enactments, also called statutory law or code law. In other words, our law comes from either judges or the legislature. However, underlying all of our law, whether case law or statutory law, is the United States Constitution which is the supreme law of the land. No law is valid if it violates the Constitution. The Supreme Court of the United States is the final arbiter as to the constitutionality of any law.

The Constitution provides that powers not delegated to the United States are reserved for the States. This means that each state may make its own laws regarding matters which are purely intrastate; however, if the state law violates the United States Constitution, it is invalid. Examples of such invalid laws can be found in the area of civil rights.

There is substantial uniformity in the laws of the various fifty states, but frequently the laws of some state will differ from the laws of other states on the very same legal point. In this situation, we refer to a majority rule and a minority rule, and sometimes to more than one minority rule. It may be interesting to note that some states can usually be relied on to represent the majority view; e.g., New York, Illinois, and Wisconsin.

Each state has a constitution supplemented by case law and a system of codes. In California, for example, there are twenty-seven codes. They are: Food and Agricultural Code, Business and Professions Code, Civil Code, Code of Civil Procedure, Corporations Code, Education Code, Elections Code, Evidence Code, Financial Code, Fish and Game Code, Government Code, Harbors and Navigation Code, Health and Safety Code, Insurance Code, Labor Code, Military and Veteran's Code, Penal Code, Probate Code, Public Resources Code, Public Utilities Code, Revenue and Taxation Code, Streets and Highways Code, Unemployment Insurance Code, Uniform Commercial Code, Vehicle Code, Water Code, and Welfare and Institutions Code.

In recent years, there has been a great effort to make the laws of the states uniform in certain areas. The most recent example is the Uniform Commercial Code.

Chapter 3

THE UNIFORM COMMERCIAL CODE

A. HISTORY AND PURPOSE

The Uniform Commercial Code (see Appendix A) is the product of many years of preparation by the joint efforts of the National Conference of Commissioners on Uniform State Laws and the American Law Institute. Both organizations include noted judges, law teachers, and law practitioners. The conference adopted a resolution in 1940 to prepare a uniform commercial code. In 1942, the institute joined in the undertaking. In 1945, with the help of a substantial grant, work on the code was underway. Between 1945 and 1952, parts of the code were drafted and redrafted by a staff and were reviewed many times by outside advisory groups as well as by the conference and the institute. In October, 1952, the first official text with explanatory comments was published. The first state to adopt the code was Pennsylvania which was in 1953. Between 1953 and 1956, the New York Law Revision Commission made an exhaustive study of the code. In 1956, many of the commission's recommendations were adopted and embodied in the 1957 official text of the code. In 1958, a third official text was adopted. The current official text was adopted in 1972 and is set forth in Appendix A of this book. The code has been adopted in 49 States (all except Louisiana), and in the District of Columbia and the Virgin Islands.

The purposes of the code are to simplify, clarify, and modernize the law governing commercial transactions; to permit the continued expansion of commercial practices through custom, usage, and agreement of the parties; and to make uniform the law among various jurisdictions.

B. SCOPE OF THE CODE

The U.C.C. consists of ten Articles (in some states called Divisions), namely:

1. General Provisions
2. Sales
3. Commercial Paper

4. Bank Deposits and Collections
5. Letters of Credit
6. Bank Transfers
7. Documents of Title
8. Investment Securities
9. Secured Transactions
10. Effective Date and Repealer

The code repealed many statutes and much case law. The important statutes repealed are: Uniform Sales Act, Uniform Conditional Sales Act, Uniform Bills of Lading Act, Uniform Negotiable Instruments Law, Uniform Stock Transfer Act, Uniform Warehouse Receipts Act, Uniform Trust Receipts Act, Factors Lien Act, and Bulk Sales Act.

The code is restricted to transactions involving various aspects of the sale, financing, and security in respect to PERSONAL property. Except for isolated instances, the code does not apply to real property.

Under the code, if the parties express intent to contract, some of the technical requirements for entering into a contract become unnecessary. The code provides rules and principles which will become part of the contract if the parties have not otherwise agreed. The parties can tailor their contract to suit their needs, however, they cannot change the code obligations of good faith, diligence, reasonableness, and due care.

The student will note in the material on contracts and sales that most contracts must still adhere to the accepted principles that a contract must be certain to be enforceable. The liberality in the area of certainty only applies to the sale of *goods*, and even in that area there can be exceptions; e. g., the sale of automobiles, and installment sales of consumer goods other than motor vehicles.

Chapter 4

THE COURT SYSTEM

There are two major court systems in the United States consisting of the broad federal system and the courts of the fifty individual states.

A. THE FEDERAL SYSTEM

The Constitution created the Supreme Court and authorized such inferior courts as Congress may from time to time establish. Congress, pursuant to this authority, has established eleven United States Courts of Appeal, the United States District Courts of which there is at least one in each state, and others such as the Court of Tax Appeals, the Court of Customs and Patent Appeals, and the Court of Claims. The following chart illustrates the federal court system.

Chart

FEDERAL COURT SYSTEM

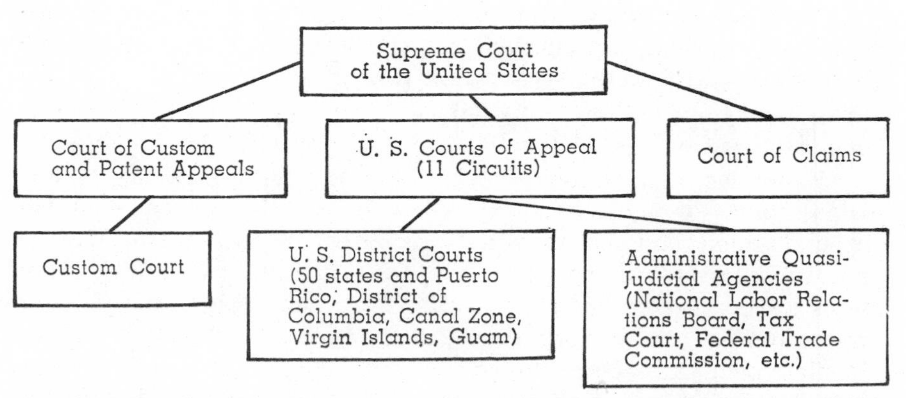

The District Courts are courts of original jurisdiction or "trial courts" (the courts in which proceedings are commenced and tried). The District Courts have jurisdiction, among other things, of cases which arise under the United States Constitution or federal laws and treaties which involve personal rights, cases involving federal crimes, and civil cases in which the matter in controversy exceeds the sum or value of $10,000.00 and is based on diversity of citizenship; e. g., citizens of different states.

The Courts of Appeal are review courts and are courts to which an appeal may be taken from the District Courts. A Court of Appeal will review the case tried in the District Court and will either affirm, reverse, or modify the judgment of the trial court.

From the Courts of Appeal, the case may then be appealed to the United States Supreme Court which has the final word on the legal problems involved. An appeal to this court is largely a matter of privilege rather than of right since this court may either allow or deny a petition for a hearing. Although the Supreme Court work is primarily appellate, it does have original jurisdiction in cases in which the states may be a party, in cases affecting ambassadors, public ministers, and consuls. The power of the Supreme Court to review the decisions of the state courts, however, is limited to those which involve a federal question. However, the Supreme Court has the power to invalidate any federal or state statute by declaring it to be contrary to the United States Constitution. It is obvious that the Supreme Court wields enormous influence and has great power. The legal principles enunciated by the Court are followed by other federal courts in controversies which come before those courts. If the decision involves a constitutional problem, the Court's decision will be followed by all of the various courts of the United States, both federal and state.

B. THE STATE SYSTEMS

Most states follow the basic federal system and have trial courts of original jurisdiction, intermediate appellate courts and the highest court of the state as the one of final appeal.

1. COURTS OF ORIGINAL LIMITED JURISDICTION

Examples of trial courts of limited jurisdiction are city or municipal courts or justices' courts whose jurisdiction is limited to the city and which may hear criminal cases involving only misdemeanors and civil cases for money damages up to a limited amount. Some states have a small claims court system in which the courts have a limited money jurisdiction; e. g., $500, and where the litigants handle their own cases since the parties may not be represented by attorneys. This has been a very useful court to relieve the municipal courts which are so crowded that it often takes up to one year to have a case tried. The small claims courts dispense justice on an assembly line basis; however, the system is surprisingly successful.

2. COURTS OF ORIGINAL UNLIMITED JURISDICTION

These are trial courts which have unlimited jurisdiction; such as, cases involving unlimited amounts of money, probate, equity, divorce, and felony cases rather than merely misdemeanors. They are called by various names: Circuit Courts (Illinois, Indiana, Michigan); Superior Courts (California, Massachusetts); Supreme Courts (New York); District Courts (Iowa, Minnesota, Oklahoma, Wyoming); Courts of Common Pleas (Ohio, Pennsylvania).

3. APPELLATE COURTS

a. Intermediate courts of appeal. These courts have been created in some states to relieve the highest state court of some of the cases which it reviews. They are usually called District Courts of Appeal or Courts of Appeal and are found in Arizona, California, Illinois, Louisiana, Michigan, New York, North Carolina, Ohio and Pennsylvania. These are the courts to which a litigant would file his initial appeal from the trial court. In general, appellate courts do not hear witnesses. They examine the record of a case on appeal to determine whether the trial court committed a prejudicial error, and if it did, to reverse the judgment.

b. Highest court. Every state has a court which it designates as its highest court of appeals. California, Illinois, and most states call it the Supreme Court. Kentucky, Maryland and New York call it the Court of Appeals. Massachusetts and Maine call it the Supreme Judicial Court. The losing litigant in the intermediate court of appeal can file an appeal in this court. An appeal from this court to the United States Supreme Court is only possible if there is a constitutional law question involved which means a state statute or decision that is asserted to be in violation of the United States Constitution.

4. ARBITRATION

Arbitration is a procedure by which a dispute is brought before one or more arbitrators who make a decision which the parties may agree to accept as final. It is encouraged as a means of avoiding expensive and timely litigation, and relieving congestion and delay in the courts. Generally speaking, virtually every state has some kind of "arbitration statute." The "modern" arbitration acts provide for the irrevocability of agreements to submit disputes to arbitration, and also provide for the means of compelling arbitration, staying suits at law and confirming awards with limited review. Thirty-one states have adopted the "modern" act. The United States Government has adopted the United States Arbitration Act which applies in any state if the transaction involves interstate commerce and there is diversity of citizenship. Information regarding the rules of arbitration and wording of arbitration clauses to be used in a contract can be obtained from the American Arbitration Association which is a private, non-profit organization founded in 1926 to foster the study of arbitration and to perfect the techniques of this method of settling disputes.

Chapter 5

HOW TO PREPARE FOR CLASS

A. IN GENERAL

You will note that a typical chapter contains text material, edited appellate cases, and problems. Before you read the cases or the problems, study the text material. This brief material will give you a summary of the law involved in the chapter. If you are familiar with this material, it will be easier to brief the cases and answer the problems. The law in your particular state may be different than the law stated in the textual material or stated in the cases. Therefore, it is extremely important that you take extensive class notes so that you can record these changes when given to you by the instructor.

B. HOW TO BRIEF A CASE

There is a standard procedure followed in reciting on a law case. The procedure is using a "brief" of the case in the book. Prior to class, the student reads the case very carefully. When he feels that he understands the case, he prepares a brief of the case. The format of the brief is below (made for the first case in the book).

RICHARDSON v. J. C. FLOOD COMPANY

190 A.2d 259 (D.C.App.1963).

ACTION: Suit for labor and material furnished for a new water line.

FACTS: Defendant (the appellant) requested the plaintiff plumbing company to correct a stoppage in the sewer line of her house. During the cleaning of the line defendant discovered that a water pipe running parallel with the sewer line was defective and had to be replaced. Defendant was informed, through her agent, of the defective water line and that it had to be replaced then or at a later date when the yard would have to be redug for that purpose. Plaintiff replaced the defective water line. Defendant and her agents, through daily inspections of the repairs, knew of the magnitude of the work required and made no objection to the replacement of the water line until after the entire job was finished at which time defendant refused to pay any part of the total bill submitted. She defends on the ground that she did not authorize the replacement of the water line.

QUESTION: Did the failure of the defendant to object to plaintiff's conduct create an implied agreement to pay for the replacement of the water line?

DECISION: Yes. Judgment for plaintiff.

RULE: A contract for work to be done is implied when arising from a mutual agreement and promise not set forth in words. A contract may be presumed from the acts and conduct of the parties.

In preparing the brief, be certain that you incorporate all of the important facts; however, remember that it is supposed to be brief. If you understand all of the important facts, you will find that the rule usually follows quite logically. If you change one important fact, you can change the result of the case.

The question or issue in the case is extremely important. Say to yourself, "What is this fight all about? Why are they in court?" If you do not know, you do not have the case.

Finally, be able to state the court's reason for the decision and be ready to defend or challenge it.

What do the numbers and abbreviations under the title of the case mean? This is called a citation. The first number means the volume in the reporter where the case can be found. The last number means the page. The letters indicate the name of the state appellate court. In our example the citation would mean "District of Columbia Court of Appeals, Volume 190 Atlantic Reporter Second Series Page 259." Thus, the entire decision in the Richardson v. Flood Company case can be found in Volume 190, Page 259 of the Second Series of the Atlantic Reporter. For purposes of classroom study, the complete decision has been edited, and this is indicated by the asterisks in the case.

Trial court decisions are generally not published as reported decisions, although there are a few exceptions; e.g., Federal Court decisions, New York decisions. Trial court decisions are only filed in the office of the clerk of the court where the trial took place.

The decisions of the *appellate* courts are found in *state* reports of that particular state *and also* in a series of reporters embracing the whole United States comprising the National Reporter System which is published by the West Publishing Company. The National Reporter System divides the states into seven regional reporter groups: Atlantic (Atl. or A.), North Eastern (N.E.), North Western (N.W.), Pacific (Pac. or P.), Southern (So.), South Eastern (S.E.), and South Western (S.W.). Consolidating reported cases by area makes it much simpler to research cases.

The Federal court decisions are found in the Federal Reporter (Fed. or F.), Federal Supplement (F.Supp.), Federal Rules Decisions (F.R.D.), and United States Supreme Court Reports (U.S.), Supreme Court Reporter (S.Ct.), Lawyers Edition (L.Ed.).

C. TAKING A CASE TO COURT

The judicial procedure which must be followed in taking a case to court varies between state and federal courts, and between the state courts. It can be complicated. Our purpose in this part of the text is to give a general summary of some of the common characteristics of judicial procedure in the United States.

1. THE PARTIES

The person who brings the lawsuit in the trial court is generally called the plaintiff or petitioner, and the person against whom the suit is brought is called the defendant or respondent.

Usually the plaintiff or petitioner is listed first in the title of the case and the defendant or respondent listed second; however, in some states the appellant is listed first even though he was the defendant in the trial court. A notation has been made in the case where this has been done so as to avoid possible confusion for the student.

2. THE PLEADINGS

The plaintiff's first pleading is generally called a complaint. The complaint alleges the facts upon which the plaintiff bases his cause of action and must be prepared pursuant to prescribed rules. The plaintiff's complaint, together with a summons, is served upon the defendant.

If the defendant desires to contest the action he must file an answer or demurrer (see dictionary in Appendix for explanation of terms). Usually the defendant files an answer rather than a demurrer. Generally the answer merely denies the allegations in the plaintiff's complaint.

After the defendant files an answer and it is served on the plaintiff or his attorney pursuant to local rules, the case is at issue and ready for pretrial proceedings.

3. PRETRIAL PROCEEDINGS

The main function of pretrial procedure is to discover the basic issues and facts prior to the trial. The theory behind discovery rules is that a lawsuit should be an intensive search for the truth, not a game to be determined in outcome by consideration of tactics and surprise. The five main discovery devices are depositions, written interrogatories, motions for inspection, physical and mental examinations, and demands for admission.

After the issues are joined it is customary for the attorneys to take depositions of the respective adverse parties and of key witnesses. The most popular type of deposition consists of oral testimony under oath given in answer to oral interrogatories of one or more attorneys which is later reduced to writing and authenticated. It is usually taken in the office of one of the attorneys. Its main function is to discover the facts upon which the opposition is relying so that preparation can be made to dispute or disprove those facts in the trial of the action. It is also useful to impeach testimony given at the trial; i. e., a statement testified to in the deposition can be used to contradict conflicting testimony given at the trial. It is extremely important for a person to be prepared as to the facts before his deposition is taken.

A deposition can also be taken upon written interrogatories. These are written questions propounded to the adverse party or to a witness which he must answer under oath. Written interrogatories are usually not as effective as oral interrogatories which provide for on-the-spot-cross-examination since the person has too much time to prepare an answer, often with the help of an attorney.

A motion for inspection permits the court to order any party to produce and permit the inspection and copying by the party bringing the motion of certain designated documents, papers, books, accounts, letters, photographs, and other objects or tangible things.

In an action in which the mental or physical condition or the blood relationship of a party, or certain other persons, is in controversy, the court may order the party to submit to a physical or mental or blood examination by a physician. This discovery device is commonly used in accident cases by insurance companies to prevent fraud on the part of claimants.

A significant tool in helping to avoid unnecessary expense and labor in trial preparation and in proof at the trial is the demand for admissions. This is a request by one party against the other to admit the genuineness of any relevant documents described in the request or of the truth of any relevant matters of fact set forth in the request.

It should be apparent that modern discovery devices provide tools for all sides to a contest which make it unnecessary to be surprised at the trial. The issues can be narrowed and practically all of the testimony of the parties elicited in advance.

In addition to the above discovery procedures a pretrial conference can be requested in many cases. At this conference, which is held before a judge or commissioner, the parties attempt to settle the case, or failing in that, to narrow the issues so that the trial can be shorter and more orderly.

4. THE TRIAL

This is the time when the witnesses, parties and attorneys congregate outside the courtroom door for amenities and last minute discussions. It is the time when the nervous wish they had settled.

Most judges want to see the attorneys in chambers before trial in an effort to make a last minute settlement. If that fails the judge wants to discuss the case in an effort to narrow the issues and thereby shorten the time of trial.

If the case is to be tried by a jury the attorneys and the judge examine the prospective jurors in an attempt to select competent and unbiased jurors. After the jury is selected each attorney makes an opening statement in which he states what he expects to prove in the trial.

The plaintiff's attorney then presents his case by examining each of his witnesses and introducing documentary evidence. As the plaintiff's attorney finishes his direct examination of each witness the defendant's attorney has the right to cross-examine. After the defendant's attorney finishes his cross-examination, the plaintiff's attorney may redirect and then the defendant's attorney may recross. After the plaintiff's attorney has presented all of his evidence he rests his case, and then the defendant puts on his case as outlined above. All of the above proceedings are subject to strict rules of procedure and evidence in order that the trial may proceed in an orderly manner.

After all of the evidence has been introduced and various motions have been made, the plaintiff's attorney makes his final argument to the jury in which he reviews the evidence and relates the evidence to the instructions which the judge will give the jury. After the plaintiff's attorney finishes his argument the defendant's attorney follows the same procedure. A short rebuttal is then available to the plaintiff's attorney.

After the arguments are concluded the judge instructs the jury on the law applicable to the case. The jury then retires to consider and render a verdict.

After the judgment is rendered the attorney for the losing party may file a motion for judgment notwithstanding the verdict; i. e., the losing party claims that the winning party did not even produce a prima facie case (insufficient evidence to support a judgment).

Either attorney can move for a new trial on one or more of several grounds; e. g., excessive or inadequate damages, irregularity in proceedings, misconduct of jury, newly discovered evidence, insufficient evidence, verdict against the law, error in the law.

5. THE APPEAL

After the judgment is entered and motions, if any, are decided, the party who feels aggrieved may appeal. This party may be the one who lost the case or the party who won the case but did not get as much as he had hoped. Some of the grounds for an appeal are that the court erred in admitting or excluding certain evidence, erred in instructing the jury, erred in refusing the appellant a directed verdict, or that the evidence was insufficient to sustain the verdict.

The appellate court hears the case without a jury and without witnesses. The attorneys for the appellant and appellee submit written briefs to the court in which they state their arguments supported by citations of previous court decisions and statutes. In addition the attorneys are usually permitted to make an oral argument to the court. The court examines the briefs of the attorneys and the record of the proceedings before the lower court including the pleadings, the testimony of the witnesses, documentary evidence, and the lower judge's instructions to the jury. After a review of the case the appellate court renders its decision and writes its opinion. These opinions are preserved in permanent bound volumes or reports. It is these opinions that we will be studying in the cases in this book. The court in its decision may affirm the lower court's decision, reverse it, or remand the case back to the lower court with directions to hold a new trial pursuant to certain instructions or with directions to enter a new judgment in accordance with the opinion that is given by the appellate court.

6. ENFORCEMENT OF THE JUDGMENT

If the losing party does not pay the judgment after it has been entered or after an appeal has been decided, the winning party must take steps to execute or carry out the judgment. Two common procedures for enforcing the judgment are the issuance of a writ of execution for the seizure and sale of property of the loser and a garnishment proceeding.

A writ of execution directs the sheriff to levy upon sufficient property of the judgment debtor to satisfy the judgment plus costs of the execution. If the sheriff finds sufficient property he will seize and sell it at public auction in accordance with state statutes. Certain property of the judgment debtor is exempt from levy and execution by statutory exemptions; e. g., furnishings, personal clothing, tools of trade, a certain amount of money. If the judgment is for the recovery of specific property, the judgment will direct the sheriff to deliver the property to the winning party.

A garnishment is a statutory proceeding whereby the judgment debtor's property, usually money, in possession or under control of another is applied to payment of the debtor's obligation. For example, the winning party may run a garnishment against the judgment debtor's employer to obtain a portion of the debtor's wages. Statutes specify the amount that can be taken under the garnishment.

Part 2

THE LAW OF CONTRACTS

Chapter 6

INTRODUCTION

A. NATURE OF CONTRACTS

A contract is an agreement, express or implied, to do or not to do a particular thing. The Restatement, Contracts, Section 1, gives the following definition: "A contract is a promise or a set of promises for the breach of which the law gives a remedy, or the performance of which the law in some recognizes as a duty." The U.C.C. definition of a contract is: " 'Contract' means the total legal obligation which results from the parties' agreement as affected by this Act and any other applicable rules of law." Section 1–201(11). Also see Section 1–201(3) for definition of "agreement".

Generally, the following elements are required in a legal contract: 1. Two or more competent parties; 2. Their consent; 3. Consideration; 4. A proper subject matter; and 5. Mutuality of obligation. These requirements will be considered in subsequent chapters.

An EXPRESS contract is one in which its terms are stated *in words*, oral or written. An IMPLIED IN FACT contract is one in which the existence and terms are manifested *by conduct*. The distinction between an express contract and an implied in fact contract relates only to the manner in which the consent was made evident by the parties. An example of an implied in fact contract would be as follows: A man waves to a taxi, gets in, and gives the driver an address. No other words are spoken. This is an implied contract that the driver will receive compensation for taking the man to the address.

Another type of contract is one that is IMPLIED IN LAW, normally referred to as a QUASI-CONTRACT. In this case, the *law* imposes an obligation on a party to prevent an *unjust enrichment*. For example, a nurse furnishes beneficial services to a person who has been insane for many years. There is no contract as such; however, if the nurse rendered the services in good faith with no intention of making a gift of such services, the nurse could recover the reasonable value of the services in quasi-contract, or as is also said, "as if" there was a contract.

A UNILATERAL contract is one in which a promise is given in exchange for an act or the forebearance of an act. There is only one promisor. An example of a unilateral contract is the reward type of case. The law enforcement agency offers a reward for the capture of a criminal. The promise is the offer of the reward, and the act is the capture of the criminal.

A BILATERAL contract is one in which there are mutual promises. One promise is given in consideration for the other promise. Most contracts are bilateral. An attorney promises to perform certain services for a client. The client promises to pay money for the services. This is a bilateral contract.

An EXECUTED contract is one in which the object of the contract is fully performed. All others are EXECUTORY; i. e., a contract which is wholly performed on one side, but unperformed on the other side, or unperformed on both sides in whole or in part. The distinction is important in certain cases; such as, illegality, modification of a written contract by executed oral agreement, consideration, and the statute of frauds. In those cases, the defenses normally available to performance of the contract are no longer available if the contract has been executed.

A VOID contract is a nullity and cannot be enforced by either party. A contract induced by fraud in the inception where the victim did not know that he was signing a legal document is a void contract. A VOIDABLE contract is void or valid at the option of the parties. For example, a contract induced by fraudulent misrepresentations would be voidable at the option of the victim. An UNENFORCEABLE contract is one that cannot be enforced because of some legal technicality; such as, the failure to satisfy the Statute of Frauds (failure to put the contract in writing which the Statute of Frauds requires of certain contracts) or because the statute of limitations has run on the contract (failure to file the law suit within the time prescribed by local statute). These contracts are referred to as unenforceable rather than as void or voidable.

A contract may also be unenforceable because it is UNCONSCIONABLE; i. e., an absence of meaningful choice on the part of one of the parties together with unreasonable contract terms favoring the other party. See the Uniform Commercial Code, Section 2–302, Appendix A. The basic test is whether the clauses involved are so one-sided as to be unconscionable under the circumstances existing at the time the contract was made and in the light of the general commercial needs of the particular trade or case. Examples of unconscionable contracts are those involving excessive prices or clauses which are hidden in fine print and which were unknown to the consumer. Most courts do not limit the test of unconscionability to the sales of goods, but will apply it to any agreement.

Revoked

B. CONFLICT OF LAWS

There is a conflict of laws when there is a difference in the laws between municipalities, between states, or between countries. The law of New York is different from the law of California regarding revocation of an offer. If the buyer (offeror) is in Los Angeles, and the seller (offeree-acceptor) is in New York, and no intent is indicated as to which law should apply, which law do we use? The validity of the contract is ordinarily determined by the law of the place where the contract was made, and this would be where the last act is necessary for its validity. This has been called the more favored rule. In our example, we would use the law of New York since the last act necessary to make the contract, namely the acceptance, would take place in New York. If the contract is entered into by telephone, the place of making is the place where the acceptor speaks.

1. Contract Implied When Failure to Object

RICHARDSON v. J. C. FLOOD COMPANY

190 A.2d 259 (D.C.App.1963).

MYERS, Judge. This is an appeal by a property owner [defendant Richardson] from a judgment against her for costs of labor and material furnished by appellee [plaintiff] plumbing company.

Appellant contends there was error in the findings of the trial court that all work done by appellee was authorized by her and that there was sufficient competent evidence to substantiate the amount of recovery.

Appellant requested appellee to correct a stoppage in the sewer line of her house. In the course of the work a "snake" used to clear the line leading to the main sewer became caught and to secure its release a portion of the sewer line in the backyard was excavated. It was then discovered that the instrument was embedded in pieces of wood which had become lodged in a sewer trap from surface debris. At this time numerous leaks were found in a rusty, defective water pipe which ran parallel with the sewer line. In order to meet District regulations, the water pipe, of a type no longer approved for such service, had to be replaced then or at a later date when the yard would have to be redug for that purpose. Appellee's agent testified he so informed appellant's agent. Appellant testified she had requested appellee to clear the sewer line but denied she was told about the need for replacement of the water line and contested the total amount of the charges for all the work done by appellee.

In the absence of a written contract, but with appellant admitting she had requested correction of a sewer obstruction but denying she had agreed to replace the water pipe, the existence of an implied agreement between the parties to replace the water pipe at the same time became an issue for the trial court.

It seems clear from the record that there was evidence to support a finding that appellant and her agents through daily inspections of the repairs knew of the magnitude of the work required and made no objection to the performance of the extra work in replacing the water pipe until after the entire job was finished when appellant refused to pay any part of the total bill submitted.

Contracts for work to be done are either express or implied—*express* when their terms are stated by the parties, *implied* when arising from a mutual agreement and promise not set forth in words. Direct evidence is not essential to prove a contract which may be presumed from the acts and conduct of the parties as a reasonable man would view them under all the circumstances. The testimony was conflicting but we cannot say that the trial court was wrong in holding that the burden of proving its right to recover had been carried by appellee.

With respect to the costs of both jobs the record reveals that no testimony was offered by appellant to show that itemized amounts for labor and materials furnished by appellee were wrong or excessive and unreasonable or that the work performed was either unnecessary or unsatisfactory. Appellee produced testimony that the charges were fair and reasonable and that the work on both the sewer and the water lines was fully completed. We find no merit in appellant's claim of error that the evidence on the costs of labor and material was insufficient to support the finding on this point.

We have frequently had occasion to state that, except for errors of law, we are expressly forbidden to set aside a judgment of the trial court, sitting without a jury, unless the judgment "is plainly wrong or without evidence to support it." D.C.Code, 1961 § 11–772 (c). We have no authority to retry issues of fact and to substitute our own findings where, as here, there is competent evidence to sustain the findings of the trial court.

Affirmed.

---

2. *Quasi-contract; Implied in Law to Prevent Unjust Enrichment*

MATARESE v. MOORE-McCORMACK LINES

158 F.2d 631 (C.C.A.N.Y., 1946).

[Action for the reasonable value of the use of certain inventive ideas.]

CLARK, Circuit Judge. This appeal raises the issue whether a corporation may be required to pay the reasonable value of the use of certain inventive ideas disclosed by an employee to an agent of the corporation in the expectation of payment where an express contract fails for want of proof of the agent's authority. [Under the law of agency, an agent cannot bind his principal to a contract unless there is authority to do so] * * * During the trial plaintiff * * amended his complaint by adding a prayer for recovery of quantum meruit [value of services rendered] upon the theory of unjust enrichment. [Judgment for plaintiff, and defendants appeal.]

The plaintiff is a man of little education, who, emigrating to this country from Italy some forty-six years ago, had always worked around the docks and in 1938 was employed as a part-time stevedore on defendants' pier. His case, which the jury quite obviously must have accepted in full, was that in August of that year he informed Furey, defendants' agent in charge of the pier, that he had something which would facilitate cargo loading and unloading, thus saving the defendants much money and preventing the numerous accidents ordinarily occurring at the pier. * * *

According to plaintiff and his witnesses, however, Furey expressed his satisfaction with the models and promised the plaintiff one-third of what the defendants would save by use of the device. He suggested that plaintiff patent his device and offered to be the plaintiff's partner in exploiting it. He also offered the plaintiff the job of supervising the construction of his devices for defendants on the defendants' premises and with the defendants' materials. * * * After a full-scale test of plaintiff's devices, defendants put a great number of them into use at the pier under Furey's charge and at other piers subsequently acquired by them. From time to time plaintiff asked Furey about his money, and Furey always assured him that he would be compensated in the future. In 1941, however, Furey sent plaintiff to another agent of the defendants, who discharged him from his job. * * * The main legal issue of the appeal turns, therefore, upon the validity of plaintiff's claim of unjust enrichment under the circumstances of this case.

* * * The doctrine of unjust enrichment or recovery in quasi-contract obviously does not deal with situations in which the party to be charged has by word or deed legally consented to assume a duty toward the party seeking to charge him. Instead, it applies to situations where as a matter of fact there is no legal contract, but where the person sought to be charged is in possession of money or property which in good conscience and justice he should not retain, but should deliver to another. * * * The doctrine is applicable to a situation where, as here, the product of an inventor's brain is knowingly received and used by another to his own great benefit without compensating the inventor. * * * Here the relationship between the parties before and after the disclosure, the seeking of disclosure by Furey, Furey's promise of compensation, the specific character, novelty, and patentability of plaintiff's invention, the subsequent use made of it by defendants, and the lack of compensation

given the plaintiff—all indicate that the application of the principle of unjust enrichment is required.

* * *

[A person shall not be allowed to enrich himself unjustly at the expense of another.]

[Judgment for plaintiff affirmed.]

---

3. Unconscionable Contracts Not Enforceable (U.C.C. 2–302)

JONES v. STAR CREDIT CORP.

59 Misc.2d 189, 298 N.Y.S.2d 264 (1969).

Action brought by buyers, welfare recipients, to reform sales contract which was allegedly unconscionable. The Supreme Court, Special Term, Sol M. Wachtler, J., held that selling for $900 ($1,439.-69 including credit charges and $18 sales tax) a freezer unit having an actual retail value of $300 was, under the Uniform Commercial Code, unconscionable as a matter of law.

SOL M. WACHTLER, Justice. On August 31, 1965 the plaintiffs, who are welfare recipients, agreed to purchase a home freezer unit for $900 as the result of a visit from a salesman representing Your Shop At Home Service, Inc. With the addition of the time credit charges, credit life insurance, credit property insurance, and sales tax, the purchase price totalled $1,234.80. Thus far the plaintiffs have paid $619.88 toward their purchase. The defendant claims that with various added credit charges paid for an extension of time there is a balance of $819.81 still due from the plaintiffs. The uncontroverted proof at the trial established that the freezer unit, when purchased, had a maximum retail value of approximately $300. The question is whether this transaction and the resulting contract could be considered unconscionable within the meaning of Section 2–302 of the Uniform Commercial Code which provides in part:

> (1) If the court as a matter of law finds the contract or any clause of the contract to have been unconscionable at the time it was made the court may refuse to enforce the contract, or it may enforce the remainder of the contract without the unconscionable clause, or it may so limit the application of any unconscionable clause as to avoid any unconscionable result.
>
> (2) When it is claimed or appears to the court that the contract or any clause thereof may be unconscionable the parties shall be afforded a reasonable opportunity to present evidence as to its commercial setting, purpose and effect to aid the court in making the determination. * * *

There was a time when the shield of "caveat emptor" would protect the most unscrupulous in the marketplace—a time when the law, in granting parties unbridled latitude to make their own contracts, allowed exploitive and callous practices which shocked the conscience of both legislative bodies and the courts.

The effort to eliminate these practices has continued to pose a difficult problem. On the one hand it is necessary to recognize the importance of preserving the integrity of agreements and the fundamental right of parties to deal, trade, bargain, and contract. On the other hand there is the concern for the uneducated and often illiterate individual who is the victim of gross inequality of bargaining power, usually the poorest members of the community.

The law is beginning to fight back against those who once took advantage of the poor and illiterate without risk of either exposure or interference. From the common law doctrine of intrinsic fraud we have, over the years, developed common and statutory law which tells not only the buyer but also the seller to beware. This body of laws recognizes the importance of a free enterprise system but at the same time will provide the legal armor to protect and safeguard the prospective victim from the harshness of an unconscionable contract.

Section 2–302 of the Uniform Commercial Code enacts the moral sense of the community into the law of commercial transactions. It authorizes the court to find, as a matter of law, that a contract or a clause of a contract was "unconscionable at the time it was made", and upon so finding the court may refuse to enforce the contract, excise the objectionable clause or limit the application of the clause to avoid an unconscionable result. "The principle", states the Official Comment to this section, "is one of the prevention of oppression and unfair surprise". It permits a court to accomplish directly what heretofore was often accomplished by construction of language, manipulations of fluid rules of contract law and determinations based upon a presumed public policy.

There is no reason to doubt, moreover, that this section is intended to encompass the price term of an agreement. In addition to the fact that it has already been so applied * * * the statutory language itself makes it clear that not only a clause of the contract, but the contract in toto, may be found unconscionable as a matter of law. Indeed, no other provision of an agreement more intimately touches upon the question of unconscionability than does the term regarding price.

Fraud, in the instant case, is not present; nor is it necessary under the statute. The question which presents itself is whether or not, under the circumstances of this case, the sale of a freezer unit having a retail value of $300 for $900 ($1,439.69 including credit charges and $18 sales tax) is unconscionable as a matter of law. The court believes it is.

Concededly, deciding the issue is substantially easier than explaining it. No doubt, the mathematical disparity between $300, which presumably includes a reasonable profit margin, and $900, which is exorbitant on its face, carries the greatest weight. Credit charges alone exceed by more than $100 the retail value of the freezer. These alone, may be sufficient to sustain the decision. Yet, a caveat is warranted lest we reduce the import of Section 2–302 solely to a mathematical ratio formula. It may, at times, be that; yet it may also be much more. The very limited financial resources of the purchaser, known to the sellers at the time of the sale, is entitled to weight in the balance. Indeed, the value disparity itself leads inevitably to the felt conclusion that knowing advantage was taken of the plaintiffs. In addition, the meaningfulness of choice essential to the making of a contract, can be negated by a gross inequality of bargaining power. * * *

Having already paid more than $600 toward the purchase of this $300 freezer unit, it is apparent that the defendant has already been amply compensated. In accordance with the statute, the application of the payment provision should be limited to amounts already paid by the plaintiffs and the contract be reformed and amended by changing the payments called for therein to equal the amount of payment actually so paid by the plaintiffs.

[Compare this case with Morris v. Capitol Furniture & Appliance Co., 280 A.2d 775 (D.C.App.1971), in which the court held that unconscionability cannot be based on excessive prices since the consumer could have done competitive shopping.]

PROBLEMS

1. Martha and her husband took plaintiff into their home when he was 6 years of age and reared him as a foster son. They had no children of their own. Plaintiff lived in the home until he was 27 years of age at which time he married and moved to a home nearby. During Martha's last few years of life she was a widow and in ill health. During this period plaintiff spent a great deal of time taking care of Martha including furnishing her with food, preparing meals, giving her insulin shots, and generally making himself the man of the house. After Martha died he brought action against her executor for the reasonable value of the services he had rendered. Decision? Reason?

2. Debtor paid money to X by mistake intending to pay the money to Creditor. X has no right to the money, but refuses to return it to Debtor. Can Debtor obtain a judgment for return of the money?

3. On February 17, 1966, Seller sold Buyer a 1959 Buick for the sum of $939.75 plus a credit service charge of $242.47. During the first week Buyer operated the automobile the steering post on the front end was loose, the wheel bearing on the right front made an unusual noise, the shock absorbers were defective, and the ignition would not always start. He spent $570 to repair the automobile. Buyer seeks your advice as to his right to relief under U.C.C. Section 2–302.

Chapter 7

REACHING THE AGREEMENT

A. INTENTION OF THE PARTIES

1. MANIFESTATION OF ASSENT

Every contract must have mutual assent or consent. Mutual assent is determined by the acts and the reasonable meaning of the words of the parties, and not from the unexpressed intentions of the parties. This is referred to as the objective test for ascertaining intent. In other words, it is not necessary to have an actual meeting of the minds of the parties to have a valid contract. It is sufficient if there is an apparent meeting of the minds.

2. NEGLIGENCE IN SIGNING OR ACCEPTING A CONTRACT

Ordinarily, one who signs or accepts a contract which on its face is a contract is deemed to assent to all of its terms. He cannot escape liability on the ground that he has not read it. Of course, if there was fraud in procuring the signature, or if a confidential relationship existed between the parties giving rise to an affirmative duty of disclosure, the signer would not be liable; however, he would probably end up in expensive litigation. One of the common complaints in a contract dispute is "I didn't read the contract" or "I didn't understand the contract". Generally this is no excuse; therefore, it is very important to remember that you should never sign a legal document of any kind unless you understand it. If you do not understand the document take it to an attorney so that he can advise you as to its legal consequences.

B. THE OFFER

1. IN GENERAL

A contract results from an offer and the acceptance thereof. No particular formality is required. An offer is a proposal to enter into a contract, and it may be expressed by acts as well as words. An offer may be a promise requesting a promise, a promise requesting an act, or an act requesting a promise. The person who makes the offer or proposal is the offeror. The person to whom it is made is the offeree.

2. OFFER IN JEST

A proposal obviously made in jest, an invitation to a purely social function, or a remark made in the course of a family discussion, which a reasonable person would not be justified in treating as an offer to enter into a contract, is not an offer. There is a conflict of authority as to whether a proposal made under *great* emotional stress is a valid offer. Some courts hold that the offeree cannot take advantage of such an offer when he knows or should know that there was no intent to make the offer. Other courts hold that the offeror is bound since to do otherwise is to open the door and permit the offeror another method of escaping from his offer.

3. PRELIMINARY NEGOTIATIONS

When a party suggests the terms of a possible contract by a letter or advertisement without making a definite proposal, the result is a mere invitation to the other party to make an offer. For example, such language as "we can quote you", without more, is considered merely a statement of terms and not an offer. However, a quotation may be sufficiently specific and promissory to constitute an offer. Thus, it may add the statement that the quotation is for "immediate wire acceptance". This would be construed as an offer.

An estimate usually does not suggest a binding proposal; however, where the word "estimate" is in the heading and not the body of the document, and the body contains words such as, "We propose to furnish to", and "The signature herein is an authorization to install such equipment as described in the above estimate", the court can call the estimate an offer.

4. CERTAINTY OF OFFER

A. In General

An offer must be sufficiently definite so that the performance required by the offeree is reasonably certain. The offer must describe the subject matter and the quantity and should state the price; however, the complete absence of any mention of the price is not necessarily fatal as the court may interpret the contract to mean the market price or a reasonable price. The offer should state the time and place; however, failure to so state does not necessarily render the contract void if the intent of the parties is otherwise ascertainable. In determining whether a contract is sufficiently enforceable, the court will liberally interpret laymen's agreements or nontechnical language. The court will attempt to make the contract valid if there is uncertainty by carrying into effect the reasonable intentions of the parties if they can be ascertained.

B. Under the U.C.C.

Under the Uniform Commercial Code, fundamental changes have been made in contracts involving the *sale of personal* property. *A word of caution*: These changes only affect personal property sales and not other contracts, such as, contracts for personal services and real estate contracts.

The most fundamental changes relaxing the requirements of certainty in a contract for the sale of goods under the U.C.C. can be found in the following sections set out in full in Appendix A:

(1) Section 2–204, *Formation in General*, which provides that a contract for sale of goods may be made in any manner sufficient *to show agreement* including conduct by the parties. In other words, if the parties act as though there is a contract, there may be one.

This section also provides that even though one or more of the terms of the contract are left open, the contract is still enforceable if the parties intended a contract and if the court can give an appropriate remedy.

(2) Section 2–305, *Open Price Term*, supplies a price if nothing is said as to price. This usually means the market price at the time and place of delivery.

(3) Section 2–306, *Output, Requirements and Exclusive Dealings*, supplies a *quantity* where the parties have not stated a definite quantity, but instead the buyer agrees to buy the seller's entire output or agrees to buy all that the buyer may "require".

In fact, under the code, if the parties agree to buy and sell all that the buyer may "desire" or "wish", the contract may be sufficiently certain to be enforceable, especially if the contract was initially entered into to fill the buyer's actual needs. See Sections 1–203 and 2–103(1) (b) and Lowell O. West Lumber Sales v. U. S. (9th Cir. 1959) 270 F.2d 12. However, in cases not within the code, a quantity stated in terms of the buyer's "desire" or "wish" would not be sufficiently certain since the buyer might not "desire" or "wish" to buy any of the subject matter of the contract; and hence the contract would be unenforceable against him, and of course, if the contract is not enforceable against one of the parties, it is not enforceable against the other party since it lacks mutuality of obligation.

(4) Section 2–308, *Absence of Specified Place for Delivery*, will supply the place of delivery if omitted in the contract.

(5) Section 2–309, *Absence of Specific Time*, will supply a time if one is omitted in the contract.

(6) Section 2–310, *Open Time for Payment or Running of Credit: Authority to Ship Under Reservation*, will supply payment terms and delivery terms if omitted in the contract.

(7) Section 2–208, *Course of Performance or Practical Construction*, provides that repeated conduct by the parties shall be relevant to determine the meaning of the agreement.

(8) Section 1–205, *Course of Dealing and Usage of Trade*, provides that a course of dealing between the parties and any usage of trade in the vocation or trade in which they are engaged shall be used to supplement or qualify the terms of the contract.

5. DURATION OF OFFER

A communicated offer continues until it lapses or expires, becomes illegal or impossible by operation of law, is revoked by the offeror, is rejected by the offeree, or is accepted by the offeree.

A. LAPSE

The offer is revoked if the offeree fails to accept the offer within the prescribed period of time stated in the offer. If the offer prescribes no particular time for its acceptance, it is revoked by the lapse of a reasonable time. What is a reasonable time is a question of fact depending upon the nature of the particular offer, the usages of business and the circumstances of the case. An offer to purchase real estate would not require as prompt an acceptance as an offer to purchase personal property of a perishable nature or of fluctuating value. The Restatement of the Law of Contracts, Section 40, cites the following illustrations regarding reasonable time: (1) whether three days is too long to accept an offer to sell land is a question of fact under the circumstances; (2) where the buyer receives the offer at the close of business hours for the sale of ordinary goods, an acceptance by letter promptly the next morning creates a contract; (3) a telegraphic offer to sell oil, which at the time is subject to rapid fluctuation in price, received near the close of business hours is not accepted in time by a telegraphic reply sent the next day.

B. ILLEGAL OR IMPOSSIBLE BY OPERATION OF LAW

If the subject matter of the contract becomes illegal, the offer is revoked, e.g., the legislature passes a law making the subject illegal.

Destruction of the subject matter prior to acceptance revokes the offer.

Death or insanity of the offeror prior to acceptance revokes the offer since at the time of acceptance, there is no offeror capable of contracting.

Death of the offeree also revokes the offer since only the person to whom the offer was made can accept it.

C. REVOCATION

The general rule is that an offer may be revoked at any time before the communication of acceptance even though the offer is stated to be good or irrevocable for a specified period.

Some of the *exceptions* are as follows:

(1) An *option* where consideration is given for an agreement to keep the offer open.

(2) A *unilateral* contract after substantial part performance by the offeree (normally in a unilateral contract, there is no acceptance until the offeree performs the act requested of him, e.g., catching the

criminal in a reward type of case; however, to prevent the injustice that would occur if the offeror revoked the offer after substantial performance on the part of the offeree, most courts will protect the offeree in some way, such as making the offer irrevocable or permitting the offeree to recover in quasi-contract for the reasonable value of his performance up to the time of revocation. To alleviate this problem *in the sale of goods*, the *U.C.C.* provides the following in *Section 2–206(2)*: "Where the beginning of a requested performance is a reasonable mode of acceptance, an offeror who is not notified of acceptance within a reasonable time may treat the offer as having lapsed before acceptance.").

(3) *Firm offers under the U.C.C. Section 2–205 of the U.C.C.* states that a *merchant's* written and signed offer to buy or sell goods which gives assurance that it will be held open is not revocable for the time stated; and if no time is stated for a reasonable time, in either case, not over three months, *even though* there is no consideration. For definition of merchant see U.C.C. Section 2–104.

The general rule is that a revocation must be communicated to the offeree before it is effective, i.e., *received* by the offeree. The minority rule, followed in California (Civil Code, Section 1587(1)), states that revocation is effective upon posting; thus, if the offeror mails the revocation before the offeree mails the acceptance, there is no contract. In the United States, posting can be effective as early as handing it to the mailman since in this country the mailman is under a duty to accept the mail. The California rule is not favored since the offeree does not know of the revocation until he receives it, and in the meantime he might have committed himself to other contracts relying on a contract that never became effective; thus, such a rule slows the economy since the offeree cannot make other contracts until he is certain that the offeror has not mailed a revocation of his offer.

D. REJECTION

From and after the effective moment of a rejection, the offeree can no longer accept the offer. A rejection is not effective until it is *received* by the offeror.

A counter-offer has the same effect as a rejection; however, if the offeree's reply does not show an unwillingness to accept the original offer, there is no rejection, e. g., a mere inquiry is not a rejection.

C. THE ACCEPTANCE

1. IN GENERAL

An offer must be accepted before there is a contract. Acceptance is an expressed or communicated overt act by the offeree indicating that he assents to the terms of the offer. It may, if the offer permits, take the form of an act (unilateral contract), a promise communicated to the offeror (bilateral contract), or the formal act of both parties signing a written document. Mere words, such as, "O. K." can constitute an acceptance. Where the offeror signs and delivers a contract to the offeree, and the latter accepts it; he will be bound even though he does not sign it, e.g., landlord hands lease to tenant who accepts it without objection.

The right to accept an offer cannot be assigned and, therefore, can only be accepted by the person to whom it was made.

The student should remember that once an offer is accepted there is a contract unless there is a valid defense. In the situation of a fluctuating market the offeree is in the better bargaining position because he can reject or accept the offer; therefore, it is usually better procedure to send out a quotation of prices (making it clear that it is not an offer) rather than an offer.

2. ACCEPTOR MUST HAVE KNOWLEDGE OF THE OFFER

The rule that the acceptor-offeree must have knowledge of the offer applies to both unilateral and bilateral contracts. In a unilateral contract, "reward" type, there can be no recovery of the reward unless the offeree knew of the reward. However, it is not necessary that he knows the precise terms of the offer or the nature of the performance requested. This is often the case when the proposed written contract is accepted without reading it; the offeree is bound. In a bilateral contract situation, identical offers to buy and sell property which cross in the mails do not create a contract when the parties are each ignorant of the other's offer.

3. ACCEPTANCE MUST BE UNQUALIFIED

In contracts where the U.C.C. is not involved the acceptance must be positive and unequivocal. It may not change any of the terms of the offer or qualify it in any way. A qualified acceptance is a new proposal and constitutes a rejection of the original offer after which the original offer cannot be accepted by the offeree.

However, *under the U.C.C., Sections 2–207(1) (2)*, the offeree may state additional terms from those contained in the offer; and the acceptance will still be valid, assuming it complies with the other requirements of a valid acceptance, as these terms are merely considered as *proposals* for additions to the contract. In other words, the offeree accepts the offer but wants the offeror to consider some additional terms; e. g., the wire of acceptance adds "ship by Thursday" or "rush". A frequent example is the exchange of printed purchase order and acceptance forms. Often the seller's form contains different terms from the buyer's form; nevertheless, the parties proceed with the transaction.

If the offeror and offeree are *both merchants*, the additional terms become part of the contract unless:

a. The offer expressly limits acceptance to its terms;

b. They materially alter the offer; or

c. The offeror objects to them within a reasonable time.

An example of a clause which "materially alters" the contract and thus not included in it unless expressly agreed to by the other party is a clause negating such standard warranties as that of merchantability or fitness for a particular purpose under circumstances in which either warranty normally attaches. An example of a clause not material is a clause fixing a reasonable time for complaints within customary limits.

In many cases goods are shipped, accepted and paid for before any dispute arises. In such a case if the writings of the parties do not establish a contract, Section 2–207(3) establishes the contract by conduct and governs the question as to what terms are included in it.

4. ACCEPTANCE BY SILENCE

In a bilateral contract, ordinarily *silence cannot constitute acceptance* of an offer, and this is true even though the offer states that silence will be taken as consent; for the offeror cannot force the offeree to make an express rejection.

There are several *exceptions* to the rule:

a. Previous dealings between the parties place the offeree under a duty to act or be bound, e.g., failure to object to a billing statement from a creditor;

b. Use of services or goods by the offeree when he had freedom to reject them amounts to an acceptance;

c. Complete performance or tender thereof by the offeree is equivalent to a promise of acceptance resulting in a contract; and

d. Under the Contracts Restatement Rule, Section 72(1) (b), if the offeror prescribes silence as the means of assent, and the offeree remains silent *intending to accept*, a contract results; however, there is little authority approving this position.

In a unilateral contract, it is ordinarily not necessary for the offeree to notify the offeror of his acceptance as the offer normally requests an act rather than a promise; and even if the offeree does give a notification, it has no legal effect.

Under the U.C.C., Section 2–206(1) (b), an order or offer to buy goods for prompt shipment may be accepted by a promise to ship the goods *or* by the prompt shipment of conforming or non-conforming goods. If the seller ships non-conforming goods (goods that deviate from the order in quality or quantity), he should notify the buyer that the shipment is an *accommodation* shipment since if he does not, he may be in breach of a contract that he accepted by shipping.

5. EFFECTIVE TIME OF ACCEPTANCE

Acceptance is effective when it is placed in the *course of transmission.* If the mails are used, it is when the offeree mails the acceptance in an envelope properly addressed and stamped. If a telegram is used, it is when the telegram is handed to the telegraph operator. It is immaterial that the letter or telegram is delayed or not received by the offeror. Once the acceptance has been completed by posting or transmitting the telegram, it cannot be countermanded or withdrawn; however, the Contracts Restatement, Section 39, and recent Federal Court of Claims cases have held to the contrary. If the acceptance is made too late or in an unauthorized manner, the offeror cannot waive the defect and treat the acceptance as valid. Instead, it is merely treated as a counter-offer which would have to be accepted by the original offeror.

The manner in which the acceptance is to be communicated can be specified in the offer, in which case no other method would be binding. If the offer does not prescribe a specified manner, any reasonable manner may be used, *Section 2–206(1) of the U.C.C.* Hence, it would be proper to answer a letter with a telegram.

An offer must be accepted within a reasonable time unless otherwise specified in the offer. An offer by telegram should be accepted by telegram rather than by letter and ordinarily sent the same day as the offer is received. If an offer by mail calls for a reply "by return mail," a letter of acceptance must be sent either by the next mail or during the day that the offer is received. If an offer states that it is "open for ten days", the ten-day period begins on the date which appears on the offer; thus, if the offer is delayed for ten days it never becomes effective. However, if the offer states that the offeree has ten days in which to accept, the ten-day period does not begin until the offer is received. In the latter case if the offer is delayed and the offeree knew or had reason to know of the delay, the offeree will have ten days less the delay in which to accept the offer. If an offer by mail does not specify "by return mail" or any other time, the offeree has a reasonable time which is determined by the type of offer, the type and usages of business, and all other surrounding circumstances.

1. *No Intent to Contract*

McCLURG v. TERRY

21 N.J.Eq. 225 (1870).

THE CHANCELLOR. The complainant seeks to have the ceremony of marriage performed between herself and the defendant, in November, 1869, declared to be a nullity. The ground on which she asks this decree is, that although the ceremony was actually performed and by a justice of the peace of the county, it was only in jest, and not intended to be a contract of marriage, and that it was so understood at the time by both parties, and the other parties present; and that both parties have ever since so considered and treated it, and have never lived together, or acted towards each other as man and wife. The bill and answer both state these as the facts of the case, and that neither party intended it as a marriage, or was willing to take the other as husband or wife. These statements are corroborated by the witnesses present. The complainant is an infant of nineteen years, and had returned late in the evening to Jersey City, from an excursion with the defendant and a number of young friends, among whom was a justice of peace, and all being in good spirits, excited by the excursion, she in jest challenged the defendant to be married to her on the spot, he in the same spirit accepted the challenge, and the justice at their request, performed the ceremony, they making the proper responses. The ceremony was in the usual and proper form, the justice doubting whether it was in earnest or in jest. The defendant escorted the complainant to her home, and left her there as usual on occasions of such excursions; both acted and treated the matter as if no ceremony had taken place. After some time the friends of the complainant, having heard of the ceremony, and that it had been formally and properly performed before the proper magistrate, raised the question and entertained doubts whether it was not a legal marriage; and the justice meditated returning a certificate of the marriage to be recorded before the proper officer. The bill seeks to have the marriage declared a nullity, and to restrain the justice from certifying it for record.

Mere words without any intention corresponding to them will not make a marriage or any other civil contract. But the words are evidence of such intention, and if once exchanged, it must be clearly shown that both parties intended and understood that they were not to have effect. In this case the evidence is clear that no marriage was intended by either party; that it was a mere jest got up in exuberance of spirits to amuse the company and themselves. If this is so, there was no marriage.

[The student should note the conflict of facts in this case; i. e., the parties went through a ceremony but did not live together, and yet the Chancellor said that the evidence is clear.]

2. *Objective Intent Determined by Words and Acts*

LUCY v. ZEHMER

196 Va. 493, 84 S.E.2d 516 (1954).

BUCHANAN, Justice. This suit was instituted by W. O. Lucy and J. C. Lucy, complainants, against A. H. Zehmer and Ida S. Zehmer, his wife, defendants, to have specific performance of a contract by which it was alleged the Zehmers had sold to W. O. Lucy a tract of land owned by A. H. Zehmer in Dinwiddie county containing 471.6 acres, more or less, known as the Ferguson farm, for $50,000.

The instrument sought to be enforced was written by A. H. Zehmer on December 20, 1952, in these words: "We hereby agree to sell to W. O. Lucy the Ferguson Farm complete for $50,000.00, title satisfactory to buyer," and signed by the defendants, A. H. Zehmer and Ida S. Zehmer.

* * *

The answer of A. H. Zehmer admitted that at the time mentioned W. O. Lucy offered him $50,000 cash for the farm, but that he, Zehmer, considered that the offer was made in jest; that so thinking, and both he and Lucy having had several drinks, he wrote out "the memorandum" quoted above and induced his wife to sign it; that he did not deliver the memorandum to Lucy, but that Lucy picked it up, read it, put in his pocket, attempted to offer Zehmer $5 to bind the bargain, which Zehmer refused to accept, and realizing for the first time that Lucy was serious, Zehmer assured him that he had no intention of selling the farm and that the whole matter was a joke. Lucy left the premises insisting that he had purchased the farm.
* * *

The discussion leading to the signing of the agreement, said Lucy, lasted thirty or forty minutes, during which Zehmer seemed to doubt that Lucy could raise $50,000. Lucy suggested the provision for having the title examined and Zehmer made the suggestion that he would sell it "complete, everything there," and stated that all he had on the farm was three heifers. * * *

Lucy took a partly filled bottle of whiskey into the restaurant with him for the purpose of giving Zehmer a drink if he wanted it. Zehmer did, and he and Lucy had one or two drinks together. Lucy said that while he felt the drinks he took he was not intoxicated, and from the way Zehmer handled the transaction he did not think he was either. * * *

The defendants insist that the evidence was ample to support their contention that the writing sought to be enforced was prepared as a bluff or dare to force Lucy to admit that he did not have $50,000; that the whole matter was a joke; that the writing was not delivered to Lucy and no binding contract was ever made between the parties. * * *

In his testimony Zehmer claimed that he "was high as a Georgia pine," and that the transaction "was just a bunch of two doggoned drunks bluffing to see who could talk the biggest and say the most." That claim is inconsistent with his attempt to testify in great detail as to what was said and what was done. * * * The record is convincing that Zehmer was not intoxicated to the extent of being unable to comprehend the nature and consequences of the instrument he executed, and hence that instrument is not to be invalidated on that ground. * * *

Not only did Lucy actually believe, but the evidence shows he was warranted in believing, that the contract represented a serious business transaction and a good faith sale and purchase of the farm. * * *

In the field of contracts, as generally elsewhere, "We must look to the outward expression of a person as manifesting his intention rather than to his secret and unexpressed intention. 'The law imputes to a person an intention corresponding to the reasonable meaning of his words and acts.' " * * *

The mental assent of the parties is not requisite for the formation of a contract. If the words or other acts of one of the parties have but one reasonable meaning, his undisclosed intention is immaterial except when an unreasonable meaning which he attaches to his manifestations is known to the other party.

* * *

Reversed and remanded [for entry of a proper decree requiring defendants to perform the contract].

---

3. *Failure to Read Contract Generally no Defense*

VARGAS v. ESQUIRE, INC.

166 F.2d 651 (C.C.A.Ill., 1948), certiorari denied 335 U.S. 813, 69 S.Ct. 29, 93 L.Ed. 36.

KERNER, Circuit Judge. Plaintiff, a citizen of Illinois, brought this action against defendant, a Delaware corporation, to cancel and set aside a contract entered into between the parties.

The trial judge * * * entered a decree setting aside and cancelling the contract. To reverse the decree, defendant appealed. * * *

Plaintiff, an artist, fifty-one years of age, is a native of Peru. He left Peru at the age of seventeen. From 1912 to 1916 he resided in continental Europe, and since 1916 he has resided in the United States. He came to Chicago in June, 1940. Defendant is engaged in the business of publishing magazines, calendars, and other printed matter. David A. Smart is its president and all of plaintiff's dealings concerning the contract were carried on with David A. Smart as defendant's agent.

In June, 1940, Vargas, then a little known artist, after a conference with Smart, entered into an employment contract with defendant, by which he agreed to furnish defendant with certain art material for use in magazines published by Esquire and for use by it. * * * We now consider what we think is the turning question in the case, that is, whether the contract is void because plaintiff failed to know what it contained. It is clear from this record and the findings of the court that Vargas understood that he was signing a contract fixing the terms and compensation under which he was to furnish pictures for defendant and that Vargas knew that Smart was representing defendant as its agent in executing the contract. There are but six paragraphs in the contract. It is written in plain and ordinary language and is readily understandable. * * *

It is a rule universally recognized that a written contract is the highest evidence of the terms of an agreement between the parties to it, and it is the duty of every contracting party to learn and know its contents before he signs it. And in the absence of fraud, which must be proved by clear and convincing evidence * * * a man in possession of all his faculties, who signs a contract, cannot relieve himself from the obligations of the contract by saying he did not read it when he signed it, or did not know or understand what it contained. * * * But the contract cannot be avoided by proof that one of the parties, if he was sound in mind and able to read, did not know the terms of the agreement. One must observe what he has reasonable opportunity for knowing; the law requires men, in their dealings with each other, to exercise proper vigilence and give their attention to those particulars which may be supposed to be within reach of their observation and judgment and not to close their eyes to the means of information which are accessible to them. A person is presumed to know those things which reasonable diligence on his part would bring to his attention. * * *

In the instant case the evidence showed and the court found that Vargas had resided in the United States since 1916; that "he writes English very well, speaks good English"; that "Vargas and his wife were both capable of reading and understanding the English language at the time of the execution of the contract"; and that "prior to the signing of the contract the plaintiff was requested * * * to read the contract, and both the plaintiff and his wife had an opportunity to read the contract."

* * * It is a well settled rule of law that when a party to a contract is able to read and has the opportunity to do so, he cannot thereafter be heard to say he was ignorant of its terms and conditions. * * *

The decree will be reversed and the cause remanded to the District Court with instructions to dismiss the complaint.

4. *Failure to Read Baggage and Claim Checks as a Defense*

KERGALD v. ARMSTRONG TRANSFER EXP. CO.

330 Mass. 254, 113 N.E.2d 53 (1953).

LUMMUS, Justice. This is an action of contract, in which the plaintiff sues for the loss of her trunk and its contents. The defendant is an intrastate common carrier. There was evidence that the plaintiff arrived with her trunk at the South Station in Boston late in an evening in May, 1949, and went to the defendant's office there. She was not asked the value of her trunk, but was given a small pasteboard check by the defendant which was not read to her and which she did not read, but put in her purse. The trunk was to be delivered at her home in Boston. The defendant failed to deliver her trunk, and admitted that it had been lost. The small check had on one side the order number and the words "Read contract on reverse side," and on the other the words, "The holder of this check agrees that the value of the baggage checked does not exceed $100 unless a greater value has been declared at time of checking and additional payment made therefor."

The defendant excepted [see dictionary in Appendix] to the denial of its motion for a directed verdict for the plaintiff in the sum of $100.

Where what is given to a plaintiff purports on its face to set forth the terms of a contract, the plaintiff, whether he reads it or not, by accepting it assents to its terms, and is bound by any limitation of liability therein contained, in the absence of fraud.

On the other hand, where as in this case what is received is apparently a means of identification of the property bailed, rather than a complete contract, the bailor is not bound by a limitation upon the liability of the bailee unless it is actually known to the bailor. * * (limitation on back of railroad ticket); * * * (schedule as to baggage, no knowledge warranting inference of assent); * * (identification check for automobile given by parking station). * * * In our opinion no error is disclosed by the record.

Exceptions overruled [judgment for plaintiff].

[Many states have statutes which limit the amount of liability on the part of the bailee. See chapters on Bailments.]

---

5. *Certainty is Required*

SHERMAN v. KITSMILLER, ADMINISTRATOR

17 Serg. & Rawle 45 (Penn., 1827).

This was an action to enforce an alleged promise to the effect that one George Sherman, now deceased and here represented by his administrator, would convey to plaintiff one hundred acres of land if plaintiff would keep house for him until her marriage. Plaintiff alleged that she performed her part of the contract fully, but that the said George Sherman refused to convey the land in accordance with the alleged contract. Defendant contended that it had never been made certain just what land plaintiff was to receive.

At the trial the court instructed the jury as follows: "There can be no recovery, unless there was a legal promise seriously made: if a promise is so vague in its terms as to be incapable of being understood, and of being carried into effect, it cannot be enforced. If George Sherman had reference to no particular lands * * * such promise would not be so perfect as to furnish the ground of an action * * *. But if George Sherman was seized of several tracts in the vicinity, and he promised her one hundred acres, in such a manner as to excite an expectation in her that it was a particular part of his lands so held by him * * * then the action might be sustained." The question submitted to the Supreme Court of Pennsylvania was whether this instruction was a correct statement of the law.

DUNCAN, J. * * * The charge of the court was * * * more favorable to the plaintiffs than their case warranted. * *

The action is brought on the express promise, and that only lies where a man * * * assumes to do a certain thing. * * * this means * * * a certainty to a common intent, giving the words a reasonable construction. But the words must show that the understanding was certain. * * * Promises or contracts ought to be certain and explicit. * * *

The jury should have been instructed that as there was nothing certain in the promise, nothing referred to to render it certain, the action could not be maintained. * * *

The promisor himself would not know what to convey, nor the promisee what to demand. * * * One hundred acres of land without locality, without estimation of value, without relation to anything which could render it certain, does appear to me to be the most vague of all promises; and if any contract can be void for its uncertainty, this must be. One hundred acres on the Rocky Mountains, or in the Conestoga manor—one hundred acres in the mountains of Hanover County, Virginia, or in the Conewango rich lands of Adams County—one hundred acres of George Sherman's mansion at eighty dollars per acre, or one hundred acres of his barren lands at five dollars? * * * The promise is as boundless as the terrestrial globe.

I am, therefore, of opinion that there was no error in the opinion of the court by which the plaintiffs have been damaged; that the law was laid down more favorably for them than the evidence warranted.

Judgment affirmed [for defendant].

[Query: could plaintiff recover for the reasonable value of her services less benefits received?]

⁎ 6. *Offer Distinguished from a Quotation of Prices*

JOHNSTON v. ROGERS

30 Ontario Reports 150 (1899).

The plaintiffs are bakers, and seek to recover damages from the defendants for breach of a contract for the sale and delivery of a quantity of flour.

The following letter is the basis of the plaintiffs' claim:

"TORONTO, APRIL 26, 1898

"*Dear Sir*—We wish to secure your patronage, and, as we have found the only proper way to get a customer is to save him money, we therefore are going to endeavor to save you money. * * *

"We quote you (* * * F.O.B.) your station, Hungarian $5.40, and strong Bakers $5.00, car lots only, and subject to sight draft with bill of lading.

"We would suggest your using the wire to order, as prices are so rapidly advancing that they may be beyond reach before a letter would reach us.

"Yours respectfully,
"ROGERS BROS."

This communication was received by the plaintiffs on the 27th of April. The plaintiffs telegraphed the defendants the same morning as follows:

"LONDON, APRIL 27, 1898

"To Rogers Bros., Confederation Life Building, Toronto.

"We will take two cars Hungarian at your offer of yesterday.

"JOHNSTON BROS."

The defendant refused to sell at the price named, and the plaintiff now sues for breach of the contract alleged by him to have arisen from this exchange of the above communications.

FALCONBRIDGE, J. * * * The real crux of the case is whether there is a contract.

I should expect to find American authority as to the phrase "we quote you," which must be in very common use amongst brokers, manufacturers, and dealers in the United States; but we were referred to no decided case, and I have found none where that phrase was used.

In the *American and English Encyclopedia of Law*, 2d ed., vol. 7, p. 138, the law is stated to be: "A quotation of prices is not an offer to sell, * * * It requires the acceptance by the one naming the price, of the order so made, to complete the transaction. Until thus completed there is no mutuality of obligation."

The meaning of "quote" is given in modern dictionaries as follows: * * *

> *Standard* (Com.)—To give the current or market price of, as bonds, stocks, commodities, etc.
>
> *Century* (Com.)—To name as the price of stocks, produce, etc.; name the current price of.
>
> *Webster* (Com.)—To name the current price of. * * *

There is little or no difference between any of these definitions. Now if we write the equivalent phrase into the letter—"We give you the current or market price, F.O.B. your station, of Hungarian Patent $5.40"—can it be for a moment contended that it is an offer which needs only an acceptance in terms to constitute a contract? * * *

I have not overlooked the concluding paragraph of the letter, viz., "We would suggest your using the wire to order, as prices are so rapidly advancing that they may be beyond reach before a letter would reach us." * * * I venture * * * to think that this suggestion is more consistent with a mere quotation of prices, which might vary from day to day or from hour to hour.

[Judgment for defendant.]

---

7. An Ad Generally Not an Offer

LOVETT v. FREDERICK LOESER & CO.

124 Misc.Rep. 81, 207 N.Y.S. 753 (1924).

SPIEGELBERG, J. The complaint alleges in substance that the defendant conducts a department store; that on September 19, 1924, it inserted an advertisement in one of the newspapers published in the city of New York to the effect that it would sell and deliver and install for any one who would purchase and pay for the same, certain "well-known standard makes of radio receivers at 25 per cent. to 50 per cent. reduction" from the advertised list prices thereof; that among the standard radio receiving sets thus advertised were those made by the makers of the "Radiola, Crosley, De Forest, Malone-Lemmon, Neutrodyne, Colon B. Kennedy, and Sleeper Monotrol" radio receiving sets. The complaint then sets forth in great detail that, among the De Forest radio receiving sets, there were types known as the "D–12 reflex radiophone receiving sets"; that on September 20, 1924, the plaintiff offered to buy two of said sets upon the terms and conditions named in the defendant's advertisement, but that the defendant repudiated its offer to sell; that thereupon on September 22, 1924, the plaintiff unconditionally accepted the defendant's said offer to sell to the plaintiff the two De Forest D–12 reflex radiophone receiving sets and tendered his certified check for the amount of the list price of said sets, less 25 per cent.

The complaint demands judgment for the damages suffered by the plaintiff by reason of the alleged breach of the defendant's contract to sell said sets.

The plaintiff's theory is that the offer of the defendant contained in the advertisement ripened into a contract by his acceptance thereof. Although the plaintiff in his complaint specifically and in great minuteness alleges that a contract of sale was made between the parties, his rights must be determined by the contents of the advertisement itself.

I am of opinion that the plaintiff sets forth no cause of action. The defendant's advertisement is nothing but an invitation to enter into negotiations, and is not an offer which may be turned into a contract by a person who signifies his intention to purchase some of the articles mentioned in the advertisement. In Georgian Company v. Bloom, 27 Ga.App. 468, 108 S.E. 813, the court says:

> "A general advertisement in a newspaper for the sale of an indefinite quantity of goods is a mere invitation to enter into a bargain, rather than an offer."

[Judgment for defendant.]

---

8. An Ad as an Offer

LEFKOWITZ v. GREAT MINNEAPOLIS SURPLUS STORE

251 Minn. 188, 86 N.W.2d 689 (1957).

This case grows out of the alleged refusal of the defendant to sell to the plaintiff a certain fur piece which it had offered for sale in a newspaper advertisement. It appears from the record that on April 6, 1956, the defendant published the following advertisement in a Minneapolis newspaper:

"Saturday 9 A.M. Sharp
3 Brand New
Fur
Coats
Worth to $100.00
First Come
First Served
$1
Each"

On April 13, the defendant again published an advertisement in the same newspaper as follows:

"Saturday 9 A.M.
2 Brand New Pastel
Mink 3-Skin Scarfs
Selling for $89.50
Out they go
Saturday. Each $1.00
1 Black Lapin Stole
Beautiful,
worth $139.50....$1.00
First Come
First Served"

The record supports the findings of the court that on each of the Saturdays following the publication of the above-described ads the plaintiff was the first to present himself at the appropriate counter in the defendant's store and on each occasion demanded the coat and the stole so advertised and indicated his readiness to pay the sale price of $1. On both occasions, the defendant refused to sell the merchandise to the plaintiff, stating on the first occasion that by a "house rule" the offer was intended for women only and sales would not be made to men, and on the second visit that plaintiff knew defendant's house rules.

The trial court properly disallowed plaintiff's claim for the value of the fur coats since the value of these articles was speculative and uncertain. The only evidence of value was the advertisement itself to the effect that the coats were "Worth to $100.00," how much less being speculative especially in view of the price for which they were offered for sale. With reference to the offer of the defendant on April 13, 1956, to sell the "1 Black Lapin Stole * * * worth $139.50 * * *" the trial court held that the value of this article was established and granted judgment in favor of the plaintiff for that amount less the $1 quoted purchase price.

The defendant contends that a newspaper advertisement offering items of merchandise for sale at a named price is a "unilateral offer" which may be withdrawn without notice. He relies upon authorities which hold that, where an advertiser publishes in a newspaper that he has a certain quantity or quality of goods which he wants to dispose of at certain prices and on certain terms, such advertisements are not offers which become contracts as soon as any person to whose notice they may come signifies his acceptance by notifying the other that he will take a certain quantity of them. Such advertisements have been construed as an invitation for an offer of sale on the terms stated, which offer, when received, may be accepted or rejected and which therefore does not become a contract of sale until accepted by the seller; and until a contract has been so made, the seller may modify or revoke such prices or terms.

On the facts before us we are concerned with whether the advertisement constituted an offer, and, if so, whether the plaintiff's conduct constituted an acceptance.

There are numerous authorities which hold that a particular advertisement in a newspaper or circular letter relating to a sale of articles may be construed by the court as constituting an offer, acceptance of which would complete a contract. [Citations]

The authorities above cited emphasize that, where the offer is clear, definite, and explicit, and leaves nothing open for negotiation, it constitutes an offer, acceptance of which will complete the contract. The most recent case on the subject is Johnson v. Capital City Ford Co., La.App., 85 So.2d 75, in which the court pointed out that a newspaper advertisement relating to the purchase and sale of automobiles may constitute an offer, acceptance of which will consummate a contract and create an obligation in the offeror to perform according to the terms of the published offer.

Whether in any individual instance a newspaper advertisement is an offer rather than an invitation to make an offer depends on the legal intention of the parties and the surrounding circumstances. We are of the view on the facts before us that the offer by the defendant of the sale of the Lapin fur was clear, definite, and explicit, and left nothing open for negotiation. The plaintiff having successfully managed to be the first one to appear at the seller's place of business to be served, as requested by the advertisement, and having offered the stated purchase price of the article, he was entitled to performance on the part of the defendant. We think the trial court was correct in holding that there was in the conduct of the parties a sufficient mutuality of obligation to constitute a contract of sale.

The defendant contends that the offer was modified by a "house rule" to the effect that only women were qualified to receive the bargains advertised. The advertisement contained no such restriction. This objection may be disposed of briefly by stating that, while an advertiser has the right at any time before acceptance to modify his offer, he does not have the right, after acceptance, to impose new or arbitrary conditions not contained in the published offer. [Citations]

Affirmed [for plaintiff.]

---

9. *A Bid as an Offer*

BERKELEY UNIFIED SCHOOL DIST. OF ALAMEDA COUNTY v. JAMES I. BARNES CONST. CO.

112 F.Supp. 396 (D.C.Cal., 1953).

OLIVER J. CARTER, District Judge. This is an action for breach of contract [for failure to construct certain school buildings]. Plaintiff is the Berkeley Unified School District, a public corporation authorized by, and organized under, laws of the State of California. Defendants are the James I. Barnes Construction Company, a copartnership hereinafter referred to as "defendant contractor," * * * Defendants now move to dismiss the "first cause of action" alleged in the complaint upon the ground that it fails to state a cause for which relief can be granted. * * *

It is contended that the allegations of the complaint fail to establish the existence of a contract. As to the existence of a contract, the complaint indicates as follows:

Plaintiff, by advertisement in a newspaper, invited the submission of bids for the construction of two public school buildings in the city of Berkeley, California. * * *

Defendant contractor submitted a bid, offering to construct the school buildings for the sum of $1,377,700. The bid was in accordance with the requirements set out in the advertisement for bids * * * The bid itself was a mimeographed form, which had been prepared by plaintiff, containing blanks to be filled in by the bidder. * * *

Thereafter, plaintiff opened all sealed bids which had been submitted, determined that the bid of defendant contractor was the lowest responsible bid, and passed a resolution accepting such bid and awarding the contract to this defendant. Plaintiff then notified the defendant construction company that it had been awarded the contract and tendered, for execution, a formal contract embodying all the terms specified in the advertisement for bids and the bid submitted by this defendant.

The defendant construction company refused to execute the tendered contract * * * The general rule is that where a public body advertises for bids, a good and binding contract is formed when the public body, acting by responsible officers, accepts a written bid of a bidder.

* * * Defendant contractor contends that it was not within the contemplation of the parties that a contract should be formed until the execution of the formal document referred to in the advertisement for bids and the bid itself. It is true that parties to an agreement may make its reduction to a formal writing and the execution of such writing a condition precedent to its effectiveness notwithstanding complete agreement to all its terms.

* * * However, the general rule is that though the parties contemplate the ultimate execution of a more formal writing, the acceptance of a bid or offer results in a binding contract when none of the material terms remain unsettled or require future determination. * * *

Since defendant contractor's bid constituted an irrevocable offer to the school district, all that was required to form a contract was a valid acceptance. The governing board of the school district determined that defendant contractor had submitted the lowest responsible bid and accepted that bid by a resolution. * * * [T]hat resolution, when communicated to defendant contractor, was effective to accept the bid and to form a contract.

For the reasons heretofore stated, the motion to dismiss the "first cause of action" of plaintiff's complaint should be denied. [Judgment for plaintiff].

---

10. *Termination of Offer by Stopping Payment on Check*

DOERFLINGER REALTY CO. v. MASERANG

311 S.W.2d 123 (Mo.App.1958).

[This is an action by sellers of certain real estate to recover from buyers (Respondents) for a forfeiture under terms of a contract which was subject to buyers' ability to procure a cash loan first deed of trust as per application with sellers' real estate agents, Doerflinger Realty Company.

Within a few days after the date of the contract, Doerflinger Realty Company informed buyers it could not procure the loan applied for but could obtain a loan only at a higher rate of interest. The buyers refused the higher rate of interest loan and stopped payment on an earnest money deposit check held by Doerflinger.

Three weeks later Doerflinger notified buyers that a loan as per their application was available; however, buyers refused to proceed with the purchase.]

In the instant case the uncertainty of respondents' ability to obtain the loan in accordance with their application then on file with Doerflinger was fully considered and expressly provided for in the purchase contract. In other words, it was, in effect, a stipulated condition precedent in their agreement that unless and until the buyers were able to get the loan on the terms of the application then on file with Doerflinger, there would be no further liability under the sale contract on the buyers' part whatsoever. Nothing could be plainer than the words mutually adopted in writing: "Undersigned purchasers make this offer subject to their ability to procure a cash loan first deed of trust against the above described property as per application for same now on file with Doerflinger Realty Company." Clearly the effect of such a provision is that if and when the loan application referred to was declined and rejected respondents' liability under the sale contract ceased, in the absence of any modification of the application or sale contract. * * *

* * * Within a few days after the date of the contract and the loan application, * * * the Doerflinger Realty Company informed respondents that it could not procure for them the loan applied for and could only obtain the loan at a higher rate of interest.

If such evidence be true, respondents then had a right either to modify their offer and agree to accept the loan at a higher rate of interest, or to terminate the application. Nothing in the sale contract required them to seek a loan elsewhere or under different terms or under a different application. Having refused to accept the more expensive loan and having been denied the loan applied for, if the evidence to that effect be true, respondents, under the terms of the sale contract, were not further liable and rightfully stopped payment on their earnest deposit check held by the sellers' agent.

It was said by Grismore on Contracts, page 55, Section 35: "A rejection of the offer by the offeree has the effect of terminating it. The reason for this is plain. When the offeror receives a rejection he naturally assumes that the offeree is no longer interested in his proposal. Consequently he would not consider it to be necessary to revoke the offer were he to change his mind in regard to it."

The fact that over three weeks after respondents terminated their loan application upon its rejection by Doerflinger, * * * and after they had cancelled their deposit check on the sales contract, Doerflinger (also the agent for the sellers in the contract) notified respondents that a loan as per their application was then available, and demanded a closing of the loan and purchase, would not, in the absence of some showing of mutual consent, thereby cause the loan application then to be revived and the sales contract to be restored.

Grismore, at the same citation, supra, further states: "It would not be just to permit the offeree to complete a contract by an acceptance after he had put the offeror off his guard by leading him to think that his proposal was no longer being considered." In view of the evidence and the law applicable thereto the court did not err in refusing to direct a verdict for appellants.

[Judgment for buyers affirmed.]

---

11. Termination by Lapse of a Specified Time

ACKERMAN v. MADDUX

26 N.D. 50, 143 N.W. 147 (1913).

This is an action to enforce an alleged contract for the sale of land. Plaintiff's offer is contained in the following letter:

"WILLISTON, N. D., SEPT. 5, 1910

"Mr. C. J. Maddux,

"New Rockford, N. Dak.

"*Dear Friend, Mr. Maddux:*

"I want to sell them lots that you sold me. I am mightly hard up for money and if I could sell them back to you I would do so at a great discount. * * * I will sell the four you sold me to you only for half price, $300.00. * * * If I could sell them * * * it would put me in better shape for next year.

"Let me know by return mail.

"Yours very truly,
"FRED ACKERMAN."

This letter was received by the defendant Maddux on September 6th or 7th. It was not until September 9th that he wrote a letter accepting plaintiff's offer. Plaintiff now seeks to hold defendant to the alleged contract. Defendant, however, no longer wishes to buy the land in question; and he now contends that his acceptance was not mailed "by return mail" as plaintiff's offer demanded, and therefore that no valid contract ever came into existence.

BRUCE, J. * * * All we find, indeed, is an offer to sell which was not accepted according to its terms. * * * It will be noticed that by its terms the offer demanded an acceptance by return mail, and there is no pretense that such was forthcoming. There was therefore no acceptance, and the offer is eliminated in law from the record and is as if it had never been made. That this is the settled law there can, we believe, be no controversy. * * * "When an individual makes an offer by post stipulating for or by the nature of the business having the right to expect an answer by return of post, the offer can only endure for a limited time, and the making of it is accompanied by an implied stipulation that the answer shall be sent by return post. If that implied stipulation is not satisfied, the person making the offer is released from it. It is clear here that the nature of the business demanded a prompt answer and the words, 'You will confer a favor by giving me your answer by return mail,' do in effect stipulate for an answer by return mail." * * *

[Judgment for defendant.]

---

12. Termination of Offer by Lapse of Reasonable Time

AKERS v. J. B. SEDBERRY

39 Tenn.App. 633, 286 S.W.2d 617 (1955).

FELTS, Judge. These two consolidated causes are before us * * to review a decree of the Chancery Court, awarding a recovery [against defds] in favor of each of the complainants, Charles William Akers and William Gambill Whitsitt, for damages for breach of a contract of employment.

* * *

The principal question presented is whether complainants resigned their employment, or were wrongfully discharged by defendants; * * *

Under Mrs. Sedberry's instructions, Akers and Whitsitt moved to Tyler, Texas, began performing their contract duties in the plant of the Jay Bee Manufacturing Company, continued working there, and were paid under the contracts until October 1, 1950, when they ceased work, Akers and Whitsitt flew to Nashville and went to Franklin to talk with Mrs. Sedberry about them. They had a conference with her at her office on Friday, September 29, 1950, lasting from 9:30 a.m. until 4:30 p.m. As they had come unannounced * * * they felt Mrs. Sedberry might mistrust them; and at the outset, to show their good faith, they offered to resign, but she did not accept their offer. Instead, she proceeded with them in discussing the operation and refinancing of the business. * * *

On Monday, October 2, 1950, Mrs. Sedberry sent to complainants similar telegrams, signed by "J. B. Sedberry, Inc., by M. B. Sedberry, President", stating that their resignations were accepted, effective immediately. * * *

An employee's tender of his resignation, being a mere offer is, of course, not binding until it has been accepted by the employer. Such offer must be accepted according to its terms and within the time fixed. The matter is governed by the same rules as govern the formation of contracts.

* * * An offer may be terminated in a number of ways, as, for example, where it is rejected by the offeree, or where it is not accepted by him within the time fixed, or, if no time is fixed, within a reasonable time. An offer terminated in either of these ways ceases to exist and cannot thereafter be accepted.

* * * The question what is a reasonable time, where no time is fixed, is a question of fact, depending on the nature of the contract proposed, the usages of business and other circumstances of the case. Ordinarily, an offer made by one to another in a face to face conversation is deemed to continue only to the close of their conversation, and cannot be accepted thereafter. * * *

Professor Corbin says:

> "When two negotiating parties are in each other's presence, and one makes an offer to the other without indicating any time for acceptance, the inference that will ordinarily be drawn by the other party is that an answer is expected at once. * * * If, when the first reply is not an acceptance, the offeror turns away in silence, the proper inference is that the offer is no longer open to acceptance." * * *

The only offer by Akers and Whitsitt to resign was the offer made by them in their conversation with Mrs. Sedberry. They made that offer at the outset, and on the evidence it seems clear that they expected an answer at once. Certainly, there is nothing in the evidence to show that they intended the offer to continue beyond that conversation; and on the above authorities, we think the offer did not continue beyond that meeting. * * *

So, we agree with the Trial Judge that when defendants sent the telegrams, undertaking to accept offers of complainants to resign, there was no such offer in existence; and that this attempt of defendants to terminate their contract was unlawful and constituted a breach for which they are liable to complainants.

[Judgment for plaintiffs].

---

13. Must Know of Offer

BROADNAX v. LEDBETTER

100 Tex. 375, 99 S.W. 1111 (1907).

Ledbetter, the sheriff of Dallas County, offered a reward of $500 for the capture and return of a certain convict who had escaped from custody. About a month after the publication of notice of this offer of reward, plaintiff discovered the fugitive and returned him to the Dallas County jail. It was proved, however, that this capture on the part of the plaintiff was not caused by the making of the offer; plaintiff had in fact not known of the existence of the offer until after he had returned the fugitive to the jail. The defendant, therefore, refused to pay the reward; and the plaintiff brought the present action to recover it. Defendant contends that there was no contract here.

WILLIAMS, J. * * * The liability for a reward of this kind must be created, if at all, by contract. There is no rule of law which imposes it except that which enforces contracts voluntarily entered into. A mere offer or promise to pay does not give rise to a contract. That requires the assent or meeting of two minds, and therefore is not complete until the offer is accepted. Such an offer as that alleged may be accepted by anyone who performs the service called for, when the acceptor knows that it has been made, and acts in performance of it, but not otherwise. He may do such things as are specified in the offer; but, in so doing, does not act in performance of it and therefore does not accept it, when he is ignorant of its having been made. * * *

Some of the authorities taking the opposite view seem to think that the principle of contracts does not control the question; and in one of them, at least, it is said that "the sum offered is but a boon, gratuity, or bounty, generally offered in a spirit of liberality * * simply for the favor or service requested * * * without regard to the motive or inducement which prompted * * * it."

But the law does not force persons to bestow boons, gratuities, or bounties merely because they have promised to do so. They must be legally bound before that can be done. * * *

Reasons have also been put forward of a supposed public policy, assuming that persons will be stimulated by the enforcement of offers of rewards in such cases to aid in the detection of crime and the arrest and punishment of criminals. But * * * it is difficult to see how the activities of people can be excited by offers of rewards of which they know nothing. If this reason had foundation in fact, it would hardly justify the courts in requiring private citizens to minister to the supposed public policy by paying rewards, merely because they have made offers to pay upon which no one has acted. Courts can only enforce liabilities which have in some way been fixed by the law. While we have seen no such distinction suggested, * * * a person might become legally entitled to a reward for arresting a criminal, although he knew nothing of its having been made, where it was offered in accordance with law by the government. A legal right might in such a case be given by law without the aid of contract. But the liability of the individual citizen must arise from a contract binding him to pay.

[Judgment for defendant.]

---

14. Silence Ordinarily Not Acceptance

PRESCOTT v. JONES

69 N.H. 305, 41 A. 352 (1898).

Defendants, who had insured plaintiff's buildings for the year 1896, wrote plaintiff an offer to furnish like insurance for the year 1897. In this communication defendants stated that if plaintiff did not notify them to the contrary they would regard him as having accepted their offer. Plaintiff, accordingly, sent no word to defendants, but assumed that the insurance had become effective. A few weeks later the buildings were destroyed by fire, but defendants refused to reimburse plaintiff for his loss. When plaintiff brought the present action, defendants contended that plaintiff had never accepted their offer, and therefore that no new contract of insurance came into existence.

BLODGETT, J. * * * An offer will not mature into a complete and effectual contract until it is acceded to by the party to whom it is made, and notice thereof, either actual or constructive, given to the maker. * * * It is well settled that "a party cannot, by the wording of his offer, turn the absence of communication of acceptance into an acceptance, and compel the recipient of his offer to refuse it at the peril of being held to have accepted it." * * * "A person is under no obligation to do or say anything concerning a proposition which he does not choose to accept. There must be actual acceptance or there is no contract." * * * And to constitute acceptance, "there must be words, written or spoken, or some other overt act." * * *

If, therefore, the defendants might and did make their offer in such a way as to dispense with the communication of its acceptance to them in a formal and direct manner, they did not and could not so frame it as to render the plaintiff liable as having accepted it merely because he did not communicate his intention not to accept it. And if the plaintiff was not bound by the offer until he accepted it, the defendants could not be, because * * * both parties are bound or neither is bound.

* * * All the plaintiff did was merely to determine in his own mind that he would accept the offer—for there was nothing whatever to indicate it by way of speech or other appropriate act. Plainly, this did not create any rights in his favor as against the defendants. From the very nature of a contract this must be so; and it therefore seems superfluous to add that the universal doctrine is that an uncommunicated mental determination cannot create a binding contract.

[Judgment for defendant].

---

15. Communication of Acceptance Required

DUNN v. SHANE

195 A.2d 409 (D.C.App., 1963).

HOOD, Chief Judge. This action was brought by a real estate broker to recover compensation for his services in allegedly obtaining a contract of sale between Mrs. Shane as seller and Mr. Sherwin as buyer. * * * The trial court denied recovery because it found there was no valid contract of sale. On this appeal the broker's entire argument is premised on the existence of a valid contract and our consideration will be confined to whether the trial court was in error in finding that no contract came into existence.

Mrs. Shane engaged the broker to sell her house for $59,500. He presented to her a proposed contract to sell to Mr. Sherwin for $50,000 all cash. She agreed to the terms and signed the paper which the broker took to Mr. Sherwin for his signature. Mr. Sherwin signed, but placed above his signature a statement that his signing was conditioned on obtaining a first trust loan of $35,000 on certain specified terms. The broker called Mrs. Shane and told her of Sherwin's conditional acceptance. In response to her inquiry he said it was not necessary for her to initial the changes made by Sherwin. * * *

Although the facts are somewhat complicated, the applicable principles of law are clear. When the proposed contract, signed by Mrs. Shane, was presented to Mr. Sherwin, it constituted an offer. When Mr. Sherwin, before signing, added a condition, he did not accept the offer but instead made a counteroffer. Until Mrs. Shane accepted the counteroffer there was no contract. Although the counteroffer was apparently acceptable to Mrs. Shane, for some reason the broker refrained from having her formally accept it until after Sherwin's oral notice of withdrawal. Then in an apparent effort to get a formal acceptance before receipt of written notice of withdrawal, the broker obtained Mrs. Shane's initials to the counteroffer.

This occurred more than two weeks after the counteroffer had been made. * * *

Assuming, but not deciding, that Sherwin's oral notice of withdrawal was ineffective, the question is whether the initialing of the changes by Mrs. Shane a few hours before receipt of the written notice of withdrawal prevented the withdrawal from becoming effective. * * * The acceptance by Mrs. Shane occurred earlier on the same day the letter of revocation was received, but her acceptance was not communicated to Sherwin until long after the letter of revocation had been received. It is our opinion that the uncommunicated acceptance did not prevent the revocation from becoming effective. The rule appears to be that, in cases like this, an acceptance is not effective until communicated to the offeree. The rule * * * is that where the offeror has specified no mode of acceptance but "the offer is of such a kind that the offeror needs to know of the acceptance in order to determine his subsequent action, and the offeree has reason to know this, a notice of acceptance must be given."

Here the offeror, Sherwin, obviously needed to know of the acceptance in order that he could proceed with assurance in his attempt to obtain a definite commitment for the required loan and it is obvious that the broker, Mrs. Shane's agent, knew this. When after a period of two weeks' waiting he had no notice of acceptance of his offer he was free to revoke it and he did so before receiving notice of acceptance. The result is that no valid agreement for sale ever came into existence and the broker's claim must fail.

Affirmed [for defendant].

---

16. Acceptance Must be Unequivocal

HEDDEN v. LUPINSKY

405 Pa. 609, 176 A.2d 406 (1962).

COHEN, Justice. In June, 1959, plaintiffs' office received a telephone call from someone purporting to act on behalf of the defendant, Lupinsky, offering to do the ceramic tile work on a proposed addition to the Wilkes-Barre General Hospital, on which plaintiffs, as general contractors, planned to bid. Plaintiffs used defendant's bid in computing their own bid for the general contract which was awarded to them the following month. In August, plaintiffs sent defendant a contract which defendant was expected to sign along with certain bond forms and a copy of the specifications. * * *

The sub-contract, which plaintiffs sent to defendant, differs in several particulars from the General Conditions and General Requirements contained in the specifications; * * *

When Lupinsky refused to sign the contract and perform the tile work in accordance with his bid, plaintiffs sued him for $6,517.00, which represents the difference between defendant's bid and the next lowest bid, plus interest. The trial court granted defendant's motion for a compulsory non-suit. * * * It would have been most helpful in deciding this appeal had the record indicated the trade custom in the building industry in Luzerne County regarding the effect given by contractors to oral bids received from sub-contractors and what actions are regarded as necessary to establish a contractual relationship. Since this information is lacking, the sole question before us is whether the provisions of the sub-contract which plaintiffs sent to defendant in response to his bid, so deviated from the General Conditions and Requirements contained in the specifications as to constitute a counter-offer rather than an acceptance of defendant's bid. * * * In our opinion, the foregoing variances constitute a counter-offer. This court has long adhered to the position * * * "a reply to an offer, though purporting to accept it, which adds qualifications or requires performance of conditions, is not an acceptance but is a counter-offer." To constitute a contract, the acceptance of the offer must be absolute and identical with the terms of the offer. * * * Assuming, as we must, that Lupinsky phoned a proposal to plaintiffs, his bid constituted an offer to perform the job for a specified amount in accordance with the specific provisions of the General Conditions and Requirements contained in the specifications. When plaintiffs sent the sub-contract to defendant with terms in variance with those in the specifications, they were actually submitting a counter-offer for his acceptance. Lupinsky chose not to accept and, consequently, no contract resulted. * * *

Judgment affirmed [for defendant].

---

17. Acceptance by Act—Unilateral Contracts

CARLILL v. CARBOLIC SMOKE BALL CO.

Law Reports, 1 Q.B.Div. 256 (1893).

The defendants, dealers in a device for the cure of influenza known as "The Carbolic Smoke Ball," to induce the sale of their remedy, offered to pay £100 to any person who contracted influenza after having used the smoke ball for two weeks in a specified manner. Mrs. Carlill, the plaintiff, on the faith of the advertisement containing this offer, bought one of these smoke balls. Although she used it as recommended three times a day for the prescribed period, she nevertheless contracted influenza. Defendants, however, refused to pay the offered reward; and Mrs. Carlill brought the present action to recover. Defendants' contention is that there is no contract with Mrs. Carlill.

LINDLEY, Lord Justice. * * * Read the advertisement how you will, and twist it about as you will, here is a distinct promise expressed in language which is perfectly unmistakable—"100 pounds reward will be paid by the Carbolic Smoke Ball Company to any person who contracts the influenza after having used the ball three times daily for two weeks according to the printed directions supplied with each ball." * * * There is the promise, as plain as words can make it.

Then it is contended that it is not binding. In the first place it is said that it is not made with anybody in particular. Now that point is common to the words of this advertisement and to the words of all other advertisements offering rewards. They are offers to anybody who performs the conditions named in the advertisement, and anybody who does perform the conditions accepts the offer. In point of law this advertisement is an offer to pay £100 to anybody who will perform these conditions, and the performance of the conditions is the acceptance of the offer. * * *

But then it is said, "Supposing that the performance of the conditions is an acceptance of the offer, that acceptance ought to have been notified". Unquestionably, as a general proposition when an offer is made, it is necessary in order to make a binding contract, not only that it should be accepted, but that the acceptance should be notified. * * * I, however, think that the true view, in a case of this kind, is that the person who makes the offer shows by his language and from the nature of the transaction that he does not expect and does not require notice of the acceptance apart from notice of the performance.

[In a unilateral contract, it is ordinarily not necessary for the offeree to notify the offeror of his acceptance.]

[Judgment for plaintiff].

---

18. Acceptance by Telegram

PICKETT v. MILLER

76 N.M. 105, 412 P.2d 400 (1966).

MOISE, Justice. Defendants appeal from a judgment which granted plaintiffs specific performance or, in the alternative, damages for breach of a contract to purchase a house and lot located in Albuquerque. Plaintiffs, Harry D. Pickett and Elizabeth R. Pickett, are husband and wife and own the property in question. Plaintiff, George A. Kloepfer, d/b/a Kloepfer Realty Co., is their real estate agent who acted in their behalf in most matters concerning the sale or rental of the property. Defendants are husband and wife and allegedly agreed to purchase the property. * * *

On October 31, 1963, defendants, through a real estate broker representing them, submitted to plaintiff real estate broker a "form" offer to purchase the property in question. * * *

Immediately upon receipt of the offer, plaintiff Kloepfer phoned the Picketts in Doylestown, Pa., where they lived, and informed them of the substance of the offer. On November 1, 1963, the following telegram was sent to Kloepfer:

> "MRS PICKETT AND I ACCEPT OFFER TO PURCHASE 1001 WALKER BY J D MILLER AT FULL PURCHASE PRICE OF $12,409 SUBJECT TO EXISTING LEASE IF LEASEE (sic) WILL RELEASE ADDITIONAL YEARS OPTION AFTER EIGHT MONTHS TENENT/SEE (sic) OR SOONER."

The communication showed the sender to be "HARRY D. PICKETT."

Kloepfer immediately notified defendants' broker of the contents of the telegraphic message. Defendants' real estate agent then prevailed upon Kloepfer to attempt to do something about the existing lease on the premises so that defendants might assume immediate occupancy. This was accomplished and the tenants vacated the premises within ten to fifteen days after the request was made. * * *

Defendants were twice notified after November 11, 1963, that the documents necessary to close the sale were ready for signing. They refused to complete the purchase and plaintiffs instigated this action.

Defendants maintain that the specified mode of acceptance was the completion of the "Purchase Agreement" by placing the names of the sellers in the blanks designated therefor, and that the attempted acceptance by wire was not a compliance with the terms of the offer. It is recognized that where an offer prescribes a manner of acceptance, that manner must be complied with in order to create a valid contract. On the other hand, if the offer only suggests a manner of acceptance, other reasonable modes of acceptance are not precluded. * * * The "Purchase Agreement" provides that the buyers' broker has three days "to complete the purchase agreement," and that if the broker is unable to complete the agreement, the offer is cancelled. In this, the transaction differs from the usual offer where the reference in the "Purchase Agreement" is to the seller's broker. Under the circumstances, we do not see in the language used a requirement that acceptance by the sellers could only be accomplished through the affixing of their signatures at the place provided therefor at the bottom of the "Purchase Agreement." When the sellers are at a considerable distance, and three days are given to complete the agreement, there are reasonable means of acceptance other than the placing of the sellers' signatures on lines in a document which is in Albuquerque, New Mexico, and there is no indication that such reasonable means of acceptance were here prohibited.

* * * A written offer does not necessarily require the signature of offeree in order to form a complete agreement. * * * Under the circumstances here present, including the distance between the parties and the limited time allowed for acceptance, it cannot be said that the use of the telegraph to manifest acceptance was not reasonable.

The judgment of the trial court is affirmed [for plaintiff.]

19. *Acceptance by Home Office*

HILL'S INC. v. WILLIAM B. KESSLER, INC.

41 Wash.2d 42, 246 P.2d 1099 (1952).

MALLERY, Justice. The plaintiff, Hill's, Inc., ordered thirty-four men's suits from the defendant, using a printed form supplied by defendant through its salesman.

The printed form provided that the order would not become a binding contract until it had been accepted by an authorized officer of the defendant at its office in Hammonton, New Jersey.

The defendant's salesman procured the order on May 16, 1950, and on May 23, 1950, the defendant, by form letter, advised the plaintiff that "You may be assured of our very best attention to this order." What occurred next is shown by the trial court's finding of fact:

> " * * * but notwithstanding, on or about July 18, 1950, defendant intentionally and deliberately, at the instigation of a large retail store selling defendant's clothing in the downtown Seattle area, wrongfully cancelled said order and breached its agreement with plaintiff to deliver said suits as ordered, or at all. That at the time defendant cancelled said order and breached its agreement, the period for placing orders for delivery of fall suits had passed, and it was impossible for plaintiff to thereafter procure comparable suits from any other source to meet its fall trade. * * * "

Thereupon, plaintiff brought this action for loss of profits in the amount of a 66⅔ per cent markup aggregating $815.83.

From a judgment in favor of the plaintiff, the defendant appeals.

The defendant contends that its letter of May 23, 1950, in which it said "You may be assured of our very best attention to this order," was not an acceptance of the plaintiff's order.

In Bauman v. McManus, 75 Kan. 106, 89 P. 15, 18, 10 L.R.A., N.S., 1138, the court said:

> " * * * The promise that the order shall receive prompt and *careful* attention seems to imply something more than that the manufacturers will quickly and cautiously investigate the advisability of accepting it. The care they might expend in that direction—in looking up the defendants' financial standing, for instance—is not presumably a matter in which any one but themselves would be greatly interested. The engagement to use care seems more naturally to relate to the manner of filling the order than to the settling of a doubt whether to fill it at all. The expression of thanks for the favor has some tendency in the same

direction. We incline strongly to the opinion that the letter standing by itself was as effectual to close a contract as though in set phrase it had said that the goods would be shipped; that to permit any other construction to be placed upon it would be to countenance the studied use of equivocal expressions, with a set purpose, if an advantage may thereby be derived, to keep the word of promise to the ear and break it to the hope."

Notwithstanding that the Bauman case is exactly in point, it is not necessary to rely upon it exclusively, for the reason that the intention of the defendant to accept the offer is shown by subsequent correspondence with the plaintiff in this case.

On July 18, 1950, defendant wrote plaintiff the following letter:

"This is to inform you we find it will be impossible to ship the Fall order which you placed with Mr. Jacobus on May 16, order #8585. We dislike very much having to inform you of this, but we trust that you will understand when we say that because of previous commitments to other stores in town it is necessary to *cancel* this order.

"We are certainly sincerely sorry if this action on our part inconveniences you at all." (Italics ours.)

This letter recognizes the existence of a contract, which it undertakes to cancel.

The judgment is affirmed.

---

20. Acceptance by Insurance Company

TURNER v. WORTH INSURANCE COMPANY

11 Ariz.App. 403, 464 P.2d 990 (1970).

HATHAWAY, Judge. This appeal arises from a declaratory judgment action initiated by Worth Insurance Company against defendants Jensen, Turner, Wilson and Farmers Insurance Group. The main issue presented to the court was whether defendant Wilson had secured automobile liability insurance from Worth on August 17, 1964, which would cover an accident Wilson was involved in on August 23, 1964.

The court on January 24, 1966, concluded that the defendant Wilson "did not secure any automobile liability insurance on August 17, 1964 from the plaintiff Worth Insurance Company which would cover, apply to or protect him in the matter of the accident on August 23, 1964." From this judgment defendants Turner and Jensen appeal.

We shall first consider the contentions made by appellant Turner, who raises three questions: (1) Was there a written binder of insurance between Worth and Wilson? (2) Was there an oral binder of insurance between Worth and Wilson? and (3) Is Worth estopped to deny coverage by reason of its agent's acts, and its retention of the premium paid by Wilson?

Wilson went to Likens Insurance Agency on August 17, 1964 to secure automobile insurance so he would be allowed to drive his car on Davis Monthan Air Force Base. Mrs. Likens is a representative of Worth Insurance in Tucson as well as a representative for six to ten other insurance companies. An application for insurance was filled out and Wilson was given a receipt which allowed him to get a permit to drive on the Air Force base. In turn he paid a premium of $30.80 to Mrs. Liken.

On August 25, 1964, Mrs. Liken wrote to Wilson saying a higher premium rate would have to be paid by him, and for him "to let us know if the policy should be issued." Not receiving any response from Mr. Wilson, on September 18, 1964, Mrs. Liken wrote to him that "* * * your application for insurance coverage with Worth Insurance Co. has been rejected, and we return herewith your deposit * * *." This check was refused by Wilson.

A.R.S. § 20–1120 states in part:

> "A. Binders or other contracts for temporary insurance may be made orally or in writing, and shall be deemed to include all the usual terms of the policy as to which the binder was given together with such applicable endorsements as are designated in the binder, except as superseded by the clear and express terms of the binder."

We conclude that a written binder of insurance was not issued to Mr. Wilson. Although Mr. Wilson states he did not read the application, a one page uncomplicated form, that application is entitled in large print "Special Risk Application for Automobile Insurance." Right below Mr. Wilson's signature the following appears in bold type: "No coverage is in effect until a binder in writing on a policy is issued by a policy writing office of International Service Group."

The evidence shows that Worth never accepted Wilson's application for insurance.

While Mr. Wilson received a written receipt from Mrs. Liken, this appears to be for the $30.80 advance payment made by Wilson in applying for the insurance and not an insurance contract itself. And even though an application for insurance is accompanied by payment of premium a contract of insurance is not consummated until the acceptance by the company, 43 Am.Jur.2d Insurance § 210, particularly where the express provisions of the application so state.

Mr. Wilson testified that he told Mrs. Liken he needed insurance coverage immediately to drive on the Air Force base, and that Mrs. Liken told him he was insured as of that date. Mrs. Liken testified that she did not bind Mr. Wilson orally or by written agreement, and although it was her intent that he be covered as of August 17, 1964, such coverage was conditional upon the company accepting his application. Mrs. Liken also denied telling Mr. Wilson on August 17, 1964 that he was insured at that time.

As in other contracts, an insurance contract must contain the requisite contractual elements. * * * One of these requisites is that there be a meeting of the minds. * * *

Mutual assent is based on objective evidence and does not depend upon the undisclosed intentions of the parties. * * * To protect one's reasonable expectances in reliance on a contract it is imperative that a contracting party be able to rely upon the apparent intentions of the other party, without concern as to his secret thoughts or mental reservations. * * * However, "there must be a distinct intention common to both and without doubt or difference and until all understand alike there can be no assent." * * * In this case each party had a different understanding of the contract, and thus there was no mutual assent.

[Judgment affirmed.]

---

21. The Problem of Conflicting Commercial Forms

APPLICATION OF DOUGHBOY INDUSTRIES, INC.

17 A.D.2d 216, 233 N.Y.S.2d 488 (1962).

Proceeding on a motion to stay arbitration proceedings.

BREITEL, Justice. This case involves a conflict between a buyer's order form and a seller's acknowledgment form, each memorializing a purchase and sale of goods. The issue arises on whether the parties agreed to arbitrate future disputes. The seller's form had a general arbitration provision. The buyer's form did not. The buyer's form contained a provision that only a signed consent would bind the buyer to any terms thereafter transmitted in any commercial form of the seller. The seller's form, however, provided that silence or a failure to object in writing would be an acceptance of the terms and conditions of its acknowledgment form. The buyer never objected to the seller's acknowledgment, orally or in writing. In short, the buyer and seller accomplished a legal equivalent to the irresistible force colliding with the immovable object.

* * *

Of interest in the case is that both the seller and buyer are substantial businesses—a "strong" buyer and a "strong" seller. This is not a case of one of the parties being at the bargaining mercy of the other.

Important case

The facts are:

During the three months before the sale in question the parties had done business on two occasions. On these prior occasions the buyer used its purchase order form with its insulating conditions, and the seller used its acknowledgment form with its self-actuating conditions. Each ignored the other's printed forms, but proceeded with the commercial business at hand.

The instant transaction began with the buyer, on May 6, 1960, mailing from its office in Wisconsin to the seller in New York City two purchase orders for plastic film. Each purchase order provided that some 20,000 pounds of film were to be delivered in the future on specified dates. In addition, further quantities were ordered on a "hold basis", that is, subject to "increase, decrease, or cancellation" by the buyer. On May 13, 1960 the seller orally accepted both purchase orders without change except to suggest immediate shipment of the first part of the order. The buyer agreed to the request, and that day the seller shipped some 10,000 pounds of film in partial fulfillment of one purchase order. On May 16, 1960, the buyer received the seller's first acknowledgment dated May 13, 1960, and on May 19, 1960 the seller's second acknowledgment dated May 16, 1960. Although the purchase orders called for written acceptances and return of attached acknowledgments by the seller no one paid any attention to these requirements. Neither party, orally or in writing, objected to the conditions printed on the other's commercial form. Later, the buyer sent change orders with respect to so much of the orders as had been, according to the buyer, on a "hold basis".

The dispute, which has arisen and which the parties wish determined, the seller by arbitration, and the buyer by court litigation, is whether the buyer is bound to accept all the goods ordered on a "hold basis". The arbitration would take place in New York City. The litigation might have to be brought in Wisconsin, the buyer's home state.

The buyer's purchase order form had on its face the usual legends and blanks for the ordering of goods. On the reverse was printed a pageful of terms and conditions. The grand defensive clause reads as follows:

> "ALTERATION OF TERMS—None of the terms and conditions contained in this Purchase Order may be added to, modified, superseded or otherwise altered except by a written instrument signed by an authorized representative of Buyer and delivered by Buyer to Seller, and each shipment received by Buyer from Seller shall be deemed to be only upon the terms and conditions contained in this Purchase Order except as they may be added to, modified, superseded or otherwise altered, notwithstanding any terms and conditions that may be contained in any acknowledgment, invoice or other form of Seller and notwithstanding

Buyer's act of accepting or paying for any shipment or similar act of Buyer."

The buyer's language is direct; it makes clear that no variant seller's acknowledgment is to be binding. But the seller's acknowledgment form is drafted equally carefully. On its front in red typography one's attention is directed to the terms and conditions on the reverse side; and it advises the buyer that he, the buyer, has full knowledge of the conditions and agrees to them unless within 10 days he objects in writing.

The seller's clause reads:

"IMPORTANT

"Buyer agrees he has full knowledge of conditions printed on the reverse side hereof; and that the same are part of the agreement between buyer and seller and shall be binding if either the goods referred to herein are delivered to and accepted by buyer, or if buyer does not within ten days from date hereof deliver to seller written objection to said conditions or any part thereof."

On the reverse side the obligations of the buyer set forth above are carefully repeated. Among the conditions on the reverse side is the general arbitration clause.

This case involves only the application of the arbitration clause. * * *

As pointed out earlier, an agreement to arbitrate must be clear and direct, and must not depend upon implication, inveiglement or subtlety * * * It follows then that the existence of an agreement to arbitrate should not depend solely upon the conflicting fine print of commercial forms which cross one another but never meet. * * *

Consequently, as a matter of law there was no agreement to arbitrate in this case, if one applies existing principles.

But the problem of conflicting commercial forms is one with which there has been much concern before this, and a new effort at rational solution has been made. The new solution would yield a similar result. The Uniform Commercial Code * * *:

"§ 2–207 Additional Terms in Acceptance or Confirmation

"(1) A definite and seasonable expression of acceptance or a written confirmation which is sent within a reasonable time operates as an acceptance even though it states terms additional to or different from those offered or agreed upon, unless acceptance is expressly made conditional on assent to the additional or different terms.

"(2) The additional terms are to be construed as proposals for addition to the contract. Between merchants such terms become part of the contract unless:

"(a) the offer expressly limits acceptance to the terms of the offer;

"(b) they materially alter it; or

"(c) notification of objection to them has already been given or is given within a reasonable time after notice of them is received.

"(3) Conduct by both parties which recognizes the existence of a contract is sufficient to establish a contract for sale although the writings of the parties do not otherwise establish a contract. In such case the terms of the particular contract consist of those terms on which the writings of the parties agree, together with any supplementary terms incorporated under any other provisions of this Act."

On this exposition, the arbitration clause, whether viewed as a material alteration under subsection (2), or as a term nullified by a conflicting provision in the buyer's form, would fail to survive as a contract term. In the light of the New York cases, at least, there can be little question that an agreement to arbitrate is a material term, one not to be injected by implication, subtlety or inveiglement. And the conclusion is also the same if the limitation contained in the offer (the buyer's purchase order) is given effect, as required by subsection 2(a) of the new section.

[Motion granted.]

PROBLEMS

1. Seller and buyer were each dealers in cattle. During an extremely hot spell, seller was worried over the fact that he had too many cattle on the market. Buyer discovering this fact jokingly offered to buy the cattle. After some dickering as to price, the parties apparently came to an agreement. Buyer later insisted that the whole transaction was a joke. Seller believed that buyer's offer to buy the cattle was made seriously. Seller sues buyer for damages. Decision?

2. Lessig discovered that an old set of harness worth about $15.00 had been stolen from his premises. Angered by the theft, in his excitement he shouted to the bystanders, "I will give $100.00 to any man who will find out who the thief is", using rough language and epithets concerning the thief. Higgins, one of the bystanders who heard the remark, caught the thief, and now sues for the $100.00. Decision?

3. Buyer, a collector of antiques, while looking about in seller's antique shop saw an ancient vase to which was tied a tag bearing the words "Genuine Chinese Vase, $125.00". Realizing that this was a bargain, buyer said to the seller, "I'll take this vase at $125.00". Seller refused to sell telling the buyer he decided to keep it for himself. Buyer contends that a contract arose from this set of facts. What should the court decide?

4. Defendant-employer promised plaintiff-employee that he would pay plaintiff in addition to his regular salary part of the profits of the business on a "very liberal basis". Plaintiff brings action for part of the profits. Decision?

5. Defendant-employer promised plaintiff-employee that he would purchase plaintiff's house. Plaintiff was unable to work at the time due to an injury so defendant promised plaintiff the sum of $15,000 for the house, and promised that plaintiff would be re-employed and given "light work" when his doctor certified he was capable of performing it. Plaintiff agreed. Defendant refuses to employ plaintiff so plaintiff brings suit for breach of contract. Decision?

6. Seller agrees to sell and buyer agrees to buy all of the steel that the buyer desires to buy for his business of making ships during the year 1968. For the first half of the year, the buyer purchased all the steel he required from the seller; however, in July, the buyer informed the seller that for the rest of the year he was going to buy his steel from another company. Seller sues for damages. Decision?

7. Buyer and seller make a contract for the purchase and sale of 1,000 bushels of wheat at a certain price. The contract is certain in all respects except that the parties forgot to discuss the place of delivery and the time of delivery. The price of wheat rises sharply so the seller refuses to deliver the wheat contending that the contract is unenforceable since it lacks certainty. Decision?

8. Seller sends a written offer to the buyer in which the seller offers to sell one thousand number 51 J coats to the buyer at a certain price. The offer states that it will be kept open for a period of sixty days. The buyer sends an acceptance ten days prior to the sixty-day period; however, the seller has sold the coats to another retailer thinking the buyer was not going to accept. Buyer sues seller for damages. Seller contends that there was no consideration paid to him by the buyer to keep the offer open; and, therefore, he could revoke the offer at any time. Decision?

9. S mailed an offer to sell certain land to B for the price of $15,000. S mailed the letter on June 4 and B received the letter on June 5. On June 5 B mailed a letter to S which contained the following language: "Will you take less?" S replied in the negative. B then mailed a letter on June 7 which stated "I accept your offer of June 4." Is there a contract?

10. On January 15 buyer mailed an offer from Los Angeles to seller in New York for the purchase of five hundred certain dresses at a certain price. On January 18 the buyer mailed a revocation of the offer. On January 19 seller received the offer and mailed an acceptance. Seller immediately purchased sufficient yardage to make the special dresses. On January 22 the seller received the revocation. Is there a contract?

11. On May 27 S, not a merchant, made an offer to sell an antique vase to B for $500. B asked S if he could have some time to think it over. S stated that he could have until June 2 to accept. On June 1 B called S and told him that he accepted the offer whereupon S said that he had sold the vase the day before. B sues for breach of contract. Decision?

12. Seller offers his hot rod to the buyer for $500.00. Buyer states that he likes the hot rod but cannot afford that much. Buyer then states

that he will give the seller $400.00. The seller tells the buyer that he cannot take the $400.00 and starts to walk away. The buyer then states, "Oh, all right, I accept your offer of $500.00". Is there a contract?

13. On June 5 B made an offer to purchase a tract of land to S. The offer stated that the deed was to be delivered to B on or before July 6. On July 10 S crossed out the date of delivery and inserted July 24. S then signed the offer indicating his acceptance. Is there a contract?

14. S mailed a letter to B on June 8 which contained an offer to sell 2,000 to 5,000 tons of 50-pound iron rails upon certain specified terms. On June 10 B received the letter and sent a telegram as follows: "Please enter an order for 1,200 tons of 50-pound iron rails on the terms specified." On receipt of the telegram S sent a telegram refusing to fulfill the order. B then sent the following telegram: "Please enter an order for 2,000 tons rails as per your letter of the eighth." Is there a contract?

15. S received an offer from B to purchase certain real estate which S owned. S sent a telegram to B which stated "Your offer accepted relative to sale of my property subject to details to be worked out by you and my attorney." The next day S sold the property to another buyer at a higher price. B sues for breach of contract. Decision?

16. Mr. Jones receives a book in the mail which he did not order. The accompanying letter states that he should either return the book in ten days or send $9.95 to the company for payment of the book. Mr. Jones does not want the book nor does he want the trouble and expense of returning the book. Is there a contract if he does not return the book?

Chapter 8

CONSIDERATION

A. NECESSITY FOR CONSIDERATION

1. IN GENERAL

In addition to the requirement of intent to contract which is evidenced by an offer and acceptance, consideration is ordinarily required in a contract.

Consideration is something of value which is a benefit to one party or a loss to the other party. It is the inducement to the contract. It is the reason, cause, motive, or price which induces a contracting party to enter into a contract. Consideration may be a benefit conferred or agreed to be conferred upon the promisor or some other person, or a detriment suffered or to be suffered by the promisee or some other person. Consideration must be bargained for; e.g., if you do something for me, I will do something for you. A promise to make a gift is not consideration and is not enforceable.

The general rule is that a contract must be supported by consideration to be valid and legally enforceable; however, the rule has received criticism and modern law tends to relax the requirement and to expand the exceptions.

2. AN ACT AS CONSIDERATION

In a unilateral contract, the promise by the offeror is the consideration for the act or forbearance by the offeree. For example, a sheriff promises a reward for the capture of a criminal. The consideration moving from the sheriff is the promise to pay the reward, and the consideration moving from the offeree is the act of capturing the criminal. Or an uncle promises his nephew the sum of $5,000 if the nephew does not smoke until he is thirty years of age. The uncle's consideration is the promise to pay $5,000, and the nephew's consideration is the giving up the legal right to smoke.

3. A PROMISE AS CONSIDERATION

In a bilateral contract, the promise of one party is the consideration for the promise of the other party. Where mutual promises are made, the one furnishes a sufficient consideration to support an action on the other. For example, S promises to sell his car to B, and B promises to pay S $400.00 for it. The agreement is binding since both sides have furnished consideration; i. e., their mutual promises.

4. ILLUSORY OFFER

A proposal by a seller to furnish to a buyer at a specified price all the goods of a certain kind which the buyer may "want" or "desire" during a certain period is considered an illusory offer (misleading) which does not, upon acceptance, result in an enforceable contract. The reason is that the offeree may not "want" or "desire" any goods during the period and hence is not bound to buy any particular amount. Thus, there is no mutuality of obligation, and hence the contract is not enforceable. However, see Chapter 7 (4.B.) for possible exception under the U.C.C.

Where the proposal is to furnish all the goods of a certain kind which the other party may "need" or "require" in a certain business for a definite period, acceptance results in a binding contract.

5. ADEQUACY OF CONSIDERATION

As a general rule, as long as the consideration is of some value, however slight, it will be sufficient to sustain a contract in the absence of fraud or unconscionable conduct. The inadequacy is for the parties to consider at the time of making the agreement, and not for the court when it is sought to be enforced. For example, an option to purchase real estate for $100,000.00 may be given for the consideration of $1.00; and a promise of a nephew to name his first son after his uncle is consideration for the uncle's promise to pay the nephew $5,000.00.

However, by statute in some states, e.g., California Civil Code, Section 3391, in specific performance cases, the consideration must be adequate or the court will not order specific performance. For example, S makes a contract to sell a parcel of real estate to B for the price of $10,000.00; however, the value of the land is really worth $25,000.00 at the time the contract is made. Later S refuses to deliver a deed to B although B is ready, willing, and able to perform his part of the bargain. B then sues S for specific performance asking the court to order S to hand over the deed since land is unique, and the remedy at law (money damages) is inadequate. The court will examine the adequacy of the consideration, and finding that the sum agreed to be paid is not sufficient will not order specific performance.

Don't worry

6. DOING WHAT ONE IS BOUND TO DO

Doing or promising to do what one is already legally bound to do cannot be consideration. For example, a police officer cannot recover a reward offered for the capture of a criminal since it is the officer's duty to capture criminals.

7. PAST CONSIDERATION

Past consideration is not sufficient to sustain a new promise. For example, S sells B a parcel of land containing an orange grove. One week after the contract is executed, B asks S if he warrants that the land is free of frost. S tells B that he so warrants. The statement

CCPA

by S is not enforceable since there is no consideration for the warranty by S.

However, if the subject of the sale was goods rather than real estate, then under the U.C.C., Section 2–209(1), the warranty would be enforceable *even though without new consideration* by B for S's warranty.

8. MORAL OBLIGATION

Generally, a moral obligation cannot be consideration. For example, a nurse cared for John Smith, an indigent who lived in Illinois, for one month prior to his death. Robert Jones, a friend from California, learned of the nurse's care at the funeral and the next day called the nurse and told her that he was going to give her $5,000.00 for her services. This promise is unenforceable since it is based on a mere moral obligation. It is merely a promise to make a gift.

There are some exceptions, however, where a moral obligation will be sufficient to sustain a promise:

a. Where the moral obligation is founded on previous benefits received by the promisor, especially if obtained by fraud or duress; e.g., a married man by fraud induces a woman to marry him, and she lives with him until she finds he was already married and then leaves him - - - she may maintain an action for her services;

b. Where by statute a moral obligation is considered sufficient consideration; however, there are only a few states having such a statute;

c. Where a promise to pay a debt is based on a pre-existing legal duty, it may be regarded as based on a moral obligation and hence enforceable; e.g., debtor owes creditor $1,000.00 for which there is no remedy since it is barred by the statute of limitations or by bankruptcy (see chapter 14). Debtor, however, writes a note to the creditor stating that he will pay the debt. This promise is binding though without new consideration (most states require that the new promise be in writing). A debt can also be revived by a mere acknowledgment in writing in most states; e. g., the debtor sends a note to the creditor stating that he knows the debt is barred by the statute of limitations, however, he acknowledges that he still owes it. Also, a debt can be revived or extended by part payment in most states.

9. LIQUIDATED DEBT

A liquidated debt is one that is for a sum certain; e. g., a patient owes a doctor $100. There is no dispute as to the amount due. In the case of a liquidated debt payment of a lesser sum will not discharge the balance since there is no consideration for the release of the balance, and this is true even though the creditor orally accepts the lesser sum in full payment. For example, the patient tells the doctor that he has only $75 and asks the doctor if he will accept that amount as payment in full. The doctor states that he will. Since there is no consideration for the release of the $25 the doctor's promise is not enforceable; thus the patient still owes $25.

A problem can arise when the debtor sends the creditor a check for a lesser sum than due marked "payment in full" or words of similar meaning. Under the U.C.C., Section 3–408, it would seem that an acceptance of such a check by the creditor discharges the balance of the debt even though there is no consideration for the discharge. Official Comment number 2 of that section states in part "an instrument given for more or less than the amount of a liquidated obligation does not fail by reason of the common law rule that an obligation for a lesser liquidated amount cannot be consideration for the surrender of a greater". Also, see Sections 1–107 and 2–209(1).

Some states have attempted to resolve the problem by statute; e. g., California Civil Code Sections 1524 and 1541 which provide that an obligation can be extinguished by a release signed by the creditor without new consideration.

A question may arise as to whether the creditor "accepted" the check. If he holds the check an unreasonable length of time without notifying the debtor that he does not accept the check in full payment, it has been held that he has accepted the check and the balance of the debt is discharged. Keeping the check after notification of refusal does not constitute an acceptance since he can keep the check until the debtor demands possession of it. Deletion of the notation "paid in full" followed by an attempt to cash the check has been held to constitute an acceptance.

10. UNLIQUIDATED DEBT

An unliquidated debt is one in which the amount is in good faith dispute. In such a case, acceptance by the creditor of the lesser sum discharges the balance *even though* the creditor protests at the time he accepts the lesser sum. For example, the patient believes he owes the doctor $75.00, but the doctor believes that the patient owes him $100.00. This is an unliquidated debt. The patient hands the doctor $75.00 cash and states that this is payment in full. The doctor takes the $75.00 but states that he will continue to look to the patient for the $25.00 balance. By taking the lesser sum, the doctor discharges the balance.

In the case of an unliquidated debt the law is clear that the acceptance of a check which bears the notation "paid in full" will release the entire debt. However, whenever such a notation is used, it should be conspicuous.

11. PART PAYMENT WITH ADDITIONAL ADVANTAGE

If a creditor accepts a lesser sum than is due, prior to due date, offered in full satisfaction of the debt, the balance is discharged because the debtor incurs a legal detriment by paying before it is due. Similarly, if the debt is not secured and the creditor accepts a lesser amount if the debtor secures the debt with a mortgage, the balance is discharged; i.e., the giving of such security is something the debtor was not legally bound to do and therefore is sufficient consideration for the creditor's promise to accept the lesser sum.

12. CHARITABLE SUBSCRIPTIONS AND PROMISSORY ESTOPPEL

Promissory estoppel arises when there is a promise which the promisor should reasonably expect to induce action or forbearance on the part of the promisee, and which does induce such action or forbearance, and such promise is binding if injustice can be avoided only by enforcement of the promise. The promisor is bound when he should *reasonably expect* a substantial *change of position* (act or forbearance) in reliance on his promise if injustice can be avoided only by its enforcement (Contracts Restatement § 90). In such a case, the promisor is estopped from pleading a lack of consideration for his promise. In other words, promissory estoppel is a substitute for consideration; i. e., the promise is binding even though the promisor received nothing in exchange for his promise.

A *subscription to a charity* is an example of the use of promissory estoppel. When the charitable institution, such as a church, makes expenditures or incurs obligations in reliance on the promise of a subscriber, he is estopped or prevented from using lack of consideration as a defense. As soon as the charity changes its position, e. g., hires an architect, in reliance on the promise of the subscriber, he can be held to his promise.

Other examples of promissory estoppel are:

a. A promise not to foreclose on a lien for one week even though the period of redemption had expired; e.g., a woman pledged her mink coat for a $270.00 loan. After the period of redemption had expired, she was notified by the lien holder that she had one week to repay and reclaim the coat. She stated that she was ready and would do so. Within the one week period, the lien holder sold the coat. The agreement was binding without consideration since the representation by the lien holder induced her to forbear redemption immediately in reliance on the promise which was calculated to induce such forbearance.

b. Where the debtor induced his creditor to postpone suit by promising not to invoke the statute of limitations, the debtor was estopped from using the statute of limitations.

c. Where the insurance adjuster promised to settle a personal injury case with the injured party as soon as the party was discharged by his doctor, the insurance company could not rely on the statute of limitations which had run after one year.

d. Where a mortgagor made improvements on his property in reliance upon the mortgagee's promise not to foreclose.

e. Where a donee (recipient of a gift) makes improvements upon land in reliance on a promised gift of the land.

In these examples, promissory estoppel is a substitute for consideration.

13. EXECUTED TRANSACTIONS

The requirement of consideration applies only to executory contracts. After a contract is fully executed (the obligations of the parties are completed so that nothing remains to be done), it is no longer possible to attack its validity on that particular ground.

14. PROMISES UNDER THE *U.C.C.* WHICH DO NOT REQUIRE CONSIDERATION

The *U.C.C.* expressly provides that consideration is not required in the following five situations:

a. Section 1–107, a claim or right arising out of a breach of contract for the sale of goods can be discharged in whole or in part without consideration by a written waiver or renunciation, signed, and delivered by the aggrieved party;

b. Section 2–205, a written offer signed by a merchant to buy or sell goods which by its terms gives assurance that it will be held open is not revocable for lack of consideration during the time stated that it is open; and if no time is stated, for a reasonable time, but in no event may the period of irrevocability exceed three months;

c. Section 3–408, no consideration is necessary when a check is accepted in full settlement of a claim;

d. Section 3–605, the holder of a promissory note or draft or check may discharge any party to the instrument without consideration by (1) intentional cancellation of the instrument; (2) striking out the signature of the party on the instrument; (3) renunciation of rights on the instrument in writing signed and delivered; or (4) surrender of the instrument to the party to be discharged;

e. Section 2–209(1), an agreement modifying a contract for the sale of goods does not need consideration to be binding, however, the modification must meet the test of good faith (§ 1–203, 2–103(1)(b)), and a mere technical consideration cannot support a modification made in bad faith; and,

f. Section 5–105, no consideration is necessary to establish a letter of credit (see Section 5–103) or to enlarge or otherwise modify its terms.

1. *Necessity for Consideration*

BROWN v. ADDINGTON

114 Ind.App. 404, 52 N.E.2d 640 (1944).

CRUMPACKER, Chief Judge. The appellant instituted this suit against the appellee in the Delaware Circuit Court to recover judgment on the following written instrument:

> "July 20, 1929
>
> "I, Claude L. Addington, remembering and appreciating the many favors and acts of kindness, rendered to me, during the years that have passed, by my beloved uncle William E. Brown, and desiring to express my gratitude to him in something more than empty words, hereby promise and pledge that I will pay to my said uncle William E. Brown, the sum of One Hundred Dollars ($100.00) during each year that the said William E. Brown shall live. Payment to be made on or about the first day of January of each said year, beginning with the year 1930.
>
> "(Signed) Claude L. Addington."

* * *

If a person has been benefited in the past by some act or forbearance for which he incurred no legal liability and "afterwards, whether from good feeling or interested motives, he makes a promise to the person by whose act or forbearance he has benefited, and that promise is made on no other consideration than the past benefit, it is gratuitous and cannot be enforced; it is based on motive and not on consideration." * * *

By the great weight of authority a past consideration, if it imposed no legal obligation at the time it was furnished, will support no promise whatever. A past consideration is insufficient, even though of benefit to the promisor, where the services rendered or things of value furnished were intended and expected to be gratuitous. * *

The facts pleaded in the appellant's * * * complaint clearly show that the appellee was taken into the decedent's family and treated as a member thereof for many years. No express contract to pay for clothing, board and lodging is pleaded and the law implies none. There being no legal obligation to pay for these necessaries imposed upon the appellee at the time they were furnished they are insufficient, as consideration, to support the contract sued upon. The demurrer [see dictionary in Appendix] * * * was properly sustained.

Judgment affirmed [for defendant].

2. *An Act as Consideration*

HAMER v. SIDWAY

124 N.Y. 538, 27 N.E. 256 (1891).

Action to recover the sum of $5,000 promised by an uncle to his nephew. The promisor had agreed with his nephew that if the latter would refrain from drinking liquor and using tobacco until he reached the age of twenty-one, the uncle would then pay his nephew $5,000. * * * [Hamer is the assignee of the nephew's claim, and Sidway is the Executor of the uncle's estate.]

PARKER, J. The trial court found as a fact that "on the 20th day of March, 1869, * * * William E. Story agreed to and with William E. Story, 2d, that if he would refrain from drinking liquor, using tobacco, swearing, and playing cards or billiards for money until he should become 21 years of age, then he, the said William E. Story, would at that time pay him, the said William E. Story, 2d, the sum of $5,000 for such refraining, to which the said William E. Story, 2d, agreed," and that he "in all things fully performed his part of said agreement."

The defendant contends that the contract was without consideration to support it and, therefore, invalid. He asserts that the promisee by refraining from the use of liquor and tobacco was not harmed but benefited; that that which he did was best for him to do independently of his uncle's promise, and insists that it follows that unless the promisor was benefited, the contract was without consideration. A contention which, if well founded, would seem to leave open for controversy in many cases whether that which the promisee did or omitted to do was, in fact, of such benefit to him as to leave no consideration to support the enforcement of the promisor's agreement. Such a rule could not be tolerated, and is without foundation in the law. * * * Courts "will not ask whether the thing which forms the consideration does in fact benefit the promisee or a third party, or is of any substantial value to anyone. It is enough that something is promised, done, forborne, or suffered by the party to whom the promise is made as consideration for the promise made to him." * * *

"In general a waiver of any legal right at the request of another party is a sufficient consideration for a promise."

* * * Consideration means not so much that one party is profiting as that the other abandons some legal right in the present or limits his legal freedom of action in the future as an inducement for the promise of the first."

Now, applying this rule to the facts before us, the promisee used tobacco, occasionally drank liquor, and he had a legal right to do so. That right he abandoned for a period of years upon the strength of the promise of the testator that for such forbearance he would give him $5,000. We need not speculate on the effort which may have been required to give up the use of those stimulants. It is sufficient that he restricted his lawful freedom of action within certain prescribed limits upon the faith of his uncle's agreement, and now having fully performed the conditions imposed, it is of no moment whether such performance actually proved a benefit to the promisor, and the court will not inquire into it * * *."

[Judgment for plaintiff.]

---

3. *Promise as Consideration*

EARLE v. ANGELL

157 Mass. 294, 32 N.E. 164 (1892).

Action by Benjamin A. Earle against Charles A. Angell, surviving executor of Mary Dewitt, deceased, to recover on a contract made by plaintiff with defendant's testatrix in her lifetime, whereby she promised to give plaintiff $500 if he would attend her funeral. Judgment for defendant. * * *

HOLMES, J. There is no difficulty in point of law in the way of a parol contract to pay a person $500, conditioned upon his attending the promisor's funeral, and in consideration of his promise to do so. It is well settled that a contract to pay money after one's own death is valid.

* * * The ruling that the plaintiff could not recover must have gone on the ground that there was no evidence of such a contract as we have supposed. According to the report, the plaintiff testified that the defendant's testatrix said, "If you will agree to come," etc., "I will give you five hundred dollars," etc., and that he promised to come if alive, and notified in time. We cannot say that this did not warrant a finding of promise for promise. It is suggested that the acceptance varied from the terms of the offer; but the parties were face to face, and separated seemingly agreed. The jury well might have found, if that was the only question, that the variation, if any, was assented to on the spot.

[In a bilateral contract, the promise of one party is the consideration for that of the other. Judgment for plaintiff.]

4. The Promise Must be Binding

UNITED BUTANE SALES v. BESSEMER–SUBURBAN GAS CO.

281 Ala. 664, 207 So.2d 416 (1968).

HARWOOD, Justice.

* * *

The alleged contract sued upon was between the plaintiff, as seller, and the defendant, as buyer, relative to the sale of butane and propane gas. In parts pertinent to this review, the purported contract reads:

> "Buyer agrees to purchase all Butane and Propane gas for the above listed points exclusively from United, its successors and assigns. However, it is understood and agreed that United, its successors and assigns, shall not be obligated to furnish buyer in any one Winter calendar month, October through February, more than one and one-half (1½) times the average monthly quantities purchased by Buyer from United during the preceding summer months, March through September. It is further understood and agreed that in the event United should have to pay a premium price for products during these Winter months that Buyer shall pay to United the same amount of increase over contract delivered price as United has to pay over market price for said products which are in excess of said guaranteed on one and one-half (1½) to one (1) ratio."

Paragraph 2 of the contract concerns the delivered prices of the gas in Bessemer, Columbiana, and Pell City.

Paragraph 3 provides that the contract shall be in effect from 20 February 1960 to 28 February 1963, and thereafter for succeeding periods of one year, with termination rights in either party on ninety days' notice prior to termination of any of the periods.

Paragraph 13 reads:

> "This contract comprises the entire agreement between United and Buyer and there are no agreements, understandings, conditions, either oral or written, expressed or implied concerning the subject matter or in consideration hereof that are not merged herein or superseded hereby, except that it is hereby expressly understood and agreed that Buyer shall hold United free against any claim of Phillips Petroleum Company or any other person or concern, to any title, mortgage, or incumbrance whatsoever, with respect to a 7200 water gallon Propane Beaird tank trailer, manufacture serial # 55223."

Among the 149 grounds on which the demurrer is based are several asserting that the contract, which as before stated is made a par. of the complaint, is void as lacking in mutuality. These grounds are well taken.

Nowhere in the purported agreement is the plaintiff-seller bound, or under any legal duty to sell to the defendant buyer gas in any quantity. No enforceable right redounds to the buyer should the seller refuse to sell gas to it.

It would also appear that the buyer is not obligated to purchase any gas if it should be so inclined.

The document sued upon is completely illusory, merely a "tinkling cymbal," conferring no legal enforceable rights upon either party. Such a contract is void, and of course unenforceable. * * *

It is to be noted that in the complaint it has been averred:

> "Plaintiff says that by the express, as well as implied, terms of said written agreement and by the valid customs and usages concerning the subject matter of the contract, of which both buyer and seller had full knowledge and well understood and were chargeable at the time of the execution thereof, said agreement, as was intended by the parties thereto, imports an obligation on the part of United to sell and on the part of Bessemer Gas and Automatic Gas to purchase all butane and propane gas for above listed points exclusively from United, its successors and assigns."

Clearly the document does not by express terms impose any enforceable rights. Able counsel for the plaintiff has, however, sought to enliven an otherwise dead instrument by breathing life into it by implying terms therein through custom and usage of the butane gas business. Counsel for the defendant below, appellee here, questions the sufficiency of the averment of custom and usage. We pretermit consideration of this contention as paragraph 13 of the document, set out above, forbids resort to anything other than the four corners of the document.

* * * [Judgment for defendant affirmed.]

+ 5. *Adequacy of Consideration*

WOLFORD v. POWERS, ADMINISTRATRIX

85 Ind. 294 (1882).

Action against the administratrix of Charles Lehman's estate to collect the sum of $10,000 upon a promissory note drawn to the plaintiff's order by the intestate some months prior to his death. Defendant contends that there was no adequate consideration for the promise of the deceased to pay plaintiff this sum. The facts are fully set forth in the opinion.

ELLIOTT, J. The * * * complaint is founded upon a promissory note * * *. The answer * * * alleges that the only consideration for the note sued on was the * * * agreement of the (plaintiff) to bestow upon one of his children the name of Charles Lehman Wolford. The (plaintiff) replied to the answer that Charles Lehman * * * was a widower, about eighty-seven years of age; that he had been the father of one boy who had died many years before the execution of the note; that on the 18th day of April, 1878, a male child was born to (plaintiff); that * * * Lehman requested that it should be given the name of Charles Lehman Wolford; that * * * the (plaintiff) did name the child Charles Lehman * * *; (and) that * * * the * * * note for $10,000 * * * "was executed in consideration of the naming of the child Charles Lehman * * *."

* * * It is the general rule that where there is no fraud, and a party gets all the consideration he contracts for, the contract will be upheld. * * *

The consideration in the case before us was * * * one which the parties alone were competent to measure and determine. Where a party contracts for the performance of an act which will afford him pleasure * * * his estimate of value should be left undisturbed, unless, indeed, there is evidence of fraud. * * * If * * * there is any legal consideration for a promise, it must be sufficient for the one made. * * *

The surrender * * * of the right or privilege of naming the * * * child was * * * consideration. The right to give his child a name was one which the father possessed * * * If the intestate chose to bargain for the exercise of this right, he should be bound; for by his bargain he limited and restrained the father's right to bestow his own or some other name upon the child. We can perceive no solid reason for declaring that the right with which the father parted at the intestate's request was of no value. * * * In yielding to the intestate's request, and in consideration of the promise accompanying it, the (plaintiff) certainly * * surrendered some right. * * * As the (plaintiff) suffered some detriment * * * there is a legal consideration.

[Judgment for plaintiff.]

6. *Forbearance to Sue as Consideration*

BOARD OF COUNTY COMMISSIONERS OF HARFORD COUNTY v. L. S. MacPHAIL

214 Md. 192, 133 A.2d 96 (1957).

Action by farm owner [MacPhail] against county commissioners to compel county to perform contract to grade, base, align, and pave remainder of county road running through farm.

HAMMOND, Judge. Once upon a time the County Commissioners of Harford County could decide calmly, as an uncomplicated part of their routine duties, what road in the county they would improve, and when and how. That was before the appellee, Larry S. MacPhail, who had retired as president of the Yankees baseball club, came down from New York in 1941 and bought some four hundred acres of farm land in the Third Election District of the county. Through the farm ran part of a county public road four miles long, a dirt road, described as "as bad a road as is possible to find in Harford County", winding, with bad curves and banks, very muddy, if not impassable in bad weather. From 1941 to the date of these presents, MacPhail has worked tirelessly getting the county bindingly to agree to pave the road, and to make it carry out the agreement. At various times from 1942 to 1951, the county has paved all of the road but a stretch, some eight-tenths of a mile long, all of it within the MacPhail farm. When no more work was done after 1951, MacPhail, just before Christmas in 1954, filed a bill to compel the county to perform the contract he alleged it made to grade, base, align and pave that last unimproved stretch of road. The chancellor decreed that the County Commissioners "immediately and forthwith fulfill such obligation", and they have appealed.

MacPhail says that in 1941 he told the Commissioners he could use his new farm and the buildings then on it as a "simple cattle farm" or, if the county would agree to pave the road, he would make substantial and expensive improvements to carry on a horse and cattle breeding operation and make the place his home. The Commissioners, he says, then promised to pave the road. In 1942, MacPhail deeded to the county the land over which the road actually ran, so as to correct the deviations from the record right-of-way, and, in addition, to give the county an extra three feet of width. He says he delivered the deed, some months after its execution, only when the Commissioners, in a meeting at the court house, gave him in return a definite assurance "that they would pave the road." Thereafter, the county did some paving until the scarcity of labor and material during the war caused an interruption in the work, in which MacPhail, who himself was in the service, acquiesced.

In 1946, MacPhail renewed his efforts. * * *

MacPhail carried out his promise substantially to improve the farm he bought. He added several hundred acres to his holdings, built thirty new buildings, rebuilt or refurbished some twenty existing buildings, built fifteen miles of fencing and a mile and a half of blacktop road, and established a large thoroughbred horse and cattle operation. * * *

The bad stretch of road cuts the farm in half and handicaps its operation. Valuable stallions and expensive vans cannot be subjected to the risks of using it. * * *

After 1951, MacPhail and his counsel, Brodnax Cameron, kept urging the Commissioners to complete the work. Legal action was threatened several times, once in writing. * * * In late March or in early April, 1954, at the direction of MacPhail, Cameron prepared suit papers for the enforcement of the agreements to pave the road, and a copy was delivered to the attorney for the County Commissioners, who was told that the suit would be filed promptly if action were not forthcoming. A few days thereafter the Commissioners asked Cameron to confer with them at their meeting of April 19–20, 1954, and he did so. Cameron testified that the Commissioners agreed to grade and base the road, if possible in 1954 or, in 1955 at the latest, and to pave it in 1955. * * *

The chancellor found, we think correctly, that the forbearance to sue in the Spring of 1954 was good consideration for the promise of the County Commissioners to base, grade and pave the final stretch of the road. It is well established that forbearance to sue for a lawful claim and demand is good consideration if the one forbearing honestly intended to prosecute litigation which is not frivolous, vexatious or unlawful, (that is, litigation that has a reasonable basis) and which he believes to be well founded even though it may in fact be unfounded.

[Decree for MacPhail affirmed.]

---

7. *Doing What One is Bound to Do is Not Consideration*

HALE v. BREWSTER

81 N.M. 342, 467 P.2d 8 (1970).

MOISE, Chief Justice. * * * The record discloses a complaint filed by appellee against appellant and Mrs. W. E. Brewster, seeking judgment for $900.53, being the unpaid balance on a promissory note for $1,000.00, plus interest and attorney fees. * * *

Appellant, for his second point, asserts a defense to the complaint in that the note sued on was lacking in consideration. The question presented concerns the right and propriety of an attorney taking compensation for representation of an indigent charged with a crime when he has been appointed by the court to represent the indigent and has been paid by the court for the services rendered.

* * *

Aside from the constitutional provision and the statute requiring that counsel be appointed for indigents charged with crime, and paid for the services rendered, it has always been considered that attorneys admitted to practice at the bar are officers of the court and have a duty and obligation to accept such appointments and to serve their clients to the best of the attorneys' abilities. * * *

The right of the courts to impose the duty on lawyers to defend indigent persons accused of crime without compensation has been upheld in all jurisdictions except four—Indiana, Iowa, New Jersey and Wisconsin. See Annot., 21 A.L.R.3d 819, 830. * * * We must decide if payment of a fee by the State makes the note executed by appellant invalid because lacking consideration. We have found only one case directly in point. It is Commonwealth v. Wormsley, 294 Pa. 495, 144 A. 428 (1928), where the court said:

> "* * * Petitioners, having been appointed by the court to represent defendant, had a duty to appeal, if they considered that course essential to protect his rights, and the fee paid them by the county must be their exclusive compensation. Under the circumstances, they had no right to contract with others for fees and expenses."

That this rule is correct would seem to follow from the duty of appellee to represent to the best of his ability plus the payment and receipt of a fee from the State. Where can the consideration be found for appellant's promise to pay an additional amount? We do not see how appellant received anything that he was not entitled to receive without payment of any amount, and accordingly there is no consideration.

[Judgment for defendant.]

---

x 8. *Payment of Lesser Sum by Check*

HORNBUCKLE v. CONTINENTAL GIN COMPANY

116 Ga.App. 449, 157 S.E.2d 829 (1967).

EBERHARDT, Judge. Hornbuckle executed two promissory notes to Continental Gin in the aggregate principal amount of $6,308 for the purchase price of ginning equipment. On June 18, 1963, when called upon to pay the matured notes, Hornbuckle claimed that he was due an adjustment on a defective "burr machine" and offered two checks in the amount of $2,000 each, one dated of even date and the other postdated to September 15, 1963, in full settlement of the indebtedness. Both checks were imprinted with a standard conditional endorsement form stating that "by endorsement this check is accepted in full payment of the following account," and, in the blanks provided in the conditional endorsement forms, the first check bore the words "on note account" and the second bore the words "balance note account in full" or "settlement of note account in full." The first check was deposited and paid and the second check was retained until September 15, 1963, when Continental Gin deposited it for payment after having first obliterated the condition without having communicated with Hornbuckle. Because of the alteration the second check was returned unpaid to Continental Gin, and one of its representatives called upon Hornbuckle on October 23, 1963. Hornbuckle then issued another check for $2,000 which, in the blank in the conditional endorsement, bore the words "settlement in full of note account." This check was delivered to the representative by Hornbuckle with the alternative of acceptance or filing suit against him on the notes, but the condition was again later struck out by Continental Gin after telephoning Hornbuckle of its intention to strike the provision, and Hornbuckle making no reply save "Well, I guess that's it," and the check was deposited for payment in its altered condition. When this check was returned unpaid Continental Gin turned the matter over to its lawyer who made demand under the promissory notes and gave notice of intention to collect attorney's fees.

Upon receipt of the demand and notice Hornbuckle tendered the $2,000 to the lawyer, which was refused. Suit was then brought for the full amount of the notes less credit of $2,000 for the first check, which had been paid. Hornbuckle filed a plea of accord and satisfaction making a continuing tender of the $2,000, * * *.

Whether an actual controversy existed between the parties or not, the conduct of Continental Gin in accepting and retaining the checks, obliterating the conditional endorsements thereon without the consent of Hornbuckle, and presenting them for payment had the legal effect of acceptance of the terms of the conditional endorsements and resulted in an accord as to the amount due under the notes * * * which it appears Hornbuckle has tendered and must pay. If Continental Gin was unwilling to accept the conditions written on the two checks tendered as a series in settlement of the notes, it was its duty promptly to return them to Hornbuckle and bring suit on the notes instead of retaining the checks and unilaterally altering the last of them by striking the condition and trying to obtain payment thereon from the bank. Under no construction of the evidence can it be said that Hornbuckle consented to the alteration of the checks.

[Judgment for plaintiff for only $2,000.]

Did Continenta accept offer?

9. Relinquishment of Right to Discharge in Bankruptcy Sufficient Consideration

MELROY v. KEMMERER

218 Pa. 381, 67 A. 699 (1907).

MITCHELL, C. J. * * *

In the present case the debtor, being in failing circumstances and contemplating bankruptcy, offered the plaintiffs 30 per cent. of his debt as a settlement in full. The plaintiffs dissuaded him from going into bankruptcy, accepted his alternative offer, received the money, and closed the account. They have now brought this suit for the balance. * * * The exact point is whether the debtor's relinquishment of his intention to seek a discharge in bankruptcy, and his payment of 30 per cent. instead, constitute a sufficient consideration to bind the creditor to the agreement. On that point we have no doubt. A valuable consideration may consist in some right, interest, or benefit to one party, or some loss, detriment, or responsibility resulting actually or potentially to the other. * * * The accord in this case was good on both branches. By it the creditors got a sum certain, instead of the chances of an uncertain dividend in bankruptcy. On the other hand, the debtor accepted the responsibility of paying a sum certain, whether his assets were sufficient or not, and gave up his right to a release of his future assets, and to a discharge from his whole debt, without regard to the sufficiency of his present assets.

[Judgment for defendant].

---

10. Consideration is Necessary for Subscription Offer

BOARD OF HOME MISSIONS, ETC. v. MANLEY

129 Cal.App. 541, 19 P.2d 21 (1933).

JAMISON, Justice pro tem. This action is upon a rejected claim against the estate of Martha D. Sanders, deceased. The claim is for a subscription or pledge by deceased for the benefit of plaintiff. * * The case was tried by the court, which found * * * in her favor upon the defense of want of consideration. Judgment was thereupon rendered for defendant, and from this judgment plaintiff appeals.

The question to be determined upon this appeal is whether or not the said claim is supported by a sufficient consideration. On October 30, 1929, the said deceased executed and delivered to appellant the following subscription or pledge: "Estate Pledge. To the Board of Home Missions and Church Extension of the Methodist Episcopal Church. In consideration of my interest in Christian Missions and of the securing by the above named Board of other pledges for its work, and for value received, I hereby promise and agree to pay to The Board of Home Missions and Church Extension of the Methodist Episcopal Church, at 1701 Arch Street, Philadelphia, Pa., the sum of Five Thousand Dollars ($5000.00) which shall become due and payable one day after my death out of my estate. * * *

A subscription is considered as a mere offer until the beneficiary has accepted it, or has acted on the faith thereof so that his conduct implies an acceptance, and until such acceptance the promisor generally has the right to revoke the subscription. The death of the subscriber before the acceptance of the subscription constitutes a revocation of the offer, and the estate of the subscriber will not be liable on the subscription. * * * An acceptance can only be shown by some act on the part of the promisee whereby some legal liability is incurred or money expended on the faith of the promise. * * * However, there is an exception to this rule, and that is that, where there is a mutual promise by several individuals to contribute to the payment of an aggregate sum for the benefit of a charitable, religious, or educational institution in which they are all interested, such mutual promise is generally held to support an adequate consideration authorizing its enforcement by the promisee. * * *

There is no evidence in the case at bar indicating that appellant performed any acts or incurred any obligations or expense in reliance upon the payment of the said subscription of deceased prior to her death, or that other individuals concurred with her in contributing to the payment of an aggregate sum for the benefit of appellant. * *

There is no showing that between the date of deceased's pledge and the date of her death, that is to say, between October 30, 1929, and June 11, 1930, appellant performed any act or incurred any obligation or expense in reliance upon the payment of the said pledge by deceased. Therefore, we are of the opinion that the said estate pledge was without consideration and was revoked by the death of the said deceased. * * *

The judgment is affirmed [for defendant].

---

11. No Consideration Needed When Contract Executed

RYE v. PHILLIPS

230 Minn. 567, 282 N.W. 459 (1938).

[This was an action by plaintiff against defendant on a promissory note. Defendant set up the defense that he had agreed with plaintiff to give plaintiff certain livestock as payment for the note. The livestock was worth less than the balance due on the note. In pursuance of the agreement the defendant turned over the livestock to the plaintiff. Defendant claims that there was an accord and satisfaction; however, plaintiff moved for a directed verdict which was granted on the ground that "a mere promise of a creditor to receive, and of the debtor to pay, a sum less than the debt in full satisfaction of it, is without consideration, and binds neither party."]

STONE, Justice.

* * *

The doctrine thus invoked is one of the relics of antique law which should have been discarded long ago. It is evidence of the former capacity of lawyers and judges to make the requirement of consideration an overworked shibboleth rather than a logical and just standard of actionability.

In Oien v. St. Paul City Ry. Co., 198 Minn. 363, 373, 270 N.W. 1, we made such observations concerning it that the bar should have been advised thereby that we were ready to label the proposition as a museum piece of the law and shelve it accordingly. As Mr. Dunnell suggests, Minn.Dig. (2 Ed.) 1932 Supp. § 39, the doctrine may have sprouted from "a mistake in reporting," in Pinnel's Case, 5 Co.Rep. 117, in 1602. It is characterized as "an artificial and groundless rule which has been consistently condemned." Allen, Law in the Making (Oxford, 1930) 189. Its true status is accurately stated in Selected Readings on the Law of Contracts (MacMillan, 1931) 325, as follows: "And the rule is commonly thought to be a corollary of the doctrine of consideration. But this is a total misconception. The rule is older than the doctrine of consideration and is simply the survival of a bit of formal logic of the mediaeval lawyers." The law has been changed by statute in at least ten of our states. Id. 328. But, being a judge made rule, no vested rights depending on it, judges are just as competent to get rid of it as the legislature.

There is more than one ground of logic and good law upon which this old and indefensible rule may be discarded. There is no reason why a person should be prevented from making an executed gift of incorporeal as well as corporeal property. Why should a receipt in full for the entire debt not be taken in a proper case as sufficient evidence of an executed gift of the unpaid portion of the debt? Again, where there is proof, or on adequate evidence a finding, that a completed legal act such as a waiver has set a matter at rest, why is it necessary to search for any consideration?

The modern view is that a new promise to pay a debt barred by the statute of limitations or discharged in bankruptcy is binding without consideration. I Restatement, Contracts, §§ 86, 87. In that field at least, judges have recognized the futility of their former efforts to create a synthetic consideration where there was no actual consideration.

What has just been said may appear mere dictum, but judicial frankness justifies it to the end that both bar and public may be advised of our attitude.

We have no hesitation in saying that * * * the answer * * * pleads a defense. It avers a new contract * * * between

Confirm

plaintiff and defendant. * * * Furthermore, it shows that the agreement was executed. * * * Insofar as defendant agreed to turn over livestock * * * he assumed new obligations which were not his as maker of the note. Hence, it is immaterial whether the obligation substituted by the new contract for the old one under the note would or would not be the latter's equivalent in money value.

For these reasons it was reversible error to exclude defendant's offered evidence in support of his defense and to direct a verdict for plaintiff.

Order reversed.

---

12. *Promissory Estoppel*

BREDEMANN v. VAUGHAN MFG. CO.

40 Ill.App. 232, 188 N.E.2d 746 (1963).

McCormick, Justice. This appeal is taken from a summary judgment entered in the Circuit Court of Cook County in favor of the defendant. The plaintiff, Marie Bredemann, had filed a complaint * * * against the defendant, Vaughan Mfg. Company. In the first count she seeks damages for the breach of an alleged oral agreement by the defendant corporation to pay her a monthly salary during her lifetime.

* * * Count I of the complaint alleges that the plaintiff was a loyal and trusted employee of defendant corporation for a period of twenty-five years immediately preceding her retirement in December 1954. It is further alleged that as a part of the consideration for the services rendered to the defendant by her, the defendant, by and through its officers, directors and agents, orally promised to pay her full salary of $375 a month as long as she lived. It is further alleged that the defendant complied with the oral agreement and paid plaintiff her full salary of $375 a month from December 23, 1954 to about June 30, 1957, and that on or about June 30, 1957 the payments were reduced, and in June 1961 the defendant stopped all payments to the plaintiff. * * * About the 15th of December, 1954 she had a conversation with a Mr. Burchill, who told her that Mr. Grace, who was then the president of the company, wanted to see her about a retirement or a pension, and she said that she could not afford to retire on a pension. Burchill then said that she did not have to worry and that Mr. Grace had said that she would receive her full pay for the rest of her life. * * *

The defendant's contention in this court is that the promises to pay the plaintiff her full salary upon retirement were without consideration and are unenforceable. * * * As the parties agree, the consideration sufficient to support a contract may be either a benefit to the promisor or a loss or detriment to the promisee. * * *

" 'It is generally true that one who has led another to act in reasonable reliance on his representations of fact cannot afterwards in litigation between the two deny the truth of the representations, and some courts have sought to apply this principle to the formation of contracts, where, relying on a gratuitous promise, the promisee has suffered detriment. It is to be noticed, however, that such a case does not come within the ordinary definition of estoppel. If there is any representation of an existing fact, it is only that the promisor at the time of making the promise intends to fulfill it. As to such intention there is usually no misrepresentation and if there is, it is not that which has injured the promisee. In other words, he relies on a promise and not on a misstatement of fact; and the term "promissory" estoppel or something equivalent should be used to make the distinction.' * * * "

[Judgment for plaintiff].

X 13. *No Failure of Consideration*

GOLD v. SALEM LUTHERAN HOME ASS'N OF BAY CITIES

53 Cal.2d 289, 1 Cal.Rptr. 343, 347 P.2d 687 (1959).

McComb, Justice. Defendant is a nonprofit corporation which maintains a licensed home for the aged. Applicants are admitted for a trial period of two months. At the end of this period, or earlier if defendant's board of directors consents, a contract may be executed under which defendant becomes obligated to provide a home for the applicant for the remainder of his life. For such life care contract the applicant pays a lump sum, determined by reference to life expectancy tables.

Plaintiffs are executors of the will of Nicholas Chouvaldjy. Mr. Chouvaldjy, 84 years of age, applied for admission to the home and was accepted on a trial basis. * * *

The contract was drawn by defendant and dated October 1, 1956. Mr. Chouvaldjy signed it September 25, 1956, and at the same time delivered to defendant a cashier's check for $8,500. On the same afternoon or the next morning the authorized officers of defendant signed the contract, and Mr. Chouvaldjy was notified that a signed copy was available for him in the office. The contract was thus executed and in force as of September 26, 1956.

Mr. Chouvaldjy suffered a stroke on September 27, 1956, and died on September 28, 1956.

Plaintiff executors brought this action to recover the payment of $8,500. After trial before the court without a jury, judgment was entered in favor of defendant, and plaintiffs appeal.

Question: *Since performance of the contract was not to commence until October 1, 1956, and Mr. Chouvaldjy died before performance was to commence, (a) was there a failure of consideration for the contract * * *? No.* (a) A life care contract is not subject to rescission or cancellation, or to recovery back of the amount paid therefor, because the beneficiary dies before performance of the contract is to commence. Defendant's promise to furnish food, lodging, and care to decedent "for the remainder of his life" constituted consideration for the agreement, and the fact that decedent died before performance of the contract was to commence did not give his estate the right to recover the amount paid under the agreement on the ground that there was a failure of consideration.

The judgment is affirmed [for defendant].

---

14. Modification Needs No Consideration Under U.C.C.

SKINNER v. TOBER FOREIGN MOTORS, INC.

345 Mass. 429, 187 N.E.2d 669 (1963).

SPALDING, Justice. In this suit the plaintiffs seek equitable replevin of an airplane alleged to belong to them and be detained against their right by the defendant; in the alternative, damages were sought.

A master, to whom the case was referred, found the following facts: * * * On October 3, 1959, the plaintiffs purchased an airplane from the defendant. * * *

The instruments executed by the parties provided for payments of $200 per month over a period of twenty-four months with a payment of $353.34 on the twenty-fifth month. Prior to the due date of the first payment the airplane developed engine trouble. This necessitated either the rebuilding of the engine or the installation of a new one at a cost of $1,400. After discussion between the plaintiffs and officers of the defendant, the plaintiffs decided that a new engine should be installed. But the necessity of replacing the engine so soon after the purchase of the plane imposed a financial burden on the plaintiffs which they would be unable to bear. Accordingly, they "offered to return the unrepaired plane to the * * * [defendant] without charge in exchange for a cancellation of all agreements." In order to alleviate the plaintiffs' burdens, and rather than accept the return of the plane, the defendant, through its officers, agreed that for the first year of the instalment contract the payments were to be $100 per month. The plaintiffs agreed to this arrangement and the new engine was installed. This agreement, which was made late in October, 1959, was oral. The defendant derived no benefit from this agreement other than the facts that the plane was not returned and the payments hereinafter mentioned were made.

Following the making of this agreement the plaintiffs, beginning in November, 1959, and continuing through May, 1960, made payments of $100 each month. * * *

In March of 1960 the defendant's president told the plaintiffs that thereafter the monthly payments would have to be increased to $200 or "he would have to take action." The plaintiffs did not agree to this proposal and, after another discussion with the defendant's president, made the April and May payments of $100 each.

On May 26, 1960, the defendant's president * * * took possession of the plane. * * * No demand for full payment was ever made. If the oral modification was controlling the plaintiffs were not in default in their payments. * * *

The defendant argues that the oral modification is unenforceable and invalid because * * * it was not supported by consideration. The short answer to the first point is that the defence of the statute of frauds is not available to the defendant, for it was not pleaded. * * * We do not, therefore, reach the question whether the transactions would be taken out of the statute by reason of delivery and acceptance of the goods, or by part payment. See § 2–201(3)(c). As to the oral modification not being supported by consideration the answer may be found in § 2–209(1) which provides that an "agreement modifying a contract within this Article needs no consideration to be binding."

If the oral modification to the written contract was valid and binding—and we hold that it was—the defendant had no right to take possession of the plane. * * *

[Judgment for plaintiffs].

PROBLEMS

1. A and B have a contract by which A is to work for B for a period of one year at a salary of $500.00 a month. Six months after A commenced working for B, he received a higher offer from another employer. B promised that if A would not leave his employment during the year, he would give him a bonus amounting to $600.00 at the end of the one-year period. A accepts the promise and does not leave the employment. At the end of the year, A requests the $600.00 bonus. Is he legally entitled to it?

2. On April 1, 1974, plaintiff leased to defendants a store for the retail merchandising of women's apparel. The term was for two years at a rental of $200 a month the first year and $250 a month the second year. Prior to the end of the first year the defendants told plaintiff that they could not meet the increased rental due to lack of business, and that if plaintiff insisted on the increased rental they would have to leave the premises. Defendants stated they would pay $200 a month until business improved. Plaintiff agreed to accept the payment of $200 a month

"on account." For eleven months of the second year defendants paid plaintiff the sum of $200 a month. Defendants left the premises at the end of the second year without paying the rent for the last month. Plaintiff sues for the rent for the last month and for the sum of $50 a month for eleven months. Decision?

3. Seller, a resident of Chicago, owned a building lot which was located in Milwaukee and which seller thought was worth $1,000.00. Buyer, who lived near the lot, knew that it was worth $5,000.00. Buyer went to the seller in Chicago and offered him $1,000.00 for the lot. In the discussion, buyer did not make any misstatements; he merely remained silent as to the true value of the lot. The parties then prepared a written contract for the sale of the real estate. Later when the buyer tendered the $1,000.00 purchase price, the seller refused the money and refused to deliver a deed. Buyer sues seller for specific performance. Decision?

4. John and Mary are brother and sister. Upon the death of their mother, it was discovered that the mother's will left the bulk of her property to Mary. John threatened to contest the will. Mary told him that if he would tell the truth in court, she would give him $10,000.00 John accepted and told the truth in court, and the will was upheld. John now demands the $10,000.00. Decision?

5. Two men robbed the First State Bank in Eubank, Kentucky. The director of the bank described the robbers to the police and testified against them at their trial. The robbers were apprehended in Pulaski County, Kentucky, by a deputy sheriff from Rockcastle County and a Kentucky state policeman. The First State Bank offered a reward for the capture and conviction of the robbers. All three men claim the reward. Decision?

6. A real estate broker found a purchaser for seller's property and then procured from the seller a written contract of employment by which the seller would pay the broker a commission. There had been some prior oral conversations between the broker and the seller, however, there had been no valid contractual relations. The sale of the property was consummated, but there was nothing the broker did regarding procuring a purchaser as that had been done prior to the contract of employment. Seller refuses to pay broker the commission pursuant to the contract of employment. Decision?

7. Defendant's son was drowning in a lake. Plaintiff, who happened to be walking beside the lake, swam out to the boy and rescued him. Defendant was so grateful that he promised to pay plaintiff $5,000. Now defendant refuses to pay. Decision?

8. Defendant owed plaintiff $10,000 which was evidenced by an unsecured note. The parties agreed that a new note in the amount of $8,000 secured by a mortgage on defendant's property would be executed in place of the note for $10,000. Defendant signed the new note and mortgage, but now plaintiff claims the defendant owes the entire $10,000 as there was no consideration for the release of the $2,000. Decision?

9. A patient owes a doctor $500.00. The patient sends the doctor a check in the amount of $400.00 which has a statement on the back as follows: "Endorsement of this check is an express release of the balance of $100.00 and is to be considered as payment in full for the obligation

between us". The doctor endorses the check. Does the doctor have a cause of action for the $100.00?

10. In February, 1974, defendant signed a pledge to his favorite college in the amount of $50,000. In March the college signed a contract to have an addition built on the law school for the amount of the pledge. In April, 1974, defendant rescinded the pledge. The college sues for the $50,000. Decision?

11. Red Owl promised plaintiffs that it would build a store building in Chilton, Wisconsin, and stock it with merchandise for plaintiffs to operate. Later plaintiffs would pay Red Owl the sum of $18,000 for a franchise agreement. In reliance on the promise of Red Owl plaintiffs sold their bakery building and business in Wautoma, Wisconsin, purchased a building site in Chilton and rented a residence there. When plaintiffs desired to enter into the franchise agreement Red Owl refused. Plaintiffs sue for damages. Red Owl defends upon the ground that there was no consideration for the promise of grant a franchise. Decision?

12. On January 1, seller sells a horse to buyer for $500.00 payable $250.00 on January 1 and $250.00 on January 10. On January 2, buyer asks the seller if he warrants the horse to be sound. The seller states that he does although there is no consideration for this warranty. If the horse is unsound, is the warranty enforceable?

Chapter 9

REALITY OF CONSENT

A. MISTAKE

To create a contract there must be mutual assent through an offer and acceptance. "Real" assent is lacking if a party is induced to contract by mistake, fraud, duress, or undue influence.

1. MUTUAL MISTAKE AS TO EXISTENCE OR IDENTITY OF SUBJECT MATTER

If both parties are mistaken, and neither is at fault or both are equally at fault, the mistake will prevent the formation of a contract. The mistake may involve the nature of the contract, the identity of the person with whom it is made, or the identity or existence of the subject matter; however, the mistake must relate to a material fact.

In the famous case of Raffles v. Wichelhaus, 2 H. & C. 906, there was a contract to sell cotton to be shipped to the buyer on the ship, "Peerless". Unknown to the parties, there were two ships of that name departing from the same port but at different times. The buyer had in mind the ship that sailed earlier; the seller had in mind the ship that sailed later. No contract resulted. Hence, if neither party is to blame, or both are to blame, there is no contract.

Similarly, where the subject matter, or something essential to performance, ceases to exist before the agreement is reached, there is no contract. Thus, S makes a contract to sell a horse to B. However, unknown to either party, the horse has been destroyed. There is no contract. The *U.C.C.* follows the same rule if the loss is total; however, if the loss is partial, the buyer may accept the partial amount of goods with due allowances from the contract price but without further right against the seller (*Section 2–613*).

2. UNILATERAL MISTAKE

Generally, a unilateral or one-sided mistake is no ground for avoiding a contract; however, it may do so when it is caused by the other party, or the other party knows or has reason to know that there is a material mistake. A common example in which relief is granted for a unilateral material mistake occurs when a contractor submits a bid for construction, and the mistake is material. In such a case, the courts rule that it would be unconscionable to hold the contractor to the bid when the other party knows of the unfairness in ample time to award the contract differently.

Duress- Recission-

3. MISTAKE AS TO VALUE

Athough a mutual mistake as to price can prevent the formation of a contract, a mutual mistake as to value will not permit recission. This is the ordinary risk in business transactions, and the courts will not grant relief. For example, a woman in Wisconsin found a rough stone which looked like a topaz. Thinking it might be worth something, she took it to a jewelry store to sell it. The jeweler did not know the true value of the stone but, nevertheless, offered her one dollar for it, which the woman accepted. Later, it was discovered that the stone was an uncut diamond of great value. The court held that the sale was valid and could not be set aside. (Wood v. Boynton, 64 Wis. 265, 25 N.W. 42).

4. NEGLIGENCE OF MISTAKEN PARTY IN FAILURE TO READ CONTRACT

Generally, a party is held to what he has signed; i.e., ignorance through negligence or inexcusable trustfulness will normally not relieve a party from his contractual obligations. However, there are exceptions:

a. Fraud or other wrongful act on the part of the other party;

b. Where the other party misrepresents the character of the paper (signer thinks he is signing an autograph book, but it is a contract); or,

c. Where a reasonable person would not think that the paper contained contractual provisions; e.g., a hat check stub containing provisions in fine print; an "Acknowledgment of Order" printed form which contained provisions for arbitration and the exclusion of warranties in fine print at the bottom of the form (Windsor Mills v. Collins & Aikman Corp., 25 C.A.3d 987, 101 Cal.Rptr. 347 (1972)).

5. MISTAKE OF LAW

In most states, a mistake of law will not afford grounds for rescission. The rule has been criticized, and there are exceptions:

a. Where there has been fraud or undue influence;

b. Where the mistake resulted in a failure of the contract to express the agreement; e.g., parties mutually agree on the terms of a contract and choose legal phrases which in legal effect express a meaning different from that agreed upon;

c. In those states where by special statute, a mistake of law is treated as a mistake of fact.

B. FRAUD AND MISREPRESENTATION

1. IN GENERAL

Fraud has been defined as "An intentional perversion of truth for the purpose of inducing another in reliance upon it to part with some valuable thing belonging to him or to surrender a legal right; a false representation of a matter of fact, whether by words or by conduct, by false or misleading allegations, or by concealment of that which should have been disclosed, which deceives and is intended to deceive another so that he shall act upon it to his legal injury". (Black's Law Dictionary, Fourth Edition.)

The essentials of fraud are:

a. A false representation of a *material fact*;

b. Made with knowledge of its falsity or made with inexcusable ignorance of its truth;

c. With intention that it be acted on *by the party deceived*;

d. That the party deceived reasonably *relied* upon the representation and acted upon it; and

e. That he was thereby injured.

2. FRAUD IN THE INDUCEMENT

In the usual case of fraud, the defrauded party knows what he is signing, but his consent has been *induced* by fraud; mutual assent is present and a contract is formed, but the contract is *voidable* due to the fraud. To avoid the contract, the party must *rescind* by prompt notice and offer to restore the consideration received, if any.

Under the U.C.C., Section 2–721, the defrauded party may rescind the contract and also recover damages, if any, resulting from the fraud.

3. FRAUD IN THE INCEPTION OR EXECUTION

In this type of case, the defrauded party does not know what he is signing due to deceit as to the nature of the document, or he does not intend to enter into a contract at all. Since mutual assent is lacking, the contract is *void* and may be disregarded without the necessity of rescission. For example, a party unable to read English signs a release relying on the representation of the insurance agent that the instrument is only a receipt. Such a contract is void.

4. INNOCENT MISREPRESENTATION

It is unjust for a person to retain the benefits of a bargain even though his misrepresentation is innocent; therefore, most courts will

Find Economis

permit rescission in this type of case; however, damages in addition to rescission would not be appropriate. In most cases, however, it would seem unnecessary to rely on the theory of fraudulent innocent misrepresentation since the facts usually establish mutual mistake; i.e., one party mistakenly representing the facts and the other believing the representation.

5. SILENCE OR CONCEALMENT AS FRAUD

Generally, silence is not fraud; however, there are several exceptions:

a. Where the parties are in a fiduciary or confidential relationship with each other, such as an attorney and client, there is a duty to speak and to make full disclosure of all facts relevant to the transaction, and failure to do so can be fraud;

b. Where there is a hidden defect, there is a duty to disclose; e.g., S sells cattle to B knowing the cattle have Texas fever, which is not easily ascertainable on inspection, without informing B of the disease;

c. Active concealment, or a half-truth, can be actionable fraud; e.g., auto dealer puts foreign substance in motor to conceal engine defect.

6. SALES TALK

Sales talk is not actionable fraud; e.g., "This is the greatest living dairy bull in Wisconsin", "This is the best car in town", etc. However, it is often difficult to distinguish between sales talk or puffing and a statement of fact. A prediction as to what will happen in the future is treated as an opinion and not as a statement of fact; e. g., A, in good faith, informs B that stock in a corporation is going to rise.

7. DECEIT OF AGENT

In some states, the innocent principal is not liable for the fraud of his agent where the contract contains a clause limiting the agent's authority to make representations. This is the rule of the Restatement of Agency, Sections 259–260. Under this rule, the innocent principal may, by such a clause, relieve himself from liability in a tort action for *damages* for fraud. However, the defrauded party may nevertheless *rescind* the contract.

If the principal is not innocent, but participates in the fraud or affirms the fraud later, the principal would be liable for damages. This is important since it is entirely possible that only the principal will have the assets to pay a judgment for damages.

To illustrate the rule, an auto salesman without the principal's knowledge (query: how could you prove knowledge?) misrepresents the auto to a trusting buyer. The buyer signs a contract containing a clause which limits the salesman's authority to make representations. In such case, the buyer is limited to the remedy of rescinding the contract as far as the principal is concerned. The agent of course would be liable in money damages for his own tort of deceit; however, he may be judgment proof.

With the exception of the rule discussed supra, a party cannot absolve himself of the effects of fraud by a stipulation in the contract that there has been no misrepresentation in the contract or that any right based on fraud has been waived. Such a clause would be against public policy and unenforceable.

C. DURESS AND UNDUE INFLUENCE

1. DURESS

Duress consists of a wrongful act which compels assent through fear. It makes the contract voidable. Duress can be of the person, i.e., unlawful confinement of the party, his spouse, child, etc.; or duress can be of goods, i. e., unlawful detention of property of the party. The modern tendency is to expand duress in the area of property to coercion in the field of business; however, to prove duress by business or economic compulsion it is generally necessary to prove that the victim would suffer irreparable loss for which he could not adequately recover from the wrongdoer.

The general rule is that the act of duress must be unlawful; i. e., it must be a tort or a crime. Threat of a civil suit is not duress.

2. UNDUE INFLUENCE

Undue influence is the unlawful control exercised by one person over another so as to substitute his will for the volition of the victim. It is a kind of mental coercion which destroys the free agency of one and constrains him to do that which is against his will and what he would not have done if left to his own judgment and volition so that his act becomes the act of the one exerting the influence rather than his own act. However, mere appeals to affection or understanding are not considered undue influence, nor mere advice or fair argument and persuasion. Normally a gift occasioned by gratitude for kindness or affection is not undue influence.

In most states, undue influence makes the contract voidable and subject to ratification; however, in some states, the remedy is limited to rescission; i.e., there can be no affirmance *and* recovery of damages.

In most states where a confidential relationship exists between the parties, e. g., attorney and client, guardian and ward, trustee and beneficiary, parent and child, etc., the confidential relationship raises a presumption of undue influence and places upon the dominant party the burden of establishing fairness of the transaction and that it was the free act of the other party. In some states, although no presumption of undue influence arises from a parent-child relationship, still if dominance of the child is found to exist in fact, the burden is on the parent to establish the fairness of the transaction. In the absence of a presumption of undue influence, the person seeking to set aside the transaction must prove that by misrepresentation and deception the alleged victim was led into doing something which he would not have done but for the misrepresentation and deception.

---

1. *Generally Unilateral Mistake Affords No Relief*

BEAVER v. ESTATE OF URBAN HARRIS

67 Wash.2d 621, 409 P.2d 143 (1965).

BRADFORD, Judge. Plaintiff brought this action against Urban Harris and Marjorie Harris, his wife, for personal injuries received in an automobile accident. Urban Harris has since died and his estate substituted as defendant. * * *

The defendant answered and alleged * * * a settlement contract with the plaintiff wherein the plaintiff received $1,750 for a full, complete and final release of the defendant for all injuries known and unknown sustained in the accident. Plaintiff presented his case on the theory there had been a mutual mistake of a material fact and the release should be rescinded. The defendant contended the release was valid and a complete defense, and the court should have determined this as a matter of law.

The primary question raised by this appeal is, can a person who has been injured in an accident caused by another's negligence rescind or set aside a general release and bring an action for damages where there is no allegation or proof of fraud, overreaching, questionable conduct, misrepresentation or any indication of incapacity of the party signing the release?

The facts are that on May 22, 1962, plaintiff was driving his automobile in a southerly direction along Aurora Avenue in Seattle. Urban Harris, at the same time, drove his car from the east side of the street to a traffic channel in the center of Aurora, stopped, and then started on across. There is a dispute as to whether the cars actually made contact. The plaintiff swerved to avoid the defendant driver, left the road, glanced off a pole, jumped the curb and ended up against a concrete abutment. The weather was misty and the pavement was wet. The plaintiff's face was bleeding and he seemed badly shaken. The plaintiff called his doctor, Virgel Anderson, on the evening of the accident and the doctor prescribed muscle relaxants, pain killers and equanil. Plaintiff complained of headaches, painful cervical spine, and pain through his low back area. * * *

Plaintiff consulted regularly with his doctor from the date of the accident until he was discharged to return to work on June 20, 1962.

Les Winder, an adjuster for defendant's insurance company, first contacted the plaintiff on May 23, 1962. He and the plaintiff had six or seven talks between this date and June 14, when plaintiff signed a settlement and release, receiving a check for $1,750. * * *

When plaintiff signed the release, he believed he had a strained back. Medical testimony, based on examinations made after August 12, indicated plaintiff had a herniated disc when he settled.

It is a well recognized principle of law that, before a plain, unambiguous instrument can be set aside on the ground of mutual mistake, the evidence must be clear and convincing. * * *

Although this specific question has not been directly decided, we have repeatedly emphasized the value of amicable settlements of claims of this character, especially when the settlement has been secured without fraud, misrepresentation or overreaching. * * *

Mutual mistake is one of the recognized grounds whereby any contract may be set aside or vacated. What constitutes a mutual mistake must be clearly established.

There is ample authority holding a mutual mistake must be one involving both parties, a mistake independently made by each party.

In the case now being considered, the only information of plaintiff's condition was from the plaintiff himself. Defendant had no independent knowledge and he accepted plaintiff's own diagnosis and opinion of his injuries. If there was a mistake, it was a unilateral mistake, rather than a mutual mistake. * * *

The judgment is reversed and plaintiff's complaint dismissed on the merits.

---

2. Fraud in General

MEYER v. BROWN

312 S.W.2d 158 (Mo.App.1959).

MAUGHMER, Commissioner. This is a suit for damages arising from alleged fraud and misrepresentation in the sale of a large lot of used storage batteries by defendant to plaintiff. There was a jury verdict for plaintiff in the sum of $2,850.

* * *

Plaintiff's petition alleged that on November 15, 1955, he purchased a number of storage batteries from defendant for the sum of $5,750; that defendant represented to plaintiff there were at least 3,000 batteries in the lot; that such representation was false and defendant knew it was false; that plaintiff relied thereon and purchased the batteries upon the assumption that defendant's statements in regard to the number were true; that in truth and fact there were only 1,786 batteries in the lot, and the reasonable value of the shortage (1,214) was $3,000. Defendant's answer was a general denial.

Plaintiff testified that he was 61 years old, had a fourth grade education, and had operated a junk yard outside of Sedalia, Missouri, since 1913. He said he formerly worked for defendant's father and "had done lots of business" with defendant. Ted Brown, the defendant, operated an automotive service business in Sedalia. This business included a machine shop, repair garage and the selling of automobile parts, including batteries. Plaintiff stated that on November 15, 1955, having learned defendant had a stock of used batteries for sale, he visited defendant's place of business for the purpose of trying to buy the batteries. He saw them in defendant's paint and body shop stacked up in a pile approximately 60 feet long, 8 feet high and 6 feet wide; that some of the batteries were so heavy one man could not lift or load them. Plaintiff then had his son Otto come over. They measured the pile and Otto, in defendant's presence said: "There ain't but about 1,800"; that defendant replied: "There was 2,800 a year ago, and we invoiced them and had 2,800 a year ago, and we have been putting more on the pile ever since; there ought to be 3,000 or 3,500". Plaintiff said he knew he could get about $2.35 apiece for the batteries and "I just took his word; that was all there was to it". The parties agreed that the sale was consummated about 2:00 or 2:30 p. m. on November 15, 1955, and at that time plaintiff gave defendant his check in the sum of $5,750, drawn on the Bank of Ionia, located in Benton County, and some miles from Sedalia. On the following day, November 16, 1955, plaintiff testified that they started loading the batteries; that by count the number totalled only 1,784; that on discovery of this fact he looked for defendant but did not find him; that he "told the bank to stop the check, but he had done took the check down that same evening I gave it to him". Plaintiff said defendant told him "lots of times" there were at least 3,000 batteries in the pile.

* * *

Defendant denied making the alleged representations as to the number of batteries and said he sold them to the plaintiff as a pile of batteries.

Defendant contends that his motion for a directed verdict should have been sustained because no submissible case was made. He says that plaintiff had the means readily within reach to determine how many batteries were in the pile; that plaintiff's son Otto actually did give a most accurate estimate; that plaintiff could have counted the batteries and that under these circumstances plaintiff had no right to rely upon the alleged misrepresentations.

* * *

The essential and fundamental elements of an action for fraud have many times been stated by our appellate courts. The rule, as stated, in 37 C.J.S. Fraud § 3, page 215, is as follows: "Comprehensively stated, the elements of actionable fraud consist of: (1) A representation. (2) Its falsity. (3) Its materiality. (4) The speaker's knowledge of its falsity or ignorance of its truth. (5) His intent that it should be acted on by the person and in the manner reasonably contemplated. (6) The hearer's ignorance of its falsity. (7) His reliance on its truth. (8) His right to rely thereon. (9) And his consequent and proximate injury".

* * * There must be substantial evidence as to each of these essential elements, otherwise a plaintiff is not entitled to go to the jury and a recovery would not be permitted to stand.

* * *

* * * We find the following statement in 37 C.J.S. Fraud § 34, pp. 279 and 280: "However, the mere presence of opportunities for investigation will not of itself preclude the right of reliance; and this is especially true where the circumstances were such that a prudent man would not have been put on inquiry, as where positive statements were made in a manner not calculated to cause inquiry, where the relations between the parties were involuntary, where, although it was possible to ascertain the facts, an investigation would have been difficult, or where there was intentional fraud, as where the representations were made for the very purpose of preventing inquiry; * * *.

"The right to rely on representations is generally conceded where the hearer lacks equal facilities for ascertaining the truth, as where the facts are peculiarly within the knowledge of the speaker and are difficult for the hearer to ascertain, as where misrepresentations relate to latent defects, where, because of the hearer's ignorance and inexperience, it would be necessary for him to employ a third person to make an examination in order to learn the truth, where the employment of an expert would be required, or where from the circumstances attending the transaction the hearer is compelled to rely on the speaker's statements".

* * *

For the plaintiff to move and count what he thought were some 3,000 batteries,—some heavier than one man could lift,—in defendant's occupied business premises, would have required the expenditure of time and money. The actual number of batteries was a latent fact not readily discoverable by plaintiff and he was not possessed of equal knowledge thereof. Moreover, he had a plain, positive and unequivocal statement and representation from the defendant that there were at least 3,000 batteries in the pile. From the record before us we believe and rule that plaintiff had the right to rely upon the alleged misrepresentations and that a submissible case was made for the jury on each of the essential elements of fraud.

[Judgment for plaintiff affirmed.]

3. *Must Intend Other Party Rely*

McCANE v. WOKOUN

189 Iowa 1010, 179 N.W. 332 (1920).

Action to enforce a contract by which defendant had agreed to buy plaintiff's farm. In 1917 plaintiff had obtained a loan upon his farm from a bank of which defendant was the cashier. To obtain the loan, plaintiff had made certain false statements to the loan committee of the bank concerning the boundaries of the farm. Defendant was present, as a member of the loan committee, when the false representations were made; and later, relying upon the supposed truth of the statements, the defendant agreed to buy the farm. He now refuses to take the property, on the ground that the contract is voidable because of the misrepresentations made to the loan committee.

WEAVER, C. J. * * * There is an utter failure of evidence on which the court or jury could base a finding of false representations by the plaintiff. It is an elementary principle of law on this subject that "No one has a right to * * * rely upon the representations of others but those to influence whose action they were made. * * * When statements are made for the express purpose of influencing the action of another * * * it is no hardship to hold the party making them to their truth. But he is morally accountable to no person whomsoever but the very person he seeks to influence, and whoever may overhear the statements and go away and act upon them can reasonably set up no claim to having been defrauded, if they prove false. Fraud implies a wrongful actor and one wrongfully acted upon * * *. One may even be the person to whom false representations are made, and yet be entitled to no remedy, if they were made to him as agent for another, and to affect the action of the other, and were not intended to influence his own action." * * * The statements which the defense attributes to the plaintiff were made to the defendant as agent for the bank in the matter of a loan upon the land, and were doubtless intended to influence the action of the bank. The loan was, in fact, made; and, if the representations were false, and the bank was thereby deceived or misled to its injury, a right of action accrued to the bank alone, and not to the agent who represented it.

There is in this case no evidence that, at the time the alleged misrepresentations were made to the loan committee of the bank, plaintiff desired to sell or was offering to sell the farm, or that defendant had any desire to purchase it, or that the idea of making such purchase ever entered his mind, until he announced his bid to the auctioneer who struck it off to him. To permit him now to repudiate his purchase, on the theory that he acted in reliance upon the statements made by plaintiff to the bank's representatives, in negotiating the loan weeks before the sale, and having no connection whatever therewith, would be a startling departure from all recognized rules and principles of the law applicable to charges of fraud and deceit.

[Judgment for plaintiff.]

4. *Failure to Reasonably Rely*

TRUSTEES OF COLUMBIA UNIVERSITY v. JACOBSEN

53 N.J.Super. 574, 148 A.2d 63 (1959), appeal dismissed 31 N.J. 221, 156 A.2d 251, certiorari denied 363 U.S. 808, 80 S.Ct. 1243, 4 L.Ed.2d 1150.

GOLDMANN, S. J. A. D. Columbia brought suit in the district court against defendant and his parents on two notes made by him and signed by them as co-makers, representing the balance of tuition he owed the University. * * * Defendant then sought to file an answer and counterclaim demanding, among other things, money damages in the sum of $7,016. The counterclaim was in 50 counts which severally alleged that plaintiff had represented that it would teach defendant wisdom, truth, character, enlightenment, understanding, justice, liberty, honesty, courage, beauty and similar virtues and qualities; that it would develop the whole man, maturity, well-roundedness, objective thinking and the like; and that because it had failed to do so it was guilty of misrepresentation, to defendant's pecuniary damage. * * *

The attempt of the counterclaim, inartistically drawn as it is, was to state a cause of action in deceit. * * *

We are in complete agreement with the trial court that the counterclaim fails to establish the very first element, false representation, basic to any action in deceit. * * *

At the heart of defendant's counterclaim is a single complaint. He concedes that

> "I have really only one charge against Columbia: that it does not teach Wisdom as it claims to do. From this charge ensues an endless number of charges, of which I have selected fifty at random. I am prepared to show that each of these fifty claims in turn is false, though the central issue is that of Columbia's pretense of teaching Wisdom."

We agree with the trial judge that wisdom is not a subject which can be taught and that no rational person would accept such a claim made by any man or institution. * * *

Defendant's extended argument lacks the element of fraudulent representation indispensable to any action of deceit. We note, in passing, that he has cited no legal authority whatsoever for his position. Instead, he has submitted a dictionary definition of "wisdom" and quotations from such works as the *Bhagavad-Gita*, the *Mundaka Upanishad,* the *Analects of Confucius* and the *Koran*; excerpts from Euripides, Plato and Menander; and references to the Bible. Interesting though these may be, they do not support defendant's indictment of Columbia. If his pleadings, affidavit and exhibits demonstrate anything, it is indeed the validity of what Pope said in his Moral Essays:

"A little learning is a dangerous thing;

Drink deep, or taste not the Pierian spring:

* * * * * * * * * *"

The papers make clear that through the years defendant's interest has shifted from civil engineering to social work, then to physics, and finally to English and creative writing. In college he became increasingly critical of his professors and his courses; in his last year he attended classes only when he chose and rejected the regimen of examinations and term papers. When his non-attendance at classes and his poor work in the senior year were called to his attention by the Columbia Dean of Students, he replied in a lengthy letter that "I want to learn, but I must do it my own way. I realize my behavior is non-conforming, but in these times when there are so many forces that demand conformity I hope I will find Columbia willing to grant some freedom to a student who wants to be a literary artist." In short, he chose to judge Columbia's educational system by the shifting standards of his own fancy, and now seeks to place his failure at Columbia's door on the theory that it had deliberately misrepresented that it taught wisdom. * * *

The judgment [for plaintiff] is affirmed.

---

5. *Active Concealment as Fraud*

DE JOSEPH v. ZAMBELLI

392 Pa. 24, 139 A.2d 644 (1958).

DANNEHOWER, President Judge. This is an action in equity by a purchaser of real estate seeking a rescission and cancellation of a deed, and the recovery of the purchase price, $18,000.00, together with costs and expenses incidental thereto, from the defendant vendors, on the grounds of false and fraudulent representations inducing the sale. * * *

The evidence discloses that the defendants' vendors had knowledge of the existence of termites in their premises as early as May, 1952, and that they persisted in attempts to check and abate them until May, 1955, when the property was sold to the plaintiff. This is established clearly by the testimony of the tenants in the second floor apartment who were disinterested parties to the controversy. * *

It was further disclosed that the basement had been given a heavy application of paint or whitewash shortly before the plaintiff first inspected the premises in February, 1955. According to the description of one witness, the basement looked like a "white sepulcher". In addition, the joists were partially obscured by shelves laden with jars and articles of clothing, and in some areas, strips of wood had been attached with the apparent purpose of concealing the more obvious termite damage. As a result of this deception and concealment the latent defects in the joists could not be detected and were not susceptible of discovery except by expert investigation.

The inference is inescapable that the defendants knew that the dwelling was infested with termites and were aware of the serious deterioration of the joists when the property was offered for sale to the plaintiff. The reply to the plaintiff's inquiry that the joists were "as good as new" was therefore a false, material and erroneous statement of fact.

* * * Where a party is induced to enter into a transaction with another by means of the latter's fraud or material misrepresentation, such a transaction can be avoided by the innocent party. Fraud arises where the misrepresentation is knowingly false, where there is a concealment calculated to deceive, or where there is a non-privileged failure to disclose. * * *

Rule

Applying the above principles to the case at bar, we are of the opinion that the defendants are guilty of fraud in the purposeful concealment of the termite condition in the premises, and in misrepresenting to the plaintiff that the joists in the basement were "as good as new". This being true we must conclude that the plaintiff is entitled to avoid the transaction and be returned to status quo.

---

6. *Failure to Read Contract Does Not Bar Relief*

SWANN v. BOB WILSON, INC.

168 A.2d 198 (D.C.Mun.App., 1961).

QUINN, Associate Judge. This appeal is from a judgment based on a jury verdict assessing against defendant, a used car dealer, $613.20 compensatory and $2,000 punitive damages for the fraudulent sale of a used car to [plaintiff.] * * *

On October 10, 1959, [plaintiff] orally agreed to purchase a 1957 Ford from [defendant.] * * *

The parties did not then execute a written contract but Swann gave a cash deposit and left his old car as a trade-in. Two days later, accompanied by his wife, daughter and son-in-law, he returned to conclude the formal arrangements. According to their testimony, [defendant's] president, Monroe Lenoff, appeared carrying a sheaf of papers and with a pencil proceeded to enter the terms of sale on the top sheet, a blank bill of sale. Finishing this task, Lenoff took the papers and left the room for a few minutes presumably to find a pen. Upon his return, Lenoff handed the pen to Swann and directed him to sign each of the papers, representing that those underneath were merely duplicates of their agreement. Without making any effort to examine the contents, Swann signed, with Lenoff pushing back the top sheets so that only the space provided for the purchaser's signature was visible on each of the forms. * * *

On October 14, Swann paid the balance due on his down payment and went with one of [defendant's] * * * salesmen to a notary public to acknowledge the papers. Recognizing his signature, he did as requested, although he did not see the figures written on the instruments. Then, before taking leave, the salesman asked Swann and his wife to indicate on the papers their satisfaction with the transaction. At his direction Swann signed across the face of the document on top and Mrs. Swann wrote in the margin, "We have read this contract it is correct and complete." Copies of the papers were placed in an envelope and given to Swann. Shortly thereafter, he inspected the papers and found that additional charges and interest totaling $613.20 had been inserted in the contract without his knowledge. * * *

Defendant denies actionable fraud on the ground that Swann unjustifiably relied on Lenoff's representations that the papers signed were copies of the original pencil agreement. Since the papers were freely accessible to Swann, it is asserted that he was bound to determine for himself whether those reputed to be copies actually conformed to the true understanding of the parties. * * *

It is settled that one who refrains from reading a contract and in conscious ignorance of its terms voluntarily assents thereto will not be relieved from his bad bargain. The question whether the same risk falls upon a person who has been disarmed by fraud has not received uniform treatment. The approach taken by some jurisdictions denies redress where the party victimized neglected available means to discover the duplicity. Other courts, adopting what commentators regard as the better view, afford relief where misrepresentation has induced a party to forego the ordinary precaution of investigation. The fact that by so doing the party exercised less vigilance than most people would have employed under the circumstances does not protect the wrongdoer. * * *

We need not consider here whether Swann was unreasonable in trusting Lenoff's representations and in failing to insist on an examination of the papers before signing. * * * The record shows that Lenoff deliberately sought to mislead Swann and was successful in the attempt. * * *

Defendant may not shield itself from the consequences of its agent's deception by saying that Swann should not have been fooled.

Affirmed.

---

7. *Silence is Fraud When Duty to Disclose*

GRIGSBY v. STAPLETON

94 Mo. 423, 7 S.W. 421 (1888).

Action to recover the contract price of 100 cattle sold by plaintiff to defendant. The defendant sets up plaintiff's failure to disclose the fact that the cattle were suffering from Texas fever, (deadly cattle fever disease, caused by tick bites, and difficult to detect) * * * and contends that silence as to this defect is fraudulent. The rest of the facts appear in the opinion.

BLACK, J. * * * Plaintiff purchased 105 head of cattle at the stock yards in Kansas City on Friday, July 25, 1884, at $3.60 per hundredweight. He shipped them to Barnard on Saturday. Mr. Ray, plaintiff's agent, attended to the shipment and accompanied the cattle. Ray says it was reported in the yards, before he left Kansas City, that the cattle were sick with Texas fever; some persons said they were sick and some said they were not. When the cattle arrived at Barnard, Ray told the plaintiff of the report, and that the cattle were in bad condition; that one died in the yards at Kansas City before loading, and another died in the cars on the way. On Sunday morning the plaintiff started with them to his home. After driving them a mile or so, he says he concluded to and did drive them back to the yards, because they were wild. One of them died on this drive, and two more died in the pen at Barnard before the sale to defendant. * * * He made no disclosure of the fact that the cattle were sick to defendant, nor that they were reported to have the fever. Defendant bargained for the cattle on Sunday afternoon and on Monday morning completed the contract at $3.75 per hundredweight, and at once shipped them to Chicago. Thirty died on the way, and twenty were condemned by the health officer. It is shown beyond all question that they all had the Texas fever. * * * If defects in the property sold are patent and might be discovered by the exercise of ordinary attention, and the buyer has an opportunity to inspect the property, the law does not require the vendor to point out defects. But there are cases where it becomes the duty of the seller to point out and disclose latent defects. * * * The sale of animals which the seller knows, but the purchaser does not, have a contagious disease, should be regarded as a fraud when the fact of the disease is not disclosed. * * *

There is no claim in this case that defendant knew these cattle were diseased. It seems to be conceded on all hands that Texas fever is a disease not easily detected, except by those having had experience with it. The cattle were sold to the defendant at a sound price. If, therefore, plaintiff knew they had the Texas fever, or any other disease materially affecting their value upon the market, and did not disclose the same to the defendant, he was guilty of a fraudulent concealment of a latent defect. * * * They were circumstances materially affecting the value of the cattle for the purposes for which they were bought, or for any other purpose, and of which defendant, on all the evidence, had no equal means of knowledge. To withhold these circumstances was a deceit * * *.

[Judgment for defendant.]

8. *Sales Talk and Opinion is Not Fraud*

CANNADAY ET UX. v. COSSEY ET UX.

228 Ark. 1119, 312 S.W.2d 442 (1958).

GEORGE ROSE SMITH, Justice. On March 1, 1956, the Cannadays bought an improved 100-acre tract of land from the Cosseys paying $2,000 down and executing an installment note for the unpaid balance of $6,000. After occupying the property for about six months the Cannadays discovered that the dwelling house had been seriously damaged by termites. They then brought this suit for a rescission of the contract, asserting that the sellers, with knowledge of the damage to the dwelling, had falsely represented it to be "a good house." Upon conflicting evidence the chancellor concluded that the Cosseys had not acted in bad faith and that the misrepresentation, even if made, was not one that the purchasers were entitled to rely upon. The court accordingly sustained the contract and granted the Cosseys' * * * prayer for foreclosure of their vendors' lien.

In our opinion the plaintiffs failed to meet the burden of proving actual fraud in the transaction. Cossey, who is seventy-five years old, had lived on the place for more than fifty years. The dwelling in question was built partly with used lumber and was twenty-eight years old at the time of the sale. Cossey considered it to be a good house for its age. He candidly admitted having seen flying ants around the farm for forty years or more, but he testified that he had had no experience with termites and did not know what a termite was. It is of course common knowledge that many species of harmless ants are temporarily able to fly.

It was evidently possible for Cossey to occupy the house without realizing its condition, for the damage, though extensive, was not easily discoverable. The floors were covered with linoleum, and the walls had been papered eight or ten years before the sale. The Cannadays themselves lived in the dwelling from March until October without suspecting the presence of termites; it was Mrs. Cannaday who first discovered the condition as she was hanging a picture. Her husband then went under the house to examine the sills. He states that the wood looked sound from the outside, but his hammer "buried up" when he tested the wood by striking it. * * *

It is insisted, however, that the purchasers were not required to prove a deliberate intention to deceive, since one may be held liable for a false statement which he honestly believed to be true. * *

Even so, the representation must amount to more than a mere expression of opinion and must involve a statement of fact that serves as an inducement to the agreement. * * *

The chancellor did not find it necessary to determine exactly what representation, if any, was made; but, in view of the conflicting versions of the incident, a finding that Cossey described the dwelling as a good house would not be against the weight of the testimony. A general statement of this kind amounts only to an expression of opinion and cannot be relied on by the purchasers as an assurance against the various defects that are apt to be found in a twenty-eight-year-old dwelling.

As Williston expresses it: "Statements that things are 'good,' or 'valuable,' or 'large,' or 'strong,' necessarily involve to some extent an exercise of individual judgment, and even though made absolutely, the hearer must know that they can be only expressions of opinion."

Affirmed [for defendants].

---

9. Duress

McINTOSH v. McINTOSH

209 Cal.App.2d 371, 26 Cal.Rptr. 26 (1962).

SHEPARD, Justice. This is an appeal from a judgment * * * in regard to enforcement of a divorce decree. * * *

During the trial, sharply conflicting testimony was had regarding whether plaintiff had written and signed an alleged waiver of alimony voluntarily or involuntarily. * * *

It appears from the record that plaintiff, about November 24, 1959, gave birth to an illegitimate child by a man named Glessner. On December 2, 1959, plaintiff wrote, signed and mailed to defendant a waiver of further alimony and a promise that when the family home (which had been awarded her by the divorce decree) was sold, she would divide the proceeds with defendant. The principal controversy between the parties involves the question of validity of said waiver. Defendant's testimony, if believed, would support the conclusion that the waiver was voluntary and for a consideration. However, plaintiff testified that on November 13, 1959, defendant beat plaintiff severely, broke part of the furniture, and threatened to kill her; that thereafter defendant made further and repeated threats to kill her, that he would burn her house down, bring her into court on a charge of adultery, and take her son and daughter away from her; that she was afraid then that if she did not send defendant the written waiver defendant would kill or injure her; that immediately prior to her writing of the waiver, defendant telephoned her and dictated its contents; that when she wrote the waiver she was worried sick and didn't know what she was doing. From the foregoing we are satisfied that the trial court was justified in finding that plaintiff was coerced into writing the waiver by fear of personal injury or death at the hands of defendant; that said fear was induced by the beating of November 13, 1959, coupled with the subsequent threats of defendant; that the waiver was not the voluntary act of plaintiff and was invalid. * *

> "Under the modern doctrine there is no standard of courage or firmness with which the victim of duress must comply at the risk of being without remedy; the question is

merely whether the pressure applied did in fact so far affect the individual concerned as to deprive him of contractual volition; if it did there is duress, if it did not there is none," * * *

The judgment is affirmed [for plaintiff].

---

10. Undue Influence

TRIGG v. TRIGG

37 N.M. 296, 22 P.2d 119 (1933).

The case was tried before the district court of San Miguel county, where the issues were found for the plaintiff from which judgment and decree the issue is here on appeal.

ZINN, Justice. The plaintiff * * * brought suit against the defendant to cancel deeds of conveyance. * * *

That conveyances and other instruments may be set aside because procured by the exercise of undue influence upon the party executing them is not questioned, and the exercise of such undue influence does not necessarily mean the infliction or threat of any physical injury or mischief. In the general sense of the term, undue influence would seem to be a species of duress, or, if this be not quite accurate, the two would at least seem to run together so that the precise line where one begins and the other stops is not easily definable. * * * Generally, the cases cited are where the husband obtained the property from the wife, where the guardian obtained property from the ward, where children obtained the property from the aged father or mother, the attorney from the client; generally the weaker or subservient having conveyed to the stronger or dominant, and equity has granted relief because of undue influence, duress, or fraud.

Here, however, we have the reverse, the clinging vine inducing the oak to convey to her all his interest in fourteen thousand broad acres on the Pablo Montoya grant, the weaker sex importuning, "nagging," and obtaining from the stronger and dominating member of the life partnership a conveyance of community real estate. She adopted the device, as alleged by the plaintiff of threatening abandonment of his bed and board, and dissolving the marriage by securing a divorce unless he gave her a deed to the ranch.

* * * The affection, confidence, and gratitude which inspires the gift from a husband to a wife, being a natural and lawful influence, does not render the gift voidable, unless the influence has been so used as to confuse the judgment and control the will of the donor.

* * * Plaintiff on cross-examination testified that the defendant abandoned him without cause, refusing to occupy the same

bed with him, that it was without reason, "just her temper and mad all the time, and she was displeased about something always, and the atmosphere she made, just made it impossible to have any affection, and she would lock her bedroom doors and if I attempted to caress or pet her, she would scream for the servants to come."

Plaintiff testified that he deemed it necessary to place the title in Mrs. Trigg, the appellant, to preserve his home and happiness, without any intention to vest the same in the * * * Domestic tranquillity, the companionship and affection of a companionable mate and a peaceful household are more priceless than jewels, and cannot be measured in dollars and cents, and a social or domestic force exercised in such a manner as might put fear into the mind of a husband that, unless a conveyance is made of property so as to vest the same in the wife, a divorce would follow, with the consequences attendant thereto upon the domestic and social affairs of the threatened husband, might be considered as such undue influence and force as preventing the true and free action of his will and consent, and, where a deed of conveyance has been made after persistent "nagging," followed by threats of divorce and abandonment unless the deed is executed, it is a legitimate inference that such deed was made under the exercise of a domestic or social force which prevented the free action of the will of the donor and that such gift was made as the result of undue influence, and, if such gift be made in consideration of the fraudulent promise of a wife to return home and live with the grantor as his wife, and such promise is not fulfilled, it will amount to fraud. * * *

Constant importunities and "nagging" amount to an undue influence which can overcome the mind of the strongest willed person, and such constant importuning and "nagging" does amount to an undue influence. Such persistent urging amounts to "nagging," and "nagging" is the exercise of a domestic force by which the mind becomes irritated, disturbed, ruffled, wearied, and troubled, so that the judgment may become confused and the free action of the will is out of normal control, and a chancellor can set aside a conveyance of property made under such improper conditions. * * *

Finding no error, the judgment of the district court is affirmed, and it is so ordered.

PROBLEMS

1. Husband had an insurance policy on his life for $10,000.00 payable to his wife as beneficiary. Husband did not return home one day and continued to be missing for two years. Wife was having trouble paying the premiums on the policy so after a discussion with the insurance company's agent decided to take a paid-up policy for $2,500.00 instead of the $10,000.00 policy. Later, it was discovered that husband was dead prior to the conversion to the $2,500.00 paid-up policy. Wife now demands the $10,000.00 payment from the insurance company; however, the insurance company will only pay her $2,500.00. Decision?

2. Builder submits a written offer to home owner to erect a building for $54,000.00, and home owner accepts the offer. Builder later discovers

that he made a mistake of $20,000.00 and that the offer should have been for $74,000.00. Builder now seeks to be allowed to withdraw his offer and to have the contract rescinded because of this mistake. Decision?

3. Mrs. Reed was injured in a train accident. The insurance agent had her examined by a company physician shortly after the accident and while she was en route to her destination. The physician told her that she was not seriously injured. The insurance agent requested her to sign a release for damages for the consideration of $100.00 which she did. After completing her journey, she discovered that she sustained serious injuries which required her hospitalization. She now seeks to have the release set aside by reason of the false representations made to her by the insurance agent and the physician. She testified that she could neither read nor write and signed the release with an X mark, that she knew little about the contents of the release, that she signed it a few hours after the accident without a chance to consult with friends, a doctor, or an attorney, and at the urgent solicitation of the claims agent who was with her on the train at the time of the accident. Decision?

4. Seller desiring to sell an orange grove told buyer that the country where the grove was situated was "absolutely free from frost" and that "a damaging frost had never been known in the neighborhood". Relying on these representations, buyer purchased the grove; however, he soon discovered that frost was quite common and that the grove in question had often been injured by frosts. Buyer seeks to have the court set aside the contract. Decision?

5. In order to induce buyer to purchase a tract of land, seller stated that the land was low enough to be readily irrigable from a nearby irrigation ditch. Seller knew that his statement was false. Buyer consulted an irrigation expert about the possibility of getting water upon the land and apparently satisfied with the expert's opinion, buyer purchased the land. Later, buyer discovered that the land was too high for irrigation from the nearby irrigation ditch and sues seller for damages for deceit. Decision?

6. To induce buyer to purchase a herd of cattle ranging over an extensive territory, seller told buyer the number of animals he had branded the preceding season; however, he failed to inform buyer that many of the cattle had since been lost or killed; and when buyer sought to determine the number in the herd for himself, seller put various obstacles in the way of buyer's inspection, as a result of which buyer was unable to learn of the extensive losses among the cattle. Buyer now sues seller for fraud. Decision?

7. Seller built a dwelling house directly over an old cesspool, and without making any reference to the unsanitary pit beneath the cellar floor sold the new house to buyer. The house soon became uninhabitable because of the odor from the hidden refuse. Buyer sues seller for the deceit. Seller contends that he was merely silent as to the cesspool, and silence is not fraud. Decision?

8. Debtor owed creditor $1,000.00. Creditor tried every friendly gesture possible to get the debtor to pay him but with no result. Finally, the creditor sent the debtor a letter as follows: "I have tried to be nice about this, but you simply will not cooperate. This is to inform you that unless I receive payment in full on or before Friday at 4:00 P.M., I am going to file a civil suit against you on Monday." Debtor claims creditor is using duress to collect the money. Decision?

9. Plaintiff leased a parcel of land from defendant for the sum of $800 a month, except that until plaintiff completed certain remodeling the rental for the parcel would be $600 a month. The remodeling took six months. During the six month period plaintiff paid $800 a month rent, but only under protest and solely because defendant made written and verbal threats that unless plaintiff paid the higher sum defendant would cancel plaintiff's lease and institute legal proceedings to evict plaintiff. Plaintiff sues for overpayment on the lease in the amount of $1,200. Decision? Plaintiff gets the sum

10. Plaintiff contracted to buy a large herd of cattle from defendant and made an initial payment of $200,000. On the day for delivery of the cattle when plaintiff was to pay the balance of the purchase price, plaintiff discovered that 460 head of cattle were missing. Plaintiff insisted on deducting the value of the missing cattle from the purchase price; however, defendant refused to deliver any of the cattle unless the entire balance called for by the contract was paid. Winter was approaching and the cattle might be exposed to great loss unless properly cared for during the winter season. To obtain the cattle and to protect his initial payment plaintiff paid the entire sum. Plaintiff now sues for the value of the missing 460 head of cattle. Defendant claims that since plaintiff paid for all of the cattle he has no claim. Decision? Plaintiff receives sum

11. Sallie Beard, 50 years of age, a widow, feeble, in ill health, and entirely without business experience, made up her mind to withdraw her extensive funds from the X bank and use them elsewhere. The bank officials, close relatives of Sallie's deceased husband, and their attorney, worried that the withdrawal would injure the bank, repeatedly urged her not to withdraw the money but instead to sign a deed of trust with the bank as trustee. She desired to see her attorney, but they persuaded her not to see him. They told her that if she withdrew the money, the bank would not survive, that if her late husband knew what she was doing he would turn over in his grave, and that her father-in-law would probably be influenced to ignore her in his will if she refused to execute the deed of trust. Finally, she executed the deed of trust. Later, she discovered that the deed she signed took away all control over the funds and deprived her forever of any power to revoke the trust. She brings an action to have the deed declared void on the grounds of undue influence. Decision?

Deed declared void

Chapter 10

THE STATUTE OF FRAUDS (WRITINGS)

A. NATURE AND EFFECT

1. IN GENERAL

Some students believe that all contracts must be in writing; otherwise, they wonder, how will the contract be proven in court? Actually, only relatively few contracts must be in writing and even to this there are exceptions.

When a contract is not in writing, it is proven in court by the testimony of the parties to the contract and by witnesses, if any. In court, there is often conflicting testimony and confusion about the actual terms of the contract, in which case it is very difficult for the judge to make a correct decision. Also, if the contract is in writing, there is much less chance of litigation on the contract.

Some contracts are so important, or there is such an opportunity for fraud in the making of the contract, that every state has a Statute of Frauds declaring which contracts must be in writing. The statutes differ only in the types of contracts which must be in writing. Below, you will find the most common and important types of these contracts.

Perhaps the Statute of Frauds is a misnomer since the statute has nothing to do with the *law of frauds* discussed supra. However, the original Statute of Frauds was passed in England in 1677 as "An Act for the Prevention of Frauds and Perjuries", and the name still continues. Perhaps a better name for this statute would be the Statute of Writings since the statute states that certain contracts must be in writing and signed by the party to be charged (always the defendant in the law suit), or the contract is unenforceable.

The writing required may be a note or memorandum, may be informal and may consist of one or more writings; e.g., separate escrow instructions and signed by one of the parties, or two letters. The writing should meet the test of reasonable certainty and should contain the names of the parties, the subject matter, and the terms and conditions of all the promises, and by whom and to whom made. Under this rule, the absence of a description of the property or the names of the parties in the sale of real estate is fatal. *Under the U.C.C.,* which is applicable to the sale of goods, the test of reasonable certainty has been greatly relaxed.

B. SALE OF GOODS

1. IN GENERAL

Section 2–201(1) of the U.C.C. states that a contract for the sale of goods for the price of $500.00 or more is not enforceable unless there is some writing sufficient to indicate that a contract for sale has been made between the parties. The writing must be signed by the party against whom enforcement is sought. The writing may be informal since the only purpose of the section is for the parties to establish that there is in fact a contract for sale and purchase. The details regarding price, place of delivery, etc., may be omitted; however, the quantity must be stated unless it is a "need" or "output" contract (see Chapter 7).

There are exceptions to the above rule.

a. *Section 2–201(2)* states that as between *merchants* an oral contract of sale is enforceable if one of the merchants sends a *written confirmation* of the contract to the other merchant, and the merchant receiving the information does not object to the contents of the confirmation within ten days after receiving it. Both merchants are bound.

b. *Section 2–201(3) (a)* states that a writing is not necessary if the goods are to be *specially manufactured* for the buyer; and before the seller receives repudiation by the buyer, he has made a substantial beginning of their manufacture or has made commitments for their procurement, and the goods are not suitable for sale to others in the ordinary course of the seller's business.

c. *Section 2–201(3) (c)* states that the contract does not have to be in writing if the goods have been *paid for*, or they have been *received* by the buyer. If the goods have been partly paid for or partially delivered, the oral contract is enforceable only to the extent of the partial payment or partial delivery.

2. MINERALS, STRUCTURES, GROWING TIMBER, CROPS

a. *Section 2–107(1)* states that a contract for the sale of minerals (including oil and gas), or the sale of a structure or its materials to be removed from the land, is a contract for the sale of *goods* IF they are to be severed by the *seller*, thus Section 2–201 applies; however, if they are to be severed by the *buyer* the contract is one affecting *land* and Section 2–201 does not apply.

b. *Section 2–107(2)* states that a contract for the sale of growing timber or growing crops is a contract for the sale of *goods* whether severed by the seller or the buyer.

3. SALE OF SECURITIES

Section 8–319 provides that every contract for the sale of securities, regardless of the amount, must be in writing and signed by the party to be charged or his authorized agent or broker. Delivery of the securities or a confirmatory writing will satisfy the statute.

4. SALES OF OTHER KINDS OF PERSONAL PROPERTY

Section 1–206 provides that other types of personal property sales, such as royalty rights, patent rights, and general intangibles in an amount over $5,000.00 are within the statute.

C. SALE OF LAND

Contracts for the sale of land, or any interest therein, must be in writing under the Statute of Frauds regardless of the amount involved. This also applies to mortgages, easements, and real estate brokers commission contracts. Most states have statutes which provide that a lease of real property for a longer period than one year must be in writing.

On occasion, a buyer and seller enter into an *oral* contract for the sale of land; and the buyer, in reliance on the oral contract, goes into possession of the land and/or makes valuable improvements on the land; in other words, the buyer, relying on the oral contract, changes his position in equity. Can the seller use the Statute of Frauds as a basis for refusal to perform the contract? Most courts will hold for the buyer under the doctrine of part performance even though there is nothing in the statute that aids the buyer in this situation. Since it would be inequitable to permit the seller to use the statute after such reliance by the buyer, the seller is estopped from using the statute as a defense to the oral contract. A few courts, relying on the literal language which provides no provisions regarding part performance, refuse to grant relief to the buyer and will not enforce the oral contract.

Most courts demand that the buyer go into possession *and* make improvements before the oral contract will be enforced. Many courts also require that the buyer make payment as required by the oral contract. Generally, payment alone is insufficient to constitute part performance.

Some courts only require that the buyer go into possession *or* make improvements in reliance on the oral contract to make the oral contract enforceable. It has been held in California that possession alone, without payment, is sufficient.

D. CONTRACT NOT TO BE PERFORMED WITHIN A YEAR

An agreement that *by its terms* is *not possible* of performance within a year *from the making thereof* is within the statute and must be in writing and signed by the party to be charged (the defendant when a lawsuit is filed).

The period commences when the agreement is *made* and not when performance begins. Thus, an agreement to perform services for exactly one year commencing on the date the contract is entered into can be oral; but if the services are to begin two days after the contract is made, then the contract is not possible to perform within a year *from its making* and hence, it is unenforceable. Most states permit one day's grace.

If it is *possible* to perform the contract within one year, then the statute does not apply. For example, A makes an oral contract with B to clear A's land in Canada of trees commencing June first. No ending date is mentioned, but the parties anticipate it will take B two years to clear the land. This contract is valid and not within the statute since B could clear the land within a year by employing more men, obtaining more equipment, etc. Even if it took B two years to clear the land, the result is the same.

There are two main *exceptions* to this section of the Statute of Frauds.

1. Where one party has fully performed in a bilateral contract most courts hold that the contract is enforceable even though the contract was not possible to perform within a year. For example, B purchases an automobile from S on a contract which provides that B will pay the price in 15 monthly payments and B is given immediate possession of the automobile. After B obtains possession of the automobile his oral promise to pay the installments is binding.

2. The modern tendency is to enforce the oral contract if the plaintiff, in reliance on the contract, has so changed his position that pecuniary or unconscionable injury would be suffered; or the defendant, having accepted the benefits of the contract, would be unjustly enriched by plaintiff's legal inability to enforce the oral contract. It has been said that part performance is available when a restitutionary remedy is wholly inadequate and the facts are "virtual fraud" for the defendant not to perform; e. g., plaintiff leased property for two years and went into possession making permanent improvements.

E. PROMISE TO PAY THE DEBT OF ANOTHER

Generally, a promise to pay the debt of another must be in writing and signed by the party to be charged. Thus, T promises C that he will pay D's debt to C. This is within the statute.

There are exceptions:

1. Where the third party makes the promise to the *debtor*. Thus, T promises D that he will pay D's debt to C. This is not within the statute.

2. Where the *leading benefit* of the transaction is for T, the statute does not apply even though the promise is made to the creditor. For example, T promised C that he would pay D's debt if C did not bid at the auction. C agreed. T was able to buy the goods at the auction at a much lower price because C did not bid. In this type of case, since the promise of T was mainly for his own pecuniary or business advantage, he is estopped from using the statute; and the oral promise is enforceable.

3. Where there has been a *novation* or substitution of debtors, the statute does not apply; and the oral arrangement is enforceable. Thus, T, D, and C agree that T will take over D's debt, and D will be discharged. T will be bound.

4. Where the promisor is the original debtor. Thus, B orally requests a jeweler to send a $400.00 watch to B's girl friend. This is an original debt of B, and he is not promising to pay the debt of another; thus, the oral promise is enforceable.

F. PROMISE MADE IN CONSIDERATION OF MARRIAGE

If a person makes a promise to pay a sum of money or to give property to another in consideration of that person's promise to marry, the agreement must be in writing. This provision of the Statute of Frauds does not apply to mutual promises to marry. It is universally held that the marriage itself does not constitute such part performance as to make the oral ante-nuptial contract valid.

G. MODIFICATION OF WRITTEN CONTRACT

Generally a contract which is required to be in writing under the Statute of Frauds cannot be modified except in writing.

Under the U.C.C., Section 2–209(3), if the contract *as modified* is within the Statute of Frauds, Section 2–201 must be satisfied. For example, buyer and seller orally agree to buy and sell certain goods for a price of $400 and later desire to increase the quantity of goods in an amount which will increase the price to $600; the modified agreement must meet the requirements of writing under the Statute of Frauds.

If the contract is in writing, but did not have to be under the Statute of Frauds, would the modification have to be in writing? In most courts it would not; however, the modification would need the essential elements of a contract to be valid. By statute in some jurisdictions the modification must be in writing, but there are exceptions; e. g., fully executed oral modification; one party induced into changing his position creating an equitable estoppel.

---

1. Written Confirmation Under U.C.C. 2–201(2)

TRAFALGAR SQUARE v. REEVES BROTHERS

35 A.D.2d 194, 315 N.Y.S.2d 239 (1970).

CAPOZZOLI, Justice. During October and November, 1967, Trafalgar Square, Ltd., petitioner-respondent, orally ordered goods from Abaco Fabrics Corp., later merged into Reeves Brothers, Inc., respondent-appellant. Following the five oral orders, each was evidenced by a written contract with its own number.

In accordance with the custom and usage prevalent in the textile industry all of these contracts were sent by Abaco to petitioner, via certified mail, return receipt requested. Across the face of each of these contracts, in bold print, the following language appears:-

> "IMPORTANT
>
> THIS CONTRACT IS SUBJECT TO ALL TERMS AND CONDITIONS INCLUDING, BUT NOT LIMITED TO ARBITRATION AS SET FORTH ON THE FACE AND SIDE HEREOF."
>
> Underneath the preceding language the following appears:-
>
> "This contract embodying the terms on the face and the reverse side hereof is hereby acknowledged to be correct by Buyer. This contract shall become binding upon the occurrence of any one of the following conditions: (1) Buyer signs and returns to Seller a signed copy of this contract or, (2) Buyer accepts delivery of all or any part of the goods herein described, or (3) Shipment by Seller to Buyer of all or any portion of the goods hereby sold, or (4) Buyer retains a copy of this contract for a period of five (5) days from date hereof. However, the Buyer's failure to sign and

> return a copy hereof within five (5) days from date shall afford Seller the right to cancel this sale without any liability to Seller resulting therefrom."

On the back of each of the contract forms the following language appears as part of paragraph (12) (a):-

> "(12) (a) * * * There are no oral understandings, options, representations or agreements relative to this contract which are not fully expressed herein."

Paragraph (15) of the contract, in part, provides as follows:

> "Any controversy arising under, or in relation to this contract, or any modification thereof, may be settled only by arbitration. Such arbitration shall be held in the City of New York, in accordance with the laws of the State of New York, and the rules then obtaining of the American Arbitration Association, or the General Arbitration Council of the Textile Industry, as the seller may determine. * * * ".

All five contracts were received by petitioner and retained without objection. Goods were delivered to petitioner and invoices were issued for each shipment. All of the invoices contained, on the face of each, a reference to the particular written contract number under which the invoice was issued. No objection was made to any of the invoices and the goods were accepted by petitioner. Petitioner has used the goods and failed to pay the invoices. Its claim that the goods were defective was rejected by Abaco.

The issue raised between the parties is whether the provision for arbitration, found in the contract forms, as above quoted, binds the petitioner.

CPLR § 7501 requires only that an agreement to submit a controversy to arbitration be "written". That section does not require that such an agreement be signed by the party to be bound.

* * *

In addition to the above, the Uniform Commercial Code, § 2–201(2) provides as follows:-

> "(2) Between merchants if within a reasonable time a writing in confirmation of the contract and sufficient against the sender is received and the party receiving it has reason to know its contents, it satisfies the requirements of subsection (1) against such party unless written notice of objection to its contents is given within ten days after it is received."

This language clearly indicates that the one who receives a "writing" in confirmation of a "contract" has the burden of objecting to its contents within ten days. There was no objection by the petitioner-respondent in this case.

Because of the foregoing reasons, the order of Special Term staying arbitration should be reversed, on the law, with costs and disbursements to appellant, and the parties directed to proceed to arbitration as prayed for in the cross-motion of respondent-appellant.

---

2. *Goods Specially Manufactured*

ADAMS v. COHEN

242 Mass. 17, 136 N.E. 183 (1922).

RUGG, C. J. This is an action of contract brought to recover damages for refusal by the defendant to accept certain shoes manufactured for him by the plaintiff. There was evidence tending to show that the plaintiff was a manufacturer of men's shoes, * * * that the defendant ordered of him one hundred dozen of "brog. oxford" shoes, * * * that the shoes ordered by the defendant "is a specially made shoe" in respect of its perforations and otherwise "very fancy," that a part of the order was for size five and one half, which was an unusual size and not commonly sold in the trade, that the order was given on April 22 for deliveries to be made in June, which was late to buy and have delivered that style of shoe; that the details of the order were: "* * * 97 perforation lace. Blind eyelets. * * * 97 perforation and pink. * * * Outside heel stay No. 4. Innersole, 'G' which means 'grain.' * * * Heel, square, No. 3. Slugging, full steel. 7—7½ E slip. White ribbon. 5:35;" that these shoes were not suitable for sale by the plaintiff in the ordinary course of his business, that these sizes and type might be salable to one concern and not salable to others, that the shoes thus ordered were extremely hard to make because of the "perforations," "pinkings or trimmings," and were not salable at that time because the oxford season had gone by. * * * The price of the entire order was more than $500.

* * * The only question presented is whether on the evidence it could have been found that the transaction was within the exception of that part of the statute of frauds contained in these words: "* * * but if the goods are to be manufactured by the seller especially for the buyer and are not suitable for sale to others in the ordinary course of the seller's business, the provisions of this section shall not apply." * * *

There was evidence sufficient to support a finding of facts to take the transaction out of the statute. It might have been found that the shoes in question were manufactured on the special order of the defendant, of a peculiar type different from that readily vendible in the general market both as to sizes and adornment, and at a time when the season for that particular style had ended.

New trial ordered.

3. *Part Payment Satisfies Statute of Frauds Under U.C.C.*

STARR v. FREEPORT DODGE, INC.

54 Misc.2d 271, 282 N.Y.S.2d 58 (1967).

BERNARD TOMSON, Judge. These cross motions for summary judgment raise, apparently for the first time in this state, the important question as to whether, under the Uniform Commercial Code, part payment exempts an indivisible contract from the operation of the statute of frauds. * * *

Plaintiff's action is for breach of contract and arises out of the attempted purchase by him of a new automobile from the corporate defendant, a car dealer, through the individual defendant, the salesman involved in the transaction. The plaintiff alleges that he signed an order form for a new automobile which described the subject matter of the sale, the price, which was in excess of $500, and the identity of both buyer and seller. The form is not signed by the dealer. * * *

It further appears that the plaintiff made a $25 down payment to the dealer, which was accepted by the dealer and for which deposit a credit was noted on the form. The plaintiff asserts that on the day scheduled for delivery of the car he was informed by the dealer's representative "that some error had been made" and that it would be necessary for the plaintiff to pay an additional $175 over and above the price previously agreed upon in order to obtain delivery of the car.

The defendants urge that there was no contract between the parties and that the order form, unsigned as it is by the dealer, falls within the purview of Section 2–201 of the Uniform Commercial Code as unenforceable since it was not signed by the party to be charged.

Section 2–201 of the U.C.C. provides in part as follows: * *

> (1) Except as otherwise provided in this section a contract for the sale of goods for the price of $500 or more is not enforceable by way of action or defense unless there is some writing sufficient to indicate that a contract for sale has been made between the parties and signed by the party against whom enforcement is sought or by his authorized agent or broker. * * *
>
> (3) A contract which does not satisfy the requirements of subsection (1) but which is valid in other respects is enforceable
>
> * * * * * * * * * *
>
> (c) with respect to goods for which payment has been made and accepted or which have been received and accepted (Section 2–606)." * * *

Under the code, part payment takes the case out of the statute only to the extent for which payment has been made. * * *

Even if subparagraph (c) validates, as the writers seem unanimously to agree, a divisible contract only for as much of the goods as have been paid for, it does not necessarily follow that such a rule invalidates an indivisible oral contract where some payment has been made and accepted. To paraphrase Hawkland—It is difficult (here) to see how the contract could have contemplated less than one (automobile), assuming as the Court did, that (automobiles) are indivisible. Any other conclusion would work an unconscionable result and would encourage rather than discourage fraud if the facts as pleaded (known as "low balling" in the trade) were proven at a trial. The statute of frauds would be used to cut down the trusting buyer rather than to protect the one who, having made his bargain, parted with a portion of the purchase price as an earnest of his good faith. Certainly here the $25 deposit was not intended as a purchase of a portion of the automobile. It was intended as payment towards the purchase of the entire article if the facts alleged in the complaint are proven at the trial.

[Part payment will take the case out of the Statute of Frauds for all of the goods when the goods are not divisible. Judgment for plaintiff.]

---

4. Delivery Satisfies Statute of Frauds Under U.C.C.

COHEN SALVAGE CORP. v. EASTERN ELECTRIC SALES CO.

205 Pa.Super. 26, 206 A.2d 331 (1965).

The opinion of Judge ETHAN ALLEN DOTY follows: * * *

In the latter part of June, 1963, plaintiff, located in Bladensburg, Maryland, and defendant, located in Philadelphia, both acting by a duly authorized agent, had a telephone conversation in which plaintiff advised defendant that it had a quantity of electric cable for sale. Arrangements were made for defendant to send one of its employees to Bladensburg, Maryland to examine the cable. After this employee examined the cable and returned to Philadelphia, another oral conversation transpired as a result of which plaintiff shipped the cable, weighing 36,440 pounds, to defendant in Philadelphia. The cable was run off plaintiff's reels to defendant's reels, and was taken by defendant's employees and placed in defendant's warehouse, where it still remains. * * *

The plaintiff brought this action in assumpsit for the cable allegedly sold and delivered. The defendant's position at trial was * * * even if there was a contract it is unenforceable because of the statute of frauds. * * *

Defendant's reliance on the Statute of Frauds to vitiate this contract is misplaced. Section 2–201(1) of the Uniform Commercial

Code provides that a contract for the sale of goods in excess of $500. is not enforceable

> "Unless there is some writing sufficient to indicate that a contract for sale has been made between the parties and signed by the party against whom enforcement is sought, or by his authorized agent or broker." * * *

In this case plaintiff introduced into evidence a written sales order which contained plaintiff's name, the notation, "SOLD TO: Eastern Electric," the date, the name of the shipper, the quantity and description of the goods, and the weight of the goods, as well as the notation, "Your Order Number," and "Our Sales Number." This form was admittedly signed by an authorized agent of the defendant's company. This writing was sufficient to satisfy the requirements of the Statute of Frauds.

> "All that is required is that the writing afford a basis that the offered oral evidence rests on a real transaction."
>
> * * *
>
> "Its object is the elimination of certain formalistic requirements adherence to which often resulted in injustice, rather than the prevention of fraud."

This writing clearly afforded a basis for believing that the oral evidence rests on a real transaction. The fact that price was omitted (and it was the only relevant term omitted) is not fatal since "A writing is not insufficient because it omits * * * a term agreed upon. * * *"

There is another reason why the Statute of Frauds does not preclude a verdict for plaintiff in this case. Section 2–201(3)(c) of the Code provides:

> "A contract which does not satisfy the requirements of subsection (1) but which is valid in other respects is enforceable with respect to goods which have been received and accepted."

That the cable was received there can be no doubt. After it was received by defendant it was run from one reel to another by several of the defendant's employees who admitted they inspected it at that time. It was then tagged and placed in the defendant's warehouse, where it remains. * * *

[Judgment for plaintiff.]

---

5. *Services Not Sale of Land*

DOBSON v. MASONITE CORP.

359 F.2d 921 (C.A.Miss., 1966).

HUTCHESON, Circuit Judge. Masonite desired to rid its Mississippi lands, consisting of some 9,200 acres, of all oak timber and undesirable and unwanted species of tree. In March, 1963, Dobson orally agreed to undertake cutting operations on Masonite's lands. Neither party disputes the existence of the oral agreement; nor is there any real quarrel regarding the basic terms of the agreement. Under the contract Dobson was (1) to cut all oak, whether dead, diseased, defective, or merchantable; (2) to have complete control over the entire cutting operation and the timber cut; (3) to sell so much of the cut timber as he could; and (4) to pay Masonite initially twelve dollars, and subsequently ten dollars, per thousand log feet of oak actually sold, and to retain all amounts received in excess thereof as compensation for his services. Dobson incurred rather heavy expenditures in preparing for operations, found buyers for much of the oak to be cut, and commenced clearing the lands. * * * Dobson continued clearing operations from March, 1963, to December, 1963, at which time Masonite unilaterally terminated the agreement and ordered Dobson to discontinue his operations. Dobson during this time cleared 4,000 acres of land, and realized a net profit, after all expenses, including payments to Masonite, of $9,383.02.

This suit was initiated by Dobson to recover the amount of net profits he would have realized had he been permitted to complete the clearing of Masonite's lands. Dobson interpreted the contract as one for services; he argued that the agreement was for clearing the land of unwanted oak trees. Masonite denied liability, interpreting the contract as one for the sale of standing timber, and invoking the Mississippi Statute of Frauds to bar Dobson's claim. The district court quite properly observed that under the Mississippi Statute of Frauds, an oral contract for the sale of standing timber is unenforceable. * * *

Counsel for Dobson is also correct in his statement of Mississippi law; an agreement for services in cutting and clearing land of timber is not within the Statute. * * * But this is of little assistance in determining *which type* of contract—sales or service—was here involved. This calls for an interpretation of the agreement between the parties to determine what they meant by the terms of that agreement. Interpretation is always a question of fact. * * * On the record before us, there is certainly ample evidence from which the jury could conclude that the contract between Dobson and Masonite was for the rendition of services, rather than for the sale of standing timber. In drawing the ultimate conclusion as to the meaning of the parties, we believe the jury was fulfilling its traditional function as the finder of the facts.

[Judgment for plaintiff.]

6. Contract Possible to Perform Within One Year

CO-OP DAIRY, INC. v. DEAN

102 Ariz. 573, 435 P.2d 470 (1967).

McFARLAND, Vice Chief Justice. Plaintiff-appellee Charles W. Dean, hereinafter referred to as Dean, sued defendant-appellant Co-Op Dairy, Inc., hereinafter referred to as Dairy, for damages for breach of an oral contract to employ Dean and to reimburse him for his moving expenses from Ardmore, Oklahoma, to Phoenix, Arizona. From a judgment on a jury verdict in Superior Court, Dairy has appealed.

START ON 13TH

The facts, stated most favorably to Dean, are as follows:

On February 12, 1962, Dairy's general manager, Gerald J. Patsey, hired Dean as sales manager at a guaranteed salary of $1,000 per month. The employment period was to be "for a minimum period of one year," and the agreement provided for the payment of Dean's moving expenses. The day after Dean was hired, he signed a one-year lease on a Phoenix apartment. He then went to Oklahoma, picked up his family, arranged to have household goods moved to Phoenix, and, on February 26, 1962, he "reported for active work." After he had worked a few days, all the delivery and supervisory personnel of Dairy resigned, and refused to return to work unless and until Patsey and Dean were fired. In order to avoid a massive loss of customers from lack of service, and a large loss of milk from spoilage, Dairy capitulated to the drivers' demands and fired the two men. For the approximately nine days that he worked, Dean was paid $1,000 "for the period ending March 8, 1962." He sued for his salary for the year, less what he was paid, and less what he earned in another job after being fired, plus his moving expenses. It was conceded that what work Dean did for Dairy was eminently satisfactory.

The jury, in addition to bringing in a general verdict for $6,000.38 for wages and $776.53 for moving expense, answered two special interrogatories by finding that there was an agreement between the parties to hire Dean for one year, and that Dairy agreed to pay Dean's moving expenses. The evidence was ample to justify the verdict and special findings.

Dairy contends that a contract of employment to start in the future, and to continue for one year, is within the Statute of Frauds, and that therefore this action cannot be maintained. As a general rule of law this is true. A.R.S. § 44–101 provides that no action shall be brought upon any oral agreement "which is not to be performed within one year from the making thereof." * * *

Dean contends that a contract for one year's employment, to commence the day following the making of the contract, is not within the Statute of Frauds, citing Columbia Pictures Corporation v. Detoth, 87 Cal.App.2d 620, 197 P.2d 580. We agree. So does Dairy in its brief. The difficulty in the instant case is that the facts are not entirely clear, and the special interrogatories submitted to the jury contained no requirement that they find when the employment contract was to begin. We know that the contract was made, orally, between Patsey and Dean on February 12, 1962. We know that the contract was to guarantee Dean $1,000 per month, and that it was to run for one year. But, nowhere in the record is there a scintilla of evidence from which one can determine when the contract was to start. It is undisputed that Dean reported for work February 26th, after having gone back to Oklahoma to get his family and to arrange for the transportation of his household goods. On cross-examination, Dean was asked whether there was any specific time that he was to start working, and he answered that there was not. However, he was also asked:

> "When you left * * * Mr. Patsey on February 12th it was understood that you would not start work until you had moved your family out from Ardmore, Oklahoma?"

and the answer was "That is correct, sir."

We need not take this statement literally. That could mean that he did not *have* to come to work until he had moved his family. It could mean that he would not come to work until he had *arranged* to move his family. However, it does not show they agreed he *could not* commence work until he had returned to Oklahoma and personally made all the arrangements. It did not mean that he could not call his wife that night, tell her to arrange for shipping the furniture and to take a plane or bus to Phoenix, so that he could start work the next day.

The conversations between Dean and Patsey, leading up to the contract of hiring, show that Dean was somewhat timid about nailing down the term of the contract. Patsey testified that Dean inquired about a contract, and Patsey told him:

> "Any man that comes in on a job like this has always got a year to prove himself. I pointed out that I had no contract with Coop Dairy. I said that I have never been too much for contracts."

Dairy argues that since Dean did not report for work until February 26, 1962, the contract was to begin on that date, and end one year later on February 26, 1963, which puts it into the Statute of Frauds. Dean argues that since he had to move here to start working, his leasing of an apartment on February 13, 1962, was one of the duties of his employment contract and hence the contract was to begin on the day after it was made, and so is not within the Statute of Frauds. We cannot agree with either position. Clearly, Dean's leasing of an apartment is no proof that the contract had begun to operate. At the same time, Dean's failure to report to work until February 26 does not prove that he could not have reported for work on February 13th.

* * * One principle that generally has been upheld is that the words "not to be performed within one year" mean *"impossible to be performed within one year."*

> "In its actual application, however, the courts have been perhaps even less friendly to this provision than to the other provisions of the statute. * * * In general, the cases indicate that there must not be the *slightest possibility* that it can be fully performed within one year. It makes no difference how long the agreed performance may be delayed or over how long a period it may in fact be continued. It makes no difference how long the parties expect performance to take, or how reasonable and accurate those expectations are, if the agreed performance can *possibly* be completed within one year." [Italics ours.] 2 Corbin on Contracts 534
>
> * * *

We therefore hold that there was nothing to prevent Dean from turning over the moving details to his wife and going to work the next day. Had he done so, the Statute of Frauds would not be applicable. Though he did not do so, the mere fact that he could have done so takes the contract out of the Statute of Frauds.

Judgment affirmed.

---

7. *Contract With Options can be Performed Within a Year*

COLUMBIA PICTURES CORP. v. DE TOTH

87 Cal.App.2d 620, 197 P.2d 580 (1948).

VALLÉE, Justice. [Action to enforce an oral contract.] By its amended complaint plaintiff-respondent, a producer of motion picture photoplays, sought a judgment declaring that on June 7, 1943, it and defendant-appellant had entered into an oral agreement whereby * * * appellant entered the employ of respondent as a director of motion picture photoplays for a term of one year immediately next ensuing to render services as such director and as respondent might designate from time to time within said term of one year; that respondent agreed to pay appellant, in consideration of said services, the sum of $250 a week for each week that he should actually render services under the contract; * * * that respondent was given the option or privilege of renewing or extending the agreement for a term of one additional year at a compensation of $350 a week, a second additional year at a compensation of $500 a week, a third additional year at a compensation of $750 a week, a fourth additional year at a compensation of $1,000 a week, a fifth additional year at a compensation of $1,250 a week, and a sixth additional year at a compensation of $1,500 a week, and that each and all of the options were to be exercised by the plaintiff before the expiration of the original or any ensuing and current yearly term thereof. * * * The court found that on June 7, 1943, Columbia and DeToth entered into an oral agreement * * * as recited above, with salaries and options as alleged by Columbia, and according to Columbia's standard form of contract for directors; * * * Judgment followed accordingly. DeToth appealed.

* * * Appellant argues that it was error to declare the entire oral agreement with the six yearly options to be valid under the statute of frauds. * * *

Appellant misconceives the effect of the statute of frauds. The oral agreement was for less than one year. Its term began June 8, 1943, one day after its date, and ended June 7, 1944. It was a valid oral agreement not affected by the statute. The fact that the agreement contained options exercisable prior to "the expiration of the original or any ensuing and current yearly term thereof" did not affect its validity. The possibility of the exercise of the options was a contingency which might never happen. Neither does the exercise of one or more of the options affect the validity of the oral agreement. * * * If the agreement can be performed within one year it is valid. It is only when it cannot be fully performed within one year that it is invalid. The statute says "by its terms is not to be performed within a year."

* * * An oral contract of employment for a period of one year "immediately next ensuing," with rendition of service to commence on the day after the agreement is entered into is not within the statute of frauds. * * *

The words "cannot be fully performed" must be taken literally. The fact that performance within a year is highly improbable or not expected by the parties does not bring a contract within the Statute. * * * The oral agreement, if valid in its inception, is valid throughout. The fact that performance may have extended over a greater period than one year does not bring the agreement within the statute. * * * The fact that option provisions, which, if exercised, enlarged the time of performance beyond a year, were included in the oral agreement did not invalidate it under the statute of frauds, "for it is nevertheless a contract which may be performed within a year from the time of its inception." * * *

Judgment affirmed.

8. *Promise to Pay for Services to be Performed for Another*

LAWRENCE v. ANDERSON

108 Vt. 176, 184 A. 689 (1936).

POWERS, Chief Justice. [Action by physician for services rendered.] Answering an emergency call from an unknown source, the plaintiff, a licensed physician, administered to John Anderson, who had suffered severe injuries in an automobile accident somewhere on the "Williston Road" outside of the city of Burlington. This was on October 1, 1933. When the plaintiff arrived at the scene of the accident, he found there the defendant, a daughter of the injured man; and when he had introduced himself to her, she directed him, as he testified, to "do everything you can under the sun to see this man is taken care of." Thereupon, the plaintiff called an ambulance, in which Anderson was taken to a hospital where the plaintiff treated him until the next morning, when he was discharged by the defendant after she had conferred with her father about it. The patient died from the effects of the injuries a few days later. The plaintiff made his charges for his services to Mr. Anderson, and sent bills to his estate. He engaged a Burlington lawyer to proceed against the estate, for the collection of his charges, and some effort in that direction was made, but nothing came of it. About a year after the accident, the plaintiff began sending bills to Anderson's widow, but nothing came from that. Finally, about a year and a half after the accident, this suit was brought. * * * At the close of the plaintiff's evidence, on motion therefor, a verdict was ordered for the defendant. * * *

But in addition to what has been recited, one Charles Brown, who was at the scene of the accident when the plaintiff arrived there, testified that in his presence the defendant said to the plaintiff, "I want my father taken care of, and give him the best care you can give him, and what the charges are * * * I will pay for it."

Ordinarily, this statement might make an entirely different case for the plaintiff. It shows that the defendant not only requested the services, but also that she made a direct promise to pay the plaintiff. Such a promise is not collateral or secondary, but primary and original. * * *

To such a contract the statute of frauds * * * does not apply, for the simple reason that it is not a promise to pay the debt of another, but is a promise to pay the debt of the promisor—one that he makes his own by force of his engagement.

But before we can apply this rule to the case in hand, we must consider the effect of the plaintiff's conduct.

When the defendant made the promise that Brown testified to, the plaintiff was at liberty to accept it and to rely upon it. But he was not obliged to do so. He could, if he chose, treat Anderson on his own credit. But he could not hold both Anderson and the defendant. If he gave the credit to Anderson, he could not hold the defendant, though she had tendered an engagement direct, in form. * * If he gave any credit to Anderson, he elected to accept the defendant's engagement as collateral to that of Anderson. Of course it is only where the promise sued on is primary and direct that this question we are now discussing arises.

* * * But in such cases, the extension of any credit to the third party involved requires a written promise on the part of the promisor. * * *

As we have seen, it appears here that the plaintiff made his original charges against Anderson. * * * No reason is given why these charges were made against Anderson. So it must be taken that it was because the plaintiff considered him responsible therefor. * * Having given credit to Anderson, the plaintiff cannot collect from the defendant. [When a third party makes a promise to pay for services to be rendered to another, but that promise is refused, the third party is not bound.]

Judgment affirmed.

---

9. Leading Benefit Rule Exception

read

NEIL B. McGINNIS EQUIPMENT CO. v. YARBRO

101 Ariz. 378, 420 P.2d 163 (1966).

BERNSTEIN, Vice Chief Justice. * * * McGinnis Equipment Co., brought suit to recover payments due it pursuant to a conditional sales contract for the sale of one used Allis-Chalmers Model HD–5G tractor. The contract was negotiated in August of 1957 and called for twenty-three monthly installments of $574.00 each. The buyer, Russell, failed to make the first monthly payment, and on his suggestion a McGinnis company representative met with the appellant, Yarbro, to ask if he would help with the payments. As a result of this meeting Yarbro agreed to, and did, pay the September installment.

In the months that followed there was a continued failure on the part of Russell to make any of the monthly installment payments. * * *

In May, 1958 when McGinnis Co. indicated that the tractor soon would have to be repossessed, Yarbro again assured the company that it would be paid as soon as two pending real estate escrows were closed. This promised payment was not made. A similar promise was made by Yarbro in July on the strength of proceeds that were to be forthcoming from an oat crop in New Mexico but again no payment was made. * * * The tractor was finally repossessed in January of 1959. Subsequently, the McGinnis Co. brought an action to recover the payments due under the conditional sales contract, naming Russell and Yarbro as defendants. A default judgment was entered against Russell and the only question before this court now concerns the liability of the defendant, Yarbro. The trial court found Yarbro liable for the entire balance under the conditional sales contract. * * *

Although the promises made by Yarbro clearly were of the type covered in [the Statute of Frauds] the plaintiff contends that the leading object or primary purpose exception is applicable. * * * Simply stated, this rule provides that where the leading object of a person promising to pay the debt of another is actually to protect his own interest, such promise if supported by sufficient consideration, is valid, even though it be oral.

* * * Although a third party is the primary debtor, situations may arise where the promisor has a personal, immediate and pecuniary interest in the transaction, and is therefore himself a party to be benefitted by the performance of the promisee. In such cases the reason which underlies and which prompted the above statutory provision fails, and the courts will give effect to the promise. Recognizing the leading object rule as a well reasoned exception, the question remains whether the facts presently before this court make the exception applicable. There are no easy, mathematical guidelines to such a determination. To ascertain the character of the promise in question and the intention of the parties as to the nature of the liability created, regard must be had to the form of expression, the situation of the parties, and to all the circumstances of each particular case. * * * Further evidence of Yarbro's interest in the tractor comes from the fact that after its purchase he had borrowed it on a series of occasions. When repairs were needed shortly after Yarbro had made the first installment payment, the McGinnis Co. repairman found the machine on Yarbro's land. * * * Yarbro had asked on several occasions that the McGinnis Co. not repossess the tractor because he needed it. These requests were usually in conjunction with a promise to pay what was owing on the tractor. * * * It is when the leading and main object of the promisor is *not* to become surety or guarantor of another, even though that may be the effect, but is to serve some purpose or interest of his own, that the oral promise becomes enforceable. * * *

[Judgment for plaintiff affirmed.]

---

10. Ante-nuptial Contract Must be in Writing

TELLEZ v. TELLEZ, ET AL.

51 N.M. 416, 186 P.2d 390 (1947).

COMPTON, Justice. This is a suit by appellee, Guadalupe Diaz Tellez, seeking relief in the nature of specific performance of an oral ante-nuptial contract. From an adverse judgment, appellants bring this appeal.

Eusebio Tellez, now deceased, in July, 1940, orally proposed marriage to appellee, then Guadalupe Diaz, now his widow, promising that if she would marry and care for him, as his wife, until death, that he would give her all his property, both real and personal. * * * Pursuant to the agreement, the deceased executed a will on or about August 1, 1940, whereby all his property was devised and bequeathed to appellee. In consideration of his promise, the marriage took place August 8, 1940.

Thereafter, while the parties were living together, and without the knowledge or consent of appellee, Eusebio Tellez conveyed the real estate here involved, to his children and grandchildren by a former marriage. This was a voluntary conveyance. Eusebio Tellez suffered a paralytic stroke on August 11, 1943, which required the constant care and attention of a nurse and other assistants. For convenience he was moved from his home to the home of a daughter, where he lived until his death, November 7, 1944. Soon after being taken to the daughter's home, difficulties arose between appellee and his children by the former marriage, causing appellee to leave the home of the daughter. She did not see her husband for about a year prior to his death. * * *

The question is whether the oral ante-nuptial contract stated in the findings may be enforced against the appellants who are the heirs at law of the deceased and grantees in a deed made by him after appellee and deceased married, by which he conveyed to them all of his property. * * *

The deceased's agreement to leave his property to appellee for the consideration stated, implied that his property would be devised and bequeathed to her, in consideration of her marrying him and caring for him until his death. * * *

The contract was within the * * * Statute of Frauds, in that it was an oral contract made upon consideration of marriage. * * *

The judgment of the district court is reversed with directions to the trial court to reinstate the case upon its docket and enter an order dismissing appellee's complaint, and it is so ordered.

PROBLEMS

1. On June 1 Buyer and Seller entered into an oral contract for the sale of 100 office chairs at $10 each. On June 3 Seller sent a signed letter to Buyer which reaffirmed the terms of the oral contract. On June 4 Seller shipped the chairs to Buyer; however, Buyer has changed his mind and wants to get out of the oral contract. Discuss.

2. Defendant made an oral contract with plaintiff for a tombstone to be made according to a pattern and design in a catalog at a price of $600. After the plaintiff selected the proper design and cut the inscription upon it the defendant refused to accept it although it was complete and ready for delivery. Defendant pleads the Statute of Frauds. Discuss.

3. Buyer and Seller entered into an oral contract for the sale of a boat at a price of $1,000. Buyer made a down payment in the amount of $50. Now Buyer desires to cancel the contract arguing that the contract should have been in writing. Discuss.

4. Buyer orally orders from the Reynolds Television Manufacturing Company a color television set for the price of $2,000.00. The set will be specially manufactured so that it will only receive educational channels and will be able to make a visual and sound tape of any program. Mr. Reynolds has personally built the chassis for the set and is about to install the fine tuning mechanism when he receives a telephone call from the buyer stating that he has lost his job at the college where he is employed and wants nothing more to do with education including the set he had ordered. Mr. Reynolds states that he has spent a lot of money on the set and must insist on payment. The buyer contends that since he has not signed anything he is not bound due to the Statute of Frauds. Decision?

5. Buyer orally contracts with seller to purchase a garage on the seller's property for the sum of $450.00. Seller is to dismantle the garage and have it ready for pickup within three months from the date of the contract. Seller dismantles the garage and has it ready for pickup within the period; however, the buyer refuses to pick up or pay for the garage. Seller brings suit, and the buyer defends on the ground that the contract was for real estate and is unenforceable under the Statute of Frauds. Decision?

6. Seller and buyer entered into an oral contract for the sale of a parcel of land for the price of $499.00 in monthly installments. In reliance on the oral contract, the buyer goes into possession and builds a cabin on the land. After the buyer has paid $200.00 in monthly installments, he discovers gold on the land. Seller brings an action to evict the buyer on the ground that the contract was for real estate, and there was nothing in writing. Decision?

7. In the middle of March, A orally employs B to manage a farm for a period of one year upon specified terms commencing April 1. In December, A discharged B without cause. B brings suit for breach of contract. Decision?

8. Buyer purchased a dry-goods and grocery business from Seller which was located in Excelsior, Wisconsin. Buyer paid $500 to Seller in addition to the purchase price for Seller's oral promise not to engage in a similar business for two years in Excelsior, Wisconsin. A few months after the sale Seller started a similar business in Excelsior. Buyer sues to enforce the oral promise. Seller pleads the one year Statute of Frauds section. Decision?

9. Employer, in California, orally promised employment to Employee in Alabama. The term of employment was two years. Employee sold his furniture at a loss, gave up his permanent employment in Alabama, moved his family to California, and worked at an "inferior job" for nine months waiting for the position to open that he had been promised. After nine months Employer discharged Employee as part of a reduction in overhead. Employee sues for breach of contract. Decision?

10. Annie and Horace Roderick are contemplating a divorce and seek your advice as to the ownership of a certain automobile which Horace purchased with his own funds shortly before marriage. Annie states that

Horace told her that if she would marry him he would give the automobile to her; however, he never gave her the automobile so she now wants either the automobile or its value. Horace admits making the statement. Decision?

Chapter 11

CAPACITY OF PARTIES

One of the requirements of a binding contract is that the parties have legal capacity to contract; i.e., that they are competent. However, many contracts involve persons under a legal disability; e.g., minors, intoxicated persons, persons of unsound mind, aliens, convicts, partnerships, and corporations. The limitations on partnerships and corporations will be found in later chapters. This chapter will consider the limitations on persons.

A. MINORS

---

1. MINOR'S RIGHT TO AVOID A CONTRACT

Under common law a person who had not attained the age of twenty-one was considered a minor. Today, by statute in many jurisdictions, persons are given adult status at the age of eighteen for most purposes; e. g., the right to make binding contracts, to make a will, and to marry without parental consent.

Unless otherwise limited by statute, a minor can avoid a contract he has entered into any time during the period of minority or within a reasonable time thereafter. What is a reasonable time depends upon the intelligence of the minor, his means of knowledge, the nature of and relation to the transaction, and the purpose to be attained thereby. There is no hard and fast rule. Three years and eight months has been held to be unreasonable, whereas fourteen years has been held to be reasonable. Generally, one or two years can be safely considered reasonable.

Until the minor avoids the contract, the adult party is bound by it.

2. RESTITUTION ON AVOIDANCE

After the minor disaffirms the contract by notice to the other party, must he return the consideration? Under the majority rule, the answer is that he does not have to return the consideration if the contract is for a luxury and he no longer has it. For example, a minor buys an automobile from a dealer and then disaffirms the contract, must he return the automobile? Most courts hold that he must return the automobile if he still has it. If he has wrecked it, he only need return the wrecked automobile. If he has sold it, but no longer has the money he received, most courts will not require its return.

By statutes, and court decisions in some states, the minor must account for its value if he cannot return the consideration.

Suppose a minor trades in his Ford automobile and purchases a new Chevrolet from a dealer, and the dealer sells the Ford to an innocent third party. Upon disaffirmance, can the minor get the Ford back from the third party? *Under Section 2–403 of the U.C.C.,* he cannot.

3. CONTRACTS FOR NECESSITIES

A minor is liable for the reasonable value of necessities that are actually furnished him by another person at the minor's request. The minor is not bound by the terms of the contract, but he is required to pay the reasonable value of the necessities on the theory of quasi-contract.

What is a necessity depends on the surrounding circumstances of the minor, such as his age, actual need, and financial or social status. Necessaries include food, clothing, shelter, medical care, tools of a trade, vocational education, and probably two years of junior college education.

4. CONTRACTS MINOR CANNOT AVOID

A minor cannot avoid a contract if he *ratifies* it when he is no longer a minor. A ratification may be made expressly by the minor or by his conduct. For example, a minor purchases an automobile and after he becomes an adult sells it; his act of selling is a ratification by conduct.

By statutes or court decisions in some states minors cannot avoid certain types of contracts; e. g., contracts for medical services; loans made for the purpose of obtaining a higher education; life insurance contracts; credit union, bank, or building and loan association contracts; contracts which involve the transfer of shares of stock; contracts for the purchase of homes and farms with the Veterans' Welfare Board; contracts for services in the field of sports or dramatics; contracts arising from a business the minor operates; and the U. S. Supreme Court has held that a minor's enlistment in the armed forces may be binding subject to statutory qualifications as to age.

5. MISREPRESENTATION OF AGE

Under the majority rule, the fact that a minor misrepresents his age will not preclude him from disaffirming the contract. This rule has been changed by statute in some states. However, the general rule is that even though the minor can disaffirm the contract, he is still liable in damages for the tort (civil or private wrong or injury not arising out of contract) of deceit on the theory that the tort is independent of the contract and that minors generally should be held liable for their torts.

By the majority view, a minor is not liable for a tort that involves a breach of a duty flowing from the contractual status; e.g., a minor rents an automobile under a contract which requires him to use reasonable care in the operation of the automobile; however, due to negligence, the minor damages it, thus breaching the contract. His contractual immunity absolves him from liability on the contract; however, can the adult recover in a suit for damages based on the minor's tort (negligence in damaging the automobile)? In most states, the adult cannot; e.g., Michigan, New Jersey. However, if the minor goes beyond the contract, by making an unauthorized use for example, and during this unauthorized use negligently damages the automobile, most courts would hold that the tort was independent of the contract and allow recovery.

6. PARENTAL LIABILITY FOR CONTRACTS

Ordinarily, a parent is not liable for the contracts of his minor child; however, the parent is liable if the child acted as his agent.

If a parent has not provided his child with necessities, the parent is liable to third persons for the reasonable value of the necessities furnished to the minor.

If a parent joins in a contract with a minor, e.g., to purchase an automobile, the parent is liable even though the minor may be able to disaffirm.

7. PARENTAL LIABILITY FOR TORTS

Generally, a parent is not liable for the tortious acts of his minor child even though the child himself may be liable. There are exceptions.

a. A parent is liable for the torts of his child when the child is acting as an agent or servant of the parent.

b. Where the negligence of the parent made the injury possible the parent is liable on the basis of the ordinary rules of negligence, but not on the parent-child relationship.

c. Where the parent directs or consents or sanctions the tort.

d. In most states by statute the parents are liable for wilful, malicious, intentional or unlawful acts of the minor child.

e. In some states the parent is liable by special statute; e. g., limited amount associated with driver's license.

B. INTOXICATED PERSONS

If a person is so intoxicated at the time he enters into a contract that he is unable to comprehend the nature and effect of the transaction, it is voidable at his option.

C. PERSONS OF UNSOUND MIND

If a person is so deranged mentally that he does not know he is making a contract or does not understand the consequences of what he is doing, the contract is voidable.

Some states by special statute, e.g., California Civil Code Sections 38–40, provide that if a person has been *judicially* declared insane, the contract is *void*; whereas, if the person is incompetent, but not judicially declared insane, the contract is voidable.

By case law in California, it has been held that where a person in a hospital signed an insurance release while in *a dazed and semi-conscious condition* as a result of injuries sustained in an automobile accident, the release was wholly void.

---

1. *Right of Minors to Rescind Contracts*

ADAMS v. BARCOMB

125 Vt. 380, 216 A.2d 648 (1966).

SHANGRAW, Justice. This is a civil action to recover the consideration paid under a contract made by plaintiff. * * * Findings of fact were made by the trial court and judgment entered in favor of the defendant. The plaintiff has appealed. * * *

The plaintiff, Rose Adams, was born August 6, 1943, and became twenty-one years of age on August 6, 1964.

In May of 1964 while the plaintiff was working in Burlington she contacted the defendant, Leonard Barcomb, concerning the purchase of an automobile. As a result she purchased a 1960 Impalla (sic) two door convertible Chevrolet. For said car she traded in a 1959 Opel and paid $975.00 in cash. Said sale was consummated on May 28, 1964.

The plaintiff operated the purchased Chevrolet for approximately two weeks and was dissatisfied with it.

* * * The defendant told her that he would not return the money and the plaintiff then contacted an attorney and suit for the return of the money was instituted by writ dated July 15, 1964.

* * * It has always been the law in this state that contracts made by a minor during infancy, if not for necessaries, may be avoided by him if disaffirmed within a reasonable time after arriving at full age.

The plaintiff became of age on August 6, 1964, and was within her rights in disaffirming the contract while under age. * * *

After disaffirmance, she was entitled to the return of the consideration paid for the automobile.

* * * It is contended by the defendant that it was a prerequisite that the plaintiff first return the automobile purchased of the defendant if liability under the contract was to be avoided by her. As a general rule, if an infant avoids his contract, he must restore the consideration that he received. * * * The defendant refused to return the money which he had received as part payment therefor. This refusal on the part of the defendant, excused the plaintiff from tendering the return of the automobile purchased by the plaintiff. The law does not require the doing of a useless act or the doing of that which would be only a vain and idle ceremony. * * *

Such use of the automobile by the plaintiff during the pendency of this action to recover what she had paid for the vehicle, after the defendant had flatly rejected her prior disaffirmance, does not constitute a ratification of the original contract as a matter of law. * * *

Judgment reversed and cause remanded for an appropriate judgment order in favor of the plaintiff.

---

2. *Minor Not Required to Restore Consideration (Majority Rule)*

ROBERTSON v. KING

225 Ark. 276, 280 S.W.2d 402 (1955).

ROBINSON, Justice. The principal issue here is whether [defendant], a minor, may rescind a contract to purchase a pick-up truck. On the 20th day of March, 1954, L. D. Robertson, a minor, entered into a conditional sales agreement whereby he purchased from Turner King and J. W. Julian, doing business as the Julian Pontiac Company, a pick-up truck for the agreed price of $1,743.85. On the day of the purchase, Robertson was 17 years of age, and did not have his 18th birthday until April 8th. Robertson traded in a passenger car for which he was given a credit of $723.85 on the purchase price, leaving a balance of $1,020 payable in 23 monthly installments of $52.66 plus one payment of $52.83. He paid the April installment of $52.66. * * *

It appears that Robertson had considerable trouble with the wiring on the truck. He returned it to the automobile dealers for repairs, but the defective condition was not remedied. On May 2nd, the truck caught fire and was practically destroyed. He notified the automobile concern and they stated that they would send the insurance man to see him. It appears that the insurance representative, upon finding out that Robertson was only 17 years of age, refused to deal with him.

On June 7th, [plaintiffs] filed suit to replevy the damaged truck from Robertson. By his father and next friend, Robertson filed a cross-complaint in which he alleged that he is a minor and asked that the contract of purchase be rescinded and sought to recover that part of the purchase price he had paid, * * * There was a judgment for King and Julian on the complaint and the cross-complaint. On appeal, Robertson contends that he was 17 years of age at the time of the alleged purchase and that he has a right under the law to rescind the contract and to recover the portion of the purchase price he has paid.

[Plaintiffs] also contend that * * * a minor cannot rescind a contract of purchase without reimbursing the seller for any loss that he may have sustained by reason of such rescission. This statute deals with situations where a minor is 18 years of age at the time of making a purchase. The statute is not applicable here because according to the undisputed evidence Robertson was only 17 years of age at the time of entering into the purchase agreement. * * *

The automobile dealers have disposed of the car they received in the trade, and cannot restore it to the minor. In a situation of this kind, the weight of authority is that the actual value of the property given as part of the purchase price by the minor is the correct measure of damages. Neither side is bound by the agreement reached as to the value of the car at the time the trade was made. * * * Hence, the court erred in finding for the automobile dealers, and the cause is therefore reversed and remanded for a new trial.

---

3. *Minors' Employment Agency Contract May be a Necessity*

GASTONIA PERSONNEL CORP. v. ROGERS

276 N.C. 279, 172 S.E.2d 19 (1970).

Defendant had graduated from high school in 1966. On May 29, 1968, he was nineteen years old, emancipated and married. He needed only "one quarter or 22 hours" for completion of the courses required at Gaston Tech for an A.S. degree in civil engineering. His wife was employed as a computer programmer at First Federal Savings and Loan. He and she were living in a rented apartment. They were expecting a baby in September. Defendant had to quit school and go to work.

For assistance in obtaining suitable employment, defendant went to the office of plaintiff, an employment agency, on May 29, 1968. After talking with Maurine Finley, a personnel counselor, defendant signed a contract containing, *inter alia*, the following: "If I ACCEPT employment offered me by an employer as a result of a lead (verbal or otherwise) from you within twelve (12) months of such lead even though it may not be the position originally discussed with you, I will be obligated to pay you as per the terms of the contract." Under the contract, defendant was free to continue his own quest for employment. He was to become obligated to plaintiff only if he accepted employment from an employer to whom he was referred by plaintiff.

After making several telephone calls to employers who might need defendant's services as a draftsman, Mrs. Finley called Spratt-Seaver, Inc., in Charlotte, North Carolina. It was stipulated that defendant, as a result of his conversation with Mrs. Finley, went to Charlotte, was interviewed by Spratt-Seaver, Inc., and was employed by that company on June 6, 1968, at an annual salary of $4,784.00. The contract provided that defendant would pay plaintiff a service charge of $295.00 if the starting annual salary of accepted employment was as much as $4,680.00.

* * *

Plaintiff sued to recover a service charge of $295.00. In his answer, defendant admitted he had paid nothing to plaintiff; alleged he was not indebted to plaintiff in any amount; and, as a further answer and defense, pleaded his infancy.

* * *

BOBBITT, Chief Justice. * * *

In general, our prior decisions are to the effect that the "necessaries" of an infant, his wife and child, include only such necessities of life as food, clothing, shelter, medical attention, etc. In our view, the concept of "necessaries" should be enlarged to include such articles of property and such services as are reasonably necessary to enable the infant to earn the money required to provide the necessities of life for himself and those who are legally dependent upon him.

* * * To hold, as a matter of law, that such a person cannot obligate himself to pay for services rendered him in obtaining employment suitable to his ability, education and specialized training, enabling him to provide the necessities of life for himself, his wife and his expected child, would place him and others similarly situated under a serious economic handicap.

In the effort to protect "older minors" from improvident or unfair contracts, the law should not deny to them the opportunity and right to obligate themselves for articles of property or services which are reasonably necessary to enable them to provide for the proper support of themselves and their dependents. The minor should be held liable for the reasonable value of articles of property or services received pursuant to such contract.

Applying the foregoing legal principles, which modify *pro tanto* the ancient rule of the common law, we hold that the evidence offered by plaintiff was sufficient for submission to the jury for its determination of issues substantially as indicated below.

To establish liability, plaintiff must satisfy the jury by the greater weight of the evidence that defendant's contract with plaintiff was an appropriate and reasonable means for defendant to obtain suitable employment. If this issue is answered in plaintiff's favor, plaintiff must then establish by the greater weight of the evidence the reasonable value of the services received by defendant pursuant to the contract. Thus, plaintiff's recovery, if any, cannot exceed the reasonable value of its services to defendant.

Accordingly, the judgment of the Court of Appeals is reversed and the cause is remanded to that Court with direction to award a new trial to be conducted in accordance with the legal principles stated herein.

Error and remanded.

---

4. *College Education Generally Not a Necessity*

JOHNSTONE v. JOHNSTONE

64 Ill.App.2d 447, 212 N.E.2d 143 (1965).

BURMAN, Presiding Justice. This suit arises out of a claim filed by petitioner, Eloise Johnstone, against the minor's estate of her stepson, Robert B. Johnstone, Jr., for amounts expended by her and obligations incurred by her in financing his college education. She based her claim upon the contention that in modern society and under the circumstances of this case a college education falls within the legal definition of a "necessary"; and that since she furnished the only funds available for her stepson's college education he is liable to her under established principles of law. The court specifically found that petitioner's expenditures were not for "necessities", and dismissed her claim. Petitioner has appealed from this ruling. * *

It is well-established, as a general rule, that a minor or his estate may be liable for necessaries furnished him.

* * * Blackstone defines necessaries to be 'necessary meat, drink, apparel, physic,' and says that an infant may bind himself to pay 'for his good teaching and instruction, whereby he may profit himself afterwards.' The articles furnished, or money advanced, must be actually necessary, in the particular case, for use, not mere ornament, for substantial good, not mere pleasure; and must belong to the class which the law generally pronounces necessary for infants. * * * The evidence in this case showed the minor was at the top of his class in high school and that there was available to the minor a full tuition scholarship to the University of Chicago. The Court could have found from the evidence that the minor might have received from Dartmouth College either a scholarship or a loan on more favorable terms than the one received from La Salle National Bank. In light of these facts and the tests for "necessaries" set forth

above, we cannot conclude that the Chancellor's findings were manifestly against the weight of the evidence, and therefore we cannot disturb his judgment. * * *

Petitioner's claim is subject to a further objection. It has been the established rule * * * that a minor is liable for necessaries furnished him only if they are furnished on his credit, and not on the credit of another.

Judgment affirmed [for defendant's estate].

---

5. *Parental Tort Liability*

GISSEN v. GOODWILL

80 So.2d 701 (Fla., 1955).

KANNER, Associate Justice.

* * *

It is averred in the second amended complaint that at the time of the appellant's injury, he was employed as a clerk at the Gaylord Hotel in the City of Miami Beach, Florida, and the appellees were residing as business invitees at the same hotel; that the minor child, Geraldine Goodwill, 8 years of age, "did wilfully, deliberately, intentionally and maliciously" swing a door "with such great force and violence against the plaintiff so that the middle finger on plaintiff's left hand was caught in the door and a portion of said finger was caused to be instantaneously severed and fell to the floor." It is further averred that

> "owing to a lack of parental discipline and neglect in the exercise of needful paternal influence and authority, the defendants, Albert Goodwill and Mrs. Albert Goodwill carelessly and negligently failed to restrain the child, Geraldine Goodwill, whom they knew to have dangerous tendencies and propensities of a mischievous and wanton disposition; that said parents had full knowledge of previous particular acts committed by their daughter about the hotel premises, such as striking, knocking down and damaging objects of furniture and furnishings and disturbing and harassing the guests and employees of the hotel and that the defendant Geraldine Goodwill did commit other wanton, wilfull and intentional acts of a similar nature to the act committed against the plaintiff, such as striking guests and employees of the aforesaid hotel, which acts were designed or resulted in injury, so that the child's persistent course of conduct would as a probable consequence result in injury to another. Said parents, nevertheless, continually failed to exercise any restraint whatsoever over the child's reckless and mischievous conduct, thereby sanctioning, ratifying and consenting

to the wrongful act committed by the defendant, Geraldine Goodwill, against the plaintiff herein."

This is a case of first incidence in this Court's jurisdiction, posing as it does the problem of whether the specific set of circumstances here can render the parents of the minor child accountable at law for the tort alleged to have been committed by the child.

It is basic and established law that a parent is not liable for the tort of his minor child because of the mere fact of his paternity. * * * However, there are certain broadly defined exceptions wherein a parent may incur liability: 1. Where he intrusts his child with an instrumentality which, because of the lack of age, judgment, or experience of the child, may become a source of danger to others. 2. Where a child, in the commission of a tortious act, is occupying the relationship of a servant or agent of its parents. 3. Where the parent knows of his child's wrongdoing and consents to it, directs or sanctions it. 4. Where he fails to exercise parental control over his minor child, although he knows or in the exercise of due care should have known that injury to another is a probable consequence. * * *

In the case of Norton v. Payne, 154 Wash. 241, 281 P. 991, 992, action was brought by infant, aged 5, by his guardian for injuries sustained when he was struck in the eyeball with a stick by defendants' child, aged 7, who had the *habit* of striking smaller children in the face with sticks. It was alleged that parents knew about and encouraged her *habit* of striking other children with sticks. The appellate court reversing the lower court's dismissal of the case said, " * * * we think parents should be held responsible and liable for a *dangerous habit* of a child of which they have knowledge and take no steps to correct, or restrain. It is that which constitutes the negligence on the part of the parent." It was pointed out by the court that, although the evidence in the case is that the father did not know that the child was committing this particular tort, the parents did nevertheless know that such child was in the habit of perpetrating this particular kind of tort and that the father encouraged her in so doing, the implication being that since he made no effort to restrain the child, he must therefore be deemed to have consented to its commission by her at any time.

* * *

In the case of Ellis v. D'Angelo, 116 Cal.App.2d 310, 253 P.2d 675, 679, it is alleged that the parents, employing plaintiff for the first time as a baby sitter for their 4 year old son and knowing that their son *habitually* engaged in violently attacking and throwing himself forcibly and violently against other people, violently shoving and knocking them, nevertheless failed to warn the plaintiff of such habitual conduct on the part of their infant; and that shortly after plaintiff entered on her duties in the home, the son attacked and injured her. The appellate court reversed the lower court's dismissal of the complaint, holding that a cause of action had been stated, and said, "While it is the rule in California, as it is generally at the common law, that there is no vicarious liability on a parent for the torts of a child there is 'another rule of law relating to the torts of minors which is somewhat in the nature of an exception, and that is that a parent may become liable for an injury caused by the child, where the parent's negligence made it possible for the child to cause the injury complained of, and probable that it would do so.' Buelke v. Levenstadt, 190 Cal. 684, 689, 214 P. 42, 44".

* * *

One common factor from the foregoing cases appears salient in the assessment of liability to the parents, that the child had the habit of doing the particular type of wrongful act which resulted in the injury complained of. In the instant case, the cause of action sought to be established fails in that the negligence charged with relation to parental restraint is not claimed to flow from the commission of an act or course of conduct which the child habitually engaged in and which led to the appellant's injury. It is nowhere claimed that the child here involved had a propensity to swing or slam doors at the hazard of persons using such doors. The deed of a child, the enactment of which results in harm to another and which is unrelated to any previous act or acts of the child, cannot be laid at the door of the parents simply because the child happened to be born theirs. However, a wrongful act by an infant which climaxes a course of conduct involving similar acts may lead to the parents' accountability. A deed brought on by a totally unexpected reaction to a situation which is isolated of origin and provocation could not have been foretold or averted and hence could not render the parents responsible.

[Judgment for defendants.]

6. *Intoxication as Grounds to Avoid Contract*

COODY v. COODY

39 Okl. 719, 136 P. 754 (1913).

SHARP, C. On September 13, 1909, plaintiff * * * brought suit against defendants * * * seeking the cancellation of certain leases, a mortgage, and a deed on lands in said county theretofore owned by him. It appears from the petition: That plaintiff was a one-fourth blood Cherokee citizen, and the lands covered by the instruments sought to be canceled constituted his allotment of lands in the Cherokee Nation. * * *

Without passing upon the sufficiency of the petition as to the other grounds upon which relief was sought, we think the court erred in sustaining the defendants' demurrers, for if, at the time the deed of August 31, 1909, was executed, plaintiff was so under the influence of intoxicants as to be wholly unable to transact business and to understand the nature of the deed which he signed, he may plead his disability from such drunkenness in an action to cancel the deed. Intoxication which is absolute and complete so that the party is for the time entirely deprived of the use of his reason and is wholly unable to comprehend the nature of the transaction and of his own acts, is a sufficient ground for setting aside or granting other appropriate affirmative relief against a conveyance or contract made while in that condition, even in the absence of fraud, procurement, or undue advantage by the other party. * * *

"A contract made by a person while he is so drunk as to be incapable of understanding its nature and effect is voidable, * * (but his intoxication) must be so excessive as to render him incapable of knowing what he is doing." * * * The rule formerly was that intoxication was no excuse and created no privilege or plea in avoidance of a contract; but it is now settled, according to the dictates of good sense and common justice, that a contract made by a person so destitute of reason as not to know the consequences of his contract, though his incompetence be produced by intoxication, is voidable and may be avoided by himself, though the intoxication was voluntary and not produced by circumvention of the other party. * * *

The judgment of the trial court should be reversed, and the cause remanded, with leave to amend, if desired.

---

7. *Insanity as Grounds to Avoid Contract*

HANKS v. McNEIL COAL CORP.

114 Colo. 578, 168 P.2d 256 (1946).

STONE, Justice. Lee A. Hanks, who was a prosperous farmer and business man in Nebraska, came to Colorado with his family in 1918, at first settling on a farm in Weld county, which included the coal lands involved in this proceeding; then, in 1920 moving to Boulder where he purchased a home, engaged in the retail coal business, and thereafter resided. His son, J. L. Hanks, continued to operate and live on the farm as a tenant. * * * Shortly after 1922 Lee Hanks discovered that he was afflicted with diabetes, and members of his family noticed a progressive change in his physical and mental condition thereafter. He became irritable and easily upset, very critical of his son's work, and increasingly interested in the emotional type of religion. He began to speculate in oil and other doubtful ventures with money needed for payment of debts and taxes. About 1934 he sent his son what he denominated a secret formula for the manufacture of medicine to cure fistula in horses, which was compounded principally of ground china, brick dust, burnt shoe leather and amber-colored glass. If the infection was in the horse's right shoulder, the mixture was to be poured in the animal's left ear, and if on the left shoulder then in the right ear. In 1937 Mr. Hanks started to advertise this medicine through the press under the name of Crown King Remedy. Thereafter he increasingly devoted his efforts and money to the compounding and attempted sale of this concoction, his business judgment became poor and he finally deteriorated mentally to the point that on May 25, 1940, he was adjudicated insane and his son was appointed conservator of his estate.

* * * Hanks learned that the defendant coal company, which had leased other lands lying to the north of his property, was extracting coal from their other leased lands and conveying it by means of the open haulage way through his lands to its shaft located to the south thereof. Hanks made demand for payment of royalty on the coal so transported across his land and there was extended argument and controversy which finally led to discussion of outright purchase of the Hanks property and the ultimate signing of the contract here involved on July 21, 1937, between Hanks and the defendant companies. * * *

The present action was brought by the conservator seeking to have the court set aside this contract. * * * The record is voluminous; the case was carefully considered by the court below and judgment of dismissal entered on findings against plaintiff on the question of insanity.

There is always in civil, as well as in criminal, actions a presumption of sanity. * * * Insanity and incompetence are words of vague and varying import. Often the definition of the psychiatrist is at variance with that of the law. The legal test of Hanks' insanity is whether "he was incapable of understanding and appreciating the extent and effect of business transactions in which he engaged." * * *

The legal rule does not recognize degrees of insanity. It does not presume to make a distinction between much and little intellect. * * * One may have insane delusions regarding some matters and be insane on some subjects, yet capable of transacting business concerning matters wherein such subjects are not concerned, and such insanity does not make one incompetent to contract unless the subject matter of the contract is so connected with an insane delusion as to render the afflicted party incapable of understanding the nature and effect of the agreement or of acting rationally in the transaction.

* * * Patently Hanks was suffering from insane delusion in 1937 with reference to the efficacy of the horse medicine, but there is no evidence of delusions or hallucinations in connection with this transaction or with his transaction of much of his other business at that time; there is no basis for holding voidable his sale here involved on the ground of his insanity, and the trial court correctly so held. * * *

Accordingly, the judgment is affirmed.

PROBLEMS

1. Buyer, a minor, purchased a used automobile for $1,000.00 from a dealer. The minor used the automobile for three months and then dam-

aged it in an accident. The automobile is now worth $250.00. Buyer takes the automobile back to the dealer and demands the return of the purchase price. Decision?

2. Buyer, a minor, badly in need of an overcoat, purchases one on credit for $100.00. The coat is really only worth $75.00. The buyer wears the coat for three months during the winter season and then attempts to return the coat and disaffirm the contract. Seller sues buyer for purchase price. Decision?

3. Buyer, a minor, purchases furniture on credit. After he becomes an adult, he sells the furniture and uses the proceeds of the sale to purchase an automobile. He defaults on the furniture payments contending that he purchased the furniture when he was a minor and therefore he can rescind the contract. Seller sues for the balance due on the contract. Decision?

4. Buyer, a minor, desires to purchase a new "Cool" automobile; however, he knows that "Cool" dealers will not sell a "Cool" to a minor so he informs the dealer that he is 22 years of age. The dealer sells the minor the automobile for cash. Six months later, and while the buyer is still a minor, he returns the automobile requesting disaffirmance of the contract. Decision?

5. A minor owns and operates a filling station. An adult drives his automobile to the station and requests an oil change and a "lube job". The minor drains the oil from the crankcase and lubricates the necessary parts of the automobile; however, due to the necessity of waiting on a gas customer, he forgets to fill the crankcase with oil. The adult pays the minor for the work and drives his car from the filling station; however, after driving a short distance, the motor becomes seriously damaged. The adult demands that the minor pay to have the motor repaired, but the minor is only willing to return the amount paid for the oil change and the "lube job". The adult sues the minor in tort for the damage. Decision?

An Adult if he is in business for himelf

6. Defendant, a minor, gave a dinner for his university friends. His father was a man of great wealth. Defendant refuses to pay for the dinner and plaintiff brings suit. Discuss.

7. Defendant, a married minor with a child, purchased certain farm machinery consisting of a tractor, disc, and cultipacker. Defendant was engaged in farming and used the machinery so that he might earn a living for himself, wife, and child. The machinery was destroyed by a fire due to no fault of defendant. Plaintiff sues for the value of the machinery. Discuss.

8. Alice, a minor, borrowed $20,000 from her aunt for the express purpose of attending the state university and obtaining a degree in Home Economics as she felt that such a degree would help her become a better home-maker. Alice, while still a minor, finished the required work and was awarded the degree. Although Alice has recently become an adult and has married a wealthy man, she refuses to repay the loan. Can Alice's aunt get a judgment against Alice?

9. Richard, a minor who likes to impress his girl friends, purchased a used automobile on an installment contract. He has defaulted in payments so the seller seeks payment from Richard's father. Discuss.

10. Two brothers, age 10 and 12, while playing football on the sidewalk collided with plaintiff who received injuries. There was no evidence that either boy had previously played with a football on the public streets or conducted himself in a disorderly manner. Plaintiff claims that a parent's failure to exercise proper supervision renders liability for acts of a minor even though there is lack of evidence of unrestrained conduct. Discuss. Have to show habitual pattern

Chapter 12

LEGALITY OF SUBJECT MATTER

A. ILLEGALITY IN GENERAL

As a general rule, contracts which involve a violation of the law or are contrary to public policy are unenforceable; e. g., gambling contracts. In West Indies v. First National Bank of Nevada, 67 Nev. 13, 214 P.2d 144, the Supreme Court of Nevada held that even though gambling is legal in Nevada, a check given in payment of a gambling debt was not enforceable because gambling is against public policy (tends to be injurious to the interests of the public).

A lottery has been defined as "a chance for a prize for a price". Lotteries are usually prohibited by statute, but there are exceptions; e. g., New York. A lottery is illegal regardless of the name attached to it since the law will look through the form to the substance; however, if participation in the game does not require the participant to purchase anything or to give anything of value then it is not a lottery.

If part of the consideration for a contract is illegal, the entire contract is unenforceable unless the contract is divisible in which case the legal part will be upheld; e. g., an employee is to receive $100 a week for sweeping the floor and for drawing beer, but the latter act is illegal because the employer does not have a license. The employee will be unable to recover any money because part of the consideration is illegal and the contract is not divisible. If he was to receive $50 for sweeping the floor and $50 for drawing the beer, he would be able to recover $50 for sweeping the floor as the contract is divisible.

This chapter will consider some of the common types of illegal contracts.

B. AGREEMENT TO COMMIT A CRIME

An agreement to commit a crime is illegal. If A promises B $5,000.00 if B will kill T and B in reliance on the promise kills T, the court will not enforce A's promise to pay the $5,000.

C. AGREEMENT NOT TO PROSECUTE FOR A CRIME

An agreement not to prosecute for a crime is not only illegal, but is a crime itself. An employer learns that E, his employee, has embezzled some of his goods and sold them to B. B and E sign a promissory note for the employer on his promise that he will not prosecute E for the crime. The employer will not be able to enforce the note in an action on it and can be held guilty of the crime of Compounding a Felony. This is based on the principle that the employee committed the crime against the state; therefore, the employer does not have the right to make an agreement to refrain from the criminal prosecution (or conceal the crime or withhold evidence) for the promise of reimbursement. The employer can also be guilty of the crime of extortion (blackmail) under these facts.

D. AGREEMENT TO COMMIT A TORT

An agreement to commit a tort (civil or private wrong or injury not arising out of contract) is illegal. A politician promises a newspaper editor that he will pay the editor $5,000 if the editor will publish a false story indicating that the politician's opponent is a communist. Such a promise is unenforceable; and if the story is published, the editor would be guilty of the tort of libel (which may also be a crime).

E. AGREEMENT INTERFERING WITH A PUBLIC DUTY

An agreement which tends to be against the public interest is unenforceable; e.g., corrupting a public official to influence legislation or to get a government contract.

Generally, lobbying contracts are upheld if the lobbyist is not to use improper methods of influencing legislation; such as, secret, personal influence; bribery; threat of loss of votes; or a contingency fee based on success.

F. FAILURE TO OBTAIN LICENSE REQUIRED BY LAW

Every state has laws requiring persons engaged in certain types of occupations to be licensed; e.g., lawyers, doctors, accountants, brokers, contractors.

These laws are either regulatory in nature or are merely for revenue purposes. If the law is *regulatory* in nature and the person does not have a license, he cannot enforce a contract he made without the license; however, if the law is merely to provide *revenue,* he can enforce the contract even though he does not have the revenue license. The occupations listed in the paragraph above all require regulatory licenses.

If a painting contractor does not have the required regulatory license and he paints your house pursuant to a contract, can he enforce the contract? The answer is "no" since the license was required so that the state could regulate the particular business. However, suppose that you pay the painter for his work and then you discover that he did not have a license; can you recover the money paid? The answer is "no" since there can be no recovery of money paid on an executed contract involving an unlicensed person. The typical city business license is one for revenue purposes only since the city does not attempt to regulate the particular business; thus, if the painter had his state regulatory license, he would be able to enforce the contract even though he did not have the revenue license.

G. STIPULATION AGAINST LIABILITY FOR NEGLIGENCE

A provision in a contract which relieves a party of liability for his own ordinary negligence is not favored by the law, is strictly construed against the party relying on it, and is often declared illegal by statutes or courts as contrary to public policy. When such a clause is declared illegal, it is usually because the public interest is involved; e. g., a charity patient in a nonprofit medical research center; release of surgeons and hospital invalid where surgeons were only ones in area capable of performing particular operation; public carrier; theatre; parking lots. Thus, if a parking lot attempts to avoid liability due to the negligence of one of the parking lot drivers, it will fail; however, it has been held that the parking lot can *limit* liability to a reasonable amount (it has been held that $1,000 was not a sufficient amount when automobile stolen from lot).

Where the public interest or some statutory limitation is not involved, the Restatement of the Law of Contracts takes the position that the clause is valid; however, there are exceptions: a person cannot contract out of *gross* negligence; an employer cannot contract to relieve himself from liability for injuries to employees (many states follow the Restatement on this point).

H. SUNDAY LAWS

Many states have enacted laws which make contracts entered into on Sunday unenforceable. These are called "blue laws". Excluded from the law, however, are acts which must be done on Sunday to protect health, life or property, and contracts entered into on a Sunday but ratified on a weekday.

I. DISCRIMINATION CONTRACTS

The Federal Civil Rights Act of 1964 provides that public accommodations and facilities (e. g., restaurants and hotels) may not discriminate on the basis of race, religion, color, or national origin.

The Fourteenth Amendment to the federal Constitution (by court interpretation) prohibits discrimination in the sale of property.

J. CONTRACT IN RESTRAINT OF TRADE

1. FEDERAL LEGISLATION

a. The *Sherman Anti-Trust Act* was passed in 1890. The United States Supreme Court stated that its object was to prohibit all "contracts or acts which it considered had a monopolistic tendency, especially those which were thought to unduly diminish competition", and to prohibit acts "producing or tending to produce the consequences of monopoly". The Court has also stated that only those contracts or combinations which impose *unreasonable* restraints upon trade and commerce are proscribed by the Act.

b. The *Clayton Anti-Trust Act* was passed in 1914. It was passed to supplement existing laws, especially the Sherman Anti-Trust Act. It prohibits price discrimination, tying restrictions (a lease of a machine which forces the lessee to use only the cards of the lessor in using the machine) and certain corporation practices.

c. The *Robinson-Patman Act* was passed in 1936 and the *Celler-Kefauver Amendment* in 1950, each of which was designed to clarify and strengthen the policy of free competition and the prevention of activities in the restraint of trade.

d. The *Miller-Tydings Act* was passed in 1937 and amended Section 1 of the Sherman Anti-Trust Act to make valid agreements fixing resale prices of competitive commodities which bear trademark or brand names. Thus, it enables manufacturers to prevent their products from being sold below a certain price. The most common "fair-traded" items are alcoholic beverages, books, sporting goods, jewelry, cosmetics, drugs, cameras, and electrical appliances.

In many states, even retail sellers who do not sign a "fair-trade" agreement with the manufacturer are bound by the established prices.

2. PROMISE NOT TO COMPETE

A promise by a seller of a business not to compete with the buyer is enforceable if it is reasonable in time and in area. Thus, if a contract for the sale of a grocery store in the city of New York contains a clause which prohibits the seller from entering into the grocery business in that city for a period of one year, the clause would be enforceable by an injunction against the seller. However, if the clause provides for a time that is too long, or an area that is too great, a problem can arise. Many courts, e. g., Pennsylvania, "blue pencil" the unreasonable part and leave the rest of the clause when the clause is divisible. For example, if the above sale had a covenant which provided that the seller could not enter into the business for a period of one year in the cities of New York, Albany, Syracuse, and Rochester, these courts would "blue pencil" the cities of Albany, Syracuse, and Rochester, and hold the rest of the clause valid. Many courts, e. g., California, Delaware, Massachusetts, Mississippi, New Jersey, New York, Texas, Washington, and Wisconsin, redo the clause by inserting *reasonable* restrictions. For example, if the clause prohibited the seller from engaging in the grocery business for thirty years in the entire state of New York, these courts would insert a reasonable time and a reasonable area. This is the modern tendency. Its objection is that it tends to encourage employers and purchasers possessing superior bargaining power over that of their employees and vendors to insist upon unreasonable and excessive restrictions, secure in the knowledge that the promise may be upheld in part, if not in full, and if not they will at least get reasonable restrictions inserted by the court. The solution to this objection can be found in McLeod v. Meyer, 237 Ark. 173, 372 S.W.2d 220, where the court held that a covenant deliberately unreasonable and oppressive, whether severable or not, is invalid. In some states the courts use all of the above rules depending upon the facts and circumstances of the case.

A clause incident to a contract of employment which restricts the employee from discussing trade secrets or engaging in competition after the employment has terminated has been a prolific source of litigation. Some of the criteria that are generally considered by the courts in determining whether or not the clause is valid are: (1) Is the restraint reasonable in the sense that it is no greater than necessary to protect the employer in some legitimate interest? (2) Is the restraint reasonable in the sense that it is not unduly harsh and oppressive on the employee? (3) Does the employee's work for the rival party irreparably injure the employer or threaten to injure him irreparably? In Washington Capitols Basketball Club, Inc. v. Barry, 304 F.Supp. 1193 (N.D.Cal., 1969), a star basketball player signed one contract too many and his original employer sought a restraining order to prevent him from playing for his new employer. The court in granting the temporary injunction held that the contract was not unconscionable, unenforceable or otherwise void, and stated "The precedents for granting injunctive relief against 'star' athletes 'jumping' their contracts—and certainly defendants do not deny that Barry is a unique, a 'star' athlete—are numerous."

K. USURY

1. IN GENERAL

Usury means an illegal contract for a loan in which illegal interest is reserved.

Most states strictly regulate the interest rates on loans by statute. The maximum chargeable interest rate allowable varies from 6% to 30% in the various jurisdictions. If the lender charges interest over the permitted maximum rate, the contract is illegal. Most states deny the lender any interest at all if he charges an illegal amount, but a few states permit him to recover the maximum legal amount that has been established by statute. In a few states the lender forfeits the entire amount of the principal and the interest. If the interest has been paid by the borrower, jurisdictions differ as to whether he recovers merely the amount of the interest paid or whether he recovers two or three times that amount as a penalty.

Most states have statutes which provide for so many exceptions to the general rule of usury that the purpose of the law, i.e., to protect debtors from excessive interest, has been largely nullified.

2. WHAT IS NOT USURY

A few of the many exceptions to the usury laws are as follows:

a. Installment sales, i.e., sales on credit, generally do not come within the usury statutes. The theory is that in such a case the seller does not lend money to the buyer but agrees that he is to be paid by the buyer later, and since no loan is made, the usury law does not apply; and the seller is free to sell for cash at one price and on credit at a different price that is much higher. However, a few states (e.g., California) have adopted statutes which regulate the differential between cash and time prices which may be charged by the seller.

b. Reasonable expenses or service fees which are incidental to the loan may be charged in addition to the maximum rate of interest; e.g., inspection of property, investigating the credit of the borrower and drawing necessary documents. Finance or carrying charges on long term loans are also allowable.

c. Most statutes provide that collecting interest in advance, compound interest, or accelerated maturity for nonpayment of installments is not usury so long as the total interest does not exceed the maximum rate per annum for the full period of the loan.

d. The purchase of a note at a discount greater than the maximum interest with no intent to evade the law is not usury.

e. Where the borrower has the option to pay the principal of the debt before due date, together with some months' unearned interest, there is no usury.

f. Most states have enacted statutes which permit licensed moneylenders, such as banks, to charge more interest than is permissible in ordinary business transactions.

3. WHAT YOU PAY FOR CREDIT

When you buy on credit, you pay an extra charge. If interest is added to the purchase price and the total is repaid in *12 equal monthly payments,* here is what you pay: if the contract provides that you pay 8% a year, you really pay 14.5% in true annual interest; if the contract provides for 1% a month, you really pay 21.5% annual interest.

If you are charged only on the unpaid balance and the contract provides that you are to pay 1½% *per month* on the unpaid balance, you really pay 18% in true annual interest. If the contract provides that you are to pay 2½% *per month* on the unpaid balance, you really pay 30% in true annual interest.

Since credit costs vary widely, the smart shopper gets credit at the lowest possible rate of interest for the shortest possible time.

L. CONSUMER PROTECTION LEGISLATION

In recent years a considerable amount of federal and state legislation has been passed to protect the consumer. In the future an expansion of this legislation can be expected. The following are examples of legislation which has already been passed for the consumer.

1. FEDERAL LEGISLATION.

a. The *Consumer Credit Protection Act* (15 United States Code 1601 et seq.), also known as the "Truth in Lending" Act, became effective July 1, 1969. It is implemented by Regulation Z, prescribed by the Board of Governors of the Federal Reserve System. For a free copy of Regulation Z, write to the Federal Trade Commission, Division of Consumer Credit, Washington, D.C. 20580, or contact your local office of the F.T.C.

The purpose of Regulation Z is to let borrowers and customers know the cost of credit so that they can compare costs with other credit sources. It does not fix maximum, minimum, or any charges for credit. The *finance charge* and the *annual percentage rate* are the two most important disclosures required by the regulation. It applies to any individual or organization which extends or arranges credit for which a finance charge is or may be payable or which is repayable in more than four installments. It is enforced by both civil and criminal penalties.

The total dollar cost of the credit and finance charge in a credit or installment transaction must be expressed as an annual rate. In a revolving credit situation, the monthly rate is also required. Exemptions not covered by the law are installment transactions not exceeding $75 with a finance charge of not over $5, and transactions above $75 with a finance charge of not more than $7.50.

In the sale of real estate, purchase money mortgage or trust deed contracts need not give the total dollar credit cost over the life of the contract; however, all other real estate contracts must comply with the law's disclosure requirements.

Life insurance premiums in a credit contract must be included as part of the finance charge unless the creditor does not require insurance. Property and liability insurance charges must be included unless the creditor does not require such insurance be purchased from him.

Advertising must include all relevant terms including an annual rate statement if any specific terms are set forth.

Garnishment is limited to the lesser of the amounts represented by 25% of the after-tax earnings of a debtor or the excess by which after-tax earnings exceed 30 times the federal minimum hourly wage.

The statute makes it a felony to extend credit where it is known by the parties that violence or criminal means will be resorted to if necessary to compel repayment.

Section 226.13, an amendment to the Act, provides that a CREDIT CARDHOLDER is liable for the unauthorized use of his credit card up to $50, and then only if: (1) the credit card is an accepted credit card (an "accepted" credit card is one that the credit cardholder has requested and received, or has signed or has used, or authorized another to use); (2) the card issuer has given adequate notice to the cardholder of his potential liability; (3) the card issuer has provided the cardholder with an addressed notification requiring no postage to be paid by him which may be mailed by him in the event of the loss, theft, or possible unauthorized use of the credit card; (4) the card issuer has provided a method whereby the user of such card can be identified as the person authorized to use it, such as by signature, photograph, or fingerprint on the credit card or by electronic or mechanical confirmation; and (5) the unauthorized use occurred before the cardholder notified the issuer that an unauthorized use occurred or may occur as a result of loss or theft. Some states have legislation which is similar to the above; e. g., New York (Section 512 of the General Business Law). In addition to statutory limitation of liability in credit card cases, courts have refused to permit the card issuer to recover any sum when the person dealing with the cardholder was negligent in assuming that the holder of the card was the lawful owner of it and in failing to take steps to identify the holder; see Gulf Refining Co. v. Williams Roofing Co., 208 Ark. 362, 186 S.W.2d 790 (1945); Union Oil Co. of California v. Lull (1945) 220 Or. 412, 349 P.2d 243 (1960); Duke v. Sears, 433 S.W.2d 919 (Tex.Civ.App.1968) reversed as to burden of proof 441 S.W.2d 521 (Tex.1969); 48 Calif.L.R. 459, 483 (1960).

b. Section 5, *Federal Trade Commission Act* (15 U.S.C.A. Section 45) gives the FTC authority to prohibit "unfair trade practices". Since criticism in "Nader Raiders' Report" in 1969 and the ABA Commission to Study FTC, the FTC has increased consumer protection considerably. These activities have been in the area of labeling, packaging, textiles, furs and wools, advertising frauds, television advertising, disclosure and collection devices, door-to-door and mail order sales, unsolicited merchandise, option plans and consumer monetary losses.

c. The *Fur Products Labeling Act* (15 U.S.C.A. Section 69–69j), *Textile Fiber Products Act* (15 U.S.C.A. Section 70–70k), and the *Wool Products Labeling Act* (15 U.S.C.A. Section 68–68j), provide standards for the labeling of the various products stated in the respective titles. The FTC has regulatory jurisdiction and has issued regulations directing the manner and form of disclosing required labeling information. The regulations are enforced by cease and desist orders, restitution, affirmative disclosure, rescission of contracts, seizure of mislabeled goods, and willful violations by criminal penalties (these methods of enforcement are generally true in all of the acts).

d. The *Flammable Fabrics Act* (15 U.S.C.A. Section 1191–1204) covers wearing apparel, fabric for wearing apparel, and household furnishings. Recent FTC activities have been in the area of carpet and rug standards, bedding and mattress standards, and children's no-burn sleepwear standards.

e. The *Federal Hazardous Substances Labeling Act* (15 U.S. C.A. Section 1261–73) through regulations issued by the Secretary of H. E. W. declares certain products to be hazardous and subject to labeling requirements to warn consumers of dangers. Some of the children's products relate to thermal, mechanical, electrical, toxicity, and eye hazard protection.

f. The *Mail Fraud Statute* (18 U.S.C. Section 1341; 26 Stat. 466; 39 U.S.C. Section 259) provides civil and criminal penalties when a party is found to be conducting a scheme or device of obtaining money or property through the mails by means of fraudulent practices.

g. The *Fair Packaging and Labeling Act* (15 U.S.C.A. Section 1451–61) assists the consumer in determining values. Foods, drugs, cosmetics and other consumer commodities must be labeled to show net quantity and other product information.

h. The *National Traffic and Motor Vehicle Safety Act* of 1966 (15 U.S.C.A. Section 1381–1425) covers motor vehicle safety standards, labeling standards relating to tires, and notification of purchasers of automobile parts, including tires, of defects discovered by the manufacturer.

i. The *Radiation Control for Health and Safety Act* (42 U.S.C.A. Section 263(b)–263(h)) provides that the Secretary of H. E. W. shall set standards for radiation emission for products covered by the statute. Standards for television receivers manufactured after January 15, 1970, have been set in addition to other electronic products.

j. The *Federal Postal Reorganization Act,* Section 3009, 1970, provides that a person who receives unsolicited goods in the mail has the right to retain, use, discard, or dispose of them in any manner he sees fit without any obligation to the sender. Some states have similar laws (see 2. c. infra).

k. Under the new *Consumer Product Safety Act* (Public Law 92–573, 1972), consumer products became subject to federal regulations. The government will have authority to set safety standards for products and to ban those products which present real hazards to the consumers. A consumer product is any article or part of an article produced or distributed for sale for personal use, consumption or enjoyment in a household, school, in recreation or otherwise, except foods, drugs, cosmetics, motor vehicles, insecticides, firearms, cigarettes, radiological hazards, and certain flammable fabrics. The exceptions are covered by the *Food, Drug and Cosmetic Act* (21 U.S.C.A. § 301), the *Poison Prevention Packaging Act of 1970* (70 U.S.C.A. § 1471), and other Acts mentioned supra or infra. The National Commission on Product Safety estimated that 20 million Americans were injured each year as a result of incidents connected with household consumer products; 30,000 were killed; 110,000 were permanently disabled; and the annual cost to the nation was set at more than $5.5 billion.

The Act provides for civil and criminal penalties. Also, in addition to the usual State court action based upon product liability, the Act provides that suit will lie in any U. S. District Court for a person injured due to a failure to knowingly observe a consumer product safety rule.

The Act grants broad power to the Consumer Product Safety Commission to preempt state or local consumer product safety standards, but allows the new agency to grant an exemption if the proposed local rule imposes a higher standard than the Federal standard.

2. STATE LEGISLATION.

a. *Guaranty and Warranty* legislation has been passed in several states; e. g., Arkansas (requirement of repair facilities in the state), California (guarantee disclosures, limitations on warranty disclaimers, requirement of repair facilities in the state), Hawaii (duty to repair within a fixed time), Illinois (guarantee disclosure area), New Hampshire (retailers repair duties), North Carolina (repair facilities in the state).

b. *Door-to-Door and Telephone Sales* legislation requires a "cooling off" period in home solicitation sales for two or three days; e. g., Alabama, California (also requires salesman to identify himself, his company, and the product he sells). Also effective in those states which have adopted the Uniform Consumer Credit Code, infra.

c. *Unsolicited Merchandise* legislation has been passed in Arizona, California, Louisiana, and Oklahoma.

d. *Unit Pricing* legislation requiring unit pricing in advertising and labeling has been passed in Alaska, California, and New York City.

e. *Product Safety* bills have been passed in California (mattress flammability standards), Illinois (regarding thermals and combustibles), Mississippi (power mower safety devices), New Hampshire (fabric flammability), New York (toy safety), and Texas (children's apparel flammability).

f. *Motor Vehicle* legislation has been passed in California (mechanic licensing and itemization of charges), Delaware (facility and mechanic licensing), and New York (facilities). Over one-half of the states have legislation against tampering with odometers with penalties which vary from a $10 fine in Connecticut to up to six months in prison in Florida.

g. *Billing Error* laws have been passed in Massachusetts, Connecticut, and New York.

h. *Repairmen* statutes have been passed licensing and regulating repairmen and others; Alaska (pharmacists), California (electronics service dealers), Illinois (interior designers), Michigan (cosmetologists), Mississippi (cosmetologists), and Ohio (home improvement contractors).

i. The *"Printer's Ink Model Statute"* has been adopted in most states, including the District of Columbia, to make an advertiser absolutely liable for what he says without proof of reliance on the part of the purchaser or an intent to deceive the purchaser.

j. The *Uniform Consumer Credit Code* (U.C.C.C.) was drafted by the National Conference of Commissioners on Uniform State Laws and approved by the Commissioners in 1968 and recommended for enactment in all states. It has also been approved by the ABA. The U.C.C.C. integrates into one document the regulation of retail installment sales, consumer credit, loans, and insurance. When a state adopts the U.C.C.C. it becomes the controlling law in that state. Many states have passed the U.C.C.C.; e. g., Colorado, Idaho, Indiana, Oklahoma, Utah, and Wyoming.

k. The *Uniform Commercial Code* contains several sections to protect the consumer; e. g., a referral sale type of contract where the buyer is given a price reduction for customers referred to the seller has been held "unconscionable" under Section 2–302 (it is expressly prohibited by Section 2.411 of the U.C.C.C.).

l. Miscellaneous Statutes. Many states have passed other types of consumer legislation; e. g., California (imitation hamburger must be advertised as such in restaurants and drive-ins, motorcycles cannot be sold without one or two headlights, snowmobile noise regulated, open dating required on all food packages), Delaware (bicycle safety standards, banning excessively leaded paint), Florida ("free" gift advertising regulation), New Hampshire (gasoline octane rating disclosure), New Jersey ("used" appliance labeling), Ohio (eyeglass marketing restriction).

1. *No Relief When Contract Illegal*

WALLACE v. OPINHAM

73 Cal.App.2d 25, 165 P.2d 709 (1946).

THOMPSON, J. * * * The cause of action alleges that plaintiff and defendant engaged in "a game of cards * * * known as Twenty-One," which is specifically prohibited by section 330 of the Penal Code. It is asserted that, at that game the plaintiff lost the total sum of $9,250 by means of the fraud of the defendant in using a deck of "marked cards," which fact was unknown to plaintiff.

The appellant contends that he was not *in pari delicto* with the defendant and that he may therefore maintain the action to recover the money of which he was thus defrauded.

The card game known and designated in the complaint as "Twenty-One" is specifically prohibited by section 330 of the Penal Code, regardless of where it is played. The plaintiff and defendant voluntarily engaged in that unlawful game, in the course of which plaintiff lost the money he now seeks to recover by this suit. * * * He could not prove the alleged fraud and deceit, by means of which he lost his bets, without evidence showing that the fraud was exercised incident to his participation in that game of cards which is prohibited by statute. It follows that the parties were *in pari delicto* with respect to their unlawful playing of that game. * * *

In substantially all jurisdictions gambling contracts are treated as unenforceable; and generally, in the absence of a statute providing for recovery or relief, the court will not, at law or in equity, * * aid or assist either party to a gambling contract or transaction to enforce any right or claim against the other growing out of the contract or transaction, but will leave the parties where they have placed themselves and the court finds them. Even though a party to an illegal betting contract seeks alleged rights against a third person, the court will not aid him where he must rely on the illegal contract. * *

* * * No California statute authorizes a party to an illegal transaction which is prohibited by law to recover gambling losses, regardless of the fact that one of them may have been the victim of fraud or deceit with respect to some incident to that illegal transaction. It has been frequently decided that courts will not become the arbiters of incidental acts of participants in gambling games which are prohibited by law. * * * Public policy prompts courts to decline to distinguish between degrees of turpitude of parties who engage in outlawed transactions. Otherwise courts might be compelled to decide which party cheated the most.

The California cases are uniform in holding that where money or property is lost in a transaction between the parties which is prohibited by law, neither of the parties has standing in a court of law or equity to recover his losses. * * *

[Case dismissed.]

2. *Mere Knowledge of Wrongful Use Will Not Preclude Recovery*

GALLICK v. CASTIGLIONE

2 Cal.App.2d 716, 38 P.2d 858 (1934).

Gallick sued for the purchase price of materials sold "for the express purpose of manufacturing intoxicating liquor," contrary to the provisions of the 18th Amendment of the Constitution of the United States and laws passed pursuant thereto. The seller knew the purpose for which the materials in question were purchased. The trial court found for plaintiff.

* * * It is claimed that this extension of credit was in aid or furtherance of the illegal purpose. We cannot hold that the trial court erred in finding that it was not. The seller did no more than to agree to sell to appellants on credit with knowledge of their illegal purpose. * * *

Appellants, however, claim further that the contract was in violation of the following section of the National Prohibition Act: "It shall be unlawful to advertise, manufacture, sell, or possess for sale any utensil, contrivance, machine, preparation, compound, tablet, substance, formula, direction, or recipe advertised, designed, or intended for use in the unlawful manufacture of intoxicating liquor." * *

In prior cases the courts held that the mere knowledge of the seller that the buyer intended to manufacture intoxicants did not bring the case within the above-quoted section of the United States Statutes, the cases holding that, in addition to knowledge, the design or intent of the seller that the materials should be so used must be established; it not being sufficient to establish the design or intent of the buyer.

---

3. *Withdrawal From Executory Illegal Contract Affords Relief*

BERNHARD v. TAYLOR

23 Or. 416, 31 P. 968 (1893).

The plaintiff and defendant agreed to conduct a bogus foot race with the purpose of inducing innocent third parties to bet with the plaintiff. It had been agreed in advance that whichever contestant the plaintiff placed his money on was always to win. Pursuant to this agreement the plaintiff had placed $560 in the hands of the defendant as stakeholders; but, before the race had actually been run, the plaintiff repented of the fraud about to be practiced and demanded that his money be returned. The defendant refused to give it back and the plaintiff sues to recover it. Defendant contends that since wagers are illegal the plaintiff must be denied relief.

LORD, C. J. * * * Of late years, by legislation and judicial decision, the hostility to wagers of every nature has been marked. This is doubtless due to the increase of betting, and the evil consequences resulting therefrom.

* * * Wagers are inconsistent with the established interests of society, and in conflict with the morals of the age; and, as such, they are void, as against public policy. In view of these considerations, we do not think that such transactions * * * are valid in this state.

There is no doubt, where money has been paid on an illegal contract, which has been executed, and both parties are *in pari delicto,* the courts will not compel the return of the money so paid. But the cases show that an important distinction is made between executory and executed illegal contracts. While the contract is executory, the law will neither enforce it nor award damages; but, if it is already executed, nothing paid or delivered can be recovered back. So that, while the contract is executory, the party paying the money or putting up the property may rescind the contract and recover back his money. The reason is that the plaintiff's claim is not to enforce, but to repudiate, an illegal agreement. * * * The wrong is not consummated, and the contract may be rescinded by either party. * * The object of the law is to protect the public, and not the parties. This is upon the principle that it best comports with public policy to arrest the illegal transaction before it is consummated.

It only remains to apply these principles to the facts. These show that the plaintiff was cognizant that the race had been fixed in advance; that one of the parties should win, and that certain other persons should lose their money; that it was a bogus race, and the arrangement based upon it corrupt, and designed to cheat and defraud the other parties; but at the same time they show that he repented, and repudiated the transaction before it was consummated, by demanding the return of his money the evening of the day before the race, and on the day of the race, but before it was to come off, and that the defendant refused to pay it back, and that he afterwards forbade the defendant to pay said money to any other person than himself. He availed himself of the opportunity which the law affords a person to withdraw from the illegal contract before it has been executed. * * * By allowing the party to withdraw, the contemplated wrong is arrested and not consummated. This the law encourages, and no obstacle should be thrown in the way of his repentance. Hence, if the plaintiff retreated before the bet had been decided, his money ought to have been returned to him; and, in default of this, he is entitled to recover. * * *

4. *Partial Illegality Will Not Avoid Severable Contract*

KEENE v. HARLING

61 Cal.2d 318, 38 Cal.Rptr. 513, 392 P.2d 273 (1964).

PETERS, Justice. Walter M. Keene and his wife brought this action against Fred Harling and Morris Blum for the balance due on a promissory note given as part of the purchase price for a business involving coin-operated machines. Defendants' sole defense was that the sales agreement was illegal. The trial court found that the transfer of a minor part of the consideration given by the Keenes in exchange for the note was, in fact, illegal, but held that the illegal portion was severable from the remaining consideration. Judgment was therefore entered in favor of the plaintiffs for the amount due on the note, less the value of the illegal consideration. Defendant Harling alone appealed.

The facts are as follows: For several years prior to September 1, 1955, Walter Keene owned and operated a coin machine route. On that date he and his wife entered into a conditional sales agreement whereby they sold the route to defendant Harling, together with all the equipment of the business. * * *

The coin machine business consisted of its goodwill and certain tangible personal property. Several "bingo-type" pinball machines were part of the tangible property. The court found that the sale of these machines was illegal under Penal Code, § 330b. None of the parties now contends otherwise. The court additionally found that the market value of the illegal machines at the time of the sale totaled $4,600. It deducted that amount from the $32,500 still owing, and entered its judgment for the balance, plus interest and costs, in favor of the Keenes. The Keenes do not object to this deduction. Thus the trial court concluded that the contract was severable. It is the correctness of this determination that is here involved.

* * * Whether a contract is entire or separable depends upon its language and subject-matter, and this question is one of construction to be determined by the court according to the intention of the parties. If the contract is divisible, the first part may stand, although the latter is illegal.

* * * Of course, if the court is unable to distinguish between the lawful part of the agreement and the unlawful part, the illegality taints the entire contract, and the entire transaction is illegal and unenforceable. * * * This finding indicates that the buyer did not enter into the transaction because of the illegal machines and that the illegal machines were of such minor importance that they did not "taint" the otherwise legal consideration. * * * Included in the legal personal property were an automobile, a truck, office furniture and equipment, repair shop equipment, approximately forty-six coin-operated phonographs, about the same number of cigarette dispensing machines, numerous legal pinball machines, eight or more coin-operated scales and several candy and popcorn dispensing machines. * * * Since the consideration on the buyer's side

was money, the court properly construed the contract by equating the established market price of the illegal machines to a portion of the money consideration. * * * The argument that the court cannot apportion because the parties did not expressly apportion is without merit. That argument exalts form over substance. * * *

The judgment appealed from by defendant Harling is affirmed.

---

5. *Agreement Violating Intra-Departmental Regulation No Defense to Third Party Contract*

VICK v. PATTERSON

158 Cal.App.2d 414, 322 P.2d 548 (1958).

DRAPER, Justice. In 1954 plaintiff, a San Francisco fireman, was employed by defendants as an announcer of Pacific Coast League baseball games televised from Oakland and San Francisco. This work was part-time only. Plaintiff was required to work only during each game and for a short time before it. No Saturday or Sunday games were televised. After he had worked for two weeks at an agreed salary which was paid, he and defendants entered into an oral contract for his services for the remainder of the season. Plaintiff performed the agreed duties through August 27, when television of the Oakland games ceased. He then requested payment of the reasonable value of his services which, in his view, defendants had agreed to pay. Defendants maintained that he had agreed to work for nothing. This action followed, and jury verdict was in favor of plaintiff for $1,200. * * *

Throughout the period he worked for defendants, plaintiff continued in the employ of the San Francisco Fire Department. At trial, defendants sought to introduce Rule 447 of that department, providing: "Members shall devote their time and attention to the best interests of the Department. They shall at no time engage in any activities that may interfere with the efficiency of the fire service, nor shall they actively participate in any other gainful occupation." * * *

It is elementary that a contract whose object is unlawful is void * * *. That is unlawful which is (1) contrary to an express provision of law, (2) contrary to the policy of express law, although not expressly prohibited, or (3) otherwise contrary to good morals. * *

The rule is settled that the courts will not enforce a contract to perform an act prohibited by statute. * * *

We find no authority extending this doctrine to the rules of a municipal department governing wholly intra-departmental administrative affairs. Our case, of course, does not involve rules prescribed by a regulatory body, such as the Division of Corporations or the Industrial Accident Commission, governing the conduct of the public in dealings with the regulated subject-matter.

Even where a statute, rather than an administrative regulation, is involved, the mere prohibition does not necessarily imply a legislative intent that agreements in contravention of it are void * * The power to invalidate agreements on the ground of public policy is so far-reaching and so easily abused that it should be called into action only in cases where the dangerous tendency clearly and unequivocally appears from the contract itself. Courts are reluctant, therefore, to declare a contract void as against public policy, and will refuse to do so if by any reasonable construction i[t] may be upheld * * * There is little doubt that within the fire department such a rule is effective, and may be enforced by disciplinary proceedings against the employee. * * * It is quite another matter to argue that the rule invalidates contracts between the employee and a third party. * * * Such intervention here would not protect the public because the employee's participation in the transaction has been completed; no serious moral turpitude is involved; and to sustain the defense of illegality would unjustly enrich the defendants. * * *

[Judgment for plaintiff.]

---

6. *Agreement Not to Prosecute Crime is Unenforceable*

GRASSO v. DEAN

171 Neb. 648, 107 N.W.2d 421 (1961).

SPENCER, Justice. This is an action by plaintiff, Grasso, against defendants, Adolph, Gladys, and Joan Dean, and defendant corporations, State Finance Company, Postal Finance Company, and First Loan Company. It seeks to foreclose a mortgage on the home owned by defendants Adolph and Gladys Dean, in which the three defendant corporations are alleged to claim some interest. The mortgage was given to secure an installment promissory note signed by the three defendants Dean.

The defense raised by defendants Adolph and Gladys Dean, is that the promissory note and mortgage * * * were obtained by the use of duress and threats. * * *

The essential facts are: Defendant Joan entered the employ of plaintiff, a dentist, in 1954 as an office clerk, receptionist, and technician. Plaintiff had been in practice but a few months. Joan was 16 years of age but represented herself to be 18. During the years 1956 and 1957, Joan embezzled funds belonging to plaintiff. According to plaintiff's testimony, Joan admitted "about the fourth or sixth month * * * of 1957," that she had been taking money, but could not give the amount. Audits were made by plaintiff's accountant. On October 24, 1957, Joan, in the office of plaintiff's accountant and in his presence, and in the presence of plaintiff, signed an "affidavit of admission," but no amount was stated. During December

1957, Joan made two payments on the obligation. Subsequent to these payments, plaintiff insisted that Joan bring her father to his office. About 2 weeks previous to February 18, 1958, Joan brought Adolph to plaintiff's office. Previous to this time, Joan had not wanted her folks informed. At this visit, plaintiff discussed Joan's difficulty with her father, who, according to plaintiff's testimony, said, "he would help her in any way he could, and he was appreciating what I was doing." On February 18, 1958, Joan and Adolph met plaintiff at the home of plaintiff's accountant, and signed a note for $7,974, and Adolph executed a mortgage on the Dean home.

* * * The evidence in this case is undisputed that Joan did embezzle funds of plaintiff. However, in considering the defense of duress herein, the question of her guilt or innocence is immaterial. The question is whether the facts and circumstances, as disclosed by the record involved, constitute duress. * * * the law is well established that where a parent or other relative is induced to execute an instrument by threats and fear of criminal punishment of a child or relative, the instrument is the result of duress and the contract may be voided. * * *

Plaintiff testified: "* * *

> Q. Just tell us what you said, just what you said in regard to paper. A. *That we wanted to try to rehabilitate her, we didn't want to persecute her, we wanted to do everything to help her. In other words, just because she is down we didn't want to trample her, we wanted to help her."* (Italics supplied.)

The word "persecute" as used by the witness would ordinarily have an entirely different meaning, but as used here could logically be calculated to induce fear of prosecution. * * * What was plaintiff doing that Joan's father appreciated? * * *

When we consider the substance of the testimony adduced by plaintiff, we can readily conclude the obvious answer must be the correct one. There was a threat of prosecution under plaintiff's evidence, and while not stated in so many words, it certainly produced the desired condition of mind. * * * We believe the consideration for the giving of the note and mortgage was the suppression of a criminal prosecution, and find the transaction illegal and void and that no recovery can be had thereon. * * *

[Judgment for defendant.]

---

7. *Agreement to Commit a Tort is Unenforceable*

ATKINS v. JOHNSON

43 Vt. 78 (1870).

The defendant had written a defamatory article about one Gregory, and to induce the plaintiff, a publisher, to print it in his newspaper, the defendant had agreed to protect him against any action for damages brought by Gregory, or any other liability that might arise from the publication. The plaintiff, having been sued successfully by Gregory, brings this action upon the defendant's promise to indemnify him.

PIERPOINT, C. J. * * * The plaintiff is here seeking to compel the defendant to indemnify him for the damage which he has sustained in consequence of publishing a libel, at the request of the defendant, and from the consequences of which the defendant agreed to save him harmless. The question is whether such an agreement as the plaintiff sets out in his declaration can be legally enforced.

In this case, these parties in the outset conspired to do a wrong to one of their neighbors, by publishing a libel upon his character. The publication of a libel is an illegal act upon its face. This both parties are presumed to have known. The publication not only subjects the party publishing to a prosecution by the person injured for damages, but also to a public prosecution by indictment. * * *

Both these parties knew that they were arranging for and consummating an illegal act, one that subjects them to legal liability, hoping, to be sure, that they might defend it; but the plaintiff, fearing they might not be able to do so, sought to protect himself from the consequences by taking a contract of indemnity from the defendant. To say under such circumstances that these parties were not joint wrongdoers, within the full spirit and meaning of the general rule, would be an entire perversion of the plainest and simplest proposition. This being so, the law will not interfere in aid of either. It will not inquire which of the two are most in the wrong, with a view of adjusting the equities between them, but regarding both as having been understandingly engaged in a violation of the law, it will leave them as it finds them, to adjust their differences between themselves as they best may. * * *

[Case dismissed.]

---

8. Agreement Interfering with a Public Duty is Unenforceable

GRIFFITH v. HARRIS

17 Wis.2d 255, 116 N.W.2d 133 (1962), certiorari denied 373 U.S. 927, 83 S.Ct. 1530, 10 L.Ed.2d 425.

This is an action by the plaintiff, Ambrose Griffith, against the defendants, William Harris and Richard Minton, to recover damages for breach of contract. The defendants demurred to the complaint on the ground that it did not state facts sufficient to constitute a cause of action. The trial court sustained the demurrer, and a judgment was entered dismissing the complaint. From this judgment the plaintiff appeals.

The contract which is alleged to have been breached is one by which the two defendants agreed to testify for the plaintiff as expert medical witnesses in a malpractice action. The following facts were alleged in the complaint:

Prior to this lawsuit the plaintiff had commenced an action against Dr. John L. Bennett to recover damages for medical malpractice. While preparing this malpractice case for trial, the plaintiff's attorneys contacted the two defendants, who are both physicians, with the intention of getting them to testify in support of the plaintiff's malpractice case. The plaintiff's attorneys furnished the two doctor-defendants with hospital records on which the malpractice charge was in part based. The hospital records were not sufficient to establish the plaintiff's case without supporting expert medical testimony. The defendants were requested to testify in response to hypothetical questions. They were told that the plaintiff's attorneys would not proceed to trial without supporting expert medical testimony. The defendants took the matter under advisement and subsequently notified the plaintiff's attorneys that they would testify favorably for the plaintiff. Later, the defendants were furnished copies of the proposed hypothetical questions. * * *

The plaintiff's attorneys noticed the malpractice action for trial, and the case was called on February 10, 1958. The trial commenced, and the plaintiff began presenting his evidence. The defendants were notified when they would be called to testify. Less than 24 hours before they were to be called to testify, the defendants informed the plaintiff's attorneys that they would not testify without a subpoena and, if subpoenaed, they would not testify in any way that would benefit the plaintiff. Because of this latter fact, the defendants were not subpoenaed. They did not appear and testify in behalf of the plaintiff. Because of the absence of favorable expert medical testimony, the plaintiff failed to establish a *prima facie* case of malpractice. As a result, the malpractice action was dismissed at the end of the plaintiff's case. * * *

GORDON, Justice. In our opinion, public policy necessitates a rejection of the cause of action alleged in the complaint. The gravamen of the complaint is that the defendants broke their contract to appear and testify in the plaintiff's favor. * * *

The plaintiff does not claim that his loss was occasioned merely by the doctors' failure to attend the trial. The complaint is not couched in terms of the burden and expense caused by the doctors' breach of an obligation to attend. On the contrary, it is their failure to give *favorable* medical evidence to establish an alleged malpractice which has prompted the plaintiff's claim that the defendants caused the plaintiff to lose his lawsuit. * * *

A litigant and a prospective witness may lawfully contract between themselves that the latter will appear at a trial; the breach of such contract would give rise to the damages which reasonably flow from a witness's failure to appear. This might include the expense involved in seeking a substitute witness or perhaps the costs incurred in procuring a postponement of the trial. However, a contract creating an obligation not only to appear but also to testify in a certain manner on behalf of a party to a lawsuit, is against public policy. * * *

Contracts which impose obligations that are contrary to public policy are unenforceable. * * *

Judgment affirmed.

---

9. *Agreement Interfering with a Private Duty is Unenforceable*

LEVY v. SPENCER

18 Colo. 532, 33 P. 415 (1893).

The plaintiff and defendant were real estate agents of Denver. Each of them had a client desiring to sell or exchange a tract of land. They agreed between themselves to endeavor to bring their principals together to effect an exchange of properties. It was further agreed that they should divide all commissions received equally between them. The exchange of land was effected, and as a result the defendant received a commission of $10,000 and the plaintiff one of $3,750. The defendant refused to divide with the plaintiff. The plaintiff sues for $3,125.

GODDARD, J. * * * This agreement comes clearly within that class of contracts that is inhibited by public policy, and consequently void. By its terms each agent was to share in the commissions paid by both principals. The compensation to be jointly shared was contingent upon the consummation of the trade or sale, and this would have a tendency to induce them to disregard, if not to sacrifice, the interests of their principals if necessary to effect that result. The fact that a sale price was fixed by the principals upon their respective properties does not answer this objection. Each was entitled to the benefit of the unbiased judgment of his agent as to the value to be placed upon the other's property, and to a reasonable effort on the part of such agent to obtain a reduction of the value to be allowed therefor in the exchange. Their pecuniary interest might have prevented such disinterested action on the part of these agents; and, it appearing from the allegations of the complaint that they "did effect the trade or sale of the property as between their respective principals," the transaction is as objectionable as those universally condemned, wherein one agent acts for both principals without their knowledge or consent. * * *

In this case (plaintiff) asserts a claim against (defendant) founded upon, and recoverable only through and by virtue of, an illegal agreement. It is therefore an action to enforce an illegal executory contract. * * * "It is quite true that a plaintiff will in no case be permitted to recover when it is necessary for him to prove his own illegal act or contract as a part of his cause of action, or when an essential element of his cause of action is his own violation of law." * * *

[Case dismissed.]

---

10. Illegal Lobbying Contracts

IN RE J. ROY BROWNING

23 Ill.2d 483, 179 N.E.2d 14 (1961).

PER CURIAM. The Committee on Grievances and the Board of Managers of the Chicago Bar Association, as Commissioners of this court, have recommended the disbarment of the respondent, J. Roy Browning, an attorney, on two charges of misconduct, and he has brought the record to this court for review.

Each of the charges relates to activities of Orville E. Hodge, formerly Auditor of Public Accounts, who embezzled substantial sums of money from the State of Illinois. * * * On April 15, 1955, Hodge, who was Auditor of Public Accounts at the time, called the respondent to ask whether he would like to represent Union Electric in "expediting" the passage of a bill through the Illinois legislature. * * * As the bill progressed through the legislature, three more checks were issued by Union Electric, making up the balance of the $35,000. They were delivered to Hodge's office in Springfield in sealed envelopes addressed to the respondent. Each was endorsed with respondent's name. * * * "All agreements whose object or tendency is improperly to interfere with or influence legislative action, either by congress, the General Assembly, or by a city council or other like body, are contrary to public policy and void. Thus contingent fee contracts for procuring favorable legislation are void since such a contract tends necessarily to influence legislation improperly, for the promise of payment of a contingent fee is a direct and strong incentive to the exertion of not merely personal but sinister influence of the legislative body." * * *

The fee was contingent, and contingent fees for services as a lobbyist are contrary to public policy and void. * * *

Not only was the fee contingent; its amount was extraordinary in view of the work to be done. The respondent was to have nothing to do with the preparation of the bill. It had already been prepared. Only a little more than two months of the legislative session remained when the respondent was retained. Despite the fact that the payment of this substantial fee was contingent upon results that he had been retained to bring about, respondent did absolutely nothing to assist in the passage of the bill. He made no attempt at any time to communicate with his client.

* * * After the bill was passed and approved, he made no inquiry as to the balance of his fee. These circumstances are hardly consistent with a good faith attorney-client relationship.

* * * He made no financial profit from either of the transactions involved, and the record suggests that his conduct was attributable to friendship for Hodge rather than to the desire for financial gain. That fact does not make his conduct less reprehensible, but it does have a bearing upon the degree of discipline that is appropriate. Upon careful consideration, we are of the opinion that the respondent should be suspended from the practice of law for a period of 3 years.

Respondent suspended.

/11. *Failure to Obtain License Required by Law*

ELEPHANT LUMBER CO. v. JOHNSON

120 Ohio App. 266, 202 N.E.2d 189 (1964).

COLLIER, Presiding Judge. The Elephant Lumber Company, a corporation, * * * herein designated the plaintiff, brought this action on June 10, 1963, in the Chillicothe Municipal Court to recover for services rendered * * * Helen Johnson, herein referred to as the defendant, in preparing and drawing plans, specifications and material lists for the erection of a building to be used as a nursing home. * * *

No answer or other pleading was filed by the defendant and, on July 15, 1963, a default judgment was entered in favor of plaintiff for the full amount claimed in the petition. * * * The defendant now seeks a reversal of that judgment. * * *

The defendant's contentions are that the petition does not state a cause of action for the reason it is not alleged in the petition that the plaintiff is an architect or has as its employee an architect authorized to draw and furnish plans and specifications and to charge for such services; that the alleged contract is in violation of statute and therefore void; that a valid default judgment may not be rendered upon such defective petition. Section 4703.18, Revised Code, provides:

> "No person shall enter upon the practice of architecture, or hold himself forth as an architect or registered architect, unless he * * * is the holder of a certificate of qualification to practice architecture issued or renewed and registered under such sections."

* * * Ohio is one of the many states that have enacted statutes regulating architects in the practice of their profession. It is generally held that designing a building for another, or furnishing the plans and specifications for such a building for another, constitutes

architectural services. It is also well settled that such legislation is a proper exercise of the police power.

* * * The general rule is that a contract entered into by a person engaged in a business without taking out a license as required by law is void and unenforceable and that where a license or certificate is required by statute as a requisite to one practicing a particular profession, an agreement of a professional character without such license or certificate is illegal and void. * * *

It is also a well established rule that a contract which cannot be performed without a violation of a statute is void. * * *

Our conclusions are that the plaintiff's claim is for services rendered as an architect; that to practice the profession of architecture in Ohio and to recover in an action for such services, it is necessary to obtain a license as prescribed by law; that a contract for such services entered into by one who is not so licensed and registered is void; that a default judgment, rendered on a petition to recover for such services in which it is not alleged that the plaintiff is a licensed and registered architect, is void. The judgment will be reversed and final judgment rendered for the defendant.

---

12. Cannot Waive Negligence When Public Interest Involved

HUNTER v. AMERICAN RENTALS, INC.

189 Kan. 615, 371 P.2d 131 (1962).

WERTZ, Justice. This was an action for damages brought by Everett L. Hunter, plaintiff against American Rentals, Inc., defendant. * * *

The petition alleged that the defendant corporation was engaged in the business of renting trailers to the general public, including trailer hitches and all other attendant equipment necessary to connect trailers to automobiles; that plaintiff went to defendant's place of business for the purpose of renting a trailer, told defendant's agent that he knew little about trailers, had never pulled a trailer behind an automobile, and that he would have to rely on defendant's agent's superior knowledge and skill to determine the size of the trailer and other necessary equipment to transport enumerated items from Wichita to Oklahoma City. * * * [T]hat defendant's agent returned to the office and advised plaintiff the trailer was ready for the trip and that it would not be necessary for plaintiff to do anything further to the trailer or the hitch. Plaintiff then paid the rental charges. * * *

Driving his automobile and the trailer loaded with the furniture and items previously described, plaintiff departed from Wichita, and when he reached a point near Edmond, Oklahoma, the trailer hitch broke, leaving the trailer and automobile attached only by the safety chain. This chain had been attached by the defendant's agent in such a manner that it permitted the trailer to start moving from one side of the highway to the other, causing plaintiff's car to overturn, and by reason thereof plaintiff received personal injury and damage to the automobile for which he seeks recovery.

* * *

By its answer defendant seeks to avoid liability to plaintiff, contending that the plaintiff entered into a written rental agreement for the use of one of defendant's trailers and at the time the rental agreement was entered into plaintiff paid the defendant the rental charge. A portion of the rental agreement reads:

> "The renter hereby absolved the AMERICAN RENTALS of any responsibility or obligation in the event of accident, regardless of causes or consequence, and that any costs, claims, court or attorney's fees, or liability resulting from the use of described equipment will be indemnified by the renter regardless against whom the claimant or claimants institute action.

* * * * * * * * * *

Contracts for exemption for liability from negligence are not favored by the law. They are strictly construed against the party relying on them. The rule is unqualifiedly laid down by many decisions that one cannot avoid liability for negligence by contract. The rule against such contracts is frequently limited to the principle that parties cannot stipulate for the protection against liability for negligence in the performance of a legal duty or a duty of public service, or where the public interest is involved or a public duty owed, or when the duty owed is a private one where public interest requires the performance thereof. * * * There is no doubt that the rule that forbids a person to protect himself by agreement against damages resulting from his own negligence applies where the agreement protects him against the consequences of a breach of some duty imposed by law.

G.S.1949, Chapter 8, Article 5, contains the uniform act regulating traffic on the highway. Section 8–5, 118 provides:

> "(a) When one vehicle is towing another the drawbar or other connection shall be of sufficient strength to pull, stop and hold all weight towed thereby, * * *. (b) In addition to the drawbar connections between any two such vehicles there shall be provided an adequate safety hitch. * * *"

* * * It is apparent that the mentioned statute was passed for the protection of the public; that the business in which the defendant is engaged, i.e., that of renting trailers to the public, is one where the interest and safety of the public must be kept in view; and, where one violates a duty owed to the public, he may not come into a court of law and ask to have his illegal contract, exempting him from liability to comply with such duty, carried out. * * *

If an agreement binds the parties, or either of them, to do something opposed to the public policy of the state, it is illegal and absolutely void. * * *

For the reasons stated, this court is of the opinion that the contract pleaded, being in contravention of the statute and the public policy of this state, is void and unenforceable and constitutes no defense to plaintiff's cause of action, * * * and the judgment must be affirmed.

---

13. *Can Waive Negligence in Private Contracts*

CIOFALO v. VIC TANNEY GYMS, INC.

10 N.Y.2d 294, 220 N.Y.S.2d 962, 177 N.E.2d 925 (1961).

FROESSEL, Judge. This action by plaintiff wife for personal injuries, and by plaintiff husband for medical expenses and loss of services, stems from injuries which the wife sustained as the result of a fall at or near the edge of a swimming pool located on defendant's premises. Plaintiff claimed that because of excessive slipperiness and lack of sufficient and competent personnel she was caused to fall and fractured her left wrist. * * *

At the time of the injury, plaintiff wife was a "member" or patron of the gymnasium operated by defendant, and in her membership contract she had agreed to assume full responsibility for any injuries which might occur to her in or about defendant's premises, "including but without limitation, any claims for personal injuries resulting from or arising out of the negligence of" the defendant.

Although exculpatory clauses in a contract, intended to insulate one of the parties from liability resulting from his own negligence, are closely scrutinized, they are enforced, but with a number of qualifications. Whether or not such provisions, when properly expressed, will be given effect depends upon the legal relationship between the contracting parties and the interest of the public therein. * * * [W]here the intention of the parties is expressed in sufficiently clear and unequivocal language * * * and it does not come within any of the * * * categories where the public interest is directly involved, a provision absolving a party from his own negligent acts will be given effect.

* * * Here there is no special legal relationship and no overriding public interest which demand that this contract provision, voluntarily entered into by competent parties, should be rendered ineffectual. Defendant, a private corporation, was under no obligation or legal duty to accept plaintiff as a "member" or patron. Having consented to do so, it had the right to insist upon such terms as it deemed appropriate. Plaintiff, on the other hand, was not required to assent to unacceptable terms, or to give up a valuable legal right, as a condition precedent to obtaining employment or being able to make use of the services rendered by a public carrier or utility. She

voluntarily applied for membership in a private organization, and agreed to the terms upon which this membership was bestowed. She may not repudiate them now. * * *

The judgment appealed from should be affirmed, without costs.

(14. *Contract in Restraint of Trade*

SIEGEL v. CHICKEN DELIGHT, INC.

448 F.2d 43 (C.A.Cal.1971).

MERRILL, Circuit Judge. This antitrust suit is a class action in which certain franchisees of Chicken Delight seek treble damages for injuries allegedly resulting from illegal restraints imposed by Chicken Delight's standard form franchise agreements. The restraints in question are Chicken Delight's contractual requirements that franchisees purchase certain essential cooking equipment, dry-mix food items, and trade-mark bearing packaging exclusively from Chicken Delight as a condition of obtaining a Chicken Delight trade-mark license. These requirements are asserted to constitute a tying arrangement, unlawful per se under § 1 of the Sherman Act, 15 U.S.C. § 1.

I. FACTUAL BACKGROUND

Over its eighteen years existence, Chicken Delight has licensed several hundred franchisees to operate home delivery and pick-up food stores. It charged its franchisees no franchise fees or royalties. Instead, in exchange for the license granting the franchisees the right to assume its identity and adopt its business methods and to prepare and market certain food products under its trade-mark, Chicken Delight required its franchisees to purchase a specified number of cookers and fryers and to purchase certain packaging supplies and mixes exclusively from Chicken Delight. The prices fixed for these purchases were higher than, and included a percentage mark-up which exceeded that of, comparable products sold by competing suppliers.

II. THE EXISTENCE OF AN UNLAWFUL TYING ARRANGEMENT

In order to establish that there exists an unlawful tying arrangement plaintiffs must demonstrate *First,* that the scheme in question involves two distinct items and provides that one (the tying product) may not be obtained unless the other (the tied product) is also purchased. * * * *Second,* that the tying product possesses sufficient economic power appreciably to restrain competition in the tied product market. * * * *Third,* that a "not insubstantial" amount of commerce is affected by the arrangement. * * * Chicken Delight concedes that the third requirement has been satisfied. It disputes the existence of the first two. * * *

A. *Two Products*

The District Court ruled that the license to use the Chicken Delight name, trade-mark, and method of operations was "a tying item in the traditional sense," the tied items being the cookers and fryers, packaging products, and mixes.

* * *

The hallmark of a tie-in is that it denies competitors free access to the tied product market, not because the party imposing the arrangement has a superior product in that market, but because of the power or leverage exerted by the tying product. * * * Rules governing tying arrangements are designed to strike, not at the mere coupling of physically separable objects, but rather at the use of a dominant desired product to compel the purchase of a second, distinct commodity. * * * In effect, the forced purchase of the second, tied product is a price exacted for the purchase of the dominant, tying product. By shutting competitors out of the tied product market, tying arrangements serve hardly any purpose other than the suppression of competition. * * *

In determining whether an aggregation of separable items should be regarded as one or more items for tie-in purposes in the normal cases of sales of products the courts must look to the function of the aggregation. Consideration is given to such questions as whether the amalgamation of products resulted in cost savings apart from those reductions in sales expenses and the like normally attendant upon any tie-in, and whether the items are normally sold or used as a unit with fixed proportions.

Where one of the products sold as part of an aggregation is a trade-mark or franchise license, new questions are injected. In determining whether the license and the remaining ("tied") items in the aggregation are to be regarded as distinct items which can be traded in distinct markets consideration must be given to the function of trade-marks.

The historical conception of a trade-mark as a strict emblem of source of the product to which it attaches has largely been abandoned. The burgeoning business of franchising has made trade-mark licensing a widespread commercial practice and has resulted in the development of a new rationale for trade-marks as representations of product quality. This is particularly true in the case of a franchise system set up not to distribute the trade-marked goods of the franchisor, but, as here, to conduct a certain business under a common trade-mark or trade name. Under such a type of franchise, the trade-mark simply reflects the goodwill and quality standards of the enterprise which it identifies. As long as the system of operation of the franchisees lives up to those quality standards and remains as represented by the mark so that the public is not misled, neither the protection afforded the trade-mark by law nor the value of the trade-mark to the licensee depends upon the source of the components.

This being so, it is apparent that the goodwill of the Chicken Delight trade-mark does not attach to the multitude of separate articles used in the operation of the licensed system or in the production of its end product. It is not what is used, but how it is used and what results that have given the system and its end product their entitlement to trade-mark protection. It is to the system and the end product that the public looks with the confidence that established goodwill has created.

Thus, sale of a franchise license, with the attendant rights to operate a business in the prescribed manner and to benefit from the goodwill of the trade name, in no way requires the forced sale by the franchisor of some or all of the component articles. Just as the quality of a copyrighted creation cannot by a tie-in be appropriated by a creation to which the copyright does not relate, * * * so here attempts by tie-in to extend the trade-mark protection to common articles (which the public does not and has no reason to connect with the trade-mark) simply because they are said to be essential to production of that which is the subject of the trade-mark, cannot escape antitrust scrutiny.

* * *

We conclude that the District Court was not in error in ruling as matter of law that the arrangement involved distinct tying and tied products.

B. *Economic Power*

Under the per se theory of illegality, plaintiffs are required to establish not only the existence of a tying arrangement but also that the tying product possesses sufficient economic power to appreciably restrain free competition in the tied product markets. * * *

The District Court ruled * * * that Chicken Delight's unique registered trade-mark, in combination with its demonstrated power to impose a tie-in, established as matter of law the existence of sufficient market power to bring the case within the Sherman Act.

We agree.

---

15. *Promise Not to Compete in Business (Modern Rule)*

HILL v. CENTRAL WEST PUBLIC SERVICE CO.

37 F.2d 451 (C.C.A.Tex., 1930).

WALKER, Circuit Judge. The appellee, a corporation, became the assignee or successor of an individual who, in May, 1928, pursuant to an option given in February, 1928, purchased the properties located in Dallas, Tex., of the Texas Ice & Cold Storage Company, and the good will of that company (herein referred to as the Ice Company), which prior to the sale of its properties was engaged in the manufacture and sale of ice. A feature of the contract of sale referred to was that the Ice Company and its officers and stockholders, one of whom was the appellant, C. B. Hill, joined in that contract, and agreed with the purchaser, his assigns or successors, that each of them will not engage, directly or indirectly, for a period of five years in the state of Texas from the date of said contract of sale in any line of business in which the company was engaged at the time of the making of the above-mentioned option agreement, either individually, or as members or employees of any copartnership, or as officers, directors, stockholders or employees in any corporation. The bill in this case was filed by the appellee against the appellant on October 1, 1928. It contained allegations to the effect that at the time the bill was filed appellant was commencing to erect in the city of Dallas an ice plant in which he intends to conduct and operate a business for manufacturing and selling ice unless he is restrained and enjoined from doing so. The bill prayed an injunction restraining appellant, his agents, employees, or associates, from erecting the plant mentioned, or any plant or building in Dallas, or elsewhere in Texas for the manufacture or sale of ice, or from engaging, in the city of Dallas or elsewhere in the state of Texas, for the above-mentioned period of five years, in any line of business in which the Ice Company was engaged on or about February 21, 1928. By his answer to the bill appellant admitted that he was engaged in the construction of an ice plant in the city of Dallas, and that he proposed to engage in the ice business. The granting of the relief sought was resisted on the grounds: (1) That the covenant not to engage in the lines of business mentioned was invalid because that covenant undertook to make the restraint operative throughout the state of Texas, though the business of the Ice Company and its good will were confined to the city of Dallas and some nearby territory * * * Provisions of the decree appealed from in effect prohibited the doing anywhere in the state of Texas what was in conflict with the terms of the above-mentioned agreement as to not engaging in any line of business in which the Ice Company was engaged.

The business of the Ice Company was predominantly local, most of its product having been sold in the city of Dallas and its vicinity. Occasionally it sold ice in other parts of Texas. It is apparent that a main purpose of this suit was to prevent the appellant from violating his agreement by engaging in the ice business in the city of Dallas. A seller of a business and its good will may validly bind himself for a reasonable time not to engage in the same business where by so doing the value of the sold business would be interfered with. When such an agreement extends the area of the restraint beyond the territory within which the engaging in the same business by a seller would be likely to affect the value of the sold business, it is unenforceable to the extent that the restraint is greater than is required to preserve to the purchaser what the latter acquired by his purchase. But we are of opinion that the restraint imposed by the provision in question was enforceable to the extent it was reasonable. For the protection of the appellant from subjecting himself to a restraint which is unreasonable, it is not necessary that he be enabled to escape compliance with his agreement in so far as the restraint of trade provided for is reasonable. The appellee would be deprived of part of the benefit of its purchase if the appellant is permitted to compete with it by engaging in an ice business in the city of Dallas. The appellant could bind himself to refrain from competition in the city of Dallas with the purchaser or his assign. Though the agreement as to not engaging in any line of business in which the Ice Company was engaged was not effective throughout the territory mentioned in the agreement, we think it was valid and effective to bar the appellant from engaging in such business in the city of Dallas, the principal place of business of the Ice Company, and the scene of the alleged and admitted violation of his agreement by the appellant. * * *

We think that in territorial scope the injunction granted went beyond what was required to protect appellee from the wrong complained of. The decree is modified by making the prohibitions of the injunction granted applicable to the city of Dallas, instead of to the entire state of Texas. This modification is to be without prejudice to the right of the appellee to seek relief for a breach of the agreement by the appellant other than the one complained of by the bill in this case. As so modified, the decree is affirmed.

---

16. Promise Not to Compete in Employment
(Blue pencil rule)

BARB–LEE MOBILE FRAME CO. v. HOOT

416 Pa. 222, 206 A.2d 59 (1965).

MUSMANNO, Justice. On September 1, 1959, Charles T. Hoot and Meyer Cohen, president of the Barb-Lee Mobile Frame Co., entered into a contract whereby Hoot agreed to work for Barb-Lee on a percentage basis, with the proviso that if he discontinued his employment he would not, for five years, compete with Barb-Lee in Pennsylvania, Delaware and New Jersey. Barb-Lee is engaged in the business of straightening and realigning damaged automobile frames by means of a portable machine which is taken to the very site of the disabled car, and, by the application of heat and pressure, realigns the damaged frame to its original dimensions and shape.

On December 21, 1961, Hoot voluntarily ceased his employment with Barb-Lee and at once proceeded to do the very thing he had said he would not do, namely, compete with his previous employer.

He solicited Barb-Lee's customers, he took business which would ordinarily go to Barb-Lee, and even sought to cloak his activities with the name of his erstwhile employer.

Barb-Lee sought and obtained in the Court of Common Pleas of Philadelphia County, an injunction restraining Hoot from violating his contract. He now appeals to this Court seeking reversal.

In its decree the lower Court narrowed the area in which the covenant was operable. It held that Barb-Lee could restrict Hoot from operating in Pennsylvania but not in Delaware and New Jersey. The appellant Hoot argues that the Court had no right to modify the contract and that since the agreement specifically covered the area of the three States, it had to stand or fall in all those three States.

The preamble of the contract stated:

> "Whereas, Company has an exclusive franchise for the operation of said frame machine within the areas of New Jersey, Pennsylvania and Delaware * * * "

The fact that there was no evidence that Barb-Lee enjoyed such an extensive franchise did not deprive it of protection in the area the Court believed to be reasonable and sustainable. The man who wildly claims that he owns all the cherry trees in the country cannot be denied protection of the orchard in his back yard. A restrictive covenant, when it comes under the scrutiny of a court of equity, will be held to reasonable geographical and chronological boundaries, according to the realities of the situation.

The record shows that Hoot performed his work inefficiently, unreliably and unsatisfactorily. In the early part of 1961 he abandoned his job and returned to his home in Texas. The president of the plaintiff company communicated with him by telephone and sent him airline transportation to come back to Philadelphia. Hoot came back to Philadelphia to realign bent automobile frames but without straightening out his bad work habits. On December 21, 1961, he left the job again, but this time, instead of returning to Texas, he went into business in the plaintiff's immediate domain, adopted the very name of his former employer and used the repair procedure in which he had been tutored while with Barb-Lee.

The unique virtue of equity is that it sometimes straightens out morally damaged frames as well as rehabilitates legally wrecked principles. The Court below properly said:

> "That Barb-Lee earned and deserved protection is record-plain. The relationship between Barb-Lee and Mr. Hoot yields readily to this conclusion. And it is the law, for it has been held 'that employment contracts containing general covenants by an employe not to compete after the termination of his employment are prima facie enforceable if they are reasonably limited as to duration of time and geographical extent.' * * *

The Chancellor, in applying equitable principles, helped the defendant by restricting the effect of the covenant to Pennsylvania. Authority supports him in this fair modification of the agreement. In Smith's Appeal, 113 Pa. 579, 6 A. 251, the covenant there in question restricted the manufacture of ochre "in the County of Lehigh or elsewhere." This Court "crossed out" the words "or elsewhere" as unreasonable and enforced the covenant as to Lehigh County, stating: "Where a county, or city or borough is named as a limit, and an unreasonable extent of territory in addition is also named, the covenant is divisible, and may be valid as to the particular place which is a reasonable limit."

* * *

Decree affirmed.

---

17. Promise not to Compete in Employment (Modern rule)

RICHMOND BROTHERS, INC. v. WESTINGHOUSE BROADCASTING COMPANY

357 Mass. 106, 256 N.E.2d 304 (1970).

SPIEGEL, Justice. This is a suit in equity seeking, inter alia, to enjoin the defendant Westinghouse Broadcasting Co., Inc. (Westinghouse) from employing the defendant Gerald Jacoby (Jacoby), also known as Jerry Williams, to "announce and broadcast over or through its Boston facilities," until October 14, 1970, and also to enjoin Jacoby from so "broadcasting and announcing." * * *

The plaintiff, operator of radio station WMEX, hired Jacoby as a radio announcer in 1957, at a starting salary of $125 a week. When Jacoby left the employ of the plaintiff on August 28, 1965, "he was earning over $40,000 per year, of which $15,000 was salary, and $25,000 were commissions on the net billings of advertisers on his show." During most of this employment period, Jacoby was employed under written contracts. "At some time during the period of his employment with the plaintiff, Jacoby became" the moderator of a "talk show," which "[a]t the time Jacoby left the plaintiff's employment * * * was on the air six days a week from 10 P.M. to 1 A.M." At the time Jacoby "left the plaintiff's employ, WMEX had one other talk show announcer, and has continued to have two ever since." There was no evidence to indicate that the talk show format was originated by either the plaintiff or Jacoby. In 1965, there were several "such shows on different Boston radio stations; * * * there are presently several such * * * shows on Boston radio and TV stations."

Jacoby's show "was popular with the listening audiences and, as indicated by * * * [his] salary and commissions," the show "was successful and profitable not only to him but to the plaintiff as well.

The popularity and profitability of Jacoby's show were due to his abilities in this particular field which he * * * developed over the years." No evidence was presented to indicate "that Jacoby's success resulted from his use of any confidential information, trade secrets, or special training furnished him by the plaintiff."

While employed by the plaintiff, Jacoby was not involved in the solicitation of advertising sponsors, and virtually his only contact with the sponsors was with regard to the advertising copy to be used during his shows.

On October 15, 1964, Jacoby and the plaintiff signed a three year contract of employment, under which Jacoby was "to be paid $300.00 per week, 15% of the net cash receipts of all advertising broadcasts by him on his show, and $50.00 per week for expenses." The contract contained a restrictive covenant which provided that "for a period of at least three years after Jacoby ceased to be employed by the plaintiff, * * * [he] would not engage in the radio, television, or advertising business anywhere in New England without the plaintiff's written permission."

In early 1965, Jacoby informed the plaintiff of his desire to terminate his contract because of an opportunity to work "for Station WBBM, Chicago, where he would * * * appear not only on radio but also on TV." On June 19, 1965, the parties, after negotiations, entered into a new contract, which terminated Jacoby's employment on August 28, 1965. Under this contract Jacoby, in addition to performing his duties was required "to introduce a new radio announcer to conduct the talk show and to train such replacement in the job." The contract also contained a covenant "that Jacoby was not to engage in any employment in radio, television, or advertising, in New England until October, 1970." On August 28, 1965, Jacoby completed his employment with the plaintiff and on August 29, 1965, "began broadcasting over Station WBBM, in Chicago. There was no evidence that after Jacoby's departure from the plaintiff's Station WMEX the plaintiff lost any advertising sponsors while its talk show was conducted by Jacoby's successor."

At the time Jacoby terminated his employment, the plaintiff owed him commissions for advertising broadcasts for June, July and up to August 6, 1965. The operating head of the plaintiff admitted "that Jacoby is owed $3,442.10 in commissions," plus an additional sum of $572.94.

On May 6, 1968, Jacoby's services with Station WBBM, Chicago, "were terminated because that station shifted to an "all news" format. Starting some weeks earlier when he knew of his impending release, * * * [Jacoby] had been in touch with representatives of * * * [Westinghouse]." Jacoby subsequently "had direct discussions concerning employment at * * * [Westinghouse's] WBZ Boston stations as a 'talk show' moderator." On July 29, 1968,

Jacoby began broadcasting for WBZ's television and radio stations. "Jacoby has not contacted any WBZ advertisers, whether or not WMEX advertisers, since his employment began, except one customer to whom he spoke regarding copy requirements." Furthermore, no evidence has been presented to indicate that the plaintiff "has sustained the loss of any advertising customers since Jacoby began his work at WBZ."

Although only one other WMEX employee was in a comparable position to Jacoby in respect to salary, length of employment and advertising commissions, the restrictive covenant in his contract "was of eighteen months' duration." In January, 1968, a contract between the American Federation of Television & Radio Artists and the plaintiff provided "that negative covenants shall not exceed sixty days in length."

* * *

The plaintiff * * * contends that the "restrictive covenant was reasonable as to time." In determining whether a restriction as to time is reasonable, we must consider the nature of the plaintiff's business and the character of the employment involved, as well as the situation of the parties, the necessity of the restriction for the protection of the employer's business and the right of the employee to work and earn a livelihood. * * * The reasonableness of the duration of a restrictive covenant "depends on the facts in each case." * * * While we recognize the unusual nature of the radio broadcasting industry, its relationship with the listening public and the unique nature of its performers, we are unable to perceive any business interest of the plaintiff which merits the length of "protection" it would receive by the enforcement of the covenant. Jacoby was not involved in the solicitation of advertisers while an employee of the plaintiff. Hence, he was not in a position whereby his competition with the plaintiff would result in any exploitation of previous contacts and thereby injure the plaintiff's established business. Moreover, there was no evidence introduced which would indicate that the plaintiff had, in fact, lost any advertisers since Jacoby returned to the Greater Boston area. * * * Furthermore, the nature of the broadcasting industry is such that Jacoby was not in possession of any of the plaintiff's trade secrets or confidential information communicated to him during the course of his employment.

The plaintiff also claims that "Jacoby's immediate success upon his return to the Greater Boston area is a direct product of the plaintiff's expenditures and promotion." It further contends that "Jacoby was a unique product of plaintiff's business established over many years." Even though a broadcasting company may have expended large sums to promote a performer's popularity with the listening public, it would indeed be difficult to determine that such expenditures and promotion have resulted in the performer's popularity. The performer's popularity may well be attributed to his own personality and ability. Even if we assume that the plaintiff's promotion of Jacoby resulted in his popularity, we believe that Jacoby's absence for almost three years from the Boston broadcasting area sufficiently protected any business interests of the plaintiff. During this period the plaintiff continued to conduct a "talk show" during the time slot previously occupied by Jacoby. Thus, during the period when the plaintiff was most vulnerable to competition from Jacoby, there was no such competition.

"[A]n employer cannot by contract prevent his employee from using the skill and intelligence acquired or increased and improved through experience or through instruction received in the course of the employment. The employee may achieve superiority in his particular department by every lawful means at hand, and then, upon the rightful termination of his contract for service, use that superiority for the benefit of rivals in trade of his former employer." * * * We are of opinion that the restrictive covenant in the 1965 contract is no longer reasonably necessary for the protection of the plaintiff's business. Enforcement of the covenant beyond the years of Jacoby's absence from Boston would merely be protecting the plaintiff against ordinary competition. It is not entitled to such protection.

[Judgment for defendant.]

---

18. Usury

C. I. T. CORP. v. EDWARDS

418 P.2d 685 (Okl., 1966).

HODGES, Justice. The action was instituted by the plaintiff, the C. I. T. Corporation, to recover the balance due on a conditional sales contract to which the defendant, Paul C. Edwards, filed a counterclaim based on usury. The trial court rendered judgment for both parties on their claims and the plaintiff appeals. * * *

The petition of the plaintiff alleged that on June 8, 1960, the defendant entered into a conditional sales contract with the A.B.C. Building Company of Tulsa, Oklahoma by which he purchased a 1959 Aero Commander airplane, that the conditional sales contract was thereafter assigned to the plaintiff, and that in January, 1962, the defendant became delinquent in making the payments as provided in the contract. Next the petition alleges that the plaintiff repossessed the aircraft and that there was then due and owing a balance of $55,180.40 in addition to interest and attorney fees. It is further alleged that the aircraft was sold at a public sale for $28,000.00, and that after deducting the costs of repossessing the aircraft, attorney fees, and certain other expenses, the defendant was credited with the sum of $16,110.70 on the contract. The petition prays for a deficiency judgment against the defendant in the amount of $39,069.70 with interest thereon at the rate of 10% per annum. * * *

The answer and counterclaim of the defendant denied the allegations of the petition and alleged that the purported conditional sales contract was a "sham and a scheme to cloak and evade a loan of money at usurious interest", that interest at a rate greater than 10% per annum was charged, and that, under the laws of the State of Oklahoma, the defendant is entitled to recover double the amount of the entire interest charged. The defendant admitted the execution of the conditional sales contract. * * * The court entered judgment in favor of the plaintiff for the sum of $39,069.70. The court further found that a greater interest rate than 10% was charged on the transaction, constituting usury, and entered an offset of twice the amount of such interest or $25,404.78 in favor of the defendant, reducing the amount of the plaintiff's judgment to $13,664.92.

* * * The plaintiff first asserts that the transaction involved in this case constituted a sale of merchandise to which usury does not attach. It has previously been determined that the usury laws of this state do not apply to sales but only to loans of money.

* * * The defendant stated that he informed the plaintiff in their discussions that he "wanted to borrow $50,000.00 on the Aero Commander" in order to (1) pay the existing mortgage on an Apache airplane that was to be used as a trade-in on the Aero Commander, (2) pay the A.B.C. Building Company the agreed cash difference between the two airplanes, and (3) provide $4,300.00 for use in his business. * * * We believe that the evidence amply supports the finding of the trial court that the transaction involved in this dispute constituted a loan of money and not a sale as contended by the plaintiff. * * *

Under the statutes of this state, interest in excess of ten per cent on a loan of money is usurious and results in the forfeiture of twice the amount of the entire interest charged. * * * The evidence establishes, and the plaintiff concedes on this appeal, that the interest charged by the plaintiff exceeds ten per cent in violation of our statutes. The judgment of the trial court is affirmed.

---

19. Referral Sale Contract Unconscionable

FROSTIFRESH CORPORATION v. REYNOSO

52 Misc.2d 26, 274 N.Y.S.2d 757 (1966).

FRANCIS J. DONOVAN, Judge.

DECISION AFTER TRIAL

Plaintiff brings this action for $1364.10, alleging that the latter amount is owed by the defendants to the plaintiff on account of the purchase of a combination-refrigerator-freezer for which they agreed to pay the sum of $1145.88. The balance of the amount consists of a claim for attorney fees in the amount of $227.35 and a late charge of $22.87. The only payment made on account of the original indebtedness is the sum of $32.00.

The contract for the refrigerator-freezer was negotiated orally in Spanish between the defendants and a Spanish speaking salesman representing the plaintiff. In that conversation the defendant husband told the salesman that he had but one week left on his job and he could not afford to buy the appliance. The salesman distracted and deluded the defendants by advising them that the appliance would cost them nothing because they would be paid bonuses or commissions of $25.00 each on the numerous sales that would be made to their neighbors and friends. Thereafter there was submitted to and signed by the defendants a retail installment contract entirely in English. The retail contract was neither translated nor explained to the defendants. In that contract there was a cash sales price set forth of $900.00. To this was added a credit charge of $245.88, making a total of $1145.88 to be paid for the appliance.

The plaintiff admitted that cost to the plaintiff corporation for the appliance was $348.00.

No defense of fraud was set forth in the pleadings and accordingly such defense is not available.

However, in the course of the trial, it did appear to the court that the contract might be unconscionable. The court therefore continued the trial at an adjourned date to afford a reasonable opportunity to the parties to present evidence as to the commercial setting, purpose and effect of the contract.

The court finds that the sale of the appliance at the price and terms indicated in this contract is shocking to the conscience. The service charge, which almost equals the price of the appliance is in and of itself indicative of the oppression which was practiced on these defendants. Defendants were handicapped by a lack of knowledge, both as to the commercial situation and the nature and terms of the contract which was submitted in a language foreign to them.

The question presented in this case is simply this: Does the court have the power under section 2–302 of the Uniform Commercial Code to refuse to enforce the price and credit provisions of the contract in order to prevent an unconscionable result.

It is normally stated that the parties are free to make whatever contracts they please so long as there is no fraud or illegality * * *

However, it is the apparent intent of the Uniform Commercial Code to modify this general rule by giving the courts power "to police explicitly against the contracts or clauses which they find to be unconscionable. * * * The principle is one of the prevention of oppression and unfair surprise." * * *

In the instant case the court finds that it was "too hard a bargain" and the conscience of the court will not permit the enforcement of the contract as written. Therefore the plaintiff will not be permitted to recover on the basis of the price set forth in the retail installment contract, namely $900.00 plus $245.85 as a service charge.

However, since the defendants have not returned the refrigerator-freezer, they will be required to reimburse the plaintiff for the cost to the plaintiff, namely $348.00. No allowance is made on account of any commissions the plaintiff may have paid to salesmen or for legal fees, service charges or any other matters of overhead.

Accordingly the plaintiff may have judgment against both defendants in the amount of $348.00 with interest, less the $32.00 paid on account, leaving a net balance of $316.00 with interest from December 26, 1964.

PROBLEMS

1. The Encino Woman's Club desires to raise scholarship money for indigent college students. The Club plans on having a party at which it will sell tickets for $100 each on a new automobile. The holder of the winning ticket will receive the automobile. The tickets will have the word DONATION at the top. What is your advice as to the legality of this transaction?

2. Las Vegas Hacienda, Inc. made a public offer to pay $5,000 to any person who, having paid 50¢ for the opportunity of attempting to do so, shot a hole in one on its golf course pursuant to certain conditions. Mr. Gibson complied with the conditions, including the payment of the money, and shot a hole in one. Hacienda refuses to pay contending the contract was a wagering contract. Gibson claims the shooting of the hole in one was a feat of skill and not a feat of chance. Decision?

3. Seller sold buyer a quantity of candy and silverware. The candy had been put up in prize packages, some of which contained tickets. The buyer was to resell the packages at a price greater than their real value each purchaser taking a chance that he would get a ticket which would entitle him to a piece of silverware. The buyer refuses to pay for the candy and the silverware contending that the contract was illegal and unenforceable. A statute provided that every lottery, game, or device of chance in the nature of a lottery, by whatsoever name it may be called, other than such as have been authorized by law, shall be deemed unlawful. Decision?

4. Defendant wished to delay action by the Board of Supervisors for the purchase of certain real estate in which defendant was interested. He made a contract with plaintiff to pay him $50,000.00 if plaintiff could get the Supervisors to postpone action. The plaintiff gave a majority of the Supervisors and their wives a party at Las Vegas at which time the plaintiff gave each of the wives a cloth coat and convinced the wives to speak to their husbands regarding a postponement of the purchase of the real estate. Subsequently, the Supervisors postponed the purchase. Defendant refuses to pay the $50,000.00. Decision?

5. Richie and Cody were the opposing nominees for the office of jailer of Knott County, Kentucky. Shortly before the election, Cody se-

cretly agreed to withdraw his candidacy if Richie would agree to appoint him his deputy and divide the fees of the office. Richie agreed; and to guarantee his performance of the contract, he deposited the sum of $500.00 with a third party with the understanding that this money was to be repaid when he had fully performed his agreement. Richie was elected and has fully complied with his obligations to Cody; and he now seeks to recover the $500.00 from the third party. The third party refuses to give Richie the $500.00. Decision?

6. The XYZ insurance company contracted to insure a surgeon against personal liability for his negligence in connection with his surgical work. During an operation, the surgeon carelessly injured a patient. The surgeon now sues the insurance company to compel it to protect him from loss as a result of such injury. The company's defense is that the surgeon's contract for protection against responsibility for his own negligence is illegal and void. Decision?

7. Lally sold his barber shop to Mattis "together with all good will." The contract contained a clause which provided that Lally would not engage in the barbering business for a period of two years in the city of Rockville where the barber shop was located. Nine months after the sale Lally set up a one-chair barbershop in his own home which was approximately 300 yards from the shop he sold to Mattis. Mattis seeks an injunction. Decision?

8. Blackman, a real estate salesman, signed an employment contract with Abramson, a real estate broker, which provided that "The salesman shall not after the termination of this contract, use to his advantage any information gained verbally or from the files of the broker." Blackman wants to leave Abramson and seeks your advice as to whether he can work for a different broker in the same area.

9. On Monday a salesman called on an elderly widow at her home and after identifying himself, the company he worked for, and the product he sold, made a contract to sell her an expensive vacuum cleaner with a lifetime guarantee. The contract provided that she pay 10% down and the balance within one year. Delivery of the vacuum cleaner was subject to the widow's credit being approved by the home office of the seller. On Tuesday the widow calls you for advice as she wants to cancel the contract.

Chapter 13

INTERPRETATION OF CONTRACTS

A. IN GENERAL

A contract should contain all of the important terms, and they should be clearly stated since ambiguous terms can result in different interpretation by the parties; and this, in turn, can result in unnecessary litigation. If the differences of the parties cannot be resolved and the case is litigated, the court applies certain principles of construction and interpretation to the contract.

1. INTENTION OF THE PARTIES

The purpose of the interpretation of a contract is to determine and give effect to the mutual intention of the parties. The modern approach is to look for the *expressed* intent, i. e., the words used, under an objective standard. The secret or undisclosed intention of a party have no effect. In other words, we are only interested in what the parties said and not their undisclosed thoughts.

An interpretation which gives a reasonable, lawful, and effective meaning to manifestations of the intent of the parties is preferred to an interpretation which makes such manifestations unreasonable, unlawful, or of no effect.

2. INTERPRETATION AS A WHOLE

A contract must be read and interpreted as a whole or in its entirety so as to give effect to every part. The intention of the parties is to be gathered from the entire instrument and not from detached or isolated words or parts.

If there are several writings between the parties regarding one transaction, they are all to be construed as one writing.

However, terms in a printed letterhead or billhead or on the reverse side of a printed contract form are not part of the contract unless a reasonable person would regard such terms as part of the contract.

3. WRITTEN AND PRINTED TERMS

When a contract is partly written and partly printed and the written part conflicts with the printed part, the written part prevails.

When there is a conflict between an amount expressed both in words and figures, the amount expressed in words prevails; e.g., One Hundred and Twenty Dollars ($1.20), the One Hundred and Twenty Dollars would prevail.

4. USAGE AND CUSTOM

Usage and custom may be used to explain the meaning of language in a contract and to imply terms when no contrary intention appears from the terms of the contract; e.g., in agency agreement to sell automobiles, custom of taking used cars as "trade-ins" established such authority of agent; in a sale of real estate, custom may properly determine details regarding opening of escrow, furnishing of deeds and title insurance and prorating of taxes.

To use a custom to interpret a contract, the parties must assent to it, or one party must know or have reason to know that the other party intends custom to govern the contract, or it must be so well known that a reasonable person would be aware of it.

5. SUBSEQUENT CONDUCT OF PARTIES

Acts of the parties that take place after the execution of the contract but before any controversy arises may be looked to in determining the meaning of the contract. The parties themselves are most likely to be correct as to their real intent.

6. PARTY CAUSING UNCERTAINTY

The language of a contract should be interpreted most strongly against the party who caused the uncertainty to exist; i.e., the person who prepared the contract. The rule is particularly applicable in the case of a contract prepared by an expert or experienced party, and especially where the party using the ambiguous language seeks to defeat the contract because of such language. The rule is also particularly applicable where the contract is on a printed form prepared by one of the parties. However, this rule of interpretation is to be used only after all other rules of interpretation have been used; and no satisfactory result has been obtained.

7. INSURANCE CONTRACTS

Insurance contracts are interpreted against the insurance company because the company prepared the contract and because the policy of the law favors coverage for losses to which the policy of insurance relates. It has been said that courts construe against insurance companies because people do not read their policies and would not understand them if they did. Whether the coverage relates to the peril insured against, the amount of liability, or the person or persons protected, the language will be interpreted in its most inclusive sense for the benefit of the insured.

Exception clauses are construed strictly. In other words, if the insurance company does not want to cover a particular loss related to the policy, the company must clearly exclude this loss or the insured will be covered. In addition, an exception clause may be held void as against public policy; e. g., automobile insurance policy excluded minor son from coverage; son, driving parent's automobile with their permission was negligent in accident, however, policy covered loss (Abbott v. Interinsurance Exchange of the Auto. Club of Southern California, 260 Cal.App.2d 528, 67 Cal.Rptr. 220; Cf. Associated Indemnity Corp. v. King, 33 Cal.App.3d 470, 109 Cal.Rptr. 190, 1973, which held exclusion valid).

SPOKEN

* B. THE PAROL EVIDENCE RULE

1. IN GENERAL

Prior to the signing of a written contract, the parties generally negotiate the various terms orally. After the oral discussion, the contract is reduced to writing and signed by the parties. All negotiations and oral understandings are merged into the written contract. It is logical that the signed written contract correctly contains the oral terms agreed upon by the parties; therefore, it does not seem reasonable for one party to claim that the parties agreed to something other than that which is stated in the written contract.

The *parol evidence rule* states that oral testimony is not admissible to vary the terms of a written contract when the oral testimony relates to oral statements made prior to the signing of the contract or at the same time as the signing of the contract.

The parol evidence rule should stand out as a *warning* to parties to a contract, especially to buyers. *Never* sign a contract unless you are certain that it contains *all* of the terms agreed upon. You may find that the salesman's oral promise will be denied when it comes time to enforce it; e.g., a warranty that he makes; and even if you can prove the promise in court, the cost of litigation might well be more than the promise involved.

There are exceptions to the parol evidence rule.

2. EXCEPTIONS TO THE PAROL EVIDENCE RULE

A. AMBIGUITY

If there is any ambiguity in any of the words of a written contract, oral testimony is admissible to explain the ambiguity; e.g., seller agreed to sell buyer a reaper which seller warranted in writing to be capable of cutting and raking from twelve to twenty acres of grain a day with one good man and a "team" of horses. Seller orally told buyer prior to the written contract that he meant a "team" *like those the buyer owned.* However, the buyer's "team" could not make the machine do the work satisfactorily. Seller claims if *any* sort of "team" can pull the machine, the buyer is bound by the contract. The buyer will be permitted to testify as to the seller's statement; i. e., that the *buyer's* "team" could pull the machine.

B. Mistake, Fraud, Duress, Undue Influence, Illegality or Lack of Capacity

If a mistake is made in reducing the contract to writing, oral testimony is admissible regarding the mistake; e.g., the typist uses the wrong figures in the written contract, and the parties do not notice the error when they sign it.

Fraud, duress, undue influence, and illegality can always be testified to in the making of a contract. Similarly, if one of the parties to the contract was a minor or insane, such testimony is admissible.

C. Incomplete Contract

If the written contract is not complete on its face, e.g., important terms are obviously missing; oral testimony is admissible to supply the missing terms.

D. Condition Precedent

If the parties orally agree that the written contract is not to be enforceable unless a certain event occurs, this condition precedent to the validity of the contract can be testified to since the party is not trying to vary or change the written contract but is attempting to prove that there is no contract since the condition precedent to its validity did not take place.

E. Later Oral Changes

The rule only applies to oral clauses made prior to or contemporaneous with the written contract and not to *later* oral changes or additions; however, although the parol evidence rule would not apply, certain other rules might prevent the later oral change or addition from being effective, e.g., statute of frauds.

F. Consideration

Frequently certain types of instruments, such as deeds, leases, notes, and bonds, will contain a statement that the consideration has been received when in fact it has not; or the instrument will contain a nominal recital of consideration whereas it is greater. Generally in these cases the courts will permit parol evidence to show that the consideration was not paid, or that it is greater than stated. This is because the document was not intended to be an integration of the agreement supplanting prior negotiations. Under this rule it would be proper to permit testimony to show that in addition to the consideration stated in the deed, there was an additional oral promise to convey certain land by a will.

However, if the terms are fully and correctly embodied in the contract, then generally parol evidence is not admissible. Under this rule if the contract sets out the purchase price, payable pursuant to certain terms, oral testimony is inadmissible to vary the contract.

G. The Uniform Commercial Code

In addition to the rules stated above the U.C.C. contains provisions relating to the interpretation of contracts for the sale of goods. *The U.C.C., Sections 1–205, 2–202, and 2–208,* provide that in a sale of goods a written contract may be explained or supplemented in four ways: (1) by a prior course of dealing between the buyer and the seller, or (2) by usage of trade, or (3) by the course of performance between the parties, or (4) by evidence of consistent additional terms used by the parties. Although a single occasion of conduct does not fall within the language of Section 2–208 relating to course of performance, other sections such as those on silence after acceptance and failure to specify particular defects can affect the parties' rights on a single occasion (see 2–605 and 2–607).

---

1. Can Presume to Contract in Reference to Custom

WALLS ET AL. v. BAILEY

49 N.Y. 464 (1872).

The plaintiffs contracted to plaster defendant's house at a specified price per square yard. In this action to recover the price, plaintiffs contend that no deduction is to be made for the area of the doors and windows. The rest of the facts appear in the opinion of the court.

FOLGER, J. The contract between the parties was in writing. By it the plaintiffs were to furnish the material for the plastering work of the defendant's house, and to do the work of laying it on. The defendant was to pay them for the work and material a price per square yard. Of course, the total of the compensation was to be got at by measurement. But when the parties came to determine how many square yards there were, they differed. The query was, the square yards of what? Of the plaster actually laid on, or of the whole side of the house, calling it solid, with no allowance for the openings by windows and doors? And it is not to be said of this contract, that it was so plain in its terms as that there could be but one conclusion as to the mode of measurement, by which the number of square yards of work should be arrived at. * * *

The meaning of words may be controlled and varied by usage; even when they are words of number, length or space, usually the most definite in language. Every legal contract is to be interpreted in accordance with the intention of the parties making it. And usage * * * when it is reasonable, uniform, well settled, not in opposition to fixed rules of law, not in contradiction of the express terms of the contract, is deemed to form a part of the contract, and to enter into the intention of the parties. * * * All men, being bound to know the law, are presumed beyond dispute, to contract in reference to it. And so they are presumed to contract in reference to the usage of the particular place or trade in or as to which they enter into agreement * * * when it is so far established and so far known to the parties that it must be supposed that their contract was made in reference to it. * * *

The jury, in the case before us, have found the existence of the usage contended for by the plaintiffs, and upon evidence which will sustain the finding. The same evidence shows that the usage was uniform, continuous and well settled. * * * The usage is not designed to obtain payment for material never furnished. It is a method devised for more conveniently and readily ascertaining the quantum of compensation for what work has been done in fact, and what material has been in fact furnished. It is agreeable with common sense that it is more difficult, asking more skill and care, requiring more time, to plaster about the frames of doors and windows, and along the edges of base boards and cornices, than over the plain uninterrupted surface of wall or ceiling. The more, then, of such openings or obstacles, the more, in proportion to the space of plaster actually laid on, should be the compensation.

[Judgment for plaintiff.]

---

2. *Interpretation by Subsequent Conduct of Parties*

CRESTVIEW CEMETERY ASS'N v. DIEDEN

54 Cal.2d 744, 8 Cal.Rptr. 427, 356 P.2d 171 (1960).

PETERS, Justice. [Action to recover legal fee paid.] The sole question presented on this appeal is whether the trial court correctly interpreted the contract admittedly existing between the parties.

The record shows that, in 1956, Crestview owned some real property in an unincorporated area of Alameda County near the city of Hayward that it desired to develop as a cemetery. This was difficult under the existing county zoning laws, which Crestview and McKeever, [counsel for Crestview] found to be confusing.

In April of 1956 Leonard Dieden was recommended to McKeever * * * as an attorney who might be able to secure the desired result. * * * As a result of several later telephone conversations the figure of $7,500 was agreed upon as the contingent fee. It was agreed that Dieden should have three months to try and secure the desired result. * * *

After the parties agreed upon the contingent fee on May 14, 1956, Dieden started to work. He prepared a letter to the Hayward Planning Commission, which was executed by McKeever, requesting a rezoning of the property. Dieden then prepared and filed an application for rezoning and actively argued in favor of the application at several hearings at which vigorous opposition to his position developed. * * * After the ordinance had passed by a vote of four to three a recess was called. At that time a woman who had opposed the rezoning ordinance told McKeever and Dieden that her group intended to continue to attack the ordinance by referendum. * * * McKeever congratulated Dieden on having completed his job so successfully and Dieden said "There's your permit. Send me a check." This McKeever promised to do. Three days later, on July 27, 1956, and after McKeever knew that the referendum was pending, he sent Dieden a check for $5,000. In determining what the parties agreed upon and intended by their agreement of May 14, 1956, we are not to determine what the words used by the parties may mean to us but if possible to ascertain what those words meant to the parties. Moreover, in interpreting those words we must keep in mind that McKeever and Dieden were not novices or inexperienced. Both are practicing attorneys.

* * * While there is substantial evidence that McKeever wanted to be assured the land would be available for cemetery purposes, the evidence is capable of being interpreted as meaning that Dieden was to secure the passage of a rezoning ordinance. While this may not be the interpretation that we might place upon the terms of the contract, it is the interpretation placed upon it by the parties before any controversy arose between them. This contract is not to be interpreted in a vacuum. These two lawyers knew what they meant and intended. By their actions, and by their performance under the contract, their intent was disclosed with crystal clarity. * *

In the first place McKeever insisted that Dieden must perform within a period of three months. That period of time may be a reasonable one for securing an amendment to an ordinance but is not reasonable if it was intended that Dieden, after passage of the ordinance, was to protect it against attacks that might be made on it. * * * Dieden, in the presence of McKeever, argued the matter before the council against strong opposition, and finally, again in the presence of McKeever, secured passage of the controversial ordinance. Then, most significantly, McKeever congratulated Dieden on a job well done. Dieden, in the obvious belief that his job was completed, requested his money. McKeever, even though he knew the opponents were contemplating a referendum, and knew the required number of signatures for a referendum, in the obvious belief that Dieden had completed the job contemplated, promised to pay. Three days later, and after McKeever knew the opponents to the ordinance were working on a referendum, McKeever sent the $5,000 check to Dieden "on account of your legal fee * * * "

The only reasonable interpretation of these actions is that both parties then believed, and acted on the belief, that the work contemplated had been completed and that Dieden had earned his fee.

* * * The trial court found that the contract of May 14, 1956, was fully performed. * * *

Certainly the parties so interpreted the contract. As already pointed out both Dieden and McKeever obviously believed the contract had been fully performed even after they knew that a referendum was to be attempted and was in process. * * *

The judgment is affirmed [for defendant.]

---

3. Exception Clause Strictly Construed

GRAY v. ZURICH INSURANCE CO.

65 Cal.2d 263, 54 Cal.Rptr. 104, 419 P.2d 168 (1966).

TOBRINER, Justice. Plaintiff, Dr. Vernon D. Gray, is the named insured under an insurance policy issued by defendant. * * *

The policy contains a provision that "[T]his endorsement does not apply * * * to bodily injury or property damages caused intentionally by or at the direction of the insured."

The suit which Dr. Gray contends Zurich should have defended arose out of an altercation between him and a Mr. John R. Jones. * * * Dr. Gray notified defendant of the suit, stating that he had acted in self-defense, and requested that the company defend. Defendant refused on the ground that the complaint alleged an intentional tort which fell outside the coverage of the policy. Dr. Gray thereafter unsuccessfully defended on the theory of self-defense; he suffered a judgment of $6,000 actual damages although the jury refused to award punitive damages.

Dr. Gray then filed the instant action charging defendant with breach of its duty to defend.

The * * * court rendered judgment in favor of defendant. * * * In interpreting an insurance policy we apply the general principle that doubts as to meaning must be resolved against the insurer and that any exception to the performance of the basic underlying obligation must be so stated as clearly to apprise the insured of its effect. * * *

These principles of interpretation of insurance contracts have found new and vivid restatement in the doctrine of the adhesion contract. As this court has held, a contract entered into between two parties of unequal bargaining strength, expressed in the language of a standardized contract, written by the more powerful bargainer to meet its own needs, and offered to the weaker party on a "take it or leave it basis" carries some consequences that extend beyond orthodox implications. Obligations arising from such a contract inure not alone from the consensual transaction but from the relationship of the parties.

Although courts have long followed the basic precept that they would look to the words of the contract to find the meaning which the parties expected from them, they have also applied the doctrine of the adhesion contract to insurance policies, holding that in view of the disparate bargaining status of the parties we must ascertain that meaning of the contract which the insured would reasonably expect.

When we test the instant policy by these principles we find that its provisions as to the obligation to defend are uncertain and undefined; in the light of the reasonable expectation of the insured, they require the performance of that duty.

* * * No one can determine whether the third party suit does or does not fall within the indemnification coverage of the policy until that suit is resolved; in the instant case, the determination of whether the insured engaged in intentional, negligent or even wrongful conduct depended upon the judgment in the Jones suit, and, indeed, even after that judgment, no one could be positive whether it rested upon a finding of plaintiff's negligent or his intentional conduct. The carrier's obligation to indemnify inevitably will not be defined until the adjudication of the very action which it should have defended * * * The insured is unhappily surrounded by concentric circles of uncertainty: the first, the unascertainable nature of the insurer's duty to defend; the second, the unknown effect of the provision that the insurer must defend even a groundless, false or fraudulent claim; the third, the uncertain extent of the indemnification coverage. Since we must resolve uncertainties in favor of the insured and interpret the policy provisions according to the layman's reasonable expectations, and since the effect of the exclusionary clause is neither conspicuous, plain nor clear, we hold that in the present case the policy provides for an obligation to defend and that such obligation is independent of the indemnification coverage.

* * * The judgment is reversed and the trial court instructed to take evidence solely on the issue of damages alleged in plaintiff's complaint including the amount of the judgment in the Jones suit, and the costs, expenses and attorney's fees incurred in defending such suit.

---

4. *Parol Evidence is Admissible to Explain Ambiguity*

NOFZIGER v. HOLMAN

61 Cal.2d 526, 39 Cal.Rptr. 384, 393 P.2d 696 (1964).

GIBSON, Chief Justice. [Action for declaratory judgment.] The principal question presented on this appeal is whether the trial court erred in refusing to admit evidence to explain the meaning of a written contract. We have concluded that the evidence should have been admitted and that the judgment must be reversed.

Plaintiffs Nofziger and Rossi employed defendant Holman as foreman to supervise the construction of houses in a certain subdivision. The contract of employment provides in part that Holman shall receive a "minimum and guaranteed" wage equal to the regular carpenter's wage scale in the area for a workweek of 40 hours and, in addition, "one-fourth of the net profit from the sale of each home constructed in said subdivision under the supervision of Employee under the terms of this agreement." Net profit is defined in the agreement as the profit to the owners after deducting a sales commission and the direct and indirect cost of the house and lot. * * *

All 63 homes constructed in the subdivision were built under Holman's supervision, and 43 were sold at a profit and 20 at a loss. After completion of construction a dispute arose as to the method of calculating Holman's share of the profits. * * *

At the trial testimony was offered by plaintiffs to show that the parties intended that Holman was to receive one-fourth of the net profit from the entire venture, including profitable and unprofitable houses, not one-fourth of the profits from the 43 houses sold at a profit without any deduction of the losses suffered on the 20 houses.

* * * The court concluded that the employment agreement was not ambiguous and that under the agreement Holman was entitled to one-fourth of the net profit on the 43 homes sold at a profit without any deduction for the losses suffered on the other 20 homes. * * *

When the language used in an agreement is fairly susceptible of two or more constructions, extrinsic evidence may be considered, not to vary or modify the terms of the agreement but to aid the court in ascertaining the true intent of the parties.

* * * Synonyms for the word "each" are "every" and "all," and the three words when applied to members of a group imply inclusion of the entire membership and admit no exceptions. (Webster's Dictionary of Synonyms (1951 ed.) pp. 280, 39). In discussing the relationship between the words, Webster's Dictionary of Synonyms also states, at page 39, that "all" implies consideration as a unit, that "every" is applied to any of the individuals comprising the group when regarded as the representative of the entire membership, and that "each," unlike "every," implies reference to a member as a distinct person or thing. Thus, "each" may have been used in the contract, as defendants urge and the trial court found, to show that the net profit of the houses was to be determined on an individual basis and that only houses sold at a profit were to be included in the computation. However, the word may also have been used, as plaintiffs urge, to stress that the understanding was that there would be no exceptions and that no home built under Holman's supervision was to be excluded from the computation of net profit. Both of these constructions are consistent with the remaining provisions of the contract. Accordingly, extrinsic evidence was admissible to aid in determining the true intent of the parties, and the court erred. * * * [Case sent back to trial court for retrial.]

---

5. *Parol Evidence is Admissible to Explain Mistake*

REDER v. KUSS

351 Mass. 15, 217 N.E.2d 904 (1966).

SPIEGEL, Justice. This is an appeal from a decree of the Probate Court ordering the defendants, who are the heirs at law of Anna Kuss, to convey to the petitioner all of their right, title and interest in certain real estate which stood in the names of the petitioner and Anna Kuss "as tenants in common."

* * * The petitioner testified through an interpreter that he spoke Polish and "[n]ot much" English. There was evidence that the petitioner was seventy-six years old and in 1914 he had come to the United States from Poland. In 1928 he went with Anna Kuss to a lawyer of "Polish extraction" to "make the agreement" concerning the premises in question and the petitioner spoke to the lawyer in Polish. He told the lawyer that he was buying the property "so that it would be him and her." The property was purchased by a deed dated June 19, 1928, for the sum of $15,200. Sixty-two hundred dollars was paid in cash, of which sum the petitioner paid $4,600 (which he withdrew from his account in a savings bank) and Anna Kuss paid $1,600. "[T]hey both assumed a mortgage for $9,000 to make the $15,200. The petitioner testified that "[t]here was talk and understanding that if he [the petitioner] died she [Anna Kuss] would get the property." After the purchase Anna lived in a tenement on the property with her mother. The petitioner also lived there. He managed the property, and paid for repairs, taxes, insurance and other costs of maintenance out of his own funds. Anna died in December, 1961. John Reder, a nephew of both the petitioner and Anna Kuss, testified that shortly before she died, Anna Kuss told him that she said to the petitioner, "After I am gone, the house is yours," and "You will have both houses when I am gone and you will have the social security to take care of yourself." Various relatives of Anna Kuss offered testimony which was inconsistent with the foregoing. * * *

The judge found that the petitioner "was certain in his own mind that having both names on the deed was all that was sufficient to insure having the property pass to him if Anna Kuss died, and that she believed the same thing." The judge further found that "there was a mutual mistake, made by non-English speaking, uneducated immigrants, who, in many respects, acted like a married couple, and both of them expected to become sole owner of the property if the other died." * * *

The respondents contend that "the lower Court was in error as a matter of law in admitting extrinsic evidence to vary, alter and contradict the terms of a complete and integrated written instrument, thus violating the parol-evidence rule."

* * * Mr. Justice Holmes said, "[I]t is settled, * * * that this particular kind of parol evidence—that is to say, evidence of mutual mistake as to the meaning of the words used—is admissible" to show "that neither party has purported or been understood to express assent to the conveyance as it stands." * * *

Decree affirmed [for plaintiff.]

6. *Parol Evidence is Admissible to Prove Condition Precedent to Validity of Written Contract*

LONG v. JONES

319 S.W.2d 292 (Ky., 1958).

MILLIKEN, Judge. The appellee, Mrs. Jones, recovered a judgment of $800, with interest, covering the down payment made by her on the proposed purchase of a house from the appellant, Dan Long, in Lexington. A written contract covering the terms of the proposed purchase was signed by her and by the vendor through his agent, and the $800 down payment was referred to therein "as evidence of good faith to bind this contract" and it was "to be applied on the purchase price upon passing of deed, or refunded, should title prove not merchantable, or acceptable, or if this offer is not accepted." * * *

As an explanation of her failure to go through with the purchase within the terms of the agreement, Mrs. Jones testified that at the time she signed the printed contract form and made the $800 down payment it was understood between her and the agent of the appellant-seller that she could not complete the proposed purchase within the time allotted unless she sold her home in Flemingsburg, and the trial court accordingly instructed the jury to find for Mrs. Jones if they believed what she said. It was proper for such testimony to be admitted for the consideration of the jury, not for the purpose of varying the terms of a written agreement, but on the issue of whether a contract in fact existed. * * *

> "Evidence is generally held admissible to show that the parties made an agreement before or at the time they entered into a written contract of sale that such contract of sale should become binding only on the happening of a certain condition or contingency, the theory being that such evidence merely goes to show that the writing never became operative as a valid agreement and that there is therefore no variance or contradiction of a valid written instrument." * * *

The motion for an appeal is overruled, and the judgment is affirmed.

PROBLEMS

1. Plaintiff was insured by the X automobile insurance company. The policy had a provision whereby the company would pay all "reasonable medical expenses" incurred by the plaintiff as a result of an automobile accident. The plaintiff was injured in an automobile accident, and his doctor prescribed medicines and an orthopedic (very hard) mattress and spring for the plaintiff's low back injury. The plaintiff submitted all medical bills as requested by the company; however, the company will not pay for the special mattress and spring. What decision?

2. L leased an apartment to T for a period of one year. The lease provided that the rent was due and payable on the first day of each and every month. Immediately prior to the signing of the lease by L and T, T informed L that he was paid every two weeks so he would usually pay his rent several days after the first of the month. L told T that this was alright with him. For several months T paid the rent several days after the first with no objection from L. Now L insists that T pay the rent on the first day of the month. If this case goes to court will T be able to testify as to the oral arrangement with L? No - Change of contract later oral change

3. Seller and buyer enter into a contract for a used automobile. As the contract was being signed, the buyer asked the seller if the automobile had a warranty. The seller stated: "It sure does. If any parts in the motor need replacing during the next 10,000 miles, bring the car in and we will furnish free labor and parts." The contract, however, stated that the automobile was being sold as is; and there were no warranties of any kind in the sale. After 8,000 miles, the automobile developed motor trouble requiring extensive repairs. Seller refuses to acknowledge the warranty. Decision?

Would your answer be different if the buyer made the inquiry during the early part of the negotiations? Fraud - reliance

If he made the inquiry five minutes after he signed the contract?

4. Seller and buyer entered into a written contract for the sale of a truck. The contract provided that the writing contained the whole agreement and that nothing not incorporated therein was to be regarded as part of the agreement between the parties. The seller fraudulently substituted a different motor for the one which he had led the buyer to believe he was buying. The buyer now sues for the fraud, but the seller contends that in view of the provisions in the written contract, oral testimony as to the alleged fraud may not be heard by the court. What should the court decide?

5. A, an architect, made a written contract with B to design a building for which A was to be paid 10% of the cost of the building. There was nothing in the written contract as to the maximum cost of the building. After A finished his work he demanded payment based on the actual cost of the building; however, B claims they had agreed on a maximum cost for the building and that A's fee could not exceed 10% of that maximum cost which was considerably lower than the actual cost. Will the court permit B to testify as to the oral agreement? ambiguous

6. C, a contractor, made a contract with O, the owner, to construct a building. The contract provided that no charges would be made for work in addition to that stated in the contract unless the additional work and the charge for it was put in writing and signed by the parties. From time to time during the construction of the building O requested certain additional work which was performed by C; however, none of this was in writing. When C finished the construction he requested payment for the additional work. O refuses on the ground it was not in writing. Decision?

Change contract

7. Seller gave buyer a deed for a tract of land. The deed stated that the consideration for the land was $5,100.00 and that the sum had been paid. Seller now contends that buyer never paid him for the land. Buyer attempts to testify to the fact that the parties had really agreed that payment was to be made in merchantable bar iron. Seller contends that this testimony should not be admitted because of the parol evidence rule. Decision? yes P. 193

Chapter 14

TERMINATION OF CONTRACTS

Ordinarily a contract is terminated by performance of the terms by the parties; however, termination may also occur by acts of the parties, by impossibility of performance, or by operation of law.

A. BY PERFORMANCE

---

1. PAYMENT

When payment is required by the contract, performance is completed by the payment of the money. Payment by check is a conditional payment and is not a discharge of the debt until it is paid; i.e., credited to the bank account of the creditor. The creditor can refuse payment by check on the ground that it is not legal tender. The *U.C.C., Sections 2–511 and 3–802(1) (b),* takes the same position.

A valid *tender* of payment consists of an unconditional offer by the debtor to the creditor of the exact amount due on the date the debt or claim is due. If the tender is refused, the debt is not discharged; however, the refusal does stop the running of interest, discharges liens, and prevents the awarding of court costs if the debtor is sued, but the debtor must keep the tender open, i. e., must keep the money available for the creditor. Statutes in some states provide that when tender is refused the debtor can deposit the money in a bank in the name of the creditor and thereafter notify the creditor at which time the obligation is extinguished (California C.C. 1500).

On occasion a debtor will owe one creditor more than one debt, and the debtor will send the creditor a partial payment. The question then arises as to which debt the payment should be applied. This may be of importance because one of the debts may be barred by the statute of limitations; and if the creditor applies the payment to that debt, it will be revived. The debtor can specify how the payment should be applied, and the creditor is bound by the debtor's selection; however, if the debtor does not specify, then the creditor may apply the payment to any one or more of the debts in such manner as he chooses.

2. TIME

If the date of performance is stated in the contract, performance should be made on that date; however, a short delay normally does not justify rescission or a suit for damages. The nature of the contract might be such that even a short delay is actionable. For example, in contracts of a mercantile nature (for manufacture and sale of goods) or where there is a sale of property of a speculative or fluctuating value (oil, gas, or mining rights), time is considered to be of the essence, and a short delay is actionable. The contract itself may contain a clause stating that "time is of the essence" in which case delayed performance is treated as a breach of contract unless to do so would be unconscionable.

In contracts for the manufacture of special products, or in building contracts, time is not of the essence; and a reasonable delay is permitted due to the great hardship that might otherwise occur. In the usual real estate contract, time is not regarded as of the essence.

3. SUBSTANTIAL PERFORMANCE

When one party fails to perform his part of the contract, the other party may terminate the contract and sue for breach of contract. In such a case, there has been a failure of consideration. However, to apply the rule strictly could result in a great hardship. For example, if a building contractor constructed a home for a party and complied with the contract except for some minor detail, it would be unfair to permit the party to rescind the contract. In this type of case the party could not rescind the contract because of substantial compliance by the builder; however, the party would be able to obtain a judgment for damages (see chapter 15 for rule of damages).

4. PERFORMANCE TO SATISFACTION OF PROMISEE OR THIRD PARTY

A. Satisfaction of Promisee

If a party contracts to personally satisfy the promisee and the promisee is not satisfied, the courts look to the type of contract to make a decision. If the contract is one in which the personal taste or fancy of the promisee is involved, e.g., painting a portrait of the promisee, the courts generally hold that the promisee has the final word; and there can be no recovery unless he is personally satisfied. However, if the contract involves operative fitness or mechanical utility, e.g., contractor agrees to build a garage to promisee's satisfaction, then the courts usually apply the term "reasonably satisfactory"; and if a reasonable person would be satisfied under the circumstances, the promisor can recover.

B. Satisfaction of Third Party

Suppose a doctor makes a contract with a contractor for the construction of his expensive home; and the doctor, realizing that he knows very little about construction, has his attorney place a clause in the contract which states that the doctor does not have to pay the contractor until the doctor's architect is satisfied with the construction and issues an architect's certificate of approval. Must the certificate be obtained before the contractor has the right of payment?

Most courts hold that the certificate is not necessary if it is unreasonably or fraudulently withheld by the architect.

B. BY ACT OF PARTIES

---

1. BY CONDITION IN CONTRACT

The contract may provide that it shall terminate upon the happening of a certain event; e.g., provision in insurance policy which provides that the insured shall give the insurance company notice of a loss by fire within a stated period and if it is not done, the right to recover on the policy is lost; a seller may sell property agreeing that it may be returned if it does not comply with certain specifications thus giving the buyer title subject to rescission; a builder agrees to perform certain construction if the city council passes a pending ordinance; a provision in the contract that either party can terminate it upon giving a thirty-day written notice.

2. BY MUTUAL RELEASE

The parties to a contract may agree to rescind it and place each other in status quo by returning any property or money that had been delivered or paid. An *oral mutual rescission* is valid except in the case of a sealed instrument or the sale of an interest in land in which case the mutual rescission must be in writing pursuant to the same formalities as required by the Statute of Frauds.

For a discussion of an oral *modification* of a written contract see Chapter 10, Section G.

3. SUBSTITUTION OF NEW AGREEMENT

The parties may agree to replace the original contract with a new one. If they do so, the original contract is terminated by substitution.

4. NOVATION

A novation is a substitution by agreement of a new obligation for an existing one with intent to extinguish the existing one. The substitution may be of a new obligation between the same parties or of new parties, either a new debtor or a new creditor. For example, debtor owes creditor $1,000.00. Third party, debtor and creditor agree that the debtor will be discharged, and the third party will be come the new debtor. No particular form is required for the novation, and it can be oral even though the original contract was written.

5. ACCORD AND SATISFACTION

An *accord* is an agreement for a substituted performance in satisfaction of the original obligation. When the accord is carried out, there is an *accord* and *satisfaction* and the original obligation is discharged. The usual purpose is to settle a claim with a different performance. Thus, debtor owes creditor $1,000.00. The parties agree that debtor shall paint creditor's house in satisfaction of the debt. The agreement is an accord. When the house is painted, there has been an accord and satisfaction; and the debt is discharged.

6. ACCOUNT STATED

An account stated is an agreement between parties who have transacted business with each other as to the amount of the final balance due from one to the other. This is a new and independent executory contract. The items in the original accounts are merged into the account stated. No right of action remains as to the items. For example, A and B have been doing business with each other over a period of time which has created a relationship of debtor and creditor between them. A and B agree that a certain amount is due and B promises to pay that amount. This is called an account stated. The agreement discharges the obligations arising under the prior transactions.

The agreement may be implied, as where a creditor renders a statement to the debtor and he fails to object within a reasonable time, there is then an account stated.

7. MATERIAL ALTERATION OF EXISTING CONTRACT

Generally a material, fraudulent alteration of a written contract by one who asserts a right under it extinguishes his right to recover on the contract. The test of materiality is whether the alteration makes any change in the meaning or legal effect of the contract. The following are exceptions to the general rule: where the alteration is not material; where it is made by a stranger to the instrument; where it is made accidentally or innocently; where made to show the actual agreement of the parties; or where the alteration is ratified by the other party. Where the alteration is intentional but not fraudulent, the effectiveness of the instrument is destroyed; however, the party who made the innocent alteration can generally recover on the original consideration; e.g., A borrowed $10,000 from B and signed a note and mortgage which created a lien on his farm. B innocently made a material alteration of the mortgage document without A's knowledge. Under the general rule B will be able to get a judgment on the note, but will not be able to enforce the mortgage lien against the farm.

Where one party signs an incomplete instrument containing blanks and the other party without authority fills them in, this is a fraudulent alteration which prevents the formation of any contract.

8. PREVENTION OR WAIVER

Where one party prevents the other party from performing, the latter is excused from performance. Also, where one party waives performance by the other, performance is excused; e.g., landlord habitually accepts rental payments many days after payments are due; in such case, before the landlord can insist that the payments be made on due date, he must give a timely notice to the tenant of the reinstatement of the requirement.

9. ANTICIPATORY BREACH

An actual breach does not take place until the time for performance has arrived; however, there may be a total breach by "anticipatory repudiation". A repudiation of a contract prior to the date fixed by the contract for performance is called an anticipatory breach. If a party to a contract informs the other party prior to performance date that he is not going to perform, the aggrieved party has an election of remedies: a. He may *wait* until the time for performance and exercise his remedies for the actual breach; or b. He may treat the repudiation as an anticipatory breach and exercise his remedies *immediately*.

The doctrine does not apply to *unilateral* contracts; e. g., debtor owes creditor $100.00 on a note that is not yet due and informs the creditor that he is not going to pay the note when it becomes due; creditor cannot bring suit until after the note is due.

The doctrine does not ordinarily apply to a *lease* between a landlord and tenant. In the absence of a special provision in the lease, the lessor cannot sue at once to recover damages based on the entire balance due when the tenant defaults.

An anticipatory breach can be retracted if the injured party has not changed his position in the meantime.

The injured party does not waive his remedies by urging performance.

Section 2–610 of the U.C.C. provides that the aggrieved party may suspend performance on his part and maintain an action for breach of contract although he has urged retraction of the repudiation.

Section 2–611 of the U.C.C. provides that if the aggrieved party has not changed his position or cancelled the contract, the repudiation may be retracted. However, although the repudiation may be retracted, the aggrieved party can demand assurance of due performance and until he receives such assurance may suspend any further performance on his part, *Section 2–609, U.C.C.*

C. BY IMPOSSIBILITY

---

1. IN GENERAL

If performance of a contract was physically impossible at the time the contract was made, and this fact was not known to the parties, performance is excused; e. g., T leases a dance hall from L, however, unknown to the parties, the building had been destroyed by fire. This is usually referred to as "objective" impossibility; i.e., impossible in the nature of things rather than because of the inability of the party to perform.

When performance becomes impossible subsequent to the making of the contract there is a conflict of authorities.

Many courts hold that impossibility arising after the contract has been made is no excuse for nonperformance, particularly when the impossibility was foreseeable; e.g., increase in cost of performance. Impossibility of performance because a party is financially unable or because he personally lacks the capability or competence is usually referred to as "subjective" impossibility. However, the modern trend is to excuse performance for supervening impossibility if the party seeking relief is not guilty of contributory fault. Under this rule the court has the problem in each case of allocating the burden of unreasonably excessive risks between the parties; risks which they did not foresee or provide for at the time the contract was made, but which *greatly* increased the burden on one of them at the time of performance. Mere increased difficulties and heightened costs of a reasonable nature, even though originally unforeseen, do not render performance of a contract impossible or impractical even under the modern trend.

2. ACT OF GOD OR NATURE

Many courts hold that an act of God or nature (flood, tornado) does not excuse performance of a contract unless performance is excused in the contract. By statute or case law in many jurisdictions, an act of God or nature which renders a contract impossible of performance is a defense to performance.

3. STRIKES AND OTHER HAZARDS

Unless provided for in the contract, strikes, picketing, riots, business threats, inevitable or unavoidable accidents, breaking of machinery or equipment, or similar hazards, generally do not constitute a defense for failure to perform.

The act of an enemy is generally no defense unless it renders performance impossible, illegal, or destroys the basis or subject matter of the contract, in which case most courts excuse performance.

Regarding strikes and other hazards constituting a defense in a contract for the sale of goods under the U.C.C., see Section 5.b. infra.

4. DESTRUCTION OF SUBJECT MATTER

When a contract requires the transfer of a *specific* thing, the destruction of the thing makes the performance impossible and excuses performance; e.g., a contract to manufacture goods in a particular factory is discharged by the destruction of the factory; a contract to paint a specific building is discharged by the destruction of the building; a contract to carry goods by a particular ship is discharged by the loss of the ship; a sale of the wheat crop growing on a specific parcel of land is discharged if the crop is destroyed.

However, if there is only a contract to sell a *given quantity* of wheat and not a *particular* crop of wheat, the seller is not discharged by the destruction of the wheat. In such a case, the seller makes an absolute undertaking to deliver the wheat which is not limited or restricted in any way to any particular wheat. Thus, if he is unable to deliver the quantity of wheat, he is liable for breach of contract. Moral: sellers, have an escape clause, e.g., destruction of the wheat excuses performance; buyers, keep it out.

5. EXTRAORDINARY DIFFICULTY OR EXPENSE

A. In General

Mere unforeseen difficulty or expense does not constitute impossibility and ordinarily is not a defense; however, the modern trend is to allow the defense of impossibility when performance is impracticable because of excessive and unreasonable expense or extraordinary difficulty which was not reasonably foreseeable (Restatement of Contracts, Section 454).

The doctrine of *commercial frustration* is similar to the doctrine of impossibility or impracticability in that both require extreme hardship in order to excuse performance; however, commercial frustration is different in that it assumes the possibility of literal performance, but excuses performance because a supervening event which was not contemplated by the parties and not reasonably foreseeable essentially *destroyed the purpose* for which the contract was made; e.g., lease of neon advertising sign followed by governmental blackout order frustrating primary purpose justified termination. However, commercial frustration cannot be used to withdraw from a poor bargain; e.g., tenant leases a gas station which does not produce the profit he anticipated due to governmental regulations.

B. Sales of Goods Under the U.C.C.

Section 2–614 of the U.C.C. provides that substituted performance is permissible when the agreed manner of shipping becomes commercially impracticable or the agreed manner of payment fails because of a governmental regulation.

Section 2–615 of the U.C.C. provides that delay in delivery or non-delivery is excused when it has been made impracticable under certain conditions. The Official Comment to this section states that the "section excuses a seller from timely delivery of goods contracted for, where his performance has become commercially impracticable because of unforeseen supervening circumstances not within the contemplation of the parties at the time of contracting. * * * Increased cost alone does not excuse performance unless the rise in cost is due to some unforeseen contingency which alters the essential nature of the performance. Neither is a rise or collapse in the market in itself a justification, for that is exactly the type of business risk which business contracts made at fixed prices are intended to cover. But a severe shortgage of raw materials or of supplies due to a contingency such as war, embargo, local crop failure, unforeseen shutdown of major sources of supply or the like, which either causes a marked increase in cost or altogether prevents the seller from securing supplies necessary to his performance, is within the contemplation of this section."

6. DEATH OR DISABILITY

When one party to a contract must perform an act which requires personal skill (author, painter, lawyer), death or disability of the person who was to perform the act discharges the contract.

But, if all the work or services are of such a character that they may be performed by others as well, the obligation will not be discharged; e.g., building contract.

D. BY OPERATION OF LAW

Common Place

1. IN GENERAL

Generally a contract is discharged and performance is excused if, after the contract has been entered into, the performance is made unlawful by a governmental order or decree since under such circumstances performance would constitute a violation of public policy; e.g., change in zoning law prior to beginning of construction prohibited construction of apartment building in that locality.

2. BANKRUPTCY

A discharge in bankruptcy is the result of a proceeding in a Federal Court by which the bankrupt is released from the obligation of certain provable debts (he is not released from such debts as taxes and wilful wrongs). However, the debt is not cancelled or extinguished. If the creditor brings suit against the debtor in a state court in a later proceeding, the debtor must plead as a defense his discharge in bankruptcy and if he fails to do this, the creditor can get a valid judgment against him. If the creditor has a claim against the debtor for a fraudulently incurred obligation, including a false financial statement in procuring a loan, or for certain other types of misconduct as stated in Section 17a of the Bankruptcy Act, he must file that claim in the bankruptcy court and be successful in that application after a hearing or the debt is automatically considered discharged.

The debtor may waive his defense of discharge in bankruptcy by *a new promise* to pay the debt after the discharge. In some states, this promise must be in writing. In most states, an oral promise is sufficient to revive the debt.

In most states, *part payment* of the debt will not revive the debt.

Although bankruptcy may discharge the remedy for the collection of certain debts, the bankruptcy of a party is no excuse for his failure to fulfill an executory contract. Unless the trustee in bankruptcy elects to assume the performance of an executory contract, the bankruptcy constitutes a breach, or an anticipatory breach, and gives rise to a provable claim in the bankruptcy.

3. STATUTE OF LIMITATIONS

Statutes provide that if you do not file the law suit within a specified time after the right accrues, you are forever barred from bringing the suit. Since the time varies, local statutes must be consulted. The *U.C.C., Section 2–725,* specifies a four-year period for actions on contracts for sales of goods.

However, in most states, the debtor may waive the Statute of Limitations by a promise to pay the debt (in most states the new promise must be in writing) or by part payment of the debt which then revives the debt. In addition, there are certain other exceptions where the statute cannot be used; e.g., cannot be used against the government; cannot be used where a party has been misled (insurance agent promises to settle suit and thereby misleads injured party into not filing law suit in time).

Some contracts, e.g., insurance contracts, contain a time limitation within which suit must be brought.

4. INSOLVENCY

Authorities differ as to whether insolvency constitutes a breach of contract. Some courts hold that there is an implied condition in every contract that the promisor will not permit himself to be disabled from making performance through insolvency, and that insolvency is a breach of the contract.

Other courts hold that insolvency does not result in a breach of contract unless there is an express provision in the contract to the contrary. In the latter courts, if the seller is selling on credit and the buyer goes insolvent, the seller must deliver the goods if the buyer can make payment; i.e., the seller is not excused from performance by the insolvency.

Under the U.C.C., Section 2–702, the seller may demand cash from an insolvent buyer prior to delivery and *may reclaim goods* sold to an insolvent buyer.

Under the U.C.C., Section 2–502, the buyer can *recover goods* from an insolvent seller when the buyer has paid all or part of the purchase price.

---

1. Tender Does Not Discharge Debt

TOWN v. TROW

41 Mass. (24 Pick.) 168 (1833).

Trow owed Town two dollars. He offered the money to Town; but, as the latter then refused to accept it, Trow placed the sum in the hands of a nearby innkeeper. In Town's presence Trow directed the innkeeper to turn the money over to Town whenever he demanded it. Town never made a demand on the innkeeper, but he later demanded payment from Trow himself. This Trow refused. In the present action upon the debt, Trow contends that his tender of the sum, and its deposit with the innkeeper, released him from all liability upon the debt.

MORTON, J. * * * In some cases, a tender of the payment of a debt or of the performance of a duty, and a refusal to accept, are deemed in law a payment of the debt or a performance of the duty; yet, ordinarily, they do not discharge the debt or duty, but only the damages which would have accrued by reason of the nonpayment of the one or the nonperformance of the other. * * * Had the defendant, when called upon for the money, offered to accompany the plaintiff to his home or place of business and there pay the money, or to pay it where they were, as soon as he could bring it, and actually used reasonable diligence for the purpose, it would have been a legal compliance with this demand. But the defendant did not adopt this course. He supposed that he had before, by the tender and by depositing the money in the hands of a stakeholder, who had agreed to perform the service, relieved himself of all responsibility on account of this debt. But we think he could not do this. If the depositary had failed, the loss would have fallen on the debtor. He had no power to transfer his liability to a third person, without the consent of the creditor. The debt is not extinguished by the tender. * * *

2. *Delayed Performance Excused When Work or Skill*

BECK & PAULI LITHOGRAPHING CO. v. COLORADO MILLING CO.

3 C.C.A. 248, 52 F. 700 (1892).

The plaintiff contracted with the defendant to furnish the latter certain fine stationery and advertising matter "in the course of the year." The work was not finished in time and delivery was not made until one week after the expiration of the year. The defendant refused to pay for the goods on the ground that they were not furnished within the time specified in the contract. Plaintiff now sues for the price [of the goods].

SANBORN, J. * * * It is a general principle governing the construction of contracts that stipulations as to the time of their performance are not necessarily of their essence, unless it clearly appears in the given case from the express stipulations of the contract or the nature of its subject matter that the parties intended performance within the time fixed in the contract to be a condition precedent to its enforcement, and, where the intention of the parties does not so appear, performance shortly after the time limited on the part of either party will not justify a refusal to perform by the party aggrieved, but his only remedy will be an action or counterclaim for the damages he has sustained from the breach of the stipulations. * * * Thus, in the ordinary contract of merchants for the sale and delivery, or the manufacture and sale, of marketable commodities within a time certain, it has been held that performance within the time is a condition precedent to the enforcement of the contract, and that a failure in this regard would justify the aggrieved party in refusing performance at a later day. * * *

On the other hand, it has been held that an express stipulation in a contract for the construction of a house that it should be completed on a certain day * * * would not justify the owner of the land on which the house was constructed in refusing to accept it for a breach of this stipulation when the house was completed shortly after the time fixed * * *.

In contracts for work or skill, and the materials upon which it is to be bestowed, a statement fixing the time of performance of the contract is not ordinarily of its essence, and a failure to perform within the time stipulated, followed by substantial performance after a short delay, will not justify the aggrieved party in repudiating the entire contract, but will simply give him his action for damages for the breach of the stipulation. * * *

These contracts were not for the sale and delivery, or the manufacture and delivery, of marketable commodities.

* * * There was nothing in the contracts or their subject matter indicating any intention of the parties that the stipulations as to time should be deemed of their essence; and the defendant was not

justified on account of the slight delay disclosed by the record in refusing to accept the goods, or in repudiating the entire contract. * * *

[Judgment for plaintiff.]

---

3. *Substantial Performance of Contract Can Be Sufficient*

SURETY DEVELOPMENT CORP. v. GREVAS

42 Ill.App.2d 268, 192 N.E.2d 145 (1963).

SMITH, Justice. When is a house a home? In our context a house is a home when it can be lived in. But when is that: When substantially completed or completely completed? We posit the question, because the answer is decisive.

Plaintiff sells prefabricated houses. Defendants selected one of their models, styled "Royal Countess, elevation 940". A contract was signed. The cost was $16,385.00; completion date September 27, 1961. Around 4:00 P.M. on that date defendants refused to accept the house asserting non-completion. Plaintiff then sued for the balance due and defendants counter-claimed for their downpayment. Both alleged performance by them and non-performance by the other. The legal issue is therefore relatively simple: Who performed and who didn't. The facts are more elusive—plaintiff at times says one thing, defendants another. We narrate them briefly.

On the morning of the twenty-seventh, "Royal Countess, elevation 940" was far from being a house, let alone a home. Racing the clock, plaintiff initiated a crash program. When defendants arrived on the scene at 4:00, at plaintiff's behest for final inspection, the crash program was still crashing—workmen were all over the place, slapping on siding, laying the floors, bulldozing the yard, hooking up the utilities, and so on. Defendants' tour was not a success, to put it mildly. Instead of a home, they found, to their dismay, a hive buzzing with activity. They did not tarry, in spite of the foreman's assurances that all would be right by 5:30. Nor did they come back. They should have. Believe it or not, the foreman was right. The job *was* substantially completed by 5:30, with only a service walk, some grading and blacktopping left undone.

The trial court found that the house had been substantially completed and concluded that there had been, therefore, substantial compliance with the contract and with this we agree. But because the house was not completely completed, it found that there had not been *complete* compliance. With this, too, we agree, but such finding is beside the point. Substantial—not complete—compliance in a construction contract is all that is required. By 5:30, there had been just that, in other words, substantial performance of the contract. Plaintiff's contretemps in having inspection set for 4:00 o'clock was hardly the way to make friends and influence people, but such happenstance is of no moment in determining whether or not there had been substantial compliance, unless such can be said to indicate bad faith. We do not think that it does. What it indicates is bad timing, not bad faith. * * *

No substantial sum was required to complete the items left undone. Nor were they of so essential a character that defendants could not have been esconced in their new home that night if they had so desired. We have thus answered our question: A house is ready to be lived in, to become a home, when it has been substantially completed.

[Judgment for plaintiff.]

---

4. *When Personal Satisfaction is Not Required*

JOHNSON v. SCHOOL DISTRICT NO. 12

210 Or. 585, 312 P.2d 591 (1957).

KESTER, Justice. This is an action to recover damages for breach of contract, in which plaintiff appeals from a judgment of nonsuit.

* * * Plaintiff was a school-bus operator in the Wallowa area, and on September 1, 1951, he entered into a contract with School District No. 4 of Wallowa county for the operation of a school bus during the two school years 1951–52–53. * * * The contract contained the following option:

> "The said second party [Johnson] is to have option the next 3 years if a bus is run and his service has been satisfactory."

It is agreed that plaintiff operated a bus during the two-year period of the contract, and for that he was fully paid.

* * * On June 9, 1953, after preliminary negotiations, plaintiff wrote to the board of District No. 12 stating that he elected to exercise his option [District No. 4 and 12 had been consolidated]. Defendant, however, refused to accept plaintiff's services, and instead defendant has operated its own bus, over the same route, since that time. * * *

In granting the nonsuit, the trial court held that the contractual provision that plaintiff's service be "satisfactory" was akin to those contracts where fancy, taste, or personal judgment are involved, and where lack of satisfaction on the part of the promisor is not reviewable. * * *

Plaintiff's option to renew the contract if his service has been satisfactory presents a question similar to those arising under contracts giving one party a right to terminate or be relieved from obligation if performance is unsatisfactory. Such contracts are generally grouped into two categories: * * *

> (1) Those which involve taste, fancy or personal judgment, the classical example being a commission to paint a portrait. In such cases the promisor is the sole judge of the

> quality of the work, and his right to reject, if in good faith, is absolute and may not be reviewed by court or jury.
>
> (2) Those which involve utility, fitness or value, which can be measured against a more or less objective standard. In these cases, although there is some conflict, we think the better view is that performance need only be "reasonably satisfactory," and if the promisor refuses the proffered performance, the correctness of his decision and the adequacy of his grounds are subject to review. * * *

Where, in a given contract, it is doubtful whether the promise is intended to be conditional on the promisor's personal satisfaction or on the sufficiency of the performance to satisfy a reasonable man, the latter interpretation is adopted.

* * * Even in cases where the right to terminate is absolute, the dissatisfaction must be actual and honest, and not merely feigned in order to escape liability. * * *

And where a right to renewal is predicated upon the existence of mutually satisfactory conditions at the expiration of the original period, one party cannot defeat the option by unreasonable refusal to cooperate in making the operation satisfactory. * * *

After study of the contract in question here, we are of the opinion that the standard of performance involved is not the mere personal satisfaction of the school board, unsupported by reason, but it is such performance as would satisfy a reasonable man under the circumstances. * * *

In our opinion, therefore, plaintiff would establish a prima facie case for renewal of the contract by proving that his performance was of a quality that should have satisfied a reasonable man under the circumstances.

[Nonsuit affirmed on procedural grounds; i. e., plaintiff should have exhausted his administrative remedies by filing his complaint with the school board before proceeding with his court action.]

---

5. *When Personal Satisfaction Required*

TOW v. MINERS MEMORIAL HOSPITAL ASS'N

305 F.2d 73 (C.A.W.Va., 1962).

BOREMAN, Circuit Judge. Dr. Abraham Tow, plaintiff, was employed in December 1958 as Chief of Pediatrics in the Man Memorial Hospital at Man, West Virginia, which was one of several hospitals owned and operated by defendant. In November 1959, defendant terminated Dr. Tow's employment and in this action plaintiff seeks to recover damages for a breach of his employment contract.

* * * Dr. Meade stated in his letter that he was "outlining * * * here the details of your appointment." It was further stated in the letter:

> "This appointment is to remain in effect *as long as you render satisfactory service in carrying out the Association's medical and hospital care program* as presently constituted." (Emphasis added.) * * *

It is plaintiff's contention that one of the binding provisions of his contract with defendant was that his employment would not be terminated except upon mutual consent or *for just cause*. Defendant contends that plaintiff's contract was consummated on the basis, and according to the terms and conditions, of the letters sent to him by Doctors Meade and Morrison on December 5, 1958; that by those terms Dr. Tow could be dismissed if his services were unsatisfactory to the Hospital Association. The District Court held that Dr. Tow was bound by the terms of the Meade-Morrison letters.

* * * We reach the conclusion that the terms stated in the Meade-Morrison letters, are, as a matter of law, the terms of the employment. * * * "[W]here a person contracts to * * * do work to the satisfaction of another, such other is * * * the sole judge of the quality of work done, and his right to accept or reject it is absolute, conclusive, and binding upon the parties, without the investigation of his reasons, unless he acts fraudulently. * *

[Judgment for defendant.]

---

6. Accord and Satisfaction Releases Debtor

OLSON v. WILSON & CO.

244 Iowa 895, 58 N.W.2d 381 (1953).

LARSON, Justice. [Action for balance due on contract.] On or about August 1, 1951, the plaintiff sold thirty head of cattle, by oral contract, to the defendant, through defendant's agent, a Mr. Johnson. Plaintiff claimed he was to receive thirty-five cents a pound for the cattle, plus the excess if they were dressed out at a better grade. Defendant admits buying the cattle but denies plaintiff's claim as to the price agreed upon and contends that the cattle were purchased from plaintiff on a grade and yield basis in compliance with O. P. S. regulations. Under plaintiff's claim they amounted to $10,725.75. Under defendant's claim the amount due was $9,372.80.

After delivery of the cattle to defendant on August 6th, plaintiff received a draft in the net sum of $9,372.80, which was marked "in full payment of the above items." * * *

On October 1, 1951, the plaintiff through counsel again wrote defendant as follows:

> "This letter is to advise you that today Myrl Olson presented for payment your draft No. 9634 in the sum of

> $9372.80. However, it is Mr. Olson's intention to consider this draft as only a partial payment on the 30 head of cattle sold to your company. It is not Mr. Olson's intention to accept this draft in full satisfaction of his claim against your company nor is the acceptance of this draft to be considered as an accord and satisfaction * * * Mr. Olson does not intend to waive any rights or claims he may have for the balance in the sum of $1351.45 * * *."

The only question before us is whether under the record there was an accord and satisfaction established as a matter of law.

* * * Obviously each case must be determined upon its own facts and circumstances. However, there are certain rules and decisions which guide and control transactions of this kind, such as those affecting liquidated and unliquidated claims, and the acts of the parties relating to intention, consideration, necessary implications, and bona fide disputes. * * *

There are many definitions of accord and satisfaction. Accord and satisfaction is a method of discharging a contract or cause of action, whereby the parties agree to give and accept something in settlement of the claim or demand of the one against the other, and perform such agreement, the "accord" being the agreement, and the "satisfaction" its execution or performance. * * * To constitute a valid accord and satisfaction, not only must it be shown that the debtor gave the amount in satisfaction, but that it was accepted by the creditor as such. * * * Where an offer of accord is made on condition that it is to be taken in full of demands, the creditor, doubtless, has no alternative but to refuse it or accept it upon such conditions.

* * * According to Webster's New International Dictionary, a claim for debt or damage is "liquidated" in law when the precise amount thereof is fixed, or has been agreed upon. * * *

> "An unliquidated claim is one, the amount of which has not been fixed by agreement or cannot be exactly determined by the rules of arithmetic or of law."

* * * True, the rule is that one cannot secure an accord and satisfaction of a liquidated or sum certain debt by the payment of a lesser amount for the reason that then there is no consideration upon which to base the accord and satisfaction.

* * * That the claim involved herein between plaintiff and defendant was unliquidated, there can be no doubt, for the exact amount due was clearly in dispute and could not be resolved except by a new agreement or the court action threatened by plaintiff. It was the proper subject of a new agreement. When defendant delivered to the plaintiff the draft for $9372.80 and made its position perfectly clear that the same was in full payment of the claim and refused to consider it otherwise on request, there was but one of two choices left to plaintiff, either, accept it as offered, or reject it, return

the draft and commence his legal action, as he had threatened to do in his correspondence.

The trial court correctly held that an accord and satisfaction had been effected, and dismissed plaintiff's petition. There is no error.

---

7. *Wrongful Alteration of Written Instrument Extinguishes Executory Obligations*

CALIFORNIA SAVINGS & COMMERCIAL BANK v. WHEELER ET AL.

216 Cal. 742, 16 P.2d 737 (1932).

Action to foreclose a mortgage in the sum of $24,500 on certain lots in Venice, Calif. Defendant proved that plaintiff had altered the mortgage. In the mortgages originally drawn up, a 12 ft. strip deeded to the city had been excluded. Later the city deeded it back to the defendants, whereupon the plaintiff took it upon itself to cross out the exclusion clause with regard to this strip in the mortgage. Presumably this was done with the approval of the defendant's husband and her agent for other purposes, but not with the consent of the defendant herself. The lower court gave judgment for defendant.

WASTE, C. J. The effect of the unauthorized alteration of an executed contract is declared in section 1700, Civil Code, in these words:

> "Extinction by unauthorized alteration. The intentional destruction, cancellation, or material alteration of a written contract by a party entitled to any benefit under it, or with his consent, extinguishes all the executory obligations of the contract in his favor, against parties who do not consent to the act."

That an alteration which results in placing property for the first time under a mortgage lien is a material one is obvious. Appellant would escape the paralyzing effect of the section by securing a finding that there was no fraud involved here, and the alterations were made to correct a mutual mistake * * * but there is no serious contention advanced that the trial court could have found, and it did not find that the northwesterly twelve feet was originally omitted through error or subsequently included to correct a mistake. The absence of a fraudulent purpose in making the alteration does not cure it of its deadening influence.

* * * obviously any unauthorized change in a material respect destroys the integrity of the instrument as the contract which the maker has executed. After the alteration, it ceases to be the maker's contract, and, as far as he is concerned, becomes void and of no legal effect. * * *

The judgment appealed from is affirmed.

8. Anticipatory Breach of Contract

KLEEB v. BURNS

5 Ariz.App. 566, 429 P.2d 453 (1967).

HATHAWAY, Chief Judge. Jeanette M. Kleeb, defendant below, has appealed from a judgment against her, awarding the full real estate broker's commission to Robert Hilgenberg dba Hilgenberg Realty Company, and ordering her to return the $1,000 earnest money to the plaintiff, Robert W. Burns. * * * The trial court found that the commission had been earned in a real estate transaction which was not carried out.

* * *

We must determine if the judgment is supported by the evidence applicable to any theory within the issues tried. Of course, the evidence will be viewed most strongly in favor of affirming the judgment. Viewing the evidence accordingly, we find that the appellee, Hilgenberg, acting under a written listing, signed by the appellant, brought the buyer and seller together.

On June 17, 1964, the appellant, Jeanette Kleeb, entered into a "DEPOSIT RECEIPT AND AGREEMENT" to sell a house in Tucson to Robert W. Burns. The pertinent provisions of the agreement provided:

> "Closing date—June 23, 1964; possession date—June 24, 1964.
>
> * * * * * * * * * *
>
> "Time is of the essence."

On June 23, a meeting relating to the closing of the transaction was held in Mr. Hilgenberg's office. Mrs. Kleeb was on a trip to Guadalajara, Mexico, but her attorney John W. Ross attended the meeting. Others present were Mr. Burns and his attorney J. Mercer Johnson, Mr. Hilgenberg and his secretary, Yvonne Hutchins.

Mr. Johnson stated that the buyer was ready and willing to complete the closing at that time, if the seller, Mrs. Kleeb, could deliver possession on June 24 according to the contract. A discussion ensued relating to Mrs. Kleeb's failure to take steps to remove any of her personal possessions and furnishings from the seven room and two and a half bath home. At this time Mr. Ross stated that he refused to take any responsibility for removing the personal property of Mrs. Kleeb from the premises. Mr. Ross then called his client in Mexico and advised her about the complication. She gave Mr. Ross authority to remove her personal possessions from the home, but left the decision up to him. An impasse developed between the parties and the closing did not take place.

Mrs. Kleeb returned from Mexico at 5 p. m. on the 24th of June and went immediately to Mr. Hilgenberg's office. Mr. Hilgenberg testified that Mrs. Kleeb told him that she was willing to do anything to complete the transaction that was not taken care of on the 23d. He further testified that he had a mover who would remove all of her property from the premises but that she refused to have this done as it would take "several days" and that "she said it is impossible to do it [to move the furniture on the 24th] at that time."

Mrs. Kleeb's testimony revealed that she had made no arrangements to have the furnishings removed as disclosed by the following cross-examination:

> "Q Was it your intention then not to make any plans to move until the closing actually had occurred on the 23d * * * ?
>
> "A Yes. I had to wait until the closing took place."

Yvonne Hutchins, Mr. Hilgenberg's secretary, testified that in talking to Mrs. Kleeb on the 24th of June, after her arrival from Mexico:

> "She [Mrs. Kleeb] said it would take about three days just packing her China alone and she couldn't do it at this time."

The buyer's attorney delivered a letter on June 24 to both Mr. Ross and the Hilgenberg Realty offering to complete the agreement on June 24. Mr. Johnson received a telephone call from Mr. Hilgenberg at his home on the evening of June 24 informing him that Mrs. Kleeb could deliver possession of the premises on June 26. * * *

The buyer brought an action against the seller and the real estate broker to rescind the contract, alleging breach by the seller, and sought to recover the $1,000 earnest money deposit. The seller counterclaimed, contending that the buyer had breached the contract and had thereby forfeited the deposit. She also cross-claimed against the real estate broker claiming that the broker was entitled to a commission of only one half of the earnest money and that she, the seller, was entitled to the other half, as provided in the deposit forfeiture clause of the contract. The broker cross-claimed against the seller for his commission, alleging breach of contract by the seller.

We believe that the evidence shows that Mrs. Kleeb anticipatorily breached the contract by putting herself in a position making it impossible for her to deliver possession of the premises on June 24. Time being of the essence of the contract, delivery of possession was required of her on the date to fulfill the performance required of her under the contract.

It is clearly the law that a party to a contract need not perform where his performance would be useless in the face of the opposite party's manifesting his inability to perform his part of the agreement.

> "No performance, tender, or demand on the part of the purchaser is necessary where the vendor is clearly unable to perform his part of the contract, within the time specified therein * * *."

In Diamos v. Hirsch, 91 Ariz. 304, 307, 372 P.2d 76, 78 (1962), our Supreme Court

> "* * * recognized that an action may be maintained for breach of contract based upon the anticipatory repudiation by one of the parties to the contract. Sarle v. School Dist. No. Twenty-Seven of Pima County, 32 Ariz. 96, 255 P. 994 [1927]. It is well established that in order to constitute an anticipatory breach of contract there must be a positive and unequivocal manifestation on the part of the party allegedly repudiating that he will not render the promised performance when the time fixed for it in the contract arrives."

* * *

From the above facts the trial court could have reasonably concluded that Mrs. Kleeb had put herself in such a position that it would have been impossible for her to perform her part of the agreement (delivering possession on June 24). As noted, Mrs. Kleeb herself made it known that it would be impossible for her to remove her possessions in such a short time on the 24th of June and that she did not intend to remove them until the closing had been completed.

For the foregoing reasons the judgment is affirmed.

---

9. *Mere Increase in Difficulty and Costs Not Impossibility*

KENNEDY v. REECE

225 Cal.App.2d 717, 37 Cal.Rptr. 708 (1964).

CONLEY, Presiding Justice. This is an appeal by the plaintiff from a judgment adverse to him on his complaint and favorable to the defendants on their counterclaim. The plaintiff, Fred Kennedy, made a contract with Reece and Thomas, mining partners, to drill a water well for them; the agreement, on the letterhead of the Fred Kennedy Company, reads as follows:

> "We propose to furnish all materials and perform all labor necessary to complete the following:
>
> "drill 12″ hole to estimated depth of 400′ — 3.50 per ft
> case with new 6″ well casing with bottom half perforated gravel pack, wash well and bail. — 1.50 per ft
>
> "All of the above work to be completed in a substantial and workmanlike manner accord-

ing to standard practices for the sum of two thousand Dollars ($2000.00)

"Payments to be made $1,000.000 on signing this agreement bal when cased $__________ as the work progresses to the value of __________ per cent (____%) of all work completed. The entire amount of contract to be paid within __________ days after completion.

"Any alteration or deviation from the above specifications involving extra cost of materials or labor will only be executed upon written orders for same, and will become an extra charge over the sum mentioned in this contract. All agreements must be made in writing.

"Respectfully submitted,
FRED KENNEDY CO.

Drilling and Sewer Contractors
By: /s/ Fred Kennedy"

An acceptance is endorsed by Louis H. Reece and Steven Thomas.

The complaint alleges with respect to the contract:

> "That on or about the 31st day of March, 1961, plaintiff and defendants entered into a written contract wherein plaintiff agreed to drill for defendants certain water well at an estimated cost of Two Thousand Dollars; that after commencing drilling operations it was determined that it was not possible to obtain water in the area selected by defendants, hence, by mutual agreements the parties discontinued drilling operations, at which time there was due to plaintiff the sum of Four Hundred Dollars, demand for which has been made and no part of which has been paid."

The answer and counterclaim avers, on the contrary, that the agreement was to drill a 12-inch hole for a water well to an estimated depth of 400 feet, case it with new 6-inch well casing with the bottom half perforated, and further to gravel pack, wash and bail the well for a fixed price of $2,000.00, payable $1,000.00 upon execution of the contract and the balance when the casing was installed; that the sum of $1,000.00 was paid upon the execution of the contract and that plaintiff "failed and refused to perform the contract and breached the same and after abandoning one hole at a depth of 130 feet, commenced a second hole, which he abandoned at 270 feet, and failed and refused and continues to fail and refuse to drill a hole to the depth of 400 feet and case the same." The pleading further alleges that the two holes in question were placed at points selected by the plaintiff as most likely to yield water; that plaintiff breached the contract by failing and refusing to complete the well; that the two holes in the ground have no value; that at the time the contract was entered into the plaintiff knew that the defendants required the well for the purpose of supplying water for their gold mining and milling operations. * * *

The cause was tried by the court sitting without a jury, and resulted in a judgment for the defendants on their counterclaim in the sum of $1,307.15, besides interest and costs.

The findings generally support the theory pleaded by the defendants. The court expressly found that the allegations in the complaint as to the contract were not true, and that the averments in the answer relative to the agreement are true except with respect to damages. * * *

The evidence shows that Mr. Kennedy was an experienced water well driller carrying on his trade in the area; that he assured Mr. Reece that he was certain of getting an acceptable well and that there would be no trouble in reaching the 400-foot level contemplated by the written contract. However, the first hole drilled by the plaintiff, after being carried to a depth of 130 feet, was abandoned at the instance of the appellant because he claimed that he had struck hard rock. The plaintiff told Mr. Reece that he would move, without charging him any additional sum, to a new point on the land of a neighbor, if Mr. Reece would dig a sump hole at the proposed location and construct a passable roadway to the place where the well was to be drilled. The defendants accordingly secured permission to drill the well on the neighbor's property, and the second hole was carried down to a depth of 270 feet; Mr. Kennedy claimed that he there struck the same hard formation, which he said was granite but which the evidence on behalf of the defendants showed was a relatively brittle rock that could be drilled through. Mr. Kennedy removed his equipment without any preliminary notice to defendants and left the area; he did not complete the well, and he did not insert any casing or cap either of the holes. No consent was given by Mr. Reece for the abandonment of the operations by Kennedy. In this respect as well as in others, there was a conflict in the testimony, but, of course, the trial court's findings, being sustained by substantial evidence, must prevail.

The defendants did not complete the well, although the evidence indicates that two contractors stated to Mr. Reece that they would be willing to drill to the 400-foot level at a cost estimated at $5.00 per foot, besides the necessary expense of setting up and taking down their equipment. The defendants arranged with their neighbor to use, in their gold-mining operations, an existing well, which was located some 4000 feet away; they connected this source of water with their mining area by a plastic pipeline and the installation of a pump of greater capacity than they would have had to use if the well drilled by plaintiff had been successful. The mining property required water for the processing of the gold, and it is claimed by defendants that a delay of approximately four months, which resulted from the failure of their hoped for source of water through Kennedy's default, caused them damage. The court, as above noted, did not make any award for the delay in carrying on their mining work, but it did give them damages for the additional cost of the pump, electrical work, plastic pipe and fittings, a pumping plant panel and labor with respect to installation, a stator, and a control switch amounting in all to the sum of $2,547.15, less an item of labor saved by the use of the plastic pipe amounting to $240.00 and the balance of $1,000.00, which would have been paid to the plaintiff had he completed his contract. This total deduction of $1,240.00 left a figure of $1,307.15 as the net damages allowed by the court.

* * *

DID THE PLAINTIFF PERFORM HIS CONTRACT?

It is obvious that the finding that the plaintiff failed to comply with the terms of his contract is supported by substantial evidence; the well driller did not dig the well to a depth of 400 feet; he did not case it; he did not gravel pack, or wash, or bail it. Appellant contends, however, that he was relieved from the duty of completing his contract because of "impossibility" resulting when he hit hard rock at the 270 foot level.

The enlargement of the meaning of "impossibility" as a defense, (which at common law originally meant literal or physical impossibility of performance) to include "impracticability" is now generally recognized * * * However, this does not mean that any facts, which make performance more difficult or expensive than the parties anticipated, discharge a duty that has been created by the contract * * * Facts which make performance harder or more costly than the parties contemplated when the agreement was made do not constitute a ground for the successful interposition of the defense of "impracticability" unless such facts are of the gravest importance. If it be noted that this is merely a difference of degree rather than a difference in kind, such notation is accurate.

* * *

Principles applicable to the present case are thus stated in Wilson v. Alcatraz Asphalt Co., 142 Cal. 182, 188–189, 75 P. 787, 789:

> "The rule is that if performance of a contract is possible, it is none the less a breach although the obligor himself may have become wholly unable to perform. The impossibility must consist in the nature of the thing to be done, and not in the inability of the party to do it. If what is agreed to be done is possible and lawful, it must be done. Difficulty of accomplishing the undertaking will not avail the party who commits a breach of the contract. If a party expressly undertakes to do a thing, lawful in itself, and not necessarily impossible under all the circumstances, and does not do it, he must make compensation in damages, though the per-

formance was rendered impracticable, or even impossible, by some unforeseen cause for which no provision is made and over which he had no control, but against which he might have provided in his contract. The rule has its foundation in common sense and honesty, and compels parties to abide by their contracts. Any other rule would leave all contracts in a sea of uncertainty, without rudder or compass."

[I]ncreased difficulties and heightened costs of a reasonable nature, even though originally unforeseen, do not render the performance of a contract "impracticable". * * * For example, if a contractor agrees to build a structure and it is destroyed by fire or other casualty when only partly completed, the contractor is not relieved from his duty to rebuild merely because of the additional expense he must incur or the added difficulties he must overcome. * * *

In the present case, neither the pleadings nor the facts as found by the court warrant the application of the doctrine of impossibility, or impracticability. * * *

More important still, the findings do not establish, but actually negate, the necessary basis for a defense of impracticability. The plaintiff testified that it would be almost impossible and extremely expensive to drill through the rock formation at the 270-foot level, but the defendants' testimony indicated that the rock encountered by the drill was not so hard a formation as plaintiff claimed and inferentially that, with some increased difficulty, it could be pierced. The evidence also showed that two other drillers had expressed to defendants a willingness to complete the well to the 400-foot level and that a charge of $5.00 per foot besides the cost of moving the drilling equipment would be adequate. Every intendment is in favor of the judgment, and the court's findings on controverted issues, if supported as here, by substantial evidence must be accepted. It is clear, therefore, that the necessary factual basis for a successful plea of impracticability was not present.

[Judgment for defendant.]

---

10. Doctrine of Commercial Frustration No Defense to Lease of Real Property

WOOD v. BARTOLINO

48 N.M. 175, 146 P.2d 883 (1944).

BRICE, Justice. The appellant leased a building to appellees "for use solely as a filling station and not for restaurant or lunch counter purposes," at a rental of $100 per month for a term of five years commencing June 1, 1939. It was operated by sub-lessees until February 1, 1941, and thereafter until July 1, 1942 by appellees, when the latter ceased its operation and offered to restore possession of the premises upon the alleged ground that the lease contract had been terminated because of "commercial frustration" resulting from government rules, regulations, and orders freezing automobiles, tires and tubes and rationing the sale of gasoline, so that it was "impossible and impracticable to use or operate the leased premises as a filling station" at any time after the first of December, 1942; and that such "impossibility and impracticability" still continued and would continue throughout the term of the lease. * * *

As a direct and proximate consequence of the governmental rules, regulations and orders concerning the "freezing" of tires, tubes and automobiles, it became and was impossible and impracticable to use or operate the leased premises as a filling station during the months of July, August, September, October and November, 1942, and by reason thereof, and of the rationing of gasoline, it became and was impossible and impracticable to use or operate the leased premises as a filling station during the months of December, 1942, January, 1943, or any time thereafter, and that such impossibility and impracticability still continues and will continue throughout the term of the lease contract.

* * *

The parties, at the time the lease contract was entered into, did not contemplate, and could not reasonably have contemplated, that such laws, rules and regulations would be enacted, promulgated or enforced, or that they would materially and substantially change the conditions of the business operated in the leased premises. * *

The doctrine of "commercial frustration," or, as more often called by the courts of this country, the doctrine of "implied condition," has been developed by a process of evolution from the rules: * * *

"(1) Impossibility due to domestic law;

"(2) Impossibility due to the death or illness of one who by the terms of the contract was to do an act requiring his personal performance.

"(3) Impossibility due to fortuitous destruction or change in character of something to which the contract related, or which by the terms of the contract was made a necessary means of performance." * * * [T]he essence of the modern defense of impossibility is that the promised performance was at the making of the contract, or thereafter became, impracticable owing to some extreme or unreasonable difficulty, expense, injury, or loss involved, rather than that it is scientifically or actually impossible. * * * The important question is whether an unanticipated circumstance has made performance of the promise vitally different from what should reasonably have been within the contemplation of both parties when they entered into the contract. If so, the risk should not fairly be thrown upon the promisor."

* * *

The courts of this country, Federal and State, have cited with approval, and generally followed, the decisions of the English courts on the doctrine of "commercial frustration," involving commercial transactions. It is held by the English courts that the doctrine has no application to an ordinary lease of real property. * * *

There are no Federal regulations prohibiting the sale of gasoline, oil, tires, tubes and other merchandise ordinarily sold at filling stations, though the enforcement of such regulations has drastically reduced appellees' income, which before was less than operating expenses; nor has any Federal law, rule or regulation deprived appellees of the use of the premises as a filling station. * * * It follows that the trial court erred in denying recovery of rent by appellant. * * *

In such cases relief lies only in the conscience of the landlord, to which in this case, it appears, fruitless appeals for relief have been made.

[Judgment for plaintiff.]

---

11. Disability of Party to Perform Affords Relief

SPALDING v. ROSA

71 N.Y. 40 (1877).

The defendants, by contract with the plaintiffs, agreed to furnish an opera troupe for certain performances at the plaintiffs' theater. A celebrated German tenor named Wachtel was the star of the troupe; but when the time for the performance drew near the famous tenor became ill and was not able to sing. The troupe was unable to stage a performance without Wachtel, and the plaintiffs now sue the defendants for failure to perform their contract. Defendants contend that the disability of Wachtel relieved them from their duty to furnish the troupe.

ALLEN, J. * * * Both the plaintiffs testified that it was Wachtel's popularity and capabilities as a singer upon which they relied to fill their theater and reimburse themselves for their expenses, and make a profit. The appearance of Wachtel in the operas was the principal thing contracted for, and the presence of the others of the company was but incidental to the employment and appearance of the "famous German tenor." The place of any other member of the company could have been supplied, but not so of Wachtel. His presence was of the essence of the contract, and his part in the performances could not be performed by a deputy or any substitute. The plaintiffs would not have been bound to accept, and would not have accepted, the services of the troupe under the contract without Wachtel; it would not have been the "Wachtel Opera Troupe" contracted for without him. There is no dispute as to the facts. The only question is one of law, as to the effect of the sickness and consequent inability of Wachtel to fulfill the engagement, upon the obligations of the defendants. So far as this question is concerned, it must be treated as if the contract was for the performance by Wachtel alone; as if he was the sole performer contracted for. This follows from the conceded fact that his presence was indispensable to the performance of the services agreed to be rendered by the entire company. In this view of the case, the legal question is very easy of solution, and can receive but one answer. The sickness and inability of Wachtel occurring without the fault of the defendants, constitutes a valid excuse for the nonperformance of the contract. Contracts of this character for the personal services, whether of the contracting party or of a third person, requiring skill and which can only be performed by the particular individual named, are not, in their nature, of absolute obligation under all circumstances. Both parties must be supposed to contemplate the continuance of the ability of the person whose skilled services are the subject of the contract as one of the conditions of the contract. Contracts for personal services are subject to this implied condition, that the person shall be able at the appointed time to perform them; and if he dies, or without fault on the part of the covenantor becomes disabled, the obligation to perform is extinguished. * * *

[Judgment for defendant.]

---

12. *New Promise Revives Debt Discharged in Bankruptcy*

DOMESTIC LOAN, INC. v. PEREGOY

116 Ohio App. 381, 184 N.E.2d 457 (1962).

KOVACHY, Presiding Judge. [Suit for money due on a promissory note.] * * * A judgment was entered against the defendant in favor of Domestic Loan, Inc. by virtue of a warrant of attorney contained in a Promissory Note on July 29, 1960 in the amount of Five Hundred Nine and 94/100 Dollars ($509.94). Thereafter the defendant filed a Voluntary Petition in bankruptcy in the United States District Court for the Northern District of Ohio and scheduled the plaintiff as one of his creditors. After the adjudication in bankruptcy and at the first meeting of creditors on February 9, 1961 the defendant and the plaintiff entered into a written agreement whereby the defendant revived said judgment obligation in the amount of Two Hundred Fifty and No/100 Dollars ($250.00) payable at the rate of Fifteen and No/100 Dollars ($15.00) per month beginning February 17, 1961.

The defendant subsequently defaulted under the terms of said agreement and plaintiff proceeded to enforce payment by filing garnishment proceedings on the judgment that had been previously entered pursuant to the terms of said revivor agreement.

* * * The law with respect to a discharge of a debt or a judgment in bankruptcy is well-settled. The debt or judgment is not paid, satisfied, extinguished or cancelled. The bankrupt is merely af-

forded the privilege to interpose the discharge as a defense against the enforcement of the debt or judgment. And, since the matter is personal with the bankrupt, he has the choice of either interposing such defense to an action on the debt or judgment or of waiving the same, as he sees fit. * * *

The Supreme Court, in a case decided in 1851, held that a *new promise* to pay a debt discharged in bankruptcy was adequate consideration to sustain a cause of action on *the old debt* for the reason that the bar to a recovery of a debt discharged in bankruptcy is "strictly a personal privilege" and is waived by a subsequent promise.

* * * It seems to us, therefore, that the defendant in the use of such clear and unmistakable language revived his obligation to the plaintiff in the sum of $250.00 and at the same time authorized the plaintiff, in case he (the defendant) defaulted on his new promise, to execute on the judgment standing against him in the Cleveland Municipal Court. * * *

We accordingly hold that the plaintiff had the right to institute proceedings in aid of execution on the existing judgment and to enforce such payments and that it is entitled to recover a total sum not exceeding $250.00 from the date of his adjudication in bankruptcy which occurred on January 5, 1961. * * *

[Judgment for plaintiff.]

PROBLEMS

1. A made a contract with B whereby A would drill a well for water 1,000 feet deep. A drilled to a depth of 800 feet without getting water and then quit because he struck granite rock. B refused to pay so A brings suit for the reasonable value of his services alleging substantial performance of the contract. Decision? see case 9

2. Mr. Moore had a fire policy on his home with the Phoenix Insurance Company which had a clause as follows: "If the above-mentioned premises shall become vacant and unoccupied for a period of more than ten days, this policy shall be void". Mr. Moore and his family left the premises for a two-week vacation. One month after their return, the home burned to the ground. The insurance company refuses to pay. Decision?

3. The XYZ Corporation had a contract with B whereby XYZ would deliver certain type motors to B on or before June 1, 1974. On February 1, 1974, XYZ informed B that it would not be able to deliver the motors as the company was having financial problems. B ignored this information. In March XYZ was able to get a governmental subsidy to continue operations. In April XYZ informed B that it was going to deliver pursuant to the contract. B, believing he can purchase the motors at a lower price, desires to cancel the contract on the grounds of anticipatory breach under U.C.C. 2–610. Decision?

4. The Weather Construction Company contracted to construct a building for O at a certain price. Due to abnormal rainfall the job site

was flooded and the contractor incurred extra expense which he now demands that O pay. O claims that Weather is bound by the contract. Decision?

5. Seller agrees to sell buyer on or before a certain date a new Chevrolet of certain specifications. Seller has ten Chevrolets with these specifications on his lot; but during the night, they are all destroyed by a fire. Seller cannot deliver, and the buyer sues for breach of contract. Decision?

6. The Mineral Park Land Company owned a bed of gravel in a ravine. One Howard, who was about to build a concrete bridge nearby, made a contract with the company by which he agreed to take from the company's gravel bed all the gravel required for the bridge at a price of five cents per cubic yard; but after he had removed about half of the total amount required for the bridge, it was discovered that the rest of the gravel was below the level of the ground water in the ravine, and that to remove it would necessitate the use of a steam dredge at an expense of ten or twelve times as much as the usual cost per yard. Howard, therefore, refused to take any more gravel; and the company sues him for his failure to go on with the performance of the contract. Decision?

7. "Whirlwind" White had a contract to fight "Madman" Morris at the Forum on June 14. On June 10, while hitting the punching bag, "Madman" sprained his wrist which has caused a postponement of the fight. The prefight ticket purchasers now sue "Madman" for spraining his wrist, "Whirlwind" for refusing to fight a man with a sprained wrist, and the Forum for postponing the fight. Result?

8. T leased a neon advertising sign from L for a period of one year. A few days after T and L entered into the lease a governmental order forbid the use of neon signs in T's area. T seeks to rescind the lease. Decision?

9. B contracts to purchase 100 copper covered tables from S. B is aware that S must obtain the copper from a certain manufacturer in a foreign country. Shortly after the contract is made the supplier of the copper is forced to shut down his factory due to a riot and a strike. B sues S for breach of contract in failing to deliver the tables contending that S should have provided an escape clause in the contract since neither a riot nor a strike is a defense. Decision?

10. Debtor filed a Petition in Bankruptcy and was discharged of his debt to his doctor-creditor. His creditor, however, filed a law suit against the debtor in a state court for the amount of the debt. Debtor, knowing that his debt had been discharged in bankruptcy, ignored the law suit. Creditor obtained a default judgment and proceeded to garnishee debtor's wages. Debtor now seeks your advice.

Chapter 15

REMEDIES IN GENERAL

A. DAMAGES

1. COMPENSATORY DAMAGES

A. In General

When one party breaches a contract, the other party may be entitled to damages. In this situation the law attempts to compensate the plaintiff so he will be placed in as good a position as if the defendant had performed the contract. The theory is *just compensation* for losses which are the immediate, direct and natural result of the act complained of, and which are usual and might have been expected.

The injured party is only entitled to damages which were *within the contemplation* of the parties at the time the contract was made. Unusual or unexpected damages resulting from facts unknown to the defendant or which he could not foresee at the time the contract was made are not recoverable.

The amount of damages recoverable is for the jury to decide, and for the court if there is no jury. Court costs, e. g., filing fees, witness fees, jury fees, deposition costs, are usually assessed against the losing party. Attorney fees are not recoverable unless provided for in the contract or by special statute; e. g., consumer protection statutes. If the plaintiff did not suffer a loss, or cannot prove a loss, the court may award him "nominal damages", e. g., one dollar, plus court costs.

Sections 2–708, 2–709, and 2–710 of the U.C.C. cover seller's damages in the sale of goods, and *2–713, 2–714, and 2–715* cover buyer's damages. Also, see *U.C.C. Section 1–106.*

In construction contracts, where the contractor breaches the contract, damages are generally measured by the reasonable cost of reconstruction and completion in accordance with the contract if this is possible and does not involve unreasonable economic waste; e. g., tearing down the building and starting over. Generally this is true whether the contractor refused to finish the work or not, and whether the breach was total or partial. However, if there would be an unreasonable economic waste, generally the damage rule is based on the difference between the value of full performance as promised and the value of the defective performance actually rendered. Some courts refuse to follow the economic waste rule if the contractor is guilty of wilful or intentional breach; thus, in those courts the contractor is liable for the actual cost of completion.

When a contractor delays in completing performance of the contract, the general rule is that the injured party may recover the cost of renting other premises. It is usually advisable in this type of contract to have a liquidated damage clause (see number 3 infra).

B. Loss of Profits

The injured party may recover for his loss of profits if he can establish them with reasonable certainty. Reasonable certainty, not mathematical certainty, is all that is required. Where there is no uncertainty as to the *fact* of damages, it is no objection that the *amount* cannot be exactly determined. Speculative profits as any speculative damages, are not recoverable; e. g., loss of future profits from a *new* business. However, loss of future profits from an established business would be recoverable if there is a reasonably certain basis for the calculation of plaintiff's probable loss resulting from the breach.

Where plaintiff is unable to prove loss of profits, courts frequently award him his amount of expenditures plus the value of his own services in preparation and performance in reliance on the contract.

C. Interest

Interest at the legal rate is recoverable from the time of breach where the amount of money is liquidated or from the time it becomes liquidated; otherwise from the date of the judgment. Even though the demand is not for a specific sum, interest may be recovered where the damages are capable of being made certain by calculation; e. g., reference to market value. If the damages are neither certain nor capable of being made certain by calculation, interest is not allowed prior to judgment.

2. PUNITIVE DAMAGES

Exemplary or punitive damages are awarded to one party in order to punish the other party and to discourage others from similar wrongful conduct. Generally, punitive damages are limited to certain situations involving willful, wanton, or malicious torts, such as fraud or libel. There are cases which have awarded punitive damages for willful breach of a fiduciary duty, persistent and repeated wrongful conduct in the operation of a business, fraud arising from a contract imposed by law, and fraud arising from a contract; however, generally punitive damages are not recoverable for breach of contract.

3. LIQUIDATED DAMAGES

The parties may stipulate in the contract that a certain amount shall be paid to the injured party in case of default. This is known as a liquidated damage clause. If the nature of the contract is such that it would be extremely difficult or impractical for the court to ascertain the actual damages, and if the amount specified is not so excessive as to be in the form of a penalty, the clause will be valid. A common example of a liquidated damage clause is found in building contracts where the contractor is required to pay a stated sum for each day of delay.

Under Section 2–718 of the U.C.C., a liquidated damage clause is valid if it is reasonable under specified circumstances.

4. DUTY TO MINIMIZE DAMAGES

The injured party is under a duty to mitigate his damages, and this duty requires that he take whatever steps are reasonably necessary to reduce the actual loss as low as possible. He cannot add to his damages when it is reasonably within his power to mitigate damages. For example, a person who is wrongfully discharged from an employment contract before the term expires must use reasonable means to find similar employment; i.e., he cannot sit idly by and expect to draw his salary. If he cannot find similar suitable employment, he is entitled to recover his full salary for the balance of the contract term. Similarly, a buyer who receives inferior goods under a contract cannot increase his damages by continuing to use the goods after learning of their unfitness.

Sections 2–602(2)(b) and 2–603(1) of the U.C.C. cover buyer's duties to minimize damages under certain conditions.

B. EQUITABLE RELIEF

---

1. SPECIFIC PERFORMANCE

There are times when a plaintiff is not interested in money damages because he feels that money per se is not the solution to the defendant's breach. For example, the plaintiff finds a rare Rembrandt painting which he desires to add to his art collection. Plaintiff makes a contract with defendant for the purchase of the painting. Later when plaintiff tenders the money, the defendant refuses to deliver the painting. In such a case, plaintiff is not interested in money damages, which could be only nominal, instead he wants the painting. Courts have the power to order the defendant to deliver the painting; and if he refuses, to sentence him to prison for contempt of court. This order is called a decree of specific performance. This decree is not granted lightly. There are five requirements to a decree for specific performance:

a. The contract must be certain;

b. Money damages must be inadequate;

c. The agreement must be legal and without fraud or immorality;

d. The decree must not work a hardship or injustice on the defendant (e. g., consideration inadequate or contract unconscionable); and

e. The court must be able to supervise the performance of the ordered act.

Courts will generally order specific performance of real estate contracts (because each parcel of real estate is unique) and contracts for unique personal property.

Contracts for ordinary personal property are not specifically enforceable because the plaintiff can purchase identical goods on the open market. If he has a loss, money damages will be adequate.

Personal services contracts are ordinarily not specifically enforceable because of the difficulty of supervision by the court and because of the Thirteenth Amendment to the Federal Constitution which prohibits involuntary servitude. However, a negative covenant in a contract, i.e., one which prohibits the athlete or singer from working for anyone else during the period of the contract, will be enforced by a court injunction. This will indirectly have the effect of compelling the defendant to work for the plaintiff.

The court will not order specific performance of a building contract because enforcement of the decree would require too much supervision of the details of construction.

Section 2–716 of the U.C.C. provides for specific performance in the sale of goods where it is equitable to do so.

2. RESCISSION

Rescission is the unmaking of the contract. A contract may not be unilaterally rescinded unless legal grounds for rescission exist. Some jurisdictions enumerate the grounds for rescission by statute.

The common grounds for rescission are: illegality, commercial frustration, fraud, undue influence and duress, mistake, insanity, intoxication, entire or substantial failure of consideration, substantial nonperformance or breach by the other party (failure of a building contractor to duly and properly perform his contract), and where one party places it out of his power to perform, the other party may treat the contract as terminated.

A right to rescind must be exercised promptly or within a reasonable time after discovery of the facts which entitle the person to rescission. Failure to act promptly can be considered a waiver of the right of rescission.

When there is a rescission, the successful party is entitled to restitution; i.e., to recover any consideration he gave plus any other compensation necessary to make him whole. Thus, a buyer who placed improvements on land was entitled to the value of the improvements when he rescinded the contract due to seller's failure to perform.

Under U.C.C. Section 2–721, a party can rescind a contract and also recover damages.

3. REFORMATION

A party may desire reformation of a contract rather than rescission; i. e., have the contract corrected to show the true intent of the parties. Typical cases of reformation are mutual mistake in the contract and fraud in the contract.

4. INJUNCTION

A contract for personal services ordinarily is not specifically enforceable. There are several reasons for the rule: difficulty of enforcement, the fact that the services would be unsatisfactory under compulsion, and where physical labor is contract for, the constitutional prohibition against involuntary servitude (13th Amendment).

However, a negative covenant in a contract may, under some circumstances, be enforced by injunction; e. g., opera singer agreed to sing at plaintiff's theatre and nowhere else for a certain time, then she contracted to sing for another; court held that she could not be forced to sing at the theatre, but could be prevented from singing anywhere else during the period. Generally an injunction in this type of case will only be granted if the services are "unique" or "extraordinary"; e. g., opera singer, ball player, actor. Also, an injunction should not be granted when it would cause unjust or harmful results; e. g., defendant is left without a reasonable means of livelihood.

The modern rule does not require an express negative covenant in a contract for injunctive relief. This is because an affirmative promise *implies* a promise not to do anything which defeats the required performance (Restatement of Contracts, Section 380, Comment a.).

---

1. *Uncertainty as to Amount of Damage Will Not Preclude Recovery*

TESSMAR v. GROSNER

23 N.J. 193, 128 A.2d 467 (1957).

OLIPHANT, J. This is an appeal from a judgment of the Superior Court, Chancery Division, in favor of the plaintiffs-respondents awarding to the plaintiff-executor the sum of $2,500 as damages for the conversion by the appellant of certain medical charts and records compiled and owned by the deceased Dr. E. L. Kadisch during his life and professional practice. * * *

Dr. Kadisch was a licensed physician and had practiced dermatology for seven years at his residence in Westwood, New Jersey. He became ill in July 1954 and was unable to practice after September 20, 1954. On that date Dr. Kadisch and the defendant entered into a written contract whereby the defendant was to take care of the practice during Dr. Kadisch's illness, seeing patients two days a week, and was to receive $40 a day for services. Dr. Kadisch died on September 28, 1954 and thereafter the defendant continued in this arrangement until November 1, 1954, and Mrs. Kadisch collected the proceeds of the medical practice and paid the defendant the stipulated sum of $40 a day. * * * Mrs. Kadisch apparently decided that he was not interested in purchasing the practice but his paramount purpose was to carry on the practice so that at the same time he could compile for his own use a list of all the patients. Under such circumstances she gave notice he should leave the premises on April 1, 1955. This he did and immediately opened an office in the Medical Arts Building in Westwood, and promptly sent out announcements to all the former patients of Dr. Kadisch from the list which he had compiled while occupying the Westwood office. * * *

The trial court held the Kadisch estate had something of value in these charts and that the appellant as effectively took them by making copies as if he had taken them away and never returned them. He got all the value out of the charts that he saw in them. The trial judge held he had no right to that, nor the right to extract such information from these charts and take them elsewhere for that purpose; * * * The judge concluded that the plaintiff-executor had suffered damages of $2,500 and ordered judgment entered in that sum payable to the executor with costs. * * *

We agree with the trial court that these charts had a value not only to Dr. Kadisch's estate but also to the appellant in his practice as a dermatologist. It is not an uncommon thing for a doctor in advanced years, prior to retirement, to dispose of a medical practice to a younger doctor, and it seems to us to be the commonsense thing that in such a disposition, if the records and charts are not included, the valuation is depreciated. * * *

The appellant then argues there was no evidence from which the court below was justified in awarding more than nominal damages against the appellant. * * * Since there is no market value, as such, for charts of this kind, the general rules of damages for the breach of contracts can be applied * * * But the general rule of damages for a breach of contract is subject to two qualifications designed to confine within reasonable limits the appraisement of the consequences of the default; (1) the damages are those arising naturally according to the usual course of things from the breach of the contract, or such as may fairly and reasonably be supposed to have been in the contemplation of the parties to the contract at the time it was made, as a probable result of the breach; and (2) there must be reasonably certain and definite consequences of the breach as distinguished from the mere quantitative uncertainty. * * * The rule relating to the uncertainty of damages applies to the uncertainty as to the fact of damage and not as to its amount, and where it is certain that damage has resulted, mere uncertainty as to the amount will not preclude the right of recovery. * * * Under the rule stated and under the proofs we do not find that the trial court erred as to the extent of the damages; they are not excessive, and there is some reasonable basis for the finding in the proofs. Under such circumstances we will not disturb the result.

[Judgment for plaintiff.]

---

2. Emotional Reaction Generally Not Recoverable in Breach of Contract

PETTAWAY v. COMMERCIAL AUTOMOTIVE SERVICE

49 Wash.2d 650, 306 P.2d 219 (1957).

FINLEY, Justice. This is an action for damages for the breach of an alleged contract for the purchase and sale of an automobile.

The defendant company displayed a special model, a 1953 Buick "Skylark," automobile in its show window. The plaintiff saw the car and discussed its purchase with a Mr. Shaw, one of defendant corporation's salesmen. Thereafter, the plaintiff signed one of the defendant corporation's order forms on which the price of the new car was stated as $5,667, and $1,500 was designated as a credit allowance for plaintiff's 1948 Chrysler.

* * * Plaintiff's testimony further indicated that, when he returned from the voyage of some two or three months' duration, he tendered a cash payment to Mr. Shaw in an amount in excess of the five hundred dollars; that he was informed the defendant corporation had sold the 1953 Buick "Skylark" model to someone else. Apparently, the manufacturer had allotted only three automobiles of the particular model to the defendant company, and defendant company failed to produce one for the plaintiff. Thereupon, plaintiff commenced this action for damages for breach of contract. * * *

The jury awarded $1,325 to plaintiff. By answer to special interrogatories, it set (a) $825 as the market value of plaintiff's Chrysler; (b) $300 for plaintiff's disappointment, mental anguish, loss of sleep, humiliation, and damages to his reputation, allegedly resulting from the breach of the contract and the deprivation of the allegedly unique chattel; and [c] $200 by reason of deprivation of use of an automobile. The defendant corporation appealed.

* * * Now, as to the question of damages: Appellant contends that the court erred in submitting to the jury the issue of damages for deprivation of the use of respondent's Chrysler. The evidence was inadequate for the jury to make an award in any amount for that item. There is testimony in the record that respondent hired a taxicab a couple of times for six dollars; but these events were not connected with the breach of the contract in question. The award is the result of pure speculation. * * *

The jury awarded respondent three hundred dollars for the mental anguish occasioned by the failure to deliver the "Skylark" for "conspicuous consumption." The appellant contends that the court erred in submitting that issue to the jury and instructing upon it. We agree. Consequential damages are sustainable if they flow naturally and inevitably from a breach of contract and are so related to it as to have been within the contemplation of the parties when they entered into it. * * * The emotional reactions peculiar to a particular individual which might flow from a breach of a contract of sale of an automobile are too subjective and variable to be contemplated prior to a breach of contract, or ascertainable afterward. Such suffering, if any, is not compensable in an action for damages for breach of contract. * * *

For the reasons stated hereinbefore, it was error to allow the respondent damages in the amounts of $300 for mental anguish and $200 for loss of use of an automobile, and the judgment must be modified and reduced in this respect. [Note: loss of use is recoverable in many jurisdictions.]

---

3. Ordinarily Attorney's Fees Not Recoverable as Damages

REID v. VALLEY RESTAURANTS

48 Cal.2d 606, 311 P.2d 473 (1957).

McComb, Justice. From a judgment denying defendant and cross-complainant attorney's fees, defendant and cross-complainant appeals.

* * * On or about July 14, 1953, plaintiffs leased to defendant a restaurant known as "The Goody-Goody Drive-In." The lease contained provisions * * * that in case suit should be brought by either party against the other by reason of the breach of any of its provisions the successful party in such suit should be entitled to a reasonable attorney's fee and costs of said action in such amount as might be fixed by the court. * * *

On December 28, 1954, plaintiffs filed a complaint against defendant for unlawful detainer and to quiet title to the property covered by the lease, alleging that defendant had violated the terms of the lease in assigning it without first obtaining the written consent of plaintiffs and failing properly to account to plaintiffs for gross profits derived from the business.

On January 3, 1955, defendant filed its answer and also a cross-complaint, by which it sought to recover attorney's fees in accordance with the provisions of the lease.

* * *

Thereupon the trial court made the following minute order: "It is stipulated that plaintiffs will dismiss their complaint and the question of whether any relief shall be granted to cross-complainant on its cross-complaint for attorney's fees, and if so the amount of same, may be determined by the Court based upon the files and depositions on file in this proceeding." * * *

On June 6, 1955, the trial judge filed a judgment ordering that defendant take nothing by its cross-complaint, and that neither party recover costs against the other.

Defendant contends on this appeal: * * * The judgment is against the law, insofar as it fails to award to defendant reasonable attorney's fees. * * *

It is the general rule that attorney's fees are not recoverable from the opposing party in the absence of an express statutory provision or a contractual agreement that they be paid. * * *

There is not any statute authorizing an attorney's fee to be paid to defendant under the facts as appear in this case. Therefore, we must look to the terms of the lease between the parties to see if there was any contractual liability upon the part of plaintiffs to pay defendant's attorney's fees. The lease provided that in case suit should be brought by either party against the other by reason of the breach of any of its provisions the successful party in such suit should be entitled to a reasonable attorney's fee in such amount as might be fixed by the court.

The stipulation entered into by the parties was not a stipulation for judgment for defendant but was a conditional stipulation in the form of a compromise providing that upon the fulfillment of certain conditions by defendant the lease might be reinstated. * * * The record supports the trial judge's implied finding that the situation was a compromise and that neither party was successful.

Since defendant was not the successful party, it was not entitled to attorney's fees under the express provisions of the lease.

---

4. Punitive Damages

BOISE DODGE, INC. v. CLARK

92 Idaho 902, 453 P.2d 551 (1969).

McQUADE, Justice. Nearly all of the facts in this case are uncontroverted. In January, 1967, the management of Boise Dodge, Inc., decided to make a special effort to sell approximately thirteen 1966 cars then held in stock as "demonstrators." * * * [T]he fact that the odometer on the car purchased by respondent Clark was set back roughly 7,000 miles (from 6,968 to 165) was stipulated by Boise Dodge and shown by an internal repair order of Boise Dodge and by the testimony of an employee of Superior Auto Products who did the work on these "demonstrators" for Boise Dodge. * * *

The "Automobile Agreement" signed by Mr. Clark clearly indicates on its face at its top in normal size print that the car was a "demonstrator" in that the word "Demo" is written in ink under the heading "Used" which appears next to an empty blank headed by

"New." Mr. Clark admits he got a copy of this agreement, but says he focused his attention only on the figures appearing on it. Clark that day (February 2nd) gave his check for $500 and the next day (February 3rd) gave his check for $1,562 when the car was delivered to his farm. These checks plus his 1963 Pontiac traded to Boise Dodge at a value of $1,100 constituted the sales price of the car. Because Clark then discovered facts which led him to believe the car was used, he stopped payment on his two checks on the next Monday, (February 5th). * * *

Boise Dodge brought suit on the checks, and Clark counterclaimed for equitable rescission or for damages for breach of contract and deceit as well as for wrongful attachment of his bank account and punitive damages. * * * The jury also awarded punitive damages to Clark in the amount of $12,500. * * *

Appellant Boise Dodge, Inc., makes several assignments of error which in essence present but a single ultimate issue: whether or not the award of punitive damages was proper. * * *

* * * [F]rom the legal point of view of the imposition of punitive damages in this case, it does not matter whether respondent's counterclaim technically sounded in contract or tort. The rule established in Idaho is that punitive damages may be assessed in contract actions where there is fraud, malice, oppression or other sufficient reason for doing so. This rule recognizes that in certain cases elements of tort, for which punitive damages have always been recoverable upon a showing of malice, may be inextricably mixed with elements of contract, in which punitive damages generally are not recoverable. In such cases, punitive damages are allowed according to the substance of a showing of willful fraud.

Various jurisdictions, including Idaho, have limited the discretion of juries in imposing punitive damages by declaring that the amount of punitive damages must bear a "reasonable relation" to the amount of actual damages. It is never made clear precisely upon what basis an amount of punitive damages will be declared "reasonable" or "unreasonable" in relation to the amount of actual damages, especially in view of the often-repeated statement that no strict mathematical ratio is to be applied. * * * [T]he true basis for an award of one amount of punitive damages as opposed to another amount lies in an overall appraisal of the circumstances of the case.

The amount of actual damages sustained by a plaintiff is one indication of the culpability of the defendant's acts, but it cannot be the sole criterion for the assessment of punitive damages. Also relevant is the prospective deterrent effect of such an award upon persons situated similarly to the defendant, the motives actuating the defendant's conduct, the degree of calculation involved in the defendant's conduct, and the extent of the defendant's disregard of the rights of others. These are legitimate concerns of the law, and the application of any fixed arithmetic ratio to all cases in which punitive damages are assessed would be arbitrary. It therefore must be recognized that the requirement of a "reasonable relation" between actual and punitive damages serves as a rough device available to trial and appellate courts for the purpose of paring down plainly extreme awards of punitive damages.

Applying these principles to the case at bar, we are satisfied that the jury's award of $12,500 punitive damages against Boise Dodge, Inc., was justified, and court below did not commit error in refusing to set aside that verdict. This is a case of calculated commercial fraud in broad disregard of the rights not only of respondent Clark but the consuming public generally. It occurs in an area of sales in which consumers are unable to gain accurate information about the product. * * *

[Judgment affirmed.]

---

5. *Liquidated Damages Recoverable When Not a Penalty*

MEDAK v. HEKIMIAN

241 Or. 38, 404 P.2d 203 (1965).

HOLMAN, Justice. Plaintiffs were real estate agents and leased from defendants in January of 1952 premises for a business office in a building on the southeast corner of Tenth and Broadway in the city of Portland. * * *

In 1954 defendants were approached by the promoters of Lloyd Center, a proposed integrated shopping complex of enormous proportions. They wished to purchase the premises, a portion of which plaintiffs occupied, for inclusion in the planned complex. * * * As a result, plaintiffs and defendants entered into another contract whereby defendants agreed to construct another building on the southwest corner of the same intersection on property also owned by them and to rent a portion of the premises to plaintiffs for a period of five years commencing in January 1957 at the expiration of plaintiffs' lease on the premises which was being sold to the Lloyd Center. * * * The agreement also provided that in the event defendants did not construct the building defendants would pay plaintiffs $5,000 as liquidated damages for their failure to perform.

Defendants failed to erect the building as agreed, and this action was brought to recover the $5,000 provided as liquidated damages for the contract's breach. The defendants appeal from a judgment of $5,000 entered upon a jury verdict. * * *

The defendants claim the provision in the contract providing they would pay to plaintiffs the sum of $5,000 as liquidated damages if defendants did not construct the building was in fact a penalty and therefore not enforceable and that the court erred in not so finding as a matter of law.

* * * Two criteria seem to be paramount in determining whether the sum provided to be paid is for the purpose of securing performance of the contract, and therefore a penalty, or whether it is intended to be paid in lieu of performance, and therefore liquidated damages. At the time of the making of the contract would the sum provided seem to bear any reasonable relationship to the anticipated damages and would the actual damages be difficult or impossible of ascertainment? If both answers are "yes," the sum provided would normally be considered liquidated damages.

* * * The agreed value of the five year extension of the lease in the old building which plaintiffs gave up was $100 per month, or a total of $6,000. Would two and one-half times the space in a new building be worth $5,000 more over the five-year period of the extension? The sum is not so grossly disproportionate to the probable actual damages resulting from failure to perform as to require it to be called a penalty. * * * Two and one-half years hence would there be other space in the same locality of like size and condition which would serve as a guide to prove plaintiffs' damage? Could the parties be sure that at that time the damage could be accurately estimated? If no space were available, it was possible plaintiffs could suffer actual damage because of loss of business which would not be compensable under the usual measure of damage. There would appear to be nothing reprehensible or unreasonable in the parties agreeing to a sum which would compensate plaintiffs for such actual anticipated loss in case of breach. * * *

These imponderables at the time of making a contract would seem to justify the use of a sum as liquidated damages as long as it was not disproportionate to actual anticipated damages.

The trial judge refused to say it was a penalty. We do not disagree. * * *

[Judgment for plaintiff.]

---

6. *Damaged Party has Duty to Mitigate Damages*

AMERICAN BROADCASTING PARAMOUNT THEATRES, INC. v. AMERICAN MFRS. MUTUAL INS. CO.

48 Misc.2d 397, 265 N.Y.S.2d 76 (1965), affirmed 24 App.Div.2d 851, 265 N.Y.S.2d 577, affirmed 17 N.Y.2d 849, 271 N.Y.S.2d 284, 218 N.E.2d 324, certiorari denied 385 U.S. 931, 87 S.Ct. 291.

ABRAHAM N. GELLER, Justice. This is an action for breach of a sponsorship contract brought by plaintiff, herein referred to as "ABC", against defendant insurance companies, collectively known as The Kemper Insurance Companies and herein referred to as "Kemper."

On August 15, 1962, the parties entered into a television network contract whereby Kemper agreed to sponsor one program per week of the ABC Evening Report news program over a 26-week period beginning October 17, 1962. On November 9, 1962, the fourth telecast under Kemper's contract, a "promotional announcement" was made at the end of the sponsored program and just before the scheduled time was up, regarding the Howard K. Smith program on November 11 entitled "The Political Obituary of Richard M. Nixon," evidently occasioned by his recent defeat in the contest for the California governorship. Alger Hiss appeared on that program and attacked Richard M. Nixon. This caused considerable public controversy.

Protesting the appearance of Hiss on the ABC–TV Network and, in particular, the promotional announcement at the close of its sponsored Evening Report program and referring to the numerous complaints received from its agents and policyholders, Kemper cancelled its participating sponsorship of Evening Report by telephone on November 13, 1962 and letter on November 14, 1962. ABC replied that same day that it intended to hold Kemper "fully responsible for any and all sums due and to become due to us under the terms of the agreement between us dated August 15, 1962." * * *

However, market value is not always the measure of recovery—as for example, where there is no market for the type of goods involved, or where it is a contract for personal services, or where the subject matter of the contract is perishable. * * *

Advertising contracts have been held to fall into the latter category, so that upon wrongful withdrawal by an advertiser the publisher is entitled to recover the contract price, reduced, as though the contract was one for services, by such amount as was or could have been obtained in the exercise of reasonable efforts to minimize damages by the use of that space for other advertisements * * * Moreover, the subject matter—commercial minutes or time—is perishable, since, if not sold in time, it has vanished and is of no value to anyone. Furthermore, there has been no showing that there is a market or market value for commercial television minutes in the same sense as there is a market and market value for goods and commodities.

* * * To keep the subject in perspective, it should be pointed out that the price in Kemper's contract dated August 15, 1962 amounted to about $7,500 net per commercial minute (after deducting 15% agency commission); that ABC's selloffs of 13½ of the 55 minutes were at an average net price of $4,080 per minute; * * *

The court determines that ABC made reasonable efforts, in light of the existent circumstances and consistent with its regular business practice, to selloff the available Kemper 55 minutes. * * *

The period from November to April is off-season for the procurement of television sponsorship. The major contracts are negotiated months before the fall season, which commences about the latter part of September. * * *

The selloffs by ABC, less the station compensation payments attributable thereto, and by its 5 owned and operated stations realized

$36,664.04. Thus, ABC's recoverable damages are in the sum of $265,047.21. * * *

---

7. *Specific Performance Proper When Property Unique*

COCHRANE v. SZPAKOWSKI

355 Pa. 357, 49 A.2d 692 (1946).

DREW, Justice. The learned court below having decreed specific performance of a written contract entered into by defendant, Mary Szpakowski, and plaintiff, John F. Cochrane, for the sale of her restaurant and retail liquor business, she took this appeal. * * * Following a verbal agreement entered into by appellant and appellee on May 18, 1945, they executed a written contract four days later for the sale on or before June 15, 1945, by appellant to appellee of this business, together with all fixtures and contents, except stock, for $7,000. The agreement also provided that appellant would transfer to appellee as part of the consideration, her liquor license, if approved by the Pennsylvania Liquor Control Board, and further that she would surrender the leased premises to him. * * *

The general rule undoubtedly is that the specific performance of contracts for the sale of personal property will not be enforced for the reason that ordinarily compensation for the breach of the contract may be had by way of damages. A well-recognized exception to the rule is where the thing contracted for cannot be purchased in the market, and, because of its nature or the circumstances, the delivery of the thing itself, and not mere pecuniary compensation, is the redress practically required. * * * In the instant case, it is obvious that equity does have jurisdiction because a similar restaurant and liquor business to the one in question could not be purchased in the market, and therefore could not be reproduced by money damages. * * * Furthermore, this contract involves the transfer and ownership of a retail liquor license, the value of which cannot be accurately determined in an action at law. It seems unrealistic to us to close our eyes to the fact that * * * retail liquor licenses cannot be issued by the Board in the City of Pittsburgh because the number allowed * * * is greatly exceeded by the existing licenses. This gives to the license, here involved a peculiar value depending upon the business ability and the popularity of the owner, which cannot be accurately or adequately measured or compensated for in an action at law. * * *

Decree affirmed, at appellant's costs.

8. *Equitable Remedies—Reformation, Rescission*

CITY OF BALTIMORE v. DE LUCA-DAVIS CONSTRUCTION CO.

210 Md. 518, 124 A.2d 557 (1956).

HAMMOND, Judge. The Bureau of Highways of the Mayor and City Council of Baltimore issued a notice of letting of a contract for the construction of the Jones Falls Expressway storm water conduits and, in response, DeLuca-Davis Construction Co., Inc., the appellee, submitted a bid that by reason of clerical error was at least $589,880 less than it intended it to be, and some $700,000 less than the engineer's estimate and the next lowest bid. * * * As soon as the bids were announced, the appellee realized that it had made a mistake. After several hours of checking the precise form of the mistake was turned up and the Director of Public Works was notified immediately. Five days after the bids were opened, DeLuca-Davis wrote the Board of Estimates, explaining in detail how the mistake had occurred and that the actual bid should be $2,385,944.25 instead of $1,769,064.25, the bid submitted. The letter requested the Board either to correct the bid accordingly or to return the bid and the certified check for $50,000, which had accompanied it pursuant to the applicable charter provisions and the notice of letting. Being advised that the Board proposed to accept the original bid, the appellee filed a bill of complaint in the Circuit Court of Baltimore City, praying a * * * decree commanding the Board of Estimates either to correct or reform its mistaken bid and to take no action thereon unless it had been corrected or, in the alternative, that the court permit the appellee to rescind the bid and have both the bid and the certified check returned. * * * In transferring the estimated unit cost for unclassified excavation of $13.34 per cubic yard from the detail work sheet to the summary sheet the estimator by mistake entered the figure of $3.34 for Item 2 and Item 11. There seems little doubt that the mistake came about because the first figure in $13.34—the figure "1" was on a vertical ruled line in the work sheet apparently accentuated by the paper having been folded. * * *

It is manifest to us that the City is correct in saying that there cannot be reformation, for at least two reasons. In the first place, to warrant the equitable remedy of reformation the mistake must have been mutual * * * Here the mistake was entirely that of the contractor and not induced by any act or omission of the City, so that it is entirely unilateral even under the perhaps fictional theory that if the act of one party is induced by the other, the mistake is mutual. More important than the first reason why there cannot be reformation is the second, namely, that a court will never in the name of reformation rewrite a contract or make a contract for the parties or act unless there is clear, convincing and satisfying proof of a mutual understanding and bargain that has not been accurately expressed. * * *

Although reformation requires that the mistake be mutual, rescission may be granted whether the mistake be that of one or both of the parties. * * * The general rule as to the conditions precedent to rescission for unilateral mistakes may be summarized thus: 1, the mistake must be of such grave consequences that to enforce the contract as made or offered would be unconscionable; 2, the mistake must relate to a material feature of the contract; 3, the mistake must not have come about because of the violation of a positive legal duty or from culpable negligence; 4, the other party must be put in status quo to the extent that he suffers no serious prejudice except the loss of his bargain. * * *

There are numerous cases in many states that have granted contractors cancellation of bids based on clerical, material, palpable, bona fide mistakes. Where, as in the case at bar, the mistake has been brought to the attention of the contracting authority before the acceptance of the bid, the courts have been almost unanimous in granting relief. * * *

We find that DeLuca-Davis is entitled to cancellation of its bid and the return of its deposit.

---

9. *Right of Buyer to Rescind for Fraud*

MYERS v. RUBIN

399 Pa. 363, 160 A.2d 559 (1960).

MUSMANNO, Justice. Murray I. Myers and the Wynnebrook Bus Lines, Inc., of which he is the president, brought an action in equity against * * * the Rubin Lines, now the County Transit Company of Glenside, to rescind a written contract wherein the plaintiffs agreed to buy their bus line. The bus line was a private business operating under the authority of the Public Utility Commission and consisted of transporting school children to and from their homes and Overbrook High School, Beeber Junior High School and Gompers Elementary School, all in the Overbrook section of the City of Philadelphia.

In their complaint the plaintiffs alleged that the defendants made untruthful statements about their business and that these statements were the inducements which caused the plaintiffs to agree to purchase the defendants' business. The Chancellor found for the plaintiffs. The defendants appealed.

* * * As late as October, 1957, the month before the sale was consummated, the defendants were deceiving the plaintiffs on the subject of fares collected. Nor were the mis-statements in question the result of ignorance or inadvertence. One of the defendants, Albert Rubin, was bookkeeper of the bus company and, therefore, had direct knowledge of the amount of business being done by his firm.

* * * The whole business structure of the country could be imperiled if the parties could supply deceptive foundations which could not be condemned and removed once the superstructure went into place. The record here reveals numerous failings on the part of the defendants. They not only misstated the total number of fares carried by them, but they were not forthright about the condition of their buses which were in such a state of disrepair that the plaintiffs were compelled to purchase three second-hand buses in order to conduct the business into which they had been led through artifice and dissimulation. * * *

We affirm the decision of the Court below in allowing rescission of the contract of sale.

---

10. Injunction Improper

FOXX v. WILLIAMS

244 Cal.App.2d 223, 52 Cal.Rptr. 896 (1966).

FILES, Presiding Justice. Plaintiff Redd Foxx, an entertainer in nightclubs and on phonograph records [and television], brought this action against Walter D. Williams, Jr., Dootone Record Manufacturing, Inc., and others, for a declaration of rights, * * * under a written contract called "ARTIST RECORDING ROYALTY AGREEMENT." Dootone cross-complained against Foxx to recover moneys paid by mistake, for damages, and for an injunction to prohibit breaches of the contract. After a court trial, judgment was entered declaring the rights of the parties, awarding a money judgment in favor of cross-complainant for overpayments, and enjoining Foxx. We have here Foxx' appeal from the judgment. * * *

In the latter part of 1955, while Foxx was performing at the Club Oasis in Los Angeles, defendant Williams suggested that he be allowed to record Foxx' comedy routine there and find out if phonograph records made therefrom would be salable. Foxx had been a performer for many years but had never made a successful phonograph record. His one previous attempt had sold about 40 copies. Williams was established in the record manufacturing and distributing business, being the president and sole stockholder of defendant Dootone Record Manufacturing, Inc. * * *

With respect to the cross-complaint the trial court found * * * that Foxx had entered into an agreement with another manufacturer to make recordings as soon as he was legally free to do so, and concluded that, unless restrained, Foxx would make records for a manufacturer other than Dootone. * * *

Civil Code section 3423 provides in part:

"An injunction can not be granted:

" * * *

> "*Fifth*—To prevent the breach of a contract, other than a contract in writing for the rendition or furnishing of personal services from one to another where the minimum compensation for such service is at the rate of not less than six thousand dollars per annum and where the promised service is of a special, unique, unusual, extraordinary or intellectual character, which gives it peculiar value the loss of which can not be reasonably or adequately compensated in damages in an action at law, the performance of which would not be specifically enforced; * * *."

It is a familiar rule that a contract to render personal services cannot be specifically enforced. * * *

It follows that the breach of such a contract may not be enjoined except in cases falling within the exception provided for in the quoted statute. The 1958 contract recites that the artist's performances "are of a special, unique, unusual, extraordinary and intellectual character which gives them a peculiar value," and at pretrial the parties agreed that such characterization was correct. There remains the question whether this is a contract "where the minimum compensation for such service is at the rate of not less than six thousand dollars per annum." * * *

We do not place our decision upon the absence of proof of the amount of royalties earned under the 1958 contract. In our opinion this royalty contract does not meet the requirements of the injunction statute even though it should ultimately appear that the royalties earned, over any given period, should exceed the rate of $6,000 per year.

An injunction which forbids an artist to accept new employment may be a harsh and powerful remedy. The monetary limitation in the statute is intended to serve as a counterweight in balancing the equities. The Legislature has concluded that an artist who is not entitled to receive a minimum of $6,000 per year by performing his contract should not be subjected to this kind of economic coercion. Under the statutory scheme, an artist who is enjoined from accepting new employment will at least have the alternative of earning $6,000 or more per year by performing his old contract. * * *

The portion of the judgment which enjoins Foxx must be deleted.

PROBLEMS

1. Plaintiff ordered from defendant two gowns for his prospective bride to be made after model 46A and to be used on the honeymoon. Plaintiff told defendant at the time that the wedding was to take place on January 10th and that he was incurring great expense for the wedding. Defendant promised to have the gowns ready on or before January 9th, but did not do so. Plaintiff alleges that as a result of the defendant's failure, his prospective bride broke the wedding date; and he suffered a loss in the amount of $1,000.00 for foods, wines, entertainment, and other expenses. Decision?

2. Plaintiff wrote a telegram in a secret code and tendered it to the telegraph company for transmission to T. Due to the carelessness of the telegraph company employee, the message never reached T. As a result of this, plaintiff lost a very valuable business deal with a profit of $10,000.00. Plaintiff now sues the telegraph company for the loss of profit. Decision?

3. Plaintiff and defendant builder contracted for defendant to build plaintiff a home for $100,000. The contract had a clause which provided that if the contractor did not have the home finished and ready for occupancy on or before May 1st, the defendant would have to pay plaintiff $10,000.00 in liquidated damages. Defendant did not have the home finished until May 10th. Plaintiff brings this action for $10,000.00. Decision?

4. Seller and buyer entered into a contract for the purchase of a truck load of tomatoes. Seller delivered the tomatoes to the buyer's warehouse pursuant to the contract, but the buyer refused them stating that he was overstocked with tomatoes. Seller drove his truck to a nearby army camp where his son was stationed and gave the tomatoes to his son; seller believing that if his son gave free tomatoes to the officers in his brigade his son would be sent to officers' candidate school. Seller now seeks the purchase price of the tomatoes from the buyer. Decision?

5. Seller and buyer entered into a written contract for the sale of real estate on certain terms. After the contract was entered into, the buyer changed his mind because of financial reverses and asked the seller to be relieved of the contract. Seller was anxious for the sale to be completed because he had tried without success to sell the property for a long time; furthermore, although the consideration for the contract was adequate, the value of the real estate dropped slightly after the contract was entered into. Seller sues buyer for specific performance. Decision?

6. "Tricky" Blowhard was a candidate in the primary election for the U. S. Senate. He had a contract with the XYZ television corporation to televise two important political speeches one week prior to the election, but through a mixup in programming the speeches were never televised. "Tricky" lost the election and now sues for breach of contract claiming damages consisting of campaign expenses and the salary he would have received as a senator. Decision?

7. Primo Carnera, a heavyweight boxer, had a contract with the Madison Square Garden Corporation to fight the winner of the Schmeling-Scribling contest. The contract provided that Carnera could not render services as a boxer in any major boxing contest pending the fight between Schmeling and Scribling. Thereafter, Carnera made a contract to fight Jack Sharkey on a date prior to the S-S fight. Madison Square Garden Corporation seeks an injunction to prevent the Carnera-Sharkey fight. Carnera claims the prohibition violates the 13th Amendment to the Federal Constitution. Decision?

8. S and B enter into a written contract whereby S agrees to sell certain real property to B; however, through a mutual mistake an incorrect description is inserted in the contract. B prefers the mistaken description because he will obtain more land for the price agreed upon; however, S seeks reformation of the contract to show the correct description. Decision?

Chapter 16

THIRD PARTIES

A. THIRD PARTY BENEFICIARIES

1. IN GENERAL

Often contracts are made between two parties for the express purpose of benefiting a third party. A common example is a contract between an insurance company and a husband under which the husband's life is insured so that on his death the amount of the policy will be paid to his wife. In such a case, his wife is the beneficiary of the contract.

There are three types of third party beneficiary contracts: a. donee; b. creditor; and c. incidental. Nearly all jurisdictions permit donee or creditor beneficiaries to bring an action to enforce a contract; however, courts will not enforce an incidental beneficiary contract.

The third party cannot enforce the contract unless it was made expressly for his benefit. Also, the beneficiary can only recover if there was an enforceable contract between the original parties to the contract; thus, any defense between the original parties will also be effective against the third party.

Section 2–318 of the U.C.C. provides that a seller's warranty whether express or implied extends to certain beneficiaries if it is reasonable to expect that such person may use, consume or be affected by the goods and who is injured in person by the breach of warranty. The beneficiary of a warranty may bring a direct action for breach of the warranty against the seller whose warranty extends to him. A seller cannot limit the operation of this section; (he cannot extend a warranty to the buyer and at the same time exclude the beneficiary); however, a proper exclusion under Section 2–316 to the buyer would also be an exclusion to the beneficiary.

2. DONEE BENEFICIARY

If the purpose of the contract is to make a gift to the third party, it is called a third party donee beneficiary contract. Thus, the insurance illustration, supra, is an example of a donee beneficiary contract.

3. CREDITOR CONTRACT

If the purpose of the contract between the original parties is to satisfy an obligation to a third party, it is a creditor beneficiary contract. A creditor beneficiary is a creditor of the promisee whose obligation will be discharged to the extent that the promisor performs his promise. Thus, where a tenant assigns a lease to a sub-tenant assignee and the assignee agrees to perform all of the terms of the lease, the agreement between the tenant and the assignee is for the benefit of the lessor (landlord); and he may sue the assignee as a creditor beneficiary (of course, he also maintains his legal rights against the original tenant). Similarly, when a business is sold and the buyer "assumes" the liabilities of the seller's business, the creditors of the business are creditor beneficiaries of the assumption agreement.

4. INCIDENTAL OR REMOTE BENEFICIARIES

A person who is only remotely benefited by a contract cannot enforce it. In such case, it is not the intention of either the promisee or the promisor that the third person benefit from the contract. Thus, where a city makes a contract with a contractor to pave Balboa Avenue, property owners living along Balboa Avenue cannot sue the contractor if he fails to perform because they are only incidental beneficiaries. The city made the contract to benefit all the members of the public and not primarily for the individual property owners on Balboa Avenue. Similarly, if Mary promises John that she will marry him if he gives her a new Cadillac and John fails to purchase and give her the Cadillac after the marriage, General Motors cannot sue John since it is only a remote or incidental beneficiary of the contract.

5. RESCISSION

A. Donee Beneficiary

It is generally held that the original parties do *not* have the right to rescind the contract without the consent of the donee beneficiary *unless the right was reserved* in the contract (Restatement of Contracts, Section 142). Some states by special statute, e.g., California Insurance Code, Section 10170(e), provide that the contract *may be rescinded* unless the rights of the beneficiary have been expressly declared *irrevocable*; thus, in California, the beneficiary of an insurance policy *can* be changed unless otherwise stated.

B. Creditor Beneficiary

The general rule is that the original parties may rescind or vary the obligation as to a creditor beneficiary until he brings suit or materially changes his position in reliance on the contract (Restatement of Contracts, Section 143). Thus, the contract can be rescinded or varied if the creditor beneficiary was unaware of the contract or did not rely on it before it was rescinded or varied.

Justifiable Reliance
shield, but not sword

B. ASSIGNMENTS

1. IN GENERAL

An assignment is a transfer by one party to a contract of some or all of his rights under the contract to a person who is not a party to the contract. The party making the assignment is called the assignor, and the party to whom the assignment is made is called the assignee.

No special language or form is necessary to make an assignment. Thus, an oral assignment is valid unless required by statute to be in writing; e.g., wage assignments generally must be in writing.

An assignment can be total or partial; e.g., a creditor may assign part of a claim and retain the remainder of the claim.

Consideration is not necessary to make an assignment; thus, an assignment may be made as a gift.

2. CONTRACTS ORDINARILY ASSIGNABLE

Whether a contract is assignable depends upon its terms and the nature of the contract. Ordinarily, a contract is assignable. Thus, a contract for the sale and delivery of all the grapes of a certain quality which the seller was to raise on a certain vineyard for ten years was assignable to the person who purchased the seller's land (La Rue v. Groezinger, 84 Cal. 281, 24 P. 42).

Under the U.C.C., Section 2–210, contracts are assignable subject to certain restrictions.

An offer is not assignable, but an option contract, which is a contract whereby the seller keeps the offer open, is assignable.

3. CONTRACTS NOT ASSIGNABLE

A. Personal Service Contracts

If the contract calls for the skill, credit, or other personal quality of the promisor, it is not assignable since the performance received from the assignee would be different from that required by the contract; e.g., a famous singer cannot assign his contract to sing at a certain night club to another singer.

B. Express Provision

If the contract contains an express provision against assignment ("This contract is not assignable by either party"), generally the provision will be upheld and the contract will not be assignable; e.g., lease containing express provision against assignment without written permission of landlord generally upheld. However, this clause can be waived; e.g., implied waiver when nonassigning party (landlord) accepted rent from assignee (new tenant).

A provision against assigning a *contract* would not prohibit an assignment of the *money due* or to *become due* under the contract, nor of money *damages* for breach of the contract.

There is a conflict of authority as to the validity of an express prohibition of an assignment of *money due* under a contract. Most jurisdictions hold the restriction invalid because it restricts the assignor's right to assign a property interest, while the others hold the prohibition valid on the theory that the parties should be free to make such a prohibition in a contract.

c. Rights Under Contract of Employment

Where there is an existing contract of employment, money to become due or other rights thereunder may be assigned (Restatement of Contracts, Section 154). However, where the contract of employment is not yet in existence, the general rule is that the assignment is not enforceable; e.g., cannot assign future wages unless employed.

d. Claims for Personal Wrongs

A right of action which is founded on a wrong of purely personal nature is not assignable; e.g., slander, assault and battery, negligent personal injuries. However, the *judgment* based on such action is assignable.

e. Under the U.C.C.

Under Section 2–210(2) an assignment may be prohibited if it treats the non-assigning party unfairly by (1) materially changing his duty, (2) materially increasing his burden or risk, or (3) materially impairing his chance of obtaining return performance.

Under Section 2–210(2) a right to *money damages* for breach of contract may be assigned despite agreement otherwise.

Under Section 9–318(4) sums due and to become due under contracts of sale can be assigned despite a provision to the contrary even if made to an assignee who took with full knowledge that the account debtor had sought to prohibit or restrict assignment of the claims. The Official Comment states "as accounts and other rights under contracts have become the collateral which secures an ever increasing number of financing transactions, it has been necessary to reshape the law so that these intangibles, like negotiable instruments and negotiable documents of title, can be freely assigned".

4. EFFECT OF ASSIGNMENT

a. Liability of Assignor

The assignor cannot escape his burdens on the contract by an assignment. He still remains liable as a surety to the promisee, and this is true even though the assignee *assumes* the obligations of the contract. In other words, he can assign the benefits of the contract but is still liable for the burdens.

U.C.C. Section 2–210(1) states "No delegation of performance relieves the party delegating of any duty to perform or any liability for breach".

B. Liability of Assignee

The assignee does not become bound to perform the obligations of the assignor by merely accepting the assignment. However, if he expressly *assumes* the assignor's promise to perform, he is liable to the creditor since the creditor would be a third party beneficiary to such an assignment if it appeared that it was made for the creditor's benefit. For example, if a tenant assigns a lease, the assignee is not liable for future rents if he vacates the property prior to the end of the term unless he expressly assumes the burdens of the lease.

Under *Section 2–210(4) of the U.C.C.*, an acceptance by the assignee of an assignment of a contract constitutes a *promise* by the assignee to perform the duties of the assignor (in the absence of language or circumstances to the contrary). The promise is enforceable by either the assignor or the other party to the original contract. This type of assignment is the normal commercial assignment (substitution of the assignee for the assignor both as to rights and duties), and should be distinguished from a financing assignment in which only the assignor's rights are transferred.

Under *Section 2–210(5) of the U.C.C.* the non-assigning original party has a stake in the reliability of the person with whom he has closed the original contract, and is therefore entitled to due assurance that any delegated performance will be properly forthcoming; thus, he may treat the assignment as creating reasonable grounds for insecurity and demand assurances from the assignee; e. g., a purchaser of goods to be specially manufactured feels insecure when the manufacturer assigns the contract to a second unknown manufacturer so the purchaser demands a provision for withholding stated amounts of the purchase price until satisfactory completion of the stated performance.

C. Rights of Assignee

After the assignment, the assignee has all of the legal rights of the assignor; however, to assert these rights, the assignee must give notice to the non-assigning original party (the obligor-debtor). After the assignee gives notice to the obligor of the assignment, payment by the obligor to the *assignor* does not extinguish the obligation; i. e., the debtor must pay the *assignee* after *actual notice* of the assignment. (For similar account debtor rule see *U.C.C. Section 9–318 (3)*).

After the assignment, the assignee "stands in the shoes" of the assignor. In other words, the assignee takes all the rights of the assignor subject to any defenses which the obligor has against the assignor prior to the notice of the assignment. For example, a painter may assign his claim for payment resulting from the painting of a home to a collection agency, but the home owner may assert against the collection agency-assignee any claims for damages sustained by the owner because the painter did not properly perform the contract which necessitated the owner paying a second painter to correct the defective work.

Clauses are frequently inserted in installment contracts which provide that the buyer will not assert any defenses he may have (such as a defective product) against an assignee of the contract (a financing company). See *U.C.C. Section 9–206(1).* These clauses have led to litigation and their present validity under case law is in confusion. In some jurisdictions they have been held void as attempts to create negotiable instruments outside the framework of Article 3, or on grounds of public policy. In some states such waivers have been invalidated by statute. In some states courts have found such waivers invalid because of the close connection the assignee of the contract has with the original transaction.

For defenses account debtor has against assignee see *U.C.C. Section 9–318(1).*

5. PRIORITIES AMONG SUCCESSIVE ASSIGNEES

Sometimes the assignor, due to mistake or fraud, assigns the same claim to more than one assignee. For example, creditor assigns a claim for $1,000.00 to A on January 10 and then assigns the same claim to B on January 12. Which assignee prevails against the debtor?

A. Assignee First in Time

The so-called American rule, adopted by the Restatement of Contracts, Section 173 and most states, including New York, gives priority to the assignee first in time on the theory that the legal title passed from the assignor after the first assignment, and thus he has nothing left to assign to the second assignee. Of course, the second assignee will have a cause of action against the assignor.

B. First Assignee to Give Notice

The minority rule, followed by California, gives priority to the assignee who first gives notice to the obligor on the theory that an assignment should be governed by equitable rules; i.e., the first assignee should perfect his right by giving notice to the debtor since if he fails to do so, he leaves the assignor with the power to deceive the second assignee, an innocent party, by another assignment.

C. The U.C.C.

In the area of accounts receivable, the *U.C.C.* (Article 9) attempts to alleviate the problem of priorities by requiring the filing of the assignment of accounts receivable in a "financing statement" (see

Chapter XXII, infra). This gives notice to all prospective purchasers of the accounts receivable that they have previously been assigned.

---

1. *Third Party Donee Beneficiary Contracts are Enforceable*

EVANS v. OTIS ELEVATOR CO.

403 Pa. 13, 168 A.2d 573 (1961).

BENJAMIN R. JONES, Justice. On July 20, 1955, Harry P. Evans [Evans], employed as a stock clerk by Sperling Tobacco Company [Sperling] in Wilkes-Barre, Pa., was operating Sperling's freight elevator which, while descending, struck something which tilted the left side of the elevator cage whereupon a board from the elevator roof fell on Evans' head, causing serious injuries. Evans instituted this trespass action * * * against Otis Elevator Company [Otis], alleging that Otis was negligent in failing to properly inspect the elevator and in failing to notify Evans or Sperling of its defective and dangerous condition. * * * After a jury trial before the Honorable Frank L. Pinola, the jury returned a verdict in Evans' favor against Otis in the amount of $65,000 * * * Otis has taken these appeals.

Otis first contends that * * * Otis owed no duty to Evans, * * * In 1953, Otis and Sperling entered in a written agreement which was in effect on the date of the accident. Under the terms of that agreement, Otis agreed to furnish to Sperling "Otis Service" on its elevator for $17.75 each month. This "Otis Service" was "to consist of a semi-monthly examination of the elevator, including oiling and cleaning machine, motor and controller; greasing or oiling bearings and guides; making necessary minor adjustments." Otis also undertook to "examine, lubricate and adjust the following necessary equipment: COA: Interlocks, Car gates, Freight gates, Hall buttons. Hoistway doors, door hinges, door latches, door knobs and when necessary: Oil, grease, rope preservatives and cleaning materials." * * *

Otis argues that this agreement imposed upon it no duty or obligation to Evans and that Evans, not a party to this agreement, has no standing to complain of an injury allegedly sustained by reason of the manner in which Otis performed this agreement. Generally a party to a contract does not become liable for a breach thereof to one who is not a party thereto. However, a party to a contract by the very nature of his contractual undertaking may place himself in such a position that the law will impose upon him a duty to perform his contractual undertaking in such manner that third persons—strangers to the contract—will not be injured thereby; * * * It is not the contract *per se* which creates the duty; it is the law which imposes the duty because of the nature of the undertaking in the contract. If a person undertakes by contract to make periodic examinations and inspections of equipment, such as elevators, he should reasonably foresee that a normal and natural result of his failure to properly perform such undertaking might result in injury not only to the owner of the equipment but also to third persons, including the owner's employees: * * * The orbit of Otis' duty to third persons is measured by the nature and scope of his contractual undertaking with Sperling and, if, as presently appears, Otis undertook to inspect the elevator at regular intervals, and, if the elevator was in a defective or dangerous condition discoverable by reasonable inspection, Otis would be liable to third persons, regardless of any privity of contract, who might be injured by Otis' failure to properly perform its contractual undertaking of inspection. Such principle finds support in reason, justice and precedent: * * *

Otis' reasons for a new trial as to Evans are without merit and the appeal from the verdict for Evans on this ground is not well taken.

[Judgment for plaintiff.]

---

2. Incidental Third Party Beneficiary Contracts Not Enforceable

COMPAGNIE NATIONALE AIR FRANCE v. PORT OF NEW YORK AUTHORITY

427 F.2d 951 (C.A.N.Y., 1970).

IRVING R. KAUFMAN, Circuit Judge. Shortly before 9 P.M. on the evening of August 13, 1964, a Boeing 707 owned by Compagnie Nationale Air France landed at John F. Kennedy International Airport in New York, after a trip from Paris. It taxied north on the outer perimeter runway until it reached Taxiway Juliet (also called Taxiway J), which permitted a left turn towards gate 21 at the International Arrivals Building, where the passengers were to disembark.

Taxiway J is divided into two parts, separated by a small island. Taxiway J North was unobstructed and led directly to gate 21; the Air France jet however, departed from the yellow line leading through J North, turned left into Taxiway J South, proceeded through a barricade marked by flags and lights, and nosed gently over into a construction ditch. Damage was considerable, and Air France instituted the instant action against the Port Authority (which maintains the airport), the United States (which employs the traffic controllers), the Lummus Company (general contractor for the construction involved) and M. Parisi & Son, Inc. (who dug the ditch). Employing considerable ingenuity as well as diligence, Air France sued all defendants for negligence in constructing and marking the ditch, the Port Authority for maintaining a nuisance, and the Authority, Lummus, and Parisi for breach of contract on the theory that Air France was a third party beneficiary to the construction contracts.

* * *

As a second cause of action, Air France alleged that it was the beneficiary of the construction contracts between the Port Authority and Lummus, and between Lummus and Parisi. It argued that it occupied the position of a third party beneficiary * * * The District Court dismissed these claims at the close of plaintiff's case. Air France, while assigning the dismissal as error, does not appear to contest the issue vigorously, and we can understand its judgment. A third party beneficiary may recover under New York law only where the parties to the contract intend to confer a benefit upon him; he may not sue on the contract when the benefit is purely incidental to the performance of the contract. * * * Air France failed to show that any of the parties intended safety features in the contract to be for its benefit, and failed to suggest any similar instances in which the New York courts have found a third party beneficiary relationship. See Prescott v. Collins, 263 App.Div. 690, 35 N.Y.S.2d 135, appeal dismissed, 290 N.Y. 811, 50 N.E.2d 232 (1942) (provision in construction contract between state and contractor requiring precautions to prevent damage to persons or property by explosives held to give injured passerby no third party beneficiary rights). * * * [D]ismissal of the third party beneficiary claim is affirmed.

---

3. Contracts Which Assignee May Perform

LA RUE v. GROEZINGER

84 Cal. 281, 24 P. 42 (1890).

HAYNE, C. This was an action for damages for the breach of a contract to buy grapes. The substance of the material portions of the contract was as follows:

One Hopper agreed to sell all the grapes which he might raise during a period of ten years * * *. In consideration whereof the defendant agreed to accept the grapes and pay for them (after delivery) at the rate of $25 per ton * * *.

The parties performed this contract for five years. At the end of that time, viz., in October, 1885, Hopper conveyed the vineyard and assigned the contract to the plaintiff. * * * The crop of the following year was grown, gathered, and tendered by the plaintiff. The defendant refused to accept it, saying that he had no contract with the plaintiff, and * * * that the contract was not assignable. * * * The Civil Code of this state provides that written contracts "for the payment of money or personal property" may be transferred * * *. It is clear, however, that the provision cannot be construed to render assignable all contracts whatever, regardless of their nature or effect, but must be taken with some qualification.

In the first place, it was not intended to render null any agreement that the parties may have made on the subject. Hence, if the contract itself provides in terms that it is not transferable, it certainly cannot be transferred, although it otherwise might be so. * * *

In the next place, although the language may not show an intention that the contract should not be assigned, yet the nature of the case may be such that performance by another would be *an essentially different thing* from that contracted for. Thus a picture by one artist is an essentially different thing from a picture on the same subject by another artist; and so of a book composed by an author, or any other act or thing where the skill, credit, or other personal quality or circumstance of the party is a distinctive characteristic of the thing contracted for, or a material inducement to the contract. * * *

If, therefore, the case before us comes within either of the qualifications above stated, then it must be conceded that the contract was not assignable. * * * There is nothing in the language which excludes the idea of performance by another * * * and * * * there is nothing in the nature or circumstances of the case which shows that the skill or other personal quality of the party was a distinctive characteristic of the thing stipulated for, or a material inducement to the contract. There is no evidence that grapes for wine-making, containing a specified amount of saccharine matter, raised upon a particular vineyard by one man, would necessarily or probably be different from grapes raised from the same vines by another man. * * *

It is not impossible that one man might have some peculiar skill or secret by which he could raise better grapes from the same vines than other men could. But there is no evidence that there was any such peculiarity about the original owner of this vineyard, and we do not think that the court will *assume* that there was. * * *
We cannot see any reason that would make this contract nonassignable * * *.

[Judgment for plaintiff.]

---

4. *Ratification of Assignment of Personal Service Contracts*

SEALE v. BATES

145 Colo. 430, 359 P.2d 356 (1961).

DOYLE, Justice. Plaintiffs in error will be referred to by name or as they were designated in the trial court where they were plaintiffs in an action against John Bates, individually, the Bates Dance Studio,

Inc. and the Dance Studio of Denver, Inc. The Seales sought to recover $2,040 which had been paid to the Bates Dance Studio to defray the cost of 300 hours of dance instruction. * * * From their complaints it would appear that the contracts which the plaintiffs entered into with the Bates Dance Studio had been assigned to the Dance Studio of Denver, doing business as Dale Dance Studio. * * * The Seales were told that the "students and the instructors, the entire organization was transferred to the Dale Studios; that we would have the same instructors, the same instruction, a continuation of what we had had at Bates." They proceeded to take lessons at Dale, but after some 30 one-half hours of instruction they became dissatisfied with the conditions. * * * This dissatisfaction arose from the fact that the room was much smaller and more crowded and the music from another room interfered with the lessons. Each of the Seales did not have his or her own instructor, Mr. Seale being required to take his lessons from a male instructor; there were difficulties in getting appointments and on some occasions when appointments were made an instructor would not be available. * * As a result of this dissatisfaction, Mr. and Mrs. Seale stopped taking lessons in May of 1957. The following August they complained to Mr. John Bates of the Bates Studio and demanded that he refund their money or make proper arrangements for completing their contract. Bates informed them that his school was then closed and that there was no money to reimburse them.

* * * The basis for dispositions as to the Bates and Dale Studios was the assent of the plaintiffs to the assumption by Dale of the obligations under the contracts; that this acceptance of Dale was apparent from the plaintiffs' conduct. * * *

In seeking reversal, plaintiffs assert that the trial court erred in: * * *

In failing to hold that the duties under these contracts were personal, therefore non-assignable.

* * * The argument of plaintiffs that this was a personal service contract and therefore non-assignable without their consent is valid. * * * This, however, does not furnish a reason for holding that plaintiffs are now entitled to recover. On the contrary, there *is* evidence to support the trial court's finding and conclusion that the plaintiffs accepted the assignment as such; they did not elect to rescind when it was brought to their attention that the contracts had been assigned to Dale Dance Studio. The undisputed evidence shows that they accepted the assignment and proceeded to take lessons from the Dale Dance Studio. This conduct is inconsistent with plaintiffs' present theory that they at all times objected to the assignment. Had they refused to receive instruction from Dale and had they taken the position that their contract was with Bates and no other, there would be substance to their present contention that this violation justified the rescission. * * * Accordingly the

trial court's finding and conclusion that the plaintiffs waived any rights which may have arisen from the assignment must be upheld. * * *

[Judgment for defendant.]

---

5. *Liability of Assignor Not Terminated by Assignment*

CRANE v. KILDORF, EXR.

91 Ill. 567 (1879).

Josiah Evans was under contract to sell and deliver certain corn to George Spurck. This contract was assigned by Spurck to the defendant, and the corn was delivered by Evans to the assignee. The assignee having refused to pay Evans the purchase price, $255, it was subsequently collected by Evans from Spurck. The present action was brought by Spurck's executor to recover the $255. Defendant [Crane] contends that Spurck was under no duty to pay Evans after he had assigned the contract, and therefore that, being a mere volunteer, Spurck had no right to recover it from defendant.

Mr. Chief Justice CRAIG. * * * It is * * * contended that the delivery of the corn by Evans to Crane & Co. was a recognition of the assignment of the contract, and in effect released Spurck from any liability to Evans on the original contract, and that Spurck's payment was that of a mere volunteer.

Under the contract, the corn was to be delivered to Spurck at Philadelphia. He had the undoubted right to direct that the corn should be delivered to any other person at the place of delivery he might name. While Spurck had this right, he could not, without the consent of Evans, release himself from that provision of the contract which obligated him to pay for the corn.

There is nothing in this record that shows that Evans agreed to release Spurck * * *. Indeed, when he commenced the delivery of the corn, he did not even know of the assignment of the contract. There is nothing in the assignment which would indicate that Crane & Co. assumed to pay Evans for the corn, and it is unreasonable to believe that he would release a man whom he doubtless knew to be responsible, and rely upon a firm who resided out of the state and with whom he had no acquaintance. The mere fact that Evans delivered the corn to Crane & Co. is of little importance. * *

Spurck was, under the contract, bound to pay for the corn; and, as he had directed the corn to be delivered to Crane & Co., no reason is perceived why he may not compel Crane & Co. to pay for the balance due on the corn they received. * * *

[The liability of an assignor is not terminated by an assignment. Judgment for Kildorf.]

6. Assignment Distinguished From Negotiation

BINGHAM v. GOSHEN NATIONAL BANK

118 N.Y. 349, 23 N.E. 180 (1890).

At the request of one Brown, Bingham cashed for him a $5,000 check certified by the defendant bank. It was later discovered that Brown had obtained the check fraudulently and that he fled with the money to Canada. Unfortunately Bingham had failed to notice that Brown had not endorsed the check, yet he now sues to recover the amount of the check from the defendant bank. The bank contends that, since Brown's fraud would prevent Brown from maintaining such an action as this, the plaintiff, who took the check from Brown, would have no greater rights than Brown himself.

PARKER, J. * * * It is too well settled by authority, both in England and in this country, to permit of questioning, that the purchaser of a draft, or check, who obtains title without an endorsement by the payee, holds it subject to all equities and defenses existing between the original parties, even though he has paid full consideration, without notice of the existence of such equities and defenses. * * *

The reasoning on which this doctrine is founded may be briefly stated as follows: The general rule is that no one can transfer a better title than he possesses. An exception arises out of the rule of the law-merchant, as to negotiable instruments. It is founded on the commercial policy of sustaining the credit of commercial paper. Being treated as currency in commercial transactions, such instruments are subject to the same rule as money. If transferred by endorsement, for value, in good faith and before maturity, they become available in the hands of the holder, notwithstanding the existence of * * * defenses which would have rendered them unavailable in the hands of a prior holder. [See Chapter 37.]

This rule is only applicable to negotiable instruments which are negotiated according to the law-merchant. When, as in this case, such an instrument is transferred but without an endorsement, it is treated as a chose in action assigned to the purchaser. The assignee acquires all the title of the assignor and may maintain an action thereon in his own name. And like other choses in action it is subject to all the equities and defenses existing in favor of the maker or acceptor against the previous holder. * * * Therefore, Bingham & Co. were subject to the defense existing in favor of the bank as against Brown * * *. Having taken title by assignment, for such was the legal effect of the transaction, * * * the defense of the bank against Brown became effectual as a defense against a recovery on the check in the hands of the plaintiffs as well * * *.

[Judgment for defendant.]

PROBLEMS

1. Mr. Smith takes out a policy of insurance on his life with his mother as the beneficiary. Several years later Mr. Smith marries and desires to change the beneficiary of the policy to his wife. Discuss his right to do so without permission of his mother.

2. S entered into a contract with B to sell a going business to him. The sales price was to be paid in installments. Shortly thereafter B assigned the contract to T who assumed all the liabilities and obligations under the contract. Prior to complete payment of the sales price, T assigned the contract to X who assumed all the liabilities and obligations. Shortly thereafter X became insolvent. S seeks a judgment against B and T. B defends on the ground he is under no obligation to pay since T assumed all liabilities and obligations. T defends on the ground that the second assignment operated as a rescission of the agreement between B and T. Decision?

3. A has been injured in an automobile accident and retains B as his attorney to represent him. Later B assigns the retainer contract to T without A's permission. A seeks your advice as to whether he must accept T as his new attorney.

4. Seller and buyer enter into a contract for the sale of a carload of tomatoes. The contract states that the right of either party to money damages in case of breach of contract cannot be assigned. The seller delivers buyer inferior goods causing him $1,000.00 in damages. Buyer assigns his action to a collection agency for collection. Seller defends on the grounds the contract prohibited assignment of the claim. Decision?

5. S sold an automobile to B by a contract which contained a clause prohibiting S from assigning the money due under the contract. S needs money and desires to assign the contract to T who knows of the prohibiting clause. Can S assign the contract without B's permission?

6. Tenant assigns the balance of his five year store lease to assignee who assumes all of the burdens of the lease. Shortly after the assignment, the assignee becomes bankrupt. The landlord seeks unpaid and future rentals for the balance of the term from the tenant. Tenant defends on the ground that he had assigned the lease and the assignee expressly assumed the burdens of the lease. Decision?

7. A contracted with B to do some plumbing work in B's home. A did not have a license although a statute required a license as a condition to recovering for plumbing work. After A completed the work he assigned the right to the money for the work to T. B refuses to pay T so T sues B on the contract between A and B. Decision?

8. Debtor owes creditor $1,000.00. Creditor assigns the claim to T who promptly mails notice to the debtor. The debtor, however, fails to read the notice of the assignment from T and pays the creditor in full without knowing of the assignment. T seeks payment from debtor, and debtor contends that his payment to creditor without notice is a defense. Decision?

9. Debtor owes creditor $1,000.00. Creditor assigns the claims to A on June 1 and then by mistake assigns the same claim to B on June 4. On June 4, B gives notice of the assignment to debtor. On June 5, A gives notice of the assignment to the debtor. Both A and B claim the $1,000.00 from debtor. Who prevails?

Part 3

THE LAW OF SALES

Chapter 17

INTRODUCTION

A. NATURE OF SALES

1. IN GENERAL

A "sale" consists of the passing of title from the seller to the buyer for a price (*U.C.C.*, Section 2–106(1)); e.g., housewife buys a bottle of milk at the store. Although the basic principles of the law of contracts apply to the law of sales, the Uniform Commercial Code contains many variations. Many of the variations were covered in Part Two, The Law of Contracts. Others will be stated in Part Three. Part Three contains the most important laws relating to sales in the following order:

1. Introduction.
2. Transfer of Title and Risk of Loss.
3. Performance of the Contract.
4. Remedies of the Seller and the Buyer.
5. Warranties and Products Liability.
6. Documents of Title and Secured Transactions.

2. CONTRACT TO SELL

There is a distinction between a "sale" and a "contract *to* sell". In a sale title can pass at the time the contract is made, whereas in a contract to sell title passes at a future time; e.g., contract to sell crops to be grown in the future. The importance of title is discussed in the next chapter.

There can be no *sale* of goods not in existence; e.g., fish to be caught in the ocean or goods to be manufactured. Such an attempted sale only operates as a contract *to* sell the goods (*U.C.C.*, Section 2–105(2)). Of course, if the seller cannot perform the contract to sell, he will be liable for breach of contract unless he has a valid and legal defense.

3. FUNGIBLE GOODS

" 'Fungible' with respect to goods or securities means goods or securities of which any unit is, by nature or usage of trade, the equivalent of any other like unit" (*U.C.C.*, Section 1–201(17)). For example, oil, corn, flour, and wheat are considered fungible goods by nature. Goods such as bales of cotton, sacks of sugar, and cases of canned goods, can be considered as fungible by usage of trade.

In the case of fungible goods where the seller purports to sell a portion of the mass to the buyer, the buyer becomes an owner in common with the seller in the proportion the amount sold bears to the amount in the mass at the time of the sale. For example, the seller has 1,000 bushels of wheat in a bin. The buyer and the seller enter into a contract whereby the buyer purchases 500 of the bushels in the bin. When the contract is entered into, the seller and the buyer own the wheat as tenants in common even though the wheat has not been divided (*U.C.C.*, Section 2–105(4)). The buyer cannot own title to a specific 500 bushels of wheat until that amount of wheat has been separated from the mass. Precisely how and when title passes to the buyer is discussed in the next chapter.

4. CONDITIONAL SALE OR SECURITY AGREEMENT

A conditional sale is a transfer of title on a condition. The condition usually is the payment of money; e.g., seller sells a television set to the buyer transferring the possession at the time of the contract but withholding the transfer of the title until the buyer makes complete payment. The contract provides the seller with the right to peaceably retake possession of the property if the buyer defaults. If the property is destroyed before full payment, the seller loses his security; and the buyer loses the property but must still pay the balance due on the contract. To cover this loss, the typical contract provides that the buyer must take out an insurance policy with a loss payable clause to the seller.

Under the Code, a conditional sales contract is known as a "security agreement" rather than as a conditional sale.

5. BULK SALES

A bulk sale is a transfer in bulk (not in the ordinary course of the transferor's business) of a substantial part of the materials, supplies, merchandise, or other inventory, including equipment, of the enterprise (*U.C.C.*, Section 6–102).

To protect the creditors of the merchant from the possibility that he may sell all of the inventory and then disappear with the money, the *U.C.C.*, Article 6, provides that advance notice of the sale must be given to the creditors; and if notice is not given, the creditors may recover the sold property in the hands of the purchaser if he knew that no notice was given or if he did not pay value.

A sale which does not comply with Article 6 is still valid, however, between the buyer and the seller as this legislation is only for the protection of the creditors of the seller.

6. SALES BETWEEN MERCHANTS OR MERCHANT A PARTY

A merchant is a person who deals in goods which are the subject of the contract, or who holds himself out as having special knowledge or skill regarding such goods or employs an agent who holds himself out as having such special knowledge or skill (*U.C.C.,* Section 2–104(1)).

The *U.C.C.* contains fifteen sections which apply to sales between merchants or when a merchant is a party; they do not apply to non-merchants. These rules demand a higher standard of conduct on the part of merchants because merchants set the standards for business practices, and they have special knowledge in the field of trade and commerce. Some of the sections have been discussed in earlier chapters; e.g., Statute of Frauds, 2–201(2), Firm Offers, 2–205. Others will be discussed in later chapters under appropriate headings. The numbers of the sections are as follows: 2–201(2) (Statute of Frauds), 2–205 (Firm Offers), 2–207(2) (Additional Terms), 2–209 (2) (Modification), 2–312(3) (Warranty of Title), 2–314(1) (Implied Warranty), 2–326(3) (Sale on Approval), 2–327(1)(c) (Special Incidents of Sale), 2–402(2) (Rights of Seller's Creditors), 2–403(2) (Entrusting of Possession), 2–509(3) (Risk of Loss), 2–603 (1)(2) (Buyer's Duties), 2–605(1)(b) (Waiver), 2–606(1)(2) (Acceptance), 2–609(2) (Assurance).

7. AUCTION SALES

Auction sales are covered by Section 2–328 of the *U.C.C.* In a sale by auction if goods are put up in separate lots each lot is the subject of a separate sale. Title passes when the auctioneer so announces by the fall of the hammer or in other customary manner.

An auction "with reserve" is the normal procedure, and in such a sale the auctioneer may withdraw the goods at any time until he announces completion of the sale. If the sale is "without reserve" the auctioneer cannot withdraw the article or lot after he calls for bids unless no bid is made within a reasonable time. An auction is "with reserve" unless the goods are in explicit terms put up "without reserve".

---

1. *Beauty Treatment Not a Sale*

EPSTEIN v. GIANNATTASIO

25 Conn.Sup. 109, 197 A.2d 342 (1963).

LUGG, Judge. On or about 5 October, 1962, the plaintiff visited a beauty parlor, conducted by the defendant Giannattasio, for the purpose of receiving a beauty treatment. During the course of that treatment, Giannattasio used a product called "Zotos 30-day Color," manufactured by defendant Sales Affiliates, Inc., and a prebleach manufactured by defendant Clairol, Inc. The plaintiff claims that as a result of the treatment she suffered acute dermatitis, disfigurement resulting from loss of hair, and other injuries and damages. * * *

The issue reduces itself to the simple one of whether or not the use of the products involved in the course of the beauty treatment amounts to a sale or a contract for sale of goods under the pertinent sections of the code. * * * " 'Goods' means all things, including specially manufactured goods, which are movable at the time of identification to the contract for sale * * *."

As the complaint alleges, the plaintiff asked Giannattasio for a beauty treatment, and not for the purchase of goods. From such language, it could not be inferred that it was the intention of either party that the transaction be a transaction in goods within the meaning of the code. This claim of the plaintiff is hence distinguished more by the ingenuity of its conception than by the strength of its persuasion. * * *

There are other cases, involving differing facts, which have decided that "when service is the predominant, and transfer of title to personal property the incidental, feature of a transaction, the transaction is not a sale of goods within the application of statutes relating to sales. * * * When this plaintiff made her arrangement with the beauty parlor, she did so as the complaint sets forth: "* * * for the purpose of receiving a beauty treatment." Obviously, the subject of the contract was not a sale of goods but the rendition of services. The materials used in the performance of those services were patently incidental to that subject, which was a treatment and not the purchase of an article. * * *

[Judgment for defendant.]

---

2. *Contract to Sell*

LOW v. PEW

108 Mass. 347 (1871).

The owner of a fishing schooner purported to make a present sale to Low of all the halibut to be caught during the next trip of the vessel to the Grand Banks. Low paid the full price of the fish at the time the contract was made. The schooner made a successful voyage, but the owner became bankrupt before the vessel returned. Low now seeks to obtain possession of the fish, contending that title passed to him when the contract was made. The defendant, who represents the bankrupt, contends that no title could pass to property not owned by the seller at the time the contract was made, and that the transaction at most was a mere contract to sell.

MORTON, J. * * * The question in the case therefore is whether a sale of halibut afterwards to be caught is valid, so as to pass to the purchaser the property in them when caught. It is an elementary principle of the law of sales, that a man cannot grant personal property in which he has no interest or title. To be able to sell property, he must have a vested right in it at the time of the sale. * * *

In the case at bar, the sellers, at the time of the sale, had no interest in the thing sold. There was a possibility that they might catch halibut; but it was a mere possibility and expectancy, coupled with no interest. We are of opinion that they had no actual or potential possession of, or interest in, the fish; and that the sale to the plaintiff was void. * * *

[Judgment for defendant.]

---

3. A Farmer is Not a Merchant Under U.C.C.

COOK GRAINS, INC. v. FALLIS

239 Ark. 962, 395 S.W.2d 555 (1965).

ROBINSON, Justice. [Suit for breach of contract.] Appellant, Cook Grains, Inc., filed this suit alleging that it entered into a valid contract with appellee, Paul Fallis, whereby Fallis sold and agreed to deliver to Cook 5,000 bushels of soybeans at $2.54 per bushel. It is alleged that Fallis breached the alleged contract by failing to deliver the beans, and that as a result thereof Cook has been damaged in the sum of $1,287.50. There was a judgment for Fallis. The grain company has appealed. * * *

Following the discussion or sale, whichever it was, between Horton and Fallis, appellant grain company prepared and mailed to Fallis a proposed contract in writing which provided that Fallis sold to the grain company 5,000 bushels of beans. The instrument was signed by the grain company and it would have been bound thereby if Fallis had signed the paper, but Fallis did not sign the instrument and did not return it to the grain company. Later, Fallis refused to deliver the beans and the grain company filed suit. * * *

The appellant grain company concedes that ordinarily the alleged cause of action would be barred by the statute of frauds, but contends that here the alleged sale is taken out of the statute of frauds by the Uniform Commercial Code. * * *

> "(2) Between merchants if within a reasonable time a writing in confirmation of the contract and sufficient against the sender is received and the party receiving it has reason to know its contents, it satisfies the requirements of subsection (1) against such party unless written notice of objection to its contents is given within ten [10] days after it is received. * * *"

Thus, it will be seen that under the statute, if appellee is a merchant he would be liable on the alleged contract because he did not, within ten days, given written notice that he rejected it.

The solution of the case turns on the point of whether the appellee Fallis is a "merchant" within the meaning of the statute. * *

> " 'Merchant' means a person who deals in goods of the kind or otherwise by his occupation holds himself out as having knowledge or skill peculiar to the practices or goods involved in the transaction or to whom such knowledge or skill may be attributed by his employment of an agent or broker or other intermediary who by his occupation holds himself out as having such knowledge or skill. * * *"

There is not a scintilla of evidence in the record, or proffered as evidence, that appellee is a dealer in goods of the kind or by his occupation holds himself out as having knowledge or a skill peculiar to the practices of goods involved in the transaction, and no such knowledge or skill can be attributed to him.

The evidence in this case is that appellee is a farmer and nothing else. He farms about 550 acres and there is no showing that he has any other occupation.

* * * There is nothing whatever in the statute indicating that the word "merchant" should apply to a farmer when he is acting in the capacity of a farmer, and he comes within that category when he is merely trying to sell the commodities he has raised. * * *

The judgment is affirmed.

---

4. Bulk Sales Law

BROOKS v. LAMBERT

10 D. & C.2d 237 (Pa., 1957).

DIGGINS, J. March 1, 1957. This is an action * * * wherein plaintiffs are judgment creditors against Louis Lambert and have two judgments against John S. McCleary Republican Club as well.

The record also discloses that on or about August 10, 1956, Louis Lambert entered into a written agreement with Isadore Gus Weinberg, transferring, for a consideration of $1,500, personal property equipment and fixtures, excluding the club liquor license, of the Delaware County Athletic Association, and these are the same goods which are the subject matter of this action. * * *

The bill of complaint seeks to set aside the * * * alleged sale by Lambert to Weinberg on the ground that neither complied with the bulk sales provisions of the Uniform Commercial Code. * * *

"(1) A 'bulk transfer' is any transfer in bulk and not in the ordinary course of the transferor's business of a major part of the materials, supplies, merchandise or other inventory. * * *

"(2) A transfer of a substantial part of the equipment of such an enterprise is a bulk transfer if it is made in connection with a bulk transfer of inventory, but not otherwise."

The question of whether or not the Uniform Commercial Code applies to a business which has a liquor license has been the subject of interpretation by lower courts during the operation of the old Bulk Sales Act * * *, of which, for all practical purposes, the pertinent sections of the Uniform Commercial Code are reenacted. These cases hold that even though the liquor inventory is not the subject of any normal sale, the other inventory is, that is to say, a restaurant business with a liquor license or a combination bar and taproom, or a combination restaurant and taproom, is within the contemplation of the act as to all save presumably the liquor itself which under the liquor control board's regulations, can only be sold to another licensee under its supervision and approval. * * * However, the Uniform Commercial Code * * * provides that a transfer of a substantial part of the equipment of such an enterprise is a bulk transfer if it is made in connection with the bulk transfer of inventory, but not otherwise. Since by its very terms, unchallenged here, this sale included only personal property, equipment and fixtures, without reference to stock in trade, which would seem normal under the circumstances, because the little stock in trade that such a business enterprise as here involved would have would consist of goods unsaleable in bulk. * * *

It therefore follows that the sale covered by the agreement dated August 10, 1956, between Louis Lambert and Isadore Gus Weinberg was not prohibited by the Uniform Commercial Code. * * *

[Judgment for defendant.]

---

5. *Sale by Auction*

HAWAII JEWELERS ASSOCIATION v. FINE ARTS GALLERY, INC.

463 P.2d 914 (Hawaii, 1970).

ABE, Justice. The defendant, Fine Arts Gallery, Inc., commenced business on July 5, 1968, at 2270 Kalakaua Avenue, in Waikiki, Honolulu, Hawaii, advertising its business as "auction." It also gave notice of "auction" to the public by bulkmail. At the premises there were several signs reading "auction."

The plaintiff, Hawaii Jewelers Association, an unincorporated trade association, brought this action against the defendant corporation and Stanton M. Bier, as principal stockholder and "auctioneer," pursuant to HRS § 445–32 to enjoin the operation by the defendants of a public auction without having first obtained a license as required by HRS § 445–7; without designating a public auction room as required by HRS § 445–29; and without obtaining a bond as required by HRS § 445–31.

The defendants contended in the trial court that the following statement or notice "OUR GOLDEN RULE 30 day money back guarantee on every sale" appearing in newspaper advertisements and on the inside back cover of the catalogue gave a buyer a right to return any article for any or no reason within 30 days and to a refund of the purchase price. Therefore, they argue that though the sale was conducted by competitive bidding, they were not conducting an auction.

The trial court on July 15, 1968, * * * issued a preliminary injunction.

Subsequently, after a hearing on October 25, 1968, the preliminary injunction was made permanent and the final order was entered on November 6, 1968. Defendants appealed.

* * *

The defendants' contention is that the "thirty day money back guarantee" postpones the transfer to purchasers of title to articles and therefore the operation was not an auction within the provisions of the Uniform Commercial Code, HRS § 490:2–328. The pertinent portion of the provision reads as follows:

> "*Sale by auction.* (1) In a sale by auction if goods are put up in lots each lot is the subject of a separate sale.
>
> (2) A sale by auction is complete when the auctioneer so announces by the fall of the hammer or in other customary manner. * * *"

The section defines sale by auction, but we believe that it does not mean that one cannot enter into a sales contract or an agreement of sale by way of an auction; or that where all other incidents of an "auction" are present, the transaction is not an auction if title to the chattel is not transferred upon the fall of the hammer.

There are cases holding that upon the acceptance of a bid by a fall of the hammer at an auction, one has contractual rights which may be enforced, but title to a chattel auctioned is not transferred to a successful bidder. The relationship between a vendor and a vendee, upon the acceptance of the vendee's bid at an auction, is the same as between a promissor and a promissee of an executory contract of sale conventionally entered into. * * *

However, for the determination of this action it is not necessary for this court to decide that point because here we hold that upon the fall of the hammer, title to a chattel auctioned was transferred to a successful bidder. We believe that defendants and successful bidders intended that title would pass upon the fall of the hammer and that purchasers could do as they pleased with the goods purchased—give or sell them to third parties. The "thirty day money back guarantee" was either an option given a successful bidder to return the goods and get a refund of money paid within 30 days or a continuing offer of defendants to repurchase the goods for a period of 30 days from the date of sale. It was similar to a satisfaction or money back guarantee given purchasers under a "sale or return" contract which gives the buyer an option or right to return the goods. * * *

As we have stated the "thirty day money back guarantee" did not prevent or postpone the transfer of the title to chattels upon the fall of the hammer and we hold that defendants were conducting a public auction within the meaning of HRS §§ 445–21 to 38, but without meeting the requirements of HRS §§ 445–7, 445–29, and 445–31. Therefore, the trial court properly issued a permanent injunction under the provisions of HRS § 445–32 to enjoin defendants from conducting an auction.

PROBLEMS

1. P was a patient in the XYZ hospital. During the course of his treatment he was given a blood transfusion. The transfusion was listed as a separate item on his hospital bill. P contracted serum hepatitis from the blood used in the transfusion which resulted in his death. P's heirs brought suit against the hospital on the theory that the transfusion was a sale of blood which carried with it an implied warranty that the blood was fit for use. XYZ does not argue the law of implied warranty but claims that the transfusion was merely a service and not a sale. Decision?

2. Seller and buyer enter into a contract whereby the buyer purchases a freezer-refrigerator combination from the seller on an installment plan. Seller is to retain the legal-security title until the appliance is paid for. Shortly after the purchase the appliance is destroyed due to a fire in the buyer's home. Buyer refuses to pay the balance contending that since the seller retained legal title he must bear the loss. Decision?

3. S made a sale of his grocery store to B which included all of the inventory. S did not notify his creditors of the sale, but he did place an advertisement in the local newspaper that he was going to sell his store to B. Neither S nor B knew of the legal requirements necessary to validate a bulk sale. B paid adequate value for the store. After S received the money he left the area and his whereabouts are unknown. The creditors seek your advice.

4. Buyer telephones seller and orders some records for the price of $1,000.00 for resale in his retail record shop. Seller sends a letter confirming the order stating the details of the agreement which the buyer receives in the ordinary course of the mails. Three weeks later pursuant to the agreement, seller ships the records; however, due to a slump in the record business, buyer refuses the records. Seller brings suit for breach of contract, and buyer defends on the ground that since he did not sign anything the agreement is unenforceable under the Statute of Frauds. Decision?

5. Seller sends a signed offer to sell 1,000 fishing rods at $10.00 each to buyer who is a retailer. Two days after the seller sends the offer, he sends a revocation of the offer to the buyer. After the buyer receives the

revocation, he mails an acceptance to the seller. Seller contends there is no contract because he can revoke his offer at any time before it is accepted and because there was no consideration paid by the buyer to keep the offer open. Buyer contends there is a contract since between merchants no consideration is necessary to keep an offer open for a reasonable time. Decision?

2-205

Chapter 18

TRANSFER OF TITLE AND RISK OF LOSS

1. When does title transfer to the buyer so that the creditors of the seller can no longer seize the goods?

2. At what point does the buyer have an insurable interest in the goods?

3. When goods are destroyed due to no fault of the buyer or seller, who must suffer the loss?

The parties can and should provide the answers to these questions by inserting appropriate clauses in the contract (*U.C.C.*, Sections 1–102(4), 2–303, 2–401(1), 2–509(4). In the absence of an explicit agreement, the *U.C.C.* attempts to provide the answers.

Under the *U.C.C.*, *title* has limited importance in determining the rights, duties and remedies of the seller and buyer. Under the *U.C.C.*, *title* and *risk of loss* are treated *separately*. Risk of loss may exist independently of ownership; e.g., buyer may have *title* to identified goods in a deliverable state in seller's possession but *risk of loss* is on seller until buyer takes physical possession of the goods (Section 2–401(3)(b)).

Title is still important, however, in determining whether the seller can recover the purchase price of the goods, which party is liable for taxes, and which creditors can seize the goods.

The *U.C.C.* states specific rules which apply to various transactions regarding the rights, duties and remedies of the buyer and the seller.

A. IDENTIFICATION

---

1. IN GENERAL

Identification means the designation of particular existing goods as the goods to which the contract refers. Goods can be identified in many ways; e.g., by being described in the contract, by shipment, by being marked, or by being set aside. In other words, identification means that the parties can say that these are the goods involved in the sale. See *U.C.C.* 2–501.

The Official Comment to Section 2–501 states "In view of the limited function of identification there is no requirement in this section that the goods be in a deliverable state or that all of the seller's duties with respect to the processing of the goods be completed in order that identification occur. For example, despite identification the risk of loss remains on the seller under the risk of loss provisions until completion of his duties as to the goods and all of his remedies remain dependent upon his not defaulting under the contract."

Identification alone does not necessarily pass title, but title cannot pass to the buyer until the goods have been identified. Identification and passage of title can occur at the same time, but often identification precedes the passage of title and gives the seller and buyer certain rights that are independent of title.

2. RIGHTS OF BUYER

Identification invests the buyer with a "*special property*" and an "*insurable interest*" in the goods (Sections 2–401(1), 2–501(1)).

The "*special property*" interest includes the right of the buyer to reclaim goods from an insolvent seller (Section 2–502), the right of the buyer to inspect the goods (Section 2–513(1)), the right of possession (Section 2–716), and the right to sue third parties for injuries to the goods (Section 2–722). These rights will be discussed in Chapter 20.

The "*insurable interest*" that is created in the buyer on identification of the goods is the interest a person must have in property to be able to insure it. Without an insurable interest, the insurance policy would be invalid as a wagering contract. The buyer can insure goods to the extent of his interest even though the goods are still in the seller's possession (Section 2–501(1)); e.g., buyer may carry insurance to protect himself from damage to his business by interruption due to nondelivery of necessary materials—this could be a loss not collectible from the seller because the seller is excused by casualty or unforeseen circumstances under Section 2–613. The practical solution regarding insurance is to have a clause in the contract stating which party is to obtain the policy and who is to pay the premiums, and such a policy should name the buyer and the seller as insureds with benefits payable according to their respective interests.

3. RIGHTS OF SELLER

If the buyer repudiates or breaches the contract after identification is made, the seller can shift to the buyer the risk of loss that occurs within a reasonable time and for which the seller is not insured (Section 2–510(3)).

Identified goods which are subsequently destroyed due to no fault of the seller prior to passage of risk of loss to the buyer, relieves the seller of liability for *breach of contract* (Section 2–613).

Identification entitles the seller to fix damages by reselling the goods at a public sale (Sections 2–706(4), 2–704(2)).

4. WHEN IDENTIFICATION OCCURS

It is important to know when identification of existing goods as the goods to which the contract refers occurs since title cannot pass to the buyer until the goods are identified to the contract, and because the buyer and the seller do not obtain the rights stated in sections 2 and 3 above until the goods are identified to the contract.

In the absence of specific agreement, identification of the goods to the contract occurs in the following ways:

a. When the contract is made if it is for the sale of goods already existing and identified: e.g., undivided shares in an identified fungible bulk (grain in an elevator or oil in a storage tank) can be sold, and the mere making of the contract would be sufficient to effect an identification even though the seller has not yet performed his duties to segregate and deliver the amount stated in the contract (Section 2–105(3)(4)).

b. If the contract is for the sale of future goods (existing goods not yet identified or not yet in existence), other than unborn young or future crops, identification occurs when the goods are shipped, marked, or otherwise designated by the seller as the goods to which the contract refers (Section 2–501(1)(b)).

c. Unborn young or future crops are identified to a contract when the crops are planted or otherwise become growing crops, or the young are conceived (Section 2–501(1)(c)). If the contract is made after the young are conceived or the crops are planted, they are identified by the making of the contract (Section 2–501(1)(a)).

B. DELIVERY REQUIRING MOVEMENT OF GOODS

The general rule is that *title* passes to the buyer at the time and place at which the seller completes his performance with reference to the *physical* delivery of the goods (Section 2–401(2)).

Additional provisions apply when the seller is to ship the goods to the buyer. The transaction may then take place either as a shipment contract or as a destination contract.

1. SHIPMENT CONTRACTS

a. *In General*

A shipment contract requires or authorizes the seller to send the goods but does not require him to deliver them to a particular place. The *shipment* contract is the *normal shipping arrangement.* The seller's duties in a shipment contract are generally stated in Section 2–504 (discussed in Chapter 19). They can be varied by the use of shipment terms; e.g., F.O.B.; or by an agreement by the parties; or by the open term provisions of the *U.C.C.,* e. g., delivery in single or multiple lots (Section 2–307), seller's choice of shipment arrangements (Section 2–311(2)), and time for delivery (Section 2–309(1)).

Title passes on completion of the seller's duty of physically putting the goods into the carrier's possession (Section 2–401(2)(a)), This duty sometimes includes actually loading the goods. The seller usually loads rail carloads, but less than carloads are usually loaded by the railroad.

Risk of loss to the buyer passes on *delivery* to the carrier (Section 2–509(1)(a)).

b. *F.O.B. (free on board) place of shipment* requires the seller to bear the expense and the risk of putting the goods into possession of the carrier, and *title* and *risk* pass when physical delivery to the carrier is completed (Section 2–319(1)(a)).

c. *F.O.B. carrier* requires the seller to bear the expense and risk of loading the goods on board the carrier (Section 2–319(1)(c)); i.e., *title* and *risk* pass after loading.

d. *F.A.S. (free alongside) vessel* requires the seller to deliver the goods alongside the vessel, and *title* and *risk* pass when that is completed (Sections 2–319(2)(a), 2–401(2)(a)).

e. *C.I.F.* (cost, insurance, freight) means that the price includes the cost of the goods, the insurance, and the freight to the named destination. *Title* and *risk* pass on shipment; i.e., when the seller com-

COD - shipment

pletes his duty of physical delivery to the carrier (Sections 2–320(1), 2–401(2)(a)).

2. DESTINATION CONTRACTS

a. *In General*

A destination contract is one that requires the seller to deliver the goods at a named destination. *Title* and *risk of loss* pass to the buyer when the goods are *tendered* at destination (Sections 2–401(2)(b), 2–509(1)(b)). It is the tender of delivery and not the delivery itself that causes title to pass. The seller must perform certain duties before title can pass at destination, and these are stated in Section 2–503; e.g., must put and hold goods at the buyer's disposition at a reasonable hour and for a reasonable time, must give buyer notice so he can take delivery, must tender appropriate documents.

b. *F.O.B. destination* requires the seller to transport the goods to the destination and tender them there in the manner required under destination contracts (Section 2–319(1)(b)). *Title* and *risk of loss* under F.O.B. destination contracts pass on *tender* at destination while in the possession of the carrier (Sections 2–401(2)(b), 2–509(1)(b)).

c. *Ex Ship* (from the carrying vessel) contracts require the buyer to receive the goods alongside the *incoming* vessel. *Risk of loss* does not pass to the buyer until the goods are off the ship at destination (Section 2–322(2)(b)). Ex ship contracts are presumably governed by the same rules as destination contracts and therefore *title* transfers to the buyer on *tender* at destination (Sections 2–401(2)(b), 2–322(2)(a)); however, it can be argued that Section 2–401(2)(a) delays passage of title until the seller unloads the goods from the ship. In ex ship contracts, it is advisable for the parties to explicitly state when title passes.

d. *No arrival, no sale* term means the seller must ship conforming goods properly and must tender them to the buyer when they arrive; however, the seller is not liable for breach of contract if they do not arrive unless he has caused the nonarrival. *Title* and *risk of loss* do not pass until the seller properly tenders the goods (Sections 2–324, 2–401(2)(b), 2–509(1)(b)).

3. COLLECT ON DELIVERY CONTRACTS

The *U.C.C.* fails to define C.O.D. or state whether it creates a shipment contract or a destination contract. The courts will probably treat C.O.D. contracts as shipment contracts which means that *title* and *risk* will pass on delivery to the carrier (see Shipment Contracts, supra). In C.O.D. contracts the parties should use a shipping term, e.g., F.O.B. place of shipment or F.O.B. destination, or insert an explicit term in the contract regarding title and risk of loss to avoid the problem.

C. DELIVERY WITHOUT MOVING GOODS

1. WITH DOCUMENT OF TITLE

When the goods are in possession of a bailee (100,000 bushels of wheat with a warehouseman), and the seller is to deliver a document of title (an instrument showing title to the wheat, such as a bill of lading or warehouse receipt), *title and risk of loss* pass to the buyer when he takes *possession* of the *document of title* (Sections 1–201(14)(15), 2–401(3)(a), and 2–509(2)(a)(c)).

For further discussion of documents of title see Chapter XXII.

2. WITHOUT DOCUMENT OF TITLE

If the goods are to be delivered without a document of title and without being moved, e.g., buyer to load and haul away without seller's help, *title* passes as soon as the goods are *identified* (Section 2–401(3)(b)), (see supra A. 4.). The goods do not have to be in a deliverable state. Thus, title to a machine to be specially manufactured may pass as soon as it is in an identifiable form even though it is not finished. Title to crops may pass as soon as they are planted (Section 2–501(1)(c)).

If the seller is to help load the goods, *title* does not pass until he completes his physical duties (Section 2–401(2)).

Risk of loss passes to the buyer on *receipt* of the goods if the seller is a merchant (usual case); if the seller is a nonmerchant, risk of loss passes on *tender* of delivery to the buyer (Section 2–509(3)).

If the goods are in possession of a bailee, *risk of loss* passes when the *bailee* acknowledges the buyer's right to possession of the goods (Section 2–509(2)(b)).

D. EFFECT OF BREACH OF CONTRACT

1. BUYER'S BREACH

a. *Risk of loss* passes to the buyer (Section 2–510(3)).

b. In the case of an anticipatory breach, *title* remains with the seller (Section 2–610).

c. In the case of a wrongful refusal to accept the goods, *title* revests in the seller (Section 2–401(4)).

d. In the case of a breach after acceptance or wrongful attempt to revoke acceptance, *title* remains in the buyer.

2. SELLER'S BREACH

If the seller breaches the contract before the buyer accepts or rejects the goods, *risk of loss* remains with the seller (*title* probably passes to the buyer pursuant to Section 2–401, subject to revesting in the seller pursuant to Sections 2–601 and 2–608).

E. SALE ON APPROVAL

In a sale on approval, neither *title* nor *risk of loss* passes to the buyer until he indicates approval of the goods (Section 2–327(1)(a)). Obviously, this is the best method of making a purchase as far as the buyer is concerned. If the buyer decides not to accept the goods, he must seasonably notify the seller of his election to return them; the risk and expense of returning them is on the seller, but a merchant buyer must follow any reasonable instructions (Section 2–327 (1)(b)(c)). "Seasonably" means an action taken at or within the time agreed or if no time is agreed at or within a reasonable time (Section 1–204(3)).

F. SALE OR RETURN

In a sale or return contract, the goods are delivered to the buyer with an option to return them. *Title* and *risk* pass to the buyer pursuant to rules stated supra under Delivery Requiring Movement of Goods and Delivery Without Moving Goods. The return of the goods is at the buyer's risk and expense (Section 2–327). Title probably revests in the seller when the goods are delivered at destination; i.e., place from which they were sent (Section 2–401(2)(b)).

Sale or return contracts are usually between a manufacturer and a dealer who will use the goods for resale.

G. CONSIGNMENT

In this type of arrangement, goods are delivered to a dealer; and the dealer is a sales agent who is empowered to sell the goods and return the proceeds, less commissions, to the principal. Title does not pass to the dealer. When the goods are sold, title passes from the principal to the buyer (Section 2–401).

H. SALE BY NON-OWNER

1. IN GENERAL

It is a fundamental rule of law that a thief, finder, or bailee of goods cannot transfer title even to a bona fide purchaser for value.

An exception as to a bailee is found in the *U.C.C.* Section 2–403 (2)(3) which provides that an owner of goods who entrusts the possession of them to a merchant who deals in goods of that kind gives the merchant the power to transfer all rights of the owner to a buyer in the ordinary course of business; e. g., B purchases a watch from a jeweler and leaves it with the jeweler to have his initials engraved on it, but the jeweler sells it to a buyer in the ordinary course of business. Some states (California U.C.C. Section 2403(3)) have enacted legislation giving greater protection to the owner by providing that the entrustment must be for the purposes of sale, obtaining offers to purchase, locating of buyer, etc., for the owner's rights to be defeated by a sale to a bona fide purchaser for value; thus in the example above, the owner could reclaim the watch.

2. RESALE BY FRAUDULENT BUYER

The general rule is that when the buyer of goods perpetrates a fraud on the seller and thereby gains possession of the goods, a sale of the goods by the fraudulent buyer to a bona fide purchaser for value passes title to the goods to the purchaser. The theory for passing a good title to the bona fide purchaser for value is that as between two innocent persons, namely the seller and the bona fide purchaser, the person who permitted the transaction to take place should suffer the loss; i. e., the innocent seller. The exception to the rule is in the case of fraud in the execution; e. g., the buyer obtains the seller's signature by trick so that the seller does not know he is signing a legal document or he believes he is signing a document which is different than the one he is actually signing.

The general rule has been expanded by Section 2–403(1) of the *U.C.C.* which provides that the bona fide purchaser prevails over the seller when the seller has been deceived as to the identity of the buyer, or when delivery of the goods was in exchange for a check which is later dishonored, or when it was agreed that the transaction was to be a "cash" sale and the buyer did not pay cash.

TRANSFER OF TITLE AND RISK OF LOSS CHART

TYPE OF DELIVERY OR SALE	WHEN TITLE PASSES	WHEN RISK PASSES
DELIVERY BY MOVEMENT OF GOODS.		
1. Shipment contract (Usual type of sale between merchants)	Delivery to carrier	Delivery to carrier
2. Destination contract	Tender at destination	Tender at destination though in possession of carrier
3. Other contracts requiring physical delivery by seller:		
a. Merchant seller (Usual type of sale between merchant and nonmerchant)	Completion of seller's duties of delivery	Buyer's taking physical possession of goods
b. Nonmerchant seller	Same as (a) above	Tender of delivery
DELIVERY WITHOUT MOVEMENT OF GOODS.		
1. Goods in seller's possession:		
a. Merchant seller (Usual type of sale between merchant and nonmerchant)	Identification of goods or making sales contract (whichever is later)	Buyer's taking physical possession of goods
b. Nonmerchant seller	Same as above	Tender of delivery
2. Goods in bailee's possession:		
a. Delivery by negotiable document of title	When buyer takes possession of document	When buyer takes possession of document
b. Delivery by non-negotiable document of title	Same as above	Honoring of document by bailee or buyer's inaction for reasonable time after receiving it
c. Delivery by procuring bailee's acknowledgment without a document of title	Identification of goods or making of contract (whichever is later)	Bailee's acknowledgment
d. Delivery by giving buyer written direction to bailee	Same as above	Honoring of document by bailee or buyer's inaction for reasonable time after receiving it
SALE ON APPROVAL	Signifies approval	Signifies approval
SALE OR RETURN	Title passes pursuant to rules above except sale on approval	Risk of loss passes pursuant to rules above except sale on approval

Risk

1. *Goods Must be Identified*

CHATHAM v. CLARK'S FOOD FAIR, INC.

106 Ga.App. 648, 127 S.E.2d 868 (1962).

CARLISLE, Presiding Judge. * * * A document which purports to be a bill of sale but which fails to identify the thing sold is not sufficient to convey title to anything * * *, and the thing sold must be so identified by the contract, agreement or bill of sale as to be capable of being separated from the mass of other similar articles and to be identified. * * *

[T]he plaintiff alleged in his petition that he purchased from the defendant "One boathouse, Model No. 924," for a stated price; that he paid the price; and that the defendant thereafter failed and refused to deliver the boathouse and further failed and refused to return to the plaintiff on demand the purchase price which he had paid. * * *

Where the plaintiff filed a petition containing allegations in the nature above indicated, and where the defendant in its answer admitted the sale and the payment of the purchase price but denied its failure to deliver the property, and where on the trial of the case the plaintiff testified that after the defendant delivered to the plaintiff the bill of sale "for: One Model 924 boathouse," that he went to take possession of the boathouse but could not take possession because of adverse weather conditions; that when he went back at a later time the defendant's agent informed him that his boathouse "had sunk"; and where he further testified that, when he first went to take possession, there were several of the particular model boathouse located at the place where delivery was expected; that the boathouse which he bought was one of a general type and had no other identifying marks on it, the evidence did not show that the plaintiff had purchased any particular boathouse and there was, therefore, no delivery either actual or constructive, effected by the delivery of the bill of sale, and the title to the boathouse, therefore, remained in the defendant vendor until such time as the particular boathouse intended to be sold was selected. * * *

[Judgment for plaintiff.]

---

2. *Transfer of Title on Delivery to Buyer*

MOTORS INSURANCE CORPORATION v. SAFECO INSURANCE COMPANY OF AMERICA

412 S.W.2d 584 (Ky., 1967).

CULLEN, Commissioner. A motion for appeal previously having been sustained, we have before us the appeal of Motors Insurance

Corporation from a judgment holding it liable to the appellees Scott Oldsmobile, Incorporated, and James C. Grugin in the amount of $1277 (less certain credits) under a collision insurance policy. The policy was issued to Scott Oldsmobile covering automobiles "owned" and "held for sale" by it. Motors Insurance Corporation maintains that the automobile in question, the damages to which furnish the basis of the claim under the policy, had been sold and delivered to appellee Grugin before it was damaged (in an accident which occurred when Grugin's son was driving the car), and therefore the automobile was not "owned" or "held for sale" by Scott Oldsmobile at the time the damage occurred.

Grugin's son smashed up the car on a Friday night. Earlier in the day Grugin and Scott Oldsmobile had agreed on a "trade," and each testified that it was understood that the trade was final and firm. Grugin turned over his old car to Scott, and Scott gave Grugin unqualified and unconditional possession of the new car. All that remained was for title papers to be processed and for Grugin to return the next day with a check for the cash due on the trade. After the accident Grugin did pay the cash and the sale and title papers were fully executed and delivered.

Grugin and Scott are in full agreement that the car was "sold" to Grugin on the day of the accident. However, Grugin's personal insurer, the appellee Safeco Insurance Company, denied coverage on the ground that "ownership" had not passed to Grugin and therefore Motors Insurance Corporation, as Scott's insurer, was liable. The instant lawsuit was brought to determine which of the two companies was liable. The circuit court adjudged that the automobile was "still owned" by Scott "despite any oral negotiations."

We think the judgment is clearly erroneous. There had been a physical delivery of the automobile to Grugin as a purchaser. Under the Uniform Commercial Code, KRS 355.2–401, title passed at the time and place of such delivery. Also under the Code, KRS 355.2–201, it is provided that it is not necessary that a contract of sale be in writing in order to be enforceable with respect to goods "which have been received and accepted."

The fact that the title *papers* had not been delivered did not require that Scott still be considered the "owner" within the meaning of the insurance policy. [citations]

* * *

Safeco maintains that Rash v. North British & Mercantile Ins. Co., Ky., 246 S.W.2d 990, is controlling. We think not. There the automobile was not delivered to the customer as a purchaser or with any intent to pass title; the customer simply was permitted to use the automobile temporarily, as a bailee, for the purpose of trying to find a source of funds which would put him in shape to become a purchaser.

If, as between Scott and Grugin, ownership had passed and an effective sale had been accomplished, obviously the automobile was not thereafter "owned" or "held for sale" by Scott within the meaning of the Motors Insurance policy. The policy does not undertake to determine what constitutes ownership; necessarily that must be determined by the law of sales.

The judgment is reversed as it relates to Motors Insurance Company with directions to enter judgment dismissing the claims against Motors Insurance Company.

---

3. Transfer of Title on Delivery to Carrier

VAL DECKER PACKING CO. v. ARMOUR AND COMPANY

184 N.E.2d 548 (Ohio Com.Pl., 1962).

GESSAMAN, Judge. Plaintiff seeks to recover from the defendant the sum of $1690.49. * * *

The facts are not in dispute. At about 5:00 P.M., December 26, 1956, a Mr. Irwin Busse, representing the defendant, called the plaintiff's office and talked with Mr. Louis B. Decker, Chairman of the Board of Directors of plaintiff. At the price of $8885.51, fixed by Mr. Decker, Mr. Busse ordered from plaintiff for defendant a truck load of dressed hogs to be shipped to Western Pork Packers, Inc. "C.A.F.", Worcester, Mass. Plaintiff engaged the Wilson Freight Forwarding Co., Cincinnati, Ohio, to transport the hogs in a refrigerated truck. The loaded truck left plaintiff's place of business in Piqua, Ohio, at 12:25 P.M., December 27, 1956. On December 28, 1956, before 3:00 P.M. the driver of the truck called Mr. Ralph Cutillo, Armour and Company manager in Worcester, Mass. and stated that his truck had developed mechanical trouble and that he could not make delivery by 3:00 P.M. that day. Mr. Cutillo authorized the driver to deliver by 6:00 A.M. December 29, 1956. The truck did not arrive by that time and did not arrive until December 31, 1956, at which time defendant refused to accept the shipment. It was sold to another company for $7203.99. The condition and quality of the merchandise is not in dispute.

After the telephone conversation between Mr. Busse and Mr. Decker, plaintiff received from defendant a "Confirmation of Purchase". In addition to the provisions to which we have already referred, there are contained in this document the shipping date, "11 P.M. 12/26/56." "Payment: S.D.B.L. (sight draft bill of lading) against documents," and the following: "Note: Please show on bill of lading in large size, bright colored print or crayon that Western Pork Packers, Inc. desire to unload these hogs not later than 3:00

P.M. Friday, 12/28 and as much sooner as possible. If delayed, truck driver to please call collect, Mr. Raph Cutillo, Mgr. Armour & Co., 219 Summit St., Worcester, Mass., tele. No. Pleasant 2–5653." This was done.

Counsel for the plaintiff contend that since the hogs were to be shipped "C.A.F." Worcester, their duty under the contract was fulfilled when the merchandise was delivered to the carrier at their place of business in Piqua, and that the risk thereafter was on the buyer, the defendant. Counsel for the defendant contend as follows:

> "The defendant takes no issue with the general legal incidents of a 'C&F' or 'C.I.F.' contract, as set forth in plaintiff's brief. It is agreed that title to the goods with the attendant risk of loss passes from the seller to the buyer upon delivery to the carrier, but only if the terms of the contract to sell are fulfilled by the seller."

In considering the questions herein, we must first examine Section 1315.19, Revised Code, which reads as follows:

> "When there is a contract to sell specific or ascertained goods, the property in them is transferred to the buyer at such time as the parties to the contract intend it to be transferred.
>
> "For the purpose of ascertaining the intention of the parties, regard shall be had to the terms of the contract, the conduct of the parties, usages of trade, and the circumstances of the case."

Consideration must also be given to Section 1315.20, Revised Code, the pertinent parts of which provide:

> "Unless a different intention appears, the following are rules for ascertaining the intention of the parties as to the time at which the property in the goods is to pass to the buyer:
>
> * * * * * * * *
>
> "(E) If a contract to sell requires the seller to deliver the goods to the buyer, or at a particular place, or to pay the freight or cost of transportation to the buyer, or to a particular place, the property does not pass until the goods have been delivered to the buyer or reached the place agreed upon."
>
> * * *

One of the terms of the contract, which also involves a usage of the trade, is the provision that the hogs were to be shipped "C.A.F. Worcester." To understand that term fully, we call attention to Madeirense Do Brasil S/A v. Stulman-Emrick Lumber Co., 147 F.2d 399 and specifically to the language of the Court at page 402 of the opinion:

> "Plaintiff argues further that it has duly performed because a c. & f. contract requires it only to deliver, or to tender

> delivery of, the lumber to a carrier in Brazil. The term 'c. & f.' means that the price includes in a lump sum 'cost' and 'freight' to the named destination. * * * The term 'c. & f.' thus either requires the seller to prepay the freight or permits the buyer after having paid the actual charges to deduct them from the price, in either case putting the seller under an ultimate obligation to pay for the transportation. Ordinarily where the seller pays the freight, there is an inference * * * that the parties intend no passage of title until the goods reach the destination to which freight is paid. But commercial usage, recognized by the courts and text writers, is that under a c. & f. contract the seller fulfills his duty on shipment of the goods, and that the risk thereafter is on the buyer unless other terms of the contract indicate a contrary intention. * * *"

Does the contract indicate such a contrary intention? We think not.

Counsel for the defendant agree, as we have hereinabove noted, that under a C.A.F. contract "title to the goods with the attendant risk of loss, passes from the seller to the buyer upon delivery to the carrier, but *only* if the terms of the contract to sell are fulfilled by the seller." They contend that while the delay in shipment was not the *fault* of the plaintiff, it "was certainly plaintiff's *default* which is the pertinent issue." Counsel for defendant conclude their brief with this statement:

> "The plaintiff materially breached the contract to sell by failing to ship the hogs at the required time. * * *

Therein their argument is summarized. Did the plaintiff fail to perform "an essential term" of the contract? To state it in another way, was the time of shipment (as contained in the contract) "of the essence of the agreement?" We think not.

"Time is not of the essence of the contract unless made so by its terms." * * * A careful examination of the contract reveals clearly that the consignee *desired* to unload the shipment by "3:00 P.M. Friday, 12/28." Whether that date was or was not of the essence, need not now be determined, but it is obvious that it was the only date in which either the defendant or Western Pork Packers, Inc. were interested. * * * Therefore, we feel that the time of shipment, mentioned in the contract, was not made of the essence "by its terms" nor was there anything in the conduct or acts of the parties that made it of the essence of the contract, nor was it an essential term thereof.

* * *

Our conclusions are: 1. that the agreement entered into between plaintiff and defendant was a C.A.F. or C. & F. contract; 2. that the shipping date was neither an essential term of nor was it of the essence of the contract; 3. that, therefore, plaintiff did not breach the contract by shipping the hogs on December 27, 1956; 4.

that when plaintiff delivered the hogs to the carrier, title passed to the defendant and the risk thereafter was on the defendant; 5. that defendant's refusal to accept the hogs when they were delivered in Worcester Mass. did not relieve it of its duty to pay plaintiff for them and, 6. that therefore the plaintiff should recover from the defendant the difference between the contract price of the hogs and the price at which it sold them, plus $8.97 expense incurred by plaintiff by reason of defendant's refusal to accept the hogs. Our finding is that the plaintiff recover from the defendant the sum of $1690.49.

---

4. *Risk of Loss Passes to Buyer on Receipt of Goods*

LAIR DISTRIBUTING CO. v. CRUMP

48 Ala.App. 72, 261 So.2d 904 (1972).

THAGARD, Presiding Judge. This is a suit seeking damages of $382.36 for materials and labor furnished by appellant, Lair Distributing Co., Inc., to appellee, Eugene Crump. * * *

According to the testimony, in September of 1968, appellee purchased from appellant a TV antenna and tower for an agreed price of $900.00 payable in consecutive monthly installments of $7.50 for ten years. To secure the payments appellee executed a conditional sales contract. The contract provided, among other things, that title remain in appellant until the purchase price was paid in full and that appellee would not move the tower and antenna from appellee's premises until the full purchase price was paid, except with the written consent of appellant.

There was no provision in the sales contract for maintenance or repairs, or for the carrying of insurance by either party. However, both appellant and appellee testified that appellant verbally agreed to maintain the system during the ten year term of the written contract. Appellant testified that he verbally agreed that in the event there was damage to the system by external forces he would pay $50.00 on the deductible portion of appellee's insurance. Appellee denied that there was any reference to insurance or a deductible during the negotiations.

In June 1969, the system was struck and so badly damaged by lightning that the entire antenna system had to be replaced. Appellee's wife telephoned appellant that the damage had occurred and requested that he make the necessary repairs immediately. Appellee does not deny that the repairs were made promptly.

It appears that the case was tried on the issue of whether the loss caused by the lightning stroke should fall upon the seller or the buyer. Appellee contends that (1) the promise by the seller to "maintain" the system for the ten year life of the contract included an implied promise to replace the system if that became necessary from any cause whatsoever, and (2) that neither the title nor the possession passed to the buyer, because (a) the seller reserved title under the terms of the conditional sales contract, and (b) the seller retained possession by denying the buyer the right to move the system from his own premises until the same was paid for.

Appellant contends that the question is one of law and points out that the instrument securing the sale price was dated September 13, 1968, wherefore the transaction was subject to the provisions of the Uniform Commercial Code, Tit. 7A, Code of Alabama (Recompiled 1958), which became effective midnight December 31, 1966. Section 2–509(3) of the Uniform Commercial Code, supra, reads as follows:

> "(3) In any case not within subsection (1) or (2), the risk of loss passes to the buyer *on his receipt* of the goods if the seller is a merchant; otherwise the risk passes to the buyer on tender of delivery." (Emphasis supplied.)

We do not think there is any merit in appellee's contention that he was not in possession because he was prohibited from moving the system from his own premises. The system was installed by appellant on the premises of appellee and appellee had the uninterrupted use thereof until the lightning struck. Furthermore, appellant had no right to remove the system from appellee's premises so long as appellee did not become delinquent in his payments, so, according to appellee's reasoning, neither was appellant in possession of the system. We hold that under the undisputed testimony appellee "received" the system on or about September 13, 1968, and continued in possession until the damage was repaired by appellant, and, for all we know, may still be in possession.

The only conflict in the testimony of appellant and appellee was whether or not the question of insurance was discussed during the negotiations and whether or not appellant limited his promise to "maintain" the system to ordinary malfunctions resulting from wear and tear and expressly excluded damage from lightning and windstorms. Appellant testified "Yes" and appellee testified "No." We think the conflict is immaterial. The appellee did not testify that appellant agreed to replace the system if it was destroyed by the elements but only that he agreed to "maintain." The intent of the parties is the decisive question. We cannot believe that appellant intended the word "maintain" to mean "replace" and we doubt that appellee so construed the promise.

There having been no material conflict in the testimony, there was no fact for the trial court to "find" but only a conclusion of law to arrive at. We are clear to the conclusion that the provision of the Uniform Commercial Code hereinabove quoted is the law applicable to this case and that the trial court erred in giving judgment for the defendant.

Reversed and remanded.

5. *Sale of Goods on Approval*

LANE FARM SUPPLY, INC. v. CROSBY

40 N.Y.Misc.2d 645, 243 N.Y.S.2d 725 (1963).

W. VINCENT GRADY, Justice (Sitting by Designation). The only articles in controversy at this time are a tractor and plow which were delivered to Mr. Crosby on trial and approval on November 7, 1960 which articles had an agreed price of $3,000. After the delivery of the tractor and plow to Mr. Crosby's farm by the Lane Farm Supply Inc., the tractor and plow were used for a period of fifty-three days, plowing and skidding logs covering land of approximately sixty acres (four fields) and were used approximately one hundred and ten hours.

It further appears that when a representative of the seller questioned Mr. Crosby about payment for the tractor and plow, the defendant stated that he did not have any money and that he had a big deal pending and when that broke, he would be able to pay for the tractor and plow. He never stated that he rejected the sale of the tractor and plow. The tractor was burned in a barn on the defendant's property on January 1, 1961.

Section 100 of the Personal Property Law provides:

> "* * * 2. When goods are delivered to the buyer on approval or on trial or on satisfaction, or other similar terms, the property therein passes to the buyer—
>
> "(a) When he signifies his approval or acceptance to the seller or does any other act adopting the transaction;
>
> "(b) If he does not signify his approval or acceptance to the seller, but retains the goods without giving notice of rejection, then if a time has been fixed for the return of the goods, on the expiration of such time, and, if no time has been fixed, on the expiration of a reasonable time. What is a reasonable time is a question of fact."

Certainly, on the evidence presented, the title to the tractor and plow passed to the defendant, as he did not reject the sale and used the articles longer than a reasonable time.

Judgment will be awarded the plaintiff accordingly in the amount of $3000.00, plus interest from January 26, 1961.

6. *Invalid Sale of Goods by Bailee*

HERTZ CORP. v. HARDY

197 Pa.Super. 466, 178 A.2d 833 (1962).

MONTGOMERY, Judge. In this action of replevin, * * * plaintiff-appellant, The Hertz Corporation, sought to recover a 1957 Oldsmobile automobile it had delivered to James Hardy, one of the defendants, under a rental agreement executed in Cleveland, Ohio. Sara Thompson and I. Edgar Thompson were added as additional defendants when the automobile was found in their possession * * At that time I. Edgar Thompson held a certificate of title for the car issued by the Pennsylvania Bureau of Motor Vehicles. Thompsons * * * defended the action, and the trial by jury resulted in a verdict in defendants' (Thompsons') favor. Hardy was not served with the writ, nor did he appear. * * *

The Hertz office at the Cleveland (Ohio) Airport, on November 24, 1957, by the customary form of written agreement, rented the vehicle involved to James Hardy for a five day rental. * * * Prior to renting the car from Hertz, on July 6, 1957, Hardy, using the address of 73 East 80th Street, New York, New York, had prepared a bill of sale for the identical automobile from a Mrs. Mary Emerson of New York, and on the same day registered this vehicle with the Bureau of Motor Vehicles of New York. On November 26, 1957, he sold the car obtained from Hertz to West Brownsville (Pa.) Iron and Metal Company, a licensed Pennsylvania motor vehicle dealer located just across the Ohio line and used the New York registration for the purpose of establishing himself as the owner and of transferring title to the vehicle. Previously, on November 25, 1957, Hardy had obtained an Ohio certificate of title for the Hertz car which he also used in selling it to the Brownsville company. There actually was a Mary Emerson, but she denied knowing Hardy or ever having owned a 1957 Oldsmobile car. How Hardy accomplished this is unexplained.

The Brownsville company resold the car on December 6, 1957, at the regular automobile auction at Manheim, Pennsylvania, to David J. Hoffman, the used car dealer from whom Thompson purchased it on January 7, 1958. * * *

It is appellant's contention that it is entitled to judgment in its favor because a purchaser from a thief, or any subsequent purchaser, has no ownership and cannot hold the property against the true owner; * * * the only issue raised by the pleadings is the legality of the title to the car claimed by I. Edgar Thompson as a bona fide purchaser for value without notice, which title was also based on a registration certificate issued by the Commonwealth of Pennsylvania, and as well on the certificate of title issued by the State of Ohio to one of its predecessors. * * *

Where a certificate of title to an automobile is fraudulently procured by false representation it is void ab initio and the title of a subsequent holder for value which arises therefrom can have no greater solemnity than its source. * * *

(a) Where the owner loses or is robbed of his property, or one who has a temporary right to its use attempts to sell or pledge it without consent, the owner may follow and reclaim it no matter in whose possession it may be found. (b) Possession of property in the bailee for hire does not clothe him with an apparent title or authority to dispose of it as to create an estoppel preventing the owner from asserting his title. (c) If the possession of the seller or pledgor is that of a bailee or a trespasser, the rule that declares where one of two innocent persons must suffer the loss must fall on him whose act or omission made the loss possible does not apply to the pledgee or vendee. The pledgee stands in no better position than a person who innocently buys, leases, or acquires property that has been stolen. The owner can follow and reclaim it no matter where it may be found. * * *

Although defendants must restore to Hertz the value of the car, they are not without rights to secure redress from the persons from whom the car was purchased, and they on back to the defrauding party.

The judgment for defendants is reversed and entered for plaintiff in the sum of $2,700, the amount of the counter-bond filed by defendants, plus interest.

---

7. *Entrusting Gives Power to Transfer Under U.C.C. 2–403*

LITCHFIELD v. DUEITT

245 So.2d 190 (Miss., 1971).

JONES, Justice. This case comes on appeal from the Circuit Court of Hancock County and is a case of first impression in this State. It involves the Uniform Commercial Code. * * * The sections involved in Mississippi are subdivisions of section 41A of our Code and title 7A of the Alabama Code, to-wit: 2–403, 2–104, and 1–201(9).

Subsections (2) and (3) of Section 2–403 read as follows:

> (2) Any entrusting of possession of goods to a merchant who deals in goods of that kind gives him power to transfer all rights of the entruster to a buyer in ordinary course of business.
>
> (3) "Entrusting" includes any delivery and any acquiescence in retention of possession regardless of any condition expressed between the parties to the delivery or acquiescence and regardless of whether the procurement of the

entrusting or the possessor's disposition of the goods have been such as to be larcenous under the criminal law.

* * *

This was a replevin suit filed by appellant to recover possession of one Lima-type 24 Crane, serial number 3330–21. * * *

The facts are substantially these. Appellee [Dueitt] was the owner of the crane hereinbefore described. He purchased same for $5,000 cash and financed $5,000 with C.I.T. evidenced by written security on the crane. Appellee was a resident of Greene County, Mississippi, and the sales contract was recorded in Greene County. In 1968 the equipment was leased to a pipeline dredging company and sent to Dyersburg, Tennessee. While on the job there, it was somehow dropped into a river and remained submerged for about ninety hours. Upon recovery from the river, it was delivered to the Allis-Chalmers Shop in Dyersburg where it remained for approximately two months. At the time of the accident, appellee was two months behind in his payments to C.I.T.

Alabama Tractor Company was an equipment company engaged in the business of supplying, selling and repairing heavy equipment and was located at Saraland, Alabama, near Mobile. Its president and general manager was W. E. Small. Appellee knew Mr. Small and talked with him several times about moving the crane from Tennessee to Saraland and making the necessary repairs. Small paid the expenses of a man to go to Dyersburg to see the crane. After the man had inspected the crane, it was moved from Dyersburg to Saraland. Prior to moving the crane, Small had agreed with Dueitt that he would pay the C.I.T. Company, which claimed that the entire amount was due and refused to release the crane for the two months back payment. Small gave appellee $240 or $245 with which to pay the back payments due the finance company before he knew they had declared the whole balance due. Small then paid to the finance company the balance due of $2,094.

* * *

After having held the equipment for some time and having it upon the sales lot, it was finally sold to appellant. We find no evidence in the record that would put Mr. Litchfield upon notice or in any way impugn his position as an innocent purchaser for value or "buyer in ordinary course of business" (UCC § 1–201(9). Sometime after the sale, Mr. Dueitt ascertained that the crane had been sold to appellant. Dueitt traced the crane and found it working on Dauphin Island off the Alabama coast. He went there during the night without knowledge of appellant and removed it to Hancock County, Mississippi. Thereafter appellant learned of its whereabouts. This replevin suit was instituted.

We are of the opinion that the evidence here is overwhelming and contradicted by no more than a scintilla, if that, that the equipment was entrusted to Mr. Small and that he is entitled to possession thereof. With this view of the case, it is unnecessary to pass upon the other questions raised or to pass upon the cross-appeal filed by appellee.

* * *

The jury, in the trial below in rendering a verdict for appellee, fixed the value of the equipment at $7,500. We are reversing the case and entering judgment here in favor of appellant and valuing the crane of $7,500, the amount found by the jury.

Reversed and judgment here for appellant.

PROBLEMS

1. Buyer and seller enter into a contract for the sale of fifty tubs of butter. The contract provides that the seller will ship the goods. Seller places the buyer's name on the fifty tubs of butter and sets them aside in his warehouse. During the evening, the butter is destroyed by a fire. Seller demands payment of the butter contending that risk of loss passed to the buyer when he put the buyer's name on them and set them aside. Decision?

2. B in New York ordered 1,000 pitons for use in mountain climbing from S in Chicago and sent a check for part payment of the purchase price with the order. S put the pitons aside in his factory and put B's name on the box containing them. Eight days later S became insolvent. B tendered the balance of the purchase price and demanded the pitons. C, a creditor of S, wants to seize all of the goods including the pitons as they have gone up in value since B's order. Who should get the pitons, and why?

3. Buyer in Illinois and seller in New York enter into a contract for the sale of 1,000 cases of dog food F.O.B. New York, C.O.D. Seller delivers the dog food to the carrier in New York, but the goods are destroyed in transit by an unusual flood in Ohio. Seller demands payment, but buyer contends that since he did not have an opportunity to inspect the goods he does not have to pay for them. Decision?

4. Buyer in Los Angeles and seller in New York enter into a contract whereby seller will ship to the buyer F.O.B. Los Angeles, 1,000 sweaters #R 15. Seller ships the sweaters, and they arrive at the freight depot in Los Angeles. The freight depot agent telephones the buyer and tenders delivery of the goods. Two days later, and before the buyer picks up the goods, an earthquake and fire destroys the freight depot and the sweaters. Seller demands payment, but buyer contends that neither title nor risk passes until the goods are delivered. Decision?

5. Buyer, a housewife, enters into a contract with the Reynolds Television retail store at 11:00 A.M. for the purchase of a radio-tape recorder combination at a price of $1,000.00. Mr. Reynolds tells the buyer that the set will have to be checked out by one of his employees and that she can pick it up the next day. She says she will bring a station wagon and asks him if she should bring someone along to help load the set. He tells her this is not necessary because his employees will load the set. She then pays him $500.00 on account and leaves the store. At 4:00 P.M.

the same day, seller calls buyer and informs her they were able to get the set ready ahead of time, and he is now tendering delivery to her. Buyer states that she cannot get the set until the next day as previously arranged. During the night, the set is stolen. Seller demands the balance of the purchase price contending that title to the set passed at the time the contract was made because the goods were identified to the contract; and if not at that time, then certainly when tender was made. Decision?

6. Buyer purchases and pays for a suit at the seller's clothing store. The seller tells the buyer that the suit will be ready for delivery the next day after some necessary alterations are made. That evening all of the suits in the store are stolen. The buyer claims that the seller is liable for breach of contract. The seller claims that the risk of loss is on the buyer. Discuss.

7. Buyer, a business law student, and seller enter into a contract whereby buyer purchases a typewriter on thirty-days approval. Twenty days after the purchase, the typewriter is stolen from the buyer's locked room due to no fault of the buyer. Buyer immediately notifies seller of the theft and states that he does not approve of the typewriter and disclaims all liability for the purchase price. Seller brings suit. Decision?

8. Mickey Smith steals a watch and sells it to a bona fide purchaser for value who has no knowledge that it has been stolen. The owner of the watch demands the return of the watch from the bona fide purchaser. Decision?

9. Buyer purchases and pays for an expensive large painting from seller who deals in goods of that kind, but since the buyer does not have the facilities to take the painting with him he leaves it with the seller with the understanding that he will pick it up the next day. Later, the same day, seller wrongfully sells the painting to a bona fide purchaser for value in the ordinary course of business. Seller absconds with the money from the two sales. Buyer sues the bona fide purchaser to recover the painting. Decision?

10. Buyer, representing himself to be Henry Ford, offers to purchase a radio from seller on credit. Seller, quite willing to sell to Ford on credit, sells the radio to buyer. Buyer then sells the radio to T, a bona fide purchaser for value, who has no knowledge of the buyer's fraud. When seller discovers the fraud, he attempts to repossess the radio. Decision?

Chapter 19

PERFORMANCE OF THE CONTRACT

In every sale, the obligation of the seller is to transfer and deliver the goods and the obligation of the buyer is to accept and pay in accordance with the contract (Section 2–301). This is true whether the sale involves a bottle of milk at the neighborhood grocery store or a sale involving millions of bushels of wheat. Section 2–301 is adequate to govern performance in almost all sales transactions. Only mercantile sales, e.g., between manufacturer and wholesaler, distributor and retailer, are likely to involve difficult problems regarding delivery, acceptance, or payment.

A. SELLER'S PERFORMANCE

---

1. DUTY TO SHIP

In a *shipment* contract, the seller's obligation is performed when he starts the goods on their way by delivery to the carrier; he does not guarantee arrival of the shipment (Section 2–504). In the absence of a provision in the contract, it will be considered a shipment contract rather than a destination contract.

In a *destination* contract, however, the seller has the duty to get the goods to their destination (Section 2–503).

The seller's duties in a shipment contract are as follows:

a. He must make a reasonable contract with a reasonable carrier (Section 2–504(a)); e.g., he cannot ship perishable goods from New York to Los Angeles by a slow freighter going around "the Horn"; he must provide for the care of the goods in transit if needed (such as refrigeration of perishables and feeding and watering of livestock);

b. He must have the goods classified and described as to their true worth;

c. He must arrange for the goods to be properly loaded;

d. He must promptly procure and offer to the buyer any document the buyer needs to obtain possession of the goods when they arrive, such as a bill of lading (Section 2–504(b));

e. He must notify the buyer that the shipment has been made (Section 2–504(c)). A standard manner of notification is sending an invoice or bill of lading to the buyer. Frequently the *agreement* expressly requires prompt notification; e. g., by wire or cable. Failure of the seller to notify the buyer that shipment has been made, or to make a reasonable contract for their transportation, is a ground for rejection of the goods if the failure results in material delay or damage.

2. SHIPMENT WITH RESERVATION

This is a shipment in which the seller reserves a security interest in the goods. For example, instead of sending the bill of lading directly to the buyer which would enable the buyer to pick up the goods when they arrive without paying the seller for them, the seller makes the bill of lading to the order of his agent located in the buyer's city or to a financing agency or bank at destination. In this situation the buyer cannot obtain the goods until he pays for and receives the bill of lading. Thus, the seller retains control of the goods in transit without paying the freight or assuming the risk of loss (Section 2–505). Title and risk pass to the buyer under the normal rules in the absence of an agreement to the contrary.

3. MERCANTILE SHIPPING TERMS

The *U.C.C.* defines mercantile shipping terms in Sections 2–319 through 2–324. Sometimes, these definitions conflict with those in the American Foreign Trade Definitions (AFTD). In case of conflict, the parties should incorporate one or the other in the contract. The AFTD definitions can be obtained from N.F.T.C., Inc., 10 Rockefeller Plaza, New York, New York 10020, for ten cents a copy.

F.O.B. shipment point, seller must arrange the shipping; buyer pays the cost of freight, cost of loading unless carrier requires the seller to load, insurance, export and import charges, custom duties, fees, and document expenses needed to bring the goods into the country (Sections 2–311(2), 2–319(1)(a), 2–504, AFTD).

F.O.B. vessel, car or other vehicle, seller must arrange the shipping and pay for the loading; buyer pays for everything else (Sections 2–311(2), 2–319(1)(a)(c), 2–504, AFTD).

F.A.S. vessel, buyer must arrange shipping and pay for everything (Sections 2–319(3), 2–319(2)(a), AFTD).

C.I.F., seller must arrange shipping and pay for everything except import duties (Sections 2–311(2), 2–504, 2–320(2)(b), 2–320(c), AFTD).

C. & F., seller must arrange shipping and pay for loading, freight, and cost of export licenses, fees, and similar exportation charges, while the buyer must pay for insurance and cost of import charges, custom duties, fees, and document expenses to bring the goods into the country (Sections 2–311(2), 2–320(2)(b), 2–320(3)).

F.O.B. destination, seller must arrange shipping and pay freight and insurance (Section 2–319(1)(b), AFTD).

No Arrival, No Sale, seller must arrange shipping and pay for everything (Section 2–324).

Ex Ship, seller must arrange shipping and pay for everything (Section 2–322(2)(a)).

4. TENDER OF DELIVERY

A. IN GENERAL

There are two requirements to a valid tender of delivery (as used in this section "tender" contemplates an offer coupled with a present ability to fulfill all the conditions resting on the tendering party and must be followed by actual performance if the other party shows himself ready to proceed):

1. The seller must put and hold conforming goods at the buyer's disposition; and

2. Must give the buyer any notification reasonably necessary to enable him to take delivery (Sections 2–503(1), 2–503(3)).

The tender must be at a reasonable hour and must be kept available for a reasonable time so the buyer can take delivery (Section 2–503(1)(a)).

The tender must be at the place stated in the contract; and if no place is stated, the seller's place of business (Sections 2–308, 2–503(1)).

B. EFFECT OF TENDER

The effect of tender of delivery is to entitle the seller to the buyer's acceptance of the goods at the place and time of tender (Section 2–507(1)).

Unless expressly stated in the contract to the contrary, tender of delivery and payment are concurrent conditions; i.e., neither party is required to perform until the other performs or tenders performance (Sections 2–507(1), 2–511(1)). Neither party can claim the other party is in default until he first tenders performance. However, if one party refuses to perform, the other party does not have to tender performance as this would be a useless act (Section 2–610).

Many contracts provide for credit; i.e., goods are to be delivered to buyer on 60 days credit. In credit cases, the seller must perform his part of the contract before he can demand performance from the buyer.

C. DELIVERY IN POSSESSION OF SELLER

The *U.C.C.* does not specifically provide rules for tender of delivery when the goods are in the possession of the seller and are not to be moved by him. For passage of *title,* see Section 2–401(3).

If the seller tenders delivery by putting and holding conforming goods for the buyer and gives him required notice, and if the buyer accepts the goods, probably the seller has completed delivery (Sections 2–503(1), 2–606).

D. Delivery Without Movement of Goods Held by Bailee

When the goods are to be picked up by the buyer from a bailee, a valid tender of delivery can be made either by tendering to the buyer a negotiable document of title (bill of lading or warehouse receipt covering the goods), or by an acknowledgment from the *bailee* that the buyer is entitled to possession of the goods (Section 2–503(4)(a)).

E. Imperfect Tender

If the goods fail to conform to the contract in any respect, e.g., greater quantity than ordered or goods of a different description mixed with the goods he ordered, the buyer may: (1) reject the whole; or (2) accept the whole; or (3) accept any commercial unit or units and reject the rest (Section 2–601). Exact performance by the seller may be tempered, however, by usage of trade, prior course of dealing, or course of performance, any one of which may permit commercial leeway in performance.

There are two important exceptions to the above rule: (1) installment contracts (buyer can reject only if non-conformity substantially impairs the value of that installment and cannot be cured), Section 2–612; and (2) limitations of remedy (parties can contract to limit the buyer's rights), Sections 2–718 and 2–719.

If the goods do not conform to the contract and the buyer refuses to accept them, the seller can "cure" his defective performance if time for performance has not yet expired by: (1) giving reasonable notice to the buyer of his intention to cure; and (2) making a conforming delivery within the contract time (Section 2–508). However, the seller does not have the right to cure unless he had reasonable grounds to believe that the tender would be accepted; such reasonable grounds can be in prior course of dealing, course of performance, usage of trade, or in the particular circumstances surrounding the making of the contract. Also, if the buyer does not inform the seller as to the nonconforming defect, he may not assert such defect as an excuse for nonperformance if the defect is one which is curable (Section 2–605).

When a *merchant* buyer rightfully rejects delivered goods, he must follow the *reasonable instructions* of the seller regarding the disposition of the goods unless the seller has an agent or place of business at the market of rejection. If the goods are perishable or threaten to decline in value speedily, the buyer must make reasonable efforts to sell them for the seller even in the absence of instructions. The buyer is entitled to reimbursement for reasonable expenses (Sections 2–603, 2–604).

When a *non-merchant* buyer rightfully rejects delivered goods, he is only under a duty to hold them with reasonable care at the seller's disposition for a time sufficient to permit the seller to remove them (Section 2–602(2)(b)(c)).

If the agreed type of carrier becomes unavailable or the agreed manner of delivery becomes commercially impracticable, and if neither party is at fault, *substituted performance* if commercially reasonable must be tendered and accepted (Section 2–614). Neither party is excused from performance because the express manner of delivery is impractical when there is a substitute available.

In case either party *repudiates* the contract before performance is due, the other party may either (1) wait for performance by the repudiating party; or (2) resort to any remedy for breach of contract; or (3) suspend his own performance (Section 2–610).

When reasonable grounds for insecurity arise with respect to the performance of either party, e.g., financial problems or strike against manufacturer-seller, the other may in writing demand *adequate assurance* of performance, and until he receives such assurance may suspend his own performance (Section 2–609). "Adequate assurance" of due performance depends on the factual situation. Where the buyer can make use of a defective delivery, a mere promise by a seller of good repute that he will give the matter his immediate attention and that the defect will not be repeated, is sufficient assurance. However, this would probably be insufficient if the statement was made by a known corner-cutter, unless accompanied by a surety bond, or if so demanded by the buyer, a speedy replacement of the defective product. If the defective product cannot be used by the buyer, a mere verbal assurance would not be adequate unless accompanied by replacement or other commercially reasonable cure.

F. Delivery Under Installment Contracts

"An 'installment contract' is one which requires or authorizes the delivery of goods in separate lots to be separately accepted" (Section 2–612(1)). The buyer may reject any installment which is non-conforming IF the non-conformity substantially impairs the value of that installment AND cannot be cured (Section 2–612(2)). If the non-conformity of an installment does not impair the value of the whole contract, the buyer must accept that installment if the seller gives adequate assurance of its cure. Impairment of the value of an installment can turn not only on the quality of the goods but also on such factors as quantity, time and assortment.

B. BUYER'S PERFORMANCE

1. PAYMENT

The buyer must tender payment before he has the right to obtain the goods (Sections 2–507(1), 2–511(1)). Unless the seller has refused to deliver, tender of payment is a prerequisite to putting the seller in default. All sales are for cash unless the seller agrees to extend credit.

Tender of payment is sufficient when made by any means or in any manner current in the ordinary course of business, including check, unless the seller demands payment in legal tender and gives the buyer a reasonable amount of time to procure it (Section 2–511(2)).

Payment by check is conditional on the check being honored by the buyer's bank (Section 2–511(3)). If the check is dishonored, the buyer has no right to retain the goods or dispose of them (Section 2–507(2)). A seller who has been paid by a dishonored check may sue for breach of contract or sue on the instrument itself (Sections 1–106(2), 3–802(1)(b)).

A good faith purchaser from a buyer who has paid for the goods with a bad check will prevail over the seller (Section 2–403(1)); however, the buyer's creditors do not prevail over the seller.

2. PAYMENT UNDER INSTALLMENT CONTRACTS

If the buyer defaults on an installment payment, *and if* the breach "substantially impairs" the value of the whole contract to the seller, there is a breach of contract (Sections 2–612(3), 2–703). What is substantial impairment is a difficult question of fact; however, it has been held that nonpayment of an installment can be a substantial impairment of the value of the contract either by creating financial difficulties for the seller or making it virtually impossible for him to assign the contract for financing, or by giving him reasonable apprehension that the buyer would not make future payments (Plotnick v. Pennsylvania Smelting & Ref. Co., C.A.Pa., 194 F.2d 859).

If the buyer fails to pay for one or more installments, the seller can stop delivery of the goods not paid for, and if the seller is uncertain about future performance can demand adequate assurances of performance from the buyer; e.g., demand that buyer post a surety bond, or submit a good credit report from his bank (Section 2–609).

If the buyer persists, over the seller's objections, in wrongfully *rejecting* installments or *failing to pay for them*, the buyer will then be held to have repudiated the contract permitting the seller to exercise his remedies (see Chapter XX, infra). However, if the seller accepts the payments without notification of cancellation of the contract, or if he brings an action with respect to past installments, or demands performance as to future installments, he reinstates the contract (Section 2–612(3)). The seller's acceptance of late payments may also be regarded as a waiver or modification of the contract (Sections 1–205(3), 2–208(3)).

3. PAYMENT AND INSPECTION

If a sale involves a documentary transaction (bill of lading) and the contract terms call for payment upon presentation of the bill of lading, or the contract calls for C.O.D., the buyer must pay for the goods before he inspects the goods (Section 2–513(3)(b)).

If the sale is F.O.B. vessel, F.A.S. vessel, C.I.F., or C.F. terms, the buyer must pay before inspection of the goods (Section 2–310(c), Section 2–319(4), and Section 2–320(4)). In a sale using C.I.F. or C.F. terms, but the documents are not to be presented for payment until after arrival of the goods, Section 2–321(3) provides for preliminary inspection before payment when this is feasible.

In all other cases, the buyer may inspect the goods before he makes payment (Section 2–513(1)). The buyer is allowed a reasonable time to inspect the goods and may test or analyze them in the process of inspecting them. The buyer must pay for the inspection; however, if the goods do not conform to the contract, the buyer may recover from the seller necessary expenses of inspection (Section 2–513(2), 2–515(a)).

If the goods are nonconforming and the buyer knows this, he does not have to pay for the goods before inspection (Section 2–512(1)). Section 2–512(1) does not provide any remedy for a seller against an alert buyer who refuses to pay for nonconforming goods. Furthermore, the seller's suit for damages would be ineffective because the seller could not prove damages. The buyer can be aware that the goods are nonconforming by simple observation (this is not considered inspection), e.g., damaged boxes that rattle, wrong quantity, or routine weighing before unloading which reveals an incorrect weight.

In cases where the buyer does not have the right of inspection before payment of the goods and the goods are nonconforming, the buyer must pay first and complain later of the defects.

C. EXCUSING PERFORMANCE

As stated in chapter 14, hazards such as strikes, financial problems, unforeseen shutdown of sources of supply, governmental regulations, and delay due to fire, generally do not excuse performance unless expressly provided for in the contract. However, it may have been within the contemplation of the parties at the time the contract was made that the goods to be manufactured and sold to the buyer were to be manufactured in a designated factory which is damaged or destroyed through an act such as an earthquake or fire. Under such circumstances, unless the seller has expressly assumed the risk of the nonhappening of the "presupposed condition", the seller is excused from performance (Section 2–615(a)).

1. *Seller's Duty to Ship*

SIMPSON FEED CO. v. CONTINENTAL GRAIN CO.

199 F.2d 284 (C.A.Ark., 1952).

SANBORN, Circuit Judge. The defendant in this action for damages for the alleged breach of a sales contract has appealed from the judgment in favor of the plaintiff. * * *

There is little dispute as to the facts which gave rise to this controversy. On October 30, 1950, the defendant had a carload of beans (about 2,000 bushels) for the plaintiff and called for shipping instructions which the plaintiff was obligated to furnish. These instructions were promptly given and the car was shipped. The defendant sent the plaintiff a draft for 90% of the purchase price, which was paid upon presentation. The balance of the purchase price, amounting to $441.87, has not been paid.

On the night of October 30, 1950, the defendant loaded another car of beans for the plaintiff, and on October 31, by telephone, asked the plaintiff's agent for shipping instructions. There is a dispute in the evidence as to this telephone conversation. The plaintiff's version is that the defendant's agent was informed that the plaintiff was seeking a permit for shipment to New Orleans, but had not yet received it; that the defendant's agent asked when the permit would be obtained and was told that it might be in thirty minutes or in a day or two; that he then said, "Let me know as soon as possible." The defendant's testimony was that the plaintiff's agent stated over the telephone that the plaintiff would furnish shipping instructions within thirty minutes, and that nothing was said about a New Orleans permit.

Shipping instructions were not received by the defendant from the plaintiff until November 2, or about 48 hours after they had been requested. When the plaintiff furnished the instructions, it was advised by the defendant that it considered the contract breached by virtue of the plaintiff's delay and that no more beans would be shipped under the contract. The plaintiff refused to accept this renunciation of the contract and insisted on performance.

It appears that there was a car shortage at the time that shipping instructions for the second carload were requested, and that the defendant was under pressure from the railroad to move the car and billed it out to another of its customers. It thereafter continued to refuse to ship any more soy beans to the plaintiff.

* * *

The District Court concluded that, under the evidence and the applicable law, the attempted renunciation of the contract because of the plaintiff's delay in giving shipping instructions was not justified; that the defendant was indebted to the plaintiff for the difference between the contract price of the beans and their market price on November 30; and that the plaintiff was indebted to the defendant for the balance due upon the carload of beans shipped on October 30, amounting to $441.87. Judgment was entered accordingly, and this appeal followed.

* * * It seems obvious to us, as it did to the District Court, that the plaintiff's delay in furnishing shipping instructions was of no serious or prejudicial consequence to the defendant, but was seized upon by it as an excuse for refusing to furnish the plaintiff with the beans at the contract price which was much lower than the market price which prevailed at the time the delay occurred. * * *

[Judgment affirmed.]

---

2. *Payment and Delivery are Concurrent*

VIDAL v. TRANSCONTINENTAL & WESTERN AIR, INC.

120 F.2d 67 (C.A.3d 1941).

GOODRICH, Circuit Judge. * * * This appeal by the plaintiffs is from the action of the trial court in dismissing their complaint. By the terms of the contract, which bears date of April 14, 1937, the defendant agreed to sell and the plaintiff agreed to buy four used airplanes of a specified type belonging to the seller. The price was stipulated and payment was to be made by certified check upon delivery of the airplanes to the buyer at the Municipal Airport, Kansas City, Missouri. The date for delivery was stated to be June 1, 1937. * * *

The trial court found as a fact that on June 1 the defendant was ready, able and willing to deliver one of the planes described in the contract to the plaintiffs at Municipal Airport in Kansas City, Missouri, and that after June 1 and on and prior to July 10 the defendant was ready, able and willing to deliver all of the four airplanes at the place specified. It was also found as a fact that the plaintiffs did not on June 1 or any other date either tender payment on any or all of the machines nor request delivery. * * *

What are the respective rights and duties of the parties in a contract of this kind? * * * [T]here was a simple contract promising delivery by the seller to the buyer of specified goods at a definite time and place and neither party demanded performance from the other or tendered his own. Has either a right against the other? Payment and delivery are concurrent conditions since both parties are bound to render performance at the same time. Restatement, Contracts, § 251. In such a case, as Williston points out, neither party can maintain an action against the other without first making an offer of performance himself. Otherwise, if each stayed at home ready and willing to perform each would have a right of action against the other. "* * * to maintain an action at law the plaintiff must not only be ready and willing but he must have manifested this before bringing his action, by some offer of performance to the defendant, * * * It is one of the consequences of concurrent conditions that a situation may arise where no right of action ever arises against either party * * * so long as both parties remain inactive, neither is liable * * *." This statement by the learned author not only has the force of his authority and that of many decisions from many states, but is also sound common sense. It is not an unfair requirement that a party complaining of another's conduct should be required to show that the other has fallen short in the performance of a legal obligation.

* * *

The conclusion is, therefore, that the defendant is not in default. Neither side having demanded performance by the other, neither side is in a position to complain or to assert any claim in an action of law against the other. This view of the case makes it unnecessary to examine the testimony which asserts that the buyers either abandoned or repudiated the contract prior to the time of the performance.

The judgment is affirmed.

---

3. *Seller's Right to Cure Non-Conforming Delivery*

WILSON v. SCAMPOLI

228 A.2d 848 (D.C.App., 1967).

MYERS, Associate Judge. This is an appeal from an order of the trial court granting rescission of a sales contract for a color television set and directing the return of the purchase price plus interest and costs.

[Plaintiff] purchased the set in question on November 4, 1965, paying the total purchase price in cash. The transaction was evidenced by a sales ticket showing the price paid and guaranteeing ninety days' free service and replacement of any defective tube and parts for a period of one year. Two days after purchase the set was delivered and uncrated, the antennae adjusted and the set plugged into an electrical outlet to "cook out." When the set was turned on, however, it did not function properly, the picture having a reddish tinge. Appellant's delivery man advised the buyer's daughter, Mrs. Kolley, that it was not his duty to tune in or adjust the color but that a service representative would shortly call at her house for that purpose.

On November 8, 1965, a service representative arrived, and after spending an hour in an effort to eliminate the red cast from the picture advised Mrs. Kolley that he would have to remove the chassis from the cabinet and take it to the shop as he could not determine the cause of the difficulty from his examination at the house. * * Mrs. Kolley refused to allow the chassis to be removed, asserting she did not want a "repaired" set but another "brand new" set. Later she demanded the return of the purchase price, although retaining the set. [Defendant] refused to refund the purchase price, but renewed his offer to adjust, repair, or, if the set could not be made to function properly, to replace it. * * * [Uniform Commercial Code, § 2–508]:

> "(1) Where any tender or delivery by the seller is rejected because non-conforming and the time for performance has not yet expired, the seller may seasonably notify the buyer of his intention to cure and may then within the contract time make a conforming delivery.
>
> "(2) Where the buyer rejects a non-conforming tender which the seller had reasonable grounds to believe would be acceptable with or without money allowance the seller may if he seasonably notifies the buyer have a further reasonable time to substitute a conforming tender."

A retail dealer would certainly expect and have reasonable grounds to believe that merchandise like color television sets, new and delivered as crated at the factory, would be acceptable as delivered and that, if defective in some way, he would have the right to substitute a conforming tender. The question then resolves itself to whether the dealer may conform his tender by adjustment of minor repair or whether he must conform by substituting brand new merchandise. * * * Here the adamant refusal of Mrs. Kolley, acting on behalf of appellee, to allow inspection essential to the determination of the cause of the excessive red tinge to the picture defeated any effort by the seller to provide timely repair or even replacement of the set if the difficulty could not be corrected. The cause of the defect might have been minor and easily adjusted or it may have been substantial and required replacement by another new set—but the seller was never given an adequate opportunity to make a determination.

We do not hold that appellant has no liability to appellee, but as he was denied access and a reasonable opportunity to repair, appellee has not shown a breach of warranty entitling him either to a brand new set or to rescission.

[Judgment for defendant.]

4. Seller's Rights on Breach of Installment Contract

REPUBLIC-ODIN APPLIANCE CORP. v. CONSUMERS PLUMBING & HEATING SUPPLY CO.

24 Ohio Opinions 2d 226, 192 N.E.2d 132 (1963).

HODDINOTT, Judge. Plaintiff is a manufacturer of home water heaters. For about seven years, it did a large-scale business with defendant, which sold at wholesale to building contractors and at retail to home owners. This dual mode of business apparently offended the notions of orderly marketing procedure held by plaintiff and plaintiff's other customers who competed with defendant, and gave rise to friction.

Defendant's dominating figure is Richard Friedman, its president. He is a skillful bargainer in a business which is highly competitive, and adept at obtaining substantial price discounts in his purchases. He is proud of taking cash discounts for prompt payment of all his bills; over the years, however, there were frequent disputes about items on the bills rendered by plaintiff. Defendant was a good, but hardly a favorite, customer of plaintiff. * * *

On December 10, a balance was due on the account and on December 12 defendant purported to pay it, except that defendant held back $7,000 which was to be paid "when instructed by R. C. Friedman."

Then, on December 19th, plaintiff's vice president and general manager, William Lennon, wrote in a letter to Friedman, the following: * * *

> "In light of your past record of arbitrary deductions, 'misunderstanding of terms,' arbitrary withholding of $7,000.00 and your violation of our selling agreement, and in keeping with our desire to improve our channels of distribution, we are hereby notifying you that we are unwilling to ship to your account for any and all of your four locations.
>
> "Unless payment for your account in full is received in this office by December 23, 1958, we will be forced to take necessary legal action to insure collection." * * *

Plaintiff brought this action on its account with defendant for heaters sold, freight and parcel post, and prayed for a judgment of $7,465.58 and interest. * * *

The failure to pay the substantial amount due on this order, following on the heels of the troubled relations of the parties and the unprecedented demands of the defendant put forth as conditions for doing business in the future, is a material breach of contract within the purview of the statute. Plaintiff was justified in repudiating this order. * * *

Plaintiff was also justified in repudiating the other unfilled orders of defendant.

* * * To state it in its simplest terms: If there is one installment contract between seller and buyer and one party breaches it under circumstances indicating he will not perform his duties in the future, then the other party is excused from further performance.

The Uniform Commercial Code, which went into effect in 1962, recognizes that a party to an installment contract has a right to "a continuing sense of reliance and security that the promised performance will be forthcoming when due," the Code makes provision for an adequate assurance of performance. * * *

Judgment shall be awarded to plaintiff against defendant on the petition for $7,465.58 with interest.

---

5. *Buyer Has Reasonable Time to Inspect Goods*

SQUARE DEAL MACHINE CO. v. GARRETT CORP.

128 Cal.App.2d 286, 275 P.2d 46 (1954).

MOSK, Justice pro tem. [Suit for damages for breach of contract.] Square Deal had received a $51,500 subcontract to perform machining operations on 500 elevating screws destined for the Army Ordnance Department. In order to meet specifications and to cut two threads to an inch on a lathe theretofore capable of cutting only as low as four threads, it became necessary to replace the standard gear assembly consisting of an 18-tooth gear with a 36-tooth gear.

On April 25, 1952, Philip Greathead, president of Square Deal, telephoned Garrett and ordered "one 36-tooth * * * and a 72-tooth gear," * * * and dispatched an employee, John Collins, with the order to pick up the two gears. Collins presented the order to Robert E. Dick, sales engineer for Garrett, and was given two gears wrapped in a paper bag. Neither party counted the teeth on the gears. * * *

Greathead received the bag from Collins, he did not note the marking on the gear and he did not count the teeth before installing the new gear train in place of the 18-tooth gear. He checked the first elevating screw threaded on the reassembled lathe, both visibly and with what instruments were available. Satisfied that the lathe was cutting two threads to the inch, he proceeded with the operation. * * * After the lathe had threaded 166 pieces during some 15 days, respondent discovered * * * that the gear contained only 35 teeth. The ultimate result was rejection and scrapping of the 166 pieces, and corresponding financial loss to Square Deal.

At the trial, Square Deal recovered a judgment in the sum of $8,267, and from it Garrett appeals, contending first that Square Deal may not prevail as a matter of law since it failed in a legal duty to examine the gear delivered to determine if it filled the contract. * * *

The buyer's right of inspection includes a reasonable time within which to make it, and imposes on him the duty to make it within that time after the goods have been received or tendered for acceptance; what is reasonable being a question of fact dependent upon the circumstances of each case, the situation of the goods, the nature of the business and the customs of the trade. * * *

If the buyer receives goods into his possession and fails to inspect them within a reasonable time after he has had opportunity to do so, he thereby loses the right to complain of their condition, and is thereafter to be treated as having assented to take or keep title to the goods. * * *

What constitutes a reasonable opportunity is always a question of fact to be determined according to the reasonable man standard by the trier of fact, in this case a jury. * * * If the seller can show that the buyer accepted the goods with actual knowledge that they did not conform to the order of purchase, he establishes an invincible defense to the buyer's action. * * *

It seems, therefore, that the test is not merely whether the purchaser laid eyes upon the object, but whether he had knowledge of the nonconformity to specification, or if he did not, were the circumstances such as required him, as a reasonable man, to have acquired such knowledge. Whether the purchaser here had or should have had such knowledge cannot be determined as a matter of law. It is clearly a factual problem, and we cannot say the jury and trial judge erroneously read the weight upon the evidentiary scales.

* * * It would be a harsh rule, indeed, if we were to hold as a matter of law that no warranties were to be implied in a purchase transaction where the purchaser's mere messenger had an opportunity of cursory inspection over the counter before he accepted the merchandise for delivery to his employer. Suffice it to say that a seller may not be so readily insulated from his legal responsibilities. * * *

That the buyer, after receiving the goods, has retained them without objection for an unreasonable period is the most frequent defense of the seller who argues an implied acceptance, * * *

What time may be deemed a reasonable one is a question of fact to be determined by the jury in view of all the circumstances of the case. * * *

The judgment is affirmed.

PROBLEMS

1. Buyer in Michigan and seller in New York enter into a contract for the sale of 1,000 coats #J 23 on credit. Nothing is stated as to whether it is a shipment or destination contract. Seller properly packs the coats and puts them in possession of the carrier, at which time he makes a proper contract for their transportation. Seller obtains a bill of lading representing title to the goods and mails it to the buyer via air mail. While the coats are in transit they are destroyed by fire. Seller demands pay-

ment for the coats citing Section 2–509(1)(a). Buyer refuses citing Section 2–504(c).

2. Seller in New York enters into a contract for the sale of 1,000 bushels of wheat with the buyer in Florida. Seller takes out a negotiable bill of lading in his own name and ships the goods by reasonable contract to the buyer in Florida by independent carrier. Seller immediately notifies buyer of the shipment. While the goods are in transit, they are destroyed. Buyer refuses to pay for the wheat on the ground that the seller reserved title in his own name by the use of the bill of lading and, therefore, the seller also retained the risk of loss. Decision?

3. Buyer in Kansas ordered a prefabricated house to be delivered "F.O.B., building site" from the seller in Minnesota. The seller brought the house to the building site and unloaded it. The state of Kansas taxed the buyer on the theory that the sale was made in Kansas. Buyer contends the sale took place in Minnesota. Decision?

4. Buyer and seller entered into a contract for the sale of sheep of specified ages. At the place of delivery in Oregon, the buyer requested that he be permitted to inspect the sheep to ascertain the age of each. The seller would not permit a detailed inspection but would permit the buyer to "gate run" them and reject the sick or crippled sheep. Buyer refuses to take the sheep without a detailed inspection. Decision?

5. Buyer and seller enter into a contract for the sale of 100 cases of Beefeater Gin. On the contracted delivery date at 4:30 P.M., the seller delivers by truck to the buyer's place of business 80 cases of Beefeater Gin and 20 cases of Gordon's Gin. The buyer tells the truck driver that he will not accept delivery because he ordered 100 cases of Beefeater Gin, and there are only 80 cases on the truck. The truck driver returns the shipment to the seller the next morning explaining to his employer why the shipment was refused. Five days later, the seller attempts to cure his improper tender by delivering 100 cases of Beefeater Gin; however, the buyer refuses the shipment stating that he has purchased the goods from someone else. Decision?

6. Buyer and seller enter into a contract for certain precision motor parts which the buyer intends to use immediately upon delivery. Prior to delivery the buyer learns that the seller is making defective deliveries of such parts to other buyers with similar needs. Buyer seeks your advice as to his right to demand adequate assurance.

7. Buyer and seller entered into a contract for the sale of oil on 30 day's credit with 2% off for payment within ten days, provided that credit was to be extended to buyer only if his financial responsibility was satisfactory to the seller. The buyer normally paid early so that he could take advantage of the discount; however, on the last sale buyer did not pay within ten days. Seller heard a rumor which was false that buyer was having financial difficulties, so seller demanded adequate assurance. Buyer sent a good credit report from his banker with a statement that he would make payments within the 30 day term and insisted on further deliveries under the contract. Seller seeks your advice.

8. Buyer and seller enter into a contract for the sale of goods. The purchase price is $4,000.00. On Friday evening, the proper time for delivery, the buyer brings his truck to seller's place of business to receive delivery of the goods and offers seller his check in the amount of $4,000.00.

Seller refuses the check demanding cash. Buyer states that the banks are closed, but he will bring the cash Monday morning. Seller refuses to give buyer the extra time to raise the cash and declares the buyer is in breach of contract. Decision?

9. Buyer and seller enter into a contract for the purchase of a television set. Payments are to be made in installments of $50.00 a month, payable on the first day of each and every month. Buyer makes his first payment on the first of the month; however, he makes his next five payments on the 10th of the month because of a change in salary payment dates. The seller does not complain about these late payments. On the seventh month, the seller repossesses the television set on the 8th day of the month. Seller claims this right because the buyer is late in his payment. Decision?

10. Buyer and seller enter into a contract whereby seller will sell and deliver to the buyer 1,000 injectors for buyer's steam boilers. While seller is in the process of manufacturing the injectors, his factory burns down. Buyer demands performance, but seller claims he is excused under Section 2–615(a) of the *U.C.C.* Decision?

Chapter 20

REMEDIES UNDER THE UNIFORM COMMERCIAL CODE

If the sales agreement does not specifically provide for remedies on breach of contract, the *U.C.C.* attempts to meet the problem in Part 7, Sections 2–701—2–724.

Some of the courses of action open to the buyer and seller have been treated previously in chapter 19; e. g., Section 2–602 (Buyer's rejection of nonconforming goods), Section 2–609 (Right to adequate assurance by either party), and Section 2–508 (Seller's right to cure an improper tender or delivery).

A. REMEDIES OF THE SELLER

---

1. WITHHOLD DELIVERY OF THE GOODS

Section 2–703(a) permits the seller to *withhold* delivery of the goods when:

a. the buyer wrongfully rejects or revokes acceptance of the goods; or

b. the buyer fails to make a payment due on or before delivery; or

c. the buyer repudiates the contract in whole or in part; or

d. the buyer fails to cooperate with the seller so as to enable the seller to perform (Section 2–311(3)(a)); or

e. if the seller discovers the buyer is insolvent, the seller can withhold delivery until he is paid cash for the goods; and if he has already delivered, he can demand cash (Section 2–702 (1)). Since the code does not state what constitutes discovery, the seller must have good evidence before he uses this remedy or he will be in breach of contract if the buyer is solvent; therefore, if the seller is not quite certain that the buyer is insolvent, it would be better for him to use the remedy of demanding assurances of performance under Section 2–609(1).

2. STOP DELIVERY WHEN GOODS IN POSSESSION OF CARRIER

The seller can *stop* delivery of goods when:

a. the buyer is insolvent (Section 2–702(1)); or

b. the buyer repudiates or fails to make a payment due before delivery (Section 2–705(1)); or

c. the seller has any other right to withhold or reclaim the goods; e.g., when the buyer fails to cooperate or when the seller is waiting for justifiably demanded assurances (Section 2–705(1)).

The right of the seller to stop delivery *ends* when:

a. the buyer or someone holding under him, such as a subpurchaser, actually receives the goods (Section 2–705(2)(a)); or

b. a bailee of the goods, except the original carrier, acknowledges to the buyer that it holds the goods for him (Section 2–705(2)(b)) (an example of such a bailee would be a warehouseman); or

c. a reshipping carrier or a carrier acting as a warehouseman acknowledges to the buyer that it holds the goods for him (Section 2–705(2)(c))—a diversion of a shipment is not a "reshipment" when it is merely an incident to the original contract of transportation, and an acknowledgment by the carrier as a "warehouseman" requires a contract of a truly different character from the original shipment, i. e., a contract not in extension of transit but as a warehouseman; or

d. a negotiable document of title covering the goods is negotiated to the buyer (Section 2–705(2)(d)).

To stop delivery, the seller must notify the carrier or other bailee so that the bailee by reasonable diligence can prevent delivery (Section 2–705(3)). To stop delivery, the seller usually notifies the freight agent who handled the shipment for him. The agent will need information from the bill of lading; such as, names of the shipper and consignee, the routing, the car number, the shipping point, and the destination point. If a negotiable bill of lading is outstanding, the carrier will probably demand a bond; however, the seller can probably avoid this by simply diverting the goods to some other destination (Section 7–303). The seller is not required to notify the buyer that he is stopping delivery; however, it is usually good practice to give such a notice.

3. RECLAIM THE GOODS

A seller can reclaim goods sold on credit to the buyer if he discovers that the buyer was insolvent when he received the goods; however, to reclaim the goods, the seller must demand return of the goods within ten days after the buyer has received them (Section 2–702(2)).

The seller loses his right to reclaim if the buyer has resold the goods to third persons in the ordinary course of business or to other good faith purchasers (Section 2–702(3)).

4. IDENTIFY GOODS TO CONTRACT ON BUYER'S BREACH

The seller may identify goods to the contract (see chapter 18) on the buyer's breach if conforming goods are in the seller's possession or control when he learns of the breach.

The *effect* of identification to the contract is that the seller can resell the goods and hold the buyer for damages (Section 2–704). If the seller cannot resell the goods, he can hold the buyer for the contract price (Section 2–709(1)(b)).

5. RESELL THE GOODS

The seller may resell the goods when the buyer wrongfully rejects them or revokes acceptance, fails to make a payment due on or before delivery, or repudiates the contract in whole or in part (Section 2–706).

The seller may recover from the buyer the difference between the resale price and the contract price together with any incidental damages (Section 2–706(1)).

The resale may be at public or private sale (Section 2–706(2)). If at *private* sale, the seller must give the buyer reasonable notice of intention to resell (Section 2–706(3)). If at *public* sale, the seller must give the buyer reasonable notice of the time and place of the resale unless the goods are perishable or threaten to decline in value speedily (Section 2–706(4)(b)).

The seller may purchase the goods at a *public* sale (Section 2–706(4)(d)). The seller is not accountable to the buyer for any profit made on a resale (Section 2–706(6)).

6. CANCEL THE CONTRACT

When the buyer wrongfully rejects the goods or revokes acceptance, fails to make a payment due, or repudiates the contract, the seller may cancel the contract (Section 2–703(f)). Cancellation permits the seller to end his obligations while retaining remedies for breach of contract.

7. RECOVER DAMAGES

The seller is entitled to recover damages after the buyer's wrongful rejection of the goods, revocation of acceptance, failure to make a payment due, or repudiation of the contract (Sections 2–703(d)(e), 2–706(1), 2–708).

The *normal* measure of damages is the difference between the contract price and the market price at the time and place for tender, plus any incidental damages sustained, less any expenses saved as a result of the buyer's breach (Section 2–708(1)).

If the seller *resells* the goods, the damages will be the difference between the contract and the resale price, plus any incidental damages, less any expense saved as a result of the buyer's breach (Section 2–706(1)).

If the measure of damages stated supra (difference between contract price and market price, or between contract price and resale price) is inadequate to put the seller in as good a position as performance would have done, the *U.C.C.* attempts to remedy the situation by providing the seller with an alternative measure of damages. Section

2–708(2) provides that the seller may recover his *profit,* including reasonable overhead, which he would have realized from full performance by the buyer, plus any incidental damages, less expenses saved as a result of the buyer's breach.

8. RECOVER PRICE OF THE GOODS

The seller can recover the price of the goods and incidental damages in three situations:

a. when the buyer has accepted the goods (Section 2–709(1)(a)); or

b. when conforming goods are lost or damaged after risk of loss has passed to the buyer (Section 2–709(1)(a)); or

c. when the goods have been identified to the contract and he is unable to resell them for a reasonable price (Section 2–709(1)(b)).

B. REMEDIES OF THE BUYER

---

1. COVER

When the seller fails to make delivery or repudiates the contract, or when the buyer rightfully rejects goods or justifiably revokes acceptance (and the seller does not cure his defective performance), the buyer has the right to "cover"; i.e., to purchase goods in substitution for those due under the contract (Sections 2–711(a), 2–712).

The buyer is not required to cover, and his failure to do so does not affect any of his other remedies under the *U.C.C.* (Section 2–712(3)).

The buyer's damages are the difference between the contract price and the cost of cover, plus incidental or consequential damages, less expenses saved (Section 2–712(2)).

2. REVOKE ACCEPTANCE

When the buyer has accepted goods that later prove to be defective, he can revoke his acceptance; i.e., withdraw his previous assent (Section 2–608). See Section 2–607(2) regarding acceptance of non-conforming goods. He can revoke his acceptance only when the non-conformity is such as will cause a substantial impairment of value to him. Generally this remedy is resorted to only after attempts at adjustment have failed.

The *effect* of a revocation of acceptance is that the buyer is in the same position as if he had rejected the goods and, therefore, has the same remedies and duties as a rejecting buyer (Section 2–608(3)).

(See Section 2–711(3)—security interest; Section 2–602(2)(b)—holding goods for seller; Section 2–603(1)—disposing of goods; Section 2–604—salvaging goods; Section 2–602(a)—using goods; Section 2–401(4)—revesting title in seller; Sections 1–201(26), 2–327(1)(c), 2–327(2)—sales on approval and sale or return, Section 2–721—remedies for fraud.)

After a proper revocation of acceptance, the buyer is not liable for the price of the goods (Section 2–607(1)).

3. OBTAIN SECURITY INTEREST

A buyer, who has rightfully rejected goods or justifiably revoked acceptance of non-conforming goods which remain in his possession, has a security interest in the goods to cover payments made on the price, and the costs of inspection, receipt, transportation, care, and custody. The buyer may resell the goods in the same manner as an aggrieved seller (Section 2–711(3)).

4. OBTAIN IDENTIFIED GOODS FROM INSOLVENT SELLER

Insolvency of the seller gives the buyer specific rights to the goods (Sections 2–502, 2–711(2)(a)). However, for the buyer to have these rights, all of the following four conditions must exist:

a. Buyer has paid all or part of the price, and if he has not paid all of the price then he has tendered the unpaid portion of the price (Section 2–502(1)).

b. Seller has failed to deliver the goods, or he has repudiated the contract (Sections 2–502(1), 2–711(2)).

c. The goods have been identified to the contract by the seller (Section 2–502(1)).

d. Seller became insolvent within ten days after receiving the first installment on the price (Section 2–502(1)).

If a buyer is concerned that the seller is having financial trouble, he should demand assurances of performance (Section 2–609).

5. DEDUCTION OF DAMAGES FROM THE PRICE

If the buyer is damaged by the seller's breach, he may, after notice to the seller, offset all or part of his damages from the price still due on the contract (Section 2–717).

6. CANCEL THE CONTRACT

The buyer, after notice to the seller, may cancel the contract if the seller fails to deliver the goods or repudiates the contract, or the buyer rightfully revokes acceptance (Section 2–711(1)). The right to cancel is subject to the seller's right to cure a defective performance.

Cancellation excuses further performance by the buyer, but does not deprive him of any remedy for past breaches; e.g., he may cover, claim damages for breach, obtain conforming goods through replevin (see 8, infra), or obtain specific performance (see 9, infra).

7. DAMAGES

On the seller's repudiation of the contract, failure to deliver the goods, non-conforming delivery, or breach of warranty, the buyer is entitled to recover damages (Sections 2–711 through 2–715).

The *normal* measure of damages is the difference between the contract price and the market price or the cost of cover, plus incidental and consequential damages, less expenses saved (Sections 2–713, 2–714, 2–715).

In case of breach of *warranty,* the buyer's measure of damages is the difference between the value of the goods accepted and the value they would have had if the goods had been as warranted (Section 2–714(2)).

Punitive or exemplary (penalty) damages are not covered in the code. Normally, such damages are not recoverable in contract cases.

8. REPLEVIN THE GOODS

Replevin is an action to recover specific goods in which the buyer has an interest and which are unlawfully withheld from him. The buyer's right to such action is stated in Section 2–716(3) of the *U.C.C.* This remedy is given the buyer in cases in which cover is reasonably unavailable and goods have been identified to the contract. This right is in addition to the buyer's right to recover identified goods on the seller's insolvency. The purpose of this section is to give a buyer rights to goods which are comparable to a seller's rights to the price.

9. SPECIFIC PERFORMANCE

The buyer can get specific performance of a contract when the goods are unique, or "in other proper circumstances" (Section 2–716(1)). Thus, the *U.C.C.* broadens the right to obtain specific performance. For example, various situations that could justify specific performance are: output and requirement contracts involving a particular or peculiarly available source or market, unavailability of cover, and insolvency of the seller.

The decree for specific performance may include such terms and conditions as to payment, damages, or other relief as the Court may deem just (Section 2–716(2)).

1. Right to Reclaim Goods from Insolvent Buyer

METROPOLITAN DISTRIBUTORS v. EASTERN SUPPLY CO.

21 D. & C.2d 128 (Pa., 1959).

On March 24, 1958, receivers for Eastern Supply Company were appointed by this court. Subsequent to that appointment and without notice or knowledge of it, Turf Man Sales Corporation contracted for the delivery of 150 lawnmowers to Eastern Supply Company. On March 28, 1958, the lawnmowers were accepted by Eastern Supply Company at its premises. Eastern Supply Company was then insolvent and was unable and did not intend to pay for the lawnmowers. The insolvency was known by the company and the receivers. On April 8, 1958, Turf Man Sales made demand upon the receivers for return of the mowers claiming that title had remained in the seller throughout this course of events.

SOFFEL, J. November 6, 1959. * * *

Since Turf Man Sales Corporation cannot rely on any rights under case law to rescind its contract and recover its lawnmowers, it must rely solely on Section 2–702(1)(*b*), Uniform Commercial Code * * * which provides: * * *

"(1) Where the seller discovers the buyer to be insolvent he may * * *

"(b) subject to the rights of a buyer in ordinary course or other good faith purchaser or lien creditor * * * and within ten days after receipt, reclaim any goods received by the buyer on credit." * * *

On its face this section would seem to give Turf Man Sales Corporation an unqualified right to recover possession of the lawnmowers, since delivery to Eastern Supply Company was made on March 28, 1958, and a telephone demand for their return was made on April 4, 1958. The receivers have, however, argued that Turf Man Sales Corporation only "demanded" the return of the goods while the code requires a physical reclamation. Such an interpretation of this section is not justified. Not only would such a conclusion force vendors to devious means to gain physical possession of goods within the 10-day period, but in a suit which invoked this section as reciting a remedy available to vendors, the very thing which is the object of the suit would be deemed to be a prerequisite to obtaining it, i.e., possession of the goods.

* * * Section 2–702(1)(*b*) of the Uniform Commercial Code, which permits a seller of goods, upon learning of the buyer's insolvency, to reclaim its goods within 10 days after receipt of the goods by the purchaser, would determine the rights of the parties here if it were not for the fact that there exists a possible conflict between that section and the provisions of the Federal Bankruptcy Act

pertaining to preferences. Because of the possible conflict it seems judicious to have the rights of the parties determined by the Federal district court before which bankruptcy proceedings are now pending.

---

2. Seller's Damages Under U.C.C. 2–708

CHICAGO ROLLER SKATE MANUFACTURING COMPANY v. SOKOL MANUFACTURING COMPANY

185 Neb. 515, 177 N.W.2d 25 (1970).

NEWTON, Justice. This is an action for damages for breach of contract. A jury was waived and trial had to the court. Defendant purchased of plaintiff truck and wheel assemblies with plates and hangers for use in the manufacture of skate boards. The skate board fad terminated and several weeks later, defendant returned, without plaintiff's consent, a quantity of the merchandise purchased. There was due plaintiff the sum of $12,860. The merchandise was not suitable for other uses and could not be resold. It was held by plaintiff for 7 months. Plaintiff offered a credit of 70 cents per unit which defendant neither accepted nor rejected. Plaintiff then disassembled, cleaned, and rebuilt the units to make them suitable for use on roller skates. The undisputed evidence shows the rebuilt units had a reasonable value of 67 cents and 69 cents. In the salvage operation plaintiff incurred an expense of $3,540.76. Profits lost amounted to an additional $2,572. Plaintiff, disregarding its expense, credited defendant with 70 cents per unit and brought suit for the balance due of $4,285 for which sum it recovered judgment in the trial court. We affirm the judgment.

Section 1–103, U.C.C., provides: "Unless displaced by the particular provisions of this act, the principles of law and equity, including the law merchant and the law relative to capacity to contract, * * * or other validating or invalidating cause shall supplement its provisions."

Section 1–106, U.C.C., provides in part: "(1) The remedies provided by this act shall be liberally administered to the end that the aggrieved party may be put in as good a position as if the other party had fully performed but neither consequential or special nor penal damages may be had except as specifically provided in this act or by other rule of law."

Section 1–203, U.C.C., states: "Every contract or duty within this act imposes an obligation of good faith in its performance or enforcement."

Section 2–718(4), U.C.C., provides: "Where a seller has received payment in goods their reasonable value or the proceeds of their resale shall be treated as payments * * *."

In accordance with section 2–709, U.C.C., plaintiff was entitled to hold the merchandise for defendant and recover the full contract price of $12,860. Plaintiff did not elect to enforce this right, but recognizing that there was no market for the goods or resale value and that they were consequently worthless for the purpose for which they were designed, it attempted to mitigate defendant's damages by converting the goods to other uses and credited defendant with the reasonable value of the goods as converted or rebuilt for use in roller skates. In so doing, plaintiff was evidencing good faith and conforming to the general rule requiring one damaged by another's breach of contract to reduce or mitigate damages. * * *

The Uniform Commercial Code contemplates that it shall be supplemented by existing principles of law and equity. It further contemplates that the remedies provided shall be liberally administered to the end that an aggrieved party shall be put in as good a position as it would have been in if the contract had been performed. Here the buyer was demanding of the seller credit for the full contract price for goods that had become worthless. The seller was the aggrieved party and a return of worthless goods did not place it in as good a position as it would have been in had the contract been performed by the buyer paying the contract price. On the other hand, the crediting to defendant of the reasonable value of the rebuilt materials and recovery of the balance of the contract price did reasonably reimburse plaintiff. This procedure appears to be contemplated by section 2–718(4), U.C.C., which requires that a seller paid in goods credit the buyer with the reasonable value of the goods.

It is the defendant's theory that since the goods were not resold or held for the buyer, the seller cannot maintain an action for the price. We agree with this proposition. We also agree with defendant in its contention that the controlling measure of damages is that set out in section 2–708(2), U.C.C. This section provides that the measure of damages is the profit which the seller would have made from full performance by the buyer, together with any incidental damages resulting from the breach and costs reasonably incurred. Defendant overlooks the provision for allowance of incidental damages and costs incurred. The loss of profits, together with the additional costs or damage sustained by plaintiff amount to $6,112.76, a sum considerably in excess of that sought and recovered by plaintiff. Although the case was tried by plaintiff and determined on an erroneous theory of damages, the error is without prejudice to defendant. There being no cross-appeal, the judgment of the district court is affirmed.

Affirmed.

3. Seller Can Recover Loss of Profits

NERI v. RETAIL MARINE CORP.

30 N.Y.2d 393, 334 N.Y.S.2d 165 (1972).

GIBSON, Judge. The appeal concerns the right of a retail dealer to cover loss of profits and incidental damages upon the buyer's repudiation of a contract governed by the Uniform Commercial Code. * * *

The plaintiffs contracted to purchase from defendant a new boat of a specified model for the price of $12,587.40, against which they made a deposit of $40. They shortly increased the deposit to $4,250 in consideration of the defendant dealer's agreement to arrange with the manufacturer for immediate delivery on the basis of "a firm sale", instead of the delivery within approximately four to six weeks originally specified. Some six days after the date of the contract plaintiffs' lawyer sent to defendant a letter rescinding the sales contract for the reason that plaintiff Neri was about to undergo hospitalization and surgery, in consequence of which, according to the letter, it would be "impossible for Mr. Neri to make any payments". The boat had already been ordered from the manufacturer and was delivered to defendant at or before the time the attorney's letter was received. Defendant declined to refund plaintiffs' deposit and this action to recover it was commenced. Defendant counterclaimed, alleging plaintiffs' breach of the contract and defendant's resultant damage in the amount of $4,250, for which sum defendant demanded judgment. Upon motion, defendant had summary judgment on the issue of liability tendered by its counterclaim; and Special Term directed an assessment of damages, upon which it would be determined whether plaintiffs were entitled to the return of any portion of their down payment.

Upon the trial so directed, it was shown that the boat ordered and received by defendant in accordance with plaintiffs' contract of purchase was sold some four months later to another buyer for the same price as that negotiated with plaintiffs. From this proof the plaintiffs argue that defendant's loss on its contract was recouped, while defendant argues that but for plaintiffs' default, it would have sold two boats and have earned two profits instead of one. Defendant proved, without contradiction, that its profit on the sale under the contract in suit would have been $2,579 and that during the period the boat remained unsold incidental expenses aggregating $674 for storage, upkeep, finance charges and insurance were incurred. Additionally, defendant proved and sought to recover attorneys' fees of $1,250.

* * *

The issue is governed in the first instance by section 2–718 of the Uniform Commercial Code which provides, among other things, that the buyer, despite his breach, may have restitution of the amount by which his payment exceeds: (a) reasonable liquidated damages stipulated by the contract or (b) absent such stipulation, 20% of the value of the buyer's total performance or $500, whichever is smaller (§ 2–718, subsection [2], pars. [a], [b]). As above noted, the trial court awarded defendant an offset in the amount of $500 under paragraph (b) and directed restitution to plaintiffs of the balance. Section 2–718, however, establishes, in paragraph (a) of subsection (3), an alternative right of offset in favor of the seller, as follows: "(3) The buyer's right to restitution under subsection (2) is subject to offset to the extent that the seller establishes (a) a right to recover damages under the provisions of this Article other than subsection (1) ".

Among "the provisions of this Article other than subsection (1)" are those to be found in section 2–708, which the courts below did not apply. Subsection (1) of that section provides that "the measure of damages for non-acceptance or repudiation by the buyer is the difference between the market price at the time and place for tender and the unpaid contract price together with any incidental damages provided in this Article (Section 2–710), but less expenses saved in consequence of the buyer's breach." However, this provision is made expressly subject to subsection (2), providing: "(2) If the measure of damages provided in subsection (1) is inadequate to put the seller in as good a position as performance would have done then the measure of damages is the profit (including reasonable overhead) which the seller would have made from full performance by the buyer, together with any incidental damages provided in this Article (Section 2–710), due allowance for costs reasonably incurred and due credit for payments or proceeds of resale."

* * * Closely parallel to the factual situation now before us is that hypothesized by Dean Hawkland as illustrative of the operation of the rules: "Thus, if a private party agrees to sell his automobile to a buyer for $2,000, a breach by the buyer would cause the seller no loss (except incidental damages, i. e., expense of a new sale) if the seller was able to sell the automobile to another buyer for $2000. But the situation is different with dealers having an unlimited supply of standard-priced goods. Thus, if an automobile dealer agrees to sell a car to a buyer at the standard price of $2000, a breach by the buyer injures the dealer, even though he is able to sell the automobile to another for $2000. If the dealer has an inexhaustible supply of cars, the resale to replace the breaching buyer costs the dealer a sale, because, had the breaching buyer performed, the dealer would have made two sales instead of one. The buyer's breach, in such a case, depletes the dealer's sales to the extent of one, and the measure of damages should be the dealer's profit on one sale. Section 2–708

recognizes this, and it rejects the rule developed under the Uniform Sales Act by many courts that the profit cannot be recovered in this case."

The record which in this case establishes defendant's entitlement to damages in the amount of its prospective profit, at the same time confirms defendant's cognate right to "any incidental damages provided in this Article (Section 2–710)" (Uniform Commercial Code, § 2–708, subsection [2]).

* * *

The trial court correctly denied defendant's claim for recovery of attorney's fees incurred by it in this action. Attorney's fees incurred in an action such as this are not in the nature of the protective expenses contemplated by the statute. * * *

It follows that plaintiffs are entitled to restitution of the sum of $4,250 paid by them on account of the contract price less an offset to defendant in the amount of $3,253 on account of its lost profit of $2,579 and its incidental damages of $674.

The order of the Appellate Division should be modified, with costs in all courts, in accordance with this opinion, and, as so modified, affirmed.

---

4. Limitations on Right of Seller to Recover Price

DENKIN v. STERNER

10 D. & C.2d 203 (Pa., 1956).

ANDERSON, J., July 16, 1956. This case comes before the court on a petition by defendants to open a judgment entered upon what is termed a "Purchase Money Security Agreement," * * *.

From the testimony and the agreement it appears that defendants agreed on April 11, 1955, to purchase from plaintiff certain refrigerated cases and equipment as specified for a food market which they were erecting in Hanover, for the total price of $35,500. Under date of June 9, 1955, defendants by letter canceled the order or agreement before delivery of any part thereof to them, and on July 28, judgment was entered on the agreement for the full amount of the purchase price.

Defendants further contend that the clause in paragraph 11 of the agreement, providing for entry of judgment for the full amount of the purchase price, is contrary to section 2–709 of the Uniform Commercial Code entitled "Action for the Price," which states:

> "(1) When the buyer fails to pay the price as it becomes due the seller may recover, together with any incidental damages under the next section, the price

"(a) of goods accepted or of conforming goods lost or damaged after risk of their loss has passed to the buyer; and

"(b) of goods identified to the contract if the seller is unable after reasonable effort to resell them at a reasonable price or the circumstances reasonably indicate that such effort will be unavailing.

"(2) Where the seller sues for the price he must hold for the buyer any goods which have been identified to the contract and are still in his control except that if resale becomes possible he may resell them at any time prior to the collection of the judgment. The net proceeds of any such resale must be credited to the buyer and payment of the judgment entitles him to any goods not resold."

While there seems little doubt from the depositions taken under the rule issued in this case that plaintiff is entitled to damages, for defendants admit that they canceled the agreement because they found out after checking that they could buy more equipment for less money elsewhere, yet it also seems evident under all the circumstances that to permit plaintiff to recover the full amount of the purchase price without showing what goods, if any, have been identified to the contract, what goods were standard items and readily salable and what goods had actually been specially manufactured prior to the cancellation by defendants, as well as what goods have been or can be readily resold, would be in effect "unreasonably large liquidated damages" and, therefore, unconscionable and void.

We therefore hold that the judgment in this case should be opened to permit defendants to defend as to the amount due plaintiff.

---

5. *Right of Buyer to Revoke Acceptance*

GRANDI v. LeSAGE

74 N.M. 799, 399 P.2d 285 (1965).

CHAVEZ, Justice. This is an appeal from a judgment ordering a rescission of plaintiffs' claim to a race horse and awarding, jointly and severally, compensatory and punitive damages.

On July 3, 1962, Henry Grandi and Kathryn Grandi, his wife, filed a complaint * * * against defendants, R. S. LeSage and H. R. Claggett, which alleged, * * * that on January 6, 1962, defendant LeSage, as owner, * * * entered a race horse named "Cur-Non" in a claiming race with a claiming price of $3,500 at Sunland Park Race Track, Sunland Park, New Mexico; that in order to enter the race and to induce qualified persons to file claims, the defendants deposited with officials of the track a "Jockey Club Certificate of Foal Registration," which represented Cur-Non as a horse and said representation was published in the official program; that defendants, in depositing said registration, knew said statement as to the sex of Cur-Non was false and was done with intent to induce plaintiffs and others to file claims on Cur-Non and thus defraud them; that plaintiffs, believing the statements, were induced to claim Cur-Non for the sum of $3,500, that plaintiffs claimed Cur-Non expressly and exclusively as a stallion for themselves and others for a fee; that, prior to January 6, 1962, Cur-Non had been gelded and made useless as a breeder, and plaintiffs were thereby damaged in the sum of $3,500; that it has been the general custom that a claimant is prohibited from making a prior inspection of an entry in a claiming race; that plaintiffs abided by said custom and, upon learning of the true sex of Cur-Non, immediately made demand upon defendants for the return of the claim price and their expenses incurred; * * *.

Sections 711(1)(b), 713 and 715(1), * * *, give a buyer, who rightfully rejects or justifiably revokes acceptance of the goods, the right not only to rescind and recover back the purchase price paid, but, in addition, the right to recover incidental damages resulting from the seller's breach, including expenses reasonably incurred in the care and custody of such goods. * * *

By his point VI, appellant LeSage argues:

> * * * the plaintiffs accepted delivery of Cur-Non after reasonable opportunity to inspect him,

Notwithstanding there may have been an acceptance * * *, a buyer who justifiably revokes his acceptance has the same right to rescission as though he had rejected the goods in the first place. Such revocation is justifiable if he accepted them:

> "(b) Without discovery of such nonconformity if his acceptance was reasonably induced either by the difficulty of discovery before acceptance or by the seller's assurances.
>
> "(2) Revocation of acceptance must occur within a reasonable time after the buyer discovers or should have discovered the ground for it and before any substantial change in condition of the goods which is not caused by their own defects. It is not effective until the buyer notifies the seller of it.
>
> "* * *"

[Judgment for plaintiff.]

6. *No Effective Revocation of Acceptance Until Seller Given Notice*

POOLE v. MARION BUICK CO.

14 N.C.App. 721, 189 S.E.2d 650 (1972).

This action was instituted for the recovery of $3,309.36 purchase price payments and $1,000.00 loss of use. The plaintiff alleged that on 8 October 1968 he had purchased a 1968 Buick GS400 automobile and had made payments therefor in the total amount of $3,309.36. * * *

The evidence on behalf of plaintiff may be summarized as follows:

On 8 October 1968 plaintiff purchased the automobile. He began having difficulty immediately after purchase. With less than 150 miles on the automobile he returned it to Marion Buick for repair of a water leak and misfiring motor. He continued to have trouble with the car, particularly a water leak, and subsequently returned the car to Marion Buick for repairs on frequent occasions. In August 1968 when the car had been driven 17,000 miles, plaintiff again returned the car to Marion Buick; and at that time Marion Buick took the motor apart and replaced a number of major parts. Plaintiff testified that the motor continued to misfire and that Marion Buick was never able to get the automobile to run properly. On 15 April 1969 after the plaintiff had had the car eighteen months and had driven it 27,000 miles, the engine "blew" at approximately 1:00 a. m. as the plaintiff was driving on Interstate Highway I–40. Plaintiff had the automobile towed to Marion Buick. Marion Buick had never charged plaintiff for any repairs made up until that time. On this occasion Marion Buick offered to dismantle the engine to determine if the cause of the engine failure was a defect in material or workmanship. If such a defect were found, repairs would be made without charge. If there were no defects in material or workmanship, plaintiff was to pay for the repairs. Plaintiff testified that he authorized Marion Buick to proceed in accordance with this offer and that he had also received a letter from Buick Motor Division of the defendant General Motors Corporation which repeated the offer made by Marion Buick and requested a reply from the plaintiff. Plaintiff testified that he never answered the letter and that the automobile is still at Marion Buick unrepaired.

* * *

The jury returned a verdict in favor of the plaintiff awarding plaintiff $2,500. The defendants moved for judgment notwithstanding the verdict, and this motion was denied. * * *

CAMPBELL, Judge. Defendants assign as error the denial of their motions for directed verdict made at the close of the plaintiff's evidence and renewed at the close of all the evidence and for judgment notwithstanding the verdict.

* * *

All of the evidence on behalf of the plaintiff is to the effect that he began having mechanical trouble with the automobile immediately after he purchased it; that he returned the automobile to Marion Buick on numerous occasions and repairs were made free of charge; that the trouble continued until the engine finally blew up eighteen months after the date of purchase and after the automobile had been driven 27,000 miles. Nowhere is there any evidence that plaintiff ever gave defendants any notice of his revocation of acceptance.

* * *

In the instant case plaintiff merely left his automobile at Marion Buick's place of business. There is a conflict in the evidence as to whether plaintiff instructed Marion Buick to determine if the cause of the engine failure was defective materials or workmanship but it is clear from the evidence that plaintiff never gave Marion Buick any notice of revocation of acceptance. Plaintiff kept and operated the automobile for eighteen months and drove it 27,000 miles. There is no construction of the evidence which would allow a jury to find that defendants had been notified of a revocation of acceptance; therefore, defendants' motions should have been allowed.

* * *

This cause is remanded to the trial court with the direction that judgment be entered in accordance with the motion of appellants for a directed verdict in their favor.

---

7. *Revocation of Acceptance Within Reasonable Time (Defective Goods)*

BIRKNER v. PURDON

27 Mich.App. 476, 183 N.W.2d 598 (1970).

J. H. GILLIS, Presiding Judge. This is an action on an oral contract for the sale of Christmas trees. Plaintiff Birkner, a grower and wholesaler of scotch pines, sued to recover an unpaid purchase price due on the contract. Defendant Purdon, a lot-retailer, counterclaimed, alleging that the trees delivered did not meet contract requirements and were of inferior quality. The case was tried by the court sitting without a jury. From a judgment awarding defendant his counterclaim, plaintiff appeals.

At trial, defendant testified that he had ordered "Number One" trees—a designation generally used in the field of Christmas tree sales. Harry Hartjen, an experienced wholesaler and retailer of Christmas trees, testified that such a tree is over 5½ feet in height, with 3 good sides, a conical shape, and a satisfactory top (one without crows' nests). A Number One tree is also free from holes or gaps.

When the trees were delivered to defendant's retail lots, defendant was of the opinion that they were not of the specified quality. He was assured by plaintiff, however, on several occasions that the trees delivered were good, saleable trees. And, because of his relative inexperience, defendant decided to retain the trees and attempt to sell them. Defendant is a teacher by profession with little experience in grading and selling Christmas trees. Plaintiff, on the other hand, is a wholesaler with 32 years of experience.

Defendant's retail lots were, according to the testimony of Hartjen, ideally located for tree sales: "The best Christmas tree lot location I have ever seen." Defendant's business records established that he incurred large expenses in an attempt to sell the trees in question, but to no avail. Of 3,555 trees delivered defendant was able to sell only 627. It was defendant's claim that the poor sales were attributable to the inferior quality of the trees.

The trial court found that the contract required the delivery of number one trees—"meaning a common description of something which is quite good." This finding is not challenged on appeal. Both parties agree that the contract excluded defective or inferior trees. The court also found the contract had been breached in that the trees delivered did not conform to contract requirements.

Plaintiff next contends that defendant failed to reject the trees in a timely manner, thus waiving any claim of nonconformity. Defendant received the first of 5 shipments of trees on November 24, 1967. On December 21, 1967, immediately after obtaining the results of the USDA inspection and consulting with his attorney, defendant sent plaintiff a telegram revoking his acceptance of the trees.

U.C.C. 2–608, M.C.L.A. § 440.2608 (Stat.Ann.1964 Rev. § 19.-2608) provides in part:

> "(1) The buyer may revoke his acceptance of a lot or commercial unit whose nonconformity substantially impairs its value to him if he has accepted it.
>
> * * * * * * * * * *
>
> "(b) [W]ithout discovery of such nonconformity if his acceptance was reasonably induced either by the difficulty of discovery before acceptance or by the seller's assurances.
>
> "(2) Revocation of acceptance must occur within a reasonable time after the buyer discovers or should have discovered the ground for it and before any substantial change in condition of the goods which is not caused by their own defects. It is not effective until the buyer notifies the seller of it."

There was testimony tending to show that immediate discovery of the defects was difficult because of the time required for the trees to open up after being flattened in transit; that on several occasions defendant had been expressly assured by plaintiff that the trees delivered were of good quality; that, because of the slow build-up of the selling season, it was difficult to judge the merchantability of the trees until the weekend of the 17th; and, finally, that defendant's relative inexperience limited his appreciation of the defects. In light of these circumstances, the question of defendant's alleged delay was one of fact for resolution by the trier. * * * The trial judge found that defendant had revoked his acceptance within a reasonable time under all the circumstances. We find no error.

Nor are we persuaded that the method utilized by the trial judge in assessing damages, including damages for lost profits, was improper. * * *

Affirmed. Costs to defendant.

---

8. Short Drive of New Automobile Not Acceptance (Buyer can Revoke Acceptance; Seller's Improper Cure)

ZABRISKIE CHEVROLET, INC. v. SMITH

99 N.J. 441, 240 A.2d 195 (1968).

DOAN, J. D. C.

[Action for purchase price of new automobile.] * * *

On February 2, 1967 defendant signed a form purchase order for a new 1966 Chevrolet Biscayne Sedan which was represented to him to be a brand-new car that would operate perfectly. On that occasion he paid plaintiff $124 by way of deposit. On February 9, 1967 defendant tendered plaintiff his check for $2069.50 representing the balance of the purchase price ($2064) and $5.50 for license and transfer fees. Delivery was made to defendant's wife during the early evening hours of Friday, February 10, 1967, at which time she was handed the keys and the factory package of printed material, including the manual and the manufacturer-dealer's warranty, none of which she or her husband ever read before or after the sale was made, nor were the details thereof specifically explained to or agreed to by defendant. While en route to her home, about 2½ miles away, and after having gone about 7/10 of a mile from the showroom, the car stalled at a traffic light, stalled again within another 15 feet and again thereafter each time the vehicle was required to stop. When about halfway home the car could not be driven in "drive" gear at all, and defendant's wife was obliged to then propel the vehicle in "low-low" gear at a rate of about five to ten miles per hour, its then maximum speed. In great distress, defendant's wife was fearful of completing the journey to her home and called her husband, who thereupon drove the car in "low-low" gear about seven blocks to his home. Defendant, considerably upset by this turn of events, thereupon immediately called his bank (which was open this Friday evening), stopped payment on the check and called plaintiff to notify them that they had sold him a "lemon," that he had stopped payment on the check and that the sale was cancelled. The next day plaintiff sent a wrecker to defendant's home, brought the vehicle to its repair shop and after inspection determined that the transmission was defective.

Plaintiff's expert testified that the car would not move, that there was no power in the transmission and in that condition the car could not move. Plaintiff replaced the transmission with another one removed from a vehicle then on plaintiff's showroom floor, notifying defendant thereafter of what had been done. Defendant refused to take delivery of the vehicle as repaired and reasserted his cancellation of the sale. Plaintiff has since kept the vehicle in storage at his place of business. Within a short period following these occurrences plaintiff and defendant began negotiations for a new 1967 Chevrolet, but these fell through when plaintiff insisted that a new deal could only be made by giving defendant credit for the previously ordered 1966 Chevrolet. This defendant refused to do because he considered the prior transaction as cancelled.

* * *

Plaintiff urges that defendant accepted the vehicle and therefore under the Code (N.J.S. 12A:2–607(1), N.J.S.A.) is bound to complete payment for it. Defendant asserts that he never accepted the vehicle and therefore under the Code properly rejected it; further, that even if there had been acceptance he was justified under the Code in revoking the same. Defendant supports this claim by urging that what was delivered to him was not what he bargained for, i. e., a new car with factory new parts, which would operate perfectly as represented and, therefore, the Code remedies of rejection and revocation of acceptance were available to him. These remedies have their basis in breach of contract and failure of consideration although they are also viewed as arising out of breach of warranty. The essential ingredient which determines which of these two remedies is brought into play is a determination, *in limine*, whether there had been an "acceptance" of the goods by the buyer. Thus, the primary inquiry is whether the defendant had "accepted" the automobile prior to the return thereof to the plaintiff.

N.J.S. 12A:2–606, N.J.S.A. states in pertinent part:

"(1) Acceptance of goods occurs when the buyer

> (a) after a reasonable opportunity to inspect the goods signifies to the seller that the goods are conforming or that he will take or retain them in spite of their nonconformity.

* * *

It is clear that a buyer does not accept goods until he has had a "reasonable opportunity to inspect." Defendant sought to purchase a new car. He assumed what every new car buyer has a right to assume and, indeed, has been led to assume by the high powered advertising techniques of the auto industry—that his new car, with the exception of very minor adjustments, would be mechanically new and factory-furnished, operate perfectly, and be free of substantial defects. The vehicle delivered to defendant did not measure up to these representations. Plaintiff contends that defendant had "reasonable opportunity to inspect" by the privilege to take the car for a typical "spin around the block" before signing the purchase order. If by this contention plaintiff equates a spin around the block with "reasonable opportunity to inspect", the contention is illusory and unrealistic. To the layman, the complicated mechanisms of today's automobiles are a complete mystery. To have the automobile inspected by someone with sufficient expertise to disassemble the vehicle in order to discover latent defects before the contract is signed, is assuredly impossible and highly impractical. * * * Consequently, the first few miles of driving become even more significant to the excited new car buyer. This is the buyer's first reasonable opportunity to enjoy his new vehicle to see if it conforms to what it was represented to be and whether he is getting what he bargained for. How long the buyer may drive the new car under the guise of inspection of new goods is not an issue in the present case. It is clear that defendant discovered the nonconformity within 7/10 of a mile and minutes after leaving plaintiff's showroom. Certainly this was well within the ambit of "reasonable opportunity to inspect." That the vehicle was grievously defective when it left plaintiff's possession is a compelling conclusion, as is the conclusion that in a legal sense defendant never accepted the vehicle.

* * *

Even if defendant had accepted the automobile tendered, he had a right to revoke under N.J.S. 12A:2–608, N.J.S.A.:

> "(1) The buyer may revoke his acceptance of a lot or commercial unit whose non-conformity *substantially impairs its value* to him if he has accepted it.

* * * Here the breach was substantial. The new car was practically inoperable and endowed with a defective transmission. This was a "remarkable defect" and justified rejection by the buyer.

Lastly, plaintiff urges that under the Code, N.J.S. 12A:2–508, N.J.S.A. it had a right to cure the nonconforming delivery. * * * The inquiry is as to what is intended by "cure," as used in the Code. This statute makes no attempt to define or specify what a "cure" shall consist of. It would appear, then, that each case must be controlled by its own facts. The "cure" intended under the cited section of the Code does not, in the court's opinion, contemplate the tender of a new vehicle with a substituted transmission, not from the factory and of unknown lineage from another vehicle in plaintiff's possession. It was not the intention of the Legislature that the right to "cure" is a limitless one to be controlled only by the will of the seller. A "cure" which endeavors by substitution to tender a chattel not within the agreement or contemplation of the parties is invalid.

For a majority of people the purchase of a new car is a major investment, rationalized by the peace of mind that flows from its dependability and safety. Once their faith is shaken, the vehicle loses not only its real value in their eyes, but becomes an instrument whose integrity is substantially impaired and whose operation is fraught with apprehension. The attempted cure in the present case was ineffective.

* * *

[Judgment for defendant.]

---

9. Retention of Goods Does Not Affect Revocation Under U.C.C. 2–602

GARFINKEL v. LEHMAN FLOOR COVERING CO.

60 Misc.2d 72, 302 N.Y.S.2d 167 (1969).

FRANCIS J. DONOVAN, Judge. Plaintiff seeks to recover the sum of $1,363.63 which was paid to the defendant for floor covering. The covering was installed on the floors March 8, 1967. Immediately the plaintiff noticed an unsightly condition and called it to the attention of the defendant.

On two occasions representatives of the defendant called at the plaintiff's home and worked on the carpet in an attempt to correct the condition.

The expert who testified on behalf of the defendant, described the condition as pressure bands caused by pressure when the carpeting was on the roller.

The expert said that the condition was corrected but that, on a later inspection, he found a condition which he attributed to wear or traffic causing differences in color or shading and perhaps a flattening out or crushed appearance. It was his opinion that the latter condition was normal with velvet carpet of the kind in suit.

The plaintiff testified that the condition which had been originally reported, examined and worked on by the defendant, continued throughout.

On this issue the court accepts the testimony of the plaintiff. Therefore it follows that the pressure band condition was never corrected and the merchandise was defective. There were continual complaints to the defendant. On April 12, 1967 plaintiff's attorney wrote to the defendant rejecting the merchandise and demanding its removal.

The defendant failed to remove it. On August 15, 1967 a formal letter was sent by certified mail to the defendant, again demanding that it be removed and the purchase price refunded. Nevertheless the defendant has failed to take any action. The merchandise is substantially defective and the plaintiff is entitled to have the purchase price refunded unless he has in some way prejudiced that right by retaining the carpet which is still on his floor and in use.

* * *

Plaintiff relies on the Uniform Commercial Code.

The cited cases antedate the enactment of the Uniform Commercial Code. Section 2–602 of the Uniform Commercial Code provides that the buyer, if he has possession of the goods, is under a duty after rejection to "hold them with reasonable care at the seller's disposition for a time sufficient to permit the seller to remove them; but the buyer has no further obligations with regard to goods rightfully rejected." It follows that the plaintiff was then permitted to retain the goods at his home awaiting removal by the seller and had no further obligation if the rejection was within a reasonable time and he had notified the seller.

The court finds as a fact that the rejection was justified; that it was made within a reasonable time and that proper notification was given to the seller.

The need for this provision of the Uniform Commercial Code has been apparent in this court for some time. Many cases were brought where a merchant delivered defective merchandise, bulky in character, expensive to transport and store. He then left the defective merchandise and refused to remove it. This placed the consumer in a dilemma. If the consumer removes and returns the goods, it is an expensive proposition. He is out of pocket money, in addition to the loss of his purchase price, in exchange for the gamble of recovering some of it by court action. On the other hand, if he retains the merchandise in his home, he loses the right to rescind the contract and his purchase money is gone. In return he has to seek the right to damage for which he will need expensive expert testimony.

It is the opinion of the court that one of the beneficial purposes intended by the new commercial code was to put the burden on the merchant where the goods are defective and he is given proper notice of the defect. He delivered the goods and it is fair that he should remove them or let them remain at his peril.

Judgment for plaintiff for the sum of $1363.63 with interest from March 8, 1967.

10. *Right of Buyer to Specific Performance*

McCORMICK DRAY LINE, INC. v. LOVELL

13 D. & C.2d 464 (Pa., 1957).

GREEVY, J., May 24, 1957. The complaint in this case was filed to compel defendants to specifically perform a contract for the sale of defendants' trucking business, its good will, a piece of real estate, and transfer of ICC and PUC certificates as owned by defendants. * * *

The present contract calls for the transfer of ICC and PUC certificates of public convenience and for the sale of a going business and its good will. The actual damages of a vendor's failure to comply with such an agreement are impossible of precise calculation so that there is no adequate remedy at law. With respect to the remedy of specific performance the Uniform Commercial Code provides (§ 2–716):

> "(1) Specific performance may be decreed where the goods are unique or in other proper circumstances."

The ICC and PUC rights are unique and therefore proper subject of a decree of specific performance.

A decree for specific performance is not a matter of right but a matter of grace, and will not be granted unless plaintiff is clearly entitled thereto, and there is no adequate remedy at law, * * *.

In our opinion, filed May 24, 1957, we stated that specific performance may be decreed where the goods are unique and that Interstate Commerce Commission and Public Utility Commission rights are unique.

The test of uniqueness must be made in terms of the total situation which characterizes the contract and here, because specific performance attaches to a material portion of the subject matter of the contract, specific performance will be allowed to the entire contract. We find that plaintiff is ready, willing, desirous, prompt, eager and able to carry out the terms of the contract.

This is clearly a case for relief by specific performance and inasmuch as the contract involves accounting and adjustment between the parties and contains a warranty upon the part of defendant, John E. Lovell, it will be necessary for the court to retain jurisdiction in order to see that the contract is carried out according to its terms.

PROBLEMS

1. Seller pursuant to a credit contract for the sale of 100 television sets, ships the sets from New York to the buyer in Chicago. Upon arrival of the goods, the freight agent for the carrier calls the buyer and acknowledges to him that they are holding the 100 television sets for him and asks him to pick them up. Before the buyer has an opportunity to pick up the sets, the seller learns that the buyer has become insolvent, so the seller calls the representative of the carrier and asks him to stop delivery. The agent of the carrier states that he has already acknowl-

edged to the buyer that they are holding the goods for him. Does the seller have the right to stop delivery?

2. Seller in Ohio ships a set of books to the buyer in San Francisco on credit. Two days after the buyer receives the books, the seller learns that the buyer was insolvent when he received them and that he will not be able to pay for them. Seller immediately demands that the buyer return the books. Buyer tells the seller that he will not return the books and that the seller can get in line with the rest of his creditors. Decision?

3. Seller in Kentucky sold to the buyer in Florida a large quantity of tobacco, but the buyer refused delivery of the tobacco. After due notice, the seller sold the tobacco for a price less than the contract price between the seller and the buyer. Seller brings suit for the difference between the resale price and the contract price, plus his expenses in the transportation, care and custody of the goods after the buyer refused delivery together with the costs of the resale. Buyer contends that seller's election to resell the property to another buyer released him from all liability on the contract. Decision?

4. Seller in Michigan sold to buyer in Indiana a large quantity of Christmas cards made to special order for the buyer; but when the cards were delivered in October pursuant to the contract, the buyer refused delivery. Seller brings suit for the price of the cards. Buyer contends that he cannot be compelled to pay the full price for the cards and that the seller must resell them to another purchaser and collect merely the difference between the sum so realized and the contract price. Seller contends that since the cards are not readily resaleable at a reasonable price so late in the season, he has no duty to attempt to resell them. Decision?

5. S, a seller of soft water equipment, sold a unit to B. Approximately two weeks after the sale, the equipment proved defective. B complained to S who attempted to fix the unit. However, the unit continued to be defective. B continued to complain and S continued to try to fix it. This procedure went on for approximately one year when B finally sent a letter to S requesting him to pick up the equipment and refund the purchase price. S refuses to do either claiming that B waited too long to revoke his acceptance. Decision?

6. B purchased a large quantity of toys from S to use as stock in his store for Christmas trade. Several shipments of toys were sent to B during October and November; however, the number was less than half of the toys ordered. B called S many times during October and November complaining that he was not receiving all of the toys, and each time was assured by S that the rest of the toys would be forthcoming. Finally, on December 1, B called S and angrily demanded the toys. When S gave B the same reply, an exasperated B said that he wanted no more toys. Apparently this call was too late as B received a large shipment of the toys on December 2. This shipment completed the entire purchase order except for one small lot which was never sent. B did not open this shipment. The other toys were priced, put on display, and sold by B. In February B sent all of the toys not sold to S and demanded S pay their value. S returned the shipment to B. Decision?

7. Buyer purchases twenty motors to be used in the construction of swimming pools. After delivery to the buyer, it is discovered that the

motors do not conform to the contract so the buyer revokes his acceptance; however, the seller refuses to recognize the revocation and refuses to take back the motors. Buyer after due notice to the seller sells the motors and sues seller for the difference between the price realized on the sale and the price he had paid the seller, plus incidental damages. Seller contends that the buyer's exercise of ownership over the goods in reselling them prevents buyer's action. Decision?

8. B purchased a new automobile from S which proved to be defective. He returned the automobile after he drove it approximately 8,000 miles, and demanded the return of his purchase price. S claims the correct measure of damages is the difference between the value the car had at the time of the transaction and the value it would have had if it had been as warranted. Decision?

9. Seller agreed to sell buyer two unusual oriental jars; but when the buyer tendered payment and demanded possession of the jars, the seller refused, stating that he intended keeping them for his wife. Buyer sues for specific performance, and the seller states that the buyer is limited to money damages for breach of contract. Decision?

Chapter 21

WARRANTIES AND PRODUCTS LIABILITY

A. WARRANTIES

1. IN GENERAL

A warranty is a promise by the seller concerning some aspect of the sale, such as the quality of the goods, the quantity, or the title.

There are two types of warranties, i.e., express and implied. An express warranty is made part of the contract by the words or conduct of the seller. An implied warranty is made part of the contract by operation of the law.

Under the *U.C.C.,* a warranty can arise by course of dealing between the parties or by usage of trade; e. g., the obligation to provide pedigree papers in the sale of a pedigreed dog or blooded bull.

The *U.C.C.'s* warranty provisions are in Sections 2–312 to 2–319.

2. EXPRESS WARRANTIES

a. By Affirmation or Promise

Section 2–313(1)(a) provides that *"any affirmation of fact or promise* made by the seller to the buyer which relates to the goods and becomes part of the basis of the bargain creates an express warranty that the goods shall conform to the affirmation or promise". (Emphasis added.)

No particular words are necessary to create a warranty. The word "guarantee" is treated as the equivalent of "warranty".

Section 2–313(2) provides that a seller's statement as to the value of the goods or a statement which purports to be merely the seller's opinion or commendation of the goods does not create a warranty as common experience discloses that such statements cannot fairly be viewed as entering into the bargain. These statements are commonly referred to as "puffing" or "sales talk". However, a statement in which the seller gives market figures relating to sales of similar goods would be a statement of fact, not of value, and hence actionable.

Not every chance remark of the seller is a warranty; however, if the statement has in the circumstances and in objective judgment become part of the basis of the bargain, it can be considered a warranty. Also, the more expert and experienced the seller, the more likely his words will be construed to be a warranty.

Examples of words construed to be warranties are as follows: the machine is "durable" is a warranty that its parts will not wear out or break when put to use; calling goods "number one" is an express warranty of good quality; seller will "stand behind the goods 100%"; oil well suspension plug is "as good as" the plug of the competition; "this cloth is all wool".

Examples of statements considered as only opinion are as follows: goods are "first class"; peach kernel oil "as good as the best grade of olive oil"; caramel coloring matter "just as good or perhaps better than any"; jukebox a "good machine" in "workable condition" and "would probably not require repair".

A warranty may be made after the transaction is completed, and it need not be supported by consideration (Section 2–209(1)); however, if the sales contract as modified is within the Statute of Frauds it must be in writing (Section 2–209(3)).

Section 2–313(1)(a) states that a warranty is made by a *seller* to a buyer. Can a buyer rely on a warranty made in a *manufacturer's* advertising so as to hold the manufacturer liable even though the buyer did not deal directly with the manufacturer? Most courts hold the manufacturer liable on the basis of an express warranty even though there is no privity of contract.

B. Warranty by Description

"Any description of the goods which is made part of the basis of the bargain creates an express warranty that the goods shall conform to the description", Section 2–313(1)(b). Thus, a descriptive name constitutes a warranty; e.g., "black grapes" warrants black-colored grapes; "Blue Goose" tomatoes; "No. 1 Saigon Long Grain Rice"; "export-cured boneless codfish".

The descriptive word or phrase can be an express warranty even though it is only in the invoice or in an advertisement and not in the sales contract.

C. Warranty by Sample or Model

"Any sample or model which is made part of the basis of the bargain creates an express warranty that the whole of the goods shall conform to the sample or model." Section 2–313(c).

If the seller used the sample merely to "suggest" the character of the subject matter of the contract, then it is not a warranty by sample; however, if the seller used the sample to indicate intent that it was to "be" the character of the subject-matter of the contract, then it is a warranty. In other words, if the contract is based on the understanding that the seller will supply goods according to a particular description or that the goods will be the same as the sample or a model, the seller is bound by an express warranty that the goods shall conform to the description, sample, or model. If the seller does not want to make this warranty, he should label his samples and models in such manner as to indicate that they are only suggestive of the material he desires to sell and that they did not come from the goods to be sold. If a sample has been drawn from an existing bulk it is considered as describing values of the goods contracted for unless it is accompanied by a denial of warranty.

3. WARRANTY OF TITLE

Every sale of goods contains a warranty of title; i.e., that the title conveyed shall be good and that the goods shall be free from any security interest or other lien of which the buyer has no knowledge (Section 2–312(1)).

4. WARRANTIES IMPLIED BY LAW

A. Warranty of Merchantability

A warranty that the goods shall be merchantable is implied in a contract for their sale if the seller is a merchant with respect to goods of that kind (Section 2–314(1)). In general, "merchantable" means of average or medium quality (see Section 2–314(2) for specific situations).

B. Warranty of Fitness for Particular Purpose

Where the seller has reason to know the particular purpose for which the goods are required and that the buyer is relying on the seller's skill or judgment to select or furnish the goods, there is an implied warranty that the goods shall be fit for such purpose (Section 2–315).

The buyer must actually rely on the seller's skill or judgment and if the buyer does not, there is no warranty for a particular purpose; however, there would still be a warranty of merchantability.

When the buyer asks for a product by trade name, there may be a warranty of fitness for a particular purpose; however, there is no such warranty if the buyer insists on a particular brand since he is not relying on the seller's skill or judgment. If the seller assures the buyer that a certain product will do a particular job, the seller is making an *express* warranty.

In *restaurant* cases, the seller can be liable if the goods are not fit for human consumption. Section 2–314(1) states that food to be consumed on or off the premises is a sale, and Section 2–315 indicates that the food must be fit for human consumption. Whether food is unfit for human consumption is a question of fact. Food for human consumption need not be actually unfit; it is sufficient if the consumer has adequate grounds for believing that it is. The fact that some person would be willing to eat the food on the witness stand would not be a defense. In many states (California, Louisiana, Massachusetts, North Carolina), the warranty of fitness for human consumption does not apply if there is an object in the food that is not foreign to the food; e. g., cherry pit in cherry pie, bone in fish chowder, oyster shell in oyster soup, chicken bone in chicken pie.

Other states (Maryland, Pennsylvania, Wisconsin) have rejected the so-called "foreign-natural" test in favor of what is known as the "reasonable expectation" test. Under this test, the jury must make a determination whether the buyer could reasonably have expected the object in the food. If he could not, the buyer will recover. Examples of recovery under this test are chicken bone in a chicken sandwich, oyster shell in canned oysters used in making oyster stew, and chicken bone in chow mein.

In *landlord-tenant* cases, many courts hold that a lease is, in essence, a sale, and thus there is an implied warranty of habitability under Section 2–315. If the tenant does not terminate the lease he remains liable for the reasonable rental value of the premises as determined by the court for such time as the premises were in violation of the housing codes. Minor housing code violations which do not affect habitability will not entitle the tenant to a reduction in rent; i. e., the violation must be relevant and affect the tenant's apartment or the common areas which he uses. The tenant must also give notice of alleged defects to the landlord and allow a reasonable time for repairs to be made. In addition to the right of rescission, the tenant has the right to damages under proper circumstances. Where material violations of the housing code existed *prior* to the agreement to lease, it has been held that the lease is void because it is in violation of the law and against public policy, and under such circumstances the tenant is not liable for the rent.

The implied warranty of habitability has been extended to the first purchaser of a new house.

5. EXCLUSION, MODIFICATION, AND DISCLAIMER

Disclaimers or exclusions of both express and implied warranties are construed against the seller.

A. Warranties of Description

A clause excluding "all warranties, express or implied" will not disclaim the warranty of *description* unless it is within the contemplation of both parties that such warranty is to be disclaimed. To make the disclaimer effective, the seller should state in conspicuous language that there is no warranty of description and place the disclaimer after the language of description.

B. Merchantability Warranty

A disclaimer of the implied warranty of merchantability must specifically mention merchantability and, if in writing, must be conspicuous (Section 2–316(2)). An effective disclaimer would state that the seller does not warrant the goods to be merchantable.

C. Particular Purpose Warranty

A disclaimer of an implied warranty for a particular purpose must be in writing and must be conspicuous (Section 2–316(2)). An effective disclaimer would be as follows: "There is no warranty that this product is fit for any particular purpose".

D. Trade Usage Warranties

An effective disclaimer in course of dealing or trade usage should be conspicuous and should state that the buyer acknowledges (1) no warranties implied by custom or usage have become part of the contract, (2) in their trade, it is customary not to give warranties, and (3) prior dealings do not imply any warranties.

E. Title Warranty

A warranty of title can only be excluded by specific language or by circumstances which give the buyer reason to know that the person selling does not claim title in himself, or that he is purporting to sell only such right or title as he or a third person may have (Section 2–312(2)). The language should include the word "title" and be conspicuous.

F. Exclusion by Inspection

(1) *Express warranties* (see #2, supra).

A buyer does not have to inspect or examine the goods, but may rely solely on the seller's express warranties. When the seller makes an *express* warranty and the buyer does not inspect although an inspection would have revealed that the seller's representations were false, the seller is liable as the buyer is justified in believing the seller's representations.

(2) *Implied warranties* (see #4, supra).

In the case of implied warranties, the seller can demand that the buyer inspect the goods or a sample or model; and if the buyer refuses, all implied warranties are disclaimed. If the buyer does examine the goods, there is no implied warranty as to defects which such examination should have revealed (Section 2–316(3)(b)).

G. Other Ways of Excluding Implied Warranties

(1) If the contract states that the buyer is taking the goods "as is" or "with all faults" or "as they stand," all implied warranties are excluded (Section 2–316(3)(a)). However, a "catch phrase" disclaimer such as, "all warranties, express or implied, are excluded" is probably ineffective to exclude express or implied warranties, especially if the words are not conspicuous (Section 2–316, Comment (1)).

(2) Usage of trade may disclaim implied warranties; e. g., a buyer who purchased from a junk dealer or at a sheriff's sale cannot

rely on implied warranties. Also, course of dealing or custom can exclude implied warranties (Section 2–316(3)(c)).

H. Automobile Warranties

Automobile disclaimers of warranties are usually so strict as to be illusory (misleading). Liability is usually limited to repair or replacement of defective parts. The *U.C.C.,* Section 2–316(4), permits contractual limitation of warranties; however, the courts treat disclaimers that are too strict as ineffective. One of the leading cases in the United States held an automobile disclaimer void on public policy grounds (because buyer has no bargaining power with automobile manufacturers as to disclaimers) and permitted the wife of the buyer of the automobile to recover for personal injury damages from the manufacturer for breach of implied warranty of merchantability (Henningsen v. Bloomfield Motors, Inc., 32 N.J. 358, 161 A.2d 69). Other courts have followed the same reasoning; e.g., General Motors Corp. v. Dodson, 47 Tenn.App. 438, 338 S.W.2d 655; State Farm Mutual Auto Ins. Co. v. Anderson-Weber, Inc., 252 Iowa 1289, 110 N.W. 2d 449; Walsh v. Ford Motor Co., 59 Misc.2d 241, 298 N.Y.S.2d 538 (1969). The California Supreme Court has held that not only was the disclaimer invalid but the manufacturer and retailer were *strictly liable in tort* for the buyer's personal injuries (Vandermark v. Ford Motor Co., 61 Cal.2d 256, 37 Cal.Rptr. 896); see B. 6., infra, for discussion of strict liability in tort.

I. Family Use of Goods

Section 2–318 provides that a seller's warranty extends to any natural person who is in the family or household of his buyer or who is a guest in his home if it is reasonable to expect that such person may use, consume or be affected by the goods and who is injured by breach of the warranty. The purpose of this section is to give a limited class of beneficiaries the benefit of the same express or implied warranty which the buyer received regardless of lack of privity of contract. Virginia adopted a provision in lieu of Section 2–318 which eliminates the requirement of privity in all actions against the manufacturer and seller of goods for negligence and breach of warranty. California and Utah did not adopt Section 2–318 since prior case law went further and did not require privity of contract in the sale of food and drugs, or in the case of an express warranty made by a manufacturer. Some states ignore the requirement that a guest must be in the buyer's home at the time of the damage.

Modern decisions permit recovery for property damage as well as for personal injuries.

The last sentence of Section 2–318 forbids the seller from excluding liability to persons to whom the warranties which benefit his buyer would extend under this section. It does not mean that a seller is precluded from excluding or disclaiming a warranty which might otherwise arise in connection with a sale if the exclusion is permitted under Section 2–316; nor does it preclude the seller from limiting the remedies of his own buyer and therefore of any beneficiaries under Section 2–718 or 2–719. Provisions which exclude or modify warranties, or limit remedies for breach of contract, apply equally to the beneficiaries under this section as well as to the buyer.

B. PRODUCTS LIABILITY

---

1. IN GENERAL

When a person is injured or his property is damaged due to the use or condition of an article, the person may be entitled to recover damages. This right may be based on breach of warranty, on negligence or misrepresentation, on a violation of a statutory duty, or on strict liability in tort.

2. BREACH OF WARRANTY

Breach of warranty has been discussed in the previous chapter and is covered in Sections 2–313 to 2–319. The seller's breach of warranty normally does not extend to subpurchasers; however, Section 2–318 extends the warranty to users other than the purchaser.

3. NEGLIGENCE

Independently of the *U.C.C.,* a manufacturer will be liable to persons injured by his product when he is negligent in the preparation or manufacture of the product and when as a reasonable man he could foresee that such negligence would injure such person or persons. Such liability extends to all persons a reasonable person could foresee would be injured regardless of their relationship to the buyer. Recoveries have been allowed against manufacturers of automobiles on behalf of buyers, users, passengers, and bystanders based on negligence resulting in defective steering wheels, axles, brakes, tires, and other operating components.

4. MISREPRESENTATION

A person selling goods to the public can be liable for fraudulent or innocent misrepresentation as to the character or quality of the goods. This misrepresentation can be made by advertising, labels, or otherwise. The liability not only extends to the buyer but to any person consuming or using the goods.

Thus, M, a manufacturer of automobiles, advertises in newspapers, magazines and an illustrated brochure that the glass in its cars is "shatter-proof". B reads this advertising and in reliance thereon purchases from a retail dealer an automobile manufactured by M. While B is driving the car, a pebble thrown by a passing truck tire strikes the windshield and shatters it, causing a splinter of glass to penetrate B's eye. The manufacturer is liable to B. Baxter v. Ford Motor Co., 168 Wash. 456, 12 P.2d 409, 88 A.L.R. 521.

5. VIOLATION OF STATUTORY DUTY

State and Federal statutes impose duties upon manufacturers of food, drugs, cosmetics, flammable materials, and toxic substances, with respect to branding, labeling, description of contents, advertising, and the selling or offering for sale of adulterated, contaminated, or unwholesome products. See Chapter 12, Section L.

These statutes provide for enforcement by criminal sanctions, seizure of goods, and injunctions. They do not expressly impose civil liability based upon injuries to the user or consumer of a product which has been sold in violation of the statute; however, in a civil action for damages, a violation of statutory duty may be alleged and if established by evidence many courts hold that it constitutes negligence by itself. Examples are: recovery for destruction of property resulting from faulty electrical wiring which did not comply with the building code, and recovery for crop damage resulting from mislabeling of packages of seed in violation of a state statute.

6. STRICT LIABILITY IN TORT

A. In General

Recent decisions in the field of products liability hold the seller on the basis of strict liability in tort (liability without proof of negligence). Liability is imposed on a person who is in the business of selling the product involved, and it applies to any product in a defective condition extending to both personal injuries and property damage suffered by the ultimate user or consumer of the product. It applies to all business sellers including manufacturers. It does not apply to the occasional seller who is not in the business of selling the product, such as a person who sells his power lawn mower to his neighbor. Neither does it apply to sales of the stock of merchants not in the usual course of business, such as a bankruptcy sale.

The requirement of privity is completely eliminated when the claim is based on strict liability in tort (liability without proof of negligence). Since liability is outside the scope of the U.C.C., the injured party does not have to give notice as he does in the case of a defect constituting a breach of warranty. Also, the plaintiff does not have to prove the defendant was negligent as is necessary when the suit is brought on the theory of negligence. Finally, since the consumer has a tort right which cannot be disclaimed, the producer of a product cannot use his superior knowledge or bargaining strength to disclaim liability.

B. Seller of Manufactured Product

(1) Dangerous Product

A retail seller of a product manufactured by a third person who knows or has reason to know that the product is dangerous, or likely to be dangerous, e.g., poison, is liable for bodily harm caused by the product *unless he warns them of the danger* (Restatement, Second, Torts, 402A).

The chattel does not have to be defective for liability to attach.

If the seller does not know nor have reason to know of the dangerous character, he is protected; e.g., sale of pre-packaged or sealed container products. However, the retailer could be liable on breach of warranty to the purchaser.

(2) Defective Product

A seller of a defective product, e.g., automobile, is held to strict liability in tort. The liability is not based on the negligence of the seller or the manufacturer. The rule is imposed by law as a matter of public policy. Liability is not confined to the buyer of the product. The seller cannot contract out of liability by a disclaimer or exclusion clause.

There are seven essential requirements to this type of liability: (a) the product was *defective*, (b) the defect was one which made the product *unreasonably dangerous* to the user, (c) the defect existed at the time it left the hands of the defendant, (d) the plaintiff sustained personal injuries or property damage by its use, (e) the defect was the *proximate cause* of the injury or damage, (f) the seller was engaged in the business of selling such product, and (g) the product was one which the seller expected to and did reach the user or consumer without substantial change in the condition it was when he sold it.

There are five reasons for the rule: (a) maximum protection should be given consumers against dangerous defects, (b) manufacturers are in the best position to prevent these hazards, (c) manufacturers realize the most profits from sales and, therefore, are best able to carry the financial burden of such liability by distributing the cost of the burden among the public, (d) manufacturers utilize wholesalers and retailers as merely conduits in the marketing of their products and should not be permitted to avoid liability simply because they have no direct contract or contact with the user or consumer, (e) liability of the manufacturer saves the time and expense otherwise necessary in multiplicity of suits; i.e., buyer sues retailer, retailer looks to wholesaler, wholesaler looks to manufacturer.

(3) Wholesaler

The Restatement of Torts, Second, Section 402A, provides that strict liability is imposed on any person engaged in the business of selling products for use or consumption who sells a defective product, and that includes not only a manufacturer or retail seller, but also a wholesaler or distributor.

(4) Suppliers of Parts

Frequently the manufacturer of a finished product purchased some of the components which went into the finished product from manufacturers of those components. Let us assume that an automobile manufacturer uses a component part for the brake system that has been made by another manufacturer, and that the component part was defective. Most courts hold that the manufacturer of the defective component part is liable for injuries sustained by the user of the finished product as a result of that defective part if no essential change has been made in it by the manufacturer of the finished product. The liability is based on strict liability in tort. It is no defense that the manufacturer of the finished product failed to discover the defect by inspection or testing.

The manufacturer of the finished product is not excused from liability because of a defective condition resulting exclusively from a defective component part. Liability is based on breach of warranty, strict liability in tort, or negligence. If the manufacturer of the component part had a good reputation and if there had been no prior complaints or defects with respect to that part, such evidence would tend to show absence of negligence on the part of the manufacturer of the finished product; however, this would not preclude recovery on the grounds of breach of warranty or strict liability in tort.

C. Lessors of Personal Property

A *lessor* of personal property is liable for injuries caused by the defective condition of goods which makes them unreasonably dangerous (Restatement of the Law of Torts, 2d, Section 408).

D. Seller of Real Property

Recent decisions in some states have extended the strict liability tort theory to the sale of real estate. In Schipper v. Levitt & Sons, Inc., 44 N.J. 70, 207 A.2d 314, the court held a home developer liable on the theories of negligence, implied warranty, and strict liability where a hot water system had been installed in an apparently defective manner resulting in the scalding of the infant plaintiff (Schipper negligence principles held applicable to all builders in Totton v. Gruzen, 52 N.J. 202, 245 A.2d 1 (1968)). In Kreigler v. Eichler Homes, Inc., 269 Cal.App.2d 224, 74 Cal.Rptr. 749 (1969), the home developer was held liable for the failure of a radiant heating system in a concrete slab foundation which failed after eight years of use. In Avner v. Longridge Estates, 272 Cal.App.2d 607, 77 Cal.Rptr. 633 (1969), the defendant was held liable for slope failure and pad subsidence due to inadequate soil compaction.

A builder-seller may be insolvent or uninsured in which case the only remedy may be against the financier of the project. The lender may be liable: (a) on the theory of negligence based on the fact that the lender exercised extensive control over the project and therefore assumed a duty of reasonable care to the ultimate purchasers (Connor v. Great Western Sav. & Loan, 69 Cal.2d 850, 73 Cal.Rptr. 369, 447 P.2d 609); or (b) as a joint venturer with the builder-developer; or (c) as an independent lot manufacturer who wholesales the subdivided lots to the developer.

E. Assumption of Risk

Historically, the law has been that the user of a product who voluntarily and unreasonably proceeds to use it in the face of danger which he knows or should know exists, is barred from recovery on the grounds he assumed the risk of danger. Thus, if there was a conspicuous warning on the label of a product, the use of such product could amount to an assumption of the risk and preclude recovery. Recent decisions in some states (e. g., California) have held that the injured person is only required to prove that he was using the product as it was intended to be used and that a defect in the design or manufacture caused the accident; hence, he does not have to prove that he was not aware of the defect. Thus, in those states the manufacturer is liable even though the user knew of the apparent defect unless the jury concludes that it would be unreasonable to require the safety devices which would have avoided the injury.

However, the law is clear that contributory negligence does not bar recovery; i. e., buyer careless in use of the product. This is because liability on the seller or manufacturer is based on strict liability in tort to which contributory negligence is not a defense.

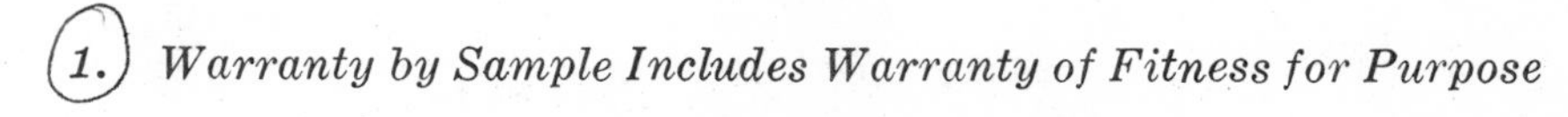

1. *Warranty by Sample Includes Warranty of Fitness for Purpose*

LOOMIS BROS. CORP. v. QUEEN ET AL.

46 Del.Cty.Rpts. 79, 17 D. & C.2d 482 (Pa., 1958).

Opinion by Diggins, J., October 15, 1958:

[Suit for price of windows.]

This is a petition to open confessed judgment based upon a contract wherein plaintiff was to install fourteen storm and screen windows in defendants' home. The defendants allege the windows were defective, useless as storm windows, and not fit for the purpose intended, and that they did not fit snug and tight and did not keep out the rain, snow and wind, and shook and rattled and were not airtight. The plaintiff admits that the storm windows did not fit the aluminum frames snug and tight and that they may let in air, and they may rattle.

The windows were purchased from an operating sample consisting of the storm window in miniature, mounted in a frame. * *

Legally we have here presented a very close question. The goods were purchased by sample, the goods conformed to the sample. Query: Must the goods also do the job for which they were designed and if not, who bears the risk? *Article 2, Section 313 of the Uniform Commercial Code,* * * * under Title "Express Warranty by affirmation, promise, description, sample", provides:

> "(c) * * * any sample or model which is made a basis of the bargain creates an express warranty that the whole of the goods should conform to the sample or model."

It would seem from a precise interpretation of this section that substantial conformity to the model constitutes performance but a reading of the cases both before and since the present Uniform Commercial Code indicates that something more is required and that is "fitness for the purpose intended" and "merchantability". All agree that here was conformity and merchantability. It is this fitness for purpose intended that presents the problem and the philosophy of the law seems to indicate that this principle is basic and must be present in the article supplied regardless of the limitations surrounding a sale by sample or by description.

The purpose of storm windows is to keep out wind and weather. These windows conformed to the sample. They are merchantable but they did not keep out wind and weather.

We are therefore of the opinion that * * * under * * [the] Uniform Commercial Code, where seller submitted sample of goods to the buyer, there was implied warranty of fitness for the purpose intended *and* that goods would be same as sample. Therefore, we think that fitness for purpose intended is the basic ingredient in every item sold, no matter by what type of bargaining the contract is reached, where the seller at the time of contracting has reason to know any particular purpose for which the goods are required and that the buyer is relying on the seller's skill or judgment to select or furnish suitable goods: *Uniform Commercial Code,* Section 315.

[Judgment for defendants.]

 *Implied Warranty that Food Fit for Human Consumption*

HUNT v. FERGUSON-PAULUS ENTERPRISES

243 Or. 546, 415 P.2d 13 (1966).

LUSK, Justice. The plaintiff bought a cherry pie from the defendant through a vending machine owned and maintained by the defendant. On biting into the pie one of plaintiff's teeth was broken when it encountered a cherry pit. He brought this action to recover damages for the injury, alleging breach of warranty of fitness of the pie for human consumption. In a trial to the court without a jury the court found for the defendant and plaintiff has appealed. * * *

In the consideration of similar cases some of the courts have drawn a distinction between injury caused by spoiled, impure, or contaminated food or food containing a foreign substance, an injury caused by a substance natural to the product sold. In the latter class of cases, these courts hold there is no liability on the part of the dispenser of the food. * * * Thus in the leading case of Mix v. Ingersoll Candy Co., 6 Cal.2d 674, 59 P.2d 144, the court held that a patron of a restaurant who ordered and paid for chicken pie, which contained a sharp sliver or fragment of chicken bone, and was injured as a result of swallowing the bone, had no cause of action against the restaurateur either for breach of warranty or negligence. * * *

The so-called "foreign-natural" test of the *Mix* case has been applied in the following cases: Silva v. F. W. Woolworth Co., 28 Cal. App.2d 649, 83 P.2d 76 (turkey bone in "special plate" of roast turkey); Musso v. Picadilly Cafeterias, Inc. (La.App.), 178 So.2d 421 (cherry pit in a cherry pie); Courter v. Dilbert Bros., Inc., 19 Misc. 2d 935, 186 N.Y.S.2d 334 (prune pit in prune butter); Adams v. Great Atlantic & Pacific Tea Co., 251 N.C. 565, 112 S.E.2d 92 (crystalized grain of corn in cornflakes); Webster v. Blue Ship Tea Room, Inc., 347 Mass. 421, 198 N.E.2d 309 (fish bone in a fish chowder). * * *

Other courts have rejected the so-called foreign-natural test in favor of what is known as the "reasonable expectation" test among them the Supreme Court of Wisconsin, which, in Betehia v. Cape Cod Corp., 10 Wis.2d 323, 103 N.W.2d 64, held that a person who was injured by a chicken bone in a chicken sandwich served to him in a restaurant, could recover for his injury either for breach of an implied warranty or for negligence. "There is a distinction," the court said, "between what a consumer expects to find in a fish stick and in a baked or fried fish, or in a chicken sandwich made from sliced white meat and in roast chicken. The test should be what is reasonably expected by the consumer in the food as served, not what might be natural to the ingredients of that food prior to preparation. What is to be reasonably expected by the consumer is a jury question in most cases; at least, we cannot say as a matter of law that a patron of a restaurant must expect a bone in a chicken sandwich either because chicken bones are occasionally found there or are natural to chicken." * * *

Among other decisions adopting the reasonable expectation test are: Bonenberger v. Pittsburgh Mercantile Co., 345 Pa. 559, 28 A.2d 913, 143 A.L.R. 1417, Annotation at page 1421 (oyster shell in canned oysters used in making oyster stew); Bryer v. Rath Packing Co., 221 Md. 105, 156 A.2d 442, 77 A.L.R.2d 1 (chicken bone in chow mein); Varone v. Calarco, 22 Misc.2d 1085, 199 N.Y.S.2d 755 (struvite in canned tuna).

* * * In view of the judgment for the defendant, we are not required in this case to make a choice between the two rules. Under the foreign-natural test the plaintiff would be barred from recovery as a matter of law. The reasonable expectation test calls for determination of a question of fact: * * * The court has found the fact in favor of the defendant and this court has no power to disturb the finding.

* * * [T]he judgment is affirmed [for defendant].

---

3. *Scope of Implied Warranty Liability under U.C.C.*

HARRIS v. THE ATLANTIC & PACIFIC TEA CO., INC.

23 Mass.App.Dec. 169 (1962).

GARVEY, J. * * * This is an action of contract or tort whereby the plaintiff seeks to recover for himself and his minor son for injury received by said minor son, Wayne Harris, *while attempting to open a beer bottle.*

I find that the plaintiff, William W. Harris, the father of Wayne Harris, purchased (on December 31, 1960 the reported evidence states) a quart bottle of beer from the defendant. He took the bottle home and that same evening asked his son, Wayne, a nine year old boy, to take the bottle out of the refrigerator and to open it. The boy did as he was requested and in the process of opening the bottle, the neck broke off inflicting a cut on the boy's finger.

The applicable sections of * * * U.C.C. relating to implied warranties and to whom they extend read:

> Sec. 2–314(1) "Unless excluded or modified by section 2–316, a warranty that the goods shall be merchantable is implied in a contract for their sale if the seller is a merchant with respect to goods of that kind. Under this section the serving for value of food or drink to be consumed either on the premises or elsewhere is a sale." The warranty applies to the bottle. * * *
>
> Sec. 2–314(2) "Goods to be merchantable must at least be such as are fit for the ordinary purposes for which such goods are used."

Sec. 2–318 "A seller's warranty whether express or implied extends to any natural person who is in the family or household of his buyer or who is a guest in his home if it is reasonable to expect that such person may *use, consume or be affected by* the goods and who is injured in person by breach of the warranty. A seller may not exclude or limit the operation of this section." (Emphasis supplied).

The plaintiff is one of the class of third parties now made beneficiaries of this warranty. * * * The trial judge's ruling that he found for the defendant on the theory that there "was no privity of contract" between the plaintiff and defendant; *was not correct.*

No case law being found or cited we are of the opinion it was also error to rule "that the defendant had no reason to expect that said minor plaintiff would be affected in any manner by the sale of the bottle of beer".

* * * Apparently the judge was of the opinion that because the bottle contained an alcoholic beverage a nine year old child wouldn't be expected to handle or be affected by it. We don't think merchants share his opinion—we don't. Children of this age are to be observed daily in modern stores handling bottled merchandise of all kinds at the invitation of sellers. It is "reasonable" to expect that they are thereby subject to being "affected" and "injured".

It was of no consequence that the bottle contained beer instead of milk, ginger ale, or one of the many kinds of beverages regularly purchased, used and consumed by members of families. There was nothing illegal, as argued by the defendant, in the plaintiff's handling of the bottle in his home. Bottled beer is part of the legal larder of many homes, and is frequently handled, and sometimes consumed with parental approval, by children. It was to be expected by the seller, in usual circumstances, that a father retained the parental prerogative of having his son fetch him a cold bottle of beer.

Prejudicial error being found, a new trial is ordered.

4. *Liability of Manufacturers and Retailers on Implied Warranty*

HENNINGSEN v. BLOOMFIELD MOTORS, INC.

32 N.J. 358, 161 A.2d 69 (1960).

FRANCIS, J. Plaintiff Clause H. Henningsen purchased a Plymouth automobile, manufactured by defendant Chrysler Corporation, from defendant Bloomfield Motors, Inc. His wife, plaintiff Helen Henningsen, was injured while driving it and instituted suit against both defendants to recover damages on account of her injuries. Her husband joined in the action seeking compensation for his consequential losses. The complaint was predicated upon breach of express and implied warranties * * *

At the trial * * * the cause was submitted to the jury for determination solely on the issues of implied warranty of merchantability. Verdicts were returned against both defendants and in favor of the plaintiffs. Defendants appealed.

The new Plymouth was turned over to the Henningsens on May 9, 1955.

* * * It had no servicing and no mishaps of any kind before the event of May 19. That day, Mrs. Henningsen drove to Asbury Park. * * * She was proceeding north on Route 36 in Highlands, New Jersey, at 20–22 miles per hour. The highway was paved and smooth, and contained two lanes for northbound travel. She was riding in the right-hand lane. Suddenly she heard a loud noise "from the bottom, by the hood." It "felt as if something cracked." The steering wheel spun in her hands; the car veered sharply to the right and crashed into a highway sign and a brick wall. No other vehicle was in any way involved. * * * In the ordinary case of sale of goods by description an implied warranty of merchantability is an integral part of the transaction.

If the buyer, expressly or by implication, makes known to the seller the particular purpose for which the article is required and it appears that he has relied on the seller's skill or judgment, an implied warranty arises of reasonable fitness for that purpose. * * *

The uniform act codified, extended and liberalized the common law of sales. The motivation in part was to ameliorate the harsh doctrine of *caveat emptor,* and in some measure to impose a reciprocal obligation on the seller to beware. The transcendent value of the legislation, particularly with respect to implied warranties, rests in the fact that obligations on the part of the seller were imposed by operation of law, and did not depend for their existence upon express agreement of the parties. * * *

Under modern conditions the ordinary layman, on responding to the importuning of colorful advertising, has neither the opportunity nor the capacity to inspect or to determine the fitness of an automobile for use; he must rely on the manufacturer who has control of its construction, and to some degree on the dealer who, to the limited extent called for by the manufacturer's instructions, inspects and services it before delivery. * * *

Accordingly, we hold that under modern marketing conditions, when a manufacturer puts a new automobile in the stream of trade and promotes its purchase by the public, an implied warranty that it is reasonably suitable for use as such accompanies it into the hands of the ultimate purchaser. * * *

The task of the judiciary is to administer the spirit as well as the letter of the law. On issues such as the present one, part of that burden is to protect the ordinary man against the loss of important rights through what, in effect, is the unilateral act of the manufacturer. The status of the automobile industry is unique. Manufacturers are few in number and strong in bargaining position. In the matter of warranties on the sale of their products, the Automotive Manufacturers Association has enabled them to present a united front. From the standpoint of the purchaser, there can be no arms length negotiating on the subject. Because his capacity for bargaining is so grossly unequal, the inexorable conclusion which follows is that he is not permitted to bargain at all. He must take or leave the automobile on the warranty terms dictated by the maker. He cannot turn to a competitor for better security.

Under all of the circumstances outlined above, the judgments in favor of the plaintiffs and against the defendants are affirmed.

5. Implied Warranty Effective When Product in Buyer's Hands

GILLISPIE v. THE GREAT ATLANTIC AND PACIFIC TEA COMPANY

14 N.C. 1, 187 S.E.2d 441 (1972).

Plaintiff's evidence tended to show that he went to defendant's store to get a carton of Coca Cola and a carton of Sprite bottle drinks. He picked up a carton of each and walked toward the checkout counter, carrying the carton of Sprite in his left hand and the carton of Coca Cola in his right hand. He was walking directly to the checkout counter where he intended to pay for the drinks. When he reached a point about 20 to 25 feet from the shelf where he had picked up the drinks and about 10 feet from the checkout counter, two of the Sprite bottles exploded and plaintiff sustained a laceration to his left wrist.

GRAHAM, Judge. Plaintiff bases his claim solely upon breach of implied warranty.

The evidence tends to show that plaintiff handled the bottles of Sprite normally from the time he took possession of them until they exploded. There is no evidence presently before us which would indicate that plaintiff's conduct contributed in any way to the explosions. Therefore, the jury would be justified in finding that the bottles exploded because they were inadequate for the purpose they were intended; namely, as containers of the Sprite soft drink.

* * *

The first question before us is whether an implied warranty of fitness has now been extended by the Uniform Commercial Code to include a product's container such as the one involved here. We hold that it has.

G.S. § 25–2–314 provides in pertinent part:

"(1) Unless excluded or modified (§ 25–2–316), a warranty that the goods shall be merchantable is implied in a contract for their sale if the seller is a merchant with respect to goods of that kind. Under this section the serving for value of food or drink to be consumed either on the premises or elsewhere is a sale.

(2) Goods to be merchantable must be at least such as . . .

(c) are fit for the ordinary purposes for which such goods are used; and . . .

(e) are adequately contained, packaged, and labeled as the agreement may require. . . ."

In the official comment following this section it is stated:

"(e) applies only where the nature of the goods and of the transaction requires a certain type of container, package or label."

The nature of bottled drinks, such as Sprite, requires a container which is adequate to contain the drink without breaking or exploding when handled with ordinary care. Another way of putting it is that under this section, soft drinks are not merchantable if inadequately contained. If they are sold in a container which is inadequate, the seller has breached his implied warranty of merchantability and he is liable for personal injury proximately caused by this breach. The fact that it is the container, rather than the product inside, which causes injury, does not make the injury any less a result of the seller's breach of warranty.

A second question presented is whether a sale had taken place at the time the bottles allegedly exploded. Warranties arise under the Uniform Commercial Code only upon a sale of goods. 46 N.C.L. Rev. 451. "A 'sale' consists in the passing of title from the seller to the buyer for a price (§ 25–2–401)." G.S. § 25–2–106(1). "Unless otherwise explicitly agreed title passes to the buyer at the time and place at which the seller completes his performance with reference to the physical delivery of the goods, despite any reservation of a security interest and even though a document of title is to be delivered at a different time or place; and in particular and despite any reservation of a security interest by the bill of lading." G.S. § 25–2–401(2).

In the case of Nationwide Mut. Insurance Co. v. Hayes, 276 N.C. 620, 632, 174 S.E.2d 511, 518, it was noted: "The most basic departure from previous law which is found in the Uniform Commercial Code is the abandonment of the concept of title as a tool for resolving sales problems. This departure is evidenced by G.S. § 25–2–401 which, in effect, holds that title to goods passes from the seller to the buyer when the goods are delivered to the buyer."

* * *

We are of the opinion that under G.S. § 25–2–401(2) the time of payment is not determinative of the question of when a sale takes place. If there has been a completed delivery by the seller, the sale has been consummated and implied warranties arise under G.S. § 25–2–314.

The presence of the drinks on the shelves in defendant's self-service store constituted an offer for sale and delivery at a stated price. If plaintiff took the drinks into his possession with the intention of paying for them at the cashier's counter, there was no further act of delivery necessary on the part of the seller. All that remained was for plaintiff to pay for the drinks—an act delayed until he reached the cashier's counter primarily for the convenience of the seller.

Defendant calls attention to the custom in self-service stores which permits a customer to return goods to the shelf without liability if he changes his mind about a purchase before reaching the checkout counter. However, even a right to return delivered goods to the seller does not necessarily delay passage of the title until that right has expired. G.S. § 25–2–401(4) provides: "A rejection or other refusal by the buyer to receive or retain the goods, whether or not justified, or a justified revocation of acceptance revests title to the goods in the seller." The result is that when a purchaser in a self-service store changes his mind and returns to the shelf a product which he has picked up with the intention of buying, title is revested in the seller. However, as long as the purchaser has the product in his possession, intending to pay for it, he has title to the product. The seller's interest at that point is not "title" but a security interest to enforce payment. "Any retention or reservation by the seller of the title (property) in goods shipped or delivered to the buyer is limited in effect to a reservation of a security interest." G.S. § 25–2–401(1).

The evidence presented would support a jury finding that plaintiff purchased the Sprite drinks by taking them into his possession with the intention of paying for them. Should the jury so find, the questions would then become: Was the warranty of implied merchantability breached by defendant, and if so, did the breach proximately cause the injuries sustained by the plaintiff? We are of the opinion the evidence is sufficient to go to the jury on these questions.

Reversed.

Why isn't the MANUFACTURER RESPONSIBLE

6. *Seller Liable Though Unable to Discover Defect*

VLASES v. MONTGOMERY WARD & COMPANY

377 F.2d 846 (C.A.Pa., 1967).

GERALD McLAUGHLIN, Circuit Judge. This case revolves around the charge that defendant-appellant, Montgomery Ward, was liable for the breach of implied warranties in the sale of one day old chickens to the plaintiff-appellee, Paul Vlases. The latter came to this country from Greece when he was sixteen and until 1954 his primary occupation was that of a coal miner. He had always raised chickens but because of his job as a miner his flocks were small, ranging from between twenty-five to one hundred chicks. In 1958 plaintiff began the construction of a two story chicken coop large enough to house 4,000 chickens and a smaller side building where he could wash, grade and sell the eggs. Vlases worked alone on the coop, twelve hours a day, fifty-two weeks a year, until its completion in 1961. In November of 1961 plaintiff placed an order at defendant's outlet store in Brownsville, Pennsylvania for the purchase of 2,000 one day old chicks. The chickens selected by the plaintiff from Ward's catalogue were hybrid Leghorns and were noted for their excellent egg production. On December 21, 1961 plaintiff received the * * * chickens and placed them on the first floor of the coop which had been equipped with new brooders, feeders and within a short time, waterers. As a further hygienic precaution wire and sugar cane were placed on the ground so the chickens would not come in contact with the dirt floor. For the first six months Vlases slept in the coop in order to give the new chicks his undivided attention.

During the first few weeks after delivery the chickens appeared to be in good health but by the third week plaintiff noticed that their feathers were beginning to fall off. This condition was brought to the attention of Mr. Howard Hamilton who represented the Agway Corporation which was supplying the plaintiff with feed on credit. In February of 1962 Mr. Hamilton took five chickens to the Bureau of Animal Industry Diagnostic Laboratory where they were examined by Dr. Daniel P. Ehlers. The examination revealed signs of drug intoxication and hemorrhagic disease involving the weakening of blood vessels. Four chicks were brought to Dr. Ehlers in May of 1962 and were found to be suffering from fatigue. On the 14th of August 1962 Mr. Hamilton brought three chickens to the laboratory where Dr. Ehlers' report noted that two of the chicks were affected with visceral leukosis, one with ocular leukosis, one had bumble foot and one had been picked. Visceral and ocular leukosis are two types of avian leukosis complex or bird cancer which disease infected plaintiff's flock either killing the chicks or causing those remaining to be destroyed.

* * *

A verdict was returned in favor of the plaintiff in the amount of $23,028.77. Montgomery Ward appeals from the resultant judgment.

I

Appellant takes the position that an action for breach of implied warranties will not lie for the sale of one day old chicks where there is no human skill, knowledge or foresight which would enable the producer or supplier to prevent the occurrence of this disease, to detect its presence or to care for the sickness if it was present. The jury was instructed by the court that recovery on behalf of the plaintiff required a finding that the chickens were afflicted with leukosis at the time defendant made delivery. The expert testimony for both sides indicated that there was no way of determining whether newly hatched chicks have leukosis and that there is no medication available to prevent the disease from occurring. Assuming the chickens were diseased upon their arrival the thrust of appellant's argument questions the sufficiency of the law to support a finding that Ward is liable under Pennsylvania law for the breach of implied warranties.

The two implied warranties before us are the implied warranty of merchantability, 12A P.S. § 2–314, and the implied warranty of fitness for a particular purpose, 12A P.S. § 2–315. Both of these are designed to protect the buyer of goods from bearing the burden of loss where merchandise, though not violating a promise expressly guaranteed, does not conform to the normal commercial standards or meeting the buyer's particular purpose, a condition upon which he had the right to rely.

Were it to be assumed that the sale of 2,000 chickens infected with avian leukosis transgressed the norm of acceptable goods under both warranties, appellant's position is that the action will not lie in a situation where the seller is unable to discover the defect or cure the damage if it could be ascertained. That theory does not eliminate the consequences imposed by the Code upon the seller of commercially inferior goods. It is without merit.

* * *

The entire purpose behind the implied warranty sections of the Code is to hold the seller responsible when inferior goods are passed along to the unsuspecting buyer. What the Code requires is not evidence that the defects should or could have been uncovered by the seller but only that the goods upon delivery were not of a merchantable quality or fit for their particular purpose. If those requisite proofs are established the only exculpatory relief afforded by the Code is a showing that the implied warranties were modified or excluded by specific language under Section 2–316. Lack of skill or foresight on the part of the seller in discovering the product's flaw was never meant to bar liability. The gravamen here is not so much with what precautions were taken by the seller but rather with the quality of the goods contracted for by the buyer. Even a provision specifically disclaiming any warrant against avian leukosis would not necessarily call for the defendant's freedom from liability. Section 1–102(3) of the Code's General Provisions states that standards which are manifestly unreasonable may not be disclaimed and prevents the enforcement of unconscionable sales where, as in this instance, the goods exchanged are found to be totally worthless.

II

Appellant contends that plaintiff failed to meet the burden of proof that the chickens were delivered with avian leukosis. * * * Upon consideration of all the trial testimony, appellant's argument must be rejected.

[Judgment for plaintiff.]

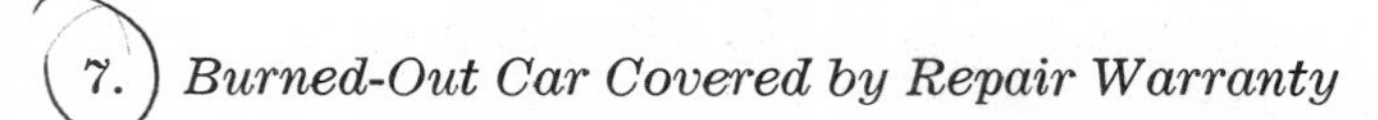

7. *Burned-Out Car Covered by Repair Warranty*

RUSSO v. HILLTOP LINCOLN–MERCURY

479 S.W.2d 211 (Mo.App., 1972).

CLEMENS, Judge (Commissioner when cause submitted).

* * *

The new automobile purchased by plaintiffs was destroyed by fire through no fault of theirs. The fire was caused by either defective wiring or workmanship and the defects were substantial, existing at the time of purchase when the value was $3,918.61 but the car was rendered worthless as a result of the fire. Plaintiffs expended $109.72 to rent an automobile and $200 interest on the financed portion of the purchase price. The car was delivered to the dealer by plaintiffs immediately after the fire in as good condition as possible in view of the defect. Defendant had expressly warranted against defects in parts or factory workmanship; had impliedly warranted the car as well and had breached the warranties given in the sale of the automobile. The total damage was $4,228.33. It was unnecessary to determine whether this is a case of rescission or a suit for damages since in either event the plaintiffs would be entitled to the same amount of damages.

We have examined the transcript and find the trial court's findings to be fully supported by plaintiffs' evidence. Defendant offered none.

The express warranty here is in a 30-page booklet of the Ford Motor Company and adopted by the defendant dealer. The pertinent parts:

> "Basic Vehicle Warranty. Ford Motor Company . . warrants to the original retail purchaser . . . each part of a new and unused 1968 model Ford-built passenger car

> . . . to be free under normal use and service from defects in factory material and workmanship . . .
>
> "General Warranty Provisions. . . . All the warranties shall be fulfilled by the Selling Dealer . . . at his place of business replacing with a genuine new Ford part . . . or repairing any such defective part, free of charge . . ."

Defendant's first Point Relied On is that "Plaintiffs failed to . . . satisfy the conditions precedent" under the warranty. The point is abstract, but reference to defendant's argument shows they contend plaintiffs failed to deliver the burned-out car to defendant for repair or replacement of defective parts. Plaintiffs did return the car immediately after the fire and we accept the trial court's finding the car was then "junk" and "worthless." Defendant argues that under the warranty its liability was limited to repairing or replacing defective parts. That provision of the warranty implies the car was repairable. Here it could not be; it was worthless junk. At trial time the defendant had the car, still not repaired. It would be ludicrous to require plaintiff to ask defendant to do the impossible. "Laws governing warranties, express and implied, should be so administered as to be fair to all parties concerned. Such warranties should be meaningful." * * *

We hold plaintiffs did meet the warranty's condition precedent and that defendant is liable for its breach.

* * *

Last, defendant contends the trial court erred in allowing plaintiffs $109.72 for cost of renting a car between two dates unspecified in the evidence, findings or judgment. This on the ground defendant's warranty expressly excludes the expense of car rental. We agree. * * * Plaintiffs' measure of damages was the $3,918.61 value of the car at the time of destruction, plus interest from the time of filing suit, September 6, 1968. The trial court erred in the $109.72 car rental allowance.

[Query: should a car rental be recoverable under Sections 1–106 and 2–715 in the absence of a valid exclusion?]

8. *Lessor's Implied Warranty of Fitness for Use*

CINTRONE v. HERTZ TRUCK LEASING AND RENTAL SERVICE

45 N.J. 434, 212 A.2d 769 (1965).

FRANCIS, J. Plaintiff Francisco Cintrone was injured while a passenger in a truck leased by his employer from the defendant. In his complaint in this action he charged that the accident in which he was injured resulted from defendant's negligent inspection or maintenance of the leased vehicle or from a breach of defendant's warranty that the vehicle was fit and safe for use. (Whether the alleged warranty was express or implied was not specified.) The trial court dismissed the warranty claim, * * *

Defendant Hertz Truck Leasing & Rental Service is in the business of leasing and renting various types of motor vehicles to the public. Plaintiff's employer, Contract Packers, Inc., had leased nine trucks from defendant for use in its business. One of them was a 1959 Ford, 22 feet long and 11 feet high. * * *

On April 3, 1961 the Ford truck was scheduled for a delivery trip. Cintrone was to be the helper that day and one Robert Sottilare, another Contract Packers employee, the driver. * * *

After leaving Dover the men headed for Suffern, New York. About noontime, as Sottilare was going along Route 202, apparently within the limits of Suffern, he came around a bend in the road and saw an overhead bridge or trestle a hundred feet or so ahead of him. It was a low bridge, the clearance only 9 feet, 6 inches. Sottilare applied his brakes; they failed. The truck "just kept going" forward until the peak of its body hit the overhead structure. As Cintrone put it, he saw "the driver pumping the brakes. And he never stopped the truck because the brakes didn't work. * * * Plaintiff seeks a reversal of the adverse judgment, however, on the ground that the contractual relationship between Hertz and his employer gave rise to an implied continuing promissory warranty by Hertz that the truck in question was fit for the purposes for which plaintiff's employer rented it, i. e., operation and transportation of goods on the public highways. He urges further that under the proof adduced the failure of the brakes and the consequent accident created a factual issue for jury determination as to whether there was a breach of the implied warranty. Therefore he claims the court erred in refusing to submit that issue for jury consideration.

* * * The nature of the U-drive-it enterprise is such that a heavy burden of responsibility for the safety of lessees and for members of the public must be imposed upon it. The courts have long accepted the fact that defective trucks and cars are dangerous instrumentalities on highways. They present great potentiality for harm to other highway users as well as to their own drivers and passengers. Therefore the offering to the public of trucks and pleasure vehicles for hire necessarily carries with it a representation that they are fit for operation. This representation is of major significance because both new and used cars and trucks are rented. * * * The nature of the business is such that the customer is expected to, and in fact must, rely ordinarily on the express or implied representation of fitness for immediate use. * * *

In the case before us, it is just as obvious that when a company like Contract Packers rents trucks for limited or extended periods for use in its occupation of transportation of goods, it too relies on the express or implied representation of the person in the business of supplying vehicles for hire, that they are fit for such use.

* * * Accordingly, we are of the opinion (1) that the leasing agreement gave rise to a continuing implied promissory warranty that the leased trucks would be fit for plaintiff's employer's use for the duration of the lease, * * *, and (3) that the evidence created a factual issue for determination by the jury as to whether defendant Hertz had been guilty of a breach of that warranty which produced the collision and plaintiff's injury. * * *

For the reasons stated, the judgment for the defendant is reversed, and the cause is remanded for a new trial to be had in accordance with the views outlined.

Employee May Recover for the Breach of an Express Warranty Made by Supplier to Employer

FROYSLAND v. LEEF BROS., INC.

293 Minn. 201, 197 N.W.2d 656 (1972).

MILTON D. MASON, Justice. This appeal followed a jury verdict awarding damages of $45,200 in favor of plaintiff against Leef Bros., Inc. * * *

This action arises out of a powder explosion on October 21, 1968, on the premises of the Federal Cartridge Company (FCC) wherein plaintiff, an employee of FCC, was severely burned. The incident occurred when the highly volatile powder that plaintiff was sifting as part of his job ignited explosively for no apparent reason, causing his clothing to catch fire. Before coworkers could remove his burning clothes and extinguish the flames, plaintiff had suffered first-, second-, and third-degree burns over the upper and lower parts of his body. * * *

This lawsuit was instituted against defendant Leef on the theory that it was negligent in treating the clothing worn by plaintiff at the time of the fire and that it had breached express and implied warranties concerning the treatment of that clothing. The issue of implied warranties was later withdrawn.

All FCC employees are furnished special flame-resistant clothing which they are required to wear while working on their employer's premises. FCC contracted with defendant Leef to treat the furnished clothing with a chemical product manufactured by duPont. The purpose of this product, referred to as X-12, is to impart to cellulosic fabrics on which it is correctly applied the ability to retard burning. It is designed so that a treated fabric will burn when exposed directly to an independent source of flame and continue to burn only as long as the exposure is continued, but will not support a flame by itself.

The fabric, if properly treated, will self-extinguish, without an after-glow, upon removal of the source of the independent flame.

The evidence indicated that defendant Leef improperly applied the duPont product to the clothing used by FCC employees, causing an insufficient level of the product to remain in the fabric following processing and thus failing to make the fabric flame-resistant. As a result, when the powder being sifted by plaintiff exploded, his clothes ignited and continued to burn after he stepped away from the burning powder, causing burns to the lower, as well as upper, parts of his body.

The issues to be resolved on this appeal are as follows:

May an employee recover for the breach of an express warranty made by a supplier to the employer with regard to a product to be used for the employee's safety? * * *

Defendant argues that the plaintiff cannot rely on contractual warranties made by defendant to plaintiff's employer relating to the flame-resistant qualities of garments supplied by defendant. Plaintiff acknowledges that he had no knowledge of the warranties expressed in the contracts, but seeks to rely thereon as the intended beneficiary. In recent decisions this court has allowed recovery despite lack of privity between plaintiff and defendant in certain situations but has not done so upon facts such as those presented herein. * * *

It is clear that even though plaintiff here was without knowledge of the warranties, he was the ultimate consumer of the treated garments and the intended beneficiary of the safety provisions provided by the express warranties in the agreement between his employer and defendant. To allow the employee to recover in such a situation is consistent with our prior decisions. We, therefore, hold that an employee may recover for breach of warranty by a supplier to an employer for a product used, as in this case, for the employee's safety.

[Judgment affirmed.]

10. Disclaimer Must be Conspicuous

HUNT v. PERKINS MACH. CO.

352 Mass. 535, 226 N.E.2d 228 (1969).

CUTTER, Justice. Hunt, an experienced commercial fisherman, got in touch with the defendant (Perkins), a distributor of Caterpillar Tractor Company's products. He was considering the purchase of a diesel engine for his fishing boat. In the fall of 1960, Perkins's sales manager, one Rideout, went to Hunt's house in Orleans to acquaint him with the various Caterpillar diesel engines available. At Rideout's suggestion, Hunt went to Maine to look at a boat equipped with such an engine. In January, 1961, Hunt signed a purchase order for one Caterpillar Model D330 engine with a 1.2 to 1 reduction gear (instead of one reduction gear ordinarily supplied by the manufacturer) and certain specified accessories. The written portion of the purchase order was prepared (except for the signatures) by Rideout. It was on a "pad of paper containing several copies separated by carbon paper."

Hunt did not read anything on the back of the order when he signed it. "The original and all * * * copies of the * * * [o]rder were taken by Rideout * * * for signature by an official" of Perkins. Hunt received a fully executed copy of the order by mail a few days later.

The face of the purchase order contains a statement of the property sold, acknowledgment of a $500 deposit, a statement of the balance ($4,095) due, and certain miscellaneous information. In the center of the face of the order in bold face type capitals appears the statement **"BOTH THIS ORDER AND ITS ACCEPTANCE ARE SUBJECT TO 'TERMS AND CONDITIONS' STATED IN THIS ORDER."** On the reverse side of the order at the top in the same bold face types capitals appear the words **"TERMS AND CONDITIONS."** Underneath those words there are eleven numbered paragraphs. Included among the numbered paragraphs are those set out in the margin.

* * *

After the engine was installed a series of mechanical problems arose, each of which was corrected by Perkins at no expense to Hunt other than the time involved while the repairs were being made. The engine, when running, gave off excessive quantities of heavy black smoke, which caused the boat to become dirty, inside and out, and rendered Hunt's work on the boat unpleasant. This condition persisted until the removal of the engine. At Hunt's request Perkins, on several occasions and by a variety of means, attempted without success to curtail the smoking.

About July 20, 1961, the engine was removed by Hunt and put on the dock at Marine's plant. Hunt called Perkins and reported that he had removed the engine and advised Perkins to get it. The engine is still on Marine's premises.

In July, 1961, Hunt purchased a new engine from another manufacturer. This new engine has performed satisfactorily.

Hunt's evidence of damages consisted of a showing of cash payments to Marine of $761.49 for installation work and testimony that he lost $250 each day when he was prevented from fishing as a result of Perkins' work on the boat. Perkins worked on the boat on about ten different occasions between the installation of the engine and June, 1961.

* * *

This case presents issues under the Uniform Commercial Code (see St.1957, c. 765, § 1) concerning excluding or modifying (a) the implied warranty of merchantability under G.L. c. 106, § 2–314, and (b) the implied warranty under c. 106, § 2–315, that goods shall be fit for a particular purpose. Section 2–316(2) reads, in part: "(2) * * * [T]o exclude or modify the implied warranty of merchantability or any part of it the language must mention merchantability *and in case of a writing must be conspicuous,* and to exclude or modify any implied warranty of fitness the exclusion must be by a writing and *conspicuous.* Language to exclude all implied warranties of fitness is sufficient if it states, for example, that 'There are no warranties which extend beyond the description *on the face hereof*'" (emphasis supplied). Section 2–316(2) must be read with § 1–201 (10) which provides, in part: " 'Conspicuous': A term * * * is conspicuous when it is so written that a reasonable person against whom it is to operate *ought to have noticed it.* A printed heading in capitals (as: NONNEGOTIABLE BILL OF LADING) is conspicuous. Language in the body of a form is 'conspicuous' if it is in larger or other contrasting type or color. * * * Whether a term or clause is 'conspicuous' * * * is for decision by the court" (emphasis supplied).

* * *

Under § 2–316(2) read with the last sentence of § 1–201(10), it is a question of law for the court whether a provision is conspicuous. We are in as good a position to decide that issue as the trial judge, for a photographic copy of both sides of the purchase order is before us. We decide the issue by applying the statutory test under § 1–201(10) of what is conspicuous, viz. whether "a reasonable person against whom * * * [the disclaimer] is to operate ought to have noticed it."

In the language of the official comment (see fn. 5 and related text) the bold face printing on the front of the purchase order (although adequate in size and contrast with the rest of the printing on the form) was not in words sufficient to call attention to the language on the back of the form. That language would naturally be concealed because the forms were part of a pad of paper when Hunt signed the paper. There was no reference whatsoever on the front of the order to the "Terms and Conditions" as being on the back of the order, and the quoted words "Terms and Conditions" might have been thought to apply to other small type provisions on the front of the order unless Hunt had happened to turn over the form and look at the back of the order. His first reasonable opportunity to do this was when the executed form was returned to him.

In the opinion of a majority of the court, the provisions on the front of the purchase order did not make adequate reference to the provisions on the back of the order to draw attention to the latter. Hence the provisions on the back of the order cannot be said to be conspicuous although printed in an adequate size and style of type. The disclaimer was not effective.

[Judgment for plaintiff in the amount of $5,357, affirmed.]

---

11. Products Liability Warranty (Based on Contract)

CHAIRALUCE v. STANLEY WARNER MANAGEMENT CORP.

236 F.Supp. 385 (D.C.Conn., 1964).

ZAMPANO, District Judge. The defendant, The Wise Shoe Company, Inc., hereinafter designated as "Wise", has moved for an order dismissing the second count of plaintiffs' amended complaint for failure to state a claim upon which relief can be granted.

* * * This action was brought to recover damages for injuries sustained by the wife-plaintiff when she fell on a stairway in a theater owned by the defendant, The Stanley Warner Management Corp. At the time of the accident she was wearing for the first time a pair of new shoes which were manufactured by Wise and purchased by the plaintiff from the mail-order retail store of the defendant, Spiegel, Inc. She alleges her fall was caused by the breaking of a defective heel on one of these shoes. * * * The second count concerns Wise and Spiegel and is founded upon the breach of express and implied warranties in the manufacture and sale of the defective shoe. As against Spiegel, the plaintiffs allege a purchase in reliance on misleading advertising contained in its mail-order catalogue. The cause of action against Spiegel is not challenged here. But, with respect to Wise, the plaintiffs merely contend there was a breach of "the warranties and duties which were owed to the plaintiff under the laws of the State of Connecticut". * * *

The obvious trend of the Connecticut law on the subject militates against defendant's position. Under the old Sales Act, § 42–16 of the Connecticut General Statutes, the protection of implied warranty of fitness of food and drink was extended to all persons for whom the purchase was intended. In 1961, the legislature enacted the Uniform Commercial Code which, by its § 42a–2–314, § 42a–2–315 and § 42a–2–318, further expands an implied warrant of merchantability and fitness for a particular purpose to any person in the family or household of the buyer, or who is a guest in his home. * * * Sound public policy requires that a manufacturer be held strictly accountable to a plaintiff who, using his product in a way it was intended, is injured as a result of a defect in manufacture of which plaintiff was not aware. * * *

In light of the evident trend of the law in Connecticut and elsewhere, this Court concludes that the plaintiffs have alleged facts sufficient to state a claim upon which relief may be granted.

Accordingly, defendant's motion to dismiss is denied.

12. Products Liability Warranty (Based on Tort)

LONZRICK v. REPUBLIC STEEL CORP.

6 Ohio St.2d 227, 218 N.E.2d 185 (1966).

O'NEILL, Judge. * * *

The allegations of the petition and all reasonable inferences therefrom will support the following statement of facts:

Defendant manufactured and sold certain steel roof joists. In selling those joists, defendant impliedly warranted that they were fit for the ordinary purposes for which such steel roof joists are used. (Section 1302.27, Revised Code, reads in part: "Goods to be merchantable must be at least such as * * * [3] are fit for the ordinary purposes for which such goods are used.") Those joists were defective because they were not fit for the ordinary purposes for which such joists are used. As a proximate result of being so defective, those joists came apart and fell on and injured plaintiff. At that time, plaintiff was working as a structural iron worker on the ground in an area where the joists had been installed directly overhead and was thus in a place where his presence was reasonably to be anticipated by defendant.

The Court of Appeals held that this petition states a good cause of action in tort, based upon the theory of breach of warranty.

This is a products liability case. In such a case, there are three possible causes of action which the plaintiff may pursue:

(1) An action in tort which is grounded upon negligence. Such cause of action does not require the allegation of a contractual relationship between the plaintiff and the defendant. The petition in this case does not allege negligence and does not state facts which constitute negligence.

(2) A cause of action which is based upon contract. Such a cause of action requires that there be a contractual relationship between the plaintiff and the defendant. The petition in this case does not allege a contract and it does not allege a breach of a contractual warranty. It does not allege any contractual relationship between the plaintiff and the defendant.

(3) An action in tort which is based upon the breach of a duty assumed by the manufacturer-seller of a product. This duty is assumed by the manufacturer by reason of his implicit representation of good and merchantable quality and fitness for intended use when he sells the product. This duty is breached when a defect in the product causes the collapse of the product and is the direct and proximate cause of injury to a person whose presence the defendant could reasonably anticipate. This is the cause of action which the petition in this case states.

In this action the plaintiff is required to allege and prove that there was a defect in the steel joists manufactured and sold by the defendant, that such defect existed at the time the joists were sold by the defendant, that the defect was the direct and proximate cause of plaintiff's injuries, and that the plaintiff, at the time he was injured, was in a place where his presence was reasonably to be anticipated by the defendant.

It is conceded by both parties that the plaintiff does not have an action based upon a contract because there was no contract of sale between the plaintiff and the defendant and, therefore, no contractual relation (privity) between the parties.

The position of the defendant is that the plaintiff's petition does not state a cause of action because it does not allege negligence, does not allege an express warranty and does not allege any contractual relationship between the plaintiff and the defendant.

The plaintiff concedes that this petition does not allege negligence, does not allege an express warranty and does not allege any contractual relationship between the plaintiff and the defendant. The plaintiff asserts that the petition states a cause of action in tort based upon an implied warranty.

* * * Is the plaintiff restricted to prosecuting his action for damages on the basis of negligence alone, or may he proceed in tort on the theory of breach of warranty?

The precise questions this court is required to determine are: (1) Where a defendant manufactures and sells steel roof joists, is there implicit in the production and sale of this product the representation that the joists are of good and merchantable quality and safe for their ordinary intended use? and (2) when, in fact, such steel joists were defective and while being devoted to their ordinary intended use collapsed because of such defect and fell to the floor and injured the plaintiff, who was working on the floor below these steel roof joists in a place where his presence was reasonably to be anticipated by the defendant manufacturer, is such innocent injured party restricted to prosecuting a tort action for damages on the basis of negligence alone, or may he proceed in tort on the theory of an implied warranty?

* * *

It is settled law in this state that there can be an action in tort, based upon breach of warranty, and no contractual relation between the plaintiff and the defendant is required.

The question which remains to be determined in this case is: Where it is conceded that a manufacturer produced and sold steel joists, implicitly representing that they were of good and merchantable quality, fit and safe for the ordinary purposes for which such steel joists are used, but without advertising the product, is an innocent plaintiff-user, whose presence the defendant could reasonably anticipate and who is injured because a defect in the joists caused them to fall upon him, restricted to an action based on negligence alone, or can he recover in an action in tort based upon breach of this implied warranty where he was not in direct contractual relation (privity) with the manufacturer-defendant?

* * *

For the plaintiff to recover, he must prove, by the required degree of proof, that the joists were defective, that they were defective at the time the manufacturer sold them, that the defect caused them to collapse while they were being used for their ordinary intended purpose, that the defect was the direct and proximate cause of the plaintiff's injury, and that the plaintiff's presence was in a place which the defendant could reasonably anticipate.

Each of these elements of the plaintiff's case is a jury question, including the question of proximate cause.

Defendant has available the opportunity to offer evidence in defense on each of these necessary elements of the plaintiff's case, and also has available the defense of assumption of risk and intervening cause.

* * *

The petition in this case states a good cause of action grounded in tort, based upon a breach of the representations which are implicit when a defendant manufactures and sells a product which, if defective, will be a dangerous instrumentality.

Judgment affirmed.

---

13. Strict Liability in Tort

VANDERMARK v. FORD MOTOR CO.

61 Cal.2d 256, 391 P.2d 168, 37 Cal.Rptr. 896 (1964).

TRAYNOR, Justice. In October 1958 plaintiff Chester Vandermark bought a new Ford automobile from defendant Lorimer Diesel Engine Company, an authorized Ford dealer doing business as Maywood Bell Ford. About six weeks later, while driving on the San Bernardino Freeway, he lost control of the car [due to a defect in the car]. It went off the highway to the right and collided with a lightpost. He and his sister, plaintiff Mary Tresham, suffered serious injuries. They brought this action for damages against Maywood Bell Ford and the Ford Motor Company, which manufactured and assembled the car. They pleaded causes of action for breach of warranty and negligence. The trial court granted Ford's motion for a nonsuit on all causes of action and directed a verdict in favor of Maywood Bell on the warranty causes of action * * *.

Plaintiffs appeal.

Ford contends, however, that it may not be held liable for negligence in manufacturing the car or strictly liable in tort for placing it on the market without proof that the car was defective when Ford relinquished control over it. * * *

Retailers like manufacturers are engaged in the business of distributing goods to the public. They are an integral part of the overall producing and marketing enterprise that should bear the cost of injuries resulting from defective products. * * * In some cases the retailer may be the only member of that enterprise reasonably available to the injured plaintiff. In other cases the retailer himself may play a substantial part in ensuring that the product is safe or may be in a position to exert pressure on the manufacturer to that end; the retailer's strict liability thus serves as an added incentive to safety. Strict liability on the manufacturer and retailer alike affords maximum protection to the injured plaintiff and works no injustice to the defendants, for they can adjust the costs of such protection between them in the course of their continuing business relationship. Accordingly, as a retailer engaged in the business of distributing goods to the public, Maywood Bell is strictly liable in tort for personal injuries caused by defects in cars sold by it. * *

Since Maywood Bell is strictly liable in tort, the fact that it restricted its contractual liability to Vandermark is immaterial. Regardless of the obligations it assumed by contract, it is subject to strict liability in tort because it is in the business of selling automobiles, one of which proved to be defective and caused injury to human beings. * * *

Accordingly, the trial court erred in directing a verdict for Maywood Bell on the so-called warranty causes of action. * * *

[Judgment for plaintiffs.]

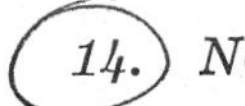

14. *No Contributory Negligence*

DE PREE v. NUTONE

422 F.2d 534 (C.A.Mich., 1970).

McCREE, Circuit Judge. Defendant appeals from a judgment rendered by the court, sitting without a jury, awarding damages of $25,000 to Mrs. Winifred DePree for the loss of part of her right index finger and $3,000 to her husband, Stanley DePree, for loss of consortium. The injury occurred when Mrs. DePree used her finger to try to remove some partially ground chicken from the bottom of the cutter plate of a vertical meat grinder operated by a counter-sunk electric motor manufactured by defendant. As a result of the accident and ensuing infections, Mrs. DePree's finger was amputated at the middle phalanx.

The District Judge in his findings of fact and conclusions of law, filed pursuant to Fed.R.Civ.P. 52(a), found that defendant had breached express warranties that the operating instructions were adequate and complete to assure safe operation of the grinder; that plaintiff could use the grinder for its intended purpose in a manner recommended by the cautions and instructions of defendant in complete safety; that the only danger in using the grinder would be from the top end and from the feed screw; and that the grinder was completely safe in all other respects. He also found that defendant was negligent in that the use of the coarse cutter plate presented a latent danger not apparent to the user; that the grinder had not been adequately tested for safety; and that adequate warning and safety devices were not provided to guard against that danger. He found that defendant's negligence and breach of warranty were proximate causes of the mishap; that Mrs. DePree was not guilty of contributory negligence; and that her use of the grinder was in the intended manner and within the scope of defendant's warranties.

Appellant contends that the representations contained in its instruction booklets and related literature were not express warranties; that if they are held to be warranties they were not breached; that the product was not negligently designed or manufactured; that any breach of warranty or negligence was not the proximate cause of the injury; and that the verdict was excessive.

Michigan law, which governs in this diversity case, permits recovery for an injury which results from a defect in a product or as a consequence of negligence in its manufacture. The development of Michigan case law makes the elements of the actions basically similar, although recovery may be had for negligence even in the absence of an identifiable defect. The measure of damages is the same whether the action is one for breach of warranty or for negligence. * * *

Here it is unnecessary to discuss all of appellant's arguments, because the verdict can be sustained on the District Court's finding of negligence. There was, first of all, evidence that appellant ignored the relevant Underwriters' Laboratories' safety standards in designing its coarse cutter plate so that the openings in the plate were large enough to permit the insertion of a human finger. Furthermore, a jury could find that appellant's warnings and instructions were misleading. These instructions emphasized the possible dangers from placing one's hand near the feed screw or into the top of the grinder, but they were silent about any danger from placing one's fingers into the easily accessible bottom end of the machine. Appellant provided a wooden spatula for use (according to the instructions) only at the top end of the machine. Appellant, at one time, provided a special spatula for use at the bottom end of the grinder, but this accessory and the requisite instructions were not included with the grinder purchased by plaintiffs.

From these facts a jury could find that appellant acted negligently. They justified a conclusion that the warnings concerning the top end of the grinder strongly implied that there was no reason for caution in using the bottom end. * * * The manufacturer of a meat grinder knows that his product can pulverize human fingers as well as chicken flesh. Appellant apparently recognized the duty to provide instructions and warnings which is imposed by Michigan law. * * * And a mechanically unsophisticated housewife (which category doubtless includes a substantial number of the likely users of the product) is entitled to rely on the completeness and accuracy of the instructions and warnings provided by a responsible manufacturer.

We also determine that the District Court did not err in finding the appellant's negligence was a proximate cause of the injury. Although the trier of fact could have found that plaintiff understood and assumed the risk, as the jury did in Barefield v. Coca-Cola Bottling Co., 370 Mich. 1, 120 N.W.2d 786 (1963), here the District Judge did not. We hold that there were sufficient facts to support his finding that plaintiff was under no duty to examine the grinder to determine its precise mechanical operation, and that she was therefore not guilty of contributory negligence or assumption of risk. On many previous occasions she had safely used her finger to scrape the bottom of the fine cutter plate, and the court could have found that there was nothing about the coarse plate, which she employed for the first time, to put her on notice of any danger.

[Judgment for plaintiff affirmed.]

PROBLEMS

1. P owned a housing for a motion picture camera; however, the recording device which showed the number of exposures per second did not accord with the number actually taken by the camera. P consulted D about the problem and D undertook to make the necessary adjustments. When D returned the camera he stated that it was now in proper working order. P used the camera to make a moving picture; however, it was spoiled due to the defective timing. P sues for breach of warranty. Decision?

2. Buyer purchased a used Mazda from a used car dealer. Later it was discovered that the Mazda was stolen. The car was returned to its rightful owner. Buyer sues the used car dealer for damages. The dealer defends on the grounds that he did not warrant good title. Decision?

3. P, the manager of a hotel, purchased on behalf of his employer four bottles of champagne produced and bottled by D. The champagne was to be consumed by guests of the hotel. While P was preparing the champagne for use, a cap from one of the bottles suddenly ejected and hit P in the eye causing serious injury. P sues D for breach of warranty. D defends on the grounds that the warranty does not extend to an employee. Decision?

4. Buyer sues the manufacturer and seller of a Mercury automobile for injuries sustained when the Mercury purchased new on the same day

went out of control due to defects in the throttle linkage and related parts. The seller admits the implied warranties of merchantability and fitness but defends on the grounds of the following disclaimer: "The warranties herein are expressly In Lieu of any other express or implied warranty, condition or guarantee on this vehicle or any part thereof, including any implied Warranty of Merchantability or Fitness". Decision?

5. Buyer tells the owner of a supermarket that she needs some wax for the vinyl tile on her kitchen floor. She asks the owner to recommend a wax that will not discolor the tile. The owner points to a shelf and tells her to select one of the brands on the shelf. She purchases one of the brands and uses it; however, it discolors her tile floor. Buyer seeks damages for breach of implied warranty of fitness for a particular purpose. Seller contends that he did not select the wax and should not be liable. Decision?

6. Buyer informed seller that he wanted a weedkiller to use on some weeds between his orange trees. Seller sold buyer a particular brand that would kill the weeds but would also damage his orange trees if used in the normal manner. Seller did not warn the buyer that the product would damage the trees if the buyer used it as he planned. Buyer used the product as he planned and damaged his trees. Decision?

7. Buyer ordered a bottle of Coca Cola at a drug store. The clerk served the buyer; but when the buyer started to drink the liquid, he discovered a dead fly in the bottle and became very ill. Buyer seeks damages from the Crystal Coca Cola Bottling Company which bottled the Coca Cola. Defendant contends it is not liable since there was no privity of contract between it and the buyer. Decision?

8. Cutter Laboratories manufactured and sold Salk polio vaccine which contained live virus instead of only inactivated virus. The vaccine was injected into children and caused the disease of poliomyelitis. In an action against the Cutter Laboratories, they defend on the ground that there was no privity of contract between the manufacturer and the buyer since the buyer purchased the vaccine from the pharmacy and not from them; and the plaintiff's children were not the actual buyers, but their doctor was. Decision?

9. Buyer of a new automobile had an accident due to a defective steering mechanism. A passenger in the automobile was injured. The manufacturer denies liability on the grounds there was no warranty in the contract of sale regarding the steering mechanism. Decision?

10. P suffered permanent skin disorders caused by the use of the defendant-manufacturer's cleaning product while working as a hotel maid. The product "Guard" was advertised as "Perfect Bathroom Sanitation". P used the product as directed by spraying it on the bathroom tile and then washing it down with water and a rag. There was no warning on the label. Plaintiff sues for the skin damage. Discuss.

11. P's wife, relying on a manufacturer's brochure, purchased a combination power tool. Due to defective design and construction, the tool could hurl a piece of wood through the air hitting the user. P was so injured and brings action for his injuries. The retailer and the manufacturer defend on the grounds that there was no breach of warranty, and that only the wife who purchased the tool can recover. Decision?

Chapter 22

DOCUMENTS OF TITLE AND SECURED TRANSACTIONS

A. DOCUMENTS OF TITLE

---

1. IN GENERAL

The document of title to goods developed so that paper representing title to the goods could be transferred between parties rather than transferring possession of the goods which was too cumbersome. They serve an important function in reserving or transferring a security interest in goods represented by the document because of the ease with which they can be handled and transferred.

The *U.C.C.* does not cover interstate shipments or foreign commerce and is expressly subject to applicable Federal statutes including the Federal Bills of Lading Act, the Interstate Commerce Act, the Harter Act of 1893 regulating offshore ocean commerce, the Carriage of Goods by Sea Act, and the United States Warehouse Act.

"Document of title" includes bill of lading, dock warrant, dock receipt, warehouse receipt, and any other document which in the regular course of business or financing is treated as adequately evidencing that the person entitled under the document has the right to receive, hold, and dispose of the document and the goods it covers. The document must represent that it was issued by a bailee, e.g., warehouse or carrier, and must purport to cover goods in the bailee's possession which are identified (Sections 1–201(15), 7–102(a)).

A bill of lading is a document evidencing the receipt of goods for shipment issued by a person engaged in the business of transporting or forwarding goods, and includes an airbill (Section 1–201(6)); i.e., it represents a right to goods from a carrier.

A warehouse receipt is a receipt issued by a person engaged in the business of storing goods for hire (Section 1–201(45)); i.e., it represents a right to goods from a warehouse.

A warehouseman is a person engaged in the business of storing goods for hire (Section 7–102(1)(h)).

A negotiable document of title is an effective tool for a seller who does not want to sell on credit. For example, a seller in New York who desires to sell goods to a buyer in California can have a bill of lading issued to the order of himself, in which case he is the consignor and the consignee (7–102(b)(c)). The buyer's name will appear on the bill of lading as the person to be notified. Next the seller draws a draft on the buyer and attaches it to the bill of lading. He then takes them to his bank in New York and indorses the draft and the bill of lading. The bank pays the seller his money and forwards the documents to its correspondent bank in California. The bank in California presents the draft to the buyer who pays for the draft and is given the bill of lading. The buyer then surrenders the bill of lading to the carrier and is given the goods.

If the seller is willing to sell to the buyer on credit, he can use a non-negotiable bill of lading, usually referred to as a "straight" bill of lading, in which the buyer is named the consignee. In this case the carrier will deliver the goods to the buyer without requiring the surrender of the bill of lading.

2. NEGOTIABILITY OF DOCUMENTS OF TITLE

Documents of title are either negotiable or non-negotiable.

A bill of lading, warehouse receipt, or other document of title is negotiable if by its terms the goods are to be delivered to the "bearer" or to the "order of" a named person. If the document does not contain these words of negotiability, it is not negotiable (Section 7–104). Thus, a bill of lading which states that the goods are consigned to "John Smith" would not be negotiable. A non-negotiable document can be assigned; however, the assignee only acquires the rights of the assignor and takes the assignment subject to defenses which are available against the assignor. In a negotiation of the document of title, the purchaser of the document takes it free from defects of his transferor's title and the claims of third persons; e. g., fraud, theft (Sections 7–501 and 7–502). The effect of due negotiation is that it creates new rights in the holder of the document.

There are two ways to negotiate a document of title depending on whether it is an "order" document or a "bearer" document. If it is an "order" document, it is negotiated by indorsement and delivery of the document. If it is a "bearer" document, it is negotiated by delivery alone. An indorsement is the placing of the transferor's signature on the document, which is usually done on the back of the document. If the indorser only signs his name and writes nothing else on the document, it is called a "blank" indorsement; and in such a case, the document can be negotiated by delivery alone. However, if the indorsement also states that the goods are to be delivered to a certain person, then it is called a special indorsement and cannot be negotiated without that person's signature; e.g., indorsement states "Deliver to John Smith" and is signed by the indorser. In such a case, if John Smith wants to negotiate the document further, he must sign the document and deliver it to his transferee. If the document states on its face that it is deliverable to "bearer," or if the indorsement is in blank or states "deliver to bearer," a thief would be able to negotiate the document.

For the transferee of the document to hold the document free from defects, he must have purchased it in good faith, without notice of a defense against it or claim to it on the part of any person; and he must have paid value for it in the regular course of business or financing. Such a holder acquires title to the document, title to the goods, and the direct obligation of the issuer (warehouseman or carrier) to hold or deliver the goods according to the terms of the document free from any defense or claim of the issuer other than those afforded him by Article 7 (Section 7–502(1)). The holder's rights cannot be defeated by a stoppage of the goods or surrender of them by the bailee (Section 7–502(2)).

3. WARRANTIES OF TRANSFEROR, INTERMEDIARY, AND INDORSER

The person negotiating or transferring a document of title for value, other than an intermediary or a secured party, warrants to his immediate purchaser only that:

a. the document is genuine; e.g., one who purchases a forged document of title may recover from the person who sold it to him;

b. he has no knowledge of any fact that would impair its validity or worth; and

c. his negotiation or transfer is rightful and fully effective with respect to the document and the goods it represents (Section 7–507).

The intermediary, e.g., collecting bank, entrusted with documents warrants only good faith and authority to act (Section 7–508).

The indorser is not liable for any default of the bailee or previous indorsers (Section 7–505). This rule is intended to avoid any reluctance on the part of the transferor about indorsing the document.

4. RIGHTS AND OBLIGATIONS OF BAILEE

A. Rights

The warehouseman and carrier are entitled to liens to guarantee the collection of unpaid charges (Sections 7–209, 7–307). The right of lien is in addition to any other rights allowed by law to a creditor against his debtor.

The bailee's lien is lost if he voluntarily delivers the goods or unjustifiably refuses to deliver (Sections 7–209(4), 7–307(3)).

B. Obligations

The duty of *care* of warehousemen and carriers requires that they act as reasonably careful men would under similar circumstances (Sections 7–204(1), 7–309(1)).

The bailee (warehouseman or carrier) must deliver the goods to the person entitled under the document who satisfies the bailee's lien and surrenders the negotiable document covering the goods (Section 7–403(1)–(3)); if he delivers to a person who holds a forged document, he will be liable for misdelivery.

Since a thief or finder of goods cannot pass title, he cannot obtain a document of title to goods and thereby defeat the true owner. For example, if a thief deposits stolen goods in a warehouse and receives a negotiable warehouse receipt, the warehouseman is not liable on the receipt if he has surrendered the goods to the true owner even though the receipt is held by a good faith purchaser since the receipt does not represent title to the goods.

B. SECURED TRANSACTIONS

---

1. IN GENERAL

Prior to the *U.C.C.*, many devices were used for the purpose of giving a creditor a security interest in personal property; i. e., to permit him to reclaim the propery on default, or to give him a preferred interest against other creditors. These security interests were known as pledges, assignments, chattel mortgages, trust receipts, trust deeds, inventory liens, equipment trusts, conditional sales, and leases and consignments intended as security. These devices have not been abolished by the *U.C.C.*, but their labels now have no legal significance. Whatever name the parties use makes no difference because the *U.C.C.* looks through the name to the substance of the transaction. Now these devices are called "security agreements", the interest created a "security interest", the borrower or credit buyer a "debtor", and the lender, credit seller, or buyer of accounts, contract rights, or chattel paper a "secured party" (Sections 1–201(37), 9–105). Though such phrases as "conditional sale" have no operative effect under the *U.C.C.*, it is probable that they will continue to be used as a brief method of describing certain types of transactions; however, it must be remembered that although legal title was retained by the seller in a conditional sales contract, under the *U.C.C.* the question of whether title to the collateral is in the secured party or the debtor is immaterial for security purposes. Under the *U.C.C.*, we look to the *method* of perfecting the security interest and the *kind of collateral* involved and its use rather than the title. Section 9–202 states as follows: "Each provision of this article with regard to rights, obligations, and remedies applies whether title to collateral is in the secured party or in the debtor."

Article 9 of the *U.C.C.* covers nearly all security interests in personal property and fixtures. The principal exceptions are: state statutes which regulate consumer installment sales and consumer loans; security interests perfected under a Federal statute; wage assignments; equipment trusts covering railway rolling stock; transfers of claims under insurance policies; transfer of deposit, savings and similar accounts maintained with a bank, a savings and loan association, credit union, or similar organization. See Sections 9–102, 9–103, 9–104.

For a secured transaction to be effective, three requirements are necessary:

a. the collateral must be in the *possession* of the secured party (lender or seller) *or* the debtor must have signed a *security agreement*;

b. there must be an *attachment* of the secured party's security interest to the collateral; and,

c. there must be a *perfection* of the security interest.

2. SECURITY AGREEMENT

"Security agreement" means an agreement between the secured party (creditor) and the debtor which creates or provides for a security interest (Section 9–105(*l*)).

The security agreement must be in writing, signed by the debtor, and contain a description of the collateral sufficient to reasonably identify it. However, if the security arrangement is a possessory one and the secured party is in possession of the collateral, it does not have to be in writing (Section 9–203). The security agreement may contain any terms and provisions that the parties desire, but the agreement must be fair to the debtor.

3. ATTACHMENT

The *U.C.C.* uses the term "attach" to indicate when the security interest in favor of a secured party is created in the debtor's property; i. e., the security agreement becomes enforceable between the parties and is said to "attach". *The security interest attaches and the lender takes a security interest in the debtor's property when three requirments have been met:*

a. there must be a security agreement signed,

b. the secured party must have given value, and

c. the debtor must have rights in the collateral (Section 9–204(1)).

These requirements may occur in any order; for example, the creditor may advance money immediately to the debtor on agreement that property to be acquired by the debtor in the future will be subject to a security interest in the creditor's favor (when the debtor acquires the rights in the collateral the security interest will attach).

Similar to the right to security in after-acquired property is the *floating lien* (Sections 9–204, 9–205). This is a security interest in constantly changing collateral. It has been called a floating lien, a lien on shifting stock, an inventory lien, a free-handed mortgage, and a floating charge. In this type of lien, the debtor has the right to use, commingle, or dispose of all or part of the collateral, or to collect or compromise accounts, contract rights, or chattel paper, or to use, commingle, or dispose of proceeds. It is not necessary for the secured party to require the debtor to account for the proceeds or to replace the collateral. The floating lien may be used only with respect to inventory or accounts receivable, but, of course, it may be used to tie up all of a debtor's assets. It is a highly useful lien in inventory and accounts receivable financing in that it permits a businessman to pledge property to be obtained in the future, permits the businessman to use the collateral to make money rather than holding it as a stationary asset, and gives the secured party an automatically perfected security interest in each item of after-acquired collateral immediately on its acquisition by the debtor.

4. PERFECTION OF SECURITY INTEREST

After the debtor and the secured party make the security agreement and after the secured party's security interest attaches to the collateral, it is necessary to *perfect* the security interest to make it valid against third parties; e.g., other secured parties, attaching creditors, a trustee in bankruptcy. Perfecting is not necessary for the secured party to enforce his interest against the *debtor*; that is done by the security agreement and the attaching of the security interest. However, it *is* necessary to perfect the security interest to make it good against *third parties*. The purpose of perfection is to give notice to all persons who may be dealing with the debtor that the secured party has or may have a security interest in the collateral.

There are three methods of perfecting a security interest. The method used depends on the kind of collateral involved.

A. Perfection by Attachment

Attachment, as described in B. 3. supra, is sufficient to constitute perfection in a limited number of transactions; e. g., installment sales to consumers, and sales of farm equipment which has a purchase price of $2,500.00 or less (Section 9–302).

Perfection by attachment gives a limited protection to the secured party. It does not give him protection against the rights of a good faith purchaser from the debtor who purchases the collateral from him without knowledge of the secured party's interest, pays value, and purchases for his own family household use or for his own farming operation (Section 9–307). Thus, a secured party should file a *financing statement* for more complete protection.

B. Perfection by Possession

Possession of the collateral (e. g., goods) by the secured party gives notice of his security interest making it unnecessary to file a financing statement (Section 9–302).

Possession is the required and exclusive method of perfecting a security interest in an *instrument*. The word "instrument" includes the following: (1) negotiable instruments (Section 3–104), (2) securities (Section 8–102), and (3) other rights to payment evidenced by writings that are in the ordinary course of business transferred by delivery with any necessary indorsement or assignment; e.g., Government warrants (Sections 9–304, 9–305).

C. Perfection by Filing a Financing Statement

The most common method of perfecting a secured party's security interest in the collateral is by filing a *financing statement* with the proper governmental agency. A financing statement is a document which is signed by both the debtor and the secured party and which contains the names and addresses of the parties and a description of the types or items of collateral covered (See Sections 9–110, 9–402). Simple forms can be purchased which are suitable for filing.

A financing statement is *not* a substitute for a security agreement. A security agreement may be filed as a financing statement, but often a security agreement contains details which the parties prefer not to reveal in a public notice so they prefer to file the simple financing statement. A person searching the records to ascertain if the debtor's property is subject to a security interest will learn very little from a financing statement except that the property may be subject to a security interest. He must, therefore, go to the parties for further information; and there is a procedure for him to follow in obtaining such information.

Must Be filed:
A- Inventory: Equipment - Business
B. Intangibles, patents, copyrights
Farm equip over $2500 is business equip

Good Faith Purchaser
Pays Value
Personal Use
No Knowledge

This **FINANCING STATEMENT** is presented for filing pursuant to the California Uniform Commercial Code

1. DEBTOR (LAST NAME FIRST) Mr. A.		1A. SOCIAL SECURITY OR FEDERAL TAX NO. 000-00-0000
1.B. MAILING ADDRESS 855 North Vermont Avenue	1C. CITY, STATE Los Angeles, California	1D. ZIP CODE 90029
1E. RESIDENCE ADDRESS (IF AN INDIVIDUAL AND DIFFERENT THAN 1B) 17000 Ventura Boulevard	1F. CITY, STATE Encino, California	1G. ZIP CODE 91316
2. ADDITIONAL DEBTOR (IF ANY) (LAST NAME FIRST)		2A. SOCIAL SECURITY OR FEDERAL TAX NO.
2B. MAILING ADDRESS	2C. CITY, STATE	2D. ZIP CODE
2E. RESIDENCE ADDRESS (IF AN INDIVIDUAL AND DIFFERENT THAN 2B)	2F. CITY, STATE	2G. ZIP CODE
3. DEBTOR(S) TRADE NAME OR STYLE (IF ANY)		3A. FEDERAL TAX NO.
4. ADDRESS OF DEBTOR(S) CHIEF PLACE OF BUSINESS (IF ANY)	4A. CITY, STATE	4B. ZIP CODE
5. SECURED PARTY NAME Mr. B. MAILING ADDRESS 46182 North Vermont Avenue CITY Los Angeles STATE California ZIP CODE 90029		5A. SOCIAL SECURITY NO., FED. TAX NO. OR BANK TRANSIT AND A.B.A. NO. 000-00-0000
6. ASSIGNEE OF SECURED PARTY (IF ANY) NAME MAILING ADDRESS CITY STATE ZIP CODE		6A. SOCIAL SECURITY NO., FED. TAX NO. OR BANK TRANSIT AND A.B.A. NO.

7. This FINANCING STATEMENT covers the following types or items of property (if crops or timber, include description of real property on which growing or to be grown).

Accounts now or later owned by debtor:

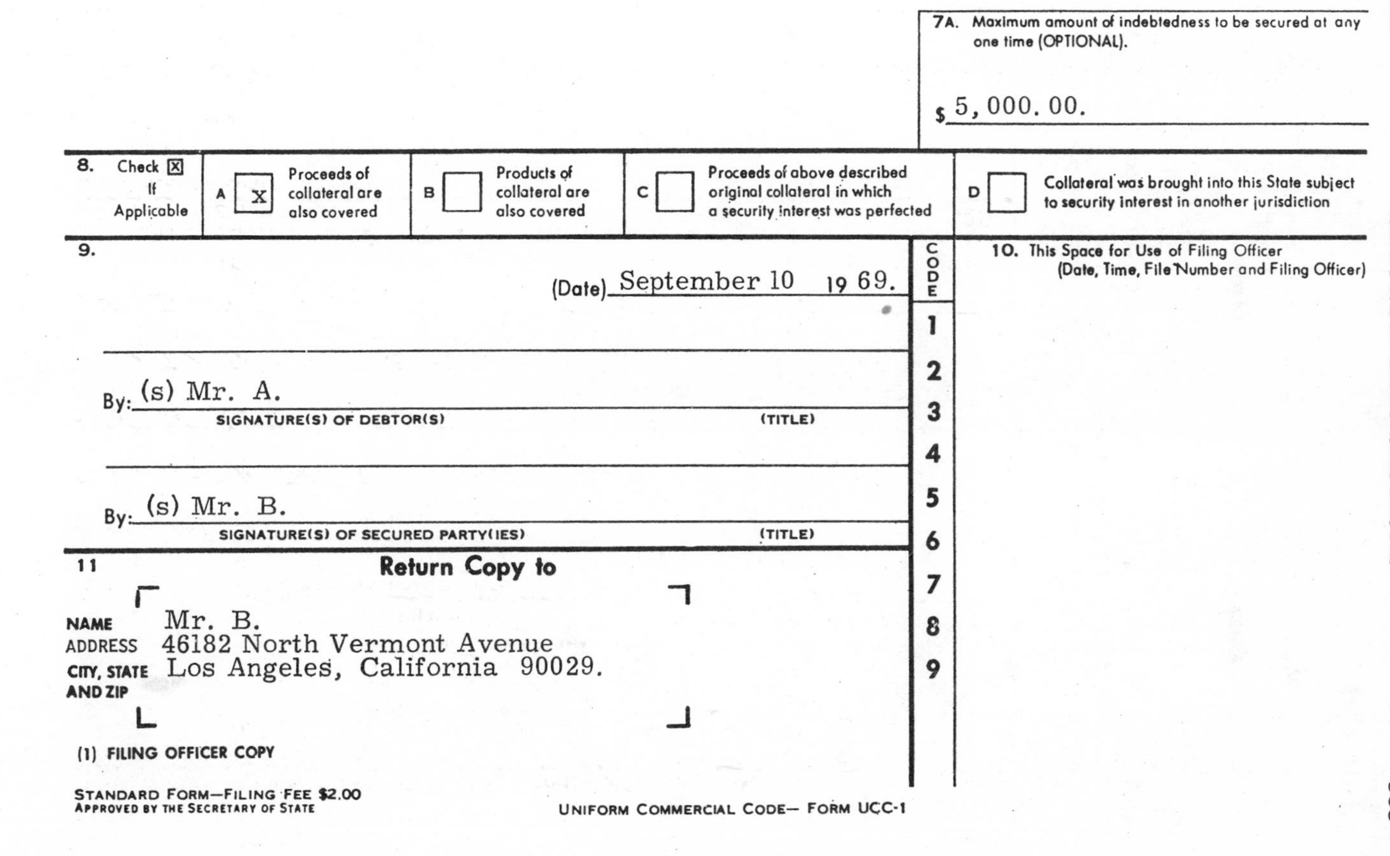

7A. Maximum amount of indebtedness to be secured at any one time (OPTIONAL).

$ 5,000.00.

8. Check [X] If Applicable

A [X] Proceeds of collateral are also covered

B [ ] Products of collateral are also covered

C [ ] Proceeds of above described original collateral in which a security interest was perfected

D [ ] Collateral was brought into this State subject to security interest in another jurisdiction

9.

(Date) September 10 19 69.

By: (s) Mr. A.
SIGNATURE(S) OF DEBTOR(S) (TITLE)

By: (s) Mr. B.
SIGNATURE(S) OF SECURED PARTY(IES) (TITLE)

CODE
1
2
3
4
5
6
7
8
9

10. This Space for Use of Filing Officer
(Date, Time, File Number and Filing Officer)

11

Return Copy to

NAME Mr. B.
ADDRESS 46182 North Vermont Avenue
CITY, STATE AND ZIP Los Angeles, California 90029.

(1) FILING OFFICER COPY

STANDARD FORM—FILING FEE $2.00
APPROVED BY THE SECRETARY OF STATE

UNIFORM COMMERCIAL CODE— FORM UCC-1

Section 9–401 provides for three alternatives regarding the place where the financing statement is to be filed; e.g., local filing (county), central filing (Secretary of State), or a combination of both local and central. States have used all three alternatives plus variations; therefore, local rules must be consulted in this area.

Filing a financing statement is required in the following secured transactions: (1) *intangible collateral;* i.e., contract rights, accounts, and general intangibles (examples of general intangibles are: any interest or claim in or under any policy of insurance; good will; literary rights; patents; and copyrights); and (2) *goods;* i.e., inventory and equipment in general (for definitions, see Sections 9–106, 9–109(1), 9–109(2)(4), and 9–109(3)).

Filing is permissive in secured transactions involving chattel paper and negotiable instruments (Section 9–304).

5. RIGHTS OF THIRD PARTIES AND DEFAULT OF DEBTOR

An in-depth discussion of the many problems which arise between competing claimants to the debtor's property (e. g., unsecured creditors of the debtor, trustees in bankruptcy of the debtor's insolvent estate, purchasers of collateral from the debtor, other parties with security interests in the same collateral), is beyond the scope of this text.

With regard to problems which arise when the debtor defaults in payment, it should be mentioned that recent decisions have generally held that repossession statutes, such as Sections 9–503 and 9–504, and lien statutes, such as garagemen's liens, are unconstitutional in that they violate the Fourteenth Amendment to the Constitution of the United States unless they provide for notice to the alleged debtor and an opportunity for a hearing.

Many competing claimant problems can be avoided by the preparation of a satisfactory security agreement. When the parties have not provided the solution in the security agreement, or when the security agreement does not apply, the *U.C.C.* sets forth applicable rules. In this area it is suggested that the student refer to Sections 9–301 through 9–507, plus local state statutes for exceptions and variations, particularly in the area of loans and retail installment sales.

---

1. Effect of Delivery without Surrender of Bill of Lading

KORESKA v. UNITED CARGO CORP.

23 App.Div.2d 37, 258 N.Y.S.2d 432 (1965).

PER CURIAM. Plaintiff, an Austrian manufacturer and seller of thermographic copying paper, appeals from an order denying his motion for summary judgment for the value of paper allegedly converted by defendant United Cargo Corporation. United, a carrier, having issued a negotiable order bill of lading for the goods, consisting of four large packages, delivered them to the New York purchaser without requiring or taking up the bill of lading, and before plaintiff had received his purchase price.

The substantial question presented is whether United has raised a triable issue of fact in contending that it was excused from its duty of requiring surrender of the bill of lading before delivering the goods. United urges that it was so excused by an oral waiver made by plaintiff's agent and also by a binding trade custom or course of dealing. * * *

A further reason why United may not avail itself of the alleged waiver, is that the waiver was oral only, and would modify the express term of the bill that delivery was to be made at the order of the New York bank consignee. One of the conditions printed on the back of the bill provides:

> "None of the terms of this bill of lading shall be deemed to have been waived by any person unless by express waiver signed by such person, or his duly authorized agent."

Ordinary prudence, moreover, would dictate that the carrier require that such instructions be noted on the bill itself (cf. U.C.C. § 7–303[2]).

For similar reasons evidence of the course of dealing or trade custom is also without significance. The express term, requiring delivery in accordance with the consignee's order, is controlling, whenever the course of dealing or trade custom is inconsistent with it * * * (U.C.C. § 1–205[4]).

In the absence of a triable issue of fact, summary judgment must be granted. Summary relief is, moreover, particularly appropriate in commercial cases, such as this, where the injured party is far away and has relied on documentary rights and evidence. If a trade custom or the oral waiver by an unknown purported agent, contrary to the plain terms of trade documents, were given the effect contended for by United, the ability of such a distant person to engage in foreign trade in reliance on negotiable documents of title would be severely and unduly handicapped. Allowance of such a practice is certainly destructive of the integrity of documents used in international trade throughout the world.

Accordingly, the order denying plaintiff Koreska's motion for summary judgment should be reversed on the law, and summary judgment for $13,939.72, the invoice price, in favor of plaintiff, granted, with costs and disbursements to plaintiff-appellant against defendant-respondent.

2. *Effect of Delivery on Forged Bill of Lading*

DAVID CRYSTAL, INC. v. CUNARD STEAM-SHIP CO.

223 F.Supp. 273 (D.C.N.Y., 1963), affirmed 339 F.2d 295, certiorari denied 380 U.S. 976, 85 S.Ct. 1339, 14 L.Ed.2d 271 and 380 U.S. 976, 85 S.Ct. 1340, 14 L.Ed.2d 271.

LEVET, District Judge. This action in admiralty, brought by the libellant, David Crystal, Inc. (Crystal), seeks to recover the value of twenty-eight of its shipment of twenty-nine cases of shirts transported by the respondent, Cunard Steam-Ship Co. (Cunard), pursuant to an ocean bill of lading consigning the goods to Crystal's customs broker in New York, Penson & Company (Penson). * * *

A single sentence suffices to express the essential facts in this case: The cargo in question was discharged from Cunard's vessel to the pier by Clark, the stevedore, and from there misdelivered by Clark upon the presentation of a forged delivery order of the customs broker, Penson, obtained by the thieves through the complicity of one of Penson's employees. While pilferage on the New York docks is not new, the cool assurance with which the conspirators completed the necessary formalities and waited at the pier almost nine hours until the cargo was finally loaded aboard their truck, gives some indication that this was a masterly executed plot to obtain the cargo by persons more than casually familiar with the procedures of the piers and the customs brokers. * * *

At the outset is the question of Cunard's liability. It was undisputed at the trial that the misdelivery occurred after the cargo had been discharged from the vessel in the same good order and condition, segregated on the pier by the stevedore, and notice given to the consignee of the time and place of the delivery.

The bill of lading provides:

> "Packages merchandise to be delivered subject to the exceptions, restrictions and conditions of the undermentioned clauses, from the ship's deck where the Shipowner's responsibility shall cease * * *."

* * *

Were a literal reading of the bill of lading permitted, the case would clearly come to a swift end in favor of the carrier. But so easy a solution is not possible. * * *

Cunard's liability as a carrier had ceased and both it and its agent Clark stood as warehouseman in relation to the cargo. The question becomes, what is the liability of a carrier, as warehouseman, for a delivery of the goods to the wrong person. * * *

The libellant argues that a warehouseman is absolutely liable for a misdelivery without any question as to his negligence. * * * As Professor Braucher of Harvard states, "Delivery to the wrong person, under the Code as under prior law, would seem to subject the bailee to an absolute liability to the person entitled under the document, even though, for example, the bailee relied on a skillfully forged delivery order."

* * * Libellant Crystal is entitled to an interlocutory decree sustaining its claim for liability against the respondent-petitioner Cunard.

---

3. Security Agreement under U.C.C.

MID-EASTERN ELECTRONICS, INC. v. FIRST NAT. BANK OF SO. MD.

380 F.2d 355 (C.A.Md., 1967).

ALBERT V. BRYAN, Circuit Judge. A security interest under the Maryland Uniform Commercial Code in personal property of its debtor, with lien primacy therefor, was denied the appellant, First National Bank of Southern Maryland, by the District Court. Instead, priority of lien was accorded Mid-Eastern Electronics, Inc., appellee, under an attachment upon its judgment against this debtor. We uphold the decision. * * *

This judgment was obtained in the District Court by Mid-Eastern (ME) against the debtor, Continental Electronics, Inc. for the sum of $30,763.32 on July 14, 1965. In seeking to collect it, ME levied upon the chattel assets, including inventory and equipment, of the judgment debtor and a garnishment was also served upon the Bank. * * * It later appeared that the Bank was asserting a security interest in the debtor's personalty for the payment of certain notes it held of the debtor. Reliance for its claim as a secured party was placed upon a financing statement filed pursuant to the UCC, § 9–302, with the appropriate State office. * * * Assuming arguendo that the financing agreement met the requisites of the UCC § 9–402, it alone did not create a security interest. It was but notice that one was claimed, a single step in the means by which the rights and priorities of a secured party are "perfected".

We begin with § 9–204(1) of the Code, which provides:

> "(1) A security interest cannot attach until there is agreement * * * that it attach and value is given and the debtor has rights in the collateral. It attaches as soon as all of the events in the preceding sentence have taken place unless explicit agreement postpones the time of attaching."

A security interest, additionally, is unenforceable unless, under the Code's statute of frauds, the "debtor has signed a security agreement which contains a description of the collateral * * *." § 9–203(1)(b). Under the UCC, " '*Collateral*' means the property subject to a security interest, and includes accounts, contract rights and chattel paper which have been sold * * *." § 9–105(1)(c). " '*Agreement*' means the bargain of the parties in fact. * * * " § 1–201(3) (Accent added). As the appellant can proffer no writing signed by the debtor giving, even sketchily, the terms of the security agreement it is unenforceable. So found the District Judge and we affirm.

---

4. Secured Transactions are Not Usurious

EQUIPMENT FINANCE, INC. v. GRANNAS

207 Pa.Super. 363, 218 A.2d 81 (1966).

JACOBS, Judge. The narrow point of law presented in this appeal is whether or not the Usury Statute applies to a sale of heavy machinery on credit when a finance company, in good faith and for value, purchases from the seller of the machinery the security agreement and accompanying note given by the buyer to the seller.

Equipment Finance, Inc., hereinafter called "Finance Co.", sued Chester E. Grannas and Paul A. Grannas, trading as Grannas Brothers, a partnership, hereinafter "Buyer", to recover three monthly payments allegedly due on the purchase of certain rock crushing equipment from Aggregates Equipment, Inc., hereinafter "Seller". In October, 1963, a jury returned a verdict of $8,062.31 for the Finance Co., which included the three monthly payments of $2,133.02 monthly, plus interest from 1959. Buyer appeals from the judgment entered on the verdict.

The main issue at trial was whether the transaction was a loan from Finance Co. to Buyer so arranged as to constitute a subterfuge to avoid the law against usury, as alleged by appellants, or a sale on credit with an assigned installment sales agreement. This was resolved against appellants. * * * Buyer made each month's payment to Finance Co. for 33 months but refused to pay the final three installments, tendering instead a check for $396.92, which it alleged was the entire balance due at the time the 34th payment was demanded in May, 1959. It contended that the credit service charge of $11,713.44 was usurious and that all it was obliged to pay was 6% interest per annum on the declining balance of the unpaid cash price, leaving $396.92 due. * * * Courts in this jurisdiction have consistently said that this act does not apply to a bona fide sale of goods on credit. Such sales are the result of a decision by a buyer to purchase property on credit at a higher price than he would pay if he paid cash. There is no loan or use of money on the part of the buyer. * * *

It being uniformly held that sellers are free to contract with buyers as to the terms and conditions of sales, the financing of sales of merchandise by the extension of credit has never been considered subject to the prohibition of usury or to regulations applicable to banking and loan transactions. * * * We agree with the jury's conclusion that even though a finance company was involved, taking an assignment of the security agreement, the primary purpose of this transaction was the purchase of goods and was not an occasion or pretext for a loan * * *

With the law thus established, the only inquiry remaining for us is to consider appellants' argument that Article 9 of the Code changes the law since a security agreement was executed here. We think not. * * * Nowhere in this article, which is a comprehensive scheme for the regulation of security interests in personal property, is any attempt made to regulate financing charges. This Buyer agreed to pay a higher price for the rock crushing equipment for the privilege of buying it on credit and using it while paying it off. He elected to enter into this financing agreement rather than attempting to secure a loan through a bank for reasons not here our concern. * *

Order and judgment affirmed [for plaintiff].

---

5. *Perfection of Security Agreement by Possession of Collateral*

IN RE MIDAS COIN CO.

264 F.Supp. 193 (D.C.Mo., 1967).

REGAN, District Judge. This petition for review of the order of Referee in Bankruptcy Brauer, denying the petition of St. John's Community Bank to foreclose a collateral note * * *, requires the construction of the Uniform Commercial Code as adopted by Missouri and its application to a security agreement involving a pledge of United States coins having an appreciated numismatic value. The facts are not in dispute. The sole issue is whether under such facts the filing of a financing statement was essential to perfect the Bank's right as against the trustee. * * *

The business of bankrupt was buying and selling coins and stamps for profit. On or about January 14, 1966 the bankrupt executed a promissory note payable to the Bank in the principal amount of $9,637.58 and pledged as collateral security therefor coins constituting part of its inventory and having a face value of $9,750.50. * * * Admittedly, no financing statement was filed.

The coins in question and others had been purchased by bankrupt either from other coin dealers or from collectors because of their numismatic value, and such coins are considered part of the bankrupt's inventory and stock in trade which it owned and intended to sell in its regular course of business. * * * The Referee held that the instant transaction was governed by Article 9 of the Code which pertains to secured transactions. * * *

Section 400.9–302(1) (a) of Article 9 provides that a financing statement must be filed to perfect all security interests, except a security interest in collateral in possession of the secured party under Section 400.9–305. The latter section authorizes the secured party to perfect a security interest in goods, instruments, negotiable documents or chattel paper (as well as letters of credit and advices of credit) by taking possession of the collateral. It is the Bank's position that having taken possession of the collateral, its security interest has thereby been perfected, so that no financing statement was required to be filed. * * *

The trustee contends, and the Referee held, that Section 400.9–305 V.A.M.S. is not here applicable, upon the theory that coins are money, and that since money is not one of the kinds of property enumerated in that section, the only method of perfecting a security interest therein is by filing a financing statement. * * *

The issue here argued by the parties is whether the pledged coins are "goods" as that term is used in Section 305. * * *

> " 'Goods' means all things (including specially manufactured goods) *which are movable* at the time of identification to the contract for sale *other than the money in which the price is to be paid,* investment securities (article 8) and things in action. 'Goods' also includes the unborn young of animals and growing crops and other identified things attached to realty as described in the section on goods to be severed from realty * * *."

In the official comment to this section it is said, * * *

> *Goods is intended to cover the sale of money when money is being treated as a commodity but not to include it when money is the medium of payment.* * * *

Hence, unless money, when used and treated as a commodity, is deemed to be "goods," as we have held, then it is not included at all in the various kinds of personal property which are governed by the provisions of Article 9 of the Code, so that in any event the Bank was not required to file a financing statement to perfect its security interest.

The petition for review is sustained and the orders of the Referee are reversed.

[Judgment for Bank.]

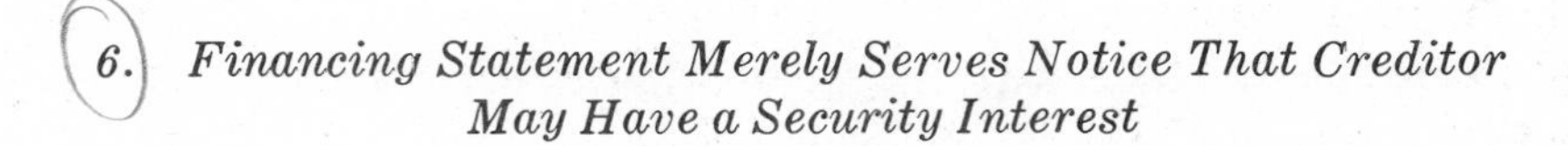

6. *Financing Statement Merely Serves Notice That Creditor May Have a Security Interest*

GENERAL ELECTRIC CREDIT CORP. v. BANKERS COMMERCIAL CORP.

244 Ark. 984, 429 S.W.2d 60 (1968).

GEORGE ROSE SMITH, Justice. This is primarily a dispute between two finance companies about their security interests in a dragline that was sold on credit by Southland Tractors, Inc., to the appellee J. T. Arnold, III. Both security agreements held by the rival finance companies are defective, that of Bankers Commercial Corporation not having met the filing requirements of the Uniform Commercial Code and that of General Electric Credit Corporation being a forgery. * * *

On April 13, 1966, Southland sold the dragline to Arnold for $33,850.04. The contract of sale was in the form of a three-year lease which recited that Arnold had paid $5,000 as advance rental and would pay the remainder in 36 equal monthly installments. Arnold was given the option of purchasing the dragline at any time during the term of the lease by paying the $33,850.04, less the total amount of rents already paid. Under the Code such a lease is treated as a security agreement. Ark.Stat.Ann. § 85–1–201(37) (Add.1961).

On the same day Southland (*a*) duly filed a financing statement showing itself as the creditor and Arnold as the debtor and (*b*) assigned the lease contract to Bankers for a cash consideration of more than $24,000.00. Bankers did not file anything to show its security interest; so Southland continued as the creditor of record.

About three months later Southland informed Arnold that it had arranged to refinance the debt with General Electric Credit Corporation. The identity of the creditor made no difference to Arnold, who readily signed another financing statement showing GECC as the creditor. Southland then forged Arnold's signature to a three-year lease, similar to the one held by Bankers, and assigned it to GECC. * * * Southland soon went into bankruptcy.

Arnold assumed that the debt had been refinanced, but he soon received demands for payment from both Bankers and GECC. * * *

This action to replevy the dragline was brought by GECC against Arnold. Bankers intervened to assert its claim. * * *

Bankers holds a valid security agreement, admittedly signed by Arnold. Bankers' failure to file any notice of its creditorship might have allowed later valid claims to take priority, but as between the two of them Bankers has an enforceable cause of action against Arnold.

By contrast, the only genuine instrument held by GECC is its financing statement. A financing statement, standing alone, does not create a security interest in the debtor's property. It merely serves notice that the named creditor may have a security interest. * * *

On cross appeal Arnold is entitled to relief. Both GECC and Bankers sought to accelerate the maturity of their total claims, but their failure to reserve that power in the contracts precluded them from exercising it. * * * At best Bankers may be entitled to damages resulting from Arnold's failure to make his payments when due—the measure of such damages presumably being interest at the legal rate and certainly not being the rents to accrue during the remaining life of the lease.

[Judgment for Bankers.]

7. *Financing Statement Effective Even Though a Minor Error*

IN THE MATTER OF, EXCEL STORES, INC.

341 F.2d 961 (C.A.Conn., 1965).

MEDINA, Circuit Judge. * * *

In the village of Pawcatuck, in the town of Stonington, Connecticut, near the Rhode Island border, lies a Shopping Center where in 1961 there was a sort of department store. Under the same management and as part of a single venture Excel Stores, Inc., a Connecticut corporation, sold "toys, domestics and other miscellaneous" articles of merchandise, and Excel Enterprises, Inc., a Massachusetts corporation, conducted "discount sales of women's and children's wear." We were told on oral argument that the name "Excel" was prominently displayed outside the store.

* * * Andrew F. Machado was in fact the Treasurer of Excel Stores, Inc., he intended to make and did make the purchase of the six cash registers on behalf of and as representing Excel Stores, Inc. and all the checks delivered from time to time in partial payment of the indebtedness to National Cash Register Company were checks of Excel Stores, Inc. But Machado inadvertently made the mistake of writing "Excel Department Stores" instead of "Excel Stores, Inc." when he filled out the security agreement, adding, after the printed word "by," his signature, "Andrew F. Machado." These names were subsequently typed by appellant in an appropriate place indicated in the agreement.

It is clear that the parties intended to execute a valid and binding contract. * * * Nor can it be doubted that any creditor of Excel or other interested person searching the record would come to the Excel Department Store at the Shopping Center of Pawcatuck, find Machado's name and be put on notice that a lien against Excel might be outstanding and that communication with Machado might be appropriate. This is precisely all that the Code requires. * * * [U.C.C. 9–402(8)]

> "A financing statement substantially complying with the requirements of this section is effective even though it contains minor errors which are not seriously misleading."

We hold the error made by Machado to be a "minor error" which is not "seriously misleading."

[Judgment for National Cash Register Company.]

8. *"Land Owned or Leased by Debtor" Insufficient Description*

CHANUTE PRODUCTION CREDIT ASS'N v. WEIR GRAIN AND SUPPLY, INC.

210 Kan. 181, 499 P.2d 517 (1972).

Creditor who held security interest on corn and soybean crops on debtor's land brought suit against purchaser of the crops for the value thereof.

PER CURIAM. In the fall of 1969, the appellee purchased corn and soy beans from Wesley Wayne Meyer, which grain was grown in Cherokee County, Kansas. Prior to the purchase of the corn and soy beans the appellant had filed in the office of the Register of Deeds of Cherokee County, Kansas, a financing statement which described the crops and the land on which the crops were grown as follows:

> "Crops: Annual and perennial crops of whatever kind and description which are now growing or are hereafter planted, grown, and produced on land owned or leased by debtor in Cherokee County, Kansas."

The Security Agreement, which was not recorded, sets out the acres, kinds of crops, name of the farms (Schultz Farm, Rotobaugh Farm, Etc.) and the legal descriptions.

This action was filed by plaintiff against the defendant for $2835.49, the value of the crops purchased from Meyer. Defendant, in its answer sets out that it had no actual knowledge of the security agreement and that the financing statement was inadequate and did not constitute a notice to the defendant as required by K.S.A. 1971 Supp. 84–9–402 and 84–9–110 and is insufficient to perfect a security interest in the crops involved.

The district court concluded as a matter of law that the financing statement is insufficient to perfect any security interest in the crops involved in this case for the reason that it does not contain a sufficient description of the real estate as required by K.S.A.1971 Supp. 84–9–402 and 84–9–110. Even though it is apparent by the amendment of K.S.A. 84–9–402 (effective July 1, 1967), the legislature intended that something less than a legal description would suffice to give notice to third persons, it is evident from reading this section, along with K.S.A. 84–9–110, that some description be given, and that a description merely stating "land owned or leased by debtor in Cherokee County, Kansas," is insufficient.

In its appeal plaintiff's main argument against the judgment below is that the financing statement gave the defendant constructive notice and the defendant was put on inquiry to ascertain whether the crops were subject to the security agreement of plaintiff.

* * * Purchaser or creditor should not be required to make a general search of the record or a general inquiry in the county as to lands leased by the debtor.

This court agrees with the district court that although the legislature, by K.S.A. 84–9–402 and 84–9–110, intended something less than a legal description, that as to purchasers and creditors, it is evident that a description merely stating "land owned or leased by the debtor in Cherokee County, Kansas," is insufficient.

The judgment is affirmed.

---

9. *Perfected Security Interest Prevails over Tax Lien*

PARAMOUNT FINANCE CO. v. UNITED STATES

379 F.2d 543 (C.A.Ohio, 1967).

NEESE, District Judge. S. & C. Tavern, Inc. procured a loan from the plaintiff [taxpayer] * * * and applied the proceeds to the purchase of a tavern business in Cleveland, Ohio. The taxpayer made its promissory note to the lender, securing the repayment of the loan with a security agreement and financing statement. The lender perfected its security interest in the collateral given by the taxpayer by filings in the respective offices of the recorder of Cuyahoga County, Ohio and the Ohio secretary of state on August 15, 1962.

Within two years therefrom the taxpayer was in default on the loan and deficient in paying its federal taxes. The defendant assessed the taxpayer on April 23, 1964 with a tax deficiency of $4,988.03. Four days afterward, the defendant's agents filed with the aforementioned recorder a lien on the taxpayer's property for federal tax liabilities, and its agents seized, * * * the tavern property, including DA–3 permit no. 3494 of the Ohio Department of Liquor Control, respecting a liquor license which had been issued theretofore to the taxpayer.

* * * The defendant was authorized to collect the tax due it from the taxpayer by levy on and seizure of the state liquor license. * * * However, such lien imposed thereon by 26 U.S.C. § 6321 was invalid against the lender's perfected purchase money security interest under the aforementioned security agreement and financing statement. * * *

The security interest acquired by the lender was a "purchase money security interest" under the Ohio Commercial Code, which applies * * * so far as concerns any personal property and fixtures within the jurisdiction of [Ohio]

> * * *: (1) to any transaction, regardless of its form, which is intended to create a security interest in personal property or fixtures including goods, documents, instruments, general intangibles, chattel paper, accounts or contract rights * *."

(A). A "* * * 'General intangible' means any personal property, including things in action, other than goods, accounts, contract rights, chattel paper, documents and instruments." * * *

The taxpayer could not transfer to the lender title to the liquor license issued to it by the Ohio Department of Liquor Control, * * * but the taxpayer could, and did, transfer to the lender a security interest in the liquor license, as constituting "property" with unique value. * * *

The fund produced by the sale by the defendant of the taxpayer's tavern and its liquor license represents the value of its business which was hypothecated to the lender under a security agreement perfected long before the taxpayer's property was seized by the defendant. We agree with District Court that the fund remaining should be applied to the satisfaction of the lender's rights thereunder.

---

10. *Oral Notice of Foreclosure Sale Sufficient*

CREST INVESTMENT TRUST, INC. v. ALATZAS

264 Md. 571, 287 A.2d 261 (1972).

Suit by lender, which held restaurant buyer's note secured by recorded financing statement, against restaurant business seller, which had repurchased such business at public sale pursuant to foreclosure proceeding against buyer, seeking damages and alleging failure of seller to give it reasonable notification of the foreclosure sale.

MCWILLIAMS, Judge. When Greek meets Greek then comes the tug of war. Triffona George Alatzas met Peter Angelides and sold him a restaurant, whence comes this tug of war. A year or so later (June 1968) Angelides borrowed $18,333 from the appellant (Crest). When Angelides defaulted Alatzas foreclosed his lien. Crest says no notice of the foreclosure was "sent" to it. Thus is presented for our consideration, for the first time it seems, the nature of the "reasonable notification" required by Code (1964 Repl. Vol.), Art. 95B, § 9–504 (3), the Uniform Commercial Code.

As we shall see, the parties are not in complete agreement in respect of what happened. In early 1967 Alatzas occupied as lessee a building in east Baltimore in which he had a restaurant-cum-bar. In March he sold it to Angelides for $33,000, $16,000 of which was evidenced by a note secured by a recorded financing statement. He assigned the lease to Angelides but, of course, his own liability to the lessor was not thereby diminished. The financing statement evidencing Crest's loan was recorded on 21 June 1968. * * *

Although Alatzas had sold him "a good business, a very good business," Angelides fell behind in his payments to Alatzas and in mid-1969 he closed his doors. The public foreclosure sale was scheduled for 28 October. The auctioneer (Billig) caused the advertisement of sale to appear in the Baltimore Sun on the two Sundays before the sale and on the day of the sale. Alatzas concedes a written notice was not sent to Crest.

Despite credible evidence to the contrary Crest insists its only notice of the sale was received during a telephone conversation between Dennis Psoras, then of counsel for Alatzas, and Irving Bowers, of counsel for Crest, around 4:00 p. m. on the day before the sale. Bowers said he and Sidney Kaplan, also of counsel for Crest, tried, without success, to inform Crest's management of the impending sale and that as a result Crest was not represented at the sale. * * *

Forty or more persons attended the sale. The bidding began at $10,000; Alatzas, at $13,000, was the highest bidder. The amount due him was $11,274.01; the expenses were $3,805; the deficiency amounted to $2,079.01. Crest does not claim the sale was not "commercially reasonable" as required by § 9–507(2) or that the collateral was not disposed of in the "good faith" required by § 1–203. The balance due it at the time, including attorney's fees of 15%, was $9,376.27.

* * *

At first glance, to be sure, one does get the impression that "send" connotes a notice in writing but, upon closer inspection, it becomes quite clear, we think, that the receipt or acquisition of actual knowledge within the time a properly sent notification could have arrived amounts to compliance with the requirement of § 9–504(3). Written notification could accomplish no more and, in this regard, it will be observed that § 9–504(3) is satisfied merely by sending the notification; there is no requirement that it be received.

* * *

Since we cannot say Judge Cardin's finding that Crest did have actual notice of the sale was clearly erroneous nor that he misapprehended the applicable law, we do not reach the question whether the notice of one day was reasonable in the circumstances. Maryland Rule 886. We shall affirm the judgment in favor of Alatzas against Crest for costs.

Judgment affirmed.

Costs to be paid by the appellant.

PROBLEMS

1. P was the holder of a warehouse receipt for a quantity of soybean oil which was stored in D's warehouse tanks. The soybean oil disappeared under circumstances which have never been explained. D has dishonored the warehouse receipt. P sues for damages. Decision?

2. C held a security agreement which covered furniture, fixtures and inventory at the bankrupt's old drugstore. The security agreement contained an after-acquired property clause. The drugstore and its contents was destroyed by fire. The bankrupt purchased a new store eight months

later in a community 270 miles away. The bankrupt has now filed bankruptcy and C claims the new inventory as against the trustee in bankruptcy. Decision?

3. C's security agreement listed the following property: one-two pc. living room suite, wine; one-five pc. chrome dinette set, yellow; one-three pc. panel bedroom suite, lime oak, matt. & spgs. The security agreement also stated the address where the items were located. The trustee in bankruptcy claims the lien is invalid because the description was insufficient since a three piece bedroom suite could be twin beds and a dresser, and a chest; a two piece living room suite could be a couch converted into a bed and a chair or overstuffed stool, or some item commonly used in a living room; and a five piece dinette, in addition to being a table and four chairs, could be a table, cabinet for dishes, or some other dining or breakfast room piece and three chairs. Decision?

4. P had a security agreement with D covering the sale of certain trailers. P did not file a financing statement or repossess the property on D's default in payments. The United States filed a tax lien on the trailers. P claims his prior security agreement prevails over the later tax lien. Decision?

Part 4

BAILMENTS

Chapter 23

NATURE AND TERMINATION

A. NATURE

1. BAILMENTS DEFINED

A bailment is the transfer of possession of personal property for a particular purpose; e.g., owner of a watch gives it to a jeweler for repair. There is no transfer of title. The owner and the transferor of the property is the bailor; the person receiving the property is the bailee. Real property cannot be the subject matter of a bailment.

2. PROPERTY CLASSIFICATION

All property is either *real* or *personal*. Real property is land and anything permanently attached thereto by man or nature. Personal property consists of moveable things, which may be tangible physical objects or intangibles such as goodwill, patent rights, trademarks, franchises, and leases.

3. ESSENTIALS OF BAILMENT

The essential elements of a bailment are:

a. Retention of title by bailor;

b. Delivery of possession to the bailee;

c. Acceptance of possession by the bailee;

d. Possession and temporary control of property by the bailee for a specific purpose;

e. Ultimate possession of the property to revert to bailor unless he orders it transferred to another person.

4. BAILMENT DISTINGUISHED

A bailment should be distinguished from a sale, a pledge or a pawn, and a lease or a license.

A. SALE

A bailment differs from a sale in three ways:

(1) A sale is a transfer of title; a bailment is a transfer only of possession (it is still a bailment even though the goods are to be returned in a different form, e.g., wheat taken to a mill to be ground into flour and returned; however, if the person to whom the goods

are given is only to return *similar* goods, the transaction may be a sale, e.g., a five-year lease of a farm and a herd of cows, with the provision that the lessee should return "cows of equal age and quality" at the expiration of the lease.

(2) A sale requires consideration; a bailment may be either for consideration or gratuitous;

(3) A sale contemplates a permanent change of possession; a bailment only a temporary change.

B. PLEDGE OR PAWN

A pledge or a pawn is a security device by which an owner of personal property gives possession of his property to secure a debt or to assure the performance of some obligation; e. g., debtor gives possession of a ring to a pawn shop owner to secure a loan. The debtor is the pledgor, and the pawnshop owner is the pledgee. A *pledge* arises when stocks, bonds, or negotiable paper is put up as security for a debtor, whereas a *pawn* exists when any other type of personal property is used as security for a loan. A pledge is similar to a bailment in that neither the pledgee nor the bailee has title to the property but merely a special interest; however, there are two differences:

(1) In a pledge, the pledgee can assign his interest in the property to another person even without permission of the pledgor; in a bailment, the bailee cannot assign the property to anyone else;

(2) In a pledge, the pledgee always has the right to sell the property if the debtor does not pay the debt; in a bailment, the bailee cannot sell the property to satisfy money due unless expressly permitted by statute. See Division 9 of the Uniform Commercial Code, Appendix A, for the pledgee's rights in the event of default by the pledgor.

C. LEASE OR LICENSE

In a lease or license, the "acceptor" of the owner's goods has neither the right to possession nor the exclusive control of the goods. The lessor or licensor is merely making space available for the lessee or licensee.

5. BAILEE'S DUTY OF CARE

The amount of care owed towards the property by the bailee depends on the type of bailment, local statutes, and the contract of bailment.

A. TYPE OF BAILMENT

(1) Gratuitous

In this type, the sole benefit of the bailment is for the bailor; e. g., bailor leaves his dog with a neighbor while bailor goes away on a vacation. In this case, the bailee only owes a duty of *slight* care towards the property.

(2) Benefit to Both Parties

In this type, both the bailor and the bailee benefit from the bailment; e.g., bailor leaves his dog with bailee with the understanding that the bailee can use the dog to go hunting while the bailor is on vacation. In this case, the bailee owes a duty of *ordinary* care. Ordinary care means reasonable care under the circumstances.

(3) Sole Benefit to Bailee

In this type, the sole benefit of the bailment is for the bailee; e. g., bailee borrows the bailor's dog to go hunting, but bailor is not going on a vacation and is receiving nothing for the use of his dog. In this type of bailment, the bailee owes a duty of *great* care.

B. LOCAL STATUTES

Many local statutes contain exemptions from, or limitations on, liability in the case of certain bailees and in certain situations; e.g., California Civil Code, Section 1840, which provides that where the bailee is informed of the value by the bailor, or has reason to assume its actual value, the liability cannot exceed such amount.

C. CONTRACT OF BAILMENT

The act of bailment may be accompanied by an agreement which enlarges the liability of the bailee; e.g., "You are responsible for any damages to any of our cylinders while they are in your possession or care"; lease of furnished house provided that lessee would redeliver furniture in good condition, and that lessee "assumes all liability", held lessee was an insurer and liable for a stolen rug.

Except where permitted by statute, contracts which attempt to *exclude or limit liability* are illegal if the bailee is *quasi-public* in character; e.g., common carrier, public parking lot, public warehouse, hotel. Even where local statutes permit limitation of liability, the amount must be reasonable or the limitation is ineffective. *Private* bailees can limit their liability if the clause does not defeat the real purpose of the contract; however, any such limitation must be brought to the attention of the bailor before the property is bailed by him. A limitation by a private bailee contained in a stub or ticket given to the bailor, or posted on a sign or on the walls of the bailee's place of business ordinarily will not bind the bailor unless the bailee calls the bailor's attention to the writing and informs him that it contains a limitation of liability. Also, see Part 2, Chapter 12, I, "Stipulation Against Liability For Negligence".

6. BAILEE'S LIEN

By statute in most states, the bailee is given the right to a lien on the goods for payment for work or services rendered in connection with the bailed goods. The lien carries with it the right to sell the goods at public sale if the bailor does not pay for the work or services.

In the absence of a statute to the contrary, the lien is lost if the bailee voluntarily returns the goods to the bailor.

No lien arises on the goods when the work is done on credit.

7. BAILEE'S DUTY TO RETURN PROPERTY

The bailee has a duty to return the bailed property to the bailor upon termination of the bailment. There are some exceptions:

a. where the goods are taken by legal process while in the bailee's possession, e.g., attached by the sheriff for a debt due by bailor;

b. where the person to whom the bailee delivers the property is better entitled to its possession than the bailor. In this situation, if the bailee is in doubt as to which of two claimants is entitled to the goods, he is protected in most states by being permitted to interplead the parties (surrendering the goods to a court and requiring the claimants to establish their rights in court) or by requiring the claimant who was not the bailor to indemnify the bailee against any liability to his bailor;

c. where the goods are lost, stolen, or destroyed due to no fault of the bailee; and,

d. if the bailee has a lien on the goods, he is entitled to keep possession of them until he has been paid the amount of the lien.

B. TERMINATION

A bailment may be terminated by performance, acts of the parties, destruction of the bailed property, or by operation of law.

1. BY PERFORMANCE

Complete performance by both parties of the bailment contract terminates the bailment. This may occur by completion of the particular purpose of the bailment, or where the bailment was created for a particular time, by the expiration of the period of time.

2. BY ACTS OF THE PARTIES

The bailment may be terminated by a subsequent agreement of the parties, or when it was created for an indefinite time by the will of either party, or when it was created for the sole benefit of one party by the will of the party receiving the benefit.

If either party causes a material breach of the bailment, the other party may terminate; e.g., bailee sells the bailed property to a third person. If the bailor elects not to terminate the bailment, the bailee remains liable for any damages caused by his breach.

3. DESTRUCTION OF BAILED PROPERTY

If the bailed property is destroyed by a third person or by an act of God, or if it becomes unfit for use for the purpose of the bailment, the bailment is terminated.

4. OPERATION OF LAW

Death terminates a bailment at will. Insanity and bankruptcy terminate a bailment at will if it becomes impossible for the bailee to perform his duties. However, if the bailment is for a definite period, death or incapacity will not terminate the bailment, but instead the rights of the deceased party pass to his estate.

---

1. *Bailment Obligation*

PHILLIPS v. CITY OF NEW YORK

71 Misc.2d 861, 337 N.Y.S.2d 303 (1972).

HARRY T. NUSBAUM, Judge. The plaintiff in this action seeks to recover the value of personal property allegedly unlawfully removed or stolen from an apartment in which it was placed by the plaintiff-tenant under the direction of the City Urban Renewal Management Company.

The question presented is whether from the facts proved a bailment resulted which placed upon the City or its employees the duty to exercise reasonable care for the safety of the tenant's property and whether the City breached that duty.

The testimony adduced at the trial established the following facts: The City of New York in its zeal to demolish the premises in which the plaintiff-tenant resided at 360 Greenwich Street, New York City, notified the tenant he must forthwith move his furniture and belongings to apartment 3A at 55 Suffolk Street under the threat that if he did not move his property, it would be seized by the Sheriff. The testimony further reveals that the tenant protested this precipitous move both because he was about to go on vacation and because the apartment at 55 Suffolk Street was not ready for occupancy. Nevertheless, he acquiesced to the City's demand some days later and proceeded to move to the emergency housing provided for him at 55 Suffolk Street under the City's relocation procedures. There he found there was no key available for the apartment and no one present to give him access. As the moving van and moving men were waiting in the street, the plaintiff with the consent of a person holding himself out to be the superintendent engaged the services of a locksmith who removed and replaced the old lock. Following the defendant's instructions he placed his belongings in one room to facilitate the painting and other repairs required to make the apartment habitable and locked the door, retaining one of the new keys for himself and turning over the other key to the person representing himself to be a Mr. Joseph Fuller, the superintendent.

When he returned from his vacation, he found the door swinging open and most of his belongings gone. The City through its witnesses denies that it received the key and states that it was unable to do the painting and other necessary repairs because it could not gain access to the apartment, although admitting that it twice found the door open which necessitated it being nailed shut. The person who held himself out to be the superintendent, Mr. Fuller, turned out to be his assistant, a Mr. MacLain.

* * *

The City Urban Renewal Management Company, as the agent of the City of New York, by forcing the plaintiff to relocate and remove his belongings to the apartment at 55 Suffolk Street which was not ready for occupancy, became the bailee of the plaintiff's personal property during the period required to make the apartment habitable. As such bailee, it was under a duty to exercise at least ordinary or reasonable care in safeguarding that property.

* * *

To determine whether a bailment has been established, the test to be applied is whether or not the person leaving the property has made such a delivery as to amount to a relinquishment of his exclusive possession, control and dominion thereof, and vested such control and dominion in the person upon whose premises the property has been left. * * *

I find from the evidence that the transaction as related by the plaintiff resulted in a relinquishment of possession and control and that a bailment resulted. Whether the bailment which resulted was a mutual benefit bailment or a gratuitous bailment or a bailment for the exclusive benefit of the City is of no importance in this case. The evidence adduced during the trial clearly indicates that the City did not use reasonable safeguards to protect the plaintiff's property and in fact could be found to have been grossly negligent in its care of the plaintiff's belongings.

Judgment is therefore awarded to the plaintiff for the sum of $2,400, plus interest.

---

2. *Bailment Distinguished from Lease*

SIMONS v. FIRST NATIONAL BANK OF DENVER

30 Colo.App. 260, 491 P.2d 602 (1971).

DUFFORD, Judge. We shall refer to the parties by their trial court positions or by name.

Plaintiff is the owner of an aircraft which he parked and tied to a ramp owned by defendant First National Bank of Denver at Jefferson County Airport and operated by the other defendant, Donald D. Estey, under an arrangement whereby plaintiff paid $15 per month. The aircraft was overturned and demolished by high winds. Plaintiff brought this action to recover the amount of $4,700 for the damage done to his aircraft and which he alleged resulted from negligence on the part of the defendants as bailees. Plaintiff alleged that defendants were bailees of his airplane and as such were responsible for its safety and had the duty of returning it to him undamaged. Defendants' answer denied that bailment was created and asserted affirmatively that the relationship which arose from the tie-down arrangement under which the plaintiff's airplane was parked on their facilities was merely a lease or a license.

The evidence at trial was uncontroverted in showing that plaintiff at all times had full control over his aircraft, tied the airplane to the ramp himself, and discouraged all parties from disturbing the aircraft. No evidence was introduced which suggested that defendants had agreed to a bailment either orally or in writing, or that they had exercised control over the aircraft at any time. Nonetheless, the trial court ruled that a bailment had been created, as a matter of law, and submitted the case to the jury solely on the issue of defendants' liability as bailees. The jury returned a verdict for plaintiff in the amount of $2,000. Defendants bring this appeal from the judgment entered on such verdict and from the trial court's ruling that a bailment existed as a matter of law.

It is the position of the defendants in this appeal that they were entitled to a judgment in their favor, and that it was error on the part of the trial court to determine that they were bailees as a matter of law, thereby allowing the jury to determine a damage award on such basis. The defendants further assert that the trial court should have held, as a matter of law, that a lease or license relationship existed between the defendants and the plaintiff, under which the defendants owed only limited duties, and as to which there was no proof given of any breach on their part. Accordingly, they claim the trial court should have directed a verdict against the plaintiff and dismissed his complaint. We find the defendants are correct in these assertions.

Bailment is the delivery of personal property by one person to another in trust for a specific purpose with a contract, express or implied, that the trust shall be faithfully executed and the property returned or duly accounted for when the special purpose is accomplished or kept until the bailor reclaims the property. * * * However, a bailment does not arise in those situations where the owner of the property retains control over his property. Consistent with these general principles of bailment law, it has been ruled that, where an aircraft is placed in an airport parking or tie-down space and the owner of the airport facility is not given and does not assert any control over the aircraft, only a lease relating to the space or facilities occupied by the aircraft is created as opposed to a bailment of the aircraft into the hands of the owner of that space. * * *

In the case before us, there is a void of any evidence which would establish that control over the plaintiff's airplane was voluntarily passed to the defendants or that they attempted to exercise any such control. As we have stated above, the evidence in this case runs the other way in that the plaintiff himself parked and tied his airplane. He locked the aircraft and retained the keys to it, and he took further steps to discourage other parties from disturbing the aircraft. Such being the case, the trial court erred in ruling, as a matter of law that a bailment existed. Additionally, there is nothing within the record of this case from which a jury might properly find that a bailment existed.

Judgment is reversed, and this cause is remanded with directions that the trial court dismiss this action.

---

3. Degrees of Liability under Bailments

PETTINELLI MOTORS, INC. v. MORREALE

39 Misc.2d 813, 242 N.Y.S.2d 76 (1963).

JOHN J. WALSH, Judge. On May 23rd, 1962, the plaintiff loaned a 1960 Cadillac hardtop automobile valued at $3,100 to defendant for the purpose of a road-test, the defendant being interested in the purchase of such an automobile. Thereafter, the plaintiff received the automobile back in such a damaged condition that it was salvaged for $400. * * *

This is obviously an action in bailment. There are three classes of bailments recognized by the law. These are: (1) a bailment for the benefit of the bailor; (2) a bailment for the mutual benefit of both parties; and (3) a bailment for the benefit of the bailee only. * * * As a general proposition, a bailee of goods is not an insurer of their safety. Negligence must be established if liability is to result. * * *

The degree of negligence required to render a bailee liable to respond in damages varies with the type of bailment. Where the bailment is gratuitous, in other words where the bailment is for the benefit of the bailor only, the bailee need exercise only slight care and is liable only for gross negligence. * * * Where the bailment is for the mutual benefit of both parties, the bailee is required to exercise ordinary care and is liable for ordinary negligence. This means that he must exercise the care and diligence which prudent men exercise in the conduct of their own affairs. * * * Where the bailment is for the sole benefit of the bailee, he is required to use great care and is liable for slight negligence. This means that he must exercise all the care and diligence that the most careful persons are accustomed to use in the conduct of their own affairs. * * *

Thus the plaintiff, the bailor seeking damages for the defendant-bailee's failure to return the automobile in its original condition had the burden of proving the bailee's negligence. * * *

The defendant testified that the automobile was delivered to him at his place of business in Rome by the plaintiff; that a Harry Faust was his supervisor at the store; that when it came time to go home, he had both the bailed car and his own; that Faust expressed an interest in the car; that defendant said that if Faust liked the car he could try it and that defendant gave him the keys and Faust and a companion Kelly took the car. * * *

It appears that later in the evening both Faust and Kelly were killed in a one-car accident which demolished the automobile. There is no evidence as to the cause of the accident.

* * * It is established that a mere bailee of a motor vehicle may give consent to others to use the same unless the terms of bailment provide otherwise. * * *

Judgment may be entered by the defendant dismissing the complaint.

* * * While this may appear an inequitable result, the law seems clear. This Court cannot hold that this bailment was for the sole benefit of the bailee which required him to use great care and rendered him liable for the slightest negligence. The bailment in this case was either a gratuitous one for the benefit of the bailor, or one for their mutual benefit and neither gross negligence nor ordinary negligence was in either event shown.

---

4. *Implied Warranty in Bailments*

MEESTER v. ROOSE

259 Iowa 357, 144 N.W.2d 274 (1966).

RAWLINGS, Justice. Plaintiff commenced an action for recovery of damages resulting from being attacked by a bull belonging to defendant.

The trial court sustained defendant's motion to dismiss and plaintiff appeals.

By his petition plaintiff alleged defendant's bull was placed on plaintiff's farm in the fall of 1960 to run with his cattle for the purpose of proving, testing or trying the animal; that the bull was mean and vicious, and in September 1962, attacked plaintiff causing him bodily injuries. He asserted breach of implied warranty that the bull was suitable for said purposes and was not of a mean or vicious disposition and dangerous.

* * * The mere fact plaintiff was injured by an animal belonging to defendant does not of itself create a good and sufficient cause of action. * * * We are persuaded the case now before us involves a bailment for mutual benefit which, in effect, makes it one for hire. * * * Under such circumstances there is ordinarily imposed on the bailor an obligation, similar to the implied warranty of fitness in the sale of personalty, that the thing is reasonably suitable for the use known to be intended.

> * * * *The warranty implied arises by operation of law and must be applied in a reasonable sense.* * * *

[P]laintiff here claims a breach of implied warranty the bull was kind, gentle, docile, tame and friendly.

We are satisfied this stretches the theory of implied warranty a bit too far.

In the first place plaintiff neither alleges nor infers by his petition the bull was vicious, mean and unmanageable at time of bailment.

Next, and even more important, the law will not lend itself to the creation of an implied warranty which patently runs counter to the experience of mankind or known forces of nature. It will not read into any sale or bailment a condition or proviso which is unreasonable, impossible or absurd.

* * * Useful and even necessary as he may be, there are few if any members of the domesticated animal kingdom more unpredictably vicious, mean and treacherous than a bull. * * *

Being neither commendable as a pet nor especially pleasing to the eye, a bull is in fact commonly recognized as fit and suitable for one purpose only—perpetuation of the species.

* * * It is to us self-evident the claim made by plaintiff could not have been and was not within the contemplation of the parties at time of the bailment.

Affirmed.

---

5. *Bailment Liens*

WM. H. WISE & CO. v. RAND McNALLY & CO.

195 F.Supp. 621 (D.C.N.Y., 1961).

DAWSON, District Judge. This action was tried by the Court without a jury. It is an action to recover damages resulting from defendant's alleged conversion of plaintiff's property. * * *

Plaintiff, Wm. H. Wise & Co., Inc. (hereinafter referred to as "Wise"), is a publishing concern. The defendant, Rand McNally & Co. (hereinafter referred to as "Rand"), is a printing establishment.

Under an agreement dated on or about July 19, 1955, Wise engaged Rand to print 25,000 copies of plaintiff's book entitled "Complete Book of Home Decorating." Under the agreement Wise was to furnish the paper stock and to pay the defendant $8,050 for making positives, color separations, engravings and press plates for printing. In addition Wise was to pay 16 cents per copy for press work and 41.1 cents for binding. Wise furnished the manuscript and art work, drawings, photographs, linotype composition, cover dies and jackets. Rand printed the work in accordance with the agreement.

* * * Rand filed a proof of claim on May 23, 1956, in which it alleged that Wise still owed it $20,335.18 for printing copies of the work and that it, Rand, held approximately 13,915 copies of the work as security for the indebtedness.

By January 14, 1958, the secured indebtedness had been reduced to $1,430.59 and Rand still had in its possession over 7,000 copies of the work. * * * In March, 1958, plaintiff sought a release of additional books. Rand then notified Wise for the first time that it had sold 7,288 books at a private sale on January 14, 1958. The books were sold to Lord & Bond Corporation for a total price of $2,550.80. At the time that they were so sold the balance of the original secured claim was only $1,430.59. * * * The sale of the books was made by Rand at a private sale without notice to Wise that the books were to be sold, and without giving Wise an opportunity to redeem them at or prior to the sale. * * *

Rand contends that the basic contract was one of sale and that it had an unpaid seller's lien which it could satisfy by selling the goods without previous notice to Wise.

* * * Rand was not selling books as books but rather was engaged to print and bind, pursuant to a contract. The contract was one of work, labor and materials and not one of sale. * * * As a result of Rand's work, pursuant to the contract for work, labor and materials, Rand became a lienor. While it is contended by Wise that Rand was a pledgee, that argument is without foundation. A pledge, in the usual or conventional sense, arises when one known as a pledgor delivers property into the possession of a pledgee, that property to be held as security for the repayment of a debt or the fulfillment of some other obligation. * * *

Rand did not obtain possession of the books for purposes of security.

Rand had a possessory lien. * * *

Rand's possessory lien might be considered one of bailment which arises when a person ordering the manufacture or production of items provides some or all of the materials pursuant to a contract for work, labor and materials. * * * Alternatively, Rand's lien might be considered an artisan's lien. Wise supplied the paper and other materials; Rand was to improve the paper by printing the book and binding it. * * *

> "A person who makes, alters, repairs or in any way enhances the value of an article of personal property, at the request or with the consent of the owner has a lien on such article, while lawfully in possession thereof, for his reasonable charges for the work done and materials furnished, and may retain possession thereof until such charges are paid."

* * * Wise supplied the bulk of the materials to Rand. It retained property in those materials, for, even if the parties had treated their transaction as one of sale and resale, still New York would consider it a bailment for the purpose of production or improvement, with title remaining in the supplier.

* * * The Court has concluded that the sale by Rand of the remaining books, which it was holding as security, to Lord & Bond, without notice to Wise, without giving Wise an opportunity to bid thereon, constituted a conversion. Accordingly, Wise may recover the fair market value of 7,288 books at the time of conversion.

---

6. *Termination of Bailment by Death*

CUTCLIFFE v. CHESNUT

126 Ga.App. 378, 190 S.E.2d 800 (1972).

CLARK, Judge. This case originated by a complaint alleging defendant Cutcliffe had received $25,000 from plaintiff's testator, John Harvey Chesnut, for the purpose of effecting a stock purchase for the latter but that the stock was never delivered to him during his lifetime nor was the money returned to Chesnut or to his executor or to anyone on his behalf.

* * *

This court then ruled a breach of contract of agency is a breach of contract for which the principal is entitled to resort to remedies provided by the law of contracts, but it was further held, in view of evidentiary deficiencies, that the trial court erred in summarily granting the plaintiff a judgment for restitution.

On return of the case to the court below a trial was had before a judge sitting without the intervention of a jury. After hearing evidence judgment was entered for plaintiff for $10,362.45. Defendant appeals, enumerating as error the denials of his motion to dismiss made at the close of the plaintiff's evidence and his motion for new trial made on the general grounds only. There is no cross appeal by the plaintiff.

Chesnut, father of the plaintiff executor, and Cutcliffe were close friends. Cutcliffe was an advisor to Chesnut and Chesnut's family. Cutcliffe had had a social and business relationship (as a Certified

Public Accountant) with the decedent since 1955; Cutcliffe testified he considered himself a "confidant" of decedent and his family. They both owned stock in a corporation known as Monterey Management Company in which Cutcliffe was a corporate officer. They decided to purchase an additional 1,500 shares to be divided between themselves from William H. Murray. It was believed the purchase could be made for $60 per share totaling $90,000. Cutcliffe was to effect the purchase. He put up $65,000 of which $40,000 was obtained through a bank loan endorsed by Chesnut. The decedent delivered his check for $25,000 to Cutcliffe who gave decedent his receipt. This receipt is contained in full in the previous opinion including the recital "that the check is one of agency for acquisition of shares of stock in Monterey Management Company . . ." Cutcliffe deposited the $25,000 check to his account and effected the purchase from Murray on February 10, 1966, the same day the check and receipt were given. Cutcliffe informed decedent that the acquisition had been made and "endorsed the certificates onto the books of the corporation." The reason Cutcliffe did not immediately issue decedent his portion amounting to 416.66 shares of the stock was because decedent specifically instructed him not to, saying that he wanted to wait until he had resolved certain family problems. Seven months later Chesnut died suddenly, without ever having given Cutcliffe directions as to how the stock should be issued.

Shortly after decedent's death Cutcliffe advised J. David Chesnut (decedent's son, executor, and plaintiff herein) that he had received $25,000 from his father for the purchase of the specified stock. Plaintiff replied he already knew of the transaction and had found Cutcliffe's receipt in a safety deposit box. Plaintiff's relationship with Cutcliffe was such that he looked upon him as a "second father." The two discussed the situation generally then and on subsequent occasions. Plaintiff testified he mentioned on one or more of these occasions a need for "the money" by his father's estate to meet anticipated taxes. But because of more important and more pressing business for each of them nothing transpired on the subject at the time nor during the following several months.

* * *

On March 28, 1969, plaintiff as executor of his father's estate through his attorneys made oral demand (confirmed in writing on that same date) for $25,000 which Cutcliffe refused. On April 23, 1969, Cutcliffe tendered a stock certificate representing 417 shares of Monterey stock to decedent's estate which plaintiff refused.

The trial judge elicited evidence of the stock's book value for the year endings of 1965, 1966, 1967, 1968 and 1969. These varied, showing an increase for the first two years and then a decline in

1968 and 1969 with Monterey Management Co. declared bankrupt on October 16, 1970. *Held:*

* * *

The evidence does show that the contract by the principal and agent for the purchase of shares of stock for decedent was completely and successfully executed before decedent's death. Thereupon Cutcliffe became the authorized custodian of decedent's stock during decedent's lifetime, he having been directed by the latter to hold the same until further instructions.

Thus the principles of bailment law are applicable and controlling under the circumstances of this case, including the duty on a bailee to return the thing bailed when the purpose of the bailment has ended. * * *

The trial judge was authorized by the evidence to find the existence of a bailment for the benefit of the bailor for an indefinite period (i. e. custody or possession of Chesnut's stock by Cutcliffe pending disposition instructions from Chesnut) which ended when Chesnut died without ever having given direction. The duty of delivering the stock to the decedent-bailor's representative arose as and when the representative qualified and was in a position to receive it. * * * A concomitant liability arose from a failure to do that which the law requires, such liability being measured as the depreciation in value of the stock from the time of the executor's qualification to the time of the tender.

Judgment affirmed [for plaintiff].

PROBLEMS

1. Plaintiff, brewery, sold cartons of beer to consumers with the understanding that there would be a refund of all deposits on returned cartons. The consumer was not required to return the cartons. The state claims that the cartons were sold to the consumers, and thus the seller owed a sales tax. The seller contends that the cartons were not sold but bailed to the consumers, and thus no sales tax was due. Decision?

2. Plaintiff left her diamond ring with the defendant, jeweler, for cleaning. Prior to closing his store, the defendant placed the ring in the safe and locked it. During the night, a burglar opened the safe and stole the contents including the plaintiff's ring. Plaintiff brings action for the value of the ring. Decision?

3. Plaintiff left her car at the defendant's garage for repairs. The shop was located in the industrial section of the city near the railroad yards. The two rear doors were locked by padlocks on hasps which were nailed to the wood. There had been prior thefts by vandals so defendant hired a night watchman; however, he often failed to report for duty. On one of the nights he failed to report for duty a thief broke the locks

and stole plaintiff's car. Plaintiff sues defendant for the resulting damages to the car. Decision?

4. Plaintiff parked his car in a parking lot operated by defendant. A sign at the entrance to the lot stated that the owner was not liable for theft or any damages to the cars from any cause and that all parking was entirely at the risk of the owner. Plaintiff did not read the sign because of the heavy traffic in getting into the lot. Defendant also handed plaintiff a parking ticket which had the same type of liability exemption on the back in small print. Plaintiff did not read the statement on the back as he believed the ticket was merely a token of identification. Plaintiff's car was stolen from the parking lot while the attendant was away from the lot aiding victims of an automobile accident that occurred nearby. Plaintiff brings action for the value of his car. Defendant contends that he is not liable due to the sign and ticket which exempted him from liability. Decision?

5. Plaintiff left his car at defendant's garage for repairs. After the repairs were completed, the defendant notified plaintiff to pick up his car. Plaintiff went to the garage and asked the defendant for ten days credit to pay the bill. Defendant refused. Plaintiff demanded his car. Defendant stated that he would not give plaintiff his car and would sell it if plaintiff did not pay the bill within a reasonable time. Plaintiff brings an action to get possession of his car and to enjoin the sale of the car. Decision?

6. Ace Rudder, while flying his private plane, had an engine failure and made an emergency landing in Rube Hayes' oat field. Ace returned to the wrecked plane to disassemble it for salvage but Rube refused to allow him to remove the plane until he paid for the damages done to Rube's field. Several days later an insurance agent, representing Ace, came by and paid the damage, whereupon Rube allowed them to remove the plane. During the interval, no watchman had been placed at the site and many people had visited the oat field to view the spot and about $2000 worth of equipment had been stolen from the plane. Ace sued Rube for the damage caused by the thefts, claiming a bailment and negligence. Decision?

7. Joe Jones, an operator of a garage for repairs and storage, contracted with Ray Rich to keep Ray's automobile under an arrangement whereby the automobile could be placed in the garage and removed at any time during the day or night. Ray drove his automobile to the garage one night about 8:30 and parked it inside. No attendant was on duty, the garage was dark, and the door was unlocked. The next morning Ray returned for his automobile and it was not in the garage, and had apparently been stolen during the night. Ray thereupon brought an action against Joe for the value of the automobile. Joe contended that, because he had no knowledge that the car was placed in the garage, he would not have become a bailee, and that he is not therefore liable. Decision?

8. Brown delivered a large quantity of wheat to the mill owned and operated by Smith. It was understood by and between the parties that the wheat would be ground into flour and that Smith would return a certain amount of flour for each bushel of wheat. The flour would not, however, necessarily be processed from the wheat of Brown since it was the custom to commingle the wheat prior to grinding it into flour. It was further agreed that Brown would call for his flour the following day. During the

night, without the fault of anyone concerned, the mill and all the wheat and flour were destroyed by fire. Brown sues Smith for the loss. Decision?

9. Marsh left a package, containing costume jewelry worth over $2,000, in a railroad station locker while he had lunch. On his return the package was gone. He sued the locker company, contending that it was under a duty to keep the package safely and had negligently failed to do so. The locker was of the common type which permits the individual user to deposit a coin and withdraw the key. The company retained a right of access to remove parcels left for more than 24 hours. Marsh sues to recover the value of the jewelry. Decision?

10. Wallace left his father's car overnight in Nickerson's garage, leaving the keys and receiving a claim check stub from the attendant. Weibers, who was familiar with the operations of the garage, falsified a claim check and put it on the windshield of the Wallace car, retaining the stub for himself. After the night man had come on duty, Weibers returned to the garage, exhibited the stub, and took the car. Wallace sued Nickerson to recoup his loss. Nickerson contended that he had not been negligent and was therefore not liable. Decision?

Chapter 24

SPECIAL BAILMENTS

A. HOTEL KEEPERS

Liability of hotel keepers is largely controlled by statute. The typical statute provides that if the proprietor provides a fireproof safe, or some similar place, for the keeping of valuable property, and if he notifies the guests of such depositary, he is not liable for the loss of any property which the guest may fail to deliver to him. If the guest delivers valuables to the proprietor, he must inform the proprietor that the articles are of unusual value, or there will not be any extraordinary liability.

When wearing apparel is left in the guest's room and it is stolen, some statutes provide that the proprietor is liable only if he was negligent. Even when the proprietor is liable, most statutes permit him to limit his liability to a certain amount which is usually rather small; e.g., $100.00 for each trunk, $50.00 for each traveling bag and contents, $10.00 for each box, bundle or package and contents, and $250.00 for all other personal property of any kind.

The hotel keeper is liable for an employee's theft of a guest's property if the theft was within the scope of the employee's employment; e.g., liable where clerk in charge of safe stole valuables deposited by guest. However, even where the theft is within the scope of the employment, the hotel keeper's liability is limited to the sums specified in the statute.

The hotel keeper has a lien on the baggage of guests for the agreed charges; and if no express agreement was made, the reasonable value of the accommodations that were furnished.

B. COMMON CARRIERS

A common carrier is one who holds himself out to the public as carrying goods and/or passengers for compensation from place to place. Common carriers are regulated by state governmental authority, e. g., Public Utilities Commission; and if engaged in interstate transportation, by the Interstate Commerce Commission.

1. LIABILITY OF COMMON CARRIERS

A common carrier is absolutely liable for any loss or damage to goods in its possession unless it can prove that the loss or damage was solely due to one of the following five exceptions:

A. Act of God

Unforeseen, unusual, violent, superhuman events or catastrophes, such as an unprecedented wind or storm, earthquake, extreme temperature, severe flood, or stroke of lightning (a fire due to human origin has been held not to be an Act of God).

B. Act of Public Enemy

Nations, persons, or groups engaged in violent activities directed at an attempt to overthrow the government are the public enemy. Thieves, rioters, arsonists, and other criminals are not included in this definition unless they are attempting to overthrow the government.

C. Acts of State or Public Authority

Seizure of narcotics by the government; attachment of goods by the sheriff.

D. Acts of Shippers

Improper packing; however, if this is apparent upon visual inspection and the carrier still accepts the goods, it has full liability for them.

E. Inherent Nature of the Goods

Carrier not liable for perishable fruits and vegetables when shipper fails to obtain refrigerated or heated cars; not liable for normal percentage of evaporation of oil or other liquids in transit.

If the carrier unnecessarily exposed the goods to damage by incorrect routing, it will be liable even though the damage was caused by one of the five exceptions stated above.

2. TERMINATION OF STRICT LIABILITY

There are three different rules followed as to when the strict liability terminates. Some states hold that it ends when the goods are unloaded from the car into the freight house at which time the duties of the warehouseman begin. Some states hold that it ends after the consignee (person to whom the shipment has been made) has had a reasonable time to inspect and remove the goods. Some states hold that the consignee has the right to notice of the arrival of the shipment and that the strict liability of the carrier does not end until after notice and after the consignee has a reasonable time in which to remove the goods.

When the goods remain in possession of the carrier after strict liability terminates, the carrier's liability is reduced to that of a warehouseman (ordinary care) until the goods are claimed.

3. LIMITATION OF LIABILITY

A carrier can limit its liability as follows:

A. Under Federal Law

Carriers in interstate commerce are subject to the Federal law. Under the Carmack Amendment to the Interstate Commerce Act, the carrier may limit its liability to a stated amount by a provision in the bill of lading provided that the shipper is allowed to obtain a higher amount at an increased rate.

B. Under State Laws

Most states provide by statute that a common carrier may, in intrastate commerce, limit its liability for injury to or loss of baggage or packages due to ordinary negligence, but not for such loss or injury caused by gross negligence. The Uniform Commercial Code, Section 7–309(2), provides that damages may be limited "if the carrier's rates are dependent upon value and the consignor by the carrier's tariff is afforded an opportunity to declare a higher value".

4. COMMON CARRIERS OF PASSENGERS

Common carriers of passengers are not insurers of the safety of the passengers; however, because of the public nature of the business, they are held to the highest degree of care, skill, and diligence. Common carriers of passengers are subject to extensive state and federal regulation.

C. WAREHOUSEMEN

A person engaged in the business of storing goods of others for compensation is a warehouseman. In the absence of special statute, the warehouseman owes a duty of *ordinary* care towards goods in his possession. Due to the public nature of the activities of warehousemen, they are subject to extensive state and federal regulation.

U.C.C. Section 7–203 places a duty on the warehouseman to deliver goods which conform to the description in the warehouse receipt or to answer in damages. The warehouseman may avoid this liability, however, by an honest disclaimer on the receipt to the effect that he does not know whether the goods conform to the description. This can be done by writing *conspicuously* such words as "said to contain", or "contents unknown."

D. LESSEE OF PERSONAL PROPERTY

In this type of bailment, e.g., automobile rental, the lessee is the bailee, and the lessor is the bailor. The bailor must deliver the personal property in a condition fit for the purpose of letting, must repair all deteriorations not due to the fault of the bailee or the natural result of use, and must secure quiet title in the bailee from any lawful claimant.

If the bailee is injured or his property is damaged due to a defective condition of the bailed property, the bailor may be liable as follows:

1. The bailor of dangerous personal property is liable to the bailee for injuries resulting from negligence (bailee may be barred by contributory negligence or assumption of the risk);

2. The bailor of personal property warrants that the property is fit for its particular use; and if it is not, the warranty is breached for failure to exercise reasonable care to ascertain that it was safe; e.g., in hiring a horse for riding purposes, there is an implied warranty that the stable-keeper used reasonable care to ascertain the habits of the horse; and if he should have discovered its dangerous propensities and he did not, he is liable (Kersten v. Young, 52 Cal.App.2d 1, 125 P.2d 501). Modern cases have extended the bailor's liability of fitness for a particular use at the time of the bailment to a fitness during the entire period of the bailment and to third persons (see Part 3, Chapter 21, 5 h., and the case in that chapter, Cintrone v. Hertz Truck Leasing and Rental Service).

Where property is leased for a particular use and the bailee uses it for another purpose, the bailor may recover damages or terminate the hiring. Also, most courts hold the bailee absolutely liable for injury or loss occurring during such unauthorized use even though he was not negligent.

E. PARKING LOTS

The courts have generally held that when the owner locks his automobile and takes the keys with him, there is no bailment since the parking lot attendant is not given sufficient physical control over the car to constitute him a bailee; however, when the owner leaves the key in the automobile at the request of the parking lot attendant, a bailment is created and the bailee owes a duty of ordinary care towards the car.

F. RESTAURANTS

The courts generally hold that when a patron hangs his coat on a hook in a restaurant, barber shop, or other similar place, no bailment is created. The reasoning is that there was no actual delivery of the coat to the proprietor. However, if the establishment provides an attendant to receive the coat, then a bailment is created. A question arises as to whether the proprietor is liable for something contained in the pocket of the coat that is lost or stolen. Courts generally hold that there is no liability for the reason that the proprietor did not intend to assume possession of the bailor's property in his pocket, unless the proprietor was advised of the contents or reasonably should have known of their existence when he accepted custody of the article.

G. SAFE DEPOSIT BOX

When a person rents a safe deposit box, he will have one key for access to the box, and the bank will retain the other. Both keys are necessary to gain admittance to the box. The bank has control of the premises. Nearly all courts hold that the customer is the bailor, and the bank is the bailee. Since this is a mutual benefit type of bailment, the bank must use ordinary care regarding the contents of the box.

H. CONTENTS OF CONTAINER

Whether the contents of a safe deposit box are bailed, whether the bailment of a coat is a bailment of the contents of the pockets, whether a bailment of an automobile is a bailment of the personal property on the seats, is a question whether the contained articles are of a nature that are reasonably or normally found within the container; if they are, it is a bailment; if they are not, it is not a bailment. Thus, a bailee of a container is not liable for the contents of a container which are not visible when the container is bailed to him unless from the nature of the container itself or from the surrounding circumstances he ought to have anticipated the presence of such contents as a reasonable man, or he had express notice of the contents.

In the case of a safe deposit box, the bank is liable as a bailee for the contents of the box because it has a high degree of control in preventing unauthorized access and because it is reasonable to anticipate that a safe deposit box might contain valuable personal property.

I. CONSTRUCTIVE BAILMENTS

The law recognizes certain types of bailments wherein the bailee's obligation is imposed by law rather than by agreement of the parties and the courts usually hold that he is a gratuitous bailee; e. g., finder of lost or misplaced property; police officer taking possession of stolen goods; animal from one farm strays upon land of adjoining farm owner; property placed on property of another by mistake; a seller of goods who has not yet delivered the goods to the buyer is a bailee of the goods if the title has passed to the buyer; and similarly, the buyer who is in possession of goods but does not have title is a bailee of the goods.

In the finder, or voluntary type of bailment, the finder must take possession of and care for the lost property; however, he will be entitled to recover for the value of his time and expense in caring for the property.

In the unwilling type of bailment, where property is thrust upon a stranger through some agency beyond the control of either party, such as a tornado or other act of God, most courts hold that the bailee only has a moral duty to care for the property; but if he undertakes to do so, he becomes a bailee and is liable for negligence in caring for the personal property. Some states, by statute, impose a duty of care on the unwilling bailee regardless of his undertaking to care for the property.

These are all constructive bailments made by law.

1. *Parking Lot Bailment*

TAYLOR v. PHILADELPHIA PARKING AUTHORITY

398 Pa. 9, 156 A.2d 525 (1959).

MCBRIDE, Justice. Plaintiffs brought suit in assumpsit against the defendant, Philadelphia Parking Authority, alleging *inter alia* that they were regular monthly parkers at a garage operated by defendant in Philadelphia; that defendants had been informed that in their business the cars of plaintiffs carried valuable jewelry samples and that such cars were equipped with burglar alarms; that plaintiffs were to park their cars in the garage and lock them retaining control of the keys thereto at all times. On or about March 8, 1957, one of plaintiffs' cars was placed in defendant's garage and locked as usual. The complaint goes on to aver that this car contained approximately $8,000 worth of samples of various types of jewelry; that on or about March 19, 1957 the car was missing from the garage and was reported to the police as stolen. On March 23, 1957 the car was found but the jewelry was missing. It is plaintiffs' contention that the defendant violated a bailment contract in failing to return the automobile and its contents and sought judgment. * * * The case was tried by the court without a jury and at the conclusion of plaintiffs' case, defendant moved for a non-suit on the ground that there was no bailor-bailee relationship but instead, a lease of parking privileges and consequently there was no liability for loss by theft in the absence of proof of culpable negligence on its part. * * *

The trial court entered a compulsory non-suit which was affirmed by the court en banc. This appeal followed. * * *

In order to fix liability upon the proprietors of an automobile parking place, it is necessary to ascertain if there is such a delivery of or assumption of control of the automobile entrusted to him as to create a bailment. One who merely leases automobile parking privileges is not the bailee of the parked car and consequently is under no duty to guard against loss by theft.

The decided cases recognize two principal classes of legal relationships in dealing with the present-day type of parking lot. The first is where an owner rents space in a parking lot, drives his automobile therein, locks it or not as he chooses, and for all practical purposes retains control thereof. The second is where the garage attendants collect fees, assume control of cars, park them and move them about within the garage as they find convenient, the keys are left in the cars and tickets are issued as means of identifying cars upon redelivery. The first class of cases has almost universally been held to be that of a mere lease of parking privileges because the owner has paid a fee only for the privilege of parking his automobile without any actual delivery to the parking lot operator and with no corresponding right to redelivery. * * *

The second class of cases has been held to constitute a bailment and the lot owner held responsible for loss of the car or damage to it. * * *

The characterization of the relationship as a bailment or a lease does not depend upon the physical structure of the place where the article is stored, as plaintiffs would have us hold, but rather it is based solely on whether the alleged bailor delivered the custody and control of the item to the bailee. * * * Since here plaintiffs reserved possession of the car at all times by retaining the keys thereto, defendant acquired no dominion over the vehicle nor any right to control removal of it; hence there was no bailment. * * *

The judgment of the court below is affirmed.

2. No Liability for Unknown Contents

ALLEN v. HOUSERMAN

250 A.2d 389 (Del.Super.1969).

QUILLEN, Judge. The plaintiff left his car in the defendant's parking lot. The keys, including the trunk key, were left in the car. The car was taken from the lot by persons unknown. The car was later recovered but the plaintiff's golf clubs, valued at $373.53, which had been locked in the trunk, were missing and not recovered. The plaintiff was not asked and did not voluntarily advise the defendant about the presence of the golf clubs when he left his car in the defendant's lot.

The plaintiff brings this civil action for the value of the golf clubs. * * *

Both [parties] agree that the duty of the bailee parking lot depends upon notice, actual or constructive, of the presence of golf clubs. It is clear under the stipulated facts that there was no actual or express notice given by the plaintiff to the defendant.

The case thus turns on constructive notice. It has been held that constructive notice may be established by the presence in a car of personal property in plain view which was or should have been seen by the employees of the parking lot. * * * This is especially true when the property is such that its presence would normally be anticipated. * * * But such authority does not help the plaintiff where the property is locked out of sight in the trunk. And, notwithstanding the growing band of golf devotees, it can hardly be reasonably said that a downtown parking lot should impliedly anticipate the presence of golf clubs in the trunk of each patron's car.

Since there is no genuine issue of fact and no evidence of actual notice and no facts which could constitute constructive notice, the defendant is entitled to judgment as a matter of law.

---

3. Check Room Bailments

JOHNSON v. B. & N., INC.

190 Pa.Super. 586, 155 A.2d 232 (1959).

HIRT, Judge. In the late afternoon or early evening of January 28, 1956, the plaintiff, with a Miss Williams, went to the defendant's restaurant for dinner, and to see a style show. There were about 200 people present, which number was about the capacity of the club. Some time after they were seated plaintiff and her companion decided to check their coats and Miss Williams took the two coats to the check room for that purpose. There, according to her testimony, the check room was filled with coats; that the attendant, referred to as

Patty, told her that there were no more checks, but that she knew both Miss Williams and the plaintiff, and for that reason would accept the coats without giving checks for their later identification when claimed. When the two women were ready to leave, there was no attendant at the check room. This was a small room, open to the restaurant, except for a "half gate" across the doorway. Patty appeared later and delivered Miss Williams' coat to her, but was unable to find the plaintiff's Persian Lamb coat. Plaintiff reported the loss of the coat to the manager of the club and to the police, but it was never recovered. In this action to recover the value of the coat, tried before a judge without a jury, the finding was for the plaintiff in the sum of $500. The lower court on entering judgment on the finding, discharged the defendant's rules * * * for a new trial; hence this appeal.

Check room service was an incident of the defendant's business and was necessary for the accommodation of its patrons. And the authority of Patty, the check room attendant, to accept plaintiff's coat, without giving her a check, must be implied from the circumstances. * * *

And in the light of the finding of the trial judge in the present case, supported as it is by the evidence, we must take it that a bailment for hire resulted—in reality a mutual benefit bailment—notwithstanding the plaintiff paid nothing for the service.

* * * In accordance with the duties of her employment Patty served the defendant as a hostess in the restaurant as well as the only check room attendant at the time. Plaintiff's evidence was to the effect that during dinner, Patty was seen moving about the restaurant and that when plaintiff and her friend came to the check room to claim their coats, no attendant was there. On this evidence the trial judge properly concluded: "The evidence was clear and precise that the cloak room attendant was absent therefrom at times, leaving it and its contents unguarded and an easy prey to the covetous eyes of a purloiner, an early departing patron perhaps or one entering, taking the coat and leaving unseen." The defendant in this instance failed to exercise ordinary care as bailee of the plaintiff's coat, and accordingly was liable for the loss. * * *

Order affirmed.

---

4. *Common Carrier Liability*

CLIFFORD W. BROWN v. BONESTEELE

218 Or. 312, 344 P.2d 928 (1959).

O'CONNELL, Justice. This is an action for damages brought by a shipper against a carrier to recover for the loss by fire of a truck load of twine while being transported in defendant's truck. The origin of the fire was not established although it is probable that it resulted from placing the twine too close to the exhaust pipe which was exposed in the interior of the truck. * * *

The complaint is drawn on the theory that the defendant had possession of the goods as a common carrier and was, therefore, absolutely liable for their loss. * * *

The case was submitted to the jury which found for the defendant. * * *

The defendant's principal business is the storage of goods. However, he is also engaged in the business of transporting goods for others, which he does under a permit from the Public Utilities Commissioner authorizing him to haul goods as a common carrier within the city of Salem and not to exceed 25 miles outside of Salem. * *

The principal question before us is whether there is any substantial evidence to submit to a jury showing that defendant had changed his status in this particular instance from that of common carrier to that of a lessor of a truck or as a carrier contracting to haul goods under a special contract of carriage. As a common carrier defendant would be liable as an insurer for the loss of plaintiff's goods. * * As a contract carrier or lessor he would be liable only if the loss resulted from his fault. * * *

It is undisputed that the defendant held himself out to the public as a common carrier. That being so, it would devolve upon him to establish that the transaction with plaintiff was not in the regular course of his ostensible calling.

* * * We can find no basis for the defendant's conclusion that the truck was leased to plaintiff. Here was a valuable piece of equipment, the use of which could create myriad legal problems. Normally, the parties to a lease of such equipment would agree upon their respective rights and liabilities; ordinarily their agreement would be reduced to writing. The parties in the instant case made no effort to resolve these problems, but instead dealt upon the basis of a conversation which amounted to nothing more than the ordinary request by a shipper for trucking service and the acceptance of the business by the carrier. * * * If a common carrier enters into a special contract to carry the same type of goods as he is authorized to carry under his permit, he does not thereby change his position as a common carrier. * * *

It is our conclusion that the defendant was a common carrier in transporting the plaintiff's goods. As a common carrier he is absolutely liable for the loss of goods entrusted to his care unless he can establish that the case falls within one of the exceptions to the general rule of strict liability, i. e., that the loss resulted from an act of God, or an act of the state, the public enemy, or the shipper, or that the damages were due to the inherent nature of the goods themselves. * * *

The trial judge should have directed a verdict for the plaintiff leaving to the jury only the question of the amount of damages.

5. *"Act of God" as Excuse for Liability*

JOSEPH RESNICK CO. v. NIPPON YUSEN KAISHA

39 Misc.2d 513, 241 N.Y.S.2d 134 (1963).

SAMUEL A. SPIEGEL, Judge. This is an action by an importer against both a steamship line and a pier operator to recover $1594.54 for flood damage to a shipment of 100 cartons of cabana sets, purchased by plaintiff and shipped from Hong Kong to New York aboard defendant's steamship. The vessel arrived in New York on or about February 12, 1960, and the cargo was discharged into the hands of defendant pier operator. The cargo was eventually delivered to plaintiff in a damaged condition.

* * * Both defendants, however, unite in the common defense that an unpredecented flood on the night of February 18, 1960 caused the damage.

* * * However, in order for this defense to be effective, it must be shown that the "act of God" was the sole and exclusive cause of the casualty and that there is no admixture of human agency.

* * * There is no question but that this flood was of itself an "act of God." Testimony showed that the flood occurred somewhat after midnight of the night of February 17, 1960. At 5 P.M. of the same day the United States Weather Bureau forecast predicted tides of only two feet above normal, a forecast which in and of itself would not have imposed a duty or placed an obligation upon the defendants to alter their normal course of operations. There was nothing contained in this official weather forecast to put the defendants on notice that the tides would rise in fact to more than five feet above normal, nor could they have reasonably foreseen this unseasonable occurrence from any of the surrounding circumstances. According to tide records kept by the United States Army Corps of Engineers and introduced at the trial, only two tides since 1893, a period of sixty-seven years, have ever reached the height and proportions of the tide of February 18, 1960. One occurred in November of 1950 and the second in November of 1953. Both tides were the result of hurricanes and both were in the fall, the traditional season for high tides. * * *

Further, to attribute liability to the defendant pier owner for not avoiding the effects of the resulting flood, in effect, would be to penalize him by making him pay a premium for the lack of superhuman qualities, in failing to envision a sudden high tide, out of season, without experience with any prior one, and without adequate notice thereof.

So far, this court has applied the traditional common law principle embodied in the tried if not tired phrase "act of God." In this nuclear age, man's unlimited capabilities and scientific advancement have brought him to the very threshold of other planets. His newly-harnessed nuclear power causes atmospheric reactions as yet unresolved and unpredicted, next to which his ability to create rain by the use of dry ice seems almost primitive. Is it not time to relieve Nature of even the formal blame for many acts which now seem to be within the scope of man's prowess? Perhaps the term "act of God" should be replaced by a concept which reflects the possibility of human causality as well as that of the Divine.

* * * The court then holds that the damage to plaintiff's goods was caused by an act over which neither defendant had the slightest control and whose effects could not have been reasonably foreseen nor avoided.

Accordingly, this court awards judgment for defendant Nippon Yusen Kaisha and defendant Universal Terminal & Stevedoring Corporation.

---

6. *Act of Shipper as Excuse*

FEDERATED DEPARTMENT STORES v. BRINKE

450 F.2d 1223 (C.A.Fla., 1971).

JOHN R. BROWN, Chief Judge. The sole issue in this case is whether the notation "shipper's load and count" (SLC) on a uniform straight bill of lading vitiates Carmack Amendment liability and exculpates the carrier from his negligence in providing an inadequate trailer for transporting a shipment in interstate commerce. * * *

Brinke had acted as a freight forwarder for Frigid for some time. Accordingly, sometime in June of 1968, Frigid requested that Brinke supply a trailer for the shipment of electric fans and stands from Frigid's Brooklyn warehouse to Consignee Burdine's Miami, Florida location. Although in the past it had always provided an enclosed van for such shipments, Brinke had no such trailer available on this occasion, and therefore delivered an open or "rag top" van to Frigid's dock. Frigid's traffic manager was apprehensive (if not upset) about the kind of trailer which had been provided, and he therefore telephoned Brinke's terminal manager to protest. The terminal manager assured the traffic manager that the canvas top trailer would be completely adequate and that the fans would arrive in Miami in good condition. To further secure the safe passage of the goods, Terminal Manager promised to place a polyethylene lining under the canvas top after the truck was loaded.

Although this added precaution was timely taken, Traffic Manager's initial anxiety turned out to be well founded and Terminal Manager's confidence in the sufficiency of the rag top van proved unfortunately misplaced. The van arrived in Miami water-logged and its contents were irreparably damaged. Understandably, everybody is looking for some other party on whom to put the loss.

Under the Carmack Amendment, which the parties have stipulated controls the liability in this case, the rule is very simple. The initial and delivering carrier is liable to the holder of a bill of lading, without proof of negligence, for all damage to the goods transported by it, unless it affirmatively shows that the damage was occasioned by the shipper, act of God, the public enemy, public authority or the inherent vice or nature of the commodity. And if goods leave the shipper's hands in good condition and arrive at their destination damaged, it is presumed that the carrier was negligent and responsible.

The presumption of liability is, of course, subject to limitation and exception. One of these relied on by Brinke is the shipper's weight, load and count exemption.

Brinke's argument is simply this—the bill of lading carried the notation "shipper's load and count," the shipper's loading of the fans onto the now-admittedly inadequate canvas top trailer was improper if not negligent, and therefore, it is not liable for the damages.

This you-should-have-known-better-than-to-rely-on-me argument completely misconstrues both the meaning and the purpose of the SLC section of the Bills of Lading Act. In the first place, Brinke's theory that placing the goods on a trailer so obviously vulnerable to water damage constituted "improper loading" requires a strained, at best, and we think unreasonable interpretation of that term. It disregards the fact that Frigid's Traffic Manager seriously questioned the propriety of using a rag top van and agreed to do so only upon receiving assurances from Brinke that it was safe and secure. And it disregards the carrier's duty to furnish suitable equipment. The carrier cannot palm off deficiencies in equipment onto the shipper. We cannot say the loading was "improper" under these circumstances. Moreover, even if Frigid was somehow negligent in acquiescing to Brinke's suggestion that the van was safe for shipping the fans—and we doubt that very much—that would have been negligence in *accepting* the trailer, not in the manner of *loading* it, as the term "loading" is contemplated by the statute. Thus, there can be no amelioration of liability on account of the SLC notation because damage did not come from loading—either "proper" or "improper." It came directly from inadequate equipment known specifically to the carrier to be deficient.

If anything further was needed to tie down an inescapable carrier liability, it came from the District Court's finding that the damage to the cargo was caused—in part at least—by the presence of holes in the inner plastic lining provided by Brinke, in accordance with their promise to Frigid, *after* the trailer had been moved to Brinke's warehouse in Jersey City. The supplying of a defective polyethylene lining constituted an independent act of negligence on the part of the carrier which contributed to causing damage to the shipment. * * *

Of course, the SLC provision has to be applied in light of the well-settled principle of law that a common carrier cannot by agreement relieve itself of liability for its own negligence. The Trial Court found, on evidence amply provided by the record, that Brinke was negligent in (i) providing a canvas top van which was inadequate for the type goods being shipped (and Brinke knew full well the contents and requirements of the shipment) and (ii) in using a defective inner plastic lining to secure the shipment. Even giving full effect to the SLC condition could not exculpate Brinke and relieve it from responsibility for these failures to exercise reasonable care, under the circumstances.

Affirmed [for plaintiff].

---

7. *Effect of Statutes on Liability of Interstate Carriers*

BLAIR v. DELTA AIR LINES, INC.

344 F.Supp. 360 (D.C.Fla., 1972).

FULTON, Chief Judge. * * * The plaintiff alleges in the original complaint that the defendant airline was negligent in shipping and transporting the casket and remains of the plaintiff's deceased wife from Miami to Vicksburg, Mississippi. Plaintiff claims that as a result of defendant's negligence in loading and unloading the shipment was damaged by rain. Damages are sought for physical damage to the casket, the attempted restoration of the deceased and great mental anguish to the plaintiff. The defendant's answer set forth as an affirmative defense the tariff filed with the Civil Aeronautics Board [hereinafter C.A.B.] as constituting an absolute bar, or alternatively a limitation upon the damages recoverable by the plaintiff. * * *

Defendant's [motion] for summary judgment [was] filed May 4, 1972, and [was] accompanied by affidavits in support thereof, a copy of the airbill under which the remains of plaintiff's deceased wife were shipped, and a copy of the tariff of Delta Air Lines on file with the C.A.B., which tariff was in effect on the date of the shipment. Airbill No. 006–MIA–1311 2712 was issued May 3, 1970, as to one casket of human remains of Agnes Blair weighing 265 pounds at a charge of $54.48. No specific value was declared. * * *

The basis for the defendant's motion for summary judgment is that the tariff filed with the C.A.B. pursuant to 49 U.S.C. § 1373 constitutes a limitation upon the damages recoverable by the plaintiff as a matter of law and that under the tariff provisions cited earlier the maximum liability of the defendant is $132.50. The plaintiff makes the following assertions: (1) that state law, not federal, is applicable to this lawsuit; (2) that this claim does not fall into the category covered by the defendant's tariff; and (3) that the tariff cannot bar a claim for gross negligence and that if such a bar exists, it is against public policy.

First, it is clear that a tariff, required by law to be filed, constitutes the law and is not merely a contract, * * * and that with respect to such tariff federal law governs the loss of or damage to baggage or freight as a result of an air carrier's negligence. * * * It is also clear that tariffs, if valid and accepted by the C.A.B., may contain exclupatory clauses for certain classes of freight and limitations of liability for loss or damage to specified property regardless of fault, and that such provisions are not prohibited by the Federal Aviation Act of 1958, 49 U.S.C. §§ 1301 et seq. * * * The established rule is that the tariffs, if valid, constitute the contract of carriage between the parties and "conclusively and exclusively govern the rights and liabilities between the parties." * * * Thus, federal, not state, law is controlling, and the tariff filed by the defendant with the C.A.B. governs the shipment in this cause.

* * *

The plaintiff asserts that he does not fall within the tariff provisions of the defendant in that the tariff is applicable only to claims of ordinary negligence and does not bar a claim of gross negligence on the part of the air carrier. It is apparent that plaintiff's contention must fail. The language of tariff Rule 30(B) does not distinguish between ordinary or gross negligence on the part of the air carrier. The Rule excludes the air carrier from liability except as to its actual negligence, of whatever degree. Further, tariff Rule 30(C) expressly states that the carrier shall not be liable in any event for special or consequential damages, and the limitation of liability provision of Rule 32(A) unambiguously states that the total liability of the carrier shall in no event exceed the value of the shipment as determined under Rule 52. The tariff provisions are clearly applicable to claims for both ordinary and gross negligence on the part of the defendant. * * *

Finally, the plaintiff asserts that the imposition of the tariff as a bar to a claim against the defendant for gross negligence is against public policy and that such a bar would deprive the plaintiff of his constitutional right of due process. * * *

The tariff limiting liability in this lawsuit is not contrary to public policy. Defendant's tariff provisions are valid and cover all aspects of this cause. Plaintiff had the opportunity to declare a higher value upon the shipment if he so desired. Failing to do so, the plaintiff's loss is subject to the limitations in the Air Tariff Rules which provide in Rule 32(A) that the total liability of the carrier shall in no event exceed the value of the shipment as determined in Rule 52. Rule 52, "Charges for Declared Value," provides that a shipment shall have a declared value of $0.50 per pound, but not less than $50.00, where a higher value is not declared. Since plaintiff did not declare a higher value, the shipment weighing 265 pounds results in a declared value of $132.50. Tariff Rule 32(C) provides that the total liability of the carrier shall not exceed either the value of the shipment under Rule 52, or the actual value of the shipment, or the amount of damages actually sustained, whichever is the least. In accord with the above provisions of the Official Air Freight Rules, Tariff No. 1–B, defendant's maximum liability in this cause is limited to $132.50 as a matter of law.

---

8. Innkeeper's Liability

NO. RIVER INS. CO. v. TISCH MANAGEMENT, INC.

64 N.J.Super. 357, 166 A.2d 169 (1960).

CONFORD, S. J. A. D. Plaintiff paid the insurance claim of Mr. and Mrs. Louis Cohen for loss of Mrs. Cohen's mink coat while guests at the Traymore Hotel in Atlantic City December 24, 1957, and now, as subrogee, brings this action to recover for the loss against the defendant operator of the hotel on its common-law liability. The Law Division of the Superior Court granted a motion for judgment in favor of the defendant at the end of the case, and plaintiff appeals therefrom.

Plaintiff's proofs were that the Cohens had been guests at the hotel since December 21, 1957, and that when they returned to the room on the evening of December 24, 1957 they discovered that the coat was missing from the hanger in the closet where it had been placed by Mr. Cohen. * * *

It has long been a principle of English law, accepted by most American jurisdictions, that in the absence of statute an innkeeper is practically the insurer of the safety of property entrusted to his care by a guest, exoneration being had only by showing the loss was due to an act of God or the public enemy, or to the fault of the guest himself. * * *

It remains to be considered whether, as argued by defendant, the result below should be confirmed because of the application to the facts of the case of the special statute affecting liability of hotels to guests. * * *

* * * This provision ordains that whenever a hotelkeeper provides a safe or other depository for safekeeping valuables of types specified in the act, including furs, and "shall place, in a conspicuous position in the room or rooms occupied by such guests, a notice stating the fact that such safe or other depository is provided" in which the valuables may be deposited, and a guest neglects so to deposit the articles, the hotelkeeper is not liable for loss of the property. If the goods are thus deposited the liability of the hotelkeeper for loss is limited to $500.

Defendant's principal dependence in this regard is upon a document which, according to its proofs, was left under the glass on a dresser in the hotel room at the time it was occupied by the Cohens. This paper is about 11½ inches square. Commanding its top-center space, in the style of a title, is the prominent designation, "The Traymore Directory." * * *

What defendant relies upon is a box of about 2½ inches in the lower righthand corner of the "Directory," bearing the caption, "Notice to Guests," in type substantially less prominent than that of the five captions for featured facilities set forth in much more prominent positions elsewhere on the paper. This notice contains the statutory information concerning the availability of a "safe" and of the absence of liability of the hotel for valuables not left there.

The question before us is whether this notice satisfied the statute as a matter of law. We hold it did not. The "notice" constituted a minor appendage of what in primary purport was a hotel directory. A guest whose eye should be caught by this document might very well stop reading it as soon as he gathered its general import, if not interested therein, and before reaching the lower corner where the "notice" is set out. The express requirement in the statute that the notice be placed "in a conspicuous position" evidences an intent that the notice itself be conspicuous and a serious question is presented as to whether this notice can be regarded as conspicuous, in the light of the diverting character of the main substance of the data on the paper on which it appears. * * *

Evidence of actual knowledge by the guest of the availability of a hotel depository and of the limited statutory liability, is, by the weight of authority, with which we agree, not an acceptable substitute for strict compliance with the statute as to notice by the hotelkeeper. * * *

Reversed and remanded for a new trial.

---

9. *Who are Innkeeper's "Guests"?*

ROSS v. KIRKEBY HOTELS

8 Misc.2d 750, 160 N.Y.S.2d 978 (1957).

HOFSTADTER, Justice. The plaintiffs, husband and wife, recovered below against the defendant, the operator of the Hotel Warwick, in the City of New York, the full value of their luggage and wearing apparel stolen from the husband's automobile. The plaintiffs were to be married at the Warwick on the day of the theft, the arrangements for the ceremony and the reception to follow at the hotel having been made by the bride's mother. The husband, accompanied by his brother, arrived at the hotel in his car the morning of his wedding day.

The trial court was justified in finding on disputed evidence that the car was placed in the care of the hotel doorman, with specific instructions to park it in the hotel garage, so that nothing would go wrong; that the doorman undertook to do so, and told the plaintiff husband to leave the keys in the ignition switch. As the husband entered the hotel with his brother, he saw the doorman drive the automobile away. * * * Later in the day, when the husband came out of the hotel to arrange for the delivery of his car, he found it in the street and discovered that it had been broken into and that all its contents were missing. The doorman admitted that he had not placed the car in a garage, but had parked it across the street from the hotel.

It is undisputed that the plaintiffs did not register as guests of the hotel, that no room was assigned to them, and that the sole purpose of their visit was to participate in the wedding ceremony and reception. * * * Leaving the car containing the plaintiffs' wardrobe in the street, especially after the explicit instructions that it be placed in a garage, likewise warranted a finding of negligence, because of the defendant's failure to exercise the care imposed on it by law as a bailee.

The defendant urges, however, that the bailment was an incident of the relation of hotel keeper and guest between it and the plaintiffs and that, because of this relation, it is entitled to the limitation of liability prescribed by section 201 of the General Business Law. This section, so far as here material, provides:

> "No hotel keeper shall be liable for damage to or loss of wearing apparel or other personal property in the room or rooms assigned to a guest for any sum exceeding the sum of five hundred dollars, * * *."

It, therefore, becomes necessary to determine whether the plaintiffs were guests of the hotel within the purview of section 201.

It is to be noted that section 201 refers at several points to "the room or rooms assigned" to the guest. * * *

This vital element of the relation is totally absent in the case at bar. The plaintiffs did not seek or receive lodging at the defendant's hotel. As stated, they came solely to attend the marriage function. * * * It follows that the defendant is not entitled to the benefit of the limitation of liability and that the plaintiffs were correctly permitted to recover the full value of their property.

Judgment affirmed, with $25 costs.

---

10. Constructive Bailment

SHAMROCK HILTON HOTEL v. CARANAS

488 S.W.2d 151 (Tex.Civ.App., 1972).

BARRON, Justice. This is an appeal in an alleged bailment case from a judgment in favor of plaintiffs below.

Plaintiffs, husband and wife, were lodging as paying guests at the Shamrock Hilton Hotel in Houston on the evening of September 4, 1966, when they took their dinner in the hotel restaurant. After completing the meal, Mr. and Mrs. Caranas, plaintiffs, departed the dining area leaving her purse behind. The purse was found by the hotel bus boy who, pursuant to the instructions of the hotel, dutifully delivered the forgotten item to the restaurant cashier, a Mrs. Luster. The testimony indicates that some short time thereafter the cashier gave the purse to a man other than Mr. Caranas who came to claim it. There is no testimony on the question of whether identification was sought by the cashier. The purse allegedly contained $5.00 in cash, some credit cards, and ten pieces of jewelry said to be worth $13,062. The misplacement of the purse was realized the following morning, at which time plaintiffs notified the hotel authorities of the loss.

Plaintiffs filed suit alleging negligent delivery of the purse to an unknown person and seeking a recovery for the value of the purse and its contents.

* * *

We find after a full review of the record that there is sufficient evidence * * * to support the jury findings on the special issues to the effect that the misdelivery was negligence and a proximate cause of the loss to appellees. Article 4592, Vernon's Tex.Rev.Civ. Stat.Ann. (1960), does not apply to limit the hotel's liability to $50.00 since its proviso declares that the loss must not occur through the negligence of the hotel, and such limiting statute is not applicable under the circumstances of this case.

Contrary to appellants' contention, we find that there was indeed a constructive bailment of the purse. The delivery and acceptance were evidenced in the acts of Mrs. Caranas' unintentionally leaving her purse behind in the hotel restaurant and the bus boy, a hotel employee, picking it up and taking it to the cashier who accepted the purse as a lost or misplaced item. The delivery need not be a knowingly intended act on the part of Mrs. Caranas if it is apparent that were she, the quasi or constructive bailor, aware of the circumstances (here the chattel's being misplaced) she would have desired the person finding the article to have kept it safely for its subsequent return to her. * * *

As stated above, the evidence conclusively showed facts from which there was established a bailment with the Caranases as bailors and the hotel as bailee. The evidence also showed that the hotel, as bailee, had received Mrs. Caranas' purse and had not returned it on demand. Such evidence raised a presumption that the hotel had failed to exercise ordinary care in protecting the appellees' property. When the hotel failed to come forward with any evidence to the effect that it had exercised ordinary care, that the property had been stolen, or that the property had been lost, damaged or destroyed by fire or by an act of God, the appellees' proof ripened into proof by which the hotel's primary liability was established as a matter of law. * * *

Further, this bailment was one for the mutual benefit of both parties. Appellees were paying guests in the hotel and in its dining room. Appellant hotel's practice of keeping patrons' lost personal items until they could be returned to their rightful owners, as reflected in the testimony, is certainly evidence of its being incidental to its business, as we would think it would be for almost any commercial enterprise which caters to the general public. Though no direct charge is made for this service there is indirect benefit to be had in the continued patronage of the hotel by customers who have lost chattels and who have been able to claim them from the management.

Having found this to have been a bailment for the mutual benefit of the parties, we hold that the appellants owed the appellees the duty of reasonable care in the return of the purse and jewelry, and the hotel is therefore liable for its ordinary negligence. * * *

Appellants urge that if a bailment is found it existed only as to "the purse and the usual petty cash or credit cards found therein" and not to the jewelry of which the hotel had no actual notice. This exact question so far as we can determine has never been squarely put before the Texas Courts, but as appellants concede, the general rule in other jurisdictions is that a bailee is liable not only for lost property of which he has actual knowledge but also the property he could reasonably expect to find contained within the bailed property. * * *

We believe appellants' contention raises the question of whether or not it was foreseeable that such jewelry might be found in a woman's purse in a restaurant of a hotel such as the Shamrock Hilton under these circumstances.

* * * It is known that people who are guests in hotels such as the Shamrock Hilton, a well-known Houston hotel, not infrequently bring such expensive jewelry with them, and it does not impress us as unreasonable under the circumstances that one person might have her jewelry in her purse either awaiting a present occasion to wear it or following reclaiming it from the hotel safe in anticipation of leaving the hotel.

* * * Appellants were on notice that recovery was sought primarily for the value of the jewelry and that the only ground for recovery was the hotel's negligence with respect to the bailment, purse and contents. * * *

* * * It follows that the findings of negligence and proximate cause of the loss of the purse apply to the jewelry as well, which is deemed to be a part of the bailment. * * *

* * *

The bus boy and cashier assumed possession and control of the purse per instructions of the hotel with respect to articles misplaced or lost by customers. The active cause which produced the loss was wholly independent of the negligence of Mrs. Caranas, and the hotel's primary duty of ordinary care to its paying guest was clear.

The judgment of the trial court is affirmed.

PROBLEMS

1. Plaintiff was a guest in the defendant's hotel. She left a valuable fur piece in her locked room when she went downstairs to dinner. On her return, she found the fur piece missing. The room had a notice posted on the inside of the entrance door which she did not read stating that the hotel provided a safe, free of charge, for the deposit of all valuable articles and that the hotel would not be liable for any valuable articles stolen from the room. Plaintiff brings action against the hotel for the value of her fur. Decision?

2. Plaintiff, shipper, sends goods from New York to Chicago by defendant's railroad. During transit, the goods are destroyed by rioters. Plaintiff sues railroad as an insurer for the value of the goods. Defendant contends that it is not liable since the damage was beyond its control. Decision?

3. Defendant rented a horse from plaintiff, a horse renting stable, to take a ride through a prescribed area in a park. While defendant was riding in the park, she decided to ride over to her friend's house which necessitated leaving the park and crossing very heavy automobile traffic. Defendant rode to her friend's house and let her friend ride the horse through the city streets. Later when defendant was attempting to cross the heavy traffic to return to the park, a hit-and-run automobile driver negligently struck the horse and killed it. Plaintiff brings action against defendant for the value of the horse. Decision?

4. Plaintiff draped her sable stole over the back of her chair in a restaurant while eating dinner. After dinner, she left the table to make a telephone call. While she was gone, a thief stole the sable. Plaintiff brings action against the owner of the restaurant for the value of the stole. Decision?

5. Plaintiff rented a safe deposit box at the defendant's bank and placed $10,000.00 in it. The bank had a key to the box, and the plaintiff had a key; both keys being necessary to open the box. During the night, burglars entered the vault and broke open the box and took plaintiff's money. The bank had all doors locked including the vault doors, had maintained lights burning throughout the night, and had a burglar alarm system, but did not maintain a night watchman. Plaintiff brings action for the $10,000.00. Decision?

6. Parris stored his car in a garage owned and operated by Jaquith. Through the negligence of Jaquith's employee, the garage burned and Parris' car was destroyed. Parris sued for the value of his car. Jaquith denied liability on the grounds that he had posted a sign over the door of the garage which stated that the garage would not be liable in case of loss by fire. There was no evidence that Parris had seen the sign or that his attention had been called to it. Parris sued for the full value of his car. Decision?

7. Carpenter sued the B. & O. Railroad Co. to recover damage to a piano which was properly crated and in good condition when delivered to the railroad. The defense of the railroad was based on the following, written in ink on the bill of lading: "Rel val 500 per cwt," which the railroad maintained meant, when interpreted, a limitation of $5 per hundredweight

on the piano. The railroad contends that its liability was thus limited. Decision?

8. A common carrier accepted a shipment of goods at Chicago for delivery to a buyer in Boston, Massachusetts. The goods were in transit between the two cities. Would the carrier be liable to the owner of the goods if they were destroyed by a discharged employee holding a grudge against the carrier, who caused a wreck which destroyed the goods?

9. Mrs. Chown saw a brood of turkeys along the highway which she believed to be hers and took them to the protection of her chicken-yard. She then learned that they belonged to Ryan, her neighbor, so she put the turkeys back on the highway where they were all killed. Ryan sues Mrs. Chown for the value of the turkeys. Decision?

10. Ike stored a sealed box in Lyons' warehouse, stating that the box contained books. Lyons issued a negotiable warehouse receipt for "books". Ike negotiated the receipt to Don, who bought in good faith for value. Don surrendered the warehouse receipt to Lyons and the warehouseman delivered the sealed box. When opened, the box was found to contain worthless pieces of wood. Don sued Lyons for the value of the "books". Decision?

Part 5

AGENCY

Chapter 25

INTRODUCTION

A. NATURE OF AGENCY

1. IN GENERAL

Agency is the fiduciary relationship between two persons in which one person (the agent) acts for or represents another (the principal) in dealings with third persons; e.g., real estate broker representing home owner.

2. SERVANT OR EMPLOYEE

Most of the laws relating to servants and employees are the same as to agents; however, the relationship is not identical. Normally, a servant or employee is one who gives personal service as a member of a business or domestic household and is subject to control by the employer as to his physical duties or activities. A servant or employee usually does work that is more ministerial in nature, has no discretion as to the means to accomplish the end for which he is employed, and seldom has authority to represent the master or employer in business dealings. A servant or employee sells or gives his time, while a non-servant agent is paid primarily for results rather than for the time which it takes to accomplish them. At times, an employee will act in a dual relationship as an agent; e.g., the store manager is an employee regarding internal affairs but is an agent when he purchases inventory. Often the lines are not clearly drawn as to whether a person is acting as an employee or as an agent.

The agency relationship is created when the servant or employee represents the employer in transactions with third persons. The employee or servant then becomes the agent and the employer or master is the principal.

3. INDEPENDENT CONTRACTOR

An independent contractor is a person who contracts to do a piece of work according to his own methods and without being subject to the control of his employer except as to the result of the work, e.g., building contractor; whereas, in an agency, the right of the principal to direct what the agent shall do or not do is basic. Also, an independent contractor does not represent the employer in business dealings.

It is important to distinguish between an agent, servant or employee on the one hand, and an independent contractor on the other hand; since under the doctrine of *respondeat superior*, the principal, master or employer is liable for the tort of his agent, servant, or employee committed while acting within the scope of his employment; whereas, the employer is not liable for the tort of an independent contractor. Also, the benefits of the Workmen's Compensation Laws do not apply to independent contractors.

B. CREATION OF AGENCY

---

1. IN GENERAL

An agency can be created by agreement, by estoppel, by ratification, or by operation of law.

Since the law treats one who acts through an agent as doing the act himself, the capacity to act by an agent depends on the capacity of the principal to do the act himself if he were present; thus, a person who has capacity to contract may appoint an agent, but an appointment by a person without capacity, e.g., a minor, would be voidable.

Any person can act as an agent except a person who does not understand the legal importance of making contracts for another; e.g., a minor can act as an agent, but not if he is an infant of tender years. Thus, agents are not required to possess the same qualifications as are principals; i.e., a person can act as an agent for someone else although he is not capable of acting for himself. The principal cannot complain of the lack of mental capacity of one whom he has chosen to represent him. Generally, anyone except a lunatic, imbecile, or infant of tender years is capable of acting as an agent.

2. BY AGREEMENT

The usual method of creating an agency is by agreement; i.e., one person expressly authorizes another to act for him. In most instances, the authorization may be oral; however, if the agent is authorized to enter into a contract for the sale of real property for the principal, most states require that such an authorization be in writing. In some states, the authorization must be in writing in any case in which the agent will enter into any of the types of contracts required by the Statute of Frauds to be in writing; e.g., sale of real property, sales of goods of a value of $500.00 or more, etc. This is called the *equal dignities* rule; i.e., if the agent is to make contracts which are required to be in writing, his authorization must be created by a method of equal dignity, namely, a written instrument.

3. BY ESTOPPEL

Agency by estoppel (apparent authority) arises when the principal intentionally, or by want of ordinary care, causes a third person to believe another to be his agent who is not really employed by him. For example, if the owner of a store places another person in charge of the store, third persons may assume that the person in charge is the agent of the owner of the store. The agent has apparent authority because he appears to be the agent and the principal is estopped from denying the agency.

The situation of agency by estoppel also exists where the actual agency exists, but the principal leads third persons to believe that the agent has greater powers than actually exist. In Leavens v. Pinkham & McKevitt, 164 Cal. 242, 128 P. 399, the principal placed limitations upon prices that its general agent could pay when he purchased fruit from the growers; however, the principal did not inform the growers of this limitation. Thereafter, the agent made contracts at prices in excess of the limitations. Held, the principal was bound since the agent continued to have ostensible authority to do what he had done in the past until the parties with whom he had regularly dealt were advised to the contrary.

Agency by estoppel should be distinguished from an implied agency. An implied agency is an actual agency while an agency by estoppel is no agency at all. An implied agency is shown or ascertained by inferences and deductions from the words and conduct of the parties and the circumstances of the particular case. If it appears that there was at least an implied intention to create the agency, the relation may be held to exist notwithstanding a denial by the principal. Some of the circumstances that may indicate an implied agency are the prior habit or conduct or course of dealings between the two persons, the family ties or relationship of the persons, the active holding out of another as agent, subsequent acts, and acquiescence or ratification of previous similar acts.

Agency by estoppel can be invoked by a third person only when he knew and relied on the conduct of the principal; however, such knowledge is not necessary in the case of an implied agency since in such case the agent is an actual agent. Also, an agent by implied appointment is a real agent with all the rights and liabilities of an agent; whereas, an apparent agent or agent by estoppel is no agent at all and as against the principal has none of the rights of an agent.

4. BY RATIFICATION

An agency may be created by ratification; i.e., acceptance by the principal of the benefits of the acts of the purported agent.

Nearly all courts hold that the agent must be purporting to act for the principal at the time of the contract with the third person as prerequisite for ratification.

Ratification may be express or implied. It is implied when the principal, with knowledge of the material facts surrounding the agent's unauthorized act, receives and retains the benefits thereof.

The principal must ratify before the third person withdraws from the transaction; and until the principal ratifies, the third person can withdraw for any reason. This is because until affirmance the third person and the purported principal are similar to an offeror and an offeree before acceptance; there is no mutuality of obligation until the principal ratifies the transaction and if the principal cannot be bound neither can the third person. Since the agent acted without authority, the principal may repudiate the act if he chooses to do so.

5. BY OPERATION OF LAW

Agency implied by law can arise by statute. For example, most states have adopted a non-resident motorist statute which provides that the operation of a motor vehicle upon the highway of a State is an appointment of the Secretary of that State as the agent of the nonresident for service of process in any action arising out of the operation of the motor vehicle in the State.

Agency can also be implied by law when the acts of a self-constituted agent are, by reason of the neglect of the principal or the act of God, necessary for the self-preservation of the principal or the well-being of society. For example, as where the principal is so incapacitated by injuries that he cannot act for himself; or where a merchant furnishes necessities to a wife and charges them to her husband's account (no agency relationship exists, but the husband is liable for the necessities by virtue of a social policy that is in furtherance of the welfare of the neglected wife and the well-being of society as a whole).

C. TERMINATION OF AGENCY

An agency may be terminated by act of the parties or by operation of law.

1. ACT OF THE PARTIES

A. MUTUAL AGREEMENT

Since the agency was created by an agreement, it can be terminated in the same manner.

B. Expiration of Contract

The contract of agency may provide that it shall terminate at a definite time, e.g., one year. In such case, the agency terminates in one year by virtue of the terms of the contract. Or the agency may be created for a particular purpose in which case the agency terminates when the agent accomplishes the particular purpose; e.g., real estate broker sells the house.

C. Revocation of Authority

The principal may at any time revoke the authority given his agent by reasonable notice with or without good cause. When the agency is created for an indefinite time, it can be revoked by either person after reasonable notice without incurring liability. If it was created for a definite period, neither person can revoke the agency without cause, or he will be liable for damages.

D. Renunciation by the Agent

The agent may also at any time renounce the power conferred upon him by reasonable notice to the principal with or without good cause. If the agency was for a definite period, renunciation by the agent prior to the expiration of the period subjects him to liability for damages for breach of contract.

E. Option of a Party

An agency agreement may provide that either party can terminate the agency by giving a specified notice or paying a specified sum of money.

2. OPERATION OF LAW

A. Death

In nearly all states, death of the principal terminates the agency. In a few states, the agency is not terminated until the agent is notified of the principal's death. Under the Uniform Commercial Code, Section 4–405, death of a customer does not revoke the authority of a bank to accept, pay, collect or account until the bank is notified of the death and has reasonable opportunity to act on it.

In many states a third person can rely on the agent's authority until the third person receives notice of the principal's death.

The authority of the agent terminates instantly on his death.

B. Insanity

Insanity of the principal or the agent generally terminates the agency. In some states, a third person who has no knowledge of the principal's insanity and who deals in good faith with the agent will be protected if it would work an injustice on him; however, if the principal has been judicially declared insane, the third person is not protected since all persons are deemed to know the status of a judicially declared incompetent. Under the Uniform Commercial Code, Section 4–405, incompetency of a customer does not revoke the authority of the bank to accept, pay, collect or account until the bank is notified of the incompetency.

C. Bankruptcy

Bankruptcy of the principal terminates the agency if the agent has notice; however, if the agent is involved in transactions which the agent believes the principal would want him to finish, the agency is not terminated until the transaction is finished. Likewise, the bankruptcy of the principal would not terminate the authority to deal with goods that are in the agent's possession.

Bankruptcy of the agent terminates the agency if the agent should realize that the state of his credit would so affect the interests of his principal that the principal, if he had knowledge of the facts, would no longer consent to the agency.

D. Impossibility

The agency terminates when it becomes impossible to perform the agency; e.g., change in the law that makes the performance of the authorized act illegal or criminal; destruction of the subject matter; death of the third person the agent has been dealing with; insanity of the third person.

E. War

If the outbreak of war places the principal and agent in the position of alien enemies, the agency is terminated or at least the agent's authority is suspended until peace is restored. War can also make it impossible or impractical for the agency to continue in which case it will terminate.

F. Change in Business Conditions

The agency is terminated by the occurrence of an unusual event or a change in value or business conditions of such a nature that the agent should reasonably infer that the principal would not desire him to continue to act under the changed circumstances; e.g., broker to sell land at a certain price should regard his authority to sell the land at that price as terminated if the land suddenly doubles in value.

D. IRREVOCABLE AGENCY

An agency coupled with an interest is irrevocable and neither the death, insanity, or bankruptcy of the principal or the agent terminates the agency. An example of an agency coupled with an interest may be a mortgage; e. g., the agent advances funds on behalf of the principal and the agent's power to act is given as security for the advance. For example, P owns real estate worth $50,000.00. He wants to borrow $15,000 from A. A wants security in the form of a mortgage on P's property. The mortgage provides that if P fails to repay the money, A may sell the property and take the money from the proceeds of the sale. If A sells the property, he will give the purchaser a deed to the property. He will do this by executing a deed in P's name by himself, A, as "agent". This arrangement is an agency or "power coupled with an interest". It is a technical legal concept of agency which has caused much confusion.

---

1. *Independent Contractor vs. Agent*

MIRTO v. NEWS-JOURNAL CO.

50 Del. (11 Terry) 103, 123 A.2d 863 (1956).

LAYTON, Judge. This is a suit by a plaintiff injured as the result of tripping over a piece of wire left on the sidewalk by a newsboy. The Complaint charges that the newsboy uncoiled the wire wrapping around a bundle of newspapers and negligently left the wire lying on the sidewalk, over which plaintiff tripped and fell, injuring himself severely. * * * The case requires a decision as to whether a newsboy is an agent of a newspaper under the doctrine of respondeat superior. * * * Defendant takes the position that the newsboy was an independent contractor, not its agent. This presents a question of first instance in this State. There are a number of decisions on the point from other jurisdictions which are not altogether harmonious. In general, Courts seem to base their decisions upon the time-honored, if not altogether satisfactory, tests governing the extent of control exercised over the newsboys. * * *

The News-Journal Company prepares its newspapers for sale and distribution by assembling them into bundles, which are bound by wire. * * * The newsboys who resell the newspapers to the public accept delivery of them at the points where they are left by the haulers. The area of circulation is divided into districts, and district managers, who are salaried employees of the publisher, are responsible for the sale of the newspapers in those districts. The district managers select the newsboys to whom they sell the newspapers at 3½ cents per copy. The newsboys resell the papers to the public for 5 cents per copy. The newsboys are not entered on the payroll records of the publisher and do not receive any salary or commission from the publisher. Their only compensation is the profit they make by selling the newspapers at a price greater than that which they paid the publisher. The newsboys settle their accounts weekly with the district managers and unsold copies are returnable for a credit of 3½ cents per copy. If the newsboys sell papers to regular customers and the customer's account is delinquent or unpaid, the loss is borne by the newsboy and not by the publisher. The newsboys do not have specifically defined territories in which to sell retail to the public, and there is nothing to prohibit the selling of newspapers wherever they choose. The newsboys are not forbidden to sell newspapers or periodicals other than those of the defendant. The publisher will sell carrying bags and covers for account books to the newsboys, but they are not required to buy them, nor are they furnished free to the newsboys. The district managers do not have any means for controlling the methods by which the newsboys resell the newspapers to the public (such as a penalty of 10 cents whenever a customer complains) except that the district managers can refuse to sell newspapers to any newsboy who proves to be unsatisfactory. Newsboys are not compelled to solicit additional customers in order to increase their territories.

Based upon facts substantially similar to these, (and in several cases considerably less favorable to the defendant's newspaper) the weight of authority is to the effect that the newsboy is an independent contractor. * * *

In my judgment, the method and manner of control over the newsboys in this case was of a most limited sort and only for the purpose of insuring in a general way that newspaper deliveries were satisfactorily made. * * *

Defendant's motion for summary judgment granted.

---

2. Agency Distinguished from Bailment

NATIONAL FARMERS UNION PROPERTY & CASUALTY CO. v. GENERAL GUARANTY INS. CO.

149 Mont. 387, 434 P.2d 708 (1967).

JAMES T. HARRISON, Chief Justice. This is an appeal by the plaintiffs from an adverse judgment in a declaratory judgment action. * * *

Lingen was insured by General Guaranty Insurance Company (hereinafter called General) and Salisbury was insured by National Farmers Union Property & Casualty Company (hereinafter called National).

The circumstances surrounding the accident are these. Clifford Lingen needed a dented fender fixed on his car. He obtained four estimates and then contacted Russell Salisbury for another. Salisbury's estimate was lower or as low as the lowest of the others. Lingen then told Salisbury to contact the insurance company which was to pay for the repairs and Salisbury did so. The insurance company approved Salisbury's estimate and told him to proceed with the work.

Within the next couple days and on March 9, 1964, Lingen drove to Salisbury's farm where Salisbury was to do the work. Lingen could not wait for the work to be done so he needed a ride home. Lingen suggested they take his car since it was already warm. Lingen drove home and while Salisbury was driving back to his farm in Lingen's car he was involved in an accident with one James Wilcox. Wilcox brought suit against Lingen and Salisbury for damages arising out of the accident. National tendered the defense of Salisbury to General on the theory that General was primarily liable. General declined but undertook the defense of Lingen. National then brought this declaratory judgment action, joining Salisbury as a co-plaintiff and Lingen as a co-defendant with General.

* * * The provision of General's insurance contract with Lingen which is in issue is as follows: * * * *The insurance* with respect to any person or organization other than the named insured or such spouse *does not apply*: * * * to any person or organization, or to any agent or employee thereof, *operating an automobile* sales agency, *repair shop*, service station, storage garage or public parking place, *with respect to any accident arising out of the operation thereof.* * * *

Appellants' * * * claim is that the court was in error in finding that Salisbury was not Lingen's agent. It is clear and admitted that as to the repairs to be done, Salisbury was not an agent of Lingen's. Consequently the determining question here is whether driving the customer's car to or from the repair shop is a relationship of a different character.

* * * Restatement of Agency 2d, § 14N, Comment b., describes a non-agent independent contractor as one "who contracts to accomplish something for another or to deliver something to another, but who is not acting as a fiduciary for the other * * *." In driving the car back to Salisbury's farm there is no fiduciary relationship. It is a bailment. A bailment is distinguished from an agency in that an agent has the power to subject the principal to personal liability. "In this respect, the agency relation differs from that arising from a bailment, since a bailee has, as such, no power to subject the bailor to liability in contract or in tort." Restatement of Agency 2d, § 12, Comment c. There was no authority given by Lingen to Salisbury to bind him to a contract with a third party. Also Lingen would not be personally liable for any damage caused by Salisbury's negligence in driving without some further act on Lingen's part. We find that the lower court was correct and that Salisbury was not Lingen's agent.

* * * For the foregoing reasons the judgment is affirmed.

3. *Agency by Estoppel*

LINDSTROM v. MINNESOTA LIQUID FERTILIZER CO.

264 Minn. 485, 119 N.W.2d 855 (1963).

MURPHY, Justice. Action for labor and materials furnished by plaintiff, Anund T. Lindstrom, to defendant Minnesota Liquid Fertilizer Company, a Minnesota corporation. The jury returned a verdict in plaintiff's favor for $2,338.90, and defendant appeals from an order denying its motion for judgment notwithstanding the verdict or for a new trial.

The labor and material furnished by plaintiff were ordered by one Hurley Weaver, who represented to plaintiff that he was acting for defendant in the transactions. Defendant denies that he was its agent or employee and contends that the evidence compelled a finding that his status was merely that of a lessee of defendant's plant and equipment, without authority to bind defendant in any way. * *

Weaver undertook to use defendant's equipment solely for the sale of defendant's products under defendant's trade name, and to maintain a sales volume in the area, which, in defendant's opinion, would represent a reasonable amount of business. He was directed to promote the sale of defendant's products in cooperation with defendant and to use defendant's equipment in applying the products sold. He agreed to furnish defendant with copies of invoices covering all sales and of contracts with the customers and to deposit the proceeds of such sales in defendant's name in the local bank. Therein defendant agreed to promote the sales of its products in Weaver's area; to act as consultant with respect thereto; and to provide sales and technical instructions therein at all reasonable times. It reserved the right to conduct an advertising program in the area and required that Weaver furnish it with a mailing list of all of his prospective customers. Any provisions in the agreement constituting a limitation on Weaver's authority were certainly unknown to the public or to plaintiff.

* * * Further, at all times its corporate name was painted in large letters on the buildings, tanks, and equipment of this branch, with nothing thereon to indicate that Weaver was lessee of such business or operated it as an independent contractor. It is well settled that, in so far as third parties are concerned, the relationship of principal and agent may be evidenced by acts on the part of the alleged principal or appearances of authority he permits another to have which lead to the belief that an agency has been created. * * * It has been held that, where a party permits his name to be used on property or equipment which is placed under the control or direction of another and thus makes such other an ostensible agent, an agency by estoppel will result. * * *

The jury's finding that a principal and agent relationship existed between defendant and Weaver would render defendant liable for acts performed by Weaver within the scope of his apparent authority as plant manager. Any secret limitations placed thereon by defendant would not absolve it from liability to third persons such as plaintiff who dealt with Weaver as defendant's manager and who were unaware of any limitations upon his authority as such. * *

Affirmed.

---

4. *Agency by Ratification*

RAKESTRAW v. RODRIGUES

8 Cal.3d 67, 104 Cal.Rptr. 57, 500 P.2d 1401.

WRIGHT, Chief Justice. Cross-defendant Sherwood T. Rodrigues (Rodrigues) appeals from a judgment upon a jury verdict for $30,000 in favor of cross-complainant Joyce Rakestraw (Joyce). His claimed liability arises out of involvement in a transaction whereby Joyce's name was forged on a promissory note and a deed of trust in order to obtain funds for a business venture of her then husband, William Rakestraw (William), who was also a cross-defendant. We have concluded that as a matter of law the alleged fraudulent acts of Rodrigues in connection with the forgeries were ratified by Joyce and that he was thereby absolved of liability to her.

The action was initiated by Acme Financial Corporation (Acme) and Security Title Insurance Company (Security) to enforce payment of a $75,000 promissory note bearing Joyce's purported signature which in fact had been forged and which was secured by a deed of trust (also forged) covering property owned by her. Joyce, Robert Ellinghouse (Ellinghouse), who affixed the notarial acknowledgment on the deed of trust and Agricultural Insurance Company (Agricultural) as surety on Ellinghouse's bond as a notary public were named defendants. Joyce asserted the forgeries as a defense to the action and cross-complained against * * * Rodrigues and William. * * *

Joyce's cross-complaint against the remaining cross-defendants, Rodrigues and William, proceeded to trial and resulted in a jury verdict in her favor. * * *

In late 1964 Joyce discussed with William the possibility of using her separate improved real property in Woodside as collateral for a loan to provide capital for the operation of a supermarket. On January 28, 1965, Joyce executed but did not deliver a promissory note in the amount of $40,000 and, as security for the obligation, a deed of trust on her Woodside property. Although at that time she expected to obtain a loan, the transaction was never completed. Joyce thereafter withdrew her consent to the use of her Woodside property as collateral. William, however, signed Joyce's name to both a promissory note for $75,000 in favor of Acme and a deed of trust on her Woodside property securing the loan. The signature on the deed of trust was notarized by Ellinghouse on February 18, 1965. * * *

William took the forged documents to Acme and arranged for the loan. A check was drawn by Acme payable to William and Joyce which she endorsed without realizing that she was purportedly liable on the note or that her property had purportedly been encumbered. The major portion of the proceeds of the loan was used to satisfy obligations incurred in connection with a supermarket which was owned and operated by the William Rakestraw Co., Inc. (the corporation).

Joyce concedes that within a few days after she endorsed the check she learned of the forgeries. Later in conversations with her husband and others she claimed that she was the owner of the supermarket since her property had been used as security to finance it. She also demanded that stock in the corporation be issued to her. William, however, refused to issue or transfer any stock to her and initially refused to permit her to take any active role in the operation of the business.

Shortly after the discovery of the forgeries Joyce consulted an attorney who advised her to report the matter to the trustee designated in the deed of trust. Joyce, however, did not follow this advice and sought no remedy until three years later when both the business and her marriage had failed and the complaint had been filed by Acme and Security. * * *

Joyce benefited financially through corporate operations made possible by the loan. * * * In addition, William's paychecks from the corporation were deposited in a joint account standing in the names of William and Joyce and all payments applied on the Acme loan (totaling $36,250) were made by the corporation. * * * Rodrigues asserts that because Joyce ratified the forgeries he is relieved from any liability in damages to her. We agree.

The issues we deal with involve the application of traditional principles of agency law. Two basic rules are involved: (1) ratification by a person of an act purportedly done on his behalf not only creates the relationship of principal and agent but also constitutes approval by the ratifier of the purported agent's act, relieving such agent of liability to the ratifier for the act; and (2) forgeries can be ratified thereby relieving the wrongdoer agent of liability to the principal.

* * *

Ratification is the voluntary election by a person to adopt in some manner as his own an act which was purportedly done on his behalf by another person, the effect of which, as to some or all persons, is to treat the act as if originally authorized by him. * * * A purported agent's act may be adopted expressly or it may be adopted by implication based on conduct of the purported principal from which an intention to consent to or adopt the act may be fairly inferred, including conduct which is "inconsistent with any reasonable intention on his part, other than that he intended approving and adopting it." * * * It is essential, however, that the act of adoption be truly voluntary in character. Moreover, there can be no adoption if the act, although voluntary, is done only because the purported principal is obligated to minimize his losses caused by the agent's wrongful act * * * or because of duress or misrepresentation by the agent.

Generally, the effect of a ratification is that the authority which is given to the purported agent relates back to the time when he performed the act. * * * Since he is considered to be an agent with authority at the time he performed the act, he does not incur liability for acts done within the scope of that authority. * * *

* * * We conclude that the ratification of an act of forgery by one held out to be a principal creates an agency relationship between such person and the purported agent and relieves the agent of civil liability to the principal which otherwise would result from the fact that he acted independently and without authority.

We now turn to the facts of this case. Joyce concedes that she became aware of the forgeries within a few days after she had endorsed the check from Acme and thereafter consulted an attorney in connection therewith. Accordingly, the requirement of knowledge of the material facts essential to voluntary ratification is satisfied. * * * Here it is clear that Joyce elected not to rescind at a time when she was fully informed and had power to do so and had been advised of her rights.

It was not until three years after discovery of the forgeries, and then only when a complaint was filed against her, that Joyce sought relief. Her conduct during the interim period has been previously set forth and is revealing. When both her marriage and the business failed she formally asserted for the first time a claim for wrongdoing against her former husband and Rodrigues. It thus appears as a matter of law that Joyce affirmatively endorsed the fraudulent acts of William and Rodrigues in anticipation of benefits to be gained, and sought to negate her indorsement thereof only when benefits failed to materialize as anticipated.

* * * At the time of discovery she had not ratified the transaction nor had she done anything to preclude her from asserting that the signatures were not hers. Had she then repudiated the forgeries, her failure to take action to force the corporation to make restitution of the proceeds of the loan would not have validated the forged signatures. * * *

As Joyce's ratification of the fraudulent transaction relieved Rodrigues of liability to her as a matter of law, the trial court improperly denied his motion for judgment notwithstanding the verdict. * * * The judgment insofar as it relates to Rodrigues is therefore reversed and the cause remanded with directions to enter judgment in his favor.

5. *Termination of Agency by Death*

MUBI v. BROOMFIELD

108 Ariz. 39, 492 P.2d 700 (1972).

UDALL, Vice Chief Justice. This case is before us on a Petition to Review a ruling by the Court of Appeals (No. 1 CA–CIV 1755) wherein the Court declined to accept jurisdiction in a special action for the reason that prior to the time of the service of the written acceptance of offer on August 11, 1970, William Mubi, plaintiff's husband, had died. The Court of Appeals ordered the petition dismissed. We also conclude the petitioner's prayer for relief must be denied.

The undisputed facts are that William Mubi, husband of petitioner in this case, commenced a civil suit in Superior Court, Maricopa County, against Walter W. Tribble and Jane Doe Tribble for personal injuries and property damages resulting from a motor vehicle collision. On August 5, 1970, after this action was filed, defendants through their attorney filed an answer and an Offer of Judgment in the amount of $3,150.

Under Rule 68, Rules of Civil Procedure, 16 A.R.S., this offer had to be accepted, if at all, within 10 days or it was deemed withdrawn. William J. Mubi died at approximately 9:00 A.M. on the 11th day of August, 1970, 6 days after the offer was made. Prior to his death he had advised his wife Sharon Mubi to accept the offer of settlement of $3,150, and she in turn advised the secretary of Mubi's attorney, Robert Spillman, that the offer was accepted. Because Spillman was out of town on vacation he did not receive the notice of the offer of judgment until 2:00 P.M. on August 11th, whereupon Spillman authorized an office associate to immediately accept the offer of judgment pursuant to Rule 68, which acceptance of offer was duly mailed to the defendants on August 11, 1970 and was received in due course. Upon Spillman's return to his office he caused an acceptance of offer of judgment to be mailed to the law firm representing defendants on August 17, 1970, which acceptance of offer was duly receipted by the attorneys for the defendants.

It appears, thus, that while the decision to accept the Offer was communicated to decedent's attorney before he died, the written acceptance as required by Rule 68 was not made until after Mubi died.

* * *

Since written acceptance as required by Rule 68 was not made prior to death, we must inquire into whether it was validly made after death in view of our holding that death did not terminate the offer. We hold that acceptance was not properly made.

The power to accept after Mubi's death was transferred to his estate and upon its command the acceptance, if made in writing and within the 10-day period would have been valid. Since this did not occur, the only question remaining is whether the decedent's attorney could accept on behalf of Mubi after his death. With very few exceptions, none of which are applicable here, the death of the principal acts as an instantaneous revocation by operation of law of the authority of the agent. * * * When a person has authority as an attorney to do an act, he must do it in the name of the one who gave him that authority. The principal appoints the attorney to act in his place and represent his person. Thus, where there is only a naked authority, not coupled with an interest, the death of the principal without notice ends the agent's authority to act in his principal behalf. In short, the agent's power is a derivative one and simply cannot last longer than the original authority except in a few unrelated instances.

Since the existence of a contingent fee contract does not create an agency coupled with an interest nor otherwise create an interest in the suit sufficient to create an exception to this rule, we hold that the power of the attorney to answer on behalf of Mubi terminated at Mubi's death. * * * Since the acceptance, made first by Mr. Spillman's office associate and then by Mr. Spillman, could not bind Mubi or his estate, the offer was not accepted within the 10-day period and pursuant to Rule 68 was "deemed withdrawn".

It is ordered that petitioner's prayer for relief be denied.

PROBLEMS

1. Defendant, a milk route distributor, struck and injured plaintiff while defendant was on his milk route. The defendant distributed milk for the Mt. Meadow Creameries, but the Mt. Meadow company had no control over the activities of the defendant. Plaintiff joins the company in the lawsuit. Company defends on the ground that the defendant was an independent contractor, and therefore the doctrine of *respondeat superior* does not apply. Decision?

2. Plaintiff, owner of an antique shop, asked his friend Richard to "mind the store" while he went to the post office to mail a package. While the plaintiff was gone, a lady came into the store and purchased a rare painting for a very low price. When the plaintiff returned, Richard told him about the sale. Plaintiff brings action against the lady for the return of the painting on the ground that Richard did not have authority to make the sale. Decision?

3. Jones, the secretary of defendant's corporation, purchases some personal property for the corporation which he knows the corporation needs. Jones does not have authority to make the purchase. Defendant, after learning of the purchase, accepts the benefits of the purchase and is pleased to get the goods. Plaintiff, seller of the goods, brings action against the corporation for the purchase price. Defendant takes the position that Jones acted without authority. Decision?

4. Plaintiff, a real estate broker, asks defendant, a home owner, if he wants to sell his house. Defendant replies that he does. Plaintiff asks defendant if he can represent him and make a sale of the house for

him. Defendant tells him that it is all right with him if the price is at least $25,000 and if the commission is not over 5%. The plaintiff agrees. A few days later, the plaintiff enters into a contract for the sale of the house with a third party; however, the defendant refuses to confirm the sale. Plaintiff brings action to force defendant to specifically perform the oral contract, the sale, and to pay the commission. Decision?

5. P, a manufacturer, employs A as a traveling salesman to contract for the sale of goods manufactured by P. P is killed, but A does not know of this and continues to make contracts. A makes a contract with T who now brings action against P's estate. Decision?

6. Plaintif's small daughter was injured as the result of negligence of a concessionaire while riding on a "kiddie ride," which was owned and operated by the concessionaire as a component part of a carnival owned and operated by the defendant. Defendant had nothing to do with the actual operation of the "kiddie ride," but did make rules and regulations for the concessionaires and had the right to require the correction of anything wrong with the equipment used or its mode of operation or to remove it entirely from the carnival. Plaintiff sues for damages. Decision?

7. Atwood employed Bade, aged 17, as an agent. Acting within the scope of his authority and on behalf of Atwood, Bade made a contract with Sibley. Sibley demanded that Atwood perform the contract. Atwood sues to rescind on the ground that Sibley's contract was made with a minor. Decision?

8. The National Life Insurance Co. employed Brown as its district agent. Brown died and in his will stated that his son was to carry on his work as district agent. When the son attempted to write an insurance policy for Sullivan, Sullivan claimed that the son could not legally do so. Decision?

9. Bill, the driver of a school bus carrying fifty small children en route to school, discovered that the brakes did not work. To avoid disaster he drove into a garage and had them repaired, then drove on to the school. The garage sues Mac, the bus owner, for the cost of the repairs. Decision?

10. Joe, a skilled photographer, was hired by the ABC company to photograph the new models of equipment they were getting ready for market. Before Joe could take the pictures, he was arrested for a felony, failed to make bail and was put in prison. ABC claims their agency contract with Joe is terminated. Decision?

Chapter 26

RELATIONSHIP BETWEEN PRINCIPAL AND AGENT

A. IN GENERAL

The agent is a fiduciary; i. e., he owes a duty of scrupulous good faith and candor to his principal. The agent-principal relationship is one of trust.

B. DUTIES OF AGENT

Generally, the agent owes the following duties to the principal:

1. DUTY OF CARE

The agent owes a duty to use reasonable care, diligence and skill in his work; however, he is not obliged to render perfect service, and errors in judgment not due to want of care, fraud or unfair dealing, are alone not actionable against him. For example, an insurance agent must not neglect to keep insurance in force for the specified amount to which he had agreed; an attorney should file a lawsuit or an appeal within the required time; an insurance broker must obtain insurance covering the designated risk.

2. DUTY OF GOOD CONDUCT

The agent owes a duty to conduct himself in such a manner so as not to bring discredit or disrepute upon the principal or his business or to make it impossible to continue friendly relations; e. g., a waitress should not become a "call girl".

3. DUTY TO GIVE INFORMATION

It is the duty of an agent to keep the principal informed of all facts relevant to the agency so that the principal can protect his interests; e. g., broker must reveal all offers to purchase property.

4. DUTY TO KEEP AND RENDER ACCOUNTS

It is the duty of an agent to account to his principal for all property or money belonging to his principal that comes into the agent's possession.

5. DUTY TO ACT ONLY AS AUTHORIZED

The agent owes a duty not to act in the principal's affairs except in accordance with all lawful instructions given to him by his principal.

6. DUTY NOT TO ATTEMPT THE IMPOSSIBLE OR IMPRACTICABLE

The agent owes a duty not to continue to render service which subjects the principal to risk of expense if it reasonably appears to him to be impossible or impracticable for him to accomplish the objects of the principal and if he cannot communicate with him.

7. DUTY TO OBEY

The agent is subject to a duty to obey all reasonable and lawful directions in regard to the manner of performing a service that he has contracted to perform. If he disobeys a reasonable order, the principal can terminate the employment.

8. DUTY OF LOYALTY

An agent must be loyal and faithful to his principal. The agent must not obtain any secret profit or advantage from the agency relationship. An agent must not enter into any transaction within the scope of the agency in which he has a personal interest unless he obtains the consent of the principal. An agent must not compete with his principal concerning the subject matter of the agency, nor represent a person whose interests conflict with his principal. Unless otherwise agreed, an agent has a duty to act in his principal's name and not to appear as the owner of the principal's property; e. g., attorney must not put money he has collected for a client in his own personal bank account. The agent's loyalty must be undivided.

9. DUTY AFTER TERMINATION OF AGENCY

An agent is subject to a duty not to act as such after the termination of his authority.

C. DUTIES OF PRINCIPAL

---

1. DUTY TO PERFORM CONTRACT

The principal has the duty to perform the contract which he has made with the agent.

2. DUTY NOT TO INTERFERE WITH AGENT'S WORK

A principal has a duty to refrain from unreasonably interfering with the agent's work; e. g., terminating the agent's authority to act; supplying him with goods which are inferior; competing with him when the agent's services are exclusive (appointing an agent to collect a debt and then collecting it himself).

3. DUTY TO GIVE AGENT INFORMATION

The principal owes a duty to use care to inform the agent of risks of physical harm or pecuniary loss which exist in the performance of authorized acts and which he has reason to know are unknown to the agent. The principal's duty to give other information to the agent depends on their agreement or on the custom of the business; e. g., furnishing list of prospective customers to selling agent.

4. DUTY TO KEEP AND RENDER ACCOUNTS

A *master* has a duty to keep and render accounts of the money due from him to a *servant*. An *agent* can sue a *principal* for an accounting as an equitable remedy; however, the extent of the principal's duty in this area depends upon the contract between them, custom of the business, method of compensation, whether the agent operates an independent business, and other similar factors.

5. DUTY OF GOOD CONDUCT

The principal owes a duty to conduct himself in such a manner so as not to harm the agent's reputation nor to make it impossible for the agent, consistent with his reasonable self-respect or personal safety, to continue in the employment; i. e., agent does not have to continue to act for one whom he discovers to be an unsavory person, nor for one who physically or verbally abuses or insults him.

6. DUTY TO INDEMNIFY

It is the duty of the principal to indemnify the agent for any losses or damages suffered without his fault; e. g., payments of damages to third persons which the agent is required to make on account of the authorized performance of an act which constitutes a tort or a breach of contract; expenses of defending actions by third persons brought because of the agent's authorized conduct, such actions being unfounded but not brought in bad faith; obligations arising from the possession of things which the agent is authorized to hold on account of the principal; authorized payments made by the agent on behalf of the principal; payments resulting in benefit to the principal made by the agent under such circumstances that it would be inequitable for indemnity not to be made; and losses caused by the failure of the principal to give the agent required information (failure to give agent proper instructions for grading a street).

7. DUTY TO COMPENSATE

The principal is under a duty to pay the agent the compensation agreed upon. If no sum was agreed upon, the agent may recover the customary compensation for such services; and if there is no customary compensation, the agent may recover the reasonable value of his services.

8. DUTY NOT TO TERMINATE

A principal has a duty not to repudiate or terminate the agency relationship in violation of the contract of employment.

---

1. Duty of Agent to Principal

GENERAL AUTOMOTIVE MANUFACTURING CO. v. SINGER

19 Wis.2d 528, 120 N.W.2d 659 (1963).

BROWN, Chief Justice. Study of the record discloses that Singer was engaged as general manager of Automotive's operations. Among his duties was solicitation and procurement of machine shop work for Automotive. Because of Singer's high reputation in the trade he was highly successful in attracting orders. * * * As time went on a large volume of business attracted by Singer was offered to Automotive but which Singer decided could not be done by Automotive at all, for lack of suitable equipment, or which Automotive could not do at a competitive price. When Singer determined that such orders were unsuitable for Automotive he neither informed Automotive of these facts nor sent the orders back to the customer. Instead, he made the customer a price, then dealt with another machine shop to do the work at a lesser price, and retained the difference between the price quoted to the customer and the price for which the work was done. Singer was actually behaving as a broker for his own profit in a field where by contract he had engaged to work only for Automotive. We concur in the decision of the trial court that this was inconsistent with the obligations of a faithful agent or employee.

Singer finally set up a business of his own, calling himself a manufacturer's agent and consultant, in which he brokered orders for products of the sort manufactured by Automotive,—this while he was still Automotive's employee and without informing Automotive of it. Singer had broad powers of management and conducted the business activities of Automotive. In this capacity he was Automotive's agent and owed a fiduciary duty to it. * * * Under his fiduciary duty to Automotive Singer was bound to the exercise of the utmost good faith and loyalty so that he did not act adversely to the interests of Automotive by serving or acquiring any private interest of his own. * * * He was also bound to act for the furtherance and advancement of the interest of Automotive.

* * * If Singer violated his duty to Automotive by engaging in certain business activities in which he received a secret profit he must account to Automotive for the amounts he illegally received. * * *

The present controversy centers around the question whether the operation of Singer's side line business was a violation of his fiduciary duty to Automotive. * * *

The trial court found that Singer's side line business, the profits of which were $64,088.08, was in direct competition with Automotive. However, Singer argues that in this business he was a manufacturer's agent or consultant, whereas Automotive was a small manufacturer of automotive parts. The title of an activity does not determine the question whether it was competitive but an examination of the nature of the business must be made. In the present case the conflict of interest between Singer's business and his position with Automotive arises from the fact that Singer received orders, principally from a third-party called Husco, for the manufacture of parts. As a manufacturer's consultant he had to see that these orders were filled as inexpensively as possible, but as Automotive's general manager he could not act adversely to the corporation and serve his own interests. * * *

Rather than to resolve the conflict of interest between his side line business and Automotive's business in favor of serving and advancing his own personal interests, Singer had the duty to exercise good faith by disclosing to Automotive all the facts regarding this matter. * * * By failing to disclose all the facts relating to the orders from Husco and by receiving secret profits from these orders, Singer violated his fiduciary duty to act solely for the benefit of Automotive. Therefore he is liable for the amount of the profits he earned in his side line business.

---

2. Nature of Fiduciary Relationship

MOON v. PHIPPS

67 Wash.2d 948, 411 P.2d 157 (1966).

HALE, Judge. Joanna Moon had never met Dr. Woolery until the day after her stroke. Sixty-one years of age, widowed, and living with her 91-year-old aunt in the latter's home, she awoke the morning of May 19, 1962, to find her entire left side paralyzed; she could move neither her left leg nor arm.

* * * Dr. Woolery sent Mrs. Moon to the hospital for four days and then transferred her to a nursing home for continuous observation, treatment and rehabilitation during the next four months. On leaving the nursing home, she continued treatments from Dr. Woolery, reporting at intervals to his office. During the course of and as a part of his therapy, he sought to alleviate her feelings of financial insecurity by advising her to sell her farm, and recommended his father-in-law as the agent to help her. * * *

Dr. Woolery's treatment included drugs and psychotherapy, for he believed her emotional symptoms were interrelated to her physical problems. * * *

He employed a kind of therapy whereby the patient is said to ventilate her feelings by talking about personal problems; and in so doing he noted that her ownership of a run-down farm was the source of several unhappy emotional responses. * * *

Mrs. Moon, acting on this suggestion, telephoned defendant Everett R. Phipps, Dr. Woolery's father-in-law, who came from his home in Portland a few days before Christmas, 1962, to look the farm over.

* * * In 1955, the land alone had been appraised at $18,-700 by three realtors. The trial court found it had a value of $25,000 in 1962.

In January, Phipps drove Mrs. Moon to his home in Portland where his wife served her coffee and cookies, and he prepared a one page written legal instrument which Mrs. Moon testified she thought to be a listing agreement. * * * The instrument, which Mrs. Moon says she thought to be simply a listing agreement, turned out to be a 60-day, irrevocable option to Mr. Phipps to buy the farm for $12,500 at $1,000 down and $150 per month. * * * Plaintiff brought this action to rescind * * *. The court did, however, grant full relief on the basis of breach of fiduciary trust * * *.

A simple reposing of trust and confidence in the integrity of another does not alone make of the latter a fiduciary. There must be additional circumstances, or a relationship that induces the trusting party to relax the care and vigilance which he would ordinarily exercise for his own protection. * * * Nor would the circumstances that plaintiff was a widow in poor health, without family, under severe emotional stress, and taking a number of powerful drugs, convert an ordinary agency into a fiduciary relationship, for every sick and emotionally dependent person of advanced years does not, merely in listing his property for sale with a real estate agent, make of the latter a fiduciary with respect to the listed property.

* * * Loyalty is the chief virtue required of an agent. * * *

The evidence in this case discloses a number of circumstances which, when added to the agency, support the court's finding of a fiduciary relationship. First, we have evidence of special trust and confidence generated by the doctor and patient relationship. Then, we have a vicarious transfer of that trust and confidence through the doctor's psychotherapy and advice from the plaintiff to defendant Phipps, and her engaging him to procure a purchaser for her property at the best price and terms obtainable. Finally, instead of employing Phipps as her agent, she unwittingly conferred upon him a temporary legal title to her farm, giving him both the power of alienation over and the profits to be derived therefrom. * * *

When, therefore, by virtue of an agency relationship, an agent, without the knowledge and consent of his principal, acquires dominion over and control of his principal's property in such a way that the agent possesses a legal power to alienate the principal's interests in or possessory rights thereto, the agent has transformed the agency into a fiduciary relationship. A fiduciary, in handling another's property, must exercise the utmost good faith, disclose fully all facts relating to his interest in and his actions affecting the property involved in the fiduciary relationship, and deliver over to the party for whom he is acting all benefits derived from or inuring to the property from the breach.

The judgment is, therefore, affirmed.

---

3. *Duty of Principal to Agent*

McKINNON AND MOONEY v. FIREMAN'S FUND INDEMNITY CO.

288 F.2d 189 (C.A.Mich., 1961).

PER CURIAM. Plaintiff-appellee, as agent for The Fireman's Fund Indemnity Company, defendant-appellant, issued a liability policy for the appellant on an automobile owned by one Fitzgerald. On October 17, 1954, it cancelled the policy for nonpayment of premium. On October 23, 1954, Fitzgerald was involved in an automobile accident in which one Davis was injured.

Davis recovered a $10,000.00 judgment in the state court against Fitzgerald, and thereafter filed a supplemental petition against the Indemnity Company asserting that Fitzgerald was covered by the insurance policy of the Indemnity Company in that the alleged cancellation of the policy was fraudulent. At the request of the Indemnity Company, appellee's employees testified in this action with respect to the cancellation of the policy. The Indemnity Company was successful in its defense of the action.

Thereafter, Davis sued appellee in the United States District Court alleging that appellee fraudulently conspired to manufacture evidence depriving him of a recovery under the supplemental petition in the state court. Appellee notified the Indemnity Company of this suit and requested it to defend the action, which the Indemnity Company refused to do. Appellee employed its own attorney and successfully defended this action on the ground of res judicata.

* * * The attorney submitted his bill for attorney's fee for his services in the matter and expenses in the amount of $5,236.09, which the appellee paid. Appellee then brought the present action against the Indemnity Company for reimbursement of this expense.

The District Judge rendered judgment for the appellee in the amounts of $4,000.00 for a reasonable attorney's fee plus $500.00 for expenses. This appeal followed.

We agree with the reasoning of the District Judge that an agent may recover from his principal any expenditures necessarily incurred in the transaction of his principal's affairs and that under this well settled rule of principal and agent, an agent, compelled to defend a baseless suit, grounded upon acts performed in his principal's business, may recover from the principal the reasonable and necessary expenses of his defense. * * * The judgment is affirmed.

PROBLEMS

1. Roumel, the owner of an apartment building, employed Robbins as manager to live in the building and, among other things, to collect rent from the tenants. Robbins kept the rental money in an unlocked desk in her apartment although banking facilities were available nearby. Tenants and workmen had frequent access to the desk. Rent money in the amount of $200.00 was left in the desk and apparently stolen. Roumel brought action against Robbins for the rent money. Decision?

2. Jackson, an agent, leased real estate for Kribbs, his principal, at $275.00 a month. When this lease terminated, Jackson and a third person, Solomon, made an agreement that if Solomon obtained a new tenant at a rental of $500.00 a month, Jackson would pay Solomon $100.00 a month. Solomon obtained a new tenant at a rental of $550.00 a month. Jackson paid Solomon $100.00 a month, Kribbs $275.00 a month, and kept the rest of the rental money for himself. When Kribbs learned of these facts, he brought action against Jackson for the entire $550.00 a month. Decision?

3. Plaintiff entrusted defendant with $1,200.00 to buy a selected parcel of land for plaintiff. Defendant secretly purchased a much larger tract, including the selected parcel, for $500.00, and attempted to keep the balance of the money and the land as a profit. Decision?

4. Home owner employed a broker to sell his home. Broker sold the home to his wife for $10,500.00. Some months later, the broker sold the home to a third person for $11,500.00. Home owner sues broker for the $1,000.00 profit. Decision?

5. Principal gave agent an exclusive territory to sell principal's products. During the exclusive contract, the principal invaded the territory and made sales of his own. Agent brings action against principal for the profits he would have made on the sales. Decision?

6. Isaacs bought chances on an automobile, which was to be presented to the winner at a picnic on a certain date. Isaacs offered Leake $25 to take his tickets to the picnic and receive the car for him if he was the winner. Leake agreed. One of Isaacs' tickets was the lucky one, and the car was turned over to Leake, but he refused to give it to Isaacs, maintaining that the lottery was illegal and that by the rules the winner had to be present. Isaacs sues for the car. Decision?

7. Dinsmore was employed by Heath to locate property in Chicago suitable for development as parking lots. Dinsmore located a lot suitable for this purpose. He had a friend purchase it in the friend's name and then informed Heath that this lot could be purchased. Heath purchased the lot from the friend. Dinsmore then divided the profit on the sale with the friend. When Heath learned of this, he sued Dinsmore for the money which the latter had secretly made on this transaction. Decision?

8. As an agent for Albert, Doyle received $1,000 from the sale of certain merchandise. He deposited this amount in his personal bank account. The bank failed, and Albert sued Doyle for the $1,000. Decision?

9. Evans, the credit manager for ABC Corp., attended a regional credit meeting held in San Francisco. He submitted an expense account including reasonable amounts for air fare, hotel, meals, taxi and registration fee. The firm's accountant questions these expenses and Evans claims he is entitled to reimbursement. Decision?

10. Moe, hired by Super T-V as a repairman, went on a house call and, while repairing the television set, received a high-voltage shock which resulted in medical care and a long period of curative treatments. Moe claims that Super T-V is liable for these expenses. Decision?

Chapter 27

RELATIONSHIP BETWEEN PRINCIPAL AND THIRD PARTIES

A. LIABILITY OF PRINCIPAL FOR AGENT'S CONTRACTS

A principal is liable to third persons on contracts made by the agent on behalf of the principal within the scope of the agent's authority. The principal is liable whether the agent's authority was actual or apparent, and whether the principal's existence was disclosed or undisclosed. Also, a principal is liable to a third party for the unauthorized transaction made by his agent if the agent was acting within his apparent authority, the principal is estopped, or the principal has been unjustly benefited. Representations, declarations, and admissions of an agent, made within his actual or apparent authority while acting on behalf of the principal, are also binding on the principal.

1. ACTUAL AUTHORITY

Actual authority is the express or implied authority that the principal intentionally confers on the agent. *Express* authority is the actual authority given to the agent in words, oral or written. *Implied* authority is the actual authority given to the agent which is *inferred* from the words of the principal or the *conduct* of the principal; e. g., principal employs agent to manage his apartment building at a certain salary per month; the agent has implied authority to employ necessary labor to keep the apartment building clean and to make minor repairs when needed, to purchase fuel for heating, and to arrange for rubbish pick-up.

2. APPARENT AUTHORITY

Apparent or ostensible authority is such authority as the principal either intentionally or by want of ordinary care causes or allows a third person to believe the agent possesses. The principal is liable to persons who have in good faith and without want of ordinary care relied upon the apparent or ostensible authority to their detriment. For example, a local manager of a business had express authority to receive checks, but no express authority to indorse and cash any checks received. However, he did so for some time without complaint from his principal. The court held that ostensible authority was established, and the principal was liable (Safeway Stores v. King Lumber Co., 45 Cal.App.2d 17, 113 P.2d 483). So we see that whether or not a principal is bound by the acts of his agent when dealing with a third person who does not know the extent of the agent's authority depends, not so much upon the actual authority given or intended to be given by his principal, but rather upon whether, as a result of the acts of the principal, the third person believed and had a right to believe that the agent had authority to act.

3. UNDISCLOSED PRINCIPAL

Where the principal is named in the contract and not excluded by its terms, and the fact of agency appears, the principal will be liable for the acts of his agent, actually or apparently authorized as a *disclosed* principal. However, on occasion, an agent may enter into a transaction on behalf of a principal without disclosing to the third party that he is acting only as an agent. For example, a movie star desires to purchase a certain house but realizes that if the owner of the house knows who the prospective purchaser is, he may raise the price. So the movie star appoints an agent to make the purchase for him without disclosing that he is an agent. This would be a transaction by an agent for an *undisclosed* principal. In the case of an undisclosed principal, the contract can be enforced by the principal against the third party; and the third party can enforce the contract against *either* the agent or the undisclosed principal, but not against both.

Suppose that an agent enters into a contract with a third party disclosing that he is an agent but not disclosing the name of his principal; e. g., agent signs contract "John Doe, agent". The general rule is that oral evidence may be introduced at the trial to show that the parties intended to bind only the principal and not the agent.

B. LIABILITY OF PRINCIPAL FOR AGENT'S TORTS

---

1. DOCTRINE OF RESPONDEAT SUPERIOR

A principal, employer, or master is liable for torts of an agent, employee, or servant committed *within the scope of his agency or employment*. This is a form of liability without fault and is based on the doctrine of respondeat superior; i. e., let the superior respond. It is immaterial that the agent acted in excess of his authority or contrary to his instructions. The main justification for the doctrine is that the employer can spread the risk of loss through insurance and carry the cost as part of his overhead.

A. WITHIN SCOPE OF EMPLOYMENT

(1) In General

To impose liability on the principal or employer, it is essential that the agent or employee be acting for the principal within the scope of the employment when the tort was committed. Scope of employment means that the act was done in the course of the agency and by virtue of the authority as agent with a view to the principal's business; the agent in performing the act is endeavoring to promote his principal's business within the scope of the actual or apparent authority conferred on him for that purpose; however, the act may be within the scope of the agent's authority and not be in the interest of the principal or in the prosecution of the principal's business and still be within the scope of employment. It is also said that the conduct of an agent is within the scope of employment if it is not a serious departure from authorized conduct in manner or space and is actuated in part by a motive to serve the principal. For example, a truck driver is delivering gasoline for his principal. The driver throws a lighted cigarette to the ground on which there is a pool of gasoline that has dripped from the truck during the process of delivery. The principal is liable for the resulting damage as it occurred within the scope of employment.

(2) Acts for Personal Convenience or Pleasure

Acts which are necessary for the comfort, convenience, health, and welfare of the employee while at work, though strictly personal, do not take him outside the scope of his employment. Cessation of work for eating, drinking, smoking, warming himself, and similar acts are necessary incidents of employment and contribute to the furtherance of his work.

(3) Deviation and Departure

Only a substantial deviation or departure to take care of his own business or engage in activities for his own pleasure will take the employee outside the scope of his employment. If the main purpose of his activity is still the employer's business, it is still within the scope of the employment even though there are incidental personal acts, slight delays, or a deviation from the most direct route; e. g., a truck driver starts out on a direct route from his employer's factory to the railroad depot to deliver some goods. On the way, he stops at his home which is one block off the direct route. As he is driving away from his home, he has an accident. The employer is liable as the deviation was slight.

(4) Going and Coming Rule

The "going and coming" rule describes the rule in which there is a substantial deviation or departure by the agent. For example, an employee going to and from work, or to meals, is considered outside the scope of his employment. However, there are some exceptions to the rule.

(a) *Bunkhouse rule.* Where the employee lives at his place of work, e. g., ranch hand lives on ranch, he is generally regarded as within the scope of his employment when he is going to or returning from the fields to his living quarters.

(b) *Traveling salesmen.* He is generally regarded within the scope of his employment the whole time that he is away even while not actually at work.

(c) *Special errand or dual purpose.* Where the employee's going or coming has some additional business purpose, he may be considered within the scope of employment during the entire trip. For example, an employee who worked nights when it was necessary to do so went home to get certain tools and then went to dinner. On the way back, he had an accident. His dual purpose was to obtain the tools and to eat and, therefore, was within the scope of his employment .

(d) *Employer provides travel.* Where the employer provides transportation to the worker, compensates him for travel time, or defrays travel expenses, the courts have held that such employee is exempt from the "going and coming" rule.

B. INTENTIONAL TORTS

(1) In General

The employer is liable for the malicious acts of the employee within the scope of employment or connected with the employment.

(2) Over Business Dispute

The employer is liable for the assault and battery by an employee committed against a third person arising over a business dispute connected with the employment. An employee, manager of a Safeway store, and a lady customer argued over an order. The customer used some abusive language towards the employee. The employee ran after the customer and struck her. Safeway argued that the employee was outside of his employment as it did not hire him to hit customers; however, the Court held Safeway liable as the assault was connected with the employment (Stansell v. Safeway Stores, 44 Cal.App.2d 822, 113 P.2d 264).

However, where the tort results from a personal grudge which is unrelated to the employment, the principal will not be liable even though the assault takes place on the employer's premises during business hours.

(3) To Maintain Order or to Protect Property

The employer is liable for the employee's torts where the employment involves the risk of force and the act is connected with the employment; e. g., "bouncer" in a night club assaulted noisy customer; employee in charge of property trying to safeguard equipment threw a stone at a boy trespassing on the property injuring the boy.

C. FRAUD

Generally, the principal is liable for fraudulent representations of a type which are normally incidental to sales; i. e., which the principal might reasonably expect would be the subject of representations by the agent. However, the principal is not liable for representations which are unusual or exceptional unless the principal with knowledge of the fraud retains the benefits of the transactions. For example, the owner of a business employs a broker to sell the business for him. The broker misrepresents to a buyer that the net income is much greater than it really is, and that Howard Hughes is purchasing the surrounding area to erect a tract of homes which will greatly increase the business. The first misrepresentation is one that a principal might reasonably expect a salesman to make, and, therefore, the principal is liable for the fraud of the agent; however, the second misrepresentation is so unusual to the sale of a business that there would be no liability on the part of the principal.

In some states, the principal is held liable for the fraud of an agent even when the fraudulent statement is unusual or extreme under the doctrine of respondeat superior.

In some states, e. g., California, the courts hold that an innocent principal is not liable for the fraud of his agent if the written contract provides that the agent has no authority to make any representations not contained in the written contract, which the seller must sign. Such a provision gives notice to the third person that the agent's representations are not authorized. In such a case, although the third party cannot hold the principal liable for fraud, he can hold the agent for fraud; and he can also rescind the contract.

D. AUTOMOBILE STATUTES

Many states have statutes which provide that the owner of an automobile who has permitted another to drive his vehicle is liable up to a certain amount of money for the negligent act of the driver as though the driver was his agent.

Many states require that parents sign the application for a minor's driver's license. In this situation, the parents undertake financial responsibility up to limited amount for the negligent acts of the minor while driving the vehicle.

In about half the states, a person who owns or supplies an automobile that he permits to be used by members of his family is liable for any damages caused by the negligent operation of the vehicle by such member of his family. This is known as the "family-purpose" doctrine. It has been repudiated in many states as illogical and contrary to the general principles of agency law.

Many states have statutes which relieve the driver of a motor vehicle from civil liability for injuries sustained by a guest in the vehicle where the driver was only guilty of ordinary negligence; i. e., failure to use ordinary care under the circumstances. However, the guest can recover if the driver was guilty of wilful, wanton, or grossly negligent conduct, e. g., driver under influence of drugs or intoxicating liquor; but even here contributory negligence or assumption of the risk is a defense, e. g., accepting a ride with a driver the guest knows is under the influence.

In the absence of statute or personal fault on the part of an owner of an automobile, he is not liable for its negligent use by (1) an employee who was not authorized to use the vehicle, (2) an employee who was not subject to control in its operation, (3) an employee who without authorization invites a person to ride with him, (4) an employee who permits another to drive the vehicle without authorization, and (5) a non-employee bailee.

However, the Supreme Court of the State of California recently invalidated its automobile guest statute as a violation of equal protection of the law guarantees of the Constitution. (Brown v. Merlo, 8 Cal.3d 855, 106 Cal.Rptr. 388, 506 P.2d 212 (1973)).

C. LIABILITY OF THIRD PERSON TO PRINCIPAL

The third person can be liable to the principal in contract or in tort.

1. IN CONTRACT

A third person who has contracted with an agent representing a disclosed principal is as liable to the principal as though the contract had been made with him personally. Where the contract was unauthorized, it is not binding on the third party until the principal ratifies it.

A third person is liable to an undisclosed principal on a contract made on his behalf by his agent unless the terms of the contract expressly bar any principal or the third party would not contract with that particular principal and the agent or the principal knows this; in such a case, it is fraudulent for the agent not to reveal his principal's identity. However, in the normal case where the agent enters into a contract in his own name, concealing the fact that he is an agent and contracting as if he were the principal, the contract inures to the benefit of his principal; and he may at any time come forward and claim all of the benefits from the third party.

2. IN TORT

A third person is liable in tort to a principal for injuries committed by him to the principal's property or interests in the hands of an agent, whether or not the principal had been disclosed at the time, in the same manner and to the same extent as though such agency did not exist and as if the third person had dealt with him directly.

A person who knowingly induces or assists an agent to violate a fiduciary duty to his principal is liable to the principal; e. g., bribe of agent for obtaining confidential information.

A third person who colludes with the agent to have the agent act for the third person rather than the principal is liable for fraud in the absence of a reasonable belief that the principal acquiesces.

A third person who causes an agent to fail in his performance, e. g., to leave his employment prematurely, will be liable to the principal for damages.

---

1. Doctrine of Respondeat Superior

MARTIN v. JOHN C. BOWERS & CO.

334 F.Supp. 5 (D.C.Ill., 1971).

PERRY, District Judge. [T]he Court having considered all the evidence offered and being fully advised in the premises,

FINDS THE FACTS TO BE AS FOLLOWS:

That the plaintiff, Howard Martin, is and was at all times relevant hereto a Negro citizen of the United States of America, who resides in Chicago, Illinois, and who has been seeking to rent a residential apartment.

That the Defendant John C. Bowers d/b/a John C. Bowers Company is real estate agent and rental agent for a multi-unit residential apartment building located at 3720–28 North Pine Grove, Chicago, Illinois, and may take rental applications for the aforementioned building, the business office of said Defendant, being located at 4628 North Broadway, Chicago, Illinois.

* * *

That Marvin Miller is an employee of Defendant John C. Bowers d/b/a John C. Bowers Company in charge of the multi-unit apartment building located at 3720–28 North Pine Grove, Chicago, Illinois, and among his duties was the recording and maintenance of apartment availability records for the aforementioned building. In the course of his employment, Marvin Miller had actual knowledge that a basement apartment was available for rental in the aforementioned building, at least sixty (60) days prior to October 1, 1971.

That Mr. John T. Woltjen is employed as a full-time investigator of housing discrimination claims, by the Leadership Council for Metropolitan Open Communities, an organization seeking to eliminate discrimination in housing.

That on September 7, 1971, at 1:50 p. m., Mr. John T. Woltjen visited the multi-unit apartment building located at 3720–28 North Pine Grove, Chicago, Illinois, and was there and then told of the availability of two apartments, one on the second floor and one on the third floor of said building. * * *

That on September 7, 1971, at 2:10 p. m. fifteen minutes after the events described * * * above the Plaintiff, Howard Martin entered the office of John C. Bowers d/b/a John C. Bowers Company and asked Marie Folta, a receptionist employed in that office, and Marvin Miller if there were any apartments for rent in the building located at 3720–28 North Pine Grove, Chicago, Illinois; Plaintiff Howard Martin was told that there were no apartments available.

* * *

The evidence does not reveal that Defendant John C. Bowers d/b/a John C. Bowers Company had any actual knowledge of any discrimination against the Plaintiff, but only his agents. The Court cannot and does not find him guilty of any wilful discrimination against the Plaintiff on account of the acts of his agents. On the contrary, he has caused an apartment to be leased to the Plaintiff Howard Martin. The Plaintiff did not prove any substantial damages that he suffered other than obligations for costs and reasonable attorney's fees which the Court finds to be $300.00. He testified that he felt bad about being turned down but his feelings were not greatly injured when he is willing to rent through Defendant John C. Bowers d/b/a John C. Bowers Company. Plaintiff's damages were de minimus and nominal at most. The Court finds such damages to be $100.00.

CONCLUSIONS OF LAW

That the experiences of John T. Woltjen established a standard as to the "same right * * * as is enjoyed by white citizens * * * to * * * lease * * * real * * * property" pursuant to 42 U.S.C. § 1982.

That on September 7, 1971, Marvin Miller told the Plaintiff Howard Martin that no apartments were available for rental or lease in the multi-unit apartment building located at 3720–28 North Pine Grove, Chicago, Illinois, when in fact Marvin Miller, as agent of John C. Bowers d/b/a John C. Bowers Company, knew of no less than two (2) such apartments which were in fact available, to-wit, the second floor apartment and the basement apartment in the aforementioned building; which conduct constituted discrimination on the basis of race toward Howard Martin in that he was denied the same right as is enjoyed by white citizens to lease real property and in that Howard Martin was refused the right to rent after making a bona fide offer on the basis of his race.

The Defendant John C. Bowers d/b/a John C. Bowers Company is liable for the acts of his agents who did in fact discriminate against the Plaintiff.

* * *

2. *Liability of Principal for Torts of Agent*

LYONS v. ZALE JEWELRY CO.

246 Miss. 139, 150 So.2d 154 (1963).

KYLE, Justice. This case is before us on appeal by Mrs. Irene Lyons, plaintiff from a judgment of the Circuit Court of the First Judicial District of Hinds County, sustaining a demurrer filed by Zale Jewelry Company, defendant, to the plaintiff's declaration in an action for damages for extreme shock, mental anguish and nervous shock and physical pain and suffering allegedly suffered by the plaintiff as the result of willful and wanton, vile and abusive language and threats used by the Company's employee and codefendant in a telephone conversation with the plaintiff for the purpose of enforcing payment of a debt claimed to be due and owing to the defendant by the plaintiff's 23-year-old son. The damages sought to be recovered were damages suffered on account of the abusive language directed to the plaintiff during a long distance telephone conversation on March 22, 1961. * * *

The plaintiff further alleged that she was a practical nurse by profession, and that at the time of the injury complained of she * * * received a telephone call about 6:30 o'clock P.M. from Jackson, Mississippi, from the defendant Welch, who represented himself as an attorney for Zale Jewelry Company, inquiring as to the whereabouts of plaintiff's son, Kenneth Lloyd Myrick, who owed a debt to Zale Jewelry Company. The plaintiff further alleged that she informed Welch that she did not know the exact whereabouts of her son, Kenneth, but he was "somewhere in Laurel, Mississippi"; that Welch then became abusive and vulgar in his language toward her and said to her, "I know damn good and well you do know where your son Kenneth is"; that plaintiff replied that she did not know where Kenneth was, and Welch then said, "What kind of a damn mother are you, not to know where your son is. Your son owes Zale Jewelry Company a large debt and I intend to collect it." * * *

* * * The plaintiff alleged that she replied that she was not responsible for the debts her son, who was 23 years of age, had incurred. Whereupon Welch became highly incensed and yelled even louder in an abusive tone of voice the following words: "Listen you, g..d..bitch, if you don't pay this bill to Zale Jewelry Store, I am going to send the law down there tonight to put both you and your son into jail."

The plaintiff alleged that, after making that statement, Welch slammed the phone down; that she then hung up the receiver, sat down in a nearby chair, and did not remember anything until three hours later when Mayor Thigpen returned to his home and found her slumped over in the chair in a state of shock; that Mayor Thigpen immediately called in Dr. William R. Eure from Bay Springs, who found the plaintiff in a state of extreme shock, writhing in bed, and in a hysterical condition. * * *

The only question presented for our decision on this appeal is whether or not the facts alleged in the plaintiff's declaration, if proved, were sufficient in law to support a recovery of damages for the alleged severe mental distress and emotional and physical injury resulting from the wrongful conduct of the defendant's employee Welch.

* * * When the creditor's agents become vindictive and abusive in their collection efforts and resort to insulting and humiliating language, whether verbally or by letter, the courts have, in many instances, held that the creditor may be obliged to respond in damages for injuries caused to the debtor thereby. * * *

After a careful review of the cases cited by the respective parties in their briefs and many other cases cited by the textwriters referred to in this opinion, we think the allegations of the plaintiff's declaration were sufficient to withstand a demurrer, and that the trial court erred in sustaining the demurrer filed by the defendant jewelry company.

---

3. Liability of Principal for Punitive Damages for Act of Agent

FISHER v. CARROUSEL MOTOR HOTEL, INC.

424 S.W.2d 627 (Tex., 1967).

GREENHILL, Justice. This is a suit for actual and exemplary damages growing out of an alleged assault and battery. The plaintiff Fisher was a mathematician with the Data Processing Division of the Manned Spacecraft Center, an agency of the National Aeronautics and Space Agency, commonly called NASA, near Houston. The defendants were the Carrousel Motor Hotel, Inc., located in Houston, the Brass Ring Club, which is located in the Carrousel, and Robert W. Flynn, who as an employee of the Carrousel was the manager of the Brass Ring Club. * * * Trial was to a jury which found for the plaintiff Fisher. The trial court rendered judgment for the defendants notwithstanding the verdict. * * * The questions before this Court are whether there was evidence that an actionable battery was committed, and, if so, whether the two corporate defendants must respond in exemplary as well as actual damages for the malicious conduct of Flynn.

The plaintiff Fisher had been invited by Ampex Corporation and Defense Electronics to a one day's meeting regarding telemetry equipment at the Carrousel. The invitation included a luncheon. The guests were asked to reply by telephone whether they could attend the luncheon, and Fisher called in his acceptance. After the morning session, the group of 25 or 30 guests adjourned to the Brass Ring Club for lunch. The luncheon was buffet style, and Fisher stood in line with others and just ahead of a graduate student of Rice University who testified at the trial. As Fisher was about to be served, he was approached by Flynn, who snatched the plate from Fisher's hand and shouted that he, a Negro, could not be served in the club. Fisher testified that he was not actually touched, and did not testify that he suffered fear or apprehension of physical injury; but he did testify that he was highly embarrassed and hurt by Flynn's conduct in the presence of his associates. * * *

The jury found that Flynn "forceably dispossessed plaintiff of his dinner plate" and "shouted in a loud and offensive manner" that Fisher could not be served there, thus subjecting Fisher to humiliation and indignity. It was stipulated that Flynn was an employee of the Carrousel Hotel and, as such, managed the Brass Ring Club. The jury also found that Flynn acted maliciously and awarded Fisher $400 actual damages for his humiliation and indignity and $500 exemplary damages for Flynn's malicious conduct.

* * * We now turn to the question of the liability of the corporations for exemplary damages. * * *

The rule in Texas is that a principal or master is liable for exemplary or punitive damages because of the acts of his agent, but only if:

(a) the principal authorized the doing and the manner of the act, or

(b) the agent was unfit and the principal was reckless in employing him, or

(c) the agent was employed in a managerial capacity and was acting in the scope of employment, or

(d) the employer or a manager of the employer ratified or approved the act.

* * * It is undisputed that Flynn was acting in the scope of employment at the time of the incident; he was attempting to enforce the Club rules by depriving Fisher of service.

* * * As applicable here, there is liability if (a) the act is authorized, or (d) the act is ratified or approved, *or* (c) the agent was employed in a managerial capacity and was acting in the scope of his employment. Since it was established that the agent was employed in a managerial capacity and was in the scope of his employment, the finding of the jury that the Carrousel did not authorize or approve Flynn's conduct became immaterial.

* * * The judgments of the courts below are reversed, and judgment is here rendered for the plaintiff for $900 with interest from the date of the trial court's judgment, and for costs of this suit.

4. Torts Which are Agent's Sole Responsibility

CITY OF GREEN COVE SPRINGS v. DONALDSON

348 F.2d 197 (C.A.Fla., 1965).

JONES, Circuit Judge. This action was brought against appellant, a Florida municipal corporation, by the appellee, Mrs. Yvonne Donaldson, to recover damages sustained as a result of the actions of an employee of the City of Green Cove Springs. Jurisdiction was based upon diversity of citizenship. A judgment was recovered in the amount of $9,000, and costs. * * * At about 9:00 o'clock in the evening of July 10, 1960, Mrs. Donaldson and a companion, Mrs. Wells, left the Donaldson home in Mayport, Florida, and drove to Green Cove Springs. After arriving there and driving around for several hours, the two women began their journey home, and were then stopped by two police officers employed by the City and driving an official vehicle. The officers were on duty at the time. The record shows that the initial reason for the arrest was that Mrs. Donaldson was slightly exceeding the speed limit, for which the officers intended to give her a mere warning. Upon further investigation it appeared that there was something irregular about the automobile license tag, and Mrs. Donaldson was requested to follow the officers to the city jail so the tag could be checked.

* * * At no time was the plaintiff booked or issued a citation; nor was she ever taken into the jail. When they arrived at the jail, Mosely said there was no one there, and drove to a point near a railroad track, a short distance away. Mosely stopped the car, "propositioned" Mrs. Donaldson several times, and then assaulted her. According to the plaintiff's testimony, she resisted for approximately forty-five minutes, until Mosely overcame her and succeeded in raping her. The next thing she remembered was driving home. The jury returned a verdict for Mrs. Donaldson, and the City has appealed from the judgment entered on the verdict. * * * Subsequent to the oral argument before this Court, the Supreme Court of Florida held that Florida municipal corporations are liable for intentional torts of their police officers to the same extent as private corporations. * * *

The imposition upon an employer of vicarious liability for the torts of its agents is limited by the proposition that the tort must have been committed while the agent was acting within the scope of his employment. * * * Although the scope of employment is considerably broader than explicitly authorized acts of the employee, it does not extend to cases in which "the servant has stepped aside from his employment to commit a tort which the master neither directed in fact, nor could be supposed, from the nature of his employment, to have authorized or expected the servant to do." * * * We hold that the acts of Officer Mosely in his assault and rape of the plaintiff were outside the scope of his employment as a police officer for the City of Green Cove Springs. Consequently, the City is not liable, as a matter of law, for her injuries.

* * * It is generally held that liability for an assault by an employee that bears no relation to the real or apparent scope of his employment or to the interest of his employer is not imposed upon the employer under the doctrine of respondeat superior. * * *

The facts, construed most favorably for the appellee, will admit of no inference other than that in his rape of the plaintiff, Officer Mosely stepped aside from his employment to accomplish his own, rather than the City's purpose. Accordingly, the judgment is reversed and the cause remanded to the district court for entry of a judgment in favor of the City of Green Cove Springs.

Reversed and remanded.

---

5. *Issue of "Scope of Employment"*

DUMAS v. LLOYD

6 Ill.App.3d 1026, 286 N.E.2d 566 (1972).

ENGLISH, Justice. This action was brought by plaintiff, William Dumas, to recover damages for personal injuries allegedly caused by the negligence of defendants, William G. Lloyd, Clarence Shaefer, Norman Oil Company, Inc., and William H. Frazier. * * * At the close of plaintiff's case at trial, verdicts were directed in favor of Norman Oil and Shaefer, and it is from the judgments entered thereon that plaintiff has appealed. * * *

Defendant Norman Oil Company owns and supplies gasoline stations in the Chicago area, one of which is located at 143 S. California Avenue, Chicago. In September, 1962, defendant Shaefer was hired by Dale Norman, an officer of Norman Oil Company, to operate that service station on behalf of Norman Oil. He was not given a written contract by the company, nor did he hold a license to operate the station or give Norman Oil money or security for the operation. Shaefer did not own anything at the station and was not permitted to sell any products other than those supplied by Norman Oil. He received a commission of four cents for each gallon of gasoline sold at the station, and each day he banked the receipts after deducting his commission, and sent copies of the deposit slips to Norman Oil.

Shaefer was empowered to hire other people to help him with work at the station but, in practice, did not hire anyone without telling Dale Norman. Defendant Frazier was one of those hired, and his employment continued at the times pertinent to this case. Each person hired by Shaefer was paid out of his own commissions.

The operating license for the service station was in the name of John Norman, president of Norman Oil Company. Each month Norman Oil paid the rent on the property, the electric bills, and sales tax on all products sold at the station. All of the equipment, such as the gas pumps, air compressor, underground tanks, and signs, including one which said "Norman Oil Products," were owned by Norman Oil, and all products sold there were furnished and delivered to the station by the company, usually through Dale Norman. Either he or John Norman would visit the station once or twice a week and would instruct Shaefer as to keeping the station clean.

The company supplied all sales books and had its name on all books and records used at the station. Shaefer had no control over the price set for gasoline, that being determined by Norman Oil. Nor could Shaefer draw on the bank account which was in the name of the company.

On various occasions Shaefer, in the presence of Dale Norman, accepted and held various items as security for products sold when the customer could not pay the full amount. On December 18 or 19, 1963, Shaefer took a revolver from a customer as security for a payment of $3.00 for gasoline. The gun had a belt wrapped around it which Shaefer did not remove, but he placed the gun with the belt in a desk drawer at the station. The desk had only one drawer and it was unlocked. He never unwrapped the belt and never looked to see if the gun was loaded.

The station was located in a rough neighborhood and almost every day at 3:30 or 4:00 P.M., a small group of friends, including plaintiff, would meet at the station and sit in the room where the desk was located, to laugh and joke and have a good time. They usually stayed there until Frazier was off work at 9:00 or 9:30 P.M.

On December 19, 1963, Preston Evans, a friend of both plaintiff and Frazier, saw Frazier in the gas station with the gun which had been taken from the desk drawer. He was playing with the revolver by spinning it on his finger. Evans said to Frazier, "You are going to shoot someone if you don't quit playing," and Frazier replied, "There is no bullets in it." When he got through playing with the gun, Frazier put it back in the scabbard in the drawer.

The next day, plaintiff came to the gas station about 3:30 P.M. to visit Frazier and to have a grease job and oil change on his car, but it turned out to be too cold to do the grease job. He and Frazier had been pretty good friends for about five years and Frazier had been driving plaintiff's car all summer. About 5:30, while both men where in the station, along with several others, a man entered and asked Frazier to help him charge the battery in his car. Frazier said he couldn't do it right away and when the man asked how long he would have to wait, Frazier refused to do it and talked to the man in rough language. Plaintiff said he would help, and left the station and got the car started.

* * *

Plaintiff, in a joking manner, "told Frazier if he talked to me like he did to that old man, I would cut his throat off, and I did like this with my keys [indicating], and I walked out the door." As he went out, Frazier, also laughing, turned to a friend and said, "Watch me scare Red" [plaintiff]. He opened the drawer, took out the gun, and said, "Red, I'm going to shoot you," and shot him. Whereupon, Frazier immediately said, "Damn, look what I done did," and ran to help plaintiff, saying, "Man, I am sorry." They brought plaintiff back into the station, where Frazier called the police and told them he had accidentally shot a man.

Plaintiff suffered severe and permanent injuries and brought an action to recover damages based on defendants' alleged negligence.

Plaintiff declared that he having proved a prima facie case of agency between Norman Oil and Shaefer, the trial court erred in directing a verdict in favor of either Norman Oil or Shaefer because the latter's negligence is a question of fact for the jury.

* * *

Of primary consideration in the determination of whether a person is acting as an independent contractor or as an agent or employee is the degree and character of control exercised over the work being done. * * * When one undertakes to produce a given result without being in any way controlled as to the method used, he is considered an independent contractor and not an employee. * * But the relationship of principal and agent exists if the principal has the right or the duty to supervise and control, and also the right to terminate the relationship at any time. * * * The test is in the right to control and is not dependent upon its exercise. * * The general rule of liability is that a principal is liable for the negligent acts of his agent, but not for those of an independent contractor. * * *

We believe that the evidence as introduced by plaintiff did establish prima facie that Shaefer was acting as Norman's agent in the operation of the service station and was not an independent contractor. Although the day-to-day operating procedures were managed by Shaefer, his authority was limited by the interest of the owner whose representative frequently visited the premises and laid down for Shaefer certain rules as to buying and distribution methods. Norman owned all of the equipment used by Shaefer and set the prices for all the products sold. Signs, records and accounts were in the name of Norman Oil and Shaefer was powerless to change them. Furthermore, on January 5, 1965, without prior notice to Shaefer, the owners closed the station and terminated their relationship with Shaefer effective at that time. * * *

However, even though a principal-agent relationship between Shaefer and Norman Oil could have been found to exist, a principal cannot be made liable through the doctrine of respondeat superior when the actions of his agent in no way constitute negligence.

Plaintiff contends that Frazier could not have discharged the gun were it not for the careless and negligent manner in which Shaefer permitted the loaded gun to remain at ready access in the desk drawer. Yet, the uncontroverted testimony of both Shaefer and Frazier discloses that Shaefer did not know if the gun was loaded, and Frazier definitely thought it was not. We believe Shaefer acted reasonably when he allowed the belt to remain wrapped around the pistol and its case and placed it in a drawer which, although unlocked, was out of sight from those persons who might enter the station. Under all the circumstances of this case, for a gas station attendant to keep a gun, whether loaded or not, in a desk of his service station is, in our opinion, ordinary care as a matter of law. We also believe that the negligent or reckless act of Frazier was clearly not of a character which could be attributed to his employer. For both these reasons, therefore, we conclude that the trial judge acted properly in directing verdicts in favor of defendants Norman Oil and Shaefer. The judgments entered thereon are affirmed.

---

6. *Issue of the "lunch hour rule"*

GIPSON v. DAVIS REALTY CO.

215 Cal.App.2d 190, 30 Cal.Rptr. 253 (1963).

MOLINARI, Justice. This is an appeal from a judgment in favor of the defendant, Davis Realty Company, a corporation, in an action for damages for personal injuries. * * *

On April 4, 1957, Mrs. Jane Gipson, who was pregnant with child, was being transported by ambulance to the Stanford Hospital where her child was to be delivered. A collision between the ambulance and an automobile owned and driven by Roland Shugg occurred at the intersection of 26th Avenue and Clement Street in San Francisco. The accident occurred at about 12:20 p. m. The child was born about 40 minutes after the accident. The child showed signs of brain damage immediately after the accident, it being subsequently determined that such damage was permanent and that the child was suffering from a disability diagnosed as cerebral palsy. * * * A personal injury action was thereafter instituted by the child's father, Edward T. Gipson, as guardian ad litem on behalf of the child, * * * and against Shugg and Davis Realty Company, a corporation, as the alleged employer of Shugg. * * *

The important question is whether, at the time of the accident in question, Shugg, as such agent, was acting within the course and scope of his employment. * * *

The facts leading up to the accident appear to be undisputed. Shugg testified: that on the morning of the accident he was at the office of Davis Realty; that he left the office for the purpose of going to 38th Avenue and Clement Street to try to obtain a listing on a house at that corner on behalf of Davis Realty; that his sole intention upon leaving the office was to look at that property; * * * that as he started out on Clement Street he noticed it was around noon, so he decided to stop by at his home for lunch and then continue out to look at the property after lunch; * * * that the respondent did not instruct its salesmen as to when or where they should eat lunch; that it was the usual practice to stop at a convenient location for lunch and then continue on with the business of Davis Realty; that he ate lunch at home if he happened to be in the area; * * *.

* * * Therefore, whether or not the principal or employer is responsible for the act of the agent or employee at the time of the injury depends upon whether the agent or employee was engaged at that time in the transaction of the business of his principal or employer, or whether he was engaged in an act which was done for his own personal convenience or accommodation and related to an end or purpose exclusively and individually his own. * * * Accordingly, it is the general rule that an employee on his way to lunch, even though he is driving an automobile which is the property of the master, is not engaged in furthering any end of the employer, and that therefore under such circumstances, the servant is not acting within the scope of his employment. * * *

The so-called "lunch hour rule," * * * is, however, subject to an exception termed the "dual or combined purpose rule." * *

> "[W]here the servant is combining his own business with that of his master, or attending to both at substantially the same time, no nice inquiry will be made as to which business the servant was actually engaged in when a third person was injured; but the master will be held responsible, unless it clearly appears that the servant could not have been directly or indirectly serving his master."

* * * In the instant case it cannot be said that at the time of the accident Shugg was engaged in an act which was done for his own personal convenience or accommodation and related to an end or purpose exclusively and individually his own. The testimony shows that, initially, his sole intent was to attend to the business of his principal at 38th Avenue and Clement Street. Enroute, he decided to combine his business with that of Davis Realty. This is the extent of his deviation. * * * The extent and substantiality of Shugg's deviation, if any, was a question of fact for the jury.

The judgment is reversed.

7. *"Actual" Authority of Agent*

COBLENTZ v. RISKIN

74 Nev. 53, 322 P.2d 905 (1958).

MERRILL, Justice. Appellants are owners of the Thunderbird Jewel Shop in Clark County, Nevada. Respondent Riskin is a diamond broker and wholesale jeweler of Los Angeles, California. In August, 1955 appellants employed Hyman Davidson for services in connection with their store. In January, 1956 Davidson entered into a consignment agreement with Riskin pursuant to which he received, for purposes of retail sale, two expensive items of jewelry. In his dealings with Riskin, Davidson represented himself as manager of the jewel shop with full authority to receive merchandise on consignment. Riskin did not check these representations with appellants but did check with others in the jewelry trade and satisfied himself as to Davidson's authority. The jewelry pieces were reconsigned by Davidson without Riskin's approval or consent. The person to whom they were reconsigned has disappeared. Riskin demanded of appellants the return of the jewelry or its agreed value pursuant to the terms of the agreement. Upon failure of appellants to comply with his demand this action was brought. Judgment in favor of Riskin was given in the sum of $16,300. * * *

Riskin testified that it was the custom in the jewelry trade to take expensive pieces of jewelry on consignment rather than by purchase at wholesale. * * * By consignment retail merchants are not financially committed to the purchase of expensive items until they have themselves resold the items. Until resale their only financial commitment is that of safekeeping. Thus there is substantial benefit to be realized at the minimum of financial commitment. It can hardly be questioned that the engaging in consignment transactions would be regarded by those in the jewelry trade as a customary, proper and necessary function of store management. * * *

Davidson testified positively that he had been employed as manager of the store with instructions to run the store as he saw fit; that he had discussed with appellants the matter of taking merchandise on consignment and that appellants had approved; * * * that appellants had indicated approval of Davidson's success in securing such quality pieces and had never said anything about restrictions upon his authority to deal on consignment.

* * * Actual authority includes both implied authority and incidental authority. * * * Implied authority is that which the agent reasonably believes himself to possess as a result of representations by the principal or of acts of the agent permitted by the principal over a course of time in which the principal has acquiesced. * * * Incidental authority is that which is reasonably necessary, proper and usual to carry into effect the main authority granted. * * *

The trial court has found that Davidson was employed to serve as manager and that he did so serve. The evidence we have recited presents a clear case of both implied authority and incidental authority. We conclude that the trial court's determination of actual authority is supported by the record and that appellants are bound by Davidson's actions in their behalf in committing them to the consignment agreement with Riskin.

Affirmed.

---

8. Requirements of "Implied" Authority of Agent

BARBER v. CAROLINA AUTO SALES

236 S.C. 594, 115 S.E.2d 291 (1960).

OXNER, Justice. This is an action to recover actual and punitive damages for the alleged conversion of an automobile. At the conclusion of plaintiff's testimony, the Court granted a motion by defendants for a nonsuit. From this order, plaintiff has appealed.

Respondents, doing business under the name and style of Carolina Auto Sales, are engaged in the business of buying and selling automobiles in Columbia, South Carolina. Appellant, who is approximately 31 years of age, was married in West Virginia. To this union were born five children, now ranging in age from one to seven. He has been in the army for twelve years and has attained the rank of sergeant. After being stationed at Fort Jackson, he bought a home in Columbia where he resided with his wife and children. He had a 1950 Oldsmobile which was registered in his name. In October, 1958, he was transferred to Germany. He left his automobile in charge of his wife for family use. On January 5, 1959, while he was still in Germany, his wife, without his knowledge or consent, traded the 1950 Oldsmobile to the Carolina Auto Sales for a 1956 Oldsmobile.

* * * Appellant testified that several months later he received information that his wife was going out with other men and neglecting his children. He secured from his commanding officer in Germany an emergency leave and returned to Columbia on March 23, 1959. He then learned for the first time that his car had been sold by his wife, who at that time was working in a Columbia restaurant, and that his children were at the home of his parents in West Virginia. On the night of his return he went to the place of business of the Carolina Auto Sales to see if he could locate his automobile but was unable to do so. The next day he asked his wife to drive him to West Virginia to see about his children who were ill. * * * Upon arriving in West Virginia he found it necessary to hospitalize his children. While there he brought suit against his wife for divorce. After a stay of approximately two and a half weeks in West Virginia, his wife drove him back to Columbia. Within about a week after his return, he consulted counsel in reference to his automobile.

Thereafter, on April 20, 1959, this suit for conversion was commenced. * * *

The nonsuit was granted upon the grounds that the wife had implied authority to trade the automobile * * *.

It is well settled that the wife is not the agent of her husband by virtue of the marital relationship between them. * * * He may, however, make her his agent and be bound by her acts as such. The agency relationship in such case ordinarily rests upon the same considerations as any other agency; she is his agent, and he is bound by her acts as his agent, only when her agency is express, implied, or ostensible. * * * There may be circumstances where an agency may arise by implication of law, ex necessitate. * * * Where the wife is left in possession of the husband's property during his absence, as where he has absconded and his whereabouts are unknown, the law will imply or presume that she is acting as his agent and that she has authority to exercise the usual and ordinary control over the property. However, the mere fact that the husband is absent does not give rise to a presumption that the wife is his agent generally; her authority springs from and is limited to what can be reasonably presumed to be the intention of the husband; it does not extend beyond the authority which is usually and customarily conferred by husbands under the same or similar circumstances.

* * * It is equally clear that the fact that the owner of an automobile has left it in the possession of another does not give the latter implied authority to sell it. * * * This is true even though the relationship between the parties is that of husband and wife. * * * Under the foregoing principles, we conclude that appellant's wife was not empowered to sell his automobile while he was stationed in Germany. It is conceded that she had no express authority. The record discloses no circumstances from which an authority to sell may be implied from necessity. Nor is such authority usually and customarily given a wife during her husband's absence. * * *

The order of nonsuit is reversed and the case remanded for a new trial.

---

9. *"Ostensible" Authority of Agent*

MIDWAY MOTORS v. PERNWORTH

141 Cal.App.2d 929, 296 P.2d 130 (1956).

PATROSSO, Judge. Action upon a sight draft drawn in favor of plaintiff's assignor, Berl Berry, Inc., by one F. H. Bradbury, purporting to act as agent for and in the name of the defendant, issued in payment for an automobile purchased from said assignor. The sole question is whether the trial court was warranted in concluding that Bradbury was not authorized to purchase and accept delivery of the automobile and to execute and deliver the draft upon behalf of the defendant.

Berl Berry, Inc., is a dealer in automobiles with its place of business in Kansas City, Missouri. Defendant is a physician having his office in Compton, California, and also was Secretary of Bradbury Motor Corporation, of which Bradbury was President. Prior to the events with which we are here concerned, the defendant established an account with funds provided by him and in his own name in the Compton National Bank for the purpose of paying for automobiles to be purchased by Bradbury who alone was authorized to draw thereon. The defendant testified that the account was opened for the purpose of providing funds for the purchase of cars by Bradbury Motor Corporation but due to the fact that it was in financial difficulties the account previously mentioned was maintained in defendant's individual name. * * *

The evidence * * * leaves no doubt but that Bradbury was authorized by defendant to purchase automobiles in the latter's name and to issue in payment thereof drafts in defendant's name drawn upon the defendant through the Compton National Bank; that Bradbury, pursuant to such authorization, proceeded to purchase automobiles, taking title thereto in the name of defendant and issuing in payment thereof drafts drawn upon the defendant which were accepted by the latter. This, if it does not establish actual authority in Bradbury to bind defendant, establishes that he was clothed with ostensible authority so to do. "Ostensible authority to do a particular act may be established by showing that the principal approved similar acts of the agent." * * *

Accepting as true defendant's statement that the purpose of establishing the account in the name of defendant individually was to permit the corporation to purchase automobiles because of the financial difficulties in which it found itself, it would be a gross fraud upon those who in good faith sold automobiles in the belief that the defendant individually was the purchaser thereof to permit defendant to say after the automobiles were purchased in his name that such cars were in fact purchased for the corporation, for it is only reasonable to assume that under the circumstances they would have refused to do so upon the credit or promise of a financially embarrassed corporation. More important, however, is the fact that, whether the automobiles were purchased for the defendant or the corporation, according to defendant's own testimony Bradbury was authorized to draw drafts on defendant in payment of such cars as he might purchase. * * *

The judgment is reversed.

PROBLEMS

1. P is a bread manufacturer. He employs A to purchase wheat for him, but he instructs A not to purchase any wheat in a quantity greater than 100 bushels without first contacting P for approval of the price. A represents to T, who knows he is P's agent, that he has authority to purchase 500 bushels of wheat for P; however, he does not inform T that he has no such authority without approval of P. Without obtaining P's

approval, A purchases 500 bushels of wheat from T. P now refuses to take the wheat so T sues him for breach of contract. Decision?

2. S, a delivery man for M's liquor store, delivers a case of whiskey to a customer's home. After leaving the customer's home, S drives five miles farther to a hospital to visit his sick mother. As he is driving out of the hospital parking lot, he negligently runs into a child in the cross-walk. The child, through her guardian ad litem, brings suit against M. Decision?

3. A is a salesman for P. He attended a banquet given by P to award service pins. P expected his employees to attend the banquet. After the banquet while A was driving directly home in his own car, he injured the plaintiff. Plaintiff brings action against P for his injuries. Decision?

4. A, authorized to sell an orange grove owned by P, sells it to T orally misrepresenting the area to be free from frost and free from incumbrances. The form sales contract provides among other things that: "The agent of the seller has no authority to make any representation not contained in this contract. If the agent makes any such representation, it shall not be binding upon the seller or in any way affect the validity of this contract or any part thereof. * * *". Shortly after the sale, T learns of the falsity of the representations and brings action against A and P for fraud. Decision?

5. A bus driver for a local bus company asked a passenger who was slightly intoxicated to please get off of the bus as he was making a general nuisance of himself. The passenger refused. The bus driver and the passenger exchanged words and tempers flared. Finally, the bus driver pushed the passenger off the bus. With that, the passenger referred to the bus driver's ancestors with some unkindly remarks. The bus driver then got off the bus and hit the passenger in the mouth breaking some front teeth. Passenger brings action against the bus company. Bus company defends on the grounds that the bus driver went beyond the scope of employment as the company does not hire bus drivers to go around hitting people. Decision?

6. Gerstein sued Adams to recover damages for assault and battery. Gerstein testified that Adams' agents and employees entered her home and forcibly took a clock from her premises and committed an assault and battery upon her. The evidence further showed that when the employees of Adam took the clock, they were attempting to collect installments due thereon which had not been paid. Decision?

7. Burkovits sued Morton Gregson Co. and Kleeburger for return of overpayments for meat. Kleeburger was a salesman for Morton Gregson Co., delivering meat to Burkovits and collecting weekly. Over a period of time Kleeburger wrongfully altered statements to Burkovits, and in consequence Burkovits made large overpayments. Burkovits sued Morton Gregson to recover the amounts overpaid, which had been retained by Kleeburger. Decision?

8. Reilly, president of Rock Wool Insulating Co., borrowed money from Huston on behalf of the corporation and executed a promissory note for the amount of the loan. The minute book of the corporation showed that Reilly had general authority to make loans for the company but indicated nothing regarding execution of notes. When Huston sued on the

note, Rock Wool Insulating Co. claimed that Reilly had no authority to execute the note. Decision?

9. Pete operated a service station for the Southern Oil Company and was one of their most successful retailers. Pete told several customers that the products of his neighboring competitors were from foreign-owned companies, were inferior, and tended to cause irreparable damage to motors when used. Southern Oil had permitted Pete to make these statements, knowing that they were false and slanderous. The competitors sued Southern Oil Company for damages due to Pete's misrepresentations. Decision?

10. The Frigid Hockey Corporation owned a professional ice hockey team that was doing poorly in league play. To strengthen the team and increase attendance, the corporation bought "Wildman" Marrs, who had a national reputation for rough and tough play. During a hard-fought game, "Wildman" intentionally threw his stick at an opponent, missed him, and hit a spectator seated in the front row, knocking out several teeth. The spectator sued the Frigid Hockey Corporation. The evidence revealed that 10–20 spectators each year were injured in the arena from flying pucks or hockey sticks. Decision?

Chapter 28

RELATIONSHIP BETWEEN AGENT AND THIRD PARTIES

A. LIABILITY OF AGENT

There are a number of situations in which an agent may become personally liable to third persons.

1. TORTS

An agent is personally liable for any torts committed by him regardless of the liability of his principal. For example, if a truck driver negligently injures a person in a crosswalk, he is liable to the injured person even though his principal may also be liable.

The agent is liable even though he acted pursuant to his principal's directions; however, where an innocent agent is required to pay damages for such a tort, he is entitled to reimbursement from the principal.

2. CONTRACT IN NAME OF AGENT

A. UNDISCLOSED AGENCY AND UNDISCLOSED PRINCIPAL

If the agent's name appears alone on the contract without either the name of the principal or a statement of the fact of agency, the agent is personally liable.

B. DISCLOSED AGENCY AND PARTIALLY DISCLOSED PRINCIPAL

Under the Restatement of Agency and the law of nearly all of the states, where the agent signs as an agent, but does not set forth the name of his principal, the agent for such a partially disclosed principal is liable on the contract unless otherwise agreed; however, extrinsic evidence is permitted to show the intent of the parties; i. e., that the agent was not to be bound.

Other courts, e. g., California, go farther and hold the agent liable regardless of the disclosure of the agency unless the name of the principal is disclosed so that it appears *on the face of the instrument that only the principal is to be bound*; e. g., plaintiff proposed a contract to "Hotel Berry Systems", and defendant Berry wrote on the contract as follows: "Signed and accepted, B. S. Berry". The plaintiff knew that the defendant was acting only as an agent. Held, defendant was personally liable as he had signed his name without disclosure of the principal or of the fact of agency. The fact that the proposed contract was submitted to the hotel company was not enough since the contract may have intended to hold the agent as well. Otis Elevator Co. v. Berry, 28 Cal.App.2d 430, 82 P.2d 704.

After the third person has discovered the identity of the undisclosed or partially disclosed principal, he may hold either the principal or the agent on the contract, but he cannot hold them both. He has a choice; and once he has made it, he is bound by it.

3. LACK OF AUTHORITY

Every agent impliedly warrants or guarantees that he is authorized by the principal to do what he is doing. If he does not have authority to bind the principal, he is bound by the contract unless the principal ratifies it.

4. INCOMPETENCY OF PRINCIPAL

Under the majority rule, the agent does not warrant the competency of his principal; e. g., that the principal is not a minor or mentally incompetent. However, the agent has a duty to inform third persons of his principal's lack of capacity and is liable for fraud in the form of non-disclosure if he does not do so.

5. WRONGFUL RECEIPT OF MONEY

If an agent obtains a payment of money from a third person by the use of illegal methods, the agent is liable to the third person. When a third person makes an overpayment to the agent or a payment when none is due, the agent is liable to the third person when he knows that the payment was not proper.

B. LIABILITY OF THIRD PERSON

An agent who makes a contract with a third person on behalf of a disclosed principal has no right of action against the third person for breach of contract, and likewise, the third person normally has no right of action against the agent; however, there are some exceptions.

1. UNDISCLOSED AND PARTIALLY DISCLOSED PRINCIPAL

If an agent executes a contract without informing the third person of the existence of the agency and the identity of the principal, the agent may maintain an action against the third person for breach of contract. Of course if the principal asserts his rights under the contract, the rights of the agent are extinguished.

2. AGENT INTENDS TO BE BOUND

If the parties intend that the agent be bound to the contract even though the third person knew the agent was acting as an agent, the agent may bring action against the third person for breach of contract.

3. TORTS

The third person is liable for fraudulent or other wrongful acts causing injury to the agent. If the third person wrongfully injures the agent's property or person, the agent has a cause of action against him. If the third person wrongfully causes the agent to be discharged, the agent has a cause of action against him.

4. AGENT AS ASSIGNEE

When the principal has assigned or otherwise transferred his claim or right to his agent, e. g., for purpose of collecting money for the principal, the agent has a cause of action against the third person for breach of his obligation to the principal.

5. FOR INJURY TO PRINCIPAL'S PROPERTY

An agent, such as a bailee, in possession of the principal's property has a general or special interest in the property and, therefore, may maintain an action against a third person who disturbs his possession or unlawfully injures the property. The third person's liability is not merely to the extent of the agent's special interest, but is also for the full measure of damages caused by the injury, the agent being liable to account to the principal for the balance beyond his own interest.

---

1. Liability of Agent Where Principal Undisclosed

ANDERSON v. SMITH

398 S.W.2d 635 (Tex., 1966).

BATEMAN, Justice. The appellees Cole Smith and Robert Ekblad sued the appellant Hal Anderson for an amount claimed to be due them for architects' services rendered to appellant under a written contract providing for certain rates of hourly compensation. Appellant defended on the grounds (a) that the alleged contract was not with him but with a Texas corporation known as Hal Anderson, Inc., * * * The jury found in response to special issues that: (1) before appellees commenced the preparations of the plans in question Hal Anderson as an individual agreed to pay them for their services on an hourly basis; * * * and (4) the amount due them by Hal Anderson was $8,312. Appellees received judgment for this amount. We affirm.

* * * Appellees received three checks, one dated April 2, 1962 for $157.12, one dated April 27, 1962 for $2,000 and the other dated May 15, 1962 for $1,750, all of which checks bear the maker's name in print as "HAL ANDERSON, INC." followed by individual

handwritten signatures. These checks all bear appellees' endorsements by rubber stamp "For deposit only." It was not shown that either of the appellees ever saw these checks or knew how they were signed. * * *

Appellant concedes that until such time as appellees received the checks in April and May 1962, as an agent for an undisclosed principal he was personally bound by the contract, but contends that after appellees had actual knowledge of his agency, or were put upon inquiry which if pursued would have revealed such agency, only the corporation was liable.

* * * Unless the parties have agreed otherwise, a person making or purporting to make a contract with another as agent for a disclosed principal is not himself a party to the contract and is not liable thereon. * * * However, if he purports to act on his own account, but is in fact contracting on account of an undisclosed principal, or even if it be known that he is acting as an agent but the identity of his principal remains undisclosed, the agent is a party to the contract and is personally bound thereby. * * *

If the agent would avoid personal liability, the duty is on him to disclose his principal; it is not upon the party with whom the agent deals to discover the principal. * * *

The agent is not relieved from personal liability merely because the person with whom he dealt had a means of discovering that the agent was acting in a representative capacity. "Knowledge of the real principal is the test, and this means actual knowledge, not suspicion." * * * There is no hardship in the rule of liability against agents. They always have it in their own power to relieve themselves, and when they do not, it must be presumed that they intend to be liable. * * *

If an agent who negotiates a contract in behalf of his principal would avoid personal liability, the burden is upon him to disclose his agency to the other contracting party. And his disclosure must include not only the fact that he is an agent, but also the identity of his principal. * * *

Applying these well settled principles of law to the facts of this case leads us to the inescapable conclusion that, since it was never established that appellees had actual knowledge that appellant was acting as agent for the corporation, if in fact he was, appellees were entitled to recover from appellant the amounts earned by them under the schedule of hourly rates of pay agreed upon between them. * * *

The judgment, being correct, is

Affirmed.

2. *Liability of Principal where Agency Disclosed*

GUILLORY v. COURVILLE

158 So.2d 475 (La., 1963).

CULPEPPER, Judge. This is a suit on an open account. From an adverse judgment the plaintiff appeals.

The substantial issue is whether defendant has proved his defense that he was acting as a disclosed agent of a corporation.

* * * There is no dispute as to the law. An agent is responsible to those with whom he contracts when he does not disclose that he is acting as an agent. * * *

Furthermore, the special defense of agency, cannot be proved by the mere testimony of defendant. He must be corroborated by other evidence. * * *

The facts show that in January of 1958 the defendant, Claude Courville, and several other parties formed a corporation known as "Basile Flying Service, Inc.", domiciled in Evangeline Parish, Louisiana, for the purpose of engaging in the business of providing flying services to farmers. This concern purchased gasoline from the plaintiff at various times, from February, 1958 down through July of 1959, on an open account. Although occasionally delinquent, the account was paid except for the sum of $1,834.48 for purchases made during the period July 4, 1959 through July 30, 1959. Plaintiff's statements of account were addressed to "Basile Flying Service."

Plaintiff testified that he did not know the business was incorporated and that he was relying on the credit of defendant, with whom he had done satisfactory business before. Defendant testified that he personally told plaintiff before the purchases in question were made, that the business was incorporated. At least one other witness corroborated defendant in this respect. Furthermore, several checks received by plaintiff's office, in payment of previous amounts on this open account, were clearly marked "Basile Flying Service, Inc.", although plaintiff denied seeing any of these checks. * * *

The record amply supports the following finding of facts by the district judge:

> "The court is of the opinion that plaintiff was informed by the defendant and other stockholders of the corporation of the fact that he was doing business with the corporation; that plaintiff cashed checks from the corporation; that an account was opened for the corporation and a credit check was made on the corporation. It is further the opinion of the court that the present action against defendant is a result of plaintiff's inability to effect collection against the corporation to whom the gasoline was originally billed or charged.

The court is of the opinion that no action of defendant in this matter created a personal obligation toward plaintiff."

* * *

For the reasons assigned the judgment appealed is affirmed.

Affirmed.

PROBLEMS

1. P employs A to manage an apartment building and keep it in repair. A manages the building but does not keep it in good repair, and as a result, an invitee is injured when part of the building falls on him. The invitee brings action against A. Decision?

2. A ordered 40 barrels of olives from T, but did not disclose that he was acting for P, although this became known later. T brings action against A for payment. Decision?

3. P gives false information to A, and A makes representations based thereon to T reasonably believing them to be true. T brings action against A for fraud. Decision?

4. A contract was put on the letterhead of a corporation principal and signed "The Feldheym Co., Inc. *Dave Schwebel*". T brings action against Dave Schwebel personally. T contends that Schwebel did not indicate by his signature that he was acting only as an agent and that he should have used the word "by" before his signature. Schwebel contends that he was acting only as an agent and that this fact is easily inferred from the letterhead and from the name of the company before the signature. Decision?

5. A, without authority and pretending to act for P, an infant, purchases goods from T who sends them to P. P refuses the goods and informs T that he is an infant. T brings action against A for damages. Decision?

6. T writes a letter to P informing P that A is a communist. This is not true as T knows. As a result of the letter, P discharges A. A brings suit against T for damages for the discharge. Decision?

7. Dawson contracted to buy a machine for the DP Corporation. The corporation preferred to remain as an undisclosed principal, so Dawson agreed to take title to the machine in his own name. The seller refused to perform the contract, so Dawson brings suit in his own name as if he were the principal. Decision?

8. Luke was fired by the ABC Company because of arguments he had with the sales manager. Shortly thereafter, Luke visited the XYZ Company, one of the accounts he had serviced for the ABC Company, and collected $250 which was due the ABC Company. Luke absconded with the money. No notice had been given to XYZ Company concerning Luke's discharge. ABC Company sues XYZ Company for the $250. Decision?

9. Bates Co. made a valid contract with Roy whereunder Roy was to sell Bates' goods on commission for one year. Roy made satisfactory sales for four months and was about to close an unusually large order when Bates Co. suddenly and without notice revoked Roy's authority to sell. Can Roy continue to sell Bates' goods to customers for the balance of the year?

10. Paul instructed Albert, his agent, to purchase a quantity of hides. Albert bought the hides from Terry on Albert's account and then delivered the hides to Paul. Terry then learned that Paul was the principal and sent the bill for the hides to Paul, who gave Albert the money to pay Terry. Albert absconds with the money. Terry sued both Albert and Paul for the purchase price. Decision?

Part 6

PARTNERSHIPS

Chapter 29

INTRODUCTION

A. NATURE OF PARTNERSHIPS

1. IN GENERAL

When a person starts a business, he is faced with a choice as to what type of business organization he should use; e.g., a sole proprietorship, partnership, or corporation. If he has sufficient money to get started, he will probably use the sole proprietorship because this form gives him absolute control of the operation of the business, and he receives all of the profits. However, if he has insufficient funds, he will probably have to choose between a partnership and a corporation.

A *partnership* is an agreement between two or more persons to carry on a business for profit (see Uniform Partnership Act, Appendix B). A *corporation* is an artificial legal being created by the government and endowed with certain powers; it is treated in the law as a separate person or legal entity separate and distinct from the shareholders who are the owners of the corporation. Following is a chart which indicates the main differences between a partnership and a corporation.

	PARTNERSHIP	*CORPORATION*
1.	Created by agreement.	Created by statutory authorization.
2.	Is not a legal, separate entity, in most states.	Is a legal entity separate and distinct from its owners; i. e., is a legal person for the ownership of property and appearance as a party to litigation.
3.	Each partner is subject to unlimited liability for the debts, contracts, and torts of the other partners arising out of the partnership business.	Shareholders not liable for the debts of the corporation.

	PARTNERSHIP	CORPORATION
4.	A partner's interest is not transferable without the consent of all of the other partners.	Shares of stock are freely transferable.
5.	Each partner has a direct and equal voice in the management of the business.	Management indirect through elected directors.
6.	The partnership is terminated by the agreement, or by the death, bankruptcy or withdrawal of a partner.	May have perpetual existence.
7.	Each partner pays an income tax on his share of the net profits whether distributed or not.	Corporation pays an income tax on net profits, and the shareholders pay an income tax on the dividends they receive. There can be a tax advantage depending on the amount of net profits distributed and the shareholder's tax bracket.

2. ELEMENTS OF A PARTNERSHIP

The elements of a partnership are:

a. an association (joining together),

b. of two or more persons having legal capacity (includes individuals, partnerships, corporations, and other associations as defined in the Uniform Partnership Act, Section 2),

c. to carry on a business (includes every trade, occupation, or profession),

d. for the purpose of making profits (profit sharing is the prima facie test of a partnership),

e. as co-owners of the business.

3. CREATION

A partnership may be created by an oral agreement except where it must be in writing due to the Statute of Frauds; e. g., most courts hold that if the partnership is to continue for more than one year, or it will buy or sell real estate, the partnership agreement must be in writing.

Even though an oral partnership agreement is usually valid, it is desirable that the agreement be in writing to avoid subsequent disputes as to mutual rights and duties.

An agreement to form a partnership may be made between parties; however, such an agreement does not of itself create a partnership; nor is a partnership created by the advancement by one party of his agreed share of the capital. Persons who have entered into a contract to become partners at a future time do not become partners until the agreed time has arrived.

B. FICTITIOUS NAME

Statutes frequently require the registration and publication of certificates setting forth the true names and addresses of the members of partnerships and preclude the use by a partnership of a fictitious name or of a designation which does not show the names of all the partners unless the certificate is filed. This can be done through the local newspaper.

The purpose of the requirement is to make a public record of the individuals in the partnership for the benefit of those who deal with the partnership.

C. PARTNERSHIP BY ESTOPPEL

One who holds himself out as a partner, or knowingly allows himself to be held out as a partner, becomes liable as such to those who deal with the firm in the belief that he is a partner. A partnership by estoppel is similar to an agency created by estoppel covered in Part 5.

D. JOINT VENTURE

A joint venture, or joint adventure, is similar to a partnership in that its members associate together as co-owners of a business enterprise, however, a partnership is usually intended to continue for a definite or indefinite period as a continuing business, while a joint venture is formed for a single transaction or single series of transactions, not requiring the entire attention of the participants, and thus is more limited in scope and duration. An example of a joint venture is an agreement between an owner of lots and a building contractor to build houses for sale and a division of the profits.

The relationship between the members in a joint venture are governed by the rules applicable to partners; e. g., Uniform Partnership Act applied to dissolution; there is a fiduciary duty to account for profits and joint property; there is a power of representation within the scope of the business; profits earned are taxable income to the members whether or not distributed; tort of one member committed in furtherance of joint enterprise causes all other members to be liable.

E. LIMITED PARTNERSHIP

A limited partnership is a statutory form of association in which there is no personal liability on the part of the limited partner. It consists of general partners who manage the business and have the same liability as in an ordinary partnership, and of limited or special partners who take no part in the management. The limited partners share in the profits but do not share losses beyond their capital investment. Limited partnership acts have been enacted in all states. Most states have enacted the Uniform Limited Partnership Act.

A limited partnership is not created by a mere informal agreement as is possible with a general partnership. It is created by a formal proceeding which must follow the statute. For example, the associates must sign, file, and record a certificate which must set forth the partnership name, charter, and location of business, the term to carry on the business, amount, and character of contributions by special or limited partners, the share of profits or compensation of each limited partner, and methods for changing personnel and continuing business after retirement of a general partner.

Limited partnerships have not been used extensively since a corporation offers a more stable and permanent form of association.

F. UNINCORPORATED ASSOCIATION

Social clubs, political parties, and fraternal organizations are common examples of unincorporated associations. No particular form of organization is required. The purpose of the organization is nonprofit. A member is not liable for the debts of the association unless he authorized or ratified the particular act which created the liability.

G. COOPERATIVE

A cooperative is a union of individuals formed for the prosecution in common of some productive enterprise, the profits being shared in accordance with the capital or labor contributed by each. Common examples of cooperatives are farmers, laborers or small capitalists. In many states, statutes regulate cooperatives. In the absence of statute, the cooperative is similar to an unincorporated association in that the rights and liabilities of the members are the same.

H. PARTNERSHIP PROPERTY

1. IN GENERAL

It is frequently important, especially when creditors of a partner are involved or upon dissolution, to ascertain exactly what property constitutes partnership property and what constitutes property of the individual partner in order to ascertain the rights of the partners and the creditors to specific property.

What constitutes partnership property is ascertained from the agreement of the partners, from their conduct, and from the purpose for and the way in which the property is used in the partnership business. The Uniform Partnership Act states that all property originally brought into the partnership or subsequently acquired by purchase or otherwise on account of the partnership is partnership property; and unless a contrary intention appears, property acquired with partnership funds is partnership property (U.P.A., Section 8(1) (2)).

Anything which is a proper subject of ownership may be partnership property. Examples of partnership property are: cash, land, goods, the rendition of personal services, corporate stock, a seat on the stock exchange, an insurance policy on the life of a partner, and a patent.

2. GOOD WILL

In the absence of an express or implied agreement to the contrary, good will is a partnership asset. Good will means the favor the owner of the business has won from the public and the probability that all customers will continue their patronage. It means every advantage that has been acquired by a proprietor in carrying on his business. Good will includes the right to use the established firm name. Whether or not good will exists as a partnership asset in any particular case depends on the particular facts and circumstances in each case. One test for determining whether or not good will exists is whether a reasonable man would pay anything for it (Spalding v. Spalding's Administrator, 248 Ky. 259, 58 S.W.2d 356).

3. CROPS

Crops growing on partnership land are considered partnership property if that is the express or implied agreement of the partners.

4. PARTNERSHIP CAPITAL

The capital of the partnership is a monetary figure which represents the total of the sums contributed by the partners as permanent investments. It represents a fixed amount which the partnership is obligated to return to the partners at the time of dissolution. Undivided profits which one of the partners may permit to be accumulated in the business do not become part of the capital. Nor do loans made by a partner to the partnership become part of the capital.

It is important for partners to make it clear whether contributions to the partnership are to become partnership property or are to remain the individual's property. This is because creditors of the partnership have first claim on the partnership property, and the creditors of the individual partner have first claim on the individual's property. Also, on dissolution it is important to be able to distinquish the property.

5. TITLE TO PARTNERSHIP PROPERTY

A. Personal Property

A partnership may hold and transfer title to personal property in the name of the partnership, whether the name is fictitious or consists of the names of the partners.

B. Real Property

Under the Uniform Partnership Act, which has been adopted by 44 states, real property may be acquired in the partnership name, whether it is fictitious or not. Title acquired in the partnership name must be conveyed in the partnership name.

Whenever real property is acquired by the partnership for partnership purposes, the rule of "out and out" conversion applies, which converts the real property to personalty for all purposes, including descent and distribution.

6. RIGHTS OF PARTNERS IN PARTNERSHIP PROPERTY

A partner is a co-owner with his partners of specific partnership property; e. g., the factory, equipment, trucks, etc. In the absence of an agreement to the contrary between the partners, each partner has an equal right with his partners to possess specific partnership property for partnership purposes; however, he has no right to possess such property for any other purpose without consent of his partners.

7. ASSIGNABILITY

A partner may sell his interest in the assets of the partnership to a third person; however, such a transfer does not pass the title of the partnership in the assets but only the interest of the individual partner. The assignee does not become a member of the firm due to the highly personal nature of a partnership; thus, he is not entitled to interfere in the management of the partnership business, nor to inspect the partnership books, nor to require any information regarding partnership transactions. He is only entitled to receive the profits to which the assignor would otherwise be entitled.

8. EXECUTION

A partner's right in specific partnership property is not subject to execution unless it is a claim against the entire partnership. In other words, a personal creditor of a particular partner cannot have that partner's interest in the partnership attached and sold to pay what is owed. The remedy of a personal creditor of a partner is to attempt to reach other assets of the partner; or if the creditor desires to proceed against partnership property, he should get a *charging order* under which a receiver will be appointed to collect from the partnership the share of profits of the debtor-partner. The U.P.A., Section 28, provides that the creditor can get a charging order whereby a receiver is appointed and the partner's interest in the profits and in the corpus upon dissolution is applied to satisfy the judgment. If the partnership is a partnership at will (no definite time limit), a dissolution can be brought about immediately.

9. DEATH OF A PARTNER

On the death of a partner, his right (not ownership) in specific partnership property vests in the surviving partner or partners, except where the deceased was the last surviving partner in which case his right in such property vests in his legal representative. This is to prevent the executor of the deceased's estate from coming into the partnership and taking custody of the deceased partner's interest, which would probably cause confusion and difficulty. The surviving partners do not become the owners of the deceased partner's interest. They merely have the right of exclusive possession during the period that the partnership is liquidated and the net assets distributed to the partners, including the representative of the deceased partner. The liquidation of the partnership and distribution of the net assets must be done immediately after death of one of the partners in the absence of an agreement to the contrary.

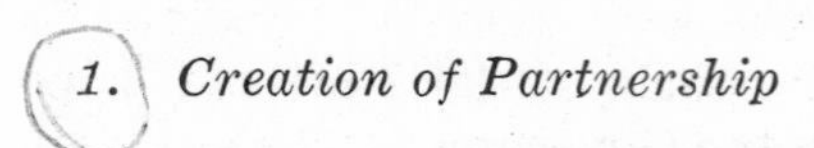

1. *Creation of Partnership*

ADAMS v. UNITED STATES

328 F.Supp. 228 (D.C.Neb., 1971).

RICHARD E. ROBINSON, Chief Judge.

* * *

On April 18, 1969, the defendant levied upon a bank account located in the First West Side Bank, Omaha, Nebraska, and as a result of this levy obtained $5,747.28. * * * This bank account was in the name of Ralph's Body Shop and was levied upon in order to satisfy a tax lien that had been levied against a business known as Ralph's Body Shop.

The tax liability for which the levy was made was for withholding and social security taxes and unemployment insurance that was withheld from the Body Shop's employees but not remitted to the Government. * * *

Prior to this levy plaintiff and a Ralph Wolff [hereinafter Wolff] had entered into a business arrangement. In accordance with this agreement plaintiff provided Wolff with a shop in which Wolff carried on a body shop business. Plaintiff paid all expenses except for the wages of employees and the monies that were left over after these expenses were split between plaintiff and Wolff. Wolff was responsible for paying the wages of employees out of his percentage. Accordingly, it was the responsibility of Wolff to pay for the employees' taxes which were not remitted to the Government. Initially, the arrangement called for plaintiff to receive 30% of the monies left after expenses and Wolff to receive 70%. These percentages were periodically adjusted so that at the time of the levy plaintiff's cut was 15% and Wolff's was 85%.

The initial capital for this venture was put up by a Mr. Richard Rogers [hereinafter Rogers]. He was referred to at the trial as a "silent partner" of plaintiff. Rogers put up $1000.00 which was used to set up the business. Rogers and plaintiff had an agreement whereby they would split fifty-fifty the monies realized from plaintiff's percentage of profits from Ralph's Body Shop.

Wolff, in addition to being responsible for the hiring of all help was also the shop foreman. He used the same tax numbers for this business as he had previously used in a similar venture.

The business was in operation from June 19, 1967, until February of 1969. During this period of time the total profit credited to Adams and his partner Rogers was $6,911.42, or $3,455.76 each. Of this amount they withdrew a total of $1600–$800 apiece. The rest was allowed to remain with the First West Side Bank account for use in the business. Both plaintiff and Rogers reported on their 1968 federal income tax returns the $3,455.76 credited to them. * * *

At the time of the levy there was $5,747.28 in the First West Side account. On the basis of the aforesaid, I have concluded that this sum levied on by the Government was not money of the deficient taxpayer, Ralph's Body Shop, but was the personal assets of the plaintiff, Robert Adams. Adams held this amount on behalf of himself and his silent partner, Rogers.

I have further concluded that plaintiff and Ralph Wolff were partners in the business known as Ralph's Body Shop. In reaching this conclusion I have carefully examined the relationship between plaintiff and Wolff and have considered the many cases in this Circuit and in other courts in determining the tests used by courts in determining the existence of a partnership.

It has been frequently stated that the existence of a partnership is a matter of contract, and that no particular form of contract is necessary to create the entity known as a partnership.

* * *

Although no one test is controlling the tests that have been found indicative of the existence of a partnership are set forth in Volume 6 of Mertens, § 35.03 p. 21. Therein the tests are stated as follows:

1. Mutual interest in profits,
2. Mutual liability, joint and several, for debts and loss of capital,
3. Mutual agency and responsibility in the conduct of the business,
4. Common contribution and ownership of the partnership property,
5. The rendition of services by all partners,
6. The nonalienability of an interest in the business.

The plaintiff and Ralph Wolff had an agreement to share in the profits of the business. Also said men were mutually liable for the debts of the enterprise. Here the liability was several. Plaintiff was responsible for the rent of the building and for equipment and Wolff was liable for the wages of any employees of the venture. There was also mutual responsibility and rendition of services by plaintiff and Wolff in the conduct of the business. Plaintiff testified that he recruited business for several months and was paid by Wolff from monies from Wolff's percentage cut of the business. Plaintiff was responsible for collecting all monies for services rendered by the business. Further his purchasing of equipment and supplies was a dividing of the services. Wolff was responsible for all repairs performed in the shop. There was also common contribution to and ownership of partnership property. Wolff testified that he used his own mechanics tools in the business and as previously pointed, plaintiff furnished all supplies and equipment.

Wolff testified at trial that he believed he was in a partnership with the plaintiff.

* * *

When plaintiff reported the income from this business on his 1968 tax return, he reported it as "undistributed share of profit" under the heading "INCOME OR LOSSES FROM PARTNERSHIP, ESTATES OR TRUSTS, ETC." I realize of course that this reporting of income as partnership profits is not controlling, but simply evidence of the intention of the parties.

Further plaintiff carried the bank account upon which the Government levied in the name of Ralph's Body Shop. Here it is obvious to me that the plaintiff and Wolff set up a business venture, wherein plaintiff provided everything but labor, and provided for this expense by allowing Wolff a large percentage of the monies left over after paying for supplies, equipment and rent.

No doubt, the employees hired by Wolff looked to all the assets as security for payment of their salaries. If I were to hold that the arrangement here under consideration did not constitute a partnership then businessmen would be limited only by their imagination in setting up liability-free arrangements.

It is now necessary to determine whether a lien filed against the property of a partnership is also a lien on the personal property of an individual partner and whether the Government may levy on said property. * * *

* * *

I am aware that one partner is not liable for the tax liability of another partner. However, I have concluded that the tax liability that was owed was the joint responsibility of plaintiff and Wolff notwithstanding the involved arrangement that existed between said parties.

* * *

[Judgment for Defendant.]

---

2. *Partnership by Estoppel*

CALADA MATERIALS CO. v. COLLINS

184 Cal.App.2d 250, 7 Cal.Rptr. 374 (1960).

VALLÉE, Justice. Appeal by defendant R. W. Walker from an adverse judgment in an action for the value of oil well drilling materials alleged to have been sold by plaintiff to defendants M. H. Collins and R. W. Walker. * * *

Plaintiff delivered mud and mud materials in connection with the drilling of two oil wells, Higdon No. 3 and C & W No. 1. Defendant concedes he is liable for an unpaid balance of $5,338.21 plus interest for materials furnished by plaintiff for Higdon No. 3. He denies he is responsible for any part of $5,795.28 for materials furnished by plaintiff for C & W No. 1. * * *

The court found that at all times mentioned in the complaint defendants Collins and Walker were doing business as a partnership under the firm name of Collins and Walker. * * * Collins and Walker testified the relationship between them was the same as to both wells. Plaintiff furnished the materials for both wells.

* * * On one occasion Walker, speaking of the lease on which C & W No. 1 was drilled, said "he was a partner with Collins and backing him and anything Collins did he was with him as long as it was all right with Mr. Collins." When Walker signed the drilling contract for C & W No. 1 he was asked, "You are partners in the deal, aren't you?" Walker replied, "Yes." During the drilling of C & W No. 1 there were signs on the rig and on trailers around the site reading, "Collins-Walker, C & W No. 1." On several occasions Collins introduced Walker as his partner with respect to C & W No. 1. Walker told plaintiff's manager that he and Collins were partners in C & W No. 1 and that plaintiff would get part of the money, if not all of it, in a few days and that Collins would pay him. * * *

A partnership need not be evidenced by a writing. It may be oral. * * *

And where there is no writing evidencing the agreement, the existence of a partnership may be evidenced by the conduct of the parties. * * *

Whether the acts and conduct of Walker were sufficient to lead plaintiff to believe he was a copartner and assumed responsibility as such was a question of fact for the trial court to determine from the evidence and the inferences to be drawn therefrom. * * *

Judgment affirmed.

---

3. Nature of Limited Partnership

BROWN v. BROWN

15 Ariz.App. 333, 488 P.2d 689.

DONOFRIO, Judge. William D. Plaster and Walter C. Brown commenced this litigation to dissolve a partnership in which they claimed to be limited partners and to obtain a distribution of the partnership assets. * * *

The pertinent facts are as follows. The parties to this action executed a certificate of limited partnership under the name of Ponderosa Land and Investment Company on or about May 1, 1960, for the purpose of subdividing 320 acres of land near Flagstaff, Arizona, to be sold as lots for summer homes. The plaintiffs were designated therein as two of the limited partners, and G. Harold Brown, defendant-appellee, (herein referred to as defendant) as the general partner. (It should be noted that plaintiff Walter C. Brown and defendant G. Harold Brown are not related.) After the instant action was commenced, the parties stipulated on February 3, 1966, that the matter be referred to a master for a certified audit. * * *

* * *

Plaintiffs contend that the defendant was not entitled to a salary subsequent to the act of dissolution. Plaintiffs argue that the dissolution occurred in September 1962, the date plaintiff Brown was excluded from the partnership, and that defendant was not entitled to a salary allowance through April 1965, the date the receiver was appointed. We do not agree.

The partnership dissolution did not occur at the time the limited partner was excluded from the partnership affairs. It is true that a general partnership dissolves when any partner ceases to be associated with the carrying on of the partnership. A limited partnership, however, is not affected in the same manner. The disassociation of a limited partner does not by itself dissolve the partnership.

* * * In September 1962, at the time plaintiff became disassociated, the partnership was viably functioning; the defendant, as general partner, was offering his services to the partnership and was entitled to remuneration for these services.

* * *

Finally, plaintiffs argue that the trial court erred in finding a limited partnership to be in existence. Plaintiffs contend that the limited partnership was never formed because the certificate of limited partnership was neither sworn to nor recorded as required by A.R.S. § 29–302. However, A.R.S. § 29–302, subsec. B states that a limited partnership is formed if there has been substantial compliance in good faith with the requirements of the statute.

The question is one of first impression in this State. New Mexico has decided this issue and reached what we believe to be a logical analysis. The cases * * * state the main purpose in requiring registration regulations is to limit the liability of limited partners. The certificate requirement is to inform third persons they are dealing with a special partnership, one in which certain partners have limited liability. It is simply a protection to third persons. The cases further state that where neither the rights of third persons nor a partner's claim of limited liability is involved, the failure to record should not affect the existence of a limited partnership as far as the parties are concerned. The parties are presumed to have had knowledge of the content of the certificate and should be bound by their contractual acts. In the present case the plaintiffs contracted to form a limited partnership and held themselves out to the community as limited partners. They are thereby estopped because of their actions to assert that, between themselves, a limited partnership was never formed.

The judgment of the trial court is affirmed [for accounting and setting fees.]

4. *Charging Order and Execution*

TUPPER v. KROC

494 P.2d 1275 (Nev., 1972).

BATJER, Justice. Lloyd G. Tupper, appellant and Ray A. Kroc, respondent, entered into three limited partnerships for the purpose of holding title to and leasing parcels of real estate. Tupper was the general partner, Kroc was the limited partner and each held a fifty percent interest.

Kroc filed an action alleging that Tupper had mismanaged and misappropriated funds from these partnerships and requested that they be dissolved and that a receiver be appointed. Pending the final outcome of that action the trial court appointed a receiver to manage the three business organizations. Prior to the date on which the complaint for dissolution had been filed, Tupper had on several occasions been unable to pay his share of the partnerships' obligations. Kroc on those occasions personally contributed the total amounts owed by the partnerships, and in return accepted interest bearing notes from Tupper in amounts equal to one-half of the partnerships' debts paid by him. Kroc thereafter filed an action against Tupper to recover on those notes and was awarded a summary judgment in the amount of $54,609.02.

In an effort to collect on that judgment, Kroc filed a motion requesting the district court to charge Tupper's interest in the partnerships with payment of the judgment and for the sale of Tupper's interest to satisfy the judgment. On June 12, 1969, a charging order was entered directing the sheriff to sell all of Tupper's "right, title and interest" in the three partnerships and to apply the proceeds against the unsatisfied amount of the judgment. Tupper was served with notice of the sale, but he took no action to redeem his interest. The sale was held on June 27, 1969, and Kroc purchased Tupper's interest for $2,500.

Kroc filed a motion to terminate the receivership on March 12, 1970, contending that he was the sole owner of the partnerships and that the need for a receiver had ceased. On May 18, 1970, the appellants filed an objection to the respondents' motion to terminate the receivership, and a motion to set aside the sale conducted pursuant to the charging order. The trial court denied the appellants' motion to set aside the sale, and granted the respondents' motion to terminate the receivership and discharge the receiver. It is from these two orders that this appeal is taken.

* * *

The charging order was properly entered by the district court against Tupper's interest in the three partnerships. * * * The district court also was authorized, in aid of the charging order, to make all orders and directions as the case required. Pursuant to the provisions of this statute the district court was authorized to appoint a receiver to act as a repository for Tupper's share of the profits and surplus for the benefit of Kroc, or as the court did hear order the sale of Tupper's interest.

* * *

The appellants' contention that the price paid by Kroc for Tupper's interest in the three partnerships is inadequate, is without merit. The mode for determining the value of Tupper's interest in the partnerships was by a public sale. * * * The fair market value of $2,500 was established by Kroc's bid at the sheriff's sale. The respondents were under no duty or obligation to support or justify that price and the entire burden was upon the appellants to prove its inadequacy. Thus it became a question of fact to be determined by the trial judge who heard the testimony and observed the witnesses.

* * *

Finally the appellants contend that because Tupper retained an equity in the partnerships' business and assets, the district court erred when it discharged the receiver. Unfortunately for the appellants this is not true. After Kroc bought all of Tupper's interest in the partnerships, i. e. all of his right and title to the profits and surplus, Kroc was entitled to all of the profits and all of the surplus. "Surplus" is the excess of assets over liabilities. * * * After the sale Tupper had no immediate or future rights to any profits or surplus or any equity whatever in the partnership property, and therefore he had no valid reason to insist on a continuation of the receivership.

Although as a matter of law the respondents were entitled to have the receivership terminated and the receiver discharged, the wisdom of that request, short of the dissolution of the partnerships, is questionable for as soon as the receiver was discharged Tupper had the authority under NRS Ch. 87, as well as the partnerships' agreements to assert his right to participate in the management. By purchasing Tupper's interest in the partnerships Kroc did not divest Tupper of his other property rights.

The receiver was appointed at the request of Kroc, now Tupper wants the receiver to be reappointed to protect Tupper as a general partner from liability that might be incurred through excessive partnership debts. At a glance it might seem that Tupper's fears have some merit. However, as a matter of law, at the moment the receiver was discharged Tupper's right to participate in the management of the partnerships was restored, and as the general partner he would, at least theoretically, be able to prevent the partnerships from incurring liabilities in excess of assets.

The orders of the district court from which these appeals have been taken are affirmed.

PROBLEMS

1. A, B, and C agree that they will form a partnership, but that C will not become a partner until he is discharged from the army which will be in one year. In the meantime, C lends the partnership $5,000.00 and agrees to take 5% of the profits as interest on the loan. A tells T, without C's knowledge, that C is a partner of the firm. T, relying on this information, sells the firm goods on credit. Six months later, the firm becomes insolvent. T brings action against C for the debt still due. Decision?

2. Defendant, a friend of the members of a partnership, was present when the partners requested goods on credit from the plaintiff and when, at the same time, they told plaintiff that defendant was a partner. Although defendant heard the statement, he remained silent. Plaintiff brings action for the goods against defendant. Decision?

3. A and B are partners in the garage business. They invest part of the profits from their business in land taking title in their names as tenants in common. The land becomes very valuable, but their business becomes insolvent. B dies leaving a wife. Creditors of the partners seek the land. B's wife and A also claim the land. Decision?

4. A, B, and C are partners. Nothing is said in the partnership agreement regarding the assignability of a partner's interest. C and A get into a dispute after which A sells his entire interest to T, a responsible and wealthy business man who is an expert in the business of the partnership. B and C refuse to permit T to participate in the management of the partnership business. Decision?

5. A and B are partners at will. C, a judgment creditor of B, wants to attach B's interest in the partnership property to collect his judgment. What advice would you give C?

6. A, B, C, and D, residents of Illinois, were partners doing business under the trade name of Morning Glory Nursery. A owned one-third interest and B, C and D, two-ninths each. The partners acquired three tracts of land in Illinois for the purpose of the partnership. Two of the tracts were acquired in the names of the partners, "trading and doing business as Morning Glory Nursery." The third was acquired in their individual names without the trade name appearing on the deed. B died intestate, leaving his wife and one son as only heirs. The widow and son sue to have B's interest in the real property transferred to them by descent. Decision?

7. Bolden, a minor, and Allen, an adult, formed a partnership for the purpose of purchasing and operating a machine-shop. They purchased the shop from plaintiff and each contributed $5,000 toward the purchase price and gave the plaintiff a note for $5,000 for the balance. The project was unsuccessful and the partnership became insolvent. Plaintiff brought an action against the partnership and Bolden and Allen individually to recover the $5,000 due on the unpaid note. Bolden claims that, as a minor, he has no liability. Decision?

8. Mather, a toy manufacturer, employed Stark as a salesman, agreeing to pay him a salary of 20% of the profits of the business. The business showed a loss of $1,500 at the end of the year. Mather claimed that since Stark was to get 20% of the profits, he was also liable for 20% of the losses. Is Mather correct?

9. Penner, Cory, and Sheldon decided to ask for contributions of food, clothing, and money from the businessmen in their town to be used for the poor. They considered themselves to be partners in the work and so identified themselves to others. All contributions made to the group were distributed by them as soon as received. Sheldon presented to Penner and Cory a bill of $25 for transportation and postage expense and insisted that, as partners, they must pay their proportionate shares. Are Penner and Cory partners with Sheldon in this enterprise?

10. Price and Mulford formed a partnership for the manufacture and sale of low-priced clocks. Price contributed $5,000, and Mulford contributed $10,000. The articles of copartnership made no provision for the division of profits. At the end of one year, the profits amounted to $8,000. How should the profits be distributed?

Chapter 30

POWERS, RIGHTS, DUTIES, AND LIABILITIES OF PARTNERS

A. POWERS OF PARTNERS

---

1. MANAGEMENT OF THE BUSINESS

Decisions on business matters of the partnership are made by the partners. "All partners have equal rights in the management and conduct of the partnership business." (U.P.A., Section 18(e)). Usually, decisions are made by majority vote.

2. POWER OF INDIVIDUAL PARTNER

Every partner is an *agent* of the partnership for the purpose of carrying on the partnership business. An individual partner may have express authority to act for the partnership through the partnership agreement or because of a majority vote of the partners. In addition, a partner has implied authority to do those acts which are customarily done in his partnership or which are usual for similar partnerships. The agreement of the partnership determines its nature and scope of the business. The agreement of the partnership can only be changed by the unanimous consent of the partners. If all of the partners agree to enlarge the scope of their business, the agreement is effective and new powers are then conferred on the partners.

A. CUSTOMARY POWERS

The customary powers of a partner to bind the partnership depend on the nature of the business. The following are examples of customary powers held to bind the partnership due to the nature of the particular partnership: contracts made by a partner necessary to the transaction of business; sales of the goods of the partnership in the regular course of business with warranties usual to such sales; purchases of property within the scope of the business including purchases on credit; hiring and firing of employees; obtaining or canceling insurance; borrowing money and execution of negotiable instruments in a trading partnership (a business of buying or selling for profit), but not in a non-trading partnership (e. g., lawyers, physicians, real estate business); compromising, adjusting or paying claims against the partnership, and compromising, adjusting and receiving payment for claims by the partnership.

B. Acts Not Within Apparent Authority

An act of a partner which is not apparently necessary for the carrying on of the business of the partnership in the usual way does not bind the partnership unless authorized by the other partners. Examples of acts which are not within the authority of a partner in the usual type of partnership are contracts in which the partner assumes the debt of another; payment of a separate debt of the partner with partnership property; pledging partnership property to secure a partner's separate debt; giving away partnership property; and selling part of the partnership capital.

C. Unauthorized Acts Under the U.P.A.

The U.P.A., Section 9(3), provides that a partner has no authority to perform the following acts unless authorized by the other partners or unless the other partners have abandoned the business:

(1) to make an assignment of the partnership property for the benefit of creditors; such an assignment may be avoided by the other creditors or by the other partners;

(2) to dispose of the good will of the business; e. g., a partner has no implied power to bind the partnership by a promise not to compete with a competitor;

(3) to do any other act which would make it impossible to carry on the ordinary business of the partnership; e. g., disposing of the stock of goods in one of the departments in a department store; agreeing not to compete with a competitor;

(4) to confess a judgment; e. g., one partner cannot abandon defenses in a lawsuit; one partner cannot permit a plaintiff to take a judgment without a contest since all partners should have the right to defend in court;

(5) to submit a partnership claim or liability to arbitration. It has been held that the partnership is not bound to perform an award unless all partners agreed to the submission; nor can it enforce an award against the third person.

B. RIGHTS OF PARTNERS

---

1. SHARE OF PROFITS

The partners are entitled to share the profits equally; however, the partners can provide by agreement that the profits shall be shared in unequal proportions. Losses are shared in the same proportion as profits.

2. CONTRIBUTIONS

Each partner shall be repaid his contributions, whether he made them by way of capital or later advances to the partnership property. Partners who have made advances beyond the amount of their agreed capital contributions are to be repaid such advances before anything is distributed to partners.

3. REIMBURSEMENT

The partnership must reimburse or indemnify every partner for all expenditures made and personal liabilities reasonably incurred by him in the ordinary and proper conduct of the partnership business, or for the preservation of its business or property.

4. MANAGEMENT

All partners have equal rights in the management and conduct of the business.

5. PARTNERSHIP BOOKS

Each partner shall at all times have access to and may inspect and copy any of the partnership books.

6. INFORMATION

Partners shall render on demand true and full information of all things affecting the partnership to any partner or to his legal representative. The partners not only have the right to demand information, but it is the duty of a partner to voluntarily give information when it affects the partnership; e. g., partner must voluntarily disclose interest he has in property that is being purchased by the partnership.

7. RIGHT TO AN ACCOUNT

A partner cannot sue his partner on an obligation due him by the partnership; e. g., reimbursement for expense incurred, or a loan to the partnership. Such items cannot be isolated from the partnership accounts and made the subject of a separate action unless the other partners consent to the suit. The proper remedy for an aggrieved partner is a suit in equity for an accounting, although this remedy is seldom permitted except on dissolution of the partnership. The U.P.A., Section 72, provides for this remedy stating that every partner has the right to a formal account as to partnership affairs:

a. if he is wrongfully excluded from the partnership business or from the possession of the partnership property by his co-partners;

b. if the right exists under any partnership agreement;

c. if a partner has breached a fiduciary duty (U.P.A., Section 21);

d. whenever other circumstances render it just and reasonable.

8. PARTNERSHIP PROPERTY

The rights of a partner regarding partnership property have been stated in Chapter 29, Section H, 6.

C. DUTIES OF PARTNERS

---

1. INFORMATION

The duty of a partner regarding information has been discussed in B. 6., supra.

2. ACCOUNTABILITY

Each partner must account to the partnership for any benefit, and hold as trustee for it any profits, derived by him without the consent of the other partners from any transaction connected with the partnership. The partners have a fiduciary relationship; i. e., a relationship of trust, loyalty, confidence and good faith which prohibits a partner from taking advantage of his co-partners in any transaction relating to the partnership business or of secretly profiting from the partnership business.

3. FULL TIME AND ENERGY

In the absence of an agreement to the contrary, it is the duty of each partner to give his entire time, skill, and energy to the partnership business. A partner is not entitled to compensation for his services unless there is an express or implied agreement for such payment.

4. REASONABLE CARE

A partner is under a duty to use reasonable care in the transaction of the partnership business. He is liable for any loss resulting from his failure to use reasonable care.

5. OBEDIENCE

A partner is under a contractual obligation to do all that is required of him by the partnership agreement; and if a loss results from his failure to comply with the agreement, he must indemnify the partnership.

D. LIABILITIES OF PARTNERS

1. TORT LIABILITY

The partnership is liable for any wrongful act or omission of any partner acting in the ordinary course of the partnership business with the authority of the co-partners; e. g., partner's negligence in the operation of an automobile during the course of the partnership business causing injury to a third person.

The partnership is bound by a partner's breach of trust, and the partnership must make good the loss; e. g., where one partner acting within the scope of his apparent authority receives money from a third person and applies it to his own use.

Tort liability of partners is *joint and several* whether for torts committed by a partner or by an employee of the partnership; i. e., they may be sued jointly or severally. Thus, an action may be brought against any partner without joining the others; however, a judgment against one partner is not generally regarded as *res judicata* (a matter settled by judgment) in a later action against his co-partners, especially when the co-partners were unknown to the third party at the time he brought his first action.

If a partner commits a tort while acting outside the partnership business, although the partnership is not liable in the absence of ratification, the individual partner is liable to the third party.

2. CONTRACTUAL LIABILITY

The contracts of a partner made for the partnership become the obligation of the partnership, and this is true even though the partner made the contract in his name instead of in the partnership name, as long as he was acting within the scope of his authority. However, if a partner personally borrows money and the loan is made solely on his personal credit, the fact that he uses the money for partnership purposes does not make the partnership liable for such personal loan.

Third party remedies for breach of contract by a partnership in general include damages, restitution, and specific performance.

Generally, in the absence of a statute to the contrary, the liability of the partners on a contractual obligation is *joint*. Thus, the action may be brought against the partnership *or* against *all* of the individual partners, naming them as defendants.

3. ADMISSION BY PARTNER

An admission or representation made by a partner concerning partnership business within the scope of his authority is evidence against the partnership; e. g., partner involved in automobile accident while on partnership business admitted it was his fault; the admission is evidence to hold the partnership liable. However, for the admission to be admissible against the co-partners, the making of the admission must be itself a partnership transaction; i. e., the partner must at the time be acting within the scope and course of partnership business. Thus, a partner who is on personal business when the automobile accident takes place cannot make an admission that will bind the partnership.

4. EXTENT OF PARTNER'S LIABILITY

Each partner has unlimited liability and is personally liable to the full extent of his personal assets for all obligations and liabilities incurred by the partnership.

A "silent partner", i. e., one who does not actively engage in the partnership business and is not known to be a partner to those dealing with the partnership, likewise has unlimited liability. Only a limited partner in a limited partnership can limit his liability.

An incoming partner who does not personally assume the prior debts is not personally liable for obligations existing at the time he came into the partnership, but all of the partnership assets continue to be liable including the share he purchased from the outgoing partner. However, if the incoming partner assumed the prior obligations of the partnership, he will be liable for them.

An outgoing partner continues to be liable for all partnership debts incurred prior to the transfer to the incoming partner, but not those after the transfer. The only way the outgoing partner can rid himself of prior debts is by a novation with the creditors; i. e., the creditors expressly agree to look to the incoming partner and to release the outgoing partner of all liability.

---

1. Scope of Partnership Liability

McKINNEY v. TRUCK INS. EXCHANGE

324 S.W.2d 773 (Mo.App., 1959).

STONE, Presiding Judge. Cut to the quick by the indignity inflicted upon him, a bull calf being castrated by one Davis, "sort of an expert" at such matters, rebelled and grievously injured his tormentor, by reason of which Davis filed a claim for benefits under the Missouri Workmen's Compensation Law against Paul McKinney, as employer, and Truck Insurance Exchange (hereinafter referred to as the Exchange), his alleged insurer. The Exchange theretofore had issued a "standard workmen's compensation and employers' liability policy" to "Ralph McKinney & Paul McKinney dba Acme Glass Co., 1647 St. Louis, Springfield, Missouri," as "employer," described in the policy declarations as a "co-partnership"; but, claimant Davis having been employed by Paul in connection with operation of a 167-acre farm in another county owned by Paul and his wife and Davis' castration of the calf having been wholly unrelated to the business conducted by Acme Glass Company (even though the castrated calf had wreaked as much havoc as the proverbial bull in a china closet), the Exchange insisted that its policy issued to Acme afforded no coverage to Paul with respect to his farm operation and refused to defend him in the compensation proceeding instituted by Davis, although Davis' joinder of the Exchange as a party to the proceeding necessitated a defense on its own behalf. After counsel employed by Paul personally and counsel for the Exchange, presenting a united front against their common antagonist, had concluded upon appeal to this court a successful defense of Davis' claim * * * and thus had put out of the way (if not out of mind) the castrated calf and the contentious claimant, Paul turned on the Exchange and brought the instant suit to recoup the expenses (primarily attorneys' fees) incurred by him personally in such defense. Cast in the trial court on the Exchange's motion to dismiss his petition, Paul appeals from the adverse judgment.

* * * Although other jurisdictions reflect a sharp conflict of authority as to whether or not a partnership is a legal or juristic entity separate and distinct from the individuals who compose it, * * * the courts of this state usually have regarded a partnership as a mere ideal entity with no legal existence apart from its members, and have followed the so-called aggregate or common-law theory of partnership rather than the entity theory. * * * However, the persuasive opinion of informed scholars is that the Uniform Partnership Act does not transform a partnership into a separate legal or juristic entity * * * but "adopts the common law approach with 'modifications' relating to partnership property" so that the Act "is consistent with the entity approach for the purposes of facilitating transfers of property, marshalling assets, and protecting the business operation against the immediate impact of personal involvements of the partners." * * *

But, grave danger lurks in unquestioning acceptance and unguarded application of potentially deceptive generalities; and, although our Missouri courts usually follow the aggregate or common-law theory as to partnerships, we think that it should not and cannot be announced, as an arbitrary, absolute, unqualified and unyielding rule, that under no circumstances and for no purposes may a partnership be considered and treated as an entity. We read that the partnership entity sometimes is recognized with reference to its contracts with third persons. * * *

Thus, in jurisdictions where, as in Missouri, the aggregate or common-law theory as to partnerships usually is followed, the courts have given effect to the intention of contracting parties by treating a partnership as an entity in determining and delimiting the coverage afforded by insurance policies issued to the partnership.

* * * The Exchange had no duty to defend Davis' claim under its policy obligation to defend even groundless, false or fraudulent claims against Acme Glass Company, the employer whose liability the Exchange undertook to insure, for Davis made no claim

against Acme but, from the outset, presented his claim as an employee of Paul individually and against Paul individually. * * *

The judgment for defendant is affirmed.

---

2. *Partner's Right to Management*

SUMMERS v. DOOLEY

94 Idaho 87, 481 P.2d 318 (1971).

DONALDSON, Justice. This lawsuit, tried in the district court, involves a claim by one partner against the other for $6,000. The complaining partner asserts that he has been required to pay out more than $11,000 in expenses without any reimbursement from either the partnership funds or his partner. The expenditure in question was incurred by the complaining partner (John Summers, plaintiff-appellant) for the purpose of hiring an additional employee. The trial court denied him any relief except for ordering that he be entitled to one half $966.72 which it found to be a legitimate partnership expense.

The pertinent facts leading to this lawsuit are as follows. Summers entered a partnership agreement with Dooley (defendant-respondent) in 1958 for the purpose of operating a trash collection business. The business was operated by the two men and when either was unable to work, the non-working partner provided a replacement at his own expense. In 1962, Dooley became unable to work and, at his own expense, hired an employee to take his place. In July, 1966, Summers approached his partner Dooley regarding the hiring of an additional employee but Dooley refused. Nevertheless, on his own initiative, Summers hired the man and paid him out of his own pocket. Dooley, upon discovering that Summers had hired an additional man, objected, stating that he did not feel additional labor was necessary and refused to pay for the new employee out of the partnership funds. Summers continued to operate the business using the third man and in October of 1967 instituted suit in the district court for $6,000 against his partner, the gravamen of the complaint being that Summers has been required to pay out more than $11,000 in expenses, incurred in the hiring of the additional man, without any reimbursement from either the partnership funds or his partner. After trial before the court, sitting without a jury, Summers was granted only partial relief and he has appealed. He urges in essence that the trial court erred by failing to conclude that he should be reimbursed for expenses and costs connected in the employment of extra help in the partnership business.

The principal thrust of appellant's contention is that in spite of the fact that one of the two partners refused to consent to the hiring of additional help, nonetheless, the non-consenting partner retained profits earned by the labors of the third man and therefore the non-consenting partner should be estopped from denying the need and value of the employee, and has by his behavior ratified the act of the other partner who hired the additional man.

The issue presented for decision by this appeal is whether an equal partner in a two man partnership has the authority to hire a new employee in disregard of the objection of the other partner and then attempt to charge the dissenting partner with the costs incurred as a result of his unilateral decision.

* * *

In the instant case the record indicates that although Summers requested his partner Dooley to agree to the hiring of a third man, such requests were not honored. In fact Dooley made it clear that he was "voting no" with regard to the hiring of an additional employee.

An application of the relevant statutory provisions and pertinent case law to the factual situation presented by the instant case indicates that the trial court was correct in its disposal of the issue since a majority of the partners did not consent to the hiring of the third man. I.C. § 53–318(8) provides:

> "Any difference arising as to ordinary matters connected with the partnership business may be decided by a *majority of the partners* * * *." (emphasis supplied)

* * * A careful reading of the statutory provision indicates that subsection 5 bestows *equal rights in the management and conduct of the partnership business* upon all of the partners. The concept of equality between partners with respect to management of business affairs is a central theme and recurs throughout the Uniform Partnership law, which has been enacted in this jurisdiction. Thus the only reasonable interpretation of I.C. § 53–318(8) is that business differences must be decided by a majority of the partners provided no other agreement between the partners speaks to the issues.

A noted scholar has dealt precisely with the issue to be decided.

> "* * * if the partners are equally divided, those who forbid a change must have their way." Walter B. Lindley, A Treatise on the Law of Partnership, Ch. II, § III, ¶ 24–8, p. 403 (1924).

* * *

In the case at bar one of the partners continually voiced objection to the hiring of the third man. He did not sit idly by and acquiesce in the actions of his partner. Under these circumstances it is manifestly unjust to permit recovery of an expense which was incurred individually and not for the benefit of the partnership but rather for the benefit of one partner.

Judgment affirmed. Costs to respondent.

3. *Tort Liability of Partners*

PHILLIPS v. COOK

239 Md. 215, 210 A.2d 743 (1965).

MARBURY, Judge. This is an appeal by Daniel Phillips individually, and trading as "Dan's Used Cars", one of the defendants below, from a judgment in favor of Delores Cook and Marshall Cook, her husband, plaintiffs below, entered upon the verdict of a jury in favor of the plaintiffs against the defendants, Isadore Harris and Daniel Phillips, individually and as co-partners trading as Dan's Used Cars, in the Superior Court of Baltimore City. The verdict was rendered in an action by the Cooks to recover damages for injuries sustained by them as a result of a collision involving a partnership automobile operated by Harris and bearing dealer plates issued to Dan's Used Cars by the Department of Motor Vehicles.

The Cooks sued Harris and Phillips, individually, and as co-partners trading as Dan's Used Cars. The accident in question occurred on January 7, 1960, at about 6:50 p. m., when a partnership automobile operated by Harris struck the rear of a vehicle driven by one Smith, which in turn hit an automobile operated by Delores Cook, at the intersection of Reisterstown Road and Quantico Avenue in Baltimore. Harris was on his way home from the used car lot when the accident occurred. He was using the most direct route from the partnership lot and was only five blocks from his home at the time of the incident.

In October 1959, Harris and Phillips entered into a partnership on an equal basis under the name of "Dan's Used Cars" for the purpose of buying and selling used automobiles. Phillips owned the lot and a gas station adjacent to it. He went into the partnership with Harris because the latter had the experience and money which he did not have to put into the business.

* * * It was agreed as a part of the partnership arrangement that Harris would use a partnership vehicle for transportation to and from his home. Under this agreement, he was authorized to demonstrate and sell such automobiles, call on dealers for the purpose of seeing and purchasing used cars, or go to the Department of Motor Vehicles on partnership business after leaving the lot in the evening and before returning the next day. Both Harris and Phillips could use a partnership automobile as desired.

* * * This car was titled in the name of the partnership and Phillips could have used it if he wanted to. After the accident, he objected to Harris using the dealer's tags because "he didn't want to get in any more accidents." About a week later, the partnership was terminated and Harris left the business. * * * In a case involving a partnership, the contract of partnership constitutes all of its members as agents of each other and each partner acts both as a principal and as the agent of the others in regard to acts done within

the apparent scope of the business, purpose and agreement of the partnership or for its benefit. It is clear that the partnership is bound by the partner's wrongful act if done within the scope of the partnership's business. * * * The extent of the authority of a partner is determined essentially by the same principles as those which measure the scope of an agent's authority. * * *

Here, the fact that the defendant partners were in the used car business; * * * and that Harris conducted partnership business both at the used car lot and from his home requires that the question of whether the use of the automobile at the time of the accident was in the partnership interest and for its benefit be submitted to the jury. * * *

It has been held that the language of the Uniform Partnership Act, in making all partners jointly and severally liable for tortious acts chargeable to the partnership (Code 1957, Article 73A, §§ 13 and 15), reaffirms the common law doctrine. * * * If the tortious act may reasonably be found to be done within the scope of the business of the partnership, the individual partner against whom judgment is obtained may have a right of contribution from the partnership and from the other partners, but that right does not limit the remedy of the plaintiff to proceed against the members of the partnership as individuals as well as co-partners. * * *

Judgment affirmed; Costs to be paid by appellant.

---

4. "Scope of Employment" Requirement for Tort Liability

DOWD v. WEBB

337 F.2d 93 (C.A.N.J., 1964).

KALODNER, Circuit Judge. These actions, arising out of an assault by the defendant, Bryan Webb, upon the Plaintiff, J. Patrick Dowd, with a four-pronged pitchfork, inflicting severe injuries later detailed, were brought in the District of New Jersey. * * *

At trial, the court dismissed as to Hesse, Stavola and Beacon Stables at the close of the plaintiff's case, and as to Savage at the close of all of the evidence. A judgment of default was entered against Webb in the amount of $18,677.00.

The plaintiff prosecutes these appeals claiming that the complaints against Hesse, Stavola, Beacon Stables and Savage were erroneously dismissed, and that the amount of the verdict against Webb was inadequate. * * *

The assault occurred on March 6, 1961, at Lincoln Downs Race Course in Lincoln, Rhode Island. Webb was a race horse trainer. He operated what he termed a "public stable", i. e., one in which he trained horses for more than one owner. He employed his own men to do the work and his foreman supervised it. He received $10.00 per day for training a horse plus 10 per cent of the horse's purses, if any. His services included feeding, caring and entering the horses in such races as he thought advisable. The owner paid for transportation, veterinary fees, jockey fees, blacksmith fees and his own license fee. Webb made all decisions concerning the services rendered. All equipment used was owned by him or leased to him.

Webb was assigned 14 stalls by the Lincoln Downs Race Course and he permitted Bernard Dowd, brother of the plaintiff, to use one of them to stable his horse. In return Bernard was to help Webb with his work. * * *

On the morning of March 6 Bernard came to the stables with the plaintiff who was then performing odd jobs around the stable area. Bernard noticed another groom rubbing down two horses assigned to him. When he sought to ascertain the reason from Webb, the latter expressed dissatisfaction with his work. * * *

Webb, using "vile language", grabbed Bernard's lapel or jacket, and said, "If you two so and so's don't get out of here and get your horse out of here I am going to knock the stuff out of both of you." The plaintiff said, "If you think you can do that, step in the stall here with me." As the plaintiff turned toward the stall, Webb stabbed him in the face with a pitchfork, blinding him in one eye, fracturing his nose, destroying his dental bridgework, and lacerating his face. * * *

The plaintiff premises his claim of liability against the other defendants on an alleged master-servant relationship between them and Webb, as their trainer. He contends that Savage and Webb were partners in the ownership of certain horses trained by Webb at Lincoln Downs; and that Webb's acts are imputable to Savage under partnership law. * * * We are of the opinion that the trial judge properly dismissed as to all of Webb's co-defendants, because Webb's act was a clear departure, as a matter of law, from both the alleged employment and partnership relationships, even assuming that either existed.

The general law applicable to the liability of a master for the acts of his servant is similarly applicable to the liability of one copartner for the acts of the other. * * * Generally, unless there is authority, either express or implied, to use force, an employer is not responsible vicariously for a wilful assault by his employee upon another. * * * But if a servant commits an assault upon an innocent invitee of his master, incident to the execution of his duties, the master may be held liable. * * * Thus, if a servant is entrusted with the duty of collecting money for his master and in doing so uses inordinate force, liability may follow. * * * Here, assuming that an employment or partnership relationship existed it cannot by any stretch of the imagination be said that the nature of Webb's work as a trainer of horses might possibly require the use of force. * * *

For the reasons stated the Judgment of the District Court will be affirmed.

5. *Liability of Partner on Contract*

COSTANZO v. LAWRENCE

64 Wash.2d 901, 395 P.2d 93 (1964).

WEAVER, Justice. Defendant Sam Lawrence appeals from a money judgment entered against him in the sum of $4,165.

March 15, 1959, defendants Lawrence and Harris formed a partnership to operate a livestock business to purchase, breed, feed and sell cattle. Defendant Lawrence purchased a substantial number of cattle and certain farm machinery from plaintiff. May 23, 1959, defendants entered into a written partnership agreement. Basically, it provided that Lawrence was to advance the money to purchase the cattle and Harris was to provide the expense of their care and maintenance and to do the work. * * *

A large quantity of chopped hay, which is the subject matter of this appeal, was stored on the ranch. The oral understanding concerning the hay is in dispute, but the written lease provided that the hay be "transferred, set-over and sold" to defendant Harris for $20 per ton if he exercised the option to purchase the ranch; otherwise he would have the option to pay for the hay consumed or to replace it.

Defendants' livestock venture was not successful. April 4, 1961, they terminated their partnership. About a month later defendant Harris exercised the option to purchase the ranch. He did not pay for the hay stored thereon.

Plaintiff brought this action against both defendants * * * for the value of the hay stored on the ranch in the spring of 1959.

The trial court found that the partnership was unjustly enriched to the extent of 199.5 tons of hay, having a market value of $3,990, which had been eaten by cattle *owned by the partnership* in the spring of 1959 and during the period between October 1, 1959, and May 1, 1960. * * *

The fact that plaintiff "transferred, set-over and sold" the hay to defendant Harris has no bearing on the question of whether the partnership was unjustly enriched. The fact remains that, to the extent found by the trial court, the hay was consumed by partnership cattle and the partnership was benefited. * * *

The judgment is affirmed.

6. *Extent of Partnership Liability*

HORN'S CRANE SERVICE v. PRIOR

182 Neb. 94, 152 N.W.2d 421 (1967).

WESTERMARK, J. Court sustained a general demurrer * * *, dismissed the action, and plaintiff appeals. We affirm the judgment.

Plaintiff, a seller of equipment and supplies, in two causes of action in his amended petition seeks a personal judgment against the defendants, and each of them, for liability arising out of specific sums due under a written contract with (first cause of action) and for supplies and services furnished (second cause of action) a partnership * * * comprised of the two defendants, Wendell H. Prior and Orie Cook, and one C. E. Piper, the manager * * *. The partnership * * * was formed for the purpose of operating a quarry and rock-crushing business for profit, and the written contract was entered into and the supplies and services furnished pursuant thereto. Defendants' ultimate liability for personal judgment flowed out of the partnership's * * * original liability as a separate entity in the transactions.

* * * In neither the original nor amended petition is it alleged, either directly or by inference, that the partnership * * * property was insufficient to satisfy its debts, or that there was no partnership property, and there is no allegation of dissolution or insolvency of said * * * partnership. This was fatal.

In an action seeking a personal judgment against the individual members of a partnership * * * the petition does not state a cause of action if it fails to state that there is no partnership property or that it is insufficient to satisfy the debts of the partnership * * *. However, the partnership relation is such that the separate property of a partner cannot be subjected to the payment of partnership debts until the property of the firm is exhausted. * * * Firm property must also be subjected to the payment of the firm debts before it can be applied to the debts of the individual members of the firm. * * * The partners are personally, jointly, and severally responsible for partnership liabilities. But the benefits and liabilities of a partner arise from and are the result of the partnership relation. * * *

There are several reasons for the rule. One of the most obvious is that credit having been extended to the partnership or firm, the members ought to have a right to insist that the partnership property be exhausted first. And to permit a firm creditor to by-pass the partnership property and exhaust the assets of an individual member leaving the partnership property extant, would be an obvious injustice, permit the other partners to profit at his expense, and place him in an adverse position with relation to his copartners. * * *

The judgment of the district court in dismissing the action is correct and is affirmed.

PROBLEMS

1. A and B are partners in the grocery business. A signed notes totaling $24,000.00 in the partnership name, giving as the reason for the loans that the partnership was expanding. A then disappeared, and the notes were discovered by B. The holder of the notes brings action against the partnership. Decision?

2. A and B are partners in a dairy. They purchase their feed from the Edwards Feed Mill. B made a purchase of feed on his own personal credit and charged to his individual personal account, separate from the partnership business, and executed a personal promissory note for its payment in his name alone. Edwards Feed Mill brings action against both partners on the note on the theory that A is also liable since the partnership received the benefit of the purchase. Decision?

3. A and B are partners. The creditors of the partnership threatened suit if the debt was not paid. B paid the debt in full from his own funds and then sued A in the name of the partnership for reimbursement. Decision?

4. A and B form a partnership to produce a play on a profit-sharing basis paying the author certain royalties. A concealed from B an agreement with the author whereby A was the assignee of a share of the royalties. B brings a suit in equity to make A account for a pro rata share of the royalties he received. Decision?

5. A and B are partners. By its contract terms, the partnership is to expire on Jan. 1. The partnership has a lease on some valuable property which will expire the following July 1. After the partnership expires and immediately prior to the end of the lease, A secures a new lease in his own name. B brings a suit for an accounting. Decision?

6. A and B are partners. A's son borrows an automobile owned by the partnership and while returning home from a dance has an accident. A's son admits to the plaintiff at the time of the accident that it was all his fault. Plaintiff brings action against the partnership and seeks to use the admission against the partnership. Decision?

7. A and B are partners. B attempts by peaceful means to get a tenant of the partnership to leave the premises; however, the tenant refuses to leave. B then uses unlawful force and bodily evicts the tenant from the premises. The tenant brings action for the unlawful eviction against the partnership. Decision?

8. A and B are partners. They desire to sell their business to T. A misrepresents the profits and the income of the business to T without B's knowledge. T purchases the business and then learns of the misrepresentations. T elects to affirm the contract of sale and sue the partners for fraud. B defends on the basis that he was innocent of the fraud. Decision?

9. A and B were partners. A spent most of his time fishing, hunting, and golfing while B took care of the business. Finally, B found it necessary to hire extra help to do the work that A was supposed to be doing. At the end of the fiscal year, B deducted the expense of the extra help from A's share of the profits. A sued B for the share of the profits which B deducted. Decision?

10. A, B, and C are partners. C is a silent or dormant partner. T sells goods to the partnership on credit not knowing that C is a partner. Later, the partnership becomes insolvent, and T brings action against the partnership, including C, for the debt. Decision?

Chapter 31

DISSOLUTION AND WINDING UP

A. IN GENERAL

1. DISSOLUTION

Dissolution designates the point in time when the partners cease to carry on the business together. It is the change in the relationship of the partners caused by a partner ceasing to be associated in the carrying on of the business. On dissolution, the partnership is not terminated, but continues until the winding up of the partnership business is completed.

2. WINDING UP

Winding up is the process of settling partnership affairs after dissolution. In the ordinary partnership when a partner ceases to be associated with the carrying on of the partnership business, it usually has the consequence of winding up the partnership or the formation of a new partnership to carry on the business. During the period of winding up a dissolved partnership, the partnership is still in existence. The property is still held by the partners as tenants. The partners can sue and be sued regarding partnership rights and obligations. However, the partners should not undertake new business after the dissolution, but should only liquidate and distribute the partnership property. Any new business transacted by a partner is solely for his own account.

B. CAUSES OF DISSOLUTION

1. WITHOUT VIOLATION OF AGREEMENT

a. Termination of Term or Undertaking

A partnership can be dissolved by the partnership agreement; e. g., partnership relation shall end on a certain date or on the happening of a certain condition.

b. Dissolution by Will in Partnership at Will

A partnership at will can be dissolved by the will of any partner.

c. Dissolution by Agreement

A partnership can be ended by the mutual unanimous agreement of the partners.

2. IN VIOLATION OF AGREEMENT

Any partner may dissolve the partnership at any time, even though it is in violation of the partnership agreement. This is because the partnership relationship is one of agency and, therefore, so personal that it cannot be specifically enforced. The partner who wrongfully causes a dissolution is subject to liability for damages. To prevent undue hardship on the other partners, the U.P.A., Section 38(2) (b), provides that they can buy out his interest.

3. SUPERVENING CAUSES FOR DISSOLUTION

a. Supervening Illegality

A partnership is dissolved, like any other contract, by supervening illegality; e. g., business becomes illegal.

b. Bankruptcy

A partnership is dissolved by the adjudication of bankruptcy or insolvency of the partnership, or an adjudication of bankruptcy or insolvency by one of the partners. Most courts hold that insolvency of the partnership or one of the partners without an adjudication will not dissolve the partnership.

c. Death

Death of one of the partners dissolves the partnership. In this area, it might be desirable to provide in the partnership agreement for continuation of the business on death of a partner and compensation to his estate.

d. War and Armed Conflict

Where partners are the respective citizens of the belligerent countries in a state of war or armed conflict, the partnership is dissolved, however, this does not affect contracts made prior to the hostilities.

4. DECREE OF COURT

A court may decree the dissolution of a partnership. The grounds are as follows:

a. where the circumstances render it just and equitable; e. g., insolvency of a partner; where it becomes unprofitable to carry on the business; or

b. misconduct of a partner to the extent that it is injurious to the partnership or to the other partners; e. g., misappropriation of funds; excluding other partner from possession of partnership property; or

c. incapacity of a partner to discharge his duties; e. g., insanity; or

d. dissension among the partners where it is so serious and persistent as to make the successful continuance of the partnership impractical.

C. EFFECT OF DISSOLUTION

---

1. IN GENERAL

Dissolution terminates the existence of the partnership except for purpose of winding up; e. g., performance of existing contracts, collection of money due, payment of debts, administering of firm assets, and the distribution of the assets in accordance with the partnership agreement. See U.P.A., Sections 33–43.

2. EFFECT ON POWERS OF PARTNERS

Normally, dissolution terminates the power of a partner to bind the partnership except for the purpose of winding up. However, he may bind the partnership to third persons as follows:

a. to those who had extended credit to the firm prior to dissolution and had no knowledge or notice of the dissolution; and

b. to those who had not extended credit but knew of the partnership prior to dissolution and had no knowledge or notice of the dissolution, and the notice of the dissolution had not been advertised in a newspaper of general circulation (U.P.A., Section 35).

3. EFFECT ON RIGHTS OF PARTNERS

A. Right to Wind Up

Unless otherwise agreed, the partners who have not caused the dissolution have the right to wind up the partnership affairs (U.P.A., Section 37).

B. Right to Application of Partnership Property

Each partner has the right to insist that all the partnership assets be used first to pay partnership debts (U.P.A., Section 38). After partnership debts are paid, remaining assets are used to return capital investments.

4. LIABILITY OF PARTNERS CONTINUING THE BUSINESS

When the membership of the partnership changes, by reason of death or retirement of a partner, or the coming in of another member, and the business is *continued*, the creditors of the first or dissolved partnership are also creditors of the partnership continuing the business, and the new member is liable for all the obligations arising before his becoming a partner; however, the liability of the new member for prior obligations shall be satisfied out of partnership property only (U.P.A., Section 41).

D. RULES FOR DISTRIBUTION

---

1. TO CREDITORS

The liabilities of the partnership are paid in the following order:

a. to creditors other than partners;

b. to partners other than for capital and profits; and

c. to partners in respect of capital (U.P.A., Section 40(b)).

If there is insufficient partnership property to satisfy the liabilities, the partners must make contribution to the extent necessary to satisfy the liabilities (U.P.A., Section 40(d)). In the absence of agreement, partners share losses in the same way as they share profits (U.P.A., Section 18(a)).

Where the partnership or a partner is insolvent or in bankruptcy, the rule of *marshaling of assets* is applied (U.P.A., Section 40(h) (i)). This rule is that *partnership* assets must be applied first to the satisfaction of the claims of the *partnership* creditors, and *individual or personal* assets of a partner to the satisfaction of his *individual or personal* creditors, any balance of the personal estate of a partner then is applied to the satisfaction of partnership creditors.

2. TO PARTNERS

The balance of the partnership property after payment of all liabilities and return of capital investment is distributed to the partners as profits pursuant to the partnership agreement.

---

1. Partnership Accounting

WEIDLICH v. WEIDLICH

147 Conn. 160, 157 A.2d 910 (1960).

SHEA, Associate Justice. The Weidlich Sterling Spoon Company, a copartnership which formerly carried on business in Bridgeport, was dissolved on January 10, 1950, by agreement of the three partners, William Weidlich, Louis Weidlich and Frank B. Weidlich. Under this agreement Louis was designated liquidating partner, and he acted in this capacity until his death on July 21, 1950. Thereafter, Frank, the plaintiff, proceeded with the liquidation as though he were the sole surviving partner. After the payment of claims, he made distribution of part of the assets to the parties interested. * * * In May, 1950, William assigned all his interest in the partnership to his son, Clifton F. Weidlich, a defendant. William died in 1955. * * *

An accounting of the transactions of the partnership for the period from January 23, 1951, to October 31, 1955, prepared by a firm of certified public accountants, was offered as Frank's final account of his liquidation of the partnership. * * * Distribution of this money was withheld by Frank pending the outcome of litigation brought by Clifton, one action being in the United States District Court for the district of Connecticut and another in the New York Supreme Court. * * *

Certain bills for legal fees and expenses incurred in connection with all of this litigation were charged against the partnership in liquidation, and the various items are reflected in the account which is presented for approval in the present action. The trial court found that all of these charges were fair and reasonable and, after directing certain minor amendments in the account, approved, accepted and allowed it as Frank's final account. From this judgment Clifton appealed, individually and as executor. * * *

Upon the termination of a partnership either by act of the parties or operation of law, an accounting usually becomes necessary. * * *

Unless there is an adjustment by agreement, an accounting must be made in court, and equity is the proper forum. * * * Equity has full jurisdiction of a suit for an accounting and settlement of partnership affairs. The petition may be brought either by the representatives of a deceased partner against the survivors or by the survivors against such representatives. * * *

Where a partner presents a petition in equity against the other partners, stating that the accounts are unsettled and praying for an account, the usual course for the court is to appoint a committee of auditors before whom the parties can produce their accounts and be heard on oath and who will conduct a minute and patient examination of their claims. * * *

After the balance due and to whom it is due is ascertained, a report is made to the court, which has power to accept it or reject it. If the report is accepted, a decree may be entered in favor of the partners who are entitled to it and executions will be issued accordingly, whether the debtors are plaintiffs or defendants in the case. * * *

Each partner owes to his associates the duty of rendering true accounts and full information about everything which affects the partnership. If he fails to perform this duty, his associates are entitled to maintain a suit for an accounting against him. * * * Any partner may bring a petition in equity for the settlement of partnership affairs.

* * * No inventory of the assets of the partnership was included in the account, nor is there any detail listed concerning the process of liquidation. The capital of the partnership and the interests of the partners in it are not revealed. Unless this information is furnished, the court is powerless to make any final order of settlement or distribution. * * * A final account is the one great occasion for a comprehensive and effective settlement of all partnership affairs. All the claims and demands arising between the partners should be settled upon such an accounting.

* * * There is error, the judgment is set aside and a new trial is ordered.

2. *Distinction Between "Dissolution" and "Termination"*

BAYER ET AL. v. BAYER

215 App.Div. 454, 214 N.Y.S. 322 (1926).

MERRELL, J. This controversy concerns the purchase made by the defendant on August 13, 1919, of 76 shares of stock of the Montville Finishing Company. * * *

For several years prior to June 11, 1919, the plaintiffs and the defendant were copartners in business, under the firm name of Bayer Bros., engaged in the purchase of cotton goods in an unfinished state, or, as they were known, "in the gray." * * *

In or about the month of September, 1913, the said copartnership acquired a two-thirds interest in the capital stock of the Montville Finishing Company, a New Jersey corporation. * * * On June 11, 1919, a meeting of the members of the copartnership was held at the office of said copartnership, * * * and at such conference Samuel Bayer, a plaintiff, announced that under no circumstances would these plaintiffs continue the partnership of Bayer Bros. as then constituted. * * *

As a result of such conference, the copartnership ceased doing business as a going concern, and from that time on the entire efforts of the partners were devoted to the closing up of the copartnership affairs and in an attempt to agree upon a distribution of the assets among themselves. * * *

The defendant purchased said shares on August 13, 1919, paying for the same from his private funds upon the terms and conditions aforesaid. It is such purchase of the said 76 shares of stock * * * that the plaintiffs in the present action attack, and which the plaintiffs claim was in violation of defendant's fiduciary obligation to the plaintiffs. * * *

The trial court has held that the defendant, in acquiring said stock, violated his fiduciary duty to his copartners; that at the time said stock was acquired the copartnership of Bayer Bros. had not been dissolved, and that the defendant's relationship to his fellow partners was such as precluded his obtaining to himself the said stock of the Montville Finishing Company. * * *

We are convinced that the facts proven by the testimony at the trial, and as found by the trial court upon the evidence, show conclusively that at the time defendant purchased the * * * stock the partnership had been fully dissolved; that such dissolution, under the statutes of this state and under the common law, occurred on June 11, 1919, at the conference between the partners. * * * Upon such dissolution of the partnership, any fiduciary duty which the defendant owed toward the plaintiffs while the copartnership existed ceased, and the defendant was free to purchase the Booth and Healion shares for his exclusive benefit, or to do anything else which he might deem prudent for his own protection. * * * At common law it is not unusual that the courts have failed carefully to distinguish between the terms "dissolution," "winding up," and "termination" of a copartnership. * * * A copartnership at will is dissolved at the moment when either of the partners expresses an intent not to continue longer, or when the partners decide to cease doing business for their mutual benefit. The partnership affairs, however, are not terminated until the winding up is completed. Their energies thereafter are devoted to the winding up of the business affairs of the copartnership and to reaching an agreement as to the distribution of its assets. * * *

For the reasons above stated, the judgment appealed from should be reversed, with costs, and plaintiffs' complaint dismissed, and judgment directed for the defendant, with costs.

3. *Reasons for Dissolution of Partnership*

JONES v. JONES

15 Misc.2d 960, 179 N.Y.S.2d 480 (1958).

JAMES S. BROWN, Jr., Justice. In this action for a dissolution of a partnership, accounting, etc., defendant moves for an order * * * dismissing the complaint on the ground that it does not set forth facts sufficient to constitute a cause of action. The action is brought by a wife against her husband. * * *

However, it appears from the complaint that the grounds upon which the action rests are that (1) one of the partners, defendant herein, is guilty of adultery and that an action for divorce has been instituted against him by the other party, and (2) defendant has refused to make a distribution of the assets or to account therefor.

Dissolutions of partnerships can only be brought about as provided by Sections 62 and 63 of the Partnership Law. An examination of Sec. 62 reveals that subdivision 1(b) is the only subdivision of this section that possibly could be applied to the situation presented herein provided the proper facts are pleaded. Subdivision 1(b) reads as follows:

> "By the express will of any partner when no definite term or particular undertaking is specified."

The courts, however, have held in order to effect a dissolution of a partnership at will

> "there must have been a mutual agreement to dissolve, *or there must have been notice by a party desiring a dissolution to his copartners 'of his election to terminate the partnership, or his election must be manifested by unequivocal acts or circumstances brought to the knowledge of the other party which signify [the exercise of] the will of the former that the partnership be dissolved'.* * * * "

Nowhere in the complaint has the plaintiff set forth such facts even though it may well be that such notice of election was given. The court, however, cannot assume from the facts as pleaded that such notice was given. In addition, while allegations of adultery and the institution of a divorce action could be the basis for terminating an alleged partnership at will, it cannot be said that these are unequivocal acts or circumstances signifying an election to dissolve for it is common knowledge that wives have divorced husbands without terminating businesses in which both parties were interested. * * * In an action for a dissolution of a partnership the accounting, impressing of a trust, appointment of a receiver, etc. are merely incidental relief sought in the dissolution of the partnership. * * *

Accordingly, the motion to dismiss is granted with leave to the plaintiff to serve an amended complaint if so advised within 20 days after service of a copy of the order to be entered herein, with notice of entry.

---

4. *Determination of Dissolution*

HAYNES v. ALLEN

482 S.W.2d 85 (Mo.App., 1972).

WEIER, Judge. Dissolution of a partnership and its consequences is the area of concern in this case. From a judgment limiting plaintiff's recovery to $7,484.83, plaintiff has appealed, contending generally that the trial court misinterpreted the partnership agreement with regard to liquidation and distribution of assets. If plaintiff prevails with his interpretation of the contract, then, by stipulation of the parties made at trial, plaintiff would be entitled to a total of $27,100.43. * * *

Dr. James W. Haynes, the plaintiff, is a medical doctor whose specialty has been pathology. In 1955, he was employed by Allen Medical Laboratories, a partnership composed of physicians who engaged in the practice of medicine and, particularly, in the operation of clinical pathological laboratories. Within six months after initial employment he became a partner. Upon admission as a partner, he paid nothing for his interest in the existing laboratory equipment, the accounts receivable, supplies and the established practice, except the sum of $2,500.00, which was stated in the partnership agreement to be his contribution as partnership capital. Under the terms of the agreement, all medical and surgical instruments, laboratory equipment, stock, medicines and medical books which the parties had previously accumulated while associated together, were delivered over to the partnership and thereupon became partnership property. Additional supplies and equipment were subsequently purchased over the years out of partnership funds and they also became partnership property.

In June of 1966, at a partnership meeting, Dr. Haynes became involved in an animated conversation with one of the partners over the productivity of one of the laboratories as it affected partnership income. He left the meeting abruptly and failed to return to any further meetings. Three were held thereafter. * * * All those present agreed to dissolve the partnership and expel Dr. Haynes. One of the partners, Dr. William L. Drake, Jr., was delegated the task of notifying Dr. Haynes that he was to be "separated" from the partnership. This notice, signed December 31, 1966, ws served on January 2, 1967.

The partnership agreement contained a clause, Article VII, which spelled out in detail the methods to be used to ascertain the value of a partner's interest upon retirement or death. Upon payment of the amount therein determined, the partnership business could be perpetuated in the remaining partners, or in those who desired to continue with its operation. The article that followed, Article VIII, because of its importance in the determination of this lawsuit, is set out verbatim:

1. Unless dissolved by the retirement or death of a partner, the partnership shall continue until dissolved by agreement of the partners. * * * The remaining assets (excluding the accounts receivable and laboratory equipment) shall be divided according to the proportionate interests of the partners on the basis of their respective pro rata proportion of the income as existed immediately prior to dissolution."

On appeal, Dr. Haynes contends the unambiguous meaning of this clause of the partnership agreement is that all partners must agree to dissolve the partnership before its terms are applicable. * * * The other partners likewise maintain the partnership agreement is clear and unambiguous, but their interpretation differs from that of plaintiff. And so, on the one hand, plaintiff asserts that the word "agreement" means unanimous agreement, or agreement of all the partners. But, on the other hand, defendants declare the word means consent of a majority of the partners.

* * *

The court below, in its memorandum opinion, gave as its reason for interpreting the phrases to call for something less than total accord and thus require distribution under its provisions, the failure of the article to require dissolution by "unanimous" agreement. By the same token, however, we note that the clause did not in plain terms provide for dissolution by "a majority" of the partners. * * * But if one is able to go beyond the plain meaning of "agreement" and add "by majority" to it, the result could be just as unreasonable or absurd, since a majority of four of the seven partners could, under that interpretation, then agree to dissolution and proceed to appropriate for themselves the greater share of the assets of the partnership. The minority of three would then have to be content with being cast out without their fair share, even though disagreeing with the dissolution.

The partnership was for an indefinite term. It was dissolved by act of the defendants and notice of dissolution served on plaintiff January 2, 1967. * * *

The judgment below is reversed and the case remanded, with instructions to enter judgment for plaintiff and against defendants in the sum of $27,100.43, together with interest thereon at the rate of six per centum per annum, commencing January 1, 1967, down to the date the judgment is entered in compliance with our mandate.

5. *Rights of Partner on Dissolution*

FORTUGNO v. HUDSON MANURE CO.

51 N.J.Super. 482, 144 A.2d 207 (1958).

GOLDMANN, S. J. A. D. This proceeding began as an action for the dissolution of a family partnership when Anthony Fortugno, one of the partners, filed his complaint * * * on January 4, 1956 against the partnership and his co-partners. * * *

Defendants are the partnership, Hudson Manure Company, and Anthony's seven co-partners: Sylvia Fortugno (mother of the seven other partners), Daniel, Arthur, Alfred and Adeline Fortugno, Connie (Fortugno) Ruble, and Ann (Fortugno) Campanella. * * * The basic dispute concerned the distribution of partnership assets. The question was whether certain corporations, five in number, were assets of the partnership or owned by the individual partners. * * * Arthur claimed the corporations were assets of the partnership and that he was entitled upon dissolution of the partnership to his proportionate share in cash, rather than to be forced to exchange his position as an equal partner for that of a minority shareholder in the family-controlled corporations whose shares would have no value on an open market. * * *

The other partners contended that distribution should be of the shares of stock. * * * The trial court held that the first four of the above-named corporations were not assets of the partnership, and ordered the equal distribution of their stock to the partners. The fifth corporation, Hudson Farms, Inc., was held to have been fraudulently formed with partnership funds; it belonged to the partnership, and was ordered sold. Arthur appeals this order (as well as all other interlocutory orders), particularly with respect to the finding that the first four corporations were not assets of the partnership. * * *

Arthur's present position, essentially, is that he is entitled to have the partnership pay him for his one-eighth interest. * * *

The partnership's original business was * * * the collection and sale of manure. * * * The partnership sold the manure to mushroom growers in southeastern Pennsylvania; it also derived an income from race tracks and other sources of supply for removing the manure. In the course of its operations the partnership found it convenient to put certain of its activities in corporate form. * * *

The reasons for Arthur's stand are readily understandable. As a member of a partnership that owns several corporations he has an effective voice in partnership policy and operation, but as a minority stockholder he could be overruled by a majority vote. * * *

Our statutes provide that all property originally brought into a partnership or subsequently acquired in any way on its behalf is partnership property and, unless a contrary intention appears, property acquired with partnership funds is partnership property. Uniform Partnership Act, 42:1–8(1) and (2) * * *

Less than all the partners in a partnership may not bind the partnership by an act or acts not performed for the purpose of carrying on the usual business of the partnership, unless authorized by the other partners. Uniform Partnership Act, R.S. 42:1–9 * * * This applies particularly to a situation where one or several partners, but not all, seek to incorporate a partnership and transfer the assets of the partnership to the new corporation. * * *

Co-partners must deal with each other with trust, confidence and good faith; there can be no secret advantages or benefits. A partner has a fiduciary duty to share with the partnership those business opportunities clearly related to the subject of its operations. * * *

Applying the principles, stated earlier, of determining what is partnership property, we conclude that the four named corporations were and presently are assets of the partnership, Hudson Manure Company. * * *

We therefore conclude that the assets of the partnership, including those of all the corporations, should be liquidated, and the proceeds distributed in cash. * * *

We cannot order the remaining partners to buy out Arthur's interest.

* * * If the opposing partners will agree to the entry of an order for the appraisal of the partnership under the direction of the court and directing them to pay Arthur one-eighth of the valuation determined upon, such an order will be entered. Otherwise, there will be a liquidation by sale of all the partnership assets, including those owned by the several corporations.

---

6. *Distribution of Assets upon Dissolution*

GLASSELL v. PRENTISS

175 Cal.App.2d 599, 346 P.2d 895 (1959).

COUGHLIN, Justice pro tem. Action for partnership accounting and dissolution, damages for breach of contract, * * * and non-payment of wages. Judgment for defendants affirmed.

This action arose out of an oral agreement entered into in November, 1954, between the plaintiff Glassell, as one party, the defendant Glen Ashurst, as a second party, and the defendant partnership, Chartier, Laufer and Prentiss, which was engaged in the painting business, as a third party. The pre-trial conference order recites that the parties agree that they entered into an oral contract to form a business for installing walls in houses under construction; that the plaintiff would be field superintendent of the business at a salary of $200 per week; that the defendant Prentiss would be office manager at a salary of $25 per week; that the defendant Ashurst would do the estimating at $25 per week; and that all profits would be divided equally between the parties. Each party contributed $3,000 to the business. * * * After the business had been in operation approximately two months, the defendants discovered that the cost of performance was exceeding the contract price payable to them by approximately $125 per house. * * * No further contracts were negotiated and the business came to an end. After March 25, 1955, the plaintiff made no request to participate in the business; to assist in its winding up; or to examine its books and records.

The plaintiff brought this action to recover his share of the partnership assets as of March 25, 1955, as well as damages for breach of the alleged contract of employment and resultant loss of wages at the rate of $200 per week.

* * * Upon dissolution, a partner has authority to wind up the partnership affairs and "complete transactions begun but not then finished". * * *

The duty of a liquidating partner is to wind up the affairs of the firm, pay its debts out of the assets, if sufficient, and divide the residue, if any, among those entitled to it. * * *

In settling accounts between partners after dissolution, the liabilities of the partnership to creditors first must be paid; secondly, the liabilities owing to partners other than for capital and profits, and thereafter the liabilities owing to partners in respect to capital and profits.

* * * If there is not sufficient partnership property to satisfy the liabilities, each partner must contribute his share towards such satisfaction, and any partner who contributes more than his share may recover from a defaulting partner the amount which was paid in excess of his liability. * * *

The plaintiff participated in a venture which proved to be unsuccessful. The defendants, in an attempt to prevent a loss greater than their investment, in good faith brought the venture to a close. The judgment of the trial court that the plaintiff is not entitled to more than his share of the remaining assets, subject to the remaining liabilities, was proper.

The judgment is affirmed.

---

7. *Distribution of Partnership Assets in Kind*

LOGOLUSO v. LOGOLUSO

233 Cal.App.2d 523, 43 Cal.Rptr. 678 (1965).

STONE, Justice. This appeal is from a judgment ordering a sale of assets in a proceeding for dissolution of a copartnership engaged in farming. All of the partnership property, both real and personal, was ordered sold as a unit. Appellants attack that part of the judgment ordering the real property sold as a unit, contending that the court erred in not approving a division in kind made by the partners.

The five Logoluso brothers, under the terms of a written copartnership agreement, owned and farmed 12 parcels of real property valued by the court at $2,000,000, subject to encumbrances of about $166,700. The partnership owns equipment valued at $100,000 and has accounts receivable and interests in revolving funds of cooperatives amounting to approximately $278,000.

Leonard Logoluso, one of the appellants herein, on September 26, 1960, gave notice in accordance with the articles of copartnership, that he was resigning from the partnership and demanded termination thereof within 90 days. * * * [T]he five partners divided the 12 parcels of real property by each making a first-choice selection, followed by a second-choice selection, and an auction of the two remaining parcels. * * *

Division in kind of partnership assets upon dissolution is conditioned, however, upon the satisfaction of all partnership obligations to third parties. Here, the partnership owed approximately $166,700, but the obligations present no obstacle to distribution in kind since there are liquid assets, aside from the real property, sufficient to satisfy all partnership obligations. * * * Thus, an executed agreement for the division of real property in kind must be honored by a court presiding over the dissolution of a partnership, unless the agreement is assailed on the ground of mistake, error or fraud.

* * * Therefore we hold that in a partnership dissolution action a court has authority to make distribution of partnership real property in kind. This power, of course, is conditioned upon a finding that it is not necessary to hold a sale in order to satisfy partnership obligations. Absent a compelling necessity to satisfy partnership obligations, a public sale of assets can be justified only if it is found that distribution in kind would result in great prejudice to the parties. This simply conforms to the tenet of equity that recognizes real property and certain kinds of personal property as unique, which, in turn, impels a court of equity to maintain the ownership of property when feasible. * * *

The judgment is reversed.

PROBLEMS

1. A and B formed a partnership for five years. In the fourth year, A fraudulently converted property of the partnership to his own use. B, on discovering this fact, ousted A from the partnership. A brings an action for dissolution of the partnership, an accounting, and for damages for the expulsion and loss of profits. Decision?

2. A and B were partners. They were performing a highway construction contract when A died. B continued performance of the contract. It was necessary for B to borrow a substantial sum of money from the bank to continue the project. When the partnership became insolvent, the bank sued the partnership. A's widow raised the defense that B could not enter into a new transaction, such as borrowing money, and, therefore, the partnership should not be liable for the new loan. Decision?

3. A, B, and C are partners. C retired from the firm. A and B assumed the debts of the firm and paid C the value of his interest. D then became a partner of the firm with A and B, and the partnership of A, B, and D continued the business. T, a creditor of the firm of A, B, and C, brings action against A, B, C, and D for the debt. Decision?

4. A, B, and C formed a partnership. The capital was $5,000.00 to which A contributed $3,000.00; B, $2,000.00; and C, nothing. It was agreed that profits would be shared equally. Later, the partnership became insolvent and was short $4,000.00 to pay the creditors. How shall the loss be adjusted?

Losses shared equally

5. A, B, and C were partners. The firm borrowed money from a bank and gave the bank the firm's note for the loan. In addition, each partner guaranteed the note personally. The partnership became insolvent. The bank claims that it has a right to file its claim as a partnership debt and has a right to a lien on the assets of the individual partners before the other general creditors of the partnership can look to the assets of the individual partners. Decision?

6. Phillips, Atkins, and Webb formed a partnership for the term of ten years. In the sixth year, Phillips withdrew without cause and Webb became bankrupt. A dispute then arose among the partners over the right to liquidate and wind up the firm's business. The exclusive right to do so was claimed by each of the partners and by Webb's trustee in bankruptcy. Who is entitled to wind up the business?

7. Golden was admitted into the partnership firm of Jackson and Smith. At the time of Golden's admission as a partner, the firm was indebted to several creditors, including Armen. The firm thereafter became insolvent, and the assets of the partnership and of the partners were insufficient to pay the partnership debts. Armen seeks to hold Golden personally liable for the deficit in his claim. Decision?

8. Riddle and Mohn form a ten-year partnership to practice surgery. During the second year, Mohn is involved in a serious motor accident which necessitates the amputation of both his arms. Riddle seeks to obtain a decree of dissolution of the partnership in a court of equity. Decision?

9. ABC partnership, and its three partners, Ace, Best, and Conn, individually, were adjudged bankrupts. No assets remained in the estates of Ace and Best after the necessary expenses of administration had been paid. As to the estate of Conn and the partnership ABC, however, there remained the sums of $1,000 and $2,000, respectively. Can the ABC partnership creditors share in the assets remaining in the estate of Conn along with Conn's personal creditors?

10. Andy, who owned and operated a variety store, formed a partnership with Bill, who agreed to manage and operate the store as a partnership for half the profits. Bill made no capital investment in the enterprise. Later the partnership was dissolved. What proportion of the business assets should have been distributed to Bill?

Part 7

CORPORATIONS

Chapter 32

INTRODUCTION, FORMATION, TERMINATION

A. INTRODUCTION

Corporations are subject to greater governmental formalities and control than any other form of business enterprise. Corporations involve the federal Constitution, federal laws, and state laws. Part 7 is not intended to be a comprehensive coverage of the law of corporations, but merely a light treatment of the subject with emphasis on material that is important to the business student.

1. NATURE

For a comparison with partnerships, the student is referred to Part 6, Chapter 29.

A corporation is a legal "person" or entity. It has an existence separate from that of its shareholders.

A corporation is a "person" within the meaning of the fifth (due process) and fourteenth (equal protection) amendments to the Constitution of the United States. It is not a "citizen" within that part of the fourteenth amendment to the Constitution of the United States which has to do with the protection of privileges and immunities; however, it is a "citizen" for the purpose of determining diversity of citizenship as a basis for jurisdiction of the Federal courts in an action to which the corporation is a party.

2. ENTITY

A corporation is a legal entity with separate rights and liabilities. It may sue or be sued. It exists in the eyes of the law as though it were a person separate and distinct from the shareholders. The debts of the corporation are not the debts of the shareholders, the directors, or the officers; thus, the corporate entity absolves the shareholders and the managers from the liability of the corporation, and this is one of the main advantages of a corporation.

However, this corporate entity or veil can be broken or disregarded in an appropriate case to hold personally liable those individuals who are attempting to use the entity to protect themselves from liability for their wrongs.

The general rule is that the corporate entity will be recognized and not disregarded. The exception is that the entity will be disregarded when it is used to defeat public convenience, protect fraud, justify a wrong, evade the law or defend crime. The courts will not recognize the entity protection to the managers or the shareholders if to do so would produce unjust or undesirable consequences inconsistent with the purpose of the entity concept. The question of disregarding the corporate entity, or as if often said "piercing the corporate veil", usually arises with a one-man or family type of corporation. The one-man or close corporation is found where one or two persons own all of the corporation stock. This type of corporation may usually afford grounds for disregarding the entity unless the following two conditions are complied with:

a. the business must be conducted on a corporate basis rather than a personal basis, and

b. the business must be established on an adequate financial basis.

3. KINDS OF CORPORATIONS

A. DE JURE

A de jure corporation is one that results from substantial compliance with the statutory requirements for incorporation. It is in all respects legal. Generally, it cannot be deprived of its corporate existence or powers contrary to its charter even by the state.

B. DE FACTO

A de facto corporation is an association which actually exists for all practical purposes but which has no right to corporate existence, as against a direct action by the state, because there has been a failure to comply with some provision in the incorporation law.

To be a de facto organization, there must be:

(1) a valid statute under which the corporation can be formed,

(2) a good faith attempt to organize under such statute, and

(3) a user of the corporate powers, i.e., business has been transacted as a corporation. A de facto corporation is entitled to act as a corporation until dissolved by direct state action.

C. CORPORATION BY ESTOPPEL

When an association represents itself to be a corporation, it cannot escape liability by denying its own corporate existence. Furthermore, if the association is not a de jure or de facto corporation, the members have unlimited liability as in a partnership. When a person contracts with an association as if it were a corporation, the general rule is that he cannot avoid liability on a contract by denying the corporate existence since he thereby admits the legal existence of the corporation for the purpose of any action that may be brought to enforce the contract.

D. Private and Public Corporations

Private corporations are those organized for private purposes. *Public* corporations are created by the people or government for public purposes, political, or otherwise; e.g., United States, states, cities, towns, counties, school districts.

E. Nonprofit

A nonprofit corporation may be formed for religious, charitable, social, educational, or cemetery purposes. The business can be carried on at a profit as an incident to the main purpose of the corporation; however, the corporation cannot distribute any gains, profits, or dividends to any of its members except upon dissolution or winding up. A nonprofit corporation is a non-stock corporation; i.e., it may have memberships, but no shares.

F. Domestic or Foreign

A *domestic* corporation is one that is created by the laws of a particular state or country in which it does business; whereas, a *foreign* corporation is one created by the laws of one state or country, but also does business in another, the "foreign" state or country. "Doing business" means that the corporation is doing a substantial amount of business with substantial regularity in the state. When it is doing business in the state, it must qualify as a foreign corporation. To qualify, it must, among other things, permit itself to be sued in the state. This is done by filing with the Secretary of State in which it is going to do business a copy of its articles of incorporation, together with a statement setting forth its home office and office within the state, and the name and address of a person or corporation within the state upon whom legal process may be served in any legal action against it. Failure to qualify as a foreign corporation can result in fines and the denial of the use of the courts of the state to enforce contracts.

4. PROMOTERS

Large corporations are usually planned and formed by promoters. Their activities include researching the economic feasibility of the new business, and assembling the necessary resource, property and personnel. Promoters often continue in control of the corporation after its formation.

A. Duty of Disclosure

Promoters are fiduciaries. They owe a duty of good faith, fair dealing, and full disclosure to the corporation. They are liable to the corporation for any secret profits.

international corp - another country

Breach of Implied Warranty of Authority

B. CONTRACTS OF PROMOTERS

The acts of the promoters do not bind the corporation prior to its legal existence since until it legally exists, there cannot be a principal-agency relationship. The corporation is not liable on promoter contracts until it adopts or ratifies them after incorporation.

The promoters themselves are liable on the contracts if they entered into them as individuals, but not if they made the contracts in the name of the *contemplated* corporation and solely on its credit. If the other party to the contract is unaware that the corporation has not come into existence at the time he contracts with the promoter, and if the promoter expressly or impliedly holds it out to him as an existing corporation and that he has the right to bind it by contract, the promoter will be personally liable on the contract on the theory that he has been guilty of a breach of warranty of his agency.

5. PREINCORPORATION STOCK SUBSCRIPTIONS

Prior to forming the corporation, the promoters may attempt to get people to pledge themselves to purchase its stock after it is formed. To take this action, the promoters must first secure a permit from the state to take preincorporation subscriptions. After they obtain the permit, they can solicit prospective investors for their promises to purchase stock.

These pledges (or offers) by the investors to purchase stock are usually revocable by the investor, in the absence of statute, until accepted by the corporation after it comes into legal existence. Modern statutes usually make preincorporation subscriptions irrevocable for a stated period of time; e.g., Model Business Corporation Act, Section 16 (six months).

Preincorporation agreements are not in common use. Modernly, it is more usual to first form the corporation and then attempt to sell the stock.

B. FORMATION

---

1. ARTICLES OF INCORPORATION

In most states, corporate existence begins with the filing of the articles of incorporation prepared by an attorney at law. In some states, corporate existence does not begin until a formal certificate of incorporation is issued by the state.

The contents of the articles of incorporation are prescribed in the general incorporation statutes of the various states. Typical requirements are found in the Model Business Corporation Act, Section 48:

a. The name of the corporation;

b. The period of duration, which may be perpetual;

c. The purpose for which it is organized;

d. The number of shares which it shall have authority to issue, and the par (equal) value of each share or a statement that the shares are without par value;

e. If the shares are to be divided into classes, the designation of each class and a statement of preferences, limitations, and relative rights of each class;

f. A statement that the corporation will not commence business until at least $1,000.00 has been received for issued shares;

g. Any provision limiting or denying to shareholders the right to acquire additional or treasury shares of the corporation on a preemptive basis;

h. Any provision the incorporators may choose to set forth for the regulation of the internal affairs of the corporation;

i. The address of its initial office and agent;

j. The number of directors constituting the original board of directors and the names and addresses of the persons who are to serve as the first board of directors until the first annual meeting of shareholders or until successors are elected.

k. The name and address of each incorporator (usually three or more and of legal capacity).

After the articles are prepared and signed by the incorporators, the attorney files them and the necessary fee with the proper state officer, usually the Secretary of State. If the articles are in order the Secretary of State issues a certificate of incorporation. The certificate and a copy of the articles are filed with the local county recorder. After they are returned by the recorder, they are placed in the corporation minute book. As soon as the corporation comes into legal existence, the directors can hold their first meeting at which time they will elect officers, adopt by-laws, choose the type of seal and minute book they desire, and conduct other business, such as, an application for permit to issue stock.

2. BY-LAWS

By-laws are the rules enacted by a corporation to regulate and govern its own affairs, and its directors, officers, and shareholders. They are not necessary in the formation of a corporation.

By-laws must conform to the articles of incorporation and local laws. States vary as to the required and the permissible content of by-laws and as to how they are to be adopted or amended. By-laws vary in content from a brief statement of rules for one corporation to a comprehensive booklet for another.

In most states, the by-laws are not filed in any public office.

C. TERMINATION

Termination of a corporation can be brought about by a reorganization or by dissolution. Local statutes vary and must be consulted.

1. REORGANIZATION

There are three common devices for the reorganization of a corporation: merger, consolidation, and sale of its assets.

A. Merger

Merger is the purchase of one corporation by another; e.g., the A Corporation buys out the B Corporation. The B Corporation is merged into the A Corporation and ceases to exist. The A Corporation continues and is known as the surviving corporation.

B. Consolidation

In the case of a consolidation, the two or more constituent corporations cease to exist, and a new corporation is formed; e.g., the A Corporation and the B Corporation consolidate with the result that A and B cease to exist, and a new corporation, C, emerges.

C. Sale of its Assets

When one corporation purchases all of the assets of another corporation, there is technically no change in the legal existence of either corporation. The purchasing corporation has acquired ownership of more physical assets, and the selling corporation has acquired cash or income for a period of years in place of the physical assets.

2. DISSOLUTION

Dissolution may be voluntary or involuntary.

A. Voluntary

Shareholders may vote to dissolve a corporation. The percentage necessary to cause a dissolution varies with local statutes from fifty per cent to two-thirds.

B. Involuntary

Forced dissolution may be caused by creditors of a corporation or by petition of a percentage of the stockholders which varies from ten to fifty per cent. Some of the reasons are fraud on the part of the directors, deadlocked factions of directors and stockholders, wasting of corporate property, misapplication of corporate property, mismanagement, abuse of authority, and unfairness to minority stockholders.

Involuntary dissolution can also be caused by the act of the state legislature in terminating the corporate existence where the right has been reserved; and can be caused by a decree of Court initiated by the Attorney General of the state of incorporation when it appears that the corporation has violated a corporation law; e.g., failure to pay franchise tax, abuse of powers.

3. WINDING UP

A. VOLUNTARY DISSOLUTION

Usually, a certificate of election to dissolve the corporation must be filed with the Secretary of State as the first step in winding up. The corporation must cease doing any business except that necessary to wind up its affairs. The directors must liquidate as much of the assets as they believe necessary to effect the winding up. After all the debts have been paid, the directors must distribute the balance of the assets to the shareholders. After distribution, the directors must file a certificate with the Secretary of State showing that the corporation has been wound up, debts paid, and the balance of the assets distributed to the shareholders. Upon the filing of this certificate, the corporation terminates.

B. INVOLUNTARY DISSOLUTION

In this case, the court decrees dissolution and orders the winding up by the directors under the supervision of the court. The procedure for winding up is similar to the voluntary dissolution.

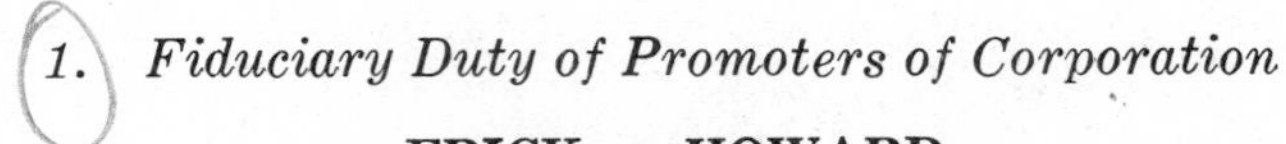

1. *Fiduciary Duty of Promoters of Corporation*

FRICK v. HOWARD

23 Wis.2d 86, 126 N.W.2d 619 (1964).

Action to foreclose a mortgage on real estate. Plaintiff-respondent is the assignee of the promoter of a corporation. The purchase money mortgage being foreclosed was executed by the corporation in favor of the promoter and his wife when they sold certain real estate located in the city of Milwaukee to the corporation. Defendant-appellant is the receiver of the corporation. * * *

From a judgment of foreclosure in favor of the plaintiff for the amount of $77,159.57 defendant appeals. * * *

BEILFUSS, Justice. *Did Preston, as a promoter, breach a fiduciary duty to the corporation?* It appears without dispute that Preston was the organizer and promoter of the Pan American Motel, Inc.

He entered into the contract to purchase land for $240,000 on January 24, 1958. * * * He organized the corporation April 1, 1958 and was its sole stockholder until September 3, 1958. After successfully bringing an action on the contract to purchase, he obtained title to the land on August 29, 1958.

* * * Three days later, September 1, 1958, the corporation offered him $350,000 for the land. The offer was accepted and

the corporation paid Preston $70,000 by cancellation of his debt of $35,000 to the corporation, issuing 35 shares of its stock to him, assuming the $170,000 mortgage, and giving him a note and mortgage for $110,000. The offer was signed by Preston as seller and Frank J. Mack for the corporation. At the time the offer to purchase was made by the corporation Preston was, as far as the record reveals, the sole stockholder and completely dominated the affairs of the corporation. There was a board of directors consisting of Preston and two others but the record does not show they owned any stock or that they were in any way independent of Preston. On April 1, 1959 the note of $110,000 and mortgage were signed by Preston as president of the corporation and by Frank J. Mack as secretary payable to Preston and his wife.

The trial court found that Preston committed a fraud upon the corporation but that the transaction was not secret.

* * * The fact that the transaction was not secret does not in all instances relieve a promoter of his fiduciary obligation to the corporation.

> "The promoters may deal with the corporation, but they must deal fairly, the burden of proof of fairness being on them. When they deal with the corporation, it must have independent directors; and the promoters cannot also be directors or dominate them as representatives of the other adversely interested parties.
>
> "Perfect candor, full disclosure, good faith, in fact, the utmost good faith, and the strictest honesty are required of promoters, and their dealings must be open and fair, or without undue advantage taken.
>
> "As a result of the fiduciary relation or relation of trust and confidence sustained by a promoter, an unfair advantage taken or secret profit gained thereby is a fraud. * * *"

It is clear that at the time of the sale of the land to the corporation, and the execution of the note and mortgage, that the corporation had no independent board of directors. The actions of the corporation were completely dominated by Preston. The transaction to sell the land held for a very short period of time was controlled by Preston both as buyer and seller. This was not an agreement between an independent buyer and seller dealing at arm's length. Preston as an individual selling the property had a personal financial interest to obtain the highest price available; Preston as the alter ego of Pan American Motel, Inc. had a financial interest to purchase the property at the lowest price available. There could be no meeting of the minds.

The fact that the land may or may not have been worth more than $240,000 cannot override Preston's fiduciary obligation as a promoter of the corporation.

* * * Judgment reversed with directions to dismiss the complaint.

2. *Corporate Entity Created by Law*

IN RE THOM LAMBDA LEGAL DEF. & ED. FUND, INC.

40 A.D.2d 787, 337 N.Y.S.2d 588 (1971).

PER CURIAM. Application for approval as a legal assistance corporation (section 495, subdivision 5, Judiciary Law; Part 608, Rules of the Appellate Division) denied and petition dismissed, without costs and without disbursements. The application states: "The attorneys employed by the Corporation will render, provide and carry out the practice of law activities of the Corporation as set forth in this paragraph. These activities include providing without charge legal services in those situations which give rise to legal issues having a substantial effect on the legal rights of homosexuals; to promote the availability of legal services to homosexuals by encouraging and attracting homosexuals into the legal profession; to disseminate to homosexuals general information concerning their legal rights and obligations, and to render technical assistance to any legal services corporation or agency in regard to legal issues affecting homosexuals." The stated purposes are on their face neither benevolent nor charitable (cited section, Judiciary Law), nor, in any event, is there a demonstrated need for this corporation. It is not shown that the private sector of the profession is not available to serve this clientele, nor that, as to indigents, the existing legal assistance corporations are not available. A supplemental affidavit does indicate a lack of desire on the part of some attorneys who work pro bono publico to take the cases of homosexuals, but this appears to be no more than a matter of taste, and it is not established that lawyers are completely lacking. The averment does not show that the persons concerned will be without legal services unless this corporation is approved for the purpose.

It is sought in the papers to demonstrate a likeness to the application of Puerto Rican Legal Defense & Education Fund, Inc., heretofore approved by us, but there is no parallel: the latter's application demonstrated clearly that indigence is rife amongst the intended clientele. It does not appear that discrimination against homosexuals, which undoubtedly exists, operates to deprive them of legal representation.

The lack of merit in this application leads us to comment further. We are not told whence the funds to finance the corporation are expected to come, except that they will be solicited. It is well known that there has not been a lack of public and private moneys available to support corporations of this nature, and this free flowing of finance has undoubtedly led to the proliferation of those similar corporations which now exist. While we have not approved any except those which in our opinion fill a real need, we shall require of each such corporation, on application for continued approval, that it demonstrate continuance of that need. Perhaps the legislature should speak again with clarity as to what the words "benevolent or charitable purposes" mean as they are used in section 495. We invite such a clarification. Meanwhile, it seems to us that we should not put our imprimatur upon any corporation which seeks approval to practice law for no more reason than that it claims to represent a minority.

3. *Corporation as a "Person"*

UNION SAVINGS ASS'N v. HOME OWNERS AID, INC.

23 Ohio St.2d 60, 262 N.E.2d 558 (1970).

DUNCAN, Justice. The record, briefs and arguments of counsel raise the question: May a corporate litigant maintain a legal action *in propria persona* through an officer of the corporation who is not a licensed attorney? If a corporation cannot appear *in propria persona* through its officer, the order of the Court of Common Pleas, striking the corporate defendant's petition to vacate judgment, was proper.

Appellant, Home Owners, contends that corporate statutes in R.C. Chapter 1701, in essence, either provide or imply that a corporation is the same as a natural person in all respects and has all the capacities of a natural person, including the right to represent itself *in propria persona* through an appointed agent who need not be an attorney at law. Home Owners asserts constitutional protection for the right to litigate in this manner pursuant to its entitlement to due process and equal protection of the law, as guaranteed by the Ohio and United States Constitutions. In addition, Home Owners urges that a denial of the maintenance of this litigation through its officer unconstitutionally impairs the obligation of contract.

We cannot agree with appellant's contentions, which appear to be based upon the premise that a corporation and a natural living person are in all respects equal. A corporation is an artificial person, created by the General Assembly and deriving its power, authority and capacity from the statutes.

It is true that certain statutes, make it appear that a corporation is to be treated as a natural person. Many other statutes, however, clearly reveal that the General Assembly did not intend a corporation to have all the attributes and powers of a natural person.

* * *

In other jurisdictions, courts have held that a corporation cannot appear *in propria persona*. * * *

The fallacy of defendant corporation's constitutional arguments is that they rest upon the faulty premise that a corporation is in all respects equal to a natural person.

* * *

Beyond what has been concluded hereinabove in importance as a basis for our decision is the statutory prohibition regarding the practice of law. R.C. 4705.01 prohibits anyone from practicing law or commencing or defending an action "in which he is not a party concerned, * * * unless he has been admitted to the bar by order of the Supreme Court * * *."

It is the responsibility of this court to provide effective standards for admission to the practice of law and for the discipline of those admitted to practice. Litigation must be projected through the courts according to established practice by lawyers who are of high character, skilled in the profession, dedicated to the interest of their clients, and in the spirit of public service. In the orderly, process of the administration of justice, any retreat from those principles would be a disservice to the public. To allow a corporation to maintain litigation and appear in court represented by corporate officers or agents only would lay open the gates to the practice of law for entry to those corporate officers or agents who have not been qualified to practice law and who are not amenable to the general discipline of the court.

Judgment affirmed.

---

4. *De Facto Corporations*

ALLEN v. THOMPSON

248 Miss. 544, 158 So.2d 503 (1963).

McElroy, Justice. Appellant filed his bill of complaint on March 28, 1962 seeking an alleged equitable claim or right to certain realty against the following parties: * * *

Lands, Inc., called Lands, the owner of the property since November 17, 1959 under a warranty deed from Thompson and Allen; * * *

The appellants' next contention is that Lands, Inc. never did come into existence, was never either a de jure or de facto corporation, and therefore could not take legal title to the land through a deed executed to them on November 17, 1959, that Lands, Inc. was not legally entitled to do any business or was not in existence for that purpose on either November 17 or November 18, 1959, or until November 26, 1959. Chapter 209, Miss.Laws 1954, now Section 5311.5 of Mississippi Code 1942, Rec., expressly forbids the doing of business by any corporation before $500 has been paid in for capital stock, and the charter of Lands, Inc. contains this provision. The $500 had not been paid in to Lands, Inc. * * *

The incorporators of Lands made a bona fide effort to organize a corporation. The Charter of Incorporation was secured on November 17, 1959, and Lands has since engaged in business as a corporation.

Five hundred shares of capital stock were subscribed for on November 17. A joint meeting of incorporators and subscribers of capital stock was held on the same date; and the organization of the corporation was carried out, officers and directors were elected and the purchase of the real estate was authorized. All of this appears from proper corporate minutes. Bylaws were adopted. The Charter was recorded on November 21 and published on November 28. The required Report of Organization was filed with the Secretary of State on December 1. Lands has since operated as a corporation in every particular and all of its relevant corporate records were examined by Allen's counsel prior to trial. * * *

A technical violation of the * * * statute would not alter the conclusion that Lands, Inc., was a de facto corporation and that Allen, as the grantor, cannot attack the corporation's legality or its ability to acquire title to land.

* * * The general rule, supported by an almost unanimous consensus of judicial opinion, and sometimes expressly declared by statute, is that the legality of the existence of a de facto corporation can be questioned only by the state in a direct proceeding, and cannot be collaterally attacked or litigated in actions or proceedings between private individuals or other corporations or between them and the alleged corporation * * *.

* * * The general rule is that there is a de facto corporation, so that the legality of its corporate existence cannot be attacked collaterally, * * * where there is a special act or general law under which such a corporation may lawfully exist, a bona fide attempt to organize under the law and colorable compliance with the statutory requirements, and actual user or exercise of corporate powers in pursuance of such law and attempted organization; * * *.

In most, if not all, instances where statutes prohibit the corporation from transacting business before the stock has been subscribed or paid for, a failure has not precluded the creation of at least a de facto corporation. * * *

Lands, under the reasonable construction of corporate law and under our own decisions, was a de facto corporation. * * *

Affirmed.

---

5. *Distinction between Public and Private Corporation*

EDSON v. GRIFFIN HOSPITAL

21 Conn.Sup. 55, 144 A.2d 341 (1958).

DEVLIN, Judge. The plaintiff, a resident of the town of Shelton, is a duly licensed physician and surgeon who has been practicing in the Naugatuck valley towns since 1938. In 1943 he became a member of the staff of the defendant hospital and treated patients as a physician and performed certain surgery with the assistance of other surgeons in the hospital until 1954. At that time, as the result of the adoption of new by-laws, rules and regulations, he was denied the right to use the facilities of the hospital in performing certain major surgical operations. These are described as cholecystectomies, abdominal hysterectomies, pelvic repairs, Caesarean sections and surgical procedures on female tubes and ovaries. * * *

In this action he seeks to restrain the defendant hospital from prohibiting him the use of its facilities in performing these operations. * * *

The basis of his * * * claim is that the defendant is a public corporation and public hospital maintained for the medical and surgical treatment of all persons who apply and that he has a right to practice therein so long as he stays within the law and conforms to all reasonable rules and regulations. In effect he contends the hospital is a public institution receiving considerable governmental and public financial assistance, some immunity from taxation, and that he and his patients are entitled to the facilities of the hospital as a matter of right.

The basic question is whether the defendant is a private corporation operating a nonprofit private hospital or is a public corporation operating a public hospital. The defendant was originally incorporated as the Derby Hospital by virtue of a special act of the General Assembly approved June 14, 1901. * * * It does not operate for profit. * * *

The distinction between a public and private corporation has long been recognized. A public corporation is an instrumentality of the state, founded and owned in the public interest, supported by public funds, and governed by those deriving their authority from the state. Public institutions such as state, county and city hospitals and asylums are owned by the public and are devoted chiefly to public purposes. * * *

On the other hand, a corporation organized by permission of the legislature, supported largely by voluntary contributions, and managed by officers and directors who are not representatives of the state or any political subdivision, is a private corporation, although engaged in charitable work or performing duties similar to those of public corporations. * * * The difference between a public and private hospital is now clearly established, the latter being one founded and maintained by private persons or a corporation, the state or municipality having no voice in the management or control of its property or the formation of rules for its government. * * * The mere fact that it is the recipient of state aid, financial assistance from the General Assembly, special grants from the surrounding towns, or contributions from the United Fund, Community Chest or New Haven Foundation does not change its status from a private to a public hospital. Ninety-five per cent of its income is derived from charges for services rendered. * * *

The original act incorporating the defendant empowered it to "make and execute such by-laws, rules, and regulations not contrary to the laws of this state as shall be deemed necessary for the proper management of the affairs of the corporation"; * * * and provided for the selection of a board of trustees who "shall have power to manage and conduct all the business and affairs of the corporation, and to appoint all necessary and proper servants, officers, attendants, and agents, and to remove the same at pleasure, and to do any and all acts necessary and proper to be done for the full and effectual carrying out of the purposes of said corporation." * * * The defendant is found to be a private hospital with the right to exercise control over its own internal operations and management.

* * * Judgment may enter for the defendant.

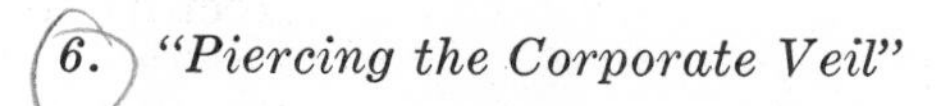

6. *"Piercing the Corporate Veil"*

CASANOVA GUNS, INC. v. CONNALLY

454 F.2d 1320 (C.A.Wis., 1972).

PER CURIAM. This is an appeal by Casanova Guns, Inc. (Casanova Guns), a Wisconsin corporation, from the denial of its application for renewal of its federal firearms license by the Wisconsin Regional Commissioner of the Treasury Department's Alcohol, Tobacco and Firearms Division. The appellant brought an action in the district court under section 102 of the Gun Control Act of 1968, 18 U.S.C. § 923(f)(3), to review the commissioner's decision not to renew the license. The district court upheld the commissioner's decision.

The license was denied because of Casanova Guns' relationship with Casanova's, Inc. (Casanova's), a convicted felon. The Gun Control Act prohibits the issuance of federal firearms licenses to convicted felons and to companies directed or controlled by convicted felons. 18 U.S.C. § 923(d)(1)(B). Based upon their findings that Casanova's controlled or had the power to control Casanova Guns, the commissioner and the district court found the appellant ineligible for a renewal license. We are asked to review the finding that Casanova's controlled Casanova Guns.

An understanding of the commissioner's decision requires an examination of the history of the respective corporations. Casanova's, although incorporated in 1959 by Clarence Casanova, has been in the sporting goods and gun business in Milwaukee for 39 years. The president and major stockholder of Casanova's, Clarence Casanova, held approximately 350 of the 500 shares. Other members of the Casanova family held the remainder of the shares and acted as minor officers in the corporation. In 1966 Casanova's was indicted for the possession of unregistered firearms. Two years later the corporation pleaded guilty and was fined the minimum amount imposed by the statute. That conviction rendered Casanova's ineligible under section 923 for renewal of its federal license.

Casanova Guns was organized in March 1967, subsequent to the indictment of Casanova's but prior to the conviction. The president and sole shareholder of Casanova Guns was John Casanova, Clarence Casanova's son and a shareholder of Casanova's. The other family members, who continued to direct Casanova's, became officers and directors of Casanova Guns. In February 1967 Casanova Guns applied for and received a federal firearms license. After the license was obtained, Casanova Guns took over the first company's entire gun business. Casanova's continued in the general sporting goods business.

On April 16, 1969, Casanova Guns purchased the entire inventory of firearms of Casanova's. In exchange for the inventory, Casanova Guns gave an unsecured promissory note for $424,000. John Casanova ran Casanova Guns in the same building and used the same display area as Casanova's. There was an informal arrangement by which Casanova Guns leased floor space and storage facilities from Casanova's. Separate books and accounts were kept for the two corporations, but John, who considered himself the sole employee of Casanova Guns, was paid his $32,710 salary by Casanova's.

In January 1969, Casanova Guns had applied for a renewal of its federal license. That renewal application was refused on May 29, 1969.

* * *

The appellant urges that Casanova Guns is not a convicted felon and therefore should not be denied a license on the basis of the felon status of Casanova's. That view ignores the express language of the licensing act. The statute explicitly prohibits the issuance of a license to a convicted felon or to a corporation, partnership or association over which a convicted felon exercises or could exercise control. Additionally, it is well settled that the fiction of a corporate entity must be disregarded whenever it has been adopted or used to circumvent the provisions of a statute. * * *

It is apparent from the record that a substantial purpose for the incorporation of Casanova Guns was the circumvention of the statute restricting issuance of firearms licenses to convicted felons. Casanova Guns was formed after Casanova's was under federal indictment. Indeed, the testimony of John Casanova at the administrative hearing is a reluctant admission that the second corporation was formed to insure the continuation of the gun business.

Further, there is a significant unity of interest between the officers and stockholders of the two corporations and the business operations were closely integrated. The four officers of each corporation were the same, the only difference being that Clarence Casanova was the president of Casanova's and John Casanova was the president of Casanova Guns. Casanova Guns operated from the same building as Casanova's and was dependent on Casanova's for light, heat, telephone, bookkeeping and additional personnel when necessary. Casanova's provided these services on an informal "fee" arrangement, but the nature of that arrangement does not destroy the interlocking relationship between the management personnel and practices of the two companies.

In addition, the total assets of Casanova Guns derived from the inventory purchased from Casanova's. That inventory was purchased on a $424,000 unsecured note which is payable on demand. We believe a debt of this nature and magnitude warrants the inference that Casanova's possessed a substantial degree of control over Casanova Guns. That belief is bolstered by the admission of Clarence Casanova that he exercised some control over Casanova Guns in order to protect his investment. That control was made possible by the fact that the two corporations operated out of the same building; also Clarence Casanova's daughter was the bookkeeper for both corporations.

Under these circumstances, although we realize the hardship the denial works upon the Casanova enterprises, we find that the commissioner's denial of the application and the district court's affirmance of that decision were not clearly erroneous. The decision below is therefore affirmed.

---

7. *Corporation cannot "Pierce Veil"*

COLIN v. ALTMAN

39 A.D.2d 200, 333 N.Y.S.2d 432 (1971).

STEUER, Justice. The petitioner herein sought a certificate of eviction for the tenant of an apartment in the building located at 130 West 112th Street. Respondent Rent Commissioner denied the request. * * *

The building is owned by 130 West 112th Street Corp., all the stock of which is owned by the petitioner. Petitioner claimed he desired the apartment for his own use. Respondent denied the application on the ground that petitioner had no standing to obtain a certificate of eviction. We believe the respondent to be correct in that ruling. No other question is involved.

The right to evict a statutory tenant is governed by Rent, Eviction and Rehabilitation Regulations section 55.a, which in pertinent part reads as follows: "A certificate shall be issued where the landlord seeks in good faith to recover possession of a housing accommodation because of immediate and compelling necessity for his own personal use and occupancy, or for the use and occupancy of his immediate family . . . " Petitioner directs attention to other sections of the Regulations where the word "landlord" is used or defined to include a corporate landlord. Such sections have no relevance. It must be obvious that the landlord referred to above is an individual owner as distinct from other legal entities. A corporation has no compelling necessity to occupy housing accommodations, nor does it have a family, immediate or otherwise. The section is limited to individual landlords * * *

A distinction is sought to be made because the petitioner is the sole stockholder. In this connection it is noteworthy that the corporate veil is never pierced for the benefit of the corporation or its stockholders. The procedure is only permissible against a purported stockholder who is using the corporate veil to defraud. Nor is some supposed principle of equity involved. The corporate method of doing business or holding property has long been recognized as a legitimate exercise of business discretion. A sole stockholder receives the same protection and immunities that stockholders of multi-owned corporations enjoy. He is also subject to the same disadvantages. He is not the corporation either in law or fact and, having elected to take the advantages, it is not inequitable to subject him to the disabilities consequent upon his election.

The judgment entered January 10, 1972 (Baer, J.), annulling, pursuant to article 78 CPLR, respondent's order denying a certificate of eviction and remanding the matter for further proceedings should be reversed and vacated on the law and the petition dismissed, without costs.

---

8. *Corporate Merger and Consolidation*

AKWELL CORP. v. EIGER

141 F.Supp. 19 (D.C.N.Y., 1956).

LEVET, District Judge. Defendant has moved to dismiss the complaint in this action to recover damages for an alleged fraud on the ground that the Court lacks jurisdiction because (a) the plaintiff is not the real party in interest; and (b) the controversy is not between citizens of different states, in that the defendant is a citizen of the State of New York and that Killashun Export Corporation, the alleged real party in interest, is also a citizen of the State of New York.

It appears from the affidavits and annexed exhibits submitted on this motion that the defendant had been a customer of Killashun Export Corporation. It also appears that pursuant to an agreement of "Merger and Consolidation" between National Hygienic Products Corporation, The J. & E. Stevens Sales Co., and Killashun Export Corporation a combination was effected which resulted in the continued existence of the National Hygienic Products Corporation. * * *

A photostatic copy of a certificate of the Secretary of State of Delaware, which is annexed to the answering affidavit, indicates that the agreement was filed in the Secretary's office on December 14, 1954.

There is also annexed a photostatic copy of a certificate of the Secretary of State of Delaware which states that on January 7, 1955 a certificate of amendment of the certificate of incorporation of National Hygienic Products Corporation was filed in the Secretary's office. Pursuant to said certificate of amendment, the name of the corporation was changed to The Akwell Corporation, the plaintiff in this action.

* * * Although the term "consolidation" is used in the agreement between the combining corporations in conjunction with the term "merger," it is manifest that the combination of corporate entities resulted in a merger. A merger consists in the uniting of two or more corporations by the transfer of all of the property to an existing corporation which survives the absorption. In this respect a merger differs from a consolidation wherein the existence of all the corporate entities terminates and a new corporation is created. * * *

It is well settled that subsequent to a merger the continuing corporation succeeds to the rights of the absorbed corporation and may itself sue on the claims of the absorbed corporation which have passed to the survivor or continuing corporation by reason of the merger. * * * Accordingly, the plaintiff, The Akwell Corporation, is a proper party to this action and, therefore, this Court has jurisdiction to entertain the suit because there is a diversity of citizenship between the plaintiff, a Delaware corporation, and the defendant, who is a citizen of the State of New York.

Defendant's motion to dismiss is denied.

---

9. Foreign Corporations "Doing Business" in State

HERALY v. VICTOR PRODUCTS CORP.

282 F.Supp. 351 (D.C.Wis., 1968).

REYNOLDS, District Judge. This is an action for personal injuries commenced April 19, 1965. Plaintiff alleges that he was injured as a result of an explosion occurring in a vending machine manufactured by defendant. Plaintiff is an employee of a bottling company which purchased some vending machines from defendant. The vending machine in question was of a type that dispensed soft drinks into a paper cup. The soft drinks are held under pressure from carbon dioxide until they are dispensed. It is alleged that the carbon dioxide regulator which was attached to the new machine as sold by Victor Products was of the wrong type. The explosion allegedly occurred when the plaintiff opened the carbon dioxide valve to allow the pressure to enter tanks where the soft drinks are stored.

Defendant has moved to dismiss the complaint on the grounds that * * * the Court has no jurisdiction over the defendant.

It is conceded by both sides that Victor Products is a Maryland Corporation and does not have a certificate of authority to transact business in Wisconsin. Service of process therefore was made by the plaintiff upon the Secretary of State pursuant to Wisconsin Statutes * * *.

The prime issue before this Court is whether the defendant Victor Products, Inc, was doing business in Wisconsin so that service pursuant to the statutes was effective to give this court jurisdiction of this case.

In considering the question of whether a foreign corporation was doing business within a state, courts view the number, type and significance of contacts a foreign corporation has with the host state.

In the instant case, Victor Products maintains no office or agency in Wisconsin. Instead, it employs salesmen who travel about the state contacting potential customers. These salesmen are also available to give technical advice to their customers and at times they have been known to make or assist in making on the spot repairs of vending machines for their customers. Defendant's affidavits also show that sales representatives do carry some small parts for vending machines with them for use in making minor repairs. * * *

Defendant puts its principal reliance upon the allegation that all contracts negotiated by its sales representatives are "subject to home office approval" before they become binding. This concept is a legal fiction at best. * * *

This court is impressed with the fact that defendant's sales representatives do more than solicit business on a regular and systematic basis in Wisconsin. They are more than "walking catalogs" of defendant's products. They aid and instruct the customer's vendor repairmen. They will aid their customers to set up and maintain a workable vendor repair program. The sales representatives sell small parts which they carry with them directly to the customer without the necessity of home office confirmation.

The Wisconsin long arm statutes have been liberally construed to provide a forum for Wisconsin residents who have been injured through the negligence of foreign corporations. * * *

Courts should determine whether a foreign corporation is doing business within a state for purposes of service of process in the illuminating light of commercial actuality. * * * With these factors in mind this court finds that the defendant had sufficient contacts with this state so that it is amenable to service of process by the methods prescribed by the Wisconsin Statutes for foreign corporations.

For the foregoing reasons the defendant's motion to dismiss should be and hereby is denied.

PROBLEMS

1. A, B, and C decide to organize a corporation for the purpose of conducting a television repair service. The articles of incorporation are prepared and signed by A and B and acknowledged by a notary public. The articles are then given to C who signs them but forgets to have his signature acknowledged by a notary which is required by statute. C files the articles and the required fee with the Secretary of State. Thereafter, A, B, and C meet as the first directors of the ABC Corporation, elect officers, adopt by-laws, purchase a truck to be used in the business, employ D to drive the truck, and conduct other necessary corporate business. While D is driving the truck during the course of his employment, he negligently runs over a pedestrian. The pedestrian brings action against A, B, C, and D individually. A, B, and C defend on the ground that the corporate liability of the ABC Corporation does not extend to them individually. Decision?

2. A entered into a contract with B. In the contract, B was identified as a corporation which was not true. A defaulted on the contract and B brought suit for breach of contract. A defends on the ground that B was not incorporated. Decision?

3. A formed a corporation for the purpose of conducting a newspaper business so that he could publish untrue stores about B, a liberal politician who held a high office. A obtained a stock permit which gave the corporation permission to issue 100 shares of stock at $5.00 a share. The corporation issued 90 shares to A, 5 shares to A's wife, and 5 shares to A's son. Thereafter, A printed a libelous story about B claiming that B was a communist sympathizer, which A knew was untrue. B brings action against A individually. A defends on the ground that only the corporation is liable. Decision?

4. A was the promoter of the D Corporation which was being organized to operate a chain of grocery stores. Prior to the incorporation, A entered into a purchase and sale agreement with S, the owner of a grocery store. The contract was in the name of the D Corporation and A signed as agent; however, A did not inform S that the corporation was not incorporated. Shortly thereafter, D was incorporated; however, the directors refused to recognize the contract with S. S brings action against D and A. Decision?

5. Mr. and Mrs. Jones and Mr. and Mrs. Smith, all ski enthusiasts, purchased a ski lodge. To avoid liability problems, they formed a corporation. Everything went fine the first year. There was plenty of snow, they all pitched in on the work around the lodge, and the corporation showed a good profit. However, the second year Mr. Smith spent more time at the ski lift than he did at the lodge. By the close of the second year, relations between the four owners of the corporation became strained. During the third year it was apparent that Mr. Smith was becoming a great skier, Mrs. Smith was becoming an alcoholic, and Mr. and Mrs. Jones were getting "housemaid's knees". At the end of the third year the corporation was still solvent; however, there was such dissension among the shareholders that there was a management deadlock and irreparable injury to the corporation was threatened. Mr. and Mrs. Jones file suit for dissolution. Decision?

6. The State of Oregon indicted the Pacific Powder Co., a corporation, for manslaughter, when a truck load of explosives belonging to the company was negligently parked and blew up during a fire, causing the death of a bystander. Oregon Criminal Statutes say: "Person' includes corporations as well as natural persons." The statutory penalty for manslaughter is: "Every person convicted of manslaughter shall be punished by imprisonment in the penitentiary for not more than 15 years and by a fine not exceeding $5,000." Can the Pacific Powder Co. be convicted of manslaughter?

7. The Columbia Chemical Company was incorporated in the State of New York. Later a group of persons filed incorporation papers in the State of New York for an organization with the name of The Columbian Chemical Company. In a law suit to prevent the issuance of a charter to the latter company, the Columbia Chemical Company contended that no other company could use the name The Columbian Chemical Company. Is Columbia correct?

8. A state law provides that any person or persons doing business under an assumed or fictitious name should file their true names in the office of the county recorder. Ace, Best and Conn owned all the stock of the ABC Company, a duly organized corporation within the state. The State prosecutes Ace, Best and Conn for failing to register their names under this statute. Decision?

9. The ABC Corporation has 20,000 shares of common stock outstanding, of which 19,000 are owned by Joe Able, 500 by his wife Betty, and 500 by his brother Bill. The three are also the directors and officers of the corporation. ABC Corporation obtained a $50,000 fire insurance policy covering a building owned by the corporation. Thereafter, Joe poured gasoline in the building, set it on fire and let it burn to the ground. The ABC Corporation now sues the insurance company to recover the $50,000 on the policy. Decision?

10. Ace and Best obtained an option upon a building which had been used as a warehouse. They acted as promoters for a corporation, and when the corporation was formed, turned over the building to it for $100,000 worth of stock. Actually, their option on the building called for a purchase price of only $60,000. The other shareholders desire to have $40,000 of Ace's and Best's stock cancelled. Can they succeed in an action to have the stock cancelled?

Chapter 33

CORPORATE MANAGEMENT

A. IN GENERAL

There are three groups which participate in the management of a corporation: the shareholders, the directors, and the officers. The powers, qualifications, functions, and procedures relating to these three groups are prescribed in part by constitutions, statutes, administrative rules and regulations, articles of incorporation, by-laws, various shareholder and director resolutions and agreements, and proxies.

B. POWERS

A corporation's powers are the things which it is authorized to do. They are derived from its articles of incorporation and the laws of the state under which it was organized. A corporation has only such powers as are expressly or impliedly conferred by its charter. There is a difference between the powers of a natural person and a corporation; a natural person can do anything not forbidden by law, but a corporation can only do what is expressly or impliedly authorized by the state.

1. EXPRESS POWERS

Express powers may be found in the corporation statutes, which are usually quite explicit and lengthy, or in the articles of incorporation.

Common express powers granted by statute are:

a. to have a corporate name;

b. to have perpetual existence;

c. to have a common seal;

d. to purchase and hold land and personal property for authorized corporate purposes;

e. to make by-laws for the governing of the corporation;

f. to borrow money when necessary to carry out the corporate purpose;

g. to sell, convey, mortgage, pledge, or lease part or all of its property;

h. to make contracts and incur liabilities;

i. to conduct its business within or outside of the state of incorporation;

j. to acquire its own shares;

k. to declare and pay dividends;

l. to amend its articles of incorporation;

m. to effect a merger or consolidation;

n. to have and exercise all powers necessary or convenient to effect any or all of the purposes for which it was formed;

o. to seize its corporate activities and surrender its corporate franchise.

2. IMPLIED POWERS

In addition to the express powers granted by the state, corporations, in the absence of limitation by statute or by the articles, have the implied powers to do all acts that may be necessary to enable them to exercise the express powers. To be implied, the act must tend directly and immediately to accomplish the purpose of the corporation's creation. Examples of implied powers are:

a. to take and hold property;

b. to borrow money, issue notes, bonds or other obligations;

c. to loan corporate funds;

d. to reacquire its own shares of stock;

e. to acquire and hold shares and other securities of other corporations;

f. to contribute to charity.

Implied powers are often made express by statute or by the articles.

3. ULTRA VIRES

An ultra vires act is one that is beyond the scope of the powers of the corporation; e.g., business corporation engaging in charitable enterprise, such as building a church; corporation in grocery business lending money to produce a stage play on broadway.

Contracts fully executed on both sides are valid, and neither the corporation nor the other contracting party can use ultra vires as a defense; however, when the contract is entirely executory, ultra vires is a good defense by either party.

The modern majority rule is that an ultra vires contract which is not illegal is not void but is enforceable under certain circumstances; e.g., where one party has received benefits under the contract he cannot set up the defense that the corporation did not have power to act.

The Model Business Corporation Act and many statutes abolish the defense of ultra vires. Even where the doctrine has been abolished as a shield against liability, it may still be used in the following ways:

a. by a shareholder against the corporation to enjoin it from further ultra vires acts;

b. by the state to enjoin further ultra vires acts or to dissolve the corporation; and

c. by the corporation or a shareholder acting on behalf of the corporation to sue the persons who committed the ultra vires act to recover damages for loss to the corporation.

Formerly, the tortious acts of the corporation's agents were ultra vires; and, therefore, the corporation was not liable. Today, a corporation is liable for the torts of its agents committed within the course of employment under the agency rule of respondeat superior; i.e., let the master answer.

Formerly, a corporation could not be guilty of a crime, but today it is well settled that a corporation can be criminally punished by fine or dissolution for the criminal conduct of its agents.

C. SHAREHOLDERS

1. IN GENERAL

A shareholder or stockholder is one who holds membership in a corporation by reason of his ownership of one or more shares of stock. He appears on the books of the corporation as owner and, therefore, is entitled to a voice in its affairs and is burdened with the liabilities incident to that of a shareholder.

In the absence of statute, shareholders cannot act for the corporation, either individually or collectively. The management of the corporation is vested in the board of directors; however, the shareholders have indirect managerial power in the form of voting at shareholder's meetings for the election or removal of directors, adoption of by-laws, shareholder resolutions, approval of changes in the articles of incorporation, and approval of transactions beyond the regular business of the corporation.

2. SHAREHOLDER MEETINGS

Shareholders must act at a regular or special meeting, or their actions have no legal effect; however, it has been held that where all of the shareholders act together on behalf of the corporation without a regular meeting or formal vote, the action is valid.

A. Place of Meeting

The articles, by-laws, or directors may prescribe the place of meeting. Most states permit a shareholders' meeting to be held outside the state of incorporation and this is the position of the Model Business Corporation Act, Section 26. Shareholders who participate in a meeting improperly held as to place or time waive their right to object to it.

B. Time of Holding

Regular meetings must be held at the time prescribed in the statute, articles, or by-laws. Statutes normally do not require notice of regular meetings; however, it is the usual practice to give notice to all shareholders.

C. Special Meetings

Special meetings are usually called by the board of directors pursuant to the by-laws, articles, or statutes for a special purpose. Notice of the day, hour, and place of the meeting must be given to all shareholders. The notice must state the nature of the business to be transacted at the meeting, and no other business may be conducted unless all of the shareholders waive this limitation. Shareholders who participate in a special meeting improperly called waive their right to object.

D. Quorum

A quorum is necessary to have a valid shareholders' meeting. Articles, by-laws, or statutes may provide that in order to constitute a quorum, a specified number of shareholders must attend; usually, this is a simple majority.

E. Vote

In the absence of restrictions, each person who is registered as a shareholder on the corporation books has the right to vote. The general rule is that each shareholder has the right to one vote for each share of stock. The common law rule that each shareholder had one vote, regardless of the number of shares he holds, has been changed by statute or court decision in practically all jurisdictions.

The most common types of voting rights are (1) straight, (2) cumulative, and (3) class.

Straight voting means that each share has one vote for each business matter including one vote for each director to be elected. Straight voting is the common method of voting on corporation business, except where cumulative voting is used in the election of directors.

Cumulative voting which is required in some states, is a system of voting which applies only to the election of the board of directors. Each share has as many votes as there are vacancies to be filled, and the votes can be distributed among the candidates in any way the shareholder desires; i.e., the shareholder can cumulate his votes. For example, if ten directors are to be elected, a shareholder who owns one share has ten votes, and he may give all ten votes to one candidate or five votes to two candidates, etc. The purpose of cumulative voting is to permit minority shareholders to combine and secure some representation on the board of directors. For this reason, it is necessary that the directors be elected as a board; i.e., all at the same time. Cumulative voting is also permitted in the removal of directors.

Class or series voting is where there are two or more classes or series of stock outstanding and where each class or series of stock votes as a separate unit for one or more purposes; e.g., a classified board of directors with one class of stock voting for its class of directors and the other class voting for its class of directors.

F. PROXY VOTING

A proxy is an authority to vote stock. In the absence of an express requirement, a person does not have to be a shareholder to act as a proxy. The person acting as proxy to vote the stock is an agent for voting purposes. Most states permit voting by proxy but require that the proxy be in writing and signed by the shareholder; however, in the absence of an express requirement, no particular formality is required.

G. VOTING AGREEMENTS

In most states, an agreement among shareholders to vote in a certain manner so as to concentrate their voting strength for the purpose of controlling the management is valid unless there is fraud or other illegal object. In most states, such agreements are valid even though they bind the directors in the exercise of their discretion as long as they do not substantially limit the discretion of the directors.

H. VOTING TRUSTS

A voting trust exists when, pursuant to an agreement, some or all of the shareholders transfer their shares to a voting trustee or trustees to hold and vote for them until the purpose of the trust is fulfilled or for a specified period. It is a device to concentrate shareholder control in one or more persons for the purpose of controlling management. Voting trusts are valid in most states, many of which have enacted statutes which provide for the procedures in setting up the trust, powers and duties of trustees, and its duration.

3. SHAREHOLDER ELECTION AND REMOVAL OF DIRECTORS

At the annual or regular shareholder meeting, shareholders participate in the management of the corporation by electing the directors. Also, in the absence of statute or by-laws to the contrary, shareholders elect directors to fill vacant and newly-created directorates.

Shareholders also have the power to remove a director for cause. A director can be removed without cause only if such right were reserved at the time the director was elected.

4. BY-LAWS AND RESOLUTIONS

Shareholders participate in management in some states by the power to adopt the initial by-laws, and in most states by the inherent power to amend or repeal the by-laws.

Shareholders may pass resolutions which will affect the management of the corporations; e.g., indorsing the administration of former president and demanding his reinstatement. Shareholder resolutions may cover a wide variety of subject matter.

5. UNUSUAL MATTERS

Shareholders exercise managerial powers in various unusual corporate business matters; e.g., approval of shareholders required for amendment of articles of incorporation, sale or lease of assets outside regular course of corporation business, merger, consolidation, or dissolution.

6. INSPECTION OF BOOKS

A shareholder personally or through an attorney or accountant, has the right to inspect the books of the corporation at reasonable times for any legitimate purposes; e.g., to ascertain the financial condition of the corporation; to compile a list of shareholders to contact them for the purchase of their stock so as to increase ownership and voting power; to obtain information in aid of bona fide litigation with the corporation. However, improper, or hostile purposes will justify a denial of inspection; e.g., to seek information to aid a competitor in business; to secure advertising lists; to secure list of shareholders to use for contact as business prospects.

7. SHAREHOLDERS' ACTIONS

A shareholder can sue his corporation in a direct action to enforce his shareholder contract. He can also sue in a derivative action on behalf of the corporation against persons who have damaged the corporation when the corporation refuses to bring an action; e.g., suit against third persons for breach of contract with corporation. Shareholders may also join in an action on behalf of the corporation when the corporation refuses to defend itself.

8. OTHER SHAREHOLDER RIGHTS

Other rights include the rights to have his shares recorded in the stock book of the corporation, to have issued to him a properly executed certificate as evidence of his ownership of shares, to transfer his shares as he chooses subject to any valid restrictions, to receive his proportion of dividends as they are declared subject to various preferences, and to receive any balance of the net corporate assets upon dissolution.

9. SHAREHOLDER LIABILITY

Ordinarily, shareholder liability is limited. See Corporations, Chapter 32, Section A, 2, supra. Thus, in the ordinary case, the shareholder is not personally liable for the debts of the corporation. The risk of the shareholder is limited to his capital investment. In some cases, the shareholder may have unlimited or further liability; e.g., when the corporate entity is broken, discussed supra; when a statute provides that a shareholder is liable for wages of corporation employees; when a shareholder has not fully paid his stock subscription; when dividends are improperly paid out of capital, the shareholders are generally liable to creditors to the extent of the depletion of the capital.

D. DIRECTORS

The management of a corporation is usually entrusted to a board of directors. Nearly all states require at least three directors. The required number is usually stated in the articles of incorporation.

1. QUALIFICATIONS

Most statutes today make no requirement regarding qualifications. Some statutes require that the directors be twenty-one years of age, be citizens of the United States, be residents of the state of incorporation, or be shareholders. Qualifications may be prescribed in the articles of incorporation or the by-laws.

2. ELECTION, TERM, AND REMOVAL

The first directors are usually named in the articles of incorporation or are elected by the incorporators.

The term of office is usually until the next annual meeting and until the successor is elected.

Directors may be removed for cause by the shareholders; e. g., insanity, conviction of a felony, fraud, or gross abuse of authority. Many states have enacted statutes which spell out the removal of directors, and which often preserve cumulative and class voting rights for the shareholders.

3. COMPENSATION

Directors are not entitled to compensation for ordinary services. If extraordinary services are performed as an officer or agent of the corporation, quasi-contractual recovery may be had. Directors have no inherent authority to vote a salary to any director; however, it is becoming more common for director compensation to be provided for by statutes, articles of incorporation, by-laws, or shareholder resolutions. Directors are usually entitled to reimbursement of expenses incurred in furtherance of corporate business.

4. FUNCTIONS AND POWERS

The function of the board of directors is to set major policies and to direct the business of the corporation. The details of the operating management is usually left in varying degrees to the officers. Some of the usual functions and powers of the board of directors are:

a. to select, supervise, remove, and fix the compensation for officers including retirement plans;

b. to determine dividend payments, financing and capital changes;

c. policy decisions regarding products, prices, services, wages, and labor relations.

The following actions by the board of directors generally require a two-thirds approval of the shareholders:

a. amendment of the articles of incorporation;

b. increase or decrease of stock;

c. consolidation, merger, sale of entire assets, or dissolution.

A director has an absolute right to inspection of the corporation books, and his right cannot be denied even though his motive is ulterior and his purpose is improper.

5. MEETINGS AND BOARD ACTION

A. NOTICE

Notice of a directors' meeting is usually necessary although it may be waived if a quorum is present, and each of the directors present signs a written approval of the meeting. It may also be waived by a director who is not notified of a special meeting, but nevertheless attends without complaint as to the illegality of the meeting. A resolution passed at an improperly called board of directors' meeting can be enforced by a third party who was unaware that the meeting was improperly called as the corporation is estopped from setting up such a defense. Innocent third persons have the right to assume that the meeting was duly held. By-laws may dispense with notice of regular meetings but not of special meetings.

B. PLACE

Regular meetings must be held at the place designated in the by-laws except when changed by approval of all the members of the board or by board resolution. *Special* meetings may be held at a place designated or at the principal office of the corporation.

Meetings usually may be held within or without the state of incorporation unless restricted by statute, the articles, or by-laws.

C. QUORUM

Unless otherwise stated by statute, the articles, or by-laws, a quorum is a majority of the whole number of directors. Board of directors action usually requires a majority vote of the directors present at a meeting at which a quorum of the directors is present.

D. MUST ACT AS A BOARD

Ordinarily, directors can only exercise their management functions when duly convened as a board. This requirement may be waived by the shareholders as it is mainly for their benefit.

E. PROXY

Directors vote personally as individuals and are not allowed to vote by proxy except in a few states by statute. This is because directors must attend personally to the business of the corporation and because of the value of their consultation and collective judgment.

6. FIDUCIARIES

Directors are fiduciaries and must exercise their powers in good faith and in the interest of the corporation. A director cannot enter into any competing business with the corporation, cannot take advantage of a business opportunity which could have been utilized by the corporation, cannot have an interest which conflicts with the interest of the corporation, cannot make secret profits, cannot oppress minority shareholders, and in a growing minority of states cannot sell stock to shareholders without revealing important inside information that he may have as to the value of the stock or as to the business of the corporation (there are three federal statutes dealing with insider trading: the Securities Exchange Act of 1934, as amended in 1964; the Public Utility Holding Company Act of 1935; and the Investment Company Act of 1940).

7. LIABILITY OF DIRECTORS

Directors owe a duty of ordinary and reasonable care to the corporation. When the required duty of care is violated, the directors are liable to the corporation for such corporate damage as was caused by the negligence. Directors are liable for losses caused by their bad faith, willful and intentional departures from their duty, and fraudulent breaches of trust. Directors are also under a duty to act within their authority and are liable for any loss to the corporation from engaging in activities which are ultra vires. Examples of actions which have caused directors to be jointly and severally liable to the corporation are as follows:

a. negligence in selecting or supervising an officer, agent, or employee;

b. participation in the wrongful act of another director or officer;

c. making false reports or entries in the corporate books;

d. improperly expending corporate funds for management compensation;

e. wrongful distribution of corporate assets among themselves or the shareholders;

f. making unauthorized loans to directors, officers, or shareholders, of corporate funds or other property;

g. unauthorized purchase of corporation's own stock;

h. unauthorized issuance of a dividend; and

i. closing down factory with loss of over one million dollars in furtherance of anti-labor policy.

E. OFFICERS

Statutes usually provide that a corporation must have specified officers. Typical are the requirement of a president, vice-president, secretary, and treasurer.

1. QUALIFICATIONS

Some statutes provide that officers must have certain qualifications. In the absence of statute, there are no particular qualifications except that an officer should have legal capacity since he is an agent of the corporation.

2. ELECTION, TERM, AND REMOVAL

The officers are usually appointed by the directors; however, in many states, by statute, officers are elected by the shareholders.

Officers usually serve at the pleasure of the board of directors.

Officers are removable with or without cause by the board of directors in most states. When an officer has a valid contract of employment with the corporation, the board of directors has the power to remove the officer without cause but must pay damages for breach of contract.

3. COMPENSATION

Officers who are not directors have the right to reasonable compensation for their services. Their compensation is normally fixed prior to the rendering of services.

Officers who are also directors are presumed to serve without compensation on usual matters, but are entitled to reasonable compensation for unusual services. It is becoming common for a director-officer to receive a fixed compensation on a pre-arranged basis. Sometimes, the compensation is ratified by the shareholders.

In addition to fixed salaries and liberal expense accounts, there are other forms of compensation; e.g., profit-sharing plans, stock bonuses, stock purchase plans, pensions, annuities, tax reimbursement plans, and deferred compensation plans.

4. FUNCTIONS AND POWERS

Officers have such management functions and powers as are given them by the board of directors. The board is limited in such delegation by statutes, articles of incorporation, and by-laws.

A. PRESIDENT

The president may also be chairman of the board of directors. If he is, he is the chief executive officer of the corporation; if he is not, he is second in command to the chairman of the board. His real power depends on the internal structure of the corporation; he may be a figurehead, or he may be the controlling power.

The president usually presides at board of directors and shareholder meetings. Modern cases hold that he has authority to act as agent on behalf of the corporation within the scope of the business of the corporation. The older cases hold that he has no authority to bind the corporation. When the president is also the general manager of the corporation, he has implied power to do such acts as are necessary to carry out the business of the corporation. In large corporations, the president is usually the presiding officer, and the detailed management of the corporate business is delegated to a general manager.

B. VICE-PRESIDENT

A vice-president assists the president and acts as his substitute when the president is unable to act. A vice-president has no authority to bind the corporation. In large corporations, there are usually several vice-presidents whose functions are to act as department heads.

C. SECRETARY

The secretary usually attends meetings of the corporation and keeps minutes and records of corporate transactions. He also gives notices, certifies corporate records and keeps the corporate seal. He cannot bind the corporation.

D. TREASURER

The treasurer has charge of the financial records and disbursement of corporate funds. In most states, he cannot bind the corporation. In large corporations, there is usually a controller in addition to the treasurer. In such case, the controller keeps the records while the treasurer handles the money.

5. FIDUCIARIES

Officers, like directors, have a fiduciary relationship with the corporation. The law on the fiduciary relationship between the directors and the corporation, supra, is applicable here; i.e., cannot make secret profits, etc.

6. LIABILITY OF OFFICERS

Officers owe a duty of ordinary and reasonable care to the corporation and are liable for willful or negligent acts that result in corporate loss.

An officer may incur personal liability when he contracts on behalf of the corporation without authority; and even when he has authority, he can be liable on a contract if he does not indicate that he is contracting as an agent for the corporation.

An officer who commits a tort is personally liable to the victim of the tort; and if the tort is committed within his scope of employment, the corporation will also be liable under the doctrine of respondeat superior.

Statutes in many states provide that officers are liable for corporate taxes, debts, wages, and crimes under specific circumstances; e. g., liable for failure to withhold taxes; liable for debts contracted before filing of certificate of paid-in capital; liable for anti-trust violation.

---

1. *Ultra Vires Acts of Corporation*

LEPPALUOTO v. EGGLESTON

57 Wash.2d 393, 357 P.2d 725 (1960).

DONWORTH, Judge. This is a derivative action brought by appellant as the owner of one half of the outstanding stock of Alaska Towing & Salvage, Inc., an Alaska corporation, against respondents Eggleston and wife as the owners of the remaining half of the corporate stock. * * *

In the case at bar there were two pivotal issues decided by the trial court:

(1) That respondent had no express or implied authority to commit the corporation (ATS) to the lighterage agreement, that is, the transaction was *ultra vires,* and (2) respondent, in chartering his own equipment to the joint venture without the knowledge or consent of appellant, breached a fiduciary obligation to ATS. Both parties to this action accept these conclusions of law as fair and accurate. The fiduciary relationship between respondent Eggleston and ATS and the above-mentioned breaches of the obligation arising therefrom are unchallenged facts as found by the trial court. The rule of law applicable to these facts is this:

> "Whether a director or other corporate officer be considered as an agent or as trustee, he is liable to the corporation * * * where he acts outside the scope of his authority to the injury of the corporation. * * *" 3 Fletcher, Cyclopedia Corporations, 526, § 1021.

Furthermore, the good motives or good intentions of the corporate officer in no way relieve him from liability. * * * If a corporate officer willfully perform an act which he knows, or ought to know, is unauthorized (an express finding in the case at bar), such person is clearly liable to the corporation for resulting damages. * * *

Summarizing, the profits gained from an unauthorized transaction, entered into by a corporate officer in behalf of the corporation, belong to the corporation, whereas the losses sustained in such a transaction are borne by the corporate officer himself. As we view the problem, the relief to which the corporation is entitled is no different whether the corporate officer engages in the unauthorized pursuit in his own behalf or whether he does so in behalf of the corporation, as in the present case. A wrong has been committed in either case. * * *

The judgment of the trial court is hereby modified by increasing the amount thereof to $18,229.37, and, as so modified, it is affirmed.

---

2. *Cumulative Voting for Directors*

BOHANNAN v. CORPORATION COMMISSION

82 Ariz. 299, 313 P.2d 379 (1957).

STRUCKMEYER, Justice. Appellants petitioned the court below for a writ of mandamus to compel the filing of the articles of incorporation of a proposed domestic company. Judgment was entered that no writ issue and this appeal followed.

* * * On the 24th of January, 1956, appellants attempted to form a corporation to be known as the Associated Mortgage and Investment Company by filing their proposed articles of incorporation with the Arizona Corporation Commission. The Commission rejected the articles, giving as its reason that Part 4 thereof provided for a system of staggered directors in violation of the Constitution. * * * Part 4 established a nine-member board of directors to be elected on a staggered basis in this manner: At the first meeting all nine to be elected, three to serve one year, three to serve two years, and three to serve three years; thereafter, at each annual election, three directors to be elected for terms of three years each. * * *

As a preliminary, it is to be observed that there is nothing contrary to the public policy of this state in the practice of classification of directors by term. It has as its aim corporate stability and continuity of experienced management.

* * * Cumulative voting for directors, on the other hand, as a somewhat more recent development in corporate practice is in

derogation of the common law and not to be permitted unless specifically authorized by constitutional, statutory or charter provisions. * * *

Article 14, Section 10, of the Arizona Constitution provides:

> "In all elections for directors or managers of any corporation, each shareholder shall have the right to cast as many votes in the aggregate as he shall be entitled to vote in same company under its charter multiplied by the number of directors or managers *to be elected* at such election; and each shareholder may cast the whole number of votes, either in person or by proxy, for one candidate, or distribute such votes among two or more such candidates; and such directors or managers shall not be elected otherwise." (Italics ours.)

* * * The Commission points out that at least one method of staggering directors by terms plainly denies to the stockholders this right; namely, where a corporation has three directors elected one each year for a three-year term. Unquestionably such a plan is illegal and void as coming within the implied prohibition of the Constitution in that it absolutely denies the mandatory right guaranteed to cumulate votes; but merely because it is possible to circumvent the Constitution by one method of staggering directors does not mean that all schemes or plans to that end are within the implied prohibition. * * *

We have been referred to the statement by Mr. E. E. Ellinwood, an illustrious attorney and member of the Bar of this state and a member of the constitutional convention. There at a meeting of the committee of the whole, he in part stated:

> "Mr. Chairman, this provision in one form or the other is in effect in California, Illinois, Idaho, Missouri, Montana, South Dakota, Pennsylvania, North Dakota, West Virginia, and it seems to me it is very essential. It gives the minority stockholder a look-in. While he cannot control the corporation he can have a member on the board so he knows what is going on, and I think if this system is adopted the minority stockholders will be protected." * * *

Plainly there is manifested an intention to protect minority stockholders, but nothing stated imports an intention to give proportional representation to them. Rather the purpose is to make it possible to have "a member on the board so that he knows what is going on." From this the least that can be said is that it contains no comfort for the argument in favor of proportional representation.

* * * The judgment of the court below is reversed with directions to grant the petition for peremptory writ of mandamus.

3. *Stockholders Right to have Shares Registered*

KEENELAND ASS'N v. PESSIN

484 S.W.2d 849 (Ky., 1972).

GARDNER, Commissioner. By summary judgment Keeneland Association was directed to register in Arnold G. Pessin's name twenty-five shares of capital stock of Keeneland Association. Keeneland appeals. We affirm.

Dr. Pessin purchased twenty-five shares of Keeneland stock from one W. T. Markey for five dollars ($5.00). The new ownership was properly authenticated but Keeneland refused to transfer the stock on the corporation books on the ground that Dr. Pessin's purpose in acquiring the stock was to wreck the corporation and to use his position as a stockholder to aid him as a competitor.

We shall not indulge in a discussion of the acrimonious relationship of Dr. Pessin and Keeneland Association, except as it might have a bearing on the legal issues involved.

Keeneland points out that it was a nonprofit corporation organized and formed for broad eleemosynary purposes. Under its articles no dividend would ever be paid to a shareholder and in the event of dissolution assets would be distributed to tax-exempt organizations. Other purposes for which Keeneland was organized were the improvement and betterment of racing in general, the improvement of a breed of thoroughbred horses and other livestock, and generally to promote the welfare of the horse industry.

Keeneland contends that Dr. Pessin and his associates not only did not share the lofty purposes expressed in the articles but, as evinced by their talk and action, were determined to do all in their power to destroy Keeneland. * * *

It is a well established rule that a corporation must transfer on its books the name of the owner of newly acquired stock. * * * And the rule holds regardless of the motive of the person acquiring the stock. * * * An exception to the rule is recognized in some jurisdictions where the new stockowner seeks the transfer for purposes seriously injurious to the corporation.

* * *

We do not find where this court has passed on the question of whether a corporation may refuse to transfer stock in the name of the transferee where it is shown there exists a conspiracy to destroy the corporation. * * * Since Dr. Pessin established the ownership of the stock, the burden of proof was on Keeneland. This was conceded by Keeneland. Dr. Pessin insisted he did not intend to destroy Keeneland or to do anything to its detriment. On the contrary, he stated in his deposition and in his affidavit that his purpose in becoming a stockholder was to help Keeneland and the horse-racing business in Central Kentucky and that he had the best interest of Keeneland at heart. * * *

Keeneland has pointed to nothing concrete in the record to substantiate the claim of conspiracy to destroy, nor has it demonstrated that such facts exist. * * *

Keeneland argues further that Dr. Pessin was in the business of buying and selling thoroughbred horses in direct competition with Keeneland (a fact admitted by Dr. Pessin) and that as a registered stockholder of Keeneland he would have access to confidential information which could be used to the detriment of Keeneland. No cases are cited holding that a stockholder of a corporation may not legitimately carry on business in competition with the corporation. * * *

As a bulwark against a stockholder's using his position to cause harm to the corporation is KRS 271.395(4), which provides: "Every shareholder shall have a right to examine, in person or by agent or attorney, at any reasonable time or times, *for any proper corporate purpose,* the share register or duplicate, and the books of account and records of the proceedings of the shareholders and directors, and to make extracts therefrom." It is noted that a shareholder may examine the books only for a "proper corporate purpose." We do not believe that an intent to destroy a corporation, to bring vexatious suits, or to take unfair advantage for competition reasons could be included in the phrase "proper corporate purpose." Even though a transferee should intend to carry out these schemes, he would be precluded, as pointed out by the trial court, from consummating them because of the statute. The question is not so much whether the stockholder is entitled to have the stock transferred on the books but whether he uses his right to examine the books for proper corporate purposes.

* * *

The judgment is affirmed.

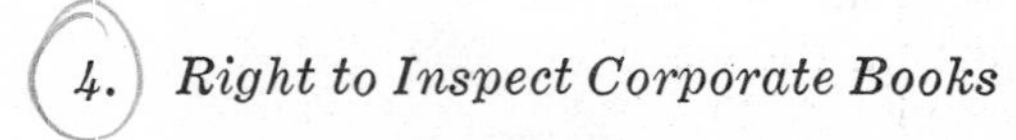

4. *Right to Inspect Corporate Books*

GOLDMAN v. TRANS-UNITED INDUSTRIES, INC.

404 Pa. 288, 171 A.2d 788 (1961).

COHEN, Justice. Appellees, collective owners of one-half of one percent of the stock in appellant corporation (Trans-United), filed a complaint in mandamus seeking inspection of the books of Trans-United. The complaint avers that the affairs of Trans-United were not being properly managed and that the books were irregular and incomplete. The complaint also states that the plaintiffs-appellees desire to ascertain: (1) salaries paid to officers and directors, (2) the value of corporate shares, and (3) the names of stockholders and the extent of their holdings, and it is concluded by an assertion that if the books of the corporation reveal irregularities and mismanagement the plaintiffs will either file a bill in equity to appoint a receiver or solicit proxies to effectuate a change in management.

Trans-United's amended answer denied these allegations and alleged as new matter that appellees' true purpose in seeking examination of all the books of Trans-United was to gain control of that corporation through a general plan designed to deflate the market value of Trans-United stock while simultaneously inflating the value of the stock of Son-Mark Industries, Inc., a holding company in which the appellees have an interest and through which they intend to gain control of Trans-United.

* * * The lower court granted judgment on the pleadings in favor of plaintiff-appellees thus permitting them to examine the books, and Trans-United appealed. * * *

The common law right of a shareholder to inspect the books of a corporation is not an absolute right—it rests on conditions of propriety and reasonableness as to time, place and purpose. * * * The requested relief will not be granted where the purpose is proven to be improper or unreasonable, but the burden of so proving is on the corporation.

* * * A distinction must be made, however, between a stockholder's right to a general inspection of the books and records and a request for inspection or a copy of the shareholders lists. It has been commonly held in this state that a request for inspection of the stockholders lists for purposes of contacting and binding together the other stockholders for such blanket reasons as voting at stockholders' meetings constitutes a proper purpose. Courts tend to be more lenient as to the inspection of stockholders lists than inspections of books and records.

The primary reason for this special treatment lies in the very nature of and purpose for obtaining the stockholders lists; i. e., to influence the vote at an impending stockholders' meeting. If the right to obtain a list of stockholders is not granted liberally by the courts, the corporation, by such simple dilatory tactics as filing an answer and submitting the case to a trial of fact, can delay the stockholder's procurement of the list beyond date of the stockholders' meeting. * * *

The right to obtain a list of stockholders nevertheless remains a qualified right, and in a proper case the corporation could sufficiently aver an improper purpose on the part of the plaintiff-stockholder to merit a trial on the factual issue. * * * However, the facts averred in the answer must indicate not merely that the purpose is improper in the same general sense that a request for an inspection of the books is proven improper, but rather that it is improper as it relates to the relatively harmless act of obtaining a list of stockholders.

* * * Accordingly, to the extent of allowing appellees to obtain a list of stockholders and their holdings, the lower court was correct in granting judgment on the pleadings. However, in respect to the appellees' request to inspect all the books of the corporation we reverse and remand to the court below for further proceedings not inconsistent with this opinion. * * *

The judgment, as modified, is affirmed.

---

5. *Corporate Management by Directors*

SAIGH EX REL. ANHEUSER-BUSCH, INC. v. BUSCH

396 S.W.2d 9 (Mo., 1965), certiorari denied 384 U.S. 942, 86 S.Ct. 1465, 16 L.Ed.2d 541.

RUDDY, Judge. This is a stockholders' derivative action.

The instant appeal before us is by plaintiffs from a judgment * * * wherein the trial court sustained the motion of defendant August A. Busch, Jr., to dismiss * * * "with prejudice."

This suit was instituted by Fred Saigh and Elizabeth Saigh as stockholders of Anheuser-Busch, Inc., as a class action against August A. Busch, Jr., an individual defendant, and Anheuser-Busch, Inc. * * *

The general nature of the allegations * * * is that August A. Busch, Jr., as president of the nominal defendant is receiving salary and perquisites which are excessive and not based on the reasonable value of his services as president of the corporation. * * *

We now review what we consider to be the fundamental principles of law involved. The management and control of the property and business of a corporation is vested * * * in the Board of Directors, and this has been a fundamental principle of our statutory corporate law for many years. * * * Essentially, a corporation should be run for the benefit of its stockholders and not for that of its directors and officers, but no individual stockholder has the authority to take over the duties of corporate management. The management and control of the corporation being vested by statute in the board of directors * * * and the stockholders cannot control the directors in the exercise of the judgment vested in them by the statute. * * * If any or all of the directors perform improperly, the corporation itself is the proper party plaintiff to bring an action to recover any losses occasioned by the wrong. * * * In the event of the failure or refusal of the directors to litigate, then the stockholders may sue, however, it must be in right of the corporation, in which their petition and proof must make a case of wrongful refusal on the part of the directors to sue. * * *

If it is necessary for a stockholder to bring a derivative action because the corporate management wrongfully refuses to do so, it is conducted by the stockholder as the representative of the corporation and in such action the corporation is the real party in interest and it is brought for the benefit of the corporation. * * *

The management of a corporation is in the directors and the establishment and fixing of remuneration and perquisites for officers and managerial duties normally and initially are in the board of directors and, as we have pointed out in this regard, such duties being in the business and management area, any decision by the board of directors in connection therewith is usually controlling and exclusive and the stockholders cannot control the exercise of the judgment vested in them, unless this judgment is exercised in an arbitrary and capricious manner or contrary to by-laws or majority stockholders' action. * * *

Plaintiffs contend that since the action desired by them was the restitution of unreasonable compensation given to defendant Busch and since the setting of his compensation was within the management area of the board of directors and was beyond the statutory power of the stockholders, that they considered it not necessary to explain their failure to apply to the stockholders for redress. We do not agree with this position taken by the plaintiffs. * * *

Therefore, we agree with defendant Busch that one could scarcely imagine an issue which would be more properly subject to resolution within the walls of a corporation than the setting of an officer's compensation, especially where, as in the instant case, it is alleged that the board of directors is controlled by the defendant Busch. The authorities * * * give support to our position that where the directors are charged to be under the influence of defendant Busch, the stockholders have the right to consider the matter and ratify, if they wish, any act of the directors, provided the act is not ultra vires, illegal or fraudulent. We rule that plaintiffs were under a duty to submit their grievance to the body of stockholders before bringing this action. * * *

The judgment of the trial court should be affirmed. It is so ordered.

---

6. *Director is not Employee*

WHARTON v. FIDELITY-BALTIMORE NATIONAL BANK

222 Md. 177, 158 A.2d 887 (1960).

EMORY H. NILES, Special Judge. The question presented in this case is whether a director of a corporation is an "employee" of, or "employed" by, or in the "employment" of the corporation. The case arises upon the interpretation of a restricted stock option agreement and related documents, under the terms of which the option is not exercisable until the holder "has been employed" by the corporation for a period of forty-eight months. * * *

In 1951 the Company was in financial straits, and it was determined to invite Wharton to be "vice president—finance" in order to take control of the management. * * * Wharton was offered a salary of $45,000. and a series of options to purchase 25,000 shares of common stock. * * * The option in the case at bar was not exercisable until Wharton had been employed for forty-eight months by the Martin Company.

* * * Wharton assumed * * * duties at the Company as of February 21, 1952. * * * Wharton was elected as a director on May 15, 1953 in addition to his office as vice president —finance. * * *

On December 24, 1954 Wharton suffered a severe illness, and * * * he * * * advised that he did not intend to resume his duties as vice president—finance after recovering from his illness, but that he intended to continue as a director of the Company. * * * Wharton thereafter continued as a director only until December 20, 1956, when he resigned.

Wharton's service as an officer was thus for approximately thirty-nine months, from February 21, 1952 until June 3, 1955. * * * The total time of his service both as officer and as director was approximately fifty-seven months, from February 21, 1952 until December 20, 1956. * * *

The position of the Company was that after his resignation as vice president—finance, and while he was merely a director, Wharton was not *"employed."* As a consequence, this suit was brought to compel the issuance of the stock covered by the option.

* * * A director occupies a special status, which has some aspects in common with that of ordinary workers variously called agents, servants and employees, and in some aspects in common with the corporate officers. * * * Whether a director is or is not an employee depends upon the nature of his duties.

* * * A director is elected by the stockholders, and his duties ordinarily consist in attending meetings, exercising his judgment on propositions brought before the board, and voting. He has no power to issue orders to any officer or employee, nor can he institute policies by himself, command or veto any other action by the board.

Ordinarily, a director is not subject to dismissal by the board or by any officer thereof, nor can he hire or discharge any employee. Nor can he be discharged by the officers, his fellow directors, by any stockholder or any employee or agent of the Company. He can be removed only through action by the stockholders.

Directors are sometimes paid and sometimes not paid. * * *

The record in the present case indicates clearly that while Wharton was vice president—finance, he gave substantially his full time to the duties of that office, exercising managerial and executive duties, presumably under the direction of the president and the board of directors.

After his resignation as vice president—finance and while he remained as director, he ceased completely to exercise the functions of an officer and performed only such duties as are customary for directors. * * * Suffice it to say that on the facts of this case and by a construction of the documents set forth above, we believe that the director herein concerned, Wharton, was not an "employee" during the time subsequent to his resignation as vice president—finance. He thus had not been "employed" continuously for forty-eight months as required by the option, and was not entitled to exercise the option involved herein.

The decree of the lower court is therefore affirmed.

7. *Liability of Corporate Officers and Directors*

PENROC OIL CORP. v. DONAHUE

476 S.W.2d 849 (Tex.Civ.App.1971).

RAMSEY, Chief Justice. This is an appeal from a summary judgment involving a suit for recission of a contract and for damages resulting from alleged fraudulent representations. * * * The trial court severed the cause of action as to the Estate of A. C. Donahue and Don Jordon and entered judgment for these two Defendants. We reverse and remand.

* * *

Plaintiff's petition alleges that the Defendants acted in concert to perpetrate a fraudulent scheme for the purpose of inducing the Plaintiff to enter into an agreement for the purchase of sulphur leases. International Sulphur & Minerals, Inc. was a corporation in which the individual Defendants owned all of the stock and were the officers and directors. There was no detailed information in the record as to the corporate structure, but it appears that the individual Defendants acquired their stock ownership from services furnished to the corporation, together with expense money and personal efforts. In the corporate operations, Defendant Jordon testified that they all worked together, with no particular assignment being delegated to any particular person.

The Defendants Jordon and Donahue contend that they are entitled to a summary judgment in that they executed the agreement only in their corporate officer capacities, and not individually. * * *

The well where the sulphur find was allegedly made was being drilled by Griggs. Each of the individual Defendants was notified about the evidence of sulphur in this well and on being so notified, they all met at the well site on Father's Day to observe the drilling and production. All of the Defendants witnessed this operation and Plaintiff's president testified that they all told Plaintiff that they all watched the sulphur being drilled. Defendant Bramlett testified that at the time of the execution of the agreement that when Jordon and Donahue were there that one of the topics of conversation was the amount of sulphur indicated in the well.

The testimony reveals that Jordon recovered a specimen of the sulphur produced from the Father's Day well. This same specimen was taken by Mr. Donahue to a laboratory for analysis to determine the percentage of sulphur content. This laboratory analysis, together with a sulphur sample, was delivered to the Plaintiff by either Whitton, Griggs or Bramlett, or all of them, when they met with the Plaintiff. To say the least, the specimen obtained by Jordon which was used by Donahue for the analysis was then used by the other three individuals to substantiate their representations to the Plaintiff.

Plaintiff's secretary was at the meeting when the contract was signed. He testified that Jordon was entering into a general discussion of the fact that it looked like there was a good sulphur find and now that they were going to get some leases from the State of Texas that they would be in an excellent position to capitalize on it. He also testified that at the time of the execution of the agreement that he talked to Mr. Donahue who stated that he (Donahue) had seen the sulphur drilled and it looked like a real good thing and that they could all make some money.

It is the law in this State that all parties to a fraudulent transaction are responsible for the acts and representations of the others done in pursuance of a mutual understanding or in furtherance of a common plan, design or scheme. * * * It is well settled that the directors or officers of a corporation are liable for their own fraudulent acts and representations to persons injured thereby. This rule is applicable even though the individuals are acting for the benefit of the corporation and the corporation is likewise liable. * * *

* * * We therefore reverse the judgment of the trial Court and remand for trial.

PROBLEMS

1. The president of a corporation engaged in the business of selling new automobiles made a contract with a stock broker on behalf of the corporation for the purchase of wheat on the stock exchange. Before the broker was able to purchase the wheat for the corporation, the manager of the corporation learned of the contract and canceled the order. The broker brings action against the corporation to enforce the contract. Decision?

2. A, B, and C, each owns ten shares of stock in the X Corporation.

   a. A demands an inspection of the corporate books so that he can compile a list of shareholders for the purpose of contacting them to sell them some speculative oil stock. Does he have the right?

   b. B demands to see the corporate books so that he can obtain information to help his brother who is a competitor of the X Corporation. Does he have the right?

c. C demands to see the corporate books so that he can compile a list of shareholders for the purpose of trying to buy shares of stock from them. Does he have the right?

3. Plaintiff, a shareholder in defendant's corporation, brings a shareholder's derivative suit against the defendant's corporation and X on the following grounds:

a. X owes the corporation $10,000.00 on an unsecured note, and the statute of limitations will run on the debt in four months;

b. Plaintiff has tried to get defendant to bring suit against X, but defendant will not;

c. Two of the three members of the board of directors of the defendant are related to X;

d. There is insufficient time to take action through the shareholders. The defendant resists the suit. Decision?

4. A, B, C, D, and E constituted the board of directors of the defendant corporation. At a duly noticed special meeting, A, B, C, and D were present; but E was absent. E had given A his written proxy so that A could vote for him. At the meeting, a resolution was presented which would authorize the corporation to purchase a parcel of land which was within the scope of the corporate business. A voted for the resolution for himself and for E; B voted for the resolution; but C and D voted against the resolution. A and B claim that the resolution is valid since a quorum was present at the duly called meeting, and a quorum voted in favor of the resolution. Decision?

5. The chairman of the board of directors of the defendant corporation called a special meeting of the board to authorize the payment of a compromise agreement regarding a tort committed by an agent of the corporation against an innocent third person. All the directors were present except the plaintiff who was not notified of the meeting. At the meeting, the board of directors unanimously voted to approve of the compromise. Plaintiff brings action to prevent payment. Decision?

6. Plaintiff, a shareholder in defendant corporation, brings a shareholder derivative action against the directors of his corporation for losses alleged to be caused by mismanagement in the following manner: the directors formulated an anti-labor policy which resulted in their closing and causing the dismantling and removal of plants and equipment of the corporation which curtailed production; this was not done for any legitimate business purpose, but only to punish and intimidate employees; the acts were illegal and intended to evade the obligations of the directors under the National Labor Relations Act and constituted unfair labor practices; and they caused corporate losses of more than one million dollars. The corporation resists the action. Decision?

7. Defendant was a director and officer in the plaintiff corporation. He was requested to locate new quarry lands as plaintiff's supply was becoming exhausted. Defendant found some good quarry land and took a lease on it in his own name. Plaintiff corporation demands that defendant assign the lease to the corporation, but defendant refuses. Decision?

8. Plaintiff was a shareholder in the defendant corporation. The corporation was in the business of making buggy whips. With the advent of the automobile, the corporation became insolvent. The creditors of the corporation seek an assessment against the stock of the shareholders

to pay off the corporate debts. Plaintiff seeks declaratory relief. Decision?

9. Plaintiff was the secretary and a director of the defendant corporation. The president and secretary of the corporation were directed by the board of directors to sign certain mortgage papers, but the plaintiff refused to sign them. Thereafter, the full board of directors at a duly called meeting by majority vote removed plaintiff from the office of secretary, but not as a director. Plaintiff brings an action to enjoin the corporation from removing her as secretary. Decision?

10. Abe, Bill, Charlie, Dave and Ernie constituted the board of directors of the XYZ Corporation. While Dave and Ernie were out of town, Abe, Bill, and Charlie held a special meeting of the board. Just prior to the meeting, Charlie became ill, gave a proxy to Abe, and went home without attending the meeting. A resolution was then adopted directing and authorizing the purchase by the XYZ Corporation of an adjoining piece of land, owned by Victor, as a site for an additional factory building. Abe and Bill voted for the resolution, and Abe, as Charlie's proxy, cast Charlie's vote in favor of the resolution. A contract was then made by the XYZ Corporation with Victor for the purchase of the land. Upon the return of Dave and Ernie, another special meeting of the board was held, with all five directors present. A resolution was unanimously adopted to cancel the contract with Victor. Victor, when notified, sued XYZ Corporation for breach of contract. Decision?

Chapter 34

CORPORATE FINANCE

A corporation initially obtains its operating capital principally from investors who receive in return securities issued by the corporation evidencing the security holders' rights in the corporation.

However, after the corporation is launched and in operation, corporate funds may be derived from many sources: retained earnings, reserves, accounts receivable, the government, short-term borrowing, accounts receivable financing, inventory financing, trust receipts financing, field warehousing, sales and leasebacks, sale of unneeded assets, reduction of working capital, leasing and installment purchasing, depreciation and depletion deductions, and acquisition of tax-loss corporations.

Today, less than 20% of all corporate funds are derived from the issue of securities, such as bonds, debentures, long-term notes, and preferred and common shares of stock.

Securities are defined in U.C.C. 8–102 as instruments which are issued in bearer or registered form; are a type commonly dealt in upon security exchanges or markets; are either one of a class or series or by their terms are divisible into a class or series of instruments; and evidence a share, participation or other interest in property or in an enterprise, or evidences an obligation of the issuer.

A. BONDS

Bonds are long term promissory notes issued by a corporation to people who lend money to it. The bonds are the evidence of the corporation's obligation to repay the bondholders at a future date. The bondholders are the *creditors* of the corporation. Bonds are described as "debt" securities because a creditor-debtor relationship is created.

Sometimes a debt security may be *convertible*, which involves a privilege, usually of the holder, of converting it into some other security. Debt securities convertible into shares of stock have been issued frequently because they combine safety (creditor status) with opportunity for possible speculative gain (increase in price of shares beyond conversion price).

The use of bonds in corporate financing is almost limited to governmental agencies, quasi-public corporations, and large industrial corporations because the sale of bonds require the debtor-corporation to have very substantial assets in order to sell the bonds.

B. STOCKS

A corporation sells its ownership to people by issuing shares of stock to them. Stock evidences the shareholder's proportionate ownership in the corporation. Whereas bondholders are creditors of the corporation, the shareholders are the *owners*. Shares of stock are described as "equity" securities because they indicate the shareholder's equitable ownership in the corporation.

The shareholders do not own the corporate property as such, the corporation owns its property; however, the shareholders do have an interest in the corporation in that they have a right to receive dividends, the right to participate in distribution of capital on dissolution, and the right to control (see Chapter 33, supra).

1. CERTIFICATE

A certificate of stock is the evidence of the ownership of the shares represented by it. The Model Business Corporation Act, Section 21, requires that the certificate include the following: (a) the state of incorporation, (b) the name of the person to whom issued, (c) the number and class of shares represented by the certificate, and the designation of the series, if any, and (d) the par value of each share represented by such certificate, or a statement that the shares are without par value.

2. AUTHORIZED, ISSUED, OUTSTANDING, AND TREASURY SHARES

Authorized shares of stock are the shares which the corporation is authorized to issue by the state of incorporation and the articles of corporation.

Issued shares of stock are authorized shares which have been issued to shareholders.

Outstanding shares of stock are issued shares that are held by the shareholders.

Shares which have been reacquired by the corporation are *treasury* shares, but are not considered outstanding. Treasury shares cannot be voted and do not participate in dividends or distribution of net assets on dissolution.

3. KINDS OF STOCK

The rights and privileges of different classes of stock are controlled by the articles of incorporation in the absence of contrary statute. The most common division of classes of stock is into *common* stock and *preferred* or *guaranteed* stock.

A. Common Stock

Common stock is the ordinary stock of the corporation. It entitles the owner to pro rata dividends, but without priority over other stock. On dissolution, common stock is entitled to participate in the distribution of the net assets.

The common stock is usually the voting stock. Thus, the common stockholders, rather than the preferred stockholders, elect the board of directors. This is because the preferred stockholders, although owners of the corporation with other stockholders, are primarily interested in a fixed return in the form of a dividend, and they are not as concerned about management as long as their dividend is paid. On the other hand, the common stockholder has a greater stake as owner of the corporation since he is taking a greater gamble on the success of the corporation and, therefore, should have the choice of management. He has a greater gamble because if the corporation is a success, he may receive the largest dividends; but if the venture fails, he must absorb the initial and the heaviest losses.

B. Preferred Stock

Preferred stock is stock which has a preference over other classes of stock. The preference is usually as to dividends; however, it can take the form of various rights, powers, and privileges, including a priority on distribution of capital on dissolution of the corporation.

Preferred stock may be made either cumulative (usual) or noncumulative (unusual). *Cumulative* stock means that if there are no distribution of profits in the form of dividends in a particular year because there are no profits or because the profits are to be used for expansion, etc., the dividends accrue and both back and current dividends must be paid in full before any dividend may be paid on common stock. In the case of *noncumulative* stock, the dividends are lost forever. Even if there is a large surplus legally available, a strong showing of fraud or abuse of discretion by the board of directors will be necessary before a court will compel a declaration of a dividend on common or preferred stock. Thus, unless the preferred stock is cumulative, or unless the noncumulative stockholders have a contract with the corporation that makes a dividend mandatory, the noncumulative stock will lose its dividend unless declared each year.

Preferred stock also may be made *participating* or *non-participating.* The usual provision for *participating* entitles the preferred shares to participate with the common shares in the annual distribution of surplus earnings after the common have received a dividend equal to that payable to the preferred.

Guaranteed stock is preferred stock on which the payment of the dividend is guaranteed.

4. CAPITAL, CAPITAL STOCK, AND STATED CAPITAL

"Capital stock", as a term used in Corporation law, has generated much confusion and misunderstanding. In common usage and even in court decisions, *"capital stock"* has been used interchangeably with *"capital"* and *"stock."* Likewise, "stock" and "shares" have been used synonomously to indicate an identical concept.

Because of this misunderstanding, the new Model Business Corporation Act and the corporation laws of some states use the term *"stated capital"* in lieu of *"capital stock."*

The basic idea of *"stated capital"* or *"capital stock"* is that it represents the money, property, or other consideration which the corporation has received from its "stockholders" or "shareholders" which is to be used in the business and which is represented by a specific number of outstanding shares of stock.

Sometimes, par value stock may be sold at a premium, or a higher price than par, in which case the excess is allocated to a "capital surplus" account.

Shares of capital stock are represented by certificates which describe a proportionate interest in the corporate enterprise, but in no way vest their owner with any title to the corporation's property.

5. CONSIDERATION FOR ISSUANCE OF STOCK

The general rule is that shares of stock cannot be issued without payment in money or money's worth or a valid obligation to pay, but in the absence of statute or articles of incorporation to the contrary, the stock can be issued without actual payment at the time of issuance. Statutes or articles of incorporation commonly provide that no stock can be issued except for money, labor done, or property actually received. - can receive for promise of money

Although there is a conflict of authority, the majority rule is that if there is no constitutional, statutory, or charter prohibition, a corporation has the power to issue shares of its stock as fully paid on payment of less than its par value and the agreement under which they are so issued will be binding as between the parties. In some states, corporations cannot legally issue stock for less than par value.

6. PAR VALUE AND WITHOUT PAR VALUE

Par value shares and shares without par value are permitted in most states. The trend has been for corporations to establish low par values; e.g., $10.00 a share valuation.

a. *Par value* means that the shares have a definite value stated on the face of the certificate; e.g., $10.00.

b. *Without par value* means that there is no definite amount stated on the certificate. The amount the stock will sell for will be determined by the board of directors.

There are three considerations in determining whether par stock or no par stock should be issued:

(1) The corporation may desire that the consideration be fixed at a certain amount per share based on a minimum capital requirement, or it may desire that the board of directors be able to fix the value from time to time depending on capital requirements, *book value* (total assets of the corporation divided by the number of outstanding shares of stock) and *market value* of the stock (the price the stock might be expected to bring if offered for sale in a fair market).

(2) In some states, there is a capital tax on the corporation's authorized shares, a tax on the issuance of shares, and a tax on the transfer of shares. The rate of these taxes on stock without par value is often arbitrarily set at a figure of $100.00 a share. If the stock is worth considerably less than that amount, the corporation and the stockholders are paying an unnecessarily high tax.

(3) Only a *capital surplus* (the excess of the net assets of a corporation over its stated capital), and not stated capital or capital, may be distributed as dividends or used by the corporation to purchase its own stock in many states; thus, in such states it is desirable to establish a capital surplus so that the corporation has greater flexibility. Capital surplus can be established by issuing par value shares for more than par value, in which case the par value received is allocated to capital and the excess to capital surplus, or by allocating a part of the money received for shares without par value to capital surplus and the excess to capital. States differ as to the amount received from shares without par value which may be allocated to capital surplus. In New York, for example, the total consideration received for shares without par value without as stated value must be allocated to capital. The Model Business Corporation Act, Section 19, provides that in the case of the issuance of shares having par value, the consideration received shall constitute stated capital to the extent of the par value of such shares, and the excess shall constitute surplus. In case of issuance of shares without par value, the entire consideration shall constitute stated capital unless the corporation shall determine that only a part thereof shall be stated capital and the rest capital surplus.

7. LIABILITY FOR SHARES

Shares which are issued for proper consideration are usually non-assessable. Shares which are issued for improper consideration or for no consideration are often declared void by state law. Where permitted by statute, shares may be issued which are only partly paid, subject to assessments until the full amount has been paid; however, most states and the Model Business Corporation Act, Section 21, take the position that a stock certificate cannot be issued for stock which is only partly paid.

When a corporation issues shares of stock as fully paid and non-assessable for less than proper consideration, the stock is often described as "watered stock". (This term evolved from an alleged practice of live-stock sellers wherein they watered thirsty cattle just before weighing in at the market so that the buyer paid extra for the water.) The record owner of such stock is usually held liable for the unpaid consideration. A good faith transferee of watered stock is not liable for any unpaid balance, and the original purchaser cannot escape liability by such a transfer. Usually a person who holds shares in a fiduciary capacity is not liable for the unpaid balance, nor is a pledgee.

8. ISSUANCE AND TRANSFER OF SHARES

A. Issuance

A person may become a shareholder in three ways: (1) by a pre-incorporation stock subscription (see Corporations, Chapter 32, Section A, 5, supra), (2) by subscribing to a share in an organized corporation, and (3) by transfer of a share from a shareholder. In the case of a pre-incorporation subscription and a transfer from a shareholder, there is no shareholder status until the stock certificate has been delivered and paid for; whereas in the case of a subscriber, there is immediate shareholder status at the time of making of the subscription, and the subscription usually does not have to be in writing pursuant to the statute of frauds. In the case of an executory contract for the purchase of a share of stock, the purchaser usually does not become a shareholder until the closing of the transaction since it is usually subject to the statute of frauds.

B. "Blue Sky" Laws

Prior to the solicitation or issuance of stock, a corporation must get a permit from the government in every state, except Delaware and Nevada. These state laws are to protect the public from stock frauds and are known as "blue sky" laws; i.e., to prevent "speculative schemes which have no more basis than so many feet of blue sky". The governmental agency, usually a Division of Corporations, will only grant the permit if it finds that the proposed corporate venture and the securities are fair, just, and equitable. Many state laws also have broker-dealer-registration provisions which regulate the persons engaged in the securities business, and registration-of-securities provisions which provide for the registration of the securities. Generally, a sale of shares made by a corporation in violation of the "blue sky" law, or other non-compliance, is voidable and may be rescinded by the purchaser.

C. Federal Regulations

In addition to the state regulations, there are many federal regulations:

(1) The Securities Act, 1933, which imposes registration and prospectus requirements, and anti-fraud provisions on securities of-

fered or sold through the mails or on radio or interstate or foreign commerce. The purpose of the Securities Act is to bring about full disclosures of relevant facts to a prospective investor.

(2) The Federal Securities Exchange Act, 1934, which requires registration with the Securities and Exchange Commission of security exchanges, filing by listed users of reports with the S.E.C., regulation of proxy solicitation regarding listed securities, limitation on inside trading, registration of over-the-counter brokers, and prohibition of fraud and manipulation of prices of stock or the selling of stock in excess of current market prices. The main purpose is to force disclosure to buyers and sellers of securities and to regulate the security market. Brokers can be expelled from an exchange and their licenses revoked for fraudulent or unethical practices.

(3) The Public Utility Holding Company Act, 1935, which regulates holding companies and their subsidiaries engaged in the interstate electric utility business or interstate distribution of gas business.

(4) The Trust Indenture Act, 1939, which requires that bonds or other debt securities offered for sale through the mails or interstate commerce be secured by an indenture qualified under the Act.

(5) The Investment Company Act, 1940, which regulates companies that invest and reinvest in the securities of other companies.

(6) The Investment Advisors Act, 1940, which regulates persons engaged for compensation in the business of rendering advice regarding securities.

(7) Under Chapter X of the Bankruptcy Act (corporate reorganization), which is administered only by the federal courts, the Securities and Exchange Commission has advisory functions.

(8) There are also several miscellaneous federal statutes which regulate the issuance of securities; e.g., Interstate Commerce Commission regulates interstate rail and motor carriers; Comptroller of the Currency regulates national banks; Federal Home Loan Bank Board regulates federal savings and loan associations; and the Federal Power Commission regulates electric utilities engaged in interstate commerce.

D. Transfer of Shares

Unless restricted by statute, the articles, or by-laws, a shareholder may freely transfer his shares. By-laws may contain reasonable restrictions on the right to transfer or hypothecate the shares. The usual restriction is for the purpose of keeping unacceptable outsiders from membership in a close corporation by requiring that the shares first be offered to existing shareholders. A restriction is ineffective unless it is stated on the face of the certificate (Uniform Commercial Code, Section 8–204).

The share is transferred by a delivery of the certificate indorsed by its owner on the back or on a separate assignment form. Usually the transfer must be recorded on the corporate stock books before the corporation must recognize the transferee as a shareholder. Today, owing to the size of the corporations and their large number of shareholders, the corporations have generally retained a "transfer agent", usually a bank or other large financial institution, to keep its stockholder records up to date. A transfer of the certificate without an indorsement is valid between the parties, but the transferee is not a bona fide purchaser for value as against third parties.

Article 8, Uniform Commercial Code, is a negotiable instrument law dealing with securities (See Appendix A). Securities have the negotiability of commercial paper; e.g., thief or finder can pass good title to a bona fide purchaser (see U.C.C., Section 8–302 for definition of bona fide purchaser), and fraud, mistake, duress, etc. in the original transfer will not prevent good title from passing to a bona fide purchaser in the next transfer as he takes the security "free of any adverse claim" (U.C.C., Section 8–301(1)). In one type of case, securities have even greater negotiability; e.g., a security with a forged indorsement is passed to a bona fide purchaser who gets a new security issued by the corporation, the bona fide purchaser gets good title to the new security (U.C.C., Section 8–311(a)), while the corporation, transfer agent, or brokerage firm must make good the loss to the rightful owner.

E. PRE-EMPTIVE RIGHTS

The common-law pre-emptive right of a shareholder is his right to purchase a pro-rata share of newly authorized issues of shares before they are offered to others. This rule has the effect of permitting a stockholder to maintain his same pro-rata interest in the corporation. There are so many exceptions to the rule today that it has lost much of its significance. Most state corporation laws permit charter provisions to either limit or deny the pre-emptive right.

C. DIVIDENDS

1. IN GENERAL

A dividend is a distribution of cash, property, or shares of stock to the shareholders in proportion to their interests. Usually, dividends are paid in cash. Property dividends, e.g., stock in subsidiary or other corporation, other securities, or products of own corporation, are rather unusual.

2. SOURCES

Dividends are payable from various limited funds as prescribed by statutes; e.g., earned surplus, net profits, and surplus.

A. Earned Surplus

All states permit dividends to be issued from earned surplus; i.e., the undistributed net profits earned by the corporation, including the gains from the sale of fixed assets, traced back to the date of incorporation. A few states restrict the issuance of dividends to the earned surplus fund.

B. Net Profits

Some statutes permit dividends to be issued from current net profits without regard to the existence of a deficit from prior years; e.g., California Corporation Code, Section 1500(b).

C. Surplus

Some statutes permit dividends out of any kind of surplus, earned or unearned.

In addition to the limitation placed on the *source* of the dividend, there are other limitations placed on the issuance of a dividend; e.g., several statutes prohibit dividends where the corporation is or might thereby become insolvent; some statutes prohibit dividends if it would impair the capital of the corporation; federal statutes place limitations on dividends, e.g., Public Utility Holding Company Act of 1935 and the Investment Company Act of 1940; limitations are frequently imposed by other jurisdictions in which the corporation is doing business; and limitations are frequently imposed by stock exchange requirements, articles of incorporation, by-laws, resolutions, and shareholder agreements.

3. DECLARATION BY BOARD

The declaration of dividends is discretionary with the board of directors. Even where there is a large surplus, the shareholders cannot compel distribution of a dividend unless there has been an obvious abuse of discretion, or there has been bad faith.

4. PERSON ENTITLED TO DIVIDEND

The right to a cash dividend vests in the shareholder as of the time it is *declared* by the corporation; therefore, it belongs to the person who is the record owner on that date even though it is to be payable at a later time. In the case of a *transfer* of stock, dividends declared before the transfer belong to the transferor, whereas those declared after the transfer belong to the transferee.

The rule that the right to a cash dividend is the date of *declaration* of the dividend is subject to modification by the corporation in most states; e.g., the corporation may make the dividend payable to those who will be *holders of record* on a later specified date; in such case, the purchaser of stock from another person would have the right to the dividend if he purchased before the record date rather than the declaration date.

If the corporation declares a stock dividend rather than a cash dividend, the ownership is determined by the *date of distribution*. This is because the declaration of a stock dividend has the effect of diluting the corporate assets among a larger number of shares so the value of the holding represented by each share is accordingly diminished and unless the person who owns the stock on the date of distribution is made receives his share of the stock dividend, the net effect will be to lessen his holdings.

The right of preferred shareholders has been discussed in Corporations, Chapter 34, Section B, 3, supra.

 1. *Pre-Incorporation Stock Subscriptions*

NEBRASKA CHICORY CO. OF SCHUYLER v. LEDNICKY

79 Neb. 587, 113 N.W. 245 (1907).

EPPERSON, C. In February, 1897, certain citizens of Schuyler, Neb., united in a movement for the organization of a company for the manufacture of chicory at that place. Articles of incorporation were prepared and discussed on one or more occasions by the interested parties, and during said month a written agreement, of which the following is a copy, was prepared and circulated and signed by a considerable number of persons; the signature of the defendant being attached thereto as below indicated: "We, the undersigned, do hereby agree to take shares of stock in the Nebraska Chicory Company of Schuyler, Nebraska, to be organized on the plan set forth in the articles of incorporation, and we agree to pay for the number of shares set opposite our respective names in accordance with the by-laws, rules and regulations of the company, which provide for a division of the capital stock of $50,000.00 in shares of $50 each, to be paid in monthly installments of 4 per cent. per month, beginning the first Saturday of March, 1897. [Signed] Anton Lednicky, 5 shares." Some time after the defendant signed the foregoing, and on or about March 8, 1897, a certificate of incorporation was filed with the county clerk, and with the Secretary of State on March 25th. * * * On June 29, 1897, the president and secretary executed and delivered to him a paper certifying that he had subscribed for five shares of the capital stock of the company and would be entitled to the same "upon the surrender of this certificate and compliance with the rules and by-laws of this company." For this "certificate of entitlement," as it was called, he subscribed and delivered to the company a written receipt. He ceased to pay on and after the ninth installment, and this is an action to recover the unpaid residue upon his promise of subscription above copied. At the close of plaintiff's evidence, the court directed a verdict for defendant. Plaintiff appeals.

* * * A subscription by a number of persons to the stock of a corporation, to be thereafter formed by them, constitutes a contract between the subscribers themselves to become stockholders

when the corporation is formed, upon the conditions expressed in the agreement, and as such it is binding and irrevocable from the date of its subscription. It is in the nature of a continuing offer to the proposed corporation, which, upon acceptance by it, becomes as to each subscriber a contract between him and the corporation. * * * Such a contract is based upon a sufficient consideration. Such subscriptions are mutual promises among the subscribers as toward each other, and this mutuality of promise among the subscribers constitutes a sufficient consideration for such a subscription. There is in the act of the particular subscriber, in subscribing with others, a mutuality of promise which obliges him to make good his promise to the corporation after it comes into its existence. * * * That "a subscription for stock implies a promise to pay for it, even though the subscription was before incorporation, is the rule sustained by the great weight of authority." * * * We gather this proposition from the decisions, and think it is sustained by the weight of authority. A subscription to corporate shares, made before the corporation comes into existence, but accepted by the corporation after coming into existence, either expressly by issuing the share certificates, or impliedly by recognizing the subscriber as a shareholder, makes him a shareholder, and the corporation may maintain an action upon the subscription against the signers. * * * For the reasons stated in the foregoing opinion, the judgment of the district court is reversed, and the cause remanded for a new trial.

---

2. *Payment for Stock Shares*

STERLING VARNISH CO. v. SONOM CO.

241 Miss. 810, 133 So.2d 624 (1961).

ETHRIDGE, Justice. This case involves a claim by a creditor of an insolvent corporation against a stockholder who purchased his stock with an assignment of an exclusive marketing contract for a manufacturing process. The issue is whether under the statute stock can be paid for in such property and contract rights, where the transaction is in good faith and there is no fraud. We hold that it can.

Appellee Sonom Company, Inc. (called Sonom) was incorporated under the laws of Mississippi in April 1957, for the general purposes of manufacturing, buying and selling paints and metal preservatives. The capitalization was $100,000, with 1,000 shares of $100 par value common stock, with a required, initial capital of $40,000. The sole stockholders and officers were Erickson, Nevins, Buntin, and S. L. Taylor who is the real appellee. Each of these persons purchased 25% of the stock. * * *

A man from Texas named Smith developed a formula for protective materials. The incorporators made a contract with him for the exclusive marketing and use of this product. When the corporation was organized, this contract was assigned by them to the corporation in consideration for the issuance of stock. * * *

Sonom purchased from appellant, The Sterling Varnish Company, of Sewickley, Pa., a large amount of paint and preservatives to be used in its manufacturing process. On April 20, 1960, Sterling obtained a default judgment against Sonom for $8,811.42. It had a writ of garnishment issued against Taylor, who answered that he did not owe Sonom anything. * * * The court held the garnishee's answer was supported by the evidence, overruled the contest of that answer, and entered an order in favor of the garnishee, dismissing him from the suit. This appeal is from that order.

Miss.Code 1942, Rec., Sec. 5332, provides that a stockholder is liable for corporate debts for the amount of any balance remaining unpaid for a stock subscription, and gives any corporate creditor a right to sue such stockholder. * * *

Appellant contends that appellee Taylor did not pay for the stock received by him; that transfer to the corporation of the Smith exclusive marketing contract was not a payment in the contemplation of the statute; and therefore under Sec. 5332 Sterling, as creditor, has a right of action against Taylor.

A corporation is not restricted to receiving money in payment for its stock, unless there is some requirement to this effect in its charter, or in the constitution or laws of the state. It may receive in payment therefor property, labor or services, provided the transaction is in good faith, and no fraud is perpetrated upon other stockholders or creditors. * * * Stock may be paid for in various kinds of property, including valuable contract rights. * * *

A payment for stock in property or services must have been made in good faith and without fraud. The testimony here shows that those conditions were met.

* * * Affirmed.

---

3. *Value of Shares of Stock*

BURTON v. BURTON

161 Cal.App.2d 572, 326 P.2d 855 (1958).

GRIFFIN, Acting Presiding Justice. In an action for divorce instituted by plaintiff-respondent against defendant-appellant, the court found that the parties owned, as community property, a one-half interest in a certain named corporation, its stock, tools, equipment and good will. * * * The court found the total value of said business, good will, etc. to be $50,000. Assets and accounts receivable were fixed at $45,112, and good will at $4,888. It held that plaintiff was entitled to one-fourth of said valuation or the sum of $12,500, as her share of the community property. * * *

The evidence shows Burton Enterprises was incorporated for $75,000 in 1956. It was owned and operated by defendant and his brother, who held the corporate stock. Each had a drawing account of $10,000 per year and shared equally in its profits. The business is the outgrowth of a family partnership and has, over the years, been quite successful from a financial standpoint. The gross sales for 1955 was $190,179.49, with a net profit of $28,195, after paying the drawing accounts. * * *

After the reception of the corporation's books in evidence defendant's bookkeeper testified from summaries taken therefrom and said that the books, as of December 31, 1955, * * * was $31,506.13. [Book value.]

Counsel for defendant, in reply to an inquiry by the court, said that in making application to the Corporation Commissioner for the approval of the corporation, a statement justifying the value of $75,000 stock capitalization was submitted. * * *

The main complaint is that * * * the record of the value, as evidenced by the books, was unimpeached and must prevail; that $31,506.13 is that value; and that plaintiff was entitled to no more than a one-fourth interest therein. It is also argued that since there was no good will and its value, if any, was not established, it was error to allow the sum indicated for that purpose.

* * * Good will has been held to be property of an intangible nature and is recognized as a thing of value. * * *

Here, the trial court had before it the fact that these two brothers had been, for many years, successfully operating this concern as a partnership. It was well known in the community; it had many employees and accumulated considerable up-to-date equipment; and the assets and property of the partnership were set forth in a statement to the Corporation Commissioner in establishing the capital stock of $75,000. Stock was conditionally issued to the partners in that sum. * * *

* * * The term "Capital Stock" is frequently used to express the property and assets of a corporation. Strictly speaking, the capital stock of a corporation is the money contributed by the corporators to the capital, and is usually represented by shares issued to subscribers to the stock on the initiation of the corporate enterprise. It consists of the consideration received or agreed to be received in exchange for all issued stock, whether the consideration takes the form of money paid, labor done, or property actually received. * * *

If the book value submitted to secure the stock was less than the $75,000 indicated, the court might well have concluded that the good will of the corporation made up a part of the difference in arriving at the value for which the corporation was capitalized. * * *

Judgment affirmed.

4. *Right to Transfer Stock*

BENSON v. BRAUN

8 Misc.2d 67, 155 N.Y.S.2d 622 (1956).

CHRIST, Justice. This is a stockholders' derivative and representative action brought by two stockholders of the Prosperity Company (hereinafter sometimes referred to as "Prosperity"), a domestic corporation engaged in the business of manufacturing commercial laundry equipment. * * *

The amended complaint alleges that the individual defendants, as officers, directors and owners of the controlling stock of Prosperity, in breach of their fiduciary duties sold their entire stock to a purchasing group dominated by two individuals for a price which, plaintiffs allege, exceeded the fair value of the stock by $800,000. * * * The general rule is that a stockholder may dispose of his stock at any time and at such price as he chooses. Recognition is given to the fact that the advantages which flow from control of a corporation may make the price paid for controlling shares greater than that paid for other shares. * * * However, the freedom of a controlling stockholder to dispose of his stock has been restricted to reduce the possibility of injustice being done to other stockholders or the corporation. The purpose of the rules restricting transfers of controlling interests is to prevent transactions tainted with bad faith, intent to defraud or negligence on the part of those possessing control. In the absence of such elements it is desirable that control of a corporation be readily transferable "so that persons with ideas for improving a business might be able to put their ability to work". * * *

Determination of the value of stock involves consideration of numerous factors. Market value, book value, capitalization of earnings are all important elements in this process. But they are not singly or in the aggregate the sole criteria in determining stock value. It is trite but true to say that each corporation whose stock is evaluated must be viewed in relation to the facts peculiar to that particular enterprise. In this case factors were present which could well have been taken into account and have led to establishing a selling price well above the market quotations on the corporation's one listed stock. * * *

Finally, the court must note the absence of any harm to Prosperity or its stockholders from the transfer of the controlling stock. The rules restricting free alienability of controlling stock have been developed, as earlier noted, to prevent injury and injustice to the corporation and its stockholders. When these restrictive rules have been applied their thrust has been at those found to be responsible for injury to the corporation, its shareholders or creditors. The transfer of control was followed by actual looting of the corporation, or the corporation was deprived of a business opportunity, or shareholders were induced to part with their stock at prices unjustifiably lower than the price received by the sellers of control. Here no damage was done to the corporation and no injury was caused to the stockholders or creditors. * * *

Judgment is accordingly awarded. [to Defendants]

5. *Limitations on Right to Transfer Stock*

CASADY v. MODERN METAL SPINNING & MANUFACTURING CO.

188 Cal.App.2d 728, 10 Cal.Rptr. 790 (1961).

LILLIE, Justice. This is an appeal by plaintiff from a judgment refusing to decree specific performance of the executory provisions of a marital property settlement agreement.

On or about May 10, 1957, plaintiff, Nevella Casady, was awarded an interlocutory decree of divorce from defendant Casady. Prior to their separation, the Casadys owned as a portion of their community property 433⅓ shares of the capital stock of defendant corporation, said shares standing of record in the name of Mr. Casady. Pursuant to pertinent addenda in a property settlement agreement, approved by the court, it was decreed that "Plaintiff shall have and she is awarded 216⅔ shares of stock of Modern Metal Spinning and Manufacturing Co., a corporation, as her sole and separate property"—the addenda also provided that defendant Casady would be entitled to a like number of shares of that company's stock. Both plaintiff and Casady were ordered to comply with all the terms of the decree. The corporation refused to issue a new certificate to Mrs. Casady for 216⅔ shares, and in October of 1959 the present action was commenced. * * *

Section 6 of the By-laws * * * provides as follows: "The shares of stock of the company shall not be transferrable or the subject of sale or pledge until first offered to the Company at the then value, as determined by a certified public accountant. If said offer is refused by the Company, then said stock shall be offered to the stockholders and if necessary prorated among them or such of them as desire to purchase. In each of the foregoing cases if such offer be made and refused by the Company, and the stockholders, the shares so offered shall be subject to sale, pledge or transfer, but not otherwise."

* * * As with other by-laws, Section 6 is made subject to amendment by written assent of two-thirds of the stockholders. * * *

Shortly after the entry of the interlocutory decree of divorce, Casady delivered his certificate for 433⅓ shares to the defendant corporation with a request for transfer and the issuance of a new certificate to plaintiff for 216⅔ shares. Defendant corporation refused to do so as no compliance had been had with the pertinent provisions of * * * Section 6 of the by-laws just quoted; specifically, plaintiff did not offer to sell the shares awarded her by the divorce decree nor did she offer to have them valued or appraised by a certified public accountant.

* * * The by-laws of a corporation constitute a contract between the shareholders and the corporation * * *; the by-laws are also a contract among the shareholders * * *; accordingly, courts have often said that a first option provision, akin to that found in Section 6, is " 'in the nature of a contract' between the corporation and its stockholders and, as such, binding upon them (citations)." * * *

Under the particular facts at bar, we are of the opinion that the trial court correctly concluded that specific performance should not be decreed. * * *

The judgment is affirmed.

6. *Right of Stockholders to Compel Dividend Payment*

DOHERTY v. MUTUAL WAREHOUSE CO.

255 F.2d 489 (C.A.Ala., 1958).

RIVES, Circuit Judge. This action is by a minority shareholder against a corporation to compel declaration and payment of dividends.

* * * In Alabama, the law is well settled that a court of equity will not interfere with the internal business management of corporate affairs by the board of directors so long as they keep within the scope of the charter powers, and are not guilty of fraud, maladministration, or abuse of discretion. * * *

The original capital of the corporation was $15,000.00, and as of the end of the year 1955 the surplus of the corporation was $188,738.-38.

Prior to the year 1955, the management of the corporation had determined that for sound business reasons the corporation should accumulate a surplus of $200,000.00. At the end of the year 1956 the surplus of the corporation, for the first time exceeded $200,000.00; the surplus being $206,314.30. Early in 1957 the directors of the corporation declared a dividend of $6,000.00 to stockholders of record—being a $40.00 dividend for each share of outstanding stock.

The decision not to declare a dividend for the year 1955 and to use the profits of the corporation in the business was not an abuse of discretion, and such refusal to declare a dividend was not arbitrary, nor was there any bad faith or fraud, or maladministration destructive or injurious to the corporation. The decision not to declare a dividend for 1955 and to accumulate surplus was consistent with the character and needs of the business. At all times here material the directors, officers and management of the corporation have acted fairly and in the utmost good faith in the handling of the business, management and corporate affairs of the corporation in the interest of the corporation. * * *

The judgment was right, and it is

Affirmed.

---

7. *Stock Dividends*

IN RE FOSDICK'S TRUST

4 N.Y.2d 646, 176 N.Y.S.2d 966, 152 N.E.2d 228 (1958).

BURKE, Judge. * * * Fosdick created two trusts for the lives, respectively, of two nieces. * * * The principals of the funds were originally made up of 300 shares of General Electric Company stock. * * * A special provision for the treatment of stock dividends, the subject of this proceeding, was inserted in the deed. It states: "Anything hereinabove contained to the contrary notwithstanding, said Trustee shall transfer to said Donor, or if he is dead, to his executor * * * free of all trusts hereby created, *any and all stock dividends* which it may from time to time receive on any stocks held by it hereunder." (Emphasis supplied.)

Fosdick died on April 6, 1926 without revoking or amending the trust. His will named the American Museum of Natural History sole residuary legatee. As such it would be entitled to any distributions of stock in the nature of stock dividends declared after the settlor's death. * * *

The problem here presented requires only a definition of the term stock dividends as used in the deed. That definition, we have seen, appears with unmistakable clarity in the decisions. * * *

The construction was sought with reference to certain stock distributions in 1954 from companies, shares in which then constituted the trust corpora. Special Term decided that distributions * * * by * * * General Electric * * * were in part stock dividends within the meaning of the trust deed. * * * By April of 1954 the trustee held 1,200 shares of General Electric no par value common stock in each trust. The increase had resulted from stock splits in 1926 and 1929, both of which split the stock 4 for 1 and both of which were unaccompanied by any transfer of accumulated earnings to capital.

* * * The lower court held that 7⁄12ths of the new stock which was attributed to the transfer from reinvested earnings to capital account constituted a stock dividend within the meaning of the trust deed and was distributable, therefore, to the residuary legatee as required by the instrument. * * *

Appellants beneficiaries assert that the substance and intent of the distribution was not to distribute earnings, but rather was merely to split up the shares and apportion the additional capital and that, therefore, it did not constitute a stock dividend. They point out that distributions of stock, like the one under discussion, which substantially increase the number of shares outstanding, ordinarily reduce both the market value of and income upon the original shares so that in a case like the present one if the additional shares are permitted to leave the trust principals it will bring about a considerable reduction in the amount of annual income distributable to the beneficiaries. * * *

The term "dividend" signifies a distribution of profits or earnings to the shareholders. In its most obvious form it consists of a distribution of cash. It may also be in shares of the corporation. When in this form it is accomplished by segregating that part of the earnings it represents. The segregation is accomplished by capitalization. Therein lies the distinction, as found in the cases, between a mere stock split and a stock dividend. The stock dividend evidences that "the company's accumulated profits have been capitalized, instead of distributed to the stockholders or retained as surplus available for distribution in money or in kind should opportunity offer" * * * A stock split, on the other hand, results from the simple increase in the number of shares without altering surplus or segregating earnings. * * *

It is the almost exceptionless holding of the later cases on this subject that the distribution of additional stock to shareholders in conjunction with the capitalization of earned surplus constitutes a stock dividend. It is established with equal clarity that in apportioning the amount of newly issued shares attributable to the new capital no reference is had to market value—that proportion of the shares whose par or stated value is represented by the new capital constitutes the stock dividend. * * *

The order of the Appellate Division should be affirmed.

8. *Stock Transfer by Forgery*

WELLER v. AMERICAN TELEPHONE AND TELEGRAPH

290 A.2d 845 (Del.Ch., 1972).

MARVEL, Vice Chancellor. Plaintiff seeks the entry of a judgment against two corporations, namely American Telephone and Telegraph Company and General Electric Company, based on her claim for injuries sustained by her as a result of the alleged unauthorized registration of stock owned by her in each such company. * * *

At the time of the acts complained of plaintiff was the registered holder of 500 shares of common stock of American Telephone and Telegraph Company and 100 shares of common stock of General

Electric. Later, the shares of the latter company were split two for one.

In 1968, Gertrude L. Weller, a 94 year old widow, was invited to live in the home of Mr. and Mrs. Kenneth Jumper. This change of residence came about because the plaintiff had known Mrs. Jumper for many years and was also acquainted with Mr. Jumper, who had performed various helpful services for her in the past. Because of her lonely circumstances and advanced age she was more than delighted to accept the Jumpers' proposal. As a token of her appreciation for their apparently unselfish gesture Mrs. Weller, after moving in with them, made a gift of 100 shares of American Telephone and Telegraph stock to Mr. Jumper.

Thereafter, because of her age and poor health, plaintiff gradually surrendered more and more responsibility concerning the details of her business affairs to Mr. Jumper. Thus, she acquiesced when he took upon himself to open her mail, being reassured by him on numerous occasions that he was sending her stock dividend checks and other income receipts to her bank. During this period Mrs. Weller evinced complete trust in the Jumpers notwithstanding momentary worries over the fact that her mail was being opened by Mr. Jumper and that she was not actually being shown the income checks which she had received in the mail. However, she was easily convinced that there was nothing to worry about.

In February, 1970, after having moved to her nephew's to live, following disclosure to some extent of Mr. Jumper's actual nature, Mrs. Weller ascertained that for over a period of almost two years she had been systematically defrauded by Mr. Jumper. In other words she became aware for the first time of the fact that Kenneth Jumper had used a form containing her signature for the purpose of opening a joint trading account with a stockbroker, namely the third party defendant Merrill Lynch, Pierce, Fenner & Smith, Inc., and that Mr. Jumper thereafter had apparently forged her name to the stock certificates here involved for the purpose of selling them on the market.

The trial evidence is to the effect that Mr. Jumper had not only forged plaintiff's name to plaintiff's stock certificates but had also closed out her savings account and terminated her checking account by means of a forged signature. Needless to say, the income checks which Mr. Jumper had removed from Mrs. Weller's mail had also been diverted to his own use.

Plaintiff thereupon notified the defendants American Telephone and Telegraph Company and General Electric Company on March 4, 1970 that the stock certificates representing her investments in such companies had been sold by means of forged signatures and requested the issuance to her of replacement certificates. The defendants having declined to issue such certificates as requested, this action ensued, the complaint naming as defendants the issuers of the certificates in question. Merrill Lynch was later joined as a third party defendant in its capacity as the broker which had guaranteed Mrs. Weller's signature.

* * *

Section 8–404(2) of the Uniform Commercial Code provides that where an issuer has registered a transfer of a security in the name of a person not entitled to it, such issuer on demand must deliver a like security to the true owner, provided, inter alia, the owner has acted pursuant to subsection (1) of the section which follows. Section 8–404(2)(b). Subsection (1) of the following section provides that the owner of such a security must notify the issuer of the wrongful taking complained of within a reasonable time after he has notice of a lost or wrongfully taken certificate, Section 8–405(1).

Defendants argue that in the case at bar plaintiff failed to notify the issuers within a "reasonable time", as such phrase is defined in the statute. It contends that plaintiff should have known some twenty-two months before she notified the issuing corporations that Mr. Jumper had converted her stock certificates. Defendants go on to point out that had plaintiff made a causal examination of her bank book or bank statement, it would have been brought to her attention that dividend checks accruing on the shares here in issue were not being deposited to her credit.

In order to determine whether or not Mrs. Weller notified the issuer within a "reasonable time" after she had "noticed" that her shares had been transferred as a result of forgery it is necessary to determine the meaning of these two phrases as employed in the statute.

The definition section of Article 8 provides inter alia: "In addition Article 1 contains general definitions and principles of construction and interpretation applicable throughout this Article." Section 8–102(6). Article 1 provides that a person has "notice" of a fact when he has actual knowledge of it, has received notification, or "* * * from all the facts and circumstances known to him at the time in question he has reason to know that it exists." Section 1–201(25). Article 1 also provides: "What is a reasonable time for taking any action depends on the nature, purpose and circumstances of such action." Section 1–204(2).

In the case at bar we are concerned with the affairs of a 94 year old woman, who while a guest in another's home, was persuaded to allow one of her hosts, whom she trusted, to handle her affairs. I am accordingly satisfied that Mrs. Weller, a lonely and trusting person of advanced years and of infirm mind and body, had every reasonable right to trust a family which took her in and which she had known intimately before she moved into its home. Furthermore, in light of her reliance on the perpetrator of the acts which deprived her of title to her securities and her own age and decrepitude, she having among other things broken a hip while at the

Jumpers, I do not think Mrs. Weller can be charged with unreasonable action in not checking her accounts from time to time. I therefore conclude in view of all of the surrounding circumstances that Mrs. Weller did not have the required statutory notice of Mr. Jumper's dishonesty until February 19 or 20, 1970, and that she thereafter notified the issuers of her stolen securities within a reasonable time.

* * *

There being no contention that the issuance of substitute certificates to plaintiff would result in an overissue of stock in this case, plaintiff's relief must be limited to the recovery by her of new certificates. * * *

Accordingly, plaintiff is entitled to the entry of an order providing for the issuance to her of 500 shares of American Telephone and Telegraph Company common stock together with accrued and unpaid dividends as well as 200 shares of General Electric Company common stock together with accrued and unpaid dividends, summary judgment having been earlier granted to the defendants American Telephone and Telegraph Company and General Electric Company on their claim against the third party defendant Merrill Lynch, Pierce, Fenner and Smith, Incorporated on the basis of the latter's guarantee of Mrs. Weller's signature.

---

9. *Rights of Stockholders upon Dissolution*

SQUIRES v. BALBACH CO.

177 Neb. 465, 129 N.W.2d 462 (1964).

BROWER, Justice. This action was brought in the district court for Douglas County, Nebraska, by Louise Kountze Squires and John C. Kirmse as plaintiffs on their own behalf and on behalf of all holders of preferred stock of The Balbach Company, against The Balbach Company, The Engler Company, and Paul E. Engler, defendants. Its object is to procure a declaratory judgment determining the amount per share they and the other preferred stockholders similarly situated should receive on winding up the affairs of the defendant, The Balbach Company, a corporation, on voluntary dissolution by action of the stockholders. The two named corporations are one and the same and will be referred to herein as the corporation or the defendant corporation. * * *

At the conclusion of the trial, the district court held that the preferred stockholders were entitled to the par value of their stock with dividends at $8 per annum from January 1, 1962, to the date of payment less $2 per share which had already been paid, and that the common stockholders were entitled to the remainder. * * *

From this judgment plaintiffs have appealed assigning as error that the judgment is contrary to the law and the evidence. * * *

On the certificates of preferred stock the following appears: * * *. The dividends on the Preferred stock shall be cumulative, and shall be paid before any dividends are paid on the Common stock, and after dividends of eight per centum (8%) per annum have been paid on the Common stock, the Preferred and Common stock shall participate equally in all further dividends.

"In the event of the winding up or dissolution of the Corporation, whether voluntary or involuntary, the holders of the Preferred stock shall receive the par value of their shares with any unpaid dividends thereon, before any payments are made to holders of the Common stock." * * *

The quoted provisions from the amended article of incorporation and the recitations set out from the preferred stock certificates are quite clear with respect to dividends which might be declared before liquidation. Each share of preferred stock was entitled to receive an 8 percent dividend. If there was an excess each share of common stock was entitled to an 8 percent dividend and if it was proper to make further distribution they were to be equally and proportionately divided between the preferred and common stock. * * *

The question of participation rights upon dissolution had been somewhat obscured by a conflict of authority on the related problem of the right of preferred shareholders to participate in additional dividend distribution beyond their stated priority before dissolution. * * *

From the cases cited and those to be cited it appears that there are certain rules which have been generally announced in certain jurisdictions relating to the distribution of assets on liquidation of a corporation.

One is that in the absence of specified rights or limitations all stockholders are entitled to share equally in liquidated surplus assets.

Another is that courts universally adhere to the rule that the rights of respective classes of stockholders are determined by the terms of the articles and memorandum of the corporation except as may be limited by statute.

* * * We conclude that provisions in corporate articles and memoranda that holders of preferred stock shall be paid the par value of their stock before any liquidation dividends are paid to the holders of common stock is exhaustive and means that the preferred stock shall have its par preference on liquidation and nothing more.

It follows that the judgment of the trial court was without error and should be and is affirmed.

PROBLEMS

1. The defendant corporation had a provision in its articles of incorporation which stated that holders of Class A preferred shares should

be entitled to a dividend of $8.00 per share payable in each and every year before any dividend should be paid on the common shares for that year, but such dividends should be noncumulative. No dividends were paid in 1968. The board of directors declared a dividend on the preferred and common shares from earned surplus in 1969 without paying a dividend to the preferred for the year 1968. A preferred shareholder brings suit to have a dividend paid for the year 1968. Decision?

2. Defendant corporation had a surplus of $112,000,000.00. Henry Ford, who controlled the board of directors, convinced the board to use the money for business expansion although it appeared that this would not increase profits but would enable the corporation to sell its products cheaper. Some of the stockholders brought an action to compel the directors to declare a cash dividend of $40,000,000.00. Decision?

3. Defendant corporation declared a dividend on June 1, payable on September 1, to shareholders of record on August 1. Seller sells 10 shares to buyer on June 10. The buyer becomes the record holder on July 15. Defendant corporation sends the dividend check to the buyer. Seller files suit. Decision?

4. Defendant corporation sold 100 shares of stock for $25,000.00 to plaintiff without having obtained a permit from the Division of Corporations as required by the Corporate Securities Act. Plaintiff knew the defendant has not obtained a permit to sell the stock. Plaintiff attended and participated in shareholder meetings for two years and accepted dividends. The defendant corporation is now insolvent and plaintiff sues to rescind the sale. Decision?

5. Buyer purchased a certificate for 100 shares of stock which had been stolen by the seller. The buyer paid value for the stock and did not know it was stolen. As between the buyer and the owner from whom the stock was stolen, who has the right to the certificate?

6. Smith signed a stock subscription agreement to buy 10 shares of stock having a par value of $100 per share of the proposed XYZ Corporation. Two weeks later the company was incorporated. A certificate for 10 shares was duly tendered to Smith but he refused to accept it. He was notified of all the shareholders meetings but never attended. A dividend check was mailed to him but he returned it. XYZ Corporation now sues Smith to recover the $1,000. Smith argues that his subscription agreement was an unaccepted offer that he had not ratified it, so he was not liable. Decision?

7. David subscribed for 200 shares of 8 per cent cumulative, participating, redeemable, convertible, preferred shares of the Atlas Hotel Company of the par value of $100 per share. The subscription agreement provided that he was to receive a bonus of one share of common stock of $100 par value for each share of preferred stock. David fully paid his subscription agreement of $20,000 and received the aforementioned 200 shares of preferred and the bonus stock of 200 shares of the par value common. Subsequently, the Hotel Company becomes insolvent. Rogers, the receiver of the corporation, brings suit for $20,000, the par value of the common stock, against David. Decision?

8. Albert owns 100 shares of stock of the Acme Steel Corporation. At a meeting of the board of directors held in January, a dividend was declared, payable April 1 to shareholders of record March 1. Albert died on March 15, leaving a will under which everything that he owned at the

time of his death was left in trust, the income thereof only to be paid to his wife during her life. When the dividend was paid to the executors of A's will on April 1, was it proper to treat it as part of the trust estate or as income payable to the wife?

9. Mac owned stock in a major oil company which declared a stock dividend. The Collector of Internal Revenue claimed that this dividend was income received by Mac and was subject to the federal income tax. Decision?

10. Ray, a shareholder in Swanson Company, a corporation, delivered his stock certificate indorsed in blank to Turpin, a purchaser for value. The following day, Ray died. His executor, believing that the certificate was lost, applied to the corporation for a new certificate, which was issued and the share transferred to the executor's name on the books. The executor sold the new certificate to Upson, an innocent purchaser, delivering the certificate to him, indorsed to his name, three weeks after Ray's death. Two days later, Turpin presented the original certificate to the corporation, asking that appropriate action be taken to reflect his ownership of the shares. Turpin brings an action against Swanson Company, demanding that he be adjudged the owner of the stock, that Swanson Company be required to issue a new certificate in his name, and that he be paid a dividend which had accrued since the certificate was transferred to him. Decision?

Part 8

NEGOTIABLE INSTRUMENTS

Chapter 35

INTRODUCTION

A. IN GENERAL

Modern commercial paper includes (1) Instruments payable in money or goods; (2) Receipts for and promises to deliver goods; (3) Instruments creating rights in personal or real property; and (4) Documents of title in goods.

Viable business requires the ready transferability of these documents from person to person without loss of attendant rights.

Such transfers may be by (1) assignment; (2) negotiation; (3) sale and delivery of goods; and (4) deeding of real property.

When one takes an assignment of such paper, he acquires all the rights of the assignor, but also he is subjected to existing defenses excepting certain equities in sales to innocent third parties. However, when such paper is negotiated, nearly all defenses are cut off.

Today's national and international commerce has dictated the need for uniformity in such paper, which has resulted in a major part of the Uniform Commercial Code. The Uniform Commercial Code, Article 3, Commercial Paper; Article 7, Warehouse Receipts, Bills of Lading and other Documents of Title; and Article 8, Investment Securities (Appendix A) set forth the statutory law of negotiable instruments.

It has been estimated that ninety per cent of all business transactions involve the use of a check; thus, it is apparent that negotiable instruments play a very important role in the business world. Most of the assets of banks, insurance companies and mortgage companies are in the form of negotiable securities. Corporations participate in the gains and losses of business by means of ownership of negotiable stocks and bonds of other companies. The amount of monetary metal in the United States is very small when compared with the total wealth represented by negotiable securities.

B. TYPES OF NEGOTIABLE INSTRUMENTS

1. PROMISSORY NOTES

A negotiable promissory note is a written unconditional promise by one person, the *maker*, to pay a sum certain in money to another person, the *payee*. It may be made payable on demand or at a stated future time. It may be made payable to order (and the payee may order that it be paid to another person) or to bearer (one who has possession). See *U.C.C.*, Section 3–104(1). It is a two party instrument.

2. DRAFTS

A draft, or bill of exchange, is an unconditional written order by one party, the *drawer,* on another party, the *drawee* to pay a certain sum in money on demand or at a stated future time to a third party, the *payee.* See *U.C.C.*, Section 3–104(2)(a).

3. CHECKS

A check is a draft drawn on a bank and payable on demand. See *U.C.C.,* Section 3–104(2) (b). A *cashier's* check is drawn by a bank on itself ordering itself to pay a sum certain to the depositor or to the person designated by him. A *certified* check is a personal check of the bank's depositor which the bank has certified that the depositor has such amount on deposit. A *bank draft* is a check drawn by one bank upon another bank in which the first bank has money on deposit.

4. CERTIFICATES OF DEPOSIT

A certificate of deposit is a written acknowledgment by a bank of receipt of a certain amount of money by a depositor and a promise to pay the holder of the certificate that amount when the certificate, properly indorsed, is surrendered. See *U.C.C.*, Section 3–104(2)(c).

C. THE PARTIES TO NEGOTIABLE INSTRUMENTS

1. PROMISSORY NOTE

A promissory note has two original parties: the maker and the payee. The *maker* is the party who promises to pay the money. The *payee* is the party entitled to receive the money.

2. DRAFT AND CHECK

The draft and check have three original parties: the drawer, the drawee, and the payee. The *drawer* is the person who executes the instrument. In the case of a check, he is sometimes called a signer. The obligation of the drawer is conditional in the sense that if the instrument is not paid by the drawee, he is promising to pay. The *drawee* is the person or institution to whom the order to pay is directed. In the case of a check, the drawee would be a banking establishment. The obligation of the drawee depends entirely upon the relationship between the drawer and the drawee. The usual checking account obligates the bank to honor all orders for payment of money as long as the account has sufficient balance. In the case of a draft or check, the obligation of the bank extends directly to the holder once the bank has *accepted* or in effect *agreed to honor it*. Where the bank has so accepted, it may be referred to as an *acceptor*. The *payee* is the party entitled to payment.

3. INDORSER

In addition to original parties, other parties may be involved in a negotiable instrument. An *indorser* is the party who transfers a negotiable instrument by signing and delivering it to another person. In the case of a check, the first indorser would be the payee. The usual method of indorsing a negotiable instrument is to sign your name on the back of it.

4. INDORSEE

The *indorsee* is the person to whom an indorsement is made. An indorsee may also indorse and negotiate the instrument in which case he is also an indorser.

5. BEARER

The *bearer* is the person who has possession of the instrument payable to bearer or indorsed in blank.

6. HOLDER

The *holder* is the person who has possession of the instrument issued or indorsed to him or to his order, or to bearer, or indorsed in blank. A *holder for value* is a holder who gives consideration for the instrument. A *holder in due course* is a person who becomes a holder for value, in good faith, and without notice of any defense to the instrument (*U.C.C.*, Section 3–302(1)).

7. ACCOMMODATION PARTY

An *accommodation party* is a person who signs the instrument for the purpose of lending his name to another party to it (*U.C.C.*, Section 3–415(1)). An accommodation party may be a co-maker, surety, or an indorser.

8. GUARANTOR

A *guarantor* is a person who signs the instrument adding a statement that he will pay the instrument under certain conditions (*U.C.C.,* Section 3–416).

D. LIABILITY OF THE PARTIES

---

1. PROMISSORY NOTE

The liability of the *maker* is primary which means that he will pay the instrument according to its terms at the time of his promise to pay (*U.C.C.,* Section 3–413(1)).

2. DRAFT OR CHECK

The liability of the *drawer* is secondary in that he promises to pay the amount of the draft or check to the holder thereof or to any indorser if the drawee (bank) does not pay *and* if he is given proper notice (*U.C.C.,* Section 3–413(2)). The *drawee or acceptor* has primary liability if the check or draft is accepted by it (*U.C.C.,* Section 3–411(1)).

3. INDORSER

The indorser promises to pay the instrument according to its terms at the time of his indorsement to the holder or to any subsequent indorser if the instrument is dishonored and proper notice has been given him (*U.C.C.,* Section 3–414).

A person who transfers the instrument without indorsing it, or who indorses it by using such words as "without recourse" above his signature, is not liable for its payment (*U.C.C.,* Sections 3–401(1), 3–414(1)); *however,* such a person may be bound by *warranties* that are involved in the transfer of negotiable instruments (*U.C.C.,* Section 3–417).

Unless otherwise agreed, indorsers are liable to one another in the order in which they indorse, which is presumed to be the order in which their signatures appear on the instrument (*U.C.C.,* Section 3–414(2)).

E. WARRANTIES OF THE PARTIES

The transferor of negotiable instruments warrants or guarantees that certain facts exist. The warranties vary according to the manner in which the negotiation is made. Where there is an indorsement, the warranty runs to subsequent holders; however, if the transfer is made by delivery alone, the warranty only runs to the immediate transferee.

1. WARRANTIES OF INDORSER

The following warranties apply where the indorser has transferred the instrument, has received consideration, and his indorsement is not without recourse; e. g., he merely signs his name as the indorsement, or he makes the following indorsement: "Pay to the order of John Smith (signed) Robert Jones":

a. That he has good title or is authorized to act for one who has such title;

b. That the signatures on the instrument are genuine or executed by authorized agents;

c. That the instrument has not been materially altered;

d. That he has no knowledge of any insolvency proceeding instituted against the maker or acceptor or the drawer of an unaccepted instrument; and

e. That no defense of any party is good against him. See *U.C.C.,* Section 3–417(2).

2. WARRANTIES OF NONRECOURSE INDORSER

A person who indorses an instrument "without recourse" is still liable for all the warranties of an indorser except that number (e), supra, is limited by the following: "that he has no knowledge of such a defense" (*U.C.C.,* Section 3–417(3)). The nonrecourse indorser may exclude *all* warranties by inserting "without warranties" above his signature.

3. WARRANTIES OF TRANSFEROR BY DELIVERY

When one transfers a negotiable instrument by delivery, the warranties are the same as those made by a nonrecourse indorser except that they extend to the transferee only if he has given consideration.

1. *Check as a Negotiable Instrument*

GARDEN CHECK CASH. SERV., INC. v. FIRST NAT. CITY BANK

25 App.Div.2d 137, 267 N.Y.S.2d 698 (1966), affirmed 18 N.Y.2d 941, 277 N.Y.S.2d 141, 223 N.E.2d 566.

BASTOW, Justice. This action was brought to recover on a written instrument, more fully hereinafter described. * * *

The proof is that any person, whether a customer or not, may purchase from defendant for twenty cents a check up to the amount of $250. The instrument when issued bears the name of defendant, an identification number and the amount is machine-imbedded thereon. * * *

On April 13, 1962 one Higgins purchased from defendant a check in the amount of $130.37. On the same date he reported to the bank that the check had been lost and requested that payment be stopped. The name of a payee, according to Higgins, had not been filled in. Defendant stopped payment and five days later delivered to Higgins a cashier's check for the amount of $130.37.

It further appears that on April 13 one Walker presented the check in its blank form to plaintiff. Upon furnishing identification satisfactory to plaintiff, Walker inserted his name as payee, signed the check with his name and received the proceeds thereof less plaintiff's fee. Following deposit the check was returned to plaintiff by defendant with the notation that payment had been stopped.

The issue presented is, whether, as plaintiff contends, the instrument is "akin to a cashier's check or a traveler's check" upon which defendant is primarily liable from the moment of issue with no right to stop payment thereon. Or, on the other hand, as defendant submits, is the instrument an unconditional order in writing addressed by the owner-drawer to the bank, requiring the latter to pay on demand the stated sum to order or to bearer with the ensuing right to the purchaser to stop payment?

A check, strictly speaking, is a negotiable instrument, i. e., a bill of exchange drawn on a bank payable on demand. * * * A bill of exchange is an unconditional order in writing addressed by one person to another, signed by the person giving it, requiring the person to whom it is addressed to pay on demand a sum certain to order or to bearer. * * *

Such a bill becomes a check when drawn on a bank payable on demand * * * The relationship between defendant and the purchaser of the check is reasonably clear. The latter deposited with defendant a sum of money and received therefor a writing in which defendant plainly appeared as drawee. The novel feature of the instrument was that the prospective names of drawer and payee were blank. * * *

Defendant was not primarily liable thereon * * * The drawee enters into no contract relations with the holder unless and until the instrument is accepted. * * * and such liability did not arise until there was certification or acceptance of the instrument.

* * * We conclude that Higgins, the purchaser of the instrument, effectively stopped payment thereon prior to its presentation to defendant by plaintiff. It follows that no cause of action has been established against defendant.

---

2. *Certified Check or Cashier's Check not Cash*

PERRY v. WEST

110 N.H. 351, 266 A.2d 849 (1970).

KENISON, Chief Justice. The issue in this case is whether a municipality can be compelled to accept a bid for property sold for taxes accompanied by a bank draft or a cashier's check when the municipal ordinance and the announced terms of the auction sale require the bid to be accompanied by "cash or certified check." The facts are not in dispute and the issues have been competently argued and briefed by the parties.

Plaintiffs submitted the highest bid at an auction sale of certain property within the City of Concord conducted by George M. West, Tax Collector, as real estate agent for the City. The City had previously acquired the property by tax sale. * * * The advertisements appearing in the *Concord Daily Monitor* * * * required that all bids be accompanied "by cash or certified check in an amount to at least 10% of the bid price." Plaintiffs' high bid was accompanied by a bank draft of the New Hampshire Savings drawn on the Mechanicks National Bank and payable to George West, Tax Collector. The second highest bid, submitted by Henry J. Love, was accompanied by a cashier's check of Concord National Bank payable to the City of Concord. The third highest bid was submitted by Pasquale Alosa and accompanied by United States currency. Lockwood Realty Company submitted the fourth highest bid accompanied by its check certified by the Mechanicks National Bank. * * *

On the day of the auction, November 17, 1969, defendant West, on the advice of the City Solicitor, sent a letter to Alosa and the Perrys advising them that Alosa was the successful bidder. On November 19, 1969, the City executed a quitclaim deed to the property in favor of Alosa, which was never recorded. After a hearing on November 20, 1969, in Merrimack County Superior Court on the petition of the Perrys, the City was ordered to execute and deliver a deed to the Perrys. None of the other bidders was made a party at this hearing. On November 21 the City executed a quitclaim deed in favor of the Perrys which was delivered and recorded.

Alosa filed a petition to enter the action as party defendant which was granted. After a hearing on November 25, 1969, the Court enjoined the Perrys from encumbering, transferring or dealing with any rights of ownership in the property. The other bidders were subsequently added as parties. Defendants' exceptions to the granting of the petition of the Perrys have been reserved and transferred by *Loughlin,* J.

Plaintiffs contend that the bank draft submitted with their bid was "cash" within the modern usage of the term and therefore their bid complied with the terms of the auction. * * *

* * *

Although the meaning of "cash" may vary with the context of its use, the common meaning is United States currency. * * * Nothing in the present case indicates that the City Council intended to expand this meaning. Indeed the term "certified check" would be unnecessary if "cash" were to include various forms of commercial paper in addition to currency.

The various commercial instruments involved in this case have definite and distinct meanings. A bank draft is merely the instrument of one bank drawing upon its deposits with another bank. A cashier's check is the instrument of a bank drawing upon its own funds. * * * Certification of a check is acceptance by the drawee.

For this case the important distinction among these instruments is the number of parties liable on the instrument. Bank drafts and cashier's checks are "one-name paper." Only the drawer bank is liable on a bank draft until accepted by the drawee. Although a cashier's check is accepted upon issuance, there is only one bank involved and therefore only one party bound on the instrument. * * * However both the drawer and drawee are bound on a certified check. * * * There are therefore accepted and reasonable distinctions among "cash," "certified check," "bank draft" and "cashier's check" upon which the City Council could base its preference for cash or certified check. Within the context of the auction of property sold for taxation the phrase "cash or certified check" had a definite, unambiguous and accepted commercial meaning. * * *

The general rule that a municipality must accept the highest bid, * * * only requires acceptance of the highest bid which conforms to the terms of the auction sale consistent with the governing municipal ordinance. * * * The City did not waive the bidding requirements. It rejected the two highest bids which did not comply with the terms of the auction and accepted the bid accompanied by currency. Subsequent compliance with a court order was not a waiver of the terms by the City. Acceptance of the Perrys' bid by defendant West could have subjected him to personal liability. * * *

Both the City and the public were entitled to rely upon the terms of the auction sale and the controlling ordinance and this Court will not compel the City to waive the conditions in the advertisements and Ordinances. * * * All bidders must have equal opportunity and the city officials must not be required to make subjective evaluations of the apparent financial integrity of the bidders. * * * Certainty in bidding procedures by which all bidders are on an equal basis should not be discouraged in the disposition and sale of municipal property.

Pasquale Alosa, the highest bidder who conformed to the terms of the auction, is therefore entitled to the property upon full payment of his bid price. * * *

Remanded.

---

3. Note Requires "words of negotiability"

HALL v. WESTMORELAND, HALL & BRYAN

123 Ga.App. 809, 182 S.E.2d 539 (1971).

Attached is Exhibit "A" consisting of an instrument in the form of a letter addressed to Westmoreland, Hall & Bryan which recited: "I agree to pay to your firm as attorney's fees for representing me in obtaining property settlement agreement and tax advice, the sum of $2,760, payable at the rate of $230 per month for twelve (12) months beginning January 1, 1970." This instrument was signed "Very truly yours, Barbara Hall Hodge."

The defendant filed defensive pleadings and a counterclaim. Defendant denied owing the plaintiff any sum whatsoever, and as her defenses set out: that she was represented by John L. Westmoreland, Jr. in a divorce proceeding under an agreement whereby he would secure attorney's fees by order of court and that he had received a sum in excess of $3,500 by court order; that Exhibit "A" was signed by her after the divorce matter had been completely settled and she received no consideration for its execution; that she did not receive any tax advice from the plaintiff or the plaintiff's firm; that she was informed that she would not be required to pay any fee, that Westmoreland would receive his fee from defendant's husband.

* * *

The trial judge entered an order granting the plaintiffs' motion for summary judgment. From this order appeal was taken.

QUILLIAN, Judge. The plaintiffs contend that the trial judge properly granted their motion for summary judgment since Exhibit "A" was a negotiable instrument and that they were holders in due course to whom any defenses interposed by the defendant were not applicable.

One of the requirements of a negotiable instrument is that it contain the time honored "words of negotiability," such as pay to the order of or pay to bearer. This was inherent in our law prior to the enactment of the Commercial Code. * * * The Commercial Code continues this practice by now stating: "Any writing to be a negotiable instrument within this Article must * * * be payable to order or to bearer." * * * In the absence of such language, Exhibit "A" would not be a negotiable instrument.

Even if Exhibit "A" be considered a negotiable instrument, plaintiffs failed to meet the requirements of a holder in due course. * * * Furthermore, even a holder in due course takes the instrument free of all defenses *only* "of any party to the instrument with whom the holder has not dealt." Here, the plaintiffs failed to show they occupied the status of a holder in due course, or to establish they were not a party with whom the defendant dealt in this transaction.

As to one who is not a holder in due course, he takes the instrument subject to "all defenses of any party which would be available in an action on a simple contract; and the defenses of want or failure of consideration, nonperformance of any condition precedent, nondelivery, or delivery for a special purpose.

While parol evidence is generally not admissible to vary the terms of a written contract, want or failure of consideration or that a contract was void ab initio may be set forth by evidence extrinsic to the instrument. * * *

It is therefore apparent that the defendant was entitled to use the defense of failure of consideration. * * * Since the defense offered by the defendant was not legally insufficient as a matter of law, the plaintiffs had the burden of establishing the insufficiency of the defense as a matter of fact. The evidence in this case failed to accomplish this and the trial judge erred in granting summary judgment.

Judgment reversed.

---

4. Accommodation Party

STATE BANK OF GREELEY v. OWENS

502 P.2d 965 (1972).

SILVERSTEIN, Chief Judge. State Bank of Greeley, (Bank) sued to recover the balance due on a note, made and executed by defendant Lemax Corporation (Lemax), and endorsed by defendants Owens, Donily and Baldwin. William R. Meller and Associates, Inc., (Meller) was also joined as a defendant. After a trial to the court, judgment was entered for the Bank against all defendants. Only Owens, Donily and Baldwin (appellants) appeal. We affirm.

The facts are not in dispute. Lemax executed a note payable to to the order of the Bank as payee, on August 3, 1966, with payment due on November 3, 1966. This note was guaranteed by Meller. On August 30, 1966, at the request of the Bank, the appellants executed an agreement guaranteeing payment of the note. The note was not paid at maturity, and on February 3, 1967, Lemax executed a new note which was due and payable on August 6, 1967. The appellants executed an endorsement on this note which read, "For value received, I/we hereby guarantee the payment of the within note at maturity. * * *" This second note was not paid, and the Bank brought this action to recover on this note. At the time of the execution of the second note, Lemax was insolvent.

Appellants contend they are not liable on their guarantee for three reasons:

* * *

3. The Bank was the party accommodated in the transaction and therefore cannot recover on the endorsement.

* * *

It is immaterial that at the time the renewal note was given Lemax Corporation was insolvent and unable to pay the obligation at its maturity. Lemax's obligation to pay the loan remained and was unaffected by its financial circumstances. * * *

Appellants contend that, because they endorsed the renewal note at the Bank's request, the Bank became the party accommodated. This contention is without merit. It is appellants' theory that if the Bank is the party accommodated, defendants are not liable to it, under [U.C.C.] 3–415(5), for their accommodation endorsement. However, the party accommodated is the one to whom the name of the accommodation party is loaned. [U.C.C.] 3–415(1). The payee may derive incidental benefit from the accommodation but that does not, ipso facto, make the payee the party accommodated. In this instance, Lemax obtained an extension of its obligation to repay the Bank as a result of the defendants' endorsement of its renewal note. The mere fact that the accommodation endorsement was made at the request of the Bank does not alter Lemax's position as the beneficiary of the defendants' endorsement. Lemax was the maker of the instrument to which the defendants lent their names. Lemax Corporation was the party accommodated in this transaction. The defendants are liable, as accommodation endorsers, to the holder of the renewal note. [U.C.C.] 3–415(2).

The judgment is affirmed.

5. *Endorser may become Guarantor*

JAMAICA TOBACCO & SALES CORP. v. ORTNER

70 Misc.2d 388, 333 N.Y.S.2d 669 (1972).

HENTEL, J. Plaintiff corporation's secretary-treasurer Froehlich testified that G & R Stationery Corporation was indebted to plaintiff for goods supplied, and on or about July 28, 1971, Froehlich arrived at G & R's place of business along with a City Marshal to replevy against the goods of G & R. At that dramatic moment, Morris Stone, the president of G & R telephoned the defendant Jerry Ortner, which thereupon led to a telephone conversation between Froehlich and the defendant.

Froehlich testified that he had never met the defendant before; that he had previously done business with him over the telephone and thus recognized his voice; that defendant told him on this occasion Stone was a friend, and that he had loaned money to Stone before; that defendant asked Froehlich to call off the replevin proceeding and stated: *"I'll guarantee you will get your money."* (emphasis supplied). Further, when defendant was asked by Froehlich "will you put it in writing?", the defendant reportedly answered "yes."

Later in this non-jury trial, defendant testified that he received a telephone call from Stone late in July 1971, to the effect that a City Marshal was at Stone's place of business and that he was going to close up his store because he owed money to the plaintiff. The defendant admittedly spoke to the Marshal who told him that Stone would be out of business if he did not pay plaintiff's outstanding bill. The defendant further stated he had done business with Stone for some six prior years, and he recalled his conversation with Froehlich on the telephone on that day and told Froehlich: "If you clean out the store, the store is finished, * * * the Stones are elderly people who are in tears, * * * *I'll sign for them* * * * they (the Stones) promised me they would make good." The defendant also stated that he felt sorry for the Stones and that he was trying to help keep them in business. All of this is corroborative of Froehlich's testimony.

In July 1971, the proof shows G & R owed the plaintiff $2439.80; and also owed the defendant approximately $400.

Following the reported telephone conversation, Froehlich released the City Marshal, the replevin proceeding was halted; and a series of six notes were executed dated July 29, 1971, each in the sum of $406.63 or $406.64, payable to the order of the plaintiff and which were signed by Stone as president of G & R, due on the first of every month commencing September 1, 1971, and concluding on February 1, 1972. After Stone signed the notes, Froehlich sent them over to the defendant by messenger for his signature pursuant to the telephone advice of the defendant. Froehlich instructed an employee to type on the reverse of each note this legend: *"In event of nonpayment then the total amount due of all notes shall become due and payable"* (emphasis supplied) over the blank, underscored line meant for defendant's signature. * * *

The six notes were introduced into evidence with defendant's signature on the back of each note immediately below the quoted italicized legend supra.

On September 1, 1971, the due date of the first of the notes, the same not being paid, an action was thereupon commenced by a complaint dated September 3, 1971, against the defendant indorser. No demand for payment was made first of G & R.

* * * With respect to the affirmative defense that the signature of the defendant on the reverse of the notes "does not legally constitute an endorsement or a promise to pay for the debt or default of the debtor herein," the court reserved decision.

The defendant's memorandum of law rightly asserts: "The controversial point involved in this action is the statement (legend) on the back (of each note)". (See italicized legend supra). The questions to be answered by the court are: Does the legend bind the defendant to do anything? Is the legend applicable to him? Does his signature make him liable as an indorser regardless of the ambiguous legend? Is the defendant an accommodation indorser? Is he a guarantor? May the plaintiff sue the defendant directly on the notes as an individual of primary liability rather than secondary thereunder without first going through the procedures of presentment, notice of dishonor and protest?

The court answers all of these questions affirmatively—yes!

In the court's opinion, we have a very strong case here in favor of the plaintiff. * * * Here we have the plaintiff-creditor actually in the midst of protecting its rights to payment by levying on the goods of the debtor under process of law. This was not an idle threat of foreclosure—the closing down of the plaintiff's business was actually in progress. At that moment of high drama, a friend of the debtor makes a plea to the creditor to exercise humane forbearance, halt the replevy proceeding and give the debtor six months to pay off the indebtedness. The creditor agrees to do so and then surrenders its immediate right to replevy relying upon the third party's extremely strong and unequivocal oral representation to guarantee payment of the indebtedness and his stated willingness to put such a guarantee in writing.

* * * It was upon defendant's promise and guarantee to pay that the plaintiff primarily relied and acted upon to its subsequent detriment. Plaintiff had already written the debtor G & R off its credit book as a bad risk, and was insuring a return on its money by levying on the goods of the debtor. That remedy came to a close when the replevin proceeding was aborted by virtue of the defend-

ant's intervention and a new and primary debt came into being upon the defendant's promise to pay. The circumstances surrounding this negotiation identify the *defendant as being more in the guise of a co-maker of these notes rather than an indorser.*

* * *

(2) Regardless of the ambiguity, artlessness and clouded meaning of the legend on the reverse side of the notes, the defendant's signature establishes him, at the very least, as an accommodation indorser with consequent liability to the plaintiff. Defendant's signature on the notes cannot be held to be an empty act without consequence or liability to the defendant. He put his signature on the notes as a guarantor of payment on condition that plaintiff would desist from exercising its swift and immediate right to replevy.

* * *

The accommodation indorser, a stranger to the instrument, i. e., not a maker, drawer, acceptor or payee, *usually* indorses his name prior to the delivery of the note to the payee in order "to give credit to the principal obligor or maker, and often is one whom the payee himself requires as security before he will take the instrument or advance the funds represented thereby."

"The liability of an indorser is not a joint obligation with the maker, and he cannot compel the holder to sue the maker first. . . . Thus, the holder may proceed against any or all indorsers." 42 N.Y.Jur. § 430, p. 52; § 433, p. 54. *"The contract of the indorser is a new and independent one, distinct from that of the maker."* 42 N.Y.Jur. § 433, p. 53. "The holder of a note may sue both the maker and the indorser or either. An indorser, sued upon his contract of indorsement, is absolutely liable therein." See U.C.C. § 3–414(1) and comment 1.

Inasmuch as the court concludes from the evidence that defendant guaranteed payment of the notes, plaintiff did not have to go through the process of presentment, dishonor and protest with the maker (G & R) of the notes.
Presentment is not necessary to charge a guarantor. * * * *Where words of guaranty are used, presentment, notice of dishonor, and protest are not necessary to charge the user."* 42 N.Y.Jur. § 440, p. 60.

The plaintiff, in the court's opinion, had the right—under the circumstances of this case—to sue the defendant directly and primarily on these notes not only as an accommodation indorser/guarantor but also as a de facto co-maker.

* * *

Keep in mind that an accommodation indorser is only secondarily liable unless he makes a special agreement (*such as proved in this case by parol evidence*) which makes him primarily liable.

* * *

"An indorser who guarantees payment waives all demand on the maker or drawee, and his liability becomes indistinguishable from that of a co-maker (Comment U.C.C. § 3–416). When words of guaranty are used, presentment, notice of dishonor, and protest are not necessary to charge the user. (U.C.C. § 3–416(5))."

The court in making its determination of the intention of the parties to this action that defendant intended to be held liable under the notes in any event, has a right to invoke the theorem of construction anent what the average businessman would have intended under the same circumstances. The court holds that the average businessman, under the same circumstances, would conclude that the guarantee of payment, in view of the forbearance of the plaintiff, was meant to create a primary obligation to pay a debt in order to induce such forbearance rather than in insulated secondary obligation of the usual indorser. The activist role of defendant in negotiating these notes imposed upon him, by operation of law, the responsibilities and obligations of a *co-maker* even though he appeared to be an indorser as a matter of form.

"An instrument should be considered as it would manifestly be understood by the *average businessman,* and the party signing it should be exonerated from liability when, according to such construction, it appears that he did not intend, and was not understood, to bind himself." Here, the court is convinced that defendant intended to bind himself on the same level as the maker of the notes.

On the basis of this reasoning of the court, the plaintiff was not required to go against the maker, G & R, first in order to trigger liability on the part of the accommodation indorser. The creditor has the right to move directly against the accommodation party as it did here.

* * *

Accordingly, the fourth affirmative defense upon which decision was reserved is dismissed, and judgment is rendered in favor of the plaintiff on the notes for $2439.80, plus interest, from September 1, 1971.

---

6. *Right to Verify Endorsements*

KLOTZ v. FIRST NATIONAL BANK OF TOLEDO

10 Ohio App.2d 62, 226 N.E.2d 804 (1967).

SKEEL, Judge. This appeal is from a judgment of dismissal of plaintiff-appellant's action seeking damages for an alleged libel. The plaintiff deposited with the defendant-appellee for collection and deposit an instrument in the nature of a bank check or sight draft in the sum of $300, drawn on The Western Federal Savings & Loan Association of Los Angeles, California. The plaintiff's petition alleges that the instrument was doubly endorsed with plaintiff's signature appearing as the second endorsement. It is alleged that the defendant was well informed of plaintiff's standing in the community, his good reputation and impeccable character, and that he was thus recognized and was known as an inventor, physicist and mathematician who has worked for the past several years as an engineering writer.

It is alleged that the defendant wrongfully and with deliberate malice caused to be typed on its (the bank's) collection request form and made known to the bank employees the words, "pay only if payee's endorsement appears genuine." In that form the collection request was sent to Los Angeles.

It is claimed that the defendant therefor and thereby imputed to plaintiff his "possible and probable" forgery of the first endorsement and the possible and probable illegal, unlawful, wrongful, dishonest, fraudulent and criminal possession of the instrument.

It is alleged that by causing such words to be placed on its collection form, the defendant acted with intent to impugn plaintiff's honesty, to ascribe to plaintiff a felonious and criminal personality, to bring plaintiff into disrepute in Toledo and its environs, and with like result in Los Angeles, California. * * * The plaintiff having failed to plead further, the court, upon motion, dismissed plaintiff's action and entered judgment against plaintiff for the costs.

* * * As indicated, this action is based on the conduct of the defendant when plaintiff deposited for collection and deposit a banker's check or sight draft upon which, as he alleged, the plaintiff was the second endorser. There is no claim that he was the payee, nor is the identity of the first endorser or payee disclosed. Without identifying the payee as an endorser, the plaintiff could not claim any clear or absolute right based upon possession of the bank check or draft. The defendant, as it was its right to do, placed on the collection request as indicated, "pay only if payee's endorsement appears genuine." * * *

These paragraphs, as indicated above, allege that the use of the words, "pay only if payee's endorsement appears to be genuine," were intended to attribute to the plaintiff the unlawful forging of the "signatures" appearing as endorsements on the instrument; that such words imputed to plaintiff his "possible and probable" illegal, unlawful, wrongful, dishonest, fraudulent and criminal possession of such instrument; that such words placed on defendant's collection request were intended to impugn plaintiff's honesty and to ascribe to plaintiff a felonious and criminal personality and to bring plaintiff into disrepute in Toledo and Los Angeles. No such interpretation could be reasonably ascribed to the use of such words as used on defendant's collection request. * * *

The possession by an agent for collection of an order for the payment of money gives him the legal right, when in doubt, to seek verification of the genuineness of all endorsers and vests the collection agent with the right to request that his agent verify the genuineness of all endorsements.

* * *

Judgment affirmed.

PROBLEMS

1. The following promissory note has just been executed:

Atlanta, Georgia
July 1, 1973

One year after date I promise to pay to the order of John Jones Three Hundred and no/100 ($300) dollars, at the First National Bank. Value received.

(signed) Richard Roe

Who is the maker and who is the payee of this note?

2. The following bill of exchange has just been executed:

Atlanta, Georgia
July 1, 1973

To Bill Brown
Augusta, Georgia
Ninety days after date pay to the order of John Jones Three Hundred and no/100 ($300) Dollars and charge the same to my account. Value received.

(signed) Richard Roe
Acct. No. 43–751–02

Identify the drawer, the drawee, and the payee of this bill.

3. Ace Holder gave Bill Betton his promissory note for money won by Bill in a game of cards. State law made notes given for gambling debts void. Bill endorsed the note in due course and for value to California Bank. After due presentment and notice of dishonor, the California Bank sues Bill for the amount of the note. Bill interposes the defense that the note was given for an amount won in an illegal gambling transaction. Decision?

4. Jenson contracted to take a correspondence course and signed an agreement: "In consideration of receiving the lessons in this course, I promise to pay to the order of the Literary Writers Correspondence School $250 in equal installments of $25 each month for ten months, starting one month from the date of this contract."

A few weeks after giving the note to the school, Jenson received a letter from the North American Bank, stating that the bank had purchased his note and instructing him to send all payments to the bank. Jenson refused, claiming that the agreement he had made was a contract with the school, not a negotiable instrument. Decision?

5. Sam Sherman, a debtor from out of town, stopped by the Ace Loan Company to make a payment. He had forgotten his checkbook, and the company had no blanks or counter checks. Sam wrote out what purported to be a check on a plain piece of typing paper, including the requisites of negotiability and his encoded number. Sam claims that this is a valid check when he signs and delivers it to Ace Loan Co. Decision?

6. Gordon received a certified check from Bain, a customer, in payment of a bill of goods. He kept the check for a week and then presented

it for payment to the bank on which it was drawn. The bank refused to pay it, claiming that Bain had become insolvent since the check was issued and they are no longer liable on the check. Decision?

7. Baker applied for a $500 loan from the Ace Loan Company. As Baker was not well known and did not own property, Ace required him to obtain a comaker on his note as added security. Able, a friend with excellent credit references and property, agreed to sign the note as an accommodation to Baker. Baker fails to pay the note when due and Ace seeks to hold Able as an accommodation indorser. Decision?

8. Richard Fay sued Harry Witte to recover on a promissory note payable to the order of Witte, and endorsed by him as follows: "I hereby assign all my right and interest in this note to Richard Fay in full. Harry Witte." The issue is whether these words make Witte liable as an unqualified endorser or whether he is an endorser without recourse and therefore not liable. Decision?

9. A promissory note was made payable to the order of Paul Payee, and Paul sold it, delivering it to the buyer without endorsement. What is the legal status of the transfer of the note?

10. The Ace Loan Company's safe contained notes that were signed as follows: (a) Al Baker, Secretary; (b) Harry Rose, cashier of the Bullway Department store; (c) Maple Furniture Company, by Moe Woods, treasurer. In reviewing the Ace assets, which, if any, of these notes, obligate the signer personally? Why?

Chapter 36

NEGOTIABILITY

Negotiable instruments are contracts for the payment of money which must meet certain formal requirements to be classified as negotiable instruments. These contracts can be freely transferred without the normal personal defenses that we find in the assignment of ordinary contracts, and it is in this respect that negotiable instruments differ from ordinary contracts. For example, a thief cannot pass title to stolen goods; however, a thief of a negotiable instrument can pass a good title to the instrument to a purchaser for value without notice of the theft. This chapter covers the requirements of negotiability, the transfer of negotiable instruments, and the holder in due course.

A. REQUIREMENTS OF NEGOTIABILITY

If a written contract is to be negotiable so that the purchaser of it takes free and clear of personal defenses of the true owner of the instrument, it must conform to the requirements set out in the *U.C.C.*, Section 3–104(1): "Any writing to be a negotiable instrument within this Article must:

(a) be signed by the maker or drawer; and

(b) contain an unconditional promise or order to pay a sum certain in money and no other promise, order, obligation or power given by the maker or drawer except as authorized by this Article; and

(c) be payable on demand or at a definite time; and

(d) be payable to order or to bearer.".

1. WRITING AND SIGNATURE

If the instrument is to be negotiable, it must be in writing. Writing includes typing, printing, and engraving. Ink or pencil may be used; however, pencil is not advisable because it is not as durable and can be easily altered.

The signature may be in one's own handwriting, or printed, engraved, or stamped. The signature may consist of initials, figures, or a mark (*U.C.C.*, Section 1–201(39)). It need not be at the end, but must appear some place on the instrument except in the case of an acceptance of a bill in a separate writing or an indorsement on a paper attached to the instrument.

2. PROMISE OR ORDER

If the instrument is a promissory note, it must contain a *promise* to pay money; if it is a draft or check, it must contain an *order* to pay money. An acknowledgment of a debt is not a promise; e. g., "I.O.U., John Smith, the sum of $10,000.00. Signed: Robert Williams.". An authorization to pay money is not an order; e. g., "We hereby authorize you to pay on our account, to the order of William Smith, the sum of $10,000.00.". Such instruments are not negotiable since there is no promise to pay and no order to pay.

3. PROMISE AND ORDER MUST BE UNCONDITIONAL

The promise and the order must not be conditional; e. g., an instrument which recites that it is "subject to" the terms of another agreement such as a contract or mortgage is conditional (*U.C.C.,* Section 3–105(2) (a)); an *order* to pay out of a particular fund is conditional (*U.C.C.,* Section 3–105(2) (b)); however, if the instrument merely *indicates* a particular account to be debited or any other fund from which reimbursement is expected it is not conditional, e. g., "charge my expense account" (*U.C.C.,* Section 3–105(1) (f)). An instrument which is limited to payment out of a particular fund is not conditional if issued by the government (*U.C.C.,* Section 3–105(1) (g)).

4. SUM CERTAIN

If the instrument is to be negotiable, it must call for the payment of a *sum certain*; i. e., definite on its face as to how much is to be paid. The sum payable is a sum certain even though it is to be paid with stated different rates of interest before and after default or a specified date (*U.C.C.,* Section 3–106(1) (b)); or with costs of collection or an attorney's fee or both upon default (*U.C.C.,* Section 3–106(1) (e)).

5. IN MONEY

The instrument must call for payment in *money.* It is payable in money if the medium of exchange in which it is payable is money at the time the instrument is made; if the instrument is payable in "currency" or "current funds"; and if it is payable in foreign currency (*U.C.C.,* Section 3–107).

6. TIME OF PAYMENT

The instrument to be negotiable must be payable on demand or at a definite time. An instrument is payable at a definite time if by its terms it is payable at a fixed period after a stated date, at a definite time subject to any acceleration, or at a definite time subject to extension at the option of the holder (*U.C.C.,* Section 3–109). It is not payable at a time certain if it is payable upon the happening of an event that may never happen; e. g., "when John is twenty-one years old".

An instrument is payable on demand if it states that it is payable on demand, or payable at sight, or on presentation, or when no time of payment is expressed (*U.C.C.,* Section 3–108).

7. ORDER AND BEARER

The instrument to be negotiable must be made payable to order or to bearer. When it is stated in the instrument that it is payable to the order of a specified person, it is an order paper; e. g., "pay to the order of John Smith", or "pay to John Smith or order". John Smith would have to deliver and indorse the instrument to negotiate it. (*U.C.C.,* Section 3–110, Section 3–202(1)).

An instrument is payable to bearer when it is payable to bearer or the order of bearer, or a specified person or bearer, or cash or the order of cash; e. g., "pay to bearer", or "pay to John Smith or bearer". (*U.C.C.,* Section 3–111). Bearer paper can be negotiated by delivery alone (*U.C.C.,* Section 3–202(1)).

8. DESIGNATION OF PARTIES

The parties to the instrument must be designated with certainty; i. e., each party must be identified, and the position he occupies on the instrument must be indicated. The use of assumed or trade names is sufficient identification.

9. ADDITIONAL RECITALS

Many promissory notes and bonds of corporations contain additional recitals which may or may not affect negotiability. Negotiability is not affected by such recitals as an authorization of a confession of judgment (debtor permits judgment to be entered against him for a stipulated sum without institution of legal proceedings; this proceeding is not permitted in many states); statement that collateral has been given for the instrument; statement that debtor waives the benefit of any law intended for his benefit (not permitted in many states); statement that the indorsement by payee is an acknowledgment of full satisfaction of the debt; notations on the check as to purpose for which the check was given or the items discharged by the check. (*U.C.C.,* Section 3–112).

However, a provision authorizing the holder of the instrument to require an act other than the payment of money, e. g., delivery of goods, makes the instrument non-negotiable (*U.C.C.,* Section 3–104(1) (b)).

It should be remembered that because an instrument is non-negotiable does not necessarily mean that it is void. It may still be the basis of a valid contract action. Non-negotiability means that the instrument is transferred with all defenses, if any, to the transferee; it is the same as an assignment of a contract.

B. TRANSFER OF NEGOTIABLE INSTRUMENTS

A negotiable instrument may be transferred from one person to another by negotiation or by an assignment. If by negotiation, the transferee may get a better legal title than the transferor; if by an assignment, the assignee gets only the title of the assignor. A negotiable instrument is *assigned* when it is an order instrument, and it has been transferred without an indorsement.

A negotiable instrument is negotiated by delivery or by delivery and indorsement. If the instrument is payable to bearer on its face, it may be negotiated by delivery alone. If the instrument is payable to order, it is negotiated by delivery with the indorsement of the holder. If it is payable to order on its face and the last indorsement is in blank (indorser only signs his name), it may be negotiated by delivery alone.

1. INDORSEMENTS

The holder of an instrument may indorse it by merely signing his name, or he may add other words to it. The indorsement must be on the back of the instrument unless it is all filled up in which case it may be written on a paper attached to the instrument. If a holder adds such words as "I hereby assign the within instrument to John Smith" to his signature, such a transfer will constitute a valid negotiation by indorsement and delivery; such language of assignment does not constitute a restrictive indorsement. When the holder signs a guaranty of payment on the back of the instrument, the character of the indorsement is not affected. The addition of a waiver of presentment and notice does not affect the character of the indorsement. *U.C.C.,* Section 3–202(4).

When an instrument is made payable to a person under a misspelled name or one other than his own, he may indorse in that name or his own or both; but signature in both names may be required by a person paying or giving value for the instrument (*U.C.C.,* Section 3–203).

The *U.C.C.,* Sections 3–204, 3–205, 3–206, 3–414(1), provides for four kinds of indorsements: special, blank, restrictive, and without recourse.

A. SPECIAL

A special indorsement specifies the person to whom or to whose order the instrument is to be payable; e. g., "Pay to John Smith (signed) Robert Jones"; "Pay to the order of John Smith (signed) Robert Jones". The special indorsee's indorsement (Robert Jones) is necessary for further negotiation of the instrument. He may also indorse specially or in any other proper form.

A special indorsement transfers title to the instrument, imposes a liability on the indorser to pay the amount of the instrument under certain conditions, and creates certain warranties (*U.C.C.,* Sections 3–414, 3–417).

B. BLANK

A blank indorsement specifies no indorsee and consists of a mere signature. An instrument so indorsed is payable to bearer and may be negotiated by delivery alone. Bearer paper may also be converted to order paper by writing a special indorsement over the blank indorsement; e. g., if John Smith endorses in blank and delivers to Richard Jones, Richard can write above John Smith's signature the words "Pay to Richard Jones". This will protect Richard Jones in case the instrument is stolen since his signature is now necessary to transfer the instrument. Although blank indorsements are common, they are dangerous to use since a finder or thief can negotiate by delivery alone.

The negotiation of a blank indorsement passes ownership of the instrument, imposes on the indorser a liability to pay the amount of the instrument under certain conditions, and creates certain warranties (*U.C.C.,* Sections 3–414, 3–417).

C. RESTRICTIVE

A restrictive indorsement specifies the use to be made of the paper. The *U.C.C.,* Section 3–205, makes the following four indorsements restrictive:

(1) Conditional

This is an indorsement which states that it is to be effective only upon the satisfaction of a specific condition; e. g., "Pay to John Smith upon completion of building".

(2) Purported Prohibition of Further Transfer

This is an indorsement which appears to prohibit further transfer but does not as it is restrictive in form only; e. g., "Pay to John Smith only". *U.C.C.,* Section 3–206(1).

(3) For Collection or Deposit

This is an indorsement which uses such words as "for collection", "for deposit", or "pay any bank" to show an intention as to the use of the instrument.

(4) Trust Indorsement

An indorsement that makes the indorsee the agent or trustee of the indorser is restrictive in that it states that the indorsement is for the benefit or use of the indorser or another person; e. g., "Pay John Smith as agent for Robert Jones (signed) Richard Paul", "Pay John Smith for account of Robert Jones (signed) Richard Paul", "Pay John Smith in trust for Robert Jones (signed) Richard Paul".

A restrictive endorsement can be ignored by a bank except when it has been made by the person presenting the instrument to the bank for payment or transferring it to the bank; however, a restrictive indorsement must be recognized by a depositary bank, i. e., one in which the customer deposits the instrument.

D. Without Recourse

A nonrecourse indorsement is made by using the following words with the signature: "without recourse"; e. g., "Without recourse (signed) Richard Paul". Such an indorsement limits the liability of the indorser; e. g., to escape liability to his transferee if the maker becomes insolvent and is not able to pay; or in the case of an attorney who is merely indorsing to his client a check made payable to the client and the attorney by a third person (in such a case the transferee of the check would not expect the attorney to guarantee the check when he is not a party to the transaction).

A nonrecourse indorsement does not affect the passage of title or the negotiable character of the instrument.

C. HOLDER IN DUE COURSE

A holder in due course is a bona fide purchaser of the instrument for value without notice of any defect in the instrument or wrongdoing in connection with it. A holder in due course takes the instrument free of all personal defense (such as lack of consideration, fraud in the inducement, or that it was stolen), but not of real defenses (such as forgery). See Chapter III for material on defenses. The *U.C.C.,* Section 3–302, establishes certain requirements for becoming a holder in due course.

1. WHO MAY BECOME A HOLDER IN DUE COURSE

A. In General

Almost anyone can become a holder in due course, even a payee; however, he must take the instrument for value, in good faith, and without notice of any defects. The *U.C.C.,* Section 3–302(2), provides that a payee may be a holder in due course; e. g., where he deals through a third person. If the payee deals directly with the drawer, as in the typical case, he would have knowledge of any defense that the drawer might have and thus could not be an H.D.C.

B. Holder Through an H.D.C.

A holder who derives his title through an H.D.C., and who is not himself a party to any fraud or illegality, has all the rights of an H.D.C. even though he cannot satisfy the requirements of an H.D.C. For example, a payee by fraud induces a drawer to issue a check to him. The payee negotiates the check to an H.D.C. The H.D.C. negotiates the check to John Smith who knows of the fraud. Since John Smith takes the rights of the H.D.C., he can enforce the check against the drawer. *U.C.C.,* Section 3–201(1).

C. Reacquirer

A reacquirer is a holder of an instrument who negotiates it and then reacquires it. A reacquirer who was an H.D.C. the first time he acquired the instrument will hold it as an H.D.C. even though he was not an H.D.C. when he reacquired it; i. e., he is remitted to his former position.

D. Those Who Cannot

A buyer who purchases goods at a sale which is not of an ordinary commercial nature cannot be an H.D.C.; e. g., purchaser at a judicial sale; sale of assets of an estate; or bulk sale not in the regular course of business (*U.C.C.,* Section 3–302(3)).

2. REQUIREMENTS OF DUE COURSE

To be a holder in due course, the person must have taken the instrument for value, in good faith, and without notice it was overdue, dishonored, or had any defense against it or claim to it (*U.C.C.,* Section 3–301(1)).

A. Value

A holder takes the instrument for value:

(1) to the extent that the agreed consideration has been performed (*U.C.C.,* Section 3–303(a)); e. g., On June 1, Payee indorses a $2,000.00 note to H for H's promise that he will pay Payee the sum of $1,000.00 on July 1 and $1,000.00 on August 1. On July 1, H pays Payee $1,000.00; at this point in time, H becomes an H.D.C. to the extent of $1,000.00. If after July 1 and prior to August 1, H should learn of a defense to the note, he will not be able to improve his position as an H.D.C.

(2) when he takes the instrument in payment of or as security for an antecedent claim whether or not it is due (*U.C.C.,* Section 3–303(b)); e. g., D owes C $1,000.00 which is due on June 1. On May 15, D receives a negotiable note for $1,000.00 from M which he transfers to C as payment for the debt. C is an H.D.C.

(3) when he gives a negotiable instrument for the instrument or makes an irrevocable commitment to a third person (*U.C.C.,* Section 3–303(c)); e. g., Payee gives Holder a $1,000.00 negotiable note in exchange for Holder's guarantee of a $1,000.00 loan by bank to P. Holder has made an irrevocable commitment to a third person (bank) and so is an H.D.C.

(4) A purchase at a discount is for value (*U.C.C.,* Section 1–201(32)). The courts do not measure the value given unless it is so

slight as to be evidence of fraud. In this respect, value in a negotiable instrument is the same as in an ordinary contract.

B. Good Faith

" 'Good faith' means honesty in fact in the conduct or transaction concerned", *U.C.C.,* Section 1–201(19). Giving a small value for the instrument can cause the question of good faith to arise. Bad faith is established by proving that the transferee knew certain facts that rendered it improper for him to acquire the instrument; e. g. knew that fraud was involved.

C. Notice it Was Overdue or Dishonored

To qualify as an H.D.C., the purchaser of an instrument must not know that it was overdue or had been dishonored (refusal to pay instrument when due). When an instrument is not paid when due, it may be for the reason that the debtor has a good defense. The H.D. C. may not know this; however, the law assumes that he knows there is a defense when the paper is overdue and hence he cannot be an H.D.C. A purchaser of an instrument with a fixed date must take it before that date arrives. A demand instrument must be purchased within a reasonable time after its issue. A reasonable time for a check drawn and payable in the United States is presumed to be thirty days (*U.C.C.,* Section 3–304(3) (c)). A holder cannot be an H. D.C. if he has reason to know that an installment of principal is delinquent, but not interest, or an acceleration of the instrument has been made (*U.C.C.,* Section 3–304(3) (a) (b)).

D. Ignorance of Defenses and Adverse Claims

A purchaser cannot be an H.D.C. if he knows of defenses or adverse claims by prior parties to the instrument; e. g., knows that defective goods were given for the instrument (failure of consideration).

The purchaser has notice of a claim or defense if the instrument is so incomplete, bears such visible evidence of forgery or alteration, or is otherwise so irregular as to call into question its validity, terms or ownership, or to create an ambiguity (*U.C.C.,* Section 3–304(1) (a)); or the purchaser has notice that the obligation of any party to the instrument is voidable in whole or in part, or that all the parties have been discharged (*U.C.C.,* Section 3–304(1)(b)); or the purchaser has notice of misappropriation by an agent or fiduciary in which case he has notice of the claim of the principal (*U.C.C.,* Section 3–304(2)).

The *U.C.C.,* Section 3–304(4), states that certain facts do not of themselves prevent a purchaser from becoming an H.D.C.:

(1) that the instrument is antedated or postdated;

(2) that consideration for the instrument remains executory; e. g., instrument given for goods not yet delivered;

(3) that a party has signed as an accommodation party;

(4) that an incomplete instrument has been properly completed;

(5) that a person negotiating the instrument is or was a fiduciary;

(6) that there has been a default in payment of interest on the instrument.

The filing or recording of a document does not of itself give such notice that would prevent a purchaser from becoming an H.D.C. (*U.C.C.,* Section 3–304(5)); e. g., recording notice of action to cancel a note and mortgage does not give notice to a purchaser.

---

1. *Signature Requirements*

McCOLLUM v. STEITZ

261 Cal.App.2d 76, 67 Cal.Rptr. 703 (1968).

CONLEY, Presiding Justice. One of the defendants, William Steitz, partner of William Hamrick in the operation of a Fresno restaurant called the "Desert Inn," appeals from a judgment against him and the partnership based on a promissory note for $6,700 principal, together with interest, attorneys' fees, and costs. For approximately 20 years, both before and after the date of the note, Messrs. Steitz and Hamrick were partners; during most of that time, Mr. Steitz was also in the automobile business for himself in Stockton and later in Salinas, while Mr. Hamrick lived in Fresno and, as manager, had charge of the restaurant business.

The promissory note in question reads as follows:

$ 6700 00 — 2-20-65 CALIFORNIA, 7/20 1965

FOR VALUE RECEIVED ______ PROMISE TO PAY TO Conrad ______ OR ORDER

AT ______ THE SUM OF 6% Int. ______ DOLLARS

PAYABLE To Donald H. McCollum or Boyd Hey

______ WITH INTEREST FROM paid

UNTIL PAID AT THE RATE OF 6% PER CENT PER ANNUM, PAYABLE ______

Should the interest not be so paid, it shall thereafter bear like interest as the principal. Should default be made in the payment of any instalment of principal or interest when due, then the whole sum of principal and interest shall become immediately due and payable at the option of the holder of this note. The undersigned (jointly and severally) further promise to pay all costs of collection, including attorney's fees, incurred in the collection of this note. Principal and interest payable in lawful money of the United States. The makers, sureties, guarantors and endorsers of this note hereby consent to extensions of time at or after the maturity hereof, and hereby waive diligence, protest, demand and notice of every kind. Should this note be signed by more than one person, firm or corporation, all of the obligations herein contained shall be considered joint and several obligations of each signer hereof.

[signature]

Desert Inn

[signature]

ADDRESS [illegible]

2281

ESC 2506 8-60 100 P.S. Customer's Note

The record shows that the note was executed to replace two promissory notes which evidenced earlier loans by Mrs. Hey and her husband to the "Desert Inn." At her request, the name of her son, Donald H. McCollum, was added as payee so that he would have an interest in the moneys represented by it, and could collect the proceeds if she were not in a position to do so. Mr. Hamrick executed the note in the normal course of business and admits that, in signing the name "Desert Inn" beneath his own signature, he intended to charge the partnership; he acquiesces in the judgment. There is no legitimate evidence leading to a contrary conclusion, and it must be held that the findings are supported by substantial evidence. Mr. Steitz at the time the note was signed, and for many years previously, had been a partner of Mr. Hamrick in the operation of the "Desert Inn," under that trade name.

We fail to find any reason why the judgment should be reversed. * * *

A general partner is the agent of the partnership and may bind the partnership. * * * Here, the partnership had been in existence and operating the "Desert Inn" for many years; appellant knew of the debt before the execution of this note; the partner of appellant testified the note was intended to be that of the "Desert Inn" as did Mrs. Hey, respondent.

The principal contention made by the appellant is that the promissory note was not executed in compliance with the requirements of the Commercial Code so as to bind Mr. Steitz as a partner.

Mrs. Hey testified that she had loaned the "Desert Inn" money on more than one occasion; she had held one note for $5,000 and another for $1,700; she asked Mr. Hamrick to combine the amounts and to make a single note for $6,700 and also to put her son's name on it with hers, as a payee, so that if she should become ill, he could collect; she agreed to return the two notes which she then held in exchange for the new note. She testified that she had never been paid any of the principal or any interest.

Sections 3401 and 3403 of the Commercial Code declare the signature and form thereof required in executing a negotiable instrument such as the one in this suit. Section 3401 reads as follows:

> "(1) No person is liable on an instrument unless his signature appears thereon.
>
> "(2) A signature is made by use of any name, including any trade or assumed name, upon an instrument, or by any word or mark used in lieu of a written signature."

Section 3403 of the Commercial Code provides in part:

> "A signature may be made by an agent or other representative, and his authority to make it may be established as in other cases of representation. No particular form of appointment is necessary to establish such authority."

In II California Commercial Law, California Continuing Education of the Bar, 1965, a proper form for a note executed on behalf of partners is given (§ 3.6); the text states that while no person is liable on an instrument unless his signature appears on it (Comm. Code § 3401, subd. (1)), "* * * a partnership is liable on a note executed on behalf of the partnership (§ 3401(2)), and all partners are jointly liable for the obligation. Corp.C. § 15015(b)."

* * * The name "Desert Inn" is on the note. One may be liable under a trade name even though one's own name is not on the instrument. (Comm.Code § 3401, subd. (2).)

The "Desert Inn" was a well-known business. Section 3403, subdivision (3), of the Commercial Code states, in part, that the name of an organization *preceded* or *followed* by the name of the authorized person is the signature made in a representative capacity. Here, Hamrick's name came before that of the "Desert Inn." The address "2445 Whites Bridge Rd." is set forth twice on the note. Respondents contend that almost every blank in the note has the wrong word on it—as it has—although the overall sense is clear and that the two addresses on the note could properly indicate that two parties are involved, that is to say, Mr. Hamrick and the partnership, and that the address of each is added. We are convinced that the evidence shows that the note was properly executed by Mr. Hamrick, who was the manager of the partnership business, and that in writing "Desert Inn" under his own name with two statements of the address, he properly included the necessary factors to make the partnership liable.

The judgment is affirmed.

---

2. *Requirement of "Sum Certain"*

BRAZOS RIVER AUTHORITY v. CARR

405 S.W.2d 689 (Tex., 1966).

STEAKLEY, Justice. This is an original proceeding in which the Relator, Brazos River Authority, seeks a writ of mandamus to require the Respondent, the Attorney General of Texas, to approve * * * two issues of bonds.

* * * We consider only the reasons which form the basis of the disapproval action of the Attorney General. * * *

The final reason assigned by the Attorney General for his disapproval rested upon the asserted nonnegotiability of the Series B Bonds supplemental coupons. The coupons in question pay to the bearer "an amount of interest (not exceeding 2½%) under the conditions and to the extent provided for in the resolution authorizing this issue of Revenue Bonds * * *." * * * Section 4.03 of the resolution of May 24, 1966, of the Authority states:

> "Supplemental coupons are payable solely from the Series B Supplemental Interest Fund established by this Resolution. To the extent that money is available in the Series B Sup-

plemental Interest Fund it shall be applied to the full or pro rata payment of the next maturing Supplemental coupons; to the extent that Supplemental coupons are not so paid they shall be cancelled."

* * * It is clear under both the Negotiable Instruments Law and the Uniform Commercial Code that the bonds and coupons in question are not negotiable instruments. * * *

As of midnight, June 30, 1966, the Texas N.I.L. was superseded by the Texas U.C.C., and Sections 3–104(1) (b) thereof * * * states:

> "(1) Any writing to be a negotiable instrument within this Article must * * * (b) contain an unconditional promise or order to pay a sum certain in money and no other promise, order, obligation or power given by the maker or drawer except as authorized by this Article * * *."

The requirement of a "sum certain" within the meaning of Section 3–104(1) (b) is defined by section 3–106, as follows:

> "(1) The sum payable is a sum certain even though it is to be paid
>
> (a) with stated interest or by stated installments; or
>
> (b) with stated different rates of interest before and after default or a specified date; or
>
> (c) with a stated discount or addition if paid before or after the date fixed for payment; or
>
> (d) with exchange or less exchange, whether at a fixed rate or at the current rate; or
>
> (e) with costs of collection or an attorney's fee or both upon default.
>
> "(2) Nothing in this section shall validate any term which is otherwise illegal."

* * * We turn, then, to Section 5–c of the statute governing the Authority to determine if the bonds with the indefinite interest rate provisions, and the interest coupons corresponding thereto, have been declared statutorily negotiable. Section 5–c, enacted in 1953, reads in part:

> "In addition to all other powers Brazos River Authority is authorized to issue its *negotiable revenue bonds* * * * payable from and secured by a pledge of its revenue to the extent and in the manner prescribed by the Board of Directors * * *." [Italics added]

* * * In our opinion the legislative history of the statutes governing the Brazos River Authority will not support the proposition that the 1953 amendment adding Section 5–c has the effect of rendering the Series B Bonds negotiable, notwithstanding the nature of the interest payment obligation. * * *

The writ of mandamus is denied. No motion for rehearing will be entertained.

3. *Requirement of Definite Time*

McLEAN v. PADDOCK

78 N.M. 234, 430 P.2d 392 (1967).

NOBLE, Justice. The circumstances giving rise to this appeal began in 1958 when Carl R. Paddock and Essie Paddock, his wife (hereafter referred to as Paddocks), executed a real estate listing authorizing Harper Realty Company, a real estate broker (hereafter referred to as Harper), to sell their motel. Harper produced a purchaser acceptable to Paddocks, and a binder agreement was executed, reciting a deposit of $1,000 and providing for a further cash down payment of $8,000 on a total price of $249,000. * * * Paddocks and the purchaser thereafter executed a real estate contract which, among other things, directed the Albuquerque National Bank, escrow agent, to pay Harper $75 per month from the purchaser's monthly installment payments. Concurrently with the execution of the real estate contract, Paddocks executed a promissory note in the principal amount of $12,388.20, payable to Harper in monthly installments of $75, representing the balance of the commission. The note was unconditional in its terms and contained no reference to the real estate contract, nor did the contract refer to the note. Harper negotiated this promissory note to Alexander and William McLean (hereafter referred to as McLeans) in May, 1959. Payments on the note becoming in default in January, 1960, McLeans elected to declare the whole balance due, as provided in the note, and sued Paddocks. * * *

The trial court found that Harper had orally agreed the note would be paid solely from the monthly installments on the purchase price of the motel, and that Paddocks were induced to sign the note by Harper's false representation that a note was required in order to authorize the escrow agent to make these monthly payments to Harper. The court concluded that McLeans were holders in due course, finding they had no knowledge of Harper's misrepresentations. Judgment was, accordingly, entered in favor of McLeans and against Paddocks.

* * * The Paddocks challenge the court's determination that the McLeans were holders in due course of a negotiable instrument on several grounds. * * * The note here involved is dated August 9, 1958, and reads:

> "For value received, I, we, or either of us promise to pay to Harper Realty, or order, the sum of Twelve Thousand Three Hundred Eighty-eight and 20/100 Dollars, said amount to be paid in equal installments of Seventy-Five and no/100 Dollars, each, payable monthly after date beginning ______ 1, 1958 and on the first day of each month thereafter until the whole amount first herein named and any interest or costs shall have been paid in full. * * *"

Two contentions arise from the failure of the note to specify, in the blank space indicated, the month in which payments were to begin. Pointing to the requirement that the instrument "[m]ust be payable on demand, or at a fixed or determinable future time," the Paddocks argue that this note lacks negotiability. Alternatively, they argue the blank space prevents the McLeans from taking an instrument "[t]hat is complete and regular upon its face" * * *

The Paddocks note is "payable monthly after date." The note is dated August 9, 1958. If the instrument had stopped at this point, it could not be doubted but that payments would have commenced September 9, 1958. The following language making payments due on the first day of each month does not create a fatal ambiguity under either theory of the Paddocks. Construing the instrument as a whole, it seems clear that the first payment was intended to be September 1, 1958. * * *

The judgment in favor of McLeans against Paddocks should be affirmed.

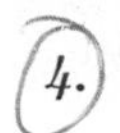

4. *Endorsements Must Be On or Attached to Instrument*

LOPEZ v. PUZINA

239 Cal.App.2d 708, 49 Cal.Rptr. 122 (1966).

MOLINARI, Justice. Plaintiffs, John and Emanuela Lopez, as holders of a promissory note, brought this action against defendants, Milo and Nora Puzina, as alleged endorsers of this note. From the judgment of nonsuit entered against them plaintiffs appeal. The sole issue presented is whether defendants are endorsers of the subject note so as to give plaintiffs a right to recover against them upon the refusal of the makers to pay.

The subject note dated July 15, 1958 in the principal sum of $4,-298.26, payable to the order of Anthony Joseph Caruso and Marie Doris Caruso, his wife, was executed by Robert W. Lesco and Willa Mae Lesco, his wife, and delivered to said payees. The note recited that it was secured by a deed of trust. The Carusos subsequently assigned the note to the Puzinas without recourse by an assignment affixed to the note. Thereafter, on July 23, 1958, the Puzinas delivered the note to plaintiffs as part payment for a parcel of real property sold by plaintiffs to the Puzinas. No endorsement or assignment was endorsed upon or physically affixed to the note. * * *

When the note became due and payable on July 15, 1963 it was presented by plaintiffs to the Lescos for payment of the face amount, plus interest then due in the sum of $1,719.30. Payment having been refused, plaintiffs brought the instant action on the subject note against the Lescos, as makers, and the Puzinas upon a complaint alleging that the Puzinas were endorsers of the note. A demurrer to the complaint, interposed by the Puzinas, was overruled and the cause proceeded to trial against them. At the conclusion of plaintiffs' case the Puzinas made a motion for nonsuit which was granted and judgment was entered thereon.

In order to hold defendants liable on the subject promissory note as endorsers thereof it was incumbent upon plaintiffs to establish that the note was endorsed by defendants. At all times relevant to this action Civil Code, section 3112 provided for the manner by which an endorsement must be made as follows: "The indorsement must be written on the instrument itself or upon a paper attached thereto." * * * In the instant case there is no endorsement on the note itself. It is contended by plaintiffs, however, that the endorsement of the note is to be found on the instrument entitled "Assignment of Deed of Trust," bearing defendants' signatures and providing in the language hereinabove set out verbatim that they had "endorsed," assigned and transferred to plaintiffs the subject deed of trust together with the promissory note therein mentioned. It should be noted here that it is not contended by plaintiffs that the subject "Assignment of Deed of Trust" was physically attached to the subject promissory note.

The crucial question presented, accordingly, is whether a promissory note can be endorsed by an instrument which is separate from the note. * * *

Plaintiffs make the further contention that, since section 3112 provides that "The signature of the indorser, without additional words, is a sufficient indorsement," the *"allonge"* provided for in that section merely refers to a paper which contains only a signature. Accordingly, they argue, an endorsement consisting of a signature with additional words may be made on a separate paper or instrument. This contention is without merit. Section 3112 specifically provides that *"The indorsement,"* if not written on the instrument itself, *"must* be written * * * upon a paper attached thereto." * * *

Having determined that under California law defendants did not effectively endorse the subject note we conclude that they are, by the terms of the "Assignment of Deed of Trust," merely assignors of the note. * * * As such they are not liable upon the note upon the obligor's failure to pay, since an assignor of a promissory note does not by the mere fact of assignment warrant that the obligor is solvent or that the assignor will perform the obligor's obligations. * * *

The judgment is affirmed.

---

5. *Effect of Special Endorsement*

FIRST TRUST & SAV. BANK OF ZANESVILLE, OHIO v. FIDELITY-PHILADELPHIA TRUST CO.

214 F.2d 320 (C.A.Pa., 1954), certiorari denied 348 U.S. 856, 75 S.Ct. 81, 99 L.Ed. 674.

GOODRICH, Circuit Judge. This case presents the often recurring situation of two people who, doing business in the ordinary course, have been fooled by a swindler. The swindler disappears or goes to jail. Which of the two parties is to bear the loss his rascality has occasioned? * * *

Our set of operative facts gets down to this comparatively simple case. A bank's customer (the bank being the defendant, Fidelity-Philadelphia Trust Company) brings to the bank what purports to be the negotiable promissory note of a whisky distiller. This note is accompanied by what purports to be a negotiable warehouse receipt evidencing a deposit of whisky, which is to be collateral security for the note. Both the note and the warehouse receipt are, in fact, spurious. * * *

The customer (Philadelphia Acceptance Corporation, hereafter called PAC) does two things. First, it deposits with the bank in its trust department the purported warehouse receipt, for which the bank issues a safekeeping receipt and puts the document in a file. * * *

Second, the customer, PAC, leaves with the collection department of the bank a draft drawn by itself in its own favor on the plaintiff, The First Trust and Savings Bank of Zanesville, Ohio, (Zanesville), which is to be the purchaser of the note. Forthwith defendant Fidelity credits its customer with the amount of the draft and charges PAC interest until the transaction is closed. It is closed by Fidelity's forwarding the draft, note and safekeeping receipt to Zanesville. This bank in turn sends Fidelity a check payable to Fidelity's order and drawn on the Chase Bank in New York. In due course of time this check clears and Fidelity is thus reimbursed for the credit it has made to its customer.

* * * The situation differs also from the sight-draft-bill-of-lading-attached transaction in that here PAC's draft was accompanied by the distilling company's note, which was the supposed thing of value given for the loan.

* * * Furthermore, it can hardly be denied that when a bank takes a document for collection advancing to its customer credit prior to the actual collection being made, the bank then becomes at least a security owner. * * *

In the case of each of the worthless notes involved in this litigation, PAC, * * * had drawn a draft in its own favor upon Zanesville. These drafts were endorsed to the order of Fidelity, without qualification. Such endorsement is a special endorsement * * * and is in no sense a restrictive endorsement. Ordinarily when a person is given physical possession of a negotiable instrument thus specially endorsed to him he becomes the owner.

* * * If Fidelity had a duty to investigate the genuineness of these documents, quite obviously it did not fulfill that duty. Likewise it did not use reasonable care to fulfill this duty, if it existed, because a small amount of inquiry would have revealed whether the distillery had the officers whose names appeared on the notes and receipts and also whether the receipt in fact had been issued by the

warehouseman. No such inquiry was made. It is also true that Zanesville could have found out with equal ease and convenience, or at least almost equal ease and convenience, about the genuineness of the documents. So our question becomes: Does a bank, when it takes a document for its safekeeping file for a customer and issues a receipt describing the document, warrant or have a duty to find out about the genuineness thereof? * * * A bank which pays in good faith against a forged bill of lading can recover from the customer for whom it issued the letter. The bank is under no duty to investigate the genuineness of the shipping document. * * * Fidelity is not liable either as a warrantor nor as one who had a duty to investigate and failed to perform it. * * *

The judgment of the district court will be affirmed.

6. *Restrictive Endorsement*

BARNES v. CHERRY CREEK NATIONAL BANK OF DENVER

163 Colo. 414, 431 P.2d 471 (1967).

MOORE, Chief Justice. J. Y. Barnes and Portland Cement Association, hereinafter referred to as Portland, brought an action in the trial court against the defendant in error, hereinafter referred to as the bank, seeking recovery of moneys paid out by the bank under the following circumstances, none of which are in dispute. * * *

"Plaintiff, J. Y. Barnes, was the payee of check # 4405 of Portland Cement Association, dated October 7, 1963, for $5,088.70. * * *

That plaintiff, J. Y. Barnes, endorsed said check as follows:

" 'J. Y. Barnes
Jack Y. Barnes
For Deposit Only'

and said check was mailed to Denver United States National Bank in a bank-by-mail envelope * * * for deposit to the account of the Portland Cement Association.

"The letter containing said check was stolen from said United States mail depository by one, Denzil Arthur Woodward, who, on October 10, 1963, opened a checking account # 22–53116 in the Cherry Creek National Bank in the name of Jack Y. Barnes; * * * that defendant, Cherry Creek National Bank of Denver, paid $250.00 in cash to Denzil Arthur Woodward, who represented himself as Jack Y. Barnes, and credited the balance of said check, $4,838.70 to checking account No. 22–53116 in the name of Jack Y. Barnes.

"That said check being plaintiffs' Exhibit 'A' from the Portland Cement Association for $5,088.70, was accepted by the drawee bank, First National Bank of Chicago, and through regular banking channels, defendant, Cherry Creek National Bank, received payment thereof in the amount of $5,088.70. That subsequent thereto, checks were drawn against said account by Denzil Arthur Woodward, representing himself to be Jack Y. Barnes, and all of the money deposited in said account, except $577.03, was withdrawn, prior to the time that defendant, Cherry Creek National Bank, had any notice that said check * * * had been stolen and prior to the time that said bank had any notice that its depositor, Denzil Arthur Woodward, was not J. Y. Barnes, the true payee of said check." * * *

The trial court, after argument on the law as applicable to the agreed facts, entered judgment in favor of the bank, except as to the amount of $577.03 admittedly due Barnes and Portland, being the sum still on deposit in the bank when the fraud of Woodward was discovered. * * *

C.R.S.1963, 14–8–5, in pertinent part provides that an endorsement,

> "* * * of an item by the payee or other depositor 'for deposit' shall be deemed a restrictive endorsement and indicate that the endorsee bank is an agent for collection of the item."
>
> "(1) (a) An indorsement is restrictive, which either:
>
> (b) Prohibits the further negotiation of the instrument; or
>
> (c) Constitutes the indorsee the agent of the indorser; or * * *."

Under these statutes by the restrictive endorsement "for deposit only" affixed to the check by the real Barnes, the negotiability of the check was destroyed and the bank became the agent of the owner of the check for the purpose of collection thereof. * * * A restrictive endorsement preserves the title of the endorser to deposited items in the absence of contrary course of dealings. The endorsement in this case "for deposit only" being restrictive, did not transfer title to the check, and the bank in receiving it became an agent for collection. In the instant case the bank became the agent of the true owner of the check, the real J. Y. Barnes who had endorsed the check "for deposit only." The bank collected the item and permitted an imposter to withdraw most of the funds in the account, notwithstanding the fact that the payee of the check was particularly described as being "District Engineer, Portland Cement Assn., 721 Boston Bldg."

Being an agent for collection of the true owner of the check, and having paid out moneys to an imposter, the bank is liable for the loss.

7. *Value Required of Holder in Due Course*

KORZENIK v. SUPREME RADIO, INC.

347 Mass. 309, 197 N.E.2d 702 (1964).

WHITTEMORE, Justice. The plaintiffs, as indorsees, brought an action in the District Court of Western Hampden to recover $1,900 on two "note[s] in the form of * * * trade acceptance[s]" given by Supreme Radio, Inc. (Supreme), to Southern New England

Distributing Corporation (Southern), dated October 16, 1961, and due, respectively, on November 1, 1961, and December 1, 1961. The plaintiffs are partners in the practice of law. The trade acceptances in suit and others, all of a total face value of about $15,000, were transferred to them on October 31, 1961, by their client Southern "as a retainer for services to be performed" by the plaintiff Korzenik. * * * The trade acceptances in suit and two others given by Supreme had been obtained by fraud. Southern had retained Korzenik on October 25, 1961, in connection with certain anti-trust litigation. Korzenik did some legal work between October 25 and October 31, but there was no testimony as to the value of the services and the trial judge was unable to determine their value. He found for the defendant. Korzenik did not know that the acceptances were obtained by fraud. "He has paid co-counsel retained in the anti-trust case part of the money he has collected" on the assigned items.

* * * Decisive of the case, as the Appellate Division held, is the correct ruling that the plaintiffs are not holders in due course under G.L. c. 106, § 3–302; they have not shown to what extent they took for value under § 3–303. That section provides:

> "A holder takes the instrument for value (a) to the extent that the agreed consideration has been performed or that he acquires a security interest in or a lien on the instrument otherwise than by legal process; or (b) when he takes the instrument in payment of or as security for an antecedent claim against any person whether or not the claim is due; or (c) when he gives a negotiable instrument for it or makes an irrevocable commitment to a third person."

Under clause (a) of § 3–303 the "agreed consideration" was the performance of legal services. It is often said that a lawyer is "retained" when he is engaged to perform services, and we hold that the judge spoke of "retainer" in this sense. The phrase that the judge used, "retainer *for services*" (emphasis supplied), shows his meaning as does the finding as to services already performed by Korzenik at the time of the assignments. Even if the retainer had been only a fee to insure the attorney's availability to perform future services * * *, there is no basis in the record for determining the value of this commitment for one week.

The Uniform Laws Comment to § 3–303 points out that in this article "value is divorced from consideration" and that except as provided in paragraph (c)

> "[a]n executory promise to give value is not * * * value * * * The underlying reason of policy is that when the purchaser learns of a defense * * * he is not required to enforce the instrument, but is free to rescind the transaction for breach of the transferor's warranty."

General Laws c. 106, § 3–307(3), provides:

> "After it is shown that a defense exists a person claiming the rights of a holder in due course has the burden of estab-

lishing that he or some person under whom he claims is in all respects a holder in due course."

The defence of fraud having been established this section puts the burden on the plaintiffs. The plaintiffs have failed to show "the extent * * * [to which] the agreed consideration * * * [had] been performed."

The only other possible issue under § 3–303 is whether, because of or in connection with taking the assignments, Korzenik made "an irrevocable commitment to a third person." There is no evidence of such a commitment. The finding as to a payment to cocounsel shows only that some of the proceeds of other assigned items have been expended by Korzenik.

Order dismissing report affirmed.

8. *"Good Faith" Required of Holder in Due Course*

U. S. FINANCE COMPANY v. JONES

285 Ala. 105, 229 So.2d 495 (1969).

MERRILL, Justice. This appeal is from a decree setting aside a mortgage given by appellee to one Bell and assigned by him to appellant, United States Finance Company, Inc.

* * *

* * *

The evidence tended to show that two salesmen from The Bell Company (hereinafter Bell), a Florida contracting company, visited appellee, an uneducated black woman and a widow, one night at her house in Baldwin County. They offered to perform certain repairs on her house. They persuaded appellee to sign a mortgage on her house and land securing a note providing for payments of $30.66 per month for 84 months ($2,575.44). Appellee could only read and write "a little bit." Three days later, Bell sold the note and mortgage to U. S. Finance.

The evidence was undisputed that Bell agreed to work on a back room of appellee's house, put aluminum siding on the outside and put a new roof on the top. It is also undisputed that Bell put tar paper on the sides of the house instead of aluminum, then sprayed it with aluminum paint, and did not adequately perform the work on the back room or roof. It is also undisputed that more harm than good was done to the house by Bell.

The undisputed evidence shows that Bell did not perform as he contracted to do, and did not provide adequate consideration under the contract, note and mortgage. It is also undisputed that the mortgage was executed in Baldwin County. The signature on the mortgage of Willie Jones was an obvious forgery. [Jones was dead on the day the mortgage was executed.] The acknowledgment of the notary on the mortgage shows that it was taken by Zack Watkins, a Notary

Public of Mobile County, in Baldwin County where he had no authority under his affixed seal. He also certified "that Evelyn Jones and Willie Jones whose name is signed to the foregoing conveyance, and who is known to me, acknowledged before me on this day that, being informed of the contents of this conveyance, she executed the same voluntarily on the day the same bears date." He could not possibly have seen Willie Jones that day or could he have been known to him as a person signing the mortgage.

The note, secured by the mortgage here involved, is not in the record, but is described in the mortgage. When a mortgage securing a note is transferred along with the note, the mortgage follows and is of the same character as the note. Birmingham Trust & Savings Co. v. Howell, 202 Ala. 39, 79 So. 377; Davies v. Simpson, 201 Ala. 616, 79 So. 48.

The main question is whether appellant was a holder in due course. The Uniform Commercial Code, Tit. 7A, § 1–101 through 10–104, applied to this transaction since it became effective midnight December 31, 1966, and the note was signed on January 23, 1967. Section 3–302(1) provides, in part, that:

> "A holder in due course is a holder who takes the instrument
>
> * * * * * * * * * *
>
> "(c) without notice that it is overdue or has been dishonored or of any defense against or claim to it on the part of any person."

Section 1–201(25) defines notice as follows:

> "A person has 'notice' of a fact when
>
> "(a) he has actual knowledge of it; or
>
> * * * * * * * * * *
>
> "(c) from all the facts and circumstances known to him at the time in question he has reason to know that it exists.
>
> "A person 'knows' or has 'knowledge' of a fact when he has actual knowledge of it. * * *"

Appellant's first witness, Bill Patterson, credit manager for appellant when the Jones transaction was handled, testified that appellant purchased the paper from Bell on February 2, 1967 for $1,360.00; that "in order for us to purchase the contract and mortgage from any of these contractors they did have to tell me the work was completed and satisfactory"; that he called appellee on the day the work was completed and she said it was satisfactory, but he did not deny her previous testimony that she told him that it had not rained and was satisfactory but later it leaked when it rained; that he "bought the mortgage, acting on her word."

But he also testified that he examined the mortgage before purchasing it, and the discrepancy as to the signing in Baldwin County before a Mobile County Notary "must have been" on the mortgage when he bought it, and that the assignment of the mortgage bore the date of January 26, 1967, but that he bought it on February 2, 1967.

* * *

This testimony smacks of bad faith on the part of appellant. Repairing houses, covering them with siding, re-roofing, and paneling rooms requires the assembling of materials and usually several days work for the amount of work and the cost on the project here involved. But from the testimony, it seems that appellant gets the mortgage executed, and requires a certificate of completion and satisfaction to be signed at the same time, or at least, on the same day. It apparently wants to guarantee, in writing, its status as a holder in due course whether or not the work is ever completed. Yet, appellant's testimony was that this procedure was "normal" not only with Bell but with other contractors.

* * *

It taxes credulity to accept the contention that appellant did not have notice of Bell's fraud and manner of dealing with people from his many transactions with appellant.

There is also the matter of the price paid by appellant for the mortgage. It was executed on January 23, 1967, assigned in writing to appellant on January 26, filed for record on February 1, and "purchased" by appellant on February 2, 1967 for $1,360.00, about fifty per cent of the face value of the mortgage.

The mere fact that a note is purchased for an amount less than its face, or that an unusually large discount is accepted, is never of itself sufficient to charge the purchaser with notice of existing equities, unless the consideration is merely nominal. However, inadequacy is always a fact to be considered by the jury as evidence of bad faith, and may, with suspicious circumstances, authorize a finding of bad faith, especially if the consideration is grossly inadequate.
* * *

In the instant case we think the trial court was justified from the evidence (all of which we have not delineated) in holding that appellant was not a holder in due course, since it, through its agents, servants or employees had knowledge, or had possession of knowledge of facts sufficient to impute knowledge, at the time appellant purchased the mortgage, of its infirmities, defects, and defenses thereto, and was not a purchaser in good faith.

Affirmed.

9. *Effect of Notice of Claim or Defense*

FIRST PENNSYLVANIA BANKING AND TRUST CO. v. DE LISE

186 Pa.Super. 398, 142 A.2d 401 (1958).

GUNTHER, Judge. This appeal is from an order of the court below discharging defendants' rule to open judgment. * * * The record discloses that on September 7, 1955, Babco Aluminum Products and defendants entered into an agreement for certain alterations to the house of the defendants, stipulating that defendants execute a promissory note to the order of Babco Aluminum Products in the amount of $2,320.66. The note was endorsed for value to the First National Bank of Philadelphia, predecessor to plaintiff.

Defendants, in their petition, claim that they were induced to sign the note by false representations as to the nature of the instrument by Babco Aluminum Products Co., Inc. It was also averred that plaintiff's predecessor in title had notice of dishonor prior to the date of the negotiation of the note. * * *

At the time of the taking of the depositions, it was stipulated that the plaintiff was a holder in due course except as to notice of dishonor and notice that a valid defense existed against the note.

Defendants testified that it was their impression that the legal size paper which they signed concerned the repairs only. They did not, according to their version, suspect that they were signing a judgment note. * * * The note in question is dated October 10, 1955, for $2,320.25 payable in thirty-six monthly installments of $64.-46 each, beginning November 15, 1955. Defendants contend that they notified the bank that they would not honor the note because the repairs were not being made in a workmanlike manner and assert that the notice to the bank took place during the first week of October, 1955.

The bank, however, maintains that it first received notice from Mrs. DeLise, one of the defendants, on December 15, 1955, when she complained that the repairs were not satisfactory. Mr. Hanson, the bank supervisor, testified that the next time he heard from the defendants was on March 2, 1956, when Mr. DeLise complained that the work was unfinished.

* * * It is our opinion that the judgment should be opened and defendants be allowed to present their defense. A holder in due course is a holder who takes the instrument without notice that it is overdue or has been dishonored or of any defense against it. Uniform Commercial Code, * * * section 3–302.

* * * Defendants contend that they were induced to sign the note by fraud and misrepresentation and that they notified the bank that they would not pay the note which Babco either intended to or did assign. Section 3–307(3) of the Uniform Commercial Code,

supra, provides that after evidence of a defense has been introduced a person claiming the rights of a holder in due course has the burden of establishing that he or some person under whom he claims is in all respects a holder in due course. Since the plaintiff introduced no testimony as to the circumstances under which the note was negotiated and since the endorsement is not dated, plaintiff has not met the burden placed upon it. * * *

Had plaintiff bank introduced evidence to the effect that it received the note for value before maturity and without notice of any claim or defense, a refusal to open judgment would have been warranted. However, the telephone call from Mrs. DeLise to the bank, advising it of her refusal to pay unless certain things were done, was sufficient. Notice may be given in any reasonable manner. It may be oral or written and in any terms which identify the instrument and states that it has been dishonored. Uniform Commercial Code, supra, section 3–508(3). As to the date of the notice, a question of fact has been raised, and this question is solely for the determination of the jury. * * *

The relevant factors and circumstances surrounding execution of the judgment note lead us to conclude that justice will be served in opening the judgment and allowing the question to be determined by a jury.

The order of the court below is reversed.

10. *Legal Effect of Post-Dated Check*

NATIONAL CURRENCY EXCHANGE, INC. #3 v. PERKINS

52 Ill.App.2d 215, 201 N.E.2d 668 (1964).

KLUCZYNSKI, Justice. This is an action on a check drawn May 14, 1960 and dated May 16, 1960. Prior to the due date of the check, on May 14, the payee, John Stauropoulos, endorsed and cashed the check at plaintiff's currency exchange. The drawer, defendant Perkins, instructed drawee bank, Commercial National Bank of Chicago, to stop payment on the check on May 16. The plaintiff presented the check to the drawee bank for payment but it was dishonored. Plaintiff secured a default judgment against Stauropoulos, the payee therein, which judgment remains unsatisfied. Consequently, plaintiff brought the instant action against the defendant, the drawer thereof. The trial court found against defendant, and entered judgment on the instrument.

The sole question presented to this court, which is one of first, and perhaps last, impression in this State is whether one who purchases for value and in good faith a postdated check before its maturity or due date is a holder in due course and does not take the check subject to whatever defenses are available as between the original parties.

The facts are uncontroverted. The defendant, Perkins, is engaged primarily in the distribution of amusement machines. On May 14 he was contacted by a customer and restaurant owner, John Stauropoulos, who informed defendant of his intention to open a second restaurant. In return for permitting defendant to install an amusement machine in his proposed restaurant, Stauropoulos asked defendant to lend him $450.00.

Desiring to obtain this business, defendant issued the check, postdating it for the purpose of investigating Stauropoulos' representations and background. Upon discovering that Stauropoulos was insolvent and about to close his one restaurant, and that he had no intention of opening a second one, defendant, at the opening of business Monday morning, May 16, instructed his bank to stop payment on the check. * * *

On May 14, Stauropoulos and another man entered plaintiff's currency exchange, and presented the check for cashing. Stauropoulos was known to the cashier, Mrs. Ross, who testified that since the amount of the check was over $250, she first cleared it with her employer, and determined that defendant's company existed. She then cashed the check. Her further testimony was that postdating would not enter into consideration in cashing a check, and that in the instant case she did not notice that the check was in fact postdated. * * *

Plaintiff deposited the check in its account at the Exchange National Bank, but it was returned with the notation that payment had been stopped on May 16. * * *

In attempting to find further support for his theory, defendant urges that a postdated check is not payable on demand with the drawee bank, and an action cannot be brought on it until the maturity date arrives. But, arguendo, it does not follow that the check is not negotiable, nor that it is invalid. Indeed, the contrary is true.

The weight of authority is that the mere fact that a postdated check is negotiated prior to the date it bears, does not prevent the transferee from becoming a holder in due course. * * *

The decisions also hold that the date on the paper is not notice of defenses, and while the question of regularity has not received serious consideration heretofore, the results of the cases are consistent with the rule that postdated checks are complete and regular. * * * Uniform Commercial Code (Chap. 26, et seq. Ill.Rev.Stat. (1963), sec. 3–304(4) (a) thereof addresses itself to the question before us. That section reads:

> "(4) Knowledge of the following facts does not of itself give the purchaser notice of a defense or claim
>
> "(a) that the instrument is antedated or postdated."

* * * The rule announced here not only favors negotiability but is consistent with sound commercial practice and experience, as

evidenced by the relevant provisions quoted above from the recently enacted Uniform Commercial Code, now the law in Illinois. Therefore, the judgment of the lower court finding plaintiff to be a holder in due course and entitled to recover on the instrument is affirmed.

---

11. Warranty on Transfer of Instruments

UNION BANK, ETC. v. JOSEPH MOBILLA

43 Erie County L.J. 45 (Pa., 1959).

LAUB, J. April 9, 1959. This is a complaint * * * for breach of warranty to which the defendant filed an answer containing new matter and a counterclaim. The plaintiff filed a reply, then moved for judgment on the pleadings. It is this latter action which is before us now.

On January 15, 1958, the defendant, a used car dealer, represented to the plaintiff bank that he had sold a used Ford automobile to one Theresa Piotrowski of 650 East 24th Street. For finance purposes, he exhibited an installment sales contract and a judgment note allegedly signed by Theresa Piotrowski as maker. There was nothing on the face of either instrument to indicate that the signatures had not been placed there by the maker or that either had been signed by someone else acting in the maker's behalf. * * * The note which was payable to defendant was endorsed by him "without recourse", and the security agreement, which was in defendant's favor as a seller of a chattel, was assigned to the bank. Both instruments, as well as the title to the vehicle in question, were turned over to the bank as part of the finance transaction.

* * * After default the bank importuned both the purported maker and the defendant to discharge the obligation but without avail, the maker having denied executing either document or having bought the vehicle from the defendant. In consequence, plaintiff instituted this action, alleging that defendant is guilty of a breach of warranty, and as part of its action, alleging a written warranty in the security agreement "that the above instrument is genuine and in all respects what it purports to be". Plaintiff also claims upon an implied warranty of the genuineness of the note.

The defendant in his answer admits that he endorsed the note and assigned the security agreement to the plaintiff. He also admits that the maker did not sign either document. It is his defense, however, that Theresa Piotrowski's signature was affixed by an authorized agent named Edward Rogalia and that he (the defendant) is not liable in any event because his endorsement of the note was "without recourse". * * *

We can see no merit whatever in the defenses offered and consider that plaintiff is entitled to the judgment which it seeks. The defendant's conception of the litigation as being a suit against an endorser who signed "without recourse", misses the point. Plaintiff is not suing on the note, but, as noted above, is claiming upon a breach of warranty. * * * While no statute is required to establish the common sense conclusion that one who presents a document for discount or otherwise, impliedly warrants its genuineness when he accepts a consideration for its transfer, the Uniform Commercial Code has such a provision. In Section 3–417(2) (a) of that Act * * * it is provided that the transferor of an instrument for consideration warrants, among other things, that all signatures are genuine or authorized. This certainly does not imply that a transferor, with knowledge that a signature is not that of the person it purports to belong to and there is no qualifying or descriptive language indicating that the signature was made by someone other than the maker, may remain silent and suppress such knowledge to the detriment of the transferee. * * *

And now, to-wit, April 9, 1959, judgment is entered on the pleadings in favor of the plaintiff.

PROBLEMS

1. Ace Holder, heavy loser in a business transaction to Willie Win, gives Willie the following instrument: "I. O. U., Willie Win, $10,000. /s/ Ace Holder." Is this a negotiable instrument that can be negotiated to a holder in due course? Why?

2. Harry John, doing business as The Star Store, signs a promissory note in the trade name of The Star Store. He now disclaims liability on the note on the basis that it does not bear his signature. Decision?

3. Robert Jones had signed the following instrument: "Los Angeles, California, 7/1/73. I promise to pay to the order of Paul Payee Ten Thousand Dollars ($10,000) one year from date with interest at the rate of 7% per annum from date. If this note is not paid at maturity, it shall bear interest at the rate of 9% per annum from maturity until paid and costs of collection and reasonable attorney fees. (Signed) Robert Jones." A dispute arises as to whether or not this is a negotiable instrument. Decision?

4. Bill Smith was the payee of a check made out to his order. Before it was endorsed, he lost the check. John Finder found it on the floor of the bank and transferred it without endorsement to Joe Brown, a holder who paid value and took it without notice that it had been lost. Joe claims that it has been transferred to him by negotiation and he is a holder in due course. Decide?

5. Morton Marker writes out in longhand, "I, Morton Marker, promise to pay to Paul Porter or order, $100.00". Does this instrument meet the requirement that a negotiable instrument must be signed?

6. Buyer purchases an automobile from Seller and executes a 90 day note for $500 payable to Seller's order. The note provides that Buyer has the option of giving Seller a color TV set in lieu of cash payment. Seller claims that this note is a negotiable instrument. Decision?

7. Maurice executes a promissory note payable in five days after the first manned landing on the planet Mars. The payee of the note contends that it is negotiable. Decision?

8. Jordan makes and signs a promissory note which states: "Thirty days after date I promise to pay to Andy Rose, or order, one thousand dollars." There is no issuance date on the face of the note and Rose claims that it is nonnegotiable because there is no certain due date. Decision?

9. Randall, a salesman on a business trip to Tokyo, called upon a client who purchased several thousand dollars worth of supplies from him and offered to Randall in payment a draft properly drawn on a San Francisco correspondent bank and made payable in yen. Randall refuses to accept, arguing that it is nonnegotiable since it is made payable in Japanese yen. Decision?

10. The payee of a check endorsed it to Hal for value. At the time of the endorsement, the payee looked like a tramp as he was dressed in old clothes and had a beard of several days growth as he had just returned from a fishing trip. Hal took the check for a 10% discount. Hal was actually innocent when he purchased the check even though the attendant circumstances looked suspicious. It is contended that Hal cannot be a holder in due course. Decision?

Chapter 37

DEFENSES

The maker or drawer of a negotiable instrument may or may not be liable to the payee; e. g., the payee may have sold and delivered the drawer defective goods which would be a defense to the instrument (failure of consideration). Similarly, the maker or drawer may or may not be liable to a holder in due course. If the maker or drawer has only a personal defense to the instrument, he must pay the H. D.C.; however, if he has a real defense, he is not liable to the H.D.C.

A. PERSONAL DEFENSES

There are five personal defenses; namely, failure of consideration, fraud in the inducement, lack of delivery, payment or cancellation, and unauthorized completion. There are two defenses which can be personal or real: illegality and duress.

1. FAILURE OF CONSIDERATION

This is the defense that is most common. It arises whenever a party to a contract receives less than he bargained for; e. g., defective goods (*U.C.C.*, Section 3–408).

2. FRAUD IN THE INDUCEMENT

When a person knows that he is signing a negotiable instrument and knows its contents, but is induced into signing it by false representations, he can only raise the defense of fraud against the party with whom he bargained and not against an H.D.C.; e. g., M signs a promissory note to P for the purchase of a used automobile relying on false representations by P as to the condition of the automobile. P negotiates the note to an H.D.C. M has no defense against the H. D.C. His remedy will be a suit for fraud against P.

3. LACK OF DELIVERY

Failure to deliver a negotiable instrument is only a personal defense and not good against an H.D.C.; e. g., drawer makes out a check to cash and leaves it on his desk, and a thief sells the check to an H.D.C. Lack of delivery of the check is not a good defense; i. e., a thief or finder can pass good title to an H.D.C. (*U.C.C.*, Sections 3–305; 3–306(c)).

4. PAYMENT OR CANCELLATION

When a person *pays* a debt which is represented by a negotiable instrument, he should always take possession of the instrument or be certain that it is destroyed. If he does not, a dishonest holder can negotiate it; and if the new holder is an H.D.C., he takes free of the defense of payment.

When a person liable on an instrument and the holder agree to *cancel* the instrument, the person liable should be certain that he takes possession of it or that it is destroyed. Otherwise, the holder can negotiate it to an H.D.C. in which case the defense of cancellation is not valid.

5. UNAUTHORIZED COMPLETION

When a person signs a check or note and leaves blank the name of the payee, or the amount, or any other term, and the instrument falls into the hands of a thief or a dishonest employee who fills it in and then negotiates it to an H.D.C., the drawer or maker has no defense (*U.C.C.*, Section 3–407(3)).

6. ILLEGALITY

If a statute declares that an instrument is void when issued in a particular type of illegal transaction, illegality is a real defense; but in the absence of such a statute, it is only a personal defense (*U.C.C.*, Section 3–305(2) (b)). For example, New York has a statute which provides that an instrument given in payment of a gambling debt is void, but California, which prohibits certain types of gambling, has nothing in its statutes declaring that instruments given in payment of a gambling debt are void. Thus, in New York, the instrument would be void, and the drawer would have a good defense; but not so in California (H.D.C. would prevail). Ordinarily, illegality is only a personal defense.

7. DURESS

Duress in the form of threatened great bodily injury or death is a real defense (contract is a nullity), but anything less is only a personal defense (contract voidable), or not a defense at all (*U.C.C.*, Section 3–305(2)(b)); e. g., payee tells drawer that if he does not sign the check he will not speak to him again (no defense at all); payee tells drawer that if he does not sign the check he will tell newspapers that his wife is a bigamist (contract voidable and only a personal defense); however, if payee tells drawer that if he does not sign the check he will shoot him in the head and he holds a revolver to his head, the instrument is void and the drawer has a good defense against an H.D.C. Duress in the law of negotiable instruments is the same as in the law of contracts. It is very hard to draw the line between duress as a personal defense and duress as a real defense.

B. REAL DEFENSES

There are four real defenses; namely, forgery, fraud in the inception or execution, incapacity, and material alteration. Also, illegality and duress can be real defenses as previously stated.

1. FORGERY

Forgery is treated in negotiable instruments the same way we treat counterfeit money; both are valueless. If a signature is forged or signed without authority, the purported drawer or maker has a real defense against the holder in due course. Forgery may be ratified in which case the drawer or maker would be liable. The defense of forgery also may be lost under the doctrine of estoppel if one permits a forgery by negligence. (*U.C.C.,* Section 4–404).

2. FRAUD IN THE INCEPTION

When a person is induced to sign a negotiable instrument by fraud and he does not know the nature of the instrument, or he does not know the essential terms, it is fraud in the inception and he has a good defense against an H.D.C.; e. g., an illiterate person signs a negotiable note on the representation it is a receipt (*U.C.C.*, Section 3–305(2) (c)). However, if a person has reasonable opportunity to obtain knowledge of the character of the instrument or its essential terms and does not do so, his defense or fraud will be personal and not available against an H.D.C.

3. INCAPACITY

A minor can avoid an obligation to an H.D.C. on a negotiable instrument as he can on a contract (*U.C.C.,* Section 3–305(2) (a)). A mentally incompetent person can avoid his obligation to an H.D.C. if state law provides that his contracts are void, but not if only voidable; e. g., California statute provides that a judicially declared incompetent's contracts are void, but if not declared so judicially, then only voidable. Thus, in California, a judicially declared incompetent would have a real defense against an H.D.C., but if incompetent and not judicially declared so, then only a personal defense (*U.C.C.*, Section 3–305(2) (b)).

4. MATERIAL ALTERATION

Where there has been a material fraudulent alteration of an instrument, e. g., raise in amount, there is a partial defense against an H.D.C.; i. e., the H.D.C. can enforce the instrument according to its original terms. The defense of material alteration can be lost by ratification or by negligence; e. g., leaving blank spaces in which words or figures may be inserted. (*U.C.C.,* Sections 3–407; 3–406).

C. ADVERSE CLAIMS

An adverse claim is a claim by a third person that he and not the holder is the real owner of the instrument; e. g., a check is made payable to Payee. Subsequently, it is indorsed to A, B, and C. A then claims that B induced him into transferring the check to him by fraud, that he rescinds said transfer, and that he is therefore the true owner of the check. A will not prevail against C, the H.D.C.

An H.D.C. takes free of all adverse claims except a forged indorsement; e. g., a thief steals a note from Payee, endorses Payee's name to it and sells it to H.D.C. Payee will be able to recover the note from H.D.C. (*U.C.C.*, Sections 3–207; 3–305(1); 3–306; 3–404 (1)).

1. *Defenses Available against Holder in Due Course*

MARINE MIDLAND TRUST COMPANY OF ROCHESTER v. BLACKBURN

50 Misc.2d 954, 271 N.Y.S.2d 388 (1966).

G. ROBERT WITMER, Justice. The plaintiff has moved for summary judgment in its action on a check made by defendant to one Vanella in payment for a used automobile. It appears that Vanella deposited the check with the plaintiff bank and received credit and cash therefor. Defendant ascertained that Vanella had misrepresented to him that the automobile was free of liens, and so defendant stopped payment upon the check. The plaintiff secured partial repayment from Vanella of the money it advanced on the check, and brings this action to collect the balance from the defendant as drawer of the check.

The defendant raises the defense of Vanella's fraud; and contends that even a holder in due course of the check, as plaintiff concededly is, takes it subject to fraud in the transaction giving rise to issuance of the check; and he relies upon Uniform Commercial Code, § 3–305(2) (c). This section provides in pertinent part as follows: * * *

> "To the extent that a holder is a holder in due course he takes the instrument free from * * *
>
> "(2) all defenses of any party to the instrument with whom the holder has not dealt except
>
> "(c) such misrepresentation as has induced the party to sign the instrument with neither knowledge nor reasonable opportunity to obtain knowledge of its character or its essential terms".

Neither counsel nor I have found any reported case in New York involving this question arising since the effective date of the U.C.C.,

September 27, 1964. The quoted section does not appear, however, to have changed the law in New York with respect to the question at bar. The comment under this section * * * indicates that the section is designed to accord with the great majority of decisions under the prior law to the effect that only fraud as to the nature of the instrument itself signed by the defendant is a defense to an action by a holder in due course. * * * It appears that the new section was designed to codify the prior case law in this respect; and that construction of it is adopted by the court.

The defense, therefore, is insufficient in law, and plaintiff's motion for summary judgment is granted.

2. *Negligence of Maker Prevents Recovery from Holder*

UNIVERSAL C. I. T. CREDIT CORP. v. CYR

160 Me. 152, 200 A.2d 213 (1964).

WILLIAMSON, Chief Justice. This is an action on a negotiable promissory note by the Universal C. I. T. Credit Corporation, an indorsee and holder in due course, against the makers. The defense is that through fraud on the part of the payee the defendants executed the note without negligence on their part. The jury found for the defendants. * * *

Apart from the alleged fraud, the plaintiff is plainly a holder in due course * * *.

The Kennebec Siding and Roofing Co. (Kennebec Venetian Blind & Window Co.) was engaged in selling and installing siding, roofing, doors, windows, and other housing materials. On February 10, 1960, the defendants, husband and wife, signed a "Contract of Sale" authorizing the installation of a garage door and siding for the barn, with other details. * * *

Under date of March 2, 1960, we find a "CUSTOMER'S COMPLETION CERTIFICATE AND AUTHORIZATION" addressed to the Universal C. I. T. Credit Corporation, in which the defendants over their signatures certified the contract had been satisfactorily completed "on premises indicated in my/our Property Improvement Statement, which material and work constitute the entire consideration for my/our Promissory Note." Opposite the signatures the certificate reads: "IMPORTANT: Do Not Sign This Certificate Until All Materials And Work Contracted For Have Been Satisfactorily Delivered And Completed."

Also under date of March 2, 1960, the defendants executed a note to the Kennebec Venetian Blind & Window Co. or order in the amount of $1807.65 payable in 60 monthly instalments. In large type at the outset of the note are the following words: "THIS IS A NEGOTIABLE PROMISSORY NOTE." At the end of the note we read:

> "Customer acknowledges receipt of a completed copy of this promissory note, including above Notice.
> s/Lawrence J. Cyr
>
> ___
>
> "Customer (Person on whose life group credit life insurance will be obtained, if applicable.)
> s/Rosalie Cyr
>
> ___
>
> (Additional Customer, if any)"

The note was indorsed by the payee to the plaintiff without recourse, and, as we have said, the plaintiff is a holder in due course. * * * In fact the "Customer's Completion Certificate and Authorization" and the promissory note were executed in blank by the defendants *before* the work was *completed.* As we may expect, the work was never completed.

The defendants stoutly assert that they did not know they were signing a note, that they thought they were signing a paper having something to do with credit or financing of the project, but in any event not a note. The evidence warranted a finding that the dealer defrauded the defendants in the execution of the note. * * *

There is no suggestion that the defendants were illiterate, or inexperienced in business matters * * *

We cannot escape the conclusion that the defendants were utterly heedless in signing the note. If they had read what was so plainly stated, no confusion could have arisen. Their trust in the salesman was misplaced. The dealer had the plaintiff's money, loaned on the strength of defendants' note. One must lose, and the loss here falls on the defendants.

On this record defendants were negligent as a matter of law. The plaintiff was entitled to the direction of a verdict in its favor. * * *

Appeal sustained. Remanded for assessment of damages and entry of judgment for the plaintiff notwithstanding the verdict.

---

3. *Fraud and Usury as a Real Defense*

MATTHEWS v. ALUMINUM ACCEPTANCE CORP.

1 Mich.App. 570, 137 N.W.2d 280 (1965).

FITZGERALD, Judge. If ever the elements of a classic case involving an aluminum siding company and its subsequent assignee were before an appellate court, that case unravels here. It could be drawn from the files of almost any practicing lawyer or it might be the complaint of the next client in the waiting room.

* * * In this action to enjoin defendant from enforcing any claims against plaintiffs and from foreclosing the mortgage upon plaintiffs' home, the questions on appeal are whether * * * constructive forgery or fraud was established. * * * and whether the entire transaction was shot through with usury.

In April of 1962, plaintiffs Robert and Katherine Matthews were approached by representatives of All-Style Builders, aluminum siding applicators. They allege that All-Style indicated that their modest home had been chosen as a demonstration site for aluminum siding for that area. New siding was to be applied over the tar paper on their home, and in addition they were to be given a loan of $650 in cash to fix their tractor and the total price for this was to be $3,250. Further, they were to receive $100 to apply against their contract for each potential customer which All-Style brought to view their newly-sided house.

To the Matthews, the alleged inducements were sufficiently alluring that they signed up for the package. The siding was applied, they were given $650, but to time of trial, no one had ever shown up to view the siding as a potential customer.

When the smoke cleared, so to speak, the Matthews learned that the instrument they had signed included a promissory note and mortgage calling for 84 equal monthly installments at the rate of $61.04 per month for a grand total of $5,127.36, not the $3,250 they had anticipated, and the instruments had been assigned to defendant Aluminum Acceptance Corporation, a firm specializing in financing siding application.

All-Style Builders is not a party to this suit and defendant Aluminum Acceptance claims it is a bona fide holder of the paper, denies fraud and further claims that the instruments are not usurious because the agreement provides for a cash price, whereas the note and mortgage represent a "time price" and are a discount transaction.

As to the transaction itself, Mr. Matthews says that he was unable to read any but the largest print, and that only with difficulty, and Mrs. Matthews was able only to read the printed portion with her glasses and that the papers were stacked one on top of another at the time of signing and with the upper portions covered, leaving visible only the area to be signed. The papers, they further allege, were blank at the time of signing.

Plaintiffs made only one payment and now seek to enjoin foreclosure of the mortgage and defendant counterclaims, seeking foreclosure, deficiency and such other relief "as shall be agreeable to equity and good conscience."

The latter phrase is a little difficult to digest when the record is studied closely.

* * * Judgment entered canceling the mortgage and giving defendant judgment on its counterclaim in the sum of $3,250. Aluminum Acceptance Corporation appeals this judgment. * * * The rule in Michigan is * * * that a signature de-

ceptively procured is in law a forgery and those who subsequently acquire interest under the forged instrument are in no better position than if they had purchased with notice.

* * * Appellant corporation also urges that if defendant is a holder in due course it is immaterial whether or not there was fraud in the inducement with respect to the promissory note. * * *

The agreement gave defendant notice of the agreed contract price of $3,250 while the note and mortgage stated the sum of $5,127.36. Such a disparity furnishes ample notice of the infirmity of the instrument and that it was usurious, rendering it impossible for defendant to be a holder in due course and to avail itself of such defenses as a holder in due course might have. * * *

The judgment of the court is affirmed.

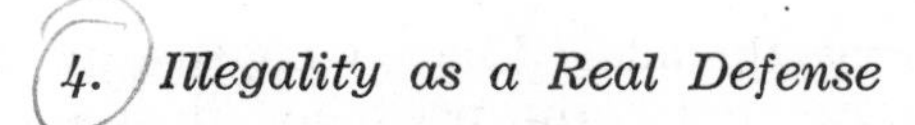

4. *Illegality as a Real Defense*

PACIFIC NATIONAL BANK v. HERNREICH

240 Ark. 114, 398 S.W.2d 221 (1966).

JOHNSON, Justice. Appellee George Hernreich, operator of a jewelry store in Fort Smith, executed three promissory notes payable to W. F. Sebel Co., Inc., a foreign corporation. Sebel Company, a wholesaler of diamond jewelry, was not qualified to do business in Arkansas. Hernreich had been doing business with Sebel Company for two decades prior to this litigation. The testimony reflects that this was their manner of doing business: Sebel Company's salesman, Sam Leibson, with his entire stock of diamond jewelry, would call on Hernreich at his Fort Smith store. Hernreich would select and receive diamond jewelry from Leibson's stock. Hernreich would sign one or more promissory notes representing the purchase price of the jewelry, which notes Leibson would then forward to Sebel Company's home office in Los Angeles. (Unknown to Hernreich, Sebel Company would then discount the notes with appellant, Pacific National Bank.) * * * When each note was due and sent to a Fort Smith bank for payment, Hernreich would pay the note with the proceeds of what he had sold * * *

On February 20 and March 14, 1963, appellee executed three notes totaling $10,611.70, due in three to five months. These notes were sent to Sebel Company by Leibson and negotiated to appellant bank a few days later. Shortly thereafter Sebel, the principal owner of Sebel Company, died and the corporation was dissolved. When the notes became due and were presented for payment at a Fort Smith bank, appellee refused to pay them. * * *

Appellant contends that a holder in due course is entitled to summary judgment against the maker of negotiable notes under the undisputed facts, even though the payee was a non-qualified foreign corporation, and the trial court erred in granting appellee's motion for summary judgment and overruling appellant's.

For reversal, appellant cites Ark.Stat.Ann. § 85–3–305 (Add. 1961) which says:

> "To the extent that a holder is a holder in due course he takes the instrument free from
>
> (2) all defenses of any party to the instrument with whom the holder has not dealt except
>
> (b) such other incapacity, or duress, or illegality of the transaction, as renders the obligation of the party a nullity; and

For affirmance of the trial court, appellee cites Ark.Stat.Ann. § 64–1202 (Repl.1957):

> "Any foreign corporation which * * * shall fail or refuse to file its articles of incorporation or certificate as aforesaid, cannot make any contract in the State which can be enforced by it either in law or in equity, and the complying with the provisions of this act after the date of any such contract, or after any suit is instituted thereon, shall in no way validate said contract."

The legislature has in the past encouraged free negotiability of commercial paper and recently * * * passed the Uniform Commercial Code, of which § 85–3–305, supra, is a part. On the other hand, the legislature passed the highly penal statute, § 64–1202, supra, on foreign corporations to protect our citizenry. * * *

To reverse this case and permit enforcement of the notes here sued on would in effect repeal our penal statute prohibiting unlicensed foreign corporations from doing business in this state. * * * Weighing the possible hampering of negotiability of commercial paper made in Arkansas against permitting fly-by-night foreign corporations to prey unimpededly on our citizens, we conclude that the better rule is that

> * * * [T]he notes and mortgage evidenced a contract made by the corporation in violation of the statute laws of the state. The defect was inherent in the notes * * *, and therefore a subsequent purchaser must take notice of the defect."

The effect of this adoption is to render a transaction of this kind not merely unenforceable but void ab initio. Accordingly, there can be no holder in due course here of a negotiable instrument arising out of this illegal transaction.

Affirmed.

PROBLEMS

1. Payee represents that certain land is readily irrigable and that the soil is good for raising oranges. M, in reliance on the representations, gives Payee his negotiable note for the purchase price. Payee

negotiates the note to an H.D.C. M learns that the property is in the desert, not irrigable, and the soil is poor for oranges. M refuses to pay the note. Decision?

2. M executes a note payable to bearer and forgets it on a counter at the bank. X finds the note and negotiates it to an H.D.C. May the H.D.C. recover from M?

3. M executed a note and left the line blank in which the amount was to be inserted. An employee of M took the note from M's desk, filled in the blank, and passed it on to an H.D.C. Can the H.D.C. recover from M?

4. Payee tells M that if M does not sign a note to Payee, he will inform the District Attorney that M's son is an escaped felon. M signs the note which Payee negotiates to an H.D.C. May the H.D.C. recover from M?

5. Payee forged M's signature to a note and then asked H to purchase it. H asked M if the note was good, and M said that it was. H then purchased the note. Can H recover on the forged note from M?

6. P represented to M that an instrument he was asking M to sign was a contract by which P was hiring M as an employee. M was unable to read, and there was no one nearby to read the instrument to him. M signed the note. P negotiated it to an H.D.C. Can the H.D.C. recover from M?

7. A minor, seventeen years of age, purchased an automobile which he did not need and gave the seller a negotiable note as payment. The seller negotiated the note to H. The minor then rescinded the contract. Can H recover from the minor on the note?

8. M signed a note on January 1, 1969, payable on June 1, 1970, and delivered it to P. P changed the date from June 1, 1970, to June 1, 1979, and on July 1, 1970, negotiated it to H. Can H recover from M?

9. D gave an order check to P for $5.00. The check was so drawn that figures could be inserted between the dollar ($) sign and the number 5. On the line where the word "five" appeared, there was room to the left to insert several words. P inserted the numbers "90" next to the number 5, and the words "nine hundred and" next to the word five. P then negotiated the check for the sum of $905.00 to H. D refused to pay H. Decision?

10. M gave an order check to P for value. P negotiated the check to a minor seventeen years of age. The minor negotiated the check to A who negotiated it to an H.D.C. The minor rescinds the transfer to A and claims the check. Decision?

Chapter 38

PRESENTMENT, DISCHARGE, AND BANKING PROCEDURES

A. PRESENTMENT

1. IN GENERAL

In Chapter 35, it was stated that the liability of the drawer of a *check* and an indorser was secondary (the drawee bank is primary). This means that they are not liable for payment on the check unless certain conditions precedent are met. If these conditions are met, the drawer or indorser must pay. Since the maker of a *note* is primarily liable, the conditions precedent to liability for the drawer and the indorser do not apply to him; i. e., in the case of a maker, payment may be demanded of him, and he may be sued by the holder as soon as the debt is due since he is under a duty to pay the note at the time and at the place named. The conditions precedent to the liability of the drawer of a check and an indorser are presentment and notice of dishonor.

2. PRESENTMENT

Presentment is a demand for payment or acceptance made upon the maker, acceptor, drawee on other payor by the holder (*U.C.C.*, Section 3–504(1)). Presentment is necessary to charge secondary parties unless excused (*U.C.C.,* Section 3–501(1)). Sections 3–503 (Time of Presentment), 3–504 (How Presentment Made), 3–505 (Rights of Party to Whom Presentment is Made), and 3–506 (Time Allowed for Acceptance or Payment) of the *U.C.C.* detail the procedures and rights of presentment. Some of the more important rules are as follows: an instrument having a fixed maturity date must be presented on or before that date; a demand instrument must be presented within a reasonable time after the party the holder seeks to hold has become liable on the instrument; a reasonable time to hold the drawer of a check is within thirty days after the check has been issued, and a reasonable time to hold an indorser is seven days after his indorsement; presentment must be made at the place specified in the instrument, and if there is none, then at the residence or place of business of the party liable; and the holder presenting the instrument for payment must be prepared to issue a receipt and to surrender the instrument.

3. NOTICE OF DISHONOR

An instrument is dishonored when presentment has been properly made and payment or acceptance is refused (*U.C.C.*, Section 3–

507(1)). Upon dishonor, the holder has an immediate right of recourse against drawers and indorsers upon giving them prompt notice of dishonor (*U.C.C.*, Section 3–508). The notice of dishonor must be given by a bank before its midnight deadline (midnight on the next banking day following the banking day on which it receives notice of dishonor, *U.C.C.*, Section 4–104(1) (h)), and by any other person before midnight of the third business day after dishonor or receipt of notice of dishonor. The holder should give notice of dishonor to all prior parties so that he preserves his rights against all of them. The notice may be oral but should be written and a copy retained with a notation as to when notice was given, to whom notice was given, and the address where the notice was given. If notice is sent by mail, it should be sent registered; and a copy should be retained noting the date it was sent and where it was posted. The notice does not have to be in any particular form, but it must identify the instrument and state that it was dishonored. Failure to give notice of dishonor releases parties secondarily liable.

4. PROTEST

A protest is a *formal* presentment and certificate of dishonor (*U.C.C.*, Section 3–509). It declares that the instrument was on a certain day presented for payment or acceptance and that such payment or acceptance was refused, stating the reasons given, if any, for the refusal, whereupon the holder protests against all parties to such instrument and declares that they will be held responsible for all loss or damage arising from its dishonor. It is only required on a draft that is drawn or payable outside the United States; however, a holder may protest a dishonor on any instrument. The advantage of a protest is that it is evidentiary in character and may save expenses in obtaining or proving evidence through such devices as depositions. In addition to protests, other documents and records are admissible in court to prove a dishonor; e. g., bank stamps and memorandums ("not sufficient funds"); bank records kept in the usual course of business.

5. WHEN PRESENTMENT AND NOTICE OF DISHONOR NOT NECESSARY

a. Presentment and notice of dishonor may be *waived* by the express or implied agreement of the secondary party (*U.C.C.*, Section 3–511(2) (a)). Waiver may be made before or after the instrument, or notice, is due. It may be oral, written, or by conduct of the party liable; e. g., party liable promises to substitute a new note. A waiver is binding on all parties if it appears on the face of the instrument; however, if the waiver if only part of an indorsement, it only binds the indorser (*U.C.C.,* Section 3–511(6)).

b. Presentment and notice of dishonor may be excused when the holder is unable through reasonable diligence to locate the person who is to make payment (*U.C.C.*, Section 3–504(2), Section 3–511(1), Section 3–511(2) (c)).

c. Presentment and notice of dishonor may be excused when the person liable has already refused to pay (*U.C.C.*, Section 3–511(3) (b), Section 3–511(2) (b)).

d. Presentment and notice of dishonor may be excused when the party to be charged has died or gone into insolvency proceedings (*U.C.C.*, Section 3–511(3) (a)).

B. DISCHARGE OF PARTIES

A party to a negotiable instrument may be discharged individually or by some act which discharges all of the parties to the instrument at one time. The Uniform Commercial Code, Section 3–601, lists the twelve grounds for the discharge of parties. These grounds have either been discussed previously or are self-explanatory. It is suggested that the students read Sections 3–601 through 3–606, plus the cited sections in Section 3–601.

C. BANKING PROCEDURES

1. COLLECTION OF CHECKS

Rarely does the holder of a check go to the drawee (payor) bank to cash it. Normally, the holder goes to his own bank (depository or collecting bank) and either cashes the check or deposits it in his account. This creates a collection situation for the depositary or collecting bank from the drawee or payor bank (a payor bank is a bank by which an item is payable as drawn or accepted, *U.C.C.*, Section 4–105(b)). A depositary bank is the first bank to which an item is transferred for collection even though it is also the payor bank, Section 4–105(a). A collecting bank is any bank handling the item for collection except the payor bank, Section 4–105(d).

The usual practice is for the depositary bank to credit the account of the depositor (holder of check) at the time of the deposit. This credit is a provisional settlement in that if the check is not good and it is dishonored, the depositary bank cancels its credit to the holder; whereas, if the check is honored by the payor bank, the settlement is final. The depositary bank may collect either directly from the drawee bank through a clearing house or through one or more intermediary banks. A clearing house is any association of banks or other payors regularly clearing items. When the check reaches the payor bank, it debits the account of the drawer of the check. The payor bank then credits the account of the presenting bank and remits the money to it.

Unless a contrary intention appears, a collecting bank is an agent for the depositor of the check (*U.C.C.,* Section 4–201(1)). Thus, the depositor of the check has the risk of loss in the event of nonpayment of the check or insolvency of one of the intermediary collecting banks before final settlement.

A depositary or collecting bank must use ordinary care in presenting the check for payment (*U.C.C.,* Section 4–202(1) (a)).

When a holder has given a depositary bank a check for collection without his indorsement, the bank can supply the indorsement to speed up the collecting process (*U.C.C.,* Section 4–205(1)).

The customer and the collecting bank make certain *warranties* to the payor bank when payment is received; e. g., good title, no knowledge signature not authorized, no material alteration, etc. (see *U.C.C.,* Section 4–207).

The collecting bank has a *security interest* in the check or proceeds to protect the bank with respect to advances and payments made in connection with the check (see *U.C.C.,* Section 4–208).

Following the receipt of the check by the *payor* bank, the check must be processed; e. g., photographed, examined as to form and signature, etc. (*U.C.C.,* Section 4–109). During this processing period, the bank may receive notice that the drawer has stopped payment on the check, that his account has been attached, or that he has gone through bankruptcy. The *U.C.C.,* Section 4–303, provides rules to govern the situation as to when checks are subject to notice, stop-order, legal process or setoff, and the order in which items may be charged or certified. Any notice or stop-order received by a payor bank, or any legal process served on it, or any setoff exercised by the bank, comes too late to prevent payment of the check if the bank has done any one of the following:

a. accepted or certified the check;

b. paid the check in cash;

c. settled for the check without having or reserving a right to revoke the settlement;

d. completed the posting of the check or otherwise has evidenced its decision to pay the check; or

e. become liable for the check because of failure to settle for or return the check in time.

2. RELATIONSHIP BETWEEN PAYOR BANK AND ITS CUSTOMER

A. In General

The *payor* bank may charge against its customer's account, i. e., drawer's account, any check which is properly payable even though it creates an overdraft (*U.C.C.,* Section 4–404(1)). If there is an overdraft, the bank has an implied promise from the customer for reimbursment. If a drawer signs his name to a check in blank and loses it, the bank may pay an unauthorized person the full amount of the check, if it pays in good faith and does not know that the completion was improper, and charge the customer the full amount of the check.

B. Duties of Bank

A bank is under a duty to honor checks drawn by its customer when there are sufficient funds in his account to cover the checks, the check is not over six months old, and the check is in proper form; and if a bank wrongfully dishonors a check, it is liable in damages to its customer (*U.C.C.,* Section 4–402, Section 4–404).

The drawer has the right to *stop payment* on checks drawn on his account (*U.C.C.,* Section 4–403). The order to stop payment must be received at such time and in such manner as to afford the bank a reasonable opportunity to act on it prior to any action by the bank with respect to the check; e. g., payment or promise to pay. An oral stop payment is binding upon the bank but only for fourteen days unless confirmed in writing within that period. A written offer is effective for only six months unless renewed in writing. A drawer cannot stop payment on a check that has been certified by the bank. A stop payment agreement between the bank and the drawer which provides that the bank shall not be liable for negligence in failing to stop payment is invalid (*U.C.C.,* Section 4–103(1)).

The death or incompetence of the drawer does not revoke the bank's authority to pay checks drawn by him until the bank knows of the death or the adjudication of incompetency and has a reasonable time to act (*U.C.C.,* Section 4–405(1)). Even though the bank knows of the death of a drawer, it may pay or certify checks for a period of ten days after the date of death unless ordered to stop payment by a person claiming an interest in the account (*U.C.C.,* Section 4–405(2)). The reason for the rule is to permit holders of checks drawn by the deceased to cash them without the necessity of filing a claim against the deceased's estate.

C. Duties of Customer

A customer (drawer) of a payor bank owes a duty to examine his bank statement and cancelled checks for forgeries or alterations within a reasonable time after they are returned to him or made available to him (*U.C.C.,* Section 4–406(1)). The *U.C.C.* does not specify the period of time within which the customer must report forgeries or alterations, but many banks attempt to limit liability by provisions in signature cards which state that errors must be reported within ten days after receipt of monthly statements and cancelled checks. Most courts hold that these provisions are invalid on one of several grounds; e. g., that ten days is not sufficient time for examination of the statement and checks; or that the provisions are too indefinite; or that the provisions were not called to the attention of the customer and that therefore he did not intend to be bound by them. If the customer does not notify the bank promptly of any forgeries or alterations after he receives his cancelled checks, *and if* the bank establishes that it suffered a loss by reason of such failure, the customer is precluded from asserting against the bank his unauthorized signature or the alteration (*U.C.C.,* Section 4–406(2)). However, if the customer notifies the bank promptly, the bank is liable to the drawer since the bank has the opportunity of examining the check when it is presented for payment and if it fails to detect the alteration of forgery, it is responsible for the loss.

If the bank did not use ordinary care in paying on a forged or altered check, the bank cannot assert the defense that the customer did not notify it promptly of the forgery or alteration, unless the customer does not notify the bank within one year of the forgery or alteration, in which case the customer must take the loss (*U.C.C.,* Section 4–406). If the bank waives its defense of late notification (perhaps for good public relations), it cannot thereafter hold the collecting bank or any prior party for the forgery or alteration (*U.C.C.,* Section 4–406(5)).

If the *customer* is negligent in permitting a forgery or an alteration, e. g., negligent in caring for an automatic check signing device, he is estopped from asserting liability against the bank (*U.C.C.,* Section 3–406).

Where there are *successive* forgeries or alterations, the failure of the customer to examine and notify the bank within a period of fourteen days after the first statement and checks were delivered or available to him would preclude him from asserting forgeries or alterations of *later* checks by the *same person* paid by the bank, and he would suffer the loss (*U.C.C.,* Section 4–406(2) (b)). This rule is intended to help prevent the forger from having an opportunity to repeat the wrongdoing. However, the bank is liable during the fourteen day period.

3. SUBROGATION RIGHTS OF PAYOR BANK

If a payor bank has paid an item, e. g., check, over the stop payment order of the drawer or maker or otherwise under circumstances giving a basis for objection by the drawer or maker, to prevent unjust enrichment and only to the extent necessary to prevent loss to the bank by reason of its payment on the item, the payor bank shall be subrogated (substituted) to the rights of the following parties against the drawer or maker:

a. any holder in due course that the bank paid on the item. Thus, when the payor bank is sued for wrongful payment, it can assert the defense that its customer (drawer) did not suffer a loss because he would have been liable to the holder in due course whether the bank had obeyed the stop payment order or not; i. e., even if payment had been stopped by the bank, the drawer would still have had to pay the holder in due course. Thus, the *U.C.C.* places the payor bank in the position of a holder in due course against the drawer.

b. the payee or any other holder. Thus, when the payor bank is sued for wrongful payment, it can assert any defense that the payee had; e. g., if the payee received the check as payment for goods which were defective and the drawer retained the goods, the payee would have a defense to the extent of the value of the goods retained by the drawer.

c. the drawer or maker against the payee or any other holder of the item with respect to the transaction out of which the item arose. Thus, the bank, which has made an improper payment on an item, is subrogated to the rights of its own customer (drawer) against the payee; e. g., payee has defrauded the drawer, the drawer stops payment on the check, the bank pays on the check wrongfully, the bank pays the drawer for the mistake, the bank sues payee and takes over the rights of the drawer in the suit against the payee. *U.C.C.,* Section 4–407(a) (b) (c).

4. OTHER RECOVERY RIGHTS OF PAYOR BANK

A. Forged Check

If a bank pays on a forged check to a holder who is innocent of the forgery, can the bank recover the money from the holder? The *U.C.C.,* Section 4–418, provides that the bank cannot.

B. Forged Indorsement

If a bank pays on a forged indorsement, can the bank recover the money from the party paid? The *U.C.C.,* Section 3–417, provides that it can.

C. Alteration

If the bank pays on an altered instrument, can the bank recover the money from the party paid? The *U.C.C.,* Section 3–417(c), provides that it can, unless the party paid purchased it after certification and was innocent of the alteration in which case the bank cannot.

D. Fictitious Payee

If the bank pays on a check made out to a fictitious payee, e. g., employee in charge of payroll checks sets up a fictitious employee and draws checks to him which he has his employer sign along with other pay checks and then indorses and cashes the checks, can the bank debit the account of the employer? The *U.C.C.,* Section 3–405(1) (c), provides that the bank can.

E. Imposter Payee

If a bank pays on a check made out to an imposter, e. g., imposter induces customer of bank to give him a check payable to the person impersonated, can the bank debit the account of the customer? The *U.C.C.,* Section 3–405(1) (a), provides that it can.

---

1. Necessity for Presentment of Dishonored Checks

DLUGE v. ROBINSON

204 Pa.Super. 404, 204 A.2d 279 (1964).

FLOOD, Judge. This is an appeal from a judgment for the plaintiffs in an action against J. Robinson as endorser of two checks, brought by Isaac Dluge, the endorsee. The checks were dishonored by the drawee bank because of insufficient funds in the maker's account. Dluge died after instituting suit and the executors of his estate have been substituted as plaintiffs.

The complaint sets forth that immediately after the bank refused payment and returned the checks to Dluge, he returned them to the defendant with a demand for payment which the defendant refused. The defendant, both in his answer and on the witness stand, denied any demand for payment at the time Dluge returned the checks. * * * If the plaintiffs were holders in due course, they would have to prove only (1) that the defendant endorsed the checks and delivered them to Dluge, and (2) that they had been presented to the endorser for payment within a reasonable time. Uniform Commercial Code, * * * § 3–501(1) (b). In the case of an uncertified check this is presumed to be within seven days after the endorsement. U.C.C., § 3–503(1) (e), § 3–503(2) (b).

* * * "Presentment is a demand for acceptance or payment * * * by or on behalf of the holder." U.C.C., § 3–504(1). The only evidence of any demand was the admission by defendant that he received a letter from Dluge's attorney demanding payment. The defendant did not state when he received this letter. The plaintiffs did not offer the letter in evidence and there is no way to determine from the record when it was sent except that it was presumably sent before the complaint was filed on September 12, 1960, seven months after the checks were dishonored by the drawee bank. Since the defendant denied any demand at the time the checks were returned to him, and the record is otherwise barren of any evidence of demand within seven days, or any reasonable time, after endorsement, the plaintiffs did not establish any right to recover even if they had been holders in due course.

* * * The plaintiffs are not holders in due course. Dluge gave the checks to the defendant without any demand for payment, so far as the record shows, and was not in possession of them when the suit was brought. Therefore he was not the holder. " 'Holder' means a person who is in possession of a document of title or an instrument or an investment security drawn, issued or indorsed to him or to his order or to bearer or in blank." U.C.C., § 1–201(20). A fortiori, he was not a holder in due course. U.C.C., § 3–302(1).

* * * In the absence of possession, ownership would usually depend upon proof that the holder did not voluntarily surrender possession unless he did so conditionally upon payment of the checks. Surrender of the checks to a prior party, without payment, and without even a demand for payment, tells against the retention of ownership, and indicates, if anything, an intention not to hold such party liable on the instrument. Cf. U.C.C., § 3–605(1) (b).

* * * More importantly, there is no proof of demand for payment by the plaintiffs when the checks were returned to the defendant. Plaintiffs have therefore failed to prove their right to recover against Robinson whether they are holders or owners of the checks.

The burden upon one not a holder who seeks to recover on a negotiable instrument is a heavy one. The plaintiffs have not sustained it. They must recover, if at all, upon the underlying obligation for which the checks were given.

Judgment reversed.

---

2. *Effect of Notice of Dishonor by Mail*

DURKIN v. SIEGEL

340 Mass. 445, 165 N.E.2d 81 (1960).

CUTTER, Justice. Promissory notes signed by one Browne were indorsed by the defendant. They were protested for nonpayment and notice of dishonor was sent on January 17, 1957, "by the plaintiffs' attorney by certified mail, return receipt requested, properly stamped and addressed to the defendant at his home * * * [in] Brookline * * *. The letter, unopened, was returned by the post office * * * with the notation 'refused' * * * across the face of the envelope. The defendant testified that he was in Canada at the time."

* * * There were verdicts for the plaintiffs. The only question argued raised by the bill of exceptions is whether it was good notice of dishonor of promissory notes * * *, to send a letter, otherwise in order, by certified mail, return receipt requested, rather than regular mail, where the letter was returned unopened and undelivered, marked "refused," with the blank form of post office receipt unsigned. * * * The holder of a dishonored negotiable instrument must give prompt notice of dishonor to those secondarily liable. * * * The provision here controlling is G.L. c. 107, § 128 (§ 105 of the original uniform act), which reads, "Where notice of dishonor is duly addressed and deposited in the post office the sender is deemed to have given due notice, notwithstanding any miscarriage in the mails." Registered and certified mail, return receipt requested, are usually regarded by careful people as preferred methods of ensuring delivery. No exception is made in § 128 with respect

to these or other types of first class mail. The section has been carried over into the Uniform Commercial Code in somewhat different language but without attempt to change its meaning. See G.L. c. 106, § 3–508, which in par. (3) provides that "[n]otice may be given in any reasonable manner" and that "[i]t may be oral or written," and in par. (4) states, "Written notice is given when sent although it is not received." * * *

The most carefully supervised available methods of mail delivery, registered and certified first class mail, are certainly a "reasonable manner" of giving notice of dishonor, for the propriety of the use of registered or certified mail for important notices has frequently been recognized in our statutes. Although some statutes permit notices by ordinary mail, in the absence of explicit language in a particular statute, a court would be slow to say that service by registered or certified mail was not a compliance with such a statutory requirement for notice by mail. Service by registered mail in probate proceedings is familiar to us all. * * *

Persons who become secondarily liable upon negotiable instruments are not unfairly burdened if they are held bound by notices sent to them by any generally used form of first class mail at a usual address. They can protect themselves by stipulating (see § 131) that a particular address be used and by arranging at that address during any absence to have their mail received, opened, forwarded, and collected (in the event of the receipt of a notification from the postal authorities that it has not been possible to deliver to them a piece of registered or certified mail). * * * Refusal of a registered or certified letter, of course, would not protect an indorser from the effect of notice. * * *

Exceptions overruled.

---

3. *Waiver of Presentment*

GERRITY CO. v. PADALINO

51 Misc.2d 928, 273 N.Y.S.2d 994 (1966).

HAROLD E. KOREMAN, Justice. In an action to recover on a promissory note, plaintiff moves for an order dismissing the defenses contained in the answer on the ground that a defense is not stated therein. (CPLR 3211[b]). Defendants, the maker and endorser, assert that the note was not presented for payment, was not protested for non-payment, and no notice of protest or non-payment was given to the endorser. Defendants also contend that they are not responsible for payment of reasonable attorney's fees, and that the note does not contain any provision for payment of such fees.

The note attached to the complaint states on its face, "protest waived". A waiver of protest is also a waiver of presentment and of notice of dishonor, and where the waiver is embodied in the instrument itself, it is binding upon all parties. (See Uniform Commercial

Code, Section 3–511[5], [6]). The note also bears on its face the words "plus costs and reasonable attorney's fees".

Accordingly, the motion is granted and the defenses are stricken.

---

4. Presentment and Notice may be Excused

TRAFALGAR SQUARE, LTD. v. GREEN

57 D. & C.2d 166 (Pa., 1972).

SHADLE, J. March 3, 1972. In this action on a promissory note, defendant has filed preliminary objections to plaintiff's complaint.

The note was executed by Crael, Inc., Robert Green, President, and was endorsed by Green, individually. It was payable to plaintiff 60 days after its date, which was May 12, 1970. Plaintiff's complaint alleges that on July 11, 1970, plaintiff requested payment of the note from "Robert Green, president of Crael, Inc., and Defendant herein," who thereupon advised plaintiff that "Crael, Inc., was unable at the time to pay the note, but requested an extension and forebearance and promised periodic payments." The complaint further alleges that on November 20, 1970, the note was presented to "Robert Green, president of Crael, Inc., for payment," and that "Again Robert Green stated that Crael, Inc., could not make payment of the note." The complaint concludes that "Robert Green was thereupon advised that because of the failure of Crael, Inc., to honor its obligation to pay the note he was personally liable in his capacity as indorser and payment from him was demanded," with which he failed to comply.

[Defendant demurs] that the complaint is fatally defective in failing to allege that * * * (2) notice of dishonor by the corporate maker was given to defendant as the individual endorser and (3) presentment for payment was made to defendant as such individual endorser.

* * *

On the second and third points, defendant refers to section 3–501 of the code, 12A P.S. § 3–501, which requires both notice of dishonor by the maker and presentment for payment to the endorser before the latter may be charged.

It will be noted initially that it is not crystal-clear from the complaint as to the capacity in which Robert Green acted in the communications. Presentment was made to, and payment was requested of, "Robert Green, president of Crael, Inc., and Defendant herein," and Robert Green stated that "Crael, Inc., could not make payment of the note" on both occasions, but he "requested an extension and forebearance and promised periodic payments." Clearly, presentment for payment was, in effect, made to defendant as an individual when he was advised that "he was personally liable in his capacity as indorser and payment from him was demanded."

In our opinion, the present situation is covered by section 3–501, supra, and section 3–511, 12A P.S. § 3–511 of the code. The former section provides that notice of dishonor and presentment for payment are necessary to charge an endorser "Unless excused (section 3–511) * * *." The latter section declares that "(2). Presentment or notice or protest as the case may be is entirely excused when (a) the party to be charged has waived it expressly or by implication * * * or (b) such party has himself dishonored the instrument * * * or otherwise has no reason to expect * * * that the instrument [will] be * * * paid * * * (and) (3) Presentment is also entirely excused when * * * (b) * * * payment is refused but not for want of proper presentment."

We simply decline to engage in the type of legerdemain and legal ballet dancing which acceptance of defendant's arguments would require. We here deal with a single corporate officer who acted both on behalf of the corporation as maker and individually on his own behalf as endorser. It is nonsense to conclude that the dishonor which he made on behalf of the corporation was not known to him individually as endorser, or that the request for extension and forebearance which he made as a corporate officer was not known or consented to by him individually. In the language of section 3–511, supra, defendant waived a second and formal (and useless) presentment and notice and protest to himself individually as endorser.

* * *

We do not question that there may be cases in which the formalistic requirements of presentment, protest and notice to a corporate maker will not constitute such as to an officer who is an individual indorser. Neither do we hold that the performance of such formalities as to a person who is both a corporate officer and individual endorser always binds him and his corporation in both capacities. We hold merely that the facts alleged in this complaint are sufficient to entitle plaintiff to prove, if it can, that defendant individually consented and agreed to the extension and forebearance granted by plaintiff to the corporate maker, and that notice of dishonor by the maker and presentment for payment to defendant either were given to him or were waived by him.

5. *Rights of Depositary Bank as Holder*

CITIZENS NAT. BANK OF ENGLEWOOD v. FORT LEE SAVINGS & LOAN ASS'N

89 N.J.Super. 43, 213 A.2d 315 (1965).

BOTTER, J. S. C. Citizens National Bank of Englewood has moved for summary judgment to recover monies advanced against a check which was deposited with the bank for collection but was later dishonored. The issue is whether the bank should be protected for advances made to its depositor before the check cleared. * *

On August 27, 1963, George P. Winter agreed to sell a house in Fort Lee, New Jersey to defendant Jean Amoroso and her husband. On the same day Amoroso requested her bank, Fort Lee Savings and Loan Association (Fort Lee Savings), to issue the bank's check to her order for $3,100 to be used as a deposit on the contract for sale. Fort Lee Savings complied by drawing the check against its account with the Fort Lee Trust Company. Later that day Amoroso indorsed and delivered the check to Winter, and he deposited the check in his account at the plaintiff bank. At that time he had a balance of $225.33. After the $3,100 check was deposited the bank cashed a $1,000 check for him against his account. * * *

The next day Amoroso discovered that Winter had previously sold the property to a third party by agreement which had been recorded in the Berger County Clerk's Office. Amoroso immediate-ately asked Winter to return her money. She claims that he admitted the fraud and agreed to return the deposit. But when Mrs. Amoroso and her husband reached Winter's office they learned that he had attempted suicide. He died shortly thereafter.

Upon making this discovery, in the afternoon of August 28, the Amorosos went to Fort Lee Savings to advise it of the fraud and request it to stop payment on the check. The bank issued a written stop payment order which was received by the Fort Lee Trust Company, the drawee, on the following day, August 29. In the meantime the $3,100 check was sent by plaintiff through the Bergen County Clearing House to the Fort Lee Trust Company. By then the stop payment order had been received. Notice of nonpayment was thereafter transmitted to plaintiff.

Plaintiff contends that, under the Uniform Commercial Code, * * * it is a holder in due course to the extent of the advances made on Winter's account and is entitled to recover these moneys from the drawer and payee-indorser of the check. * * * The definition of "holder" includes a person who is in possession of an instrument indorsed to his order or in blank. * * * It is clear that the bank is a holder of the check notwithstanding that it may have taken the check solely for collection and with the right to charge back against the depositor's account in the event the check is later dishonored. * * * Moreover, a depositary bank may properly charge an account by honoring a check drawn by a depositor even though it creates an overdraft. * * *

It would be anomalous for a bank to lose its status as a holder in due course merely because it has notice that the account of its depositor is overdrawn.

* * * This result is continued by provisions of the Uniform Commercial Code which give plaintiff a security interest in the check and the monies represented by the check to the extent that credit given for the check has been withdrawn or applied. * * *

It would hinder commercial transactions if depositary banks refused to permit withdrawal prior to clearance of checks. Apparently banking practice is to the contrary. It is clear that the Uniform Commercial Code was intended to permit the continuation of this practice and to protect banks who have given credit on deposited items prior to notice of a stop payment order or other notice of dishonor.

* * * Accordingly both Fort Lee Savings as drawer and Amoroso as indorser of the check are liable to plaintiff.

---

6. *Right of Bank to Supply Customer's Indorsement*

COLE v. FIRST NATIONAL BANK OF GILLETTE

433 P.2d 837 (Wyo., 1967).

Mr. Chief Justice HARNSBERGER delivered the opinion of the court.

As a down payment upon a purchase contract with Wyoming Homes, Wilma Cole delivered to a Wyoming Homes salesman appellants' check, payable to Wyoming Homes, in the sum of $4,000 drawn upon appellants' account held under the name "Buffalo Auto Supply," in The First National Bank of Buffalo, Wyoming. Without there being any endorsement on the check, the salesman took it to The First National Bank of Gillette, the appellee. The Gillette bank, thereupon, deposited $4,000 to the credit of Wyoming Homes without the check having any endorsement other than there being stamped thereon "First National Bank Gillette, Wyoming For Deposit Only," together with the Gillette bank's own transferring endorsement to the order of any bank. Through banking channels, the check came to The First National Bank of Buffalo, and the $4,000 was then charged to and deducted from the appellants' Buffalo Auto Supply account.

Claiming there was failure of consideration for the check and that it was fraudulently obtained, appellants sought recovery from appellee on the theory the Gillette bank was a transferee with only the rights possessed by Wyoming Homes, and the bank was not a holder in due course or even a holder as defined by statute and decision of this court and consequently subject to defenses of failure of consideration and fraud.

* * * After hearing upon the motion, summary judgment was rendered in favor of defendant, and the Coles have appealed contending this court, as a matter of law, should reverse.

* * * Section 4–205 clearly authorized the Gillette bank, as the depositary bank taking the check for collection, to place a statement on the check to the effect that the item was credited to the account of a customer, which statement is said to be as effective as the customer's endorsement. This was done. The section is as follows:

> "(1) A depositary bank which has taken an item for collection may supply any indorsement of the customer which is necessary to title unless the item contains the words 'payee's endorsement required' or the like. In the absence of such a requirement a statement placed on the item by the depositary bank to the effect that the item was deposited by a customer or credited to his account is effective as the customer's indorsement.
>
> "(2) An intermediary bank, or payor bank which is not a depositary, is neither given notice nor otherwise affected by a restrictive indorsement of any person except the bank's immediate transferor."

Any question as to whether Wyoming Homes was such a "customer" * * * is answered by § 4–104(e), * * * reading, " 'Customer' means any person having an account with a bank or for whom a bank has agreed to collect items and includes a bank carrying an account with another bank".

It follows that the Gillette bank having credited the amount of the check to the account of its payee and a final settlement of the item having been made, the bank did not step into the shoes of the payee or become subject to any equities between the check's maker or its payee. Thus matters of possible failure of consideration or of fraud relate solely to matters between the Coles and Wyoming Homes to which transactions the appellee was not a party.

The judgment of the trial court is affirmed.

Affirmed.

7. *Respective Rights on Stop Payment Order*

CICCI v. LINCOLN NAT. BANK & TRUST CO. OF CENTRAL N. Y.

46 Misc.2d 465, 260 N.Y.S.2d 100 (1965).

TONY MANCUSO, Judge. * * * This is an action by the plaintiff depositor against the defendant bank for wrongful payment of a check drawn by the plaintiff in favor of one Joseph Santo in the amount of $3,000.00 after receipt by the defendant bank of a timely stop payment order. The action is grounded upon Section 4–403 of the New York U.C.C.

The answer of the defendant bank denies the allegations of the complaint except jurisdiction and pleads two affirmative defenses: First, that the check was given by the plaintiff to Joseph Santo as a loan which has not been repaid or discharged and the plaintiff has, therefore, suffered no loss by reason of the defendant's having paid the check * * * Plaintiff made and delivered his check drawn on the defendant bank payable to the order of one Joseph Santo for $3,000.00 on or about November 10, 1964. On December 10, 1964 plaintiff gave written notice to defendant to stop payment on said check. No question appears to be raised as to the form or timeliness of the plaintiff's stop payment order to the bank or to the timely receipt thereof by the defendant bank. U.C.C. § 4–403(1). Also, that on or about December 24, 1964 the defendant paid said check contrary to the stop payment order of the plaintiff and charged plaintiff's account with the sum of $3,000.00 and has refused to credit the plaintiff's account after demand. * * *

Prior to the adoption of the Uniform Commercial Code in New York (effective Sept. 27, 1964) there was no question that a depositor who issued to his bank a timely stop payment order could recover against the bank for a breach of the depositor's order by payment of the check in absence of any ratification of the bank's payment by the depositor. * * *

Section 4–403 subdivision (3) of the Uniform Commercial Code provides

> "The burden of establishing the fact and amount of loss resulting from the payment of an item contrary to a binding stop payment order is on the customer."

* * * By reason of the foregoing the plaintiff's motion for summary judgment herein is denied inasmuch as the defendant's first affirmative defense, that the plaintiff suffered no loss by reason of the defendant's payment of said check, makes out a triable issue of fact as to the liability herein. Any triable issue of fact, of course, compels a denial of a motion for summary judgment. I am deciding herein only that where a depositor and maker of a check moves for summary judgment pursuant to Section 4–403 of the Uniform Commercial Code it is part of the plaintiff's prima facie case to allege and

thereafter, of course, to prove that he has been damaged by reason of the bank's wrongful payment of a check after receipt of a timely and proper stop payment order and absent ratification. U.C.C. § 4–403(3).

---

8. *Bank's Liability to Customers*

JEWETT v. MANUFACTURERS HANOVER TRUST CO.

48 Misc.2d 1094, 266 N.Y.S.2d 607 (1965).

ARNOLD L. FEIN, Judge. On July 13, 1964, plaintiff and defendant Drake, partners in a dry cleaning business, opened a checking account, requiring the signature of both partners to all checks, in a branch of defendant Manufacturers Hanover Trust Company, pursuant to a bank account agreement and authorized signature card furnished by defendant bank. The funds were provided by plaintiff. The first five checks were properly signed by both.

Plaintiff sues to recover $623.30, charged to the account by the bank, representing twelve checks signed by defendant Drake only, and paid by the bank between July 21, 1964 and September 4, 1964, including one undated check, bearing an illegible endorsement, drawn to the order of a payee whose first name was omitted, only the title "Mr." being shown.

The oral complaint alleges breach of contract and "unauthorized taking and paying by the defendants of * * * the property of the plaintiff * * *."

The relationship between the bank and its depositor being that of debtor and creditor, the bank cannot charge the account of the depositor with moneys paid out without authority. * * * Although research has failed to disclose any New York cases directly in point, it is obvious that a check signed by one of two depositors, where both signatures are required, is not authority for such payment. * * * The bank could only pay on the order of its depositor. The depositor here consisted of both parties to the contract with the bank. * * * The bank breached its contract by paying only on the signature of one.

It is undisputed that: (1) the bank's statements, dated respectively July 31, August 31, and September 30, 1964, together with the cancelled checks for each month were mailed to defendant Drake and not to plaintiff, pursuant to the bank account agreement, and (2) plaintiff failed to notify the bank of the absence of her signature until December 1964, far more than thirty days after such mailing and delivery. The bank pleads that (1) the bank account agreement relieves it of liability because of the failure to notify it within thirty days; * * * and (4) plaintiff's loss was caused by her negligence in failing to notify the bank within thirty days and not any negligence on its part, entitling defendant to judgment on its counterclaim for negligence to the extent of any judgment granted plaintiff for bank's breach of contract. * * *

It is palpable that in forgery, alteration or other fraud cases the depositor is more likely to be in a position to detect the fraud and be chargeable with negligence in failing to do so and notify the bank. In the present case the bank already and at all times knew two signatures were required. This is the only notice plaintiff could give the bank, knowledge it already had from the bank account agreement and signature cards in its possession. The bank was palpably negligent as to each check. It was not the failure of notice which caused the repetition of the fraud. * * * After trial, judgment for the plaintiff in the sum of $623.30, together with interest from September 4, 1964, against both defendants.

---

9. *Duty of Customer to Notify Bank of Error*

HUBER GLASS CO. v. FIRST NATIONAL BANK OF KENOSHA

29 Wis.2d 106, 138 N.W.2d 157 (1965).

Respondent, Huber Glass Co., Inc., maintained a checking account with the appellant, The First National Bank of Kenosha. R. C. Huber, respondent's president, and his wife, Bertha, were the only ones authorized to sign checks in respondent's behalf. Kenneth J. Miller began working in respondent's bookkeeping department in 1959 and became head of that department some time in 1960. Miller was discharged on April 25, 1963, and committed suicide the next day. It was later discovered that certain checks, signed "R. C. Huber" and made out to and endorsed by Miller, had been drawn on respondent's account in the appellant bank since August of 1960. Huber denied actually signing any of the checks.

On May 2, 1963, respondent brought suit against appellant to recover $23,875.42, which had been paid on 38 of these checks returned within the prior year as allowed by sec. 116.28, Stats. Judgment was rendered for respondents, Huber Glass Co., Inc., and appellant appeals. * * *

WILKIE, Justice. * * * Since their relationship is grounded in contract, a bank can only make payments from a depositor's account in accordance with proper authorization and is bound to restore any amount paid out on forged checks. A bank can only avoid this strict liability where the "depositor is in equity estopped to assert that the bank is absolutely liable."

* * * In the instant case the trial court found as a matter of fact that (1) the bank "was negligent in not detecting the forgeries," and (2) that the depositor "was not negligent." To enable the bank to prevail against the depositor's claim it must, on this appeal, demonstrate that both of these findings are against the great weight

and clear preponderance of the evidence. * * * As to the forgeries themselves, an examination of the bogus checks, respondent's signature card, and several genuine checks which were introduced into evidence, demonstrates that "each forged signature was a reasonable facsimile of the genuine signature." * * * Consequently there is no evidence to support the finding that the bank was negligent.

* * * Even if the bank is not guilty of negligence in failing to uncover the forgery, the depositor is nonetheless entitled to a restoration of the funds paid out in the absence of negligence on its own part. Thus, the crucial question here is whether or not the depositor was negligent. * * *

It has been held that the reconciliation should include, as a minimum, the following steps: (1) A comparison of the cancelled checks with the check stubs, (2) a comparison of the statement balance with the checkbook balance, and (3) a comparison of the returned checks with the checks listed on the statement.

There is no question that in the case at bar the procedure employed by the respondent in checking the returned checks and bank statements did not comply with these suggested steps. On the contrary, the undisputed evidence showed that the checks returned to respondent by appellant were received by Miller who made a preliminary examination of the statement. Presumably, the forged checks were removed from the others at this point. * * *

Miller's methods were such that a comparison of the statement balance with the checkbook balance or a matching of the cancelled checks with the actual charges on the statement would have quickly disclosed a discrepancy. Likewise, a perusal of the cancelled checks, which were numbered consecutively, would have revealed that certain checks were missing and had been missing for some time. Yet Huber admittedly never complied with any of the suggested reconciliation practices, and, in fact, left full responsibility to Miller. * * Under the circumstances, entrusting Miller alone with the job of reconciling the statements for three years, when a simple spot check of the records would have uncovered the forgeries, was unreasonable and the trial court's finding of no negligence is contrary to the great weight and clear preponderance of the evidence. * * *

Judgment reversed.

---

10. Liability of Bank Customer for Negligence

PARK STATE BANK v. ARENA AUTO AUCTION, INC.

59 Ill.App.2d 235, 207 N.E.2d 158 (1965).

PETERSEN, Justice. This case comes into Court by reason of certain mistakes made by employees of the involved parties following the normal routine of customary business details so characteristic of the rapidly changing society and world in which we live.

Defendant-Appellant, Arena Auto Auction, Inc., created the problem brought to court by the issuance of its check dated December 17, 1963, and by the mailing of it to Plunkett Auto Sales, Rockford, Illinois. For clarity's sake, we will refer to the Rockford Plunkett and the Alabama Plunkett by these geographic designations rather than by their corporate names which, to this Court, are almost identical. Rockford Tom Plunkett might well have felt, upon receiving said check, that he was the recipient of some give-away or promotional scheme, for it later appears that he had sold no merchandise, a fact of which he was well aware, to the Defendant-Appellant. We might visualize Rockford Tom Plunkett as a fast-thinking, old-time horse trader, now engaged in the business of buying and selling used automobiles. He, being well known to the Plaintiff-Appellee Bank * * * signed his name to the check and presented it for payment to Charlotte Parish, head teller, who, promptly and without question, turned over to him the check-designated sum of $1,435.00.

On January 9, 1964, the said check was returned to the Plaintiff-Appellee Bank by reason of a stop-payment order by the maker, and came into the hands of the Assistant Vice-President, Mr. Marconi, whose duties are to assist in the operation of a financial institution, to know its customers, and, equally, to earn a profit for the Plaintiff-Appellee. * * * Vice-President Marconi promptly called his personal friend, Jack Clark of the Arena Auto Auction, Inc., who, * * * to explain the error, commented thus: "This guy here (meaning Rockford Tom Plunkett) wasn't supposed to get the check. It was another Plunkett in Alabama. But Alabama Plunkett wasn't on our books, so that's why our gals sent the check to Rockford Plunkett, and that's why we stopped payment on our check."

But, to put the frosting on the cake, or as Counsel put it, to add insult to injury, Defendant-Appellant, Arena Auto Auction, Inc., issued their second check in the same amount to the same payee, and again sent the check to Rockford Tom Plunkett. Again we can visualize quick-thinking Rockford Tom Plunkett's surprise, for this truly must come from the money tree. He loses no time in going to the same financial institution as before. * * *

Mindful of the first experience, the Vice-President * * * informed poor Tom that he was in difficulty. Rockford Tom Plunkett, seeing that the Vice-President could be right, promptly left the State of Illinois and established his abode in a more sunny climate. * * *

So now we find the Plaintiff-Appellee Bank in the embarrassing position of having cashed a check and having had payment of that check stopped. Desirous of not losing money, they start suit to recover from the Arena Auto Auction. Judge Dusher of the Circuit Court of Winnebago decided in favor of the Plaintiff and against the Arena Auto Auction, Inc., who appeals to this Court. * * *

The Plaintiff-Appellee Bank relies upon * * * our Commercial Code, is as follows:

> "Any person who by his negligence substantially contributes * * * to the making of an unauthorized signature is precluded from asserting the * * * lack of authority against a holder in due course or against a drawee or other payor who pays the instrument in good faith in accordance with the reasonable commercial standards of the drawee's or payor's business."

Hence, we may have a case of first impression in construing the latter section of our statutory law. * * *

Secondly, bearing in mind the erroneous sending of a second check to the same payee, * * * it is our considered conclusion that to require the recipient Bank to stop and question persons known to that Bank and presenting checks in routine business and issued by makers likewise known to the Bank, would be placing cogs in the wheels of business, which, in turn, would bring those wheels of the banking business to an astounding and abrupt halt. * * *

We, therefore and accordingly, do conclude that the Trial Court was correct.

---

11. Authority of Bank to Cash Overdraft

CITY BANK OF HONOLULU v. TENN

469 P.2d 816 (Hawaii, 1970).

RICHARDSON, Chief Justice. In this case, City Bank of Honolulu, plaintiff-appellee, sued its depositor, defendant-appellant Harry Tenn, to recover $6000 that it paid out on an overdraft drawn by Tenn. Tenn contends that City Bank had no authorization to pay a check in excess of the funds he had on deposit. City Bank argues that the check itself authorized it to pay, and that it is now entitled to reimbursement from Tenn for the full amount of the check.

In July, 1964, Tenn left Honolulu for a mainland vacation. In Los Angeles, he met one Gene Hawley, who represented Sonic Educational Products, Inc. Hawley offered Tenn a business deal in which Tenn showed interest. The two were to meet again later to finalize the deal, but Hawley demanded an advance of $6000. Tenn drew a check payable to the order of Sonic Educational Products, Inc., in the amount of $6000, on his personal account at City Bank in Honolulu. Tenn knew when he drew the check that it was approximately $4700 in excess of the funds on deposit in his personal account, and he told Hawley so. He gave the check to Hawley on the express oral understanding that Hawley would not present the check for payment, but would merely hold it as evidence of Tenn's good faith.

* * *

In any event, while Tenn was still away on vacation the check was deposited in San Diego. When it reached City Bank in Honolulu, City Bank cashed the check, after trying and failing to reach Tenn by telephone in Honolulu. The operations manager transferred $4700 from Tenn's business account (Ala Moana Motel, Ltd.) to Tenn's personal account to cover the amount of the check, which was then charged against Tenn's personal account. Tenn's signature was the only one authorized for either account. * * *

Tenn attempted to get repayment of the $6000 from Sonic in California, and Sonic did repay $600, which Tenn turned over to City Bank. However, no further payments were made by Sonic, and when Tenn refused to reimburse City Bank for the remaining $5400, the bank brought this action to collect it.

* * *

The main issue in this appeal is whether the bank had the authority to cash the check drawn by Tenn, in the absence of express authorization to do so. We agree with the trial court that the bank had such authority. The authority was impliedly given by the drawing of the check and its delivery to the payee. This result is in accord with the majority of cases in the United States. Furthermore, it is the view taken by the Uniform Commercial Code, Section 4–401 (1), adopted in Hawaii and applicable to all transactions arising after January 1, 1967.

* * *

Affirmed.

PROBLEMS

1. D drew a check on June 1 payable to P. P negotiated to an H.D.C. The H.D.C. presented the check to the drawee bank on June 10. The drawee dishonored the check. The H.D.C. did not give D or P notice of dishonor. D and P claim that failure to give due notice of dishonor is an absolute discharge of their liability. Decision?

2. The H.D.C. of a check that had been dishonored sent notice of the dishonor to the drawer by a properly stamped and addressed envelope deposited in a United States Post Office Department box. The drawer states that he never received the notice. Was the notice valid?

3. The drawer of a check had it certified and then delivered it to P. P negotiated it to H.D.C. The drawer and P now claim they are discharged of liability by the certification. Decision?

4. The payee of a note indorsed it to H. H, without consent of the payee, extended the time for payment of the note. The maker failed to pay so H looks to the payee for payment. Decision?

5. The drawer of a check for $50.00 delivered it to P. P negotiated it to H. H fraudulently altered the check by raising it to $500.00 and negotiated it to H.D.C. What are the rights of the parties?

6. A check was forged, negotiated, and paid by the drawee. The drawee debited the account of the purported drawer. A few days after the purported drawer received his bank statement and checks, he noticed

the forgery and complained to the bank demanding that the bank remove the debt. Decision?

7. The drawer of a check gave it to the payee in payment of some goods which proved defective. The payee had it certified and negotiated it to an H.D.C. The drawer then requested the bank to stop payment. The H.D.C. demands payment from the bank. Decision?

8. F, an employee in charge of payrolls at the X corporation, sets up a fictitious employee by the name of Robert Paul and makes out checks to him each month for six months. F signs the checks as Robert Paul and cashes them. The payor bank debits the X corporation's account not knowing of the forgeries. The X corporation claims the bank has no right to debit its account on forged checks. Decision?

9. The drawer of a check delivered it to the payee who negotiated it to H. H altered the check by increasing the amount from $50.00 to $500.00 and cashed it at the payor bank. The payor bank made a debit of the drawer's account in the amount of $500.00. The drawer promptly notified the bank of the alteration after he received his bank statement and checks. Does the bank have the right to debit the drawer's account for $500.00?

10. The drawer of a check in the amount of $5,000.00 delivered it to P who indorsed it to H. H took the check to the payor bank for collection. The drawer had only $4,000.00 in his account, but the bank paid H the sum of $5,000.00. The drawer refuses to pay the bank $1,000.00 since the bank had no authority to pay the additional sum. Decision?

APPENDIX A

THE UNIFORM COMMERCIAL CODE

(Adopted in 51 jurisdictions: District of Columbia, Virgin Islands, and 49 States, all except Louisiana)

The Code consists of 10 Articles as follows:

Art.
1. General Provisions
2. Sales.
3. Commercial Paper
4. Bank Deposits and Collections
5. Letters of Credit
6. Bulk Transfers
7. Warehouse Receipts, Bills of Lading and Other Documents of Title
8. Investment Securities
9. Secured Transactions: Sales of Accounts, Contract Rights and Chattel Paper
10. Effective Date and Repealer

1972 OFFICIAL TEXT

[Including all Amendments to July 1, 1972]

ARTICLE 1

GENERAL PROVISIONS

PART 1

SHORT TITLE, CONSTRUCTION, APPLICATION AND SUBJECT MATTER OF THE ACT

§ 1—101. Short Title.

This Act shall be known and may be cited as Uniform Commercial Code.

§ 1—102. Purposes; Rules of Construction; Variation by Agreement.

(1) This Act shall be liberally construed and applied to promote its underlying purposes and policies.

(2) Underlying purposes and policies of this Act are

(a) to simplify, clarify and modernize the law governing commercial transactions;

(b) to permit the continued expansion of commercial practices through custom, usage and agreement of the parties;

(c) to make uniform the law among the various jurisdictions.

(3) The effect of provisions of this Act may be varied by agreement, except as otherwise provided in this Act and except that the obligations of good faith, diligence, reasonableness and care prescribed by this Act may not be disclaimed by agreement but the parties may by agreement determine the standards by which the performance of such obligations is to be measured if such standards are not manifestly unreasonable.

(4) The presence in certain provisions of this Act of the words "unless otherwise agreed" or words of similar import does not imply that the effect of other provisions may not be varied by agreement under subsection (3).

(5) In this Act unless the context otherwise requires

(a) words in the singular number include the plural, and in the plural include the singular;

(b) words of the masculine gender include the feminine and the neuter, and when the sense so indicates words of the neuter gender may refer to any gender.

§ 1—103. Supplementary General Principles of Law Applicable.

Unless displaced by the particular provisions of this Act, the principles of law and equity, including the law merchant and the law relative to capacity to contract, principal and agent, estoppel, fraud, misrepresentation, duress, coercion, mistake, bankruptcy, or other validating or invalidating cause shall supplement its provisions.

§ 1—104. Construction Against Implicit Repeal.

This Act being a general act intended as a unified coverage of its subject matter, no part of it shall be deemed to be impliedly repealed by subsequent legislation if such construction can reasonably be avoided.

§ 1—105. Territorial Application of the Act; Parties' Power to Choose Applicable Law.

(1) Except as provided hereafter in this section, when a transaction bears a reasonable relation to this state and also to another state or nation the parties may agree that the law either of this state or of such other state or nation shall govern their rights and duties. Failing such agreement this Act applies to transactions bearing an appropriate relation to this state.

(2) Where one of the following provisions of this Act specifies the applicable law, that provision governs and a contrary agreement is effective only to the extent permitted by the law (including the conflict of laws rules) so specified:

Rights of creditors against sold goods. Section 2—402.

Applicability of the Article on Bank Deposits and Collections. Section 4—102.

Bulk transfers subject to the Article on Bulk Transfers. Section 6—102.

Applicability of the Article on Investment Securities. Section 8—106.

Perfection provisions of the Article on Secured Transactions. Section 9—103.

§ 1—106. Remedies to Be Liberally Administered.

(1) The remedies provided by this Act shall be liberally administered to the end that the aggrieved party may be put in as good a position as if the other party had fully performed but neither consequential or special nor penal damages may be had except as specifically provided in this Act or by other rule of law.

(2) Any right or obligation declared by this Act is enforceable by action unless the provision declaring it specifies a different and limited effect.

§ 1—107. Waiver or Renunciation of Claim or Right After Breach.

Any claim or right arising out of an alleged breach can be discharged in whole or in part without consideration by a written waiver or renunciation signed and delivered by the aggrieved party.

§ 1—108. Severability.

If any provision or clause of this Act or application thereof to any person or circumstances is held invalid, such invalidity shall not affect other provisions or applications of the Act which can be given effect without the invalid provision or application, and to this end the provisions of this Act are declared to be severable.

§ 1—109. Section Captions.

Section captions are parts of this Act.

PART 2

GENERAL DEFINITIONS AND PRINCIPLES OF INTERPRETATION

§ 1—201. General Definitions.

Subject to additional definitions contained in the subsequent Articles of this Act which are applicable to specific Articles or Parts thereof, and unless the context otherwise requires, in this Act:

(1) "Action" in the sense of a judicial proceeding includes recoupment, counterclaim, set-off, suit in equity and any other proceedings in which rights are determined.

(2) "Aggrieved party" means a party entitled to resort to a remedy.

(3) "Agreement" means the bargain of the parties in fact as found in their language or by implication from other circumstances including course of dealing or usage of trade or course of performance as provided in this Act (Sections 1—205 and 2—208). Whether an agreement has legal consequences is determined by the provisions of this Act, if applicable; otherwise by the law of contracts (Section 1—103). (Compare "Contract".)

(4) "Bank" means any person engaged in the business of banking.

(5) "Bearer" means the person in possession of an instrument, document of title, or security payable to bearer or indorsed in blank.

(6) "Bill of lading" means a document evidencing the receipt of goods for shipment issued by a person engaged in the business of transporting or forwarding goods, and includes an airbill. "Airbill" means a document serving for air transportation as a bill of lading does for marine or rail transportation, and includes an air consignment note or air waybill.

(7) "Branch" includes a separately incorporated foreign branch of a bank.

(8) "Burden of establishing" a fact means the burden of persuading the triers of fact that the existence of the fact is more probable than its non-existence.

(9) "Buyer in ordinary course of business" means a person who in good faith and without knowledge that the sale to him is in violation of the ownership rights or security interest of a third party in the goods buys in ordinary course from a person in the business of selling goods of that kind but does not include a pawnbroker. All persons who sell minerals or the like (including oil and gas) at wellhead or minehead shall be deemed to be persons in the business of selling goods of that kind. "Buying" may be for cash or by exchange of other property or on secured or unsecured credit and includes receiving goods or documents of title under a pre-existing contract for sale but does not include a transfer in bulk or as security for or in total or partial satisfaction of a money debt.

(10) "Conspicuous": A term or clause is conspicuous when it is so written that a reasonable person against whom it is to operate ought to have noticed it. A printed heading in capitals (as: NON-NEGOTIABLE BILL OF LADING) is conspicuous. Language in the body of a form is "conspicuous" if it is in larger or other contrasting type or color. But in a telegram any stated term is "conspicuous". Whether a term or clause is "conspicuous" or not is for decision by the court.

(11) "Contract" means the total legal obligation which results from the parties' agreement as affected by this Act and any other applicable rules of law. (Compare "Agreement".)

(12) "Creditor" includes a general creditor, a secured creditor, a lien creditor and any representative of creditors, including an assignee for the benefit of creditors, a trustee in bankruptcy, a receiver in equity and an executor or administrator of an insolvent debtor's or assignor's estate.

(13) "Defendant" includes a person in the position of defendant in a cross-action or counterclaim.

(14) "Delivery" with respect to instruments, documents of title, chattel paper or securities means voluntary transfer of possession.

(15) "Document of title" includes bill of lading, dock warrant, dock receipt, warehouse receipt or order for the delivery of goods, and also any other document which in the regular course of business or financing is treated as adequately evidencing that the person in possession of it is entitled to receive, hold and dispose of the document and the goods it covers. To be a document of title a document must purport to be issued by or addressed to a bailee and purport to cover goods in the bailee's possession which are either identified or are fungible portions of an identified mass.

(16) "Fault" means wrongful act, omission or breach.

(17) "Fungible" with respect to goods or securities means goods or securities of which any unit is, by nature or usage of trade, the equivalent of any other like unit. Goods which are not fungible shall be deemed fungible for the purposes of this Act to the extent that under a particular agreement or document unlike units are treated as equivalents.

(18) "Genuine" means free of forgery or counterfeiting.

(19) "Good faith" means honesty in fact in the conduct or transaction concerned.

(20) "Holder" means a person who is in possession of a document of title or an instrument or an investment security drawn, issued or indorsed to him or to his order or to bearer or in blank.

(21) To "honor" is to pay or to accept and pay, or where a credit so engages to purchase or discount a draft complying with the terms of the credit.

(22) "Insolvency proceedings" includes any assignment for the benefit of creditors or other proceedings intended to liquidate or rehabilitate the estate of the person involved.

(23) A person is "insolvent" who either has ceased to pay his debts in the ordinary course of business or cannot pay his debts as they become due or is insolvent within the meaning of the federal bankruptcy law.

(24) "Money" means a medium of exchange authorized or adopted by a domestic or foreign government as a part of its currency.

(25) A person has "notice" of a fact when

(a) he has actual knowledge of it; or

(b) he has received a notice or notification of it; or

(c) from all the facts and circumstances known to him at the time in question he has reason to know that it exists.

A person "knows" or has "knowledge" of a fact when he has actual knowledge of it. "Discover" or "learn" or a word or phrase of similar import refers to knowledge rather than to reason to know. The time and circumstances under which a notice or notification may cease to be effective are not determined by this Act.

(26) A person "notifies" or "gives" a notice or notification to another by taking such steps as may be reasonably required to inform the other in ordinary course whether or not such other actually comes to know of it. A person "receives" a notice or notification when

(a) it comes to his attention; or

(b) it is duly delivered at the place of business through which the contract was made or at any other place held out by him as the place for receipt of such communications.

(27) Notice, knowledge or a notice or notification received by an organization is effective for a particular transaction from the time when it is brought to the attention of the individual conducting that transaction, and in any event from the time when it would have been brought to his attention if the organization had exercised due diligence. An organization exercises due diligence if it maintains reasonable routines for communicating significant information to the person conducting the transaction and there is reasonable compliance with the routines. Due diligence does not require an individual acting for the organization to communicate information unless such communication is part of his regular duties or unless he has reason to know of the transaction and that the transaction would be materially affected by the information.

(28) "Organization" includes a corporation, government or governmental subdivision or agency, business trust, estate, trust, partnership or association, two or more persons having a joint or common interest, or any other legal or commercial entity.

(29) "Party", as distinct from "third party", means a person who has engaged in a transaction or made an agreement within this Act.

(30) "Person" includes an individual or an organization (See Section 1—102).

(31) "Presumption" or "presumed" means that the trier of fact must find the existence of the fact presumed unless and until evidence is introduced which would support a finding of its nonexistence.

(32) "Purchase" includes taking by sale, discount, negotiation, mortgage, pledge, lien, issue or re-issue, gift or any other voluntary transaction creating an interest in property.

(33) "Purchaser" means a person who takes by purchase.

(34) "Remedy" means any remedial right to which an aggrieved party is entitled with or without resort to a tribunal.

(35) "Representative" includes an agent, an officer of a corporation or association, and a trustee, executor or administrator of an estate, or any other person empowered to act for another.

(36) "Rights" includes remedies.

(37) "Security interest" means an interest in personal property or fixtures which secures payment or performance of an obligation. The retention or reservation of title by a seller of goods notwithstanding shipment or delivery to the buyer (Section 2—401) is limited in effect to a reservation of a "security interest". The term also includes any interest of a buyer of accounts or chattel paper which is subject to Article 9. The special property interest of a buyer of goods on identification of such goods to a contract for sale under Section 2—401 is not a "security interest", but a buyer may also acquire a "security interest" by complying with Article 9. Unless a lease or consignment is intended as security, reservation of title thereunder is not a "security interest" but a consignment is in any event subject to the provisions on consignment sales (Section 2—326). Whether a lease is intended as security is to be determined by the facts of each case; however, (a) the inclusion of an option to purchase does not of itself make the lease one intended for security, and (b) an agreement that upon compliance with the terms of the lease the lessee shall become or has the option to become the owner of the property for no additional consideration or for a nominal consideration does make the lease one intended for security.

(38) "Send" in connection with any writing or notice means to deposit in the mail or deliver for transmission by any other usual means of communication with postage or cost of transmission provided for and properly addressed and in the case of an instrument to an address specified thereon or otherwise agreed, or if there be none to any address reasonable under the circumstances. The receipt of any writing or notice within the time at which it would have arrived if properly sent has the effect of a proper sending.

(39) "Signed" includes any symbol executed or adopted by a party with present intention to authenticate a writing.

(40) "Surety" includes guarantor.

(41) "Telegram" includes a message transmitted by radio, teletype, cable, any mechanical method of transmission, or the like.

(42) "Term" means that portion of an agreement which relates to a particular matter.

(43) "Unauthorized" signature or indorsement means one made without actual, implied or apparent authority and includes a forgery.

(44) "Value". Except as otherwise provided with respect to negotiable instruments and bank collections (Sections 3—303, 4—208 and 4—209) a person gives "value" for rights if he acquires them

(a) in return for a binding commitment to extend credit or for the extension of immediately available credit whether or not drawn upon and whether or not a charge-back is provided for in the event of difficulties in collection; or

(b) as security for or in total or partial satisfaction of a pre-existing claim; or

(c) by accepting delivery pursuant to a pre-existing contract for purchase; or

(d) generally, in return for any consideration sufficient to support a simple contract.

(45) "Warehouse receipt" means a receipt issued by a person engaged in the business of storing goods for hire.

(46) "Written" or "writing" includes printing, typewriting or any other intentional reduction to tangible form.

§ 1—202. Prima Facie Evidence by Third Party Documents.

A document in due form purporting to be a bill of lading, policy or certificate of insurance, official weigher's or inspector's certificate, consular invoice, or any other document authorized or required by the contract to be issued by a third party shall be prima facie evidence of its own authenticity and genuineness and of the facts stated in the document by the third party.

§ 1—203. Obligation of Good Faith.

Every contract or duty within this Act imposes an obligation of good faith in its performance or enforcement.

§ 1—204. Time; Reasonable Time; "Seasonably".

(1) Whenever this Act requires any action to be taken within a reasonable time, any time which is not manifestly unreasonable may be fixed by agreement.

(2) What is a reasonable time for taking any action depends on the nature, purpose and circumstances of such action.

(3) An action is taken "seasonably" when it is taken at or within the time agreed or if no time is agreed at or within a reasonable time.

§ 1—205. Course of Dealing and Usage of Trade.

(1) A course of dealing is a sequence of previous conduct between the parties to a particular transaction which is fairly to be regarded as establishing a common basis of understanding for interpreting their expressions and other conduct.

(2) A usage of trade is any practice or method of dealing having such regularity of observance in a place, vocation or trade as to justify an expectation that it will be observed with respect to the transaction in question. The existence and scope of such a usage are to be proved as facts. If it is established that such a usage is embodied in a written trade code or similar writing the interpretation of the writing is for the court.

(3) A course of dealing between parties and any usage of trade in the vocation or trade in which they are engaged or of which they are or should be aware give particular meaning to and supplement or qualify terms of an agreement.

(4) The express terms of an agreement and an applicable course of dealing or usage of trade shall be construed wherever reasonable as consistent with each other; but when such construction is unreasonable express terms control both course of dealing and usage of trade and course of dealing controls usage of trade.

(5) An applicable usage of trade in the place where any part of performance is to occur shall be used in interpreting the agreement as to that part of the performance.

(6) Evidence of a relevant usage of trade offered by one party is not admissible unless and until he has given the other party such notice as the court finds sufficient to prevent unfair surprise to the latter.

§ 1—206. Statute of Frauds for Kinds of Personal Property Not Otherwise Covered.

(1) Except in the cases described in subsection (2) of this section a contract for the sale of personal property is not enforceable by way of action or defense beyond five thousand dollars in amount or value of remedy unless there is some writing which indicates that a contract for sale has been made between the parties at a defined or stated price, reasonably identifies the subject matter, and is signed by the party against whom enforcement is sought or by his authorized agent.

(2) Subsection (1) of this section does not apply to contracts for the sale of goods (Section 2—201) nor of securities (Section 8—319) nor to security agreements (Section 9—203).

§ 1—207. Performance or Acceptance Under Reservation of Rights.

A party who with explicit reservation of rights performs or promises performance or assents to performance in a manner demanded or offered by the other party does not thereby prejudice the rights reserved. Such words as "without prejudice", "under protest" or the like are sufficient.

§ 1—208. Option to Accelerate at Will.

A term providing that one party or his successor in interest may accelerate payment or performance or require collateral or additional collateral "at will" or "when he deems himself insecure" or in words of similar import shall be construed to mean that he shall have power to do so only if he in good faith believes that the prospect of payment or performance is impaired. The burden of establishing lack of good faith is on the party against whom the power has been exercised.

ARTICLE 2

SALES

PART 1

SHORT TITLE, CONSTRUCTION AND SUBJECT MATTER

§ 2—101. Short Title.

This Article shall be known and may be cited as Uniform Commercial Code—Sales.

§ 2—102. Scope; Certain Security and Other Transactions Excluded From This Article.

Unless the context otherwise requires, this Article applies to transactions in goods; it does not apply to any transaction which although in the form of an unconditional contract to sell or present sale is intended to operate only as a security transaction nor does this Article impair or repeal any statute regulating sales to consumers, farmers or other specified classes of buyers.

§ 2—103. Definitions and Index of Definitions.

(1) In this Article unless the context otherwise requires

(a) "Buyer" means a person who buys or contracts to buy goods.

(b) "Good faith" in the case of a merchant means honesty in fact and the observance of reasonable commercial standards of fair dealing in the trade.

(c) "Receipt" of goods means taking physical possession of them.

(d) "Seller" means a person who sells or contracts to sell goods.

(2) Other definitions applying to this Article or to specified Parts thereof, and the sections in which they appear are:

"Acceptance". Section 2—606.
"Banker's credit". Section 2—325.
"Between merchants". Section 2—104.
"Cancellation". Section 2—106(4).
"Commercial unit". Section 2—105.
"Confirmed credit". Section 2—325.
"Conforming to contract". Section 2—106.
"Contract for sale". Section 2—106.
"Cover". Section 2—712.
"Entrusting". Section 2—403.
"Financing agency". Section 2—104.
"Future goods". Section 2—105.
"Goods". Section 2—105.
"Identification". Section 2—501.
"Installment contract". Section 2—612.
"Letter of Credit". Section 2—325.
"Lot". Section 2—105.
"Merchant". Section 2—104.
"Overseas". Section 2—323.
"Person in position of seller". Section 2—707.
"Present sale". Section 2—106.
"Sale". Section 2—106.
"Sale on approval". Section 2—326.
"Sale or return". Section 2—326.
"Termination". Section 2—106.

(3) The following definitions in other Articles apply to this Article:

"Check". Section 3—104.
"Consignee". Section 7—102.
"Consignor". Section 7—102.
"Consumer goods". Section 9—109.
"Dishonor". Section 3—507.
"Draft". Section 3—104.

(4) In addition Article 1 contains general definitions and principles of construction and interpretation applicable throughout this Article.

§ 2—104. Definitions: "Merchant"; "Between Merchants"; "Financing Agency".

(1) "Merchant" means a person who deals in goods of the kind or otherwise by his occupation holds himself out as having knowledge or skill peculiar to the practices or goods involved in the transaction or to whom such knowledge or skill may be attributed by his employment of an agent or broker or other intermediary who by his occupation holds himself out as having such knowledge or skill.

(2) "Financing agency" means a bank, finance company or other person who in the ordinary course of business makes advances against goods or documents of title or who by arrangement with either the seller or the buyer intervenes in ordinary course to make or collect payment due or claimed under the contract for sale, as by purchasing or paying the seller's draft or making advances against it or by merely taking it for collection whether or not documents of title accompany the draft. "Financing agency" includes also a bank or other person who similarly intervenes between persons who are in the position of seller and buyer in respect to the goods (Section 2—707).

(3) "Between merchants" means in any transaction with respect to which both parties are chargeable with the knowledge or skill of merchants.

§ 2—105. Definitions: Transferability; "Goods"; "Future" Goods; "Lot"; "Commercial Unit".

(1) "Goods" means all things (including specially manufactured goods) which are movable at the time of identification to the contract for sale other than the money in which the price is to be paid, investment securities (Article 8) and things in action. "Goods" also includes the unborn young of animals and growing crops and other identified things attached to realty as described in the section on goods to be severed from realty (Section 2—107).

(2) Goods must be both existing and identified before any interest in them can pass. Goods which are not both existing and identified are "future" goods. A purported present sale of future goods or of any interest therein operates as a contract to sell.

(3) There may be a sale of a part interest in existing identified goods.

(4) An undivided share in an identified bulk of fungible goods is sufficiently identified to be sold although the quantity of the bulk is not determined. Any agreed proportion of such a bulk or any quantity thereof agreed upon by number, weight or other measure may to the extent of the seller's interest in the bulk be sold to the buyer who then becomes an owner in common.

(5) "Lot" means a parcel or a single article which is the subject matter of a separate sale or delivery, whether or not it is sufficient to perform the contract.

(6) "Commercial unit" means such a unit of goods as by commercial usage is a single whole for purposes of sale and division of which materially impairs its character or value on the market or in use. A commercial unit may be a single article (as a machine) or a set of articles (as a suite of furniture or an assortment of sizes) or a quantity (as a bale, gross, or carload) or any other unit treated in use or in the relevant market as a single whole.

§ 2—106. Definitions: "Contract"; "Agreement"; "Contract for Sale"; "Sale"; "Present Sale"; "Conforming" to Contract; "Termination"; "Cancellation".

(1) In this Article unless the context otherwise requires "contract" and "agreement" are limited to those relating to the present or future sale of goods. "Contract for sale" includes both a present sale of goods and a contract to sell goods at a future time. A "sale" consists in the passing of title from the seller to the buyer for a price (Section 2—401). A "present sale" means a sale which is accomplished by the making of the contract.

(2) Goods or conduct including any part of a performance are "conforming" or conform to the contract when they are in accordance with the obligations under the contract.

(3) "Termination" occurs when either party pursuant to a power created by agreement or law puts an end to the contract otherwise than for its breach. On "termination" all obligations which are still executory on both sides are discharged but any right based on prior breach or performance survives.

(4) "Cancellation" occurs when either party puts an end to the contract for breach by the other and its effect is the same as that of

"termination" except that the cancelling party also retains any remedy for breach of the whole contract or any unperformed balance.

§ 2—107. Goods to Be Severed From Realty: Recording.

(1) A contract for the sale of minerals or the like (including oil and gas) or a structure or its materials to be removed from realty is a contract for the sale of goods within this Article if they are to be severed by the seller but until severance a purported present sale thereof which is not effective as a transfer of an interest in land is effective only as a contract to sell.

(2) A contract for the sale apart from the land of growing crops or other things attached to realty and capable of severance without material harm thereto but not described in subsection (1) or of timber to be cut is a contract for the sale of goods within this Article whether the subject matter is to be severed by the buyer or by the seller even though it forms part of the realty at the time of contracting, and the parties can by identification effect a present sale before severance.

(3) The provisions of this section are subject to any third party rights provided by the law relating to realty records, and the contract for sale may be executed and recorded as a document transferring an interest in land and shall then constitute notice to third parties of the buyer's rights under the contract for sale.

PART 2

FORM, FORMATION AND READJUSTMENT OF CONTRACT

§ 2—201. Formal Requirements; Statute of of Frauds.

(1) Except as otherwise provided in this section a contract for the sale of goods for the price of $500 or more is not enforceable by way of action or defense unless there is some writing sufficient to indicate that a contract for sale has been made between the parties and signed by the party against whom enforcement is sought or by his authorized agent or broker. A writing is not insufficient because it omits or incorrectly states a term agreed upon but the contract is not enforceable under this paragraph beyond the quantity of goods shown in such writing.

(2) Between merchants if within a reasonable time a writing in confirmation of the contract and sufficient against the sender is received and the party receiving it has reason to know its contents, it satisfies the requirements of subsection (1) against such party unless written notice of objection to its contents is given within ten days after it is received.

(3) A contract which does not satisfy the requirements of subsection (1) but which is valid in other respects is enforceable

(a) if the goods are to be specially manufactured for the buyer and are not suitable for sale to others in the ordinary course of the seller's business and the seller, before notice of repudiation is received and under circumstances which reasonably indicate that the goods are for the buyer, has made either a substantial beginning of their manufacture or commitments for their procurement; or

(b) if the party against whom enforcement is sought admits in his pleading, testimony or otherwise in court that a contract for sale was made, but the contract is not enforceable under this provision beyond the quantity of goods admitted; or

(c) with respect to goods for which payment has been made and accepted or which have been received and accepted (Sec. 2—606).

§ 2—202. Final Written Expression: Parol or Extrinsic Evidence.

Terms with respect to which the confirmatory memoranda of the parties agree or which are otherwise set forth in a writing intended by the parties as a final expression of their agreement with respect to such terms as are included therein may not be contradicted by evidence of any prior agreement or of a contemporaneous oral agreement but may be explained or supplemented

(a) by course of dealing or usage of trade (Section 1—205) or by course of performance (Section 2—208); and

(b) by evidence of consistent additional terms unless the court finds the writing to have been intended also as a complete and exclusive statement of the terms of the agreement.

§ 2—203. Seals Inoperative.

The affixing of a seal to a writing evidencing a contract for sale or an offer to buy or sell goods does not constitute the writing a sealed instrument and the law with respect to sealed instruments does not apply to such a contract or offer.

§ 2—204. Formation in General.

(1) A contract for sale of goods may be made in any manner sufficient to show agreement, including conduct by both parties which recognizes the existence of such a contract.

(2) An agreement sufficient to constitute a contract for sale may be found even though the moment of its making is undetermined.

(3) Even though one or more terms are left open a contract for sale does not fail for indefiniteness if the parties have intended to make a contract and there is a reasonably certain basis for giving an appropriate remedy.

§ 2—205. Firm Offers.

An offer by a merchant to buy or sell goods in a signed writing which by its terms gives assurance that it will be held open is not revocable, for lack of consideration, during the time stated or if no time is stated for a reasonable time, but in no event may such period of irrevocability exceed three months; but any such term of assurance on a form supplied by the offeree must be separately signed by the offeror.

§ 2—206. Offer and Acceptance in Formation of Contract.

(1) Unless otherwise unambiguously indicated by the language or circumstances

(a) an offer to make a contract shall be construed as inviting acceptance in any manner and by any medium reasonable in the circumstances;

(b) an order or other offer to buy goods for prompt or current shipment shall be construed as inviting acceptance either by a prompt promise to ship or by the prompt or current shipment of conforming or nonconforming goods, but such a shipment of non-conforming goods does not constitute an acceptance if the seller seasonably notifies the buyer that the shipment is offered only as an accommodation to the buyer.

(2) Where the beginning of a requested performance is a reasonable mode of acceptance an offeror who is not notified of acceptance within a reasonable time may treat the offer as having lapsed before acceptance.

§ 2—207. Additional Terms in Acceptance or Confirmation.

(1) A definite and seasonable expression of acceptance or a written confirmation which is sent within a reasonable time operates as an acceptance even though it states terms additional to or different from those offered or agreed upon, unless acceptance is expressly made conditional on assent to the additional or different terms.

(2) The additional terms are to be construed as proposals for addition to the contract. Between merchants such terms become part of the contract unless:

(a) the offer expressly limits acceptance to the terms of the offer;

(b) they materially alter it; or

(c) notification of objection to them has already been given or is given within a reasonable time after notice of them is received.

(3) Conduct by both parties which recognizes the existence of a contract is sufficient to establish a contract for sale although the writings of the parties do not otherwise establish a contract. In such case the terms of the particular contract consist of those terms on which the writings of the parties agree, together with any supplementary terms incorporated under any other provisions of this Act.

§ 2—208. Course of Performance or Practical Construction.

(1) Where the contract for sale involves repeated occasions for performance by either party with knowledge of the nature of the performance and opportunity for objection to it by the other, any course of performance accepted or acquiesced in without objection shall be relevant to determine the meaning of the agreement.

(2) The express terms of the agreement and any such course of performance, as well as any

course of dealing and usage of trade, shall be construed whenever reasonable as consistent with each other; but when such construction is unreasonable, express terms shall control course of performance and course of performance shall control both course of dealing and usage of trade (Section 1—205).

(3) Subject to the provisions of the next section on modification and waiver, such course of performance shall be relevant to show a waiver or modification of any term inconsistent with such course of performance.

§ 2—209. Modification, Rescission and Waiver.

(1) An agreement modifying a contract within this Article needs no consideration to be binding.

(2) A signed agreement which excludes modification or rescission except by a signed writing cannot be otherwise modified or rescinded, but except as between merchants such a requirement on a form supplied by the merchant must be separately signed by the other party.

(3) The requirements of the statute of frauds section of this Article (Section 2—201) must be satisfied if the contract as modified is within its provisions.

(4) Although an attempt at modification or rescission does not satisfy the requirements of subsection (2) or (3) it can operate as a waiver.

(5) A party who has made a waiver affecting an executory portion of the contract may retract the waiver by reasonable notification received by the other party that strict performance will be required of any term waived, unless the retraction would be unjust in view of a material change of position in reliance on the waiver.

§ 2—210. Delegation of Performance; Assignment of Rights.

(1) A party may perform his duty through a delegate unless otherwise agreed or unless the other party has a substantial interest in having his original promisor perform or control the acts required by the contract. No delegation of performance relieves the party delegating of any duty to perform or any liability for breach.

(2) Unless otherwise agreed all rights of either seller or buyer can be assigned except where the assignment would materially change the duty of the other party, or increase materially the burden or risk imposed on him by his contract, or impair materially his chance of obtaining return performance. A right to damages for breach of the whole contract or a right arising out of the assignor's due performance of his entire obligation can be assigned despite agreement otherwise.

(3) Unless the circumstances indicate the contrary a prohibition of assignment of "the contract" is to be construed as barring only the delegation to the assignee of the assignor's performance.

(4) An assignment of "the contract" or of "all my rights under the contract" or an assignment in similar general terms is an assignment of rights and unless the language or the circumstances (as in an assignment for security) indicate the contrary, it is a delegation of performance of the duties of the assignor and its acceptance by the assignee constitutes a promise by him to perform those duties. This promise is enforceable by either the assignor or the other party to the original contract.

(5) The other party may treat any assignment which delegates performance as creating reasonable grounds for insecurity and may without prejudice to his rights against the assignor demand assurances from the assignee (Section 2—609).

PART 3

GENERAL OBLIGATION AND CONSTRUCTION OF CONTRACT

§ 2—301. General Obligations of Parties.

The obligation of the seller is to transfer and deliver and that of the buyer is to accept and pay in accordance with the contract.

§ 2—302. Unconscionable Contract or Clause.

(1) If the court as a matter of law finds the contract or any clause of the contract to have been unconscionable at the time it was made

the court may refuse to enforce the contract, or it may enforce the remainder of the contract without the unconscionable clause, or it may so limit the application of any unconscionable clause as to avoid any unconscionable result.

(2) When it is claimed or appears to the court that the contract or any clause thereof may be unconscionable the parties shall be afforded a reasonable opportunity to present evidence as to its commercial setting, purpose and effect to aid the court in making the determination.

§ 2—303. Allocation or Division of Risks.

Where this Article allocates a risk or a burden as between the parties "unless otherwise agreed", the agreement may not only shift the allocation but may also divide the risk or burden.

§ 2—304. Price Payable in Money, Goods, Realty, or Otherwise.

(1) The price can be made payable in money or otherwise. If it is payable in whole or in part in goods each party is a seller of the goods which he is to transfer.

(2) Even though all or part of the price is payable in an interest in realty the transfer of the goods and the seller's obligations with reference to them are subject to this Article, but not the transfer of the interest in realty or the transferor's obligations in connection therewith.

§ 2—305. Open Price Term.

(1) The parties if they so intend can conclude a contract for sale even though the price is not settled. In such a case the price is a reasonable price at the time for delivery if

(a) nothing is said as to price; or

(b) the price is left to be agreed by the parties and they fail to agree; or

(c) the price is to be fixed in terms of some agreed market or other standard as set or recorded by a third person or agency and it is not so set or recorded.

(2) A price to be fixed by the seller or by the buyer means a price for him to fix in good faith.

(3) When a price left to be fixed otherwise than by agreement of the parties fails to be fixed through fault of one party the other may at his option treat the contract as cancelled or himself fix a reasonable price.

(4) Where, however, the parties intend not to be bound unless the price be fixed or agreed and it is not fixed or agreed there is no contract. In such a case the buyer must return any goods already received or if unable so to do must pay their reasonable value at the time of delivery and the seller must return any portion of the price paid on account.

§ 2—306. Output, Requirements and Exclusive Dealings.

(1) A term which measures the quantity by the output of the seller or the requirements of the buyer means such actual output or requirements as may occur in good faith, except that no quantity unreasonably disproportionate to any stated estimate or in the absence of a stated estimate to any normal or otherwise comparable prior output or requirements may be tendered or demanded.

(2) A lawful agreement by either the seller or the buyer for exclusive dealing in the kind of goods concerned imposes unless otherwise agreed an obligation by the seller to use best efforts to supply the goods and by the buyer to use best efforts to promote their sale.

§ 2—307. Delivery in Single Lot or Several Lots.

Unless otherwise agreed all goods called for by a contract for sale must be tendered in a single delivery and payment is due only on such tender but where the circumstances give either party the right to make or demand delivery in lots the price if it can be apportioned may be demanded for each lot.

§ 2—308. Absence of Specified Place for Delivery.

Unless otherwise agreed

(a) the place for delivery of goods is the seller's place of business or if he has none his residence; but

(b) in a contract for sale of identified goods which to the knowledge of the parties at the time of contracting are in some other place, that place is the place for their delivery; and

(c) documents of title may be delivered through customary banking channels.

§ 2—309. Absence of Specific Time Provisions; Notice of Termination.

(1) The time for shipment or delivery or any other action under a contract if not provided in this Article or agreed upon shall be a reasonable time.

(2) Where the contract provides for successive performances but is indefinite in duration it is valid for a reasonable time but unless otherwise agreed may be terminated at any time by either party.

(3) Termination of a contract by one party except on the happening of an agreed event requires that reasonable notification be received by the other party and an agreement dispensing with notification is invalid if its operation would be unconscionable.

§ 2—310. Open Time for Payment or Running of Credit; Authority to Ship Under Reservation.

Unless otherwise agreed

(a) payment is due at the time and place at which the buyer is to receive the goods even though the place of shipment is the place of delivery; and

(b) if the seller is authorized to send the goods he may ship them under reservation, and may tender the documents of title, but the buyer may inspect the goods after their arrival before payment is due unless such inspection is inconsistent with the terms of the contract (Section 2—513); and

(c) if delivery is authorized and made by way of documents of title otherwise than by subsection (b) then payment is due at the time and place at which the buyer is to receive the documents regardless of where the goods are to be received; and

(d) where the seller is required or authorized to ship the goods on credit the credit period runs from the time of shipment but post-dating the invoice or delaying its dispatch will correspondingly delay the starting of the credit period.

§ 2—311. Options and Cooperation Respecting Performance.

(1) An agreement for sale which is otherwise sufficiently definite (subsection (3) of Section 2—204) to be a contract is not made invalid by the fact that it leaves particulars of performance to be specified by one of the parties. Any such specification must be made in good faith and within limits set by commercial reasonableness.

(2) Unless otherwise agreed specifications relating to assortment of the goods are at the buyer's option and except as otherwise provided in subsections (1) (c) and (3) of Section 2—319 specifications or arrangements relating to shipment are at the seller's option.

(3) Where such specification would materially affect the other party's performance but is not seasonably made or where one party's cooperation is necessary to the agreed performance of the other but is not seasonably forthcoming, the other party in addition to all other remedies

(a) is excused for any resulting delay in his own performance; and

(b) may also either proceed to perform in any reasonable manner or after the time for a material part of his own performance treat the failure to specify or to cooperate as a breach by failure to deliver or accept the goods.

§ 2—312. Warranty of Title and Against Infringement; Buyer's Obligation Against Infringement.

(1) Subject to subsection (2) there is in a contract for sale a warranty by the seller that

(a) the title conveyed shall be good, and its transfer rightful; and

(b) the goods shall be delivered free from any security interest or other lien or encumbrance of which the buyer at the time of contracting has no knowledge.

(2) A warranty under subsection (1) will be excluded or modified only by specific language or by circumstances which give the buyer reason to know that the person selling does not

claim title in himself or that he is purporting to sell only such right or title as he or a third person may have.

(3) Unless otherwise agreed a seller who is a merchant regularly dealing in goods of the kind warrants that the goods shall be delivered free of the rightful claim of any third person by way of infringement or the like but a buyer who furnishes specifications to the seller must hold the seller harmless against any such claim which arises out of compliance with the specifications.

§ 2—313. Express Warranties by Affirmation, Promise, Description, Sample.

(1) Express warranties by the seller are created as follows:

(a) Any affirmation of fact or promise made by the seller to the buyer which relates to the goods and becomes part of the basis of the bargain creates an express warranty that the goods shall conform to the affirmation or promise.

(b) Any description of the goods which is made part of the basis of the bargain creates an express warranty that the goods shall conform to the description.

(c) Any sample or model which is made part of the basis of the bargain creates an express warranty that the whole of the goods shall conform to the sample or model.

(2) It is not necessary to the creation of an express warranty that the seller use formal words such as "warrant" or "guarantee" or that he have a specific intention to make a warranty, but an affirmation merely of the value of the goods or a statement purporting to be merely the seller's opinion or commendation of the goods does not create a warranty.

§ 2—314. Implied Warranty: Merchantability; Usage of Trade.

(1) Unless excluded or modified (Section 2—316), a warranty that the goods shall be merchantable is implied in a contract for their sale if the seller is a merchant with respect to goods of that kind. Under this section the serving for value of food or drink to be consumed either on the premises or elsewhere is a sale.

(2) Goods to be merchantable must be at least such as

(a) pass without objection in the trade under the contract description; and

(b) in the case of fungible goods, are of fair average quality within the description; and

(c) are fit for the ordinary purposes for which such goods are used; and

(d) run, within the variations permitted by the agreement, of even kind, quality and quantity within each unit and among all units involved; and

(e) are adequately contained, packaged, and labeled as the agreement may require; and

(f) conform to the promises or affirmations of fact made on the container or label if any.

(3) Unless excluded or modified (Section 2—316) other implied warranties may arise from course of dealing or usage of trade.

§ 2—315. Implied Warranty: Fitness for Particular Purpose.

Where the seller at the time of contracting has reason to know any particular purpose for which the goods are required and that the buyer is relying on the seller's skill or judgment to select or furnish suitable goods, there is unless excluded or modified under the next section an implied warranty that the goods shall be fit for such purpose.

§ 2—316. Exclusion or Modification of Warranties.

(1) Words or conduct relevant to the creation of an express warranty and words or conduct tending to negate or limit warranty shall be construed wherever reasonable as consistent with each other; but subject to the provisions of this Article on parol or extrinsic evidence (Section 2—202) negation or limitation is inoperative to the extent that such construction is unreasonable.

(2) Subject to subsection (3), to exclude or modify the implied warranty of merchantability or any part of it the language must mention merchantability and in case of a writing

must be conspicuous, and to exclude or modify any implied warranty of fitness the exclusion must be by a writing and conspicuous. Language to exclude all implied warranties of fitness is sufficient if it states, for example, that "There are no warranties which extend beyond the description on the face hereof."

(3) Notwithstanding subsection (2)

(a) unless the circumstances indicate otherwise, all implied warranties are excluded by expressions like "as is", "with all faults" or other language which in common understanding calls the buyer's attention to the exclusion of warranties and makes plain that there is no implied warranty; and

(b) when the buyer before entering into the contract has examined the goods or the sample or model as fully as he desired or has refused to examine the goods there is no implied warranty with regard to defects which an examination ought in the circumstances to have revealed to him; and

(c) an implied warranty can also be excluded or modified by course of dealing or course of performance or usage of trade.

(4) Remedies for breach of warranty can be limited in accordance with the provisions of this Article on liquidation or limitation of damages and on contractual modification of remedy (Sections 2—718 and 2—719).

§ 2—317. Cumulation and Conflict of Warranties Express or Implied.

Warranties whether express or implied shall be construed as consistent with each other and as cumulative, but if such construction is unreasonable the intention of the parties shall determine which warranty is dominant. In ascertaining that intention the following rules apply:

(a) Exact or technical specifications displace an inconsistent sample or model or general language of description.

(b) A sample from an existing bulk displaces inconsistent general language of description.

(c) Express warranties displace inconsistent implied warranties other than an implied warranty of fitness for a particular purpose.

§ 2—318. Third Party Beneficiaries of Warranties Express or Implied.

A seller's warranty whether express or implied extends to any natural person who is in the family or household of his buyer or who is a guest in his home if it is reasonable to expect that such person may use, consume or be affected by the goods and who is injured in person by breach of the warranty. A seller may not exclude or limit the operation of this section.

§ 2—319. F.O.B. and F.A.S. Terms.

(1) Unless otherwise agreed the term F.O.B. (which means "free on board") at a named place, even though used only in connection with the stated price, is a delivery term under which

(a) when the term is F.O.B. the place of shipment, the seller must at that place ship the goods in the manner provided in this Article (Section 2—504) and bear the expense and risk of putting them into the possession of the carrier; or

(b) when the term is F.O.B. the place of destination, the seller must at his own expense and risk transport the goods to that place and there tender delivery of them in the manner provided in this Article (Section 2—503);

(c) when under either (a) or (b) the term is also F.O.B. vessel, car or other vehicle, the seller must in addition at his own expense and risk load the goods on board. If the term is F.O.B. vessel the buyer must name the vessel and in an appropriate case the seller must comply with the provisions of this Article on the form of bill of lading (Section 2—323).

(2) Unless otherwise agreed the term F.A.S. vessel (which means "free alongside") at a named port, even though used only in connection with the stated price, is a delivery term under which the seller must

(a) at his own expense and risk deliver the goods alongside the vessel in the manner usual in that port or on a dock designated and provided by the buyer; and

(b) obtain and tender a receipt for the goods in exchange for which the carrier is under a duty to issue a bill of lading.

(3) Unless otherwise agreed in any case falling within subsection (1) (a) or (c) or subsection (2) the buyer must seasonably give any needed instructions for making delivery, including when the term is F.A.S. or F.O.B. the loading berth of the vessel and in an appropriate case its name and sailing date. The seller may treat the failure of needed instructions as a failure of cooperation under this Article (Section 2—311). He may also at his option move the goods in any reasonable manner preparatory to delivery or shipment.

(4) Under the term F.O.B. vessel or F.A.S. unless otherwise agreed the buyer must make payment against tender of the required documents and the seller may not tender nor the buyer demand delivery of the goods in substitution for the documents.

§ 2—320. C.I.F. and C. & F. Terms.

(1) The term C.I.F. means that the price includes in a lump sum the cost of the goods and the insurance and freight to the named destination. The term C. & F. or C.F. means that the price so includes cost and freight to the named destination.

(2) Unless otherwise agreed and even though used only in connection with the stated price and destination, the term C.I.F. destination or its equivalent requires the seller at his own expense and risk to

(a) put the goods into the possession of a carrier at the port for shipment and obtain a negotiable bill or bills of lading covering the entire transportation to the named destination; and

(b) load the goods and obtain a receipt from the carrier (which may be contained in the bill of lading) showing that the freight has been paid or provided for; and

(c) obtain a policy or certificate of insurance, including any war risk insurance, of a kind and on terms then current at the port of shipment in the usual amount, in the currency of the contract, shown to cover the same goods covered by the bill of lading and providing for payment of loss to the order of the buyer or for the account of whom it may concern; but the seller may add to the price the amount of the premium for any such war risk insurance; and

(d) prepare an invoice of the goods and procure any other documents required to effect shipment or to comply with the contract; and

(e) forward and tender with commercial promptness all the documents in due form and with any indorsement necessary to perfect the buyer's rights.

(3) Unless otherwise agreed the term C. & F. or its equivalent has the same effect and imposes upon the seller the same obligations and risks as a C.I.F. term except the obligation as to insurance.

(4) Under the term C.I.F. or C. & F. unless otherwise agreed the buyer must make payment against tender of the required documents and the seller may not tender nor the buyer demand delivery of the goods in substitution for the documents.

§ 2—321. C.I.F. or C. & F.: "Net Landed Weights"; "Payment on Arrival"; Warranty of Condition on Arrival.

Under a contract containing a term C.I.F. or C. & F.

(1) Where the price is based on or is to be adjusted according to "net landed weights", "delivered weights", "out turn" quantity or quality or the like, unless otherwise agreed the seller must reasonably estimate the price. The payment due on tender of the documents called for by the contract is the amount so estimated, but after final adjustment of the price a settlement must be made with commercial promptness.

(2) An agreement described in subsection (1) or any warranty of quality or condition of the goods on arrival places upon the seller the risk of ordinary deterioration, shrinkage and the like in transportation but has no effect on the place or time of identification to the contract for sale or delivery or on the passing of the risk of loss.

(3) Unless otherwise agreed where the contract provides for payment on or after arrival of the goods the seller must before payment allow such preliminary inspection as is feasible; but if the goods are lost delivery of the documents and payment are due when the goods should have arrived.

§ 2—322. Delivery "Ex-Ship".

(1) Unless otherwise agreed a term for delivery of goods "ex-ship" (which means from the carrying vessel) or in equivalent language is not restricted to a particular ship and requires delivery from a ship which has reached a place at the named port of destination where goods of the kind are usually discharged.

(2) Under such a term unless otherwise agreed

(a) the seller must discharge all liens arising out of the carriage and furnish the buyer with a direction which puts the carrier under a duty to deliver the goods; and

(b) the risk of loss does not pass to the buyer until the goods leave the ship's tackle or are otherwise properly unloaded.

§ 2—323. Form of Bill of Lading Required in Overseas Shipment; "Overseas".

(1) Where the contract contemplates overseas shipment and contains a term C.I.F. or C. & F. or F.O.B. vessel, the seller unless otherwise agreed must obtain a negotiable bill of lading stating that the goods have been loaded on board or, in the case of a term C.I.F. or C. & F., received for shipment.

(2) Where in a case within subsection (1) a bill of lading has been issued in a set of parts, unless otherwise agreed if the documents are not to be sent from abroad the buyer may demand tender of the full set; otherwise only one part of the bill of lading need be tendered. Even if the agreement expressly requires a full set

(a) due tender of a single part is acceptable within the provisions of this Article on cure of improper delivery (subsection (1) of Section 2—508); and

(b) even though the full set is demanded, if the documents are sent from abroad the person tendering an incomplete set may nevertheless require payment upon furnishing an indemnity which the buyer in good faith deems adequate.

(3) A shipment by water or by air or a contract contemplating such shipment is "overseas" insofar as by usage of trade or agreement it is subject to the commercial, financing or shipping practices characteristic of international deep water commerce.

§ 2—324. "No Arrival, No Sale" Term.

Under a term "no arrival, no sale" or terms of like meaning, unless otherwise agreed,

(a) the seller must properly ship conforming goods and if they arrive by any means he must tender them on arrival but he assumes no obligation that the goods will arrive unless he has caused the non-arrival; and

(b) where without fault of the seller the goods are in part lost or have so deteriorated as no longer to conform to the contract or arrive after the contract time, the buyer may proceed as if there had been casualty to identified goods (Section 2—613).

§ 2—325. "Letter of Credit" Term; "Confirmed Credit".

(1) Failure of the buyer seasonably to furnish an agreed letter of credit is a breach of the contract for sale.

(2) The delivery to seller of a proper letter of credit suspends the buyer's obligation to pay. If the letter of credit is dishonored, the seller may on seasonable notification to the buyer require payment directly from him.

(3) Unless otherwise agreed the term "letter of credit" or "banker's credit" in a contract for sale means an irrevocable credit issued by a financing agency of good repute and, where the shipment is overseas, of good international repute. The term "confirmed credit" means that the credit must also carry the direct obli-

gation of such an agency which does business in the seller's financial market.

§ 2—326. Sale on Approval and Sale or Return; Consignment Sales and Rights of Creditors.

(1) Unless otherwise agreed, if delivered goods may be returned by the buyer even though they conform to the contract, the transaction is

(a) a "sale on approval" if the goods are delivered primarily for use, and

(b) a "sale or return" if the goods are delivered primarily for resale.

(2) Except as provided in subsection (3), goods held on approval are not subject to the claims of the buyer's creditors until acceptance; goods held on sale or return are subject to such claims while in the buyer's possession.

(3) Where goods are delivered to a person for sale and such person maintains a place of business at which he deals in goods of the kind involved, under a name other than the name of the person making delivery, then with respect to claims of creditors of the person conducting the business the goods are deemed to be on sale or return. The provisions of this subsection are applicable even though an agreement purports to reserve title to the person making delivery until payment or resale or uses such words as "on consignment" or "on memorandum". However, this subsection is not applicable if the person making delivery

(a) complies with an applicable law providing for a consignor's interest or the like to be evidenced by a sign, or

(b) establishes that the person conducting the business is generally known by his creditors to be substantially engaged in selling the goods of others, or

(c) complies with the filing provisions of the Article on Secured Transactions (Article 9).

(4) Any "or return" term of a contract for sale is to be treated as a separate contract for sale within the statute of frauds section of this Article (Section 2—201) and as contradicting the sale aspect of the contract within the provisions of this Article on parol or extrinsic evidence (Section 2—202).

§ 2—327. Special Incidents of Sale on Approval and Sale or Return.

(1) Under a sale on approval unless otherwise agreed

(a) although the goods are identified to the contract the risk of loss and the title do not pass to the buyer until acceptance; and

(b) use of the goods consistent with the purpose of trial is not acceptance but failure seasonably to notify the seller of election to return the goods is acceptance, and if the goods conform to the contract acceptance of any part is acceptance of the whole; and

(c) after due notification of election to return, the return is at the seller's risk and expense but a merchant buyer must follow any reasonable instructions.

(2) Under a sale or return unless otherwise agreed

(a) the option to return extends to the whole or any commercial unit of the goods while in substantially their original condition, but must be exercised seasonably; and

(b) the return is at the buyer's risk and expense.

§ 2—328. Sale by Auction.

(1) In a sale by auction if goods are put up in lots each lot is the subject of a separate sale.

(2) A sale by auction is complete when the auctioneer so announces by the fall of the hammer or in other customary manner. Where a bid is made while the hammer is falling in acceptance of a prior bid the auctioneer may in his discretion reopen the bidding or declare the goods sold under the bid on which the hammer was falling.

(3) Such a sale is with reserve unless the goods are in explicit terms put up without reserve. In an auction with reserve the auctioneer may withdraw the goods at any time until he announces completion of the sale. In an auction without reserve, after the auctioneer calls for bids on an article or lot, that article or lot cannot be withdrawn unless no bid is made within a reasonable time. In either case a bidder may retract his bid until the auction-

eer's announcement of completion of the sale, but a bidder's retraction does not revive any previous bid.

(4) If the auctioneer knowingly receives a bid on the seller's behalf or the seller makes or procures such a bid, and notice has not been given that liberty for such bidding is reserved, the buyer may at his option avoid the sale or take the goods at the price of the last good faith bid prior to the completion of the sale. This subsection shall not apply to any bid at a forced sale.

PART 4

TITLE, CREDITORS AND GOOD FAITH PURCHASERS

§ 2—401. Passing of Title; Reservation for Security; Limited Application of This Section.

Each provision of this Article with regard to the rights, obligations and remedies of the seller, the buyer, purchasers or other third parties applies irrespective of title to the goods except where the provision refers to such title. Insofar as situations are not covered by the other provisions of this Article and matters concerning title became material the following rules apply:

(1) Title to goods cannot pass under a contract for sale prior to their identification to the contract (Section 2—501), and unless otherwise explicitly agreed the buyer acquires by their identification a special property as limited by this Act. Any retention or reservation by the seller of the title (property) in goods shipped or delivered to the buyer is limited in effect to a reservation of a security interest. Subject to these provisions and to the provisions of the Article on Secured Transactions (Article 9), title to goods passes from the seller to the buyer in any manner and on any conditions explictly agreed on by the parties.

(2) Unless otherwise explicitly agreed title passes to the buyer at the time and place at which the seller completes his performance with reference to the physical delivery of the goods, despite any reservation of a security interest and even though a document of title is to be delivered at a different time or place; and in particular and despite any reservation of a security interest by the bill of lading

(a) if the contract requires or authorizes the seller to send the goods to the buyer but does not require him to deliver them at destination, title passes to the buyer at the time and place of shipment; but

(b) if the contract requires delivery at destination, title passes on tender there.

(3) Unless otherwise explicitly agreed where delivery is to be made without moving the goods,

(a) if the seller is to deliver a document of title, title passes at the time when and the place where he delivers such documents; or

(b) if the goods are at the time of contracting already identified and no documents are to be delivered, title passes at the time and place of contracting.

(4) A rejection or other refusal by the buyer to receive or retain the goods, whether or not justified, or a justified revocation of acceptance revests title to the goods in the seller. Such revesting occurs by operation of law and is not a "sale".

§ 2—402. Rights of Seller's Creditors Against Sold Goods.

(1) Except as provided in subsections (2) and (3), rights of unsecured creditors of the seller with respect to goods which have been identified to a contract for sale are subject to the buyer's rights to recover the goods under this Article (Sections 2—502 and 2—716).

(2) A creditor of the seller may treat a sale or an identification of goods to a contract for sale as void if as against him a retention of possession by the seller is fraudulent under any rule of law of the state where the goods are situated, except that retention of possession in good faith and current course of trade by a merchant-seller for a commercially reasonable time after a sale or identification is not fraudulent.

(3) Nothing in this Article shall be deemed to impair the rights of creditors of the seller

(a) under the provisions of the Article on Secured Transactions (Article 9); or

(b) where identification to the contract or delivery is made not in current course of trade but in satisfaction of or as security for a pre-existing claim for money, security or the like and is made under circumstances which under any rule of law of the state where the goods are situated would apart from this Article constitute the transaction a fraudulent transfer or voidable preference.

§ 2—403. Power to Transfer; Good Faith Purchase of Goods; "Entrusting".

(1) A purchaser of goods acquires all title which his transferor had or had power to transfer except that a purchaser of a limited interest acquires rights only to the extent of the interest purchased. A person with voidable title has power to transfer a good title to a good faith purchaser for value. When goods have been delivered under a transaction of purchase the purchaser has such power even though

(a) the transferor was deceived as to the identity of the purchaser, or

(b) the delivery was in exchange for a check which is later dishonored, or

(c) it was agreed that the transaction was to be a "cash sale", or

(d) the delivery was procured through fraud punishable as larcenous under the criminal law.

(2) Any entrusting of possession of goods to a merchant who deals in goods of that kind gives him power to transfer all rights of the entruster to a buyer in ordinary course of business.

(3) "Entrusting" includes any delivery and any acquiescence in retention of possession regardless of any condition expressed between the parties to the delivery or acquiescence and regardless of whether the procurement of the entrusting or the possessor's disposition of the goods have been such as to be larcenous under the criminal law.

(4) The rights of other purchasers of goods and of lien creditors are governed by the Articles on Secured Transactions (Article 9), Bulk Transfers (Article 6) and Documents of Title (Article 7).

PART 5

PERFORMANCE

§ 2—501. Insurable Interest in Goods; Manner of Identification of Goods.

(1) The buyer obtains a special property and an insurable interest in goods by identification of existing goods as goods to which the contract refers even though the goods so identified are non-conforming and he has an option to return or reject them. Such identification can be made at any time and in any manner explicitly agreed to by the parties. In the absence of explicit agreement identification occurs

(a) when the contract is made if it is for the sale of goods already existing and identified;

(b) if the contract is for the sale of future goods other than those described in paragraph (c), when goods are shipped, marked or otherwise designated by the seller as goods to which the contract refers;

(c) when the crops are planted or otherwise become growing crops or the young are conceived if the contract is for the sale of unborn young to be born within twelve months after contracting or for the sale of crops to be harvested within twelve months or the next normal harvest season after contracting whichever is longer.

(2) The seller retains an insurable interest in goods so long as title to or any security interest in the goods remains in him and where the identification is by the seller alone he may until default or insolvency or notification to the buyer that the identification is final substitute other goods for those identified.

(3) Nothing in this section impairs any insurable interest recognized under any other statute or rule of law.

§ 2—502. Buyer's Right to Goods on Seller's Insolvency.

(1) Subject to subsection (2) and even though the goods have not been shipped a buyer who has paid a part or all of the price of goods in which he has a special property under the provisions of the immediately preceding section may on making and keeping good a tender of any unpaid portion of their price recover them from the seller if the seller becomes insolvent within ten days after receipt of the first installment on their price.

(2) If the identification creating his special property has been made by the buyer he acquires the right to recover the goods only if they conform to the contract for sale.

§ 2—503. Manner of Seller's Tender of Delivery.

(1) Tender of delivery requires that the seller put and hold conforming goods at the buyer's disposition and give the buyer any notification reasonably necessary to enable him to take delivery. The manner, time and place for tender are determined by the agreement and this Article, and in particular

(a) tender must be at a reasonable hour, and if it is of goods they must be kept available for the period reasonably necessary to enable the buyer to take possession; but

(b) unless otherwise agreed the buyer must furnish facilities reasonably suited to the receipt of the goods.

(2) Where the case is within the next section respecting shipment tender requires that the seller comply with its provisions.

(3) Where the seller is required to deliver at a particular destination tender requires that he comply with subsection (1) and also in any appropriate case tender documents as described in subsections (4) and (5) of this section.

(4) Where goods are in the possession of a bailee and are to be delivered without being moved

(a) tender requires that the seller either tender a negotiable document of title covering such goods or procure acknowledgment by the bailee of the buyer's right to possession of the goods; but

(b) tender to the buyer of a non-negotiable document of title or of a written direction to the bailee to deliver is sufficient tender unless the buyer seasonably objects, and receipt by the bailee of notification of the buyer's rights fixes those rights as against the bailee and all third persons; but risk of loss of the goods and of any failure by the bailee to honor the non-negotiable document of title or to obey the direction remains on the seller until the buyer has had a reasonable time to present the document or direction, and a refusal by the bailee to honor the document or to obey the direction defeats the tender.

(5) Where the contract requires the seller to deliver documents

(a) he must tender all such documents in correct form, except as provided in this Article with respect to bills of lading in a set (subsection (2) of Section 2—323); and

(b) tender through customary banking channels is sufficient and dishonor of a draft accompanying the documents constitutes non-acceptance or rejection.

§ 2—504. Shipment by Seller.

Where the seller is required or authorized to send the goods to the buyer and the contract does not require him to deliver them at a particular destination, then unless otherwise agreed he must

(a) put the goods in the possession of such a carrier and make such a contract for their transportation as may be reasonable having regard to the nature of the goods and other circumstances of the case; and

(b) obtain and promptly deliver or tender in due form any document necessary to enable the buyer to obtain possession of the goods or otherwise required by the agreement or by usage of trade; and

(c) promptly notify the buyer of the shipment.

Failure to notify the buyer under paragraph (c) or to make a proper contract under paragraph (a) is a ground for rejection only if material delay or loss ensues.

§ 2—505. Seller's Shipment Under Reservation.

(1) Where the seller has identified goods to the contract by or before shipment:

(a) his procurement of a negotiable bill of lading to his own order or otherwise reserves in him a security interest in the goods. His procurement of the bill to the order of a financing agency or of the buyer indicates in addition only the seller's expectation of transferring that interest to the person named.

(b) a non-negotiable bill of lading to himself or his nominee reserves possession of the goods as security but except in a case of conditional delivery (subsection (2) of Section 2—507) a non-negotiable bill of lading naming the buyer as consignee reserves no security interest even though the seller retains possession of the bill of lading.

(2) When shipment by the seller with reservation of a security interest is in violation of the contract for sale it constitutes an improper contract for transportation within the preceding section but impairs neither the rights given to the buyer by shipment and identification of the goods to the contract nor the seller's powers as a holder of a negotiable document.

§ 2—506. Rights of Financing Agency.

(1) A financing agency by paying or purchasing for value a draft which relates to a shipment of goods acquires to the extent of the payment or purchase and in addition to its own rights under the draft and any document of title securing it any rights of the shipper in the goods including the right to stop delivery and the shipper's right to have the draft honored by the buyer.

(2) The right to reimbursement of a financing agency which has in good faith honored or purchased the draft under commitment to or authority from the buyer is not impaired by subsequent discovery of defects with reference to any relevant document which was apparently regular on its face.

§ 2—507. Effect of Seller's Tender; Delivery on Condition.

(1) Tender of delivery is a condition to the buyer's duty to accept the goods and, unless otherwise agreed, to his duty to pay for them. Tender entitles the seller to acceptance of the goods and to payment according to the contract.

(2) Where payment is due and demanded on the delivery to the buyer of goods or documents of title, his right as against the seller to retain or dispose of them is conditional upon his making the payment due.

§ 2—508. Cure by Seller of Improper Tender or Delivery; Replacement.

(1) Where any tender or delivery by the seller is rejected because non-conforming and the time for performance has not yet expired, the seller may seasonably notify the buyer of his intention to cure and may then within the contract time make a conforming delivery.

(2) Where the buyer rejects a non-conforming tender which the seller had reasonable grounds to believe would be acceptable with or without money allowance the seller may if he seasonably notifies the buyer have a further reasonable time to substitute a conforming tender.

§ 2—509. Risk of Loss in the Absence of Breach.

(1) Where the contract requires or authorizes the seller to ship the goods by carrier

(a) if it does not require him to deliver them at a particular destination, the risk of loss passes to the buyer when the goods are duly delivered to the carrier even though the shipment is under reservation (Section 2—505); but

(b) if it does require him to deliver them at a particular destination and the goods are there duly tendered while in the possession of the carrier, the risk of loss passes to the buyer when the goods are there duly so tendered as to enable the buyer to take delivery.

(2) Where the goods are held by a bailee to be delivered without being moved, the risk of loss passes to the buyer

(a) on his receipt of a negotiable document of title covering the goods; or

(b) on acknowledgment by the bailee of the buyer's right to possession of the goods; or

(c) after his receipt of a non-negotiable document of title or other written direction to deliver, as provided in subsection (4) (b) of Section 2—503.

(3) In any case not within subsection (1) or (2), the risk of loss passes to the buyer on his receipt of the goods if the seller is a merchant; otherwise the risk passes to the buyer on tender of delivery.

(4) The provisions of this section are subject to contrary agreement of the parties and to the provisions of this Article on sale on approval (Section 2—327) and on effect of breach on risk of loss (Section 2—510).

§ 2—510. Effect of Breach on Risk of Loss.

(1) Where a tender or delivery of goods so fails to conform to the contract as to give a right of rejection the risk of their loss remains on the seller until cure or acceptance.

(2) Where the buyer rightfully revokes acceptance he may to the extent of any deficiency in his effective insurance coverage treat the risk of loss as having rested on the seller from the beginning.

(3) Where the buyer as to conforming goods already identified to the contract for sale repudiates or is otherwise in breach before risk of their loss has passed to him, the seller may to the extent of any deficiency in his effective insurance coverage treat the risk of loss as resting on the buyer for a commercially reasonable time.

§ 2—511. Tender of Payment by Buyer; Payment by Check.

(1) Unless otherwise agreed tender of payment is a condition to the seller's duty to tender and complete any delivery.

(2) Tender of payment is sufficient when made by any means or in any manner current in the ordinary course of business unless the seller demands payment in legal tender and gives any extension of time reasonably necessary to procure it.

(3) Subject to the provisions of this Act on the effect of an instrument on an obligation (Section 3—802), payment by check is conditional and is defeated as between the parties by dishonor of the check on due presentment.

§ 2—512. Payment by Buyer Before Inspection.

(1) Where the contract requires payment before inspection non-conformity of the goods does not excuse the buyer from so making payment unless

(a) the non-conformity appears without inspection; or

(b) despite tender of the required documents the circumstances would justify injunction against honor under the provisions of this Act (Section 5—114).

(2) Payment pursuant to subsection (1) does not constitute an acceptance of goods or impair the buyer's right to inspect or any of his remedies.

§ 2—513. Buyer's Right to Inspection of Goods.

(1) Unless otherwise agreed and subject to subsection (3), where goods are tendered or delivered or identified to the contract for sale, the buyer has a right before payment or acceptance to inspect them at any reasonable place and time and in any reasonable manner. When the seller is required or authorized to send the goods to the buyer, the inspection may be after their arrival.

(2) Expenses of inspection must be borne by the buyer but may be recovered from the seller if the goods do not conform and are rejected.

(3) Unless otherwise agreed and subject to the provisions of this Article on C.I.F. contracts (subsection (3) of Section 2—321), the buyer is not entitled to inspect the goods before payment of the price when the contract provides

(a) for delivery "C.O.D." or on other like terms; or

(b) for payment against documents of title, except where such payment is due only after the goods are to become available for inspection.

(4) A place or method of inspection fixed by the parties is presumed to be exclusive but un-

less otherwise expressly agreed it does not postpone identification or shift the place for delivery or for passing the risk of loss. If compliance becomes impossible, inspection shall be as provided in this section unless the place or method fixed was clearly intended as an indispensable condition failure of which avoids the contract.

§ 2—514. When Documents Deliverable on Acceptance; When on Payment.

Unless otherwise agreed documents against which a draft is drawn are to be delivered to the drawee on acceptance of the draft if it is payable more than three days after presentment; otherwise, only on payment.

§ 2—515. Preserving Evidence of Goods in Dispute.

In furtherance of the adjustment of any claim or dispute

(a) either party on reasonable notification to the other and for the purpose of ascertaining the facts and preserving evidence has the right to inspect, test and sample the goods including such of them as may be in the possession or control of the other; and

(b) the parties may agree to a third party inspection or survey to determine the conformity or condition of the goods and may agree that the findings shall be binding upon them in any subsequent litigation or adjustment.

PART 6

BREACH, REPUDIATION AND EXCUSE

§ 2—601. Buyer's Rights on Improper Delivery.

Subject to the provisions of this Article on breach in installment contracts (Section 2—612) and unless otherwise agreed under the sections on contractual limitations of remedy (Sections 2—718 and 2—719), if the goods or the tender of delivery fail in any respect to conform to the contract, the buyer may

(a) reject the whole; or

(b) accept the whole; or

(c) accept any commercial unit or units and reject the rest.

§ 2—602. Manner and Effect of Rightful Rejection.

(1) Rejection of goods must be within a reasonable time after their delivery or tender. It is ineffective unless the buyer seasonably notifies the seller.

(2) Subject to the provisions of the two following sections on rejected goods (Sections 2—603 and 2—604),

(a) after rejection any exercise of ownership by the buyer with respect to any commercial unit is wrongful as against the seller; and

(b) if the buyer has before rejection taken physical possession of goods in which he does not have a security interest under the provisions of this Article (subsection (3) of Section 2—711), he is under a duty after rejection to hold them with reasonable care at the seller's disposition for a time sufficient to permit the seller to remove them; but

(c) the buyer has no further obligations with regard to goods rightfully rejected.

(3) The seller's rights with respect to goods wrongfully rejected are governed by the provisions of this Article on Seller's remedies in general (Section 2—703).

§ 2—603. Merchant Buyer's Duties as to Rightfully Rejected Goods.

(1) Subject to any security interest in the buyer (subsection (3) of Section 2—711), when the seller has no agent or place of business at the market of rejection a merchant buyer is under a duty after rejection of goods in his possession or control to follow any reasonable instructions received from the seller with respect to the goods and in the absence of such instructions to make reasonable efforts to sell them for the seller's account if they are perishable or threaten to decline in value speedily. Instructions are not reasonable if on demand indemnity for expenses is not forthcoming.

(2) When the buyer sells goods under subsection (1), he is entitled to reimbursement from the seller or out of the proceeds for reasonable expenses of caring for and selling them, and if the expenses include no selling commission then to such commission as is usual in the trade or if there is none to a reasonable sum not exceeding ten per cent on the gross proceeds.

(3) In complying with this section the buyer is held only to good faith and good faith conduct hereunder is neither acceptance nor conversion nor the basis of an action for damages.

§ 2—604. Buyer's Options as to Salvage of Rightfully Rejected Goods.

Subject to the provisions of the immediately preceding section on perishables if the seller gives no instructions within a reasonable time after notification of rejection the buyer may store the rejected goods for the seller's account or reship them to him or resell them for the seller's account with reimbursement as provided in the preceding section. Such action is not acceptance or conversion.

§ 2—605. Waiver of Buyer's Objections by Failure to Particularize.

(1) The buyer's failure to state in connection with rejection a particular defect which is ascertainable by reasonable inspection precludes him from relying on the unstated defect to justify rejection or to establish breach

(a) where the seller could have cured it if stated seasonably; or

(b) between merchants when the seller has after rejection made a request in writing for a full and final written statement of all defects on which the buyer proposes to rely.

(2) Payment against documents made without reservation of rights precludes recovery of the payment for defects apparent on the face of the documents.

§ 2—606. What Constitutes Acceptance of Goods.

(1) Acceptance of goods occurs when the buyer

(a) after a reasonable opportunity to inspect the goods signifies to the seller that the goods are conforming or that he will take or retain them in spite of their nonconformity; or

(b) fails to make an effective rejection (subsection (1) of Section 2—602), but such acceptance does not occur until the buyer has had a reasonable opportunity to inspect them; or

(c) does any act inconsistent with the seller's ownership; but if such act is wrongful as against the seller it is an acceptance only if ratified by him.

(2) Acceptance of a part of any commercial unit is acceptance of that entire unit.

§ 2—607. Effect of Acceptance; Notice of Breach; Burden of Establishing Breach After Acceptance; Notice of Claim or Litigation to Person Answerable Over.

(1) The buyer must pay at the contract rate for any goods accepted.

(2) Acceptance of goods by the buyer precludes rejection of the goods accepted and if made with knowledge of a non-conformity cannot be revoked because of it unless the acceptance was on the reasonable assumption that the non-conformity would be seasonably cured but acceptance does not of itself impair any other remedy provided by this Article for nonconformity.

(3) Where a tender has been accepted

(a) the buyer must within a reasonable time after he discovers or should have discovered any breach notify the seller of breach or be barred from any remedy; and

(b) if the claim is one for infringement or the like (subsection (3) of Section 2—312) and the buyer is sued as a result of such a breach he must so notify the seller within a reasonable time after he receives notice of the litigation or be barred from any remedy over for liability established by the litigation.

(4) The burden is on the buyer to establish any breach with respect to the goods accepted.

(5) Where the buyer is sued for breach of a warranty or other obligation for which his seller is answerable over

(a) he may give his seller written notice of the litigation. If the notice states that the seller may come in and defend and that if the seller does not do so he will be bound in any action against him by his buyer by any determination of fact common to the two litigations, then unless the seller after seasonable receipt of the notice does come in and defend he is so bound.

(b) if the claim is one for infringement or the like (subsection (3) of Section 2—312) the original seller may demand in writing that his buyer turn over to him control of the litigation including settlement or else be barred from any remedy over and if he also agrees to bear all expense and to satisfy any adverse judgment, then unless the buyer after seasonable receipt of the demand does turn over control the buyer is so barred.

(6) The provisions of subsections (3), (4) and (5) apply to any obligation of a buyer to hold the seller harmless against infringement or the like (subsection (3) of Section 2—312).

§ 2—608. Revocation of Acceptance in Whole or in Part.

(1) The buyer may revoke his acceptance of a lot or commercial unit whose non-conformity substantially impairs its value to him if he has accepted it

(a) on the reasonable assumption that its non-conformity would be cured and it has not been seasonably cured; or

(b) without discovery of such non-conformity if his acceptance was reasonably induced either by the difficulty of discovery before acceptance or by the seller's assurances.

(2) Revocation of acceptance must occur within a reasonable time after the buyer discovers or should have discovered the ground for it and before any substantial change in condition of the goods which is not caused by their own defects. It is not effective until the buyer notifies the seller of it.

(3) A buyer who so revokes has the same rights and duties with regard to the goods involved as if he had rejected them.

§ 2—609. Right to Adequate Assurance of Performance.

(1) A contract for sale imposes an obligation on each party that the other's expectation of receiving due performance will not be impaired. When reasonable grounds for insecurity arise with respect to the performance of either party the other may in writing demand adequate assurance of due performance and until he receives such assurance may if commercially reasonable suspend any performance for which he has not already received the agreed return.

(2) Between merchants the reasonableness of grounds for insecurity and the adequacy of any assurance offered shall be determined according to commercial standards.

(3) Acceptance of any improper delivery or payment does not prejudice the aggrieved party's right to demand adequate assurance of future performance.

(4) After receipt of a justified demand failure to provide within a reasonable time not exceeding thirty days such assurance of due performance as is adequate under the circumstances of the particular case is a repudiation of the contract.

§ 2—610. Anticipatory Repudiation.

When either party repudiates the contract with respect to a performance not yet due the loss of which will substantially impair the value of the contract to the other, the aggrieved party may

(a) for a commercially reasonable time await performance by the repudiating party; or

(b) resort to any remedy for breach (Section 2—703 or Section 2—711), even though he has notified the repudiating party that he would await the latter's performance and has urged retraction; and

(c) in either case suspend his own performance or proceed in accordance with the provisions of this Article on the seller's right to identify goods to the contract notwithstanding breach or to salvage unfinished goods (Section 2—704).

§ 2—611. Retraction of Anticipatory Repudiation.

(1) Until the repudiating party's next performance is due he can retract his repudiation unless the aggrieved party has since the repudiation cancelled or materially changed his position or otherwise indicated that he considers the repudiation final.

(2) Retraction may be by any method which clearly indicates to the aggrieved party that the repudiating party intends to perform, but must include any assurance justifiably demanded under the provisions of this Article (Section 2—609).

(3) Retraction reinstates the repudiating party's rights under the contract with due excuse and allowance to the aggrieved party for any delay occasioned by the repudiation.

§ 2—612. "Installment Contract"; Breach.

(1) An "installment contract" is one which requires or authorizes the delivery of goods in separate lots to be separately accepted, even though the contract contains a clause "each delivery is a separate contract" or its equivalent.

(2) The buyer may reject any installment which is non-conforming if the non-conformity substantially impairs the value of that installment and cannot be cured or if the non-conformity is a defect in the required documents; but if the non-conformity does not fall within subsection (3) and the seller gives adequate assurance of its cure the buyer must accept that installment.

(3) Whenever non-conformity or default with respect to one or more installments substantially impairs the value of the whole contract there is a breach of the whole. But the aggrieved party reinstates the contract if he accepts a non-conforming installment without seasonably notifying of cancellation or if he brings an action with respect only to past installments or demands performance as to future installments.

§ 2—613. Casualty to Identified Goods.

Where the contract requires for its performance goods identified when the contract is made, and the goods suffer casualty without fault of either party before the risk of loss passes to the buyer, or in a proper case under a "no arrival, no sale" term (Section 2—324) then

(a) if the loss is total the contract is avoided; and

(b) if the loss is partial or the goods have so deteriorated as no longer to conform to the contract the buyer may nevertheless demand inspection and at his option either treat the contract as avoided or accept the goods with due allowance from the contract price for the deterioration or the deficiency in quantity but without further right against the seller.

§ 2—614. Substituted Performance.

(1) Where without fault of either party the agreed berthing, loading, or unloading facilities fail or an agreed type of carrier becomes unavailable or the agreed manner of delivery otherwise becomes commercially impracticable but a commercially reasonable substitute is available, such substitute performance must be tendered and accepted.

(2) If the agreed means or manner of payment fails because of domestic or foreign governmental regulation, the seller may withhold or stop delivery unless the buyer provides a means or manner of payment which is commercially a substantial equivalent. If delivery has already been taken, payment by the means or in the manner provided by the regulation discharges the buyer's obligation unless the regulation is discriminatory, oppressive or predatory.

§ 2—615. Excuse by Failure of Presupposed Conditions.

Except so far as a seller may have assumed a greater obligation and subject to the preceding section on substituted performance:

(a) Delay in delivery or non-delivery in whole or in part by a seller who complies with paragraphs (b) and (c) is not a breach of his duty under a contract for sale if performance as agreed has been made impracticable by the occurrence of a contingency the non-occurrence of which was a basic assumption on which the contract was made or by compliance in good faith with any applicable foreign or domestic governmental regulation or order whether or not it later proves to be invalid.

(b) Where the causes mentioned in paragraph (a) affect only a part of the seller's capacity to perform, he must allocate production and deliveries among his customers but may at his option include regular customers not then under contract as well as his own requirements for further manufacture. He may so allocate in any manner which is fair and reasonable.

(c) The seller must notify the buyer seasonably that there will be delay or non-delivery and, when allocation is required under paragraph (b), of the estimated quota thus made available for the buyer.

§ 2—616. Procedure on Notice Claiming Excuse.

(1) Where the buyer receives notification of a material or indefinite delay or an allocation justified under the preceding section he may by written notification to the seller as to any delivery concerned, and where the prospective deficiency substantially impairs the value of the whole contract under the provisions of this Article relating to breach of installment contracts (Section 2—612), then also as to the whole,

(a) terminate and thereby discharge any unexecuted portion of the contract; or

(b) modify the contract by agreeing to take his available quota in substitution.

(2) If after receipt of such notification from the seller the buyer fails so to modify the contract within a reasonable time not exceeding thirty days the contract lapses with respect to any deliveries affected.

(3) The provisions of this section may not be negated by agreement except in so far as the seller has assumed a greater obligation under the preceding section.

PART 7

REMEDIES

§ 2—701. Remedies for Breach of Collateral Contracts Not Impaired.

Remedies for breach of any obligation or promise collateral or ancillary to a contract for sale are not impaired by the provisions of this Article.

§ 2—702. Seller's Remedies on Discovery of Buyer's Insolvency.

(1) Where the seller discovers the buyer to be insolvent he may refuse delivery except for cash including payment for all goods theretofore delivered under the contract, and stop delivery under this Article (Section 2—705).

(2) Where the seller discovers that the buyer has received goods on credit while insolvent he may reclaim the goods upon demand made within ten days after the receipt, but if misrepresentation of solvency has been made to the particular seller in writing within three months before delivery the ten day limitation does not apply. Except as provided in this subsection the seller may not base a right to reclaim goods on the buyer's fraudulent or innocent misrepresentation of solvency or of intent to pay.

(3) The seller's right to reclaim under subsection (2) is subject to the rights of a buyer in ordinary course or other good faith purchaser under this Article (Section 2—403). Successful reclamation of goods excludes all other remedies with respect to them.

§ 2—703. Seller's Remedies in General.

Where the buyer wrongfully rejects or revokes acceptance of goods or fails to make a payment due on or before delivery or repudiates with respect to a part or the whole, then with respect to any goods directly affected and, if the breach is of the whole contract (Section 2—612), then also with respect to the whole undelivered balance, the aggrieved seller may

(a) withhold delivery of such goods;

(b) stop delivery by any bailee as hereafter provided (Section 2—705);

(c) proceed under the next section respecting goods still unidentified to the contract;

(d) resell and recover damages as hereafter provided (Section 2—706);

(e) recover damages for non-acceptance (Section 2—708) or in a proper case the price (Section 2—709);

(f) cancel.

§ 2—704. Seller's Right to Identify Goods to the Contract Notwithstanding Breach or to Salvage Unfinished Goods.

(1) An aggrieved seller under the preceding section may

(a) identify to the contract conforming goods not already identified if at the time he learned of the breach they are in his possession or control;

(b) treat as the subject of resale goods which have demonstrably been intended for the particular contract even though those goods are unfinished.

(2) Where the goods are unfinished an aggrieved seller may in the exercise of reasonable commercial judgment for the purposes of avoiding loss and of effective realization either complete the manufacture and wholly identify the goods to the contract or cease manufacture and resell for scrap or salvage value or proceed in any other reasonable manner.

§ 2—705. Seller's Stoppage of Delivery in Transit or Otherwise.

(1) The seller may stop delivery of goods in the possession of a carrier or other bailee when he discovers the buyer to be insolvent (Section 2—702) and may stop delivery of carload, truckload, planeload or larger shipments of express or freight when the buyer repudiates or fails to make a payment due before delivery or if for any other reason the seller has a right to withhold or reclaim the goods.

(2) As against such buyer the seller may stop delivery until

(a) receipt of the goods by the buyer; or

(b) acknowledgment to the buyer by any bailee of the goods except a carrier that the bailee holds the goods for the buyer; or

(c) such acknowledgment to the buyer by a carrier by reshipment or as warehouseman; or

(d) negotiation to the buyer of any negotiable document of title covering the goods.

(3) (a) To stop delivery the seller must so notify as to enable the bailee by reasonable diligence to prevent delivery of the goods.

(b) After such notification the bailee must hold and deliver the goods according to the directions of the seller but the seller is liable to the bailee for any ensuing charges or damages.

(c) If a negotiable document of title has been issued for goods the bailee is not obliged to obey a notification to stop until surrender of the document.

(d) A carrier who has issued a non-negotiable bill of lading is not obliged to obey a notification to stop received from a person other than the consignor.

§ 2—706. Seller's Resale Including Contract for Resale.

(1) Under the conditions stated in Section 2—703 on seller's remedies, the seller may resell the goods concerned or the undelivered balance thereof. Where the resale is made in good faith and in a commercially reasonable manner the seller may recover the difference between the resale price and the contract price together with any incidental damages allowed under the provisions of this Article (Section 2—710), but less expenses saved in consequence of the buyer's breach.

(2) Except as otherwise provided in subsection (3) or unless otherwise agreed resale may be at public or private sale including sale by way of one or more contracts to sell or of identification to an existing contract of the seller. Sale may be as a unit or in parcels and at any time and place and on any terms but every aspect of the sale including the method, manner, time, place and terms must be commercially reasonable. The resale must be reasonably identified as referring to the broken contract, but it is not necessary that the goods be in existence or that any or all of them have been identified to the contract before the breach.

(3) Where the resale is at private sale the seller must give the buyer reasonable notification of his intention to resell.

(4) Where the resale is at public sale

(a) only identified goods can be sold except where there is a recognized market for a public sale of futures in goods of the kind; and

(b) it must be made at a usual place or market for public sale if one is reasonably available and except in the case of goods which are perishable or threaten to decline in value speedily the seller must give the buyer reasonable notice of the time and place of the resale; and

(c) if the goods are not to be within the view of those attending the sale the notification of sale must state the place where the goods are located and provide for their reasonable inspection by prospective bidders; and

(d) the seller may buy.

(5) A purchaser who buys in good faith at a resale takes the goods free of any rights of the original buyer even though the seller fails to comply with one or more of the requirements of this section.

(6) The seller is not accountable to the buyer for any profit made on any resale. A person in the position of a seller (Section 2—707) or a buyer who has rightfully rejected or justifiably revoked acceptance must account for any excess over the amount of his security interest, as hereinafter defined (subsection (3) of Section 2—711).

§ 2—707. "Person in the Position of a Seller".

(1) A "person in the position of a seller" includes as against a principal an agent who has paid or become responsible for the price of goods on behalf of his principal or anyone who otherwise holds a security interest or other right in goods similar to that of a seller.

(2) A person in the position of a seller may as provided in this Article withhold or stop delivery (Section 2—705) and resell (Section 2—706) and recover incidental damages (Section 2—710).

§ 2—708. Seller's Damages for Non-acceptance or Repudiation.

(1) Subject to subsection (2) and to the provisions of this Article with respect to proof of market price (Section 2—723), the measure of damages for non-acceptance or repudiation by the buyer is the difference between the market price at the time and place for tender and the unpaid contract price together with any incidental damages provided in this Article (Section 2—710), but less expenses saved in consequence of the buyer's breach.

(2) If the measure of damages provided in subsection (1) is inadequate to put the seller in as good a position as performance would have done then the measure of damages is the profit (including reasonable overhead) which the seller would have made from full performance by the buyer, together with any incidental damages provided in this Article (Section 2—710), due allowance for costs reasonably incurred and due credit for payments or proceeds of resale.

§ 2—709. Action for the Price.

(1) When the buyer fails to pay the price as it becomes due the seller may recover, together with any incidental damages under the next section, the price

(a) of goods accepted or of conforming goods lost or damaged within a commercially reasonable time after risk of their loss has passed to the buyer; and

(b) of goods identified to the contract if the seller is unable after reasonable effort to resell them at a reasonable price or the circumstances reasonably indicate that such effort will be unavailing.

(2) Where the seller sues for the price he must hold for the buyer any goods which have been identified to the contract and are still in his control except that if resale becomes possible he may resell them at any time prior to the collection of the judgment. The net proceeds of any such resale must be credited to the buyer and payment of the judgment entitles him to any goods not resold.

(3) After the buyer has wrongfully rejected or revoked acceptance of the goods or has failed to make a payment due or has repudiated

(Section 2—610), a seller who is held not entitled to the price under this section shall nevertheless be awarded damages for non-acceptance under the preceding section.

§ 2—710. Seller's Incidental Damages.

Incidental damages to an aggrieved seller include any commercially reasonable charges, expenses or commissions incurred in stopping delivery, in the transportation, care and custody of goods after the buyer's breach, in connection with return or resale of the goods or otherwise resulting from the breach.

§ 2—711. Buyer's Remedies in General; Buyer's Security Interest in Rejected Goods.

(1) Where the seller fails to make delivery or repudiates or the buyer rightfully rejects or justifiably revokes acceptance then with respect to any goods involved, and with respect to the whole if the breach goes to the whole contract (Section 2—612), the buyer may cancel and whether or not he has done so may in addition to recovering so much of the price as has been paid

(a) "cover" and have damages under the next section as to all the goods affected whether or not they have been identified to the contract; or

(b) recover damages for non-delivery as provided in this Article (Section 2—713).

(2) Where the seller fails to deliver or repudiates the buyer may also

(a) if the goods have been identified recover them as provided in this Article (Section 2—502); or

(b) in a proper case obtain specific performance or replevy the goods as provided in this Article (Section 2—716).

(3) On rightful rejection or justifiable revocation of acceptance a buyer has a security interest in goods in his possession or control for any payments made on their price and any expenses reasonably incurred in their inspection, receipt, transportation, care and custody and may hold such goods and resell them in like manner as an aggrieved seller (Section 2—706).

§ 2—712. "Cover"; Buyer's Procurement of Substitute Goods.

(1) After a breach within the preceding section the buyer may "cover" by making in good faith and without unreasonable delay any reasonable purchase of or contract to purchase goods in substitution for those due from the seller.

(2) The buyer may recover from the seller as damages the difference between the cost of cover and the contract price together with any incidental or consequential damages as hereinafter defined (Section 2—715), but less expenses saved in consequence of the seller's breach.

(3) Failure of the buyer to effect cover within this section does not bar him from any other remedy.

§ 2—713. Buyer's Damages for Non-Delivery or Repudiation.

(1) Subject to the provisions of this Article with respect to proof of market price (Section 2—723), the measure of damages for non-delivery or repudiation by the seller is the difference between the market price at the time when the buyer learned of the breach and the contract price together with any incidental and consequential damages provided in this Article (Section 2—715), but less expenses saved in consequence of the seller's breach.

(2) Market price is to be determined as of the place for tender or, in cases of rejection after arrival or revocation of acceptance, as of the place of arrival.

§ 2—714. Buyer's Damages for Breach in Regard to Accepted Goods.

(1) Where the buyer has accepted goods and given notification (subsection (3) of Section 2—607) he may recover as damages for any non-conformity of tender the loss resulting in the ordinary course of events from the seller's breach as determined in any manner which is reasonable.

(2) The measure of damages for breach of warranty is the difference at the time and place of acceptance between the value of the goods accepted and the value they would have had if they had been as warranted, unless special circumstances show proximate damages of a different amount.

(3) In a proper case any incidental and consequential damages under the next section may also be recovered.

§ 2—715. Buyer's Incidental and Consequential Damages.

(1) Incidental damages resulting from the seller's breach include expenses reasonably incurred in inspection, receipt, transportation and care and custody of goods rightfully rejected, any commercially reasonable charges, expenses or commissions in connection with effecting cover and any other reasonable expense incident to the delay or other breach.

(2) Consequential damages resulting from the seller's breach include

(a) any loss resulting from general or particular requirements and needs of which the seller at the time of contracting had reason to know and which could not reasonably be prevented by cover or otherwise; and

(b) injury to person or property proximately resulting from any breach of warranty.

§ 2—716. Buyer's Right to Specific Performance or Replevin.

(1) Specific performance may be decreed where the goods are unique or in other proper circumstances.

(2) The decree for specific performance may include such terms and conditions as to payment of the price, damages, or other relief as the court may deem just.

(3) The buyer has a right of replevin for goods identified to the contract if after reasonable effort he is unable to effect cover for such goods or the circumstances reasonably indicate that such effort will be unavailing or if the goods have been shipped under reservation and satisfaction of the security interest in them has been made or tendered.

§ 2—717. Deduction of Damages From the Price.

The buyer on notifying the seller of his intention to do so may deduct all or any part of the damages resulting from any breach of the contract from any part of the price still due under the same contract.

§ 2—718. Liquidation or Limitation of Damages; Deposits.

(1) Damages for breach by either party may be liquidated in the agreement but only at an amount which is reasonable in the light of the anticipated or actual harm caused by the breach, the difficulties of proof of loss, and the inconvenience or nonfeasibility of otherwise obtaining an adequate remedy. A term fixing unreasonably large liquidated damages is void as a penalty.

(2) Where the seller justifiably withholds delivery of goods because of the buyer's breach, the buyer is entitled to restitution of any amount by which the sum of his payments exceeds

(a) the amount to which the seller is entitled by virtue of terms liquidating the seller's damages in accordance with subsection (1), or

(b) in the absence of such terms, twenty per cent of the value of the total performance for which the buyer is obligated under the contract or $500, whichever is smaller.

(3) The buyer's right to restitution under subsection (2) is subject to offset to the extent that the seller establishes

(a) a right to recover damages under the provisions of this Article other than subsection (1), and

(b) the amount or value of any benefits received by the buyer directly or indirectly by reason of the contract.

(4) Where a seller has received payment in goods their reasonable value or the proceeds of their resale shall be treated as payments for the purposes of subsection (2); but if the seller has notice of the buyer's breach before reselling goods received in part performance, his resale is subject to the conditions laid down in this Article on resale by an aggrieved seller (Section 2—706).

§ 2—719. Contractual Modification or Limitation of Remedy.

(1) Subject to the provisions of subsections (2) and (3) of this section and of the preceding section on liquidation and limitation of damages,

(a) the agreement may provide for remedies in addition to or in substitution for those provided in this Article and may limit or alter the measure of damages recoverable under this Article, as by limiting the buyer's remedies to return of the goods and repayment of the price or to repair and replacement of non-conforming goods or parts; and

(b) resort to a remedy as provided is optional unless the remedy is expressly agreed to be exclusive, in which case it is the sole remedy.

(2) Where circumstances cause an exclusive or limited remedy to fail of its essential purpose, remedy may be had as provided in this Act.

(3) Consequential damages may be limited or excluded unless the limitation or exclusion is unconscionable. Limitation of consequential damages for injury to the person in the case of consumer goods is prima facie unconscionable but limitation of damages where the loss is commercial is not.

§ 2—720. Effect of "Cancellation" or "Rescission" on Claims for Antecedent Breach.

Unless the contrary intention clearly appears, expressions of "cancellation" or "rescission" of the contract or the like shall not be construed as a renunciation or discharge of any claim in damages for an antecedent breach.

§ 2—721. Remedies for Fraud.

Remedies for material misrepresentation or fraud include all remedies available under this Article for non-fraudulent breach. Neither rescission or a claim for rescission of the contract for sale nor rejection or return of the goods shall bar or be deemed inconsistent with a claim for damages or other remedy.

§ 2—722. Who Can Sue Third Parties for Injury to Goods.

Where a third party so deals with goods which have been identified to a contract for sale as to cause actionable injury to a party to that contract

(a) a right of action against the third party is in either party to the contract for sale who has title to or a security interest or a special property or an insurable interest in the goods; and if the goods have been destroyed or converted a right of action is also in the party who either bore the risk of loss under the contract for sale or has since the injury assumed that risk as against the other;

(b) if at the time of the injury the party plaintiff did not bear the risk of loss as against the other party to the contract for sale and there is no arrangement between them for disposition of the recovery, his suit or settlement is, subject to his own interest, as a fiduciary for the other party to the contract;

(c) either party may with the consent of the other sue for the benefit of whom it may concern.

§ 2—723. Proof of Market Price: Time and Place.

(1) If an action based on anticipatory repudiation comes to trial before the time for performance with respect to some or all of the goods, any damages based on market price (Section 2—708 or Section 2—713) shall be determined according to the price of such goods prevailing at the time when the aggrieved party learned of the repudiation.

(2) If evidence of a price prevailing at the times or places described in this Article is not readily available the price prevailing within any reasonable time before or after the time described or at any other place which in commercial judgment or under usage of trade would serve as a reasonable substitute for the one described may be used, making any proper allowance for the cost of transporting the goods to or from such other place.

(3) Evidence of a relevant price prevailing at a time or place other than the one described in this Article offered by one party is not admissible unless and until he has given the other party such notice as the court finds sufficient to prevent unfair surprise.

§ 2—724. Admissibility of Market Quotations.

Whenever the prevailing price or value of any goods regularly bought and sold in any established commodity market is in issue, reports in official publications or trade journals or in newspapers or periodicals of general circulation published as the reports of such market shall be admissible in evidence. The circumstances of the preparation of such a report may be shown to affect its weight but not its admissibility.

§ 2—725. Statute of Limitations in Contracts for Sale.

(1) An action for breach of any contract for sale must be commenced within four years after the cause of action has accrued. By the original agreement the parties may reduce the period of limitation to not less than one year but may not extend it.

(2) A cause of action accrues when the breach occurs, regardless of the aggrieved party's lack of knowledge of the breach. A breach of warranty occurs when tender of delivery is made, except that where a warranty explicitly extends to future performance of the goods and discovery of the breach must await the time of such performance the cause of action accrues when the breach is or should have been discovered.

(3) Where an action commenced within the time limited by subsection (1) is so terminated as to leave available a remedy by another action for the same breach such other action may be commenced after the expiration of the time limited and within six months after the termination of the first action unless the termination resulted from voluntary discontinuance or from dismissal for failure or neglect to prosecute.

(4) This section does not alter the law on tolling of the statute of limitations nor does it apply to causes of action which have accrued before this Act becomes effective.

ARTICLE 3

COMMERCIAL PAPER

PART 1

SHORT TITLE, FORM AND INTERPRETATION

§ 3—101. Short Title.

This Article shall be known and may be cited as Uniform Commercial Code—Commercial Paper.

§ 3—102. Definitions and Index of Definitions.

(1) In this Article unless the context otherwise requires

(a) "Issue" means the first delivery of an instrument to a holder or a remitter.

(b) An "order" is a direction to pay and must be more than an authorization or request. It must identify the person to pay with reasonable certainty. It may be addressed to one or more such persons jointly or in the alternative but not in succession.

(c) A "promise" is an undertaking to pay and must be more than an acknowledgment of an obligation.

(d) "Secondary party" means a drawer or endorser.

(e) "Instrument" means a negotiable instrument.

(2) Other definitions applying to this Article and the sections in which they appear are:

"Acceptance". Section 3—410.
"Accommodation party". Section 3—415.
"Alteration". Section 3—407.
"Certificate of deposit". Section 3—104.
"Certification". Section 3—411.
"Check". Section 3—104.
"Definite time". Section 3—109.
"Dishonor". Section 3—507.
"Draft". Section 3—104.
"Holder in due course". Section 3—302.
"Negotiation". Section 3—202.
"Note". Section 3—104.
"Notice of dishonor". Section 3—508.
"On demand". Section 3—108.
"Presentment". Section 3—504.
"Protest". Section 3—509.

"Restrictive Indorsement". Section 3—205.
"Signature". Section 3—401.

(3) The following definitions in other Articles apply to this Article:
"Account". Section 4—104.
"Banking Day". Section 4—104.
"Clearing house". Section 4—104.
"Collecting bank". Section 4—105.
"Customer". Section 4—104.
"Depositary Bank". Section 4—105.
"Documentary Draft". Section 4—104.
"Intermediary Bank". Section 4—105.
"Item". Section 4—104.
"Midnight deadline". Section 4—104.
"Payor bank". Section 4—105.

(4) In addition Article 1 contains general definitions and principles of construction and interpretation applicable throughout this Article.

§ 3—103. Limitations on Scope of Article.

(1) This Article does not apply to money, documents of title or investment securities.

(2) The provisions of this Article are subject to the provisions of the Article on Bank Deposits and Collections (Article 4) and Secured Transactions (Article 9).

§ 3—104. Form of Negotiable Instruments; "Draft"; "Check"; "Certificate of Deposit"; "Note".

(1) Any writing to be a negotiable instrument within this Article must

(a) be signed by the maker or drawer; and

(b) contain an unconditional promise or order to pay a sum certain in money and no other promise, order, obligation or power given by the maker or drawer except as authorized by this Article; and

(c) be payable on demand or at a definite time; and

(d) be payable to order or to bearer.

(2) A writing which complies with the requirements of this section is

(a) a "draft" ("bill of exchange") if it is an order;

(b) a "check" if it is a draft drawn on a bank and payable on demand;

(c) a "certificate of deposit" if it is an acknowledgment by a bank of receipt of money with an engagement to repay it;

(d) a "note" if it is a promise other than a certificate of deposit.

(3) As used in other Articles of this Act, and as the context may require, the terms "draft", "check", "certificate of deposit" and "note" may refer to instruments which are not negotiable within this Article as well as to instruments which are so negotiable.

§ 3—105. When Promise or Order Unconditional.

(1) A promise or order otherwise unconditional is not made conditional by the fact that the instrument

(a) is subject to implied or constructive conditions; or

(b) states its consideration, whether performed or promised, or the transaction which gave rise to the instrument, or that the promise or order is made or the instrument matures in accordance with or "as per" such transaction; or

(c) refers to or states that it arises out of a separate agreement or refers to a separate agreement for rights as to prepayment or acceleration; or

(d) states that it is drawn under a letter of credit; or

(e) states that it is secured, whether by mortgage, reservation of title or otherwise; or

(f) indicates a particular account to be debited or any other fund or source from which reimbursement is expected; or

(g) is limited to payment out of a particular fund or the proceeds of a particular source, if the instrument is issued by a government or governmental agency or unit; or

(h) is limited to payment out of the entire assets of a partnership, unincorporated association, trust or estate by or on behalf of which the instrument is issued.

(2) A promise or order is not unconditional if the instrument

(a) states that it is subject to or governed by any other agreement; or

(b) states that it is to be paid only out of a particular fund or source except as provided in this section.

§ 3—106. Sum Certain.

(1) The sum payable is a sum certain even though it is to be paid

(a) with stated interest or by stated installments; or

(b) with stated different rates of interest before and after default or a specified date; or

(c) with a stated discount or addition if paid before or after the date fixed for payment; or

(d) with exchange or less exchange, whether at a fixed rate or at the current rate; or

(e) with costs of collection or an attorney's fee or both upon default.

(2) Nothing in this section shall validate any term which is otherwise illegal.

§ 3—107. Money.

(1) An instrument is payable in money if the medium of exchange in which it is payable is money at the time the instrument is made. An instrument payable in "currency" or "current funds" is payable in money.

(2) A promise or order to pay a sum stated in a foreign currency is for a sum certain in money and, unless a different medium of payment is specified in the instrument, may be satisfied by payment of that number of dollars which the stated foreign currency will purchase at the buying sight rate for that currency on the day on which the instrument is payable or, if payable on demand, on the day of demand. If such an instrument specifies a foreign currency as the medium of payment the instrument is payable in that currency.

§ 3—108. Payable on Demand.

Instruments payable on demand include those payable at sight or on presentation and those in which no time for payment is stated.

§ 3—109. Definite Time.

(1) An instrument is payable at a definite time if by its terms it is payable

(a) on or before a stated date or at a fixed period after a stated date; or

(b) at a fixed period after sight; or

(c) at a definite time subject to any acceleration; or

(d) at a definite time subject to extension at the option of the holder, or to extension to a further definite time at the option of the maker or acceptor or automatically upon or after a specified act or event.

(2) An instrument which by its terms is otherwise payable only upon an act or event uncertain as to time of occurrence is not payable at a definite time even though the act or event has occurred.

§ 3—110. Payable to Order.

(1) An instrument is payable to order when by its terms it is payable to the order or assigns of any person therein specified with reasonable certainty, or to him or his order, or when it is conspicuously designated on its face as "exchange" or the like and names a payee. It may be payable to the order of

(a) the maker or drawer; or

(b) the drawee; or

(c) a payee who is not maker, drawer or drawee; or

(d) two or more payees together or in the alternative; or

(e) an estate, trust or fund, in which case it is payable to the order of the representative of such estate, trust or fund or his successors; or

(f) an office, or an officer by his title as such in which case it is payable to the principal but the incumbent of the office or his successors may act as if he or they were the holder; or

(g) a partnership or unincorporated association, in which case it is payable to the partnership or association and may be indorsed or transferred by any person thereto authorized.

(2) An instrument not payable to order is not made so payable by such words as "payable upon return of this instrument properly indorsed."

(3) An instrument made payable both to order and to bearer is payable to order unless the bearer words are handwritten or typewritten.

§ 3—111. Payable to Bearer.

An instrument is payable to bearer when by its terms it is payable to

(a) bearer or the order of bearer; or

(b) a specified person or bearer; or

(c) "cash" or the order of "cash", or any other indication which does not purport to designate a specific payee.

§ 3—112. Terms and Omissions Not Affecting Negotiability.

(1) The negotiability of an instrument is not affected by

(a) the omission of a statement of any consideration or of the place where the instrument is drawn or payable; or

(b) a statement that collateral has been given to secure obligations either on the instrument or otherwise of an obligor on the instrument or that in case of default on those obligations the holder may realize on or dispose of the collateral; or

(c) a promise or power to maintain or protect collateral or to give additional collateral; or

(d) a term authorizing a confession of judgment on the instrument if it is not paid when due; or

(e) a term purporting to waive the benefit of any law intended for the advantage or protection of any obligor; or

(f) a term in a draft providing that the payee by indorsing or cashing it acknowledges full satisfaction of an obligation of the drawer; or

(g) a statement in a draft drawn in a set of parts (Section 3—801) to the effect that the order is effective only if no other part has been honored.

(2) Nothing in this section shall validate any term which is otherwise illegal.

§ 3—113. Seal.

An instrument otherwise negotiable is within this Article even though it is under a seal.

§ 3—114. Date, Antedating, Postdating.

(1) The negotiability of an instrument is not affected by the fact that it is undated, antedated or postdated.

(2) Where an instrument is antedated or postdated the time when it is payable is determined by the stated date if the instrument is payable on demand or at a fixed period after date.

(3) Where the instrument or any signature thereon is dated, the date is presumed to be correct.

§ 3—115. Incomplete Instruments.

(1) When a paper whose contents at the time of signing show that it is intended to become an instrument is signed while still incomplete in any necessary respect it cannot be enforced until completed, but when it is completed in accordance with authority given it is effective as completed.

(2) If the completion is unauthorized the rules as to material alteration apply (Section 3—407), even though the paper was not delivered by the maker or drawer; but the burden of establishing that any completion is unauthorized is on the party so asserting.

§ 3—116. Instruments Payable to Two or More Persons.

An instrument payable to the order of two or more persons

(a) if in the alternative is payable to any one of them and may be negotiated, discharged or enforced by any of them who has possession of it;

(b) if not in the alternative is payable to all of them and may be negotiated, discharged or enforced only by all of them.

§ 3—117. Instruments Payable With Words of Description.

An instrument made payable to a named person with the addition of words describing him

(a) as agent or officer of a specified person is payable to his principal but the agent or officer may act as if he were the holder;

(b) as any other fiduciary for a specified person or purpose is payable to the payee and may be negotiated, discharged or enforced by him;

(c) in any other manner is payable to the payee unconditionally and the additional words are without effect on subsequent parties.

§ 3—118. Ambiguous Terms and Rules of Construction.

The following rules apply to every instrument:

(a) Where there is doubt whether the instrument is a draft or a note the holder may treat it as either. A draft drawn on the drawer is effective as a note.

(b) Handwritten terms control typewritten and printed terms, and typewritten control printed.

(c) Words control figures except that if the words are ambiguous figures control.

(d) Unless otherwise specified a provision for interest means interest at the judgment rate at the place of payment from the date of the instrument, or if it is undated from the date of issue.

(e) Unless the instrument otherwise specifies two or more persons who sign as maker, acceptor or drawer or indorser and as a part of the same transaction are jointly and severally liable even though the instrument contains such words as "I promise to pay."

(f) Unless otherwise specified consent to extension authorizes a single extension for not longer than the original period. A consent to extension, expressed in the instrument, is binding on secondary parties and accommodation makers. A holder may not exercise his option to extend an instrument over the objection of a maker or acceptor or other party who in accordance with Section 3—604 tenders full payment when the instrument is due.

§ 3—119. Other Writings Affecting Instrument.

(1) As between the obligor and his immediate obligee or any transferee the terms of an instrument may be modified or affected by any other written agreement executed as a part of the same transaction, except that a holder in due course is not affected by any limitation of his rights arising out of the separate written agreement if he had no notice of the limitation when he took the instrument.

(2) A separate agreement does not affect the negotiability of an instrument.

§ 3—120. Instruments "Payable Through" Bank.

An instrument which states that it is "payable through" a bank or the like designates that bank as a collecting bank to make presentment but does not of itself authorize the bank to pay the instrument.

§ 3—121. Instruments Payable at Bank.

Note: *If this Act is introduced in the Congress of the United States this section should be omitted.*
(States to select either alternative)

Alternative A—

A note or acceptance which states that it is payable at a bank is the equivalent of a draft drawn on the bank payable when it falls due out of any funds of the maker or acceptor in current account or otherwise available for such payment.

Alternative B—

A note or acceptance which states that it is payable at a bank is not of itself an order or authorization to the bank to pay it.

§ 3—122. Accrual of Cause of Action.

(1) A cause of action against a maker or an acceptor accrues

(a) in the case of a time instrument on the day after maturity;

(b) in the case of a demand instrument upon its date or, if no date is stated, on the date of issue.

(2) A cause of action against the obligor of a demand or time certificate of deposit accrues upon demand, but demand on a time certificate may not be made until on or after the date of maturity.

(3) A cause of action against a drawer of a draft or an indorser of any instrument accrues upon demand following dishonor of the instrument. Notice of dishonor is a demand.

(4) Unless an instrument provides otherwise, interest runs at the rate provided by law for a judgment

(a) in the case of a maker, acceptor or other primary obligor of a demand instrument, from the date of demand;

(b) in all other cases from the date of accrual of the cause of action.

PART 2

TRANSFER AND NEGOTIATION

§ 3—201. Transfer: Right to Indorsement.

(1) Transfer of an instrument vests in the transferee such rights as the transferor has therein, except that a transferee who has himself been a party to any fraud or illegality affecting the instrument or who as a prior holder had notice of a defense or claim against it cannot improve his position by taking from a later holder in due course.

(2) A transfer of a security interest in an instrument vests the foregoing rights in the transferee to the extent of the interest transferred.

(3) Unless otherwise agreed any transfer for value of an instrument not then payable to bearer gives the transferee the specifically enforceable right to have the unqualified indorsement of the transferor. Negotiation takes effect only when the indorsement is made and until that time there is no presumption that the transferee is the owner.

§ 3—202. Negotiation.

(1) Negotiation is the transfer of an instrument in such form that the transferee becomes a holder. If the instrument is payable to order it is negotiated by delivery with any necessary indorsement; if payable to bearer it is negotiated by delivery.

(2) An indorsement must be written by or on behalf of the holder and on the instrument or on a paper so firmly affixed thereto as to become a part thereof.

(3) An indorsement is effective for negotiation only when it conveys the entire instrument or any unpaid residue. If it purports to be of less it operates only as a partial assignment.

(4) Words of assignment, condition, waiver, guaranty, limitation or disclaimer of liability and the like accompanying an indorsement do not affect its character as an indorsement.

§ 3—203. Wrong or Misspelled Name.

Where an instrument is made payable to a person under a misspelled name or one other than his own he may indorse in that name or his own or both; but signature in both names may be required by a person paying or giving value for the instrument.

§ 3—204. Special Indorsement; Blank Indorsement.

(1) A special indorsement specifies the person to whom or to whose order it makes the instrument payable. Any instrument specially indorsed becomes payable to the order of the special indorsee and may be further negotiated only by his indorsement.

(2) An indorsement in blank specifies no particular indorsee and may consist of a mere signature. An instrument payable to order and indorsed in blank becomes payable to bearer and may be negotiated by delivery alone until specially indorsed.

(3) The holder may convert a blank indorsement into a special indorsement by writing over the signature of the indorser in blank any contract consistent with the character of the indorsement.

§ 3—205. Restrictive Indorsements.

An indorsement is restrictive which either

(a) is conditional; or

(b) purports to prohibit further transfer of the instrument; or

(c) includes the words "for collection", "for deposit", "pay any bank", or like terms signifying a purpose of deposit or collection; or

(d) otherwise states that it is for the benefit or use of the indorser or of another person.

§ 3—206. Effect of Restrictive Indorsement.

(1) No restrictive indorsement prevents further transfer or negotiation of the instrument.

(2) An intermediary bank, or a payor bank which is not the depositary bank, is neither given notice nor otherwise affected by a restrictive indorsement of any person except the bank's immediate transferor or the person presenting for payment.

(3) Except for an intermediary bank, any transferee under an indorsement which is conditional or includes the words "for collection", "for deposit", "pay any bank", or like terms (subparagraphs (a) and (c) of Section 3—205) must pay or apply any value given by him for or on the security of the instrument consistently with the indorsement and to the extent that he does so he becomes a holder for value. In addition such transferee is a holder in due course if he otherwise complies with the requirements of Section 3—302 on what constitutes a holder in due course.

(4) The first taker under an indorsement for the benefit of the indorser or another person (subparagraph (d) of Section 3—205) must pay or apply any value given by him for or on the security of the instrument consistently with the indorsement and to the extent that he does so he becomes a holder for value. In addition such taker is a holder in due course if he otherwise complies with the requirements of Section 3—302 on what constitutes a holder in due course. A later holder for value is neither given notice nor otherwise affected by such restrictive indorsement unless he has knowledge that a fiduciary or other person has negotiated the instrument in any transaction for his own benefit or otherwise in breach of duty (subsection (2) of Section 3—304).

§ 3—207. Negotiation Effective Although It May Be Rescinded.

(1) Negotiation is effective to transfer the instrument although the negotiation is

(a) made by an infant, a corporation exceeding its powers, or any other person without capacity; or

(b) obtained by fraud, duress or mistake of any kind; or

(c) part of an illegal transaction; or

(d) made in breach of duty.

(2) Except as against a subsequent holder in due course such negotiation is in an appropriate case subject to rescission, the declaration of a constructive trust or any other remedy permitted by law.

§ 3—208. Reacquisition.

Where an instrument is returned to or reacquired by a prior party he may cancel any indorsement which is not necessary to his title and reissue or further negotiate the instrument, but any intervening party is discharged as against the reacquiring party and subsequent holders not in due course and if his indorsement has been cancelled is discharged as against subsequent holders in due course as well.

PART 3

RIGHTS OF A HOLDER

§ 3—301. Rights of a Holder.

The holder of an instrument whether or not he is the owner may transfer or negotiate it and, except as otherwise provided in Section 3—603 on payment or satisfaction, discharge it or enforce payment in his own name.

§ 3—302. Holder in Due Course.

(1) A holder in due course is a holder who takes the instrument

(a) for value; and

(b) in good faith; and

(c) without notice that it is overdue or has been dishonored or of any defense against or claim to it on the part of any person.

(2) A payee may be a holder in due course.

(3) A holder does not become a holder in due course of an instrument:

(a) by purchase of it at judicial sale or by taking it under legal process; or

(b) by acquiring it in taking over an estate; or

(c) by purchasing it as part of a bulk transaction not in regular course of business of the transferor.

(4) A purchaser of a limited interest can be a holder in due course only to the extent of the interest purchased.

§ 3—303. Taking for Value.

A holder takes the instrument for value

(a) to the extent that the agreed consideration has been performed or that he acquires a security interest in or a lien on the instrument otherwise than by legal process; or

(b) when he takes the instrument in payment of or as security for an antecedent claim against any person whether or not the claim is due; or

(c) when he gives a negotiable instrument for it or makes an irrevocable commitment to a third person.

§ 3—304. Notice to Purchaser.

(1) The purchaser has notice of a claim or defense if

(a) the instrument is so incomplete, bears such visible evidence of forgery or alteration, or is otherwise so irregular as to call into question its validity, terms or ownership or to create an ambiguity as to the party to pay; or

(b) the purchaser has notice that the obligation of any party is voidable in whole or in part, or that all parties have been discharged.

(2) The purchaser has notice of a claim against the instrument when he has knowledge that a fiduciary has negotiated the instrument in payment of or as security for his own debt or in any transaction for his own benefit or otherwise in breach of duty.

(3) The purchaser has notice that an instrument is overdue if he has reason to know

(a) that any part of the principal amount is overdue or that there is an uncured default in payment of another instrument of the same series; or

(b) that acceleration of the instrument has been made; or

(c) that he is taking a demand instrument after demand has been made or more than a reasonable length of time after its issue. A reasonable time for a check drawn and payable within the states and territories of the United States and the District of Columbia is presumed to be thirty days.

(4) Knowledge of the following facts does not of itself give the purchaser notice of a defense or claim

(a) that the instrument is antedated or postdated;

(b) that it was issued or negotiated in return for an executory promise or accompanied by a separate agreement, unless the purchaser has notice that a defense or claim has arisen from the terms thereof;

(c) that any party has signed for accommodation;

(d) that an incomplete instrument has been completed, unless the purchaser has notice of any improper completion;

(e) that anv person negotiating the instrument is or was a fiduciary;

(f) that there has been default in payment of interest on the instrument or in payment of any other instrument, except one of the same series.

(5) The filing or recording of a document does not of itself constitute notice within the provisions of this Article to a person who would otherwise be a holder in due course.

(6) To be effective notice must be received at such time and in such manner as to give a reasonable opportunity to act on it.

§ 3—305. Rights of a Holder in Due Course.

To the extent that a holder is a holder in due course he takes the instrument free from

(1) all claims to it on the part of any person; and

(2) all defenses of any party to the instrument with whom the holder has not dealt except

(a) infancy, to the extent that it is a defense to a simple contract; and

(b) such other incapacity, or duress, or illegality of the transaction, as renders the obligation of the party a nullity; and

(c) such misrepresentation as has induced the party to sign the instrument with neither knowledge nor reasonable opportunity to obtain knowledge of its character or its essential terms; and

(d) discharge in insolvency proceedings; and

(e) any other discharge of which the holder has notice when he takes the instrument.

§ 3—306. Rights of One Not Holder in Due Course.

Unless he has the rights of a holder in due course any person takes the instrument subject to

(a) all valid claims to it on the part of any person; and

(b) all defenses of any party which would be available in an action on a simple contract; and

(c) the defenses of want or failure of consideration, nonperformance of any condition precedent, non-delivery, or delivery for a special purpose (Section 3—408); and

(d) the defense that he or a person through whom he holds the instrument acquired it by theft, or that payment or satisfaction to such holder would be inconsistent with the terms of a restrictive indorsement. The claim of any third person to the instrument is not otherwise available as a defense to any party liable thereon unless the third person himself defends the action for such party.

§ 3—307. Burden of Establishing Signatures, Defenses and Due Course.

(1) Unless specifically denied in the pleadings each signature on an instrument is admitted. When the effectiveness of a signature is put in issue

(a) the burden of establishing it is on the party claiming under the signature; but

(b) the signature is presumed to be genuine or authorized except where the action is to enforce the obligation of a purported signer who has died or become incompetent before proof is required.

(2) When signatures are admitted or established, production of the instrument entitles a holder to recover on it unless the defendant establishes a defense.

(3) After it is shown that a defense exists a person claiming the rights of a holder in due course has the burden of establishing that he or some person under whom he claims is in all respects a holder in due course.

PART 4

LIABILITY OF PARTIES

§ 3—401. Signature.

(1) No person is liable on an instrument unless his signature appears thereon.

(2) A signature is made by use of any name, including any trade or assumed name, upon an instrument, or by any word or mark used in lieu of a written signature.

§ 3—402. Signature in Ambiguous Capacity.

Unless the instrument clearly indicates that a signature made in some other capacity it is an indorsement.

§ 3—403. Signature by Authorized Representative.

(1) A signature may be made by an agent or other representative, and his authority to make it may be established as in other cases of representation. No particular form of appointment is necessary to establish such authority.

(2) An authorized representative who signs his own name to an instrument

(a) is personally obligated if the instrument neither names the person represented nor shows that the representative signed in a representative capacity;

(b) except as otherwise established between the immediate parties, is personally obligated if the instrument names the person represented but does not show that the representative signed in a representative capacity, or if the instrument does not name the person represented but does show that the representative signed in a representative capacity.

(3) Except as otherwise established the name of an organization preceded or followed by the name and office of an authorized individual is a signature made in a representative capacity.

§ 3—404. Unauthorized Signatures.

(1) Any unauthorized signature is wholly inoperative as that of the person whose name is signed unless he ratifies it or is precluded from denying it; but it operates as the signature of the unauthorized signer in favor of any person who in good faith pays the instrument or takes it for value.

(2) Any unauthorized signature may be ratified for all purposes of this Article. Such ratification does not of itself affect any rights of the person ratifying against the actual signer.

§ 3—405. Impostors; Signature in Name of Payee.

(1) An indorsement by any person in the name of a named payee is effective if

(a) an impostor by use of the mails or otherwise has induced the maker or drawer to issue the instrument to him or his confederate in the name of the payee; or

(b) a person signing as or on behalf of a maker or drawer intends the payee to have no interest in the instrument; or

(c) an agent or employee of the maker or drawer has supplied him with the name of the payee intending the latter to have no such interest.

(2) Nothing in this section shall affect the criminal or civil liability of the person so indorsing.

§ 3—406. Negligence Contributing to Alteration or Unauthorized Signature.

Any person who by his negligence substantially contributes to a material alteration of the instrument or to the making of an unauthorized signature is precluded from asserting the alteration or lack of authority against a holder in due course or against a drawee or other payor who pays the instrument in good faith and in accordance with the reasonable commercial standards of the drawee's or payor's business.

§ 3—407. Alteration.

(1) Any alteration of an instrument is material which changes the contract of any party thereto in any respect, including any such change in

(a) the number or relations of the parties; or

(b) an incomplete instrument, by completing it otherwise than as authorized; or

(c) the writing as signed, by adding to it or by removing any part of it.

(2) As against any person other than a subsequent holder in due course

(a) alteration by the holder which is both fraudulent and material discharges any party whose contract is thereby changed unless that party assents or is precluded from asserting the defense;

(b) no other alteration discharges any party and the instrument may be enforced according to its original tenor, or as to incomplete instruments according to the authority given.

(3) A subsequent holder in due course may in all cases enforce the instrument according to its original tenor, and when an incomplete instrument has been completed, he may enforce it as completed.

§ 3—408. Consideration.

Want or failure of consideration is a defense as against any person not having the rights of a holder in due course (Section 3—305), except that no consideration is necessary for an instrument or obligation thereon given in payment of or as security for an antecedent obligation of any kind. Nothing in this section shall be taken to displace any statute outside this Act under which a promise is enforceable notwithstanding lack or failure of consideration. Partial failure of consideration is a defense pro tanto whether or not the failure is in an ascertained or liquidated amount.

§ 3—409. Draft Not an Assignment.

(1) A check or other draft does not of itself operate as an assignment of any funds in the hands of the drawee available for its payment, and the drawee is not liable on the instrument until he accepts it.

(2) Nothing in this section shall affect any liability in contract, tort or otherwise arising from any letter of credit or other obligation or representation which is not an acceptance.

§ 3—410. Definition and Operation of Acceptance.

(1) Acceptance is the drawee's signed engagement to honor the draft as presented. It must be written on the draft, and may consist of his signature alone. It becomes operative when completed by delivery or notification.

(2) A draft may be accepted although it has not been signed by the drawer or is otherwise incomplete or is overdue or has been dishonored.

(3) Where the draft is payable at a fixed period after sight and the acceptor fails to date his acceptance the holder may complete it by supplying a date in good faith.

§ 3—411. Certification of a Check.

(1) Certification of a check is acceptance. Where a holder procures certification the drawer and all prior indorsers are discharged.

(2) Unless otherwise agreed a bank has no obligation to certify a check.

(3) A bank may certify a check before returning it for lack of proper indorsement. If it does so the drawer is discharged.

§ 3—412. Acceptance Varying Draft.

(1) Where the drawee's proferred acceptance in any manner varies the draft as presented the holder may refuse the acceptance and treat the draft as dishonored in which case the drawee is entitled to have his acceptance cancelled.

(2) The terms of the draft are not varied by an acceptance to pay at any particular bank or place in the United States, unless the acceptance states that the draft is to be paid only at such bank or place.

(3) Where the holder assents to an acceptance varying the terms of the draft each drawer and indorser who does not affirmatively assent is discharged.

§ 3—413. Contract of Maker, Drawer and Acceptor.

(1) The maker or acceptor engages that he will pay the instrument according to its tenor at the time of his engagement or as completed pursuant to Section 3—115 on incomplete instruments.

(2) The drawer engages that upon dishonor of the draft and any necessary notice of dishonor or protest he will pay the amount of the draft to the holder or to any indorser who takes it up. The drawer may disclaim this liability by drawing without recourse.

(3) By making, drawing or accepting the party admits as against all subsequent parties including the drawee the existence of the payee and his then capacity to indorse.

§ 3—414. Contract of Indorser; Order of Liability.

(1) Unless the indorsement otherwise specifies (as by such words as "without recourse") every indorser engages that upon dishonor and any necessary notice of dishonor and protest he will pay the instrument according to its tenor at the time of his indorsement to the holder or to any subsequent indorser who takes it up, even though the indorser who takes it up was not obligated to do so.

(2) Unless they otherwise agree indorsers are liable to one another in the order in which they indorse, which is presumed to be the order in which their signatures appear on the instrument.

§ 3—415. Contract of Accommodation Party.

(1) An accommodation party is one who signs the instrument in any capacity for the purpose of lending his name to another party to it.

(2) When the instrument has been taken for value before it is due the accommodation party is liable in the capacity in which he has signed even though the taker knows of the accommodation.

(3) As against a holder in due course and without notice of the accommodation oral proof of the accommodation is not admissible to give the accommodation party the benefit of discharges dependent on his character as such. In other cases the accommodation character may be shown by oral proof.

(4) An indorsement which shows that it is not in the chain of title is notice of its accommodation character.

(5) An accommodation party is not liable to the party accommodated, and if he pays the instrument has a right of recourse on the instrument against such party.

§ 3—416. Contract of Guarantor.

(1) "Payment guaranteed" or equivalent words added to a signature mean that the signer engages that if the instrument is not paid when due he will pay it according to its tenor without resort by the holder to any other party.

(2) "Collection guaranteed" or equivalent words added to a signature mean that the signer engages that if the instrument is not paid when due he will pay it according to its tenor, but only after the holder has reduced his claim against the maker or acceptor to judgment and execution has been returned unsatisfied, or after the maker or acceptor has become insolvent or it is otherwise apparent that it is useless to proceed against him.

(3) Words of guaranty which do not otherwise specify guarantee payment.

(4) No words of guaranty added to the signature of a sole maker or acceptor affect his liability on the instrument. Such words added to the signature of one of two or more makers or acceptors create a presumption that the signature is for the accommodation of the others.

(5) When words of guaranty are used presentment, notice of dishonor and protest are not necessary to charge the user.

(6) Any guaranty written on the instrument is enforcible notwithstanding any statute of frauds.

§ 3—417. Warranties on Presentment and Transfer.

(1) Any person who obtains payment or acceptance and any prior transferor warrants to a person who in good faith pays or accepts that

(a) he has a good title to the instrument or is authorized to obtain payment or acceptance on behalf of one who has a good title; and

(b) he has no knowledge that the signature of the maker or drawer is unauthorized, except that this warranty is not given by a holder in due course acting in good faith

(i) to a maker with respect to the maker's own signature; or

(ii) to a drawer with respect to the drawer's own signature, whether or not the drawer is also the drawee; or

(iii) to an acceptor of a draft if the holder in due course took the draft after the acceptance or obtained the acceptance without knowledge that the drawer's signature was unauthorized; and

(c) the instrument has not been materially altered, except that this warranty is not given by a holder in due course acting in good faith

(i) to the maker of a note; or

(ii) to the drawer of a draft whether or not the drawer is also the drawee; or

(iii) to the acceptor of a draft with respect to an alteration made prior to the acceptance if the holder in due course took the draft after the acceptance, even though the acceptance provided "payable as originally drawn" or equivalent terms; or

(iv) to the acceptor of a draft with respect to an alteration made after the acceptance.

(2) Any person who transfers an instrument and receives consideration warrants to his transferee and if the transfer is by indorsement to any subsequent holder who takes the instrument in good faith that

(a) he has a good title to the instrument or is authorized to obtain payment or acceptance on behalf of one who has a good title and the transfer is otherwise rightful; and

(b) all signatures are genuine or authorized; and

(c) the instrument has not been materially altered; and

(d) no defense of any party is good against him; and

(e) he has no knowledge of any insolvency proceeding instituted with respect to the maker or acceptor or the drawer of an unaccepted instrument.

(3) By transferring "without recourse" the transferor limits the obligation stated in subsection (2) (d) to a warranty that he has no knowledge of such a defense.

(4) A selling agent or broker who does not disclose the fact that he is acting only as such gives the warranties provided in this section, but if he makes such disclosure warrants only his good faith and authority.

§ 3—418. Finality of Payment or Acceptance.

Except for recovery of bank payments as provided in the Article on Bank Deposits and Collections (Article 4) and except for liability for breach of warranty on presentment under the preceding section, payment or acceptance of any instrument is final in favor of a holder in due course, or a person who has in good faith changed his position in reliance on the payment.

§ 3—419. Conversion of Instrument; Innocent Representative.

(1) An instrument is converted when

(a) a drawee to whom it is delivered for acceptance refuses to return it on demand; or

(b) any person to whom it is delivered for payment refuses on demand either to pay or to return it; or

(c) it is paid on a forged indorsement.

(2) In an action against a drawee under subsection (1) the measure of the drawee's liability is the face amount of the instrument. In any other action under subsection (1) the measure of liability is presumed to be the face amount of the instrument.

(3) Subject to the provisions of this Act concerning restrictive indorsements a representative, including a depositary or collecting bank, who has in good faith and in accordance with the reasonable commercial standards applicable to the business of such representative dealt with an instrument or its proceeds on behalf of one who was not the true owner is not liable in conversion or otherwise to the true owner beyond the amount of any proceeds remaining in his hands.

(4) An intermediary bank or payor bank which is not a depositary bank is not liable in conversion solely by reason of the fact that proceeds of an item indorsed restrictively (Sections 3—205 and 3—206) are not paid or applied consistently with the restrictive indorsement of an indorser other than its immediate transferor.

PART 5

PRESENTMENT, NOTICE OF DISHONOR AND PROTEST

§ 3—501. When Presentment, Notice of Dishonor, and Protest Necessary or Permissible.

(1) Unless excused (Section 3—511) presentment is necessary to charge secondary parties as follows:

(a) presentment for acceptance is necessary to charge the drawer and indorsers of a draft where the draft so provides, or is payable elsewhere than at the residence or place of business of the drawee, or its date of payment depends upon such presentment. The holder may at his option present for acceptance any other draft payable at a stated date;

(b) presentment for payment is necessary to charge any indorser;

(c) in the case of any drawer, the acceptor of a draft payable at a bank or the maker of a note payable at a bank, presentment for payment is necessary, but failure to make presentment discharges such drawer, acceptor or maker only as stated in Section 3—502(1) (b).

(2) Unless excused (Section 3—511)

(a) notice of any dishonor is necessary to charge any indorser;

(b) in the case of any drawer, the acceptor of a draft payable at a bank or the maker of a note payable at a bank, notice of any dishonor is necessary, but failure to give such notice discharges such drawer, acceptor or maker only as stated in Section 3—502(1) (b).

(3) Unless excused (Section 3—511) protest of any dishonor is necessary to charge the drawer and indorsers of any draft which on its face appears to be drawn or payable outside of the states, territories, dependencies, and possessions of the United States, the District of Columbia and the Commonwealth of Puerto Rico. The holder may at his option make protest of any dishonor of any other instrument and in the case of a foreign draft may on insolvency of the acceptor before maturity make protest for better security.

(4) Notwithstanding any provision of this section, neither presentment nor notice of dishonor nor protest is necessary to charge an indorser who has indorsed an instrument after maturity.

§ 3—502. Unexcused Delay; Discharge.

(1) Where without excuse any necessary presentment or notice of dishonor is delayed beyond the time when it is due

(a) any indorser is discharged; and

(b) any drawer or the acceptor of a draft payable at a bank or the maker of a note payable at a bank who because the drawee or payor bank becomes insolvent during the delay is deprived of funds maintained with the drawee or payor bank to cover the instrument may discharge his liability by written assignment to the holder of his rights against the drawee or payor bank in respect of such funds, but such drawer, acceptor or maker is not otherwise discharged.

(2) Where without excuse a necessary protest is delayed beyond the time when it is due any drawer or indorser is discharged.

§ 3—503. Time of Presentment.

(1) Unless a different time is expressed in the instrument the time for any presentment is determined as follows:

(a) where an instrument is payable at or a fixed period after a stated date any presentment for acceptance must be made on or before the date it is payable;

(b) where an instrument is payable after sight it must either be presented for acceptance or negotiated within a reasonable time after date or issue whichever is later;

(c) where an instrument shows the date on which it is payable presentment for payment is due on that date;

(d) where an instrument is accelerated presentment for payment is due within a reasonable time after the acceleration;

(e) with respect to the liability of any secondary party presentment for acceptance or payment of any other instrument is due within a reasonable time after such party becomes liable thereon.

(2) A reasonable time for presentment is determined by the nature of the instrument, any usage of banking or trade and the facts of the particular case. In the case of an uncertified check which is drawn and payable within the United States and which is not a draft drawn by a bank the following are presumed to be reasonable periods within which to present for payment or to initiate bank collection:

(a) with respect to the liability of the drawer, thirty days after date or issue whichever is later; and

(b) with respect to the liability of an indorser, seven days after his indorsement.

(3) Where any presentment is due on a day which is not a full business day for either the person making presentment or the party to pay or accept, presentment is due on the next following day which is a full business day for both parties.

(4) Presentment to be sufficient must be made at a reasonable hour, and if at a bank during its banking day.

§ 3—504. How Presentment Made.

(1) Presentment is a demand for acceptance or payment made upon the maker, acceptor, drawee or other payor by or on behalf of the holder.

(2) Presentment may be made

(a) by mail, in which event the time of presentment is determined by the time of receipt of the mail; or

(b) through a clearing house; or

(c) at the place of acceptance or payment specified in the instrument or if there be none at the place of business or residence of the party to accept or pay. If neither the party to accept or pay nor anyone authorized to act for him is present or accessible at such place presentment is excused.

(3) It may be made

(a) to any one of two or more makers, acceptors, drawees or other payors; or

(b) to any person who has authority to make or refuse the acceptance or payment.

(4) A draft accepted or a note made payable at a bank in the United States must be presented at such bank.

(5) In the cases described in Section 4—210 presentment may be made in the manner and with the result stated in that section.

§ 3—505. Rights of Party to Whom Presentment Is Made.

(1) The party to whom presentment is made may without dishonor require

(a) exhibition of the instrument; and

(b) reasonable identification of the person making presentment and evidence of his authority to make it if made for another; and

(c) that the instrument be produced for acceptance or payment at a place specified in it, or if there be none at any place reasonable in the circumstances; and

(d) a signed receipt on the instrument for any partial or full payment and its surrender upon full payment.

(2) Failure to comply with any such requirement invalidates the presentment but the person presenting has a reasonable time in which to comply and the time for acceptance or payment runs from the time of compliance.

§ 3—506. Time Allowed for Acceptance or Payment.

(1) Acceptance may be deferred without dishonor until the close of the next business day following presentment. The holder may also in a good faith effort to obtain acceptance and without either dishonor of the instrument or discharge of secondary parties allow postponement of acceptance for an additional business day.

(2) Except as a longer time is allowed in the case of documentary drafts drawn under a letter of credit, and unless an earlier time is agreed to by the party to pay, payment of an instrument may be deferred without dishonor

pending reasonable examination to determine whether it is properly payable, but payment must be made in any event before the close of business on the day of presentment.

§ 3—507. Dishonor; Holder's Right of Recourse; Term Allowing Re-Presentment.

(1) An instrument is dishonored when

(a) a necessary or optional presentment is duly made and due acceptance or payment is refused or cannot be obtained within the prescribed time or in case of bank collections the instrument is seasonably returned by the midnight deadline (Section 4—301); or

(b) presentment is excused and the instrument is not duly accepted or paid.

(2) Subject to any necessary notice of dishonor and protest, the holder has upon dishonor an immediate right of recourse against the drawers and indorsers.

(3) Return of an instrument for lack of proper indorsement is not dishonor.

(4) A term in a draft or an indorsement thereof allowing a stated time for re-presentment in the event of any dishonor of the draft by nonacceptance if a time draft or by nonpayment if a sight draft gives the holder as against any secondary party bound by the term an option to waive the dishonor without affecting the liability of the secondary party and he may present again up to the end of the stated time.

§ 3—508. Notice of Dishonor.

(1) Notice of dishonor may be given to any person who may be liable on the instrument by or on behalf of the holder or any party who has himself received notice, or any other party who can be compelled to pay the instrument. In addition an agent or bank in whose hands the instrument is dishonored may give notice to his principal or customer or to another agent or bank from which the instrument was received.

(2) Any necessary notice must be given by a bank before its midnight deadline and by any other person before midnight of the third business day after dishonor or receipt of notice of dishonor.

(3) Notice may be given in any reasonable manner. It may be oral or written and in any terms which identify the instrument and state that it has been dishonored. A misdescription which does not mislead the party notified does not vitiate the notice. Sending the instrument bearing a stamp, ticket or writing stating that acceptance or payment has been refused or sending a notice of debit with respect to the instrument is sufficient.

(4) Written notice is given when sent although it is not received.

(5) Notice to one partner is notice to each although the firm has been dissolved.

(6) When any party is in insolvency proceedings instituted after the issue of the instrument notice may be given either to the party or to the representative of his estate.

(7) When any party is dead or incompetent notice may be sent to his last known address or given to his personal representative.

(8) Notice operates for the benefit of all parties who have rights on the instrument against the party notified.

§ 3—509. Protest; Noting for Protest.

(1) A protest is a certificate of dishonor made under the hand and seal of a United States consul or vice consul or a notary public or other person authorized to certify dishonor by the law of the place where dishonor occurs. It may be made upon information satisfactory to such person.

(2) The protest must identify the instrument and certify either that due presentment has been made or the reason why it is excused and that the instrument has been dishonored by nonacceptance or nonpayment.

(3) The protest may also certify that notice of dishonor has been given to all parties or to specified parties.

(4) Subject to subsection (5) any necessary protest is due by the time that notice of dishonor is due.

(5) If, before protest is due, an instrument has been noted for protest by the officer to make protest, the protest may be made at any time thereafter as of the date of the noting.

§ 3—510. Evidence of Dishonor and Notice of Dishonor.

The following are admissible as evidence and create a presumption of dishonor and of any notice of dishonor therein shown:

(a) a document regular in form as provided in the preceding section which purports to be a protest;

(b) the purported stamp or writing of the drawee, payor bank or presenting bank on the instrument or accompanying it stating that acceptance or payment has been refused for reasons consistent with dishonor;

(c) any book or record of the drawee, payor bank, or any collecting bank kept in the usual course of business which shows dishonor, even though there is no evidence of who made the entry.

§ 3—511. Waived or Excused Presentment, Protest or Notice of Dishonor or Delay Therein.

(1) Delay in presentment, protest or notice of dishonor is excused when the party is without notice that it is due or when the delay is caused by circumstances beyond his control and he exercises reasonable diligence after the cause of the delay ceases to operate.

(2) Presentment or notice or protest as the case may be is entirely excused when

(a) the party to be charged has waived it expressly or by implication either before or after it is due; or

(b) such party has himself dishonored the instrument or has countermanded payment or otherwise has no reason to expect or right to require that the instrument be accepted or paid; or

(c) by reasonable diligence the presentment or protest cannot be made or the notice given.

(3) Presentment is also entirely excused when

(a) the maker, acceptor or drawee of any instrument except a documentary draft is dead or in insolvency proceedings instituted after the issue of the instrument; or

(b) acceptance or payment is refused but not for want of proper presentment.

(4) Where a draft has been dishonored by nonacceptance a later presentment for payment and any notice of dishonor and protest for nonpayment are excused unless in the meantime the instrument has been accepted.

(5) A waiver of protest is also a waiver of presentment and of notice of dishonor even though protest is not required.

(6) Where a waiver of presentment or notice or protest is embodied in the instrument itself it is binding upon all parties; but where it is written above the signature of an indorser it binds him only.

PART 6

DISCHARGE

§ 3—601. Discharge of Parties.

(1) The extent of the discharge of any party from liability on an instrument is governed by the sections on

(a) payment or satisfaction (Section 3—603); or

(b) tender of payment (Section 3—604); or

(c) cancellation or renunciation (Section 3—605); or

(d) impairment of right of recourse or of collateral (Section 3—606); or

(e) reacquisition of the instrument by a prior party (Section 3—208); or

(f) fraudulent and material alteration (Section 3—407); or

(g) certification of a check (Section 3—411); or

(h) acceptance varying a draft (Section 3—412); or

(i) unexcused delay in presentment or notice of dishonor or protest (Section 3—502).

(2) Any party is also discharged from his liability on an instrument to another party by

any other act or agreement with such party which would discharge his simple contract for the payment of money.

(3) The liability of all parties is discharged when any party who has himself no right of action or recourse on the instrument

(a) reacquires the instrument in his own right; or

(b) is discharged under any provision of this Article, except as otherwise provided with respect to discharge for impairment of recourse or of collateral (Section 3—606).

§ 3—602. Effect of Discharge Against Holder in Due Course.

No discharge of any party provided by this Article is effective against a subsequent holder in due course unless he has notice thereof when he takes the instrument.

§ 3—603. Payment or Satisfaction.

(1) The liability of any party is discharged to the extent of his payment or satisfaction to the holder even though it is made with knowledge of a claim of another person to the instrument unless prior to such payment or satisfaction the person making the claim either supplies indemnity deemed adequate by the party seeking the discharge or enjoins payment or satisfaction by order of a court of competent jurisdiction in an action in which the adverse claimant and the holder are parties. This subsection does not, however, result in the discharge of the liability

(a) of a party who in bad faith pays or satisfies a holder who acquired the instrument by theft or who (unless having the rights of a holder in due course) holds through one who so acquired it; or

(b) of a party (other than an intermediary bank or a payor bank which is not a depositary bank) who pays or satisfies the holder of an instrument which has been restrictively indorsed in a manner not consistent with the terms of such restrictive indorsement.

(2) Payment or satisfaction may be made with the consent of the holder by any person including a stranger to the instrument. Surrender of the instrument to such a person gives him the rights of a transferee (Section 3—201).

§ 3—604. Tender of Payment.

(1) Any party making tender of full payment to a holder when or after it is due is discharged to the extent of all subsequent liability for interest, costs and attorney's fees.

(2) The holder's refusal of such tender wholly discharges any party who has a right of recourse against the party making the tender.

(3) Where the maker or acceptor of an instrument payable otherwise than on demand is able and ready to pay at every place of payment specified in the instrument when it is due, it is equivalent to tender.

§ 3—605. Cancellation and Renunciation.

(1) The holder of an instrument may even without consideration discharge any party

(a) in any manner apparent on the face of the instrument or the indorsement, as by intentionally cancelling the instrument or the party's signature by destruction or mutilation, or by striking out the party's signature; or

(b) by renouncing his rights by a writing signed and delivered or by surrender of the instrument to the party to be discharged.

(2) Neither cancellation nor renunciation without surrender of the instrument affects the title thereto.

§ 3—606. Impairment of Recourse or of Collateral.

(1) The holder discharges any party to the instrument to the extent that without such party's consent the holder

(a) without express reservation of rights releases or agrees not to sue any person against whom the party has to the knowledge of the holder a right of recourse or agrees to suspend the right to enforce against such person the instrument or collateral or otherwise discharges such person, except that failure or delay in effecting any required presentment, protest or notice of dishonor with respect to any such person does not discharge any party as to whom presentment, protest or notice of dishonor is effective or unnecessary; or

(b) unjustifiably impairs any collateral for the instrument given by or on behalf of the party or any person against whom he has a right of recourse.

(2) By express reservation of rights against a party with a right of recourse the holder preserves

(a) all his rights against such party as of the time when the instrument was originally due; and

(b) the right of the party to pay the instrument as of that time; and

(c) all rights of such party to recourse against others.

PART 7

ADVICE OF INTERNATIONAL SIGHT DRAFT

§ 3—701. Letter of Advice of International Sight Draft.

(1) A "letter of advice" is a drawer's communication to the drawee that a described draft has been drawn.

(2) Unless otherwise agreed when a bank receives from another bank a letter of advice of an international sight draft the drawee bank may immediately debit the drawer's account and stop the running of interest pro tanto. Such a debit and any resulting credit to any account covering outstanding drafts leaves in the drawer full power to stop payment or otherwise dispose of the amount and creates no trust or interest in favor of the holder.

(3) Unless otherwise agreed and except where a draft is drawn under a credit issued by the drawee, the drawee of an international sight draft owes the drawer no duty to pay an unadvised draft but if it does so and the draft is genuine, may appropriately debit the drawer's account.

PART 8

MISCELLANEOUS

§ 3—801. Drafts in a Set.

(1) Where a draft is drawn in a set of parts, each of which is numbered and expressed to be an order only if no other part has been honored, the whole of the parts constitutes one draft but a taker of any part may become a holder in due course of the draft.

(2) Any person who negotiates, indorses or accepts a single part of a draft drawn in a set thereby becomes liable to any holder in due course of that part as if it were the whole set, but as between different holders in due course to whom different parts have been negotiated the holder whose title first accrues has all rights to the draft and its proceeds.

(3) As against the drawee the first presented part of a draft drawn in a set is the part entitled to payment, or if a time draft to acceptance and payment. Acceptance of any subsequently presented part renders the drawee liable thereon under subsection (2). With respect both to a holder and to the drawer payment of a subsequently presented part of a draft payable at sight has the same effect as payment of a check notwithstanding an effective stop order (Section 4—407).

(4) Except as otherwise provided in this section, where any part of a draft in a set is discharged by payment or otherwise the whole draft is discharged.

§ 3—802. Effect of Instrument on Obligation for Which It Is Given.

(1) Unless otherwise agreed where an instrument is taken for an underlying obligation

(a) the obligation is pro tanto discharged if a bank is drawer, maker or acceptor of the instrument and there is no recourse on the instrument against the underlying obligor; and

(b) in any other case the obligation is suspended pro tanto until the instrument is due or if it is payable on demand until its presentment. If the instrument is dishonored action may be maintained on either the instrument or the obligation; discharge of the underlying obligor on the instrument also discharges him on the obligation.

(2) The taking in good faith of a check which is not postdated does not of itself so extend the time on the original obligation as to discharge a surety.

§ 3—803. Notice to Third Party.

Where a defendant is sued for breach of an obligation for which a third person is answerable over under this Article he may give the third person written notice of the litigation, and the person notified may then give similar notice to any other person who is answerable over to him under this Article. If the notice states that the person notified may come in and defend and that if the person notified does not do so he will in any action against him by the person giving the notice be bound by any determination of fact common to the two litigations, then unless after seasonable receipt of the notice the person notified does come in and defend he is so bound.

§ 3—804. Lost, Destroyed or Stolen Instruments.

The owner of an instrument which is lost, whether by destruction, theft or otherwise, may maintain an action in his own name and recover from any party liable thereon upon due proof of his ownership, the facts which prevent his production of the instrument and its terms. The court may require security indemnifying the defendant against loss by reason of further claims on the instrument.

§ 3—805. Instruments Not Payable to Order or to Bearer.

This Article applies to any instrument whose terms do not preclude transfer and which is otherwise negotiable within this Article but which is not payable to order or to bearer, except that there can be no holder in due course of such an instrument.

ARTICLE 4

BANK DEPOSITS AND COLLECTIONS

PART 1

GENERAL PROVISIONS AND DEFINITIONS

§ 4—101. Short Title.

This Article shall be known and may be cited as Uniform Commercial Code—Bank Deposits and Collections.

§ 4—102. Applicability.

(1) To the extent that items within this Article are also within the scope of Articles 3 and 8, they are subject to the provisions of those Articles. In the event of conflict the provisions of this Article govern those of Article 3 but the provisions of Article 8 govern those of this Article.

(2) The liability of a bank for action or non-action with respect to any item handled by it for purposes of presentment, payment or collection is governed by the law of the place where the bank is located. In the case of action or non-action by or at a branch or separate office of a bank, its liability is governed by the law of the place where the branch or separate office is located.

§ 4—103. Variation by Agreement; Measure of Damages; Certain Action Constituting Ordinary Care.

(1) The effect of the provisions of this Article may be varied by agreement except that no agreement can disclaim a bank's responsibility for its own lack of good faith or failure to ex-

ercise ordinary care or can limit the measure of damages for such lack or failure; but the parties may by agreement determine the standards by which such responsibility is to be measured if such standards are not manifestly unreasonable.

(2) Federal Reserve regulations and operating letters, clearing house rules, and the like, have the effect of agreements under subsection (1), whether or not specifically assented to by all parties interested in items handled.

(3) Action or non-action approved by this Article or pursuant to Federal Reserve regulations or operating letters constitutes the exercise of ordinary care and, in the absence of special instructions, action or non-action consistent with clearing house rules and the like or with a general banking usage not disapproved by this Article, prima facie constitutes the exercise of ordinary care.

(4) The specification or approval of certain procedures by this Article does not constitute disapproval of other procedures which may be reasonable under the circumstances.

(5) The measure of damages for failure to exercise ordinary care in handling an item is the amount of the item reduced by an amount which could not have been realized by the use of ordinary care, and where there is bad faith it includes other damages, if any, suffered by the party as a proximate consequence.

§ 4—104. Definitions and Index of Definitions.

(1) In this Article unless the context otherwise requires

(a) "Account" means any account with a bank and includes a checking, time, interest or savings account;

(b) "Afternoon" means the period of a day between noon and midnight;

(c) "Banking day" means that part of any day on which a bank is open to the public for carrying on substantially all of its banking functions;

(d) "Clearing house" means any association of banks or other payors regularly clearing items;

(e) "Customer" means any person having an account with a bank or for whom a bank has agreed to collect items and includes a bank carrying an account with another bank;

(f) "Documentary draft" means any negotiable or nonnegotiable draft with accompanying documents, securities or other papers to be delivered against honor of the draft;

(g) "Item" means any instrument for the payment of money even though it is not negotiable but does not include money;

(h) "Midnight deadline" with respect to a bank is midnight on its next banking day following the banking day on which it receives the relevant item or notice or from which the time for taking action commences to run, whichever is later;

(i) "Properly payable" includes the availability of funds for payment at the time of decision to pay or dishonor;

(j) "Settle" means to pay in cash, by clearing house settlement, in a charge or credit or by remittance, or otherwise as instructed. A settlement may be either provisional or final;

(k) "Suspends payments" with respect to a bank means that it has been closed by order of the supervisory authorities, that a public officer has been appointed to take it over or that it ceases or refuses to make payments in the ordinary course of business.

(2) Other definitions applying to this Article and the sections in which they appear are:

"Collecting bank"	Section 4—105.
"Depositary bank"	Section 4—105.
"Intermediary bank"	Section 4—105.
"Payor bank"	Section 4—105.
"Presenting bank"	Section 4—105.
"Remitting bank"	Section 4—105.

(3) The following definitions in other Articles apply to this Article:

"Acceptance"	Section 3—410.
"Certificate of deposit"	Section 3—104.
"Certification"	Section 3—411.
"Check"	Section 3—104.
"Draft"	Section 3—104.
"Holder in due course"	Section 3—302.
"Notice of dishonor"	Section 3—508.

"Presentment" Section 3—504.
"Protest" Section 3—509.
"Secondary party" Section 3—102.

(4) In addition Article 1 contains general definitions and principles of construction and interpretation applicable throughout this Article.

§ 4—105. "Depositary Bank"; "Intermediary Bank"; "Collecting Bank"; "Payor Bank"; "Presenting Bank"; "Remitting Bank".

In this Article unless the context otherwise requires:

(a) "Depositary bank" means the first bank to which an item is transferred for collection even though it is also the payor bank;

(b) "Payor bank" means a bank by which an item is payable as drawn or accepted;

(c) "Intermediary bank" means any bank to which an item is transferred in course of collection except the depositary or payor bank;

(d) "Collecting bank" means any bank handling the item for collection except the payor bank;

(e) "Presenting bank" means any bank presenting an item except a payor bank;

(f) "Remitting bank" means any payor or intermediary bank remitting for an item.

§ 4—106. Separate Office of a Bank.

A branch or separate office of a bank [maintaining its own deposit ledgers] is a separate bank for the purpose of computing the time within which and determining the place at or to which action may be taken or notices or orders shall be given under this Article and under Article 3.

Note: *The brackets are to make it optional with the several states whether to require a branch to maintain its own deposit ledgers in order to be considered to be a separate bank for certain purposes under Article 4. In some states "maintaining its own deposit ledgers" is a satisfactory test. In others branch banking practices are such that this test would not be suitable.*

§ 4—107. Time of Receipt of Items.

(1) For the purpose of allowing time to process items, prove balances and make the necessary entries on its books to determine its position for the day, a bank may fix an afternoon hour of two P.M. or later as a cut-off hour for the handling of money and items and the making of entries on its books.

(2) Any item or deposit of money received on any day after a cut-off hour so fixed or after the close of the banking day may be treated as being received at the opening of the next banking day.

§ 4—108. Delays.

(1) Unless otherwise instructed, a collecting bank in a good faith effort to secure payment may, in the case of specific items and with or without the approval of any person involved, waive, modify or extend time limits imposed or permitted by this Act for a period not in excess of an additional banking day without discharge of secondary parties and without liability to its transferor or any prior party.

(2) Delay by a collecting bank or payor bank beyond time limits prescribed or permitted by this Act or by instructions is excused if caused by interruption of communication facilities, suspension of payments by another bank, war, emergency conditions or other circumstances beyond the control of the bank provided it exercises such diligence as the circumstances require.

§ 4—109. Process of Posting.

The "process of posting" means the usual procedure followed by a payor bank in determining to pay an item and in recording the payment including one or more of the following or other steps as determined by the bank:

(a) verification of any signature;

(b) ascertaining that sufficient funds are available;

(c) affixing a "paid" or other stamp;

(d) entering a charge or entry to a customer's account;

(e) correcting or reversing an entry or erroneous action with respect to the item.

PART 2

COLLECTION OF ITEMS: DEPOSITARY AND COLLECTING BANKS

§ 4—201. Presumption and Duration of Agency Status of Collecting Banks and Provisional Status of Credits; Applicability of Article; Item Indorsed "Pay Any Bank".

(1) Unless a contrary intent clearly appears and prior to the time that a settlement given by a collecting bank for an item is or becomes final (subsection (3) of Section 4—211 and Sections 4—212 and 4—213) the bank is an agent or sub-agent of the owner of the item and any settlement given for the item is provisional. This provision applies regardless of the form of indorsement or lack of indorsement and even though credit given for the item is subject to immediate withdrawal as of right or is in fact withdrawn; but the continuance of ownership of an item by its owner and any rights of the owner to proceeds of the item are subject to rights of a collecting bank such as those resulting from outstanding advances on the item and valid rights of setoff. When an item is handled by banks for purposes of presentment, payment and collection, the relevant provisions of this Article apply even though action of parties clearly establishes that a particular bank has purchased the item and is the owner of it.

(2) After an item has been indorsed with the words "pay any bank" or the like, only a bank may acquire the rights of a holder

- (a) until the item has been returned to the customer initiating collection; or
- (b) until the item has been specially indorsed by a bank to a person who is not a bank.

§ 4—202. Responsibility for Collection; When Action Seasonable.

(1) A collecting bank must use ordinary care in

- (a) presenting an item or sending it for presentment; and
- (b) sending notice of dishonor or non-payment or returning an item other than a documentary draft to the bank's transferor [or directly to the depositary bank under subsection (2) of Section 4—212] (*see note to Section 4—212*) after learning that the item has not been paid or accepted as the case may be; and
- (c) settling for an item when the bank receives final settlement; and
- (d) making or providing for any necessary protest; and
- (e) notifying its transferor of any loss or delay in transit within a reasonable time after discovery thereof.

(2) A collecting bank taking proper action before its midnight deadline following receipt of an item, notice or payment acts seasonably; taking proper action within a reasonably longer time may be seasonable but the bank has the burden of so establishing.

(3) Subject to subsection (1) (a), a bank is not liable for the insolvency, neglect, misconduct, mistake or default of another bank or person or for loss or destruction of an item in transit or in the possession of others.

§ 4—203. Effect of Instructions.

Subject to the provisions of Article 3 concerning conversion of instruments (Section 3—419) and the provisions of both Article 3 and this Article concerning restrictive indorsements only a collecting bank's transferor can give instructions which affect the bank or constitute notice to it and a collecting bank is not liable to prior parties for any action taken pursuant to such instructions or in accordance with any agreement with its transferor.

§ 4—204. Methods of Sending and Presenting; Sending Direct to Payor Bank.

(1) A collecting bank must send items by reasonably prompt method taking into consideration any relevant instructions, the nature of the item, the number of such items on hand, and the cost of collection involved and the method generally used by it or others to present such items.

(2) A collecting bank may send

(a) any item direct to the payor bank;

(b) any item to any non-bank payor if authorized by its transferor; and

(c) any item other than documentary drafts to any non-bank payor, if authorized by Federal Reserve regulation or operating letter, clearing house rule or the like.

(3) Presentment may be made by a presenting bank at a place where the payor bank has requested that presentment be made.

§ 4—205. Supplying Missing Indorsement; No Notice from Prior Indorsement.

(1) A depositary bank which has taken an item for collection may supply any indorsement of the customer which is necessary to title unless the item contains the words "payee's indorsement required" or the like. In the absence of such a requirement a statement placed on the item by the depositary bank to the effect that the item was deposited by a customer or credited to his account is effective as the customer's indorsement.

(2) An intermediary bank, or payor bank which is not a depositary bank, is neither given notice nor otherwise affected by a restrictive indorsement of any person except the bank's immediate transferor.

§ 4—206. Transfer Between Banks.

Any agreed method which identifies the transferor bank is sufficient for the item's further transfer to another bank.

§ 4—207. Warranties of Customer and Collecting Bank on Transfer or Presentment of Items; Time for Claims.

(1) Each customer or collecting bank who obtains payment or acceptance of an item and each prior customer and collecting bank warrants to the payor bank or other payor who in good faith pays or accepts the item that

(a) he has a good title to the item or is authorized to obtain payment or acceptance on behalf of one who has a good title; and

(b) he has no knowledge that the signature of the maker or drawer is unauthorized, except that this warranty is not given by any customer or collecting bank that is a holder in due course and acts in good faith

(i) to a maker with respect to the maker's own signature; or

(ii) to a drawer with respect to the drawer's own signature, whether or not the drawer is also the drawee; or

(iii) to an acceptor of an item if the holder in due course took the item after the acceptance or obtained the acceptance without knowledge that the drawer's signature was unauthorized; and

(c) the item has not been materially altered, except that this warranty is not given by any customer or collecting bank that is a holder in due course and acts in good faith

(i) to the maker of a note; or

(ii) to the drawer of a draft whether or not the drawer is also the drawee; or

(iii) to the acceptor of an item with respect to an alteration made prior to the acceptance if the holder in due course took the item after the acceptance, even though the acceptance provided "payable as originally drawn" or equivalent terms; or

(iv) to the acceptor of an item with respect to an alteration made after the acceptance.

(2) Each customer and collecting bank who transfers an item and receives a settlement or other consideration for it warrants to his transferee and to any subsequent collecting bank who takes the item in good faith that

(a) he has a good title to the item or is authorized to obtain payment or acceptance on behalf of one who has a good title and the transfer is otherwise rightful; and

(b) all signatures are genuine or authorized; and

(c) the item has not been materially altered; and

(d) no defense of any party is good against him; and

(e) he has no knowledge of any insolvency proceeding instituted with respect to the maker or acceptor or the drawer of an unaccepted item.

In addition each customer and collecting bank so transferring an item and receiving a settlement or other consideration engages that upon dishonor and any necessary notice of dishonor and protest he will take up the item.

(3) The warranties and the engagement to honor set forth in the two preceding subsections arise notwithstanding the absence of indorsement or words of guaranty or warranty in the transfer or presentment and a collecting bank remains liable for their breach despite remittance to its transferor. Damages for breach of such warranties or engagement to honor shall not exceed the consideration received by the customer or collecting bank responsible plus finance charges and expenses related to the item, if any.

(4) Unless a claim for breach of warranty under this section is made within a reasonable time after the person claiming learns of the breach, the person liable is discharged to the extent of any loss caused by the delay in making claim.

§ 4—208. Security Interest of Collecting Bank in Items, Accompanying Documents and Proceeds.

(1) A bank has a security interest in an item and any accompanying documents or the proceeds of either

(a) in case of an item deposited in an account to the extent to which credit given for the item has been withdrawn or applied;

(b) in case of an item for which it has given credit available for withdrawal as of right, to the extent of the credit given whether or not the credit is drawn upon and whether or not there is a right of charge-back; or

(c) if it makes an advance on or against the item.

(2) When credit which has been given for several items received at one time or pursuant to a single agreement is withdrawn or applied in part the security interest remains upon all the items, any accompanying documents or the proceeds of either. For the purpose of this section, credits first given are first withdrawn.

(3) Receipt by a collecting bank of a final settlement for an item is a realization on its security interest in the item, accompanying documents and proceeds. To the extent and so long as the bank does not receive final settlement for the item or give up possession of the item or accompanying documents for purposes other than collection, the security interest continues and is subject to the provisions of Article 9 except that

(a) no security agreement is necessary to make the security interest enforceable (subsection (1) (b) of Section 9—203); and

(b) no filing is required to perfect the security interest; and

(c) the security interest has priority over conflicting perfected security interests in the item, accompanying documents or proceeds.

§ 4—209. When Bank Gives Value for Purposes of Holder in Due Course.

For purposes of determining its status as a holder in due course, the bank has given value to the extent that it has a security interest in an item provided that the bank otherwise complies with the requirements of Section 3—302 on what constitutes a holder in due course.

§ 4—210. Presentment by Notice of Item Not Payable by, Through or at a Bank; Liability of Secondary Parties.

(1) Unless otherwise instructed, a collecting bank may present an item not payable by, through or at a bank by sending to the party to accept or pay a written notice that the bank holds the item for acceptance or payment. The notice must be sent in time to be received on or before the day when presentment is due and the bank must meet any requirement of the party to accept or pay under Section 3—505 by the close of the bank's next banking day after it knows of the requirement.

(2) Where presentment is made by notice and neither honor nor request for compliance

with a requirement under Section 3—505 is received by the close of business on the day after maturity or in the case of demand items by the close of business on the third banking day after notice was sent, the presenting bank may treat the item as dishonored and charge any secondary party by sending him notice of the facts.

§ 4—211. Media of Remittance; Provisional and Final Settlement in Remittance Cases.

(1) A collecting bank may take in settlement of an item

(a) a check of the remitting bank or of another bank on any bank except the remitting bank; or

(b) a cashier's check or similar primary obligation of a remitting bank which is a member of or clears through a member of the same clearing house or group as the collecting bank; or

(c) appropriate authority to charge an account of the remitting bank or of another bank with the collecting bank; or

(d) if the item is drawn upon or payable by a person other than a bank, a cashier's check, certified check or other bank check or obligation.

(2) If before its midnight deadline the collecting bank properly dishonors a remittance check or authorization to charge on itself or presents or forwards for collection a remittance instrument of or on another bank which is of a kind approved by subsection (1) or has not been authorized by it, the collecting bank is not liable to prior parties in the event of the dishonor of such check, instrument or authorization.

(3) A settlement for an item by means of a remittance instrument or authorization to charge is or becomes a final settlement as to both the person making and the person receiving the settlement

(a) if the remittance instrument or authorization to charge is of a kind approved by subsection (1) or has not been authorized by the person receiving the settlement and in either case the person receiving the settlement acts seasonably before its midnight deadline in presenting, forwarding for collection or paying the instrument or authorization,—at the time the remittance instrument or authorization is finally paid by the payor by which it is payable;

(b) if the person receiving the settlement has authorized remittance by a non-bank check or obligation or by a cashier's check or similar primary obligation of or a check upon the payor or other remitting bank which is not of a kind approved by subsection (1) (b),—at the time of the receipt of such remittance check or obligation; or

(c) if in a case not covered by sub-paragraphs (a) or (b) the person receiving the settlement fails to seasonably present, forward for collection, pay or return a remittance instrument or authorization to it to charge before its midnight deadline,—at such midnight deadline.

§ 4—212. Right of Charge-Back or Refund.

(1) If a collecting bank has made provisional settlement with its customer for an item and itself fails by reason of dishonor, suspension of payments by a bank or otherwise to receive a settlement for the item which is or becomes final, the bank may revoke the settlement given by it, charge back the amount of any credit given for the item to its customer's account or obtain refund from its customer whether or not it is able to return the items if by its midnight deadline or within a longer reasonable time after it learns the facts it returns the item or sends notification of the facts. These rights to revoke, charge-back and obtain refund terminate if and when a settlement for the item received by the bank is or becomes final (subsection (3) of Section 4—211 and subsections (2) and (3) of Section 4—213).

[(2) Within the time and manner prescribed by this section and Section 4—301, an intermediary or payor bank, as the case may be, may return an unpaid item directly to the depositary bank and may send for collection a draft on the depositary bank and obtain reimbursement. In such case, if the depositary bank has received provisional settlement for the item, it must reimburse the bank drawing the draft and any provisional credits for the item between banks shall become and remain final.]

Note: *Direct returns is recognized as an innovation that is not yet established bank practice, and therefore, Paragraph 2 has been bracketed. Some lawyers have doubts whether it should be included in legislation or left to development by agreement.*

(3) A depositary bank which is also the payor may charge-back the amount of an item to its customer's account or obtain refund in accordance with the section governing return of an item received by a payor bank for credit on its books (Section 4—301).

(4) The right to charge-back is not affected by

- (a) prior use of the credit given for the item; or
- (b) failure by any bank to exercise ordinary care with respect to the item but any bank so failing remains liable.

(5) A failure to charge-back or claim refund does not affect other rights of the bank against the customer or any other party.

(6) If credit is given in dollars as the equivalent of the value of an item payable in a foreign currency the dollar amount of any charge-back or refund shall be calculated on the basis of the buying sight rate for the foreign currency prevailing on the day when the person entitled to the charge-back or refund learns that it will not receive payment in ordinary course.

§ 4—213. Final Payment of Item by Payor Bank; When Provisional Debits and Credits Become Final; When Certain Credits Become Available for Withdrawal.

(1) An item is finally paid by a payor bank when the bank has done any of the following, whichever happens first:

- (a) paid the item in cash; or
- (b) settled for the item without reserving a right to revoke the settlement and without having such right under statute, clearing house rule or agreement; or
- (c) completed the process of posting the item to the indicated account of the drawer, maker or other person to be charged therewith; or
- (d) made a provisional settlement for the item and failed to revoke the settlement in the time and manner permitted by statute, clearing house rule or agreement.

Upon a final payment under subparagraphs (b), (c) or (d) the payor bank shall be accountable for the amount of the item.

(2) If provisional settlement for an item between the presenting and payor banks is made through a clearing house or by debits or credits in an account between them, then to the extent that provisional debits or credits for the item are entered in accounts between the presenting and payor banks or between the presenting and successive prior collecting banks seriatim, they become final upon final payment of the item by the payor bank.

(3) If a collecting bank receives a settlement for an item which is or becomes final (subsection (3) of Section 4—211, subsection (2) of Section 4—213) the bank is accountable to its customer for the amount of the item and any provisional credit given for the item in an account with its customer becomes final.

(4) Subject to any right of the bank to apply the credit to an obligation of the customer, credit given by a bank for an item in an account with its customer becomes available for withdrawal as of right

- (a) in any case where the bank has received a provisional settlement for the item,—when such settlement becomes final and the bank has had a reasonable time to learn that the settlement is final;
- (b) in any case where the bank is both a depositary bank and a payor bank and the item is finally paid,—at the opening of the bank's second banking day following receipt of the item.

(5) A deposit of money in a bank is final when made but, subject to any right of the bank to apply the deposit to an obligation of the customer, the deposit becomes available for withdrawal as of right at the opening of the bank's next banking day following receipt of the deposit.

§ 4—214. Insolvency and Preference.

(1) Any item in or coming into the possession of a payor or collecting bank which suspends payment and which item is not finally paid shall be returned by the receiver, trustee or agent in charge of the closed bank to the presenting bank or the closed bank's customer.

(2) If a payor bank finally pays an item and suspends payments without making a settlement for the item with its customer or the presenting bank which settlement is or becomes final, the owner of the item has a preferred claim against the payor bank.

(3) If a payor bank gives or a collecting bank gives or receives a provisional settlement for an item and thereafter suspends payments, the suspension does not prevent or interfere with the settlement becoming final if such finality occurs automatically upon the lapse of certain time or the happening of certain events (subsection (3) of Section 4—211, subsections (1) (d), (2) and (3) of Section 4—213).

(4) If a collecting bank receives from subsequent parties settlement for an item which settlement is or becomes final and suspends payments without making a settlement for the item with its customer which is or becomes final, the owner of the item has a preferred claim against such collecting bank.

PART 3

COLLECTION OF ITEMS: PAYOR BANKS

§ 4—301. Deferred Posting; Recovery of Payment by Return of Items; Time of Dishonor

(1) Where an authorized settlement for a demand item (other than a documentary draft) received by a payor bank otherwise than for immediate payment over the counter has been made before midnight of the banking day of receipt the payor bank may revoke the settlement and recover any payment if before it has made final payment (subsection (1) of Section 4—213) and before its midnight deadline it

(a) returns the item; or

(b) sends written notice of dishonor or nonpayment if the item is held for protest or is otherwise unavailable for return.

(2) If a demand item is received by a payor bank for credit on its books it may return such item or send notice of dishonor and may revoke any credit given or recover the amount thereof withdrawn by its customer, if it acts within the time limit and in the manner specified in the preceding subsection.

(3) Unless previous notice of dishonor has been sent an item is dishonored at the time when for purposes of dishonor it is returned or notice sent in accordance with this section.

(4) An item is returned:

(a) as to an item received through a clearing house, when it is delivered to the presenting or last collecting bank or to the clearing house or is sent or delivered in accordance with its rules; or

(b) in all other cases, when it is sent or delivered to the bank's customer or transferor or pursuant to his instructions.

§ 4—302. Payor Bank's Responsibility for Late Return of Item.

In the absence of a valid defense such as breach of a presentment warranty (subsection (1) of Section 4—207), settlement effected or the like, if an item is presented on and received by a payor bank the bank is accountable for the amount of

(a) a demand item other than a documentary draft whether properly payable or not if the bank, in any case where it is not also the depositary bank, retains the item beyond midnight of the banking day of receipt without settling for it or, regardless of whether it is also the depositary bank, does not pay or return the item or send notice of dishonor until after its midnight deadline; or

(b) any other properly payable item unless within the time allowed for acceptance or payment of that item the bank either accepts or pays the item or returns it and accompanying documents.

§ 4—303. When Items Subject to Notice, Stop-Order, Legal Process or Setoff; Order in Which Items May Be Charged or Certified.

(1) Any knowledge, notice or stop-order received by, legal process served upon or setoff exercised by a payor bank, whether or not effective under other rules of law to terminate, suspend or modify the bank's right or duty to pay an item or to charge its customer's account for the item, comes too late to so terminate, suspend or modify such right or duty if the knowledge, notice, stop-order or legal process is received or served and a reasonable time for the bank to act thereon expires or the setoff is exercised after the bank has done any of the following:

(a) accepted or certified the item;

(b) paid the item in cash;

(c) settled for the item without reserving a right to revoke the settlement and without having such right under statute, clearing house rule or agreement;

(d) completed the process of posting the item to the indicated account of the drawer, maker or other person to be charged therewith or otherwise has evidenced by examination of such indicated account and by action its decision to pay the item; or

(e) become accountable for the amount of the item under subsection (1) (d) of Section 4—213 and Section 4—302 dealing with the payor bank's responsibility for late return of items.

(2) Subject to the provisions of subsection (1) items may be accepted, paid, certified or charged to the indicated account of its customer in any order convenient to the bank.

PART 4

RELATIONSHIP BETWEEN PAYOR BANK AND ITS CUSTOMER

§ 4—401. When Bank May Charge Customer's Account.

(1) As against its customer, a bank may charge against his account any item which is otherwise properly payable from that account even though the charge creates an overdraft.

(2) A bank which in good faith makes payment to a holder may charge the indicated account of its customer according to

(a) the original tenor of his altered item; or

(b) the tenor of his completed item, even though the bank knows the item has been completed unless the bank has notice that the completion was improper.

§ 4—402. Bank's Liability to Customer for Wrongful Dishonor.

A payor bank is liable to its customer for damages proximately caused by the wrongful dishonor of an item. When the dishonor occurs through mistake liability is limited to actual damages proved. If so proximately caused and proved damages may include damages for an arrest or prosecution of the customer or other consequential damages. Whether any consequential damages are proximately caused by the wrongful dishonor is a question of fact to be determined in each case.

§ 4—403. Customer's Right to Stop Payment; Burden of Proof of Loss.

(1) A customer may by order to his bank stop payment of any item payable for his account but the order must be received at such time and in such manner as to afford the bank a reasonable opportunity to act on it prior to any action by the bank with respect to the item described in Section 4—303.

(2) An oral order is binding upon the bank only for fourteen calendar days unless confirmed in writing within that period. A written order is effective for only six months unless renewed in writing.

(3) The burden of establishing the fact and amount of loss resulting from the payment of an item contrary to a binding stop payment order is on the customer.

§ 4—404. Bank Not Obligated to Pay Check More Than Six Months Old.

A bank is under no obligation to a customer having a checking account to pay a check, other than a certified check, which is presented more than six months after its date, but it may charge its customer's account for a payment made thereafter in good faith.

§ 4—405. Death or Incompetence of Customer.

(1) A payor or collecting bank's authority to accept, pay or collect an item or to account for proceeds of its collection if otherwise effective is not rendered ineffective by incompetence of a customer of either bank existing at the time the item is issued or its collection is undertaken if the bank does not know of an adjudication of incompetence. Neither death nor incompetence of a customer revokes such authority to accept, pay, collect or account until the bank knows of the fact of death or of an adjudication of incompetence and has reasonable opportunity to act on it.

(2) Even with knowledge a bank may for ten days after the date of death pay or certify checks drawn on or prior to that date unless ordered to stop payment by a person claiming an interest in the account.

§ 4—406. Customer's Duty to Discover and Report Unauthorized Signature or Alteration.

(1) When a bank sends to its customer a statement of account accompanied by items paid in good faith in support of the debit entries or holds the statement and items pursuant to a request or instructions of its customer or otherwise in a reasonable manner makes the statement and items available to the customer, the customer must exercise reasonable care and promptness to examine the statement and items to discover his unauthorized signature or any alteration on an item and must notify the bank promptly after discovery thereof.

(2) If the bank establishes that the customer failed with respect to an item to comply with the duties imposed on the customer by subsection (1) the customer is precluded from asserting against the bank

(a) his unauthorized signature or any alteration on the item if the bank also establishes that it suffered a loss by reason of such failure; and

(b) an unauthorized signature or alteration by the same wrongdoer on any other item paid in good faith by the bank after the first item and statement was available to the customer for a reasonable period not exceeding fourteen calendar days and before the bank receives notification from the customer of any such unauthorized signature or alteration.

(3) The preclusion under subsection (2) does not apply if the customer establishes lack of ordinary care on the part of the bank in paying the item(s).

(4) Without regard to care or lack of care of either the customer or the bank a customer who does not within one year from the time the statement and items are made available to the customer (subsection (1)) discover and report his unauthorized signature or any alteration on the face or back of the item or does not within three years from that time discover and report any unauthorized indorsement is precluded from asserting against the bank such unauthorized signature or indorsement or such alteration.

(5) If under this section a payor bank has a valid defense against a claim of a customer upon or resulting from payment of an item and waives or fails upon request to assert the defense the bank may not assert against any collecting bank or other prior party presenting or transferring the item a claim based upon the unauthorized signature or alteration giving rise to the customer's claim.

§ 4—407. Payor Bank's Right to Subrogation on Improper Payment.

If a payor bank has paid an item over the stop payment order of the drawer or maker or otherwise under circumstances giving a basis for objection by the drawer or maker, to prevent unjust enrichment and only to the extent necessary to prevent loss to the bank by reason of its payment of the item, the payor bank shall be subrogated to the rights

(a) of any holder in due course on the item against the drawer or maker; and

(b) of the payee or any other holder of the item against the drawer or maker either on the item or under the transaction out of which the item arose; and

(c) of the drawer or maker against the payee or any other holder of the item with respect to the transaction out of which the item arose.

PART 5

COLLECTION OF DOCUMENTARY DRAFTS

§ 4—501. Handling of Documentary Drafts; Duty to Send for Presentment and to Notify Customer of Dishonor.

A bank which takes a documentary draft for collection must present or send the draft and accompanying documents for presentment and upon learning that the draft has not been paid or accepted in due course must seasonably notify its customer of such fact even though it may have discounted or bought the draft or extended credit available for withdrawal as of right.

§ 4—502. Presentment of "On Arrival" Drafts.

When a draft or the relevant instructions require presentment "on arrival", "when goods arrive" or the like, the collecting bank need not present until in its judgment a reasonable time for arrival of the goods has expired. Refusal to pay or accept because the goods have not arrived is not dishonor; the bank must notify its transferor of such refusal but need not present the draft again until it is instructed to do so or learns of the arrival of the goods.

§ 4—503. Responsibility of Presenting Bank for Documents and Goods; Report of Reasons for Dishonor; Referee in Case of Need.

Unless otherwise instructed and except as provided in Article 5 a bank presenting a documentary draft

(a) must deliver the documents to the drawee on acceptance of the draft if it is payable more than three days after presentment; otherwise, only on payment; and

(b) upon dishonor, either in the case of presentment for acceptance or presentment for payment, may seek and follow instructions from any referee in case of need designated in the draft or if the presenting bank does not choose to utilize his services it must use diligence and good faith to ascertain the reason for dishonor, must notify its transferor of the dishonor and of the results of its effort to ascertain the reasons therefor and must request instructions.

But the presenting bank is under no obligation with respect to goods represented by the documents except to follow any reasonable instructions seasonably received; it has a right to reimbursement for any expense incurred in following instructions and to prepayment of or indemnity for such expenses.

§ 4—504. Privilege of Presenting Bank to Deal With Goods; Security Interest for Expenses.

(1) A presenting bank which, following the dishonor of a documentary draft, has seasonably requested instructions but does not receive them within a reasonable time may store, sell, or otherwise deal with the goods in any reasonable manner.

(2) For its reasonable expenses incurred by action under subsection (1) the presenting bank has a lien upon the goods or their proceeds, which may be foreclosed in the same manner as an unpaid seller's lien.

ARTICLE 5

LETTERS OF CREDIT

§ 5—101. Short Title.

This Article shall be known and may be cited as Uniform Commercial Code—Letters of Credit.

§ 5—102. Scope.

(1) This Article applies

(a) to a credit issued by a bank if the credit requires a documentary draft or a documentary demand for payment; and

(b) to a credit issued by a person other than a bank if the credit requires that the draft or demand for payment be accompanied by a document of title; and

(c) to a credit issued by a bank or other person if the credit is not within subparagraphs (a) or (b) but conspicuously states that it is a letter of credit or is conspicuously so entitled.

(2) Unless the engagement meets the requirements of subsection (1), this Article does not apply to engagements to make advances or to honor drafts or demands for payment, to authorities to pay or purchase, to guarantees or to general agreements.

(3) This Article deals with some but not all of the rules and concepts of letters of credit as such rules or concepts have developed prior to this act or may hereafter develop. The fact that this Article states a rule does not by itself require, imply or negate application of the same or a converse rule to a situation not provided for or to a person not specified by this Article.

§ 5—103. Definitions.

(1) In this Article unless the context otherwise requires

(a) "Credit" or "letter of credit" means an engagement by a bank or other person made at the request of a customer and of a kind within the scope of this Article (Section 5—102) that the issuer will honor drafts or other demands for payment upon compliance with the conditions specified in the credit. A credit may be either revocable or irrevocable. The engagement may be either an agreement to honor or a statement that the bank or other person is authorized to honor.

(b) A "documentary draft" or a "documentary demand for payment" is one honor of which is conditioned upon the presentation of a document or documents. "Document" means any paper including document of title, security, invoice, certificate, notice of default and the like.

(c) An "issuer" is a bank or other person issuing a credit.

(d) A "beneficiary" of a credit is a person who is entitled under its terms to draw or demand payment.

(e) An "advising bank" is a bank which gives notification of the issuance of a credit by another bank.

(f) A "confirming bank" is a bank which engages either that it will itself honor a credit already issued by another bank or that such a credit will be honored by the issuer or a third bank.

(g) A "customer" is a buyer or other person who causes an issuer to issue a credit. The term also includes a bank which procures issuance or confirmation on behalf of that bank's customer.

(2) Other definitions applying to this Article and the sections in which they appear are:

"Notation of Credit".	Section 5—108.
"Presenter".	Section 5—112(3).

(3) Definitions in other Articles applying to this Article and the sections in which they appear are:

"Accept" or Acceptance".	Section 3—410.
"Contract for sale".	Section 2—106.
"Draft".	Section 3—104.
"Holder in due course".	Section 3—302.
"Midnight deadline".	Section 4—104.
"Security".	Section 8—102.

(4) In addition, Article 1 contains general definitions and principles of construction and interpretation applicable throughout this Article.

§ 5—104. Formal Requirements; Signing.

(1) Except as otherwise required in subsection (1) (c) of Section 5—102 on scope, no particular form of phrasing is required for a credit. A credit must be in writing and signed by the issuer and a confirmation must be in writing and signed by the confirming bank. A modification of the terms of a credit or confirmation must be signed by the issuer or confirming bank.

(2) A telegram may be a sufficient signed writing if it identifies its sender by an authorized authentication. The authentication may be in code and the authorized naming of the issuer in an advice of credit is a sufficient signing.

§ 5—105. Consideration.

No consideration is necessary to establish a credit or to enlarge or otherwise modify its terms.

§ 5—106. Time and Effect of Establishment of Credit.

(1) Unless otherwise agreed a credit is established

(a) as regards the customer as soon as a letter of credit is sent to him or the letter of credit or an authorized written advice of its issuance is sent to the beneficiary; and

(b) as regards the beneficiary when he receives a letter of credit or an authorized written advice of its issuance.

(2) Unless otherwise agreed once an irrevocable credit is established as regards the customer it can be modified or revoked only with the consent of the customer and once it is established as regards the beneficiary it can be modified or revoked only with his consent.

(3) Unless otherwise agreed after a revocable credit is established it may be modified or revoked by the issuer without notice to or consent from the customer or beneficiary.

(4) Notwithstanding any modification or revocation of a revocable credit any person authorized to honor or negotiate under the terms of the original credit is entitled to reimbursement for or honor of any draft or demand for payment duly honored or negotiated before receipt of notice of the modification or revocation and the issuer in turn is entitled to reimbursement from its customer.

§ 5—107. Advice of Credit; Confirmation; Error in Statement of Terms.

(1) Unless otherwise specified an advising bank by advising a credit issued by another bank does not assume any obligation to honor drafts drawn or demands for payment made under the credit but it does assume obligation for the accuracy of its own statement.

(2) A confirming bank by confirming a credit becomes directly obligated on the credit to the extent of its confirmation as though it were its issuer and acquires the rights of an issuer.

(3) Even though an advising bank incorrectly advises the terms of a credit it has been authorized to advise the credit is established as against the issuer to the extent of its original terms.

(4) Unless otherwise specified the customer bears as against the issuer all risks of transmission and reasonable translation or interpretation of any message relating to a credit.

§ 5—108. "Notation Credit"; Exhaustion of Credit.

(1) A credit which specifies that any person purchasing or paying drafts drawn or demands for payment made under it must note the amount of the draft or demand on the letter or advice of credit is a "notation credit".

(2) Under a notation credit

(a) a person paying the beneficiary or purchasing a draft or demand for payment from him acquires a right to honor only if the appropriate notation is made and by transferring or forwarding for honor the documents under the credit such a person warrants to the issuer that the notation has been made; and

(b) unless the credit or a signed statement that an appropriate notation has been made accompanies the draft or demand for payment the issuer may delay honor until evidence of notation has been procured which is satisfactory to it but its obligation and that of its customer continue for a reasonable time not exceeding thirty days to obtain such evidence.

(3) If the credit is not a notation credit

(a) the issuer may honor complying drafts or demands for payment presented to it in the order in which they are presented and is discharged pro tanto by honor of any such draft or demand;

(b) as between competing good faith purchasers of complying drafts or demands the person first purchasing has priority over a subsequent purchaser even though the later purchased draft or demand has been first honored.

§ 5—109. Issuer's Obligation to Its Customer.

(1) An issuer's obligation to its customer includes good faith and observance of any general banking usage but unless otherwise agreed does not include liability or responsibility

(a) for performance of the underlying contract for sale or other transaction between the customer and the beneficiary; or

(b) for any act or omission of any person other than itself or its own branch or for loss or destruction of a draft, demand or document in transit or in the possession of others; or

(c) based on knowledge or lack of knowledge of any usage of any particular trade.

(2) An issuer must examine documents with care so as to ascertain that on their face they appear to comply with the terms of the credit but unless otherwise agreed assumes no liability or responsibility for the genuineness, falsification or effect of any document which appears on such examination to be regular on its face.

(3) A non-bank issuer is not bound by any banking usage of which it has no knowledge.

§ 5—110. Availability of Credit in Portions; Presenter's Reservation of Lien or Claim.

(1) Unless otherwise specified a credit may be used in portions in the discretion of the beneficiary.

(2) Unless otherwise specified a person by presenting a documentary draft or demand for payment under a credit relinquishes upon its honor all claims to the documents and a person by transferring such draft or demand or causing such presentment authorizes such relinquishment. An explicit reservation of claim makes the draft or demand non-complying.

§ 5—111. Warranties on Transfer and Presentment.

(1) Unless otherwise agreed the beneficiary by transferring or presenting a documentary draft or demand for payment warrants to all interested parties that the necessary conditions of the credit have been complied with. This is in addition to any warranties arising under Articles 3, 4, 7 and 8.

(2) Unless otherwise agreed a negotiating, advising, confirming, collecting or issuing bank presenting or transferring a draft or demand for payment under a credit warrants only the matters warranted by a collecting bank under Article 4 and any such bank transferring a document warrants only the matters warranted by an intermediary under Articles 7 and 8.

§ 5—112. Time Allowed for Honor or Rejection; Withholding Honor or Rejection by Consent; "Presenter".

(1) A bank to which a documentary draft or demand for payment is presented under a credit may without dishonor of the draft, demand or credit

(a) defer honor until the close of the third banking day following receipt of the documents; and

(b) further defer honor if the presenter has expressly or impliedly consented thereto.

Failure to honor within the time here specified constitutes dishonor of the draft or demand and of the credit [except as otherwise provided in subsection (4) of Section 5—114 on conditional payment].

Note: *The bracketed language in the last sentence of subsection (1) should be included only if the optional provisions of Section 5—114(4) and (5) are included.*

(2) Upon dishonor the bank may unless otherwise instructed fulfill its duty to return the draft or demand and the documents by holding them at the disposal of the presenter and sending him an advice to that effect.

(3) "Presenter" means any person presenting a draft or demand for payment for honor under a credit even though that person is a confirming bank or other correspondent which is acting under an issuer's authorization.

§ 5—113. Indemnities.

(1) A bank seeking to obtain (whether for itself or another) honor, negotiation or reimbursement under a credit may give an indemnity to induce such honor, negotiation or reimbursement.

(2) An indemnity agreement inducing honor, negotiation or reimbursement

(a) unless otherwise explicitly agreed applies to defects in the documents but not in the goods; and

(b) unless a longer time is explicitly agreed expires at the end of ten business days following receipt of the documents by, the ultimate customer unless notice of objection is sent before such expiration date. The ultimate customer may send notice of objection to the person from whom he received the documents and any bank receiving such notice is under a duty to send notice to its transferor before its midnight deadline.

§ 5—114. Issuer's Duty and Privilege to Honor; Right to Reimbursement.

(1) An issuer must honor a draft or demand for payment which complies with the terms of the relevant credit regardless of whether the goods or documents conform to the underlying contract for sale or other contract between the customer and the beneficiary. The issuer is not excused from honor of such a draft or demand by reason of an additional general term that all documents must be satisfactory to the issuer, but an issuer may require that specified documents must be satisfactory to it.

(2) Unless otherwise agreed when documents appear on their face to comply with the terms of a credit but a required document does not in fact conform to the warranties made on negotiation or transfer of a document of title (Section 7—507) or of a security (Section 8—306) or is forged or fraudulent or there is fraud in the transaction

(a) the issuer must honor the draft or demand for payment if honor is demanded by a negotiating bank or other holder of the draft or demand which has taken the draft or demand under the credit and under circumstances which would make it a holder in due course (Section 3—302) and in an appropriate case would make it a person to whom a document of title has been duly negotiated (Section 7—502) or a bona fide purchaser of a security (Section 8—302); and

(b) in all other cases as against its customer, an issuer acting in good faith may honor the draft or demand for payment despite notification from the customer of fraud, forgery or other defect not apparent on the face of the documents but a court of appropriate jurisdiction may enjoin such honor.

(3) Unless otherwise agreed an issuer which has duly honored a draft or demand for payment is entitled to immediate reimbursement of any payment made under the credit and to be put in effectively available funds not later than the day before maturity of any acceptance made under the credit.

[(4) When a credit provides for payment by the issuer on receipt of notice that the required documents are in the possession of a correspondent or other agent of the issuer

(a) any payment made on receipt of such notice is conditional; and

(b) the issuer may reject documents which do not comply with the credit if it does so within three banking days following its receipt of the documents; and

(c) in the event of such rejection, the issuer is entitled by charge back or otherwise to return of the payment made.]

[(5) In the case covered by subsection (4) failure to reject documents within the time specified in sub-paragraph (b) constitutes acceptance of the documents and makes the payment final in favor of the beneficiary.]

Note: *Subsections (4) and (5) are bracketed as optional. If they are included the bracketed language in the last sentence of Section 5—112(1) should also be included.*

§ 5—115. Remedy for Improper Dishonor or Anticipatory Repudiation.

(1) When an issuer wrongfully dishonors a draft or demand for payment presented under a credit the person entitled to honor has with respect to any documents the rights of a person in the position of a seller (Section 2—707) and may recover from the issuer the face amount of the draft or demand together with incidental damages under Section 2—710 on seller's incidental damages and interest but less any amount realized by resale or other use or disposition of the subject matter of the transaction. In the event no resale or other utilization is made the documents, goods or other subject matter involved in the transaction must be turned over to the issuer on payment of judgment.

(2) When an issuer wrongfully cancels or otherwise repudiates a credit before presentment of a draft or demand for payment drawn under it the beneficiary has the rights of a seller after anticipatory repudiation by the buyer under Section 2—610 if he learns of the repudiation in time reasonably to avoid procurement of the required documents. Otherwise the beneficiary has an immediate right of action for wrongful dishonor.

§ 5—116. Transfer and Assignment.

(1) The right to draw under a credit can be transferred or assigned only when the credit is expressly designated as transferable or assignable.

(2) Even though the credit specifically states that it is nontransferable or nonassignable the beneficiary may before performance of the conditions of the credit assign his right to proceeds. Such an assignment is an assignment of an account under Article 9 on Secured Transactions and is governed by that Article except that

(a) the assignment is ineffective until the letter of credit or advice of credit is delivered to the assignee which delivery constitutes perfection of the security interest under Article 9; and

(b) the issuer may honor drafts or demands for payment drawn under the credit until it receives a notification of the assignment signed by the beneficiary which reasonably identifies the credit involved in the assignment and contains a request to pay the assignee; and

(c) after what reasonably appears to be such a notification has been received the issuer may without dishonor refuse to accept or pay even to a person otherwise entitled to honor until the letter of credit or advice of credit is exhibited to the issuer.

(3) Except where the beneficiary has effectively assigned his right to draw or his right to proceeds, nothing in this section limits his right to transfer or negotiate drafts or demands drawn under the credit.

§ 5—117. Insolvency of Bank Holding Funds for Documentary Credit.

(1) Where an issuer or an advising or confirming bank or a bank which has for a customer procured issuance of a credit by another bank becomes insolvent before final payment under the credit and the credit is one to which this Article is made applicable by paragraphs (a) or (b) of Section 5—102(1) on scope, the receipt or allocation of funds or collateral to secure or meet obligations under the credit shall have the following results:

(a) to the extent of any funds or collateral turned over after or before the insolvency as indemnity against or specifically for the purpose of payment of drafts or demands for payment drawn under the designated credit, the drafts or demands are entitled to payment in preference over depositors or other general creditors of the issuer or bank; and

(b) on expiration of the credit or surrender of the beneficiary's rights under it unused any person who has given such funds or collateral is similarly entitled to return thereof; and

(c) a charge to a general or current account with a bank if specifically consented to for the purpose of indemnity against or payment of drafts or demands for payment drawn under the designated credit falls under the same rules as if the funds had been drawn out in cash and then turned over with specific instructions.

(2) After honor or reimbursement under this section the customer or other person for whose account the insolvent bank has acted is entitled to receive the documents involved.

ARTICLE 6

BULK TRANSFERS

§ 6—101. Short Title.

This Article shall be known and may be cited as Uniform Commercial Code—Bulk Transfers.

§ 6—102. "Bulk Transfer"; Transfers of Equipment; Enterprises Subject to This Article; Bulk Transfers Subject to This Article.

(1) A "bulk transfer" is any transfer in bulk and not in the ordinary course of the transferor's business of a major part of the materials, supplies, merchandise or other inventory (Section 9—109) of an enterprise subject to this Article.

(2) A transfer of a substantial part of the equipment (Section 9—109) of such an enterprise is a bulk transfer if it is made in connection with a bulk transfer of inventory, but not otherwise.

(3) The enterprises subject to this Article are all those whose principal business is the sale of merchandise from stock, including those who manufacture what they sell.

(4) Except as limited by the following section all bulk transfers of goods located within this state are subject to this Article.

§ 6—103. Transfers Excepted From This Article.

The following transfers are not subject to this Article:

(1) Those made to give security for the performance of an obligation;

(2) General assignments for the benefit of all the creditors of the transferor, and subsequent transfers by the assignee thereunder;

(3) Transfers in settlement or realization of a lien or other security interest;

(4) Sales by executors, administrators, receivers, trustees in bankruptcy, or any public officer under judicial process;

(5) Sales made in the course of judicial or administrative proceedings for the dissolution or reorganization of a corporation and of which notice is sent to the creditors of the corporation pursuant to order of the court or administrative agency;

(6) Transfers to a person maintaining a known place of business in this State who becomes bound to pay the debts of the transferor in full and gives public notice of that fact, and who is solvent after becoming so bound;

(7) A transfer to a new business enterprise organized to take over and continue the business, if public notice of the transaction is given and the new enterprise assumes the debts of the transferor and he receives nothing from the transaction except an interest in the new enterprise junior to the claims of creditors;

(8) Transfers of property which is exempt from execution.

Public notice under subsection (6) or subsection (7) may be given by publishing once a week for two consecutive weeks in a newspaper of general circulation where the transferor had its principal place of business in this state an advertisement including the names and addresses of the transferor and transferee and the effective date of the transfer.

§ 6—104. Schedule of Property, List of Creditors.

(1) Except as provided with respect to auction sales (Section 6—108), a bulk transfer subject to this Article is ineffective against any creditor of the transferor unless:

(a) The transferee requires the transferor to furnish a list of his existing creditors prepared as stated in this section; and

(b) The parties prepare a schedule of the property transferred sufficient to identify it; and

(c) The transferee preserves the list and schedule for six months next following the transfer and permits inspection of either or both and copying therefrom at all reasonable hours by any creditor of the transferor, or files the list and schedule in (*a public office to be here identified*).

(2) The list of creditors must be signed and sworn to or affirmed by the transferor or his agent. It must contain the names and business addresses of all creditors of the transferor, with the amounts when known, and also the names of all persons who are known to the transferor to assert claims against him even though such claims are disputed. If the transferor is the obligor of an outstanding issue of bonds, debentures or the like as to which there is an indenture trustee, the list of creditors need include only the name and address of the indenture trustee and the aggregate outstanding principal amount of the issue.

(3) Responsibility for the completeness and accuracy of the list of creditors rests on the transferor, and the transfer is not rendered ineffective by errors or omissions therein unless the transferee is shown to have had knowledge.

§ 6—105. Notice to Creditors.

In addition to the requirements of the preceding section, any bulk transfer subject to this Article except one made by auction sale (Section 6—108) is ineffective against any creditor of the transferor unless at least ten days before he takes possession of the goods or pays for them, whichever happens first, the transferee gives notice of the transfer in the manner and to the persons hereafter provided (Section 6—107).

[§ 6—106. Application of the Proceeds.

In addition to the requirements of the two preceding sections:

(1) Upon every bulk transfer subject to this Article for which new consideration becomes payable except those made by sale at auction it is the duty of the transferee to assure that such consideration is applied so far as necessary to pay those debts of the transferor which are either shown on the list furnished by the transferor (Section 6—104) or filed in writing in the place stated in the notice (Section 6—107) within thirty days after the mailing of such notice. This duty of the transferee runs to all the holders of such debts, and may be enforced by any of them for the benefit of all.

(2) If any of said debts are in dispute the necessary sum may be withheld from distribution until the dispute is settled or adjudicated.

(3) If the consideration payable is not enough to pay all of the said debts in full distribution shall be made pro rata.]

Note: *This section is bracketed to indicate division of opinion as to whether or not it is a wise provision, and to suggest that this is a point on which State enactments may differ without serious damage to the principle of uniformity.*

In any State where this section is omitted, the following parts of sections, also bracketed in the text, should also be omitted, namely:

Section 6—107(2)(e).
6—108(3)(c).
6—109(2).

In any State where this section is enacted, these other provisions should be also.

Optional Subsection (4)

[(4) The transferee may within ten days after he takes possession of the goods pay the consideration into the (specify court) in the county where the transferor had its principal place of business in this state and thereafter may discharge his duty under this section by giving notice by registered or certified mail to all the persons to whom the duty runs that the consideration has been paid into that court and that they should file their claims there. On motion of any interested party, the court may order the distribution of the consideration to the persons entitled to it.]

Note: *Optional subsection (4) is recommended for those states which do not have a general statute providing for payment of money into court.*

§ 6—107. The Notice.

(1) The notice to creditors (Section 6—105) shall state:

(a) that a bulk transfer is about to be made; and

(b) the names and business addresses of the transferor and transferee, and all other business names and addresses used by the transferor within three years last past so far as known to the transferee; and

(c) whether or not all the debts of the transferor are to be paid in full as they fall due as a result of the transaction, and if so, the address to which creditors should send their bills.

(2) If the debts of the transferor are not to be paid in full as they fall due or if the transferee is in doubt on that point then the notice shall state further:

(a) the location and general description of the property to be transferred and the estimated total of the transferor's debts;

(b) the address where the schedule of property and list of creditors (Section 6—104) may be inspected;

(c) whether the transfer is to pay existing debts and if so the amount of such debts and to whom owing;

(d) whether the transfer is for new consideration and if so the amount of such consideration and the time and place of payment; [and]

[(e) if for new consideration the time and place where creditors of the transferor are to file their claims.]

(3) The notice in any case shall be delivered personally or sent by registered or certified mail to all the persons shown on the list of creditors furnished by the transferor (Section 6—104) and to all other persons who are known to the transferee to hold or assert claims against the transferor.

§ 6—108. Auction Sales; "Auctioneer".

(1) A bulk transfer is subject to this Article even though it is by sale at auction, but only in the manner and with the results stated in this section.

(2) The transferor shall furnish a list of his creditors and assist in the preparation of a schedule of the property to be sold, both prepared as before stated (Section 6—104).

(3) The person or persons other than the transferor who direct, control or are responsible for the auction are collectively called the "auctioneer". The auctioneer shall:

(a) receive and retain the list of creditors and prepare and retain the schedule of property for the period stated in this Article (Section 6—104);

(b) give notice of the auction personally or by registered or certified mail at least ten days before it occurs to all persons shown on the list of creditors and to all other persons who are known to him to hold or assert claims against the transferor; [and]

[(c) assure that the net proceeds of the auction are applied as provided in this Article (Section 6—106).]

(4) Failure of the auctioneer to perform any of these duties does not affect the validity of the sale or the title of the purchasers, but if the auctioneer knows that the auction constitutes a bulk transfer such failure renders the auctioneer liable to the creditors of the transferor as a class for the sums owing to them from the transferor up to but not exceeding the net proceeds of the auction. If the auctioneer consists of several persons their liability is joint and several.

§ 6—109. What Creditors Protected; [Credit for Payment to Particular Creditors].

(1) The creditors of the transferor mentioned in this Article are those holding claims based on transactions or events occurring before the bulk transfer, but creditors who become such after notice to creditors is given (Sections 6—105 and 6—107) are not entitled to notice.

[(2) Against the aggregate obligation imposed by the provisions of this Article concerning the application of the proceeds (Section 6—106 and subsection (3) (c) of 6—108) the transferee or auctioneer is entitled to credit for sums paid to particular creditors of the transferor, not exceeding the sums believed in good faith at the time of the payment to be properly payable to such creditors.]

§ 6—110. Subsequent Transfers.

When the title of a transferee to property is subject to a defect by reason of his non-compliance with the requirements of this Article, then:

(1) a purchaser of any of such property from such transferee who pays no value or who takes with notice of such non-compliance takes subject to such defect, but

(2) a purchaser for value in good faith and without such notice takes free of such defect.

§ 6—111. Limitation of Actions and Levies.

No action under this Article shall be brought nor levy made more than six months after the date on which the transferee took possession of the goods unless the transfer has been concealed. If the transfer has been concealed, actions may be brought or levies made within six months after its discovery.

Note to Article 6: *Section 6—106 is bracketed to indicate division of opinion as to whether or not it is a wise provision, and to suggest that this is a point on which State enactments may differ without serious damage to the principle of uniformity.*

In any State where Section 6—106 is not enacted, the following parts of sections, also bracketed in the text, should also be omitted, namely:

Sec. 6—107(2)(e).
6—108(3)(c).
6—109(2).

In any State where Section 6—106 is enacted, these other provisions should be also.

ARTICLE 7

WAREHOUSE RECEIPTS, BILLS OF LADING AND OTHER DOCUMENTS OF TITLE

PART 1

GENERAL

§ 7—101. Short Title.

This Article shall be known and may be cited as Uniform Commercial Code—Documents of Title.

§ 7—102. Definitions and Index of Definitions.

(1) In this Article, unless the context otherwise requires:

(a) "Bailee" means the person who by a warehouse receipt, bill of lading or other document of title acknowledges possession of goods and contracts to deliver them.

(b) "Consignee" means the person named in a bill to whom or to whose order the bill promises delivery.

(c) "Consignor" means the person named in a bill as the person from whom the goods have been received for shipment.

(d) "Delivery order" means a written order to deliver goods directed to a warehouseman, carrier or other person who in the ordinary course of business issues warehouse receipts or bills of lading.

(e) "Document" means document of title as defined in the general definitions in Article 1 (Section 1—201).

(f) "Goods" means all things which are treated as movable for the purposes of a contract of storage or transportation.

(g) "Issuer" means a bailee who issues a document except that in relation to an unaccepted delivery order it means the person who orders the possessor of goods to deliver. Issuer includes any person for whom an agent or employee purports to act in issuing a document if the agent or employee has real or apparent authority to issue documents, notwithstanding that the issuer received no goods or that the goods were misdescribed or that in any other respect the agent or employee violated his instructions.

(h) "Warehouseman" is a person engaged in the business of storing goods for hire.

(2) Other definitions applying to this Article or to specified Parts thereof, and the sections in which they appear are:

"Duly negotiate". Section 7—501.

"Person entitled under the document". Section 7—403(4).

(3) Definitions in other Articles applying to this Article and the sections in which they appear are:

"Contract for sale". Section 2—106.

"Overseas". Section 2—323.

"Receipt" of goods. Section 2—103.

(4) In addition Article 1 contains general definitions and principles of construction and interpretation applicable throughout this Article.

§ 7—103. Relation of Article to Treaty, Statute, Tariff, Classification or Regulation.

To the extent that any treaty or statute of the United States, regulatory statute of this State or tariff, classification or regulation filed or issued pursuant thereto is applicable, the provisions of this Article are subject thereto.

§ 7—104. Negotiable and Non-Negotiable Warehouse Receipt, Bill of Lading or Other Document of Title.

(1) A warehouse receipt, bill of lading or other document of title is negotiable

(a) if by its terms the goods are to be delivered to bearer or to the order of a named person; or

(b) where recognized in overseas trade, if it runs to a named person or assigns.

(2) Any other document is non-negotiable. A bill of lading in which it is stated that the goods are consigned to a named person is not made negotiable by a provision that the goods are to be delivered only against a written order signed by the same or another named person.

§ 7—105. Construction Against Negative Implication.

The omission from either Part 2 or Part 3 of this Article of a provision corresponding to a provision made in the other Part does not imply that a corresponding rule of law is not applicable.

PART 2

WAREHOUSE RECEIPTS: SPECIAL PROVISIONS

§ 7—201. Who May Issue a Warehouse Receipt; Storage Under Government Bond.

(1) A warehouse receipt may be issued by any warehouseman.

(2) Where goods including distilled spirits and agricultural commodities are stored under a statute requiring a bond against withdrawal or a license for the issuance of receipts in the nature of warehouse receipts, a receipt issued for the goods has like effect as a warehouse receipt even though issued by a person who is the owner of the goods and is not a warehouseman.

§ 7—202. Form of Warehouse Receipt; Essential Terms; Optional Terms.

(1) A warehouse receipt need not be in any particular form.

(2) Unless a warehouse receipt embodies within its written or printed terms each of the following, the warehouseman is liable for damages caused by the omission to a person injured thereby:

(a) the location of the warehouse where the goods are stored;

(b) the date of issue of the receipt;

(c) the consecutive number of the receipt;

(d) a statement whether the goods received will be delivered to the bearer, to a specified person, or to a specified person or his order;

(e) the rate of storage and handling charges, except that where goods are stored under a field warehousing arrangement a statement of that fact is sufficient on a non-negotiable receipt;

(f) a description of the goods or of the packages containing them;

(g) the signature of the warehouseman, which may be made by his authorized agent;

(h) if the receipt is issued for goods of which the warehouseman is owner, either solely or jointly or in common with others, the fact of such ownership; and

(i) a statement of the amount of advances made and of liabilities incurred for which the warehouseman claims a lien or security interest (Section 7—209). If the precise amount of such advances made or of such liabilities incurred is, at the time of the issue of the receipt, unknown to the warehouseman or to his agent who issues it, a statement of the fact that advances have been made or liabilities incurred and the purpose thereof is sufficient.

(3) A warehouseman may insert in his receipt any other terms which are not contrary to the provisions of this Act and do not impair his obligation of delivery (Section 7—403) or his duty of care (Section 7—204). Any contrary provisions shall be ineffective.

§ 7—203. Liability for Non-Receipt or Misdescription.

A party to or purchaser for value in good faith of a document of title other than a bill of lading relying in either case upon the description therein of the goods may recover from the issuer damages caused by the non-receipt or misdescription of the goods, except to the extent that the document conspicuously indicates that the issuer does not know whether any part or all of the goods in fact were received or conform to the description, as where the description is in terms of marks or labels or kind, quantity or condition, or the receipt or description is qualified by "contents, condition and quality unknown", "said to contain" or the like, if such indication be true, or the party or purchaser otherwise has notice.

§ 7—204. Duty of Care; Contractual Limitation of Warehouseman's Liability.

(1) A warehouseman is liable for damages for loss of or injury to the goods caused by his failure to exercise such care in regard to them as a reasonably careful man would exercise under like circumstances but unless otherwise agreed he is not liable for damages which could not have been avoided by the exercise of such care.

(2) Damages may be limited by a term in the warehouse receipt or storage agreement limiting the amount of liability in case of loss or damage, and setting forth a specific liability per article or item, or value per unit of weight, beyond which the warehouseman shall not be liable; provided, however, that such liability may on written request of the bailor at the time of signing such storage agreement or within a reasonable time after receipt of the warehouse receipt be increased on part or all of the goods thereunder, in which event increased rates may be charged based on such increased valuation, but that no such increase shall be permitted contrary to a lawful limitation of liability contained in the warehouseman's tariff, if any. No such limitation is effective with respect to the warehouseman's liability for conversion to his own use.

(3) Reasonable provisions as to the time and manner of presenting claims and instituting actions based on the bailment may be included in the warehouse receipt or tariff.

(4) This section does not impair or repeal . . .

Note: *Insert in subsection (4) a reference to any statute which imposes a higher responsibility upon the warehouseman or invalidates contractual limitations which would be permissible under this Article.*

§ 7—205. Title Under Warehouse Receipt Defeated in Certain Cases.

A buyer in the ordinary course of business of fungible goods sold and delivered by a warehouseman who is also in the business of buying and selling such goods takes free of any claim under a warehouse receipt even though it has been duly negotiated.

§ 7—206. Termination of Storage at Warehouseman's Option.

(1) A warehouseman may on notifying the person on whose account the goods are held and any other person known to claim an inter-

est in the goods require payment of any charges and removal of the goods from the warehouse at the termination of the period of storage fixed by the document, or, if no period is fixed, within a stated period not less than thirty days after the notification. If the goods are not removed before the date specified in the notification, the warehouseman may sell them in accordance with the provisions of the section on enforcement of a warehouseman's lien (Section 7—210).

(2) If a warehouseman in good faith believes that the goods are about to deteriorate or decline in value to less than the amount of his lien within the time prescribed in subsection (1) for notification, advertisement and sale, the warehouseman may specify in the notification any reasonable shorter time for removal of the goods and in case the goods are not removed, may sell them at public sale held not less than one week after a single advertisement or posting.

(3) If as a result of a quality or condition of the goods of which the warehouseman had no notice at the time of deposit the goods are a hazard to other property or to the warehouse or to persons, the warehouseman may sell the goods at public or private sale without advertisement on reasonable notification to all persons known to claim an interest in the goods. If the warehouseman after a reasonable effort is unable to sell the goods he may dispose of them in any lawful manner and shall incur no liability by reason of such disposition.

(4) The warehouseman must deliver the goods to any person entitled to them under this Article upon due demand made at any time prior to sale or other disposition under this section.

(5) The warehouseman may satisfy his lien from the proceeds of any sale or disposition under this section but must hold the balance for delivery on the demand of any person to whom he would have been bound to deliver the goods.

§ 7—207. Goods Must Be Kept Separate; Fungible Goods.

(1) Unless the warehouse receipt otherwise provides, a warehouseman must keep separate the goods covered by each receipt so as to permit at all times identification and delivery of those goods except that different lots of fungible goods may be commingled.

(2) Fungible goods so commingled are owned in common by the persons entitled thereto and the warehouseman is severally liable to each owner for that owner's share. Where because of overissue a mass of fungible goods is insufficient to meet all the receipts which the warehouseman has issued against it, the persons entitled include all holders to whom overissued receipts have been duly negotiated.

§ 7—208. Altered Warehouse Receipts.

Where a blank in a negotiable warehouse receipt has been filled in without authority, a purchaser for value and without notice of the want of authority may treat the insertion as authorized. Any other unauthorized alteration leaves any receipt enforceable against the issuer according to its original tenor.

§ 7—209. Lien of Warehouseman.

(1) A warehouseman has a lien against the bailor on the goods covered by a warehouse receipt or on the proceeds thereof in his possession for charges for storage or transportation (including demurrage and terminal charges), insurance, labor, or charges present or future in relation to the goods, and for expenses necessary for preservation of the goods or reasonably incurred in their sale pursuant to law. If the person on whose account the goods are held is liable for like charges or expenses in relation to other goods whenever deposited and it is stated in the receipt that a lien is claimed for charges and expenses in relation to other goods, the warehouseman also has a lien against him for such charges and expenses whether or not the other goods have been delivered by the warehouseman. But against a person to whom a negotiable warehouse receipt is duly negotiated a warehouseman's lien is limited to charges in an amount or at a rate specified on the receipt or if no charges are so specified then to a reasonable charge for storage of the goods covered by the receipt subsequent to the date of the receipt.

(2) The warehouseman may also reserve a security interest against the bailor for a maximum amount specified on the receipt for charges other than those specifed in subsection (1), such as for money advanced and interest. Such a security interest is governed by the Article on Secured Transactions (Article 9).

(3) (a) A warehouseman's lien for charges and expenses under subsection (1) or a security interest under subsection (2) is also effective against any person who so entrusted the bailor with possession of the goods that a pledge of them by him to a good faith purchaser for value would have been valid but is not effective against a person as to whom the document confers no right in the goods covered by it under Section 7—503.

(b) A warehouseman's lien on household goods for charges and expenses in relation to the goods under subsection (1) is also effective against all persons if the depositor was the legal possessor of the goods at the time of deposit. "Household goods" means furniture, furnishings and personal effects used by the depositor in a dwelling.

(4) A warehouseman loses his lien on any goods which he voluntarily delivers or which he unjustifiably refuses to deliver.

§ 7—210. Enforcement of Warehouseman's Lien.

(1) Except as provided in subsection (2), a warehouseman's lien may be enforced by public or private sale of the goods in bloc or in parcels, at any time or place and on any terms which are commercially reasonable, after notifying all persons known to claim an interest in the goods. Such notification must include a statement of the amount due, the nature of the proposed sale and the time and place of any public sale. The fact that a better price could have been obtained by a sale at a different time or in a different method from that selected by the warehouseman is not of itself sufficient to establish that the sale was not made in a commercially reasonable manner. If the warehouseman either sells the goods in the usual manner in any recognized market therefor, or if he sells at the price current in such market at the time of his sale, or if he has otherwise sold in conformity with commercially reasonable practices among dealers in the type of goods sold, he has sold in a commercially reasonable manner. A sale of more goods than apparently necessary to be offered to insure satisfaction of the obligation is not commercially reasonable except in cases covered by the preceding sentence.

(2) A warehouseman's lien on goods other than goods stored by a merchant in the course of his business may be enforced only as follows:

(a) All persons known to claim an interest in the goods must be notified.

(b) The notification must be delivered in person or sent by registered or certified letter to the last known address of any person to be notified.

(c) The notification must include an itemized statement of the claim, a description of the goods subject to the lien, a demand for payment within a specified time not less than ten days after receipt of the notification, and a conspicuous statement that unless the claim is paid within the time the goods will be advertised for sale and sold by auction at a specified time and place.

(d) The sale must conform to the terms of the notification.

(e) The sale must be held at the nearest suitable place to that where the goods are held or stored.

(f) After the expiration of the time given in the notification, an advertisement of the sale must be published once a week for two weeks consecutively in a newspaper of general circulation where the sale is to be held. The advertisement must include a description of the goods, the name of the person on whose account they are being held, and the time and place of the sale. The sale must take place at least fifteen days after the first publication. If there is no newspaper of general circulation where the sale is to be held, the advertisement must be posted at least ten days before the sale in not less than six conspicuous places in the neighborhood of the proposed sale.

(3) Before any sale pursuant to this section any person claiming a right in the goods may pay the amount necessary to satisfy the lien and the reasonable expenses incurred under this section. In that event the goods must not be sold, but must be retained by the warehouseman subject to the terms of the receipt and this Article.

(4) The warehouseman may buy at any public sale pursuant to this section.

(5) A purchaser in good faith of goods sold to enforce a warehouseman's lien takes the goods free of any rights of persons against whom the lien was valid, despite noncompliance by the warehouseman with the requirements of this section.

(6) The warehouseman may satisfy his lien from the proceeds of any sale pursuant to this section but must hold the balance, if any, for delivery on demand to any person to whom he would have been bound to deliver the goods.

(7) The rights provided by this section shall be in addition to all other rights allowed by law to a creditor against his debtor.

(8) Where a lien is on goods stored by a merchant in the course of his business the lien may be enforced in accordance with either subsection (1) or (2).

(9) The warehouseman is liable for damages caused by failure to comply with the requirements for sale under this section and in case of willful violation is liable for conversion.

PART 3

BILLS OF LADING: SPECIAL PROVISIONS

§ 7—301. Liability for Non-Receipt or Misdescription; "Said to Contain"; "Shipper's Load and Count"; Improper Handling.

(1) A consignee of a non-negotiable bill who has given value in good faith or a holder to whom a negotiable bill has been duly negotiated relying in either case upon the description therein of the goods, or upon the date therein shown, may recover from the issuer damages caused by the misdating of the bill or the non-receipt or misdescription of the goods, except to the extent that the document indicates that the issuer does not know whether any part or all of the goods in fact were received or conform to the description, as where the description is in terms of marks or labels or kind, quantity, or condition or the receipt or description is qualified by "contents or condition of contents of packages unknown", "said to contain", "shipper's weight, load and count" or the like, if such indication be true.

(2) When goods are loaded by an issuer who is a common carrier, the issuer must count the packages of goods if package freight and ascertain the kind and quantity if bulk freight. In such cases "shipper's weight, load and count" or other words indicating that the description was made by the shipper are ineffective except as to freight concealed by packages.

(3) When bulk freight is loaded by a shipper who makes available to the issuer adequate facilities for weighing such freight, an issuer who is a common carrier must ascertain the kind and quantity within a reasonable time after receiving the written request of the shipper to do so. In such cases "shipper's weight" or other words of like purport are ineffective.

(4) The issuer may by inserting in the bill the words "shipper's weight, load and count" or other words of like purport indicate that the goods were loaded by the shipper; and if such statement be true the issuer shall not be liable for damages caused by the improper loading. But their omission does not imply liability for such damages.

(5) The shipper shall be deemed to have guaranteed to the issuer the accuracy at the time of shipment of the description, marks, labels, number, kind, quantity, condition and weight, as furnished by him; and the shipper shall indemnify the issuer against damage caused by inaccuracies in such particulars. The right of the issuer to such indemnity shall in no way limit his responsibility and liability under the contract of carriage to any person other than the shipper.

§ 7—302. Through Bills of Lading and Similar Documents.

(1) The issuer of a through bill of lading or other document embodying an undertaking to be performed in part by persons acting as its agents or by connecting carriers is liable to anyone entitled to recover on the document for any breach by such other persons or by a connecting carrier of its obligation under the document but to the extent that the bill covers an undertaking to be performed overseas or in territory not contiguous to the continental United States or an undertaking including matters other than transportation this liability may be varied by agreement of the parties.

(2) Where goods covered by a through bill of lading or other document embodying an undertaking to be performed in part by persons other than the issuer are received by any such person, he is subject with respect to his own performance while the goods are in his possession to the obligation of the issuer. His ob-

ligation is discharged by delivery of the goods to another such person pursuant to the document, and does not include liability for breach by any other such persons or by the issuer.

(3) The issuer of such through bill of lading or other document shall be entitled to recover from the connecting carrier or such other person in possession of the goods when the breach of the obligation under the document occurred, the amount it may be required to pay to anyone entitled to recover on the document therefor, as may be evidenced by any receipt, judgment, or transcript thereof, and the amount of any expense reasonably incurred by it in defending any action brought by anyone entitled to recover on the document therefor.

§ 7—303. Diversion; Reconsignment; Change of Instructions.

(1) Unless the bill of lading otherwise provides, the carrier may deliver the goods to a person or destination other than that stated in the bill or may otherwise dispose of the goods on instructions from

(a) the holder of a negotiable bill; or

(b) the consignor on a non-negotiable bill notwithstanding contrary instructions from the consignee; or

(c) the consignee on a non-negotiable bill in the absence of contrary instructions from the consignor, if the goods have arrived at the billed destination or if the consignee is in possession of the bill; or

(d) the consignee on a non-negotiable bill if he is entitled as against the consignor to dispose of them.

(2) Unless such instructions are noted on a negotiable bill of lading, a person to whom the bill is duly negotiated can hold the bailee according to the original terms.

§ 7—304. Bills of Lading in a Set.

(1) Except where customary in overseas transportation, a bill of lading must not be issued in a set of parts. The issuer is liable for damages caused by violation of this subsection.

(2) Where a bill of lading is lawfully drawn in a set of parts, each of which is numbered and expressed to be valid only if the goods have not been delivered against any other part, the whole of the parts constitute one bill.

(3) Where a bill of lading is lawfully issued in a set of parts and different parts are negotiated to different persons, the title of the holder to whom the first due negotiation is made prevails as to both the document and the goods even though any later holder may have received the goods from the carrier in good faith and discharged the carrier's obligation by surrender of his part.

(4) Any person who negotiates or transfers a single part of a bill of lading drawn in a set is liable to holders of that part as if it were the whole set.

(5) The bailee is obliged to deliver in accordance with Part 4 of this Article against the first presented part of a bill of lading lawfully drawn in a set. Such delivery discharges the bailee's obligation on the whole bill.

§ 7—305. Destination Bills.

(1) Instead of issuing a bill of lading to the consignor at the place of shipment a carrier may at the request of the consignor procure the bill to be issued at destination or at any other place designated in the request.

(2) Upon request of anyone entitled as against the carrier to control the goods while in transit and on surrender of any outstanding bill of lading or other receipt covering such goods, the issuer may procure a substitute bill to be issued at any place designated in the request.

§ 7—306. Altered Bills of Lading.

An unauthorized alteration or filling in of a blank in a bill of lading leaves the bill enforceable according to its original tenor.

§ 7—307. Lien of Carrier.

(1) A carrier has a lien on the goods covered by a bill of lading for charges subsequent to the date of its receipt of the goods for storage or transportation (including demurrage and terminal charges) and for expenses necessary for preservation of the goods incident to their transportation or reasonably incurred in their sale pursuant to law. But against a purchaser for value of a negotiable bill of lading a carrier's lien is limited to charges stated in

the bill or the applicable tariffs, or if no charges are stated then to a reasonable charge.

(2) A lien for charges and expenses under subsection (1) on goods which the carrier was required by law to receive for transportation is effective against the consignor or any person entitled to the goods unless the carrier had notice that the consignor lacked authority to subject the goods to such charges and expenses. Any other lien under subsection (1) is effective against the consignor and any person who permitted the bailor to have control or possession of the goods unless the carrier had notice that the bailor lacked such authority.

(3) A carrier loses his lien on any goods which he voluntarily delivers or which he unjustifiably refuses to deliver.

§ 7—308. Enforcement of Carrier's Lien.

(1) A carrier's lien may be enforced by public or private sale of the goods, in bloc or in parcels, at any time or place and on any terms which are commercially reasonable, after notifying all persons known to claim an interest in the goods. Such notification must include a statement of the amount due, the nature of the proposed sale and the time and place of any public sale. The fact that a better price could have been obtained by a sale at a different time or in a different method from that selected by the carrier is not of itself sufficient to establish that the sale was not made in a commercially reasonable manner. If the carrier either sells the goods in the usual manner in any recognized market therefor or if he sells at the price current in such market at the time of his sale or if he has otherwise sold in conformity with commercially reasonable practices among dealers in the type of goods sold he has sold in a commercially reasonable manner. A sale of more goods than apparently necessary to be offered to ensure satisfaction of the obligation is not commercially reasonable except in cases covered by the preceding sentence.

(2) Before any sale pursuant to this section any person claiming a right in the goods may pay the amount necessary to satisfy the lien and the reasonable expenses incurred under this section. In that event the goods must not be sold, but must be retained by the carrier subject to the terms of the bill and this Article.

(3) The carrier may buy at any public sale pursuant to this section.

(4) A purchaser in good faith of goods sold to enforce a carrier's lien takes the goods free of any rights of persons against whom the lien was valid, despite noncompliance by the carrier with the requirements of this section.

(5) The carrier may satisfy his lien from the proceeds of any sale pursuant to this section but must hold the balance, if any, for delivery on demand to any person to whom he would have been bound to deliver the goods.

(6) The rights provided by this section shall be in addition to all other rights allowed by law to a creditor against his debtor.

(7) A carrier's lien may be enforced in accordance with either subsection (1) or the procedure set forth in subsection (2) of Section 7—210.

(8) The carrier is liable for damages caused by failure to comply with the requirements for sale under this section and in case of willful violation is liable for conversion.

§ 7—309. Duty of Care; Contractual Limitation of Carrier's Liability.

(1) A carrier who issues a bill of lading whether negotiable or non-negotiable must exercise the degree of care in relation to the goods which a reasonably careful man would exercise under like circumstances. This subsection does not repeal or change any law or rule of law which imposes liability upon a common carrier for damages not caused by its negligence.

(2) Damages may be limited by a provision that the carrier's liability shall not exceed a value stated in the document if the carrier's rates are dependent upon value and the consignor by the carrier's tariff is afforded an opportunity to declare a higher value or a value as lawfully provided in the tariff, or where no tariff is filed he is otherwise advised of such opportunity; but no such limitation is effective with respect to the carrier's liability for conversion to its own use.

(3) Reasonable provisions as to the time and manner of presenting claims and instituting actions based on the shipment may be included in a bill of lading or tariff.

PART 4

WAREHOUSE RECEIPTS AND BILLS OF LADING: GENERAL OBLIGATIONS

§ 7—401. Irregularities in Issue of Receipt or Bill or Conduct of Issuer.

The obligations imposed by this Article on an issuer apply to a document of title regardless of the fact that

(a) the document may not comply with the requirements of this Article or of any other law or regulation regarding its issue, form or content; or

(b) the issuer may have violated laws regulating the conduct of his business; or

(c) the goods covered by the document were owned by the bailee at the time the document was issued; or

(d) the person issuing the document does not come within the definition of warehouseman if it purports to be a warehouse receipt.

§ 7—402. Duplicate Receipt or Bill; Overissue.

Neither a duplicate nor any other document of title purporting to cover goods already represented by an outstanding document of the same issuer confers any right in the goods, except as provided in the case of bills in a set, overissue of documents for fungible goods and substitutes for lost, stolen or destroyed documents. But the issuer is liable for damages caused by his overissue or failure to identify a duplicate document as such by conspicuous notation on its face.

§ 7—403. Obligation of Warehouseman or Carrier to Deliver; Excuse.

(1) The bailee must deliver the goods to a person entitled under the document who complies with subsections (2) and (3), unless and to the extent that the bailee establishes any of the following:

(a) delivery of the goods to a person whose receipt was rightful as against the claimant;

(b) damage to or delay, loss or destruction of the goods for which the bailee is not liable [, but the burden of establishing negligence in such cases is on the person entitled under the document];

Note: *The brackets in (1)(b) indicate that State enactments may differ on this point without serious damage to the principle of uniformity.*

(c) previous sale or other disposition of the goods in lawful enforcement of a lien or on warehouseman's lawful termination of storage;

(d) the exercise by a seller of his right to stop delivery pursuant to the provisions of the Article on Sales (Section 2—705);

(e) a diversion, reconsignment or other disposition pursuant to the provisions of this Article (Section 7—303) or tariff regulating such right;

(f) release, satisfaction or any other fact affording a personal defense against the claimant;

(g) any other lawful excuse.

(2) A person claiming goods covered by a document of title must satisfy the bailee's lien where the bailee so requests or where the bailee is prohibited by law from delivering the goods until the charges are paid.

(3) Unless the person claiming is one against whom the document confers no right under Sec. 7—503(1), he must surrender for cancellation or notation of partial deliveries any outstanding negotiable document covering the goods, and the bailee must cancel the document or conspicuously note the partial delivery thereon or be liable to any person to whom the document is duly negotiated.

(4) "Person entitled under the document" means holder in the case of a negotiable document, or the person to whom delivery is to be made by the terms of or pursuant to written instructions under a non-negotiable document.

§ 7—404. No Liability for Good Faith Delivery Pursuant to Receipt or Bill.

A bailee who in good faith including observance of reasonable commercial standards has received goods and delivered or otherwise disposed of them according to the terms of the document of title or pursuant to this Article is not liable therefor. This rule applies even though the person from whom he received the goods had no authority to procure the document or to dispose of the goods and even though the person to whom he delivered the goods had no authority to receive them.

PART 5

WAREHOUSE RECEIPTS AND BILLS OF LADING: NEGOTIATION AND TRANSFER

§ 7—501. Form of Negotiation and Requirements of "Due Negotiation".

(1) A negotiable document of title running to the order of a named person is negotiated by his indorsement and delivery. After his indorsement in blank or to bearer any person can negotiate it by delivery alone.

(2) (a) A negotiable document of title is also negotiated by delivery alone when by its original terms it runs to bearer.

(b) When a document running to the order of a named person is delivered to him the effect is the same as if the document had been negotiated.

(3) Negotiation of a negotiable document of title after it has been indorsed to a specified person requires indorsement by the special indorsee as well as delivery.

(4) A negotiable document of title is "duly negotiated" when it is negotiated in the manner stated in this section to a holder who purchases it in good faith without notice of any defense against or claim to it on the part of any person and for value, unless it is established that the negotiation is not in the regular course of business or financing or involves receiving the document in settlement or payment of a money obligation.

(5) Indorsement of a non-negotiable document neither makes it negotiable nor adds to the transferee's rights.

(6) The naming in a negotiable bill of a person to be notified of the arrival of the goods does not limit the negotiability of the bill nor constitute notice to a purchaser thereof of any interest of such person in the goods.

§ 7—502. Rights Acquired by Due Negotiation.

(1) Subject to the following section and to the provisions of Section 7—205 on fungible goods, a holder to whom a negotiable document of title has been duly negotiated acquires thereby:

(a) title to the document;

(b) title to the goods;

(c) all rights accruing under the law of agency or estoppel, including rights to goods delivered to the bailee after the document was issued; and

(d) the direct obligation of the issuer to hold or deliver the goods according to the terms of the document free of any defense or claim by him except those arising under the terms of the document or under this Article. In the case of a delivery order the bailee's obligation accrues only upon acceptance and the obligation acquired by the holder is that the issuer and any indorser will procure the acceptance of the bailee.

(2) Subject to the following section, title and rights so acquired are not defeated by any stoppage of the goods represented by the document or by surrender of such goods by the bailee, and are not impaired even though the negotiation or any prior negotiation constituted a breach of duty or even though any person has been deprived of possession of the document by misrepresentation, fraud, accident, mistake, duress, loss, theft or conversion, or even though a previous sale or other transfer of the goods or document has been made to a third person.

§ 7—503. Document of Title to Goods Defeated in Certain Cases.

(1) A document of title confers no right in goods against a person who before issuance of the document had a legal interest or a perfected security interest in them and who neither

(a) delivered or entrusted them or any document of title covering them to the bailor or his nominee with actual or apparent authority to ship, store or sell or with power to obtain delivery under this Article (Section 7—403) or with power of disposition under this Act (Sections 2—403 and 9—307) or other statute or rule of law; nor

(b) acquiesced in the procurement by the bailor or his nominee of any document of title.

(2) Title to goods based upon an unaccepted delivery order is subject to the rights of anyone to whom a negotiable warehouse receipt or bill of lading covering the goods has been duly negotiated. Such a title may be defeated under the next section to the same extent as the rights of the issuer or a transferee from the issuer.

(3) Title to goods based upon a bill of lading issued to a freight forwarder is subject to the rights of anyone to whom a bill issued by the freight forwarder is duly negotiated; but delivery by the carrier in accordance with Part 4 of this Article pursuant to its own bill of lading discharges the carrier's obligation to deliver.

§ 7—504. Rights Acquired in the Absence of Due Negotiation; Effect of Diversion; Seller's Stoppage of Delivery.

(1) A transferee of a document, whether negotiable or nonnegotiable, to whom the document has been delivered but not duly negotiated, acquires the title and rights which his transferor had or had actual authority to convey.

(2) In the case of a non-negotiable document, until but not after the bailee receives notification of the transfer, the rights of the transferee may be defeated

(a) by those creditors of the transferor who could treat the sale as void under Section 2—402; or

(b) by a buyer from the transferor in ordinary course of business if the bailee has delivered the goods to the buyer or received notification of his rights; or

(c) as against the bailee by good faith dealings of the bailee with the transferor.

(3) A diversion or other change of shipping instructions by the consignor in a non-negotiable bill of lading which causes the bailee not the deliver to the consignee defeats the consignee's title to the goods if they have been delivered to a buyer in ordinary course of business and in any event defeats the consignee's rights against the bailee.

(4) Delivery pursuant to a non-negotiable document may be stopped by a seller under Section 2—705, and subject to the requirement of due notification there provided. A bailee honoring the seller's instructions is entitled to be indemnified by the seller against any resulting loss or expense.

§ 7—505. Indorser Not a Guarantor for Other Parties.

The indorsement of a document of title issued by a bailee does not make the indorser liable for any default by the bailee or by previous indorsers.

§ 7—506. Delivery Without Indorsement: Right to Compel Indorsement.

The transferee of a negotiable document of title has a specifically enforceable right to have his transferor supply any necessary indorsement but the transfer becomes a negotiation only as of the time the indorsement is supplied.

§ 7—507. Warranties on Negotiation or Transfer of Receipt or Bill.

Where a person negotiates or transfers a document of title for value otherwise than as a mere intermediary under the next following section, then unless otherwise agreed he warrants to his immediate purchaser only in addition to any warranty made in selling the goods

(a) that the document is genuine; and

(b) that he has no knowledge of any fact which would impair its validity or worth; and

(c) that his negotiation or transfer is rightful and fully effective with respect to the title to the document and the goods it represents.

§ 7—508. Warranties of Collecting Bank as to Documents.

A collecting bank or other intermediary known to be entrusted with documents on behalf of another or with collection of a draft or other claim against delivery of documents warrants by such delivery of the documents only its own good faith and authority. This rule applies even though the intermediary has purchased or made advances against the claim or draft to be collected.

§ 7—509. Receipt or Bill: When Adequate Compliance With Commercial Contract.

The question whether a document is adequate to fulfill the obligations of a contract for sale or the conditions of a credit is governed by the Articles on Sales (Article 2) and on Letters of Credit (Article 5).

PART 6

WAREHOUSE RECEIPTS AND BILLS OF LADING: MISCELLANEOUS PROVISIONS

§ 7—601. Lost and Missing Documents.

(1) If a document has been lost, stolen or destroyed, a court may order delivery of the goods or issuance of a substitute document and the bailee may without liability to any person comply with such order. If the document was negotiable the claimant must post security approved by the court to indemnify any person who may suffer loss as a result of non-surrender of the document. If the document was not negotiable, such security may be required at the discretion of the court. The court may also in its discretion order payment of the bailee's reasonable costs and counsel fees.

(2) A bailee who without court order delivers goods to a person claiming under a missing negotiable document is liable to any person injured thereby, and if the delivery is not in good faith becomes liable for conversion. Delivery in good faith is not conversion if made in accordance with a filed classification or tariff or, where no classification or tariff is filed, if the claimant posts security with the bailee in an amount at least double the value of the goods at the time of posting to indemnify any person injured by the delivery who files a notice of claim within one year after the delivery.

§ 7—602. Attachment of Goods Covered by a Negotiable Document.

Except where the document was originally issued upon delivery of the goods by a person who had no power to dispose of them, no lien attaches by virtue of any judicial process to goods in the possession of a bailee for which a negotiable document of title is outstanding unless the document be first surrendered to the bailee or its negotiation enjoined, and the bailee shall not be compelled to deliver the goods pursuant to process until the document is surrendered to him or impounded by the court. One who purchases the document for value without notice of the process or injunction takes free of the lien imposed by judicial process.

§ 7—603. Conflicting Claims; Interpleader.

If more than one person claims title or possession of the goods, the bailee is excused from delivery until he has had a reasonable time to ascertain the validity of the adverse claims or to bring an action to compel all claimants to interplead and may compel such interpleader, either in defending an action for non-delivery of the goods, or by original action, whichever is appropriate.

ARTICLE 8

INVESTMENT SECURITIES

PART 1

SHORT TITLE AND GENERAL MATTERS

§ 8—101. Short Title.

This Article shall be known and may be cited as Uniform Commercial Code—Investment Securities.

§ 8—102. Definitions and Index of Definitions.

(1) In this Article unless the context otherwise requires

(a) A "security" is an instrument which

(i) is issued in bearer or registered form; and

(ii) is of a type commonly dealt in upon securities exchanges or markets or commonly recognized in any area in which it is issued or dealt in as a medium for investment; and

(iii) is either one of a class or series or by its terms is divisible into a class or series of instruments; and

(iv) evidences a share, participation or other interest in property or in an enterprise or evidences an obligation of the issuer.

(b) A writing which is a security is governed by this Article and not by Uniform Commercial Code—Commercial Paper even though it also meets the requirements of that Article. This Article does not apply to money.

(c) A security is in "registered form" when it specifies a person entitled to the security or to the rights it evidences and when its transfer may be registered upon books maintained for that purpose by or on behalf of an issuer or the security so states.

(d) A security is in "bearer form" when it runs to bearer according to its terms and not by reason of any indorsement.

(2) A "subsequent purchaser" is a person who takes other than by original issue.

(3) A "clearing corporation" is a corporation all of the capital stock of which is held by or for a national securities exchange or association registered under a statute of the United States such as the Securities Exchange Act of 1934.

(4) A "custodian bank" is any bank or trust company which is supervised and examined by state or federal authority having supervision over banks and which is acting as custodian for a clearing corporation.

(5) Other definitions applying to this Article or to specified Parts thereof and the sections in which they appear are:

"Adverse claim".	Section 8—301.
"Bona fide purchaser".	Section 8—302.
"Broker".	Section 8—303.
"Guarantee of the signature".	Section 8—402.
"Intermediary Bank".	Section 4—105.
"Issuer".	Section 8—201.
"Overissue".	Section 8—104.

(6) In addition Article 1 contains general definitions and principles of construction and interpretation applicable throughout this Article.

§ 8—103. Issuer's Lien.

A lien upon a security in favor of an issuer thereof is valid against a purchaser only if the right of the issuer to such lien is noted conspicuously on the security.

§ 8—104. Effect of Overissue; "Overissue."

(1) The provisions of this Article which validate a security or compel its issue or reis-

sue do not apply to the extent that validation, issue or reissue would result in overissue; but

(a) if an identical security which does not constitute an overissue is reasonably available for purchase, the person entitled to issue or validation may compel the issuer to purchase and deliver such a security to him against surrender of the security, if any, which he holds; or

(b) if a security is not so available for purchase, the person entitled to issue or validation may recover from the issuer the price he or the last purchaser for value paid for it with interest from the date of his demand.

(2) "Overissue" means the issue of securities in excess of the amount which the issuer has corporate power to issue.

§ 8—105. Securities Negotiable; Presumptions.

(1) Securities governed by this Article are negotiable instruments.

(2) In any action on a security

(a) unless specifically denied in the pleadings, each signature on the security or in a necessary indorsement is admitted;

(b) when the effectiveness of a signature is put in issue the burden of establishing it is on the party claiming under the signature but the signature is presumed to be genuine or authorized;

(c) when signatures are admitted or established production of the instrument entitles a holder to recover on it unless the defendant establishes a defense or a defect going to the validity of the security; and

(d) after it is shown that a defense or defect exists the plaintiff has the burden of establishing that he or some person under whom he claims is a person against whom the defense or defect is ineffective (Section 8—202).

§ 8—106. Applicability.

The validity of a security and the rights and duties of the issuer with respect to registration of transfer are governed by the law (including the conflict of laws rules) of the jurisdiction of organization of the issuer.

§ 8—107. Securities Deliverable; Action for Price.

(1) Unless otherwise agreed and subject to any applicable law or regulation respecting short sales, a person obligated to deliver securities may deliver any security of the specified issue in bearer form or registered in the name of the transferee or indorsed to him or in blank.

(2) When the buyer fails to pay the price as it comes due under a contract of sale the seller may recover the price

(a) of securities accepted by the buyer; and

(b) of other securities if efforts at their resale would be unduly burdensome or if there is no readily available market for their resale.

PART 2

ISSUE—ISSUER

§ 8—201. "Issuer."

(1) With respect to obligations on or defenses to a security "issuer" includes a person who

(a) places or authorizes the placing of his name on a security (otherwise than as authenticating trustee, registrar, transfer agent or the like) to evidence that it represents a share, participation or other interest in his property or in an enterprise or to evidence his duty to perform an obligation evidenced by the security; or

(b) directly or indirecting creates fractional interests in his rights or property which fractional interests are evidenced by securities; or

(c) becomes responsible for or in place of any other person described as an issuer in this section.

(2) With respect to obligations on or defenses to a security a guarantor is an issuer

to the extent of his guaranty whether or not his obligation is noted on the security.

(3) With respect to registration of transfer (Part 4 of this Article) "issuer" means a person on whose behalf transfer books are maintained.

§ 8—202. Issuer's Responsibility and Defenses; Notice of Defect or Defense.

(1) Even against a purchaser for value and without notice, the terms of a security include those stated on the security and those made part of the security by reference to another instrument, indenture or document or to a constitution, statute, ordinance, rule, regulation, order or the like to the extent that the terms so referred to do not conflict with the stated terms. Such a reference does not of itself charge a purchaser for value with notice of a defect going to the validity of the security even though the security expressly states that a person accepting it admits such notice.

(2) (a) A security other than one issued by a government or governmental agency or unit even though issued with a defect going to its validity is valid in the hands of a purchaser for value and without notice of the particular defect unless the defect involves a violation of constitutional provisions in which case the security is valid in the hands of a subsequent purchaser for value and without notice of the defect.

(b) The rule of subparagraph (a) applies to an issuer which is a government or governmental agency or unit only if either there has been substantial compliance with the legal requirements governing the issue or the issuer has received a substantial consideration for the issue as a whole or for the particular security and a stated purpose of the issue is one for which the issuer has power to borrow money or issue the security.

(3) Except as otherwise provided in the case of certain unauthorized signatures on issue (Section 8—205), lack of genuineness of a security is a complete defense even against a purchaser for value and without notice.

(4) All other defenses of the issuer including nondelivery and conditional delivery of the security are ineffective against a purchaser for value who has taken without notice of the particular defense.

(5) Nothing in this section shall be construed to affect the right of a party to a "when, as and if issued" or a "when distributed" contract to cancel the contract in the event of a material change in the character of the security which is the subject of the contract or in the plan or arrangement pursuant to which such security is to be issued or distributed.

§ 8—203. Staleness as Notice of Defects or Defenses.

(1) After an act or event which creates a right to immediate performance of the principal obligation evidenced by the security or which sets a date on or after which the security is to be presented or surrendered for redemption or exchange, a purchaser is charged with notice of any defect in its issue or defense of the issuer

(a) if the act or event is one requiring the payment of money or the delivery of securities or both on presentation or surrender of the security and such funds or securities are available on the date set for payment or exchange and he takes the security more than one year after that date; and

(b) if the act or event is not covered by paragraph (a) and he takes the security more than two years after the date set for surrender or presentation or the date on which such performance became due.

(2) A call which has been revoked is not within subsection (1).

§ 8—204. Effect of Issuer's Restrictions on Transfer.

Unless noted conspicuously on the security a restriction on transfer imposed by the issuer even though otherwise lawful is ineffective except against a person with actual knowledge of it.

§ 8—205. Effect of Unauthorized Signature on Issue.

An unauthorized signature placed on a security prior to or in the course of issue is ineffective except that the signature is effective in favor of a purchaser for value and without notice of the lack of authority if the signing has been done by

(a) an authenticating trustee, registrar, transfer agent or other person entrusted by the issuer with the signing of the security or of similar securities or their immediate preparation for signing; or

(b) an employee of the issuer or of any of the foregoing entrusted with responsible handling of the security.

§ 8—206. Completion or Alteration of Instrument.

(1) Where a security contains the signatures necessary to its issue or transfer but is incomplete in any other respect.

(a) any person may complete it by filling in the blanks as authorized; and

(b) even though the blanks are incorrectly filled in, the security as completed is enforceable by a purchaser who took it for value and without notice of such incorrectness.

(2) A complete security which has been improperly altered even though fraudulently remains enforceable but only according to its original terms.

§ 8—207. Rights of Issuer With Respect to Registered Owners.

(1) Prior to due presentment for registration of transfer of a security in registered form the issuer or indenture trustee may treat the registered owner as the person exclusively entitled to vote, to receive notifications and otherwise to exercise all the rights and powers of an owner.

(2) Nothing in this Article shall be construed to affect the liability of the registered owner of a security for calls, assessments or the like.

§ 8—208. Effect of Signature of Authenticating Trustee, Registrar or Transfer Agent.

(1) A person placing his signature upon a security as authenticating trustee, registrar, transfer agent or the like warrants to a purchaser for value without notice of the particular defect that

(a) the security is genuine; and

(b) his own participation in the issue of the security is within his capacity and within the scope of the authorization received by him from the issuer; and

(c) he has reasonable grounds to believe that the security is in the form and within the amount the issuer is authorized to issue.

(2) Unless otherwise agreed, a person by so placing his signature does not assume responsibility for the validity of the security in other respects.

PART 3

PURCHASE

§ 8—301. Rights Acquired by Purchaser; "Adverse Claim"; Title Acquired by Bona Fide Purchaser.

(1) Upon delivery of a security the purchaser acquires the rights in the security which his transferor had or had actual authority to convey except that a purchaser who has himself been a party to any fraud or illegality affecting the security or who as a prior holder had notice of an adverse claim cannot improve his position by taking from a later bona fide purchaser. "Adverse claim" includes a claim that a transfer was or would be wrongful or that a particular adverse person is the owner of or has an interest in the security.

(2) A bona fide purchaser in addition to acquiring the rights of a purchaser also acquires the security free of any adverse claim.

(3) A purchaser of a limited interest acquires rights only to the extent of the interest purchased.

§ 8—302. "Bona Fide Purchaser."

A "bona fide purchaser" is a purchaser for value in good faith and without notice of any adverse claim who takes delivery of a security in bearer form or of one in registered form issued to him or indorsed to him or in blank.

§ 8—303. "Broker."

"Broker" means a person engaged for all or part of his time in the business of buying and selling securities, who in the transaction concerned acts for, or buys a security from or sells a security to a customer. Nothing in this Article determines the capacity in which a person acts for purposes of any other statute or rule to which such person is subject.

§ 8—304. Notice to Purchaser of Adverse Claims.

(1) A purchaser (including a broker for the seller or buyer but excluding an intermediary bank) of a security is charged with notice of adverse claims if

(a) the security whether in bearer or registered form has been indorsed "for collection" or "for surrender" or for some other purpose not involving transfer; or

(b) the security is in bearer form and has on it an unambiguous statement that it is the property of a person other than the transferor. The mere writing of a name on a security is not such a statement.

(2) The fact that the purchaser (including a broker for the seller or buyer) has notice that the security is held for a third person or is registered in the name of or indorsed by a fiduciary does not create a duty of inquiry into the rightfulness of the transfer or constitute notice of adverse claims. If, however, the purchaser (excluding an intermediary bank) has knowledge that the proceeds are being used or that the transaction is for the individual benefit of the fiduciary or otherwise in breach of duty, the purchaser is charged with notice of adverse claims.

§ 8—305. Staleness as Notice of Adverse Claims.

An act or event which creates a right to immediate performance of the principal obligation evidenced by the security or which sets a date on or after which the security is to be presented or surrendered for redemption or exchange does not of itself constitute any notice of adverse claims except in the case of a purchase

(a) after one year from any date set for such presentment or surrender for redemption or exchange; or

(b) after six months from any date set for payment of money against presentation or surrender of the security if funds are available for payment on that date.

§ 8—306. Warranties on Presentment and Transfer.

(1) A person who presents a security for registration of transfer or for payment or exchange warrants to the issuer that he is entitled to the registration, payment or exchange. But a purchaser for value without notice of adverse claims who receives a new, reissued or re-registered security on registration of transfer warrants only that he has no knowledge of any unauthorized signature (Section 8—311) in a necessary indorsement.

(2) A person by transferring a security to a purchaser for value warrants only that

(a) his transfer is effective and rightful; and

(b) the security is genuine and has not been materially altered; and

(c) he knows no fact which might impair the validity of the security.

(3) Where a security is delivered by an intermediary known to be entrusted with delivery of the security on behalf of another or with collection of a draft or other claim against such delivery, the intermediary by such delivery warrants only his own good faith and authority even though he has purchased or made advances against the claim to be collected against the delivery.

(4) A pledgee or other holder for security who redelivers the security received, or after payment and on order of the debtor delivers that security to a third person makes only the warranties of an intermediary under subsection (3).

(5) A broker gives to his customer and to the issuer and a purchaser the warranties provided in this section and has the rights and privileges of a purchaser under this section.

The warranties of and in favor of the broker acting as an agent are in addition to applicable warranties given by and in favor of his customer.

§ 8—307. Effect of Delivery Without Indorsement; Right to Compel Indorsement.

Where a security in registered form has been delivered to a purchaser without a necessary indorsement he may become a bona fide purchaser only as of the time the indorsement is supplied, but against the transferor the transfer is complete upon delivery and the purchaser has a specifically enforceable right to have any necessary indorsement supplied.

§ 8—308. Indorsement, How Made; Special Indorsement; Indorser Not a Guarantor; Partial Assignment.

(1) An indorsement of a security in registered form is made when an appropriate person signs on it or on a separate document an assignment or transfer of the security or a power to assign or transfer it or when the signature of such person is written without more upon the back of the security.

(2) An indorsement may be in blank or special. An indorsement in blank includes an indorsement to bearer. A special indorsement specifies the person to whom the security is to be transferred, or who has power to transfer it. A holder may convert a blank indorsement into a special indorsement.

(3) "An appropriate person" in subsection (1) means

(a) the person specified by the security or by special indorsement to be entitled to the security; or

(b) where the person so specified is described as a fiduciary but is no longer serving in the described capacity,—either that person or his successor; or

(c) where the security or indorsement so specifies more than one person as fiduciaries and one or more are no longer serving in the described capacity,—the remaining fiduciary or fiduciaries, whether or not a successor has been appointed or qualified; or

(d) where the person so specified is an individual and is without capacity to act by virtue of death, incompetence, infancy or otherwise,—his executor, administrator, guardian or like fiduciary; or

(e) where the security or indorsement so specifies more than one person as tenants by the entirety or with right of survivorship and by reason of death all cannot sign,—the survivor or survivors; or

(f) a person having power to sign under applicable law or controlling instrument; or

(g) to the extent that any of the foregoing persons may act through an agent,—his authorized agent.

(4) Unless otherwise agreed the indorser by his indorsement assumes no obligation that the security will be honored by the issuer.

(5) An indorsement purporting to be only of part of a security representing units intended by the issuer to be separately transferable is effective to the extent of the indorsement.

(6) Whether the person signing is appropriate is determined as of the date of signing and an indorsement by such a person does not become unauthorized for the purposes of this Article by virtue of any subsequent change of circumstances.

(7) Failure of a fiduciary to comply with a controlling instrument or with the law of the state having jurisdiction of the fiduciary relationship, including any law requiring the fiduciary to obtain court approval of the transfer, does not render his indorsement unauthorized for the purposes of this Article.

§ 8—309. Effect of Indorsement Without Delivery.

An indorsement of a security whether special or in blank does not constitute a transfer until delivery of the security on which it appears or if the indorsement is on a separate document until delivery of both the document and the security.

§ 8—310. Indorsement of Security in Bearer Form.

An indorsement of a security in bearer form may give notice of adverse claims (Section

8—304) but does not otherwise affect any right to registration the holder may possess.

§ 8—311. Effect of Unauthorized Indorsement.

Unless the owner has ratified an unauthorized indorsement or is otherwise precluded from asserting its ineffectiveness

(a) he may assert its ineffectiveness against the issuer or any purchaser other than a purchaser for value and without notice of adverse claims who has in good faith received a new, reissued or re-registered security on registration of transfer; and

(b) an issuer who registers the transfer of a security upon the unauthorized indorsement is subject to liability for improper registration (Section 8—404).

§ 8—312. Effect of Guaranteeing Signature or Indorsement.

(1) Any person guaranteeing a signature of an indorser of a security warrants that at the time of signing

(a) the signature was genuine; and

(b) the signer was an appropriate person to indorse (Section 8—308); and

(c) the signer had legal capacity to sign. But the guarantor does not otherwise warrant the rightfulness of the particular transfer.

(2) Any person may guarantee an indorsement of a security and by so doing warrants not only the signature (subsection 1) but also the rightfulness of the particular transfer in all respects. But no issuer may require a guarantee of indorsement as a condition to registration of transfer.

(3) The foregoing warranties are made to any person taking or dealing with the security in reliance on the guarantee and the guarantor is liable to such person for any loss resulting from breach of the warranties.

§ 8—313. When Delivery to the Purchaser Occurs; Purchaser's Broker as Holder.

(1) Delivery to a purchaser occurs when

(a) he or a person designated by him acquires possession of a security; or

(b) his broker acquires possession of a security specially indorsed to or issued in the name of the purchaser; or

(c) his broker sends him confirmation of the purchase and also by book entry or otherwise identifies a specific security in the broker's possession as belonging to the purchaser; or

(d) with respect to an identified security to be delivered while still in the possession of a third person when that person acknowledges that he holds for the purchaser.

(e) appropriate entries on the books of a clearing corporation are made under Section 8—320.

(2) The purchaser is the owner of a security held for him by his broker, but is not the holder except as specified in subparagraphs (b), (c) and (e) of subsection (1). Where a security is part of a fungible bulk the purchaser is the owner of a proportionate property interest in the fungible bulk.

(3) Notice of an adverse claim received by the broker or by the purchaser after the broker takes delivery as a holder for value is not effective either as to the broker or as to the purchaser. However, as between the broker and the purchaser the purchaser may demand delivery of an equivalent security as to which no notice of an adverse claim has been received.

§ 8—314. Duty to Deliver, When Completed.

(1) Unless otherwise agreed where a sale of a security is made on an exchange or otherwise through brokers

(a) the selling customer fulfills his duty to deliver when he places such a security in the possession of the selling broker or of a person designated by the broker or if requested causes an acknowledgment to be made to the selling broker that it is held for him; and

(b) the selling broker including a correspondent broker acting for a selling customer fulfills his duty to deliver by placing the security or a like security in the possession of the buying broker or a person designated by him or by effecting clearance of the sale in accordance with the rules of the exchange on which the transaction took place.

(2) Except as otherwise provided in this section and unless otherwise agreed, a transferor's duty to deliver a security under a contract of purchase is not fulfilled until he places the security in form to be negotiated by the purchaser in the possession of the purchaser or of a person designated by him or at the purchaser's request causes an acknowledgment to be made to the purchaser that it is held for him. Unless made on an exchange a sale to a broker purchasing for his own account is within this subsection and not within subsection (1).

§ 8—315. Action Against Purchaser Based Upon Wrongful Transfer.

(1) Any person against whom the transfer of a security is wrongful for any reason, including his incapacity, may against any one except a bona fide purchaser reclaim possession of the security or obtain possession of any new security evidencing all or part of the same rights or have damages.

(2) If the transfer is wrongful because of an unauthorized indorsement, the owner may also reclaim or obtain possession of the security or new security even from a bona fide purchaser if the ineffectiveness of the purported indorsement can be asserted against him under the provisions of this Article on unauthorized indorsements (Section 8—311).

(3) The right to obtain or reclaim possession of a security may be specifically enforced and its transfer enjoined and the security impounded pending the litigation.

§ 8—316. Purchaser's Right to Requisites for Registration of Transfer on Books.

Unless otherwise agreed the transferor must on due demand supply his purchaser with any proof of his authority to transfer or with any other requisite which may be necessary to obtain registration of the transfer of the security but if the transfer is not for value a transferor need not do so unless the purchaser furnishes the necessary expenses. Failure to comply with a demand made within a reasonable time gives the purchaser the right to reject or rescind the transfer.

§ 8—317. Attachment or Levy Upon Security.

(1) No attachment or levy upon a security or any share or other interest evidenced thereby which is outstanding shall be valid until the security is actually seized by the officer making the attachment or levy but a security which has been surrendered to the issuer may be attached or levied upon at the source.

(2) A creditor whose debtor is the owner of a security shall be entitled to such aid from courts of appropriate jurisdiction, by injunction or otherwise, in reaching such security or in satisfying the claim by means thereof as is allowed at law or in equity in regard to property which cannot readily be attached or levied upon by ordinary legal process.

§ 8—318. No Conversion by Good Faith Delivery.

An agent or bailee who in good faith (including observance of reasonable commercial standards if he is in the business of buying, selling or otherwise dealing with securities) has received securities and sold, pledged or delivered them according to the instructions of his principal is not liable for conversion or for participation in breach of fiduciary duty although the principal had no right to dispose of them.

§ 8—319. Statute of Frauds.

A contract for the sale of securities is not enforceable by way of action or defense unless

(a) there is some writing signed by the party against whom enforcement is sought or by his authorized agent or broker sufficient to indicate that a contract has been made for sale of a stated quantity of described securities at a defined or stated price; or

(b) delivery of the security has been accepted or payment has been made but the contract is enforceable under this provision only to the extent of such delivery or payment; or

(c) within a reasonable time a writing in confirmation of the sale or purchase and sufficient against the sender under paragraph (a) has been received by the party against whom enforcement is sought and he has failed to send written objection to its contents within ten days after its receipt; or

(d) the party against whom enforcement is sought admits in his pleading, testimony or otherwise in court that a contract was made for sale of a stated quantity of described securities at a defined or stated price.

§ 8—320. Transfer or Pledge within a Central Depository System.

(1) If a security

(a) is in the custody of a clearing corporation or of a custodian bank or a nominee of either subject to the instructions of the clearing corporation; and

(b) is in bearer form or indorsed in blank by an appropriate person or registered in the name of the clearing corporation or custodian bank or a nominee of either; and

(c) is shown on the account of a transferor or pledgor on the books of the clearing corporation;

then, in addition to other methods, a transfer or pledge of the security or any interest therein may be effected by the making of appropriate entries on the books of the clearing corporation reducing the account of the transferor or pledgor and increasing the account of the transferee or pledgee by the amount of the obligation or the number of shares or rights transferred or pledged.

(2) Under this section entries may be with respect to like securities or interests therein as a part of a fungible bulk and may refer merely to a quantity of a particular security without reference to the name of the registered owner, certificate or bond number or the like and, in appropriate cases, may be on a net basis taking into account other transfers or pledges of the same security.

(3) A transfer or pledge under this section has the effect of a delivery of a security in bearer form or duly indorsed in blank (Section 8—301) representing the amount of the obligation or the number of shares or rights transferred or pledged. If a pledge or the creation of a security interest is intended, the making of entries has the effect of a taking of delivery by the pledgee or a secured party (Sections 9—304 and 9—305). A transferee or pledgee under this section is a holder.

(4) A transfer or pledge under this section does not constitute a registration of transfer under Part 4 of this Article.

(5) That entries made on the books of the clearing corporation as provided in subsection (1) are not appropriate does not affect the validity or effect of the entries nor the liabilities or obligations of the clearing corporation to any person adversely affected thereby.

PART 4

REGISTRATION

§ 8—401. Duty of Issuer to Register Transfer.

(1) Where a security in registered form is presented to the issuer with a request to register transfer, the issuer is under a duty to register the transfer as requested if

(a) the security is indorsed by the appropriate person or persons (Section 8—308); and

(b) reasonable assurance is given that those indorsements are genuine and effective (Section 8—402); and

(c) the issuer has no duty to inquire into adverse claims or has discharged any such duty (Section 8—403); and

(d) any applicable law relating to the collection of taxes has been complied with; and

(e) the transfer is in fact rightful or is to a bona fide purchaser.

(2) Where an issuer is under a duty to register a transfer of a security the issuer is also liable to the person presenting it for registration or his principal for loss resulting from any unreasonable delay in registration or from failure or refusal to register the transfer.

§ 8—402. Assurance that Indorsements Are Effective.

(1) The issuer may require the following assurance that each necessary indorsement (Section 8—308) is genuine and effective

(a) in all cases, a guarantee of the signature (subsection (1) of Section 8—312) of the person indorsing; and

(b) where the indorsement is by an agent, appropriate assurance of authority to sign;

(c) where the indorsement is by a fiduciary, appropriate evidence of appointment or incumbency;

(d) where there is more than one fiduciary, reasonable assurance that all who are required to sign have done so;

(e) where the indorsement is by a person not covered by any of the foregoing, assurance appropriate to the case corresponding as nearly as may be to the foregoing.

(2) A "guarantee of the signature" in subsection (1) means a guarantee signed by or on behalf of a person reasonably believed by the issuer to be responsible. The issuer may adopt standards with respect to responsibility provided such standards are not manifestly unreasonable.

(3) "Appropriate evidence of appointment or incumbency" in subsection (1) means

(a) in the case of a fiduciary appointed or qualified by a court, a certificate issued by or under the direction or supervision of that court or an officer thereof and dated within sixty days before the date of presentation for transfer; or

(b) in any other case, a copy of a document showing the appointment or a certificate issued by or on behalf of a person reasonably believed by the issuer to be responsible or, in the absence of such a document or certificate, other evidence reasonably deemed by the issuer to be appropriate. The issuer may adopt standards with respect to such evidence provided such standards are not manifestly unreasonable. The issuer is not charged with notice of the contents of any document obtained pursuant to this paragraph (b) except to the extent that the contents relate directly to the appointment or incumbency.

(4) The issuer may elect to require reasonable assurance beyond that specified in this section but if it does so and for a purpose other than that specified in subsection 3(b) both requires and obtains a copy of a will, trust, indenture, articles of co-partnership, by-laws or other controlling instrument it is charged with notice of all matters contained therein affecting the transfer.

§ 8—403. Limited Duty of Inquiry.

(1) An issuer to whom a security is presented for registration is under a duty to inquire into adverse claims if

(a) a written notification of an adverse claim is received at a time and in a manner which affords the issuer a reasonable opportunity to act on it prior to the issuance of a new, reissued or re-registered security and the notification identifies the claimant, the registered owner and the issue of which the security is a part and provides an address for communications directed to the claimant; or

(b) the issuer is charged with notice of an adverse claim from a controlling instrument which it has elected to require under subsection (4) of Section 8—402.

(2) The issuer may discharge any duty of inquiry by any reasonable means, including notifying an adverse claimant by registered or certified mail at the address furnished by him or if there be no such address at his residence or regular place of business that the security has been presented for registration of transfer by a named person, and that the transfer will be registered unless within thirty days from the date of mailing the notification, either

(a) an appropriate restraining order, injunction or other process issues from a court of competent jurisdiction; or

(b) an indemnity bond sufficient in the issuer's judgment to protect the issuer and any transfer agent, registrar or other agent of the issuer involved, from any loss which it or they may suffer by complying with the adverse claim is filed with the issuer.

(3) Unless an issuer is charged with notice of an adverse claim from a controlling instrument which it has elected to require under subsection (4) of Section 8—402 or receives notification of an adverse claim under subsection (1) of this section, where a security presented for registration is indorsed by the appropriate person or persons the issuer is under no duty to inquire into adverse claims. In particular

(a) an issuer registering a security in the name of a person who is a fiduciary or who is described as a fiduciary is not bound to inquire into the existence, extent, or correct description of the fiduciary relationship and thereafter the issuer may assume without inquiry that the newly registered owner continues to be the fiduciary until the issuer receives written notice that the fiduciary is no longer acting as such with respect to the particular security;

(b) an issuer registering transfer on an indorsement by a fiduciary is not bound to inquire whether the transfer is made in compliance with a controlling instrument or with the law of the state having jurisdiction of the fiduciary relationship, including any law requiring the fiduciary to obtain court approval of the transfer; and

(c) the issuer is not charged with notice of the contents of any court record or file or other recorded or unrecorded document is in its possession and even though the transfer is made on the indorsement of a fiduciary to the fiduciary himself or to his nominee.

§ 8—404. Liability and Non-Liability for Registration.

(1) Except as otherwise provided in any law relating to the collection of taxes, the issuer is not liable to the owner or any other person suffering loss as a result of the registration of a transfer of a security if

(a) there were on or with the security the necessary indorsements (Section 8—308); and

(b) the issuer had no duty to inquire into adverse claims or has discharged any such duty (Section 8—403).

(2) Where an issuer has registered a transfer of a security to a person not entitled to it the issuer on demand must deliver a like security to the true owner unless

(a) the registration was pursuant to subsection (1); or

(b) the owner is precluded from asserting any claim for registering the transfer under subsection (1) of the following section; or

(c) such delivery would result in overissue, in which case the issuer's liability is governed by Section 8—104.

§ 8—405. Lost, Destroyed and Stolen Securities.

(1) Where a security has been lost, apparently destroyed or wrongfully taken and the owner fails to notify the issuer of that fact within a reasonable time after he has notice of it and the issuer registers a transfer of the security before receiving such a notification, the owner is precluded from asserting against the issuer any claim for registering the transfer under the preceding section or any claim to a new security under this section.

(2) Where the owner of a security claims that the security has been lost, destroyed or wrongfully taken, the issuer must issue a new security in place of the original security if the owner

(a) so requests before the issuer has notice that the security has been acquired by a bona fide purchaser; and

(b) files with the issuer a sufficient indemnity bond; and

(c) satisfies any other reasonable requirements imposed by the issuer.

(3) If, after the issue of the new security, a bona fide purchaser of the original security presents it for registration of transfer, the insurer must register the transfer unless registration would result in overissue, in which event the issuer's liability is governed by Section 8—104. In addition to any rights on the indemnity bond, the issuer may recover the new security from the person to whom it was issued or any person taking under him except a bona fide purchaser.

§ 8—406. Duty of Authenticating Trustee, Transfer Agent or Registrar.

(1) Where a person acts as authenticating trustee, transfer agent, registrar, or other agent for an issuer in the registration of transfers of its securities or in the issue of new securities or in the cancellation of surrendered securities

(a) he is under a duty to the issuer to exercise good faith and due diligence in performing his functions; and

(b) he has with regard to the particular functions he performs the same obligation to the holder or owner of the security and has the same rights and privileges as the issuer has in regard to those functions.

(2) Notice to an authenticating trustee, transfer agent, registrar or other such agent is notice to the issuer with respect to the functions performed by the agent.

ARTICLE 9

SECURED TRANSACTIONS; SALES OF ACCOUNTS AND CHATTEL PAPER

PART 1

SHORT TITLE, APPLICABILITY AND DEFINITIONS

§ 9—101. Short Title.

This Article shall be known and may be cited as Uniform Commercial Code—Secured Transactions.

§ 9—102. Policy and Subject Matter of Article.

(1) Except as otherwise provided in Section 9—104 on excluded transactions, this Article applies

(a) to any transaction (regardless of its form) which is intended to create a security interest in personal property or fixtures including goods, documents, instruments, general intangibles, chattel paper or accounts; and also

(b) to any sale of accounts or chattel paper.

(2) This Article applies to security interests created by contract including pledge, assignment, chattel mortgage, chattel trust, trust deed, factor's lien, equipment trust, conditional sale, trust receipt, other lien or title retention contract and lease or consignment intended as security. This Article does not apply to statutory liens except as provided in Section 9—310.

(3) The application of this Article to a security interest in a secured obligation is not affected by the fact that the obligation is itself secured by a transaction or interest to which this Article does not apply. Amended in 1972.

Note: *The adoption of this Article should be accompanied by the repeal of existing statutes dealing with conditional sales, trust receipts, factor's liens where the factor is given a non-possessory lien, chattel mortgages, crop mortgages, mortgages on railroad equipment, assignment of accounts and generally statutes regulating security interests in personal property.*

Where the state has a retail installment selling act or small loan act, that legislation should be carefully examined to determine what changes in those acts are needed to conform them to this Article. This Article primarily sets out rules defining rights of a secured party against persons dealing with the debtor; it does not prescribe regulations and controls which may be necessary to curb abuses arising in the small loan business or in the financing of consumer purchases on credit. Accordingly there is no intention to repeal existing regulatory acts in those fields by enactment or re-enactment of Article 9. See Section 9—203(4) and the Note thereto.

§ 9—103. Perfection of Security Interests in Multiple State Transactions.

(1) Documents, instruments and ordinary goods.

(a) This subsection applies to documents and instruments and to goods other than those covered by a certificate of title described in subsection (2), mobile goods described in subsection (3), and minerals described in subsection (5).

(b) Except as otherwise provided in this subsection, perfection and the effect of perfection or non-perfection of a security interest in collateral are governed by the law of the jurisdiction where the collateral is when the last event occurs on which is based the assertion that the security interest is perfected or unperfected.

(c) If the parties to a transaction creating a purchase money security interest in goods in one jurisdiction understand at the time that the security interest attaches that the goods will be kept in another jurisdiction, then the law of the other jurisdiction governs the perfection and the effect of perfection or non-perfection of the security interest from the time it attaches until thirty days after the debtor receives possession of the goods and thereafter if the goods are taken to the other jurisdiction before the end of the thirty-day period.

(d) When collateral is brought into and kept in this state while subject to a security interest perfected under the law of the jurisdiction from which the collateral was removed, the security interest remains perfected, but if action is required by Part 3 of this Article to perfect the security interest,

(i) if the action is not taken before the expiration of the period of perfection in the other jurisdiction or the end of four months after the collateral is brought into this state, whichever period first expires, the security interest becomes unperfected at the end of that period and is thereafter deemed to have been unperfected as against a person who became a purchaser after removal;

(ii) if the action is taken before the expiration of the period specified in subparagraph (i) the security interest continues perfected thereafter;

(iii) for the purpose of priority over a buyer of consumer goods (subsection (2) of Section 9—307), the period of the effectiveness of a filing in the jurisdiction from which the collateral is removed is governed by the rules with respect to perfection in subparagraphs (i) and (ii).

(2) Certificate of title.

(a) This subsection applies to goods covered by a certificate of title issued under a statute of this state or of another jurisdiction under the law of which indication of a security interest on the certificate is required as a condition of perfection.

(b) Except as otherwise provided in this subsection, perfection and the effect of perfection or non-perfection of the security interest are governed by the law (including the conflict of laws rules) of the jurisdiction issuing the certificate until four months after the goods are removed from that jurisdiction and thereafter until the goods are registered in another jurisdiction, but in any event not beyond surrender of the certificate. After the expiration of that period, the goods are not covered by the certificate of title within the meaning of this section.

(c) Except with respect to the rights of a buyer described in the next paragraph, a security interest, perfected in another jurisdiction otherwise than by notation on a certificate of title, in goods brought into this state and thereafter covered by a certificate of title issued by this state is subject to the rules stated in paragraph (d) of subsection (1).

(d) If goods are brought into this state while a security interest therein is perfected in any manner under the law of the jurisdiction from which the goods are removed and a certificate of title is issued by this state and the certificate does not show that the goods are subject to the security interest or that they may be subject to security interests not shown on the certificate, the security interest is subordinate to the rights of a buyer of the goods who is not in the business of selling goods of that kind to the extent that he gives value and receives delivery of the goods after issuance of the certificate and without knowledge of the security interest.

(3) Accounts, general intangibles and mobile goods.

(a) This subsection applies to accounts (other than an account described in subsection (5) on minerals) and general intangibles and to goods which are mobile and which are of a type normally used in more than one jurisdiction, such as motor vehicles, trailers, rolling stock, airplanes, shipping containers, road building and construction machinery and commercial harvesting machinery and the like, if the goods are equipment or are inventory leased or held for lease by the debtor to others, and are not covered by a certificate of title described in subsection (2).

(b) The law (including the conflict of laws rules) of the jurisdiction in which the debtor is located governs the perfection and the effect of perfection or non-perfection of the security interest.

(c) If, however, the debtor is located in a jurisdiction which is not a part of the United States, and which does not provide for perfection of the security interest by filing or recording in that jurisdiction, the law of the jurisdiction in the United States in which the debtor has its major executive office in the United States governs the perfection and the effect of perfection or non-perfection of the security interest through filing. In the alternative, if the debtor is located in a jurisdiction which is not a part of the United States or Canada and the collateral is accounts or general intangibles for money due or to become due, the security interest may be perfected by notification to the account debtor. As used in this paragraph, "United States" includes its territories and possessions and the Commonwealth of Puerto Rico.

(d) A debtor shall be deemed located at his place of business if he has one, at his chief executive office if he has more than one place of business, otherwise at his residence. If, however, the debtor is a foreign air carrier under the Federal Aviation Act of 1958, as amended, it shall be deemed located at the designated office of the agent upon whom service of process may be made on behalf of the foreign air carrier.

(e) A security interest perfected under the law of the jurisdiction of the location of the debtor is perfected until the expiration of four months after a change of the debtor's location to another jurisdiction, or until perfection would have ceased by the law of the first jurisdiction, whichever period first expires. Unless perfected in the new jurisdiction before the end of that period, it becomes unperfected thereafter and is deemed to have been unperfected as against a person who became a purchaser after the change.

(4) Chattel paper.

The rules stated for goods in subsection (1) apply to a possessory security interest in chattel paper. The rules stated for accounts in subsection (3) apply to a non-possessory security interest in chattel paper, but the security interest may not be perfected by notification to the account debtor.

(5) Minerals.

Perfection and the effect of perfection or non-perfection of a security interest which is created by a debtor who has an interest in minerals or the like (including oil and gas) before extraction and which attaches thereto as extracted, or which attaches to an account resulting from the sale thereof at the wellhead or minehead are governed by the law (including the conflict of laws rules) of the jurisdiction wherein the wellhead or minehead is located. Amended in 1972.

§ 9–104. Transactions Excluded From Article.

This Article does not apply

(a) to a security interest subject to any statute of the United States, to the extent that such statute governs the rights of parties to and third parties affected by transactions in particular types of property; or

(b) to a landlord's lien; or

(c) to a lien given by statute or other rule of law for services or materials except as provided in Section 9—310 on priority of such liens; or

(d) to a transfer of a claim for wages, salary or other compensation of an employee; or

(e) to a transfer by a government or governmental subdivision or agency; or

(f) to a sale of accounts or chattel paper as part of a sale of the business out of which they arose, or an assignment of accounts or chattel paper which is for the purpose of collection only, or a transfer of a right to payment under a contract to an assignee who is also to do the performance under the contract or a transfer of a single account to an assignee in whole or partial satisfaction of a preexisting indebtedness; or

(g) to a transfer of an interest in or claim in or under any policy of insurance, except as provided with respect to proceeds (Section 9—306) and priorities in proceeds (Section 9—312); or

(h) to a right represented by a judgment (other than a judgment taken on a right to payment which was collateral); or

(i) to any right of set-off; or

(j) except to the extent that provision is made for fixtures in Section 9—313, to the creation or transfer of an interest in or lien on real estate, including a lease or rents thereunder; or

(k) to a transfer in whole or in part of any claim arising out of tort; or

(*l*) to a transfer of an interest in any deposit account (subsection (1) of Section 9—105), except as provided with respect to proceeds (Section 9—306) and priorities in proceeds (Section 9—312).

Amended in 1972.

§ 9—105. Definitions and Index of Definitions.

(1) In this Article unless the context otherwise requires:

(a) "Account debtor" means the person who is obligated on an account, chattel paper or general intangible;

(b) "Chattel paper" means a writing or writings which evidence both a monetary obligation and a security interest in or a lease of specific goods, but a charter or other contract involving the use or hire of a vessel is not chattel paper. When a transaction is evidenced both by such a security agreement or a lease and by an instrument or a series of instruments, the group of writings taken together constitutes chattel paper;

(c) "Collateral" means the property subject to a security interest, and includes accounts and chattel paper which have been sold;

(d) "Debtor" means the person who owes payment or other performance of the obligation secured, whether or not he owns or has rights in the collateral, and includes the seller of accounts or chattel paper. Where the debtor and the owner of the collateral are not the same person, the term "debtor" means the owner of the collateral in any provision of the Article dealing with the collateral, the obligor in any provision dealing with the obligation, and may include both where the context so requires;

(e) "Deposit account" means a demand, time, savings, passbook or like account maintained with a bank, savings and loan association, credit union or like organization, other than an account evidenced by a certificate of deposit;

(f) "Document" means document of title as defined in the general definitions of Article 1 (Section 1—201), and a receipt of the kind described in subsection (2) of Section 7—201;

(g) "Encumbrance" includes real estate mortgages and other liens on real estate and all other rights in real estate that are not ownership interests;

(h) "Goods" includes all things which are movable at the time the security interest attaches or which are fixtures (Section 9—313), but does not include money, documents, instruments, accounts, chattel paper, general intangibles, or minerals or the like (including oil and gas) before extraction. "Goods" also includes standing timber which is to be cut and removed under a conveyance or contract for sale, the unborn young of animals, and growing crops;

(i) "Instrument" means a negotiable instrument (defined in Section 3—104), or a security (defined in Section 8—102) or any other writing which evidences a right to the payment of money and is not itself a security agreement or lease and is of a type which is in ordinary course of business transferred by delivery with any necessary indorsement or assignment;

(j) "Mortgage" means a consensual interest created by a real estate mortgage, a trust deed on real estate, or the like;

(k) An advance is made "pursuant to commitment" if the secured party has bound himself to make it, whether or not a subsequent event of default or other event not within his control has relieved or may relieve him from his obligation;

(*l*) "Security agreement" means an agreement which creates or provides for a security interest;

(m) "Secured party" means a lender, seller or other person in whose favor there is a security interest, including a person to whom accounts or chattel paper have been sold. When the holders of obligations issued under an indenture of trust, equipment trust agreement or the like are represented by a trustee or other person, the representative is the secured party;

(n) "Transmitting utility" means any person primarily engaged in the railroad, street railway or trolley bus business, the electric or electronics communications transmission business, the transmission of goods by pipeline, or the transmission or the production and transmission of electricity, steam, gas or water, or the provision of sewer service.

(2) Other definitions applying to this Article and the sections in which they appear are:

"Account".	Section 9—106.
"Attach".	Section 9—203.
"Construction mortgage".	Section 9—313(1).
"Consumer goods".	Section 9—109(1).
"Equipment".	Section 9—109(2).
"Farm products".	Section 9—109(3).
"Fixture".	Section 9—313(1).
"Fixture filing".	Section 9—313(1).
"General intangibles".	Section 9—106.
"Inventory".	Section 9—109(4).
"Lien creditor".	Section 9—301(3).
"Proceeds".	Section 9—306(1).
"Purchase money security interest".	Section 9—107.
"United States".	Section 9—103.

(3) The following definitions in other Articles apply to this Article:

"Check".	Section 3—104
"Contract for sale".	Section 2—106.
"Holder in due course".	Section 3—302.
"Note".	Section 3—104.
"Sale".	Section 2—106.

(4) In addition Article 1 contains general definitions and principles of construction and interpretation applicable throughout this Article. Amended in 1966, 1972.

§ 9—106. Definitions: "Account"; "General Intangibles".

"Account" means any right to payment for goods sold or leased or for services rendered which is not evidenced by an instrument or chattel paper, whether or not it has been earned by performance. "General intangibles" means any personal property (including things in action) other than goods, accounts, chattel paper, documents, instruments, and money. All rights to payment earned or unearned under a charter or other contract involving the use or hire of a vessel and all rights incident to the charter or contract are accounts. Amended in 1966, 1972.

§ 9—107. Definitions: "Purchase Money Security Interest".

A security interest is a "purchase money security interest" to the extent that it is

(a) taken or retained by the seller of the collateral to secure all or part of its price; or

(b) taken by a person who by making advances or incurring an obligation gives value to enable the debtor to acquire rights in or the use of collateral if such value is in fact so used.

§ 9—108. When After-Acquired Collateral Not Security for Antecedent Debt.

Where a secured party makes an advance, incurs an obligation, releases a perfected security interest, or otherwise gives new value which is to be secured in whole or in part by after-acquired property his security interest in the after-acquired collateral shall be deemed to be taken for new value and not as security for an antecedent debt if the debtor acquires his rights in such collateral either in the ordinary course of his business or under a contract of purchase made pursuant to the security agreement within a reasonable time after new value is given.

§ 9—109. Classification of Goods; "Consumer Goods"; "Equipment"; "Farm Products"; "Inventory".

Goods are

(1) "consumer goods" if they are used or bought for use primarily for personal, family or household purposes;

(2) "equipment" if they are used or bought for use primarily in business (including farming or a profession) or by a debtor who is a non-profit organization or a governmental subdivision or agency or if the goods are not included in the definitions of inventory, farm products or consumer goods;

(3) "farm products" if they are crops or livestock or supplies used or produced in farming operations or if they are products of crops or livestock in their unmanufactured states (such as ginned cotton, wool-clip, maple syrup, milk and eggs), and if they are in the possession of a debtor engaged in raising, fattening, grazing or other farming operations. If goods are farm products they are neither equipment nor inventory;

(4) "inventory" if they are held by a person who holds them for sale or lease or to be furnished under contracts of service or if he has so furnished them, or if they are raw materials, work in process or materials used or consumed in a business. Inventory of a person is not to be classified as his equipment.

§ 9—110. Sufficiency of Description.

For the purposes of this Article any description of personal property or real estate is sufficient whether or not it is specific if it reasonably identifies what is described.

§ 9—111. Applicability of Bulk Transfer Laws.

The creation of a security interest is not a bulk transfer under Article 6 (see Section 6—103).

§ 9—112. Where Collateral Is Not Owned by Debtor.

Unless otherwise agreed, when a secured party knows that collateral is owned by a person who is not the debtor, the owner of the collateral is entitled to receive from the secured party any surplus under Section 9—502(2) or under Section 9—504(1), and is not liable for the debt or for any deficiency after resale, and he has the same right as the debtor

(a) to receive statements under Section 9—208;

(b) to receive notice of and to object to a secured party's proposal to retain the collateral in satisfaction of the indebtedness under Section 9—505;

(c) to redeem the collateral under Section 9—506;

(d) to obtain injunctive or other relief under Section 9—507(1); and

(e) to recover losses caused to him under Section 9—208(2).

§ 9—113. Security Interests Arising Under Article on Sales.

A security interest arising solely under the Article on Sales (Article 2) is subject to the provisions of this Article except that to the extent that and so long as the debtor does not have or does not lawfully obtain possession of the goods

(a) no security agreement is necessary to make the security interest enforceable; and

(b) no filing is required to perfect the security interest; and

(c) the rights of the secured party on default by the debtor are governed by the Article on Sales (Article 2).

§ 9—114. Consignment.

(1) A person who delivers goods under a consignment which is not a security interest and who would be required to file under this Article

by paragraph (3) (c) of Section 2—326 has priority over a secured party who is or becomes a creditor of the consignee and who would have a perfected security interest in the goods if they were the property of the consignee, and also has priority with respect to identifiable cash proceeds received on or before delivery of the goods to a buyer, if

(a) the consignor complies with the filing provision of the Article on Sales with respect to consignments (paragraph (3) (c) of Section 2—326) before the consignee receives possession of the goods; and

(b) the consignor gives notification in writing to the holder of the security interest if the holder has filed a financing statement covering the same types of goods before the date of the filing made by the consignor; and

(c) the holder of the security interest receives the notification within five years before the consignee receives possession of the goods; and

(d) the notification states that the consignor expects to deliver goods on consignment to the consignee, describing the goods by item or type.

(2) In the case of a consignment which is not a security interest and in which the requirements of the preceding subsection have not been met, a person who delivers goods to another is subordinate to a person who would have a perfected security interest in the goods if they were the property of the debtor. Added in 1972.

PART 2

VALIDITY OF SECURITY AGREEMENT AND RIGHTS OF PARTIES THERETO

§ 9—201. General Validity of Security Agreement.

Except as otherwise provided by this Act a security agreement is effective according to its terms between the parties, against purchasers of the collateral and against creditors. Nothing in this Article validates any charge or practice illegal under any statute or regulation thereunder governing usury, small loans, retail installment sales, or the like, or extends the application of any such statute or regulation to any transaction not otherwise subject thereto.

§ 9—202. Title to Collateral Immaterial.

Each provision of this Article with regard to rights, obligations and remedies applies whether title to collateral is in the secured party or in the debtor.

§ 9—203. Attachment and Enforceability of Security Interest; Proceeds; Formal Requisites.

(1) Subject to the provisions of Section 4—208 on the security interest of a collecting bank and Section 9—113 on a security interest arising under the Article on Sales, a security interest is not enforceable against the debtor or third parties with respect to the collateral and does not attach unless

(a) the collateral is in the possession of the secured party pursuant to agreement, or the debtor has signed a security agreement which contains a description of the collateral and in addition, when the security interest covers crops growing or to be grown or timber to be cut, a description of the land concerned; and

(b) value has been given; and

(c) the debtor has rights in the collateral.

(2) A security interest attaches when it becomes enforceable against the debtor with respect to the collateral. Attachment occurs as soon as all of the events specified in subsection (1) have taken place unless explicit agreement postpones the time of attaching.

(3) Unless otherwise agreed a security agreement gives the secured party the rights to proceeds provided by Section 9—306.

(4) A transaction, although subject to this Article, is also subject to ....*, and in the case of conflict between the provisions of this Article and any such statute, the provisions of such statute control. Failure to comply with any applicable statute has only the effect which is specified therein. Amended in 1972.

Note: *At * in subsection (4) insert reference to any local statute regulating small loans, retail installment sales and the like.*

The foregoing subsection (4) is designed to make it clear that certain transactions, although subject to this Article, must also comply with other applicable legislation.

This Article is designed to regulate all the "security" aspects of transactions within its scope. There is, however, much regulatory legislation, particularly in the consumer field, which supplements this Article and should not be repealed by its enactment. Examples are small loan acts, retail installment selling acts and the like. Such acts may provide for licensing and rate regulation and may prescribe particular forms of contract. Such provisions should remain in force despite the enactment of this Article. On the other hand if a retail installment selling act contains provisions on filing, rights on default, etc., such provisions should be repealed as inconsistent with this Article except that inconsistent provisions as to deficiencies, penalties, etc., in the Uniform Consumer Credit Code and other recent related legislation should remain because those statutes were drafted after the substantial enactment of the Article and with the intention of modifying certain provisions of this Article as to consumer credit.

§ 9—204. After-Acquired Property; Future Advances.

(1) Except as provided in subsection (2), a security agreement may provide that any or all obligations covered by the security agreement are to be secured by after-acquired collateral.

(2) No security interest attaches under an after-acquired property clause to consumer goods other than accessions (Section 9—314) when given as additional security unless the debtor acquires rights in them within ten days after the secured party gives value.

(3) Obligations covered by a security agreement may include future advances or other value whether or not the advances or value are given pursuant to commitment (subsection (1) of Section 9—105). Amended in 1972.

§ 9—205. Use or Disposition of Collateral Without Accounting Permissible.

A security interest is not invalid or fraudulent against creditors by reason of liberty in the debtor to use, commingle or dispose of all or part of the collateral (including returned or repossessed goods) or to collect or compromise accounts or chattel paper, or to accept the return of goods or make repossessions, or to use, commingle or dispose of proceeds, or by reason of the failure of the secured party to require the debtor to account for proceeds or replace collateral. This section does not relax the requirements of possession where perfection of a security interest depends upon possession of the collateral by the secured party or by a bailee. Amended in 1972.

§ 9—206. Agreement Not to Assert Defenses Against Assignee; Modification of Sales Warranties Where Security Agreement Exists.

(1) Subject to any statute or decision which establishes a different rule for buyers or lessees of consumer goods, an agreement by a buyer or lessee that he will not assert against an assignee any claim or defense which he may have against the seller or lessor is enforceable by an assignee who takes his assignment for value, in good faith and without notice of a claim or defense, except as to defenses of a type which may be asserted against a holder in due course of a negotiable instrument under the Article on Commercial Paper (Article 3). A buyer who as part of one transaction signs both a negotiable instrument and a security agreement makes such an agreement.

(2) When a seller retains a purchase money security interest in goods the Article on Sales (Article 2) governs the sale and any disclaimer, limitation or modification of the seller's warranties. Amended in 1962.

§ 9—207. Rights and Duties When Collateral is in Secured Party's Possession.

(1) A secured party must use reasonable care in the custody and preservation of collateral in his possession. In the case of an instrument or chattel paper reasonable care includes

taking necessary steps to preserve rights against prior parties unless otherwise agreed.

(2) Unless otherwise agreed, when collateral is in the secured party's possession

(a) reasonable expenses (including the cost of any insurance and payment of taxes or other charges) incurred in the custody, preservation, use or operation of the collateral are chargeable to the debtor and are secured by the collateral;

(b) the risk of accidental loss or damage is on the debtor to the extent of any deficiency in any effective insurance coverage;

(c) the secured party may hold as additional security any increase or profits (except money) received from the collateral, but money so received, unless remitted to the debtor, shall be applied in reduction of the secured obligation;

(d) the secured party must keep the collateral identifiable but fungible collateral may be commingled;

(e) the secured party may repledge the collateral upon terms which do not impair the debtor's right to redeem it.

(3) A secured party is liable for any loss caused by his failure to meet any obligation imposed by the preceding subsections but does not lose his security interest.

(4) A secured party may use or operate the collateral for the purpose of preserving the collateral or its value or pursuant to the order of a court of appropriate jurisdiction or, except in the case of consumer goods, in the manner and to the extent provided in the security agreement.

§ 9—208. Request for Statement of Account or List of Collateral.

(1) A debtor may sign a statement indicating what he believes to be the aggregate amount of unpaid indebtedness as of a specified date and may send it to the secured party with a request that the statement be approved or corrected and returned to the debtor. When the security agreement or any other record kept by the secured party identifies the collateral a debtor may similarly request the secured party to approve or correct a list of the collateral.

(2) The secured party must comply with such a request within two weeks after receipt by sending a written correction or approval. If the secured party claims a security interest in all of a particular type of collateral owned by the debtor he may indicate that fact in his reply and need not approve or correct an itemized list of such collateral. If the secured party without reasonable excuse fails to comply he is liable for any loss caused to the debtor thereby; and if the debtor has properly included in his request a good faith statement of the obligation or a list of the collateral or both the secured party may claim a security interest only as shown in the statement against persons misled by his failure to comply. If he no longer has an interest in the obligation or collateral at the time the request is received he must disclose the name and address of any successor in interest known to him and he is liable for any loss caused to the debtor as a result of failure to disclose. A successor in interest is not subject to this section until a request is received by him.

(3) A debtor is entitled to such a statement once every six months without charge. The secured party may require payment of a charge not exceeding $10 for each additional statement furnished.

PART 3

RIGHTS OF THIRD PARTIES; PERFECTED AND UNPERFECTED SECURITY INTERESTS; RULES OF PRIORITY

§ 9—301. Persons Who Take Priority Over Unperfected Security Interests; Rights of "Lien Creditor".

(1) Except as otherwise provided in subsection (2), an unperfected security interest is subordinate to the rights of

(a) persons entitled to priority under Section 9—312;

(b) a person who becomes a lien creditor before the security interest is perfected;

(c) in the case of goods, instruments, documents, and chattel paper, a person who is not a secured party and who is a transferee in bulk or other buyer not in ordinary course of business or is a buyer of farm products in ordinary course of business, to the extent that he gives value and receives delivery of the collateral without knowledge of the security interest and before it is perfected;

(d) in the case of accounts and general intangibles, a person who is not a secured party and who is a transferee to the extent that he gives value without knowledge of the security interest and before it is perfected.

(2) If the secured party files with respect to a purchase money security interest before or within ten days after the debtor receives possession of the collateral, he takes priority over the rights of a transferee in bulk or of a lien creditor which arise between the time the security interest attaches and the time of filing.

(3) A "lien creditor" means a creditor who has acquired a lien on the property involved by attachment, levy or the like and includes an assignee for benefit of creditors from the time of assignment, and a trustee in bankruptcy from the date of the filing of the petition or a receiver in equity from the time of appointment.

(4) A person who becomes a lien creditor while a security interest is perfected takes subject to the security interest only to the extent that it secures advances made before he becomes a lien creditor or within 45 days thereafter or made without knowledge of the lien or pursuant to a commitment entered into without knowledge of the lien. Amended in 1972.

§ 9—302. When Filing Is Required to Perfect Security Interest; Security Interests to Which Filing Provisions of This Article Do Not Apply.

(1) A financing statement must be filed to perfect all security interests except the following:

(a) a security interest in collateral in possession of the secured party under Section 9—305;

(b) a security interest temporarily perfected in instruments or documents without delivery under Section 9—304 or in proceeds for a 10 day period under Section 9—306;

(c) a security interest created by an assignment of a beneficial interest in a trust or a decedent's estate;

(d) a purchase money security interest in consumer goods; but filing is required for a motor vehicle required to be registered; and fixture filing is required for priority over conflicting interests in fixtures to the extent provided in Section 9—313;

(e) an assignment of accounts which does not alone or in conjunction with other assignments to the same assignee transfer a significant part of the outstanding accounts of the assignor;

(f) a security interest of a collecting bank (Section 4—208) or arising under the Article on Sales (see Section 9—113) or covered in subsection (3) of this section;

(g) an assignment for the benefit of all the creditors of the transferor, and subsequent transfers by the assignee thereunder.

(2) If a secured party assigns a perfected security interest, no filing under this Article is required in order to continue the perfected status of the security interest against creditors of and transferees from the original debtor.

(3) The filing of a financing statement otherwise required by this Article is not necessary or effective to perfect a security interest in property subject to

(a) a statute or treaty of the United States which provides for a national or international registration or a national or international certificate of title or which specifies a place of filing different from that specified in this Article for filing of the security interest; or

(b) the following statutes of this state; [list any certificate of title statute covering automobiles, trailers, mobile homes, boats, farm tractors, or the like, and any central filing statute *.]; but during any period in which collateral is inventory held for sale by a person who is in the business of selling goods of that kind, the filing provisions of this Article (Part 4) apply to a security interest in that collateral created by him as debtor; or

(c) a certificate of title statute of another jurisdiction under the law of which indication of a security interest on the certificate is required as a condition of perfection (subsection (2) of Section 9—103).

(4) Compliance with a statute or treaty described in subsection (3) is equivalent to the filing of a financing statement under this Article, and a security interest in property subject to the statute or treaty can be perfected only by compliance therewith except as provided in Section 9—103 on multiple state transactions. Duration and renewal of perfection of a security interest perfected by compliance with the statute or treaty are governed by the provisions of the statute or treaty; in other respects the security interest is subject to this Article. Amended in 1972.

* **Note:** *It is recommended that the provisions of certificate of title acts for perfection of security interests by notation on the certificates should be amended to exclude coverage of inventory held for sale.*

§ 9—303. When Security Interest Is Perfected; Continuity of Perfection.

(1) A security interest is perfected when it has attached and when all of the applicable steps required for perfection have been taken. Such steps are specified in Sections 9—302, 9—304, 9—305 and 9—306. If such steps are taken before the security interest attaches, it is perfected at the time when it attaches.

(2) If a security interest is originally perfected in any way permitted under this Article and is subsequently perfected in some other way under this Article, without an intermediate period when it was unperfected, the security interest shall be deemed to be perfected continuously for the purposes of this Article.

§ 9—304. Perfection of Security Interest in Instruments, Documents, and Goods Covered by Documents; Perfection by Permissive Filing; Temporary Perfection Without Filing or Transfer of Possession.

(1) A security interest in chattel paper or negotiable documents may be perfected by filing. A security interest in money or instruments (other than instruments which constitute part of chattel paper) can be perfected only by the secured party's taking possession, except as provided in subsections (4) and (5) of this section and subsections (2) and (3) of Section 9—306 on proceeds.

(2) During the period that goods are in the possession of the issuer of a negotiable document therefor, a security interest in the goods is perfected by perfecting a security interest in the document, and any security interest in the goods otherwise perfected during such period is subject thereto.

(3) A security interest in goods in the possession of a bailee other than one who has issued a negotiable document therefor is perfected by issuance of a document in the name of the secured party or by the bailee's receipt of notification of the secured party's interest or by filing as to the goods.

(4) A security interest in instruments or negotiable documents is perfected without filing or the taking of possession for a period of 21 days from the time it attaches to the extent that it arises for new value given under a written security agreement.

(5) A security interest remains perfected for a period of 21 days without filing where a secured party having a perfected security interest in an instrument, a negotiable document or goods in possession of a bailee other than one who has issued a negotiable document therefor

(a) makes available to the debtor the goods or documents representing the goods for the purpose of ultimate sale or exchange or for the purpose of loading, unloading, storing, shipping, transshipping, manufacturing, processing or otherwise dealing with them in a manner preliminary to their sale or exchange, but priority between conflicting security interests in the goods is subject to subsection (3) of Section 9—312; or

(b) delivers the instrument to the debtor for the purpose of ultimate sale or exchange or of presentation, collection, renewal or registration of transfer.

(6) After the 21 day period in subsections (4) and (5) perfection depends upon compliance with applicable provisions of this Article. Amended in 1972.

§ 9—305. When Possession by Secured Party Perfects Security Interest Without Filing.

A security interest in letters of credit and advices of credit (subsection (2) (a) of Section 5—116), goods, instruments, money, negotiable documents or chattel paper may be perfected by the secured party's taking possession of the collateral. If such collateral other than goods covered by a negotiable document is held by a bailee, the secured party is deemed to have possession from the time the bailee receives notification of the secured party's interest. A security interest is perfected by possession from the time possession is taken without relation back and continues only so long as possession is retained, unless otherwise specified in this Article. The security interest may be otherwise perfected as provided in this Article before or after the period of possession by the secured party. Amended in 1972.

§ 9—306. "Proceeds"; Secured Party's Rights on Disposition of Collateral.

(1) "Proceeds" includes whatever is received upon the sale, exchange, collection or other disposition of collateral or proceeds. Insurance payable by reason of loss or damage to the collateral is proceeds, except to the extent that it is payable to a person other than a party to the security agreement. Money, checks, deposit accounts, and the like are "cash proceeds". All other proceeds are "non-cash proceeds".

(2) Except where this Article otherwise provides, a security interest continues in collateral notwithstanding sale, exchange or other disposition thereof unless the disposition was authorized by the secured party in the security agreement or otherwise, and also continues in any identifiable proceeds including collections received by the debtor.

(3) The security interest in proceeds is a continuously perfected security interest if the interest in the original collateral was perfected but it ceases to be a perfected security interest and becomes unperfected ten days after receipt of the proceeds by the debtor unless

(a) a filed financing statement covers the original collateral and the proceeds are collateral in which a security interest may be perfected by filing in the office or offices where the financing statement has been filed and, if the proceeds are acquired with cash proceeds, the description of collateral in the financing statement indicates the types of property constituting the proceeds; or

(b) a filed financing statement covers the original collateral and the proceeds are identifiable cash proceeds; or

(c) the security interest in the proceeds is perfected before the expiration of the ten day period.

Except as provided in this section, a security interest in proceeds can be perfected only by the methods or under the circumstances permitted in this Article for original collateral of the same type.

(4) In the event of insolvency proceedings instituted by or against a debtor, a secured party with a perfected security interest in proceeds has a perfected security interest only in the following proceeds:

(a) in identifiable non-cash proceeds and in separate deposit accounts containing only proceeds;

(b) in identifiable cash proceeds in the form of money which is neither commingled with other money nor deposited in a deposit account prior to the insolvency proceedings;

(c) in identifiable cash proceeds in the form of checks and the like which are not deposited in a deposit account prior to the insolvency proceedings; and

(d) in all cash and deposit accounts of the debtor in which proceeds have been commingled with other funds, but the perfected security interest under this paragraph (d) is

(i) subject to any right to set-off; and

(ii) limited to an amount not greater than the amount of any cash proceeds received by the debtor within ten days before the institution of the insolvency proceedings less the sum of (I) the payments to the secured party on account of cash proceeds received by the debtor during such period and (II) the cash proceeds received by the debtor during such period to which the secured party is entitled under paragraphs (a) through (c) of this subsection (4).

(5) If a sale of goods results in an account or chattel paper which is transferred by the seller to a secured party, and if the goods are returned to or are repossessed by the seller or the secured party, the following rules determine priorities:

(a) If the goods were collateral at the time of sale, for an indebtedness of the seller which is still unpaid, the original security interest attaches again to the goods and continues as a perfected security interest if it was perfected at the time when the goods were sold. If the security interest was originally perfected by a filing which is still effective, nothing further is required to continue the perfected status; in any other case, the secured party must take possession of the returned or repossessed goods or must file.

(b) An unpaid transferee of the chattel paper has a security interest in the goods against the transferor. Such security interest is prior to a security interest asserted under paragraph (a) to the extent that the transferee of the chattel paper was entitled to priority under Section 9—308.

(c) An unpaid transferee of the account has a security interest in the goods against the transferor. Such security interest is subordinate to a security interest asserted under paragraph (a).

(d) A security interest of an unpaid transferee asserted under paragraph (b) or (c) must be perfected for protection against creditors of the transferor and purchasers of the returned or repossessed goods.

Amended in 1972.

§ 9—307. Protection of Buyers of Goods.

(1) A buyer in ordinary course of business (subsection (9) of Section 1—201) other than a person buying farm products from a person engaged in farming operations takes free of a security interest created by his seller even though the security interest is perfected and even though the buyer knows of its existence.

(2) In the case of consumer goods, a buyer takes free of a security interest even though perfected if he buys without knowledge of the security interest, for value and for his own personal, family or household purposes unless prior to the purchase the secured party has filed a financing statement covering such goods.

(3) A buyer other than a buyer in ordinary course of business (subsection (1) of this section) takes free of a security interest to the extent that it secures future advances made after the secured party acquires knowledge of the purchase, or more than 45 days after the purchase, whichever first occurs, unless made pursuant to a commitment entered into without knowledge of the purchase and before the expiration of the 45 day period. Amended in 1972.

§ 9—308. Purchase of Chattel Paper and Instruments.

A purchaser of chattel paper or an instrument who gives new value and takes possession of it in the ordinary course of his business has priority over a security interest in the chattel paper or instrument

(a) which is perfected under Section 9—304 (permissive filing and temporary perfection) or under Section 9—306 (perfection as to proceeds) if he acts without knowledge that the specific paper or instrument is subject to a security interest; or

(b) which is claimed merely as proceeds of inventory subject to a security interest (Section 9—306) even though he knows that the specific paper or instrument is subject to the security interest.

Amended in 1972.

§ 9—309. Protection of Purchasers of Instruments and Documents.

Nothing in this Article limits the rights of a holder in due course of a negotiable instrument (Section 3—302) or a holder to whom a negotiable document of title has been duly negotiated (Section 7—501) or a bona fide purchaser of a security (Section 8—301) and such holders or purchasers take priority over an earlier security interest even though perfected. Filing under this Article does not constitute notice of the security interest to such holders or purchasers.

§ 9—310. Priority of Certain Liens Arising by Operation of Law.

When a person in the ordinary course of his business furnishes services or materials with respect to goods subject to a security interest, a lien upon goods in the possession of such person given by statute or rule of law for such materials or services takes priority over a perfected security interest unless the lien is statutory and the statute expressly provides otherwise.

§ 9—311. Alienability of Debtor's Rights: Judicial Process.

The debtor's rights in collateral may be voluntarily or involuntarily transferred (by way of sale, creation of a security interest, attachment, levy, garnishment or other judicial process) notwithstanding a provision in the security agreement prohibiting any transfer or making the transfer constitute a default.

§ 9—312. Priorities Among Conflicting Security Interests in the Same Collateral.

(1) The rules of priority stated in other sections of this Part and in the following sections shall govern when applicable: Section 4—208 with respect to the security interests of collecting banks in items being collected, accompanying documents and proceeds; Section 9—103 on security interests related to other jurisdictions; Section 9—114 on consignments.

(2) A perfected security interest in crops for new value given to enable the debtor to produce the crops during the production season and given not more than three months before the crops become growing crops by planting or otherwise takes priority over an earlier perfected security interest to the extent that such earlier interest secures obligations due more than six months before the crops become growing crops by planting or otherwise, even though the person giving new value had knowledge of the earlier security interest.

(3) A perfected purchase money security interest in inventory has priority over a conflicting security interest in the same inventory and also has priority in identifiable cash proceeds received on or before the delivery of the inventory to a buyer if

(a) the purchase money security interest is perfected at the time the debtor receives possession of the inventory; and

(b) the purchase money secured party gives notification in writing to the holder of the conflicting security interest if the holder had filed a financing statement covering the same types of inventory (i) before the date of the filing made by the purchase money secured party, or (ii) before the beginning of the 21 day period where the purchase money security interest is temporarily perfected without filing or possession (subsection (5) of Section 9—304); and

(c) the holder of the conflicting security interest receives the notification within five years before the debtor receives possession of the inventory; and

(d) the notification states that the person giving the notice has or expects to acquire a purchase money security interest in inventory of the debtor, describing such inventory by item or type.

(4) A purchase money security interest in collateral other than inventory has priority over a conflicting security interest in the same collateral or its proceeds if the purchase money security interest is perfected at the time the debtor receives possession of the collateral or within ten days thereafter.

(5) In all cases not governed by other rules stated in this section (including cases of purchase money security interests which do not quality for the special priorities set forth in subsections (3) and (4) of this section), priority between conflicting security interests in the same collateral shall be determined according to the following rules:

(a) Conflicting security interests rank according to priority in time of filing or perfection. Priority dates from the time a filing is first made covering the collateral or the time the security interest is first perfected, whichever is earlier, provided that there is no period thereafter when there is neither filing nor perfection.

(b) So long as conflicting security interests are unperfected, the first to attach has priority.

(6) For the purposes of subsection (5) a date of filing or perfection as to collateral is also a date of filing or perfection as to proceeds.

(7) If future advances are made while a security interest is perfected by filing or the taking of possession, the security interest has the same priority for the purposes of subsection (5) with respect to the future advances as it does with respect to the first advance. If a commitment is made before or while the security interest is so perfected, the security interest has the same priority with respect to advances made pursuant thereto. In other cases a perfected security interest has priority from the date the advance is made. Amended in 1972.

§ 9—313. Priority of Security Interests in Fixtures.

(1) In this section and in the provisions of Part 4 of this Article referring to fixture filing, unless the context otherwise requires

(a) goods are "fixtures" when they become so related to particular real estate that an interest in them arises under real estate law

(b) a "fixture filing" is the filing in the office where a mortgage on the real estate would be filed or recorded of a financing statement covering goods which are or are to become fixtures and conforming to the requirements of subsection (5) of Section 9—402

(c) a mortgage is a "construction mortgage" to the extent that it secures an obligation incurred for the construction of an improvement on land including the acquisition cost of the land, if the recorded writing so indicates.

(2) A security interest under this Article may be created in goods which are fixtures or may continue in goods which become fixtures, but no security interest exists under this Article in ordinary building materials incorporated into an improvement on land.

(3) This Article does not prevent creation of an encumbrance upon fixtures pursuant to real estate law.

(4) A perfected security interest in fixtures has priority over the conflicting interest of an encumbrancer or owner of the real estate where

(a) the security interest is a purchase money security interest, the interest of the encumbrancer or owner arises before the goods become fixtures, the security interest is perfected by a fixture filing before the goods become fixtures or within ten days thereafter, and the debtor has an interest of record in the real estate or is in possession of the real estate; or

(b) the security interest is perfected by a fixture filing before the interest of the encumbrancer or owner is of record, the security interest has priority over any conflicting interest of a predecessor in title of the encumbrancer or owner, and the debtor has an interest of record in the real estate or is in possession of the real estate; or

(c) the fixtures are readily removable factory or office machines or readily removable replacements of domestic appliances which are consumer goods, and before the goods become fixtures the security interest is perfected by any method permitted by this Article; or

(d) the conflicting interest is a lien on the real estate obtained by legal or equitable proceedings after the security interest was perfected by any method permitted by this Article.

(5) A security interest in fixtures, whether or not perfected, has priority over the conflicting interest of an encumbrancer or owner of the real estate where

(a) the encumbrancer or owner has consented in writing to the security interest or has disclaimed an interest in the goods as fixtures; or

(b) the debtor has a right to remove the goods as against the encumbrancer or owner. If the debtor's right terminates, the priority of the security interest continues for a reasonable time.

(6) Notwithstanding paragraph (a) of subsection (4) but otherwise subject to subsections (4) and (5), a security interest in fixtures is subordinate to a construction mortgage recorded before the goods become fixtures if the goods become fixtures before the completion of the construction. To the extent that it is given to refinance a construction mortgage, a mortgage has this priority to the same extent as the construction mortgage.

(7) In cases not within the preceding subsections, a security interest in fixtures is subordinate to the conflicting interest of an encumbrancer or owner of the related real estate who is not the debtor.

(8) When the secured party has priority over all owners and encumbrancers of the real estate, he may, on default, subject to the provisions of Part 5, remove his collateral from the real estate but he must reimburse any encumbrancer or owner of the real estate who is not the debtor and who has not otherwise agreed for the cost of repair of any physical injury, but not for any diminution in value of the real estate caused by the absence of the goods removed or by any necessity of replacing them. A person entitled to reimbursement may refuse permission to remove until the secured party gives adequate security for the performance of this obligation. Amended in 1972.

§ 9—314. Accessions.

(1) A security interest in goods which attaches before they are installed in or affixed to other goods takes priority as to the goods installed or affixed (called in this section "accessions") over the claims of all persons to the whole except as stated in subsection (3) and subject to Section 9—315(1).

(2) A security interest which attaches to goods after they become part of a whole is valid against all persons subsequently acquiring interests in the whole except as stated in subsection (3) but is invalid against any person with an interest in the whole at the time the security interest attaches to the goods who has not in writing consented to the security interest or disclaimed an interest in the goods as part of the whole.

(3) The security interests described in subsections (1) and (2) do not take priority over

(a) a subsequent purchaser for value of any interest in the whole; or

(b) a creditor with a lien on the whole subsequently obtained by judicial proceedings; or

(c) a creditor with a prior perfected security interest in the whole to the extent that he makes subsequent advances

if the subsequent purchase is made, the lien by judicial proceedings obtained or the subsequent advance under the prior perfected security interest is made or contracted for without knowledge of the security interest and before it is perfected. A purchaser of the whole at a foreclosure sale other than the holder of a perfected security interest purchasing at his own foreclosure sale is a subsequent purchaser within this section.

(4) When under subsections (1) or (2) and (3) a secured party has an interest in accessions which has priority over the claims of all persons who have interests in the whole, he may on default subject to the provisions of Part 5 remove his collateral from the whole but he must reimburse any encumbrancer or owner of the whole who is not the debtor and who has not otherwise agreed for the cost of repair of any physical injury but not for any diminution in value of the whole caused by the absence of the goods removed or by any necessity for replacing them. A person entitled to reimbursement may refuse permission to remove until the secured party gives adequate security for the performance of this obligation.

§ 9—315. Priority When Goods Are Commingled or Processed.

(1) If a security interest in goods was perfected and subsequently the goods or a part thereof have become part of a product or mass, the security interest continues in the product or mass if

(a) the goods are so manufactured, processed, assembled or commingled that their identity is lost in the product or mass; or

(b) a financing statement covering the original goods also covers the product into which the goods have been manufactured, processed or assembled.

In a case to which paragraph (b) applies, no separate security interest in that part of the original goods which has been manufactured, processed or assembled into the product may be claimed under Section 9—314.

(2) When under subsection (1) more than one security interest attaches to the product or mass, they rank equally according to the ratio that the cost of the goods to which each interest originally attached bears to the cost of the total product or mass.

§ 9—316. Priority Subject to Subordination.

Nothing in this Article prevents subordination by agreement by any person entitled to priority.

§ 9—317. Secured Party Not Obligated on Contract of Debtor.

The mere existence of a security interest or authority given to the debtor to dispose of or use collateral does not impose contract or tort liability upon the secured party for the debtor's acts or omissions.

§ 9—318. Defenses Against Assignee; Modification of Contract After Notification of Assignment; Term Prohibiting Assignment Ineffective; Identification and Proof of Assignment.

(1) Unless an account debtor has made an enforceable agreement not to assert defenses or claims arising out of a sale as provided in Section 9—206 the rights of an assignee are subject to

(a) all the terms of the contract between the account debtor and assignor and any defense or claim arising therefrom; and

(b) any other defense or claim of the account debtor against the assignor which accrues before the account debtor receives notification of the assignment.

(2) So far as the right to payment or a part thereof under an assigned contract has not been fully earned by performance, and notwithstanding notification of the assignment, any modification of or substitution for the contract made in good faith and in accordance with reasonable commercial standards is effective against an assignee unless the account debtor has otherwise agreed but the assignee acquires corresponding rights under the modified or substituted contract. The assignment may provide that such modification or substitution is a breach by the assignor.

(3) The account debtor is authorized to pay the assignor until the account debtor receives notification that the amount due or to become due has been assigned and that payment is to be made to the assignee. A notification which does not reasonably identify the rights assigned is ineffective. If requested by the account debtor, the assignee must seasonably furnish reasonable proof that the assignment has been made and unless he does so the account debtor may pay the assignor.

(4) A term in any contract between an account debtor and an assignor is ineffective if it prohibits assignment of an account or prohibits creation of a security interest in a general intangible for money due or to become due or requires the account debtor's consent to such assignment or security interest. Amended in 1972.

PART 4

FILING

§ 9—401. Place of Filing; Erroneous Filing; Removal of Collateral.

First Alternative Subsection (1)

(1) The proper place to file in order to perfect a security interest is as follows:

(a) when the collateral is timber to be cut or is minerals or the like (including oil and gas) or accounts subject to subsection (5) of Section 9—103, or when the financing statement is filed as a fixture filing (Section 9—313) and the collateral is goods which are or are to become fixtures, then in the office where a mortgage on the real estate would be filed or recorded;

(b) in all other cases, in the office of the [Secretary of State].

Second Alternative Subsection (1)

(1) The proper place to file in order to perfect a security interest is as follows:

(a) when the collateral is equipment used in farming operations, or farm products, or accounts or general intangibles arising from or relating to the sale of farm products by a farmer, or consumer goods, then in the office of the .... in the county of the debtor's residence or if the debtor is not a resident of this state then in the office of the .... in the county where the goods are kept, and in addition when the collateral is crops growing or to be grown in the office of the

.... in the county where the land is located;

(b) when the collateral is timber to be cut or is minerals or the like (including oil and gas) or accounts subject to subsection (5) of Section 9—103, or when the financing statement is filed as a fixture filing (Section 9—313) and the collateral is goods which are or are to become fixtures, then in the office where a mortgage on the real estate would be filed or recorded;

(c) in all other cases, in the office of the [Secretary of State].

Third Alternative Subsection (1)

(1) The proper place to file in order to perfect a security interest is as follows:

(a) when the collateral is equipment used in farming operations, or farm products, or accounts or general intangibles arising from or relating to the sale of farm products by a farmer, or consumer goods, then in the office of the .... in the county of the debtor's residence or if the debtor is not a resident of this state then in the office of the .... in the county where the goods are kept, and in addition when the collateral is crops growing or to be grown in the office of the .... in the county where the land is located;

(b) when the collateral is timber to be cut or is minerals or the like (including oil and gas) or accounts subject to subsection (5) of Section 9—103, or when the financing statement is filed as a fixture filing (Section 9—313) and the collateral is goods which are or are to become fixtures, then in the office where a mortgage on the real estate would be filed or recorded;

(c) in all other cases, in the office of the [Secretary of State] and in addition, if the debtor has a place of business in only one county of this state, also in the office of .... of such county, or, if the debtor has no place of business in this state, but resides in the state, also in the office of .... of the county in which he resides.

Note: *One of the three alternatives should be selected as subsection (1).*

(2) A filing which is made in good faith in an improper place or not in all of the places required by this section is nevertheless effective with regard to any collateral as to which the filing complied with the requirements of this Article and is also effective with regard to collateral covered by the financing statement against any person who has knowledge of the contents of such financing statement.

(3) A filing which is made in the proper place in this state continues effective even though the debtor's residence or place of business or the location of the collateral or its use, whichever controlled the original filing, is thereafter changed.

Alternative Subsection (3)

[(3) A filing which is made in the proper county continues effective for four months after a change to another county of the debtor's residence or place of business or the location of the collateral, whichever controlled the original filing. It becomes ineffective thereafter unless a copy of the financing statement signed by the secured party is filed in the new county within said period. The security interest may also be perfected in the new county after the expiration of the four-month period; in such case perfection dates from the time of perfection in the new county. A change in the use of the collateral does not impair the effectiveness of the original filing.]

(4) The rules stated in Section 9—103 determine whether filing is necessary in this state.

(5) Notwithstanding the preceding subsections, and subject to subsection (3) of Section 9—302, the proper place to file in order to perfect a security interest in collateral, including fixtures, of a transmitting utility is the office of the [Secretary of State]. This filing constitutes a fixture filing (Section 9—313) as to the collateral described therein which is or is to become fixtures.

(6) For the purposes of this section, the residence of an organization is its place of business if it has one or its chief executive office if it has more than one place of business. Amended in 1962 and 1972.

Note: *Subsection (6) should be used only if the state chooses the Second or Third Alternative Subsection (1).*

§ 9—402. Formal Requisites of Financing Statement; Amendments; Mortgage as Financing Statement.

(1) A financing statement is sufficient if it gives the names of the debtor and the secured party, is signed by the debtor, gives an address of the secured party from which information concerning the security interest may be obtained, gives a mailing address of the debtor and contains a statement indicating the types, or describing the items, of collateral. A financing statement may be filed before a security agreement is made or a security interest otherwise attaches. When the financing statement covers crops growing or to be grown, the statement must also contain a description of the real estate concerned. When the financing statement covers timber to be cut or covers minerals or the like (including oil and gas) or accounts subject to subsection (5) of Section 9—103, or when the financing statement is filed as a fixture filing (Section 9—313) and the collateral is goods which are or are to become fixtures, the statement must also comply with subsection (5). A copy of the security agreement is sufficient as a financing statement if it contains the above information and is signed by the debtor. A carbon, photographic or other reproduction of a security agreement or a financing statement is sufficient as a financing statement if the security agreement so provides or if the original has been filed in this state.

(2) A financing statement which otherwise complies with subsection (1) is sufficient when it is signed by the secured party instead of the debtor if it is filed to perfect a security interest in

(a) collateral already subject to a security interest in another jurisdiction when it is brought into this state, or when the debtor's location is changed to this state. Such a financing statement must state that the collateral was brought into this state or that the debtor's location was changed to this state under such circumstances; or

(b) proceeds under Section 9—306 if the security interest in the original collateral was perfected. Such a financing statement must describe the original collateral; or

(c) collateral as to which the filing has lapsed; or

(d) collateral acquired after a change of name, identity or corporate structure of the debtor (subsection (7)).

(3) A form substantially as follows is sufficient to comply with subsection (1):

Name of debtor (or assignor) ....
Address ....
Name of secured party (or assignee) .....
Address ....

1. This financing statement covers the following types (or items) of property:
   (Describe) ....
2. (If collateral is crops) The above described crops are growing or are to be grown on:
   (Describe Real Estate) ....
3. (If applicable) The above goods are to become fixtures on *

* Where appropriate substitute either "The above timber is standing on . . . ." or "The above minerals or the like (including oil and gas) or accounts will be financed at the wellhead or minehead of the well or mine located on . . . ."

(Describe Real Estate) ....
and this financing statement is to be filed [for record] in the real estate records. (If the debtor does not have an interest of record) The name of a record owner is ....

4. (If products of collateral are claimed) Products of the collateral are also covered.

(use whichever is applicable)
....
Signature of Debtor (or Assignor)
....
Signature of Secured Party (or Assignee)

(4) A financing statement may be amended by filing a writing signed by both the debtor and the secured party. An amendment does not extend the period of effectiveness of a financing statement. If any amendment adds collateral, it is effective as to the added collateral only from the filing date of the amendment. In this Article, unless the context otherwise requires, the term "financing statement" means the original financing statement and any amendments.

(5) A financing statement covering timber to be cut or covering minerals or the like (including oil and gas) or accounts subject to subsection (5) of Section 9—103, or a financing

statement filed as a fixture filing (Section 9—313) where the debtor is not a transmitting utility, must show that it covers this type of collateral, must recite that it is to be filed [for record] in the real estate records, and the financing statement must contain a description of the real estate [sufficient if it were contained in a mortgage of the real estate to give constructive notice of the mortgage under the law of this state]. If the debtor does not have an interest of record in the real estate, the financing statement must show the name of a record owner.

(6) A mortgage is effective as a financing statement filed as a fixture filing from the date of its recording if

(a) the goods are described in the mortgage by item or type; and

(b) the goods are or are to become fixtures related to the real estate described in the mortgage; and

(c) the mortgage complies with the requirements for a financing statement in this section other than a recital that it is to be filed in the real estate records; and

(d) the mortgage is duly recorded.

No fee with reference to the financing statement is required other than the regular recording and satisfaction fees with respect to the mortgage.

(7) A financing statement sufficiently shows the name of the debtor if it gives the individual, partnership or corporate name of the debtor, whether or not it adds other trade names or names of partners. Where the debtor so changes his name or in the case of an organization its name, identity or corporate structure that a filed financing statement becomes seriously misleading, the filing is not effective to perfect a security interest in collateral acquired by the debtor more than four months after the change, unless a new appropriate financing statement is filed before the expiration of that time. A filed financing statement remains effective with respect to collateral transferred by the debtor even though the secured party knows of or consents to the transfer.

(8) A financing statement substantially complying with the requirements of this section is effective even though it contains minor errors which are not seriously misleading. Amended in 1972.

Note: *Language in brackets is optional.*

Note: *Where the state has any special recording system for real estate other than the usual grantor-grantee index (as, for instance, a tract system or a title registration or Torrens system) local adaptations of subsection (5) and Section 9—403(7) may be necessary. See Mass.Gen.Laws Chapter 106, Section 9—409.*

§ 9—403. What Constitutes Filing; Duration of Filing; Effect of Lapsed Filing; Duties of Filing Officer.

(1) Presentation for filing of a financing statement and tender of the filing fee or acceptance of the statement by the filing officer constitutes filing under this Article.

(2) Except as provided in subsection (6) a filed financing statement is effective for a period of five years from the date of filing. The effectiveness of a filed financing statement lapses on the expiration of the five year period unless a continuation statement is filed prior to the lapse. If a security interest perfected by filing exists at the time insolvency proceedings are commenced by or against the debtor, the security interest remains perfected until termination of the insolvency proceedings and thereafter for a period of sixty days or until expiration of the five year period, whichever occurs later. Upon lapse the security interest becomes unperfected, unless it is perfected without filing. If the security interest becomes unperfected upon lapse, it is deemed to have been unperfected as against a person who became a purchaser or lien creditor before lapse.

(3) A continuation statement may be filed by the secured party within six months prior to the expiration of the five year period specified in subsection (2). Any such continuation statement must be signed by the secured party, identify the original statement by file number and state that the original statement is still effective. A continuation statement signed by a person other than the secured party of record must be accompanied by a separate written statement of assignment signed by the secured party of record and complying with subsection (2) of Section 9—405, including payment of the required fee. Upon timely filing of the

continuation statement, the effectiveness of the original statement is continued for five years after the last date to which the filing was effective whereupon it lapses in the same manner as provided in subsection (2) unless another continuation statement is filed prior to such lapse. Succeeding continuation statements may be filed in the same manner to continue the effectiveness of the original statement. Unless a statute on disposition of public records provides otherwise, the filing officer may remove a lapsed statement from the files and destroy it immediately if he has retained a microfilm or other photographic record, or in other cases after one year after the lapse. The filing officer shall so arrange matters by physical annexation of financing statements to continuation statements or other related filings, or by other means, that if he physically destroys the financing statements of a period more than five years past, those which have been continued by a continuation statement or which are still effective under subsection (6) shall be retained.

(4) Except as provided in subsection (7) a filing officer shall mark each statement with a file number and with the date and hour of filing and shall hold the statement or a microfilm or other photographic copy thereof for public inspection. In addition the filing officer shall index the statement according to the name of the debtor and shall note in the index the file number and the address of the debtor given in the statement.

(5) The uniform fee for filing and indexing and for stamping a copy furnished by the secured party to show the date and place of filing for an original financing statement or for a continuation statement shall be $.......... if the statement is in the standard form prescribed by the [Secretary of State] and otherwise shall be $.........., plus in each case, if the financing statement is subject to subsection (5) of Section 9—402, $.......... The uniform fee for each name more than one required to be indexed shall be $.......... The secured party may at his option show a trade name for any person and an extra uniform indexing fee of $.......... shall be paid with respect thereto.

(6) If the debtor is a transmitting utiltiy (subsection (5) of Section 9—401) and a filed financing statement so states, it is effective until a termination statement is filed. A real estate mortgage which is effective as a fixture filing under subsection (6) of Section 9—402 remains effective as a fixture filing until the mortgage is released or satisfied of record or its effectiveness otherwise terminates as to the real estate.

(7) When a financing statement covers timber to be cut or covers minerals or the like (including oil and gas) or accounts subject to subsection (5) of Section 9—103, or is filed as a fixture filing, [it shall be filed for record and] the filing officer shall index it under the names of the debtor and any owner of record shown on the financing statement in the same fashion as if they were the mortgagors in a mortgage of the real estate described, and, to the extent that the law of this state provides for indexing of mortgages under the name of the mortgagee, under the name of the secured party as if he were the mortgagee thereunder, or where indexing is by description in the same fashion as if the financing statement were a mortgage of the real estate described. Amended in 1972.

Note: *In states in which writings will not apear in the real estate records and indices unless actually recorded the bracketed language in subsection (7) should be used.*

§ 9—404. Termination Statement.

(1) If a financing statement covering consumer goods is filed on or after ...., then within one month or within ten days following written demand by the debtor after there is no outstanding secured obligation and no commitment to make advances, incur obligations or otherwise give value, the secured party must file with each filing officer with whom the financing statement was filed, a termination statement to the effect that he no longer claims a security interest under the financing statement, which shall be identified by file number. In other cases whenever there is no outstanding secured obligation and no commitment to make advances, incur obligations or otherwise give value, the secured party must on written demand by the debtor send the debtor, for each filing officer with whom the financing statement was filed, a termination statement to the effect that he no longer claims a security interest under the financing statement, which shall be identified by file number. A termination statement signed by a person other than the secured party of record must be

accompanied by a separate written statement of assignment signed by the secured party of record complying with subsection (2) of Section 9—405, including payment of the required fee. If the affected secured party fails to file such a termination statement as required by this subsection, or to send such a termination statement within ten days after proper demand therefor, he shall be liable to the debtor for one hundred dollars, and in addition for any loss caused to the debtor by such failure.

(2) On presentation to the filing officer of such a termination statement he must note it in the index. If he has received the termination statement in duplicate, he shall return one copy of the termination statement to the secured party stamped to show the time of receipt thereof. If the filing officer has a microfilm or other photographic record of the financing statement, and of any related continuation statement, statement of assignment and statement of release, he may remove the originals from the files at any time after receipt of the termination statement, or if he has no such record, he may remove them from the files at any time after one year after receipt of the termination statement.

(3) If the termination statement is in the standard form prescribed by the [Secretary of State], the uniform fee for filing and indexing the termination statement shall be $......, and otherwise shall be $......, plus in each case an additional fee of $...... for each name more than one against which the termination statement is required to be indexed. Amended in 1972.

Note: *The date to be inserted should be the effective date of the revised Article 9.*

§ 9—405. Assignment of Security Interest; Duties of Filing Officer; Fees.

(1) A financing statement may disclose an assignment of a security interest in the collateral described in the financing statement by indication in the financing statement of the name and address of the assignee or by an assignment itself or a copy thereof on the face or back of the statement. On presentation to the filing officer of such a financing statement the filing officer shall mark the same as provided in Section 9—403(4). The uniform fee for filing, indexing and furnishing filing data for a financing statement so indicating an assignment shall be $...... if the statement is in the standard form prescribed by the [Secretary of State] and otherwise shall be $......., plus in each case an additional fee of $...... for each name more than one against which the financing statement is required to be indexed.

(2) A secured party may assign of record all or part of his rights under a financing statement by the filing in the place where the original financing statement was filed of a separate written statement of assignment signed by the secured party of record and setting forth the name of the secured party of record and the debtor, the file number and the date of filing of the financing statement and the name and address of the assignee and containing a description of the collateral assigned. A copy of the assignment is sufficient as a separate statement if it complies with the preceding sentence. On presentation to the filing officer of such a separate statement, the filing officer shall mark such separate statement with the date and hour of the filing. He shall note the assignment on the index of the financing statement, or in the case of a fixture filing, or a filing covering timber to be cut, or covering minerals or the like (including oil and gas) or accounts subject to subsection (5) of Section 9—103, he shall index the assignment under the name of the assignor as grantor and, to the extent that the law of this state provides for indexing the assignment of a mortgage under the name of the assignee, he shall index the assignment of the financing statement under the name of the assignee. The uniform fee for filing, indexing and furnishing filing data about such a separate statement of assignment shall be $...... if the statement is in the standard form prescribed by the [Secretary of State] and otherwise shall be $......, plus in each case an additional fee of $...... for each name more than one against which the statement of assignment is required to be indexed. Notwithstanding the provisions of this subsection, an assignment of record of a security interest in a fixture contained in a mortgage effective as a fixture filing (subsection (6) of Section 9—402) may be made only by an assignment of the mortgage in the manner provided by the law of this state other than this Act.

(3) After the disclosure or filing of an assignment under this section, the assignee is the secured party of record. Amended in 1972.

§ 9—406. Release of Collateral; Duties of Filing Officer; Fees.

A secured party of record may by his signed statement release all or a part of any collateral described in a filed financing statement. The statement of release is sufficient if it contains a description of the collateral being released, the name and address of the debtor, the name and address of the secured party, and the file number of the financing statement. A statement of release signed by a person other than the secured party of record must be accompanied by a separate written statement of assignment signed by the secured party of record and complying with subsection (2) of Section 9—405, including payment of the required fee. Upon presentation of such a statement of release to the filing officer he shall mark the statement with the hour and date of filing and shall note the same upon the margin of the index of the filing of the financing statement. The uniform fee for filing and noting such a statement of release shall be $...... if the statement is in the standard form prescribed by the [Secretary of State] and otherwise shall be $......, plus in each case an additional fee of $...... for each name more than one against which the statement of release is required to be indexed. Amended in 1972.

[§ 9—407. Information From Filing Officer].

[(1) If the person filing any financing statement, termination statement, statement of assignment, or statement of release, furnishes the filing officer a copy thereof, the filing officer shall upon request note upon the copy the file number and date and hour of the filing of the original and deliver or send the copy to such person.]

[(2) Upon request of any person, the filing officer shall issue his certificate showing whether there is on file on the date and hour stated therein, any presently effective financing statement naming a particular debtor and any statement of assignment thereof and if there is, giving the date and hour of filing of each such statement and the names and addresses of each secured party therein. The uniform fee for such a certificate shall be $...... if the request for the certificate is in the standard form prescribed by the [Secretary of State] and otherwise shall be $....... Upon request the filing officer shall furnish a copy of any filed financing statement or statement of assignment for a uniform fee of $...... per page.] Amended in 1972.

Note: *This section is proposed as an optional provision to require filing officers to furnish certificates. Local law and practices should be consulted with regard to the advisability of adoption.*

§ 9—408. Financing Statements Covering Consigned or Leased Goods.

A consignor or lessor of goods may file a financing statement using the terms "consignor," "consignee," "lessor," "lessee" or the like instead of the terms specified in Section 9—402. The provisions of this Part shall apply as appropriate to such a financing statement but its filing shall not of itself be a factor in determining whether or not the consignment or lease is intended as security (Section 1—201 (37)). However, if it is determined for other reasons that the consignment or lease is so intended, a security interest of the consignor or lessor which attaches to the consigned or leased goods is perfected by such filing. Added in 1972.

PART 5

DEFAULT

§ 9—501. Default; Procedure When Security Agreement Covers Both Real and Personal Property.

(1) When a debtor is in default under a security agreement, a secured party has the rights and remedies provided in this Part and except as limited by subsection (3) those provided in the security agreement. He may reduce his claim to judgment, foreclose or otherwise enforce the security interest by any available judicial procedure. If the collateral is documents the secured party may proceed either as to the documents or as to the goods covered thereby. A secured party in possession has the rights, remedies and duties provided in Section 9—207. The rights and remedies referred to in this subsection are cumulative.

(2) After default, the debtor has the rights and remedies provided in this Part, those provided in the security agreement and those provided in Section 9—207.

(3) To the extent that they give rights to the debtor and impose duties on the secured party, the rules stated in the subsections referred to below may not be waived or varied except as provided with respect to compulsory disposition of collateral (subsection (3) of Section 9—504 and Section 9—505) and with respect to redemption of collateral (Section 9—506) but the parties may by agreement determine the standards by which the fulfillment of these rights and duties is to be measured if such standards are not manifestly unreasonable:

(a) subsection (2) of Section 9—502 and subsection (2) of Section 9—504 insofar as they require accounting for surplus proceeds of collateral;

(b) subsection (3) of Section 9—504 and subsection (1) of Section 9—505 which deal with disposition of collateral;

(c) subsection (2) of Section 9—505 which deals with acceptance of collateral as discharge of obligation;

(d) Section 9—506 which deals with redemption of collateral; and

(e) subsection (1) of Section 9—507 which deals with the secured party's liability for failure to comply with this Part.

(4) If the security agreement covers both real and personal property, the secured party may proceed under this Part as to the personal property or he may proceed as to both the real and the personal property in accordance with his rights and remedies in respect of the real property in which case the provisions of this Part do not apply.

(5) When a secured party has reduced his claim to judgment the lien of any levy which may be made upon his collateral by virtue of any execution based upon the judgment shall relate back to the date of the perfection of the security interest in such collateral. A judicial sale, pursuant to such execution, is a foreclosure of the security interest by judicial procedure within the meaning of this section, and the secured party may purchase at the sale and thereafter hold the collateral free of any other requirements of this Article. Amended in 1972.

§ 9—502. Collection Rights of Secured Party.

(1) When so agreed and in any event on default the secured party is entitled to notify an account debtor or the obligor on an instrument to make payment to him whether or not the assignor was theretofore making collections on the collateral, and also to take control of any proceeds to which he is entitled under Section 9—306.

(2) A secured party who by agreement is entitled to charge back uncollected collateral or otherwise to full or limited recourse against the debtor and who undertakes to collect from the account debtors or obligors must proceed in a commercially reasonable manner and may deduct his reasonable expenses of realization from the collections. If the security agreement secures an indebtedness, the secured party must account to the debtor for any surplus, and unless otherwise agreed, the debtor is liable for any deficiency. But, if the underlying transaction was a sale of accounts or chattel paper, the debtor is entitled to any surplus or is liable for any deficiency only if the security agreement so provides. Amended in 1972.

§ 9—503. Secured Party's Right to Take Possession After Default.

Unless otherwise agreed a secured party has on default the right to take possession of the collateral. In taking possession a secured party may proceed without judicial process if this can be done without breach of the peace or may proceed by action. If the security agreement so provides the secured party may require the debtor to assemble the collateral and make it available to the secured party at a place to be designated by the secured party which is reasonably convenient to both parties. Without removal a secured party may render equipment unusable, and may dispose of collateral on the debtor's premises under Section 9—504.

§ 9—504. Secured Party's Right to Dispose of Collateral After Default; Effect of Disposition.

(1) A secured party after default may sell, lease or otherwise dispose of any or all of the collateral in its then condition or following any commercially reasonable preparation or processing. Any sale of goods is subject to the Article on Sales (Article 2). The proceeds of

disposition shall be applied in the order following to

(a) the reasonable expenses of retaking, holding, preparing for sale or lease, selling, leasing and the like and, to the extent provided for in the agreement and not prohibited by law, the reasonable attorneys' fees and legal expenses incurred by the secured party;

(b) the satisfaction of indebtedness secured by the security interest under which the disposition is made;

(c) the satisfaction of indebtedness secured by any subordinate security interest in the collateral if written notification of demand therefor is received before distribution of the proceeds is completed. If requested by the secured party, the holder of a subordinate security interest must seasonably furnish reasonable proof of his interest, and unless he does so, the secured party need not comply with his demand.

(2) If the security interest secures an indebtedness, the secured party must account to the debtor for any surplus, and, unless otherwise agreed, the debtor is liable for any deficiency. But if the underlying transaction was a sale of accounts or chattel paper, the debtor is entitled to any surplus or is liable for any deficiency only if the security agreement so provides.

(3) Disposition of the collateral may be by public or private proceedings and may be made by way of one or more contracts. Sale or other disposition may be as a unit or in parcels and at any time and place and on any terms but every aspect of the disposition including the method, manner, time, place and terms must be commercially reasonable. Unless collateral is perishable or threatens to decline speedily in value or is of a type customarily sold on a recognized market, reasonable notification of the time and place of any public sale or reasonable notification of the time after which any private sale or other intended disposition is to be made shall be sent by the secured party to the debtor, if he has not signed after default a statement renouncing or modifying his right to notification of sale. In the case of consumer goods no other notification need be sent. In other cases notification shall be sent to any other secured party from whom the secured party has received (before sending his notification to the debtor or before the debtor's renunciation of his rights) written notice of a claim of an interest in the collateral. The secured party may buy at any public sale and if the collateral is of a type customarily sold in a recognized market or is of a type which is the subject of widely distributed standard price quotations he may buy at private sale.

(4) When collateral is disposed of by a secured party after default, the disposition transfers to a purchaser for value all of the debtor's rights therein, discharges the security interest under which it is made and any security interest or lien subordinate thereto. The purchaser takes free of all such rights and interests even though the secured party fails to comply with the requirements of this Part or of any judicial proceedings

(a) in the case of a public sale, if the purchaser has no knowledge of any defects in the sale and if he does not buy in collusion with the secured party, other bidders or the person conducting the sale; or

(b) in any other case, if the purchaser acts in good faith.

(5) A person who is liable to a secured party under a guaranty, indorsement, repurchase agreement or the like and who receives a transfer of collateral from the secured party or is subrogated to his rights has thereafter the rights and duties of the secured party. Such a transfer of collateral is not a sale or disposition of the collateral under this Article. Amended in 1972.

§ 9—505. Compulsory Disposition of Collateral; Acceptance of the Collateral as Discharge of Obligation.

(1) If the debtor has paid sixty per cent of the cash price in the case of a purchase money security interest in consumer goods or sixty per cent of the loan in the case of another security interest in consumer goods, and has not signed after default a statement renouncing or modifying his rights under this Part a secured party who has taken possession of collateral must dispose of it under Section 9—504 and if he fails to do so within ninety days after he takes possession the debtor at his option may recover in conversion or under Section 9—507(1) on secured party's liability.

(2) In any other case involving consumer goods or any other collateral a secured party in possession may, after default, propose to retain the collateral in satisfaction of the obligation. Written notice of such proposal shall be sent to the debtor if he has not signed after default a statement renouncing or modifying his rights under this subsection. In the case of consumer goods no other notice need be given. In other cases notice shall be sent to any other secured party from whom the secured party has received (before sending his notice to the debtor or before the debtor's renunciation of his rights) written notice of a claim of an interest in the collateral. If the secured party receives objection in writing from a person entitled to receive notification within twenty-one days after the notice was sent, the secured party must dispose of the collateral under Section 9—504. In the absence of such written objection the secured party may retain the collateral in satisfaction of the debtor's obligation. Amended in 1972.

§ 9—506. Debtor's Right to Redeem Collateral

At any time before the secured party has disposed of collateral or entered into a contract for its disposition under Section 9—504 or before the obligation has been discharged under Section 9—505(2) the debtor or any other secured party may unless otherwise agreed in writing after default redeem the collateral by tendering fulfillment of all obligations secured by the collateral as well as the expenses reasonably incurred by the secured party in retaking, holding and preparing the collateral for disposition, in arranging for the sale, and to the extent provided in the agreement and not prohibited by law, his reasonable attorneys' fees and legal expenses.

§ 9—507. Secured Party's Liability for Failure to Comply With This Part.

(1) If it is established that the secured party is not proceeding in accordance with the provisions of this Part disposition may be ordered or restrained on appropriate terms and conditions. If the disposition has occurred the debtor or any person entitled to notification or whose security interest has been made known to the secured party prior to the disposition has a right to recover from the secured party any loss caused by a failure to comply with the provisions of this Part. If the collateral is consumer goods, the debtor has a right to recover in any event an amount not less than the credit service charge plus ten per cent of the principal amount of the debt or the time price differential plus 10 per cent of the cash price.

(2) The fact that a better price could have been obtained by a sale at a different time or in a different method from that selected by the secured party is not of itself sufficient to establish that the sale was not made in a commercially reasonable manner. If the secured party either sells the collateral in the usual manner in any recognized market therefor or if he sells at the price current in such market at the time of his sale or if he has otherwise sold in conformity with reasonable commercial practices among dealers in the type of property sold he has sold in a commercially reasonable manner. The principles stated in the two preceding sentences with respect to sales also apply as may be appropriate to other types of disposition. A disposition which has been approved in any judicial proceeding or by any bona fide creditors' committee or representative of creditors shall conclusively be deemed to be commercially reasonable, but this sentence does not indicate that any such approval must be obtained in any case nor does it indicate that any disposition not so approved is not commercially reasonable.

ARTICLE 10

EFFECTIVE DATE AND REPEALER

§ 10—101. Effective Date.

This Act shall become effective at midnight on December 31st following its enactment. It applies to transactions entered into and events occurring after that date.

§ 10—102. Specific Repealer; Provision for Transition.

(1) The following acts and all other acts and parts of acts inconsistent herewith are hereby repealed:

(Here should follow the acts to be specifically repealed including the following:

Uniform Negotiable Instruments Act
Uniform Warehouse Receipts Act
Uniform Sales Act
Uniform Bills of Lading Act
Uniform Stock Transfer Act
Uniform Conditional Sales Act
Uniform Trust Receipts Act

Also any acts regulating:

Bank collections
Bulk sales
Chattel mortgages
Conditional sales
Factor's lien acts
Farm storage of grain and similar acts
Assignment of accounts receivable)

(2) Transactions validly entered into before the effective date specified in Section 10—101 and the rights, duties and interests flowing from them remain valid thereafter and may be terminated, completed, consummated or enforced as required or permitted by any statute or other law amended or repealed by this Act as though such repeal or amendment had not occurred.

Note

Subsection (1) should be separately prepared for each state. The foregoing is a list of statutes to be checked.

§ 10—103. General Repealer.

Except as provided in the following section, all acts and parts of acts inconsistent with this Act are hereby repealed.

§ 10—104. Laws Not Repealed.

(1) The Article on Documents of Title (Article 7) does not repeal or modify any laws prescribing the form or contents of documents of title or the services or facilities to be afforded by bailees, or otherwise regulating bailees' businesses in respects not specifically dealt with herein; but the fact that such laws are violated does not affect the status of a document of title which otherwise complies with the definition of a document of title (Section 1—201).

[(2) This Act does not repeal ....*, cited as the Uniform Act for the Simplification of Fiduciary Security Transfers, and if in any respect there is any inconsistency between that Act and the Article of this Act on investment securities (Article 8) the provisions of the former Act shall control.]

Note: *At * in subsection (2) insert the statutory reference to the Uniform Act for the Simplification of Fiduciary Security Transfers if such Act has previously been enacted. If it has not been enacted, omit subsection (2).*

ARTICLE 11

EFFECTIVE DATE AND TRANSITION PROVISIONS

This material has been numbered Article 11 to distinguish it from Article 10, the transition provision of the 1962 Code, which may still remain in effect in some states to cover transition problems from pre-Code law to the original Uniform Commercial Code. Adaptation may be necessary in particular states. The terms "[old Code]" and "[new Code]" and "[old U.C.C.]" and "[new U.C.C.]" are used herein, and should be suitably changed in each state.

This draft was prepared by the Reporters and has not been passed upon by the Review Committee, the Permanent Editorial Board, the American Law Institute, or the National Conference of Commissioners on Uniform State Laws. It is submitted as a working draft which may be adapted as appropriate in each state. The "Discussions" in the Appendix were written by the Reporters to assist in understanding the purpose of the drafts.

§ 11—101. Effective Date.

This Act shall become effective at 12:01 A. M. on ________, 19__.

§ 11—102. Preservation of Old Transition Provision.

The provisions of [here insert reference to the original transition provision in the particular state] shall continue to apply to [the new U.C.C.] and for this purpose the [old U.C.C. and new U.C.C.] shall be considered one continuous statute.

§ 11—103. Transition to [New Code]—General Rule.

Transactions validly entered into after [effective date of old U.C.C.] and before [effective date of new U.C.C.], and which were subject to the provisions of [old U.C.C.] and which would be subject to this Act as amended if they had been entered into after the effective date of [new U.C.C.] and the rights, duties and interests flowing from such transactions remain valid after the latter date and may be terminated, completed, consummated or enforced as required or permitted by the [new U.C.C.]. Security interests arising out of such transactions which are perfected when [new U.C.C.] becomes effective shall remain perfected until they lapse as provided in [new U.C.C.], and may be continued as permitted by [new U.C.C.], except as stated in Section 11—105.

§ 11—104. Transition Provision on Change of Requirement of Filing.

A security interest for the perfection of which filing or the taking of possession was required under [old U.C.C.] and which attached prior to the effective date of [new U.C.C.] but was not perfected shall be deemed perfected on the effective date of [new U.C.C.] if [new U.C. C.] permits perfection without filing or authorizes filing in the office or offices where a prior ineffective filing was made.

§ 11—105. Transition Provision on Change of Place of Filing.

(1) A financing statement or continuation statement filed prior to [effective date of new U.C.C.] which shall not have lapsed prior to [the effective date of new U.C.C.] shall remain effective for the period provided in the [old Code], but not less than five years after the filing.

(2) With respect to any collateral acquired by the debtor subsequent to the effective date of [new U.C.C.], any effective financing statement or continuation statement described in this section shall apply only if the filing or filings are in the office or offices that would be appropriate to perfect the security interests in the new collateral under [new U.C.C.].

(3) The effectiveness of any financing statement or continuation statement filed prior to [effective date of new U.C.C.] may be continued by a continuation statement as permitted by [new U.C.C.], except that if [new U.C.C.] requires a filing in an office where there was no previous financing statement, a new financing statement conforming to Section 11—106 shall be filed in that office.

(4) If the record of a mortgage of real estate would have been effective as a fixture filing of goods described therein if [new U.C.C.] had been in effect on the date of recording the mortgage, the mortgage shall be deemed effective as a fixture filing as to such goods under subsection (6) of Section 9—402 of the [new U.C.C.] on the effective date of [new U.C.C.].

§ 11—106. Required Refilings.

(1) If a security interest is perfected or has priority when this Act takes effect as to all persons or as to certain persons without any filing or recording, and if the filing of a financing statement would be required for the perfection or priority of the security interest against those persons under [new U.C.C.], the perfection and priority rights of the security interest continue until 3 years after the effective date of [new U.C.C.]. The perfection will then lapse unless a financing statement is filed as provided in subsection (4) or unless the security interest is perfected otherwise than by filing.

(2) If a security interest is perfected when [new U.C.C.] takes effect under a law other than [U.C.C.] which requires no further filing, refiling or recording to continue its perfection, perfection continues until and will lapse 3 years after [new U.C.C.] takes effect, unless a financing statement is filed as provided in subsection (4) or unless the security interest is perfected otherwise than by filing, or unless under subsection (3) of Section 9—302 the other law continues to govern filing.

(3) If a security interest is perfected by a filing, refiling or recording under a law repealed by this Act which required further filing, refiling or recording to continue its perfection, perfection continues and will lapse on the date provided by the law so repealed for such further filing, refiling or recording unless a financing statement is filed as provided in subsection (4) or unless the security interest is perfected otherwise than by filing.

(4) A financing statement may be filed within six months before the perfection of a security interest would otherwise lapse. Any such financing statement may be signed by either the debtor or the secured party. It must identify the security agreement, statement or notice (however denominated in any statute or other law repealed or modified by this Act), state the office where and the date when the last filing, refiling or recording, if any, was made with respect thereto, and the filing number, if any, or book and page, if any, of recording and further state that the security agreement, statement or notice, however denominated, in another filing office under the [U.C.C.] or under any statute or other law repealed or modified by this Act is still effective. Section 9—401 and Section 9—103 determine the proper place to file such a financing statement. Except as specified in this subsection, the provisions of Section 9—403(3) for continuation statements apply to such a financing statement.

§ 11—107. Transition Provisions as to Priorities.

Except as otherwise provided in [Article 11], [old U.C.C.] shall apply to any questions of priority if the positions of the parties were fixed prior to the effective date of [new U.C. C.]. In other cases questions of priority shall be determined by [new U.C.C.].

§ 11—108. Presumption that Rule of Law Continues Unchanged.

Unless a change in law has clearly been made, the provisions of [new U.C.C.] shall be deemed declaratory of the meaning of the [old U.C. C.].

APPENDIX B

UNIFORM PARTNERSHIP ACT

(Adopted in 43 jurisdictions: Alaska, Arizona, Arkansas, California, Colorado, Connecticut, Delaware, District of Columbia, Guam, Idaho, Illinois, Indiana, Kentucky, Maryland, Massachusetts, Michigan, Minnesota, Missouri, Montana, Nebraska, Nevada, New Jersey, New Mexico, New York, North Carolina, North Dakota, Ohio, Oklahoma, Oregon, Pennsylvania, Rhode Island, South Carolina, South Dakota, Tennessee, Texas, Utah, Vermont, Virginia, Virgin Islands, Washington, West Virginia, Wisconsin, and Wyoming.)

An Act to Make Uniform the Law of Partnerships

Be it enacted, etc.,

PART I

Preliminary Provisions

Sec. 1. (Name of Act.) This act may be cited as Uniform Partnership Act.

Sec. 2. (Definition of Terms.) In this act, "Court" includes every court and judge having jurisdiction in the case.

"Business" includes every trade, occupation, or profession.

"Person" includes individuals, partnerships, corporations, and other associations.

"Bankrupt" includes bankrupt under the Federal Bankruptcy Act or insolvent under any state insolvent act.

"Conveyance" includes every assignment, lease, mortgage, or encumbrance.

"Real property" includes land and any interest or estate in land.

Sec. 3. (Interpretation of Knowledge and Notice.) (1) A person has "knowledge" of a fact within the meaning of this act not only when he has actual knowledge thereof, but also when he has knowledge of such other facts as in the circumstances shows bad faith.

(2) A person has "notice" of a fact within the meaning of this act when the person who claims the benefit of the notice

(a) States the fact to such person, or

(b) Delivers through the mail, or by other means of communication, a written statement of the fact to such person or to a proper person at his place of business or residence.

Sec. 4. (Rules of Construction.) (1) The rule that statutes in derogation of the common law are to be strictly construed shall have no application to this act.

(2) The law of estoppel shall apply under this act.

(3) The law of agency shall apply under this act.

(4) This act shall be so interpreted and construed as to effect its general purpose to make uniform the law of those states which enact it.

(5) This act shall not be construed so as to impair the obligations of any contract existing when the act goes into effect, nor to affect any action or proceedings begun or right accrued before this act takes effect.

Sec. 5. (Rules for Cases Not Provided for in this Act.) In any case not provided for in this act the rules of law and equity, including the law merchant, shall govern.

PART II

Nature of Partnership

Sec. 6. (Partnership Defined.) (1) A partnership is an association of two or more persons to carry on as co-owners a business for profit.

(2) But any association formed under any other statute of this state, or any statute adopted by authority, other than the authority of this state, is not a partnership under this act,

unless such association would have been a partnership in this state prior to the adoption of this act; but this act shall apply to limited partnerships except in so far as the statutes relating to such partnerships are inconsistent herewith.

Sec. 7. (Rules for Determining the Existence of a Partnership.) In determining whether a partnership exists, these rules shall apply:

(1) Except as provided by Section 16 persons who are not partners as to each other are not partners as to third persons.

(2) Joint tenancy, tenancy in common, tenancy by the entireties, joint property, common property, or part ownership does not of itself establish a partnership, whether such co-owners do or do not share any profits made by the use of the property.

(3) The sharing of gross returns does not of itself establish a partnership, whether or not the persons sharing them have a joint or common right or interest in any property from which the returns are derived.

(4) The receipt by a person of a share of the profits of a business is prima facie evidence that he is a partner in the business, but no such inference shall be drawn if such profits were received in payment:

(a) As a debt by installments or otherwise,

(b) As wages of an employee or rent to a landlord,

(c) As an annuity to a widow or representative of a deceased partner,

(d) As interest on a loan, though the amount of payment vary with the profits of the business.

(e) As the consideration for the sale of a good-will of a business or other property by installments or otherwise.

Sec. 8. (Partnership Property.) (1) All property originally brought into the partnership stock or subsequently acquired by purchase or otherwise, on account of the partnership, is partnership property.

(2) Unless the contrary intention appears, property acquired with partnership funds is partnership property.

(3) Any estate in real property may be acquired in the partnership name. Title so acquired can be conveyed only in the partnership name.

(4) A conveyance to a partnership in the partnership name, though without words of inheritance, passes the entire estate of the grantor unless a contrary intent appears.

PART III

Relations of Partners to Persons Dealing with the Partnership

Sec. 9. (Partner Agent of Partnership as to Partnership Business.) (1) Every partner is an agent of the partnership for the purpose of its business, and the act of every partner, including the execution in the partnership name of any instrument, for apparently carrying on in the usual way the business of the partnership of which he is a member binds the partnership, unless the partner so acting has in fact no authority to act for the partnership in the particular matter, and the person with whom he is dealing has knowledge of the fact that he has no such authority.

(2) An act of a partner which is not apparently for the carrying on of the business of the partnership in the usual way does not bind the partnership unless authorized by the other partners.

(3) Unless authorized by the other partners or unless they have abandoned the business, one or more but less than all the partners have no authority to:

(a) Assign the partnership property in trust for creditors or on the assignee's promise to pay the debts of the partnership,

(b) Dispose of the good-will of the business,

(c) Do any other act which would make it impossible to carry on the ordinary business of a partnership,

(d) Confess a judgment,

(e) Submit a partnership claim or liability to arbitration or reference.

(4) No act of a partner in contravention of a restriction on authority shall bind the partnership to persons having knowledge of the restriction.

Sec. 10. (Conveyance of Real Property of the Partnership.) (1) Where title to real property is in the partnership name, any partner may convey title to such property by a conveyance executed in the partnership name; but the partnership may recover such property unless the partner's act binds the partnership under the provisions of paragraph (1) of section 9 or unless such property has been conveyed by the grantee or a person claiming through such grantee to a holder for value without knowledge that the partner, in making the conveyance, has exceeded his authority.

(2) Where title to real property is in the name of the partnership, a conveyance executed by a partner, in his own name, passes the equitable interest of the partnership, provided the act is one within the authority of the partner under the provisions of paragraph (1) of section 9.

(3) Where title to real property is in the name of one or more but not all the partners, and the record does not disclose the right of the partnership, the partners in whose name the title stands may convey title to such property, but the partnership may recover such property if the partners' act does not bind the partnership under the provisions of paragraph (1) of section 9, unless the purchaser or his assignee, is a holder for value, without knowledge.

(4) Where the title to real property is in the name of one or more or all the partners, or in a third person in trust for the partnership, a conveyance executed by a partner in the partnership name, or in his own name, passes the equitable interest of the partnership, provided the act is one within the authority of the partner under the provisions of paragraph (1) of section 9.

(5) Where the title to real property is in the names of all the partners a conveyance executed by all the partners passes all their rights in such property.

Sec. 11. (Partnership Bound by Admission of Partner.) An admission or representation made by any partner concerning partnership affairs within the scope of his authority as conferred by this act is evidence against the partnership.

Sec. 12. (Partnership Charged with Knowledge of or Notice to Partner.) Notice to any partner of any matter relating to partnership affairs, and the knowledge of the partner acting in the particular matter, acquired while a partner or then present to his mind, and the knowledge of any other partner who reasonably could and should have communicated it to the acting partner, operate as notice to or knowledge of the partnership, except in the case of a fraud on the partnership committed by or with the consent of that partner.

Sec. 13. (Partnership Bound by Partner's Wrongful Act.) Where, by any wrongful act or omission of any partner acting in the ordinary course of the business of the partnership or with the authority of his co-partners, loss or injury is caused to any person, not being a partner in the partnership, or any penalty is incurred, the partnership is liable therefor to the same extent as the partner so acting or omitting to act.

Sec. 14. (Partnership Bound by Partner's Breach of Trust.) The partnership is bound to make good the loss:

(a) Where one partner acting within the scope of his apparent authority receives money or property of a third person and misapplies it; and

(b) Where the partnership in the course of its business receives money or property of a third person and the money or property so received is misapplied by any partner while it is in the custody of the partnership.

Sec. 15. (Nature of Partner's Liability.) All partners are liable

(a) Jointly and severally for everything chargeable to the partnership under sections 13 and 14.

(b) Jointly for all other debts and obligations of the partnership; but any partner may enter into a separate obligation to perform a partnership contract.

Sec. 16. (Partner by Estoppel.) (1) When a person, by words spoken or written or by conduct, represents himself, or consents to another representing him to any one, as a partner in an existing partnership or with one or more persons not actual partners, he is liable to any such person to whom such representation has been made, who has, on the faith of such representation, given credit to the actual or apparent partnership, and if he has made such representation or consented to its being made in a public manner he is liable to such person, whether the representation has or has not been made or communicated to such person so giving credit by or with the knowledge of the apparent partner making the representation or consenting to its being made.

(a) When a partnership liability results, he is liable as though he were an actual member of the partnership.

(b) When no partnership liability results, he is liable jointly with the other persons, if any, so consenting to the contract or representation as to incur liability, otherwise separately.

(2) When a person has been thus represented to be a partner in an existing partnership, or with one or more persons not actual partners, he is an agent of the persons consenting to such representation to bind them to the same extent and in the same manner as though he were a partner in fact, with respect to persons who rely upon the representation. Where all the members of the existing partnership consent to the representation, a partnership act or obligation results; but in all other cases it is the joint act or obligation of the person acting and the persons consenting to the representation.

Sec. 17. (Liability of Incoming Partner.) A person admitted as a partner into an existing partnership is liable for all the obligations of the partnership arising before his admission as though he had been a partner when such obligations were incurred, except that this liability shall be satisfied only out of partnership property.

PART IV

Relations of Partners to One Another

Sec. 18. (Rules Determining Rights and Duties of Partners.) The rights and duties of the partners in relation to the partnership shall be determined, subject to any agreement between them, by the following rules:

(a) Each partner shall be repaid his contributions, whether by way of capital or advances to the partnership property and share equally in the profits and surplus remaining after all liabilities, including those to partners, are satisfied; and must contribute towards the losses, whether of capital or otherwise, sustained by the partnership according to his share in the profits.

(b) The partnership must indemnify every partner in respect of payments made and personal liabilities reasonably incurred by him in the ordinary and proper conduct of its business, or for the preservation of its business or property.

(c) A partner, who in aid of the partnership makes any payment or advance beyond the amount of capital which he agreed to contribute, shall be paid interest from the date of the payment or advance.

(d) A partner shall receive interest on the capital contributed by him only from the date when repayment should be made.

(e) All partners have equal rights in the management and conduct of the partnership business.

(f) No partner is entitled to remuneration for acting in the partnership business, except that a surviving partner is entitled to reasonable compensation for his services in winding up the partnership affairs.

(g) No person can become a member of a partnership without the consent of all the partners.

(h) Any difference arising as to ordinary matters connected with the partnership business may be decided by a majority of the partners; but no act in contravention of any agreement between the partners may be done rightfully without the consent of all the partners.

Sec. 19. (Partnership Books.) The partnership books shall be kept, subject to any agreement between the partners, at the principal place of business of the partnership, and every partner shall at all times have access to and may inspect and copy any of them.

Sec. 20. (Duty of Partners to Render Information.) Partners shall render on demand true and full information of all things affecting the partnership to any partner or the legal representative of any deceased partner or partner under legal disability.

Sec. 21. (Partner Accountable as a Fiduciary.) (1) Every partner must account to the partnership for any benefit, and hold as trustee for it any profits derived by him without the consent of the other partners from any transaction connected with the formation, conduct, or liquidation of the partnership or from any use by him of its property.

(2) This section applies also to the representatives of a deceased partner engaged in the liquidation of the affairs of the partnership as the personal representatives of the last surviving partner.

Sec. 22. (Right to an Account.) Any partner shall have the right to a formal account as to partnership affairs:

(a) If he is wrongfully excluded from the partnership business or possession of its property by his co-partners,

(b) If the right exists under the terms of any agreement,

(c) As provided by section 21,

(d) Whenever other circumstances render it just and reasonable.

Sec. 23. (Continuation of Partnership Beyond Fixed Term.) (1) When a partnership for a fixed term or particular undertaking is continued after the termination of such term or particular undertaking without any express agreement, the rights and duties of the partners remain the same as they were at such termination, so far as is consistent with a partnership at will.

(2) A continuation of the business by the partners or such of them as habitually acted therein during the term, without any settlement or liquidation of the partnership affairs, is prima facie evidence of a continuation of the partnership.

PART V

Property Rights of a Partner

Sec. 24. (Extent of Property Rights of a Partner.) The property rights of a partner are (1) his rights in specific partnership property, (2) his interest in the partnership, and (3) his right to participate in the management.

Sec. 25. (Nature of a Partner's Right in Specific Partnership Property.) (1) A partner is co-owner with his partners of specific partnership property holding as a tenant in partnership.

(2) The incidents of this tenancy are such that:

(a) A partner, subject to the provisions of this act and to any agreement between the partners, has an equal right with his partners to possess specific partnership property for partnership purposes; but he has no right to possess such property for any other purpose without the consent of his partners.

(b) A partner's right in specific partnership property is not assignable except in connection with the assignment of rights of all the partners in the same property.

(c) A partner's right in specific partnership property is not subject to attachment or execution, except on a claim against the partnership. When partnership property is attached for a partnership debt the partners, or any of them, or the representatives of a deceased partner, cannot claim any right under the homestead or exemption laws.

(d) On the death of a partner his right in specific partnership property vests in the surviving partner or partners, except where the deceased was the last surviving partner, when his right in such property vests in his legal representative. Such surviving partner or partners, or the legal representative of the last surviving partner, has no right to possess the partnership property for any but a partnership purpose.

(e) A partner's right in specific partnership property is not subject to dower, curtesy, or allowances to widows, heirs, or next of kin.

Sec. 26. (Nature of Partner's Interest in the Partnership.) A partner's interest in the partnership is his share of the profits and surplus, and the same is personal property.

Sec. 27. (Assignment of Partner's Interest.) (1) A conveyance by a partner of his interest in the partnership does not of itself dissolve the partnership, nor, as against the other partners in the absence of agreement, entitle the assignee, during the continuance of the partnership to interfere in the management or administration of the partnership business or affairs, or to require any information or account of partnership transactions, or to inspect the partnership books; but it merely entitles the assignee to receive in accordance with his contract the profits to which the assigning partner would otherwise be entitled.

(2) In case of a dissolution of the partnership, the assignee is entitled to receive his assignor's interest and may require an account from the date only of the last account agreed to by all the partners.

Sec. 28. (Partner's Interest Subject to Charging Order.) (1) On due application to a competent court by any judgment creditor of a partner, the court which entered the judgment, order, or decree, or any other court, may charge the interest of the debtor partner with payment of the unsatisfied amount of such judgment debt with interest thereon; and may then or later appoint a receiver of his share of the profits, and of any other money due or to fall due to him in respect of the partnership, and make all other orders, directions, accounts and inquiries which the debtor partner might have made, or which the circumstances of the case may require.

(2) The interest charged may be redeemed at any time before foreclosure, or in case of a sale being directed by the court may be purchased without thereby causing a dissolution:

(a) With separate property, by any one or more of the partners, or

(b) With partnership property, by any one or more of the partners with the consent of all the partners whose interests are not so charged or sold.

(3) Nothing in this act shall be held to deprive a partner of his right, if any, under the exemption laws, as regards his interest in the partnership.

PART VI

Dissolution and Winding up

Sec. 29. (Dissolution Defined.) The dissolution of a partnership is the change in the relation of the partners caused by any partner ceasing to be associated in the carrying on as distinguished from the winding up of the business.

Sec. 30. (Partnership Not Terminated by Dissolution.) On dissolution the partnership is not terminated, but continues until the winding up of partnership affairs is completed.

Sec. 31. (Causes of Dissolution.) Dissolution is caused: (1) Without violation of the of the agreement between the partners,

(a) By the termination of the definite term or particular undertaking specified in the agreement,

(b) By the express will of any partner when no definite term or particular undertaking is specified,

(c) By the express will of all the partners who have not assigned their interests or suffered them to be charged for their separate debts, either before or after the termination of any specified term or particular undertaking.

(d) By the expulsion of any partner from the business bona fide in accordance with such a power conferred by the agreement between the partners;

(2) In contravention of the agreement between the partners, where the circumstances do not permit a dissolution under any other provision of this section, by the express will of any partner at any time;

(3) By any event which makes it unlawful for the business of the partnership to be carried on or for the members to carry it on in partnership;

(4) By the death of any partner;

(5) By the bankruptcy of any partner or the partnership;

(6) By decree of court under section 32.

Sec. 32. (Dissolution by Decree of Court.) (1) On application by or for a partner the court shall decree a dissolution whenever:

(a) A partner has been declared a lunatic in any judicial proceeding or is shown to be of unsound mind,

(b) A partner becomes in any other way incapable of performing his part of the partnership contract,

(c) A partner has been guilty of such conduct as tends to affect prejudicially the carrying on of the business,

(d) A partner wilfully or persistently commits a breach of the partnership agreement, or otherwise so conducts himself in matters relating to the partnership business that it is not reasonably practicable to carry on the business in partnership with him,

(e) The business of the partnership can only be carried on at a loss,

(f) Other circumstances render a dissolution equitable.

(2) On the application of the purchaser of a partner's interest under sections 27 or 28:

(a) After the termination of the specified term or particular undertaking,

(b) At any time if the partnership was a partnership at will when the interest was assigned or when the charging order was issued.

Sec. 33. (General Effect of Dissolution on Authority of Partner.) Except so far as may be necessary to wind up partnership affairs or to complete transactions begun but not then finished, dissolution terminates all authority of any partner to act for the partnership,

(1) With respect to the partners,

(a) When the dissolution is not by the act, bankruptcy or death of a partner; or

(b) When the dissolution is by such act, bankruptcy or death of a partner, in cases where section 34 so requires.

(2) With respect to persons not partners, as declared in section 35.

Sec. 34. (Right of Partner to Contribution From Copartners After Dissolution.) Where the dissolution is caused by the act, death or bankruptcy of a partner, each partner is liable to his copartners for his share of any liability created by any partner acting for the partnership as if the partnership had not been dissolved unless

(a) The dissolution being by act of any partner, the partner acting for the partnership had knowledge of the dissolution, or

(b) The dissolution being by the death or bankruptcy of a partner, the partner acting for the partnership had knowledge or notice of the death or bankruptcy.

Sec. 35. (Power of Partner to Bind Partnership to Third Persons After Dissolution.) (1) After dissolution a partner can bind the partnership except as provided in Paragraph (3)

(a) By any act appropriate for winding up partnership affairs or completing transactions unfinished at dissolution;

(b) By any transaction which would bind the partnership if dissolution had not taken place, provided the other party to the transaction

(I) Had extended credit to the partnership prior to dissolution and had no knowledge or notice of the dissolution; or

(II) Though he had not so extended credit, had nevertheless known of the partnership prior to dissolution, and, having no knowledge or notice of dissolution, the fact of dissolution had not been advertised in a newspaper of general circulation in the place (or in each place if more than one) at which the partnership business was regularly carried on.

(2) The liability of a partner under paragraph (1b) shall be satisfied out of partnership assets alone when such partner had been prior to dissolution.

(a) Unknown as a partner to the person with whom the contract is made; and

(b) So far unknown and inactive in partnership affairs that the business reputation of the partnership could not be said to have been in any degree due to his connection with it.

(3) The partnership is in no case bound by any act of a partner after dissolution

(a) Where the partnership is dissolved because it is unlawful to carry on the business, unless the act is appropriate for winding up partnership affairs; or

(b) Where the partner has become bankrupt; or

(c) Where the partner has no authority to wind up partnership affairs; except by a transaction with one who

(I) Had extended credit to the partnership prior to dissolution and had no knowledge or notice of his want of authority; or

(II) Had not extended credit to the partnership prior to dissolution, and, having no knowledge or notice of his want of authority, the fact of his want of authority has not been advertised in the manner provided for advertising the fact of dissolution in paragraph (1bII).

(4) Nothing in this section shall affect the liability under section 16 of any person who after dissolution represents himself or consents to another representing him as a partner in a partnership engaged in carrying on business.

Sec. 36. (Effect of Dissolution on Partner's Existing Liability.) (1) The dissolution of the partnership does not of itself discharge the existing liability of any partner.

(2) A partner is discharged from any existing liability upon dissolution of the partnership by an agreement to that effect between himself, the partnership creditor and the person or partnership continuing the business; and such agreement may be inferred from the course of dealing between the creditor having knowledge of the dissolution and the person or partnership continuing the business.

(3) Where a person agrees to assume the existing obligations of a dissolved partnership, the partners whose obligations have been assumed shall be discharged from any liability to any creditor of the partnership who, knowing of the agreement, consents to a material

alteration in the nature or time of payment of such obligations.

(4) The individual property of a deceased partner shall be liable for all obligations of the partnership incurred while he was a partner but subject to the prior payment of his separate debts.

Sec. 37. (Right to Wind Up.) Unless otherwise agreed the partners who have not wrongfully dissolved the partnership or the legal representative of the last surviving partner, not bankrupt, has the right to wind up the partnership affairs; provided, however, that any partner, his legal representative or his assignee, upon cause shown, may obtain winding up by the court.

Sec. 38. (Rights of Partners to Application of Partnership Property.) (1) When dissolution is caused in any way, except in contravention of the partnership agreement, each partner as against his co-partners and all persons claiming through them in respect of their interests in the partnership, unless otherwise agreed, may have the partnership property applied to discharge its liabilities, and the surplus applied to pay in cash the net amount owing to the respective partners. But if dissolution is caused by expulsion of a partner, bona fide under the partnership agreement and if the expelled partner is discharged from all partnership liabilities, either by payment or agreement under section 36(2), he shall receive in cash only the net amount due him from the partnership.

(2) When dissolution is caused in contravention of the partnership agreement the rights of the partners shall be as follows:

(a) Each partner who has not caused dissolution wrongfully shall have,

(I) All the rights specified in paragraph (1) of this section, and

(II) The right, as against each partner who has caused the dissolution wrongfully, to damages for breach of the agreement.

(b) The partners who have not caused the dissolution wrongfully, if they all desire to continue the business in the same name, either by themselves or jointly with others, may do so, during the agreed term for the partnership and for that purpose may possess the partnership property, provided they secure the payment by bond approved by the court, or pay to any partner who has caused the dissolution wrongfully, the value of his interest in the partnership at the dissolution, less any damages recoverable under clause (2aII) of the section, and in like manner indemnify him against all present or future partnership liabilities.

(c) A partner who has caused the dissolution wrongfully shall have:

(I) If the business is not continued under the provisions of paragraph (2b) all the rights of a partner under paragraph (1), subject to clause (2aII), of this section,

(II) If the business is continued under paragraph (2b) of this section the right as against his co-partners and all claiming through them in respect of their interests in the partnership, to have the value of his interest in the partnership, less any damages caused to his co-partners by the dissolution, ascertained and paid to him in cash, or the payment secured by bond approved by the court, and to be released from all existing liabilities of the partnership; but in ascertaining the value of the partner's interest the value of the good-will of the business shall not be considered.

Sec. 39. (Rights Where Partnership is Dissolved for Fraud or Misrepresentation.) Where a partnership contract is rescinded on the ground of the fraud or misrepresentation of one of the parties thereto, the party entitled to rescind is, without prejudice to any other right, entitled,

(a) To a lien on, or right of retention of, the surplus of the partnership property after satisfying the partnership liabilities to third persons for any sum of money paid by him for the purchase of an interest in the partnership and for any capital or advances contributed by him; and

(b) To stand, after all liabilities to third persons have been satisfied, in the place of the creditors of the partnership for any payments made by him in respect of the partnership liabilities; and

(c) To be indemnified by the person guilty of the fraud or making the representation against all debts and liabilities of the partnership.

Sec. 40. (Rules for Distribution.) In settling accounts between the partners after dissolution, the following rules shall be observed, subject to any agreement to the contrary:

(a) The assets of the partnership are;

(I) The partnership property,

(II) The contributions of the partners necessary for the payment of all the liabilities specified in clause (b) of this paragraph.

(b) The liabilities of the partnership shall rank in order of payment, as follows:

(I) Those owing to creditors other than partners,

(II) Those owing to partners other than for capital and profits,

(III) Those owing to partners in respect of capital,

(IV) Those owing to partners in respect of profits.

(c) The assets shall be applied in the order of their declaration in clause (a) of this paragraph to the satisfaction of the liabilities.

(d) The partners shall contribute, as provided by section 18(a) the amount necessary to satisfy the liabilities; but if any, but not all, of the partners are insolvent, or, not being subject to process, refuse to contribute, the other parties shall contribute their share of the liabilities, and, in the relative proportions in which they share the profits, the additional amount necessary to pay the liabilities.

(e) An assignee for the benefit of creditors or any person appointed by the court shall have the right to enforce the contributions specified in clause (d) of this paragraph.

(f) Any partner or his legal representative shall have the right to enforce the contributions specified in clause (d) of this paragraph, to the extent of the amount which he has paid in excess of his share of the liability.

(g) The individual property of a deceased partner shall be liable for the contributions specified in clause (d) of this paragraph.

(h) When partnership property and the individual properties of the partners are in possession of a court for distribution, partnership creditors shall have priority on partnership property and separate creditors on individual property, saving the rights of lien or secured creditors as heretofore.

(i) Where a partner has become bankrupt or his estate is insolvent the claims against his separate property shall rank in the following order:

(I) Those owing to separate creditors,

(II) Those owing to partnership creditors,

(III) Those owing to partners by way of contribution.

Sec. 41. (Liability of Persons Continuing the Business in Certain Cases.) (1) When any new partner is admitted into an existing partnership, or when any partner retires and assigns (or the representative of the deceased partner assigns) his rights in partnership property to two or more of the partners, or to one or more of the partners and one or more third persons, if the business is continued without liquidation of the partnership affairs, creditors of the first or dissolved partnership are also creditors of the partnership so continuing the business.

(2) When all but one partner retire and assign (or the representative of a deceased partner assigns) their rights in partnership property to the remaining partner, who continues the business without liquidation of partnership affairs, either alone or with others, creditors of the dissolved partnership are also creditors of the person or partnership so continuing the business.

(3) When any partner retires or dies and the business of the dissolved partnership is continued as set forth in paragraphs (1) and (2) of this section, with the consent of the retired partners or the representative of the deceased partner, but without any assignment of his right in partnership property, rights of creditors of the dissolved partnership and of the creditors of the person or partnership continuing the business shall be as if such assignment had been made.

(4) When all the partners or their representatives assign their rights in partnership property to one or more third persons who promise to pay the debts and who continue the business of the dissolved partnership, creditors of the dissolved partnership are also creditors of the person or partnership continuing the business.

(5) When any partner wrongfully causes a dissolution and the remaining partners continue the business under the provisions of section 38(2b), either alone or with others, and without liquidation of the partnership affairs, creditors of the dissolved partnership are also creditors of the person or partnership continuing the business.

(6) When a partner is expelled and the remaining partners continue the business either

alone or with others, without liquidation of the partnership affairs, creditors of the dissolved partnership are also creditors of the person or partnership continuing the business.

(7) The liability of a third person becoming a partner in the partnership continuing the business, under this section, to the creditors of the dissolved partnership shall be satisfied out of partnership property only.

(8) When the business of a partnership after dissolution is continued under any conditions set forth in this section the creditors of the dissolved partnership, as against the separate creditors of the retiring or deceased partner or the representative of the deceased partner, have a prior right to any claim of the retired partner or the representative of the deceased partner against the person or partnership continuing the business, on account of the retired or deceased partner's interest in the dissolved partnership or on account of any consideration promised for such interest or for his right in partnership property.

(9) Nothing in this section shall be held to modify any right of creditors to set aside any assignment on the ground of fraud.

(10) The use by the person or partnership continuing the business of the partnership name, or the name of a deceased partner as part thereof, shall not of itself make the individual property of the deceased partner liable for any debts contracted by such person or partnership.

Sec. 42. (Rights of Retiring or Estate of Deceased Partner When the Business is Continued.) When any partner retires or dies, and the business is continued under any of the conditions set forth in section 41(1, 2, 3, 5, 6), or section 38(2b), without any settlement of accounts as between him or his estate and the person or partnership continuing the business, unless otherwise agreed, he or his legal representative as against such persons or partnership may have the value of his interest at the date of dissolution ascertained, and shall receive as an ordinary creditor an amount equal to the value of his interest in the dissolved partnership with interest, or, at his option or at the option of his legal representative, in lieu of interest, the profits attributable to the use of his right in the property of the dissolved partnership; provided that the creditors of the dissolved partnership as against the separate creditors, or the representative of the retired or deceased partner, shall have priority on any claim arising under this section, as provided by section 41(8) of this act.

Sec. 43. (Accrual of Actions.) The right to an account of his interest shall accrue to any partner, or his legal representative, as against the winding up partners or the surviving partners or the person or partnership continuing the business, at the date of dissolution, in the absence of any agreement to the contrary.

PART VII

Miscellaneous Provisions

Sec. 44. (When Act Takes Effect.) This act shall take effect on the ——— day of ——— one thousand nine hundred and ———.

Sec. 45. (Legislation Repealed.) All acts or parts of acts inconsistent with this act are hereby repealed.

APPENDIX C

DICTIONARY OF LEGAL TERMS

(Abridged and Adapted from Black's Law Dictionary.)

A

AB INITIO. Latin. From the beginning. E. g., void ab initio. An agreement is said to be "void ab initio" if it has at no time had any legal validity.

ABROGATE. To annul; to repeal. A statute may abrogate a rule of the common law.

ABSTRACT OF TITLE. A condensed history of the title to land, consisting of a synopsis or summary of the material or operative portion of all the conveyances, of whatever kind or nature, which in any manner affect said land, or any estate or interest therein, together with a statement of all liens, charges, or liabilities to which the same may be subject, and of which it is in any way material for purchasers to be apprised.

ACCEPTANCE. **In contracts and sales.** The act of a person to whom a thing is offered or tendered by another, whereby he receives the thing with the intention of retaining it, such intention being evidenced by a sufficient act.

In negotiable instruments. Acceptance of a bill of exchange. The act by which the person on whom a bill of exchange is drawn (called the "drawee") assents to the request of the drawer to pay it, or, in other words, engages, or makes himself liable to pay it when due. 2 Bl.Comm. 469. Under the negotiable Instruments Law, "the acceptance must be in writing and signed by the drawee."

ACCESSION. An addition to one's property by increase of the original property or by production from such property. Instances are: The growth of a tree on A.'s land, although the tree overhangs the land of B.; the birth of a calf to the cow of A.; the innocent conversion of B.'s material by A. into a thing of different kind, so that its former identity no longer exists, as where A. innocently converts the wheat of B. into bread.

ACCIDENT. An unusual event, not expected by the person affected by it.

In equity. "An occurrence in relation to a contract which was not anticipated by the parties when the same was entered into, and which gives an undue advantage to one of them over the other in a court of law. Jeremy, Eq. 358. This definition is objected to, because, as accidents may arise in relation to other things besides contracts, it is inaccurate in confining accidents to contracts; besides, it does not exclude cases of unanticipated occurrence resulting from the negligence or misconduct of the party seeking relief. In general, courts of equity will relieve a party who cannot obtain justice at law in consequence of an accident which will justify the interposition of a court of equity. The jurisdiction which equity exerts in case of accident is mainly of two sorts: Over bonds with penalties to prevent a forfeiture where the failure is the result of accident, as sickness, or where the bond has been lost, but, if the penalty be liquidated damages, there can be no relief; and, second, where a negotiable or other instrument has been lost, in which case no action lay at law, but where equity will allow the one entitled to recover upon giving proper indemnity. In some states it has been held that a court of law can render judgment for the amount, but requires the defendant to give a bond of indemnity. Relief against a penal bond can now be obtained in almost all common-law courts." Bouvier, Law Dict.

ACCOMMODATION PAPER. An accommodation bill or note is one to which the accommodating party, be he acceptor, drawer, or indorser, has put his name, without consideration, for the purpose of benefiting or accommodating some other party who desires to raise money on it and is to provide for the bill or note when due.

ACCORD AND SATISFACTION. An agreement between two persons, one of whom has a right of action against the other, that the latter should do or give, and the former accept, something in satisfaction of the right of action different from, and usually less than, what might be legally enforced. When the agreement is executed, and satisfaction has been made, it is called "accord and satisfaction." Accord and satisfaction is the substitution of another agreement between the parties in satisfaction of the former one, and execution of the latter agreement. Such is the definition of this sort of defense usually given. But a broader application of the doctrine has been made in later times, where one promise or agreement is set up in satisfaction of a prior one, unless it has been expressly accepted as such; as, where a new promissory note has been given in lieu of a former one, to have the effect of a satisfaction of the former, it must have been accepted on an express agreement to that effect.

ACCOUNT. A detailed statement of the mutual demands in the nature of debt and credit between parties, arising out of contracts or some fiduciary relation.

Account closed. An account to which no further additions can be made on either side, but which remains still open for adjustment and set-off, which distinguishes it from account stated.

Account current. An open or running or unsettled account between two parties.

Account rendered. An account made out by the creditor, and presented to the debtor for his examination and acceptance. When accepted, it becomes an account stated.

Account stated. The settlement of an account between the parties, with a balance struck in favor of one of them; an account rendered by the creditor, and by the debtor assented to as correct, either expressly or by implication of law from the failure to object.

ACKNOWLEDGMENT. In conveyancing. The act by which a party who has executed an instrument of conveyance as grantor goes before a competent officer, or court, and declares or acknowledges the same as his genuine and voluntary act and deed. The certificate of the officer on such instrument that it has been so acknowledged.

The term is also used of the act of a person who avows or admits the truth of certain facts which, if established, will entail a civil liability upon him. Thus, the debtor's acknowledgment of the creditor's demand or right of action will revive the enforceability of a debt barred by the statute of limitations.

ACTION. A lawsuit. A right of action; i. e., a right to bring suit.

ACT OF GOD. Any misadventure or casualty is said to be caused by the "act of God," when it happens by the direct, immediate, and exclusive operation of the forces of nature, uncontrolled and uninfluenced by the power of man, and without human intervention, and is of such a character that it could not have been prevented or escaped from by any amount of foresight or prudence, or by any reasonable degree of care or diligence, or by the aid of any appliances which the situation of the party might reasonably require him to use. Any accident produced by any physical cause which is irresistible, such as lightning, tempests, perils of the seas, inundations, earthquakes; and also the sudden death or illness of persons.

ADJUDICATION. The giving or pronouncing of a judgment in a case; also the judgment given. The term is principally used in bankruptcy proceedings; the adjudication being the order which declares the debtor to be a bankrupt.

ADMINISTRATION. The management and settlement of the estate of an intestate decedent.

ADMINISTRATOR. In the most usual sense, is a person to whom letters of administration—that is, an authority to administer the estate of a deceased person—have been granted by the proper court. He resembles an executor, but is appointed by the court, without any nomination by the deceased. An administrator of the estate is appointed, if the deceased has made no will, or has named no executor in his will.

ADMIRALTY. That system of law governing civil and criminal maritime cases.

ADVERSE POSSESSION. The actual, open, and notorious possession and enjoyment of real property, or of any estate lying in grant, continued for a certain length of time, held adversely and in denial and opposition to the title of another claimant, or under circumstances which indicate an assertion or color of right or title on the part of the person maintaining it, as against another person who is out of possession.

AFFIANT. The person who makes and subscribes an affidavit. The word is used, in this sense, interchangeably with "deponent." But the latter term should be reserved as the designation of one who makes a deposition.

AFFIDAVIT. A written or printed declaration or statement of facts, made voluntarily, and confirmed by the oath or affirmation of the party making it. taken before an officer having authority to administer such oath.

A FORTIORI. Latin. By a stronger reason.

AGENCY. A relation, created either by express or implied contracts or by law, whereby one party (called the principal) delegates the transaction of some lawful business or the power to do certain acts for him or in relation to his rights or property, with more or less discretionary power, to another person (called the agent, attorney in fact, or proxy) who undertakes to manage the affair and render him an account thereof.

AGENT. One who represents and acts for another under the relation of agency.

ALIAS. Latin. At other times.

In practice. An alias writ is one issued in a case wherein another writ the same in substance has been issued before. For instance, there may be an alias attachment, an alias summons, etc.

The word commonly precedes the assumed names under which a party to an action, usually a defendant in a criminal action, is known as the names are stated in the pleadings. For instance, "John Jones, alias John Smith," would indicate "John Jones, at other times known as John Smith."

ALIBI. Latin. Elsewhere. In criminal cases, the defendant frequently pleads that he was elsewhere at the time of the perpetration of the alleged crime. In such a case, he is said to plead an alibi.

Apparently through the ignorance of some of those persons reporting court news to the daily papers, the word has been often very incorrectly and inexcusably used to signify a justification or an excuse.

ALIENATION. The transfer of property from one person to another.

ALLEGATION. The assertion, declaration, or statement of a party to an action, made in a pleading, setting out what he expects to prove.

ALLEGE. To state, recite, assert, or charge; to make an allegation.

ANIMO CONTRAHENDI. Latin. With the intention of contracting.

ANIMUS TESTANDI. Latin. An intention to make a last will and testament.

ANNUL. To cancel; make void; destroy. To annul a judgment or judicial proceeding is to deprive it of all force and operation, either ab initio or prospectively as to future transaction.

ANSWER. **In pleading.** Any pleading setting up matters of facts by way of defense. In chancery pleading, the term denotes a defense in writing, made by a defendant to the allegations contained in a bill or information filed by the plaintiff against him. In pleading, under the Codes of Civil Procedure, the answer is the formal written statement made by a defendant setting forth the ground of his defense; corresponding to what, in actions under the common-law practice, is called the "plea."

ANTENUPTIAL CONTRACT. A contract made prior to marriage, usually between the prospective wife and the prospective husband, under which the wife gains certain advantages or suffers certain detriments. In some instances, the prospective wife, in consideration of the settling of a certain amount of real estate or of personalty upon her, gives up her right of dower in the property of the husband.

APPEAL. **In civil practice.** The complaint to a superior court of an injustice done or error committed by an inferior one, whose judgment or decision the court above is called upon to correct or reverse. The removal of a cause from a court of inferior to one of superior jurisdiction, for the purpose of obtaining a review and retrial.

APPEARANCE. A technical coming into court as a party to an action, as plaintiff or as defendant. The party may actually appear in court, or he may, by his attorney, enter his appearance by filing written pleadings in the case, or by filing a formal written entry of appearance. The term first came into use at a time when the only appearance known was the actual physical appearance of a party in court.

APPELLANT. A party who takes an appeal from one court to another.

APPELLEE. The party in a cause against whom an appeal is taken; that is, the party who has an interest adverse to setting aside or reversing the judgment.

APPRAISE. **In practice.** To fix or set a price or value upon; to fix and state the true value of a thing, and, usually, in writing.

APPURTENANCES. Things that belong to another thing regarded as the principal thing. Things appurtenant pass as incident to the principal thing. Sometimes an easement consisting of a right of way over one piece of land will pass with another piece of land as being appurtenant to it.

ARBITRATION. **In practice.** The investigation and determination of a matter or matters of difference between contending parties, by one or more unofficial persons, chosen by the parties, and called "arbitrators," or "referees."

ARREST OF JUDGMENT. **In practice.** The act of staying a judgment, or refusing to render judgment in an action at law, after verdict, for some matter intrinsic appearing on the face of the record, which would render the judgment, if given, erroneous or reversible.

ASSUMPSIT. Latin. He undertook; he promised. A promise or engagement by which one person assumes or undertakes to do some act or pay something to another. It may be either oral or in writing, but is not under seal. It is express, if the promisor puts his engagement in distinct and definite language; it is implied, where the law infers a promise (though no formal one has passed) from the conduct of the party or the circumstances of the case.

In practice. A form of action which lies for the recovery of damages for the non-performance of a parol or simple contract, or a contract that is neither of record nor under seal.

The ordinary division of this action is into (1) common or indebitatus assumpsit, brought for the most part on an implied promise; and (2) special assumpsit, founded on an express promise.

The action of assumpsit differs from trespass and trover, which are founded on a tort, not upon a contract; from covenant and debt, which are appropriate where the ground of recovery is a sealed instrument, or special obligation to pay a fixed sum; and from replevin, which seeks the recovery of specific property, if attainable, rather than of damages.

ASSURANCE. **In conveyancing.** A deed or instrument of conveyance. The legal evidences of the transfer of property are in England called the "common assurances" of the kingdom, whereby every man's estate is assured to him, and all controversies, doubts, and difficulties are either prevented or removed.

ATTACHMENT. The act or process of taking, apprehending, or seizing a person's property, by virtue of a writ, and bringing the same into the custody of the law, used either for the purpose of bringing a person before the court, of acquiring jurisdiction over the property seized, to compel an appearance, to furnish security for debt or costs, or to arrest a fund in the hands of a third person who may become liable to pay it over. Also the writ or other process for the accomplishment of the purposes above enumerated, this being the more common use of the word.

ATTESTATION. The act of witnessing an instrument in writing, at the request of the party making the same, and subscribing it as a witness. Execution and attestation are clearly distinct formalities; the former being the act of the party, and the latter of the witnesses only.

Attestation clause. The clause commonly placed at the conclusion of an instrument, in which clause the witnesses certify that the instrument has been executed before them.

ATTESTING WITNESS. One who signs his name to an instrument as a witness thereto at the request of the parties, for the purposes of proof and identification.

ATTORNEY. In the most general sense, this term denotes an agent or substitute, or one who is appointed and authorized to act in the place or stead of another.

It is "an ancient English word, and signifieth one that is set in the turne, stead, or place of another; and of these some be private * * * and some be publike, as attorneys at law." Co. Litt. 51b.

One who is appointed by another to do something in his absence, and who has authority to act in the place and turn of him by whom he is delegated.

When used with reference to the proceedings of courts, the term always means "attorney at law."

AUCTION. A sale of property, conducted in public or after a notice to the general public, to the highest bidder.

AUCTIONEER. One who conducts an auction.

AUTHORITIES. Legislative enactments, judicial opinions, legal textbooks, and articles in law periodicals are recognized as authorities on the law. The weight given each of these classes of authorities is far from being equal to that given each of the others. Legislative enactments, if valid under the Constitution, represent the final word on what the present law is. Judicial opinions, until overruled, constitute another primary authority. Textbooks and legal articles, though important, are only secondary authorities, guiding into and interpreting the primary authorities, the statutes and decisions.

AWARD, v. To grant, concede, adjudge to. Thus, a jury awards damages; the court awards an injunction.

AWARD, n. The decision or determination rendered by arbitrators or commissioners, or other private or extrajudicial deciders, upon a controversy submitted to them; also the writing or document embodying such decision.

B

BAGGAGE. Such articles of necessity or convenience as are carried by passengers for their general use. It includes clothing, books of the student, tools of the workman, etc.

BAIL, v. To procure the release of a person from legal custody, by undertaking that he shall appear at the time and place designated and submit himself to the jurisdiction and judgment of the court.

BAIL, n. **In practice.** The sureties who procure the release of a person under arrest, by becoming responsible for his appearance at the time and place designated. Those persons who become sureties for the appearance of the defendant in court.

BAILEE. In the law of contracts, one to whom goods are bailed; the party to whom personal property is delivered under a contract of bailment.

BAILMENT. A delivery of goods or personal property, by one person to another in trust for the execution of a special object upon or in relation to such goods, beneficial either to the bailor or bailee or both, and upon a contract, express or implied, to perform the trust and carry out such object, and thereupon either to redeliver the goods to the bailor or otherwise dispose of the same in conformity with the purpose of the trust.

BAILOR. The party who bails or delivers goods to another, in the contract of bailment.

BANKRUPT. A person who has committed an act of bankruptcy; one who has done some act or suffered some act to be done in consequence of which, under the laws of his country, he is liable to be proceeded against by his creditors for the seizure and distribution among them of his entire property.

BARTER. A contract by which parties exchange goods or commodities for other goods. It differs from sale, in this: That in the latter transaction goods or property are always exchanged for money.

BATTERY. Any unlawful beating, or other wrongful physical violence or constraint, inflicted on a human being without consent.

BENEFICIARY. A person having the enjoyment of property of which a trustee, executor, etc., has the legal possession. The person to whom a policy of insurance is payable.

BEQUEATH. To give personal property by will to another.

BEQUEST. A gift by will of personal property; a legacy.

BID. An offer by an intending purchaser to pay a designated price for property which is about to be sold at auction.

BILL. A formal declaration, complaint, or statement of particular things in writing. As a legal term, this word has many meanings and applications, the more important of which are enumerated below.

BILL IN EQUITY. The first written pleading in a proceeding in equity. The complaint in a suit in equity.

BILL OF LADING. **In common law.** The written evidence of a contract for the carriage and delivery of goods sent by sea for a certain freight. The term is often applied to a similar receipt and undertaking given by a carrier of goods by land. A bill of lading is an instrument in writing, signed by a carrier or his agent, describing the freight so as to identify it, stating the name of the consignor, the terms of the contract for carriage, and agreeing or directing that the freight be delivered to the order or assigns of a specified person at a specified place.

BILL OF PARTICULARS. **In practice.** A written statement or specification of the particulars of the demand for which an action at law is brought, or of a defendant's set-off against such demand (including dates, sums, and items in detail), furnished by one of the parties to the other, either voluntarily or in compliance with a judge's order for that purpose.

BILL OF SALE. **In contracts.** A written agreement under seal, by which one person assigns or transfers his right to or interest in goods and personal chattels to another. An instrument by which, in particular, the property in ships and vessels is conveyed.

BONA FIDE. Latin. In good faith.

C

CAPITAL. **Partnership.** "The capital of a partnership is the aggregate of the sums contributed by its members to establish or continue the partnership business." Gilmore on Partnership, p. 132.

Corporations. In reference to a corporation, it is the aggregate of the sum subscribed and paid in, or secured to be paid in, by the shareholders, with the addition of all gains or profits realized in the use and investment of those sums, or, if loss have been incurred, then it is the residue after deducting such losses.

CAPITAL STOCK. The common stock or fund of a corporation. The sum of money raised by the subscriptions of the stockholders, and divided into shares. It is said to be the sum upon which calls may be made upon the stockholders, and dividends are to be paid.

CARRIER. One who carries passengers or the goods of another. See **Common Carrier; Private Carrier.**

CAUSE OF ACTION. Matter for which an action may be brought. The ground on which an action may be sustained. The right to bring a suit.

CAVEAT EMPTOR. Latin. Let the buyer take care. This maxim summarizes the rule that the purchaser of an article must examine, judge, and test it for himself, being bound to discover any obvious defects or imperfections.

CERTIFICATE OF DEPOSIT. **In the practice of bankers.** This is a writing acknowledging that the person named has deposited in the bank a specified sum of money, and that the same is held subject to be drawn out on his own check or order, or that of some other person named in the instrument as payee.

CERTIFICATE OF STOCK. A certificate of a corporation of joint-stock company that the person named is the owner of a designated number of shares of its stock; given when the subscription is fully paid and the "scrip certificate" taken up.

CERTIORARI. A discretionary writ of review or inquiry. It is an appellate proceeding for reexamination and review of actions of an inferior court or tribunal or as auxiliary process to enable an appellate court to obtain further information in a pending cause. It is available for review of official, judicial or quasi-judicial actions.

CESTUI QUE TRUST. Anglo-French. He who has a right to a beneficial interest in and out of an estate the legal title to which is vested in another. The person who possesses the equitable right to property and receives the rents, issues, and profits thereof, the legal estate of which is vested in a trustee. It has been proposed to substitute for this uncouth term the English word "beneficiary," and the latter has come to be quite frequently used.

CHAMPERTY. A bargain made by a stranger with one of the parties to a suit, by which such third person undertakes to carry on the litigation at his own cost and risk, in consideration of receiving, if he wins the suit, a part of the land or other subject sought to be recovered by the action.

CHANCELLOR. In American law, this is the name given in some states to the judge (or the presiding judge) of a court of chancery. In England, besides being the designation of the chief judge of the Court of Chancery, the term is used as the title of several judicial officers attached to bishops or other high dignitaries and to the universities.

CHANCERY. Equity; equitable jurisdiction; a court of equity; the system of jurisprudence administered in courts of equity.

CHARTER. An instrument emanating from the sovereign power, in the nature of a grant, authorizing the formation of a corporation. Under modern statutes, a charter is usually granted by the state secretary of state, who acts under general statutory authority conferred by the state legislature.

CHARTER PARTY. A contract by which an entire ship, or some principal part thereof, is let to a merchant for the conveyance of goods on a determined voyage to one or more places.

CHATTEL. An article of personal property; any species of property not amounting to a freehold or fee in land.

CHATTEL MORTGAGE. An instrument of sale of personalty conveying the title of the property to the mortgagee with terms of defeasance; and, if the terms of redemption are not complied with, then, at common law, the title becomes absolute in the mortgagee.

CHECK. A draft or order upon a bank or banking house, purporting to be drawn upon a deposit of funds, for the payment at all events of a certain sum of money to a certain person therein named, or to him or his order, or to bearer, and payable instantly on demand.

CHOSE IN ACTION. A right to personal things of which the owner has not the possession, but merely a right of action for their possession. 2 Bl.Comm. 389, 397; 1 Chit.Pr. 99.

A right to receive or recover a debt, demand, or damages on a cause of action ex contractu, or for a tort connected with contract, but which cannot be made available without recourse to an action.

CHOSE IN POSSESSION. A thing in possession, as distinguished from a thing in action.

CIVIL. In contradistinction to "criminal," it indicates the private rights and remedies of men, as members of the community, in contrast to those which are public and relate to the government; thus, we speak of civil process and criminal process, civil jurisdiction and criminal jurisdiction.

CIVIL LAW. The "Roman law" and the "civil law" are convertible phrases, meaning the same system of jurisprudence; it is now frequently denominated the "Roman civil law."

CLIENT. A person who employs or retains an attorney, or counsellor, to appear for him in courts, advise, assist, and defend him in legal proceedings, and to act for him in any legal business.

CLOSE. A portion of land, as a field, inclosed, as by a hedge, fence, or other visible inclosure.

CODE. A collection or compendium of laws. A complete system of positive law, scientifically arranged, or promulgated by legislative authority.

COGNOVIT. Latin. He knew. The written authority of a debtor and his direction for entry of judgment against him. Defendant has confessed judgment and justice of the claim against him.

COLLATERAL. By the side; at the side; attached upon the side. Not lineal, but upon a parallel or diverging line. Additional or auxilliary; supplementary; co-operating.

COLLATERAL SECURITY. A security given in addition to the direct security, and subordinate to it, intended to guarantee its validity or convertibility or insure its performance; so that, if the direct security fails, the creditor may fall back upon the collateral security. Collateral security, in bank phraseology, means some security additional to the personal obligation of the borrower.

COLOR. An appearance or semblance, as distinguished from a reality. Hence, color of title.

COMITY OF NATIONS AND STATES. The most appropriate phrase to express the true foundation and extent of the obligation of the laws of one nation within the territories of another. It is derived altogether from the voluntary consent of the latter; and it is inadmissible when it is contrary to its known policy, or prejudicial to its interest. In the silence of any positive rule affirming or denying or restraining the operation of foreign laws, courts of justice presume the tacit adoption of them by their own government, unless repugnant to its policy, or prejudicial to its interests. It is not the comity of the courts, but the comity of the nation, which is administered and ascertained in the same way and guided by the same reasoning, by which all other principles of the municipal law are ascertained and guided.

COMMERCIAL LAW. A phrase used to designate the whole body of substantive jurisprudence applicable to the rights, intercourse, and relation of persons engaged in commerce, trade, or mercantile pursuits. It is not a very scientific or accurate term. As foreign commerce is carried on by means of shipping, the term has come to be used occasionally as synonymous with "maritime law;" but, in strictness, the phrase "commercial law" is wider, and includes many transactions or legal questions which have nothing to do with shipping or its incidents.

COMMERCIAL PAPER. The term "commercial paper" means bills of exchange, promissory notes, bank checks, and other negotiable instruments for the payment of money, which, by their form and on their face, purport to be such instruments as are, by the law-merchant, recognized as falling under the designation of "commercial paper."

COMMISSION. A warrant or authority or letters patent, issuing from the government, or one of its departments, or a court, empowering a person or persons named to do certain acts, or to exercise jurisdiction, or to perform the duties and exercise the authority of an office (as in the case of an officer in the army or navy).

Also, in private affairs, it signifies the authority or instructions under which one person transacts business or negotiates for another.

In a derivative sense, a body of persons to whom a commission is directed. A board or committee officially appointed and empowered to perform certain acts or exercise certain jurisdiction of a public nature or relation; as a "commission of assize."

In commercial law. The recompense or reward of an agent, factor, broker, or bailee, when the same is calculated as a percentage on the amount of his transactions or on the profit to the principal. But in this sense the word often occurs in the plural.

COMMISSION MERCHANT. A factor.

COMMITTEE. A term applied, in some states, to the guardian of an insane person.

COMMODATUM. Latin. A loan of goods for use without pay, the goods to be returned in kind.

COMMON CARRIER. **Of goods.** "One who holds himself out to transport for hire the goods of such as choose to employ him." Goddard on Bailments and Carriers, § 191.

Of passengers. "Such as hold themselves out for hire to carry all persons indifferently who apply for passage." Id. § 317.

COMMON COUNTS. Certain general counts or forms inserted in a declaration in an action to recover a money debt not founded on the circumstances of the individual case, but intended to guard against a possible variance, and to enable the plaintiff to take advantage of any ground of liability which the proof may disclose within the general scope of the action. In the action of assumpsit, these counts are as follows: For goods sold and delivered, or bargained and sold; for work done; for money lent; for money paid; for money received to the use of the plaintiff; for interest, or for money due on an account stated.

COMMON LAW. As distinguished from the Roman law, the modern civil law, the canon law, and other systems, the common law is that body of law and juristic theory which was originated, developed, and formulated and is administered in England, and has obtained among most of the states and peoples of Anglo-Saxon stock.

As distinguished from law created by the enactment of legislatures, the common law comprises the body of those principles and rules of action, relating to the government and security of persons and property, which derive their authority solely from usages and customs of immemorial antiquity, or from the judgments and decrees of the courts recognizing, affirming, and enforcing such usages and customs, and in this sense, particularly the ancient unwritten law of England.

As distinguished from equity law, it is a body of rules and principles, written or unwritten, which are of fixed and immutable authority, and which must be applied to controversies rigorously and in their entirety, and cannot be modified to suit the peculiarities of a specific case, or colored by any judicial discretion, and which rests confessedly upon custom or statute, as distinguished from any claim to ethical superiority.

COMPLAINANT. The plaintiff in code pleading or in equity.

COMPLAINT. **In civil practice.** In those states having a Code of Civil Procedure, the complaint is the first or initiatory pleading on the part of the plaintiff in a civil action. It corresponds to the declaration in the common law practice.

In criminal law. A charge, preferred before a magistrate having jurisdiction, that a person named (or a certain person whose name is unknown) has committed a certain offense, with an offer to prove the fact, to the end that a prosecution may be instituted. It is a technical term, descriptive of proceedings before a magistrate.

COMPOSITION. An agreement, made upon a sufficient consideration between an insolvent or embarrassed debtor and his creditors, whereby the latter, for the sake of immediate payment, agree to accept a dividend less than the whole amount of their claims, to be distributed pro rata, in discharge and satisfaction of the whole.

COMPOS MENTIS. Latin. Sound of mind.

COMPOUNDING A FELONY. The offense committed by a person who, having been directly injured by a felony, agrees with the criminal that he will not prosecute him, on condition of the latter's making reparation, or on receipt of a reward or bribe not to prosecute.

The offense of taking a reward for forbearing to prosecute a felony; as where a party robbed takes his goods again, or other amends, upon an agreement not to prosecute.

COMPROMISE. An arrangement arrived at, either in court or out of court, for settling a dispute upon what appears to the parties to be equitable terms, having regard to the uncertainty they are in regarding the facts or the law and the facts together.

CONDITIONAL SALE. A sale under the terms of which the passage of title is made to depend upon the performance of a condition. Usually the condition precedent to the passage of title is payment of the purchase price by the purchaser.

CONFESSION OF JUDGMENT. The act of a debtor in permitting judgment to be entered against him by his creditor, for a stipulated sum, by a written statement to that effect or by warrant of attorney, without the institution of legal proceedings of any kind.

CONFLICT OF LAWS. An opposition, conflict, or antagonism between different laws of the same state or sovereignty upon the same subject-matter.

A similar inconsistency between the municipal laws of different states or countries, arising in the case of persons who have acquired rights or a status, or made contracts, or incurred obligations, within the territory of two or more states.

That branch of jurisprudence, arising from the diversity of the laws of different nations in their application to rights and remedies, which reconciles the inconsistency, or decides which law or system is to govern in the particular case, or settles the degree of force to be accorded to the law of a foreign country (the acts or rights in question having arisen under it), either where it varies from the domestic law, or where the domestic law is silent or not exclusively applicable to the case in point. In this sense it is more properly called "private international law."

CONNIVANCE. The secret or indirect consent or permission of one person to the commission of an unlawful or criminal act.

CONSANGUINITY. Kinship; blood relationship; the connection or relation of persons descended from the same stock or common ancestor.

CONSERVATOR. A guardian of an insane person's estate.

CONSIDERATION. The inducement to a contract. The cause, motive, price, or impelling influence which induces a contracting party to enter into a contract.

Any benefit conferred, or agreed to be conferred, upon the promisor, by any other person, to which the promisor is not lawfully entitled, or any prejudice suffered, or agreed to be suffered, by such person, other than such as he is at the time of consent lawfully bound to suffer, as an inducement to the promisor, is a good consideration for a promise.

CONSIGNEE. **In mercantile law.** One to whom a consignment is made. The person to whom goods are shipped for sale.

CONSIGNMENT. The act or process of consigning goods; the transportation of goods consigned; an article or collection of goods sent to a factor to be sold; goods or property sent, by the aid of a common carrier, from one person in one place to another person in another place.

CONSIGNOR. One who sends or makes a consignment. A shipper of goods.

CONSPIRACY. **In criminal law.** A combination or confederacy between two or more persons formed for the purpose of committing, by their joint efforts, some lawful or criminal act, or some act which is innocent in itself, but becomes unlawful when done by the concerted action of the conspirators, or for the purpose of using criminal or unlawful means to the commission of an act not in itself unlawful.

CONSTRUCTIVE. That which is established by the mind of the law in its act of construing facts, conduct, circumstances, or instruments; that which has not the character assigned to it in its own essential nature, but acquires such character in consequence of the way in which it is regarded by a rule or policy of law; hence, inferred, implied, made out by legal interpretation.

Constructive assent. An assent or consent imputed to a party from a construction or interpretation of his conduct; as distinguished from one which he actually expresses.

CONTRA. Latin. Opposite, contrary. Where a decision is said to be contra, it is on the opposite side of the question.

CONTRACT. "In its broadest sense, an agreement whereby one or more of the parties acquire a right, in rem or in personam, in relation to some person, thing, act, or forbearance." Clark on Contracts (3d Ed.) p. 1.

CONTRIBUTION. The sharing of a loss or payment among several. The act of any one or several of a number of codebtors, cosureties, etc., in reimbursing one of their number, who has paid the whole debt or suffered the whole liability, each to the extent of his proportionate share. In equity, a bill is brought by a surety that has paid the whole debt, for contribution by his cosureties. Such an action is also had at law.

CONVERSION. An unauthorized assumption and exercise of the right of ownership over goods or personal chattels belonging to another, to the alteration of their condition or the exclusion of the owner's rights.

Constructive conversion. An implied or virtual conversion, which takes place where a person does such acts in reference to the goods of another as amount in law to the appropriation of the property to himself.

CONVICT. Under the criminal law, to find guilty of an offense as charged in the indictment or information.

CORPORATION. An artificial person or legal entity, created by or under the authority of the laws of a state or nation, composed in same rare instances of a single person and his successors, being the incumbents of a particular office, but ordinarily consisting of an association of numerous individuals, who subsist as a body politic under a special denomination, which is regarded in law as having a personality and existence distinct from that of its several members, and which is, by the same authority, vested with the capacity of continuous succession, irrespective of changes in its membership, either in perpetuity or for a limited term of years, and of acting as a unit or single individual in matters relating to the common purpose of the association, within the scope of the powers and authorities conferred upon such bodies by law.

CORPOREAL PROPERTY. Such as affects the senses, and may be seen and handled by the body, as opposed to incorporeal property which cannot be seen or handled, and exists only in contemplation. Thus, a house is corporeal, but the annual rent payable for its occupation is incorporeal. Corporeal property is, if movable, capable of manual transfer; if immovable, possession of it may be delivered up. But incorporeal property cannot be so transferred, but some other means must be adopted for its transfer, of which the most usual is an instrument in writing.

CORPUS. Latin. Body.

CORPUS DELICTI. Latin. The body of the wrong; the essential fact of the crime. The general rule is that no one can be convicted of a crime unless the actual doing of the crime has been proved. Laymen are accustomed to regard the requirements of this general rule as being much more rigid than they really are, and some convictions are on record in which the proof of the corpus delicti, while not entirely absent, was comparatively slight.

COSTS. A pecuniary allowance, made to the successful party (and recoverable from the losing party), for his court costs in prosecuting or defending a suit or a distinct proceeding within a suit. Costs do not include attorney's fees, excepting where the parties have stipulated for them, or where a statute provides for their being included in costs.

COUNSEL. The one or more attorneys or counselors appearing for a party in a cause. Both theoretically and actually, attorneys are officers of the court, and, by virtue of their office, are expected to give advice to the court, through their briefs and arguments, as to the law involved in the case in hand. Thus they are, in a very real sense, counsel.

COUNT, n. **In pleading.** The different parts of a declaration, each of which, if it stood alone, would constitute a ground for action, are the counts of the declaration. Used also to signify the several parts of an indictment, each charging a distinct offense.

COUNTERCLAIM. A claim presented by a defendant in opposition to or deduction from the claim of the plaintiff. A species of set-off or recoupment introduced by the codes of civil procedure in several of the states, of a broad and liberal character.

COURT. In practice. An organ of the government, belonging to the judicial department, whose function is the application of the laws to controversies brought before it and the public administration of justice.

COURT ABOVE—COURT BELOW. In appellate practice, the "court above" is the one to which a cause is removed for review, whether by appeal, writ of error, or certiorari; while the "court below" is the one from which the case is being removed.

COVENANT. An agreement, convention, or promise of two or more parties, by deed in writing, signed, sealed, and delivered, by which either of the parties pledges himself to the other that something is either done or shall be done, or stipulates for the truth of certain facts. A promise contained in such an agreement.

COVERT. Covered, protected, sheltered. A pound covert is one that is closed or covered over, as distinguished from pound overt, which is open overhead. A feme covert is so called, as being under the wing, protection or cover of her husband.

COVERTURE. The condition or state of a married woman.

CRIME. A crime is an act committed or omitted, in violation of a public law, either forbidding or commanding it; a breach or violation of some public right or duty due to a whole community, considered as a community in its social aggregate capacity, as distinguished from a civil injury.

D

DAMAGE. Loss, injury, or deterioration, caused by the negligence, design, or accident of one person to another, in respect of the latter's person or property.

DAMAGES. 1. The plural of damage.

2. Compensation claimed or awarded in a judicial proceeding for damage or for the invasion of a legal right. Bauer on Damages, p. 1.

DEBT. A sum of money due to certain and express agreement; as by bond for a determinate sum, a bill or note, a special bargain, or a rent reserved on a lease, where the amount is fixed and specific, and does not depend upon any subsequent valuation to settle it.

DECEIT. A fraudulent and cheating misrepresentation, artifice, or device, used by one or more persons to deceive and trick another, who is ignorant of the true facts, to the prejudice and damage of the party imposed upon.

DECLARATION. The complaint in a civil proceeding at common law. It is the first pleading filed by the plaintiff upon beginning his action.

DECREE. **In practice.** The judgment of a court of equity or admiralty, answering to the judgment of a court of common law.

DEED. A sealed instrument, containing a contract or covenant, delivered by the party to be bound thereby, and accepted by the party to whom the contract or covenant runs.

DE FACTO. Latin. In fact; in deed; actually.

DEFENDANT. The party sued in an action. The person against whom the declaration or complaint is filed, and who is so named in such declaration or complaint.

DE JURE. Latin. Of right; legitimate; lawful; by right and just title.

DEL CREDERE. An agreement by which a factor, when he sells goods on credit, for an additional commission (called a "del credere commission"), undertakes that the purchase price will be paid the seller. The del credere factor is usually held to have undertaken a primary and absolute liability, but some cases hold that he is a mere surety.

DELICTUM. Latin. A tort.

DELIVERY. The physical or constructive transfer of an instrument or of goods from the hands of one person to those of another.

DEMISE. 1. A conveyance of an estate to another for life, for years, or at will; a lease.

2. Death or decease.

DEMURRER. **In pleading.** The formal mode of disputing the sufficiency in law of the pleading of the other side. In effect it is an allegation that, even if the facts as stated in the pleading to which objection is taken be true, yet their legal consequences are not such as to put the demurring party to the necessity of answering them or proceeding further with the cause.

An objection made by one party to his opponent's pleading, alleging that he ought not to answer it, for some defect in law in the pleading. It admits the facts, and refers the law arising thereon to the court.

It imports that the objecting party will not proceed, but will wait the judgment of the court whether he is bound so to do.

In equity. An allegation of a defendant, which, admitting the matters of fact alleged by the bill to be true, shows that as they are therein set forth they are insufficient for the plaintiff to proceed upon or to oblige the defendant to answer, or that, for some reason apparent on the face of the bill, or on account of the omission of some matter which ought to be contained therein, or for want of some circumstances which ought to be attendant thereon, the defendant ought not to be compelled to answer to the whole bill, or to some certain part thereof.

DE NOVO. Latin. Anew.

DEPONENT. One who makes oath to a written statement.

DEPOSIT. **In banking law.** The act of placing or lodging money in the custody of a bank or banker, for safety or convenience, to be withdrawn at the will of the depositor or under rules and regulations agreed on; also the money so deposited.

DEPOSITION. The testimony of a witness taken upon interrogatories, not in court, but intended to be used in court.

DEPOSITUM. Latin. A bailment having for its purpose that the bailee keep the goods for the bailor without reward.

DESCENT. Hereditary succession.

DESCRIPTIO PERSONÆ. Latin. Description of the person.

DETUR DIGNIORI. Latin. Let it be given to him who is more worthy.

DEVASTAVIT. Latin. He laid waste. The allegation, "He laid waste," in a suit brought against executor, administrator, guardian, or trustee, gave rise to the naming of the wrong "devastavit." In such a case, the defendant is alleged to have mismanaged and wasted assets of the estate intrusted to him and thereby caused a loss.

DEVISE. A testamentary disposition of land or realty; a gift of real property by the last will and testament of the donor.

DICTUM. Latin. The word is generally used as an abbreviated form of obiter dictum, "a remark by the way;" that is, an observation or remark made by a judge in pronouncing an opinion upon a cause, concerning some rule, principle, or application of law, or the solution of a question suggested by the case at bar, but not necessarily involved in the case or essential to its determination; any statement of the law enunciated by the court merely by way of illustration, argument, analogy, or suggestion.

DISCOUNT. In a general sense, an allowance or deduction made from a gross sum on any account whatever. In a more limited and technical sense, the taking of interest in advance. By the language of the commercial world and the settled practice of banks, a discount by a bank means a drawback or deduction made upon its advances or loans of money, upon negotiable paper or other evidences of debt payable at a future day, which are transferred to the bank.

DISHONOR. **In mercantile law and usage.** To refuse or decline to accept a bill of exchange, or to refuse or neglect to pay a bill or note at maturity.

DIVIDEND. A fund to be divided. The share allotted to each of several persons entitled to share in a division of profits or property. Thus, dividend may denote a fund set apart by a corporation out of its profits, to be apportioned among the shareholders, or the proportional amount falling to each. In bankruptcy proceedings, a dividend is a proportional payment to the creditors out of the insolvent estate.

DOMICILE. That place in which a man has voluntarily fixed the habitation of himself and family, not for a mere special or temporary purpose, but with the present intention of making a permanent home, until some unexpected event shall occur to induce him to adopt some other permanent home.

DORMANT PARTNER. See **Partners.**

DOWER. The provision which the law makes for a widow out of lands or tenements of her husband, for her support and the nurture of her children. Co. Litt. 30a. Dower is an estate for life of the widow in a certain portion of the estate of her husband, to which she has not relinquished her right during the marriage.

DRAWEE. A person to whom a bill of exchange is addressed, and who is requested to pay the amount of money therein named.

DRAWER. The person drawing a bill of exchange and addressing it to the drawee.

DUEBILL. A brief written acknowledgment of a debt. It is not made payable to order, like a promissory note.

DURESS. Unlawful constraint exercised upon a person, whereby he is forced to do some act against his will.

E

EARNEST. The payment of a part of the price of goods sold, or the delivery of part of such goods, for the purpose of binding the contract.

EASEMENT. A right in the owner of one parcel of land, by reason of such ownership, to use the land of another for a special purpose not inconsistent with a general property in the owner. 2 Washb. Real Prop. 25.

A private easement is a privilege, service, or convenience which one neighbor has of another, by prescription, grant, or necessary implication, and without profit; as a way over his land, a gateway, watercourse, and the like. Kitch. 105.

EJECTMENT. An action of which the purpose is to determine whether the title to certain land is in the plaintiff or is in the defendant.

ELECTION. The act of choosing or selecting one or more from a greater number of persons, things, courses, rights, or remedies.

EMANCIPATION. The act by which an infant is set at liberty from the control of parent or guardian and made his own master.

EMBEZZLEMENT. The fraudulent appropriation to his own use or benefit of property or money intrusted to him by another, by a clerk, agent, trustee, public officer, or other person acting in a fiduciary character.

EMBLEMENTS. The vegetable chattels called "emblements" are the corn and other growth of the earth which are produced annually, not spontaneously, but by labor and industry, and thence are called "fructus industriales."

EMINENT DOMAIN. Eminent domain is the right of the people or government to take private property for public use.

ENTIRETY. The whole, in contradistinction to a moiety or part only. When land is conveyed to husband and wife, they do not take by moieties, but both are seised of the entirety. Parceners, on the other hand, have not an entirety of interest, but each is properly entitled to the whole of a distinct moiety.

The word is also used to designate that which the law considers as one whole, and not capable of being divided into parts. Thus, a judgment, it is held, is an entirety, and, if void as to one of the two defendants, cannot be valid as to the other. So, if a contract is an entirety, no part of the consideration is due until the whole has been performed.

EO NOMINE. Latin. By that name.

EQUITABLE. Just, fair, and right. Existing in equity; available or sustainable only in equity, or only upon the rules and principles of equity.

EQUITABLE ASSIGNMENT. An assignment which, though invalid at law, will be recognized and enforced in equity; e. g., an assignment of a chose in action, or of future acquisitions of the assignor.

EQUITY. In one of its technical meanings, equity is a body of jurisprudence, or field of jurisdiction, differing in its origin, theory, and methods from the common law.

In a still more restricted sense, it is a system of jurisprudence, or branch of remedial justice, administered by certain tribunals, distinct from the common-law courts, and empowered to decree "equity" in the complex of well-settled and well-understood rules, principles, and precedents.

Equity also signifies an equitable right; i. e., a right enforceable in a court of equity. Hence a bill of complaint which did not show that the plaintiff had a right entitling him to relief was said to be demurrable for want of equity; and certain rights now recognized in all the courts are still known as "equities," from having been originally recognized only in the court of chancery.

EQUITY OF REDEMPTION. The right of the mortgagor of an estate to redeem the same after it has been forfeited, at law, by a breach of the condition of the mortgage, upon paying the amount of debt, interest and costs.

ERROR. A mistaken judgment or incorrect belief as to the existence or effect of matters of fact, or a false or mistaken conception or application of the law.

Such a mistaken or false conception or application of the law to the facts of a cause as will furnish ground for a review of the proceedings upon a writ of error; a mistake of law, or false or irregular application of it, such as vitiates the proceedings and warrants the reversal of the judgment.

"Error" is also used as an elliptical expression for "writ of error"; as, in saying that error lies; that a judgment may be reversed on error.

Assignment of errors. In practice. The statement of the plaintiff's case on a writ of error, setting forth the errors complained of; corresponding with the declaration in an ordinary action. A specification of the errors upon which the appellant will rely, with such fullness as to give aid to the court in the examination of the transcript.

Harmless error. In appellate practice. An error committed in the progress of the trial below, but which was not prejudicial to the rights of the party assigning it, and for which, therefore, the court will not reverse the judgment; as, where the error was neutralized or corrected by subsequent proceedings in the case, or where, notwithstanding the error, the particular issue was found in that party's favor, or where, even if the error had not been committed, he could not have been legally entitled to prevail.

Reversible error. In appellate practice. Such an error as warrants the appellate court in reversing the judgment before it.

ESCROW. The state or condition of a deed which is conditionally held by a third person, or the possession and retention of a deed by a third person pending a condition; as when an instrument is said to be delivered "in escrow."

ESTATE. The interest which any one has in lands, or in any other subject of property.

In another sense, the term denotes the property (real or personal) in which one has a right or interest; the subject-matter of ownership; the corpus of property.

In a wider sense, the term "estate" denotes a man's whole financial status or condition—the aggregate of his interests and concerns, so far as regards his situation with reference to wealth or its objects, including debts and obligations, as well as possessions and rights.

ESTOPPEL. A bar or impediment raised by the law, which precludes a man from alleging or from denying a certain fact or state of facts, in consequence of his previous allegation or denial or conduct or admission, or in consequence of a final adjudication of the matter in a court of law.

EVICTION. Dispossession by process of law; the act of depriving a person of the possession of lands which he has held, in pursuance of the judgment of a court.

EVIDENCE. Any species of proof, or probative matter, legally presented at the trial of an issue, by the act of the parties and through the medium of witnesses, records, documents, concrete objects, etc., for the purpose of inducing belief in the minds of the court or jury as to their contention.

EXCEPTION. In practice. A formal objection to the action of the court, during the trial of a cause, in refusing a request or overruling an objection; implying that the party excepting does not acquiesce in the decision of the court, but will seek to procure its reversal, and that he means to save the benefit of his request or objection in some future proceeding.

EXCHANGE. In conveyancing. A mutual grant of equal interests (in lands or tenements), the one in consideration of the other.

In commercial law. A negotiation by which one person transfers to another funds which he has in a certain place, either at a price agreed upon or which is fixed by commercial usage.

In law of personal property. Exchange of goods is a commutation, transmutation, or transfer of goods for other goods, as distinguished from "sale," which is a transfer of goods for money.

EX CONTRACTU. Latin. From or out of a contract. In both the civil and common law, rights and causes of action are divided into two classes—those arising ex contractu (from a contract); and those arising ex delicto (from a delict or tort).

EX DELICTO. Latin. From a delict, tort, fault, crime, or malfeasance. In both the civil and the common law, obligations and causes of action are divided into two great classes—those arising ex contractu (out of a contract); and those ex delicto.

EX DOLO MALO NON ORITUR ACTIO. Latin. Out of fraud no action arises; fraud never gives a right of action. No court will lend its aid to a man who founds his cause of action upon an immoral or illegal act.

EXECUTED. Completed; carried into full effect; already done or performed; taking effect immediately; now in existence or in possession; conveying an immediate right or possession. The opposite of executory.

EXECUTION. **In contracts.** (1) The signing of a contract not under seal, or the signing, sealing, and delivering of a contract under seal. (2) The doing or accomplishing of the things stipulated in a contract to be done.

In criminal law. The legal putting to death of a convict, in conformity with the terms of his sentence.

In civil practice. The writ in which the court authorizes and orders the sheriff or similar officer to put into effect the court's final decree or judgment.

"Final execution is one which authorizes the money due on a judgment to be made out of the property of the defendant." Bouvier's Law Dictionary.

EXECUTOR. A person appointed by a testator to carry out the directions and requests in his will, and to dispose of the property according to his testamentary provisions after his decease.

EXECUTORY. That which is yet to be executed or performed; that which remains to be carried into operation or effect; incomplete; depending upon a future performance or event. The opposite of executed.

EXEMPLARY. Punitive, punitory, for punishment.

EXEMPLARY DAMAGES. Damages on an increased scale, awarded to the plaintiff over and above what will barely compensate him for his property loss, where the wrong done to him was aggravated by circumstances of violence, oppression, malice, fraud, or wanton and wicked conduct on the part of the defendant, and are intended to punish the defendant for his evil behavior.

EXEMPTION. A privilege allowed by law to a judgment debtor, by which he may hold property to a certain amount, or certain classes of property, free from all liability to levy and sale on execution or attachment.

EX GRATIA. Latin. Out of grace; as a matter of favor or indulgence; gratuitous.

EX MERO MOTU. Latin. Of his own mere motion; of his own accord.

EXONERATION. Latin, exonere; disburden; take the load off of. The lifting of a burden from a person or property.

In administration of estates. The taking of the burden of a mortgage debt, in certain instances, from mortgaged real estate, and the placing of the burden upon personalty.

In suretyship. The right of exoneration is an equitable right of a surety to have the burden of the debt lifted from his shoulders and placed upon those of the principal debtor. When a surety is sued by the creditor, he has sometimes filed a bill in equity, asking that the creditor be enjoined from prosecuting the action at law against the surety before suing the principal, and offering a bond to indemnify the creditor against loss.

EX PARTE. Latin. On one side only; by or for one party; done for, in behalf of, or on the application of, one party only.

EXPRESS. Made known distinctly and explicitly, and not left to inference or implication. Declared in terms; set forth in words. Manifested by direct and appropriate language, as distinguished from that which is inferred from conduct. The word is usually contrasted with "implied."

EX TURPI CONTRACTU NON ORITUR ACTIO. Latin. Out of an immoral or illegal contract an action does not arise. A contract founded upon an illegal or immoral consideration cannot be enforced by action. 2 Kent, Comm. 466.

F

FACTOR. A commercial agent, employed by a principal to sell merchandise consigned to him for that purpose, for and in behalf of the principal, but usually in his own name, being intrusted with the possession and control of the goods, and being remunerated by a commission.

FEE SIMPLE. **In English law.** A freehold estate of inheritance, absolute and unqualified. It stands at the head of estates as the highest in dignity and the most ample in extent; since every other kind of estate is derivable thereout, and mergeable therein.

FEE TAIL. An estate of inheritance, descending only to a certain class or classes of heirs; e. g., an estate is conveyed or devised "to A. and the heirs of his body," or "to A. and the heirs male of his body," or "to A., and the heirs female of his body." Such estates have been common in England, but never very common in the United States. State statutes have dealt variously with estates tail, some statutes converting them into estates in fee simple. The entire plan of the estate tail is contrary to the spirit of American progress, contemplating, as the plan does, the continuance of the tenure in one class of persons, regardless of the changes in ownership often required by the progress of the community as a whole.

FELONY. **In American law.** The term has no very definite or precise meaning, except in some cases where it is defined by statute. For the most part, the state laws, in describing any particular offense, declare whether or not it shall be considered a felony. Apart from this, the word seems merely to imply a crime of a graver or more atrocious nature than those designated as "misdemeanors."

FEME. L. Fr. A woman.

Feme covert. A married woman.

Feme sole. A single woman.

FICTION. An assumption or supposition of law that something which is or may be false is true, or that a state of facts exists which has never really taken place.

FIDUCIARY. As an adjective it means of the nature of a trust; having the characteristics of a trust; Analogous to a trust; relating to or founded upon a trust or confidence.

FINAL PROCESS. A writ of execution. Such process is final, as contrasted with earlier process in the action. Process prior to judgment is known as mesne process.

FINAL SETTLEMENT. The rendering of a final account by an executor or an administrator, at the closing of the business of the estate, approved by the probate court, and followed by the discharge of the executor or administrator.

FIRE INSURANCE. A contract under the terms of which the insurer agrees to indemnify the insured against loss caused by fire during a period specified in the contract.

FIXTURES. (Authorities differ so much in their definitions of this term that it is deemed best to include several definitions, presenting varying conceptions.)

"A fixture is a thing which, though originally a chattel, is, by reason of its annexation to land, regarded as a part of the land, partaking of its character and belonging to its owner. Whether a chattel annexed to land is, in a particular case, to be so regarded as a part thereof, is determined usually by the mode of its attachment to the land, and the character of the chattel, as indicating the presumed intention of the annexor." Tiffany on Real Property, c. 9 (IV).

"Personal chattels affixed to real estate, which may be severed and removed by the party who has affixed them, or by his personal representative, against the will of the owner of the freehold. There is much dispute among the authorities as to what is a proper definition." Bouvier's Law Dict.

F. O. B. Free on board. "If a quotation is f. o. b., the seller undertakes for the price named to deliver the goods on board car or ship at a designated place, free of charges to the buyer." Whitaker's Foreign Exchange, p. 335.

FORCIBLE DETAINER. The offense of violently keeping possession of lands and tenements, with menaces, force, and arms, and without the authority of law.

FORCIBLE ENTRY. An offense against the public peace, or private wrong, committed by violently taking possession of lands and tenements with menaces, force, and arms, against the will of those entitled to the possession, and without the authority of law.

FORECLOSURE. A proceeding by which the rights of the mortgagee of real property are enforced. This procedure varies greatly in different states. The property is commonly put up at public auction and sold to the highest bidder. The mortgagee gets out of the proceeds the amount of his debt, with costs. The remaining portion of the proceeds, if any, goes to the debtor, the mortgagor. If the property sells at a price less than the amount of the debt and costs, judgment is given against the mortgagor for the deficiency.

Foreclosure is now generally by court proceeding in the case of real estate mortgages, though formerly all mortgages were subject to "strict foreclosure"; i. e., foreclosure without judicial process.

FORFEITURE. **In bonds.** A bond is given as the absolute and sealed promise of the obligor to pay a certain sum of money, with a defeasance clause following the obligation. This clause states that, upon the happening of a certain event, such as the conveying of certain land or the faithful performance of the duties of a certain office during a specified term, the bond is to become null and void. If the condition subsequent stated in such defeasance clause does not occur, the obligor has forfeited his bond.

In insurance. In a fire insurance policy, it is often stated that the policy shall be forfeited upon the occurrence of a certain event, such as nonpayment of the premium, storage of gasoline on the premises, vacancy of the premises, etc. A life insurance policy usually provides that it shall be forfeited for nonpayment of premiums. In the event of the happening of such a condition subsequent in an insurance policy, the insurer may declare a forfeiture or may waive the forfeiture and permit the insurance to continue.

FORGERY. **In criminal law.** The falsely making or materially altering, with intent to defraud, any writing which, if genuine, might apparently be of legal efficacy or the foundation of a legal liability.

FORMS OF ACTION. Classes or kinds of action under the common law. "This term comprehends the various classes of personal action at common law, viz. trespass, case, trover, detinue, replevin, covenant, debt, assumpsit, scire facias, and revivor, as well as the nearly obsolete actions of account and annuity, and the modern action of mandamus. They are now abolished in England by Judicature Acts of 1873, and 1875, and in many of the states of the United States, where a uniform course of proceeding under codes of procedure has taken their place. But the principles regulating the distinctions between the common-law actions are still found applicable even where the technical forms are abolished." Bouvier's Law Dict.

FRANCHISE. A special privilege conferred by government upon an individual or corporation, and which does not belong to the citizens of the country generally, of common right.

FRAUD. Fraud consists of some deceitful practice or willful devise, resorted to with intent to deprive another of his right, or in some manner to do him an injury. As distinguished from negligence, it is always positive, intentional.

FREEHOLD. An estate in land or other real property, of uncertain duration; that is, either of inheritance or which may possibly last for the life of the tenant at the least (as distinguished from a leasehold), and held by a free tenure.

FRUCTUS INDUSTRIALES. Latin. Industrial fruits or fruits of industry. Those fruits of a thing, as of land, which are produced by the labor and industry of the occupant, as crops of grain; as distinguished from such as are produced solely by the powers of nature.

FRUCTUS NATURALES. Latin. Those products which are produced by the powers of nature alone; as wool, metals, milk, the young of animals.

FUNGIBLE THINGS. Movable goods, which may be estimated and replaced according to weight, measure, and number, things belonging to a class, which do not have to be dealt with in specie.

FUTURE ESTATE. An estate to begin in possession at or after the termination of the present estate; e. g., A. holds a life estate in a tract of land, and B. has a reversion therein, B.'s possession to begin on the termination of A.'s estate. B.'s reversion is one kind of future estate. The remainder is another common species of future estate.

G

GARNISH, v. To issue process of garnishment against a person.

GARNISHEE, n. One garnished.

GARNISHMENT. In the process of attachment. A warning to a person in whose hands the effects of another are attached not to pay the money or deliver the property of the defendant in his hands to him, but to appear and answer the plaintiff's suit.

GENERAL AND SPECIAL ISSUE. The former is a plea which traverses and denies, briefly and in general and summary terms, the whole declaration, indictment, or complaint, without tendering new or special matter.

GENERAL VERDICT. A verdict whereby the jury find either for the plaintiff or for the defendant in general terms; the ordinary form of verdict.

GRATIS DICTUM. Latin. A voluntary assertion; a statement which a party is not legally bound to make, or in which he is not held to precise accuracy.

GRAVAMEN. Latin. The burden or gist of a charge.

GUARANTY, n. A promise to answer for the payment of some debt, or the performance of some duty, in case of the failure of another person, who, in the first instance, is liable to such payment or performance.

GUARDIAN. A guardian is a person lawfully invested with the power, and charged with the duty, of taking care of the person and managing the property and rights of another person, who, for some peculiarity of status, or defect or age, understanding, or self-control, is considered incapable of administering his own affairs.

H

HEARSAY. A term applied to that species of testimony given by a witness who relates, not what he knows personally, but what others have told him, or what he has heard said by others.

HEIR. At common law. A person who succeeds, by the rules of law, to an estate in lands, tenements, or hereditaments, upon the death of his ancestor, by descent and right of relationship.

HEREDITAMENTS. Things capable of being inherited, be it corporeal or incorporeal, real, personal, or mixed, and including not only lands and everything thereon, but also heirlooms, and certain furniture which, by custom, may descend to the heir together with the land.

I

IMPLIED. This word is used in law as contrasted with "express"; i. e., where the intention in regard to the subject-matter is not manifested by explicit and direct words, but is gathered by implication or necessary deduction from the circumstances, the general language, or the conduct of the parties.

INCHOATE. Imperfect; unfinished; begun, but not completed; as a contract not executed by all the parties.

INCORPOREAL. Without body; not of material nature; the opposite of "corporeal."

INDEMNITY. An indemnity is a collateral contract or assurance, by which one person engages to secure another against an anticipated loss or to prevent him from being damnified by the legal consequences of an act or forbearance on the part of one of the parties or of some third person.

INDENTURE. A deed to which two or more persons are parties, and in which these enter into reciprocal and corresponding grants or obligations towards each other; whereas a deed poll is properly one in which only the party making it executes it, or binds himself by it as a deed, though the grantors or grantees therein may be several in number.

INDICIA. Latin. Signs; indications.

INDICTMENT. The formal written accusation of a crime, as presented by a grand jury. The indictment holds a place, in criminal pleading, analogous to the place held, in a civil case, by the declaration or complaint. The plaintiff, in a criminal case, is the state, and the proof introduced by the state must, in order to convict, sustain one or more of the counts named in the indictment, just as, in a civil case, the proof introduced by the plaintiff must sustain one or more counts in the declaration or complaint. In a criminal case, the state must sustain its case by proof beyond a reasonable doubt; in a civil case, the plaintiff need prove his case only by a preponderance of the evidence.

INDORSEE. The person to whom a bill of exchange, promissory note, bill of lading, etc., is assigned by indorsement, giving him a right to sue thereon.

INDORSEMENT. The act of a payee, drawee, accommodation indorser, or holder of a negotiable instrument in writing his name upon the back of same, with or without further words, whereby the property in same is transferred to another.

INDORSER. He who makes an indorsement.

INFANT. A person within age, not of age, or not of full age; a person under the age of twenty-one years; a minor.

INFORMATION. In the criminal law, an accusation made the basis of a prosecution for a crime, but not itself the result of a finding by a grand jury.

IN HÆC FŒDERA NON VENIMUS. Latin. We did not enter into these bonds; we did not make this contract.

IN INVITUM. Latin. Against an unwilling party.

INIQUUM EST INGENUIS HOMINIBUS NON ESSE LIBERAM RERUM SUARUM ALIENATIONEM. Latin. Literally, it is unjust to freeborn men that the alienation of their own property should not be free. A better and freer translation would be: It is unjust that freeborn men should be unable freely to alienate their own property. This maxim states a reason underlying the rule against restraints upon alienation.

INJUNCTION. A prohibitive writ issued by a court of equity, at the suit of a party complainant, directed to a party defendant in the action, or to a party made a defendant for that purpose, forbidding the latter to do some act, or to permit his servants or agents to do some act, which he is threatening or attempting to commit, or restraining him in the continuance thereof, such act being unjust and inequitable, injurious to the plaintiff, and not such as can be adequately redressed by an action at law.

INJURY. Any wrong or damage done to another, either in his person, rights, reputation, or property.

IN LIMINE. Latin. On or at the threshold; at the very beginning; preliminarily.

INNKEEPER. The proprietor or keeper of a hotel or inn.

IN PARI DELICTO. Latin. In equal fault; equally culpable or criminal.

In pari delicto, potior est conditio possidentis [defendentis]. In a case of equal or mutual fault (between two parties), the condition of the party in possession [or defending] is the better one. This maxim is often applied to cases in which a plaintiff seeks to procure, under an illegal contract, money or other property in the possession of the defendant, or to get a judgment or decree of any kind, under such a contract.

IN PERSONAM. Latin. Against the person. Actions or rights in personam are contrasted with actions or rights in rem, which are directed at specific property or at a specific right or status. A. sues B., in an action at law, for $100. This is one instance of an action in personam. All suits in equity were originally in personam, the bill and the decree being addressed directly to the person of the defendant and seeking to control his conduct.

IN RE. Latin. In the matter; e. g., "In re Jones" means "in the matter of Jones."

IN REM. Latin. Against a thing; against the status; directed at specific property, or at a specific right or status. An action in admiralty against a certain vessel is in rem. A suit for the foreclosure of a mortgage is, in a sense, in rem. A divorce suit, while in a certain sense in personam, is actually directed against the status of marriage and is, in part, a suit in rem.

INSOLVENCY. The condition of a person who is insolvent; inability to pay one's debts; lack of means to pay one's debts. Such a relative condition of a man's assets and liabilities that the former, if all made immediately available, would not be sufficient to discharge the latter. Or the condition of a person who is unable to pay his debts as they fall due, or in the usual course of trade and business.

INSOLVENT. Latin, insolvens; not paying.

In bankruptcy. In the federal Bankruptcy Act the following rule is stated: "A person shall be deemed insolvent within the provisions of this act whenever the aggregate of his property, exclusive of any property which he may have conveyed, transferred, concealed or removed, or permitted to be concealed or removed, with intent to defraud, hinder or delay his creditors, shall not, at a fair valuation, be sufficient in amount to pay his debts." Section 1, cl. 15.

In sales. The Uniform Sales Act gives the following rule: "A person is insolvent within the meaning of this act who either has ceased to pay his debts in the ordinary course of business or cannot pay his debts as they fall due, whether he has committed an act of bankruptcy or not, and whether he is insolvent within the meaning of the federal bankruptcy law or not." Section 76.

IN SPECIE. Latin. In kind. Specific; specifically.

IN STATU QUO. Latin. In the condition or state (in which it was).

INSURABLE INTEREST. Such a real and substantial interest in specific property as will sustain a contract to indemnify the person interested against its loss. If the assured had no real interest, the contract would be a mere wager policy.

INSURANCE. A contract whereby, for a stipulated consideration, one party undertakes to compensate the other for loss on a specified subject by specified perils. The party agreeing to make the compensation is usually called the "insurer" or "underwriter"; the other, the "insured" or "assured"; the written contract, a "policy"; the events insured against, "risks" or "perils"; and the subject, right, or interest to be protected, the "insurable interest." Insurance is a contract whereby one undertakes to indemnify another against loss, damage, or liability arising from an unknown or contingent event.

INSURED. In fire and other property insurance. The person whose property interest is insured.

In life insurance. The person whose life is insured.

INSURER. The underwriter or insurance company with whom a contract of insurance is made.

INTERPLEADER. When two or more persons claim the same thing (or fund) of a third, and he, laying no claim to it himself, is ignorant which of them has a right to it, and fears he may be prejudiced by their proceeding against him to recover it, he may file a bill in equity against them, the object of which is to make them litigate their title between themselves, instead of litigating it with him, and such a bill is called a "bill of interpleader."

INTER ALIA. Among other things. A term anciently used in pleading, especially in reciting statutes, where the whole statute was set forth at length. Inter alia enactatum fuit. Among other things it was enacted.

INTER SE, or INTER SESE. Latin. Between or among themselves.

INTERSTATE COMMERCE COMMISSION. A commission appointed by the President of the United States by authority of the Interstate Commerce Act of 1887. It is a corporate body, so that it may sue or be sued in the courts, and, by court action, its decisions, when valid, are enforced. Its work involves the rates and practices of interstate carriers.

INTERVENER. An intervener is a person who voluntarily interposes in an action or other proceeding with the leave of the court.

INTESTATE. Without making a will.

J

JOINT. United; combined; undivided; done by or against two or more unitedly; shared by or between two or more.

A "joint" bond, note, or other obligation is one in which the obligors or makers (being two or more in number) bind themselves jointly, but not severally, and which must therefore be prosecuted in a joint action against them all. A "joint and several" bond or note is one in which the obligors or makers bind themselves both jointly and individually to the obligee or payee, and which may be enforced either by a joint action against them all or by separate actions against any one or more at the election of the creditor.

JOINTLY. Acting together or in concert or co operation; holding in common or interdependently, not separately. Persons are "jointly bound" in a bond or note when both or all must be sued in one action for its enforcement.

Jointly and severally. Persons who bind themselves "jointly and severally" in a bond or note may all be sued together for its enforcement, or the creditor may select any one or more as the object of his suit.

JOINT-STOCK COMPANY. A partnership with a capital divided into transferable shares.

JOINT TENANCY. "Exists when a single estate in land is owned by two or more persons claiming under one instrument; its most important characteristic being that, unless the statute otherwise provides, the interest of each joint tenant, upon his death, inures to the benefit of the surviving joint tenant or tenants, to the exclusion of his own heirs, devisees, or personal representatives." Tiffany on Real Property, p. 368.

JUDGMENT. The official and authentic decision of a court of justice upon the respective rights and claims of the parties to an action or suit therein litigated and submitted to its determination.

JUDGMENT DEBTS. Debts, whether on simple contract or by specialty, for the recovery of which judgment has been entered up, either upon a cognovit or upon a warrant of attorney or as the result of a successful action.

JUDGMENT IN PERSONAM. A judgment against a particular person, as distinguished from a judgment against a thing or a right or status. The former class of judgments are conclusive only upon parties and privies; the latter upon all the world.

JUDGMENT IN REM. A judgment in rem is an adjudication, pronounced upon the status of some particular subject-matter, by a tribunal having competent authority for that purpose. It differs from a judgment in personam, in this: That the latter judgment is in form, as well as substance, between the parties claiming the right; and that it is so inter partes appears by the record itself.

JUDGMENT NOTE. A promissory note, embodying an authorization to any attorney, or to a designated attorney, or to the holder, or the clerk of the court, to enter an appearance for the maker and confess a judgment against him for a sum therein named, upon default of payment of the note.

JUDGMENT N. O. V. Judgment non obstante verdicto in its broadest sense is a judgment rendered in favor of one party notwithstanding the finding of a verdict in favor of the other party. Originally, at common law, judgment non obstante verdicto was a judgment entered for plaintiff "notwithstanding the verdict" for defendant. The generally prevailing rule now is that either plaintiff or defendant may have a judgment non obstante verdicto.

JUDICIAL. Belonging to the office of a judge; as judicial authority.

JURAT. The clause written at the foot of an affidavit, stating when, where, and before whom such affidavit was sworn.

JURISDICTION. The power and authority constitutionally conferred upon (or constitutionally recognized as existing in) a court or judge to pronounce the sentence of the law, or to award the remedies provided by law, upon a state of facts, proved or admitted, referred to the tribunal for decision, and authorized by law to be the subject of investigation or action by that tribunal, and in favor of or against persons (or a res) who present themselves, or who are brought, before the court in some manner sanctioned by law as proper and sufficient.

JURY. (From the Latin jurare, to swear.) A body of persons selected and summoned by law and sworn to try the facts of a case and to find according to the law and the evidence. In general, the province of the jury is to find the facts in a case, while the judge passes upon pure questions of law. As a matter of fact, however, the jury must often pass upon mixed questions of law and fact in determining the case, and in all such cases the instructions of the judge as to the law become very important.

K

KIN. Relationship; relationship by blood or marriage. The term is sometimes restricted to relationship by blood.

KNOWLEDGE. Information. "Knowledge" is a broader term than "notice," including, not only facts of which one is put on notice, but also facts of which one gets knowledge by means other than notice.

L

LACHES. Negligence, consisting in the omission of something which a party might do, and might reasonably be expected to do, towards the vindication or enforcement of his rights. The word is generally the synonym of "remissness," "dilatoriness," "unreasonable or unexcused delay"; the opposite of "vigilance"; and means a want of activity and diligence in making a claim or moving for the enforcement of a right (particularly in equity) which will afford ground for presuming against it, or for refusing relief, where that is discretionary with the court.

LANDLORD. He of whom lands or tenements are holden. He who, being the owner of an estate in land, has leased the same for a term of years, on a rent reserved, to another person, called the "tenant."

LAPSE, n. **In the law of wills.** The failure of a testamentary gift in consequence of the death of the devisee or legatee during the life of the testator.

LARCENY. **In criminal law.** The wrongful and fraudulent taking and carrying away by one person of the mere personal goods of another from any place, with a felonious intent to convert them to his (the taker's) use, and make them his property, without the consent of the owner.

LAW MERCHANT. The system of rules, customs, and usages generally recognized and adopted by merchants and traders, and which either in its simplicity or as modified by common law or statutes, constitutes the law for the regulation of their transactions and the solution of their controversies.

LEASE. A conveyance of lands or tenements to a person for life, for a term of years, or at will, in consideration of a return of rent or some other recompense. The person who so conveys such lands or tenements is termed the "lessor," and the person to whom they are conveyed, the "lessee"; and when the lessor so conveys lands or tenements to a lessee, he is said to lease, demise, or let them.

LEASEHOLD. An estate in realty held under a lease; an estate for a fixed term of years.

LEGACY. A bequest or gift of personal property by last will and testament.

LEGAL TENDER. That kind of coin, money, or circulating medium which the law compels a creditor to accept in payment of his debt, when tendered by the debtor in the right amount.

LESSEE. He to whom a lease is made.

LESSOR. He who grants a lease.

LET, v. In conveyancing. To demise or lease. "To let and set" is an old expression.

LETTERS OF ADMINISTRATION. The formal instrument of authority and appointment given an administrator by the proper court, empowering him to enter upon the discharge of his duties as administrator.

LETTERS TESTAMENTARY. The formal instrument of authority and appointment given to an executor by the proper court, empowering him to enter upon the discharge of his office as executor.

LEVY, v. To raise; execute; exact; collect; gather; take up; seize. Thus, to levy (raise or collect) a tax; to levy (raise or set up) a nuisance; to levy (acknowledge) a fine; to levy (inaugurate) war; to levy an execution—i. e., to levy or collect a sum of money on an execution.

LIEN. A qualified right of property which a creditor has in or over specific property of his debtor, as security for the debt or charge or for performance of some act.

LIFE ESTATE. An estate whose duration is limited to the life of the party holding it, or of some other person; a freehold estate, not of inheritance.

LIFE TENANT. One who holds an estate in lands for the period of his own life or that of another certain person.

LIMITATION. In conveyances. A defining or limiting, either by express words or by implication of law, of the time during which the estate granted is to be enjoyed; e. g., "to A. and his heirs forever," limits an estate in fee simple to A.; "to B. for life, remainder to C. and his heirs," limits a life estate to B., with a remainder in fee simple to C.

In statutes of limitation. Under statutes of limitation, a certain limit of time is set, after the running of which, subsequent to the accruing of a cause of action, no action can be brought successfully, if the statute is pleaded.

LIMITED PARTNERSHIP. A partnership consisting of one or more general partners, jointly and severally responsible as ordinary partners, and by whom the business is conducted, and one or more special partners, contributing in cash payments a specific sum as capital to the common stock, and who are not liable for the debts of the partnership beyond the fund so contributed.

LIQUIDATED. Ascertained; determined; fixed; settled; made clear or manifest. Cleared away; paid; discharged.

LIQUIDATED ACCOUNT. An account whereof the amount is certain and fixed, either by the act and agreement of the parties or by operation of law; a sum which cannot be changed by the proof; it is so much or nothing; but the term does not necessarily refer to a writing.

LIQUIDATED AND UNLIQUIDATED DAMAGES. The former term is applicable when the amount of the damages has been ascertained by the judgment in the action, or when a specific sum of money has been expressly stipulated by the parties to a bond or other contract as the amount of damages to be recovered by either party for a breach of the agreement by the other.

LIS PENDENS. Latin. A suit pending; that legal process. in a suit regarding land, which amounts to legal notice to all the world that there is a dispute as to the title. In equity the filing of the bill and serving a subpœna creates a lis pendens, except when statutes require some record.

LOCATIO. Latin. A hiring of goods for a reward.

LOCUS PŒNITENTIÆ. Latin. A place for repentance; an opportunity for changing one's mind; a chance to withdraw from a contemplated bargain or contract before it results in a definite contractual liability. Also used of a chance afforded to a person, by the circumstances, of relinquishing the intention which he has formed to commit a crime, before the perpetration thereof.

LODGING HOUSE. A private house at which lodging is given for a consideration, as contrasted with a public house or inn or hotel.

L. S. An abbreviation for "locus sigilli," the place of the seal; i. e., the place where a seal is to be affixed, or a scroll which stands instead of a seal.

M

MAINTENANCE. An unauthorized and officious interference in a suit in which the offender has no interest, to assist one of the parties to it, against the other, with money or advice to prosecute or defend the action.

MALFEASANCE. The wrongful or unjust doing of some act which the doer has no right to perform, or which he has stipulated by contract not to do. It differs from "misfeasance" and "nonfeasance" (which titles see).

MALUM IN SE. Latin. A wrong in itself; an act or case involving illegality from the very nature of the transaction, upon principles of natural, moral, and public law. An act is said to be malum in se when it is inherently and essentially evil—that is, immoral in its nature and injurious in its consequences—without any regard to the fact of its being noticed or punished by the law of the state. Such are most or all of the offenses cognizable at common law (without the denouncement of a statute); as murder, larceny, etc.

MALUM PROHIBITUM. Latin. A wrong prohibited; a thing which is wrong because prohibited; an act which is not inherently immoral, but becomes so because its commission is expressly forbidden by positive law; an act involving an illegality resulting from positive law. Contrasted with malum in se.

MANDAMUS. Latin, we command. A legal writ compelling the defendant to do an official duty.

MANDATE. A bailment of property in regard to which the bailee engages to do some act without reward. Story, Bailm. § 137.

MATERIALMAN. One who furnishes materials to be used in the construction or repair of ships or houses.

MATURITY. **In mercantile law.** The time when a bill of exchange or promissory note becomes due.

MECHANIC'S LIEN. A species of lien created by statute in most of the states, which exists in favor of persons who have performed work or furnished material in and for the erection of a building. Their lien attaches to the land as well as the building, and is intended to secure for them a priority of payment.

MERGER. The fusion or absorption of one thing or right into another; generally spoken of a case where one of the subjects is of less dignity or importance than the other. Here the less important ceases to have an independent existence.

MESNE. Intermediate.

Mesne process. Process issued between the beginning of a suit and final process.

Mesne profits. Profits from the use of land during wrongful occupancy, recovered, in ejectment or trespass, by the owner from the defendant in the action.

MINOR. An infant or person who is under the age of legal competence. A term derived from the civil law, which described a person under a certain age as less than so many years. Minor viginti quinque annis, one less than twenty-five years of age.

MISDEMEANOR. **In criminal law.** A general name for criminal offenses of every sort, punishable by indictment or special proceedings, which do not in law amount to the grade of felony.

MISFEASANCE. A misdeed or trespass. The doing what a party ought to do improperly. The improper performance of some act which a man may lawfully do.

Misfeasance, strictly, is not doing a lawful act in a proper manner, omitting to do it as it should be done, while malfeasance is the doing an act wholly wrongful, and nonfeasance is an omission to perform a duty, or a total neglect of duty. But "misfeasance" is often carelessly used in the sense of "malfeasance."

MISREPRESENTATION. An intentional false statement respecting a matter of fact, made by one of the parties to a contract, which is material to the contract and influential in producing it.

MORTGAGE. An estate created by a conveyance absolute in form, but intended to secure the performance of some act, such as the payment of money, and the like, by the grantor or some other person, and to become void if the act is performed agreeably to the terms prescribed at the time of making such conveyance.

A conditional conveyance of land, designed as a security for the payment of money, the fulfillment of some contract, or the performance of some act, and to be void upon such payment, fulfillment, or performance.

A debt by specialty, secured by a pledge of lands, of which the legal ownership is vested in the creditor, but of which, in equity, the debtor and those claiming under him remain the actual owners, until debarred by judicial sentence or their own laches.

The foregoing definitions are applicable to the common-law conception of a mortgage. But in many states, in modern times, it is regarded as a mere lien, and not as creating a title or estate. It is a pledge or security of particular property for the payment of a debt, or the performance of some other obligation, whatever form the transaction may take, but is not regarded as a conveyance in effect, though it may be cast in the form of a conveyance.

MUTUUM. Latin. In the law of bailments. A loan for consumption; a loan of chattels, upon an agreement that the borrower may consume them, returning to the lender an equivalent in kind and quantity.

N

NEGLIGENCE. The omission to do something which a reasonable man, guided by those considerations which ordinarily regulate the conduct of human affairs, would do, or doing something which a prudent and reasonable man would not do. It must be determined in all cases by reference to the situation and knowledge of the parties and all the attendant circumstances.

Negligence, in its civil relation, is such an inadvertent imperfection, by a responsible human agent, in the discharge of a legal duty, as immediately produces, in an ordinary and natural sequence, a damage to another.

NEGLIGENCE VEL NON. (A phrase of mixed English and Latin.) Negligence or not.

NEGOTIABLE. An instrument embodying an obligation for the payment of money is called "negotiable" when the legal title to the instrument itself and to the whole amount of money expressed upon its face, with the right to sue therefor in his own name, may be transferred from one person to another without a formal assignment, but by mere indorsement and delivery by the holder or by delivery only.

NEMO PLUS JURIS AD ALIUM TRANSFERRE POTEST QUAM IPSE HABERET. Latin. No one can transfer to another more of right than he himself has. This maxim, like most maxims, must not be taken as true without any limitations. It is well known that the bona fide purchaser of real or personal property, or the holder in due course of a negotiable instrument, does in many cases take a greater right than his transferor has had.

NIL DEBET. Latin. He owes nothing. A plea that the defendant owes nothing.

NISI PRIUS. Latin. Literally, unless before. The expression has now so far departed from its original Latin signification as to mean substantially "at the trial." The words were originally words of some importance in the writ directing the sheriff to summon jurors. "A practice obtained very early, * * * in the trial of trifling causes, to continue the cause in the superior court from term to term, provided the justices in eyre did not sooner (nisi prius justiciari) come into the county where the cause of action arose, in which case they had jurisdiction when they so came." Bouvier's Law Dict.

NOMINAL AND SUBSTANTIAL DAMAGES. Nominal damages are a trifling sum awarded to a plaintiff in an action, where there is no substantial loss or injury to be compensated, but still the law recognizes a technical invasion of his rights or a breach of the defendant's duty; or in cases where, although there has been a real injury, the plaintiff's evidence entirely fails to show its amount.

NOMINAL PARTNER. A person who appears to be a partner in a firm, or is so represented to persons dealing with the firm, or who allows his name to appear in the style of the firm or to be used in its business, in the character of a partner, but who has no actual interest in the firm or business.

NON ASSUMPSIT. Latin. The general issue in the action of assumpsit, being a plea by which the defendant avers that "he did not undertake" or promise as alleged.

NON COMPOS MENTIS. Latin. Not sound of mind; insane.

NON EST FACTUM. Latin. It was not made.

NONFEASANCE. The neglect or failure of a person to do some act which he ought to do.

NON SEQUITUR. Latin. It does not follow. An inference which does not follow from the premise.

NONSUIT. Not following up the cause; failure on the part of a plaintiff to continue the prosecution of his suit. An abandonment or renunciation of his suit, by a plaintiff, either by omitting to take the next necessary steps, or voluntarily relinquishing the action, or pursuant to an order of the court. An order or judgment, granted upon the trial of a cause, that the plaintiff has abandoned, or shall abandon, the further prosecution of his suit.

NOTARY PUBLIC. A public officer whose function is to attest and certify, by his hand and official seal, certain classes of documents, in order to give them credit and authenticity in foreign jurisdictions; to take acknowledgments of deeds and other conveyances, and certify the same; and to perform certain official acts, chiefly in commercial matters.

NUDUM PACTUM. Latin. A naked pact; a bare agreement; a promise or undertaking made without any consideration for it.

NUISANCE. That class of wrongs that arise from the unreasonable, unwarrantable, or unlawful use by a person of his own property, either real or personal, or from his own improper, indecent, or unlawful personal conduct, working an obstruction of or injury to the right of another or of the public, and producing such material annoyance, inconvenience, discomfort, or hurt that the law will presume a consequent damage.

O

OATH. An external pledge or asseveration, made in verification of statements made or to be made, coupled with an appeal to a sacred or venerated object, in evidence of the serious and reverent state of mind of the party, or with an invocation to a supreme being to witness the words of the party and to visit him with punishment if they be false.

OBITER DICTUM. Latin. A remark made, or opinion expressed, by a judge, in his decision upon a cause, "by the way"; that is, incidentally or collaterally, and not directly upon the question before him, or upon a point not necessarily involved in the determination of the cause, or introduced by way of illustration, or analogy or argument.

OMNIS RATIHABITIO RETROTRAHITUR ET MANDATO PRIORI ÆQUIPARATUR. Latin. Every ratification relates back and is equivalent to a prior authority. Broom, Max. 757, 871.

ORDINANCE. The term is used to designate the enactments of the legislative body of a municipal corporation.

OSTENSIBLE AGENCY. An implied or presumptive agency, which exists where one, either intentionally or from want of ordinary care, induces another to believe that a third person is his agent, though he never in fact employed him.

OSTENSIBLE PARTNER. A partner whose name is made known and appears to the world as a partner, and who is in reality such.

OUTLAWED. When applied to a promissory note, means debarred by the statute of limitations.

OYER. **In modern practice.** A copy of a bond or specialty sued upon, given to the opposite party, in lieu of the old practice of reading it.

P

PAR. **In commercial law.** Equal; equality. An equality subsisting between the nominal or face value of a bill of exchange, share of stock, etc., and its actual selling value. When the values are thus equal, the instrument or share is said to be "at par"; if it can be sold for more than its nominal worth, it is "above par"; if for less, it is "below par."

PARI PASSU. Latin. By an equal progress; ratably; without preference.

PARTICEPS. Latin. A participant; a sharer; anciently, a part owner, or parcener.

PARTICEPS CRIMINIS. Latin. A participant in a crime; an accomplice. One who shares or co-operates in a criminal offense, tort, or fraud.

PARTITION. The dividing of lands held by joint tenants, coparceners, or tenants in common, into distinct portions, so that they may hold them in severalty. And, in a less technical sense, any division of real or personal property between co-owners or co-proprietors.

PARTNERSHIP. A voluntary contract between two or more competent persons to place their money, effects, labor, and skill, or some or all of them, in lawful commerce or business, with the understanding that there shall be a proportional sharing of the profits and losses between them.

PART PERFORMANCE. The doing some portion, yet not the whole, of what either party to a contract has agreed to do.

PATENT, n. A grant of some privilege, property, or authority, made by the government or sovereign of a country to one or more individuals.

In English law. A grant by the sovereign to a subject or subjects, under the great seal, conferring some authority, title, franchise, or property; termed "letters patent" from being delivered open, and not closed up from inspection.

In American law. The instrument by which a state or government grants public lands to an individual.

A grant made by the government to an inventor, conveying and securing to him the exclusive right to make and sell his invention for a term of years.

PAWN, n. A bailment of goods to a creditor, as security for some debt or engagement; a pledge. Story, Bailm. art. 7.

PAYEE. The person in whose favor a negotiable instrument is made or drawn; the person to whom a negotiable instrument is made payable.

PAYER, or **PAYOR.** One who pays, or who is to make a payment; particularly the person who makes or is to make payment of a negotiable instrument.

PERFORM. To perform an obligation or contract is to execute, fulfill, or accomplish it according to its terms. This may consist either in action on the part of the person bound by the contract or in omission to act, according to the nature of the subject-matter; but the term is usually applied to any action in discharge of a contract other than payment.

PERFORMANCE. The fulfillment or accomplishment of a promise, contract, or other obligation according to its terms.

Part performance. The doing some portion, yet not the whole, of what either party to a contract has agreed to do.

Specific performance. Performance of a contract in the specific form in which it was made, or according to the precise terms agreed upon. This is frequently compelled by a bill in equity filed for the purpose. 2 Story, Eq. Pl. § 712 et seq. The doctrine of specific performance is that, where damages would be an inadequate compensation for the breach of an agreement, the contractor will be compelled to perform specifically what he has agreed to do. Sweet.

PERJURY. **In criminal law.** The willful assertion as to a matter of fact, opinion, belief, or knowledge, made by a witness in a judicial proceeding as part of his evidence, either upon oath or in any form allowed by law to be substituted for an oath, whether such evidence is given in open court, or in an affidavit, or otherwise, such assertion being known to such witness to be false, and being intended by him to mislead the court, jury or person holding the proceeding.

PERPETUITY. "A future limitation, whether executory or by way of remainder, and of real or personal property, which is not to vest till after the expiration of, or which will not necessarily vest within, the period prescribed by law for the creation of future estates, and which is not destructible by the person for the time being entitled to the property subject to the future limitation, except with the concurrence of the person interested in the contingent event." Lewis, Perp. c. 12.

PER SE. Latin. By himself or itself; in itself; taken alone; inherently; in isolation; unconnected with other matters.

PERSONALTY. Personal property; movable property; chattels.

PERSONAL PROPERTY. See **Personalty.**

PIGNUS. Latin. A pledge. A collateral pledge.

PLAINTIFF. A person who brings an action; the party who complains or sues in a personal action and is so named on the record.

PLAINTIFF IN ERROR. The party who sues out a writ of error to review a judgment or other proceeding at law.

PLEA. **In common-law practice.** A pleading; any one in the series of pleadings. More particularly, the first pleading on the part of the defendant. In the strictest sense, the answer which the defendant in an action at law makes to the plaintiff's declaration, and in which he sets up matter of fact as defense, thus distinguished from a demurrer, which interposes objections on grounds of law.

In equity. A special answer showing or relying upon one or more things as a cause why the suit should be either dismissed or delayed or barred.

PLEAD. To make, deliver, or file any pleading; to conduct the pleadings in a cause. To interpose any pleading in a suit which contains allegations of fact; in this sense the word is the antithesis of "demur." More particularly, to deliver in a formal manner the defendant's answer to the plaintiff's declaration, or to the indictment, as the case may be.

PLEADING. The peculiar science or system of rules and principles, established in the common law, according to which the pleadings or responsive allegations of litigating parties are framed, with a view to preserve technical propriety and to produce a proper issue.

The process performed by the parties to a suit or action, in alternately presenting written statements of their contention, each responsive to that which precedes, and each serving to narrow the field of controversy, until there evolves a single point, affirmed on one side and denied on the other, called the "issue," upon which they then go to trial.

The act or step of interposing any one of the pleadings in a cause, but particularly one on the part of the defendant; and, in the strictest sense, one which sets up allegations of fact in defense to the action.

PLEDGE, n. A bailment of goods to a creditor, as security for some debt or engagement; a pawn. Story, Bailm. art. 7.

PLEDGEE. The party to whom goods are pledged, or delivered in pledge.

PLEDGOR. The party delivering goods in pledge; the party pledging.

POLICE POWER. The power vested in a state to establish laws and ordinances for the regulation and enforcement of public order and tranquillity. The power vested in the legislature to make, ordain, and establish all manner of wholesome and reasonable laws, statutes, and ordinances, either with penalties or without, not repugnant to the constitution, as they shall judge to be for the good and welfare of the commonwealth, and of the subjects of the same. The police power of the state is an authority conferred by the American constitutional system upon the individual states, through which they are enabled to establish a special department of police; adopt such regulations as tend to prevent the commission of fraud, violence, or other offenses against the state; aid in the arrest of criminals; and secure generally the comfort, health, and prosperity of the state, by preserving the public order, preventing a conflict of rights in the common intercourse of the citizens, and insuring to each an uninterrupted enjoyment of all the privileges conferred upon him by the laws of his country. It is true that the legislation which secures to all protection in their rights, and the equal use and enjoyment of their property, embraces an almost infinite variety of subjects. Whatever affects the peace, good order, morals, and health of the community comes within its scope; and every one must use and enjoy his property subject to the restrictions which such legislation imposes. What is termed the "police power" of the state, which, from the language often used respecting it, one would suppose to be be an undefined and irresponsible element in government, can only interfere with the conduct of individuals in their intercourse with each other, and in the use of their property, so far as may be required to secure these objects.

POLICY OF INSURANCE. A mercantile instrument in writing, by which one party, in consideration of a premium, engages to indemnify another against a contingent loss, by making him a payment in compensation, whenever the event shall happen by which the loss is to accrue.

POST-DATE. To date an instrument as of a time later than that at which it is really made.

POWER OF APPOINTMENT. A power or authority conferred by one person by deed or will upon another (called the "donee") to appoint, that is, to select and nominate, the person or persons who are to receive and enjoy an estate or an income therefrom or from a fund, after the testator's death, or the donee's death, or after the termination of an existing right or interest.

POWER OF ATTORNEY. An instrument authorizing a person to act as the agent or attorney of the person granting it.

PREFERENCE. The payment of money or the transfer of property to one creditor in preference to other creditors. Where the debtor is solvent, he may legally make such a preference. Under the federal Bankruptcy Act, a debtor is said to have made a preference if, being insolvent, he has made a transfer of any of his property and the effect of the enforcement of such transfer will be to enable any one of his creditors to obtain a greater percentage of his debt than any other of such creditors of the same class.

PREMIUM. The sum paid or agreed to be paid by an assured to the underwriter as the consideration for the insurance; being a certain rate per cent. on the amount insured.

PRESCRIPTION. The acquisition of incorporeal hereditaments by user or enjoyment for a very long time; i. e. "from time immemorial," or for a certain time set by a statute of limitations. For instance, A. continues to cross the land of B. by a certain path each day for twenty years, the period within which an action must be brought or other means taken to cause a discontinuance of A.'s user, under the laws of the state in which B.'s land lies. A. then has the right "by prescription" to continue to cross the land of B. His easement is complete.

PRESENTMENT. The production of a bill of exchange to the drawee for his acceptance, or to the drawer or acceptor for payment; or of a promissory note to the party liable, for payment of the same.

PRESUMPTION. An inference affirmative or disaffirmative of the truth or falsehood of any proposition or fact drawn by a process of probable reasoning in the absence of actual certainty of its truth or falsehood, or until such certainty can be ascertained.

PRIMA FACIE. Latin. At first sight; on the first apearance; on the face of it; so far as can be judged from the first disclosure; presumably.

A litigating party is said to have a prima facie case when the evidence in his favor is sufficiently strong for his opponent to be called on to answer it.

PRINCIPAL. In the law of agency. The employer or constitutor of an agent; the person who gives authority to an agent or attorney to do some act for him.

PRIVATE CARRIER. One who carries passengers or the goods of another without holding himself out to the general public as serving all persons that apply. The private carrier is contrasted with the common or public carrier.

PROBATE. The act or process of proving a will. The proof before an ordinary, surrogate, register, or other duly authorized person that a document produced before him for official recognition and registration, and alleged to be the last will and testament of a certain deceased person, is such in reality.

PROCEDURE. The method and mechanism, so to speak, by which proceedings in a court are conducted.

PROCESS. In practice. This word is generally defined to be the means of compelling the defendant in an action to appear in court.

PROCURATION. Agency; proxy; the act of constituting another one's attorney in fact; action under a power of attorney or other constitution of agency. Indorsing a bill or note "by procuration" (or per proc.) is doing it as proxy for another or by his authority.

PROMISSORY NOTE. A promise or engagement, in writing, to pay a specified sum at a time therein limited, or on demand, or at sight, to a person therein named, or to his order, or bearer.

PROMOTERS. In the law relating to corporations, those persons are called the "promoters" of a company who first associate themselves together for the purpose of organizing the company, issuing its prospectus, procuring subscriptions to the stock, securing a charter, etc.

PROSECUTE. To follow up; to carry on an action or other judicial proceeding; to proceed against a person criminally.

PRO TANTO. Latin. For so much; as far as it goes.

PROTEST. A notarial act, being a formal statement in writing made by a notary under his seal of office, at the request of the holder of a bill or note, in which such bill or note is described, and it is declared that the same was on a certain day presented for payment (or acceptance, as the case may be), and that such payment or acceptance was refused, and stating the reasons, if any, given for such refusal, whereupon the notary protests against all parties to such instrument, and declares that they will be held responsible for all loss or damage arising from its dishonor.

PROXY. A person who is substituted or deputed by another to represent him and act for him, particularly in some meeting or public body. Also the instrument containing the appointment of such person.

Q

QUA. Latin. As; in the character or capacity of. E. g., "the trustee qua trustee."

QUANTUM MERUIT. Latin. As much as he deserved.

In pleading. The common count in an action of assumpsit for work and labor, founded on an implied assumpsit or promise on the part of the defendant to pay the plaintiff as much as he reasonably deserved to have for his labor.

QUASI. Latin. As if; as it were; analogous to. This term is used in legal phraseology to indicate that one subject resembles another, with which it is compared, in certain characteristics, but that there are also intrinsic differences between them.

QUASI CONTRACT. In the civil law. A contractual relation arising out of transactions between the parties which give them mutual rights and obligations, but do not involve a specific and express convention or agreement between them.

QUIA EMPTORES. Latin. The English statute (18 Edw. I) prohibiting subinfeudation.

QUIET, v. To pacify; to render secure or unassailable by the removal of disquieting causes or disputes. This is the meaning of the word in the phrase "action to quiet title," which is a proceeding to establish the plaintiff's title to land by bringing into court an adverse claimant and there compelling him either to establish his claim or be forever after estopped from asserting it.

QUITCLAIM DEED. A deed of conveyance operating by way of release; that is, intended to pass any title, interest, or claim which the grantor may have in the premises, but not professing that such title is valid, nor containing any warranty or covenants for title.

QUO WARRANTO. Latin. By what warrant? A name commonly applied, in the United States, to an "information in the nature of a quo warranto," an action compelling the defendant to show by what warrant he exercises certain powers or privileges. The proceeding is used to test the right of a person to public office, or the right of a private or public corporation to exercise certain franchises.

R

RATIFICATION. The confirmation of a previous act done either by the party himself or by another; confirmation of a voidable act.

REAL ESTATE. See **Real Property.**

REALTY. See **Real Property.**

REAL PROPERTY. A general term for lands, tenements, and hereditaments; property which, on the death of the owner intestate, passes to his heir. Real property is either corporeal or incorporeal.

RECEIPT. A receipt is the written acknowledgment of the receipt of money, or a thing of value, without containing any affirmative obligation upon either party to it; a mere admission of a fact in writing.

Also the act or transaction of accepting or taking anything delivered.

RECEIVER. A receiver is an indifferent person between the parties appointed by the court to collect and receive the rents, issues, and profits of land, or the produce of personal estate, or other things which it does not seem reasonable to the court that either party should do; or where a party is incompetent to do so, as in the case of an infant. The remedy of the appointment of a receiver is one of the very oldest in the court of chancery, and is founded on the inadequacy of the remedy to be obtained in the court of ordinary jurisdiction.

RECOGNIZANCE. An obligation of record, entered into before some court of record, or magistrate duly authorized, with condition to do some particular act; as to appear at the assizes, or criminal court, to keep the peace, to pay a debt, or the like. It resembles a bond, but differs from it in being an acknowledgment of a former debt upon record.

RECOUPMENT. Recoupment is a right of the defendant to have a deduction from the amount of the plaintiff's damages, for the reason that the plaintiff has not complied with the cross-obligations or independent covenants arising under the same contract.

"Recoupment" differs from "set-off" in this respect: that any claim or demand the defendant may have against the plaintiff may be used as a set-off, while it is not a subject for recoupment unless it grows out of the very same transaction which furnishes the plaintiff's cause of action.

RECOVERY. The collection of a debt through an action at law.

Right of recovery. A plaintiff is said to have a right of recovery when he has a right of action under the facts of a given case.

REDEMPTION. (From the Latin, redemptio; a buying back.) A buying back of property from the original purchaser by the original seller. A mortgage purports to convey title to the mortgagee, subject to a right of redemption in the mortgagor; i. e., the mortgagor has an "equity of redemption" in the property. The mortgagor has a right and a power to defeat the efficacy of his mortgage as a complete conveyance of the title, by paying the amount of the debt secured by the mortgage, thus meeting the condition subsequent stated in the "defeasance clause" of the mortgage.

REIMBURSEMENT. The equitable and legal right of reimbursement of a surety is the surety's right to be reimbursed by his principal in the amount of the principal's debt paid by the surety.

RELATOR. The person upon whose complaint, or at whose instance, an information or writ of quo warranto is filed, and who is quasi the plaintiff in the proceeding.

RELEASE. The relinquishment, concession, or giving up of a right, claim, or privilege, by the person in whom it exists or to whom it accrues, to the person against whom it might have been demanded or enforced.

REMAINDER. An estate limited to take effect and be enjoyed after another estate is determined. As, if a man seised in fee-simple grants lands to A. for twenty years, and, after the determination of the said term, then to B. and his heirs forever, here A. is tenant for years, remainder to B. in fee.

REMAND. Where a decision of a trial court is reversed in an appellate court, it is frequently sent back or "remanded" to the trial court for a new trial. In some cases, as where the plaintiff has been given judgment on a state of facts that could not, in any view, justify such judgment, the appellate court may reverse the judgment without remanding.

REMEDIAL. Of or pertaining to the legal remedy, or to the form or procedural details of such remedy.

REMEDY. The means by which the violation of a right is prevented, redressed, or compensated. Though a remedy may be by the act of the party injured, by operation of law, or by agreement between the injurer and the injured, we are chiefly concerned with one kind of remedy, the judicial remedy, which is by action or suit.

REMITTITUR DAMNA. Latin. Usually shortened to **Remittitur.** An entry made on record, in cases where a jury has given greater damages than a plaintiff has declared for, remitting the excess.

RENT. The compensation, either in money, provisions, chattels, or labor, received by the owner of the soil from the occupant thereof.

REPLEVIN. A personal action ex delicto brought to recover possession of goods unlawfully taken (generally, but not only, applicable to the taking of goods distrained for rent), the validity of which taking it is the mode of contesting, if the party from whom the goods were taken wishes to have them back in specie, whereas, if he prefer to have damages instead, the validity may be contested by action of trespass or unlawful distress.

REPLEVIN BOND. A bond executed to indemnify the officer who executed a writ of replevin and to indemnify the defendant or person from whose custody the property was taken for such damages as he may sustain.

RESCISSION. Rescission, or the act of rescinding, is where a contract is canceled, annulled, or abrogated by the parties, or one of them.

RESIDENCE. Living or dwelling in a certain place permanently or for a considerable length of time. The place where a man makes his home, or where he dwells permanently or for an extended period of time.

RESIDUARY. Pertaining to the residue; constituting the residue; giving or bequeathing the residue; receiving or entitled to the residue.

RESIDUARY DEVISEE. The person named in a will, who is to take all the real property remaining over and above the other devises.

RESIDUARY ESTATE. The remaining part of a testator's estate and effects, after payment of debts and legacies; or that portion of his estate which has not been particularly devised or bequeathed.

RESIDUARY LEGATEE. The person to whom a testator bequeaths the residue of his personal estate, after the payment of such other legacies as are specifically mentioned in the will.

RESPONDEAT SUPERIOR. Latin. Let the master answer. This maxim means that a master is liable in certain cases for the wrongful acts of his servant, and a principal for those of his agent.

RESPONDENT. The party who makes an answer to a bill or other proceeding in chancery.

The party who appeals against the judgment of an inferior court is termed the "appellant"; and he who contends against the appeal, the "respondent."

REVERSE. An appellate court uses the term "reversed" to indicate that it annuls or avoids the judgment, or vacates the decree, of the trial court.

REVOCATION. The recall of some power, authority, or thing granted, or a destroying or making void of some deed that had existence until the act of revocation made it void. It may be either general, of all acts and things done before; or special, to revoke a particular thing.

RIGHT OF ACTION. The right to bring suit; a legal right to maintain an action, growing out of a given transaction or state of facts and based thereon.

RIGHT OF ENTRY. A right of entry is the right of taking or resuming possession of land by entering on it in a peaceable manner.

RIGHT TO REDEEM. The term "right of redemption" or "right to redeem," is familiarly used to describe the estate of the debtor when under mortgage, to be sold at auction, in contradistinction to an absolute estate, to be set off by appraisement. It would be more consonant to the legal character of this interest to call it the "debtor's estate subject to mortgage."

S

SATISFACTION. The act of satisfying a party by paying what is due to him (as on a mortgage, lien, or contract), or what is awarded to him, by the judgment of a court or otherwise. Thus, a judgment is satisfied by the payment of the amount due to the party who has recovered such judgment, or by his levying the amount.

SCIENTER. Latin. Knowingly.

SCINTILLA. Latin. A spark; a remaining particle; the least particle.

SCIRE FACIAS. Latin. You may cause to know. In practice, a judicial writ, founded upon some record, and requiring the person against whom it is brought to show cause why the party bringing it should not have advantage of such record, or (in the case of a scire facias to repeal letters patent) why the record should not be annulled and vacated.

The most common application of this writ is as a process to revive a judgment, after the lapse of a certain time, or on a change of parties, or otherwise to have execution of the judgment, in which cases it is merely a continuation of the original action.

SCROLL or SCRAWL. A mark intended to supply the place of a seal, made with a pen or other instrument of writing.

SEAL. An impression upon wax, wafer, or some other tenacious substance capable of being impressed.

SEISIN. Possession with an intent on the part of him who holds it to claim a freehold interest.

SET-OFF. A counterclaim or cross-demand; a claim or demand which the defendant in an action sets off against the claim of the plaintiff, as being his due, whereby he may extinguish the plaintiff's demand, either in whole or in part, according to the amount of the set-off.

SET UP. To bring forward or allege, as something relied upon or deemed sufficient; to propose or interpose, by way of defense, explanation, or justification; as, to set up the statute of limitations—i. e., offer and rely upon it as a defense to a claim.

SEVERANCE. The cutting of the crops, such as corn, grass, etc., or the separating of anything from the realty. Brown.

SHELLEY'S CASE, RULE IN. "That rule is that, where a life estate is given to A. with a future interest to A.'s heirs (the use of the particular word 'heirs' being necessary), the whole gift is construed as one 'to A. and his heirs,' at once giving an estate to A. in fee." Albert M. Kales, in 5 Am.Law & Proced. 105.

SILENT PARTNER. Popular name for dormant partners or special partners.

SIMPLE CONTRACT. A contract based upon consideration and not upon form.

SPECIAL INDORSEMENT. An indorsement in full, which specifically names the indorsee.

SPECIAL PARTNER. A member of a limited partnership, who furnishes certain funds to the common stock, and whose liability extends no further than the fund furnished.

SPECIAL PROPERTY. Property of a qualified, temporary, or limited nature; as distinguished from absolute, general, or unconditional property. Such is the property of a bailee in the article bailed, of a sheriff in goods temporarily in his hands under a levy, of the finder of lost goods while looking for the owner, of a person in wild animals which he has caught.

SPECIALTY. A writing sealed and delivered, containing some agreement.

SPECIAL VERDICT. A special finding of the facts of a case by a jury, leaving to the court the application of the law to the facts thus found.

SPOLIATION. In torts. Destruction of a thing by the act of a stranger, as the erasure or alteration of a writing by the act of a stranger, is called "spoliation." This has not the effect to destroy its character or legal effect.

SS. An abbreviation used in that part of a record, pleading, or affidavit, called the "statement of the venue." Commonly translated or read "to wit," and supposed to be a contraction of "scilicet."

STATUS. The status of a person is his legal position or condition.

STATUTE, n. An act of the legislature.

STATUTE OF FRAUDS. A celebrated English statute, passed in 1677, and which has been adopted, in a more or less modified form, in nearly all of the United States. Its chief characteristic is the provision that no action shall be brought on certain contracts unless there be a note or memorandum thereof in writing, signed by the party to be charged or by his authorized agent.

STATUTE OF LIMITATION. A statute prescribing limitations to the right of action on certain described causes of action; that is, declaring that no suit shall be maintained on such causes of action unless brought within a specified period after the right accrued.

STATUTORY UNDERTAKING. A penal bond, given, as required by statute, in connection with certain legal proceedings. "Common examples of statutory undertaking are: The bond given by a plaintiff in an injunction suit, as security to the defendant for damages caused by the issuance of an interlocutory injunction, such damages, within the amount of the penalty, to be collected by the defendant if the injunction is found to have been wrongfully issued; and the bond given for a very similar purpose in attachment or replevin." Bauer on Damages, p. 98, note.

STOCK. **In corporation law.** The capital or principal fund of a corporation or joint-stock company, formed by the contributions of subscribers or the sale of shares, and considered as the aggregate of a certain number of shares severally owned by the members or stockholders of the corporation; also the proportional part of the capital which is owned by an individual stockholder; also the incorporeal property which is represented by the holding of a certificate of stock, and in a wider and more remote sense, the right of a shareholder to participate in the general management of the company and to share proportionally in its net profits or earnings or in the distribution of assets on dissolution.

STOPPAGE IN TRANSITU. The act by which the unpaid vendor of goods stops their progress and resumes possession of them, while they are in course of transit from him to the purchaser, and not yet actually delivered to the latter.

STRICTISSIMI JURIS. Latin. Of the strictest right or law.

SUBAGENT. An under-agent; a substituted agent; an agent appointed by one who is himself an agent.

SUBINFEUDATION. Under the feudal system, an inferior lord sometimes carved out of an estate which he held of a superior lord, a part which he granted to an inferior tenant, whose lord he in turn became. This under-feudalizing, so to speak, used in order to evade restraints on alienation, was known as subinfeudation, and was prohibited by the Statute of Quia Emptores (St. 18 Edw. I).

SUBPŒNA. Latin. Sub, under, and pœna, punishment or penalty. In the Latin writs early used in England, one was commanded to appear "sub pœna," and these words have given the name to writs of those types in which they appeared.

Of a witness. A process commanding a witness to appear in court at a certain time to testify in a given cause.

In chancery practice. A process commanding a party or parties to a suit in equity to appear and answer matters alleged against them in the bill.

SUBROGATION. The substitution of one thing for another, or of one person into the place of another with respect to rights, claims, or securities.

Subrogation denotes the putting a third person who has paid a debt in the place of the creditor to whom he has paid it, so that he may exercise against the debtor all the rights which the creditor, if unpaid, might have done.

SUBSCRIBE. **In the law of contracts.** To write under; to write the name under; to write the name at the bottom or end of a writing.

SUBSTANTIVE LAW. The part of the law which the courts are established to administer, as opposed to the rules according to which the substantive law itself is administered. That part of the law which creates, defines, and regulates rights, as opposed to adjective or remedial law, which prescribes the method of enforcing rights or obtaining redress for their invasion.

SUI GENERIS. Latin. Of its own kind or class.

SUI JURIS. Latin. Of his own right; having legal capacity to manage his own affairs.

SUIT. "Suit" is a generic term, of comprehensive signification, and applies to any proceeding in a court of justice in which the plaintiff pursues, in such court, the remedy which the law affords him for the redress of an injury or the recovery of a right.

SUMMARY, adj. Immediate; peremptory; off-hand; without a jury; provisional; statutory.

SUMMON. **In practice.** To serve a summons; to cite a defendant to appear in court to answer a suit which has been begun against him; to notify the defendant that an action has been instituted against him, and that he is required to answer to it at a time and place named.

SUMMONS. **In practice.** A writ, directed to the sheriff or other proper officer, requiring him to notify the person named that an action has been commenced against him in the court whence the writ issues, and that he is required to appear, on a day named, and answer the complaint in such action.

SURETY. A surety is one who at the request of another, and for the purpose of securing to him a benefit, becomes responsible for the performance by the latter of some act in favor of a third person, or hypothecates property as security therefor.

T

TENANCY IN COMMON. A tenancy under which each cotenant has a distinct and several estate in the property. Under such a tenancy, the survivor from among the cotenants does not take the entire property as in the case of a joint tenancy.

TENANT. In the broadest sense, one who holds or possesses lands or tenements by any kind of right or title, whether in fee, for life, for years, at will, or otherwise. Cowell.

In a more restricted sense, one who holds lands of another; one who has the temporary use and occupation of real property owned by another person (called the "landlord"), the duration and terms of his tenancy being usually fixed by an instrument called a "lease."

TENDER. An offer of money; the act by which one produces and offers to a person holding a claim or demand against him the amount of money which he considers and admits to be due, in satisfaction of such claim or demand, without any stipulation or condition.

Also, there may be a tender of performance of a duty other than the payment of money.

TENOR. In pleading the "tenor" of a document is sometimes said to be shown when an exact copy is set out in the pleading. Also, the word is often used to denote the true meaning or purport of an instrument.

TENURE. **In the law of public officers.** The period during which an officer holds office.

In the law of real property. The legal mode in which one owns an estate in lands.

TERM. **Of court.** The word "term" when used with reference to a court, signifies the space of time during which the court holds a session. A "session" signifies the time during the term when the court sits for the transaction of business, and the session commences when the court convenes for the term, and continues until final adjournment, either before or at the expiration of the term. The "term" of the court is the time prescribed by law during which it may be in "session." The "session" of the court is the time of its actual sitting.

TESTATOR. One who makes or has made a testament or will; one who dies leaving a will.

TITLE. The means whereby the owner of lands or of personalty has the just possession of his property. See Co. Litt. 345; 2 Bl.Comm. 195.

TORT. Wrong; injury; the opposite of right. So called, according to Lord Coke, because it is "wrested," or crooked, being contrary to that which is right and straight. Co. Litt. 158b.

In modern practice, "tort" is constantly used as an English word to denote a wrong or wrongful act, for which an action will lie, as distinguished from a "contract." 3 Bl.Comm. 117.

A tort is a legal wrong committed upon the person or property independent of contract. It may be either (1) a direct invasion of some legal right of the individual; (2) the infraction of some public duty by which special damage accrues to the individual; (3) the violation of some private obligation by which like damage accrues to the individual. In the former case, no special damage is necessary to entitle the party to recover. In the two latter cases, such damage is necessary. Code Ga.1882, § 2951.

TORT-FEASOR. One who commits or is guilty of a tort.

TORTIOUS. Wrongful; of the nature of a tort. Formerly certain modes of conveyance (e. g., feoffments, fines, etc.) had the effect of passing not merely the estate of the person making the conveyance, but the whole fee simple, to the injury of the person really entitled to the fee; and they were hence called "tortious conveyances." Litt. par. 611; Co. Litt. 271b, note 1; 330b, note 1. But this operation has been taken away. Sweet.

TRANSITORY ACTION. An action that is personal—i. e., brought against the person of the defendant —and possible to be brought in any county in which service of process upon the defendant is obtained.

TRESPASS. Any misfeasance or act of one man whereby another is injuriously treated or damnified. 3 Bl.Comm. 208.

An injury or misfeasance to the person, property, or rights of another person, done with force and violence, either actual or implied by law.

In the strictest sense, an entry on another's ground, without a lawful authority, and doing some damage, however inconsiderable, to his real property. 3 Bl. Comm. 209.

In practice. A form of action, at the common law, which lies for redress in the shape of money damages for any unlawful injury done to the plaintiff, in respect either to his person, property, or rights, by the immediate force and violence of the defendant.

Trespass de bonis asportatis. (Trespass for goods carried away.) In practice. The technical name of that species of trespass for injuries to personal property which lies where the injury consists in carrying away the goods or property.

Trespass on the case. The form of action, at common law, adapted to the recovery of damages for some injury resulting to a party from the wrongful act of another, unaccompanied by direct or immediate force, or which is the indirect or secondary consequence of such act. Commonly called "case," or "action on the case."

Trespass quare clausum fregit. (Trespass wherefore he broke the close, or trespass for breaking the close.) The common-law action for damages for an unlawful entry or trespass upon the plaintiff's land.

TROVER. In common-law practice, the action of trover (or trover and conversion) is a species of action on the case, and originally lay for the recovery of damages against a person who had "found" another's goods and wrongfully converted them to his own use. Subsequently the allegation of the loss of the goods by the plaintiff and the finding of them by the defendant was merely fictitious, and the action became the remedy for any wrongful interference with or detention of the goods of another.

TRUST. An equitable or beneficial right or title to land or other property, held for the beneficiary by another person, in whom resides the legal title or ownership, recognized and enforced by courts of chancery.

TRUST DEED. An instrument in use in many states, taking the place and serving the uses of a common-law mortgage, by which the legal title to real property is placed in one or more trustees, to secure the repayment of a sum of money or the performance of other conditions.

TRUSTEE. The person appointed, or required by law, to execute a trust; one in whom an estate, interest, or power is vested, under an express or implied agreement to administer or exercise it for the benefit or to the use of another.

TRUSTEE PROCESS. The name given in the New England states, to the process of garnishment or foreign attachment.

U

ULTRA VIRES. Latin. Beyond the powers. A term used to express the action of a corporation which is beyond the powers conferred upon it by its charter, or the statutes under which it was instituted. 13 Am.Law Rev. 632.

UNDERTAKING. A promise, engagement, or stipulation. Each of the promises made by the parties to a contract, considered independently and not as mutual, may, in this sense, be denominated an "undertaking."

UNDERWRITER. The person who insures another in a fire or life policy; the insurer.

A person who joins with others in entering into a marine policy of insurance as insurer.

UNIFORM STATUTES. In general, statutes of substantially uniform substance, passed by various states, with the purpose of making the law of the subject uniform throughout the country. Such statutes have been drafted by the Commission on Uniform State Laws of the American Bar Association, and recommended for passage by the Legislatures of the various states. The most important of such statutes are the Negotiable Instruments Act, the Sales Act, and the Partnership Act, which have all been enacted in many of the states.

UNILATERAL. One-sided; ex parte; having relation to only one of two or more persons or things.

USURY. Unlawful interest; a premium or compensation paid or stipulated to be paid for the use of money borrowed or returned, beyond the rate of interest established by law. Webster.

V

VALID. Of binding force. A deed, will, or other instrument, which has received all the formalities required by law, is said to be valid.

VALIDITY. This term is used to signify legal sufficiency, in contradistinction to mere regularity.

VENDEE. A purchaser or buyer; one to whom anything is sold. Generally used of the transferee of real property, one who acquires chattels by sale being called a "buyer."

VENDITIONI EXPONAS. Latin. You may expose to sale. This is the name of a writ of execution, requiring a sale to be made, directed to a sheriff when he has levied upon goods under a fieri facias, but returned that they remained unsold for want of buyers; and in some jurisdictions it is issued to cause a sale to be made of lands, seized under a former writ, after they have been condemned or passed upon by an inquisition. Frequently abbreviated to "vend. ex."

VENDOR. The person who transfers property by sale, particularly real estate, "seller" being more commonly used for one who sells personalty.

VENIRE. Latin. To come; to appear in court. This word is sometimes used as the name of the writ for summoning a jury, more commonly called a "venire facias."

VENIRE FACIAS DE NOVO. Latin. A fresh or new venire, which the court grants when there has been some impropriety or irregularity in returning the jury, or where the verdict is so imperfect or ambiguous that no judgment can be given upon it, or where a judgment is reversed on error, and a new trial awarded.

VERDICT. The formal and unanimous decision or finding of a jury, impaneled and sworn for the trial of a cause, upon the matters or questions duly submitted to them upon the trial.

VESTED. Accrued; fixed; settled; absolute; having the character or giving the rights of absolute ownership; not contingent; not subject to be defeated by a condition precedent.

VINDICTIVE DAMAGES. Exemplary damages are damages on an increased scale, awarded to the plaintiff over and above what will barely compensate him for his property loss, where the wrong done to him was aggravated by circumstances of violence, oppression, malice, fraud, or wanton and wicked conduct on the part of the defendant, and are intended to solace the plaintiff for mental anguish, laceration of his feelings, shame, degradation, or other aggravations of the original wrong, or else to punish the defendant for his evil behavior or to make an example of him, for which reason they are also called "punitive" or "punitory" damages or "vindictive" damages, and (vulgarly) "smart money."

VOID. Null; ineffectual, nugatory; having no legal force or binding effect; unable, in law, to support the purpose for which it was intended.

VOIDABLE. That may be avoided, or declared void; not absolutely void, or void in itself. Most of the acts of infants are "voidable" only, and not absolutely void.

VOLUNTARY. Free; without compulsion or solicitation.

Without consideration; without valuable consideration; gratuitous.

VOLUNTEER. **In conveyancing,** one who holds a title under a voluntary conveyance; i. e., one made without consideration, good or valuable, to support it.

A person who gives his services without any express or implied promise of remuneration in return is called a "volunteer," and is entitled to no remuneration for his services, nor to any compensation for injuries sustained by him in performing what he has undertaken. Sweet. Also one who officiously pays the debt of another.

W

WAGER. A wager is a contract by which two or more parties agree that a certain sum of money or other thing shall be paid or delivered to one of them on the happening of an uncertain event or upon the ascertainment of a fact which is in dispute between them.

WAIVER. The renunciation, repudiation, abandonment, or surrender of some claim, right, privilege, or of the opportunity to take advantage of some defect, iregularity, or wrong.

WARD. An infant or insane person placed by authority of law under the care of a guardian.

WARRANT, v. **In contracts.** To engage or promise that a certain fact or state of facts, in relation to the subject-matter, is, or shall be, as it is represented to be.

WARRANT, n. A writ or precept from a competent authority in pursuance of law, directing the doing of an act, and addressed to an officer or person competent to do the act, and affording him protection from damage, if he does it.

WARRANTY. **In real property law.** A real covenant by the grantor of lands, for himself and his heirs, to warrant and defend the title and possession of the estate granted, to the grantee and his heirs, whereby either upon voucher, or judgment in the writ of warrantia chartæ, and the eviction of the grantee by paramount title, the grantor was bound to recompense him with other lands of equal value.

In sales of personal property. A warranty is a statement or representation made by the seller of goods, contemporaneously with and as a part of the contract of sale, though collateral to the express object of it, having reference to the character, quality, or title of the goods, and by which he promises or undertakes to insure that certain facts are or shall be as he then represents them.

A warranty is an engagement by which a seller assures to a buyer the existence of some fact affecting the transaction, whether past, present, or future.

In contracts. An undertaking or stipulation, in writing, or verbally, that a certain fact in relation to the subject of a contract is or shall be as it is stated or promised to be.

A warranty differs from a representation in that a warranty must always be given contemporaneously with, and as part of, the contract; whereas, a representation precedes and induces to the contract. And, while that is their difference in nature, their difference in consequence or effect is this: that, upon breach of warranty (or false warranty), the contract remains binding, and damages only are recoverable for the breach; whereas, upon a false representation, the defrauded party may elect to avoid the contract, and recover the entire price paid. Brown.

WILL. A will is the legal expression of a man's wishes as to the disposition of his property after his death.

An instrument in writing, executed in form of law, by which a person makes a disposition of his property, to take effect after his death.

WRIT OF ENTRY. A real action to recover the possession of land where the tenant (or owner) has been disseised or otherwise wrongfully dispossessed.

WRIT OF ERROR. A writ issued from a court of appellate jurisdiction, directed to the judge or judges of a court of record, requiring them to remit to the appellate court the record of an action before them, in which a final judgment has been entered, in order that examination may be made of certain errors alleged to have been committed, and that the judgment may be reversed, corrected, or affirmed, as the case may require.

A writ of error is defined to be a commission by which the judges of one court are authorized to examine a record upon which a judgment was given in another court, and, on such examination, to affirm or reverse the same, according to law.

Y

YEAR BOOKS. Books made up of reports of English cases from Edward II, 1292, to Henry VIII, early in the sixteenth century. They constitute an important source of information on the early English common law.

TABLE OF CASES

References are to Pages

INDEX

References are to Pages

INDEX

References are to Pages

References are to Pages

References are to Pages

END OF VOLUME